A CENTURY OF
CANADIAN GRAIN

C F WILSON

Government Policy to 1951

A Century
of
Canadian Grain

A Century
of
Canadian Grain

Government Policy
to 1951

C. F. Wilson

Western Producer Prairie Books
Saskatoon, Saskatchewan

Cover designed by Warren Clark

Printed and bound in Canada by
Modern press

Saskatoon, Saskatchewan

Western Producer Prairie Books publications are produced and manufactured in the middle of western Canada by a unique publishing venture
owned by a group of prairie farmers who are members of Saskatchewan
Wheat Pool. Our first book in 1954 was a reprint of a serial originally
carried in *The Western Producer*, a weekly newspaper providing news and
information to western farm families since 1923. We continue the tradition
of providing enjoyable and informative reading for all Canadians.

Canadian Cataloguing in Publication Data

Wilson, Charles F., 1907-
A century of Canadian grain

Bibliography: p.
Includes index.
ISBN 0-919306-79-9 pa.

1. Grain trade - Canada - Hist. I. Title.
HD9044.C22W54   380.1'41'310971   C78-002009-X

To Otto Lang,
and all his predecessors and successors
as grain-policy makers

TABLE OF CONTENTS

LIST OF CHARTS

LIST OF TABLES

PREFACE

Anyone concerned with the formulation or study of government policy related to the Canadian grain industry should be able to have at his command a continuous record of the background, interplay and historical development of the basic elements in the industry. These elements include land settlement and land use; transportation; grain elevation, storage, handling and forwarding; marketing methods and opportunities; income security; and the ramifications of international competition and the search it has generated for international co-operation in the sale of grain.

In order to assemble a complete record of the evolution of government policy in relation to the grain industry, one must rely mainly upon published records for almost the first two-thirds of the relevant period. Fortunately the available material is not only adequate, but it provides rewarding reading to anyone interested in the decision-making process. Students need only to be directed to the sources. For example, parliamentary debates and the statutes pertaining to the industry are available for the whole of its relevant history. Similarly, the reports of the successive royal commissions are available. By themselves, these sources afford less than an adequate explanation of the issues which gave rise to the debates, commissions and legislation, and it is helpful to turn to other sources for a better comprehension of the events.

Much fuller accounts are, in fact, available for the earlier period in newspapers such as *The Manitoba Free Press* and in such books as Hopkins Moorhouse's *Deep Furrows,* Toronto, 1918; L. A. Wood's *A History of Farmers' Movements in Canada,* Toronto, 1924; W. A. Mackintosh's *Agricultural Co-operation in Western Canada,* (Queen's University, Kingston, The Ryerson Press, Toronto, 1924); and articles and bulletins such as W. C. Clark's *The Country Elevator in the Canadian West,* Queen's University, Kingston, 1916 and J. F. Booth's *Co-operative Marketing of Grain in Western Canada,* USDA technical bulletin No. 63, 1928. Unpublished sources, notably Sir George Foster's diaries and papers, the Bennett papers, the W. L. MacKenzie King papers and correspondence, and certain departmental files are to be found in the public archives of Canada.

For the policy-maker or adviser who has limited time there are two books written in the earlier period which should still be regarded as indispensable reading; the first is D. A. MacGibbon's *The Canadian Grain Trade,* MacMillan, Toronto, 1932; the second is Harald S. Patton's *Grain Growers' Co-operation in Western Canada,* Harvard University Press, Cambridge, 1928.

Dr. MacGibbon, a professor of political economy at the University of Alberta, was appointed a member of the royal grain inquiry commission, 1923-24, and was subsequently appointed as a commissioner of the board of grain commissioners for Canada, in which capacity he served from 1929 until his retirement in 1949. MacGibbon's work, *The Canadian Grain Trade,* is an excellent primer on the industry. Its historical section is sketchier than will satisfy the serious student, but it serves as a useful introduction. Other parts of the book describe the mechanics of the trade and its components, the country elevator and terminal elevator systems, the line elevator companies, the United grain growers, the Canadian wheat pools, the banks, the milling industry, and the role of the board of grain commissioners for Canada.

Because he was a member of the board, MacGibbon made very guarded references to the controversial issues that highlighted relations among the producers, the railways, and the line elevators throughout this fascinating earlier period. Nevertheless, MacGibbon's first book on *The Canadian Grain Trade* remains unique as the only comprehensive attempt to describe the functions of every sector of the industry. It should be read in preparation for the much more detailed account of the ascendency of the co-operative movement by Harald S. Patton who, like MacGibbon, was a professor of political economy at the University of Alberta when he submitted *Grain Growers' Co-operation in Western Canada* as his doctoral thesis at Harvard in 1925, and updated it for publication in 1928. It survives as a painstaking and authoritative publication. Even it must be accepted, however, for what it professes to be: a history of grain growers' co-operation as distinct from a history of the industry as a whole. For example, a more complete record of the railways and their contribution can be found in H. A. Innis's *History of the Canadian Pacific Railway,* London, 1923, and in the more recent histories of the companies. Also, by confining his study to the history of the co-operative movement, Patton fails to reflect the totality of the agrarian movement by underplaying its political involvement in the formation of the Progressive party.

In more recent years, writers have directed their attention increasingly to the exposition and appraisal of government grain policy, as exemplified in MacGibbon's second book, *The Canadian Grain Trade, 1931-1951,* and in the several contributions of Professors Vernon C. Fowke and George E. Britnell of the University of Saskatchewan.[1] Nevertheless, for example,

[1]Vernon C. Fowke, *Canadian Agricultural Policy, The Historical Pattern,* (University of Toronto Press, 1946).

The National Policy and the Wheat Economy (University of Toronto Press, 1957).

"The National Policy - Old and New," *Canadian Journal of Economics and Political Science,* Vol. XVIII, Aug. 1952, pp. 271-286.

"Royal Commissions and Canadian Agricultural Policy," *Canadian Journal of Economics and Political Science,* Vol. XIV, May 1948, pp. 163-175.

G. E. Britnell and V. C. Fowke, "Development of Wheat Marketing Policy in Canada," *Journal of Farm Economics,* Vol. XXXI, Nov. 1949, pp. 627-642.

Fowke's treatise on *The National Policy and the Wheat Economy* subordinates his extremely competent analysis of some aspects of government grain policy to the development of his thesis in respect of the implementation of the national policy. In so doing, he falls short of providing a continuous account of the grain policy-making process.

Over the years, especially those in which wheat was Canada's leading export commodity, the industry attracted the attention of economists and economic historians. In fact, in those days, any Canadian economist worth his salt wrote upon some aspect of it. Such illustrious Canadians as O. D. Skelton, W. C. Clark, W. A. Mackintosh and Mitchell Sharp exemplify this group. Their published contributions predated their careers in the public service. Innis and Fowke typify the economic historians who made notable contributions and who remained in academic careers. During the second world war, George Britnell served as a member of the Ottawa "establishment" before returning to the academic life and collaborating with Fowke in the preparation of *Canadian Agriculture in War and Peace*. At the time they published, none of these writers was directly involved in grain policy formulation and, as economists, they were as much preoccupied with policy analysis and appraisal as they were with its exposition.

Thus there is still room for a single, continuous account of policy formulation written from the policy-maker's standpoint and for the use of future policy-makers and advisers, as well as students embarking on careers in various sectors of the industry. Such a review should concentrate on exposition which, if adequately descriptive of events, cannot be controversial, whereas the appraisal of many policy decisions seems predestined to remain controversial, no matter how exhaustive the analysis. Only in the few instances where the published accounts appear to have left a one-sided legacy should there be occasion in an expository review to attempt to rectify the balance.

My purpose in writing such a review was to compile a continuous record of the decision-making process, and thereby to make the background material readily available for the policy-maker. The reasons a record from this standpoint has not already been written are fairly obvious. The qualities which produce a policy-maker are not those which produce an historian nor a diarist. Moreover, policy-advisers have respected their oaths of secrecy. In the past the lack of written material has not been of vital consequence to incoming ministers because they were supported by permanent bureaucrats embarked on life-time careers. Now that interchange of business and public service personnel is being encouraged it is not so likely that an incoming minister will inherit such continuity of staff. In any case, the passage of time is eroding older experts' memories and producing new policy-makers and advisers younger than the industry itself. Because their responsibility is to innovate and improve, it should be helpful to them to understand the basic structure of the industry and how it originally took shape.

In organizing this policy review, I had intended to commence with the events of 1930 and to pursue the record through the following two decades using material not only from published sources such as committee hearings, royal commissions and house of commons debates, but increasingly from official files and from personal recollection. The destruction of files has already begun; hence the urgency to salvage the remainder. The attempt, however, to set out the record of the government's price-support operations during 1931-1935 period encountered so many references to the previously developed fabric of the industry that there appeared to be obvious advantages in commencing with the earlier history, firstly, to place under one cover the available references to the entire history of government policy-making and, secondly, to facilitate cross-reference between the earlier and later developments.

Part I of the review, therefore, presents developments up to 1930 with particular attention to events of interest to the policy-maker; otherwise, where the narrative includes an account of the origins and development of the various segments of the industry, it is because their origins should be understood in relation to their subsequent involvement in government policy issues. Part II deals with the prolific period of policy formation in the depression years, 1930 to 1935. Part III covers the period of transition from a voluntary to a compulsory wheat board from 1935 to 1943 which was so markedly affected by the resumption of hostilities in 1939. Part IV is concerned with the assurance of markets during the transition period from war to peace. It deals with the Canada-United Kingdom wheat contract, the international wheat agreement and the placing of oats and barley marketing under control of the Canadian wheat board. By 1950, the basic structure of today's industry had been established.

A word might be said about policies and the people responsible for them, because the two are inseparable. Even if an attempt were made to divorce the evolution of policy from the people who were responsible for it, the exercise would detract from the value of the review. Little would have happened had it not been for the conflicts of view and abrasion of personalities. In the heat of action some derogatory remarks have been written or said, and descendants of the principal characters can possibly still take umbrage at repetition of what is already historical record. This need not be, however, for there comes a time when an adversary's confrontation is transformed into an enduring compliment. In instances set out here, that metamorphosis should already have taken place. In the diaries and correspondence of the principal personalities, there are many entries which the writers might have altered upon mature consideration, or omitted entirely had it been foreseen that they might be published. Yet history is all the richer for the record they left of their immediate personal reactions. Where comments on personalities are quoted, such references have been included because of their bearing on some turn or phase of policy. Many of the more colorful references to be found in the original sources have been omitted because they lack that justification. As it is, in my opinion, the review is enhanced by the intimate identification of people with policies. Moreover, history so far has tended to overlook the remarkable contributions of some of the policy-makers and advisers, because the recollection of the policy decisions has become detached from that of the persons who made them.

Throughout the review, extensive resort is made to quotations from original sources. At times the presentation is primarily a selection of relevant reading from such material. This has been done for the purpose of making such sources readily accessible to the more serious students of policy. Of course what can be rewarding reading to some can be tedious to others. Therefore, the reader should exercise his options to read, to scan or to skip the quotations entirely. The quotations all appear in their original form; spelling, punctuation and grammatical construction have not been altered.

CHARLES F. WILSON
Ottawa, March, 1978

ACKNOWLEDGMENTS

The inspiration for this review came from Mr. Rod Bryden, first coordinator of the Grains Group, whom I needled almost constantly with my recollections of past policy crises and their resolution. Upon my retirement Mr. Bryden recommended to the chairman of the Grains Group, the Honourable Otto Lang, the retention of my services to prepare for others, including themselves, a continuous record of the development of government grain policy. The minister not only endorsed the project but followed it with great interest to its completion. Thus this review is warmly dedicated to Otto Lang, his predecessors and successors as grain policy-makers.

I am very grateful to Dr. Gertrude Dunn, librarian of the Harriet Irving Library, University of New Brunswick, for her permission to search the Bennett Papers, and also to the Honourable Jack Pickersgill, a literary executor of the King Papers, for having archivists search the relevant portions of the King Diary for me. I am very appreciative also of the permission granted to me by officials of the Privy Council Office and of the Department of Industry, Trade and Commerce to search the relevant departmental files.

A special word of acknowledgment and appreciation is due some fifty or more of my friends in, or retired from, the grain industry and the public service who read the original manuscript and offered their comments and suggestions. Their contributions have helped very substantially to make the review as authentic a record as was possible.

I wish also to thank Mrs. Joan Hadlow for the thorough quality of her research assistance, and Mrs. Verna Moss who bore the brunt of the typing.

C.F.W.

I
SUMMARY OF EVENTS TO 1930

1

ORIGINS OF THE GRAIN INDUSTRY

The early history of the grain trade in western Canada has been well chronicled. These histories have been written from the standpoint of the political development of the country or the farmers' movements or the railways. In contrast, in this review emphasis is upon the contribution of government to the development of the grain industry. Governmental inputs included the acquisition of land and the establishment of local government, first under federal and then under provincial jurisdiction. A land survey had to be made to facilitate land settlement. Exploratory expeditions traversed the prairies to establish that a fertile soil and climate amenable to agriculture existed. Early maturing wheat varieties of high milling quality were also a prerequisite, as was a procedure for inspecting and grading grain. Even with these contributions, land settlement could not have been effectively accomplished without provision of a transportation system to facilitate migration and to move the produce of the newly opened land.

RAILWAYS

In its concern to create a dominion from sea to sea, the government of Sir John A. Macdonald committed itself to construction of a railway across western Canada as one of the key inducements to the government of British Columbia to enter confederation in 1871. Article II of the terms of union stated:

The Government of the Dominion undertake to secure the commencement simultaneously, within two years from the date of union, of the construction of a railway from the Pacific towards the Rocky Mountains, and from such point as may be selected east of the Rocky Mountains towards the Pacific, to connect the seaboard of British Columbia with the railway system of Canada; and further, to secure the completion of such railway within ten years from the date of union.

Between the commitment and its accomplishment lay a great passage in Canadian history. The Macdonald government's policy was that the undertaking should be accomplished by private enterprise but with financial and land-grant assistance from the government. Initial negotiations with a group headed by Sir Hugh Allan of the Allan Steamship Line, Montreal, foundered and culminated in the "Pacific Scandal", the downfall of the Macdonald government and an attempt by the successor Mackenzie administration to undertake construction by public enterprise. Later, upon Macdonald's return to office, a new company was formed under the leadership of George Stephen of the Bank of Montreal. All these developments highlighted the problem of implementing the commitment to British Columbia which was eventually resolved by the agreement the government entered into with the Canadian Pacific Railway.

An act of parliament respecting the Canadian Pacific Railway, assented to on February 15, 1881, confirmed the agreement. The initial government commitment to the new railway company included subsidies of $25,000,000 and 25,000,000 acres of land to be paid and conveyed to the company under prescribed terms and conditions.[1] Construction proceeded forthwith in different segments across northern Ontario, the prairies and in British Columbia. Some sections already begun under other auspices were taken over and the first Canadian transcontinental line was completed in 1885.

Of principal interest to the opening up of the west to settlement and agriculture was the construction of the main line of the Canadian Pacific across the prairies.[2] Until 1881, the federal government had tried to get a line built west of Winnipeg by letting its own contracts and when the Canadian Pacific took over, rails had already been laid from Winnipeg to Portage la Prairie. In 1881 the Canadian Pacific extended the line to Flat Creek (now known as Oak Lake), Manitoba. Land speculators and settlers preceded the extension of the line and the new company selected its divisional points and townsites with a view toward the enhancement of its newly-acquired land holdings. Thus the town of Brandon was created from open space in 1881.

Commencing in 1882, a drive was mounted to extend the line as far west as Fort Calgary, a distance of 675 miles. Altogether that year 417 miles of track were laid, which was a phenomenal record for railway construction. En route, the divisional points of Moosomin, Broadview, Regina, Moose Jaw and Swift Current were created, with the additional interest that Regina was to become the new capital of the North West Territories. In between the divisional points, the sidings constructed at six-mile intervals became potential townsites where settlers detrained and shipped their first harvests. The remainder of the main line to Fort Calgary was completed by the end of June, 1883.

Railway development continued with the construction of subsidiary lines and with the entry of two other companies in the development of transcontinental lines. Two of the key subsidiary lines of the Canadian Pacific Railway were the "Soo" line which enabled the company to compete for a share of the American transcontinental traffic from Chicago to the west coast, and also the Crow's Nest line from Lethbridge to Nelson. The latter line facilitated the development of the coal and other mineral resources of southern British Columbia and discouraged the construction of competing American branch lines into that area.

---

[1]Other federal and provincial grants to the Canadian Pacific and to railway companies Canadian Pacific acquired, brought the Company's total land grants to 36,370,828 acres. See J. L. McDougall, *Canadian Pacific,* (McGill University Press, 1968), p. 127.

[2]This has been graphically described by Pierre Burton [*The Last Spike,* (McClelland and Stewart, Limited Toronto, 1971), Chapters 1-3].

The Canadian portion of the "Soo" line was built in 1893 from the junction of Pasqua near Moose Jaw to North Portal on the border where it joined up with a branch of the Minneapolis, St. Paul and Sault Ste. Marie Railway which was controlled by the Canadian Pacific. This afforded a more direct route from Vancouver to Chicago and improved the company's ability to compete with American lines.

The Crow's Nest line project led to an agreement of historic importance between the railway and the federal government. This agreement was confirmed by legislation, which authorized a subsidy of up to $3,400,000 for the construction of the necessary links from Lethbridge via Fort Macleod through the Crow's Nest Pass to connect with other lines already built to complete the route to Nelson.[3] Lethbridge had already been connected to the Canadian Pacific main line at Dunmore, just south east of Medicine Hat. The connecting rail lines the railway acquired in British Columbia carried with them a substantial land subsidy from the provincial government.

In return for the federal subsidy the railway committed itself to approval, revision and control by the governor in council (or by a railway commission when one was created) of all its tariffs, thereby introducing for the first time the principle of rate regulation.

Secondly, the railway agreed to reduce existing tariffs on the westward movement of a list of articles covering the food, housing, implement and livestock needs of the prairie settlers. These reduced rates, effective from January 1, 1898, were to remain in effect "hereafter".

Thirdly, the company agreed to a reduction of three cents per one hundred pounds from its existing rates on grain and flour from all points west of the lakehead to Fort William/Port Arthur and all points east. Half of the reduction was to take effect on September 1, 1898 and remainder a year later. The act specified "that no higher rates than such reduced rates on tolls shall be charged after the dates mentioned. . ."[4] This had the effect of fixing such rates, for example, in perpetuity:

> Winnipeg to Thunder Bay,   14 cents per 100 lbs.
> Regina to Thunder Bay,   20 cents per 100 lbs.
> Calgary to Thunder Bay,   26 cents per 100 lbs.

The Crow's Nest Pass rates which took effect from September 1, 1899, were superseded by lower competitive rates secured by the government of Manitoba in its agreement with the Canadian Northern Railway in 1903. In 1918, the Crow's Nest Pass rates were suspended as a result of wartime inflation, but they were·restored in 1922 and were embodied in the railway act of 1925.[5]

While the Canadian Pacific Railway turned to the construction of branch lines to feed its main line, two competing transcontinental lines were in process of formation, In 1896, the team of William Mackenzie and Donald Mann undertook the construction of the Manitoba and Northwestern

---

[3] *Statutes of Canada,* 60-61 Vict., Chap. 5, 1897.
[4] *Ibid.,* Section (e).
[5] For a much fuller account of the history of the Crow's Nest Pass rates up to 1960, see E. P. Reid, *Statutory Grain Rates,* Royal Commission on Transportation, 1962, Vol. III, pp. 367-407.

Railway from Gladstone to Dauphin and Winnipegosis. From then on, through bond issues, they raised the capital to construct and acquire a network of lines in Manitoba. They built a line along the Dawson route to the lakehead. They obtained a charter to build a line to Prince Albert and thence to Edmonton. They took over from the Manitoba government a long-term lease of the Northern Pacific branch lines in Manitoba, in return for which Canadian Northern undertook to reduce general freight rates by 15 percent. The reduction included a corresponding drop in the Crow's Nest Pass rates on grain to the lakehead.[6] The completion of the Canadian Northern as a transcontinental line, and branch line construction and acquisition in western Canada continued up to 1916. The Ottawa-Port Arthur section of the Canadian Northern was completed on January 1, 1914. Its full access to the Dorchester Street station in Montreal, which required a tunnel under Mount Royal, was not completed until 1918.[7]

Many years previously Sir Wilfrid Laurier, as prime minister, had become preoccupied with railway policy and he sponsored the development of a northerly transcontinental route. At that time Sir Charles Rivers Wilson, president of the Grand Trunk, and his general manager, Charles Hays, had become interested in the extension of that railroad into western Canada. They envisaged a deal with Mackenzie and Mann, who were more noted as contractors and financiers than as railway operators. After preliminary unsuccessful negotiations to acquire the Canadian Northern properties, which would have joined the Canadian Northern and the Grand Trunk into a transcontinental system, Wilson and Hays negotiated in earnest with Sir Wilfrid on construction of a separate transcontinental route. Although Wilson and Hays were interested in constructing a line from Callander, Ontario, across northern Ontario north of the lakehead into Winnipeg, and thence through Saskatoon, Edmonton and Jasper to Port Simpson or Prince Rupert on the west coast, Sir Wilfrid favored a line from Moncton to Quebec, and thence by northern Quebec and northern Ontario through Sioux Lookout to Winnipeg. Although the Grand Trunk built the line from Moncton to Winnipeg, the federal government paid for it and leased the line to the railway. The western division, from Winnipeg to Prince Rupert was built by the Grand Trunk Pacific Railway Company, a subsidiary, under federal guarantee of construction bonds. The agreement was confirmed by passage of the national transcontinental act, assented to on July 18, 1903. The prairie section of the western division was completed by 1910, as was a branch to the lakehead.

The three railways, over a span of 25 years from 1885 to 1910, had built or acquired a myriad of branch lines through the western provinces which facilitated land settlement and served as a gathering system for shipment of grain to the lakehead.[8] The Pacific grain route through the ports of Vancouver, New Westminster and Prince Rupert awaited construction of the Panama canal and did not come into general use until after World War I.

[6]G. R. Stevens, *Canadian National Railways,* (Clark, Irwin, Toronto, 1962), Vol. II, pp. 43-56.

[7]For the cost to the federal and provincial governments in subsidies and land grants to the Canadian Northern Railway, see Stevens, *op.cit.,* p. 116.

[8]D. A. MacGibbon in *The Canadian Grain Trade,* MacMillan, Toronto, 1932, p. 40, summarized the expansion in the following terms:

HUDSON'S BAY COMPANY AND THE
NORTH-WEST TERRITORIES

At the time of confederation, the land lying between the Red River and the Rockies was the property of the Hudson's Bay Company. Ownership of this land was a pre-confederation issue, and the fathers of confederation were well aware that title to Rupert's land and the North-West territories must be acquired by the government of Canada if it were to be master of its own house. The lands, however, represented valuable property rights. Negotiations were conducted in London between representatives of the new government and the Hudson's Bay Company. The Canadian government passed enabling legislation in 1868,[9] and the agreement was confirmed by order in council of the British government on June 23, 1870, which had its own responsibility for legislation respecting the Hudson's Bay Company.[10] The order in council provided that upon surrender of title of Rupert's Land and the North-West Territories to the governor-general of Canada, the Canadian government would pay the company a sum of £300,000. In addition, the agreement provided that the land within the specified limits which surrounded the company's posts would be retained by the company and also that throughout the fertile belt bounded on the south by the United States boundary, on the west by the Rocky Mountains, on the north by the northern branch of the Saskatchewan River, and on the east by Lake Winnipeg and the Lake of the Woods, the company would retain title to one-twentieth of the total land. As the land surveys of Manitoba and the North-West Territories were completed, the Hudson's Bay Company lands were identified as sections 8 and 26 in each township of the fertile belt. Except for existing settlements along the Red River and for lands set aside for Indian reservations, the remainder of Rupert's Land became federal crown land.

NORTH-WEST TERRITORIES, MANITOBA AND
THE MOUNTED POLICE

To be ready for the projected takeover of the Hudson's Bay Company lands, the Canadian parliament passed an act to provide for the temporary government of that land.[11] The act named the land the "North-West Territories", and provided for the appointment of a lieutenant-governor

"In 1900 the total railway mileage in Manitoba amounted to 1,815 miles, and in the territories, to 1,901 miles. This represented the main line of the Canadian Pacific westward, several short railways in Manitoba and scarcely anything in the new provinces except lines from Regina to Prince Albert, and from Moose Jaw to the American boundary in the province of Saskatchewan, and rail connections in Alberta with the main line of the Canadian Pacific Railway from Lethbridge, Macleod and Edmonton. Fourteen years later, railway mileage for Manitoba was 4,076 miles, for Saskatchewan, 5,089 miles, and for Alberta, 2,545 miles, or a total for the three provinces, of 11,710 miles. All the main arteries had been constructed, or were in process of completion; there remained only to fill in here and there gaps in the railway net."

[9]See *Rupert's Land Act, Statutes of Canada,* 31-32, Vict., Chap. CV, assented to July 1, 1868.

[10]See *Charters, Statutes and Orders-in-Council, Etc., relating to the Hudson's Bay Company,* London, 1931, pp. 171-177.

[11]*Statutes of Canada,* 31-32 Vict., Chap. III, assented to 26th June, 1869.

whose responsibility was to administer the government of the territories under instructions issued from time to time by order in council. The lieutenant-governor was advised by an appointed council which had authority to appoint officials. The act was to have expired at the end of the next session of parliament, but it was amended and extended from time to time as new provinces were created, commencing with Manitoba.

The province of Manitoba was established by federal statute in 1870.[12] This act amended the 1869 act and provided for the government of the province, including appointment of a lieutenant-governor and an executive council, the election of a legislature, and representation in the senate and the house of commons. The boundaries of the province were defined, and its seat of government was located at Fort Garry.

While the foregoing acts provided for government of the North-West Territories, another act creating the North-West Mounted Police provided for the maintenance of law and order.[13] This was an essential prerequisite to land settlement in the wake of the Riel rebellion, and it contributed to the opening up of the west. The first recruiting officers of the new force travelled west in September, 1873.

EXPLORATION AND THE LAND SURVEYS

Much valuable information on the resources of the north-west had been gathered by explorers in the years preceding confederation. Captain John Palliser, an Englishman, had been commissioned in 1857 by the Royal Geographical Society to traverse the west and to report on its agricultural and mineral potential as well as upon possible transportation routes. Although Palliser reported on the fertility of the park belt, his name is historically associated with his description of the infertile triangle south of the Saskatchewan River. In the same year a party of three Canadians, George Gladman, a retired Hudson's Bay Company official, Henry Youle Hind, a geologist, and Simon James Dawson, a civil engineer, undertook a similar expedition. Still other explorers, Sandford Fleming, an engineer, John Macoun, a botanist, and George Grant, a minister, made expeditions through the west. Macoun's contribution was his claim that Palliser's triangle was in fact a fertile plain amenable to agriculture.   Dawson's name became identified with the first attempt to establish an all-Canadian transportation route from Thunder Bay to Fort Garry. John W. Dafoe described the route:

> Communication by the south, through the United States, was regarded, however, by the Canadian authorities as a mere makeshift until direct communication with the east could be secured over Canadian territory. The first attempt to secure this was the opening of the Dawson route. This was planned by Simon J. Dawson, who had been chief of staff for Henry Youle Hind in his exploratory journey through the west in the late fifties. This amphibious highway ran from Thunder Bay to Fort Garry, a distance of 499 miles. Of this, only 131 miles were covered by wagon road, the rest of the

[12]*Statutes of Canada - First Parliament,* 1870. 33 Vict., Chap. III, assented to 12th May, 1870.

[13]See *Act respecting the Administration of Justice and for the establishment of a Police Force in the North-West Territories, Statutes of Canada,* 36 Vict., Chap. 35, assented to 23rd May, 1873.

route being made up of water stretches. Although the Dominion government spent something like a million and a quarter on the road, it was not a success. The few settlers who used it suffered great hardships, and it was finally abandoned. Not until the completion of the railroad between Winnipeg and Lake Superior, over ten years later, did the currents of trade and commerce between east and west flow through Canadian channels.[14]

In 1869, Dawson also reported to the minister of public works the results of his survey of a route for a transcontinental railroad.[15] The land survey, however, was the responsibility of the secretary of state department until the department of the interior was established in 1873 and the dominion lands branch was transferred to it.[16] The surveyor-general of the dominion lands branch was Lt. Col. J. Stoughton Dennis who, with a party of surveyors, arrived at Fort Garry in August, 1869, and commenced field work at Pembina in September to determine the exact position of the 49th parallel. Dennis's detailed survey reports are to be found in appendices to the annual reports of the secretary of state and of the department of the interior.[17] Dafoe described the progress of the survey in the following account:

While these preliminary steps were being taken, to make access to the new Canadian territory easier, the government was steadily pursuing its object of securing control of the public domain, in readiness for the expected immigration. The Hudson's Bay control having been removed by the transfer of the lands to the Dominion government, there existed no legal means of acquiring lands or of securing legal transfers by purchase. Pending the necessary legislation and the surveying of the lands, the Dominion government announced that bona fide settlers would have the rights to their lands recognized upon completion of the survey; which resulted in large amounts of land being taken up by the squatters in 1871. To meet the demands of the half-breeds who, by reason of their Indian descent, had an interest in the soil, the Dominion government set aside 1,400,000 acres as a half-breed reserve. With the summer of 1871 the surveying of the prairie began in earnest. The narrow river lot surveys were recognized and legalized, but for the new surveys a block system was adapted from the Western States. The unit was the section of 640 acres, one mile square, divided into four quarter-sections of 160 acres. Each township was six miles square, divided into thirty-six sections, which were numbered from the right-hand bottom corner across the base of the township and back again. The survey began at the international boundary by the Winnipeg meridian, which divided the ranges of townships into east and west. The ranges from this meridian were numbered east and west, and the townships north from the international boundary. The whole country was thus laid out in checker-boards, by a regular system which made location and reference easy. Due provision was made for the jog resulting from the narrowing of the meridians as the lines ran north. These surveys were pushed forward with so much zeal that the whole of the Province of Manitoba and a good portion of the adjacent territories were surveyed and ready for settlement by the autumn of 1873. The survey in Manitoba and the older portions of the territories allowed a ninety-nine feet road appropriation round each section; but the new survey which has been in operation now for some years, gives only a sixty-six feet road round each two

---

[14]J.W. Dafoe, *Canada and its Provinces*, Vol. XX, Toronto, 1914, p. 288.
[15]*Sessional Papers*, 33 Vict., (No. 12) A. 1870, Report dated May 1st, 1869.
[16]*Statutes of Canada*, 36 Vict., Chap. IV, which came into force July 1st, 1873.
[17]See *Reports of the Secretary of State*, 1868-1877.

adjoining sections. This system of survey has been a great success, and has been a considerable factor in encouraging settlement in the West. Of the thirty-six sections in each township, two, sections 8 and 26, were from the outset given to the Hudson's Bay Company, in conformity with the terms of the transfer. Subsequently, by an act passed in 1879, two additional sections in each township, Nos. 11 and 29, were reserved from homesteading and set apart as an endowment for common school education in the provinces.[18]

WHEAT VARIETIES

The contributions of Red Fife and Marquis wheat to the development of the west were especially significant. David Fife, a Scottish immigrant farming in Peterborough County, Ontario, in the 1840's, secured a sample of a Galician wheat variety which he reproduced. Quality selection was common among Ontario farmers of those days, who used their names to identify the wheat they sold as seed. Because of its hardiness, use of the Red Fife variety spread through Ontario and eventually to Manitoba by way of Wisconsin, Minnesota and the Dakotas. The recent introduction of the roller process in milling, which operated best with a hard wheat, greatly enhanced the demand for Red Fife wheat which had not only a hard kernel but also a high gluten content. It was this variety which interested Canadian and British millers, and which helped to develop an overseas market for Canadian wheat. The first shipment of wheat from Manitoba was made in 1876. This was the parcel purchased for use as seed in Ontario. The first shipment to Britain occurred in 1878. These left Winnipeg via the Red River for transit through the United States. The first shipment of wheat to Britain via the Canadian route through the lakehead was made in 1883.

In 1886 the federal government established the dominion experimental farm system and appointed as its first director, Dr. William Saunders, a pharmacist-botanist who as early as 1868 had become interested in the plant breeding of wheat. Prior to appointment as director, Dr. Saunders had been commissioned by the government to report on experimental research methods already introduced in the United States. Under his direction, experimental farms were established at Ottawa in the east, and at Brandon, Indian Head and Agassiz in the west, where Dr. Saunders sent his son Percy, in 1892, to cross Red Fife with Indian and other world varieties in continuation of the work under western climatic conditions which the father had been conducting at Ottawa.

Cross-breeding was continued for years by Dr. William Saunders and his sons, Percy and Charles. The latter was eventually knighted for his identification of the Marquis variety which, as he recorded in his 1904 notebook, was "not to be retained at all unless it is *earlier* or *stronger* than Red Fife." This new wheat came into general use in 1909; it has served since as the standard of comparison in wheat breeding. Its appearance and high milling characteristics established Marquis as a top premium wheat, and its early maturity made possible the extension of wheat cultivation to the northern limits of the fertile belt.[19]

[18]*Canada and its Provinces*, Vol. XX, pp. 288-289.
[19]J. W. Morrison, *Marquis Wheat — A Triumph of Scientific Endeavor*, Agricultural History, Vol. 34, No. 4, pp. 182-188.

GRAIN REGULATION

The antecedents of the Canada grain act predate confederation and the opening of the west. The parent legislation was a simple act of the legislative council and assembly of Upper Canada passed in 1835, which established standard weights for the different kinds of grain and provided that "the bushel shall be taken and intended to mean the weight of a bushel as regulated by this Act, and not a bushel in measure, . . ."[20] The standard weights of the Winchester bushel were set at 60 pounds for wheat, 56 pounds for rye, 48 pounds for barley and 34 pounds for oats, which have remained in effect through the years. The 1835 act was re-enacted and slightly amended by the legislative council and assembly in 1853.[21]

The first legislation concerning the inspection of wheat and other grain was passed in 1863.[22] This act provided for appointment of boards of examiners by boards of trade in eastern cities where they existed. The boards of examiners were responsible for appointment of inspectors and assistant inspectors, for approving standard samples and for arbitrating disputes. Standard qualities of wheat and other grains were defined. The wheat grades for Nos. 1 and 2 White and Red Winters, and for Extra Spring, No. 1 Spring, and No. 2 Spring, were defined. For example, the act provided that Extra Spring "shall be sound, plump, and free from admixture of other Grain, and weigh not less than 61 lbs, per Winchester bushel." Inspectors were required to issue bills of inspection, but inspection was not compulsory.

The first federal grain inspection legislation was passed in 1874.[23] Its full title was "An Act to make better provision, extending to the whole of the Dominion of Canada, respecting the Inspection of certain Staple Articles of Canadian produce." Its provisions covered a list of staples, and those concerning grain remained essentially the same as in the 1863 act. Boards of examiners were authorized for nine cities in eastern Canada and the inspectors they appointed reported to the minister of inland revenue. The grades of spring wheat were defined as follows:

No. 1 Spring Wheat shall be plump and well cleaned,

No. 2 Spring Wheat shall be sound, reasonably clean, and weighing not less than fifty-eight pounds to the measured Imperial bushel,

No. 3 Spring Wheat shall be reasonably clean, not good enough for No. 2, weighing not less than fifty-five and a half pounds to the measured Imperial bushel.[24]

For some unexplained reason the test weight for the top grade was omitted.

This act was amended by the general inspection act of 1886,[25] which authorized appointment of boards of examiners in Winnipeg, Port Arthur and Victoria, as well as in the eastern cities, with power to appoint inspectors. Provision was made for a chief inspector whose responsibilities

[20] *Statutes of the Province of Upper Canada,* 5 William IV, Chap. VII, assented to 16th April, 1835.

[21] *Statutes of the Province of Canada,* 16 Vict., Cap. CXCIII, assented to 14th June, 1853.

[22] *Ibid.,* 26 Vict., Cap. III, assented to 5th May, 1863.

[23] *Statutes of Canada,* 37 Vict., 1874, Chap. 45, assented to 26th May, 1874.

[24] *Ibid.*

[25] *Revised Statutes of Canada,* 49 Vict., 1886, Chap. 99.

included arbitration of disputes referred to him by the boards of examiners. Manitoba grades based on Red Fife wheat were established for the first time by this act which provided, for example, that "Extra Manitoba hard wheat shall be sound and well cleaned, weighing not less than sixty-two pounds to the bushel, and shall be composed of Red Fife wheat grown in Manitoba or the North-West Territories of Canada."

Section 45 of the act became a matter of contention. The section provided that uniform standards of grain be set by representatives of boards of examiners who were to meet in Toronto to choose samples by which inspectors of grain throughout Canada were to be governed. MacGibbon refers to a dispute which arose in 1888 over the standards for Manitoba wheat recommended by the western members of the standards board meeting in Toronto.[26] The board could not agree and no standards for Manitoba wheat were set in that year.

In response to western representations, the government introduced a bill to repeal section 45 of the 1886 act and to replace it with a new section which related the provisions to both eastern and western Canada. The new section 45 (3) provided that

> The standards in respect of grain grown west of Port Arthur shall be chosen by a Board of persons not exceeding eleven in number, annually appointed by the Governor in Council, . . . selected from the boards of examiners . . . resident at Port Arthur or west thereof. . . . By standards so chosen, inspectors of grain throughout Canada shall be governed in the work of inspection as respects grain grown west of Port Arthur.[27]

In this manner the Winnipeg board of trade, which had taken the initiative in pressing for the change, established western control over western grain standards for the first time.

From then until 1900, there were three additional amendments to the general inspection act. The first arose out of the need for special grading provisions to deal with situations where, because of special conditions, only a small portion of the crop was eligible for the regular grades. An 1891 amendment provided that "if a considerable portion of the crop of any one year has any marked characteristics which exclude it, to the prejudice of the producer, from the grade to which it otherwise belongs, the examiners may establish a special grade, and choose a sample of such grade to be the standard therefor."[28] As a safeguard, the governor in council was given authority to veto standards so set.

An amendment to the grain inspection act in 1892 concerned grain only insofar as the general provisions affecting the choice and distribution of standard samples were further clarified.[29] The amendment read:

> 2. Section fifteen of the said Act is hereby repealed, and the following substituted therefor:
>
> "15. The Governor in Council may appoint such persons as he deems properly qualified for the purpose of choosing samples of any of the said articles subject to inspection under this Act. The standards by which the inspectors of such articles throughout Canada shall be governed in the work

[26]D. A. MacGibbon, *op. cit.,* pp. 32-33.
[27]*Statutes of Canada,* 52 Vict., Chap. 16, assented to 2nd May, 1889.
[28]*Ibid.,* 54-55 Vict., Chap. 48, assented to 28 August, 1891.
[29]*Ibid.,* 55-56 Vict., Chap. 23, assented to 9 July, 1892.

of inspection; and the persons so appointed shall distribute a portion of each of the standards so chosen to the councils of the boards of trade of the several cities in and for which inspectors of such articles have been appointed and to such elsewhere as are designated for the purpose by the Governor in Council;"

In 1899 another amendment to the general inspection act revised the statutory spring wheat grades, the top grades of which were defined as follows:

Extra Manitoba hard wheat shall consist of wheat grown wholly in Manitoba or the North-West Territories of Canada and shall weigh not less than sixty-two pounds per bushel, shall be plump, sound and well cleaned, and shall contain not less than eighty-five per cent of hard Red Fife wheat.

No. 1 Manitoba hard shall consist wholly of wheat grown in Manitoba or the North-West Territories of Canada and shall be plump, sound, and well cleaned, weighing not less than sixty pounds to the bushel, and shall be composed of at least seventy-five per cent of hard Red Fife wheat.

No. 1 Manitoba northern wheat shall consist wholly of wheat grown in Manitoba or the North-West Territories of Canada, and shall be sound and well cleaned, weighing not less than sixty pounds to the bushel and shall be composed of at least fifty per cent of hard Red Fife wheat.[30]

The schedule to the act terminated the inspection divisions of Winnipeg, Brandon and Port Arthur and created the inspection district of Manitoba. The new district included Port Arthur, Ontario west thereof, Manitoba and the North-West Territories, or the western division as it is now known. The schedule also provided for the first compulsory inspection at Winnipeg or Emerson of all wheat grown in the North-West Territories and Manitoba passing through these points. The act remained under the jurisdiction of the minister of inland revenue.

LINE ELEVATOR COMPANIES

The first wheat shipment from Manitoba to Toronto was made as a result of the spring wheat crop failure in Ontario when R. C. Steele, founding partner of a seed company, travelled to Manitoba in the autumn of 1876 to purchase seed. He secured only 857 bushels which was transported to Fisher's Landing, Minnesota, on the Red River and thence by rail to Duluth, by water to Sarnia, and by rail to Toronto. By 1879 when Winnipeg was connected by rail to Minneapolis, isolated commercial shipments of wheat from Manitoba began, and they were established on a continuous basis after the Canadian Pacific line was completed from Winnipeg to Port Arthur in 1883. The first lake shipment from Port Arthur was effected by James Richardson & Sons, before the terminal elevators had been completed. The Canadian Pacific built two terminals at the lakehead which were ready for use in 1884. Before that time grain was shipped in bags. The introduction of bulk handling of grain coincided with the construction of country elevators and the railway connection to the lakehead.[31]

Methods of loading bulk grain to railway cars at country points were adopted from those already in use in the United States. The earliest structures were flat warehouses which provided covered storage bins at

[30]*Ibid.,* 62-63 Vict., Chap. 25, assented to 11 August, 1899.
[31]MacGibbon, *op. cit.,* pp. 25-28.

trackside but which lacked any machinery for elevation. Usually the floor of the flat warehouse was level with the floor of the boxcars into which bagged grain was placed by hand or bulk grain shovelled. The first grain elevators were powered by blind horses circling a structure of primitive type, built by flour milling companies.

Although terminal elevators had elevation machinery, the first of these being built in Buffalo in 1841, it was not until the endless cup conveyor, called a "leg", was invented that the country elevator as it is now known came into existence. Elevators powered by gasoline or steam with cleaning machinery were already in use in the United States. Their efficiency in loading cars and speeding up their turn around, thereby economizing on the use of limited railway rolling stock, attracted the attention of the Canadian Pacific Railway. Although the railway might have built and operated its own elevator system, its limited capital resources induced it to attract outside capital into country elevator construction.[32] In the process, the company defined a "standard" elevator as having not less than 25,000 bushels of capacity, equipped with cleaning and elevation machinery and powered by a gasoline or steam engine. It offered a free lease of site on railway sidings to companies prepared to build such elevators. This offer was accompanied by an undertaking by the railway not to allow competitive loading from flat warehouses or from farmers' wagons at points where elevators were located.[33]

The first firms attracted into this business were flour mills. The Ogilvie Milling Company built the first country elevator in Canada at Gretna in 1881, and continued with the construction of a line of country elevators. The Lake of the Woods Milling Company was founded in 1887. George Stephen and Sir William Van Horne of the Canadian Pacific Railway were among the original subscribers to its share capital. The mill built at Keewatin was supplied through its own line of country elevators. James Richardson & Sons and the Bawlf Grain company are representative of firms whose founders first established themselves as grain merchants, and came to appreciate the advantage of adding a line of country elevators to their operations, which they did after 1900. James Richardson founded his firm at Kingston, Ontario, in 1857. It had the distinction of moving the first shipment of grain via the newly completed Canadian Pacific line from Winnipeg to the lakehead in the autumn of 1883. The grain had to be tranferred by wagon from railway cars at the lakehead to a lake vessel because the first terminal elevator built by the Canadian Pacific Railway at the lakehead was not yet completed. This first shipment of Manitoba Red Fife wheat arrived in Liverpool early in 1884. Similarly, the N. Bawlf Grain Company began as a small grain, hay and feed store which Nicholas Bawlf opened at Winnipeg in 1881. He established a reputation as a grain merchant and became one of the founders of the Winnipeg grain exchange.

[32]W. C. Clark found it remarkable that the C.P.R. was prepared to farm the elevator business out, while it retained in its own hands almost all other services subsidiary to railroading. See *The Country Elevator in the Canadian West*, (Queen's University, Kingston, 1916), pp. 4-5.

[33]*Report of the Royal Commission on Shipment and Transportation of Grain*, 63 Vict., Sessional Paper No. 81a, A. 1900, p. 7.

Apart from the line elevators operated by the two mills, the Northern Elevator Company founded in 1893 was the first line elevator company to be formed in response to the railway's solicitation. It was subsequently acquired by the Peavey interests and integrated into National Grain (1968) Limited which, in turn, was recently purchased by Cargill Grain Canada Limited. It was followed by formation of the Farmers' Elevator Company in 1896, by the Manitoba Elevator Company and the Dominion Elevator Company in 1897, and by the partnership of Bready, Love and Tryon in 1899.[34] These were the companies which came to be referred to in the contemporary press and in parliamentary debates as the "syndicates", and their association as the "syndicate of syndicates", because of the monopoly loading-rights conferred upon them by the railway.[35]

The report of the royal grain commission listed the number of country elevators in operation in the Manitoba inspection district in 1900 and their ownership as follows:[36]

Three line elevator companies[37]	206
The Lake of the Woods Milling Company	50
The Ogilvie Milling Company	45
Farmers' Elevator Company	26
Individual millers and grain dealers	120
	447[38]

After 1900, a new wave of country elevator construction followed the opening up of the Canadian Northern Railway. As the Canadian Pacific had done, Messrs. Mackenzie and Mann aggressively sought investment in elevator construction and approached, among others, the Peavey and Searle interests in Minneapolis. An interesting account appears in *The Peavey Story*[39] of the way in which Canadian Northern placed a special car at the disposal of Frank T. Heffelfinger and Frederick D. Wells, sons-in-law of

[34]H. G. L. Strange, *A Short History of Prairie Agriculture*, (Searle, 1954), p. 39.
[35]See pp. 26-27.
[36]*Report on The Royal Commission*, 63 Vict., Sessional Paper No. 81a, A. 1900, p. 9.
[37]The Report does not identify the names of these three companies. However, the *Annual Report of the Winnipeg Grain and Produce Exchange, 1900*, published a list of country elevators and their capacities, among which those of the Lake of the Woods and the Manitoba Elevator Company do not appear as such. By then the Bready, Love and Tryon elevators had been renamed the Winnipeg Elevator Company. According to this list the larger companies were as follows:

	Standard Elevators of 25,000 bu. Capacity or more	Elevators of less than 25,000 bu. Capacity	Ware- houses
Northern Elevator Co.	67	25	13
Dominion Elevator Co.	50	14	12
Winnipeg Elevator Co.	35	10	—
Ogilvie Milling Co.	32	12	—
Farmers' Elevator Co.	25	1	2

[38]The early records of the Canadian Grain Commission listed only 421 country elevators in 1900.
[39]Published by The Peavey Company, Minneapolis, 1963.

Frank Peavey. Their tour of the Canadian Northern lines led to formation of the British-American Elevator Company Limited in 1906. This company operated, as did the Searle Grain Company, on Canadian Northern lines. Later, in 1909, the Peavey interests formed the National Grain Company to operate on Canadian Pacific lines. They also acquired six other companies which were eventually consolidated into the National Grain Company Limited in 1940. Other companies formed in the earlier period included The Alberta Pacific Grain Company, The Pioneer Grain Company, which was one of the Richardson enterprises, The Norris Grain Company, The Paterson Grain Company, The British Co-operative Wholesale Society, The Scottish Co-operative Wholesale Society, Parrish & Heimbecker, and the McCabe Brothers Grain Company. At one stage or another, all of these companies became incorporated.

In the period of the 1920's a series of mergers took place, including that of the Reliance Grain Company, which was formed in 1927 to take over the Smith-Murphy Grain Company, the Province Elevator Company and the Reliance Terminal Elevator at Port Arthur. The Western Grain Company was organized in 1928 and merged the operations of six companies. In 1929 the Federal Grain Company Limited took over nine grain companies and the country elevators operated by the Maple Leaf Milling Company. Another merger led to formation of the Canadian Consolidated Grain Company.

A distinguishing feature of the line elevator companies is their family character which is well illustrated by the names associated with them. For example, great grandsons of James Richardson, who founded James Richardson & Sons at Kingston, Ontario, in 1857, have continued to operate the firm of that name. The firm was incorporated in 1909. When the Honourable James A. Richardson joined the federal cabinet in 1968 he resigned from his position as chief executive officer of the firm; it is now headed by his brother, George T. Richardson. For many years the Richardson firm operated a large line of country elevators, and still does through its subsidiary, the Pioneer Grain Company Limited.

Nicholas Bawlf, who founded a grain company, gradually extended his operations into the country elevator business which was carried on by his son, W. R. Bawlf.

The Honourable Norman M. Paterson, founder of the N. M. Paterson and Sons Limited, still sits in the senate today, and his company is directed by his sons, Donald and John Paterson. George Heffelfinger, grandson of Frank T. Heffelfinger, one of the founders of the National Grain Company in Canada, was president of National Grain (1968) Limited, until the company was sold to Cargill. He is also a great grandson of Frank Peavey, founder of the Peavey company. William B. Parrish, secretary-treasurer of Parrish and Heimbecker Limited today, is a grandson of William L. Parrish who was a charter member of the Winnipeg grain exchange and later a co-founder of the firm in 1909. Fred W. Parrish, a son of William L., and father of William B., was also a director of the firm. Herbert C. Heimbecker, president of the firm, is a son of Clayton W. Heimbecker who served as a director, and also a nephew of Norman Heimbecker, one of the co-founders.

TABLE 1:1
LICENSED COUNTRY ELEVATORS BY COMPANIES, 1971 AND 1975

LINE ELEVATOR COMPANIES	August 1, 1971	August 1, 1975
Federal Grain Limited	1,092	—
Pioneer Grain Company Limited	435	444
National Grain Limited	308	—
Cargill Grain Company Limited	—	267
N.M. Paterson & Sons Limited	94	90
Parrish & Heimbecker Limited	62	69
Inter-Ocean Grain Company Limited	25	—
Ellison Milling and Elevator Company Limited	18	2
Scottish Co-operative Wholesale Society Limited	9	—
Other licensed companies	14	20
Sub-total	2,057	892
PRODUCER-OWNED COMPANIES		
United Grain Growers Limited	793	720
Manitoba Pool Elevators	314	298
Saskatchewan Wheat Pool	1,181	1,436
Alberta Wheat Pool	504	818
Sub-total	2,792	3,272
Total	4,849	4,164

SOURCE: *Grain Elevators in Canada, 1971-72 and 1975-76,* compiled by the Canadian Grain Commission.

The Searle family, who commenced operating in Canada after becoming established in the United States, is still represented by Stewart A. Searle, Sr., in Winnipeg, who is the son of Augustus L. Searle of Minneapolis. Sons-in-law of Augustus L. Searle, Norman L. Leach and J. M. Gilchrist, were associated with Stewart A. Searle, Sr., in the Searle Grain Company of Winnipeg. The Searle Grain Company and the Alberta Pacific Grain Company were merged with Federal Grain Limited in 1967, which brought the Searle family into association with the Sellers family. Stewart A. Searle, Sr., and Henry E. Sellers became honorary chairmen, A. Searle Leach, chairman, George H. Sellers, president, and Stewart A. Searle, Jr., executive vice-president of the reconstituted Federal Grain Company Limited before it sold its elevator facilities to the Pools. This firm had as its president for many years, Henry E. Sellers, father of George, who established himself as a grain merchant and became interested in several line elevator companies which were amalgamated into Federal Grain Limited in 1929.

The company amalgamations, which had proceeded rapidly in the 1920's, were resumed after the second world war, as exemplified by the case of Federal Grain Limited just mentioned.

Historically, the line elevator companies have made a unique contribution to the industry. They were the first to provide elevator facilities in the west. Their experience in finding avenues of profitability by combining country and terminal elevator storage and handling operations with the merchandising function was emulated by the farmer-owned companies as they came into operation. By the time the pool elevator system had reached maturity in the late twenties, the farmer-owned companies, including United Grain Growers Limited, owned about 38 percent of the total number of country elevators. Since World War II, the farmer-owned share rose to as much as 58 percent in 1971. Then, with the sale in March, 1972, of Federal Grain Limited's grain assets to the three pools, the figure reached 79 percent. Thus, for the first time, the line elevator companies are in a distinctly residual position in the merchandising and handling of western grain.

Table 1:1 shows the number of licensed country elevators by companies, as at August 1, 1971, and 1975. The table reflects the Federal Grain sale to the pools in March, 1972, the sale of Inter-Ocean Grain Company Limited later that year to the Pioneer Grain Company Limited, and the National Grain Limited to Cargill Grain Company Limited in 1974.

WINNIPEG GRAIN EXCHANGE AND THE CLEARING ASSOCIATION

Heads of the grain merchandising and elevator companies became members of the Winnipeg board of trade which took steps to form a grain exchange. W. A. Mackintosh describes the origins of summerfallow and of the grain exchange almost in the same breath:

> As early as 1881 a Grain Exchange was established by a few commission merchants,[6] but it did not survive the bad crops of the middle of the decade which, however, had the good result of improving methods of cultivation.[7] With the re-establishment of the Grain Exchange in 1887 and its incorporation in 1891,[8] it may be said that the Canadian West began to assume importance as a wheat producing area even though the total production given in the census of 1890 did not quite reach 17 million bushels.[40]

Although the Winnipeg grain exchange had been in continuous operation since 1887, its function was that of a trading center for transactions in cash grain until steps were taken in 1903 to organize a futures market. Trading commenced in options for future delivery on January 29, 1904. Dr. Mackintosh had indicated that futures trading had commenced in 1903, but it was only in process of organization at that stage. When actual trading in futures began, the *Manitoba Free Press* described modestly the event: "Trade was a little stimulated by the opening of the local option board today, in advance of February 1, as originally proposed. There were not many transactions, however."[41]

[40]W.A. Mackintosh, *Agricultural Cooperation in Western Canada*, (Queen's University, 1924), p. 5. Mackintosh's footnote references:

[6]Begg, *Ten Years in Winnipeg*, p.170, cited E. Cora Hind, *The Grain Trade: The Prairie Provinces of Canada*, (London, 1914).

[7]More or less accidentally the practice of "summer fallowing" was started. Some farmers of the Indian Head and Qu'Appelle districts were assigned transport duty with the force sent out to suppress the Rebellion of 1885 and returned too late to put in the crops. During the remaining summer they tilled their land for next year's harvest and found the advantage of "summer fallowing" in a return of 23 bushels to the acre when the crop generally was a failure. W. J. Rutherford, "Economic Resources of Saskatchewan," *Canada and its Provinces*, Vol. XX, p. 560.

[8]*Statutes of Manitoba*, 54, Vict., c. 31, 1891. A Futures Market was opened in 1903 (previously "hedging" had been carried on through Minneapolis and Chicago), and a Clearing House was opened the same year. *Statutes of Manitoba*, 3 Ed. VII, c. 70, 1903.

[41]*Manitoba Free Press*, January 30, 1904, (reporting the market on Friday, January 29, 1904.)

The importance of futures trading to the development of the industry can scarcely be overstated. Use of futures contracts reduced the price risk involved in the purchase and sale of cash wheat, and thereby reduced the margins which the elevator companies or other buyers charged to producers. Such reductions were possible because the price fluctuations in futures contracts tended to move in harmony with the fluctuations in cash grain prices. Thus, by selling futures in the same quantity as their cash grain purchases, merchants could "hedge" the latter and avoid price risk to the extent that if prices of cash grain fell and were sold at a loss, it could be offset by a corresponding profit on the buying back of the futures contracts at a lower price than they had earlier been sold. In the reverse manner, a profit on the sale of cash grain would be foregone if prices rose. Because of the price security afforded by the futures market to the merchandising of grain, the banks could safely lend money to the elevator companies to finance their purchases of grain in the country, with the hedged grain serving as a stable collateral for the loans. The contribution to the efficiency of grain merchandising was considerable. By competition, these savings were reflected back to the producer.

To facilitate operation of the futures market, the Winnipeg grain exchange organized the Winnipeg grain and produce clearing association whose membership was open to the members of the exchange. The function of the clearing association included daily clearing of the members' long and short positions in the various grain futures. Payments from or to the members were required according to the positions held. The totals of members' long and short positions remained in balance, so that the clearing association carried no position. Because the risk of daily price fluctuations was small in relation to the total value of the futures contracts, the association permitted members to carry their accounts on margin at prescribed rates. But at the daily clearing, members had to deposit funds to maintain the required margins, or could withdraw funds if their margin requirements were exceeded. Also, when the delivery period fell due, a buyer of futures could either sell them or demand delivery of cash grain. A seller, in turn, could buy the futures back or exercise his right to deliver cash grain. By the end of each delivery period, all outstanding futures obligations had to be liquidated by offsetting purchase or sale or by delivery. Mr. Frank O. Fowler who was instrumental in organizing the clearing association, became its manager and presided over its operations for many years.

Until the facilities of the Winnipeg clearing house were provided in 1904, any hedging of Manitoba wheat in the Minneapolis and Chicago markets, where they were not deliverable on the contracts, was at best a makeshift price protection. The prices of such contracts reflected the demand and supply conditions for other types of wheat. Thus, the magnitude of price risk to Canadian grain firms was greatly reduced by the commencement of futures trading at Winnipeg in 1904. This safety factor, in turn, helped to attract more firms into the business. "Hedge or sell all grain as soon as it is bought, take in the hedge instantly when the grain is sold" became a business axiom.[42]

[42]The Peavey Story, p. 18.

Although the futures market helped to maximize the net return to producers obtainable from the market price on any given day, it offered producers no guarantee of price stability for any longer period. Futures trading did, in fact, help to reduce the magnitude of price fluctuations, but it reflected promptly any change in demand and supply conditions. Thus, producers had no assurance of price stability through the crop-marketing season unless they decided at any given day's price to hedge their harvests by selling futures until their crops were delivered. The tendency among producers to "miss the market" gave rise to a demand for alternative marketing systems. Such alternatives were developed many years later but, in the meantime, the futures marketing system made a unique contribution through the earlier years in the marketing of western grain.

SETTLEMENT OF WESTERN CANADA

In its earlier stages, land settlement in western Canada was slow to develop in the wake of the elaborate provisions made for it. As already mentioned, when the dominion government took over the Hudson's Bay Company lands there were no legal means by which settlers could acquire or purchase land pending legislation and the survey, although the government did undertake to protect the land rights of bona fide settlers upon completion of the survey, with the result that settlement got under way in 1871. Dafoe has provided a vivid description of the reasons for the slow rate of settlement over the next ten years:

> With the surveys completed and the Indian and half-breed titles removed, the land became available for settlement. The lure of free land brought immigration to Western Canada within a year of the transfer. On April 26, 1871, eight men, after a four weeks' journey from Ontario, arrived in Winnipeg, having floated down the Red River in a scow — the first ripple of that mighty flood which was later to transform the prairie. For many years, however, settlement was retarded by the constant changing and restricting of the land regulations, due principally to the meddlesomeness of officials in Ottawa, who failed entirely to appreciate the difficulties inherent in the settlement of a new and remote country. The public domain, while open to settlement, had certain preliminary charges to carry. First there was the half-breed scrip, to which allusion has already been made. Then there was the heavy burden of providing funds for building the Canadian Pacific Railway. The government changed its railroad policy from time to time, but all policies had one unchanging feature; this was that the cost of the road was to be met out of the proceeds of the sales of lands in Western Canada. All sorts of whimsical and fantastic plans for securing the necessary money were promulgated, only to be abandoned.

> The bureaucrats at Ottawa by these means plagued the settlers and checked immigration, to the incalculable injury of the West. Some of these progressive follies may be here noted. The Railway Act of 1874 provided for locking up large blocks of land along the proposed railway route, in which settlement was absolutely prohibited. As this included most of the land then available for settlement, there resulted, inevitably, a large amount of squatting. It took

three years of vigorous agitation before the government could be induced to recognize the right of these squatters to buy their farms. Then the government provision was that each squatter must pay an instalment of a dollar per acre and become responsible for the balance of any price which the government might see fit to fix. This gave rise to a second agitation, which continued until more reasonable provisions were conceded. In 1879 the Macdonald government, then new to office, evolved its famous plan of land belts. A series of five belts, along each side of the main line of the railway, covering, in all, a strip of country 140 miles wide, were set aside, with descending rates for pre-emption and purchase, with the right to homestead on even numbers. This evoked furious protests, again compelling modifications. Then the government decided to set aside one hundred million acres of land as reserve for building the Canadian Pacific Railway. All ungranted lands within twenty miles of the main line were withdrawn from homesteading. Indeed, the settlers had no peace until, finally, after the arrangement had been made with the Canadian Pacific Railway syndicate, the government reserved all the odd-numbered sections throughout the West for railway purposes, and threw all the remaining, even-numbered sections open for homesteading. These blunders undoubtedly kept the settlement of the country back for ten years, and were responsible for much subsequent ill-feeling and agitation.[43]

By 1875, however, a sizable settlement from eastern Canada located in the Pembina Mountain district 80 miles south-west of Winnipeg. Later that summer, 6,000 Mennonites took up homesteads in the valley between Pembina and the Red River. These were the first European immigrants to settle in western Canada. They were German Quakers who had migrated to Russia and had later left that country when their exemption from military service was withdrawn. The 1881 census showed that the population of Manitoba had grown from 18,995 in 1871 to 62,660, while Winnipeg had increased from a hamlet of 200 souls to 7,985. The English-speaking settlers, who had numbered barely 5,000 when the territory was taken over, amounted in 1881 to 38,182; while the beginnings of foreign settlements were shown by the record in the census returns of 8,652 Germans, 773 Icelanders, 250 Scandinavians, and 24 Russians and Poles. In the territories there was a population of 56,446, of which 49,742 were Indians, 2,896 half-breeds, and about 4,000 whites. By 1881 the homestead entries had reached the total of 13,750, while the area surveyed and ready for settlement amounted to about 26,000,000 acres.[44]

A short-lived land boom developed around Winnipeg and along the existing railway lines in 1881, but it collapsed in 1882. In the depression that followed, low grain prices were a deterrent to settlement, as was the rebellion of 1885, and also the early frost of 1888. Even after the completion of the main line of the Canadian Pacific Railway the rate of migration remained slow, and the company suffered financial hardship as a result. To stimulate the flow, the company established a colonization department.

After its first unsuccessful attempt to finance migration from Ireland, the railway succeeded in bringing out colonies of Hungarians, Danes, Germans, Mennonites, Moravians and Ruthenians.[45] Dafoe adds that "the first American immigration came in 1896, when 142 homestead entries were

[43] *Canada and its Provinces,* Vol. XX, pp. 291-293.
[44] *Ibid.,* p. 298.
[45] *Ibid.,* p. 302.

made by residents of the United States. The influx of Americans grew with such rapidity that in 1901 it was estimated that there were already 50,000 Americans of all ages in Western Canada."[46]

Patton also referred to the federal government's homestead regulations as a deterrent to settlement, and observed that:

> The United States, with its earlier national momentum, with its more accessible resources and more attractive climate, and with its high tide of enterprise and the expansion following the Civil War, dominated the calculations of the great majority of European people desirous of seeking opportunities in the New World. The surveyed homestead areas of Western Canada were bound to remain relatively vacant until the free and more accessible wheat land of the American Northwest had become fairly completely appropriated.[47]

The federal government also pursued an active immigration policy. As minister of the interior in the Laurier government, the Honourable Clifford Sifton established a reputation for his vigorous immigration activities. He greatly augmented the network of Canadian immigration agencies in the United States and abroad, and the government made sizable expenditures on advertising and literature. These efforts generated an influx of American settlers which the government turned to good advantage by stimulating competitive migration from eastern Canada and from the British Isles. In the first decade of the present century, the numbers of immigrants gained momentum and reached a peak in 1913 and 1914, after which the inflow subsided, but by that time the primary settlement of the western provinces had been accomplished.

The results of the migration, its ethnic pattern and its contribution to wheat cultivation which established Canada as the leading exporter of wheat following World War I, are summarized from census data. Table 1:2 shows the expansion of grain cultivation by census periods from 1901 to 1921. Table 1:3 shows the growth of population from 1871 to 1921. Tables 1:4 and 1:5 describe the origins of the population as reported in the 1921 census.

[46]*Ibid.*, p. 304.

[47]H. S. Patton, *Grain Growers' Co-operation in Western Canada,* Harvard University Press, Cambridge, 1928, p. 9.

TABLE 1:2
AREA OF FIELD CROPS PRAIRIE PROVINCES, CENSUS YEARS 1901 - 1921
(in 1000's of acres)

Year	Province	Wheat	Oats	Barley	Rye	Flaxseed	Total
1901	Manitoba	1,965	574	140	1	14	2,694
	Territories	530	260	23	2	—	815
	Total	2,495	834	163	3	14	3,509
1906	Manitoba	2,720	931	337	4	17	4,009
	Saskatchewan	2,116	902	78	3	109	3,208
	Alberta	224	477	108	7	6	822
	Total	5,060	2,310	523	14	132	8,039
1911	Manitoba	3,095	1,207	448	5	80	4,835
	Saskatchewan	5,256	2,333	274	2	1,154	9,019
	Alberta	1,640	1,221	164	14	107	3,146
	Total	9,991	4,761	886	21	1,341	17,000
1916	Prairie Provinces	13,815	6,481	1,171	35	458	21,960
1921	Manitoba	2,819	1,792	823	175	44	5,653
	Saskatchewan	11,684	4,860	420	275	369	17,608
	Alberta	4,886	2,546	391	209	33	8,065
	Total	19,389	9,198	1,634	659	446	31,326

TABLE 1:3
POPULATION BY PROVINCES AND TERRITORIES, CENSUS YEARS 1871 - 1921

Province	1871	1881	1891	1901	1911	1921
Manitoba	25,228	62,260	152,506	255,211	461,394	610,118
Saskatchewan	—	—	—	91,279	492,432	757,510
Alberta	—	—	—	73,022	374,295	588,454
N. W. Territories	48,000	56,446	98,967	20,129	6,507	7,988
Total	73,228	118,706	251,473	439,641	1,334,628	1,964,070

PERCENTAGE OF POPULATION OF CANADA

1.98	2.74	5.21	8.18	18.52	22.35

TABLE 1:4

MIGRANTS AND IMMIGRANTS PRAIRIE PROVINCES, ENUMERATED IN THE 1921 CENSUS

Provinces	From Eastern Canada	%	From United States	%	From Overseas	%	Total	%
Manitoba	85,099	27.68	21,644	7.04	200,728	65.28	307,471	100
Saskatchewan	133,015	30.74	87,617	20.25	212,060	49.01	432,692	100
Alberta	97,811	26.35	99,879	26.91	173,485	46.74	371,175	100
Prairie Provinces	315,925	28.42	209,140	18.82	586,273	52.76	1,111,338	100

TABLE 1:5
ORIGINS OF THE POPULATION OF THE PRAIRIE PROVINCES, 1921 CENSUS

Actual or Ancestral Origin	Manitoba	Saskatchewan	Alberta	Total Prairie Provinces	Percentage Distribution
Britain					
(Sub-total)...................	(350,992)	(400,416)	(351,820)	(1,103,228)	56.41
England.....................	170,286	206,472	180,478	557,236	
Scotland....................	105,034	104,678	96,062	305,774	
Ireland......................	71,414	84,786	68,246	224,446	
Other British..............	4,258	4,480	7,034	15,772	
France...........................	40,638	42,152	30,913	113,703	5.81
Low Countries					
(Sub-total)...................	(26,048)	(20,116)	(12,080)	(58,244)	2.97
Netherlands................	20,728	16,639	9,490	46,857	
Belgium......................	5,320	3,477	2,590	11,387	
Scandinavia					
(Sub-total)...................	(27,204)	(60,319)	(47,471)	(134,994)	6.91
Iceland......................	11,043	3,593	507	15,143	
Sweden......................	8,023	19,064	15,943	43,030	
Norway......................	4,203	31,438	21,323	56,964	
Denmark....................	3,429	4,287	6,772	14,488	
Finland......................	506	1,937	2,926	5,369	
Austria.........................	31,035	39,738	19,430	90,203	4.61
Germany.......................	19,444	68,202	35,333	122,979	6.29
Italy.............................	1,933	689	4,028	6,650	.33
Eastern Europe					
(Sub-total)...................	(19,480)	(26,153)	(13,543)	(59,176)	3.03
Poland.......................	16,594	8,161	7,172	31,927	
Czechoslovakia...........	1,028	2,574	2,537	6,139	
Roumania...................	919	5,645	2,017	8,581	
Hungary.....................	828	8,946	1,015	10,789	
Serbo-Croatia.............	111	827	802	1,740	
Russia..........................	58,138	73,440	45,039	176,617	9.03
Asia					
(Sub-total)...................	(1,384)	(2,776)	(4,054)	(8,214)	.42
Japan.........................	53	109	473	635	
China........................	1,331	2,667	3,581	7,579	
Other............................	33,822	23,509	24,743	82,074	4.19
TOTAL.......................	610,118	757,510	588,454	1,956,082	100.0

2

PRODUCERS' GRIEVANCES AND THEIR REDRESS

As mentioned in the previous chapter, one line elevator company had been founded in 1893 and three others by 1897. It was then that the Canadian Pacific Railway began to enforce its undertaking to provide exclusive loading rights to elevator companies at points where their elevators were located. Although the mechanized country elevator had rendered the flat warehouse and the loading platform technically obsolete, the latter retained their economic justification as long as there was no other means of competing with the elevators in the handling of grain. In later years competition would come from farmer-owned elevator companies but, until they were formed, farmers pressed for continuation of the right to load grain from flat warehouses and for the construction and use of loading platforms.

Grain dealers had built up a considerable business by buying grain delivered to their flat warehouses. When the warehousemen were told that they would not be supplied cars, and therefore could not do business, their customers shared their alarm because the only source of competition with the elevators was being destroyed. Farmers protested as strongly as the displaced warehousemen because they were being forced to deal with what they regarded as a monopoly. Their members of parliament took up their cause.

The circumstances under which grain was delivered aggravated the situation. After each harvest the objective was to move the entire surplus to the lakehead so that it could be moved down the lakes before the close of navigation. This placed an extraordinarily high seasonal pressure upon available rolling stock and on elevator facilities from September to November. If the grain could not arrive at the lakehead in time for shipment before freeze-up, the elevator companies deducted a carrying charge from the price to cover the cost of winter storage. In their concern to alleviate the seasonal car shortage, the railways were satisfied that elevators could load cars with more dispatch than could the warehouses, which was an additional reason for their preferential allotment of cars to the elevators.

1898 BILL

On February 14, 1898, James M. Douglas (East Assiniboia) moved first reading of private member's bill No. 19 to regulate the transit of grain in

Manitoba and the North-West Territories.[1] In the debate on second reading on March 17, Mr. Douglas cited the agreement between the Canadian Pacific Railway and the elevator companies, and the notification the railway had given to the operators of flat warehouses in 1897 that they would no longer be supplied with cars. He described the producers' grievances arising therefrom. He also drew attention to producer dissatisfaction with the weighing of grain at country elevators and with the practice of mixing grain after it had been received in the elevators. Mr. Douglas said:

> Prior to the time when elevators were built, men engaged in the purchasing and shipping of grain through flat warehouses; but there are now in the country a number of elevators in full operation, and an understanding has been reached between the Canadian Pacific Railway and the elevator syndicate that all such flat warehouses must pass out of existence; so that in the province of Manitoba and a portion of the North-West Territories, the business has been wholly absorbed by the elevator syndicate, and men who have been engaged for years in purchasing grain and shipping it through flat warehouses have been obliged to go out of business. This is felt to be a hardship, not only on the part of these men, but on the part of the producers themselves.[2]

He then proceeded to estimate the financial loss to producers which resulted from the removal of competition by the flat warehousemen.

The bill was supported by Mr. R. L. Richardson (Lisgar) who complained at length about the inability to move pure Red Fife hard wheat from Manitoba to Ontario because merchants could not obtain cars and Ontario buyers had to purchase mixed grain shipped through the elevator system.[3] In supporting Mr. Douglas's charge of an elevator monopoly, Mr. Richardson said:

> On the main question, I wish to go over the ground in some little detail, giving the facts. In the province of Manitoba and the North-West, we have not had such serious trouble in years gone by in handling our grain as we have had the past season, because we have had competition at nearly all the important market points, active competition, there being from one to five or six buyers at these various points. But a new condition of things has arisen. The elevator system has been enlarged, and today is a fairly complete system throughout Manitoba and the North-West Territories. These elevators are controlled largely by syndicates — the Northern Elevator Company, the Manitoba Elevator Company, and others. In addition to these there are the elevators owned by the Ogilvie Milling Company and the Lake of the Woods Milling Company. So long as there was no combination, there was real competition in the buying of wheat. But these various syndicates put their heads together last

[1]James M. Douglas, (born in Scotland, educated in Upper Canada) was a Presbyterian minister. From 1876 to 1882 he served as a missionary in India. On his return to Canada he held charges at Brandon and Moosomin from which he retired in 1893 to take up farming. He became a spokesman for the short-lived Patrons of Industry, an agrarian protest movement. He was elected to the house of commons in 1896 as an Independent Liberal with Patron support and was re-elected in 1900. In 1906 he was appointed to the senate.

[2]*House of Commons Debates*, 1898, cols. 2059-2060.

[3]Robert L. Richardson, born in Lanark County, was a journalist. He worked in Toronto until 1882 when he moved to Winnipeg. In 1889 he founded the *Winnipeg Tribune* which he edited for many years. He represented the federal constituency of Lisgar as a Liberal from 1896 to 1900.

season, and, seeing that the price of wheat has considerably advanced, they decided to corral a larger share of the profit than was their legitimate due. So they formed what is popularly known in that country as a "syndicate of syndicates". Instead of each syndicate sending out a bulletin to their buyers at the various points throughout the province and the territories, stating the price at which they wanted them to buy, the "syndicate of syndicates" meets in its little room in Winnipeg, each morning, and decides what price they propose, in their majesty, to allow the farmer for his wheat. Instead of various telegrams being sent out, the "syndicate of syndicates" sends out one telegram to each important point, and the buyer who receives it goes to the others, and the result is, that no one buyer at any station will pay more than the price which has been decided upon by this clique in Winnipeg.[4]

At the conclusion of the debate, Mr. Douglas moved that the bill be referred to the railway committee. In doing so, he expressed a wish that his private member's bill be made a government measure. This was declined by the minister of trade and commerce, Sir Richard Cartwright, who tartly observed that the government were not in the habit of sponsoring measures unless introduced and considered by themselves.

The proceedings and evidence before the railway committee on this subject were not printed, but from other sources it is known that the Canadian Pacific Railway representatives appeared as witnesses and acknowledged the conflict between their undertaking to the elevator companies and the provisions of the railway act which imposed upon them the responsibility as a common carrier to supply cars to persons prepared to pay the tariff for their services. In their dilemma, the company representatives undertook to furnish cars to individual farmers desiring to load their own grain over loading platforms and this undertaking was implemented. As a result, Mr. Douglas withdrew his bill but introduced it again early in the following session.

1899 BILL

The reintroduced bill became bill No. 15 in the 1899 session. In moving second reading on April 20, 1899, Mr. Douglas acknowledged that the railway company had allowed the direct loading of railway cars, but he considered that the use of flat warehouses was necessary, not only as a matter of right of the operators, but in order to maintain competition. He also repeated the complaint that it was impossible to preserve the identity and quality of seed grain when it was shipped through the elevator system.

An important new feature in the bill was the provision for appointment of a chief inspector to oversee the entire grain trade in Manitoba and the North-West Territories. In justifying such an appointment, Mr. Douglas referred to producer concern over weights, as he had done the year before, and on this occasion expressed concern also over the allowances taken for dockage.

The bill was supported by several western members including Mr. J. G. Rutherford (Macdonald), Mr. Nicholas F. Davin (West Assiniboia), and Mr. R. L. Richardson, who seconded the bill. At the conclusion of the debate, the minister of the interior, the Honourable Clifford Sifton,

[4]*House of Commons Debates,* 1898, col. 2065.

accepted the bill in principle and indicated that the government favored its passage. He did not endorse its provisions in detail, however, and proposed its reference to a special committee. It was contended that the bill should be referred to the railway committee but Prime Minister Laurier supported the view that the railway committee was too preoccupied to give the bill adequate consideration. The proceedings of the special committee were not printed. Wood described its meetings as "tempestuous and distinctly unpleasant."[5]

The provision for appointment of a chief grain inspector and the remainder of the draft bill were approved, with the exception of the clause relating to flat warehouses, which was voted down in the committee. The continued operation of flat warehouses, however, was the principal point at issue and the main object of the bill. As a result Mr. Douglas fell out with the minister of the interior, Mr. Sifton.

On June 21, Mr. Nicholas F. Davin, the Conservative member for West Assiniboia, repeated charges in the house which had been levelled at Mr. Sifton in an editorial in the June 3rd issue of the *Winnipeg Tribune,* and which alleged:

> The elevator-owning grain buyers, however, sent representatives to Ottawa, or rather, the chief members of those combines went there in person. What means they used to secure the support of politicians and of the Canadian Pacific Railway, we have nothing but circumstantial evidence to tell us. That the representations they made in private were more potent than their public representation of familiar sophistry, is evident from the result.[6]

The Tribune editorial went on to quote Mr. Douglas, according to an interview published in the *Toronto Telegram*: "It was a terrible blow to the whole west and of course we know where to place the blame. It was the cold steel of Clifford Sifton that did it; it was nothing else." In reply to the charge Mr. Sifton said:

> I was present at the first two or three meetings and listened carefully to the discussion which took place. The result of the information I derived there, in addition to what I knew about the subject before, brought me to the conclusion that I was prepared to support strongly the features of the Bill relating to the regulation and inspection of elevators, but I was not prepared to support that provision which provided for the unrestricted erection of flat warehouses upon the railway property and alongside the elevators.[7]

There the matter rested until early autumn when the government, taking cognizance of the dissatisfaction created by the rejection of the warehouse provision, appointed a royal commission on the shipment and transportation of grain.

ROYAL COMMISSION ON THE SHIPMENT AND TRANSPORTATION OF GRAIN

This was the first of several royal commissions appointed over the course of the years to inquire into producers' complaints. The commission (appointed

---

[5]L. A. Wood, *A History of Farmers' Movements in Canada*, Toronto, 1924, p. 164.

[6]Undoubtedly the writer of the editorial was R. L. Richardson, who, as owner of the *Tribune*, was needling his rival, Clifford Sifton, owner of the *Free Press*. On the other hand, as a backbencher, Richardson was criticizing a minister in his own party.

[7]*House of Commons Debates,* June 21, 1899, cols. 5498-5499.

on October 7, 1899) was headed by Judge E. J. Senkler of St. Catharines, Ontario, with three western farmers as members, Messrs. W. F. Sirett, William Lothian, and Charles C. Castle. Judge Senkler died during the course of the hearing and he was succeeded by Judge A. Elswood Richards of Winnipeg. Investigation of the following grievances was referred to the commission:

First, that a vendor of grain is at present subjected to an unfair and excessive dockage of his grain at the time of sale;

Second, that doubts exist as to the fairness of the weights allowed or used by owners of elevators; and

Third, that the owners of elevators enjoy a monopoly in the purchase of grain by refusing to permit the erection of flat warehouses where standard elevators are situated, and are able to keep the price of grain below its true market value to their own benefit and the disadvantage of others who are especially interested in the grain trade, and of the public generally.

The commission proceeded to take evidence from 238 witnesses at 21 points in the west. It also sent one of its commissioners, Charles C. Castle, to Duluth and Minneapolis to investigate grain regulatory legislation in Minnesota.

In its report of March 19, 1900, the commission found that

The grievances complained of have arisen largely from the above mentioned protection offered by the railway company to elevator owners to induce them to build elevators, which resulted in placing the shipping of grain at elevator points in the hands solely of the elevator owners. Owners of flat warehouses were practically done away with. No one desiring to ship grain in bulk could get it on cars otherwise than by having it handled through elevators. . . .

As a result of the refusal of the railway companies to take grain from a flat warehouse (which resulted in driving many small buyers out of the market) and of their refusal until 1898, to furnish cars to farmers desirous of doing their own shipping, and of the consequent necessity of shipping through elevators, or of selling to the operators thereof, and of lack of competition between buyers, the elevator owners have had it in their power to depress prices below what in our opinion farmers should realize for their grain. It would naturally be to their interest to so depress prices; and when buying, to dock as much as possible. . . .

The evidence shows that doubts have arisen as to the correctness of the weights given in some instances at the elevators in the weighing of grain. Recommendations as to the same are submitted with our suggestions as to legislation.

A cause that has depressed prices a great deal, has been the annual shortage of car supply during the months of October and November, during which months most of the wheat is marketed. As a result of this shortage, elevators have been offered wheat during said months faster than they could forward it to terminal points before the close of navigation. In case of a car shortage, therefore, or a threatened shortage, prices of grain have been depressed, owing to elevator owners having to consider, in buying same, that they would either have to pay all rail rates in shipping same, or the "carrying charges" to the following May. This has, in our opinion, been a serious cause of depression in prices, which should be remedied as far as possible by increase of transportation facilities during these months.

There being no rules laid down for the regulation of the grain trade other than those made by the railway companies and the elevator owners, we think it of great importance that the laws should be enacted and that rules should be made under power given by such laws, which will properly regulate the trade.[8]

The commission also recognized the operating difficulties of the elevator companies and pointed out that it was impossible at that time for the companies to remain solvent if their only source of earnings was from handling charges. As mentioned in the previous chapter, it was only by combining their warehousing operations with their merchandising business as grain dealers that the companies could operate at a profit and provide essential elevator service. This continued to be the experience in later years. It was a lesson quickly learned, and it was demonstrated in subsequent attempts at government ownership and operation, and in the formation of the farmer-owned elevator companies. The commission report said:

> The evidence shows that a standard elevator operated at the price of one and one-half cents per bushel (the present rate charged for handling, cleaning and giving fifteen days' storage) and at which no grain bought by the owner is handled, would require to be filled three times in each season to make a profitable investment to the party erecting and working it. There are too many standard country elevators in Manitoba and the North-West Territories to allow of each being so filled three times in a season. This will be apparent when it is stated that the total capacity of the country elevators in the Manitoba inspection district is 15,000,000 bushels or thereabouts. There are, therefore, more elevators than can be operated at a profit if they handle and store grain for other parties only.
>
> This inability to make a profit without three fillings per season is partly owing to the great cost of building and operating such elevators as the railway company require to be erected. As a result of the above, a country elevator can, as a rule, only be operated at a profit in Manitoba and the North-West Territories when the owner, in addition to storing and handling the grain for others, is himself largely a buyer of grain and in that way makes a buyer's profit on grain handled by himself in addition to the profit on storing and handling.
>
> The parties, therefore, who built the standard elevators were chiefly, if not entirely themselves grain dealers, whose interest it was to buy grain rather than simply handle it for others.[9]

As a guide for the use of the federal government, the commission filed a schedule of draft legislation based upon legislation already in force in Minnesota but modified to meet the circumstances of Manitoba and the North-West Territories. This schedule concerned the licensing and regulation of terminal and country elevators.

Another schedule set out additional recommendations which the commission deemed advisable. These included the appointment of a warehouse commissioner who would have broad supervisory powers over elevator operations including the right to investigate complaints. Secondly, the schedule recommended that existing flat warehouses be allowed to continue in business, and that railways be required to provide loading platforms at sites requested by producers. Further recommendations concerned dockage and the weighing of grain.[10]

---

[8] *Report and Evidence of the Royal Commission on the Shipment and Transportation of Grain*, 63 Victoria, *Sessional Paper No. 81a*, A, 1900, pp. 8-12.
[9] *Ibid.*, p. 8.
[10] *Ibid.*, Schedules D and E.

The report of the first royal commission on grain and the ensuing legislation which gave effect to all of its recommendations stand as landmarks commemorating the federal government's adoption of a policy of regulation of the grain trade. This regulation was of a different type from that involved in the general inspection act which remained as separate legislation. The latter met the requirements of the trade and producers alike. The Manitoba grain act regulated the trade in the interest of producers.

MANITOBA GRAIN ACT, 1900

With a general election pending that year, the federal government moved quickly to implement the report's recommendations. The report was dated March 19, 1900. On May 1, the minister of inland revenue, Sir Henry Joly de Lotbiniere, moved first reading of a government bill (No. 141) entitled *An Act respecting the grain trade in the Inspection District of Manitoba*, from which it derived its short title, *The Manitoba Grain Act, 1900*. On second reading a two-day debate took place, May 21-22, with another full day's debate on third reading, May 30. Douglas, Richardson and Davin were active participants in the debate, as was also the prime minister, Sir Wilfrid Laurier. Douglas gave the bill his enthusiastic endorsement, although he took issue with the prime minister over the latter's insistence that flat warehouses should pay site rentals; otherwise the legislation would be confiscatory of railway property. Douglas contended that site rentals would impede the construction of flat warehouses and thereby restrict producers' freedom of choice in the method of delivery, but Sir Wilfrid's view prevailed. The act received royal assent on July 7, 1900.

The act reflected in detail the recommendations made by the royal commission. It provided for the appointment of a warehouse commissioner responsible to the department of inland revenue.[11] Section 4 set out his duties:

(a) to require all elevators, warehouses, mills, and grain commission merchants to take out an annual license;

(b) to fix the amount of bonds to be given by the different owners and operators of elevators, mills, and flat warehouses and by grain commission merchants;

(c) to require the persons so licensed to keep books in forms approved of by the commissioner or by the Governor in Council;

(d) to supervise the handling and storage of grain, in and out of elevators, warehouses and cars;

(e) to receive and investigate all complaints made in writing, under oath, of undue dockage, improper weights or grading, refusal or neglect to furnish cars within a reasonable time, all complaints of fraud or oppression by any person, firm or corporation, owning or operating any elevator, warehouse, mill or railroad, or by any grain commission merchant, and to apply such remedy as is provided by statute;

(f) to enforce rules and regulations made under this Act, and to report to the Minister of Inland Revenue such changes therein as he deems advisable;

(g) to institute prosecutions at the Government expense whenever he considers a case proper therefor.

[11]P. C. 1509 of July 26, 1901, transferred to the department of trade and commerce the responsibility for administration of this act and also the general inspection act.

Provision was also made for the appointment of a chief weighmaster with supervisory powers over the weighing of grain. Lengthy provisions applied to the operation of terminal and country elevators. Terminal elevators, for example, were forbidden to mix grain of different grades. Country elevators equipped with grain cleaners were required to clean grain before weighing if requested to do so, thereby determining the amount of dockage, and persons selling grain were to be given free access to the scales during weighing. Maximum tariff rates, subject to revision by the governor in council, were to be filed each year by both terminal and country elevators.

A further clause allowed for the erection of flat warehouses of not less than 3,000-bushel capacity on railway property at appropriate site rentals, if farmers so petitioned. The railways were prohibited from refusing to supply cars to existing warehouses. They were also required to provide loading platforms within their station yards on the petition of ten farmers. Whether from flat warehouses or loading platforms, farmers were required to load cars within 24 hours of their placement on the railway siding.[12]

Producers reflected their satisfaction with the new legislation to a substantial degree in the 1900 election returns.[13] The appointment of Mr. Douglas to the senate in 1906 was a timely and appropriate recognition of his contribution as a pioneer spokesman for producers. For the flat warehouses, however, which symbolized the farmer's struggle for freedom of choice in the marketing of their grain, it was a pyrrhic victory. Very few new flat warehouses were built after 1900 and the existing ones gradually disappeared. Mr. Charles C. Castle, a member of the royal commission who had prepared the study of Minnesota legislation and had worked on the draft legislation incorporated in the Manitoba grain act, was chosen to become the warehouse commissioner. This appointment was very acceptable because of Mr. Castle's experience and background as a western farmer.

WHEAT BLOCKADE OF 1901

The peace which came in the wake of the Manitoba grain act was short-lived. The 1900 crop was relatively light but, in 1901, heavy yields on an expanded acreage produced a record wheat crop of 62,820,000 bushels, the harvesting of which was delayed by wet weather. By the close of navigation more than half the crop was still on farms because the Canadian Pacific lacked the car supply needed to cope with a crop of that size. When the railway could not spot enough cars to fill the orders from elevators that offered prompt loading, its agents refused to supply cars to farmers shipping from flat warehouses or loading platforms. As the car shortage developed, the elevator companies lowered their street prices, and reduced them substantially as soon as they realized that the wheat they were buying at country points could not reach the lakehead in time to be loaded out before the close of navigation. By lowering street prices in relation to those at the terminals, the elevator companies were trying to cover the costs of storage until the grain could be forwarded to terminals in the spring. In delivering

---

[12]*Statutes of Canada,* 63-64 Vict., Chap. 39, assented to July 7th, 1900.

[13]Patton states that "the Manitoba Grain Act was hailed by western grain growers as a veritable agrarian Magna Charta", *op. cit.,* p. 30.

their grain to the country elevators, farmers had to accept the street prices offered, because they could not obtain cars for their own loading. In some cases the elevator companies offered to buy top-grade wheat at lower-grade prices, by claiming that space was available only in their lower-grade bins. Farmers complained bitterly of the "wheat blockade." As it intensified, they realized that not more than half the crop could be delivered before the close of navigation, and that they must take extraordinary measures to improvise farm storage.

Earlier that year the line elevator companies organized the North-West elevator association which was to make purchases of elevator supplies and reduce telegraphic expenses of its members. But it symbolized what farmers had called "the syndicate of syndicates." In the wake of their delivery problems in the autumn of 1901, a few farmers took the first steps to organize the Territorial grain growers' association in December of that year. Both associations are described in more detail in the following chapter. Meanwhile, repercussions of the blockade echoed in the press and in parliament.

On March 10, 1902, James Douglas introduced a motion for the production of papers relating to the blockade and a full day's debate ensued. Mr. Douglas read into Hansard a report which Charles C. Castle, warehouse commissioner, had submitted on January 15 to the deputy minister of trade and commerce. To handle the 1901 crop, Mr. Castle reported that the Canadian Pacific had 3,000 cars and 236 locomotives in the western division. He believed that the critical shortage was that of engines. The railway's largest weekly shipment to the lakehead that autumn had been 1,335,414 bushels, and the total autumn movement amounted to 14,281,401 bushels. No progress was apparent in relieving the congestion, even by November. When, at the beginning of that month, the elevator companies realized it would be impossible to ship out all October purchases in time to reach the lakehead before the close of navigation, they commenced to deduct six cents from their street prices to cover winter storage costs.

On the basis of Mr. Castle's statement, Mr. Douglas calculated that producers had lost $5,000,000, and other members suggested a higher figure. Douglas reported that the congestion was particularly acute along the Canadian Pacific main line from Moosomin to Moose Jaw in which area alone he claimed producers had lost $1,500,000. Other speakers alleged that the Canadian Pacific had refused to divert traffic to the Canadian Northern Railway and to Duluth to relieve the congestion. During the debate, Douglas claimed that he was not inveighing against the line elevator companies as such, but that he was fighting for freedom of choice by the farmer in forwarding his grain whether by warehouse, loading platform, or by the elevator companies.

William J. Roche (Marquette) alleged that an elevator combine existed; Walter Scott (West Assiniboia) agreed, adding that the combine had been made possible by the congestion.[14] Scott also alleged that the railway had refused to furnish cars to farmers, and said:

The Canadian Pacific Railway Company last season more than once issued

[14]Mr. Scott became Saskatchewan's first premier in 1905.

instructions to their agents not to furnish cars to farmers; and these were cases in which they could have done so. For instance, a farmer would go to an agent at a station where cars were standing idle, and the agent would tell him that he had instructions not to allow farmers to load their grain on to the cars. The railway company denied that they had issued such instructions; but I have good reason for stating that at the present time there exists an order issued from the headquarters of the company at Winnipeg to the agents throughout the North-West Territories, not to give a car to a farmer to be loaded with wheat. That being the case, it behooves the government and parliament to take some notice of the matter.[15]

Mr. A. A. C. LaRiviere (Provencher) recommended that the government take over the elevator system, a suggestion which gained wide support in later years.

Sir Wilfrid Laurier spoke at the end of the debate and supported the motion, but suggested that western members be specific in the remedies they wished to recommend by way of amendment to the Manitoba grain act. He said, "It is only for our friends of the North-West to point out the remedy and the government will be only too glad to give them every assistance to make the Act as effective as it can be made."[16]

MANITOBA GRAIN AMENDMENT ACT, 1902

Sir Richard Cartwright, minister of trade and commerce, moved first reading of bill 162, to amend the Manitoba grain act, on May 6, 1902. On second reading, May 7, he read the amendments into Hansard, and they were debated on May 9 in committee. The amendments liberalized the provisions in the 1900 act for the erection of flat warehouses and loading platforms, which producers still regarded as their guarantee of freedom in marketing. The minimum size requirement for flat warehouses was rescinded and siding locations were now to be furnished by the railway. Moreover, farmers could now apply for loading platforms to be built by the railways at sidings where there was no station yard.

These changes did little more than meet producers' residual criticisms of the 1900 act, whereas a really new departure was made in the introduction of the car order book. An amendment made it mandatory for every railway agent to maintain such a book open to anyone desiring to ship grain, and required the distribution of cars in strict rotation of applications entered in the book. The full text of this amendment, which was soon found to be ambiguous and in need of clarification by further amendment, is as follows:

> At each station where there is a railway agent and where grain is shipped under such agent, an order book for cars shall be kept for each shipping point under such agent, open to the public, in which applicants for cars shall make order. Applicants may make order according to their requirements; cars so ordered shall be awarded to applicants according to the order in time in which such orders appear on the order book, without discrimination between elevator, flat warehouse, loading platform or otherwise, and any applicant who fails to load the said car or cars within twenty-four hours from the time such cars are furnished by the railway company, shall lose his right so far as concerns the car or cars not so loaded.

[15]*House of Commons Debates,* March 10, 1902, col. 926.
[16]*Ibid.,* col. 960.

When the railway company is unable, from any reasonable cause, to furnish cars at any shipping point to fill all orders as aforesaid, such cars as are furnished shall be apportioned to the applicants in the order of application as appearing in the said order book, until each applicant has received one car, after which the surplus cars, if any, shall be apportioned ratably according to the requirements of each applicant.[17]

SINTALUTA CASE

Only a few months after the car order book became a statutory requirement, another large harvest was in progress. Again the crop was too big to be handled even with expanded rolling stock. Railway traffic, generally, was developing so rapidly that the railway was hard pressed to keep up with the demand. In this vexing situation farmers found to their dismay that the railway was ignoring the car distribution provisions in the 1902 amendment and that because of the congestion, street prices of wheat were dropping as the close of navigation approached. Feelings ran so high that brawls broke out as cars arrived at country points.[18]

When it became evident that the car order book provisions were being disregarded, the newly formed Territorial grain growers' association ventured to take action. Two of its members, W. R. Motherwell and Peter Dayman, went to Winnipeg to draw to the attention of the western division headquarters of the Canadian Pacific Railway that its agents were violating the provisions of the act.[19] When their intervention went unheeded, the association laid a formal complaint before the warehouse commissioner that the Canadian Pacific Railway agent at Sintaluta had violated the provisions of the act in his allotment of cars at that station. On November 28, Mr. Castle and a justice department representative visited Sintaluta to investigate the complaint and they decided that a charge should be laid against the agent on behalf of the crown. The case was tried before three magistrates and evidence was produced that farmers whose applications had been duly entered in the car order book had been bypassed in the distribution of cars to the elevators. The magistrates found in favor of the plaintiff and a fine was assessed. Although the Canadian Pacific Railway appealed the case, the supreme court of Canada upheld the verdict which the company acknowledged by effective compliance thenceforth.

MANITOBA GRAIN AMENDMENT ACT, 1903

As Patton points out, the 1902 amendments had been hastily enacted to meet emergency conditions which accounted in part for the Canadian Pacific Railway's concern to test their validity.[20] In the 1903 session, a delegation of four representatives of producers, Messrs. Motherwell and Gillespie of the Territories, and Messrs. McCuaig and Henders of Manitoba, were sent to Ottawa to confer with representatives of the grain dealers and railways on further amendments. This process of consultation

---

[17]*Statutes of Canada,* 2 Edward VII, Chap. 19, assented to 15 May, 1902.
[18]L. A. Wood, *op.cit.,* pp. 178-179.
[19]W. R. Motherwell, a farmer at Abernethy, became the first minister of agriculture of Saskatchewan in 1905, and later became federal minister of agriculture in the King administrations, 1921-1930.
[20]Patton, *op.cit.,* p. 38.

among the interested parties was a new and useful departure. As a result, the 1903 amendments set forth more workable procedures to be followed in the allotment of cars. For example, each applicant, whether an elevator company or an individual farmer, was to be given a number in the book in the order of application. Where an applicant required two or more cars he was required to make two or more applications, and cars were to be allotted strictly in order of the time of application. If the railway could not fill all orders, the agent was to begin at the top of the list and to proceed downwards, allotting each applicant one car and, as cars became available, applicants would receive a second car in the second run down, and so on until the orders were filled.

As Patton observed, by 1903 the producers' struggle for direct shipment and equality in car distribution had succeeded, but it remained for the Canadian Pacific and its two competitors, the Canadian Northern and the Grand Trunk Pacific, to so increase their rolling stock and elevator services on their rights of way that the wheat blockades of 1901 and 1902 were not again repeated.[21]

GRAIN INSPECTION ACT, 1904

The grain inspection act, assented to 10th August, 1904, was a useful consolidation into one act of the portions of the general inspection act of 1886 and subsequent amendments which were concerned with grain standards and inspection. The act confirmed, as the act to amend the Manitoba grain act, 1902, had done, the combination of administrative responsibility for the two acts under the department of trade and commerce, which had been effected by order in council in 1901.

ROYAL COMMISSION ON THE GRAIN TRADE OF CANADA, 1906

Even with the two statutes newly enacted for their protection, producers remained unconvinced that they were protected in practice as well as in law, and they continued to voice their grievances. There was concern that the terminal elevators were dealt with more leniently in matters of grading than were the producers and they believed that the Winnipeg grain exchange and the North-West grain dealers' association, as the elevator association was now called, were operating a combine. In 1906 another deputation of grain growers appeared before the agricultural committee of the house of commons to air its members' complaints, and to request the appointment of a new grain inquiry commission, to which the government agreed. Three farmers were appointed as commissioners, including Mr. John Millar of Indian Head, one of the organizers of the Territorial grain growers' association, as the senior commissioner. The terms of reference of this second royal commission on the grain trade of Canada were set out by order in council in July, 1906, as follows:

> To take into consideration all or any matters connected with the Inspection and Sale Act and the Manitoba Grain Act; and in connection therewith shall have power to visit the grain growers, the elevators all over the wheat-growing region, the methods of handling the grain at the various stations, farmers'

[21]*Ibid.*, pp. 39-40.

elevators, as well as companies' elevators, the distribution of cars, methods of the grain dealers in Winnipeg, Toronto and Montreal, and the system of government inspection and collection of fees, selection of grades, and the methods of handling the grain at Fort William and Port Arthur, at the lake ports, at Montreal, St. John and Halifax, and also the conditions existing as to the manner of handling the grain upon its arrival in England.[22]

The commission submitted its report in October, 1907. With reference to improper weighing, it recommended that when the warehouse commissioner has investigated and substantiated a complaint, he should have the power to order appropriate redress to the injured party, and also to order the dismissal of the offending operator. Regarding the common complaints of excessive dockage, the commission said that the farmer was protected by section 65 of the Manitoba grain act to which it proposed certain amendments.

On the subject of screenings, the commission said that the question was one for the provincial governments, which should deal vigorously with the problem of discouraging growth of weeds on farms. It also recommended a system of compensation to shippers by the terminal elevators for the value of domestic grain contained in the screenings.

On special binning, the commission recommended that samples be kept of all special binned grain which could be used for checking receipts at terminals.

The commission rejected a proposal for government-built interior storage elevators on grounds that the scheme was impracticable because of expense and the stopover charges involved. While acknowledging that there was practically no relation between street and track prices during periods of car shortage, the commission felt that the remedy lay in a plentiful supply of cars, and not in further regulation. It recognized that there were problems of car distribution, as well as of car shortage, and proposed that the warehouse commissioner be given additional power to direct the railways to make an equitable distribution. It even went so far as to propose that the railways pay reverse demurrage when they failed to furnish cars ordered.

To correct abuses of the car order book, including the entering of fictitious names, the commission recommended a fee of $2 for every application.

Concerning proposals frequently advanced that a sample grain market should be established at Winnipeg, the commission held that such a market would create confusion in the existing grading and inspecting system and they did not recommend it. The commissioners claimed that a sample market would entail mixing in practically every grade whereas the existing inspection system had evolved from efforts to eliminate the practice of mixing.

The only "important" complaint regarding inspection came from the bay ports and from overseas buyers who found excessive quantities of dirt and foreign seeds in arrivals due to:

1st. The lack of proper cleaning machinery in Fort William and Port Arthur;

---

[22]*Report of the Royal Commission on the Grain Trade of Canada, 1906,* Sessional Paper No. 59, 1908, p. 3.

2nd. The manner of taking the sample of grain as it runs from the spout into the hold of the vessel does not necessarily give a true sample;

3rd. The lack of supervision of the channels of transportation eastward from Fort William and Port Arthur.[23]

It was concluded there was not sufficient supervision of grain cleaning operations, many machines being inadequate. There were considerable shortages (and sometimes overages) in cargo shipments which indicated irregular weighing.

As a result, it was suggested that the inspection department should be placed in full control of cleaning and binning of all grain passing through terminal elevators at Fort William and Port Arthur and also through the eastern transfer elevators. Weighing should be transferred from the inspection department to a new department under the direction of a chief weighmaster.

On the other hand, the inspection department complained that railroads did not allow sufficient time for the sampling of cars. The commission recommended that inspectors have power to hold cars until they could be sampled properly.

The commission investigated complaints regarding the handling of cars by commission merchants in Winnipeg and recommended that all consignments be reported to the consignee on a prescribed form in order that the latter might have a complete report on the disposition of his grain.

With regard to complaints against members of the Winnipeg grain exchange, the commission noted that these had become the subject of judicial inquiry and were still before the courts but, nevertheless, it made certain observations and recommendations.[24] The latter included a reduction, in the case of oats, from the one-cent per bushel commission applicable to all grain. On issues raised by the newly-formed Grain Growers' Grain Company over exchange rules which prohibited the rebate of commissions and the payment of elevator agent salaries of less than $50 per month, the commission found that there were valid arguments on both sides of the fixed commission rule but that maintenance of a fixed salary for elevator agents had the effect of driving track-buying business into the hands of the larger dealers. Accordingly, they recommended that the minimum wage

---

[23]*Ibid.,* p. 13.

[24]The report observed as follows:

"The Winnipeg Grain Exchange is a non-trading body which provides facilities for its members in doing business and makes by-laws and regulations for the systematizing of trade amongst its members. It provides a public trading room in which its members buy and sell grain. The prices at which transactions are made are officially posted on a blackboard by a man provided by the Exchange. These prices we find are made in open competition, and are beyond doubt the full value of the grain as based on the world's markets.

The work of the Grain Exchange in establishing and systematizing a market in Winnipeg for the handling of the crops of the West has been a great benefit to the country. The restrictions placed upon its members in providing for the fulfilment of contracts, the establishment of a clearing house in which contracts are protected day by day give the banks the necessary confidence and surety in advancing money to the trade with which to handle the crop. This has brought the producer much nearer to the consumer than he at one time was and no doubt is of great financial benefit to him." (*Ibid.,* p. 14)

requirement be dropped. The problem lay in the fact that in many cases the agent was required to be on duty only a few days a month which made the monthly minimum rate of compensation onerous for the smaller firms.

On the charge that the North-West grain dealers' association was operating a combine in restraint of trade, the commission noted that this question was before the courts. Producers' representatives had claimed that the setting of uniform daily street prices at country points constituted restraint. Elsewhere, the courts found against this view. The commission observed that spreads between street and track prices were usually a function of the car supply. Some agreements had been made among members of the North-West grain dealers' association to pool receipts or earnings at country points where their elevators were in competition, although the practice had been discontinued by the companies. Nevertheless, the commission recommended that such pooling be prohibited by the Manitoba grain act.

The commission also considered proposals that terminal elevators at Fort William and Port Arthur be taken over and operated by the government. Several members of parliament had addressed a petition to the prime minister requesting that the commission investigate the public interest in this regard. Their petition was referred to the commission, which submitted an interim reply:

> To prevent the evils that are made possible by the operation of terminal elevators under the present system, we do not think it wise to advise the government to go to the length of taking over the terminal elevators or of prohibiting persons engaged in the grain trade being interested in such terminals. We believe it is possible to obtain a good service from these elevators under the present ownership by having a more thorough system of supervision and control.[25]

In its report the commission added:

> Requests were made of us in the country that the elevators at Fort William and Port Arthur should be taken over and operated by the government in view of the fact that so many of them were operated by private corporations interested in the grain trade. We also had a communication from the department under date January 23, 1907, enclosing a petition of members of parliament addressed to the Right Honourable the Premier, requesting that we be instructed to specifically "inquire into and report whether it is in the public interest that terminal elevators ... continue to be operated by the common carriers or allowed to pass into the hands of or be operated by persons, firms or corporations engaged in the grain business."
>
> In reply to this communication we addressed to the Right Honourable Sir Richard Cartwright, Minister of Trade and Commerce, a letter dated February 1, a copy of which is appended hereto. We can see no reason for changing the conclusions arrived at at that time, and we believe if our recommendations are carried out they will give the public the same confidence and protection in the operation of these terminal elevators as if they were owned by the Government.[26]

Lastly, the commission drew attention to the lack of a Pacific coast outlet for grain and suggested that a trade with the Orient could be developed to the benefit of producers in Alberta and western Saskatchewan, if the

[25] *Ibid.*, p. 39.
[26] *Ibid.*, p. 19.

government could provide assistance in the building of a terminal elevator on the Pacific coast.

MANITOBA GRAIN AND GRAIN INSPECTION AND SALE AMENDMENT ACTS, 1908

The appendix to the commission's report contained 50 proposed amendments to the existing regulatory acts, which were used as the basis for new legislation.[27] In the amendments to the grain inspection and sale act, the inspection department was given full control over grain in terminal elevators, including the cleaning, binning and shipping out of grain, and was required to keep detailed records by grade of all grain received into and shipped from terminals. The inspection department was also required to take stock in August each year of each grade of grain held in the terminal elevators. The chief inspector was authorized to prepare regulations for the satisfactory identification of outward inspection certificates with the lake or rail shipping bills for the grain covered by such certificates.

Other recommendations of the commission were reflected in the amendments to the Manitoba grain act. Control of all transfer elevators east of Port Arthur, with respect to the handling of western grain, was placed under the Manitoba inspection division. Provisions for the weighing, preservation of identity, and maintenance of records were set out for the eastern transfer elevators. All public terminals in the Manitoba inspection division were subject to new regulations against mixing, new cleaning arrangements and payment by the public terminals of an allowance to the shipper for the commercial value of screenings. Detailed provisions were made for the issuance of warehouse receipts and for the maintenance of records of grain handled. Special provisions were made for the handling of grain in danger of going out of condition. The car order book provisions were further refined. Commission merchants were required to issue detailed statements of sale to the persons consigning grain to them, and track buyers were required to provide detailed grain purchase notes. Country elevators and warehouses were required to report monthly on receipts, stocks and shipments. Pooling of earnings among country elevators was prohibited. Provision was made for preservation of identity of grain in transit from Winnipeg to points of consumption in eastern Canada or for export shipment.[28]

TERMINAL ELEVATOR PROSECUTIONS

In little more than a year after the new legislation was in force, the warehouse commissioner used his authority to make a surprise inspection of three terminal elevators at the close of navigation. The inspectors produced evidence to show that in the case of two of the elevators, shipments and holdings of No. 1 Northern exceeded their recorded receipts by 1,035,786 bushels, while shortages of 832,806 bushels were found in Nos. 2, 3, and 4

---

[27] *Statutes of Canada,* 7-8 Edward VII, Chaps. 36 and 45, assented to July 20th, 1908.

[28] On the government's appointment of the 1899 and 1906 royal commissions, Fowke dryly observed:

"Governments used royal commissions in the early years of the present century, therefore, chiefly for the purpose of getting this (agrarian) protest on the record and for

Northern. It was obvious that promotion of grades by mixing had taken place on a large scale, and that the excess of overages over shortages had resulted from cleaning below the amounts of dockage assessed. The two companies were fined and threatened with loss of their licenses. Such practices played into the hands of the grain growers' associations which pressed demands for public ownership and operation of terminal elevators.[29]

PRIME MINISTER'S TOUR OF THE WEST, 1910

In the summer of 1910, Sir Wilfrid Laurier embarked on an extended tour of the west. It was his first visit since he took office in 1896. By present day standards his absence from Ottawa was extraordinarily long, for the trip lasted from early July until early September. His personal popularity ran high and he delivered addresses in all the main centres and made stops in the smaller communities. Farm organizations and individuals made representations and presented memorials, many of which were concerned with tariff reductions on farm machinery and other production items. They asked for freer trade with Britain and the United States. They also urged the public ownership and operation of terminal elevators and the prevention of the mixing of wheat. Alberta farmers wanted an interior terminal elevator at Calgary and a terminal elevator at Vancouver. Saskatchewan farmers sought the construction of the Hudson Bay Railway.

The western position on tariff reduction strengthened the prime minister's hand in proceeding with the trade reciprocity negotiations with the United States. On the question of public ownership of terminal elevators, the prime

educating public and Parliament to the need for curbing monopoly in the grain trade. So sure was the Dominion government of what it wanted to be forced to do that it would entrust to no one but farmers the task of manning its early agricultural commissions.

It would be difficult to find commissions anywhere whose recommendations were more promptly or more completely enacted than those of the farmer-dominated royal grain inquiry commissions of 1899 and 1906. The central items for investigation by the commission of 1899 were farmers' complaints that monopoly conditions among marketing agencies at local assembly points permitted exploitation of farmer shippers. ... (The commission's) recommendations were put into law immediately, "on the eve of a general election," and constituted the Manitoba Grain Act of 1900. By 1906 the centre of attention had shifted from the local to the teminal field and to the place of the Winnipeg Grain Exchange in the marketing picture. The Millar commission, appointed in 1906, and with a membership of three farmers including the chairman, had nothing but commendation for the Grain Exchange. They outlined, however, fifty detailed changes to be made in the Manitoba Grain Act and the Grain Inspection Act. A large proportion of these recommendations were immediately incorporated into legislation, again on the eve of a general election. ...

Farmers and governments were agreed that private monopolies should go, but governments could not accept the opinion which became prevalent among farmers in favour of replacing private monopoly by state monopoly. The contest was sharp by 1906 when the Dominion government appointed three farmers as a grain inquiry commission. They were not just *any* farmers, however; they were "sound" people according to governmental standards. Replying early in 1907 to a specific inquiry of Sir Richard Cartwright on the terminal elevator question they said, "we do not think it wise to advise the Government to go to the length of taking over the teminal elevators." In their final report which was published in 1908 they reaffirmed this opinion."

(V. C. Fowke, "Royal Commissions and Canadian Agricultural Policy," *The Canadian Journal of Economics and Political Science,* Volume XIV, May, 1948, pp.169-170.)

[29]Patton, *op. cit.,* p. 135.

minister indicated that he was prepared to consider additional terminal facilities where needed and that he would be prepared to receive further representations from the grain growers' associations on the subject in Ottawa. The latter organizations decided, thereupon, to join forces through the Canadian council of agriculture in the presentation of a major petition covering a number of agricultural issues.

SIEGE OF OTTAWA, 1910

Through the active promotion of the grain growers' associations in the west, and the grange in Ontario, the council of agriculture rallied some 500 western grain growers and 300 Ontario farmers, with some representation from Quebec and the maritime provinces, to converge on Ottawa in December, 1910. After a meeting among the provincial delegations on December 15, the group marched en masse to the house of commons on the morning of December 16 to present their memorial and other resolutions, known as the farmers' platform. This covered several issues including tariff reduction, an increase in the British preference, reciprocity with the United States, federal ownership and operation of terminal elevators, government construction and operation of a Hudson Bay Railway and terminal, and assistance to livestock producers by developing a chilled-meat industry. On the subject of elevators, the memorial asked

> that the Dominion government take steps to acquire and operate as a public utility, under an independent commission, the terminal elevators at Fort William and Port Arthur, and immediately establish similar terminal facilities and conditions at the Pacific coast, and provide the same at Hudson Bay when necessary; also, such transfer and other elevators as are necessary to safeguard the quality of export grain.[30]

In respect to the terminals, the deputation was supported by representatives of the Dominion millers' association and the Toronto board of trade.

This was the first among several mass demonstrations in Ottawa which have been made by farmers over the years. On this first occasion the prime minister and his cabinet received the deputation on the floor of the house of commons, a courtesy not since repeated. The direct result of the "siege" was another revision and expansion of the grain regulatory legislation.

CANADA GRAIN ACT, 1912

On February 7, 1911, Sir Richard Cartwright, who had been minister of trade and commerce and was now a member of the senate, moved first reading of bill Q, which was a consolidation of the Manitoba grain act and the inspection and sale act, with several important additions. These included replacement of the office of warehouse commissioner by a board of three commissioners reporting to the department of trade and commerce. The new board of grain commissioners would have complete responsibility for the inspection, weighing and supervisory functions administered until then under authority of the two acts. For administrative purposes two inspection divisions were created, the eastern division including all of

---

[30]For the complete text of the Farmers' Platform, see W. L. Morton, *The Progressive Party in Canada,* (Univ. of Toronto Press, 1950), Appendix A, pp. 297-299.

Canada east of Port Arthur, and the western division including Port Arthur, which correspond with the boundaries of the Manitoba inspection division extending across western Canada.

The foregoing provisions were not controversial, but Sir Richard drew attention to others which might cause debate. Under section 13 the government could construct, acquire, lease or expropriate any terminal elevator if funds were granted by parliament. Although the provision was not mandatory, it gave the government power to implement recommendations of the grain growers' associations for public ownership if it saw fit.

Secondly, section 123 of the bill provided that "No person owning, managing, operating or otherwise interested in any public terminal shall buy or sell or be interested in any other form of storage of grain."

If enacted, as had been recommended by the grain growers' associations, this section would have eliminated the profitable combination of country and terminal elevator operations.

Section 242 provided penalties for breach of the provisions in section 123.

Section 57 authorized establishment of sample markets at Winnipeg, Fort William and Calgary, in which mixing of grain would be permitted under regulations established by the board. Section 126 (8) prohibited the mixing of grades in terminal elevators.

During the debate, senators urged the appointment of a special committee to hear evidence from interested parties, to which Sir Richard reluctantly acceded. The committee met and heard evidence from the grain growers' associations, the grain dealers and railway representatives and the mills. Over strong objections from senators Douglas, Davis and Talbot, the committee voted to delete the controversial clause 123. After it was passed by the senate, the bill advanced to second reading in the house on May 19. Because public concern over deletion of section 123 had not subsided, the house realized that it had before it an unwieldy bill which could not be disposed of in the hectic days remaining before the pending dissolution of parliament. Accordingly, its sponsor, the Honourable Frank Oliver, minister of the interior, agreed to withdraw the bill.

Meanwhile, during the election campaign fought on the reciprocity issue, Mr. Robert L. Borden, leader of the Liberal-Conservative party, toured the west, in the course of which he advocated government ownership of terminals and immediate construction of the Hudson Bay Railway. With both parties vying for western support in the matter of grain legislation, the decisive factor was the tariff issue which resulted in a few Liberal gains from Conservatives in the west; but in Ontario the Conservative sweep was substantial, and Mr. Borden formed the new government with a comfortable majority.

With the change in government, western producers now looked to the new administration to give effect to its leader's campaign promises. In December, 1911, the Honourable George E. Foster, the new minister of trade and commerce, moved first reading of a new grain bill. In summing up his motion on second reading January 30, 1912, the minister said, with as much perception as whimsy:

This is not my Bill particularly, nor the Bill of any party; it is, as nearly as possible, a non-partisan Bill. I am its foster-father, at the present moment, but the child is much the same as when it came from its original parents; a little better dressed up it may be, but still it is intrinsically the same child, and I take it that the parent of that child was not a Liberal government or a Liberal-Conservative government, but it was the product of conferences of all the interests in the matter after successive years of examination and discussion.[31]

Although Mr. Foster had declared that the new bill was almost a replica of bill 209 which had been withdrawn by his predecessor in the 1911 session, farm leaders were disappointed over the failure of the bill to provide mandatory government ownership of terminals. A delegation from the grain growers' organizations came to Ottawa to watch the passage of the bill and repeatedly made representations to the minister, but Mr. Foster maintained the new government's decision to allow the terminals owned by the railways and those owned or leased by the grain companies to continue in business. On the other hand, as provided in section 13, the government would be empowered to build public terminals, and it was the government's intention to build one or two and have them operated as an experiment by the new board of grain commissioners. This was clearly a compromise solution, designed to placate the contending advocates of public and private ownership.

To add to their disappointment, producers' representatives learned that mixing of grades would not be effectively prohibited. On the one hand, section 57 of the bill authorized establishment of sample markets at Winnipeg, Fort William and Calgary which, if implemented, would involve mixing of grades. The grain growers' organizations had advocated sample markets, but in a situation where operation of country elevators would be taken out of the hands of the private trade. Moreover, the bill made an exception from the mixing prohibition in the case of treatment of out-of-condition grain in hospital elevators, and mixing could also take place in private terminals.

Lastly, the producers' representatives objected to a provision for suspension of the car order provisions whenever the board of grain commissioners might deem it "necessary and advisable in order to relieve congestion and dispatch of grain", and after a contentious debate extending over ten days' sittings, the house passed the bill in that form.

However, when the bill came up for debate in the senate it became apparent that the grain growers' associations had succeeded in their representations. The contentious provisions concerning the car order book were dropped and the provision for sample markets was rendered temporarily inoperative. The act received royal assent on April 1, 1912. The board of grain commissioners was immediately appointed, and the government chose as its first chief commissioner, Dr. Robert Magill, a professor of political economy at Dalhousie University, who had been chairman of the Saskatchewan elevator commission. As chairman of that commission, Magill had recommended against public ownership of country elevators and in favor of a provincially-assisted co-operative system.

---

[31]*House of Commons Debates,* January 30, 1912, col. 2174.

Under the provisions of the new act, the government built its first public terminal elevator at Port Arthur in 1913 with a capacity of 2,500,000 bushels. In 1914-1915 the government also built three large interior terminal elevators at Saskatoon, Moose Jaw and Calgary. Then followed construction in 1916 of a small transfer elevator at Vancouver as the Panama Canal began to come into use. It will be recalled that the 1906 royal commission had recommended against the construction of interior terminal elevators on grounds of expense and stopover charges. The new board of grain commissioners devoted six pages of its first annual report to a justification of the construction of the interior terminals.[32] Their use has been intermittent since. They have been valuable in years of congested storage space, in cleaning and treating out-of-condition grain, but they do not fit into the ordinary pattern of grain handling by the investor- and farmer-owned elevator companies. When they are used, higher transportation charges are entailed.

Although section 123 (1) of the act went through the formality of prohibiting any person having an interest in a terminal elevator from buying and selling grain, subsection 2 rendered the principle nugatory by permitting terminal elevator operations by any "persons approved by the Board".

Despite the inoperative provisions relating to sample markets, the grain companies were permitted by the act to operate hospital elevators for the treatment of tough, damp, rejected or otherwise damaged grain. Mixing of grades was permitted in such operations, and grain delivered from hospital elevators could be regraded.

Apart from its controversial features, the act accomplished the consolidation of all supervisory functions; it established statutory grades and made very detailed provision for the supervision of cleaning, binning and shipping of grain, documentation of receipts and shipments, and strict supervision over the annual weigh-up in each elevator, with penalties for shortages found in any grade.

SUMMARY

In this chapter emphasis has been placed upon redress of producers' grievances by the responsible ministers, whether they acted directly in response to the representations of producers and the trade, or upon the advice of royal commissions appointed to investigate grievances.

Throughout this period producers had made considerable progress in organizing among themselves and had formed not only growers' associations but growers' grain companies as well. By the time the Canada grain act of 1912 was enacted, farmer-owned companies had placed themselves effectively in competition with the privately owned grain companies. The origins of these farmer-owned companies will be reviewed in the next chapter.

In the transition from the first producer reaction to the "syndicate of syndicates" in 1897, to the passage of the grain act in 1912, which roughly coincided with the span of the Laurier administration, the federal government had developed an increasingly sensitive response to producers'

[32]*Sessional Paper No. 10d*, A. 1913, pp. 28-34.

representations as reflected in the cumulative progress of the regulatory legislation. Early issues, such as the producers' right to freedom of choice among marketing channels, had been resolved. Many of them had disappeared because of increasingly efficient regulation provided by legislation, and also because competition from farmer-owned country elevator systems and their extension into terminal elevator operations effectively removed the earlier but deep-rooted fears of an elevator monopoly. Over the same span, increasing competition among railway companies and the expansion of their rolling stock had overcome the worst of the evils that arose in the early years of car shortage. Public ownership of elevators, which remained an issue, would soon find a solution through experiment and compromise.

3

TRADE AND FARM ORGANIZATIONS

While the previous chapter reviewed government involvement in regulatory legislation in its most formative period from 1898 to 1912, it made only minimal reference to the trade and farm organizations which were formed in that period. For the record, the origins of these organizations should be set out. This will be done in summary fashion because, as mentioned in the introduction, detailed histories of the farmers' organizations and the development of their co-operative enterprises have already been written.

The bibliography includes *Deep Furrows,* in which Hopkins Moorhouse dramatized the events of which he was contemporary, and in which he had the benefit of personal acquaintance with the leaders who formed the farm organizations. His position as private secretary to Premier Roblin of Manitoba placed him in touch with all the principal performers. He was a journalist by training and his real name was Herbert Joseph Moorhouse. *A History of Farmers' Movements in Canada,* was written by L. A. Wood, a professor of economics who knew the leaders of farmers' movements in eastern Canada, and who used Moorhouse as a source for his account of the western farm movement. There are, in addition, three treatises, each in some debt to Moorhouse, including W. A. Mackintosh's *Agricultural Cooperation in Western Canada,* published in 1924, Harald S. Patton's *Grain Growers' Cooperation in Western Canada,* and J. F. Booth's *Cooperative Marketing of Grain in Western Canada,* both published in 1928. A more recent source is that of R. D. Colquette, *The First Fifty Years: A History of United Grain Growers Limited,* published in 1957. With such material readily available, there is no need to dwell upon the origins of the farm organizations, but rather to record their formation and early progress for purposes of ready reference in this study.

NORTH-WEST GRAIN DEALERS' ASSOCIATION

In 1901 the North-west elevator association was formed by the companies operating line elevators, with the object of promoting co-operation in matters such as the purchase of elevator supplies, and in pooling the cost of the daily price telegrams to agents at each shipping point. This association was reorganized in 1903 as the North-west grain dealers' association. Although its functions were wholly legitimate and served a useful purpose, the association quickly became identified in producers' minds as a combine. It became the target of numerous producer representations to government, and the object of attack by western members of parliament. Its formation in 1901 barely preceded the "wheat blockade". Charges of a combine reverberated when the association's members lowered street prices in consequence of the blockade. The members could not reasonably have been expected, however, to bear the extra costs of carrying grain which arose from the railway's car shortage.

TERRITORIAL GRAIN GROWERS' ASSOCIATION

This association stemmed from an indignation meeting organized by John A. Millar and John Gifford at Indian Head in the autumn of 1901 which about fifty farmers attended, including W. R. Motherwell and Peter Dayman. The latter called a larger meeting on the afternoon of December 18, 1901, when a good attendance was assured because farmers from the surrounding district were coming into town to hear a debate scheduled for that evening between Premiers Roblin of Manitoba and Haultain of the North-West Territories on the question of annexation of East Assiniboia by the province of Manitoba. A third meeting was held on January 6, 1902, at which formal organization of the association and approval of its constitution took place. Its first board of directors confirmed Motherwell as president and Millar as secretary-treasurer. Matthew Snow of Wolseley became first vice-president and G. W. Brown of Regina, second vice-president. Directors included Walter Govan and M. M. Warden of Indian Head and Peter Dayman and Elmer Shaw of Abernethy. By February of that year, 38 locals had been formed and the association's first annual convention was held at Indian Head later that month. It was this newly-organized association which sent Motherwell and Dayman to Winnipeg to complain to the CPR about car distribution, and which laid the complaint in the Sintaluta case.

In 1906, in deference to the newly-formed provinces, the parent grain growers' association changed its name to the Saskatchewan Grain Growers' Association.

MANITOBA GRAIN GROWERS' ASSOCIATION

The Sintaluta case and the Manitoba grain act amendment of 1902 stimulated the membership campaign of the Territorial association, and Motherwell was invited to address a gathering of Manitoba farmers at Virden on January 3, 1903. Following that meeting, the Manitoba group, under the leadership of J. W. Scallion, held a provincial convention at Brandon March 3-4, 1903, at which the Manitoba grain growers' association was formally organized and a constitution similar to that of the Territorial association was adopted.

The names and addresses of the first board of directors of the Manitoba grain growers' association were as follows: J. W. Scallion (Virden), president; R. C. Henders (Culross), vice-president; Roderick McKenzie (Brandon) secretary-treasurer; Donald McEwen (Brandon), William Ryan (Boissevain), W. A. Robinson (Elva), D. H. McCuaig (Portage la Prairie), John Wilson (Lenore), and H. A. Fraser (Hamiota), directors.

Some years later the Manitoba association was renamed the United Farmers of Manitoba.

UNITED FARMERS OF ALBERTA

In 1904 the Alberta branches of the American Society of Equity reorganized under the name of the Canadian Society of Equity. In 1905 several branches of the new Canadian society united with Alberta locals of the Territorial grain growers' association under the name of the Alberta farmers' association. In 1909, the main body of the Canadian society of equity formally united with the Alberta farmers' association to form the United Farmers of Alberta. Its first executive included James Bower (Red Deer), president; Rice Sheppard (Strathcona), vice-president; Edward J. Fream (Calgary), secretary; G. A. Dixon (Fishburn), A. von Mielecki (Calgary), George Long (Edmonton), George McDonald (Olds), Thomas Balaam (Vegreville), L. H. Jelliffe (Spring Coulee), E. Carswell (Penhold), and H. Jamieson (Red Deer), directors.

CANADIAN COUNCIL OF AGRICULTURE

The three provincial growers' associations had good reason to organize themselves interprovincially in presentation of a common front on issues of mutual concern. This they did by forming the interprovincial council in 1907. Two years later the council joined forces with farm associations in eastern Canada, notably the grange in Ontario, to create a national organization which was named the Canadian Council of Agriculture and which, after a hiatus in the thirties, was replaced by today's Canadian Federation of Agriculture. The history of the Ontario grange has been recorded in detail by L. A, Wood. Its metamorphosis in the form of the United Farmers of Ontario provided the power base for a provincial political movement which elected a farmer-labour government on October 20, 1919, with E. C. Drury becoming premier of Ontario.[1]

As an opening venture, the Canadian council of agriculture organized, as mentioned in the last chapter, the "Siege of Ottawa" in 1910. It played an active role in presenting the views of organized farmers to government during the enactment of the 1912 Canada grain act.

GRAIN GROWERS' GRAIN COMPANY LIMITED

After the grain growers' associations had succeeded in obtaining amendments to the Manitoba grain act in 1902 and in 1903 and in having the royal commission appointed in 1906, they became involved in an internal issue as to whether they should enter into business on their own account. One of their members E. A. Partridge, who migrated from England to settle in the Qu'Appelle Valley in 1883, had developed an exceptional talent for organization inspired by the socialist philosophy of Ruskin. He was active in the Territorial grain growers' association and inveighed against the "combine" vested in the Winnipeg grain exchange and the North-west grain dealers' association. In the interest of the association he spent a month in Winnipeg in the autumn of 1905 in a personal observation of the operations of the exchange, in the course of which he made more enemies than friends. But he convinced himself that farmers' interests would be well served by

---

[1]L. A. Wood, *op. cit.,* pp. 282-283. For an account of the E. C. Drury administration, *ibid.,* pp. 331-337.

organizing a farmer-owned company to operate as a commission merchant on the exchange. He shrewdly identified that sector of the trade as the place for a farm organization to start, because of the relatively small investment required, and this was an important consideration for a farmer-backed enterprise.

On his return from Winnipeg, Partridge addressed the third annual convention of the Manitoba grain growers' association at Brandon and shortly afterwards a convention of the Territorial association at Moose Jaw. In both cases, members expressed genuine misgivings over the proposal to enter into a business venture because earlier attempts, under the aegis of the Patrons of industry, had failed. As a result, the associations took no formal action as sponsors.

Nevertheless, individual members who supported Partridge joined with him to form a joint stock company to be operated on co-operative principles and in which the stockholders must be bona fide farmers. At an organizational meeting held at the town hall in Sintaluta on January 27, 1906, the first 200 shares of the Grain Growers' Grain Company were subscribed, and a stock selling campaign was begun. The campaign continued through the spring and summer of 1906, and a Manitoba charter was obtained. E. A. Partridge was elected president; John Kennedy, vice-president; and John Spencer, secretary-treasurer. The executive engaged as the company's manager, Thomas Coulter of the Independent Grain company, an experienced grain man who impressed Partridge during the latter's visit to Winnipeg the previous autumn. The company commenced operations on September 5, 1906, when it opened a small office in Winnipeg.

GRAIN GROWERS' GRAIN COMPANY VS THE WINNIPEG GRAIN EXCHANGE

The new company had operated for only six weeks when an issue arose which brought the company and the exchange into direct confrontation. A pamphlet circulated by the company which indicated its intention to distribute its net profits on a patronage basis was drawn to the attention of the council of the exchange. Because such action would have been in violation of an exchange bylaw which prohibited the splitting of commissions, the council summoned Partridge to answer a charge of intended violation. At the meeting, Partridge contended that the bylaws of his company contained no provision for patronage distribution, but in response to the council's request he refused to bring his directors to Winnipeg to explain the discrepancy between the company's bylaws and the statement in the pamphlet. Shortly thereafter, the council concluded that a violation of the exchange's bylaws was, in fact, intended, and it decided to withdraw the company's trading privileges, and to notify other members not to deal with it.

The withdrawal of trading privileges was a punitive blow which resulted in acute financial embarrassment to the company and might have driven it out of business. But grain already consigned to it was arriving at Winnipeg in increasing volume, on the handling of which the company now had no ready means of earning an income. If it sold its grain by payment of the mandatory one-cent per bushel commission to a firm of good standing, this would leave no income whatever for the Grain Growers' Grain Company.

Nevertheless, the company made some direct sales to mills in eastern Canada, and before long the Scottish Co-operative Wholesale Society which was operating in Winnipeg, took compassion on the fledgling co-operative by buying from it and allowing it the full commission despite the exchange's prohibition. By December, 1906, the company had incurred a net overdraft of $356,000 with its bank, which the three officers of the company (Partridge, Kennedy and Spencer) secured by personal bond.

The plight of the company had provoked widespread resentment in the country, and the Manitoba grain growers' association decided to come to its aid by retaliating against the exchange on three separate fronts. The association made representations to the Manitoba government, it gave evidence before the royal commission, and it instituted court action against the exchange.

In its appearance before the Manitoba house committee on agriculture. the Manitoba grain growers' association made representations against the practices of exchange, and the exchange representatives presented their side of the issue. In the hope of resolving the impasse, Premier Roblin offered to convene a conference of all interested parties, including representatives of the grain growers, grain exchange, government, railroads and banks. The association also testified before the royal commission, and on the basis of evidence it had adduced, it persuaded the crown to prosecute members of the council of the exchange on a charge of having "unlawfully conspired, combined or arranged with each other, to restrain or injure trade or commerce in relation to grain". This the crown did by entering an action in the assize court.

While all this pressure was being exerted against the exchange, the Grain Growers' Grain Company and the exchange made a serious and successful attempt to settle their differences. First, the Grain Growers' Grain Company at a special meeting removed the contentious issue by resolving that the company would not pay patronage dividends, but would distribute net profits to its shareholders instead. Shares of the company had been offered exclusively to producers. Then, President McCuaig of the Manitoba grain growers' association prevailed upon the acting premier to intercede with the exchange. As a result, the exchange called a general meeting at which reinstatement of the Grain Growers' Grain Company was approved. To facilitate the decision, the company agreed to place its membership in the name of John Spencer, its secretary-treasurer, instead of in Partridge's, whose public denunciations of the exchange had also provoked resentment. Restoration of the company's trading privileges took place on April 27, 1907.

The confrontation might well have ended there, except that the legal and political processes engendered by the Manitoba grain growers' association were still in train. Shortly afterward, the crown's case under section 498 of the criminal code failed in the assize court. Mr. Justice Phippen's decision stated that:

> The evidence offered assumed the form of an investigation into the conditions governing the grain trade of the west, rather than a trial of the charges

specified in the indictment. . . . With all the evidence before me, I am forced
to the opinion that not only was no undue restraint of trade disclosed, but that
the very acts complained of, taken in connection with their surrounding
conditions, made on the whole for a more stable market at the fullest values
and so for the public good.[2]

A year later, when the royal commission on the grain trade of Canada,
1906, submitted its report in 1908, it also exonerated the exchange by
concluding that no "undue" restraint of trade had been proved.

Meanwhile, the provincial conference on the grain trade which Premier
Roblin had promised was held in June, 1907, and the participants
represented a broad cross section of the industry. But, the Manitoba grain
growers' association pressed the issue by moving a resolution to the effect
that the bylaws, rules and regulations of the exchange should be subject to
approval by the lieutenant-governor in council. Such action was feasible
under provincial law because the exchange was incorporated under a
provincial charter. Over the objections of exchange representatives, the
resolution was pressed to a vote and it carried, whereupon the exchange
representatives withdrew from the conference. In response to the resolution,
however, Premier Roblin introduced a bill in the legislature in January,
1908, which was duly enacted and which subjected the bylaws of the
exchange to the supervision of the court of king's bench.

At a general meeting held after the legislation was enacted, the exchange
decided to cease operations under its existing charter. The immediate effect
of this decision was the termination of futures trading on February 26, 1908.
From then until September, only informal curb trading was carried on in
the absence of the discipline of the exchange's bylaws. The disruption to the
whole marketing system was only tempered by the fact that it occurred
within a period of light country deliveries. After its charter was cancelled,
when the next harvest got underway, the exchange reopened as a voluntary
association, and it has continued to operate on that basis since. Futures
trading was resumed in September, 1908.[3]

PUBLIC OWNERSHIP OF COUNTRY ELEVATORS

Although the Manitoba grain growers' association had failed in its
immediate endeavour to subject the bylaws of the Winnipeg grain exchange
to approval by the provincial government, the confrontation had undoubtedly strengthened the support for the farm organizations in the country. In
the matter of grain handling, however, the growers' net accomplishment to
date was the establishment of the grain growers' commission firm. Capital
requirements entailed in establishing a farmer-owned country system were a
genuine deterrent in that direction so, until producers found an effective
alternative marketing system, they remained dependent upon the use of flat
warehouses and loading platforms and the physical effort involved in those
alternatives. Because they lacked sufficient resources to build their own
elevators, the grain growers' associations began to agitate for public
ownership of country elevators.

---

[2] *Western Law Reporter 19* (1907), cited in Patton *op. cit.*, p. 59.
[3] For a more detailed account of these events, see Patton, *op. cit.*, Chap. V.

They first recommended to the royal commission of 1906 that the government should erect a system of interior elevators. When this proposal was discouraged by the commission, the grain growers' associations recommended to all three provincial governments an interprovincial system of public ownership of country elevators. The provincial premiers sought to head off the issue by proposing that the railways should enter into country elevator operations, with managers appointed and controlled by the grain growers' associations. The growers' associations were not impressed, and maintained their pressure upon the provincial governments. As a result, the Manitoba government agreed to embark upon a public system in 1909. The government acquired 174 elevators, but after only two years abandoned the scheme as a failure. It was alleged that the prices paid for elevators were too high and that patronage had entered into the appointment of elevator agents. In addition, the system's earnings were derived from storage and handling charges only, and it could not compete effectively with line elevator companies which operated also as grain merchants. In the combination of circumstances, serious operating deficits accrued.

Although the other grain growers' associations had endeavored to persuade the Saskatchewan and Alberta governments to acquire and operate country elevators in those provinces, their governments circumvented the public ownership issue by providing alternatives referred to below. In 1912 the Manitoba government withdrew from the venture by leasing its elevators to the Grain Growers' Grain Company Limited. The leasing arrangements preceded eventual purchase. On the Grain Growers' Grain Company's part, the company fully appreciated the competitive advantages the line companies enjoyed from the combination of warehousing and merchandising operations, and concluded that if the solution were not to be found through public ownership, a farmers' company should enter the field. Thus the Manitoba government's experiment in public ownership played into the hands of the farmer-owned company by its leasing arrangement, which permitted the company to proceed on a pay-as-you-go basis in the development of its own system of country elevators.

SASKATCHEWAN CO-OPERATIVE ELEVATOR COMPANY LIMITED

Instead of yielding to pressure from the Saskatchewan grain growers' association for a system of provincially-owned elevators in that province, the Saskatchewan government, in February, 1910, appointed an elevator commission to study the problem. The commission recommended against direct government operation of elevators; instead, it recommended creation of a farmer-owned and operated co-operative elevator system, in which the government would provide major financial assistance.[4] In conformity with

[4]V. C. Fowke commented on the findings of the elevator commission, as follows:

"The Saskatchewan government met the demand for public ownership by appointing a royal commission to investigate and report. This commission was headed by Robert Magill, Professor of Political Economy at Dalhousie. The scholarly reasoning by means of which he demonstrated in his report that public ownership of elevators would not work suggests strongly that he was opposed to public ownership in principle, and an inference hard to escape is that the Saskatchewan government was aware of that opposition before he was appointed. The positive recommendation of the Magill commission was that a co-operative

the commission's recommendation, the Saskatchewan government incorporated the Saskatchewan Co-operative Elevator Company Limited in 1911. The act of incorporation provided that 25 locals must be organized before the company could commence business. At the company's first general meeting held on July 6, 1911, 46 locals had been formed. The general meeting elected as the company's president, J. A. Maharg of Moose Jaw, who was also president of the Saskatchewan grain growers' association. George Langley (Maymont) was elected vice-president, and Charles A. Dunning (Beaverdale), secretary-treasurer.[5] In addition, James Robinson (Walpole), W. C. Sutherland (Saskatoon), N. E. Baumunk (Dundurn), A. G. Hawkes (Percival), J. E. Paynter (Tantallon), and Dr. E. J. Barrick were elected as directors.

ALBERTA FARMERS' CO-OPERATIVE ELEVATOR COMPANY LIMITED

In Alberta, a company similar to the one formed in Saskatchewan was incorporated by act of the provincial parliament in 1913. Although its organizers sought a guarantee of the company's bonded indebtedness by the government, this was not forthcoming because the organizers had proposed to place the company's management in the hands of the Grain Growers' Grain Company which operated outside the province. In the end the Grain Growers' Grain Company guaranteed the new company's account with the bank. At its first general meeting held on August 19, 1913, W. J. Tregillus of Calgary was elected president; J. Quinsey (Noble), vice-president; E. J. Fream (Calgary), secretary-treasurer, and E. Carswell (Red Deer), Rice Sheppard (Edmonton), P. D. Austin (Ranfurly), J. G. McKay (Provost), R. A. Parker (Winnifred), and C. Rice-Jones (Veteran), were elected directors.

UNITED GRAIN GROWERS LIMITED

With three provincial farmer-owned elevator systems in operation it was natural that the three companies should seek to amalgamate. Support for the move came from the organizations in Manitoba and Alberta. However, the Saskatchewan Co-operative Elevator Company executives pointed up several problems related to the sales subsidiaries of the elevator companies and in the end the Saskatchewan company opted against the proposal. The other two companies agreed to proceed, however, and the Alberta Farmers' Co-operative Elevator Company Limited and the Grain Growers' Grain Company Limited amalgamated in 1917, forming the United Grain Growers Limited, in which organizational form it operates today. United Grain Growers, in fact, sprang from the cluster of aggrieved farmers who

system of elevators be established with government loan support up to 85 per cent of the capital required. This recommendation was adopted in Saskatchewan and the example was followed in Alberta.

The Saskatchewan Elevator Commission of 1910 (the Magill commission), then, enabled both Saskatchewan and Alberta to avert the state ownership threat."

(*Royal Commissions and Canadian Agricultural Policy*, loc. cit., pp.170-171).

[5]The Honourable Charles A. Dunning, premier of Saskatchewan and later minister of finance in Ottawa, was thus identified in his early career with the farmers' co-operative movement.

met at Indian Head in 1901. Out of the membership of that group, the Grain Growers' Grain Company was formed a few years later under the inspiring but provocative leadership of its first president, E. A. Partridge. Then the company came under the presidency of T. A. Crerar, who contributed years of outstanding service to the developing company. Not long after the formation of the Grain Growers' Grain Company on a commission basis, its officers and shareholders recognized the need to open export sales agencies and, in order to compete effectively with the line elevator companies, to acquire and operate a system of country and terminal elevators.

DEVELOPMENT OF UNITED GRAIN GROWERS LIMITED AND THE SASKATCHEWAN CO-OPERATIVE ELEVATOR COMPANY LIMITED

As in the case of United Grain Growers Limited, the Saskatchewan company also extended its operations into the terminal elevator field. Both companies conducted their business operations in the same way as did the line elevator companies. They paid no patronage dividends but earnings were reinvested or paid out as stock dividends. They used the facilities of the grain exchange either by hedging the grain they carried or by immediate sale in the cash market.

As these companies achieved full status as operators of country and terminal elevators and as grain merchants operating their own domestic and export sales agencies, they were in a position to compete in all respects with the existing investor-owned companies. In this way they furnished producers for the first time with an effective alternative in the choice of elevator facilities. Although the Saskatchewan company limited its operations to grain marketing and handling, United Grain Growers Limited extended its activities into the co-operative purchase of farm supplies and machinery. It established a livestock department, a publishing company, and for a time engaged in a sawmill business to meet farmers' requirements.

TABLE 3:1
COMPARATIVE BUSINESS DEVELOPMENT OF UNITED GRAIN GROWERS (LTD.)
AND OF ITS PREDECESSORS

Company and Year	Paid-up Capital	Grain Receipts	Profits
Grain Growers' Grain Co. (Ltd.):		*Bushels*	
1906	$ 5,000		
1907	11,795	2,340,000	$ 790
1908	20,385	4,990,541	30,190
1909	120,708	7,643,146	52,902
1910	292,957	16,332,645	95,663
1911	494,062	18,845,305	69,575
1912	586,472	27,775,000	121,614
1913	645,362	29,975,000	164,333
1914	771,409	29,920,225	151,081
1915	867,422	18,821,402	226,963
1916	1,073,180	48,375,420	572,804
1917	1,357,382	27,722,552	607,899

TABLE 3:1 — *continued*

Alberta Farmers' Co-op. Elevator Co. (Ltd.):		*Bushels*	
1914	$ 101,639	3,774,396	$ 17,216
1915	163,869	5,039,100	28,826
1916	301,737	19,320,556	282,484
1917	563,689	16,375,333	236,502
United Grain Growers (Ltd.):			
1918	2,159,763	29,879,672	441,760
1919	2,415,185	22,203,007	148,549
1920	2,608,547	24,503,237	463,675
1921	2,765,685	36,581,371	233,743
1922	2,810,561	31,545,776	118,350
1923	2,821,305	32,944,668	532,171
1924	2,857,984	47,163,179	552,433
1925	2,809,627	30,855,532	418,574
1926	2,920,620	43,013,807	676,378
Total		575,940,870	6,007,775

SOURCE: J. F. Booth, *Cooperative Marketing of Grain in Western Canada*, USDA Technical Bulletin No. 63, 1928, p. 21.

TABLE 3:2
COMPARATIVE FINANCIAL POSITION OF THE
SASKATCHEWAN CO-OPERATIVE ELEVATOR CO. (LTD.)

Fiscal Year Ended July 31	Paid-Up Capital	Value of Land Bldg. and Equipt.	Government Loans and Accrued Interest	Reserves	Net Profit
1912	$ 176,580	$ 479,702	$ 393,694	$ —	$ 52,461
1913	227,152	1,290,228	1,205,843	51,726	167,926
1914	382,461	1,684,090	1,436,031	116,250	285,181
1915	503,116	1,866,099	1,569,808	286,834	133,745
1916	627,342	2,045,621	1,639,267	322,973	557,795
1917	938,932	3,032,456	1,794,108	612,436	350,752
1918	1,104,560	4,172,765	1,737,442	979,831	124,811
1919	1,112,312	4,728,799	2,176,960	1,069,591	193,599
1920	1,132,737	5,157,398	3,150,684	1,233,119	224,988
1921	1,408,136	5,160,271	3,256,164	1,190,622	279,413
1922	1,451,306	5,202,067	3,305,228	1,434,359	463,056
1923	1,719,952	5,431,981	3,346,855	1,624,094	442,212
1924	1,956,930	6,248,708	2,570,658	2,284,463	475,534
1925	2,396,633	6,785,781	2,466,801	2,378,439	377,872
1926	2,608,412	7,560,871	2,336,743	2,608,412	825,547

SOURCE: J. F. Booth *Cooperative Marketing of Grain in Western Canada*, USDA Technical Bulletin No. 63, 1928, p. 21.

4

THE GREAT WAR AND THE OPEN MARKET

The passage of the Canada grain act presaged a perceptible lull, at least, in producer grievances over the next few years. There were now three competing transcontinental railways with their main and branch lines serving the west, and this helped the car supply. The bitter prospect of bankruptcy attributable to over-capitalization of the two more recently built lines was looming, and their nationalization became a wartime reality. Although the debate over their social cost had begun with the formation of these lines, the full evidence was still coming in. Meanwhile western farmers, unquestionably, were to be counted among the beneficiaries of the railway expansion. Terminal elevator capacity at the lakehead was considerably extended. In this the federal government played a part, on a trial basis, as well as building interior terminal elevators and a small terminal at Vancouver. It was a mild and very partial response to the clamor for public ownership and, except for the interior elevators, the terminals were eventually leased to country elevator companies which sought to add terminal operations to their grain-handling systems. Farmer-owned companies, meanwhile, had entered the grain-handling business. By these several means, including the enactment of the Canada grain act, the major sources of producer discontent had been ameliorated.

EXPORT CONTROL

When war was declared in 1914, wheat growers experienced for the first time the concern of wartime governments with production, direction and assurance of food supplies.

To understand the working relations which existed between governments at the time, it is necessary to recall that Canada had not yet emerged from colonial status in its formal relations with Britain. Official communication between the two governments was through the governor-general in Ottawa and the colonial office in London. A Canadian high commissioner resident in London provided a second, but subordinate, line of communication. Contemporary pages of the house of commons debates abound with references to the mother country, to the imperial government, and to the virtue of the united foreign policy in which the British government spoke not only for itself but for all the dominions. The formal line of communication between the Canadian and United States governments was through the colonial office in London to the British embassy in Washington. One Canadian official served as an adviser in the British embassy, and it was not until the end of the war that the question of posting a Canadian minister to Washington was mooted. This background is essential to an appreciation of the fact that the Canadian government did not negotiate then on a basis of equal status with either the British or United States governments and that Canadian interests were prone to become a pawn in direct negotiations between Britain and the United States. In general, however, and especially under wartime conditions, the working relations among the three governments were conducted in an atmosphere of co-operation and accommodation.

A first example lay in the wartime control over the movement of wheat. The British government immediately established a committee to deal with the question of prohibition of exports from Britain, from any dominion or British possession, of articles, including foofstuffs, which could be of use to the enemy. In response to representations from that committee, as Sir Robert Borden explained to the house, the Canadian government passed an order in council on October 29, 1914, which prohibited the exportation from Canada of a long list of articles including wheat, flour and other grains to all foreign ports in Europe and on the Mediterranean and Black Seas, with the exception of those of France, Spain and Portugal, and certain Russian ports. Apart from Spain and Portugal, this order effectively cut off Canadian exports to all other European neutral countries.[1] The order was soon extended to include neutral destinations whether in Europe or elsewhere (apart fron the United States) so placing in effect an embargo on Canadian grain exports except to Britain, France and the United States. This restriction of markets was not onerous, however, due to the relatively light 1914 crop. When British and French buyers came into the market, their purchases brought about a substantial price increase.

But the fact remained that from the beginning of the war the Canadian government placed wheat and flour under export license and did not issue licenses without the approval of the British government. When it later became necessary to seek additional outlets, the Canadian government asked the British government for consideration and assistance. In this way the Canadian government was drawn, for the first time, and almost imperceptibly, into the area of wheat marketing policy, as distinct from the regulatory function it had hitherto performed in respect of grain.

On the question of price policy, Sir Robert Borden made it clear that the Canadian government would not interfere with open market prices. Farmers had been forced to accept low peacetime prices, and were therefore entitled to any higher prices the market might realize in wartime.[2] This remained the Canadian government's price policy until the market encountered difficulties of its own in 1917. In the same fashion as it left prices to be determined by the open market, the Canadian government left merchandising to the private trade, which operated within the government-imposed export restrictions. Canadian wheat prices had traded around the

[1] *House of Commons Debates,* March 1, 1915, p. 553.
[2] *Ibid.*

90 cent level prior to the outbreak of war, and had risen to a peak of $1.62 for No. 1 Northern in store Fort William by May, 1915. Then, in anticipation of the record harvest of 393,000,000 bushels in 1915, prices dropped below the dollar level again in September of that year.

EARLY SALES PROBLEMS

With the prospect of a bumper crop, whose movement was fettered by export restrictions and falling prices, the farm organizations and the trade made strong representations to the Canadian government. Moreover the British trade, finding themselves in a buyers' market, behaved as sensible buyers would do, by staying out of the market.

This was the setting in which the Canadian government became directly involved in wheat marketing policy. Its first step was to make government-to-government representations, which eventually culminated in the commandeering of available wheat stocks before the close of navigation in 1915. Within a very few years it would become even more deeply involved in marketing through the fixation of prices, the direction of exports, and in the selling of wheat on behalf of producers.

At this initial stage, however, there was considerable doubt in Sir Robert Borden's mind over which minister should be chosen to assume the wheat marketing responsibility. Although Sir George Foster (by then knighted), had been appointed by Borden on the formation of his cabinet as minister of trade and commerce, and was responsible for the administration of the Canada grain act which he had piloted through the house in 1912, the prime minister held Foster's business ability in low regard. Borden had already placed the responsibility for procuring oats for the British army under the minister of agriculture, the Honourable Martin Burrell, and wheat could be handled in the same way. Moreover, the Honourable Arthur Meighen and the Honourable Robert Rogers represented Manitoba constituencies and were more conversant with the grain industry than was Foster. As a New Brunswick-born student of the classics, politics and international affairs, wheat was far from being Foster's principal preoccupation, but the record of the next few years shows how tenaciously Foster worked to establish and retain the responsibility for wheat marketing which he considered to be within his departmental jurisdiction. In his diaries and papers relating to the critical periods for wheat policy which occurred during his administration, Foster preserved a highly enlightening record of his policy innovations, several of which became precedents for policies in effect today.

Among his papers covering the first critical period, Foster had collected 33 telegrams relating to the sale of wheat, which passed between the governor-general and the colonial secretary from June to December, 1915, and seven supplementary telegrams which passed between the office of the prime minister and the Canadian high commissioner in London. At that time, the governor-general was Prince Arthur, a younger son of Queen Victoria, who had become Field Marshall H.R.H. The Duke of Connaught, K.G. The colonial secretary was the Right Honourable Andrew Bonar Law (Canadian-born leader of the British Conservative party who joined the wartime coalition cabinet and won office for his party in 1922, when he served briefly as prime minister prior to his death in 1923). Although the telegrams are too numerous for full reproduction here, the key ones give the flavor of the representations. The cramped position in which the wheat industry had been placed by the export restrictions is reflected in the initial telegram of the series forwarded by the governor-general to the colonial secretary on June 16, 1915:

> Confidential. My advisers are receiving very strong representations respecting limitation of market for food stuffs which may be summarized as follows:
>
> First. There is a large supply of food stuffs such as flour and oats and their products now available in Canada and a very large crop is expected for the current year which will create a great exportable surplus.
>
> Second. A similar condition prevails in the United States which competes with Canada in the sale of such products.
>
> Third. The markets of the world are open to the United States producer and exporter while the markets hitherto available to the Canadian producer and exporter are excluded.
>
> Fourth. It is represented that orders from Great Britain and France to Canada have practically ceased and that such orders particularly from France are being filled by United States exporters to whom the world's markets are open and not by Canadian exporters whose markets are exceedingly circumscribed under prohibition created by Order in Council.
>
> Fifth. Large orders could be filled in Dutch West Indies, in South America and elsewhere if permission were granted.
>
> My advisers thoroughly realize the vital importance of preventing food products reaching enemy countries but on the other hand they are confronted with a large exportable surplus of food products for which apparently there is little or no market in Great Britain or allied countries or other countries to which export is permitted. They submit these conditions for consideration of His Majesty's Government and would be grateful for their suggestions at earliest opportunity.[3]

The telegrams bore the signature "ARTHUR". On July 2 a reply was made to the effect that the army council would be prepared not only to continue receiving 4,000 tons of Canadian oats weekly, but to consider the question of taking larger quantities, if they were to become available from the new crop. In response the Canadian government furnished the information requested on oats, but added rather poignantly that its telegram of June 16 had been primarily concerned with flour and cereal products as articles of chief importance. The original telegram would have been more effective, had it referred specifically to wheat. Then came a rejoinder on July 20 that His Majesty's government did not see their way clear to purchase even a part of that year's Canadian wheat crop. In the circumstances, they had no objection to the enlargement of the existing market for Canadian wheat by the establishment of a liberal system of licenses to destinations where there were adequate guarantees against shipments reaching enemy hands.

Canadian newspapers pursued the debate. An article in the *Toronto World,* August 26, 1915, stated that:

> The Canadian farmer has only one customer, England. He cannot ship to any neutral country. He certainly cannot sell to Russia. Will he be able to sell to France or Italy?

[3] *Sir George Foster's Papers,* Public Archives of Canada.

The French and Italians are not buying wheat in Canada, and they are likely to supply their needs in the United States. Just now the Bank of France has arranged with Brown Brothers of New York for credit of 20 million dollars. We are told that: "the purpose of this credit is to enable the American exporters to be paid in dollars in the United States, eliminating any risk of exchange and thus facilitating exports."

If any Canadian wheat goes to France or Italy it will go by England or be purchased through the British government. We hope that Britain is buying no wheat in the United States. We have the moral right to insist that all her wheat be purchased here and purchased at a fair price. We have no hesitation in saying that the British government should buy the entire Canadian crop of 1915 available for export. In no other way can our farmers be assured of getting the cash quickly for their wheat. In no other way can many of them avoid serious loss.

In the highly unsatisfactory position which persisted while British buyers remained out of the market, the Canadian government dispatched another telegram on September 10, 1915, through the governor-general to the colonial secretary:

Secret. My advisers find it necessary to press upon the serious consideration of His Majesty's Government the very difficult conditions confronting Canadian producers of food products. Under existing Orders in Council exportation of wheat and other grains and their products is prohibited to all neutral countries except the United States. Exportation to United States is permitted when for consumption in the United States only or when shipped to specified consignees in the United Kingdom via United States or when exported via United States under license or dispensation from Canada. Recent Order in Council also permits exportation of wheat and wheat flour when consigned to Netherlands Government. Exportable surplus of United States probably five hundred million bushels and in Canada nearly two hundred million bushels. Producers in United States which is chief competitor of Canada have access to all neutral markets from which however Canadian producer is entirely excluded except under license. These conditions have depressed and will continue to depress prices to Canadian producer as compared with United States producer. Considering the enormous exportable surplus of United States which has access to all neutral markets Canadian farmers unable to understand (what) possible detriment can arise (if) our exportable surplus amounting to about one third of theirs placed on the same footing. They naturally consider that this additional one third cannot (possibly) affect situation as United States surplus is more than sufficient of itself to supply requirements of all neutral countries. They thus conclude that present restrictions are of no advantage to Imperial interests but of marked disadvantage to their individual interest. Western Canada Provinces have displayed not only willingness, but eagerness to make highest sacrifices but in the face of oppressive competition from the United States they will be most unfavourably influenced by demand for sacrifices which appear to them absolutely futile. Under these circumstances my advisers will feel themselves constrained in immediate future to consider the removal of the restrictions hitherto established unless they are convinced that such removal would be detrimental to Imperial interests. The proposed licensing system especially under the conditions expressed in your telegram 20th July is of little advantage as prompt decision and reply in such business transactions is imperatively necessary to ensure fair competition in neutral markets.[4]

4*Ibid.*

FIRST CABINET WHEAT COMMITTEE

While the Canadian representations to the British government continued, other problems had also arisen from the shortage of shipping and rising freight costs. Sir Robert Borden recalled the situation in his memoirs as he wrote on September 10, 1915:

> To add to all these difficulties and complexities there arose trouble and controversy as to the grain situation, due to Foster's (Sir George Foster — Minister of Trade and Commerce) lack of business sense and inexperience and his keen desire to undertake tasks of a practical nature for which he was entirely unfitted.[5]

Borden resolved the ministerial issue by appointing a cabinet committee with the Honourable Robert Rogers, minister of public works, as chairman, and Foster, Burrell, Reid and Meighen as members. The importance Borden attached to the committee is reflected in his letter of September 16, 1915, to Rogers:

> As you may remember, a Committee was appointed immediately after my return from England for the purpose of considering the situation with regard to the transportation of wheat and other agricultural products across the Atlantic during the present season. That committee consisted of you as Chairman, Sir George Foster, Mr. Burrell, Dr. Reid and Mr. Meighen.
>
> I am convinced that the urgency and importance of the question make it essential that unremitting attention should be given to it from day to day. Your knowledge of conditions in the Western Provinces and your study of the problem involved in the question now under consideration make it exceedingly important that you should give your personal and undivided attention thereto. In this all the members of the Committee will I am sure second and aid your efforts in every way that you may desire. I understand that the nature of your Departmental duties at the present will permit you to undertake this work. Sir George Foster to whom I spoke on the subject yesterday is entirely willing that you should do so and he will of course assist in every possible way.
>
> It is desirable I think that the Committee should have a Secretary who will give the whole of his time and energies to his duties as such. I would suggest that Mr. Sanford Evans who has made a very wide study of problems of transportation and marketing should act as Secretary.[6]

Although Borden referred to the committee as concerned with the transportation of wheat and other agricultural products across the Atlantic, and Foster referred to it in his diary as the Atlantic grain transport committee, its terms of reference were sufficiently general to make it comparable with the cabinet wheat committee established many years later in 1935. This first cabinet wheat committee did not enjoy a long life, however. It was active in the autumn of 1915, but further references to it disappeared after Foster established himself more firmly in his responsibility for wheat policy. It did occur to Borden, however, to name a secretary to the committee; the second cabinet wheat committee functioned for its first seven years without one.

Few references were made in Foster's diary to the work of the committee; in fact, his reference of September 23, 1915, was the most expansive, in which lake transportation and congestion at the seaboard were the issues.

[5] *Robert Laird Borden: His Memoirs*, (Macmillan, Toronto, 1930), p. 510.
[6] *Foster Papers*, Public Archives of Canada.

Foster wrote:

> Deputation of Canadian Lake Marine Association met me at noon as to capacity for grain cargoes from head of the Lakes to lower lake ports and Montreal. Seems to be sufficient. Meeting of Atl. Grain Transport Committee and discussed matters. . . . We are able to do little for scarcity of tonnage and quantity of products makes costs of transport high and world wide. Council, but little done.[7]

The committee functioned only that autumn, after which it fell into disuse.

COMMANDEERING OF WHEAT

In the continuing communications between the Canadian and British governments on the sale of wheat, there followed during October and November, 1915, a considerable exchange of telegrams in which the British government proposed that the Canadian government sell wheat and oats to the Swiss and Italian governments and wheat to Portugal. These eventually shaped up as firm commitments when, early in November, the British authorized the sale to Italy of 4,000 metric tons of wheat monthly and also a total of 2,000,000 bushels of oats. The British government acted as intermediary in the negotiations during the course of which the Italians kept revising their requirements upward, and in the end approved a firm commitment for the Canadian government to buy for Italian account, at best prices obtainable, 150,000 metric tons of wheat monthly for a period of five months, and somewhat more than half that quantity of oats. As the Italians were unable to arrange their own shipping for a movement of this volume, the Canadian government was requested to charter the freight, which was under control of the British admiralty. The order for the Italian wheat was placed on November 23, 1915. At the same time, the British and French governments made known their requirements for Canadian wheat in the immediate future, amounting to some 50,000,000 bushels between them. Thus ended the period of long anxiety for the Canadian government about its ability to move the large 1915 crop; the tables were turned, for there was now considerable doubt about whether enough was in forward position to meet the newly-scheduled export shipments.

Immediately upon receipt of the firm order from Italy and the indication of British and French requirements, the cabinet wheat committee considered the merits of purchasing through the open market the wheat to fulfill these commitments, as against the alternative of commandeering all the top grades of wheat in terminal and eastern positions in order to avoid a price upheaval. Foster called in a group of advisers from the trade, shippers, and the Grain Growers' Grain Company. After consulting the experts and raising the matter in cabinet with the prime minister, on November 27 the members of the cabinet wheat committee wired the terminal elevator authorities at the lakehead and in the east, the government's decision to commandeer existing wheat stocks. These amounted to 13,621,806 bushels of which 10,300,364 were at the lakehead and the balance in the east.[8] Prices at which the wheat was commandeered were the closing levels on

[7] *Foster Diaries*, Public Archives of Canada.
[8] This was the official figure furnished in reply to a question (*House of Commons Debates*, February 3, 1916, p. 544). Somewhat higher figures were mentioned in the memorandum reproduced on p. 71.

November 27 of $1.04¾ for No. 1 Northern, $1.03⅛ for No. 2 Northern, and 98¾ cents for No. 3 Northern. The commandeered stocks were turned over to the allies and mills at the same prices.

Sir Robert Borden recalled the whole chain of events in his memoirs:

Toward the end of November there was tremendous excitement occasioned by the Order-in-Council commandeering grain. During the summer a very difficult problem had arisen with regard to wheat supply. A huge prospective Canadian crop, shortage in transport, steady increase in freight rates and a current lowering in prices together with the possible opening of the Dardenelles to Russian wheat combined to create this situation. Although every possible assistance was given to the release of ships for transport, the supply did not meet the demand and congestion of freight at all ports, increasing rates and the holding through the winter of 100,000,000 bushels of wheat resulted. By Order-in-Council in April of this year the export of wheat to any except British countries and the Allies and to the United States under bond had been prohibited. Special permission for export to neutral countries could be obtained after application and arrangements for delivery had been made. On September 20th, a Committee of the Cabinet composed of Rogers (chairman) Sir George Foster, Reid, Burrell and Meighen, with Sanford Evans as secretary, was appointed, to deal with the whole question of marketing the grain crop. As a result of the findings of the Commission, Mr. Meighen on November 29th, issued the following official statement: "The phenomenal crop of wheat in the Canadian west has brought upon the Government the duty of assisting to the farthest extent possible in the marketing. The supply of wheat the world over is known to have been abundant, and the importance of taking advantage of every opportunity to provide for the disposing of our grain is on that account the greater. For many months, the Government has been in touch with the British authorities with a view to procuring orders from the United Kingdom and the Allied Governments in order that the utmost share of the consuming demand of those countries may be turned toward our Canadian surplus. As a consequence of this, the British Government had required the Canadian Government to provide within a short time a very large supply of Nos. 1, 2 and 3 Northern Wheat.

The problem of meeting these requirements and of doing so at such prices as would induce the repetition of orders in Canada, then confronted the Government. The effect of Government purchases in the open market, such as were made by different countries a year ago, is well known to the public. The market rises abnormally, adding to the profits of the grain dealers and speculators who have purchased the grain that the Government require. The advance in price of the large amounts of grain in store becomes the loss of the owner of the stored grain. To secure the desired end this year the Government determined Saturday November 27th, to commandeer all Nos. 1, 2 and 3 Northern wheat at the head of the Lakes and eastward. This involves the purchase of anywhere from 12 to 15 million bushels. The price paid has not yet been settled by the Government but will shortly be fixed on a fair basis.

Much controversy and discussion resulted from this announcement; and the members of the Government were deluged with telegrams and messages. Differences of opinion arose between Rogers and Meighen. However, on December 1st, Meighen reported that he thought it would all work out satisfactorily.[9]

[9]*Robert Laird Borden: His Memoirs,* pp. 524-526.

It is interesting that the Honourable Arthur Meighen was chosen to make the official announcement. Apparently the Honourable Robert Rogers, as chairman of the cabinet wheat committee, was not prepared to announce a policy with which he found himself in disagreement. On the other hand, Borden appeared to be unprepared to have it made either by Foster or by Burrell.

The sequence of events was also well recorded in Foster's diary:

November 8, 1915: the day brought its grist of work — Italian boots — Italian wheat, Swiss oats, and Wheat and Transport, all pitched in at once. We shall have plenty of call for wheat, oats and flour. Council in afternoon.

November 13, 1915: Into arrears of work. Busy in S.S. matters. Transport Grain — Italian Contract and Boot prospect. Council at 12 — most unsatisfactory!

November 20, 1915: Had conference with Crothers, Stewart and Harling, and then with Burrell, when I found that the whole wheat business had been transferred by Prime Minister to Agriculture. To say I was vexed is too mild a characterization. The action is a fair sample of Borden's methods. I shall of course hand it over but shall not be caught that way again. I shall simply keep out of things suggested by him.[10]

This reference to the transfer of wheat to the department of agriculture appears to have been a transfer of the purchasing responsibilities for commitments undertaken by the Canadian government at the request of other governments. Agriculture had already been referred to in cables passing between the governor-general and the colonial secretary as the department responsible for the purchase of oats. A few days after this diary notation the cables mentioned that the department of agriculture was prepared to purchase wheat on behalf of the British and French governments. Nevertheless, the November 20th diary notation did not signify any change in the membership of the wheat committee nor in Foster's share of the responsibility therein. Foster continued to be active in the administration of wheat marketing policy and eventually gained full responsibility for it. It is interesting that the controversy which prevailed intermittently between successive ministers of trade and commerce and of agriculture over the years originated with Foster and Burrell. On the other hand, the diary notation points up the tenuous personal relation which existed between Foster and the prime minister, of whom he was never a confidant, however much he was a tower of strength in Borden's cabinet. Foster had reason to feel hurt by learning only through Burrell that Borden had reassigned the responsibility for wheat purchasing. His diary continued:

November 22, 1915: Had Lionel Clarke here and discussed the wheat purchase. Decided to get Matthews and advise with both. Clarke in favour of commandeering.

[10]*Foster Diaries,* Public Archives of Canada. "Crothers" and "Stewart" were undoubtedly Carruthers and Stuart. James Carruthers was a grain exporter and president of Canada Steamship Lines. A. P. Stuart of Montreal was a grain shipper. Thomas Harling was a Montreal steamship agent who did a forwarding business on behalf of the British, French and Canadian Governments. The Honourable Martin Burrell was Foster's colleague, the minister of agriculture.

November 23, 1915: Matthews and Clarke came. Conference with Prime Minister. Came to conclusion best way was for Govt. to commandeer. Matthews went to Montreal to consult Shaughnessy.

November 24, 1915: Conference with first Minister re Railway situation which is bad enough surely. Got order from Bonar Law to purchase for Italian Govt.

November 25, 1915: Decided to commandeer unless opinion changed. Summoned Crowe and Crerar to conference first and get views as to disturbance in market either plan.

November 26, 1915: Preparing for work of purchase and getting views. White ready to issue loan — it will succeed.

November 27, 1915: Conference with Clarke and then called in Crowe and Crerar and got their views. They varied. Agreed that Govt. buying would raise market — that other method drastic but honest — that advice on price fix would not help in readjustment but were not quite at one. Decided to commandeer and order went into effect at 11:30 p.m. I left for Toronto night train.

November 28, 1915, (Toronto): At 11 went with Clarke and Matthews and had a conference. These men do not want to do the work of buying — could only buy through exchange — commission would have to be paid. Would help in any other way. Commandeer order got out and telegrams bother me all day.

November 29, 1915: Arrived in the morning — went to office and was all day busy on the details of the commandeer. Matthews came up, but his advice was not really of much use. Stuart and Carruthers came up in the evening and Norcross joined them. Meighen and myself stayed with them until late at night and together eliminated some difficulties. Decided to base *exports* on bona fide contracts — replacement at Fort William by February 1st and 10 cts. deposit, and millers grain in Eastern elevators on same. The world seems today to be made up of telegrams. Certainly the button when pressed set many wheels going — wheat went up two or three cents.[11]

In commandeering the wheat it was not the government's intention to break existing contracts for exports to allied and other destinations, nor to Canadian millers who had held wheat for milling for export and domestic consumption. To fill such contracts wheat would be surrendered from the commandeered stocks at the price at which it had been taken over. Pro forma contracts were drawn up for the release of such wheat to shippers and to the mills. The 10-cent per bushel deposit was simply a bond to insure that companies obtaining release of wheat in performance of contracts would use it for the approved purpose. A special agreement had to be drawn up with a United States firm, Barnes-Ames Company of New York and Duluth, which had acted as agent for the Hudson's Bay Company, London,

---

[11]*Ibid.* Among the names mentioned in these entries, Lionel H. Clarke was a grain merchant and president of the Canada Malting Company, Ltd. He later became a member of the Board of Grain Supervisors and in 1919 was appointed Lieutenant-Governor of Ontario. He had been a business associate of W. D. Matthews, a Toronto grain dealer whose mission to Lord Shaughnessy was to persuade the Canadian Pacific Railway to handle the commandeered wheat account, in which mission he failed. Foster eventually turned over this responsibility to James Carruthers and Company. George R. Crowe was president of the British Empire Grain Company, Ltd., and the Northern Elevator Company; and Thomas A. Crerar was president of the Grain Growers' Grain Company, Limited. More than a year later he joined Borden's coalition government. Joseph W. Norcross was vice-president and managing director, Canada Steamship Lines, Ltd.

in the purchase of 1,794,715 bushels of wheat on behalf of the French Government.

The diary went on:

November 30, 1915: Negotiations for loan $10,000,000 with Bank of Montreal began. Loading goes on briskly at Fort William. Telegrams come thick and fast. Rogers comes back with a cry of ruin and desolation but he reports mainly the exchange operators.[12]

December 1, 1915: Still the storm rages. Decide to give the millers release from Eastern Elevators without return. The exporters are going on with exports on our basis. The price goes up two points or thereabouts. We meet a condition of French contract with H. B. Co. by agreeing to loan a part and sell a part with replacement at Buffalo and Fort William respectively. Got Harling at work on Charters. The C.P.R. have declined to take on the work.

December 2, 1915: The press have taken the action pretty favourably. The Grits have not opposed or criticized.

December 3, 1915: The labour does not diminish — and the complexities of a widely distributed business are demonstrated.

December 4, 1915: The turmoil re grain business is not lessened. It is shaping out however. I spent the entire day and night at work.

December 6, 1915: Protests come in from London Exchange from H. B. Co. and inquiries from Bonar Law and Perley. Every speculator wants to cover himself and presses for loans and releases.

December 7, 1915: The wheat market slackened off. The U.S. flurry calming down. Have arranged loan and parties are being paid off. Millers are fully satisfied, and exporters generally.[13]

December 8, 1915: Arranged H. B.-French Govt. affair. No bother now from any but some British buyers — two mainly. Opinion favourable with farmers. Have given management of business to Carruthers & Co. from lake ports to sea ports.

December 13, 1915: The usual routine with wheat added. Now comes the difficulty of transport and the great congestion of Italian ports which makes it impossible to ship thither for several weeks.

[12]A letter from Sir Robert Borden to Foster written on December 4, 1915, included in the Foster Papers, elaborated on the Honourable Robert Roger's concern:

"Mr. Rogers, who still seems greatly disturbed with regard to the appropriation of grain, calls my attention to an interview of Mr. A. G. Thompson of Montreal which is reported in the Montreal Gazette about the 2nd instant. He also gave me copy of a communication from a Winnipeg gentleman to an eastern grain dealer. He further says that a Mr. Gardner of Winnipeg came all the way to Ottawa to make him acquainted with the rage of the grain men and the epithets which they are bestowing upon the Government and upon himself. He further alleges that the result of our action has been to create a spread between our prices and that in the United States whereas previously the price had been about the same; also, that grain dealers previously operating in Canada are now transferring their operations to the United States.

It occurred to me that you should be made acquainted with these representations in order that they may be met if later they should be made in a more public way."

[13]In order to pay for the wheat retained from the November 29 takeover for resale on its commitments, the government required a revolving credit which Sir Thomas White, minister of finance, negotiated with the Bank of Montreal under government guarantee of repayment. P.C. 2874 of December 4, 1915, authorized the 10 million dollar loan, out of which Dr. Robert Magill, chairman of the board of grain commissioners, was authorized to countersign cheques issued in payment of the appropriated wheat. Belatedly, the appropriation itself was approved by another order in council dated December 8 and passed under the authority of the war measures act.

December 13, 1915: Today the last lake grain boats sail. Since Sept. over 170 m. bushels grain have come through the terminus and nearly as much gone out.

December 15, 1915: The usual work in office. *The Citizen* makes a diabolical insinuation re wheat commandeer and I write a letter — not too sharp but sharp enough for the purpose I hope.

December 20, 1915: Magill came down today and I took up the wheat business with him and got at the other end of it. On the whole it has worked out pretty well. Carruthers is working the details at this end.

December 21, 1915: Have seen Harling as to transport and it is not very encouraging. The Italian ports are congested and B.G. is unwilling to license ships to go thither.[14]

As might be expected in the wake of such unprecedented and temporarily disruptive action, protests poured in from all and sundry caught unaware, the penalized and the beneficiaries. Both Crowe and Crerar declared that they had advised against commandeering. James Richardson deplored the action, and when asked how the grain could have been purchased without raising prices, he replied "by the use of brains" and cited previous government purchases of oats and his own skill in buying "two and a half millions of durum wheat when there were only four millions available".[15]

While such reaction from the trade at home was predictable, the criticism in Britain was more difficult to understand. An official statement released by the Canadian government had declared that "the British government has requested the Canadian government to provide within a short time a very large supply of one, two and three Northern wheat."

This provoked a tart denial by the other government:

> With reference to the announcement from Ottawa on November 28, that the Canadian government had commandeered 16,000,000 bushels of wheat at the request of the British government, the Board of Agriculture state that the British government have made no such request, and that at present they have no such request, and at the present they have no information on the subject.[16]

The colonial secretary also cabled the governor-general secretly and urgently, although a copy of this telegram does not appear on Foster's file. A telegram from Sir George Perley, Canadian high commissioner, to the prime minister in Ottawa on November 30, 1915, however, reflected the general concern:

> Your cable 29th. Much apprehension exists here concerning the effect which the commandeering of wheat by your Government will have. At the earnest request of the Corn Trade Association received a deputation from them today and they expressed the fear that the action would interfere with the normal flow of wheat to this country. Hudson's Bay Company represent that the requistion will seriosly interfere with purchases for the French Government. Think it well to advise you of the above as indicative of the trend of feeling here. You have no doubt considered the effect upon the existing trade contracts.

Before he had a reply to this telegram, Perley cabled the prime minister again on December 1: "Confidential. Comandeering wheat has caused

[14]*Foster Diaries.*
[15]*House of Commons Debates,* January 17, 1916, p. 21.
[16]*Ibid.,* January 21, 1916, p. 170.

much criticism here. Personally regret that such action should have been found necessary, particularly on behalf one ally only but of course don't know arguments in favour that plan." The prime minister responded to the high commissioner immediately:

> Confidential. Your cable today. Please ask Law show you our secret cable this date respecting commandeering of wheat. Foster informs me situation working out without any difficulty whatever, and that apprehension or excitement in British Islands quite unnecessary.

The secret cable from the governor-general to the colonial secretary, Mr. Bonar Law, to which Borden referred in the foregoing cable, also went forward on December 1:

> SECRET. In reply to your secret and urgent telegram the Prime Minister submits the following report from the Minister of Trade and Commerce. Begins. In view of your telegram of November 23rd and Sir George Perley's cable of November 18th, consideration was given as to the best and cheapest way in which the initial portion of the purchases contemplated therein could be made. After taking the best available advice and giving careful consideration to the matter, the Government decided to requisition the grades of wheat Nos. 1, 2 and 3 Northern in store in the public elevators at the head of the Lakes and Eastward. This was accordingly done and at midnight on November 29th, the Government took possession of all grains of the above named to about fifteen million bushels.
>
> The purchase in this way was accomplished at lower prices than could have been secured had the Government gone upon the market and bought the large quantity required from day to day. Such a course would have enhanced prices very materially and therefore disturbed the market very widely. In purchasing in this way we secured the advantage of saving all commissions and of transporting wheat by the cheaper lake navigation before the lakes closed. The amount of grain commandeered bears a very small proportion to the enormous surplus which is still left in the Canadian North-West and which is coming out at a rapid and continuous rate.
>
> It was not the intention of the Government to place any difficulties in the way of the execution of bona fide contracts for sale and purchase of wheat for export, nor will this effect take place as the Government has made all necessary arrangements for release of commandeered grain previously held for such contracts.
>
> The action of the government will not have the least possible deterrent effect on supplies destined for the United Kingdom but was in fact designed to increase the flow thereto and to secure an initial reserve of moderate priced wheat in connection with the larger purchases contemplated in the cables referred to.[17]

The remainder of Foster's file on this episode includes summaries of the telegrams exchanged and the action taken on the Swiss and Italian purchases, and an accounting of the commandeered wheat, including a sheaf of worksheets setting out the amounts of wheat released to the exporters and mills. Although the details of the amounts released by individual companies are of no permanent interest, the tables list the names of 63 flour mills which were operating in eastern Canada at that time. The tables attempted to apportion by specific grades 1, 2 and 3 Northern, the total amount of wheat surrendered to each of the mills, but the grade

---

[17] *Foster Papers.*

reconciliation did not tally with the totals. A handwritten note from a distraught deputy minister, F. C. T. O'Hara, working to a deadline at Foster's request on March 10, 1916, labored the point:

> I am sorry to say a further complication has developed. The statement herewith prepared as desired does not agree *by grades*. The *total* does. In the previous statement handed down by you, the 3 grades unconditionally released are shown. The statement agrees in the total, but not by grades. There is no way in which we can make it agree.
>
> If the enclosed be prepared leaving out the grades, it will agree, so I am having it written out that way at once, but fear I cannot let you have it before 4 o'clock as the whole thing has to be rewritten.[18]

More importantly, however, the files include several drafts and the final version of a memorandum which Foster prepared in defence of the operation, which he tabled in response to Sir Wilfrid Laurier's motion for the production of papers on the incident. The memorandum reads:

> The Western Canada wheat crop 1915 is variously estimated at from 350 to 400 million bushels. The United States wheat crop is placed at somewhere in the neighborhood on One Billion Bushels. Other wheat growing countries report large crops as well, making the total world production the largest by a substantial margin yet on record.
>
> In the presence of these conditions the efforts of the Government to secure as rapid disposition as possible of Canadian wheat offered for marketing, met with response from the Colonial Office in the form of an order to secure on account of the Italian Government 750,000 tons at the best price obtainable, such wheat to be delivered in quantities of 150,000 tons per month, commencing at once.
>
> At the same time cables from the Colonial Office indicated the likelihood of orders on account of the British and French Governments amounting to about 50,000,000 bushels and necessitating very large deliveries in the immediate future. Conferences were held with business men of large experience in the grain trade. Two methods only, appeared available for securing the wheat required.
>
> 1. By purchase through the medium of a Government agent or Government agents.
> 2. To appropriate by Government Act.
>
> The merits of each course were exhaustively discussed. The prevailing opinion was that it was impossible to adopt the first course without the fact being almost immediately known, and without the result of very seriously inflating values to the advantage of dealers and speculators who held the grain in store and at the cost of our customers.
>
> Importance was attached to the experience of a year ago, when under the stimulus of Governmental buying on the part of European countries, the price advanced to what is now considered a purely artificial elevation much to the disadvantage of the purchasing Governments and of their peoples and mainly to the advantage of large holders of grain and speculators in the United States and Canada. The producers having in the main sold their crops, received comparatively little benefit.
>
> It was also urged that the method of buying in the market was on the part of the Government open to objection in that as between the two camps of dealers and speculators contending hourly for supremacy in the wheat market, it placed the Government as a substantial factor on the side of one,

[18]*Ibid.*

and put the Government in the position of being compelled to either authorize through its agents the various manoevres adopted in the trade to keep market conditions in hand, or possibly to let such conditions get out of hand, resulting in an inflation of price.

The method of securing wheat by appropriation had not been previously tried in Canada. It was of course not without objectionable features. Various opinions were offered as to its effect upon understanding contracts and upon the option market in general. The prevailing opinion was however, that a way might be found for respecting bona fide contracts with results carrying relatively little if any detriment. This way we believe has been found and will be explained below.

The securing of grain by appropriation would fix once and for all the price at which the appropriated grain would be purchased. That price would be fair in every respect to the purchasing Government or Governments and would obviously be fair also, to the owners of the grain appropriated, aside from the consideration of outstanding contracts. Commissions on purchases which would amount to a very large total would be avoided. All danger of delay in securing grain would be removed.

Such increase of price as would naturally result, temporarily at all events, from the appropriating of a large quantity of grain by the Government, not to the holders of grain in store and to the speculators, who it was estimated were the owners of 75% of the Fort William and Port Arthur wheat, and of practically all the stored wheat east of Port Arthur, but to the benefit of the owners of grain undelivered, who were very largely the producers themselves. These producers or grain farmers, were it was felt, entitled if anyone was, to the advantage of price that might accrue.

Accordingly, all numbers one, two and three Northern grades of wheat in store at Fort William and Port Arthur and in the public elevators eastward in Canda, were appropriated by the Government on November 27th last. The appropriated grain amounted to about 12,183,118 bushels at Fort William and Port Arthur and about 3,429,563 bushels eastward. Orders were immediately given authorizing the Board of Grain Commissioners at Fort William who had charge of the appropriated grain at the head of the lakes, to continue and to expedite to the utmost, all outgoing shipments. Loading and despatching was accordingly hurried forward, and with the advantage of control exercised by the Board of Grain Commissioners, the shipments of grain between Sunday morning the 28th inst., and Tuesday night the 30th. inst., out of Fort William and Port Arthur, reached the enormous total of 10,000,000 bushels, a substantial advance on all previous records.

The requirements of the European orders made it desirable on the part of the Government to procure the shipment of a large share of the appropriated grain from the head of the lakes before the close of navigation. . . .

There followed a list of the types of contracts covering wheat appropriated at the lakehead and eastern positions, which had been surrendered in turn to the shippers and mills. Then the memorandum concluded:

While the entire transaction has not been without its difficulties, and did at the same time cause more or less uneasiness particularly among large dealers in grain, still the difficulties have been worked out and overcome with a minimum of inconvenience to all concerned. There is some tendency to attribute loss caused by increases in values to the action of the Government, but it must be remembered that such losses perhaps in greater degree though possibly not to the same persons, would have accrued anyway had any other course been pursued.

²⁰See pp. 95, 103.

The market rose from 8 to 10¢ within a week succeeding the appropriation but such a rise is not abnormal and market conditions have since settled down materially. They were indeed at no time very seriously affected.[19]

The commandeering of wheat came up in the debate on the speech from the throne in January, 1916, and again during consideration of the departmental estimates in May. All the arguments for the action taken in an emergency situation were restated and it was just as strongly contended by opposition members that the situation could have been met by prudent purchasing in the open market. Mr. J. G. Turriff, the member for Assiniboia, added a political note, alleging that Meighen rather than Foster was the real culprit, by his suggestion that the former had sought a coup to relieve the pressure for "free wheat" (about which more will be said shortly). It remained for Turriff, however, to score the obvious point that the government had catered to the interests of overseas consumers and not to those of western farmers, some of whose wheat had been confiscated and a low price fixed.

Whatever its merits, the commandeering drew Foster closer to assumption of full responsibility for wheat marketing policy. As problems mounted with port congestion, lack of buyers and the harvesting of a record crop in 1915, Borden had displayed his lack of confidence in Foster's capacity to handle the situation by appointing a cabinet wheat committee. But toward the end of the commandeering episode, he informed the British that Foster had the situation in hand and he allowed Foster to answer for the government's decision in the house. The existence of the cabinet wheat committee, as such, appears to have terminated together with the commandeering incident. Foster had shared in the responsibility to commandeer, but out of experience with it, he was determined not to repeat the performance. Nevertheless, as a precautionary measure, when the board of grain supervisors was established in 1917, authority to commandeer wheat in country and terminal elevator positions was one of the standby powers assigned to it.[20]

ROYAL COMMISSION ON WHEAT SUPPLIES

The British government's declared policy upon the outbreak of war was one of non-interference with the private trade. In practice, importers' freedom of action was proscribed only to the extent necessary by requisitioning, and by import and shipping controls. The government made some secret purchases of wheat for reserve stocks during the first two years but these were not of a magnitude that interfered with purchases by the trade. In contrast, the French government created a purchasing agency which operated alongside the private trade, and the Italian government established a buying monopoly which replaced the trade. In the winter of 1915-1916 the three governments formed a joint committee to purchase limited amounts of wheat for reserves; this was the first experiment in the coordination of purchases by the allied governments.

For the first two years of the war British reliance upon the trade sufficed, in the main, despite the fact that traditional sources of supply had been

[19]*Ibid.*
[20]See pp. 95, 105.

materially distorted by the war. Closing of the Dardanelles in 1914 by Turkey cut off Russian, Romanian and Bulgarian supplies and resulted in much greater dependence upon North American sources. United States stocks were adequate in 1914-15 to permit a record export in that crop year and, in 1915-16, the all-time record harvest in both Canada and the United States eliminated concern over the adequacy of supplies.

In 1916, however, the position altered suddenly. To make the most effective use of ocean tonnage, the British admiralty had given preference to the North Atlantic route over those from Australia, India and Argentina but, by 1916, the German submarine fleet had been greatly enlarged, and losses of ships on the North Atlantic were rapidly mounting. To compound these problems the wheat crops in Canada and the United States were sharply reduced in yield. Rust had hit the Canadian crop and reduced quality as well as yield. The rapidly deteriorating supply situation was reflected in the futures markets in Liverpool, Chicago and Winnipeg. In 1916, Winnipeg cash prices rose from a low point of $1.09¼ in June to a peak of $1.98⅞ in November.

As public concern mounted in Britain over the assurance of basic food supplies, the British government acted by closing the Liverpool futures market and by appointing, on October 10, 1916, a royal commission on wheat supplies whose terms of reference were "to inquire into the supply of wheat, and flour in the United Kingdom; to purchase, sell and control the delivery of wheat and flour on behalf of His Majesty's government; and generally to take such steps as may seem desirable for maintaining the supply."[21]

Thus, the responsibilities of the royal commission were two-fold; first, to investigate all aspects of maintaining an adequate wheat supply, and second, to undertake its actual procurement. Although the British government subsequently created a ministry of food and appointed a food controller, the royal commission was not subject to that ministry. Wheat procurement remained the responsibility of the royal commission until it was able to effect decontrol of its operations after the end of the war. Its authority was gradually extended to cover all grains and pulses and it controlled the use of other grains as diluents of wheat in order to avoid the wartime rationing of bread. One of the objectives of the commission was to assure at all times a 13-week supply of wheat in Britain.

The appointment of the royal commission was also followed by formalizing and enlarging arrangements which had been initiated in the previous winter through the joint committee to coordinate purchasing by the allied governments. This was accomplished by negotiating the wheat executive agreement, signed on November 29, 1916, by Britain, France and Italy. The undertaking required the allies to impose uniform domestic controls, to accept allocation of supplies by the executive and to average procurement costs, thereby eliminating any national advantage through buying in the cheapest market. The royal commission did the actual

[21] *First Report of the Royal Commission on Wheat Supplies*, H. M. Stationary Office, London, 1921, p. 1. For a much fuller account of these developments, see Mitchell W. Sharp, "Allied Wheat Buying in Relationship to Canadian Marketing Policy, 1914-18," *Canadian Journal of Economics and Political Science*, Vol. VI, No. 3, Aug., 1940, pp. 372-389.

purchasing for the wheat executive, and a member of the commission represented the British government on the executive, which gradually extended its activities to making provision for other governments, including Greece, Portugal, Belgium and the commission for relief in Belgium, Norway, Sweden, the Netherlands, Iceland and Switzerland. At the height of its activities, the royal commission could claim with pride authority of the wheat executive for "world-wide supply and international distribution, unity of control from the producing market to the final destination; upon these fundamental principles the executive authority of the instrument was based."[22]

In order to proceed immediately with overseas purchases, the newly-appointed royal commission used the overseas offices of K. B. Stoddart and Company which placed its facilities at the disposal of the British government; its offices were incorporated as the Wheat Export Company (under New York state charter), with headquarters at New York, and the Wheat Export Company, Limited (under federal charter), with headquarters at Winnipeg. The Winnipeg company was operated as a subsidiary of the New York company, which reflected the working arrangements of the K. B. Stoddart firm. All shipping arrangements from North America were made by the New York office and as much as 60 percent of Canadian wheat shipments moved in wartime through United States ports. The royal commission appointed from its members' resident commissioners abroad, two in New York, one in Buenos Aires, and one in Australia. Messrs. Alan G. Anderson and Herbert T. Robson (who subsequently received knighthoods for their services) were the resident commissioners in New York. Mr. K. B. Stoddart continued to work with the Wheat Export Company in New York. The New York company, in turn, appointed Mr. James Stewart, head of the K. B. Stoddart subsidiary in Winnipeg, as president of the Wheat Export Company there. The Winnipeg company became the sole grain buyer in Canada for the allied governments. The establishment of the royal commission's own purchasing agency in Winnipeg obviated further need for the procurement of wheat and oats by the department of agriculture on behalf of the British government.

NEGOTIATIONS FOR THE PURCHASE OF CANADA'S EXPORTABLE SURPLUS

A year after the commandeering action, Foster's next major move in connection with wheat marketing was unsuccessful — an attempt to conclude a bulk contract with the royal commission for the whole of the Canadian exportable surplus. Although the Canadian government had raised the issue immediately after the appointment of the royal commission in October, 1916, it was not pursued until Sir George Foster's arrival in London in December of that year. His arrival was timely in view of the fact that the royal commission was in the midst of negotiations for the wheat surpluses in Australia, India and Egypt.

At a much later date, and several months after the British-Canadian negotiations fell through, Foster offered a condensed summary of the developments during the course of a debate in the house of commons:

[22]Royal Commission on Wheat Supplies, *op. cit.*, p. 15.

I think the facts can be very simply stated. The Canadian Government have been anxious, since the beginning of the war, that Canada should have all possible opportunity of supplying the demands of Great Britain and the Allies for such things as Canada produces. We have always been in touch with the British government and its different departments in regard to all kinds of supplies that are required and that can be produced in Canada. We are kept up to the mark in that respect by the people in Canada who have these things to sell and who are anxious to dispose of them. In carrying out that line of communication, which had never been interrupted from the time the war began, the question was mooted as to the crop of 1916-17. The British Government were asked whether they had any proposals to make with reference to the securing of that crop. Different communications took place. I was in London for a little while; I met the Export Wheat Buying Commission there, and talked the matter over with them. The result was that they made an offer for the whole crop suplus for 1916-17, the offer running at about $1.20 or $1.22 a bushel at Fort William. Ultimately they raised the offer to about $1.30 or $1.32. I simply did what I thought was my duty; I passed that offer on to persons who appeared to be representative farmers who could take hold of and decide upon any such offer — the Council of Agriculture of the West. I asked these gentlemen to come down and see me. They came, and I told them frankly and fully what had taken place. They discussed the question with me, went back, and then decided that the terms were not high enough. Consequently, the thing fell through.[23]

This account, given at a time when Foster would have been happier had the whole incident been forgotten, acknowledges that the initiative had been taken by the Canadian government. During the course of the London discussions, other evidence indicates that the royal commission expressed interest in assuring supplies from empire sources for as much as a year ahead.[24] Agreements had just been concluded for the 1917 exportable surpluses of Australia, India and Egypt, and the commission was prepared to negotiate a similar arrangement with Canada.

From the available evidence, there remains some doubt over the period the proposal covered, and also some doubt as to whether it had ever been precisely defined in the London discussions. Foster's reference in the foregoing quotation to "the 1916-1917 crop", when taken in the context of the immediately preceding debate, was clearly a reference to the 1916 crop and to its exportable surplus. Yet when Foster discussed the proposal with representatives of the Canadian council of agriculture, he created the impression that the period included the exportable surplus from the 1917 crop.[25] What is most probable is that, as indicated in Foster's press statement of March 17, the period related to the exportable surplus in the calendar year 1917, as was the case in the agreements concluded with Australia, India and Egypt.

Similar confusion remains over the actual position regarding the price negotiations. Foster's statement to the house of commons, quoted above, which he made several months after the event, indicates that the British had started negotiating at $1.20 or $1.22 and that they had "raised the offer to about $1.30 or $1.32". Yet in his press statement of March 22, Foster

[23] *House of Commons Debates,* July 23, 1917, p. 3693.
[24] See Foster's press statement of March 22, 1917, pp. 77-79 below.
[25] See the *Grain Growers' Guide,* Wednesday, March 21, 1917, and M. W. Sharp *Allied Wheat Buying in Relationship to Canadian Marketing Policy, 1914-18,* p. 380.

disclosed that, "whilst no price was definitely fixed upon in the communications with the British government, yet a possible rate was canvassed taking as a basis the price paid the British farmer, with adjustments and deductions for freight and cost . . . ."[26] This admission led the press of declare at once, "that the price of $1.30 was not fixed by the British authorities, but by the minister himself". [27]

Foster had sent a telegram on February 16 to the Canadian council of agriculture, which responded by sending a delegation to Ottawa on March 3, 1917. At that conference Foster explained the concern of the British government to have an assured supply of wheat, and also the relation of the $1.30 offer to the British farm price. At the time, the May future was at the $1.90 level and, although the October future was trading at $1.40, the price reduction for a long-term commitment weighed heavily with Foster's advisers. The delegation's immediate reaction, however, was that the $1.30 Foster proposed did not reflect the quality differentials for Canadian over British and American wheat, nor the immediate availability of Canadian wheat for shipping reasons, whereas the Australian wheat probably could not be shipped until after the end of the war. Eventually, the delegation reported to the annual meeting of the council held in Regina later that month.

On March 16, 1917, the council issued the following press statement which included the text of a telegram sent to Sir George Foster on March 13:

> The first intimation that the western farmers received that the Dominion government was considering taking over the 1917 crop at a fixed price was on February 16. On that date, Roderick McKenzie, secretary of the Canadian Council of Agriculture, received a telegram from Sir George Foster, the minister of trade & commerce, asking that representatives of the Canadian Council of Agriculture meet him in Ottawa for a confidential conference on the subject. The conference was held on March 3, the western farmers being represented by Roderick McKenzie, secretary of the council, H. W. Wood, president of the United Farmers of Alberta, C. Rice Jones, president of the Alberta Farmers' Co-operative Elevator Company, J. A. Maharg, president of the Saskatchewan Grain Growers' association, R. C. Henders, president of the Manitoba Grain Growers' association, and T. A. Crerar, president of the Grain Growers' Grain company.
>
> At that conference, Sir George Foster pointed out that the British government was anxious to have an adequate supply of wheat guaranteed for the coming year. Canada was in the best position, geographically, to provide this wheat as it was much nearer than either Argentina or Australia, and consequently, would require less shipping tonnage to transport. Sir George Foster had been in conference with the British government and proposed that the Canadian government should take over the entire surplus of the 1917 crop at a fixed price of $1.30 per bushel in store Fort William on the basis of No. 1

[26]See p. 78.

[27]*Manitoba Free Press*, March 23, 1917, p. 3. Regardless of whether Foster had a firm offer in hand when he left London in December, it remains difficult to understand why he delayed his request for consultation with producer representatives until February 16, in view of the fact that both governments were anxious to conclude an agreement. Of course consultations, of whatever nature, were more leisurely then than now. In Foster's diaries and papers there is no evidence that he ever made a telephone call. Inter-city communication was by letter or telegram.

Northern. The conference discussed the matter at considerable length but the delegates from the west were not prepared to agree to this price. It was decided to leave the matter over until it was discussed by the Canadian Council of Agriculture at their annual meeting in Regina this week. As a result of that discussion, the Canadian Council unanimously decided that the price of $1.30 per bushel could not be accepted, and they therefore sent the following wire to Sir George Foster:

"Respecting the matter of fixing or guaranteeing a price for the surplus crop of Canadian wheat, for the year 1917, discussed with you at your request in Ottawa on March 3, by representatives of the Canadian Council of Agriculture, your suggestion that a price be fixed about $1.30 per bushel, basis 1 Northern, Fort William, for the entire crop, was considered by the full meeting of the council here today and after full deliberation upon the matter, the council, having in view the present high cost of production, believe that to ensure maximum production of wheat for the coming year it is advisable to fix a minimum price covering all of this year's crop, and this council therefore recommends that a minimum price at Fort William of $1.50 per bushel, basis 1 Northern grade, be guaranteed and that maximum price of $1.90 basis 1 Northern, Fort William, be fixed. Spreads in price on grades lower than 1 Northern to be fixed on the actual difference in value between such grades, as determined by milling and baking tests, or, if a flat price be decided upon, such price should be $1.70 per bushel, basis 1 Northern, Fort William; this being less than the average price of 1 Northern at Fort William during the last six months."[28]

Foster duly reported the council's counter-proposal to the royal commission, which declined to negotiate further. His disappointment over the council's rejection of his price proposal is reflected in Foster's long statement to the press on March 22:

The situation in brief is as follows:

The government of Great Britain has purchased the whole available surplus crop of Australia, for both the past and current year. The price paid to the Australian farmer is in the neighborhood of $1.12 per bushel, delivered at the port of export.

When I was in London in December last, an urgent desire was expressed to secure the wheat surplus of Canada for 1917, and I discussed the matter thoroughly with the wheat commission which is charged with the purchase of wheat necessities of Great Britain, France and Italy.

The British government is not only anxious that Canada shall grow the largest possible crop of wheat this year, but it desires to know now that it can depend on getting all that Canada has to export and to be relieved to that extent from some of its anxiety as to sources of supply.

It has sought to secure as far as possible its supply from Empire sources, and stated to me that it relies largely on the patriotism and power of production of Empire farmers to contribute their full measure of output this year and to sell it to the government at reasonably remunerative rates.

The geographical position of Canada, taken in connection with sea war dangers and shortage of transport tonnage, makes it of great importance that its surplus supply should be at the sole disposal of the British government. Under certain conditions it might mean the salvation of the British people and the decisive factor in the decision of the war.

One vessel of the Atlantic route is nearly equal in carrying capacity to three on the India and Australian routes.

[28]*Manitoba Free Press*, March 16, 1917.

The fixing of the price has, in the cases above mentioned, been a matter of agreement, as in Australia, or of decision by the British government based on a reasonable price to the producer. Each of these countries might have said: "We will produce all we can and when we have it in hand, we will sell it to you if you will give as much or more than any other competitor?"This would not, however, have given any guarantee to the British government of a certain supply and of a reasonable price. Nor was any such demand made. The reasonable margin over cost of production was figured out, the price was fixed, the farmer has marketed his crop before it was grown, and the government knows just where the supply is to be got and the cost.

The same is desired by the British government in relation to the Canadian surplus. Whilst no price was definitely fixed upon in the communications with the British government, yet a possible rate was canvassed by taking as a basis the price paid the British farmer, with adjustments and deductions for freight and cost, etc., from Fort William to Europe. One can come pretty closely to it by taking that price as being about $1.82 to the British farmer and making his own calculations. The British government, of course, very largely controls freight. We manifestly cannot do so.

Desiring information as to what would be a reasonable price in the minds of the western producers, I sought, among other sources, the views of the Council of Agriculture, which represents large associations of growers chiefly in the west.

It advised that the lowest possible price acceptable would be a flat rate of $1.75 (sic) per bushel for No. 1 Northern at Fort William, or, preferably, a guarantee of prices from a minimum of $1.50 to a maximum of $1.90. This latter appears very much like making the price $1.90 for all, or defeating the purpose of the government in obtaining certain supply.

There are some considerations which will naturally suggest themselves to the farmers in coming to conclusions as to what constitutes a reasonable and safe price.

1. The rate paid for No. 1 Northern does not indicate the price which the farmer will get for his whole crop. He is likely to have all grades from No. 1 Northern to No. 6 commercial. On an average he will have far less of No. 1 than of the lower grades. The farmer well knows the spreads to which, under the present method of purchase, he is subject on wheat of good milling value, but of inferior grades as certified.

If, on the other hand, the British government buys all his millable wheat in terms of its millable value and buys it from the farmer himself and not from the speculator, the farmer gets the full price for all. He does not have to divide with anyone.

In selling to the British government, the farmer gets the base price for his No. 1 Northern and gets for his other millable wheat a price determined by its value, as compared with No. 1 for baking and milling purposes. He is saved from the arbitrary spreads which rob him of his due and inure to the benefit of the middleman.

2. There are also chances to be taken in respect to price in the open market. The farmer cannot market this year's crop until the late fall of 1917 or the winter of 1918. Many things may happen between now and then. The price may be higher, if the war continues for another year; the price may break lower if war ceases before this year closes.

If he sells now to the British government, he knows that all his wheat is marketed at a good profit before he puts a seed into the ground. He may gamble, if he chooses, on chances, but before he takes that risk, he should carefully consider the alternative — a profitable sale made now, and sure pay, and the full worth of all his wheat coming to himself.

3. There are in addition uncertainties of transport from Fort William to Europe. At this very moment all British liners sailing from Canadian ports or from United States ports have from 75 to 100 per cent of their space requisitioned for war and army food supplies. This leaves from 25 per cent to nothing available for commercial freight offering.

As the war goes on this condition of things will not be likely to grow better — it may probably grow worse. Even if war ceases the demand for tonnage to transport to their homes the men and equipment released from the front will, for many months, be little less urgent than now. The uncertainty of transport will surely affect prices and may very seriously effect them. But if the farmers sell now to the British government his money is sure and he need trouble nothing about transport — the British government will attend to that.

It must be remembered that the British government cannot wait until next autumn to look out for its food supplies. It must make certain of all possible as soon as possible. That is why it has arranged already for the British, Australian, Indian and Egyptian surplus. That is why it wishes to secure the Canadian surplus and secure it now.[29]

Foster's statement, which was an appeal from the council's position directly to producers in favour of state marketing in lieu of the open market, drew an immediate response from Henry Wise Wood, the council's new president, J. A. Maharg, its past president, and Roderick McKenzie, its secretary. Wood pointed out that it would be more profitable to feed wheat than to sell it as grain at $1.30. Maharg and McKenzie dwelt on the failure of that price to take into account the quality of Canadian wheat and its immediate availability, as well as on certain anomalies in the freight deductions.[30]

Although negotiations lapsed, subsequent events demonstrated that the British had foregone a major bargain in declining the council's offer of $1.70 and that Foster's proposal of $1.30 was even further out of line. Events moved so swiftly, however, from that moment forward that Foster escaped any serious criticism for having tried to promote the bulk sale.[31] Meanwhile the Germans were pursuing their unrestricted submarine campaign, the Americans were locked in congressional debate over arming their merchant marine, the Czar abdicated, the Russian revolution began and, in April, the United States formally declared war.

FREE WHEAT

The British attempt to secure all its supplies from "empire sources" at patriotic prices related to the price it had set for its own farmers, had obviously been an attempt to isolate itself from the volatile force of the open markets in North America. In the circumstances, it is remarkable that Foster and the Canadian government were convinced that they could have

[29]*Ibid.*, March 23, 1917.

[30]*Ibid.*, March 23 and April 6, 1917.

[31]When the board of grain supervisors fixed a maximum price on the balance of the 1916 crop at $2.40, the Honourable Frank Oliver, who had been minister of the interior in the Laurier government, reminded Foster that "the farming interests would have accepted a basic price of $1.70 for No. 1 Northern, as against $1.30 offered on behalf of the government through the minister of trade and commerce" (*House of Commons Debates,* July 23, 1917, p. 3693).

lived with a fixed price system alongside an open market system south of the border, and it is even more remarkable that the spokesmen for the Canadian council of agriculture failed to raise this issue of equity rather than the one they did about quality and transportation costs vis-a-vis the British and Australian farmers. But the issue of Canadian-American wheat price relations had been a political one in western Canada ever since the Conservative government gained office by opposing the reciprocity agreement.

In the context of all the other events in March-April, 1917, the conservative government reacted in a most unusual manner to the breakdown in the negotiations with the British on the bulk purchase proposal. It decided upon an alternative measure understandably resisted until that time. When the Borden administration took office, it left dangling an offer in the Wilson-Underwood tariff act of 1913 to permit free entry of wheat and flour from countries allowing reciprocal access. Although the Wilson-Underwood act had reduced the tariff on wheat from 25 cents to 10 cents per bushel, United States prices had led the way in the recent price rise, and producers on the Canadian side of the international boundary demanded access to those higher prices. Thus began an agitation by producers which was supported in parliament by western Liberal members for "free wheat". Motions to that effect were voted down on January 28 and April 23, 1914, and on February 23, 1916. Nevertheless, in the void created by the unsuccessful negotiations, the government passed and order in council under authority of the war measures act, on April 16, 1917, which permitted duty-free entry of wheat and wheat products into Canada, thereby automatically obtaining duty-free entry into the United States.[32] By taking this step to create an alternative export market for the benefit of producers, the government tacitly informed the British that, if not prepared to negotiate, they must be prepared to compete for Canadian supplies. Producers' representatives heralded the decision and prices rose into alignment with those in the United States. This upward thrust came on the eve of a market crisis of major proportions.

WARTIME CORNER

After the failure of the negotiations (which, had they succeeded, would have resulted in the closing of the futures market), the royal commission continued to purchase its requirements from the balance of the 1916 crop in the normal way. This was done through the Wheat Export Company in Winnipeg, whose president, Mr. James Stewart, was now the sole buyer in Canada for the allied governments. To make purchases, Mr. Stewart bought futures, which priced the wheat. He could later exchange futures for cash wheat as it came into position or he could await delivery against the contracts.

[32]Another reason for passage of the order in council was imputed to Mr. Arthur Meighen, M.P., by Mr. John G. Turriff, M.P., when he said: "My honourable friend went west to ostensibly look into the question of penitentiaries, and while he was there he was told emphatically by his own friends that unless wheat were placed on the free list his candidates would have very little chance of returning to this house" (*House of Commons Debates*, April 24, 1917, p. 751).

Not only was the 1916 crop reduced very much in size from the record level of 1915 but, because of wet weather, the crop was rusted and a high proportion of it fell into the tough, rejected and lower grades. In order to finance their purchases at country points, the elevator companies had to hedge their purchases of all grades, despite the fact that the futures contracts they sold were obligations to deliver wheat of the top three straight grades. Stewart became a steady buyer of all contracts offered, and the elevator companies became increasingly aware of their predicament in not having wheat of the required quality to fulfill their contracts, which left them with the only alternative of bidding competitively to buy their contracts back. Stewart was not prepared to sell his holdings at a profit to relieve the hedges, because his principals had every reason to want delivery of wheat of contract quality. Before the situation could be resolved, May futures had risen from the $1.90 level in February to a peak of $3.05 on May 3.[33]

The council of the Winnipeg grain exchange went into session with Mr. Stewart, and took the first overt action on April 28, 1917, when trading was halted at 10:30 and the president read the following statement addressed to himself by Stewart on behalf of the royal wheat commission: "This is your authority to announce that no buying of Winnipeg wheat futures has taken place by the Allied Governments during the last 40 odd cents advance and that we have sufficient bought for present requirements."

The president also stated that the council would, while trading remained halted, immediately resume its session "with a view to censorship of trades, and I give you this warning so that you may not be entirely unprepared".[34]

At 11:15 President Gage announced to the exchange the council's decision that no trade in any grain future would be executed without the prior consent of a censoring committee on which Messrs. R. Magill, F. O. Fowler, and T. Brodie would serve.[35] A desk was placed at the end of the pit at which the committee commenced authorizing trades. Within 15 minutes after trading resumed, May futures were down 20 cents. Comparable declines occurred in Minneapolis and to a lesser extent in Chicago.[36]

[33]For the benefit of its lay readers, the *Winnipeg Evening Tribune*, May 3, 1917, explained:

"Shorts frantic to level up May sales kept the prices soaring. Their situation was explained as similar to a "man who had sold a horse and had only a goat to deliver when a horse was the only thing to fill the shafts." Scarcity of "horses" to plug the gap compelled the traders to offer the amazing prices."

[34]*Manitoba Free Press*, April 30, 1917.

[35]Dr. Robert Magill, formerly chief commissioner of the board of grain commissioners, had now accepted a position as secretary of the Winnipeg grain exchange. Frank O. Fowler was manager of the Winnipeg grain and produce clearing association.

[36]The censorship issue was described by the *Free Press*, May, 5, 1917, as follows:

"As the buyer for the Allied Governments was not in the market and, as far as the Council could gather, the millers were not buying, the question arose as to the quality of the trading that was actually going on. It is inconceivable to the Council that the people of Canada have not the right to get a correct answer to this question, or that the members of the Exchange would hesitate to give a correct answer.

In the few days that it operated, the committee did not disclose any trades of questionable "quality". In any event, its function was to prevent them from taking place."

The market action for Saturday, April 28, and until trading was finally suspended before the opening on May 4, was as follows:

WINNIPEG MAY WHEAT FUTURES, 1917

	SAT. APR. 28	MON. APR. 30	TUE. MAY 1	WED. MAY 2	THU. MAY 3
OPEN	2.71 @ 2.82	2.70	2.68	2.54 @ 2.50	2.80 @ 2.80½
HIGH	2.86	2.72	2.68⅜	2.80½	3.05
LOW	2.66	2.63a	2.54	2.47	2.75½
CLOSE	2.67⅝	2.68⅛b	2.54b	2.80½	2.94b

By Wednesday, May 2, the May futures traded over a range of 33½¢, and the following day's action was headlined in the *Free Press* as the "Wildest Market in the History of Winnipeg". Throughout the week the council of the exchange had remained in session and in conference with Stewart. The pressure the council exerted upon him, and through him by cable upon the royal commission to negotiate a settlement is graphically described in a boxed article on the front page of the Thursday morning, May 3, edition of the *Free Press* under the heading of "Relief for May Shorts":

Agents of the Royal Wheat Commission will buy No. 4 wheat, Nos. 1, 2, and 3 Northern Tough and Tough 4 wheat, giving back the May.

The very serious market situation which developed yesterday morning when Winnipeg May wheat fluctuated 33½ between opening and closing, and closed at an advance of 26½ to 30½, caused grave anxiety to many members of the trade, revealing as it did the tremendous short interest which apparently they saw no means at hand to satisfy.

The council of the Exchange which has been continuously in session, spent practically all afternoon in seeking a reasonable solution to the problem with a view to steadying the market. The censorship has performed its function in showing very definitely how small was the speculation element in the trade and how very genuine was the shortage of May to fill contracts.

With this knowledge to go upon, the whole matter was taken up with the government agent who is the principal long in the market. His refusal to give back May on any purchases of wheat other than Nos. 1, 2 and 3 Northern, had undoubtedly precipitated the crisis yesterday. The agent was quite ready to go into the matter and quickly ascertained the willingness of his principals for him to negotiate with a committee named by the President of the Exchange. The committee consists of Capel Tilt of James Carruthers Company; George Fisher of the Scottish Co-operative; F. O. Fowler, head of the Clearing House; T. A. Crerar, President of the Grain Growers' Grain Company; President Gage, and Secretary, Dr. Robert Magill.

There is no manner of doubt that the Royal Wheat Commission want the actual wheat. That is what they bought for; and they want, in view of the present shipping conditions, to have it in the most concentrated form, namely, the grades of wheat which will make the most flour. But as it was pointed out to the agent, much of the wheat against which May had been sold as a hedge, had gone out of condition, and it was not possible to procure all of the contract wheat required, especially in view of the small forward movement at the present time.

After a lengthy discussion, the following was agreed to, namely that for a few days the agent of the Royal Commission will be prepared to purchase certain lower grade wheats at certain penalties, giving back May for them. The grades and penalties agreed upon are:

No. 4 wheat .... 30¢ under May
No. 1 Northern Tough .... 15¢ under May
No. 2 Northern Tough .... 18¢ under May
No. 3 Northern Tough .... 30¢ under May
No. 4 Tough Wheat .... 40¢ under May

This is preliminary to an attempt by the committee to ascertain the exact position of the various shorts and to arrange a basis whereby lower grades than contract will be taken by the government agent and May given in exchange. It is understood that if the government agent can be assured of getting a fair proportion of the contract grades as they come forward, concessions will be made with respect to lower grades.

No doubt the beneficial effect of this temporary arrangement will be seen in the market this morning.

Even after this accommodation, announced on the afternoon of May 2, the market on the following day continued in disarray and the council of the exchange responded by advising at the opening on May 4, its decision to discontinue trading in May and July wheat futures. The gravity of the situation had been underlined in the *Winnipeg Telegram* that morning whose lead story began:

With at least $60,000,000 indirectly jeopardized the gravest financial crisis that has ever threatened any financial or commercial community in Canada has obtained in Winnipeg for several weeks. It reached a super-climax yesterday when dozens of responsible and old established firms and banking institutions were threatened with losses aggregating millions.

In the house of commons that day, Sir Thomas White, minister of finance, indicated that the Canadian government had interceded with the British government on the grain companies' behalf, and gave a guarded undertaking to assure that there would be no financial collapse when he said:

I yesterday cabled Sir George Perley to take the question (of the British Wheat Commission accepting lower grades of wheat) and today cabled him further in the matter. If, as a result of those cables relief is not afforded to the situation, the government will have to consider such further action as may be expedient to the public interest.

In retrospect, it is difficult to understand why the royal commission allowed its corners in Winnipeg and Chicago to develop so long without volunteering a settlement. From the commission's standpoint, its loss in failing to negotiate a bulk purchase in Canada was only compounded by the dramatic price rise in response to the corner.

An immediate result of the suspension of trading at Winnipeg was to halt country buying because the companies had no means of hedging their purchases. Over the weekend the exchange committee continued to meet with Stewart who consulted the royal commission by cable. By Tuesday, May 8, they were able to sign an agreement on a basis for settlement of the Wheat Export Company's outstanding May and July contracts. As predicted, narrower spreads than first agreed upon were set for the non-contract grades, and the list included a larger category of non-contract grades. Moreover, the royal commission offered a scale of premiums for early delivery on the July contracts which underlined the urgency they placed upon obtaining delivery. However, there was now no market indicator for the basic price of No. 1 Northern. To meet this void, the agreement provided for the appointment of a price committee whose function would be to set the contract price for No. 1 Northern on a daily basis. Although its immediate improvisation was essential, its solution was unique in the history of Canadian wheat pricing, expressed in the following terms:

> Mills represented and Allied Governments agree to accept from day to day on basis No. 1 Northern contract, all millable wheat at above specified spreads.
>
> May, June and July contracts basis 1 Northern will be established and spread prices will be quoted daily.
>
> Grain will be accepted on the prices quoted each day until the opening of the market the following day.
>
> The prices to be paid must be fair and reasonable and the mills and Allied Governments, while following their judgments in buying, must consider both market conditions generally and the prices paid in other markets.
>
> The prices so reached will be recorded by a price committee and will form the basis of clearing these contracts from day to day.[37]

However cryptic the text, its meaning was clear. The price spreads applicable to all grades below No. 1 Northern had been set out in a long list earlier in the text of the agreement. Having been fixed by the agreement, the spreads would not change. But in order to arrive at the basic price for No. 1 Northern to which the spreads for the lower grades would apply, the mills and the Wheat Export Company as buyers undertook to negotiate each morning with the elevator companies as sellers, the price of No. 1 Northern applicable to new contracts entered into up until 9:30 the following morning. Then a newly-negotiated price for No. 1 Northern valid for the next 24 hours would be announced. The buyers and sellers were constituted as a price committee charged with the responsibility of publishing the daily price.

The foregoing agreement was not without obligation by the grain companies, however, who for their part undertook to deliver to Canadian mills and to the Wheat Export Company 90 percent of their receipts. This put an effective limit upon the amount of Canadian wheat that could be sold in the United States markets which had just been opened up. A clause in the agreement reflected the British government's response to the free wheat decision:

> We, the undersigned this 5th day of May, nineteen hundred and seventeen, in order to conserve the food supplies of the empire and to assure the Allied Governments that for the balance of this crop the wheat over which we have control will not be diverted to other channels than those controlled by the Allied Governments, do hereby agree in consideration of the buying agency of the Allied Governements giving us its assurance that it will take all grades of wheat in exchange for the Winnipeg May and July futures at spreads to be subsequently fixed, which spreads will be satisfactory and equitable to all interests, to deliver through said buying agency and to the Canadian Mills, in proportion to the allotment to them by agreement, at least ninety (90) per cent

[37] *Manitoba Free Press*, May 9, 1917.

of the grain owned or controlled by us, and that we will further exercise our influence to direct the farmers' wheat which we may handle through our warehouses into the hands of those representing the Allied Governments or the Canadian mills as agreed upon.[38]

The agreement was signed by the following buyers and by the seller who had been authorized to sign on behalf of the elevator companies:

James Stewart, Royal Wheat Commission
Andrew Kelly, Western Canadian Flour Milling Co.
R. R. Dobell, Ogilvie Milling Co.
W. A. Matheson, Lake of the Woods Milling Co.
W. E. Milner, Maple Leaf Flour Mills

W. R. Bawlf, Grain collecting agencies on behalf of all the elevator companies.

The immediate impact of the agreement was amply reflected in the *Manitoba Free Press* news report of May 9, which said:

The agreement signed yesterday is a document the like of which the grain trade of Canada has never seen before. It is doubtful if the grain trade in any part of the world has ever seen its like. It will become an historic document and grain trade events will date form the 8th day of May, 1917, when it was signed. The effect of this agreement will be to supply to the Allied Governments the greatest percentage of wheat in the shortest possible time. . . .

It was a gigantic task. Hardly anyone outside the committee believed it could be done. Today it is an accomplished fact and the whole exchange, the banking interests and milling interests owe to them a debt it will be difficult to pay.

While all the committee have worked unceasingly with one accord, they declare the end could never have been accomplished had it not been for the patience, tact and wide knowledge of the grain trade shown by President Gage.

REPORT OF THE CENSORING COMMITTEE

A by-product of the foregoing events was the report of the committee appointed on April 28 to censor trades. The work of the committee and the measure of its effectiveness is reflected in the following report submitted to the president and council of the Winnipeg grain exchange by its members, Messrs. Magill, Fowler and Brodie on May 2, 1917:

On the 28th April, 1917, you appointed us a Committee "to censor all trades for the next two or three days and report at a later meeting of the Council".

We began the work immediately during the Saturday session of the market and we have censored all orders submitted to us since.

On Saturday we had no time to secure an office and we placed a desk by the side of the pit. In order to protect the privacy of trading, we had built during the week end a temporary office in the trading room. On Monday we required slips of all approved orders, which slips were sent to the Clearing House for the purpose of checking the trades.

For the week of censoring we had no precedents to guide us and we had no written instructions from the Council. All we had consisted of certain oral

[38]*Ibid.*

instructions or explanations, and these we endeavored to conform with. We found it impracticable for the three of us to work together on each order, as that would have delayed trading unduly. Each of us, therefore, acted upon his own judgment on each order, consulting with the others in doubtful cases and endeavoring to act along the same lines.

We interpreted your explanations of the work entrusted to us as mainly that of endeavoring to ascertain whether there was any illegitimate trading going on in the pit which might unduly inflate or depress prices or cause violent fluctuations, and we understand that along with that we were authorized by you to refuse to approve trading of such character. In the orders submitted to us we have found very little, if any, of such trading. In the main we have had occasion to refuse approval of only a very small number of trades, and in regard to these trades which we refused, the ground of our refusal was, in most cases, that information for which we asked was not furnished.

In the main, we have not found it necessary to withhold approval in regard to trading in oats, barley and flax. This holds also of October wheat. Such restrictions as we have imposed were mainly if not wholly, on trades in May and July wheat.

We have permitted all old trades in May and July wheat to be closed or unwound, and of course we have permitted all trades that were of legitimate character. Apart from these two classes of trades in May and July, few orders were submitted to us, and in regard to these few our refusals to (approve) were as a rule due to the fact above stated that information we asked for was not furnished us.

We do not conceive it to be our function to express an opinion as to the effect of our work.[39]

In his presidential address to the exchange on September 12, 1917, Gage dwelt on the corner and the exchange's initiative in resolving the crisis. He referred to the negotiations with the longs and the shorts, and also with the scalpers and spreaders, but said that the censors had found very little evidence of "illegitimate speculating". Foster's diaries refer to the scalpers, but these were small-scale traders and it is remarkable that there were no substantiated charges of large-scale speculative positions at Winnipeg. As will be shown below, Foster was very much concerned that there should be no future scope for "manipulators". His concern appeared to be much greater than the facts warranted.[40]

CHICAGO SUSPENSION

A week later, in response to the chaotic market situation and to pressure exerted by the Washington administration, the Chicago board of trade followed suit by ordering discontinuation of trading in May wheat. Existing contracts were either to be filled by delivery or adjusted on the basis of a selling price determined by a committee, as was done in Winnipeg. In the week preceding this action, representatives of the royal commission had conferred in Washington and Chicago, because buyers on behalf of the commission had also taken a substantial long position at Chicago. Apparently, however, the Chicago market had experienced much more speculative activity. Although it is difficult to understand why so much speculation was alleged at Chicago and so little at Winnipeg, one is left to

[39] *Foster Papers.*
[40] *Ibid.*

conclude that the large American operators found sufficient scope for their activities at Chicago and therefore had no need to resort to Winnipeg.

The suspension of trading in May futures at Chicago is colorfully described by a special correspondent in the May 12 issue of *Manitoba Free Press:*

> Chicago, May 11: Trading in May wheat was stopped short today by Chicago Board of Trade. It is the first time that such a step has ever been taken on the Chicago Board of Trade, which fixes the price of wheat for the world. It is regaded as possibly the first step toward a predicted regulation and limitation of maximum prices for basic food products.
>
> At a meeting of the directors of the Board, it was decided existing contracts must be adjudicated by delivery of the wheat or by a settling price to be agreed upon by a committee.
>
> A federal official said the action of the Board prevented a flight which might have brought $10 wheat.
>
> The action that led to the closing of the May market came swiftly. Early in the day Alan G. Anderson, Vice Chairman of the Royal Food Commission, and H. T. Robson, chief buyer of foods for the Commission "pot" that feeds England, France and Italy, called upon Charles F. Cline, United States District Attorney. Robert W. Childs, Special Assistant Attorney General in charge of food investigations was called in.
>
> What happened at this conference not a man present would divulge. But it is known the Englishmen came to America on a mission and they have found all information. Also, they came to Chicago direct from Washington.
>
> When the secret conference was over, Mr. Cline sent for officials of the Board of Trade. Those who appeared were: John R. Mouff, lst Vice President; J. J. Stream, 2nd Vice President; J. C. Merrill, J. Hubert Ware, and Roderick McKinnon. For three hours they were closeted with Cline and Childs.
>
> Again the veil of mystery is drawn over the actual words submitted. It is not known whether threats were used or whether pleas to patriotism were made. The men went out. Joseph P. Griffin, President of the Board of Trade, who earlier in the day was ordered to bed by his physician, was called.
>
> With his own hand he signed the notice stopping the trading. Also he appointed a committee composed of James A. Patten, A. Stanford White and Hiram N. Sager, to fix the settlement price. It is probable that another meeting of the directors will be held today. What brought about the unprecedented action is supposed to be this: Vast quantities of wheat have been bought that do not exist and are unprocurable. Investors have bought wheat that cannot be found. Eastern financiers knowing the true conditions, have "mopped" up millers, mulcting the westerners who are credited with having sold to the European governments and others, wheat they could not get.
>
> One story is that Joseph Leiter has at last got his revenge, winning from $2,000,000 to $3,000,000 on the long side of wheat, and partly evening the score for his unmerciful losses at the wind-up of the famous wheat deal in 1898.
>
> Jesse Livermore, the New York stock plunger, is said to have profited $1,000,000 on the bulls with a coterie of eastern speculators also backing winners. A number of cotton traders close to the eastern financial interests that have been handling the buying for the allies, are said to have found millions by breaking through into the wheat pastures.
>
> It is possible that both the Rockefeller and Morgan interests pocketed huge sums, trading on a larger scale then ever before known to the trade. The

rumour was that "financial giants of the east plunged in with an inside knowledge of the needs of the allies, not only now but in months to come." Several weeks ago a number of Chicago's biggest traders including Arthur Cutten and James A. Patten, sold out their wheat and corn. It is understood that this was taken by the eastern clique who thereby tightened their grip and the price went up $1 a bushel more.

Buying of futures on an unprecedented scale, selective manipulation, and operations that have dwarfed anything in the history of the pit, and rendered all the old financial romances commonplace, are blamed for the existing situation by many traders.

So far as the Winnipeg wheat futures market was concerned, the mechanism had broken down under wartime conditions in which an import buyer's monopoly had been established. Such a monopoly permitted a corner which normal competition among buyers and sellers would have prevented. The council of the Winnipeg grain exchange freely admitted that a futures market could not be operated successfully under such conditions. Thus it was the council of the exchange, rather than the government, which terminated wheat futures trading on that first occasion.

5

BOARD OF GRAIN SUPERVISORS

The need for a wartime government body to determine fair prices for wheat and to regulate its trade arose primarily out of the existence of an importers' monopoly which placed the competitive export trade in jeopardy. The need for it became critical, however, when the Winnipeg grain exchange terminated wheat futures trading in order to protect the solvency of its principal member firms. As a temporary measure, the exchange had appointed a price committee which made a daily determination of the price at which wheat could be traded. From May 4, 1917, until the board of grain supervisors for Canada assumed the responsibility for price determination on July 20, the prices committee of the exchange fulfilled this role. The daily prices set by the committee ranged from a high of $3.00 at the outset on May 4 to a low of $2.15 at the end of June, after which the daily prices rose again to $2.48 by mid-July. The price committee was a creature of the exchange, itself an unincorporated association. Exchange bylaws permitted it to enforce contracts among members through the power of suspension from trading privileges, but it had no legal authority to enforce contracts with non-members.

No one was more aware of the tenuous legal basis upon which the price committee operated than were the members of the council of the exchange, who promptly drew their concern to the government's attention. In fact, the government would have found itself in an untenable position had it allowed the situation to continue. It was one thing for the exchange to direct its committee to set prices which were "fair and reasonable" but quite another matter for the government to satisfy producers that their interests were being protected, and to satisfy wage-earners, as well, that they were not being gouged by the price of bread. In addition, the United States had declared war just prior to the debacle in its futures markets, and the need to coordinate Canadian and United States wheat-pricing policies had become manifest to both governments.

At the outset of this temporary, but unique, price-making mechanism, Mr. John Charlie Gage, president of the exchange, sent a telegram to Sir Thomas White, minister of finance, on May 15, 1917, to stress the importance of the crisis which had reduced sound firms to the point of bankruptcy and had disrupted the buying of grain in the country through lack of hedging facilities. In his telegram the president proposed that the

Canadian and British governments should fix a minimum-maximum range of prices or, as an alternative, should confirm the prices determined daily by the price committee of the exchange. President Gage's telegram read as follows:

Concentrated buying by Allied interests and mills has in effect cornered May and July. Mills virtually out of May leaving large holdings Allied Governments with contract grades unavailable by heavy proportion. Situation accentuated transportation due late opening navigation now closed and terminals blocked and by original contract grade going out of condition country elevators. Line elevators followed usual hedging custom in conformity bank policy relying on Allied buyer taking all millable wheat and exchanging futures in line with past policy. Suddenly buyer ceased exchanging futures in effect demanding contract grades. This precipitated panic advancing May twenty-five and forty cents over Chicago and Minneapolis May respectively. With no protective hedge available practically all buying ceased at country points thus preventing further supplies for Allies. We believe if market left open no limit to advance, serving no useful pupose and against public and Allies interests. By closing May and July clearing price remained stationary and consequent probable failures of sound companies avoided. Exchange meeting unanimously endorsed action and clothed special committee extraordinary powers to adjust relations shorts with principal longs. The machinery of this Exchange cannot be easily restored. If Governments concerned fixed maximum and minimum price this will be effective. If the Governments do not see their way clear to do so, there must be a re-consideration of the method of buying for the Allied Governments. We are not attacking the firm doing the buying now. The question is one of method, not personnel. We consider that the agent of the Allied Governments, the mills and a committee of this exchange should agree upon marketing methods for May and July and that the agreement so reached should be confirmed by the Governments concerned and should not be altered without the knowledge of the other parties.[1]

When Sir Thomas White and the government failed to react favorably to either of President Gage's price proposals, the exchange's secretary, Dr. Robert Magill, requested an interview with Sir George Foster. Because Magill has been in and out of the narrative so far and is about to emerge more prominently as an adviser to Foster, it will be recalled that Magill began his career as a professor of political economy at Dalhousie University. He was appointed chairman of the Saskatchewan elevator commission which had recommended against the public ownership of country elevators. In 1912, Magill was appointed by the Borden government as the first chief commissioner of the board of grain commissioners for Canada, which was the body created by the Canada grain act for purposes of its administration under Sir George Foster's departmental responsibility. The board of grain commissioners should in no way be confused with the board of grain supervisors now about to be created as a purely wartime pricing and marketing body. Magill resigned from the board of grain commissioners to accept an appointment as secretary of the Winnipeg grain exchange, and in the corner which had just taken place, he became a member of the censoring committee, and in due course he became chairman of the board of grain supervisors.

[1] *Foster Papers.*

During the futures market crisis, Foster had been in Washington. Upon the entry of the United States into the war, Foster was honored by an invitation to serve as a member of the British mission to Washington. The mission, headed by the Right Honourable Arthur Balfour, foreign secretary (and a former prime minister), was for the purpose of arranging wartime co-operation between the two governments on a broad front, including food supply. Foster remained in Washington from April 21 to May 3 in an understandable atmosphere of entente. Among other matters, he discussed food issues with members of the British mission which included a representative of the royal wheat commission, and in meetings of the mission with American officials. According to his diary, he conferred for two hours on May 3 with the United States secretary of agriculture on matters of food supply, the regulation of prices, and export policy relating to neutral countries. In the policy decisions which remained to be faced in Canada, the need for coordination with British and American policies was one of the primary considerations.

ORIGIN OF THE BOARD

Upon his return to Ottawa, Foster wrote to Magill on May 14, to acknowledge the representations made by the exchange and to invite recommendations. Magill replied on May 21 submitting a long survey, calculated to assuage Foster's apprehensions, in which he reviewed the mechanics of the futures market, defended the speculative activities therein, and downplayed the elements of gambling and manipulation. He underlined the difficulty of operating a futures market under wartime distortion of normal competitive conditions. In all of his communications at that time, Magill went to great lengths to dispel from Foster's mind that there could be any room for manipulation or speculative abuse in the arrangements the government might have to adopt. However groundless Foster's fears were in that respect, they were genuine. The last thing Foster wanted was anything savoring of a trading scandal under his administration. In the present predicament Magill foresaw two alternatives: the first, a government preemption of country and terminal elevator operations under which the government could determine the price to be paid to the producer; and second, a government price-fixing agency through which country elevator buyers operating in their own right could be protected. He favored the latter and recommended the creation of a board located at Winnipeg to fix prices and to direct the distribution of supplies.[2] In his covering letter, Magill added a request that Foster receive a delegation from the exchange.

To underline the urgency, Magill followed up his letter and report immediately by sending telegrams to the minister, and through the exchange's law firm in Ottawa, requesting an interview with the exchange's representatives. Foster wired back, "Glad to see delegation immediately."[3]

The exchange delegation and Magill remained in Ottawa for a series of conferences, extending over several weeks, during which time Magill

[2] Magill's memorandum on *The Wheat Problem,* May 21, 1917, Foster Papers.
[3] *Foster Papers.*

worked in the Chateau Laurier and prepared a first draft, dated May 26, of a proposal to establish a "Grain Council of Canada". He recommended that the council be comprised of eastern and western committees of grain men with authority to direct the price and consignment of all grain in terminal elevators, to fix prices daily in parity with other markets, and to requisition elevator space and direct cars to prevent hoarding.[4] While the delegation remained in Ottawa, Foster also invited Messrs. Alan G. Anderson and Herbert T. Robson, members of the royal commission on wheat supplies resident in New York, and Mr. James Stewart of the Wheat Export Company, Winnipeg, to Ottawa to take part in the discussions. Anderson had specific proposals to offer in which the British objectives were very clear. In a period of intensifying shortage, British interests could best be served by a system which would remove the risk of continuing price fluctuations, and which would authorize the control of distribution in a way that the whole of the exportable surplus could be directed to the royal commission. The format of the board which Anderson proposed was limited to these two provisions. His advice fortified Magill's recommendation that a price-fixing agency would be preferable to government operation of country and terminal elevator facilities.

After the conference with Anderson, Magill prepared another memorandum, headed "Board of Grain Supervisors" in which he referred to the scheme proposed by Anderson as something fully understood by Foster, and he addressed himself at length to allaying the latter's concern that grain men appointed to a price-fixing board could take financial advantage of their positions. Magill used the memorandum as a draft for a more concise letter which he addressed to Foster from the Chateau Laurier on June 7, 1918:

> In regard to the Board of Grain Supervisors, I venture to ask your consideration of the following:
>
> (1) *The interest of the producer.*
> The supply of wheat available for the Allied peoples is practically limited to the surplus which North America has to export. This fact, of itself, will secure for the grain growers of Canada a good price for their wheat. In addition to this, it is the policy of the Wheat Commission to pay such prices as will stimulate production and sale on this continent. Finally, it is proposed to give the grain growers of Western Canada ample representation on the Board of Supervisors.
>
> (2) *The interest of the consumer.*
> The price of wheat at Fort William is fixed by the demand for export. The Wheat Commission representing the Allied Governments buy Canadian wheat at as low a price as is possible, consistent with the principle of stimulating production and securing the grain. The interest of the Canadian consumer is to get flour as cheaply as possible. In this respect, the interest of Canadian consumers is identical with that of the Allied peoples. There can, therefore, be no stronger representative of the Canadian consumer upon the proposed Board than the buyer for the Allied Governments. In addition to this, the purpose is to give special representation on the Board to the Canadian consumers.

[4]*Ibid.*

(3) *Fear of manipulation.*

It may be suggested that if any grain dealers are appointed to the proposed Board, they will gain inside information which would enable them in some way or other to make personal gains, or which, at least, if they continue to buy and sell grain, would influence their judgment.

But the scheme that is proposed provides against this danger.[5] There is, as you know, a Wheat Commission representing the Allied Governments. In the United States there is organized a Grain Executive, consisting of grain men, and it is proposed to create a Board of Grain Supervisors for Canada. These three Boards, or Commissions, will act in harmony and co-operation. They will have the same object in view, pursue the same policy and con-jointly, or in close co-operation, regulate prices. So far as this continent is concerned, they will pay substantially identical prices for the same grades of grain relative to the position of the grain. This would constitute a strong safeguard against attempted manipulations. Further, the proposed Board of Supervisors includes diverse interests, and any proposition made by any individual member will be keenly scrutinized by men who know all the moves of the trade. Further, if the Board of Supervisors is established in Canada, its work will be subjected to an hourly scrutiny by the trade, the farmers' organizations and the consumers, a scrutiny which, in itself would render practically impossible any attempt at making personal gain. Further, should the three bodies named decide upon a flat price, manipulation of the kind suggested would be impossible. Further, speculation in futures has been eliminated, so far as wheat is concerned, already, and it is unthinkable that the proposed Board would restore it.

The Grain Exchange at Winnipeg took the lead in restricting or eliminating what is ordinarily known as speculation in wheat. If the members of that Exchange were actuated at the present moment, mainly, by the motive of making money, they would arrange to make all grades of wheat deliverable on their future contracts, and then open the market for free and untrammelled dealing in the new crop. They believe, however, that this would militate against the interests of the people of Canada and against the interests of the Allied peoples, because, in their judgment, it would result in abnormally high prices for wheat and flour. They are anxious to avoid this, and they have shown their anxiety and their good faith by their attempted regulation of the market. The Exchange, however, has no legal right or power to limit the prices. They have accordingly asked the Government of Canada to undertake such regulation. They offer their elevators, their organizations and their experience to the Government, not to enable them to make money out of the war conditions, but in the interest of the people of the Dominion and the Allied peoples.

I do not claim any special knowledge. I have had, however, considerable experience in matters pertaining to grain in Canada, and my conscientious conviction is that while a Board of Grain Supervisors would have a very difficult task to perform, the least danger to be feared is attempts on the part of any of the trade members of the Board to further their own personal interests.[6]

On May 31, Foster's diary entry noted that he was "busy on grain control". On June 8 an entry read "Advisory Board interview took up Grain

---

[5]The memorandum referred specifically to the scheme "as understood and proposed by Mr. Anderson".

[6]*Foster Papers.*

Supervisors question but failed to reach conclusion. Objection to so many grain men."

On June 11 he recorded "We are now making some headway. The grain Supervisor passed, the Fuel Controller as well — both attached to my department."

In the light of Borden's earlier hesitation, Foster was justifiably elated that the cabinet had now agreed to assign him full responsibility for the wheat administration. In the enthusiasm of his new responsibility for the board of grain supervisors, Foster carefully did his homework to ensure that he had a complete grasp of the problem. With Magill as his tutor, Foster pencilled the following undated notes:

Line decided upon for 1917 crop:

1. Fix a price on *each grade* — Take the place of hedging. Diminish suspicion of manipulation.
Premiums usually paid by mills west of Ft. Wm. for privileges of diverting grain billed to Ft. Wm. to their mills.
Carry over charges are incurred by keeping grain at Ft. Wm. from close of Dec. till April.

2. Defer naming price until U.S. acts. Premiums and carry over charge must be taken into account.

3. Future trading was restricted by Exchange in May. Anyone could sell but not buy for future delivery except to fulfill old contracts — reduced to vanishing point. A fixed price is the substitute for future trading as it eliminates risk of fluctuations in prices.

4. Street & track prices would be regulated by fixed price at Ft. Wm. were it not that car shortages & delay in transport to terminal. The price would be the fixed price less freight, handling, storage and int., and fair profit. Board working out a systematic basis.

5. Export = *Wheat & Flour*
If U.S. put out a 2 lb. loaf for 10 cts. made of present grades there will not be much saving in consumption — consequently not a large surplus to export.
Therefore all our surplus should go to Allies — a little higher rate here would encourage this. *This done as to Flour.*

6. *Flour for Allies.*
Wheat Export Co. should have buyer in Canada. Board should know how flour orders are being placed, so as to regulate the distribution.
In Canada spreads and prices are wider than in U.S. — only by having similar spread fixations in both countries can we have similar prices. Our mills would fight this as wider spreads here favour them. So if Board fix spread prices it must get Wheat Export Co. to buy a fair share for Allied needs.[7]

ESTABLISHMENT OF THE BOARD

Foster's June 11 diary notation that "the Grain Supervision passed" was in reference to the two orders in council approved on that date under authority of the war measures act. He tabled them in the house on June 12 and commented briefly:

I just desire to say in reference to these Orders in Council that the government has passed them after consultation and consideration, first, in the interest of

---

[7] *Ibid.*

Canadian producers of wheat, and consumers of flour made therefrom to regulate and control in an intelligent and reasonable way the price at which wheat shall be sold, and the methods of dealing therein, and the transportation thereof; secondly, to assure for Great Britain and the Allies the total exportable surplus of Canadian wheat and flour at a time of great exigency, from a source which geographically and in regard to the safety and facility for transport, is most available of all overseas countries; thirdly, to act in conjunction and to co-operate with the authorities of the United States who, for similar reasons are arranging for a like arrangement and control in that country.[8]

The first paragraph of P.C. 1604, June 11, 1917, provided for the creation of a board of grain supervisors consisting of not more than 12 members who would serve in an honorary capacity. The board was given full power of enquiry to ascertain available supplies of grain, their location and ownership and the transportation and elevator facilities available to move them. Then came the key provisions:

4. The board shall have power from time to time to fix the price at which grain stored in any elevator may be purchased, and the conditions as to price, destination or otherwise under which grain may be removed from such elevator and may also prescribe what grain shall be sold to millers or milling firms in Canada or elsewhere (hereinafter called "Millers") and what grain shall be sent to the United Kingdom and the Allied powers and it shall be the duty of the Board to issue such orders and take action as it deems necessary to facilitate at all times the transportation and delivery of grain in excess of domestic requirements to the United Kingdom and the Allied powers. . . .

5. The Board shall have power to receive offers for the purchase of grain from millers and from the Wheat Export Company Limited, or from any other person or body corporate, hereinafter referred to as "Overseas Purchasers" representing or acting for the Government of the United Kingdom or for any combination of the same, and from time to time to fix the prices at which such grain shall be sold.

6. The Board shall have power to take possession of and sell and deliver to millers or to overseas purchasers at the prices so fixed grain stored in any elevator, and to account and pay over to the owners thereof the proceeds of such sales after deducting all expenses connected with the taking possession, sale and delivery.

7. The Board shall, as far as possible, and having regard to position and the cost of transportation, fix a uniform price throughout Canada for grain of the same kind, quality and grade.

8. Notwithstanding anything in the Grain Act or in the Railway Act, the Board of Railway Commissioners for Canada shall have power to order any railway company to provide cars and other transportation facilities for handling grain and to transport as directed, grain taken possession of or owned by the Board.[9]

P. C. 1605 of June 11 named the members who, together with their affiliations, indicated the representative character of the board:

Robert Magill, of Winnipeg, Manitoba, Chairman,
    Secretary, Winnipeg Grain Exchange;
H. W. Wood of Carstairs, Alberta
    President, United Farmers of Alberta;

[8]*House of Commons Debates*, June 12, 1917, p. 2236.
[9]*Ibid.*, pp. 2236-2237.

Samuel J. Rathwell of Moose Jaw, Saskatchewan,
    Grain producer;
Thomas A. Crerar of Winnipeg, Manitoba,
    President, Grain Growers' Grain Co. Ltd;
William L. Best of Ottawa, Ontario,
    Labour leader;
John Charlie Gage of Winnipeg, Manitoba,
    President, Winnipeg Grain Exchange;
William R. Bawlf of Winnipeg, Manitoba,
    President, N. Bawlf Grain Co. Ltd;
William A. Matheson of Winnipeg, Manitoba,
    General Manager, Lake of the Woods Milling Co. Ltd;
Lionel Clarke of Toronto, Ontario,
    Chairman, Toronto Harbour Commission;
Joseph Ainey of Montreal, Quebec,
    Controller, City of Montreal, and labour leader;
James Stewart of Winnipeg, Manitoba,
    President, Wheat Export Co. Ltd.[10]

POWERS OF ENQUIRY

The board exercised its powers of enquiry at the outset by holding public meetings in Montreal, Toronto and Winnipeg at which it discussed its proposed methods of operation with the trade, and at which representations were made to it on the cost of producing wheat, wartime cost increases, labor shortages, the high cost of flour and bread, and the need for stimulating production to meet British and allied needs. All of these considerations were related to the level at which the wheat price should be set, but in the end the board accepted the recommendation which emanated from an investigating committee in the United States as to what constituted a fair price in the circumstances.

PRICE REGULATION

Foster had already discussed the price issue during his visit to Washington, and two months later a committee of the new board including Messrs. Magill, Stewart, Gage and Best followed suit by visiting New York and Washington. There they held discussions with representatives of the royal commission and with Mr. Julius Barnes who was slated to become president of the food administration grain corporation when it was formed later that year.[11] On July 9, the committee of the board also met with Mr. Herbert Hoover, the United States food administrator, who obtained the consent of his Canadian visitors to bring Canadian prices into line with whatever price level might be settled upon by the United States administration.[12] This was a rather surprisingly open-ended commitment in view of the fact that the enabling legislation to create the grain corporation had not yet been enacted by congress, nor were the American officials at that time able to indicate the price they would recommend. After the committee's return to Canada, and

---

[10]*Ibid.,* p. 2237.

[11]The Food Administration Grain Corporation was created by executive order on August 14, 1917. It was renamed the United States Grain Corporation on June 30, 1919.

[12]Frank M. Surface, *The Grain Trade During the War,* (Macmillan, N.Y., 1928), p. 276.

while the board was awaiting formal price action in the United States, a speculative price rise occurred in American markets. Primarily to protect the British who were trying to move every available bushel from the remainder of the 1916 crop to the Atlantic seaboard for August shipment, the board acted unilaterally by setting a maximum price of $2.40 applicable to wheat from the 1916 crop, as indicated in the following order:

It is hereby ordered by the Board of Grain Supervisors for Canada that so far as the balance of the present crop is concerned and until further notice, the maximum price of wheat, Basis No. 1 Northern in store Fort William, shall not exceed two dollars and forty cents ($2.40) per bushel effective the first August, 1917, inclusive, from 9:30 a.m. o'clock. Winnipeg, Man., 20th July, 1917.[13]

The maximum price order effectively curbed rising price pressures in Canada at a time when prices were still uncontrolled in the United States. Shortly afterward, the board made a public appeal to all grain growers and dealers owning wheat to sell their stocks so that admiralty ships arriving at the Atlantic seaboard during August could be loaded and it repeated the plea of the royal commission that the flow of grain to the allies be maintained.[14] By mid-August wheat prices in the United States had tumbled in anticipation of congressional price legislation. To protect Canadian producers whose prices had been restricted by the maximum price order, the board made the $2.40 a minimum as well as a maximum price, effective from August 17 to August 31, 1917. Mr. H. W. Wood, a member of the board, gave a graphic account of the developments in a statement he issued to his United Farmers of Alberta executive:

Our board was practically, if not entirely, unanimous in the opinion that about $2.25 was the proper price for this year's crop, basis No. 1 Northern at Fort William. We were given to understand from Mr. Hoover that the United States would soon be ready to co-operate with us. But unforeseen events delayed them very much longer than they anticipated. The bill creating their board of grain supervisors was very much delayed in congress. In the meantime the wheat being practically all out of the hands of the farmers and in the hands of the speculators and other interests, an attempt was made to take advantage of the situation and launch a boom in wheat prices. Our board being in session at this time felt in duty bound to check this unjustified manipulation of the markets, notwithstanding we had fully intended not to fix prices till the 1917 crop began to run. To this end we put a maximum price of $2.40 on the Canadian wheat, believing that it was only a matter of a very few days until the United States would be ready to co-operate with us by protecting the market on the other side. In this we were disappointed and the price of wheat over there being uncontrolled, was rapidly pushed up beyond the $3.00 mark. Thereby the price of wheat that was stored in the mills, elevators and elsewhere, as well as all of the flour that was put out by the mills during this time was very materially raised, and the whole consuming public was bled to the extent of this raise in prices, while very little wheat actually changed hands at the advanced price. There is no good reason to believe that the legitimate law of supply and demand had anything to do with this invasion of the market.

A few of our farmers still had some wheat left over, and, of course, were anxious to get the highest price possible for it. A great deal of dissatisfaction

[13]*Department of Trade and Commerce File T-14-144,* Public Archives of Canada.
[14]Frank M. Surface, *op. cit.,* pp. 64-72.

was thereby engendered by the action of our board in setting the maximum price of $2.40 on the remnant of the old crop. This was aggravated as much as possible by a few irresponsible parties who seemed to want to destroy this board in order that the wheat market might be unprotected, and become a prey to their piracy. Incidentally, they seemed to hope that they would be able to destroy the farmers' organization by creating dissatisfaction among individual farmers against their own organization.

When the act was finally passed in the United States and the buyers at the Northern United States markets, thinking that the price would be set at about $2.00 in a few days, began to run the price of wheat down as rapidly as it had been run up, and it looked as if wheat at those points would be down to $2.00 in a few days. Our board felt that inasmuch as we had put a maximum price on our wheat and held it down while wheat had gone higher in the States, it would be nothing more than right to hold our wheat up to the maximum until the United States board took final action in setting the price. Consequently we made $2.40 a minimum as well as a maximum price, and held it at that until they finally set their prices across the line for the 1917 crop.[15]

On August 30, 1917, the fair price committee, which President Wilson had appointed a fortnight earlier to investigate and to recommend a fair price, completed a hurried study and arrived at a compromise agreement to recommend that the price for No. 1 Northern Spring wheat at Chicago be $2.20 for the 1917 crop. President Wilson immediately accepted the committee's recommendation and instructed the food administration to adhere to that price. It remained for the grain corporation to set equivalents for other grades and types of wheat at Chicago and other delivery points. Thus No. 1 Dark Northern Spring was assigned a premium of 4 cents over No. 1 Northern Spring, and Duluth prices were set at a discount of 3 cents under Chicago, so that the price for No. 1 Dark Northern Spring at Duluth was fixed at $2.21.

Having committed itself beforehand to acceptance of an equivalent price basis in Canada, the board of grain supervisors welcomed the recommendation of the fair price committee as having taken into consideration all relevant matters including increased costs of production. Having already admitted the overriding necessity for a parity of prices in both countries, the board acknowledged the fair price as determined in the United States as being equally fair for Canada. It also recognized No. 1 Northern at Fort William and No. 1 Dark Northern at Duluth as representing equivalent values. Consequently, the board issued an order on September 12, 1917, which set the price for deliveries from the 1917 crop effective until August 31, 1918 at $2.21 for No. 1 Manitoba Northern with appropriate discounts for lower grades. In his statement, (just quoted), to the United Farmers of Alberta executive, Wood recorded that at the board's first meeting in June:

> After a considerable discussion of the matter it seemed to be the unanimous opinion of the board that about $2.25 . . . would be as near an equitable price, considering all other conditions as we could determine.

Then, in relation to the board's first price of $2.40 and the United States fair price committee's $2.20, Wood added:

> I just want to draw your attention to one fact in regard to this $2.40 price. It is the highest price that has been fixed by any authority in the Empire, or in

[15]*The Grain Growers' Guide*, October 3, 1917.

any one of the Allied governments up to the present time. . . . Just how much influence our action in setting this price had on the United States board in raising their price above the $2.00 mark, above which they seemed determined not to go, I do not know. But that it did have some influence I do not doubt.[16]

On the other hand, Surface records that the fair price committee was aware of the understanding that the Canadian price "would finally be determined in accordance with prices in the United States" and that, as recording in its minutes, the $2.20 price was a compromise between the opposing views of Committee members who represented farmers and labour.[17]

When the board issued its new order setting the price for the 1917 crop, Magill prepared the following release issued on September 12:

> The Board of Grain Supervisors for Canada carried on enquiries during the weeks between the date of its creation and the date on which the United States authorities fixed prices for United States wheat with the view of being in a position to fix fair and just prices for Canadian wheat.
>
> The Board heard a very considerable amount of argument turning on such important matters as the cost of producing wheat in western Canada, the increase in the cost of production since the war broke out, the shortage of labor, the increased cost of living and more especially the increased cost of flour and bread, the shortage of the supply of wheat available for Great Britain and her Allies, the necessity of stimulating production for next year and the probable effect of the cessation of war upon the price of wheat.
>
> The commission appointed by President Wilson to fix the price of wheat in the United States undoubtedly took into consideration such matters as these, and the prices set by that commission embody their conclusions on all such matters.
>
> When the Board of Grain Supervisors met to decide the prices for Canadian wheat, they considered that they had there a definite starting point. It is needless to illustrate the argument that the prices of Canadian wheat, if fixed by law at all, should be fixed with close reference to the prices fixed in the United States. Even in normal times producers of grain in western Canada seemed to think that if they got the prices that obtained in the United States, they should be satisfied. Under the present conditions, there is, however, an argument that is perhaps stronger than that, namely, the advisability of setting prices that would not make it impossible for the Unied States to assist Great Britain and her Allies in financing the war should assistance be desired in the matter of financing wheat supplies.
>
> The Board of Grain Supervisors consider that the prices fixed in the United States could not be seriously objected to from the point of view of the producers and the endeavor of the Board of Grain Supervisors was to adapt as far as possible the prices fixed in the United States to Canadian grades and the Canadian conditions of handling.[18]

The release continued in much greater detail on the pricing arrangements entered into between the royal commission and the grain corporation in the United States, the desirability of price parity in North America, and the problem of carrying charges. Nowhere in the statement, however, was there

[16]*Ibid.*
[17]Surface, *op. cit.,* p. 20.
[18]Included in *Memoranda of the Board of Grain Supervisors for Canada,* issued at Winnipeg, 15th November, 1917, Trade and Commerce File T-14-144.

an explanation of why the price was fixed in advance for the whole crop year. It will be recalled that in his early draft on the "Grain Council of Canada", Magill had proposed the daily fixing of prices in parity with other prices, and that the order in council creating the board had allowed for flexibility in fixing the price "from time to time". Thus the setting of a price effective from September 12, 1917, to August 31, 1918, evokes some interest. Undoubtedly, one consideration was that the grain corporation established its buying price for the whole of the crop year and that the parity principle required that the Canadian price be fixed for the same period. It was only after the operations of the board had been terminated, however, that Magill provided a very convincing justification of the action in his final report:

> Naming a price is one thing — it is quite another to find a purchaser who will contract to take the article at the price fixed throughout the whole of the twelve months. For the crop of 1917 there was no difficulty in this respect. The Allies needed the whole exportable surplus wheat of Canada. They were willing to buy the whole surplus at the price fixed, and they gave a guarantee to that effect. In this respect, wheat was in a different position from coarse grains.[19]

CARRYING CHARGES

In fixing the price at Fort William, the board considered that street prices at country elevators (of direct concern to the farmers) should also be fixed. This it did by deducting from the Fort William price the applicable freight rate from the country point plus a maximum of five cents a bushel to cover elevator handling costs. But carrying costs which the board variously estimated at one-half cent per bushel every ten days, or at two cents per bushel per month also had to be covered if street prices were to be kept at the same level through the crop year. To accomplish this the board considered raising its fixed price by two cents per bushel per month from January through May, but this would have raised Fort William prices over those at Duluth by as much as ten cents per bushel by spring, to which the director of the grain corporation, Mr. Julius Barnes, took exception. Magill met with Barnes in New York at the end of August, and Barnes confirmed by his letter of August 31, 1917, to Magill the position he had taken; the relevant excerpts are quoted:

> Referring to our conversation of today, I wish to record the suggestion I made of a way to absorb the undoubtedly proper accumulating charges on wheat held in country elevators and warehouses because of car congestion.
>
> I agree with you that the equivalent of one-half a cent (½¢) per bushel for each ten days is a fair expression of this charge, and probably less than the grain could actually be cared for by an independent carrier. I agree with you that this charge should properly be returned in some form to the country elevator, in order to avoid having it taken out of the track or farmers' price.
>
> I urge strongly that some method be devised other than the method of adding this to the terminal price period by period, for the main reason that this accumulative advance soon puts your relative basis, as compared with our stabilized basis, so far out of line that it will lead to a great deal of agitation on the part of our growers.

[19]*Operations of the Board of Grain Supervisors for Canada, June 11th, 1917 to January 31st, 1920*, p. 8, Trade and Commerce File T-14-144, reproduced in Appendix 1.

I suggest, instead, that an effort be made to arrange with the Allies' representative a contract by which the Allies will pay these accumulating charges in country elevators as an outright allowance to the elevators themselves month by month. I am sure a form of weekly report showing the quantity in store each day, could be devised and so properly safe-guarded that such payments could be made without abuse. The system would be much like the allowance of interest on daily balances as inaugurated by banks. . . .

I hope you will not discard this suggestion as impracticable without attempting to arrange it, for it bridges over so many difficulties, allowing you to maintain a stabilized and uniform price at your country buying stations, and the Allies could well afford to assume this obligation and expense in the interest of the general operation.

If for any reason this seems impracticable, I would urge you most strongly, if any advancing scale of price, to start your terminal price at what you feel is low compared with ours, figuring it on the average of the period of advancing prices; and again urge that such period of advancing charges be broken at the time of the close of navigation and a fresh lower start made, which will again make the average not so unfavourable in comparison with ours. This has been the custom of trade for years in reflecting the decline in premiums because of the close of navigation. . . .[20]

Although Barnes urged Magill to negotiate with the Wheat Export Company for the payment of carrying charges, he did not let matters rest there, but followed up directly with the British authorities. Surface has given an account of this approach in which it will be noted that Barnes failed to mention his concern over dissatisfaction by American growers but argued instead that an escalating price would delay farm deliveries to the disadvantage of the British. Surface wrote:

At this time a point of considerable importance came up in that the Canadian Board wanted a basic price which would increase one-half cent for each ten days up to May 1 in order to take care of carrying charges. Mr. Barnes strongly opposed this method because of the effect it would have on delaying farm marketing. With a small crop in this country and urgent demands by the Allies it was important to secure as early marketing as possible. An unchanging price would in reality put a premium on early marketing and that was what was desired. Mr. Barnes asked the Wheat Export Company to undertake to absorb these carrying charges since it would in the end be much to their advantage. This they agreed to do by paying the Canadian Board of Grain Supervisors four cents a bushel on all wheat taken by them and the Canadian Board then agreeing to absorb all storage charges in terminal and country elevators, thus making a stable and unchanging price.[21]

Negotiations between the board of grain supervisors and the Wheat Export Company were concluded in time for the board's price announcement of September 12, at which time the arrangements for the carrying charge fund were also announced. The fund was subsequently authorized by P. C. 2867 of October 12, 1917, which amended the board's original order in council P. C. 1604 of June 11, 1917. In his "Report on Price of Wheat" released on September 12, Magill said:

The matter of carrying charges on wheat in Canada is a much more important one from the point of view of the producers than it is in the United States, and a system of fixed prices that did not take into account the carrying charges at

[20]*Ibid.*
[21]F. M. Surface, *op. cit.,* p. 276.

country points might easily work out a great injustice to the producers. The Board have had under consideration the advisability of adding an increment period by period to the fixed price at the terminal point. Mr. Julius Barnes, however, who has charge of the wheat operations of the United States Grain Corporation took very strong objection to that method of meeting the charges. He did not object to the charges being met, but he objected to that particular method on the ground that it would put the terminal price at Fort William entirely out of line with the price at Duluth and Minneapolis, and would thus lead to discontent and agitation among producers in the United States. He suggested, therefore, and indeed strongly advocated, that a fund be created by the Board of Grain Supervisors for Canada out of which the carrying charges on street wheat should be met, and that that fund be created by an assessment upon the Allies for the wheat they purchased. He pointed out that the United States Grain Corporation was levying a tax of 1% upon the United States millers and the Allies, and also had a contract which enables it to levy a further assessment upon the Allies, thus creating a fund out of which to pay administration expenses and any other necessary expenditures. To meet the objections of Mr. Barnes, the Board of Grain Supervisors, therefore, decided to adopt this method, hence the Board decided to collect from Canadian millers and the Allies the 2¢ per bushel above referred to, and further, a sum not exceeding 2¢ per bushel from the Allies, and the Board proposed to meet the carrying charges on street wheat out of this fund thus created.

In his final report written in March, 1920, Magill added the following:

It may be said that the Board could have added 2¢ a bushel per month to the terminal price, and have met the carrying charges in that way. And in fact this was the method which the Board at first contemplated. This plan would have followed commercial practice, as in normal times the price of May wheat at Fort William is higher than the price of previous December wheat by the cost of carrying. While the Board contemplated this method favorably, however, there was a very serious objection from the United States. If the Fort William price in November was $2.21½, and if 2¢ a bushel per month were added to it, the Fort William price in May would be some ten cents per bushel higher than the price in Duluth, grade for grade, because the United States authorities had determined to maintain the same nominal price for wheat at the same point the year through. The United States authorities recognized that carrying charges in Western Canada were an important thing. The Board, on the other hand, recognized the desirability of keeping the prices on the two sides of the boundary in line, and a way out was found by separating the carrying charges from the price of wheat, and handling them through the Board's offices by means of a special fund.

This was not a method which the Board ever regarded with pleasure. It was an untried method for which there was little or no guidance in previous commercial experience. It meant imposing an assessment on the wheat sold to millers and exporters. It meant the creation of Collecting and Disbursing Departments. It meant elaborate and accurate records of all purchases of wheat at every country elevator, of all quantities sold to exporters, and of all quantities ground into flour at the mills. It meant a system of checks and a machinery to enforce payment. It meant a heartbreaking audit of the books of all the elevators, grain companies and millers of the Dominion. It meant the possibility of misunderstandings about the nature of the tax; of litigation about payments, and worst of all it meant the possibility of the abuse of public money.

It is a method which should not be tolerated, or should be tolerated only so long as it is forced by imperative conditions. It has no other defence. It was adopted by the Board because there was no other way out. To maintain an identical price for twelve months at the terminal point meant that the carrying charges must be either assessed on the buyer in the form of a special payment to the Board, or taken out of the producer by giving him a lower price for his wheat. After considerable hesitation, therefore, the plan was adopted. The consumer paid and the producer benefited.[22]

Payments into the fund at the outset were assessed against millers at the rate of two cents per bushel upon the amount of wheat ground. By agreement with the wheat export company exporters paid four cents per bushel upon wheat exported. In practice, these charges were assessed before shipments were made either to mills or for export. The reason for charging a higher assessment against the Wheat Export Company was because the grain corporation in the United States had charged the Export Company not only the one percent paid by the mills and exporters alike but also an additional unspecified amount levied by agreement with the company. As for the board's carrying charge fund, the Wheat Export Company agreed to pay at the rate of four cents after assurance that any surplus accruing in the fund from its contributions would be repaid to the company. According to departmental information furnished to the select standing committee on agriculture and colonization on June 23, 1931, the carrying charge fund operations were summarized as follows:

The total revenue of the Board of Grain Supervisors amounted to $10,478,259.02 and was obtained from a levy on the Wheat Export Company of 4¢ per bushel on all wheat exported during the year 1917-1918, and two to two and a half cents per bushel from all local wheat used in Canada, which levy during the year 1918-1919 was reduced to 3¢ per bushel on wheat exported, and raised to 3¢ per bushel on local wheat handled. This levy was over and above the price fixed which was the net price paid to the farmer.

At the winding up of the operations of the Board of Grain Supervisors, the sum of $2,500,000 was returned to the Wheat Export Company, being an amount in excess of all requirements for the operations of the Board.

There was also paid into the Consolidated Fund of Canada a sum of $428,781.94 on the following dates:

November 19,1919	$300,000.00
January 31, 1920	50,000.00
July 13, 1920	25,000.00
October 20, 1920	25,000.00
December 9, 1920	28,781.94[23]

As for disbursements from the fund, Mr. H. Tooley, secretary of the board, submitted an unpublished report to the minister in April, 1918, which explained that:

The rate per bushel to be paid to the elevators called for considerable argument, such as the increased cost of money and the desirability to guard against establishing a figure which might include an earning to the elevator, which would be an inducement to hold back the wheat to create an earning and yet it was essential that the elevator would not be required to suffer a loss

[22]*Operations of the Board of Grain Supervisors for Canada, June 11, 1917 to January 31, 1920,* p. 8, Trade and Commerce File T-14-144.
[23]*Journals of the House of Commons,* June 23, 1931, p. 387.

as it might result in them being closed up. A conclusion was finally reached that the carrying charge on street wheat should be one twenty fifth (1/25¢) per bushel per day, accruing from the time the wheat is purchased until it is delivered at the Terminal Elevator or Mill.[24]

In the autumn of 1917, eastern millers contended that they were being discriminated against in relation to western millers who had access to wheat in country elevators at a net price exclusive of carrying charges, whereas the eastern mills had to pay the charges on wheat stored for their account. To remove this discrimination the board increased the assessment on all Canadian mills to 2½ cents per bushel out of which additional revenue the board paid for storage on wheat held in eastern public elevators for mill account at a rate of 1/22 cent per bushel per day, and in winter storage boats at eastern lake port 1/25 cent per bushel per day.

In January, 1918, the board responded to a request from the office of the food controller to assist in the establishment of a fixed price for flour for the time that the board's fixed price for wheat would remain in force. In order to do so, the board had to anticipate the full carrying charges that wheat used by the mills would bear during the remainder of the crop year. To cover these carrying charges the board assessed the mills an additional 1½ cents per bushel on wheat ground to August 31, 1918, and paid carrying charges on wheat held in public terminals at the rate of 1/14 cent per bushel per day, winter storage boats, interior terminals and flour mill bins 1/25 cent, and country elevators, where ordered to be held by the board for the benefit of western mills, 1/13 cent per day.[25]

COARSE GRAINS

Section 4 of the order in council creating the board, authorized it to regulate the prices of coarse grains, but this authority was not implemented. In his final report, Magill offered a convincing explanation:

> The Board did not market oats, barley, flax and rye. Its reason was not that these grains are not human food, or that they are unimportant, or that the Board wished to leave something to private enterprise. The reason was that it could not find buyers who would agree to accept the surpluses of these grains at fixed prices satisfactory to the Board. It would have been as easy to fix the prices for these grains as it was to fix the price of wheat. But to fix the prices without the certainty that the whole of the grains would be sold at the prices fixed would have incurred a risk of serious financial loss which the Board would not face.
>
> The coarse grains, therefore, were not marketed by the Board, but by private enterprise, and difficult as were the conditions of trading during the years of 1917 and 1918, the grain trade were able to market the coarse grains successfully.[26]

By way of supplementary information, a departmental report mentions that the board "worked in harmony with the Food Controller for Canada, the Dominion Government Seed Commissioner, The Grain Exchanges, and

---

[24]*The Board of Grain Supervisors for Canada, Report by the Secretary,* Trade and Commerce File T-14-144.

[25]*Annual Report of the Department of Trade and Commerce,* 1920, p. 26.

[26]*Operations of the Board of Grain Supervisors for Canada* pp. 5-6.

the authorities in the United States with respect to prices, distribution and conservation of oats, barley and flax".[27]

The continuation of futures trading in oats, barley and flax was essential to the marketing of these grains by the private trade. In his presidential address delivered at the annual meeting of the Winnipeg grain exchange on September 11, 1918, Mr. W. R. Bawlf referred to the exchange's co-operation with the board, and added that the council of the exchange had taken its own steps to prevent undue speculative trading.[28]

DISTRIBUTION

With reference to the powers conferred upon the board (paragraph 4 of its order in council) to direct the distribution of grain between the Canadian millers and the United Kingdom and allied powers, Magill recounted in his final report that Canadian requirements for bread and seed were the first priority. Seed shortages in Alberta and Saskatchewan developed both in 1917 and 1918, and the board had to make special arrangements to retain local supplies. The mills were protected on wheat supplies to meet domestic, Newfoundland, West Indies and royal commission flour orders. At times the board diverted mill supplies, with millers' concurrence and subject to replacement, to meet urgent wheat requirements for the royal commission.

Paragraph 6 of the order in council which conferred upon the board "power to take possession of and sell" was a limited provision which excluded authority to purchase. The phrase "take possession" was a legal expression for "commandeering" and in order to expedite an all-rail movement on behalf of the royal commission at a time of critical shortage during the winter of 1917-18, the board actually did commandeer wheat stored in country elevators by farmers who had not voluntarily offered it for sale. Bawlf described the action, including the all-rail winter movement to seaboard:

> During the winter months there was an insistent call from the Allied communities for wheat. The Board of Grain Supervisors commandeered wheat at various points in the West, ordered it into the Government elevators at Calgary, Saskatoon, Moose Jaw and Winnipeg, to be delivered there to the Wheat Export Company for shipment to the seaboard. Although the climatic conditions were not favourable for rail transportation, a considerable quantity of wheat was in this way forced to the seaboard and shipped across the ocean.[29]

While no questions were raised concerning the board's authority to direct the distribution of grain, its powers were preempted from time to time by actions taken both by the British and the American authorities. As for British intervention, Bawlf offered a good description in the process of contrasting the broader powers of the United States grain corporation with the more limited powers of the board when he said:

[27] *Report of the Department of Trade and Commerce for the fiscal years ended March 31, 1917 and 1918,* p. 21.

[28] W. R. Bawlf, *The Marketing of Canadian Grain under War Conditions,* (The Winnipeg Grain Exchange, 1918), pp. 5-6.

[29] W. R. Bawlf, *op.cit.,* p. 8. See also *Operations of the Board of Grain Supervisors for Canada,* p. 19.

In Canada, on the other hand, apart from the fixing of the price by the Board of Grain Supervisors and from such arrangements as are made necessary by the fixing of the price, there was during the past year no body competent to perform the functions performed by the United States Grain Corporation. The result is that apart from the fixing of the price, the control of the marketing of Canadian grain was not in Canadian hands. It was in the hands of the Wheat Export Company, acting under instructions received from either the British Royal Commission or some other body in England.

This led to some rather strange developments during the past year. Through the winter months it became practically impossible for any shipper other than the Wheat Exporting Company to get a car for the hauling of wheat east all-rail. Just how this situation arose it is difficult to say, but the result of it was not hard to understand. The result was that Canadian firms who had been in the business of shipping and forwarding grain for many years could no longer ship a carload of Canadian wheat to a Canadian mill east of the Great Lakes, and this domestic business fell into the hands of the company representing the Allied Governments. . . .

When navigation opened there was not a large quantity of wheat and the arrangement made for the supply of wheat to the eastern mills through the Wheat Exporting Company was continued, so that for the first time in the history of the Dominion, and for the first time since the war broke out four years ago, Canadian firms could not sell a cargo of wheat to Canadian mills east of the lakes.[30]

In a letter dated September 27, 1918, from Mr. Robson to Mr. Julius Barnes, the Wheat Export Company stated that "during the early part of this year, for convenience sake and at the express request of the Canadian Board of Grain Supervisors, the Wheat Export Company undertook the distribution of wheat to millers in Canada."[31]

What began as a matter of convenience, however, ended up as a source of contention, so much so, in fact, that at the outset of the 1918 crop movement the board sought and obtained additional powers which, among other things, strengthened its jurisdiction over distribution and helped to restore to the Canadian trade the handling of domestic grain shipments to mills and an opportunity to sell to the Wheat Export Company at lower lake ports and the seaboard rather than at Fort William.[32] The altered basis of delivery had, of course, to be negotiated with the British.

With regard to United States intervention in the distribution of Canadian wheat, the co-operative arrangements between the Canadian and American authorities began in evident harmony. One of the board's first acts was to issue an order on July 27, 1917, which prohibited the sale and shipment of Canadian wheat, without the consent of the board, to parties in the United States.[33] Shortly afterward Magill explained the action:

The Board of Grain Supervisors are in harmony with the United States Grain Corporation in believing that the first call upon the surplus of wheat in Canada is from the European Allies, and prices being fixed as they are, producers in Canada have nothing to lose by such regulation of exports to the United States as will result in very little wheat being shipped to the United

[30]W. R. Bawlf, *op. cit.,* pp. 8-9.
[31]F. M. Surface, *op. cit.,* p. 286.
[32]*Order of Council P.C. 2153,* September 5, 1918.
[33]Order No. 2, included in *Memoranda of the Board of Grain Supervisors for Canada,* issued at Winnipeg, Man., 15th November, 1917, Trade and Commerce File T-14-144.

States for consumption there. The understanding between the Board and the United States Grain Corporation is as follows: It may be advisable to permit a certain amount of Canadian wheat to be shipped to the United States in the common cause, but for all such shipments Mr. Barnes will take the responsibility. He must approve, he must purchase the wheat and distribute it, and the Board of Grain Supervisors, at his request, will permit the wheat to be exported; in a word, wheat shipments across the line either way must be subject to the approval and permission of the United States Grain Corporation and the Board of Grain Supervisors for Canada.[34]

The export prohibition was subsequently amended to confine its application to wheat shipped by lake or rail. A customs order of October 4, 1917, exempted wheat exports conveyed in farmers' vehicles and consigned to country elevators in the United States. Thus Canadian farmers residing close enough to haul their grain across the border could continue to take advantage of any premiums for quality wheat which American mills were willing to pay above the fixed prices for the standard grades.

In other reports, including his final report, Magill tended to gloss over the friction which developed between the Canadian and American authorities over questions of distribution. This was related more clearly by Dr. Frank M. Surface, an economist in the United States grain corporation, who recounted the American influence upon Canadian wheat distribution at that time.[35] The basic problem stemmed from the small wheat harvest in the United States in 1917, which compelled the Americans to give first priority to meeting their own domestic requirements.[36] Added to the domestic shortage of wheat was a wartime transportation problem in which the demands of military traffic left insufficient lake and rail facilities for the normal grain movement from the midwest to the eastern mills served through the port of Buffalo.

As Surface relates, Messrs. Hoover and Barnes had dwelt on the need to marshall the whole of the North American wheat supply as a unit. Competition must be ended between Canadian and American flour mills, and flour trade between the two countries would not be permitted without explicit approval. Because of the difficulty of moving wheat from the midwest to Buffalo where idle mill capacity was developing, the American authorities persuaded their British counterparts to accept flour from American mills ground from Canadian wheat in lieu of the wheat. Although this switch was defended as a means of economizing ocean tonnage, its purpose was to accommodate the American mills in the face of internal transportation congestion, and Canadian interests therein were disregarded.

Late in 1917, when the British turned to the Americans for a loan to finance the purchasing of wheat in a way that the Canadian government had been doing since 1914, the Americans drove a hard bargain, mainly at

---

[34]*Report on Price of Wheat, Board of Grain Supervisors for Canada*, p. 6, Trade and Commerce File T-14-144.

[35]F. M. Surface, *op. cit.*, p. 277.

[36]Surface reproduced a shipping program from North America to the Allies for the period December, 1917, to July, 1918, which showed 33 million bushels of wheat and flour equivalent to be shipped from the United States, and 100 million bushels from Canada. For the months of March though July, no exports of American wheat or flour were scheduled (*Ibid.*, p. 189). A similar shortage in feed grains occurred in the United States during World War II.

Canadian expense, as reflected by a memorandum of agreement concluded among the three governments under the heading of "Finance of Canadian Cereal Export" and dated October 23, 1917:

Canada to find ——	$50,000,000	November 1917
Canada to find ——	$50,000,000	During Spring of 1918

U.S.A. to advance to British Government, for purposes of buying in Canada, wheat, wheat flour, and oats, (oats limited to $20,000,000), for export to European Allies, up to $250,000,000 on following conditions:

I. Canada to cease export of flour
(a) to neutrals (especially South American and West Indian)
(b) to U. S. A.

II. Canadian mills to grind wheat up to the average output of the past three years, ending 30 September, 1917.

III. Wheat Export Company to hand over to U. S. F. A. Canadian wheat as required from time to time by U. S. F. A., receiving in exchange equivalent quantities of flour for export to Allies, made from such Canadian or other wheat. Equivalent quantity of flour to be returned to Wheat Export Company without delay and at latest within three weeks of handing over Canadian wheat.[37]

In contrast with this subordination of the mill grind in Canada and of Canadian flour export, the Canadian government's loan of $100,000,000 stood up handsomely in comparison with the United States loan of $250,000,000. The grain corporation also agreed with the Wheat Export Company of New York on the amount of Canadian wheat to be furnished daily at Buffalo for the mills in the eastern United States. As Surface commented:

These arrangements were to a very large extent made between the United States and Great Britain with the Wheat Export Company as an intermediary. Although the agreement had a very important effect upon Canada her grain officials were apparently only consulted incidentally in the matter. This caused considerable ill feeling in certain Canadian quarters for a time and there was even a refusal to abide by the agreement that Canada was not to ship flour into the United States. This difficulty was of short duration and the Canadian officials soon came to realize the desirability of the arrangements made and the justice of the demands by the United States.[38]

The extent to which Canadian wheat distribution was used to serve purely American interests is reflected in a portion of a letter which Mr. Julius Barnes addressed on March 16, 1918, to Mr. Robson, requesting the right of replacement from Canadian supplies when, as a result of current shipments to Britain, the United States found itself running short of wheat for home consumption. The relevant paragraph reads:

There are certain sections of the U.S. which will produce a surplus of flour on the equitable operation of mills, something as the Pacific Coast does; while there are other sections, viz., the Buffalo district, and the Minneapolis district, that apparently lack sufficient supplies to operate their mills on a just percentage. What we want to work out with you is such reassurance as will

---

[37] *Ibid.*, p. 278.
[38] *Ibid.*, p. 279. Small wonder that members of parliament representing milling interests (including Mr. James A. Robb, subsequently minister of trade and commerce under the King administration) demanded emphatically that all wheat provided from Canada should be shipped to Britain in the form of flour.

allow us, in case of need, to draw on Canadian supplies, to be furnished to these particular sections especially.[39]

So far as Canadian-United States co-operation was concerned in the wartime administration of wheat supplies, it was pretty much a one-sided operation.

One notable transaction of no direct concern to Canada but of passing interest since it was reckoned as a wheat transaction of record size up to that time, was the bulk purchase early in 1918 by the royal commission, of 100 million bushels of wheat at a provisional price of $2.00 per bushel from the grain corporation. As the commission revealed later, this purchase was made to accommodate the grain corporation which lacked congressional authority for replenishment of depleted capital funds. Consequently the corporation negotiated with the royal commission a bulk purchase of 100 million bushels of wheat against drawing rights of $200,000,000 of commission funds which were available to it from credits extended by the United States government to Britain. The commission, in turn, took delivery of the wheat at its discretion and as it would have done in the absence of the bulk sale.[40]

BOARD PRICE FOR THE 1918 CROP

That all was not the harmony and co-operation originally envisaged among the three government agencies is borne out by another passage in Surface's account of the setting of the board's fixed price for the 1918 crop. Although the board had willingly consented to a policy of price uniformity with the United States with respect to the 1917 crop, the experience in the distribution of that crop had created sufficient dissatisfaction to leave some doubt as to whether the Canadians would continue to co-operate through 1918. On this occasion, Barnes drew the attention of the Wheat Export Company to the fact that it would be embarrassing not only to the British but might also be regarded as discrimination against American farmers if the board of grain supervisors were to fix a Canadian price at a premium over American wheat. To make his point, Barnes was again prepared to exert financial pressure to produce the desired result. As indicated in his letter of June 21, 1918, to Mr. Herbert Hoover, Barnes wrote:

> I think it is very important that Mr. Crosby (Assistant Secretary of the Treasury) should in some manner get an indication from you that before the Canadian financing is agreed to there are some points which must be provided for in all justice to your own operations. These points I have emphasized in the past two weeks as including the following:
>
> 1. Priority in taking any Canadian wheat under the direction of the Allies wherever it may be for the purposes of the Belgian Relief Commission or other urgent needs of the Grain Corporation.
>
> 2. Some provision by which no advances shall be made if the Canadian price of wheat should by any authority be fixed at excessive premiums, in the judgment of the Food Administrator, over the prices ruling for similar qualities in similar positions, in the United States or of United States origin. . . .[41]

[39]*Ibid.*, p. 282.
[40]*First Report of the Royal Commission on Wheat Supplies,* London, 1921, pp. 66-67.
[41]Surface, *op. cit.,* p. 284.

How much pressure was brought to bear remains obscure, but the fact was that for the 1918 crop the board of grain supervisors fixed a slightly higher basic price at $2.24½ per bushel effective from August 26, 1918, to August 31, 1919. Toward the end of that crop year when other arrangements were made to handle the 1919 crop, the board terminated its fixed price for deliveries from the 1918 crop as of August 15, 1919. Fixing the price for the whole of the crop year, as was done a year earlier, led to certain marketing difficulties, however, as soon as the armistice was signed.

MARKETING OF THE 1918 CROP

It has been frequently, but inaccurately, stated that the functions of the board of grain supervisors were limited to the regulation of prices and to the direction of distribution. While this might have been an appropriate description of its first year's operations, the board's authority was expanded at the outset of the 1918-19 crop year. The need for additional powers sprang not only from the problems which arose in connection with the Wheat Export Company's preemption of grain handling from Fort William east, but more importantly from the fact that the royal commission was not prepared to guarantee the purchase of the exportable surplus from the 1918 crop, as it had done a year previously. As Magill explained:

> It was different with the crop of 1918. No guarantee was obtained from the representatives of the British Royal Commission with regard to the surplus of the crop of 1918, and when the Armistice was signed there was considerable difficulty in selling the balance of wheat still remaining in Canada. Having, however, fixed a price for 1918, and having arranged for the purchase of wheat from the farmer by the trade on that basis, a guarantee was necessary and it was given by the Dominion Government. Fortunately, the Allied countries needed the wheat, and in the end the balance of the crop of 1918 was sold at the fixed price.[42]

The enlarged authority was provided by P. C. 2153 of September 5, 1918, which amended the original order in council in the following manner:

> By adding as paragraphs 6A, 6B, 6C, the following;
> 6.(A) The Board shall have power to determine or specify the quantity and grade of grain (and the grain) to be allotted to, and to fix the commission, if any, to be paid by millers in respect of such allotments, other than as fixed by the Board of Grain Commissioners for Canada, to purchase grain and sell same to millers, and to effect arrangements for delivery of such grain to millers, such powers to include the allocation for this purpose of Canadian lake tonnage and the distribution of cars for rail shipments.
> 6.(B) The Board shall have power to effect arrangements for the export of grain to the United Kingdom or the Allied Powers, to purchase grain for such export, and to sell same to Overseas purchasers, to specify the places at which it should be delivered to Overseas purchasers, the quantities and grades of grain to be delivered, the price to be paid for same, and the commission, if any to be paid in respect of such deliveries other than as fixed by the Board of Grain Commissioners for Canada, such powers to include the allocation for this purpose of Canadian lake tonnage, and the distribution of cars for rail shipments.
> 6.(C) The Board shall have power, subject to the approval of and to financial provision being made therefore, by the Governor in Council, to

[42]*Operations of the Board of Grain Supervisors for Canada*, p. 8.

purchase grain for account of the Government of Canada and to sell same to millers or to Overseas purchasers. . . .[43]

At the same time, a press release was issued to explain the new policy:

Ottawa, Sept. 4. Complete control of the purchase and sale for export of Canadian wheat has been assumed by the Government. The control of the methods of exports has also been assumed.

Under the new arrangement the situation will be:

(1) The price for wheat for the crop of 1918 has been fixed and will be maintained for the crop year.

(2) The purchase of wheat and grains for export and for internal demands will be thrown open to dealers and shippers as before the war, subject, however, to supervision and control by the Government.

(3) The Government will guarantee the purchase of all surplus merchantable wheat raised by Canadian farmers in the year 1918 at the price already fixed.

(4) The apportionment and distribution of wheat for Canadian mills and for export will be made under Government control, as also will be the supervision and allotment of cars and lake tonnage, arrangements for lake insurance and shortages, and the mechanism for insuring the steady, speedy and effective transport of wheat from the head of the lakes to the seaboard.

(5) The board of grain supervisors, whose members represent the interests of grain producers, of shipping and forwarding agencies, of the millers and consumers of grain products, has been entrusted by the Government with the carrying out of the above programme and clothed with full powers for executing the same.

Under the arrangement of last year, the sole purchase of wheat for export was placed in the hands of the Wheat Export Company, whose headquarters are in London with branches in New York and Winnipeg.

The result was that the normal and usual Canadian agencies for the purchasing, selling and forwarding of wheat across the lakes and by rail to the seaboard were practically excluded from doing this. Incident to this control of purchase by the Wheat Export Company, the business of internal distribution to the mills and the control of shipping tonnage across the lakes gradually fell under the control of the same company. Now that the price of wheat has been fixed and speculation therein eliminated, it is not considered necessary to continue such arrangements to the exclusion and detriment of Canadian dealers and shippers.

By reason of its intimate relations to the ocean transport system, and owing to the cooperation of Canadian agencies, the Wheat Export Company was able efficiently to carry on the work of transport to destination. It is not proposed to relax in any particular the central supervision and direction necessary to secure efficient handling from the head of the lakes to the port of delivery on the Atlantic seaboard.[44]

As a result of this policy announcement the Canadian exporters and mills gradually resumed the purchase of wheat at Fort William and exporters were able to earn commissions again on the forwarding of wheat from the lakehead to seaboard. The 1918 crop was a disappointing one of 164 million bushels. Fall deliveries fell behind the royal commission's expectations, and shipping furnished by the admiralty could not find sufficient Canadian

---

[43]*Trade and Commerce File T-14-144.*
[44]*Manitoba Free Press,* September 5, 1918.

cargo. As a result, the Wheat Export Company ordered American wheat and oats to be shipped through Canadian lake ports. At the time this movement was ordered, the board of grain supervisors lacked the authority to control it, and the necessary powers were provided by order in council on November 19, 1918, only three weeks before lake navigation closed. During that autumn, from September 1 to December 12, 41,535,561 bushels of Canadian wheat, 23,896,372 bushels of United States wheat and 31,509,287 bushels of United States oats were moved through Canadian lake ports, but it had proved impossible to move any Canadian oats through the same channels.[45] Complaints were made about the blockade against Canadian oats resulting from the congestion caused by the movement of American grain, and Magill commented upon them in his letter of November 9, 1918, to Foster in which he also expressed his wish to resign:[46]

Very many thanks for your letters of November 4th and 5th about my resignation.

I did not act under any sudden impulse, as I have been wanting to get out for some months; and the criticisms of certain papers has not influenced me, as I was aware that in the main the methods and policies of the Board had the cordial approval of the representatives of the farmers and the majority of the grain and milling trades. It would be impossible for anyone to do the work of the Chairmanship of a Board like ours and escape all criticism.

In view of all the facts, I have decided, with your approval, to remain just as I am until the close of navigation, and without any change either in the matter of my relation to the Exchange or the matter of salary. Between now and then I will give the matter my best consideration and take it up with you before navigation closes, more especially with reference to the contents of your letter of November 5th.

I wired to you in this sense to-day, and I enclose copy of the telegram. I hope this will be satisfactory.

With regard to the moving of the grain, of course we are disappointed. Buffalo, however, and the United States outlet have been closed to us this year, and that has made a big difference. Then oats were needed for the armies, and the Wheat Export Company shipped a quantity of oats through Canadian ports. Only the last three million bushels of this, however, affected our movement.

Then the Admiralty had placed boats for wheat, and as our wheat was not available at the time, we permitted five million bushels of American wheat to

---

[45] *The Globe,* February 13, 1919.

[46] Magill did not resign until the board's operations were finally terminated. Other correspondence indicates that he had hoped to wind up the board's operations immediately after the armistice. Since the board, including the chairman, served in an honorary capacity, Magill was simultaneously secretary of the grain exchange and chairman of the board. During its first year and a half of operations, Magill undoubtedly devoted the major part of his time to the board. After that, as secretary of the exchange, he appears to have given almost his entire attention to ensuring the resumption of private trading. In 1919, he spent most of the first six months in Britain on matters of direct concern to the exchange, so much so, in fact, that he considered it inappropriate to accompany Canadian officials making representations on behalf of the exchange to their British counterparts. His return from Britain was delayed because he lacked priority which would have been his due as board chairman. Copies of orders in council replacing other members of the board appear on file but they do not refer to the appointment of a successor to Magill. On the other hand, P.C. 2518 of December 20, 1919, which implemented Foster's recommendation to pay an honorarium to Magill, referred to the whole period of his service including the winding-up operations after July 31, 1919.

be shipped through Canadian ports. This is the only permit our Board gave for the export of American grain through Canadian channels.

The total amount of American grain shipped through Canadian ports for the whole months of September and October was about twenty million bushels. Very little Canadian grain could be shipped during that period. This American grain included the oats above referred to and the five million bushels of wheat, and during the whole of the two months the railways were forwarding to the seaboard. It is absurd to say that this of itself would have blocked the movement of Canadian wheat.

I have no doubt we shall get all the wheat that reaches the Head of the Lakes shipped out before navigation closes.

I see you are going to England and I am very glad of the fact. I wonder if you will be able to do anything about Canadian wheat for next year.[47]

Magill replied to his critics in a pamphlet issued by the board on March 19, 1919. The booklet referred to an attempt to get the American and the Canadian lake carriers' associations to agree on a pooling of lake tonnage which had not succeeded. Magill acknowledged that the board had been accused of giving preferential treatment to the movement of American oats and to the use of American vessels, which he denied as nonsense.[48] Partly, however, as a result of the movement of American grain through Canadian ports, the royal commission had accumulated a 20-week supply of grain in Britain for the first time since the submarine campaign began and, understandably, it withdrew from the market. As a consequence, the board intervened as a buyer, under government guarantee, to sustain the delivery of wheat from farms. An account of the board's new role was furnished in a letter of September 11, 1919, from Mr. H. Tooley, secretary of the board, to Foster, in response to the latter's request for explanation of an item appearing in the board's financial statement. Tooley wrote:

During the marketing of the 1918-19 crop a period occurred when there were no buyers for wheat, which was being daily out-turned at the head of the lakes owing to the cessation of buying on the part of the Wheat Export Company and the mills who were unable to secure export orders and were consequently out of the market, it became incumbent upon the Board to arrange with the shippers and exporters of the grain trade to provide a market for the wheat arriving at the head of the lakes. As a result of this, approximately twenty-six million bushels of wheat were purchased during the closed season of navigation by the trade of which twenty million bushels were sold at the opening of navigation to the Wheat Export Company, who took delivery of same at Seaboard, at the fixed price plus three cents per bushel, plus all carrying charges and commission accrued on the wheat from the time of its purchase by the trade for account of the Board. On the balance of the wheat, approximately six million bushels two million bushels were sold to the Unites States and four million bushels to eastern Canadian mills, where the item referred to was incurred, the wheat sold to the mills being at the fixed price plus three cents per bushel, the Board of Grain Supervisors paying the cost of carrying the wheat form the time of its purchase by the shippers and

[47] *Trade and Commerce File T-14-144.*

[48] *Movement of the Grain Crop, 1918-1919,* The Board of Grain Supervisors for Canada, Winnipeg, Manitoba, March 9, 1919, pp. 28-30, (located in Trade and Commerce File T-14-144).

exporters for account of the Board. These charges, as stated, consisted of storage, interest and commission charges.[49]

In this operation, the board acted under authority of paragraph 6.(C) of P. C. 2153 which had been passed at the beginning of the crop year. In doing so the board had indeed become a marketing agency, and it differed from its successor, the Canadian wheat board, only in respect of pricing. Whereas in this instance the government had adopted a policy of fixing the price for a crop year ahead, primarily to conform with British and American interests at the time, the principal change involved in creating the wheat board was the replacement of the fixed-price policy by one of selling to best advantage.

Just at the time when the powers of the board of grain supervisors were extended and it became, in fact, a government grain marketing agency, Magill temporarily abondoned his board responsibilities by departing for London where he spent the spring and early summer months on matters of exclusive concern to the exchange. What ensued from his mission was a contretemps over government policy regarding the resumption of futures trading. Foster had never been averse to reopening the market as soon as it was capable of assuring a continuous and adequate outlet for deliveries from the western crop. The issue became one of whether and when that vital condition could be met; on these Foster and Magill disagreed. It is remarkable that their differing views failed to engender any personal animosity. In the process, Magill explained Foster's unavailability at critical periods and defended him against any suggestion that he might have acted on his own responsibility in deciding government policy without full cabinet support. A short time later Foster acknowledged Magill's contribution as board chairman and invited him to prepare for the permanent record a short history of the board's operations. Magill wrote a report and forwarded it to Foster with a covering letter on March 18, 1920:

I enclose as a separate and registered package the report on the work of the Board of Grain Supervisors for which you asked. It is somewhat less than twenty-three typed pages, and is as brief as I could make it without sacrificing intelligibility. I make no pretence to give a full and detailed report, as I conceived from our conversation about it that what you wanted was a brief and intelligible account of the policy and methods and work of the Board.

You may recall the fact that in London we discussed the advisability of having prepared an adequate account of the handling of our cereals during the war, and that as the outcome of that conversation Lord Crawford was asked for answers to a series of questions.

While Lord Crawford prepared answers, he never sent them. I do not know why.

I think it would be a great pity if some such account was not prepared and placed on the files of your Department. True enough, English-speaking people are supposed to be very quick to forget their war experiences, and some are optimistic enough to believe that the League of Nations will render all such war lessons useless in the future. I am sure you will agree with the opinion that it would be a wise provision to have accurate and comprehensive

---

[49]*Ibid.* Years later Tooley's letter of September 11, 1919, was submitted as evidence to the select standing committee on agriculture and colonization on June 23, 1931, and appears in the Committee's *Minutes of Proceedings and Evidence* of that date.

information in proper form upon the commercial side of the war, available in the Departments.

There is only one thing more that I want to suggest to you, and that is this: The Executive of the Board of Supervisors did a lot of work. We met twice a day six days in the week, for months. This applies to Messrs. Gage, Bawlf, Matheson and Stewart particularly. Of course, Mr. Stewart was acting on behalf of the British authorities, but the others were acting on behalf of the Canadian Government. Mr. Gage gave his whole time to it for a year, and a very large percentage of his time for the second year. Messrs. Bawlf and Matheson did practically the same.

I think it would be a very graceful thing if you took some opportunity to acknowledge their work. Later in the history of the Board Mr. Riddell became a member of the Executive, and then Mr. Jones of Fort William. Both of these helped us, but the main burden fell upon those who were residing in Winnipeg, and those who were on the Executive from the first.

I make this suggestion to you and leave it with you.

I expect to be in Ottawa within a few days, and if so, will call upon you in case you want to discuss the report.[50]

Although there are no copies of the correspondence on the departmental file, Foster undoubtedly acknowledged the contributions of Messrs. Gage, Bawlf, Matheson and Stewart, and the government had already recognized Magill's contribution by order in council P. C. 2518 of December 20, 1919, which eulogized his performance and authorized an honorarium of $10,000, which was paid to him out of the board's surplus. All members of the board had served in an honorary capacity, and the Winnipeg grain exchange had continued to pay Magill's salary throughout the period.

MAGILL'S REPORT

In his report, which contained no hint of interest in its publication, Magill intimated that he had prepared it for departmental reference on wartime procedures. Evidently it did not occur to Foster that the board should have issued a report with supporting financial statements in public right. Had publication been intended, Magill would undoubtedly have written in more expository style. But as it was drafted with restricted official readership in mind, the report was remarkable for brevity of style, without sacrifice of literary quality. The report has remained on file since and, in 1931, it was introduced as evidence to the select committee of the house on agriculture and colonization in response to a charge that the two boards had improperly disposed of producers' funds.[51] Magill wrote the report when the successor board's operations were in full swing. While he did not refer to the latter, the content of the report suggests some concern over the way in which the public might compare the performance of the two boards.

[50]*Trade and Commerce File T-14-144.*

[51]*Ibid.* It remains difficult to ascertain whether Magill's report was ever published in any form. It was furnished to the select standing committee on agriculture and colonization in 1931, and the minutes of that committee show that the minister, the Honourable H. H. Stevens, quoted liberally from it, but did not have the report printed. What were probably typewritten copies were distributed and the report could readily have been circulated in that form. Mitchell Sharp's article an "Allied Wheat Buying in Relationship to Canadian Marketing Policy, 1914-18" quotes by page reference from the typewritten report, but does not attribute it to any source. It deserves to be accessible as an historic document, so the report is reproduced in Appendix 1.

From the outset, Magill described his board as a marketing agency, and he repeatedly claimed that "the Board marketed the balance of the wheat crop of 1916, and the whole of the wheat crops of 1917 and 1918, making a total of about 350 million bushels of wheat".[52] He recited (too briefly) the circumstances in which the board had been created, but he recounted its early operations, including the first determination of the fixed price, and the relevance of a guaranteed market to it. He was convinced that a fixed price at Fort William should be reflected back in terms of a fixed price on street sales at country points and explained his procedures for doing so, including the cumbersome system involved in the operations of the carrying charge fund. He stressed that the charges were paid by the consumer and not by the producer. In this instance the economic argument as well as the mechanics he improvised were on his side. After describing some of the problems which arose in the distribution of wheat, he devoted more detail to an analysis of the board's impact upon the operations of the trade, and to its marketing responsibility, which he characterized as "national selling". He demonstrated that the board had enabled all segments of the trade to operate normally with the exception of the exporters and shippers whose operations and earnings had suffered from the intrusion of the Wheat Exporting Company into control of the internal and export movement.

Having predicted when the board was created that the agencies of the three governments would work in harmony, Magill wrote a concluding section on the subject of international co-operation in wheat which considerably understated the American intervention in the movement of Canadian wheat but emphasized the problems which inevitably arise between buyer and seller in intergovernmental negotiations, and he concluded with an expression of his personal conviction that only deleterious consequences could follow in the wake of government preemption of commercial affairs. He said:

> The Board were desirous of working in close harmony with the representatives of Great Britain and the authorities in the United States. And on the whole, considering the nature of the work and the conditions under which it was done, there was very little friction. It would however, be a grave mistake to ignore the fact that there were difficulties in attaining harmony, and that these difficulties were by no means unimportant, and might have led to serious trouble.
>
> Taking the two crops as a whole, the United States did not purchase a large quantity of Canadian wheat or flour, while the British Royal Commission did. The relation of the United States authorities to the Canadian method of handling the wheat was therefore different from that of the British authorities. The former were rather spectators, though deeply interested spectators — the latter were the buyers, and the interests of buyer and seller cannot be made identical. The United States authorities obviously could not approve of a higher price being paid for Canadian than for American wheat of the same grade and in the same relative position, especially as they assisted in the financing of the British purchases of Canadian wheat. This was fully recognized in Canada, and the price basis adopted was the same in the two countries. . . .

[52]Apart from this quotation from his report, see also Magill's evidence before the *Select Standing Committee on Agriculture and Colonization,* April 25, 1922, p. 193.

The British buyers were naturally eager to make the best bargain possible. The Board felt that the price being fixed at a point much below what it would otherwise have been, the buyer's interest was provided for. As time went on it became clear that so long as the British buyers took delivery of the wheat at Fort William and negotiated with the transportation companies for cars and vessels, they could control the domestic business in wheat at the expense of Canadian shippers. It is not a secret that after the year's experience the Board sought additional powers from the Government, with the result that the British buyers took delivery at the seaboard and that Canadian firms were to a limited extent enabled to do business.

It is a very superficial mind that can entertain the belief that international trading is an easy matter, or that it can be carried on without serious difficulties. In ordinary times when trading is done along commercial lines these difficulties are worked out in keen and open competition. When commercial methods are displaced, and when the trading is done by Government representatives, the difficulties still appear, but they no longer work out by competition; they become subjects of diplomatic negotiations. They are taken from the commercial into the political arena, and sooner or later they will result in bad feeling between the governments concerned, if not in the complete surrender of commercial independence on the part of the selling country, especially if it happens to be a weaker power selling to powers very much stronger and wealthier.[53]

This last succinct brief on behalf of an open market should be read with its timing and audience in mind. Magill wrote the paragraph in January, 1920, when the successor Canadian wheat board's operations were just at their height, a board whose creation Magill had assiduously opposed in his crusade to restore private trading as quickly as possible after the war. In submitting his report to the minister as a departmental reference on wartime procedures, he was writing primarily for the benefit of the minister who had frustrated his cause when he established the wheat board, and admonishing him concerning the dire consequences which would ensue if that board were to remain in existence. As for the substance of Magill's contention, there is ample evidence of the disadvantage Canada, the "weaker power", had suffered from its ebbing colonial status in relation to the two "stronger and wealthier powers". As for the ultimate consequences of "national selling" or government-to-government trading, the permanent result of this wartime procedure was by no means a surrender of Canada's commercial independence. Despite the fact that both government sellers and buyers on occasion made errors of market judgment before fixed prices were set, and had provoked the other side, Canadian and British interests alike had been remarkably well served by the board of grain supervisors.

In the wake of the appointment of the new board, the board of grain supervisors terminated its price jurisdiction on August 15 over deliveries from the 1918 crop. It continued to pay carrying charges up to August 31 of that year, after which it confined its activity to the winding up of operations. In its two years of jurisdiction over the marketing of the 1917 and 1918 crops, the board had priced and directed the distribution of 350 million bushels of wheat. The board was formally dissolved on January 31, 1920.

More than two years later Magill volunteered his own summary of the reasons for the creation of the board of grain supervisors and of its

[53] *Ibid.*

operations. In his evidence before the select standing committee on agriculture and colonization on April 15, 1922, he offered a fairly glib account. Speaking as secretary of the grain exchange, he said:

> We closed the market ourselves. The Government did not know anything about it; they were too busy with other matters. The Allied Governments then agreed to take our "no-grade" grain, our tough grain, on the contracts, at proper prices, and a settlement was made on that basis.
>
> But that was enough for the Grain Exchange. Between the German submarine on the one side and the one buyer on the other, we had enough of an open market under such world war conditions; and we came down to Ottawa and said "Our machinery is a peace-developed machinery, it is not a war machinery. We have closed the Exchange, and we want the Government to take control." That is what literally happened. The Balfour Mission was in this country at that time; the Vice-Chairman of the British Commission on the Purchase of Royal Grain Supplies, Sir Alan Anderson, was here when our delegation came down. He supported us in asking for a regulation, with the result that the Government took control and created the first war wheat board, the Supervisors' Board, which remained in existence until the war was over, and which marketed, as the cant phrase goes, 350 million bushels of wheat, in round figures, in that time. That is the story of that situation.[54]

More prosaically, the board had been improvised to replace the price committee of the Winnipeg grain exchange which itself had been improvised when futures trading had broken down under abnormal conditions. At British instigation, the government created a board with powers limited to price-fixing and distribution which were adequate as long as the British government guaranteed to purchase the exportable surplus. But when it withdrew its purchase guarantee, the Canadian government was compelled to enlarge the board's powers to create, in effect, a marketing board to implement the government's price guarantee. To fix a price for a crop year ahead, either one government or the other had to guarantee a market and to assume the accompanying financial risk. To reconcile the conflicting interests of producers, domestic consumers, importers and competitors in one fixed price was in itself a remarkable feat; the chances of success would have been infinitesimal except in the exceptional circumstances of the wartime period in which it was done. In the two years of the board's operation it was evident that the United States authorities displayed more concern than the British or Canadians over the precise levels at which Canadian prices were fixed. This was because the Americans were operating a grain corporation whose capitalization and financial risk in guaranteeing a fixed price was substantially greater than Canada's. The grain corporation and the board had been differently devised to meet the same emergency situation. While both were adequate to cope with that situation, they were equally inadequate as permanent marketing systems.

---

[54]*Minutes of Proceedings and Evidence of the Select Standing Committee on Agriculture and Colonization,* Tuesday, April 25, 1922, pp. 192-193.

6

ATTEMPT TO DECONTROL

Following the armistice of November 11, 1918, the concern of the trade, of governments and their control agencies alike on both sides of the Atlantic, was directed toward the restoration of wheat marketing to the private trade. A first small step in that direction was taken in December, 1918, when the board of grain supervisors persuaded the royal commission on wheat supplies to permit the Wheat Export Company to accept delivery of Canadian wheat at the seaboard instead of at the lakehead. Until then the Wheat Export Company, by taking delivery of wheat at the lakehead, had displaced Canadian shippers and exporters in the forwarding of grain to the seaboard and to eastern mills. In Britain, the royal commission also gave prompt consideration to decontrol measures designed on the one hand to restore to the private trade the responsibility for grain purchases and, on the other, to give back to the countries for which the royal commission had been buying, the responsibility for their own procurement arrangements. By agreement, the wheat executive discontinued purchasing on behalf of the French, Italian and other governments, but this attempt to decontrol intergovernmental purchasing arrangements proved premature. By early summer in 1919, when Canadian decontrol policy had to be decided in respect to the marketing of the 1919 crop, the wheat executive reverted to centralized purchasing on behalf of the allied and neutral governments.

INTERGOVERNMENTAL ARRANGEMENTS ON PURCHASING

A more detailed account of the intergovernmental arrangements of the time can be found in the report of the royal commission on wheat supplies.[1] At meetings of the allied food controllers in London, held during July-August, 1918, an agreement was concluded among the British, French, Italian and United States governments on an interallied food council whose responsibility was to coordinate food policy and procurement. The wheat executive, in turn, served the food council as its procurement agency. As the armistice approached, the wheat needs of the recovered territories and of southern, central and eastern Europe had to be taken into account. A supreme council of supply and relief was soon merged into the supreme economic council, which worked as an adjunct to the peace conference in Paris. As these

[1] *First Report of the Royal Commission in Wheat Supplies*, London, 1921, Appendix 39.

organizations took shape, the wheat executive became a committee of the food section of the supreme economic council. By August, 1919, a consultative food committee was established in London by the supreme economic council which had no direct purchasing authority but whose function was to eliminate unnecessary competition among buyers. While these represented the formal arrangements, the experience was that shortly after the armistice there was an understandable tendency to relax the coordinated procurement arrangements and, for a period, the French and Italian governments resumed their own independent purchasing.

CANADIAN TRADE MISSION

Canadian concern over markets in Britain and Europe in the wake of the armistice permeated the minds of industrial and government leaders and the public. For this reason, Foster organized a trade delegation to London to establish new working relations with the British government respecting trade between the two countries in the areas of food, clothing, and raw material supplies. The trade delegation included Mr. Lloyd Harris, a Massey-Harris executive, Dr. Robert Magill, who represented the grain industry, Mr. W. A. Dryden, the livestock industry, and Messrs. James Fisher and Norman P. Lambert, the Canadian council of agriculture. Mr. Henry Wise Wood was invited to join the delegation as a representative of grain producers, but he declined. As a result of the delegation's consultations with British officials, the Canadian government appointed a trade mission resident in London under the chairmanship of Mr. Harris. At the same time, when the inter-allied food council was established, Dr. J. W. Robertson was appointed to represent Canada on that body.

BRITISH WHEAT PURCHASING POLICY

With Foster already in London in connection with arrangements for the trade mission, the prime minister, Sir Robert Borden, also embarked overseas, while Sir Thomas White, minister of finance, presided in an acting capacity over wheat policy matters at home. White received a memorandum from the Winnipeg grain exchange which stressed the importance of obtaining clarification in regard to British purchasing intentions from the 1919 crop, and advocated the return of grain marketing to the private trade as quickly as possible. In response, White cabled to Borden on November 29, 1918, as follows:

> Have received important memorandum from Winnipeg Grain Exchange urging that question of guaranteed price of wheat for nineteen nineteen be at once taken up with Imperial Government and finally dealt with so that farmers may determine their policy respecting next year's production and purchase their seed grain accordingly. It is pointed out that uncertainty is creating a critical situation in middle West which may have a most injurious effect upon immigration. The grain dealers also strongly urge that operations of Wheat Export Company be now terminated and that handling of grain should be brought back to pre-war basis as quickly as possible so that Canada's grain may be marketed through usual channels. It is also strongly urged that two representative men of West should be added to your Advisory Committee in London in order that they with full knowledge of all the conditions may place facts of situation before you for presentation to Imperial

Government and Allies. I am strongly of view that it would be advisable to meet suggestion that two western men should be sent overseas as part of your Advisory Committee. This will meet situation for some time and divide responsibility for whatever policy may be finally determined. Please cable reply as soon as possible.[2]

In response to White's cable, Borden elicited the information through Robertson that the British had formulated no plans to ensure their supply from the 1919 crop, and that purchasing would probably revert to the private trade, as indicated in his cabled reply of December 3:

Robertson has ascertained from Allied Food Council that no arrangement has been formulated or proposed for purchase next year's wheat crop. It is uncertain whether any such arrangement will be made or carried out. It seems probable that purchase of wheat for European countries in nineteen nineteen will be on commercial basis as between different sources of supply. Therefore, no European buyers would pay more for wheat from United States than price at which similar supplies could be obtained in Canada. On the other hand United States being in position to advance money and give credits, loans etc., might stipulate as condition that all exportable United States' wheat should be purchased at price fixed by United States Government. We see no objection to bringing operations of Wheat Export Company to conclusion and we are willing that two representative men from West should be added to advisory committee in London, although at the moment we do not know of any useful service that they could perform as Robertson is doing everything that is necessary. If any such representatives are sent please select strong, capable men such as Doctor Rutherford and Wood.[3]

Meanwhile, Robertson and Harris negotiated with governments on the sale of wheat as opportunities arose, and Sir George Foster's diary reveals his own direct involvement therein with representatives of the French, Belgian, Romanian and Greek governments:

London, November 25, 1918: Doherty and Harris landed in yesterday and now we are trying to get on a working basis with the B.G. in respect of imports and exports — food and clothing supply, raw materials and reconstruction. I am conducting the preliminaries and though it goes slowly, the feeling is thoroughly sympathetic and we shall get a working plan in time.

London, January 8, 1919: The morning passed in conferences with Prime Minister and Wheat Delegation from Canada re marketing and prices.

London, January 10: Had the usual business of the morning and a consultation with Magill, Fisher and Robertson in which we thrashed over the wheat situation. Little can be done until we know the result of the deliberations of the Inter-Allied Food Commission.

Paris, January 30: The usual routine. At 12 noon I had a conference with Bratiano, Prime Minister of Roumania, the Roumanian Ministers at London and Washington, who are now both here. They were most grateful for the credit we gave them — they manufacture nothing and need all kinds of manufactured articles from food to clothing, implements, Railway Equipment, etc. Their climate and seasons are very like ours. They raise chiefly winter wheat. Now oil is their only exportable article. It will take time to build up their agriculture — need seed for this season's sowing. Are most anxious to make permanent connections with Canada. I have wired Harris to come at once and take their orders. We could do big business with them if they had the finances.

[2]*Sir Thomas White Papers*, Public Archives of Canada.
[3]*Ibid.*

Paris, February 6: A long conference with Mr. Clementel and other Ministers. Harris, Roy and myself went over the contract and purchase conditions. Changes are necessary and I have undertaken to have them made.

Paris, February 7: We are conferring with the French government as to contract and methods of carrying out purchases. Also with Roumanians to whom a credit of $25 million has been granted. We can do a large business with the latter permanently, not so with the former. The food supply and release of restrictions are still in course of decision and undecided. Ultimately restrictions will be largely taken off to neutrals and re-established anti-German nationalities and before long I think. The delay in information from Ottawa is terrific.

Paris, February 11: I have sent in the final agreement of contract with France and a draft to Roumania. Hope to get both through by end of week. Pourparlers with Greeks proceeding well.

Paris, February 14: In the morning I revised draft contracts with Roumanian ministers.

Paris, March 4: Busy on Belgian and Roumanian credit contracts. ... A Roumanian arrangement sent me by Harris which may result in increased trade with Canada.

Paris, March 11: A busy day with Belgian contract terms and French objections to credit conditions.

Paris, March 18: The Greek negotiations came to a head today and I am arranging a contract for signature. We have to make provisions for Roumanian Credit temporarily, for expenses of freight until peace signature gives government certainty of territory and enables loans to be made. The Belgian contract is nearing completion. The French wish to purchase little or no manufactured goods.

Paris, March 20: I hope the finishing touches have been given to the Greek and Belgian credit contracts. The French remains, and until Robertson comes to talk over the cattle situation not much more can be done.

Paris, March 26: I have finished the Belgian contract and now only the French one is left.[4]

As Foster pressed his sales efforts abroad and encountered massive requests for credit to enable the wheat sales, he received support at home from his colleague, Sir Thomas White, minister of finance, who declared that the government would continue to extend credit to finance exports as a means of warding off unemployment in Canada. Credits were negotiated with the British, French, Belgian, Romanian and Greek governments to a total of $250,000,000 in 1919.[5]

In response to questions put to him in the house, White made another effort to ascertain British purchasing policy for the 1919 crop. On April 1, 1919, he sent the following cable to Sir George Perley, the Canadian high commissioner:

B179. From White. Make inquiry and cable whether any likelihood British Government making offer of fixed price for exported surplus of this years Canadian wheat crop. ... If no offer likely will there be free market for wheat and flour or will Canadian credits be necessary for their purchase. Important to have information soon as possible so as to arrange finances and answer questions in House.[6]

[4] *Foster Diaries.*
[5] *House of Commons Debates,* April 10, 1919, pp. 1353-1358.
[6] *White Papers.*

Perley elicited a formal reply from Lord Crawford, chairman of the royal commission on wheat supplies, which he reported in his cable of April 12, 1917, to White:

> P289. For White. Your B179. Put forward to Wheat Commission. Following is Lord Crawford's answer verbatim Begins. I am desired by my colleagues on Royal Commission on Wheat supplies to state that it is not proposed to offer a fixed price for the surplus of the 1919 wheat crop of the Dominion. The Royal Commission on Wheat supplies will probably buy Canadian grain during the early part of the next cereal year but it is contemplated or at least it is hoped that before the conclusion of the cereal year conditions will permit a free market and the revival of private enterprise together with the demobilization of the Wheat Export Company of Canada when it would no longer be necessary for the British Government to undertake grain purchases as proved imperative during the war. As to whether Canadian credits will be necessary to finance the Canadian crop it is difficult for the Royal Commission to offer any prediction but it is generally to be presumed that by the coming winter financial stability may be so far re-established as to effect the movement of the crop without the intervention of the Dominion or Imperial Government. On this point, however, it would be imprudent to offer any final opinion while the general outlook remains so obscure. The Royal Commission, however, hopes that circumstances may justify the re-establishment of a free market which it is understood will be generally welcomed in the Dominion. Ends.[7]

Thus, even at that date, the British were still anticipating the return of wheat purchasing to the private trade. The royal commission had recently given an undertaking to purchase 30 million bushels from the 1918 crop, which was believed to be the remaining exportable surplus from the old crop, but it was not in a position to make any commitment respecting purchases from the 1919 crop.

In its concern to restore wheat marketing to the trade in Canada, the Winnipeg grain exchange sent a mission to London in May, 1919. The mission consisted of Mr. F. J. Anderson, president of the exchange, Dr. Robert Magill, secretary and Mr. A. P. Stuart. It made representations to Mr. Lloyd Harris and Dr. J. W. Robertson, and it also interviewed Sir Robert Borden as he returned from Paris through London for Ottawa and Sir George Foster who visited London briefly from Paris. The tenor of the exchange mission's representations was set out in the following letter it addressed to Harris on May 15, 1919:

> On behalf of the organised grain trade of the Dominion of Canada we desire to inform you that up to the present moment no policy has been formulated regarding the marketing of grain crops of Canada during the coming twelve months. In contrast with this is the position in the United States. There legislation has already been enacted, an organisation has already been created, requisite appropriations have been made and an accredited agent despatched to Europe, all with a view to successful marketing of wheat or grain of the United States during the coming twelve months.
>
> On behalf of the grain trade of Canada we desire to submit to you these proposals:
>
> 1. That if there is no price fixed or guaranteed by the Government of Canada there should be as near an approach to free and open competitive markets as is possible.

[7] *Ibid.*

2. That Canada has the right and should be permitted to market her grain in European markets directly without the intervention of agents created by the Imperial Government.

3. That with regard to the United Kingdom the British Government should not make commercial agreements with France and Italy, or any other European Power, affecting Canadian commerce, without a full consideration of the consequences of such agreements by Canadian authorities; and more particularly that the British Government should not undertake to buy Canadian wheat or grain through a Government agency, for France and Italy with the object of buying such wheat as cheaply as possible.

4. That if the British Government maintains an agency for the purpose of purchasing Canadian grain for the United Kingdom, as it has the right to do, such agency should not be located within the Dominion of Canada, but that Canadian grain trade should be permitted to sell and deliver the grain to the British agency, either Liverpool or London, or in the event of shipping being still under control, at Canadian Atlantic Ports.

The Canadian grain trade has been out of business now for between two and three years, not because there was no business to be done, but because the British authorities were permitted to create their own agency for the purchase of Canadian grain, and to place such agency in Canada, while by this step the Canadian grain trade was put and kept out of business. The British Government subsidised the grain trade of the United Kingdom, making a generous contribution to the grain trade in the United Kingdom in order to preserve the trade till the end of the war, the contribution amounting to 3d. per quarter to importers and an additional 3d a quarter to brokers. This payment is still being continued.

The Canadian grain trade desire no subsidy but they do desire, and feel that they are entitled to, an opportunity of marketing Canadian produce in the markets of the world without being subject to such drastic pecuniary losses as have been imposed upon them by the Imperial authorities during the last three years. The Canadian grain trade also maintains that they are quite able to market Canadian produce and that neither as regards experience, ability, nor any other qualifications are they inferior to the Wheat Export Company, a company British alike in its personnel, appointment, and its whole financial structure.[8]

Further reference to the exchange mission's activities in London is made in Magill's report, quoted below, to the exchange after he returned to Winnipeg.

Another visitor to London that spring was Mr. J. A. Maharg, M.P., who was seeking information on British marketing intentions on behalf of the farm organizations with which he was associated. He returned to Canada with a much less sanguine assessment of the immediate prospects for the overseas decontrol of wheat purchases than did the mission from the grain exchange.

Foster returned from London to Ottawa only briefly that spring before he accompanied the prime minister to the Paris peace negotiations. In April, Foster presided at the meetings of the supreme economic council. When Sir Robert found it necessary to return to Canada in late May, Foster remained to head the Canadian delegation and he looked forward to signing the peace treaty on behalf of Canada on June 28, but he was prevented from doing so when he too was called home, urgently, because of the illness of his wife. He

[8]*Ibid.*

returned from Paris, arrived back in Ottawa on June 21, and spent only a few hours daily in his office or in cabinet for almost a month.

CANADIAN MARKETING POLICY

With Borden and Foster both overseas, the brunt of the policy decisions in Canada respecting wheat was borne by the minister of finance, Sir Thomas White, who was directly concerned over the financial implications therein. To a less extent, the Honourable A. K. Maclean, acting minister of trade and commerce, was also involved. Reference has already been made to Sir Thomas's efforts to elicit British purchasing intentions, during which time he was being pressed by the grain exchange, the mills, the banks, the railways and the Canadian council of agriculture to come to some decision on the assurance of satisfactory marketing arrangements for the 1919 crop.

The particular interests of these various organizations were at variance with one another as the grain exchange sought the earliest practicable return to prewar marketing methods, while the Canadian council of agriculture as vigorously recommended the retention of controls with a guaranteed price to producers, and assurance of financing for the movement of the crop. The banks, in turn, were concerned about the vulnerability of prices in an open market without adequate price support from the government; in such circumstances they were reluctant to finance the hedging transactions essential to the movement of the crop. If the movement was disrupted, the railways would be affected. The mills were in a special predicament because decontrol of wheat purchasing (under which governments had bargained on the quantities of flour to be included in the wheat transactions) would leave the mills on their own to negotiate flour sales directly. When buying was partially and prematurely restored to the private trade, the mills immediately experienced difficulty in getting flour orders. From January to April, 1919, the royal commission had placed almost no flour orders through the Wheat Export Company with the Canadian mills which had been forced to reduce operations to only one-third of their capacity. The curtailed mill run had also reduced the supply of millfeeds to the domestic market.

Representatives of millers complained to Sir Thomas White that American mills were, nevertheless, heavily booked, because American officials in Europe had been successful in obtaining orders on the continent. White reacted by eliciting, through Stewart, advice that all trade in cereals and cereal products was now free to Holland, Denmark, Finland, Portugal, Switzerland and Spain. Although the Canadian milling companies attempted to sell directly by renewing contacts with their agents in those countries, the situation remained confused and the results were desultory. Thereupon, the millers asked White to receive a deputation from them.

There were, in fact, several millers' associations in existence including the Canadian millers' committee chaired by Mr. D. A. Campbell with Mr. W. Sanford Evans serving in Ottawa as secretary, the Dominion millers' association, of which Mr. C. B. Watts was secretary in Toronto, and the western millers' association of Canada of which Mr. James A. Robb was secretary-treasurer in Winnipeg. The millers' associations arranged a meeting with White on April 9, 1919, at which they presented a memorandum setting forth the problems their members had encountered, and they asked that the Wheat Export Company under Stewart be retained as exclusive export sales agent for the mills, so that the facilities of the royal commission abroad could continue to be used to obtain flour orders for them. Pursuant to these representations, Mr. C. B. Watts wrote to Sir Thomas White on several occasions, and circulated throughout the milling industry a scheme by which the federal government would guarantee an initial payment for deliveries from the 1919 crop and establish an agency by which the wheat would be sold to best advantage with any surplus from sales prorated to producers on the basis of their wheat deliveries. The agency Watts recommended was the Wheat Export Company, whose experience might now effectively be used to sell on behalf of Canada. Watts's proposals are presented in greater detail below in connection with the establishment of the first Canadian wheat board. As a result of the millers' representations, White asked Stewart to act on behalf of the mills, which he did with such success that within a month the mills were running at full capacity again.

Wheat sales policy for the 1919 crop still remained to be determined by early June, and White requested through the Canadian high commissioner, for a third time, information from the British regarding their buying intentions. In reply to White's cable of June 5, 1919, Perley sent the following message on June 18:

> Yours 5th. Had conference with Wheat Commission at which it was evident they had not contemplated necessity any change in their policy of inaction. Placed Canadian position strongly before them, pressed for decision. Pointed out to Commission serious political situation likely arise unless Canadian farmer is placed in position to satisfactorily market his grain. Have now received reply regretting impossible at present outline any specific buying policy partly owing crop situation both of consuming and producing countries still subject large variations partly because not yet known how far responsibility Royal Commission may extend in making purchases on behalf of allies. Therefore unable state what proportion new Dominion crop they will desire to buy. They desire however revive activity of commercial enterprise and to remove one obstacle they propose liquidate Wheat Export Company Winnipeg as trading concern so that complete (freedom) may be restored to Dominion grain trade sell its produce in simplest manner without restriction destination during ensuing year. Royal Commission as at present advised will probably make its purchases on f.o.b. basis as and when stocks are wanted and expect find advisable establish office Canadian seaboard ensure promptness in correspondence. They add that although for reasons indicated impracticable say how much Canadian grain will be bought by Great Britain between September 1919 and September 1920, early announcement that Wheat Export Company Winnipeg will cease operate and that trade able to resume more normal courses will remove an element of uncertainty which we (deprecate) and give adequate time for dominion interests concerned make fresh arrangements for next harvest. Seems to me considerable advantage lies in procuring the decision. Believe it will give great satisfaction to wheat trade allowing Canadian interests take steps deal with situation for which little enough time left.[9]

[9]*Ibid.*

Unlike the milling associations which had asked for retention of the Wheat Export Company, the grain exchange mission to London had worked assiduously for the termination of the company. Perley's telegram confirmed how well the mission had succeeded in that regard, and the news was by no means unwelcome to White and Maclean.

On the same day that Perley's cable was received, Mr. A. K. Maclean held a meeting to which he had invited representatives of the Winnipeg and the Fort William and Port Arthur grain exchanges, of the lake carriers' association, of the railways, of the Canadian millers' committee, and Sir Thomas White. After presenting the government's problem to the meeting and hearing the views of the invited representatives, Maclean appointed a committee of the delegates to prepare a formal report on their recommendations. The committee divided on the issue, however, and the grain exchange and mill representatives submitted separate reports. In their letter of June 19, 1919, to Maclean the grain exchange representatives wrote as follows:

> The undersigned, summoned by you for the purpose of discussion of the methods under which the 1919 crop of wheat might best be handled, beg to report as follows: —
>
> 1. The facilities of the various sections of the organized grain trade of Canada have been utilized and have proved themselves of material assistance even under Government control, and these organizations are ready to perform their legitimate functions in the same manner as in pre-war days.
>
> 2. Our representatives recently returned from Overseas, and the Dominion Government's Representatives, namely Dr. Robertson and Mr. Lloyd Harris, have confirmed our belief that Great Britain and Our Allies are anxious for all markets, dealing in food stuffs, to be free and open.
>
> Notwithstanding that the British Government are temporarily committed to bread subsidy by guaranteeing the nine penny loaf, there is no assurance that this will be continued much longer. Indeed, we would not be surprised to learn that this subsidy will be discontinued at an early date in which case, undoubtedly, the British Importers will be free to deal in every market of the world, and it may be a serious handicap to the Canadian Grain Trade, if it is not able to do business direct with its British correspondents.
>
> 3. Immediately the Peace Treaty is signed, it is our opinion that the law of supply and demand should be permitted to come into effect, as fixed prices are regarded by large classes of society, as contributing largely to the present unfortunate unrest.
>
> 4. At the present time we admit that there may not be any prospective purchasers in sight, but we believe that this is caused by the fact that the wheat prices are fixed, but if the importing countries of the world are informed that wheat is now de-controlled, that sufficient demand would develop to absorb our surplus. We would point out that only a month or two ago, when barley and oats were de-controlled in importing countries, that a good demand was created for these grains. Further, it developed during the discussion yesterday, at the conference held by you, that even if Canada fixed the price of the 1919 wheat crop, the Government were doubtful whether under controlled conditions, they could dispose of it, even at a loss.
>
> 5. As Great Britain controls the bulk of ocean tonnage, and is desirous of giving Canadian products a full preference, there is no doubt she would place facilities at the disposal of her grain merchants, whereby such preference became an accomplished fact.

In conclusion, in view of the foregoing, we respectfully submit that in our opinion an open market is desirable and necessary and in the best interests of Canada.[10]

The letter was signed by F. J. Anderson and N. W. E. Botterell, president and vice-president respectively of the Winnipeg grain exchange, N. M. Paterson and C. Birkett, vice-president and secretary respectively of the Fort William and Port Arthur grain exchange, and by A. O. Hogg on behalf of the grain section of the Toronto board of trade.

Another letter was written on the same date by W. A. Black, Ogilvie Flour Mills Company, Limited, D. A. Campbell, The Campbell Flour Mills Company, and A. George Burton, Canadian American Grain Limited, which presented an alternative view as follows:

The committee appointed by you for the purpose of discussing methods under which the 1919 crop of wheat might best be handled, have been unable, we regret to say, to agree upon a unanimous report.

Delegates from the Winnipeg and Fort William Grain Exchange, have come down with resolutions favouring return to open market conditions, and are therefore unable to subscribe to any other plan until the Government have given a decision on the open market proposal, as embodied in the respective resolutions of their exchanges.

The balance of the representatives, while desirous that de-controlled conditions should be re-installed at the earliest possible moment are unable to see how under present international conditions control could possibly be removed and submit the following reasons for this belief:

1. With high prices still prevailing as a relic of the war period financing purchases of wheat would be hazardous and large margins necessary to protect hedges.

2. Canadian Bankers have expressed the opinion that they could scarcely be expected to risk large credits when violent unprecedented declines in the value of wheat might at any time take place and at this time of prospective record production throughout the whole North American Continent. Liberal individual credits are essential.

3. With a probable congestion of wheat supplies in Canada later in the season when the crop movement reached its height it may become impossible to dispose of stocks of wheat at any price that happen to be located in such a position as to make early movement to the seaboard impossible. This enforced depression would react on the producer who by reasons of remoteness from an elevator was unable to deliver his wheat as early as others.

4. The price of wheat in the United States is guaranteed, and it is quite conceivable that under the congestion of stocks as above referred to, the Canadian producer would be forced to accept as much as from 50 cents to $1.00 per bushel less than the American farmer.

For these reasons we are opposed to a return to open market conditions at the present time, and respectfully suggest the following plans under which with only a reasonable risk, the Government, in our opinion, might control the marketing of the crop.

1. *A Guaranteed and Fixed Price Basis.*

This method would in our opinion involve the formation of a controlling organization, an outline of the scope of which is attached herewith.

[10]*Ibid.*

2. *A Pooling or Minimum Price Basis.*

Under this plan the controlling corporation would also be necessary, but while the plan suggested as No. 1 offers a first and final cash price basis to be paid the producer, this plan would permit the fixing of a minimum price only, and would permit participation by the farmer in the surplus (if any) that might be earned by the controlling corporation. This plan we may say, is the one adopted in 1915 by the Australian Government and subsequently enlarged and continued into the 1916-17-18 crops. Quantity receipts are given the producer as he delivers his grain, and at the end of the season he would participate on a pro rata basis upon the surrender of his vouchers.

We are prepared to assist the Government in any manner they may desire in determining the details of these plans once they have made a decision in regard to the matter.

In closing we beg to urge the Government to immediate action. At the present time there is no basis of working, and action on the part of the Government is necessary as we are now on the eve of the harvest.[11]

The letter just quoted anticipated the wheat board principle, and its writers were indebted to Mr. C. B. Watts who had been actively promoting the scheme, but it did not appeal to Sir Thomas White who in his letter of June 24, 1919, to the prime minister expressed the opinion that the reopening of the futures market was the best alternative, and he asked that the matter be raised in cabinet:

I have given much thought to the question of the handling of our western wheat crop. Three proposals have been put forward, as follows:

1. That the Dominion Government should fix a price and purchase the wheat at such price, trusting to sell it without loss. I am opposed to this plan for many reasons.

2. That the wheat should be pooled and the Dominion Government through a commission sell it for the benefit of the producers. In connection with this proposal it is suggested that we might make an advance of $1.50 a bushel to the farmers, giving them in addition a certificate of participation in any net profits which might result from the whole transaction. I am opposed to this because I do not believe we could create the necessary machinery to handle it successfully. Any such plan would meet with considerable opposition, both domestic and foreign, and we should find ourselves in early difficulties. From the financial standpoint it is also objectionable, as we should have to bargain for the sale of our wheat with European countries who would demand large credits which we are not in a position to afford. Our wheat this year should bring cash outside of Canada.

3. Open market, with exchanges at work as before the war. Personally I favour this plan. It will relieve the Government of the handling of the crop and will ensure its sale for cash. The objection which has been put forward is that there will be violent fluctuations in wheat. This is probably so but is not a sound ground of objection. It may be desirable to avoid fluctuations by fixing a minimum price which would ensure that the wheat, while it might sell considerably above, would not sell below the figure so fixed. I am informed that there is no danger of wheat falling below $1.75. We might therefore be justified in establishing an open market and announcing that the Government would take all wheat offered at $1.75. The objection to this is that we might be criticized for depressing the price through fixing a low figure as wheat will probably open in the trading around $2.00. Before determining upon this course it would be well to consult with the parties interested. If a minimum

[11]*Ibid.*

price is not fixed then I am strongly in favour of open trading; in fact I do not believe any other plan will be at all satisfactory or indeed possible of financing.

P.S. No doubt you will bring this matter to Council for consideration.[12]

DECISION TO OPEN THE MARKET

As a result of White's recommendation and Maclean's support, cabinet decided to let the market reopen, and Maclean issued a guarded press statement to that effect on July 6 in which he was reported as saying:

At the present time it is not the intention of the government to prohibit or control trading in wheat in the cereal year 1919/20 on the grain exchanges in Canada. If the grain exchanges deal in wheat it is to be expected, owing to the fact that grain is not traded in upon the leading grain exchanges of the world, that regulations will be made operative so as to restrict purely speculative transactions.

The press report continued:

Mr. Maclean being further asked as to the probable disposition of this year's wheat crop, stated that the question was much complicated by the delay in the United Kingdom and allied European countries, in determining whether they are to permit open markets for the future, or whether control would be further continued. The exchange conditions, the American fixed price for wheat, shipping, the problem of exportable surplus of wheat-producing countries, and the general and world-wide financial and economic conditions, are all very important and uncertain factors complicating the situation. "Conceivably", he said, "the future might develop conditions in Canada, necessitating direct and positive action, but in the meanwhile it is the view of the government that the open market should prevail".[13]

As the *Free Press* reported from the floor of the exchange next day, members of the exchange were elated by the announcement, but it later reported an opposite reaction from the Canadian council of agriculture which, in session on July 11 under the chairmanship of Henry Wise Wood, adopted the following resolution in respect of the marketing of the 1919 wheat crop:

Understanding that the Government of Canada has taken no action to control the marketing of the Canadian wheat crop of 1919, and in view of the following facts:

1. That, the entire importation of wheat into European countries is under Governmental control,

2. That the United States, Canada's principal competitor in the sale of wheat, has created a highly organised and well financed Corporation under Government direction, to dispose of its exportable surplus of wheat,

3. That it is imperative in the national interest that Canada should secure the maximum return for its wheat crop,

And further —

1. That the opening of the markets for unrestricted trading in wheat on the Canadian grain exchanges, as (is) in immediate prospect, would promote speculative rather than legitimate trading,

2. That because the true function of grain exchanges can be performed only when international operations are completely possible in an unrestricted

[12] *Ibid.*
[13] *Manitoba Free Press,* July 8, 1919.

way, they would entirely fail to provide means for disposing successfully of the wheat crop,

3. That trading under such conditions with their attendant risks would provide a market at country points for the farmers wheat only at prices much below its real value, and at times would be bound to result in (there) being no country market at all,

Therefore, the Canadian Council of Agriculture is strongly opposed to the opening of the Canadian markets for unrestricted trading in wheat and would reiterate its recommendation of August 1918, that the Government of Canada create, without delay, a body similar to the United States Grain Corporation, with like powers and functions and with the financial accommodation adequate to its operations.[14]

In support of its resolution, the council added six pages of recommendations which noted the decision of the council of the Winnipeg grain exchange to reopen futures trading, and the admonition Maclean had made about the need for restricting speculative transactions. The council painted a gloomy picture of the chaos that would prevail in the handling of the 1919 crop because of the prospective inability of Canadian exporters to find ready cash markets abroad or sufficient ocean shipping, either of which would create elevator congestion and prompt the railways to embargo grain shipments from the west, and the banks to withhold credit to the elevator companies under such conditions. As an alternative, the report recommended that;

> Undoubtedly the best solution to these problems that beset the marketing of the 1919 wheat crop is the creation of a centralized Government agency endowed with such credit and powers as to overcome financial difficulties, control transportation and ensure a continuous export outlet for the Canadian wheat surplus, also such an agency would, by permitting greater business freedom, preserve and offer fair remuneration to the existing organisations and machinery of the grain trade and at the same time safeguard the Dominion's economic welfare.[15]

The council's recommendation of August, 1918, referred to at the end of its formal resolution had been embodied in a document entitled "General Details Covering Operations of the Canadian Grain Corporation as recommended by the Grain Committee of the Canadian Council of Agriculture".[16] The scheme proposed therein was modeled upon the United States grain corporation but, in its adaptation, it bore some resemblance to the Canadian wheat board which was eventually created, and it is referred to in more detail in the following chapter.

Neither the Canadian council of agriculture nor the banks had been invited to attend the meeting which Maclean had convened on June 18. Meanwhile, the banks remained apprehensive about the reopening of the market without a floor price guarantee by the government, and they made their representations to Sir Thomas White individually, and through the secretary of the Canadian bankers' association, Mr. H. T. Ross. Since the successful operation of the futures market involving bank credit appeared to turn on the bankers' demand for a government guarantee, White proceeded

[14]*Ibid.*

[15]*Recommendation by the Grain Committee of the Canadian Council of Agriculture as to the marketing of the wheat crop of 1919*, Manitoba Free Press, July 8, 1919.

[16]*Trade and Commerce File T-14-144.*

to draft a submission to council for its authority. In his letter of June 24 to Borden, he had already requested authority to do so. On July 14, White wired to Mr. H. Tooley, secretary of the board of grain supervisors: "Please have Board of Grain Supervisors consider and wire me immediately what spreads should be for several grades of western wheat assuming we fix minimum price of say one seventy-five, one sixty or one fifty."[17]

Meanwhile the bankers consulted among themselves, following which Mr. H. T. Ross telephoned to White's private secretary, Mr. B. J. Roberts the following message:

> Bankers here in Montreal and the bankers in Toronto independently fixed upon $1.75 as minimum price. They suggest that instead of 1st day of June, 1920, the date in the Order in Council should be February 1st, 1920, as that is the date of which the Government might be called upon to take over the wheat. They think the other date is too remote and that the trend of the market would be ascertained long before that. . . .

In his memo to White, Roberts added: "Mr. Ross stated that the bankers found that both Stewart and Carruthers, expert grain men, were absent and could not be consulted."[18]

Although Tooley had replied to White's wire of July 14, White sent another telegram to Tooley on July 15:

> Not all info given. Assuming minimum price for number one hard wheat to be fixed at one dollar seventy-five please wire prices relative grades. When I receive this info shall be in position to complete Order in Council which has to be passed and must be specific as to prices.[19]

At the same time a speculative news report appeared in the *Manitoba Free Press:*

> Ottawa, July 15. — In order to give stability to the financing of the Canadian wheat crop of the present year, and safeguard prices from too violent speculation, due to the opening of the grain exchanges in the present uncertain and unsettled conditions, it is probable that the Dominion Government will fix a minimum price which it will guarantee to dealers, bankers and others interested in the crop movement. It is not the intention that this minimum price shall be the price at which wheat must be sold in Canada. Trading may also take place freely on the exchanges at any higher price or prices which may be offered.
>
> The purpose will be to fix a minimum price at which the government will be prepared to take the wheat should the price fall to this minimum figure. The fixing of a minimum appears necessary to ensure stability and bring about the movement of the crop.[20]

In the depleted state of the cabinet, White still sought to consult Meighen, but on the morning of July 14, he held a long discussion with Mr. Sanford Evans who was evidently taken by surprise by the floor price proposal. That afternoon, Evans addressed a lengthy, but cogent, letter to White expressing his reservations over the proposal because of the following considerations (a) although the government could not set a higher minimum without great financial risk, there was no precedent for setting a minimum so far out of

---

[17]*White Papers.*
[18]*Ibid.* The reference to "Stewart" was undoubtedly to Mr. A. P. Stuart, Montreal, and not to James Stewart.
[19]*Ibid.*
[20]*Manitoba Free Press,* July 16, 1919.

line with the market, (b) the minimum would be regarded by the world as the actual value and would become the ruling price, (c) although the guarantee was required by the banks before they would assist in the movement of the crop, there were other ways of assuring that movement, but not under conditions of open trading, (d) instead of pursuing the bank policy which would force prices down to the minimum, the government should secure for Canadian wheat its full value under prevailing world conditions, (e) there was doubt about the effectiveness of open trading under existing conditions in which the wheat trade in practically all other countries remained under government control.[21]

Similar reservations were expressed by the Canadian council of agriculture in the wake of the press report, as it stated:

> The Canadian Council of Agriculture views with some degree of satisfaction the press announcements of July 15th and 16th 1919 that the Canadian Government will guarantee a minimum price for the 1919 wheat crop, but the Council is of the opinion that, while this is possibly a step in the right direction, it does not go far enough. Assuming that the minimum price is fair, the Canadian Government in announcing a guaranteed minimum price, has not as yet given assurance of arrangements for the purchase of wheat at such price whenever offered to it, or in other words guaranteed a continuous market. Further announcements are awaited with interest. In the absence of such information the Canadian Council of Agriculture is still of the firm opinion that its recommendation for the creation of a Canadian Grain Corporation to control the marketing, transportation and exporting of the 1919 Canadian wheat crop, with powers to grant credits to other countries for the purchase of Canadian wheat, and all other powers necessary for the successful disposal of the 1919 Canadian wheat crop, should be acted on immediately.[22]

In the end, White resigned without getting his submission to council approved on the floor price guarantee. Mr. B. J. Roberts noted that he had "told Mr. Ross by telephone 2:30 p.m. July 25 that action, favorable or unfavorable to fixing minimum price, would be taken, probably on Monday and that in meantime, there was no assurance as to what would be done."[23] Mr. Ross complained that the banks had been acting upon the assumption the order would pass and, if this were not so, the banks should be told. By that time Foster had taken matters in hand.

A different step which could readily have compromised the restoration of wheat marketing to the private trade was taken by Borden on July 14, 1919, when he cabled through the Canadian high commissioner to his minister of customs, the Honourable Arthur L. Sifton, who was then in London:

> For Sifton. Question of marketing wheat crop most urgent. Suggest that you and Robertson see British authorities immediately and impress upon them necessity in Imperial interest of making arrangement to purchase in Canada. We could furnish part credit but most desirable that as much outside money should be provided as possible as our Exchange with United States becoming serious. Unless action taken at once railway companies will be most seriously affected in their earnings as crop will not be moved to seaboard. Ascertain if

[21] *Recommendation by the Grain Committee of the Canadian Council of Agriculture as to the marketing of the wheat crop of 1919*, White Papers.
[22] *White Papers.*
[23] *Ibid.*

> British Government would make offer for, say, fifty or seventy-five million bushels at fixed price or at price to be fixed later on agreed basis such as price paid United States. Cable reply soon as possible.[24]

This was an attempt to conclude a bulk sale of more modest proportions than Foster had recommended in the winter of 1916-17 but, in the light of subsequent price developments, it would also have resulted in a bargain for the British, had they accepted the offer.

In the meantime, the Winnipeg grain exchange had been informed by telegram and by Maclean's public announcement that the resumption of futures trading could take place, and the exchange announced arrangements for the market to reopen on Monday, July 21, 1919. Trading commenced on that date and continued through Monday, July 28, when it was suspended at the request of Sir George Foster. In the first three days there had been only a thin volume of trading, but the pace accelerated as it became apparent that the wheat crops in both Canada and the United States would fall below expectations. An upward trend developed and by Monday, July 28, prices had risen by 25½ cents since trading had begun the previous Monday. Prices ranged as follows in the brief period during which trading was permitted:

OCTOBER WHEAT FUTURES, 1919

	MON. JULY 21	TUE. JULY 22	WED. JULY 23	THU. JULY 24
OPEN	2.20	2.24¾	2.25⅛	2.28
HIGH	2.25	2.25	2.26¾ b	2.30⅝
LOW	2.20	2.24¾	2.25⅛	2.28
CLOSE	2.24⅝ b	2.24¾ b	2.25½ b	2.30⅝ b

	FRI. JULY 25	SAT. JULY 26	MON. JULY 28	TUE. JULY 29
OPEN	2.34	2.40	2.40	Trading suspended
HIGH	2.39 b	2.41¼	2.45½ b	
LOW	2.33	2.40	2.40	
CLOSE	2.39 b	2.40	2.45½ b	

DECISION TO CLOSE THE MARKET

It will be recalled that Foster returned from the peace conference in June because of his wife's illness and that for nearly a month he was absent from his official duties. He returned to his office in July just as Sir Thomas White, who had carried the main responsibility for wheat policy in Foster's protracted absence overseas and at home, was relinquishing his cabinet post. At that particular moment, the cabinet was in some disarray as Maclean also resigned and Crerar had left the government a short time earlier. Borden devoted his time primarily to the selection of cabinet replacements.

Even after the decision had been made to reopen the market White's endeavor to establish a floor price, and Borden's attempt to make a bulk sale, indicated the government's continuing uneasiness over wheat policy.

[24]*Trade and Commerce File T-14-144.*

Matters were not helped by what appeared to be a speculative surge in the newly reopened futures market as Foster hastily convened a meeting of a selected list of advisers on July 28. In advance of the meeting, Foster invited Mr. James Stewart to confer with him on the structure of a new marketing plan. Foster's diary entries at the time are particularly revealing. Although they referred primarily to Lady Foster's illness, to changes in the cabinet and to the need for new ministers with administrative capacity to meet the impending challenge of the Liberal leadership convention, the following entries are relevant;

July 8, 1919: The N.W. crops will not be average and in places a failure. East the crops promise well.

July 10: Am going each day for two hours to the office. Have not yet been to Council.

July 12: Was an hour or so in office and at Council. Ministers have scattered and strikes are everywhere and troubles loom up on all sides.

July 18: A Council meeting at 4 discusses wheat price fixing but decides nothing. White being absent and some disagreeing with his recommendations.

July 21: The usual work in office and Council over the wheat question and the drought in west and the pig iron problem and other things. We have so small a Council to deal with them.

July 22: The usual routine morning in office and afternoon in Council.

July 23: Usual routine of work at office and in Council.

July 24: At office in morning. Most of the invited wheat and mill men have accepted invitation to conference.

July 26: The acceptances for wheat conference are coming in fairly well. Had long conference with Stewart on the modus operandi of carrying out the purchasing plan.

July 28: Borden is at his post again — helped by his holiday, but Lady Borden has not been out of bed for three weeks — is very weak. . . . So he has trouble at home as well as I. . . . We are struggling with the problem of wheat handling.

July 30: Decide on a Wheat Board after conference with representatives east and west — an initial payment and a final distribution of the full realized price expenses deducted. It is a trifle paternal but seems necessary.[25]

The July 28 conference lasted through the morning, afternoon and evening, and was attended by Sir Robert Borden, the prime minister, Sir Thomas White, the retiring minister of finance; Honourable Arthur Meighen, Honourable J. A. Calder, Honourable T. A. Crerar, president of united grain growers; J. A. Maharg, M.P., president, Saskatchewan grain growers' association; James Stewart, buyer for the royal commission in Canada; C. B. Watts, secretary of the dominion millers' association Toronto; H. T. Robson, British export mission, New York; James Carruthers, grain dealer, Montreal; E. W. Beatty, president of the Canadian Pacific Railway, and Dr. J. W. Robertson, Canadian representative on the food committee of the supreme allied council. Although the list included members of the grain trade and of the farmer-owned companies, neither the Winnipeg grain exchange nor the Canadian council of agriculture was invited as such. Although Crerar and Maharg were directors of the council, they had been included in their other capacities.

[25] *Foster Diaries.*

At the conclusion of the meeting, at midnight on July 28 Foster sent a short wire to the president of the grain exchange which read "Please see that facilities of trading in wheat futures be withdrawn immediately". Foster followed up his telegram with an explanatory letter to the president of the exchange. It still took a day or two to settle with Stewart the details of a marketing organization to replace the futures market, and Foster issued a cryptic announcement on July 30 of the decision to create the Canadian wheat board and the reasons for it:

The particular conditions of the wheat market in Europe and the United States, where government agencies are almost exclusively employed in, and where government credits had to be provided for the purchase of wheat, rendered it necessary to provide a similar agency in Canada, or to run the risk of being faced with an absence of adequate cash markets for Canadian wheat and a speedy and uniform movement of the same.

The government, after very careful inquiring consideration, has therefore decided to appoint a Board of experienced men invested with adequate powers to conduct the purchase and sale of the Canadian wheat crop of 1919, both for export and domestic purposes.

An initial cash payment by way of advance will be made by the Board to the farmers for each bushel sold, based on the No. 1 Northern Fort William. At the conclusion of the season's sale, after the deduction of necessary expenses, the total excess realized over and above the first payment made to the farmers will be divided among the original sellers in proportion to the grade and quantities sold. The farmer will thus receive the best world price for his wheat in a cash payment at the time of his sale and the final payment when the wheat crop has been disposed of.

A complete system of record, under the provisions of the Canada Grain Act and the regulations made thereunder, will be kept, which will enable the Board to determine with accuracy and pay with certainty the exact proportion of the surplus due to each original seller.

The Grain Exchanges will not give facilities for the buying and selling of futures in wheat during the crop season of 1919.

The Board will utilize, so far as available and necessary, the existing facilities for the purchase, transport and handling of wheat with the view of disturbing as little as possible the existing and ultimate methods of trade.

The government has been actuated in its decision by desire to secure for the Canadian farmer the best possible price for his product and, at the same time, to ensure to the home consumer that his flour shall not cost more than is necessary by actual world prices. Such action has also been made necessary in order to secure the early marketing and speedy movement of Canada's surplus wheat, thus making it possible for the farmer to realize at once a substantial cash price for his wheat, and ultimately the fullest possible return on the balance of price realized by the season's sales.

The establishment of this Board does not interfere with the work of the Board of Grain Supervisors in respect to that portion of the crop of 1918 delivered by August 15. Their powers and functions are continued in full force so far as that crop is concerned. A new Board will have sole authority to deal with the crop of 1919, and with that portion of the crop of 1918 which will be undelivered by August 15.[26]

[26]*Manitoba Free Press*, July 31, 1919.

REACTION OF THE CANADIAN COUNCIL OF AGRICULTURE

Because of the brevity of detail provided in Foster's announcement, the Canadian council of agriculture inferred that the new board's initial payment would be at the floor price of $1.75 which had been rumored on July 15. In fact, the *Manitoba Free Press* had headlined its speculative report on the floor price guarantee with an indication that the initial payment would be $1.75. On the basis of that report, the council was upset by Foster's announcement, as the *Free Press* reported on July 31:

> That a minimum price of $1.75 per bushel on the basis of No. I Northern wheat at Fort William, as now forecast by dispatches from Ottawa as being the probable figure the government will set in the adoption of their new plans for handling this year's wheat crop, will be entirely unsatisfactory to the western grain growers, was the opinion expressed by Norman Lambert, secretary of the Dominion Council of Agriculture on Wednesday afternoon. Mr. Lambert and R. McKenzie, also a member of the Council, expressed surprise and regret that the government had seen fit to take such drastic action in the handling of the wheat crop without calling representatives of the Council to the conference held at Ottawa Monday and Tuesday of this week. Both gentlemen expressed the fear that the government was too solicitous to supply the British government with cheap wheat at the expense of the Canadian producer and although it is proposed to sell wheat at the world's highest market price, yet there is grave danger that the British government will be enabled to buy a portion of the Canadian crop at perhaps a small advance on that paid to the farmers, while the balance of the crop will be sold to neutral countries at a higher figure with the result that when the whole proceeds are pooled and the whole cost of handling is deducted, there will be little if any return to the farmers as an increase on that already paid at time of delivery.
>
> Continuing, Mr. Lambert said that in accordance with the action, the Canadian Council of Agriculture, in opposing the opening of the wheat market, he believed were still in favour of the closed market under present conditions which are abnormal in regard to demand, financing and transportation. The upward trend of the market during the seven days it was opened for dealing in futures on the Winnipeg Exchange, did not, in Mr. Lambert's opinion, reflect the true values and that prices would have receded later when the western crop began to move.[27]

REACTION OF THE WINNIPEG GRAIN EXCHANGE

Members of the Winnipeg grain exchange received the order to close the futures market with even more disappointment and resentment as they saw their efforts to resume normal trading come to naught; the *Free Press* reported their reaction:

> Resentment and considerable anger was expressed yesterday afternoon by several prominent members of the Grain Exchange at the action of the government in taking away the handling of grain from the regular trade and placing it in the hands of a Commission with a guaranteed minimum price. It is claimed that the trade is being discriminated against by the action of the government, and not only will the trade be practically put out of business, but that the farmers of western Canada will be heavy losers as it will be impossible to secure the full value of the wheat without the open market.

[27]*Ibid.*, July 31, 1919.

The plan, which, it is believed the government is now adopting for the handling of the price of wheat, is, it is said by members of the Exchange, one that was formulated some months ago and placed before the government by C. B. Watts, Secretary of the Dominion Millers Association, Headquarters at Toronto. The plan at that time was not looked upon with favour by the majority of the government, who considered plans for the handling of the new crop, the decision then being reached to open the wheat market and permit trading in futures. However, the personnel of the Cabinet has changed somewhat from that time. Sir George E. Foster, Minister of Trade and Commerce, has returned from England, and Honourable A. K. Maclean who was acting minister during Sir George's absence, has retired, as has also Sir Thomas White, Minister of Finance, and Honourable T. A. Crerar, Minister of Agriculture, all of whom were in favour of the open markets.[28]

The full extent of Magill's chagrin at the turn of events was reserved for his report to a general meeting of the Winnipeg grain exchange held on August 20, 1919. He had accompanied Messrs. F. J. Anderson and A. P. Stuart to London that spring in an abortive attempt to restore private trading, as he reported:

Your instructions to your delegates were clear. There was no ambiguity about them. You wanted an open market for the coming year. By that you meant an open cash market and an open market for trading for future delivery. In that sense I understood your instructions, and it was because I understood your instructions in that sense that I was willing to go.

I was one of those who believed then (and I still believe it) that the sooner we could get back to commercial methods in handling our business, the better it would be for our country, ourselves and everybody concerned.

I went ahead, and was followed at a later date by your President, Mr. F. J. Anderson, and Mr. A. P. Stuart, of Montreal, who had the same instructions. At that time the Canadian ministers were not in London. They were at the Peace Conference in Paris. The High Commissioner for Canada and Dr. Robertson and Mr. Harris of the War Trade Mission were the only officials for Canada in London. I went to the High Commissioner. He said it was not in his hands to negotiate with the Imperial authorities. I then went to Dr. Robertson. Dr. Robertson saw me every day for about two hours a day and for a considerable number of days. He discussed the whole business of handling wheat. He got our point of view as thoroughly as I could put it; and then he told me that if he could get the authority from the Canadian Government he would take it up with the Imperial authorities, but that his instructions limited him to last year's crop. Therefore, the first thing I set myself to do was to get authority for Dr. Robertson to take up the matter with the Imperial authorities. Then Messrs. Anderson and Stuart arrived, and the three of us went to the High Commissioner again. The three of us interviewed Dr. Robertson day after day, and we saw the War Trade Mission day after day, and we put up the same case, and we made the same request that Dr. Robertson should get authority from the Canadian Government to take up the matter of handling the new crop and formally appealed to the High Commissioner for Canada to cable to Ottawa for instructions to authorize him to take up the matter with the Imperial authorities.

Now, all this time, what about the Canadian Ministers? They were very busy in Paris. I had written to the Minister of Trade and Commerce, Sir George Foster, saying that I was in London, and that my colleagues were

[28]*Ibid.*

coming, and that we would like to see him about the handling of the grain crop.

He replied that he would see us, but could make no appointment then. When your President and Mr. Stuart were in London along with me, Sir Robert Borden appeared in London on his way to Canada. He gave us half an hour and the three of us put our case before him. Sir George Foster also came to London, and he gave us an interview at Claridge's Hotel and at the War Trade Mission offices. Sir George went back to Paris. His plans were to stay there while the Peace Conference was in session. At the end of our interview with him he suggested that I stay on, and that he would take it up again, and he said that it might be advisable for me to go to Paris. He went to Paris, and the next thing that happened was, cablegrams came announcing that his wife, Lady Foster, was dangerously ill. He left Paris and went to Ottawa. After that interview with him, at which Mr. Stuart of Montreal your President and myself were present, I never saw him again. I have not seen him since, nor have I written to him or wired him. The Canadian ministers were therefore eliminated, but the Canadian Government instructed the High Commissioner and Dr. Robertson to take the matter up with the British authorities, and they did so. They had an interview with the Royal Wheat Commission on June 13th. I want to speak on that interview for a moment. There were present on behalf of the Government of Canada, Sir George Perley, and his Secretary, Mr. Griffith, and Dr. Robertson, and on the other hand the Royal Wheat Commission. I was not there, as I was not asked to be there. I had no right to be there. I was not an official of the Government and did not expect to be there. That interview was on June 13th. What happened? Mr. Griffith sent me a letter stating what happened. I will read it to you. This letter contains the proposals of the Royal Wheat Commission to Sir George Perley, the High Commissioner for Canada. The letter is dated London, June 19, 1919:

"Dear Dr. Magill: Following the conference with the Wheat Commission a letter has been received from the Secretary stating that it is impossible at present to outline any specific buying policy, partly owing to the crop situation in both consuming and producing countries still being subject to large variations, and partly because it is not yet known how far the responsibility of the Royal Commission may extend in making purchases on behalf of the Allies. The Royal Commission, therefore, is unable to state what proportion of the new Dominion crop it will desire to buy, but as the Commission is alive to the fact that the Wheat Export Company was necessarily a hindrance to the normal conduct of the export trade during the war, and they desire to revive the activity of commercial enterprise, they propose to liquidate the Wheat Export Company (Winnipeg) as a trading concern, so that complete freedom may be restored to the Dominion grain trade to sell its produce in the simplest manner, without restriction of destination, during the ensuing year.

"It is added that the Commission, as at present advised, will probably make its purchases on an f.o.b. basis as and when stocks are wanted, and it will probably prove advisable to establish an office at the Canadian Seaboard to ensure promptness in the correspondence which must take place between London and Canada. The Commission believes that an early announcement that the Wheat Export Company (Winnipeg) will cease to operate and that trade will be able to resume some normal courses, will remove the element of uncertainty which we deprecated. Yours faithfully, W. N. Griffith."

That is from the High Commissioner's office. What does it mean? It means that the Royal Wheat Commission, on behalf of the British Government undertook to buy our crop from the Canadian Grain Trade at the Atlantic seaboard f.o.b. I think the reason that they wanted to buy it at the seaboard was that they are still controlling the shipping. Not only are they controlling the amount of tonnage available for grain, but they also control the unloading of it. Let me point out that if one of our Canadian exporters chartered a boat for Glasgow, and if they ordered it unloaded at Plymouth, he would be up against it. So they said in substance: "We will buy your wheat for the next twelve months at the seaboard. We will buy it in quantities as we need it. As we need it we will furnish the ships and pay for it f.o.b. We will not interfere with your selling to neutral countries — sell to them on a commercial basis." These neutral countries have their own tonnage and they are wealthy. They have money to pay for wheat without credits, and Germany is said to be buying through them. That was the proposal of the Commission — that we should sell to neutral and enemy countries direct and to the Royal Wheat Commission at the Canadian seaboard f.o.b. As to France and Italy, their view was this—they preferred that France and Italy should make their own arrangements for purchasing our wheat, but they did not know whether that would be done under the Supreme Council of the Allied Governments or not.

When I got that letter I believed that our work was well done. I believed that we had an export outlet for our fifty or sixty million bushels of wheat. I believed Europe would need it. I believed that no other country would have any considerable quantity of hard spring wheat to export, and that the Canadian grain trade would have no difficulty in selling the wheat. I have this to say about it also — the Royal Wheat Commission made great concessions to us. They wanted our trade to get back to more normal conditions and to commercial methods. They met us more than half way. They gave us everything we had a right to ask for. Mr. J. Stewart has been their representative here for three or four years, and the fact that they knew he was in favour of the open market was, I am certain, one of the reasons why they made these splendid concessions to us.

What about the Canadian Government? That interview took place on June 13th. On June 18th, five days later, the Acting Minister of Trade and Commerce called a conference in Ottawa. The Government of Canada then knew of these proposals; they knew that there would be an export outlet provided. On July 7th the Government of Canada, through the Acting Minister of Trade and Commerce, announced that the markets would be opened. The conference began on June 18th, and on June 21st Sir George Foster reached Ottawa. Sir George was there two weeks before the Government's policy was announced. The market was opened on the 21st July. Sir George Foster was there a month before the market was opened. It has been rumored that Sir George Foster came over to kill the market. There is not a shadow of evidence for that. In my experience, I never knew a case where a very vital problem like that of the Canadian grain trade was decided by one minister. The whole Government decided to open the market, and the whole Government at a later date decided to close the market. One man cannot be credited with opening it and one man cannot be discredited with closing it. Sir George Foster was in Ottawa a month before the market was opened. He never intimated to me that he had any hostility to the open market. He never suggested that to the delegates when we met him. I believe that when the market was opened he was as much in favor of it as any minister in Ottawa — but I don't know; I have never seen him since that interview in May, and I have never written to him or communicated with him one way or another.

After I received that letter from the High Commissioner's office, I went to a shipping office and asked about the possibility of getting back to Canada. I was told that thousands were on the waiting list and that I could not get back for two months. I took the opportunity of having an operation performed, and on recovering I went to Mr. Harris's office. He told me he had been at the conference in Ottawa, that he knew all that had gone on, and had talked with grain men, and that he came back to London believing that it was his duty to sell Canadian wheat to England and to neutral countries. Mark you, after the market had been opened, Mr. Harris, Chairman of the War Trade Mission, believed it was his duty to sell Canadian wheat to England and to neutral countries. He also told me that a cablegram had been sent by Sir Robert Borden to Mr. Arthur Sifton, telling him among other things, to sell fifty to seventy-five million bushels of our wheat. That puzzled me. How could we have an open market if the Government sold 50 to 75 million bushels? I thought something was wrong. I sent the following cablegram from London on July 27, 1919, to your President, when I got all the information:

Puzzled. Harris believes, first, authorized sell here and neutrals; second, Winnipeg trade approve; third, trade satisfied with last year's plan including Commission forwarding seaboard; fourth, opening market advertisement Canada has grain sell; fifth, wanted Stewart, Lambert come here help sale. Borden cabled Sifton sell fifty to seventy-five million bushels here. Harris trying effect sale. This is inconsistent with your cables. Suggest you cable Harris direct detail re open market, proposed sale and how protect trade if sale effected including seaboard delivery and commission to Winnipeg and Montreal shippers. Robertson recommended conference Supreme Council. French want continuation last year's plan; trade here favoring control. Maclean at Ritz. Under these conditions find I can do little; fear trade will be injured; looking for berth back. Please cable immediately and say whether open market succeeding. . . .[29]

The rest of Dr. Magill's report was devoted to speculation on the government's motives for closing the market. His explanation in that respect was somewhat wide of the mark, according to the government's own account of its action.

GOVERNMENT'S EXPLANATION

The official explanation of the government's about face in closing the market after allowing it to reopen and in replacing it by a government board is to be found in the preamble of P.C. 1589 of July 31, 1919, which created the wheat board under authority of the war measures act. The preamble stated:

For some time, owing to the war, overseas purchases have been conducted largely, and for two seasons wholly, through government organizations, and by reason of such conditions, the crop of Canada for the past two seasons, has been placed under the control of the Board of Grain Supervisors of Canada, which body has been invested with and has exercised powers conferred upon it by the Order in Council of 11th June, 1917, and by subsequent Orders. The said Board of Grain Supervisors are still exercising and purpose to continue exercising their powers with relation to the crop of 1918, to the extent delivered up to and inclusive of the 15th day of August, 1919, and provision is adequate for the final disposition of same.

As regards the crop of 1919, and any other wheat undelivered on the 15th day of August, 1919, it does not appear that there will exist in importing

[29]*The Secretary's Report on Wheat Situation,* Winnipeg Grain Exchange, August 20, 1919.

countries likely to require or purchase same, any organized buying at fixed prices such as prevailed in recent years, nor any open and stable market of the character that obtained prior to the war.

The United States Government has through a constituted agency undertaken many months ago and during the continuance of active hostilities in the present war, the purchase at a fixed price, of the crop of that country for the year 1919, and the marketing of same at home and abroad.

Under these abnormal conditions, resulting in uncertainty of price and instability of market, it would appear that in order to secure that early movement of the Canadian crop which is so essential, and that fair distribution among our wheat producers of the actual value of their product, as determined by the world demand for same throughout the entire season of marketing, which is equally desirable, action should be taken by the Government, looking to the purchase, storage, movement, financing and marketing of the wheat grown in Canada in 1919, and other wheat undelivered in Canada on the 15th of August, 1919.

Although the preamble attributed the decision to the lack of organized buying by overseas governments which remained in control of purchases, to the lack of overseas private trading and to the existence of a price support board in the United States which was Canada's principal competitor, the preamble failed to reveal the extent to which the Canadian banks and railways were exercised over the prospect that the commercial system for the movement, handling and marketing of the 1919 crop would break down in the absence of government intervention. These points were made more clearly by ministers during the course of subsequent debates in the house. On October 9, 1919, Sir George Foster delivered an eloquent speech as he moved second reading of bill 21 respecting the Canadian Wheat Board. The speech ran over eight pages of Hansard, which he delivered from pencilled notes to be found in the Foster papers. The relevant passages of Foster's speech are quoted:

In the first place, the question is put as to why the exchange market was opened up in Winnipeg, and why it was afterwards closed. A great many opinions have been expressed as to the reasons for both steps. I am free to say that if the Government had had the same information before the market was opened up as it had shortly afterwards, probably the market would not have been opened up at all; but we all depend for our sources of information on agencies, and we have to take from them what information we get from time to time, and in these confused and abnormal conditions information sometimes develops quite rapidly and changes the point of view of the seeker for enlightenment on the general question. As far as I am myself concerned, as the head of the Department of Trade and Commerce, and as far as the Government is concerned, there is no doubt that we were not at all anxious to undertake any controlled system of the marketing of wheat this year. We had experience of the controlled system of marketing during the two preceding years when the war was on, and when I think by general consent, even though some felt that their business and their privileges were largely curtailed by the fact of Government control and operation, it was conceded that nothing else was possible during those times. When the Armistice was declared and peace came in sight the natural desire, both of the Government and of the grain trade, reverted again with all its force that the shackles should be taken off and control should not be exercised, and I was of the opinion, as was the Government, that quite probably very great freedom, if not complete freedom, might be given to the Grain Trade, so that it could resume its normal and accustomed channels for carrying on its various operations. A delegation was sent by the Winnipeg Grain Exchange, which visited London while I was there, and I was in communication with that delegation. The opinion of that delegation was entirely in favour of the open market, of resuming the former methods of carrying on the grain business in this country and for export purposes. . . .

I may say that the grain trade in Great Britain and also the Royal Wheat Commission were favourable to that idea if it could possibly be carried out.
. . .

However, as matters progressed, it became more and more evident that if there were an open market and normal methods were reverted to, there would be slight prospect of a speedy sale for the farmers' wheat — if, indeed, it would be possible in the lapse of time to market the wheat at all by the old methods. This condition arose from several considerations. In the first place, there was a lack of speedy decision amongst the purchasing powers of the Allies, and several considerations contributed to that lack of speedy decision. Two or three of these are the following: Until the crops attained a certain state of maturity it was impossible to estimate what would be the requirements of the European countries, measured by what quantities these countries could produce for their own needs. Until the crops had progressed to a certain stage towards maturity no one could make a fair estimate of what amount would be contributed by the production of the European countries themselves towards their own possible consumption. On the other hand, it was impossible to estimate accurately what would be the surplus of wheat in the producing and exporting countries until a certain stage of maturity had been reached. Consequently, the British Government, the Wheat Commission, the Allies themselves, did not go into the market; they held off on account of the two very important considerations which I have mentioned before making contracts or entering into arrangements for the supplying of their needs.

There was also the consideration of finance, which I spoke of the other day. It was impossible for them to gather up a sufficient amount of cash with which to buy for their needs. Credits were necessary and those credits had to be arranged as between Governments. The question of the wherewithal to pay and the credits to be made where cash payments were impossible — as they would be in the majority of cases — was, therefore, a third and very important consideration in coming to a conclusion in the matter. All these considerations had the direct effect of keeping out of contracts and actual engagements those European countries which would ultimately require more or less, the quantity to be determined later.

The impression being entertained that it was possible to carry on the business of the grain trade in Canada and for export by a reversion to the old methods, permission was given for the opening of the exchange and it was opened. Subsequent information led the Government, after careful consideration, to the conclusion that it was impossible satisfactorily to market the grain crop of the farmers of Canada on the old open system. Practically without exception, the European countries, as they did last year, make their purchases of grain and the necessary arrangements in connection therewith under Government control. There are no open exchanges in Europe where prices are fixed. There was and is no organized system of individual or corporate buying, owing to the conditions to which I have already referred. The Government, therefore, came to the conclusion that we would have to revert to control; that Government supervision would have to be exercised and that Government facilities for moving the crop would have to be made available. The grain exchange was open for a short time; then it was closed at the request of the Government. Hon. members connected with the grain trade are quite familiar with what took place at that time. There was a speculative rise in the price of grain. I do not know how far that advance went, but it was continuous and it was considerable, and the Government felt that those speculative advances and the conditions under which they were brought about produced an unhealthy situation as well for the farmer who wished to market his grain as in respect of the possible buying sources in the Old Country. If one looks into the transactions during that time in the Exchange, he will find that the number and amount of actual sales were very small indeed. The price went up and that gave the farmer the idea that that was an indication of the price at which he could sell his product. We did not think that it was an indication of the price, and if it was not an indication of the real price that the farmer could get, the running up of prices by speculative operations was not in the interests of the farmer; it tended to create erroneous impressions on the part of the farmer as to what he would ultimately get and to bring about discontent when those anticipations were disappointed. . . .

To-day, under the conditions I have just mentioned, it is difficult to get an order for wheat flour for export from Canada at all and the Canada Wheat Board are putting forth some of their best and shrewdest efforts in order to mingle certain of the orders for flour along with orders for wheat as well so as to provide some export market for the Canadian millers and help them in that direction. But if, in the open market, the millers were left to find a market for themselves in European countries for flour, it would be very difficult indeed for them to do so. . . .

If you sum up the trend of these observations the situation sizes itself up in this way: Here is your Canadian farmer with his wheat threshed out in September and October. He wants an immediate market for that wheat. He wants as large a price as possible and he wants cash payment for his wheat. Under the conditions which existed there was no source from which this cash might be expected. I was at the centre of operations there for several months and I never could get the buying authorities, or the prospective buying authorities, in European countries to make any decision as to when they would be in the market or as to the price they would be willing to offer. Therefore, you have this situation, that unless somebody came to the front and supplied a method by which the cash was ready for the immediate purchase of the grain, and the immediate payment to the farmer, you would have a condition of things which would be very detrimental to the farmers themselves.

Their crop was garnered, their sales would be few and far between, comparatively, and the cash they demanded would be difficult to find. In that position you would have no work for your railways for, unless the grain starts to go out promptly upon its being ready for sale, the railways lose their best opportunity for carrying. That was another item which led up to the conclusion reached by the Government. As it is the Government steps in and cash for the immediate purchase of the wheat is provided for. The banks take on the payments, the purchases are made promptly and they are paid for in cash. Up to the present moment, I think I am justified in saying that at least 50 per cent of the total surplus of the Canadian farmers has already been sold and to that extent the money is provided in so far as it is required for prompt and speedy payment when the farmer sells his grain. I am satisfied that with no organized buying with credits, under the conditions that existed and with all these things government controlled on the other side of the water, which in the main they were, it would have been impossible to have had speedy and cash transactions in the wheat of the Canadian farmer under any other system than that which has been provided by the Government. . . .[30]

The explanation of the government's decision to close the market and to create a wheat board was put much more succinctly by the Honourable Arthur Meighen in the course of a debate on the Canadian wheat board bill of 1920, just a few days before he was sworn in as prime minister. Mr. Maharg had accused the government of running scared as prices rose when the market was reopened. Mr. Meighen replied:

> The hon. member as a supporter of the legislation is hardly fair in saying that last year the Government got scared. He intimated that the Government was afraid of high prices for wheat, and consequently stepped in when the exchanges opened. The hon. member knows that those were not the circumstances at all. The circumstances were these: After the Government had decided last year that we were in a position to go back to normal trading, and after trading was in operation, it transpired that by reason of the attitude of overseas governments and because of overseas control, associated with the fact of American control, no orders were coming for our wheat. Consequently, no banking facilities were available. Consequently, no wheat was going to move. As a result it appeared that the wheat was going to stack back in the West, and that the whole season of navigation would be lost on that account. On that account alone the Government stepped in — not because of any apprehensions as to the price of wheat going up. Indeed, we had the matter under consideration before the grain exchanges opened, but we could not get far enough to decide not to let them open. The advance of wheat on the exchange had not one whit to do with the Government's decision, and I think my hon. friend's intimacy with the facts and circumstances ought to have prevented his giving that impression by his statement. It was merely the fact, as I have stated over and over again, that the situation in Europe, the market for our wheat was such that no orders were coming and no finances were available to move the wheat. Not only the bankers but the railway companies made it clear to us that something had to be done or our wheat was not going to move. Those were the only circumstances that moved the Government to act.[31]

Thus it transpired that in the considerable uncertainty about decontrol abroad, and in the concern over the banks' preparedness to finance the movement of the crop under open market conditions, the government reluctantly opted for retention of control over the marketing of the 1919 crop. The decision did not represent acceptance of the principle of government control as a continuing policy; on the contrary Foster declared elsewhere in his speech that it was the government's intention to retain the controls for one year only. Although the attempt to decontrol had proved abortive, it was destined to succeed after the first Canadian wheat board had operated for a year.

---

[30]*House of Commons Debates,* October 9, 1919, pp. 910-914.
[31]*Ibid.,* June 28, 1920, p. 4346.

7

THE CANADIAN WHEAT BOARD

The Canadian wheat board was formally established, under the authority of the war measures act, by P. C. 1589 of July 31, 1919, although its personnel still remained to be appointed. On the following day, Foster and Stewart conferred at length and Stewart accepted Foster's offer of the chairmanship. Thus the Scottish-born Winnipeg grain merchant who had been appointed by the British royal commission to head its Winnipeg Export Company, had come into prominence by cornering the market, had since served as a member of the board of grain supervisors, as sales agent for the Canadian flour mills, as adviser to Foster, now became the chairman of the new board. Foster and Stewart agreed upon a list of other appointees who were immediately approached by letter or wire. Mr. F. W. Riddell, general manager of the Saskatchewan Co-operative Elevator Company, was chosen to be the assistant-chairman. It was agreed that the positions of chairman and assistant-chairman should be salaried, whereas other members of the board, selected in a representative capacity, should serve as honorary members as all the board of grain supervisors had done. Within a few days the roster was completed, including the following members:

H. W. Wood, Carstairs, Alberta;
W. A. Black, Montreal, Quebec;
Norman McLeod Paterson, Fort William, Ontario;
Wm. L. Best, Ottawa, Ontario;
C. B. Watts, Toronto, Ontario;
Frank O. Fowler, Winnipeg, Manitoba;
William Henry McWillaims, Winnipeg, Manitoba;
Joseph Quintal, Montreal, Quebec;
Lieut.-Col. John Z. Fraser, Burford, Ontario;
William A. Matheson, Winnipeg, Manitoba.

All of these appointments had been made by telegram, with the exception of Mr. Best, the legislative representative of the brotherhood of locomotive firemen and enginemen, who resided in Ottawa. Although Best was only a few blocks away, Foster addressed the following letter to him on August 1, 1919:

With reference to the composition of the Canadian Wheat Board, I would be very glad to have your services as a member thereof. Please let me have an immediate answer.

I sincerely hope that you will be able to accept this appointment.

In a classic example of leaping first and looking afterward, Best replied on August 2:

> Replying to your communication of the 1st instant, containing request that I accept appointment on the Canadian Wheat Board, I shall be glad to accept such appointment, having regard, of course, to present obligations.
>
> May I ask what are the functions of the Canadian Wheat Board and is it an honorary Body.

Foster's only reply was to send Best a copy of P. C. 1589.[1]

These and the immediate following events were recorded in Foster's diary as follows:

> August 1: Had long conference with Stewart who accepts the chairmanship of Canadian Wheat Board. Make choice of the majority of Board and telegraph for their acceptance. Find that Julius Barnes is not so optimistic about keeping price up to $2.26 in face of the pressure for lower cost of living or higher cost of service and production. He is not enamoured with our plan — too communistic. Borden appears to be incubating on some of the Cabinet eggs.
>
> August 2: Office and Council in morning. There is an offer in prospect for our surplus wheat or a portion. Had some consultation about Board. Some of the invited have accepted — others will and gradually all will come in I think and help to work the plan put. Our crop will be small and more's the pity — for us and the world. U.S. crop has gradually dwindled also. The bread basket will not overflow.
>
> August 6: Long hard day with leather and hides, W. Bd., cheese deputation and grain and other matters in afternoon conference. What the U.S. may do with its wheat — keep fixed price or sell lower and foot the loss, or as Barnes now intimates, reduce price of flour and keep wheat up and stand the loss on flour cost makes it difficult for W.B. to offer at a fixed price. Our surplus, however, we shall sell easily I think.
>
> August 20: The Government's Wheat Commission is now under way — prices fixed and methods of operation laid out. Do not understand the widespread and obstinate misunderstanding of the plan by western farmers — propaganda or prejudice or what?

POWERS OF THE BOARD

The key provisions of the order in council setting out the powers of the board were as follows:

4. The Board shall have power from time to time,

(a) To take delivery of wheat in Canada at any point.

(b) To pay, by way of advance, to the producers or other persons delivering wheat to the Board, such price per bushel according to grade or quality and place of delivery for price purposes as shall be set our in schedule to be prepared by the Board and approved by the Governor in Council, and to provide for the issue of participation certificates to persons entitled thereto.

(c) To sell wheat so delivered to millers in Canada for milling purposes at such prices and subject to such conditions as the Board sees fit, the price of sale to millers being governed as nearly as may be by the price obtainable at the same time in the world's markets for wheat of equal value, regard being had to the cost of transport, handling and storage.

(d) To store and transport such wheat with a view to marketing of same.

(e) To sell wheat so delivered in excess of domestic requirements to

---

[1] *Department of Trade and Commerce File 24181A*, Public Archives of Canada.

purchasers Overseas or in other countries, for such prices as may be obtainable.

(f) In co-operation with the Seed Purchasing Commission of the Department of Agriculture, and by sale to such Commission or otherwise, to provide for the retention or distribution in various parts of Canada of such wheat as may be necessary for seed in 1920.

(g) To fix maximum prices or margins of profit at which flour and other products made from wheat delivery to millers, may be sold, and to fix standards of quality of such flour.

(h) To purchase flour from millers at prices to be fixed by the Board and to sell same in Canada or in other countries.

(i) To take possession of and to sell and deliver to millers, or to purchasers in other countries, wheat stored in any elevator, warehouse, or on railway cars or Canadian boats and to deal with the same as to payment of advance and otherwise in the same way as if it had been otherwise delivered to the Board, and to move grain into and out of or through any elevator and to or from any car or boat.

(j) To control, by license or otherwise, the export and sales of flour out of Canada.

(k) For the purpose of performing its duties under this Order, to allocate Canadian lake tonnage and to distribute cars for rail shipments.

(l) To pay necessary expenses incident to the operations of the Board.

5. Deliveries of wheat may be taken from, through or by the use of such agents or grain companies or organizations as the Board may see fit, and may be at such points in Canada, at the seaboard or otherwise, as the Board may direct, and the Board may pay to such agents or grain companies or organizations handling wheat, or delivering wheat to the Board, such commissions, storage and other charges as the Board with the approval of the Governor in council may deem proper.

6. The Board may make payment by authorization to a chartered bank or to chartered banks to pay under such conditions and on production of such vouchers as the Board may by regulation provide, and the Governor in Council guarantees repayment of any monies so paid by a bank or banks, with interest at a rate not exceeding six per cent of which guarantee the evidence shall be this Order.

7. As soon as the Board have received payment in full for all wheat delivered to the Board, there shall be deducted from same all monies disbursed by or on behalf of the Board for expenses or otherwise connected with or incident to the operations of the Board, and the balance shall be disbursed pro rata among all producers and others holding participation certificates.

8. Notwithstanding anything in the Grain Act or in the Railway Act, the Board of Railway Commissioners for Canada shall have power to order any railway company to provide cars and other transportation facilities for handling grain, and to transport as directed wheat delivered to or by the Board, or in which the Board is interested, and at the request of the Board to withhold transport of any other wheat or grain for a fixed time.[2]

A subsequent order in council (P. C. 1751, August 22, 1919) established the following schedule of cash payments:

Manitoba, Alberta and Saskatchewan No. 1 Hard..................................$2.15
No. 1 Manitoba Northern $2.15

[2]*P.C. 1589*, July 31, 1919, reproduced in the Canadian Wheat Board, *Chairman's Report, 1919-1921,* (Winnipeg), pp. 25-29.

No. 2 Manitoba Northern $2.12
No. 3 Manitoba Northern $2.08
No. 1 Alberta Red Winter..$2.15
No. 2 Alberta Red Winter..$2.12
No. 3 Alberta Red Winter..$2.08
  Cash payments basis in store Fort William and Port Arthur.
British Columbia No. 1 wheat $2.10½
    No. 2 wheat $2.07½
    No. 3 wheat $2.03½
  Basis in store Vancouver.
Ontario and Quebec wheat, No. 1 grade...................................$2.18
    No. 2 grade...$2.15
    No. 3 grade...$2.11
  Basis in store Montreal.[3]

In devising the board, the government had introduced three policy innovations, namely, the payment of an initial advance; selling to best advantage; and the pro rata distribution of any resulting profits to producers by means of participation certificates. These three features were later adopted by the three provincial wheat pools and still later by the second Canadian wheat board, with the result that they are now basic to Canadian wheat marketing policy. For this reason, the origin of this concept for the wheat board's operation merits attention.

ORIGIN OF THE BOARD CONCEPT

The idea for the pooled marketing of wheat on the basis of an initial payment and the subsequent distribution of profits resulting from sales had originated in Australia in connection with the wartime wheat policy of that government, and had applied to the 1915 and subsequent crops. The Australian system was known to the Canadian government, the grain trade, the millers' associations and the Canadian council of agriculture. In Stewart's report on the operations of the Canadian wheat board, he acknowledged the experiment that had been tried in Australia.[4] A claim subsequently made that the board's plan of operations "was almost identical with that submitted by the Canadian Council of Agriculture" is rather difficult to substantiate.[5] The council's proposal to which reference was made had been advanced in August, 1918, (by the grain committee of the council) and recommended the establishment of a Canadian grain corporation modeled upon the United States grain corporation. More specifically, the grain committee recommended:

 4. The Corporation, through its authorized agents, to buy all wheat, when offered to it, either in store Fort William or Port Arthur, or c.i.f. Bay Ports or Atlantic seaboard, at a fixed minimum price, basis 1 Northern in store Fort William. Government grades and dockage to govern and spreads on lower grades to be based on fair milling discounts.

 5. The Corporation to arrange for the sale and export of the wheat so bought and any profit accruing therefrom after disposal of Canada's

[3]*Ibid.* p. 33.
[4]*Ibid.* p. 9.
[5]*The Grain Growers Record 1906 to 1943,* (Public Press Limited, Winnipeg, 1944), p. 25.

exportable surplus, shall be distributed pro rata to the producers, after deducting the Corporation's administrative and other expenses.

6. Canadian millers and other buyers will not be permitted to export wheat or wheat products but may buy for home consumption.

In explanation of these clauses the memorandum continued:

Clauses 4, 5 & 6 — These clauses provide for what is really the setting of a minimum price basis One Northern in store Fort William or Port Arthur, on which basis the authorized agents of the Grain Corporation would accept delivery of all wheat, in any position in Canada, when offered to it, Government grade and dockage to govern. The minimum price takes the nature of an advance. Fixed spreads, based on milling values, would also be made to cover grades lower than One Northern. The Grain Corporation would not enter any Canadian wheat market as a competitive buyer and would not buy wheat through its agents unless offered, and then only at the set minimum price. At such time as the Grain Corporation had disposed of the surplus Canadian wheat and wheat products a further payment to the producers would be made, pro rata, of any net profits. The producers by this means would receive a return for their wheat at the average price realised on the Canadian exportable surplus, less expenses, assuming that the average export sale price would be greater than the set minimum price. In other words the producers would receive whatever value the Canadian wheat surplus realised in competition with the wheat crops of other countries, which has always been the basis of Canadian wheat markets.

The pro rata distribution of profits to be made at a stated price per bushel over the minimum price. The distribution to the producers could be made through commission merchants and track buyers on car lot shipments and by line elevator companies on less than car lots bought at street price.

The operation of the Grain Corporation in immediately accepting all offerings of wheat would measurably ensure continuous marketing and transportation of the wheat crop and stabilise financing.

The Grain Corporation, not entering any Canadian market as a competitive buyer, permits of open markets and competitive buying by millers and others to the extent of the requirements for Canadian home consumption and also permits shippers and exporters to carry on business and make deliveries of wheat to the Canadian Corporation at points East of Fort William and Port Arthur even to the Atlantic seaboard, but Canadian shippers and exporters would not be permitted to do business outside the Dominion of Canada, it having previously been shown that the Canadian exporter could not adequately and successfully carry on business with other countries under existing conditions; the Canadian Grain Corporation being created primarily for this important purpose.

Thus the existing machinery and organizations of the grain trade would be preserved, the producer would be safeguarded, no extra charges would be added to the cost of wheat and flour to the consumer, and the welfare of the Dominion's commerce would be ensured.[6]

In the foregoing text, certain of the operating features of the Canadian wheat board are identifiable, such as the initial payment or floor price and the distribution of profits to producers. But the scheme was for a voluntary corporation as distinct from a monopoly board, in which producers would have the option to deliver wheat to the board on the basis of an initial

---

[6]*General Details Covering Operations of the Canadian Grain Corporation as recommended by the Grain committee of the Canadian Council of Agriculture,* Trade and Commerce File 24181A.

payment plus participation or to sell on the open market if prevailing prices were more attractive. This was the system adopted in the United States, except that its grain corporation offered producers a fixed price as an alternative to open market prices, but any profits or losses on the corporation's handlings accrued to the government.

It should be recalled also, that when the Winnipeg market was closed on July 28, 1919, the exchange members ascribed the board's plan to Mr. C. B. Watts, secretary of the Dominion millers' association, who shortly thereafter was appointed as one of the honorary members of the board. It should also be recalled that the millers that spring had been highly apprehensive over the restoration of marketing to the private trade because of their difficulties in making export flour sales. To head off the restoration of the open market, Watts had taken the initiative in proposing to Sir Thomas White the retention of marketing control, and in carrying on a propaganda campaign within the industry to that end. Watts wrote a series of letters to White on April 10, April 12, May 23 and June 16. The first of his letters ran as follows:

> The United States Grain Corporation announce they had advised European nations the U.S. could not supply them with any more wheat or flour from the 1918 crop.
>
> This is Canada's golden opportunity to merchandise her exportable surplus of the 1918 crop.
>
> This must be sold before the 1st of July when the U.S. winter wheat crop of over 800,000,000 bushels will be ready to market.
>
> The Government took the risk of guaranteeing the price, let it take the profit instead of allowing individual brokers and millers who have run no risk make profits reported to be several dollars per barrel on sales to neutral countries who have the gold.
>
> RE 1919 CROP: No Canadian grain or milling firm, no matter how big, can successfully compete against the U.S. Government in marketing Canadian wheat and flour, so it must be done *nationally*.
>
> Wheat prices should not be fixed, but the Government should provide every facility to sell Canada's wheat and flour in the best markets at the maximum prices and the minimum of expense.
>
> Adopt for this purpose tried machinery as in the United States.
>
> Utilize the Canadian Wheat Export Company under Mr. James Stewart, whose experience, strength, ability and fairmindedness, make him preeminently fitted for the position.
>
> This proposal would receive the full endorsement of the Dominion Millers' Association, and I believe of the Western Millers Association, and is the only feasible plan by which the best interests of the farmers of Canada can be served.
>
> Even the biggest millers would have to acknowledge that this plan is in the best interests of the country, although two or three of them might make more money by individually marketing their product abroad.[7]

In his letter of May 23 to White, Watts considerably refined his proposal. In his original letter of that date, he had suggested an initial payment of $1.00 plus a 50 cents per bushel government bond maturing in five years, to which White took exception, and Watts redrafted his letter as follows:

> OPTION MARKET: It is claimed by the line elevator Companies that they

[7] *White Papers.*

cannot buy wheat from the farmers unless the price is fixed or they have an option market in which to sell against it.

It is said that the bankers would also refuse to advance the necessary credits unless one or the other is done.

Mr. Jas. A. Richardson was in Chicago, the end of April and operators on the Chicago Board of Trade, told him that if the Winnipeg market was open, they would sell October wheat down to $1.40.

This, no doubt is what would happen. It would be (disastrous) for Canada to run the risk of having the actual value of her wheat depreciated in this way, by speculators selling wild, so the Winnipeg Option market for wheat should not be opened.

Canda is not in a position financially to follow the example of the United States and fix the price of wheat.

Some steps must be taken immediately to provide for the marketing of Canada's wheat crop, in such a way as will give the farmers every dollar that can be made out of it and at the same time not place any financial burden on the Canadian tax-payer for the benefit of the wheat farmers. This can be best done in two ways.

(1) Instead of making a fixed price on wheat, the Government should buy the Wheat crop, utilizing the ordinary trade channels as far as the seaboard. The grain dealers and the millers would act as agents for the Government in buying from the farmers and would sell the wheat on Government account to millers and others at prices fixed by the Government from time to time, according to its value in the markets of the world.

(2) Payment of wheat would be made to the farmers as follows:

(a) $1.50 per bushel cash, to cover approximately the cost of the wheat.

This would enable the farmer to pay his labor, threshing expenses, store bills, etc.

(b) A wheat certificate for the number of bushels each farmer sold, would be issued to him.

This would entitle him to his pro rata share of any profit made over the $1.50 per bushel which he has already been paid.

(c) Payment of cash and issue of certificate would be made through the banks on Warehouseman's Receipt.

The Government would sell the wheat at the highest market price obtainable from time to time, all the profit over the cost of the wheat including carrying charges and expense of operation, would be placed in a pool which would be divided at the end of the year 1920 in accordance with the total bushels represented by the wheat certificates issued.

As the prices no doubt will be higher immediately the wheat is harvested than later on, this method would place the new settler with a small crop, located a long distance back from the railroad, in a position to get the same price for his wheat as the farmer operating on a large scale, with his own threshing machinery and near to the railroad, where he could make early delivery.

MARKETING CROP: As our wheat will have to be sold in competition with the United States, this can only be done to the best advantage, by following the example of the United States and utilizing the machinery which has been so satisfactory used by the Allies during the war and is now used by the Government, to market the balance of the 1918 wheat crop, through the Wheat Export Company, under Mr. Jas. Stewart, as selling agents for the Government.

Also, appoint an Advisory Board, composed of not more than three representatives each of the farmers, grain dealers and millers, who could make representations to Mr. Stewart, from time to time, as circumstances required or with whom he could consult, when needful.

This whole question is one of too vital importance to the future prosperity of Canada, to allow any influence to sway the Government in the appointment of any but the most experienced and thoroughly practical men, to handle the situation. To gain the best results, the selling of our wheat should be left as free from red tape as apparently the buying of our wheat and flour by the Allies was.

Trusting you will find these suggestions of some assistance in solving this most difficult problem.[8]

Watts distributed his proposals within the industry, and Mr. James A. Robb, M.P., secretary-treasurer of the western millers' association of Canada endorsed them in a letter of April 21, 1919 to White (Robb would subsequently hold the portfolios successively of trade and commerce and finance in the King administration). Watts also sent his proposals to Dr. J. W. Robertson to counter the representations the grain exchange mission had made to Harris and Robertson in London. It will be noted from Watts's letters to White that he envisaged a Canadian board as a continuation of the Wheat Export Company with Stewart continuing as chairman, but under Canadian auspices. The board would take delivery of all wheat against an initial payment, sell to best advantage, and prorate any profits to producers through participation certificates. Thus, Watts's proposals anticipated the three key elements in the board's method of operation. Although Watts had originally suggested a Canadian grain corporation modeled on that of the United States as the grain committee of the Canadian council of agriculture had done, he altered his recommendation along the lines of the Australian government pool. Even if the concept of the Canadian wheat board originated in Australia, it was due to Watts's persistent advocacy that the scheme came to be adopted in Canada.

DETAILS OF BOARD OPERATIONS

At its inception the board held a series of public meetings, (as the board of grain supervisors had done), in Winnipeg, Toronto, Regina, Calgary, Vancouver, Montreal and Fort William, to discuss its methods of operation with the various interested parties. In particular, it was necessary to establish working relations with the trade which, as a matter of policy, it employed as agents to handle wheat in the normal way, except that the agents were now instructed by the board on buying and selling prices and on the movement of the wheat to fill the board's sales contracts.

The trade facilities were used to the extent that the grain companies accepted delivery of the wheat at country points on their own financing with the banks, whose loans were protected by government guarantee. When the companies sold the wheat, either to mills or for export, at prices determined by the board, they simply paid into a board account the difference between the buying and selling price less agreed handling charges. This method of operation is revealed in a pencilled memorandum which Foster wrote for his own guidance, under Stewart's advice:

Buyer must be licensed — person — firm — corporation; pays price fixed by Board ($2.15) gives participation certif. receipt to seller, at time of issue of

[8]*Ibid.*

cash ticket (when cash ticket is issued) or at time of purchase by com. merchant or other licensed agent completing sale.

2. *Does this include millers?* Yes — dealer has to remit 15¢ of $2.30 to C.W.B.

Exporter must pay fixed price to farmer, say $2.15 plus 15¢ to Wheat Board.

Any licensee *selling* wheat for domestic use pays 15¢ to C.W. Board. He has already bought the wheat and paid $2.15 or $2.30, and given a participation receipt. When he sells it he pays 15¢ to W. Board — so he has paid $2.30 in all. . . .

Every mill licensee who grists wheat for farmers or owners thereof shall for purpose of part. certif. and the 15¢, treat all wheat as a purchase — deliver partic. certif. for each bushel received and remit 15¢ to the C.W.B.

An agreement exists between C.W.B. and millers as to prices of wheat, bran and shorts. Millers asked for increase owing to increased cost of production of 15¢. This was not granted. Millers agree not to advance beyond price at time Board formed. . . .

The Board does not interfere unnecessarily.

Special committee of Board in Ontario and Quebec to adjust this.

Fraser — Watts and Goldie, Ont.

Black — Quintal, Goldie, Que.

Carrying Charges — for interest, storage, etc., on grain from delivey at country elev. till it reaches F.W.

1917 — 4¢ was set for this — surplus — quick delivery.

1918 — 3¢ do. Actual cost 5¢.

1919 — 5¢ set apart as carrying charge.

This leaves 10¢ of millers' 15¢ to go to farmer. . . .

Wagon load lots — how handled — C.W.B.

gives permit to Jones for certain exports.[9]

Unlike the present board which accepts delivery of wheat through its agents and incurs its own bank liability while carrying the wheat, the first board acted strictly as a custodian of funds, which it recovered from the trade on the basis of the net differences between the board's initial advance and its various selling prices, and which, in turn, it paid out in participation payments.

Foster's reference to the dealers' and millers' payments of 15 cents per bushel to the board had to do with the domestic price maintained for wheat at $2.30 per bushel, including carrying charges from August 26 until December 27, 1919, when it was raised to $2.80. The board also controlled domestic flour and millfeed prices, consistent with its wheat prices to the mills.

Initial payments were determined for Ontario, Quebec and British Columbia wheat as well as for wheat grown in the prairie provinces. The rates of carrying charges referred to by Foster were also set by regulation of the board, and were paid to the handling companies out of board receipts (which method obviated the cumbersome system of recovering carrying charges employed by the board of grain supervisors at American insistence).

THE BOARD'S EXPORT SALES POLICY

Although the board undertook to stabilize domestic wheat and flour prices,

[9]*Foster Papers.*

it raised them substantially after export prices had risen. It is primarily to its sales efforts abroad, however, that one must look for the first illustration of a board selling to best advantage.

Among the Foster papers is to be found a sheaf of telegrams which reveals how Stewart insisted upon implementing his instructions to sell to best advantage in the face of Harris's endeavors in London and Paris to sell the whole of the 1919 exportable surplus at fixed prices.

It will be recalled that in mid-July, 1919, the royal wheat commission rejected, out of hand, Borden's request that they bid on 50 to 75 million bushels at a fixed price or at a price to be based later on the price to be paid in the United States. Only a few weeks elapsed however before the commission came into the market. Foster recorded in his diary on August 2 that "there is an offer in prospect for our surplus wheat, or a portion". Mr. Lloyd Harris, who headed the Canadian trade mission in London, pursued negotiations (undertaken unsuccessfully in the first instance by Sifton and Robertson) with the royal commission, and cabled the prime minister on August 2, 1919:

> Confidential. Your cable 2nd received on return from Paris. Have been working on disposal exportable surplus 1919 crop and believe can now arrange disposal of entire surplus at fixed prices. This would necessitate government fixing price but presume this would be satisfactory. Important conference on Tuesday when matter will be discussed and perhaps settled. Important reply immediately.

Borden replied to Harris on August 3:

> Confidential. Your cable yesterday reached me this afternoon. Have conference on Tuesday when matter will be discussed and perhaps settled. Council tomorrow and telegraph you more fully. Meantime your proposal seems quite satisfactory, subject to following considerations: First. Our farmers would expect same price as United States farmers. Second. It is highly important that we should sell as far as possible to countries that can pay in real money and will not require credits. I should be glad to have a message as early as possible tomorrow giving any available information on these two points.[10]

With the prospect of a sale at hand, Foster asked for advice from his board chairman, and Stewart replied by drawing the minister's attention to the small prospective crop and to his belief that it would now be safe for the government to fix the initial advance at last year's price of $2.24½. The board could probably sell a fair sized block even up to 50 percent of the surplus to neutral countries at that price, but he thought it unwise to sell too much because, if prices in the United States were to go up, Canadian farmers were entitled to expect that part of their crop should also be sold at higher prices. Foster's telegram of August 3, to Stewart in Winnipeg, read as follows:

> Confidential. Harris believes possible arrange prices surplus wheat 1919 last year's fixed prices. Conference Tuesday, London. Would this work in with our scheme or necessitate fixed price? Wire views tomorrow. . . .

Stewart replied to Foster by telegram on August 4:

> Unfortunately crop prospects seem very materially reduced even during last fortnight and government might not be taking very great risk fix minimum at

10*Ibid.*

last year's price. Fair sized block could then possibly be disposed of or thereabouts in lieu of tonnage to avoid possible congestion at seaboard during fall and early winter months. It should be possible dispose about fifty per cent of surplus for cash to neutral countries and if prices in United States did remain high an unfavorable impression might be created among our producers if we did not also have something sold around corresponding level. However, if surplus sold now price would have to be fixed but present scheme of handling excepting the rebating of any difference to the producers would be applicable and would generally be much more simple for Board.[11]

Thus from the outset of his sales responsibility, Stewart took a constructive view of the market, which contrasted with that of the royal commission. On August 5, however, Harris transmitted the first firm offer that season from the royal commission and addressed it to the prime minister:

Sifton and I had conference Royal Wheat Commission today in order to make necessary shipping arrangements immediately for moving during open navigation. They now offer as follows: First. To contract for 1,000,000 Tons wheat. Second. Price to be definitely fixed when United States export price is fixed and to be on same basis, but in no event to be higher than last year's Canadian fixed price of two dollars 24 and half cents. Third. To pay Canadian minimum price of one dollar 75 cents against shipping documents and balance when U.S. export price is fixed definitely. Fourth. Price to be paid based on number on Northern Fort William and all customary charges free on board to be added. Relative price for lower grades. Fifth. To receive proper proportion of each grade according to crop yield. Sixth. Option to defer payments six months on 500,000 tons. Seventh. Expressing opinion would require probably entire available surplus if prices not excessive and finance can be arranged.

Harris followed up his first cable of August 5 by a second, explanatory message on the same date:

For Prime Minister. Telegraphing you today offer made by Royal Wheat Commission. Situation here is that government is uncertain as to United States action reference their Wheat arrangements. They are under the impression that United States may be forced reduce price of wheat in United States on account of internal situation and if this is done it will result in lower price than United States fixed price for export. They have expressed themselves as wanting entire Canadian surplus and as it is necessary to immediately arrange for shipping are anxious to have preliminary arrangement made whereby shipping could be arranged. It is very important from Canadian standpoint that we meet them in every way possible as if shipping is withdrawn from Canada for movement of our crop there would be great difficulty in handling same. They express opinion that in the event of United States lowering their fixed price to the consumer, the British government should not be expected to pay difference between the fixed price and lower price to the Canadian farmer who we think you will agree we cannot criticize. In order to prepare for movement of crop their offer has been made and they are unwilling to agree to pay higher price than American fixed price. You state your telegram of third that our farmers would expect same price as U.S. farmers but if U.S. only sell below their fixed price, their Government would pay difference while we cannot expect the British government to pay difference. Matter has been complicated by minimum price fixed by Canada

[11]*Ibid.*

but we think such an arrangement as they suggest would eventually give us the American fixed price for the Canadian farmers as personally we do not think U.S. will fix lower price for export. Reference Greek contract they now advise they will require a maximum amount of 32,500 tons monthly but are anxious to know something about probable prices. Would it be satisfactory arrangement with Greece that the maximum they would have to pay would be basis for last year's Canadian fixed price and give them an undertaking that in the event of price being reduced for export we will pay difference. They are very anxious about situation and to have some definite idea. Have negotiations with Belgians and they want 40,000 tons wheat per month for six months total 240,000 tons for which they can pay cash and we think could arrange to sell this quantity on condition that they take in addition flour to value of $10,000,000 which they wish to purchase under Canada credit authorized. France has advised it would not purchase cattle for $10,000,000 under the credit arrangement and as Belgium has right to purchase $5,000,000 foodstuffs under her credit I think it would be in order to allow her to purchase extra quantity making $10,000,000 in all. Without having a price it is difficult to close such a contract and would like to suggest to Belgium that they pay last year's fixed price for wheat and in the event of there being a reduction later in export price we will refund them difference. Belgians here tomorrow and important that we should have something definite as to your views.[12]

On August 6, the United States wheat director, Julius Barnes, cleared up the question of the United States price level by announcing the grain corporation's buying price of $2.26 per bushel. Harris's cables reflected the common misconception that the Canadian wheat board's initial advance had been set at $1.75. The prime minister expressed concern about this, and asked that Harris and Stewart communicate with each other directly. Borden's cable of August 16 to Harris read as follows:

Your telegrams 523 and 529 received through Canada Trade Board. Both messages together with this reply have been telegraphed to James Stewart, chairman of Canadian Wheat Board, at Winnipeg. He has been asked to communicate with you direct. That Board has complete direction of disposal of our wheat surplus. We cannot understand your reference to the fixing of a minimum price by Canadian government. Apparently you have been misled by unauthorized announcements in press. My telegram of August 1st clearly stated that the proposed advance payment was on account and that farmers would fully participate in price finally obtained for wheat in world's market. No price has been fixed by the Canadian government at present time. The amount of payment on account has not yet been fixed but will be determined as soon as possible upon the recommendation of the Canadian Wheat Board. We think the sales to Greece out of 1919 crop, and the proposed sales to Belgium, should be carried out by the Canadian Wheat Board, to whom all relevant documents are being transmitted today. We hope you will communicate direct with Stewart and that you will use every possible effort to secure tonnage.[13]

Foster wired Stewart that he was sending three coded telegrams from Harris through the Winnipeg military authorities, the first two of which were the telegrams quoted immediately above. The third telegram is not on the departmental file, but its substance was summarized in Stewart's report

[12]*Ibid.*
[13]*Ibid.*

and it stressed the fixed price basis, subject to adjustment, on which Harris was concerned that the Canadian government should negotiate:

August 7th. In order to keep purchasers interested ... definite contract is possible for their supply at last year's fixed price with an understanding to refund any difference between such price which may eventually be definitely fixed by American Government for export. ... are in market for further quantities but have considerably lower quotations for Australian wheat. ... here and they would contract I think on basis of paying last year's Canadian fixed price if we agree to refund any difference should American export price be lowered later. ....[14]

Because of his own assessment of the market, Stewart did not accept Harris's recommendation, although Borden's cablegram of August 3 to Harris, and Foster's telegram of the same date to Stewart, implied that the government would have been prepared to accept. Stewart sent a telegram to Foster on August 9:

Have cabled Harris along lines indicated to you suggesting tentative offer of certain proportion of our wheat in lieu of tonnage minimum to be three million bushels monthly. Price indicated by him seems low. Have proposed we take risk of market not declining and in lieu of their sending tonnage to Canada we are prepared fix a reasonable maximum. Will be glad to send copy of my cable if sufficiently interested.[15]

Negotiations continued between Stewart and the royal commission through Harris and by August 28, Stewart reported to Foster sales of 19,000,000 bushels to Britain and 4,750,000 bushels to Greece. The price on the British contract was $2.44 f.o.b. Montreal, or $2.36 in store Fort William. Foster recorded the transaction in his diary:

Ottawa, August 28, 1919: Have conference with Stewart re Wheat Board's work. Sales slow — about 24 million bushels to G.B. and Greece, $2.44 Montreal, $2.36 F.W. All arrangements perfected west of Lakes. In U.S. cost of living legislation to the front. Barnes has been selling wheat to Belgians under U.S. fixed price. What is done on H.C.L. may affect U.S. wheat price fixed. The exchange situation is affecting U.S. exports and all the trouble is not with G.B. and Allies.

The $2.36 received on the first sale, basis Fort William, compared favorably with the earlier price proposals based on the previous year's $2.24½, subject to adjustment to the board's initial advance ($2.15) or to the U.S. price ($2.26), whichever turned out to be lower. As Stewart noted later in his published report, this "first sale made by the Board represented the lowest price at which any of our wheat was sold during the year". Stewart also mentioned in his report that the tone of the cables from Harris continued to be depressing, primarily because Australia and the United States were underquoting Canadian prices. Nevertheless, he persisted in maintaining a constructive view of the market and, as he entered into negotiations through Harris with other governments, he raised his offering prices. This was consistent with his mandate to sell to best advantage, but it was very upsetting to Harris who protested against the new price policy. He had been accustomed to negotiating on the basis of prices fixed by the board

[14]The Canadian Wheat Board, *Chairman's Report*, (Winnipeg, January 28, 1921), p. 13.

[15]*Foster Papers.*

of grain supervisors, and he wanted the new board's price to be constant so that when other governments came into the market they could buy from Canada at the same price as had been initially negotiated with the British. A feud developed between Stewart and Harris which is highlighted by the following cables which Harris despatched to the department of trade and commerce:

M-657. September 5th. For Prime Minister.
Am much perturbed as to the policy being adopted in selling exportable surplus wheat. After negotiations with Royal Wheat Commission extending over month have finally closed contract with them to take 500,000 tons at $2.44 F.O.B.seaboard. Prices quoted Belgium F.O.B. seaboard is $2.47 and other prices quoted for European Government purchases are as high as $2.55. Greek contract calls for market prices and suggestion is to ask them $2.50 F.O.B. seaboard. Discussed matter with Maclean before his departure and he feels as I do that inasmuch as these are all Government purchases the price will be made public and if not uniform impression will be unfavourable. I have asked Stewart, Chairman, Canadian Wheat Board, to discuss matter of policy with Government. Think that you will realize effect such policy may have. Personally do not wish to conduct further negotiations unless government policy is for uniform price. Great Britain will purchase flour from outside to extent of 40,000 tons monthly and we should get bulk of this if competitive price quoted. Lowest price quoted by Canadian Wheat Board is $12.00 per barrel which will not secure this business.

M-728. September 26th. M-717, Belgium has confirmed purchase 200,000 tons wheat but have deferred their decision with reference to meat. Negotiations pending between Belgium and British Government to have British purchase meat for Belgium. If this arrangement made will be able to I think arrange for meat purchases. My reference to plan proposed of being held up by Canada referred to wheat quotations not meat. Will telegraph quoting particulars of wheat negotiations to Prime Minister showing position which is entirely untenable.

Prime Minister, September 27. Refer my M-657, September 6th, which remains unanswered. Present situation connection negotiations account wheat Board as follows. We closed with British Government for five hundred thousand tons wheat at two forty-four f.o.b. Montreal, for which they had arranged tonnage. French Government then asked British Government to purchase one hundred forty thousand tons for Spain. French officials then approached me requesting privilege of using credit granted by Canada to France to pay for same. Amount involved would be approximately fourteen million dollars. In order save use of Canadian credits I then negotiated with Hudson Bay Company and finally arranged with them to finance purchase on behalf French Government for fifty thousand tons, this taking care of one-third amount of French requirements, for cash. For balance one hundred thousand tons French applied for right to use Canadian credit as under their agreement they are permitted to use ten million dollars for purchase cattle and food stuffs. Matter submitted to Ottawa and Wheat Board advised me credit would be granted on condition France purchases two-thirds of one hundred thousand tons in flour and one-third in wheat. Submitted this proposal to French was advised on account of their political and economic situation they cannot do this, but intimated they might arrange take one-third flour and two-thirds wheat. Wheat Board now advise they insist on French taking two-thirds flour and quote two fifty for wheat, as against British price two forty-four. Italians also asked British Government purchase in Canada one hundred and fifty thousand tons wheat and then approached me for Canadian credit which I advised them we cannot do. After further negotiations I have been able to arrange with them to use credits they have established in United States and now agree to purchase one hundred and fifty thousand tons Canadian wheat and pay in New York funds. They have depended on securing this quantity from Canada and have made arrangements for necessary tonnage to take delivery October and November but Wheat Board now advise price to Italians is two fifty and will not agree to Italians receiving benefit of exchange on New York funds, which would increase their price by eight to ten cents. Some weeks ago I quoted Belgians for two hundred thousand tons wheat two forty-seven, payable cash, which was authorized by Wheat Board. This offer now accepted by Belgians and contract closed at price stated. Greek contract for wheat you are familiar with. This contract was made last May and is for their entire requirements until July 1st next, and as there was no price fixed at that date, they agreed to pay ruling market price and are taking their shipments monthly and paying cash. Am now authorized quote price two forty-seven which should be satisfactory and hope to close this basis. We have negotiations pending for small quantity wheat for Poland for which cash payments would be arranged and Wheat Board quote two fifty-five. You will see Canada's position as Governments with whom we are dealing recognize only Canadian Government in these negotiations and for this reason think your Government should decide policy. No criticism can be made on any price we may desire to make to Great Britain and their price need not be basis for other countries. For sales to other Governments, however, Canada's policy should be equal treatment for all on wheat and flour. I have not suggested what uniform price should be but cannot see just reason why price to France, Italy, Poland should exceed price to Belgium and Greece, as, when dealing with Governments, all information is made public and prices and details of such transactions are known to everybody. Such discrimination untenable. Answering my repeated requests for uniformity in price, Stewart cabled September 25th as follows. Begins. We are charged by Government to dispose of crop to best advantage. They have not attempted in any way to influence our actions and our understanding was such, when we accepted our positions. At this stage we don't propose invite them to change this principle. Ends. If Wheat Board insists on discrimination I cannot continue to act for them, as I consider policy wrong and will go far to destroy Canada's reputation and impair results of work we have been carrying on in establishing trade relations and confidence with various Governments. Am advising Wheat Board this effect. In meantime negotiations with France and Italy at standstill and they are depending on securing portion their supplies from Canada. As negotiations have been pending for thirty days, while price continued to advance, it may be that we can squeeze price from them but with disastrous results for future relations. You will appreciate my attitude is based entirely on my desire to serve best interests Canada and will appreciate immediate reply.[16]

It would not be too difficult to infer from the telegrams that Harris had resented being told to deal directly with Stewart rather than with the prime minister. When he fell out with Stewart and appealed to the prime minister, Foster publicly supported Stewart. In response to Harris's representation that other governments recognized only the Canadian government in the

[16]*Ibid.*

negotiations and thought that the government should decide policy, Foster came down firmly on the side of Stewart by declaring in the house that "if representations are made to the government, they will be submitted to the Canada wheat board, by whom they will be considered" [17] Whether this directly prompted his departure, or not, Harris left London later in October to return to private business in Canada. On December 3 he met with the prime minister and several members of the cabinet to present a memorandum on the future of the trade mission in London, and recommended to a government already overburdened financially a large revolving credit to facilitate sales to other governments. Foster wrote in his diary:

> Ottawa, December 5, 1919: We had Harris verbal report hazy — optimistic — indefinite — in part absurd. The Mission is practically closed in London. We seem to be getting nowhere as to substitute. Meanwhile exchange conditions growing worse. The embargo off in U.S. may help our coal dealings and our price if wheat goes there — but if they take only wheat and no flour, what of our mills and our feeds for stock?

As for his feud with the wheat board, Harris remained implacable and he expressed his views in public. Remarks in Hamilton attributed to him were read into Hansard several months later during the debate on the wheat board resolution by Mr. P. F. Casgrain:

> Mr. Harris alluded to the Board of Commerce being appointed to check profiteering, and stated that while it was at this duty, the Wheat Board was profiteering to "beat the band." If he were allowed to control the entire steel output of Canada he could make all kinds of money, and the situation regarding wheat was like this. The board made wheat prices that were a crime. [18]

With Harris's departure from London, Stewart sent Mr. Sanford Evans there as representative of the board, primarily to negotiate flour sales, but also to keep the board informed on other conditions in Europe. As for Stewart, (the man engaged by the royal commission as its Winnipeg buyer, who had precipitated the termination of futures trading May, 1917, and who continued as buyer for the commission until May, 1919), he had transferred his responsibilities from buying to selling. In his new role, his intimate knowledge of the market mentality and methods of the British buyers stood him in good stead. When ministers appeared ready to accept the British offer of August 2 to buy the 1919 surplus on the previous year's price basis of $2.24½, subject to downward adjustment, Stewart demurred. Had the British made their offer two weeks earlier they could, by hindsight, have allayed the Canadian government's concern over financing the movement of the unsold crop, covered their requirements more cheaply and removed the justification for the wheat board. As chairman of the new board, Stewart proved to be an astute salesman. His success was recorded in one of Foster's pencilled memoranda:

---

[17] *House of Commons Debates,* October 9, 1919, p. 915.
[18] *Ibid.,* June 24, 1920, p. 4129.

Sold for delivery prior to December 1:

(U.K.	19,000,000 bushels	
(Belgium	2,250,000 bushels	
(Greece	4,750,000 bushels	26,000,000
	26,000,000	
(Switzerland	4,500,000 bushels	
(France plus		
(Italy	11,250,000 bushels	15,750,000
	15,750,000	
(Belgium	5,250,000 bushels	
(Greece	5,000,000 bushels	
(Near boundary		
wagon lots	4,000,000 bushels	14,250,000
	14,250,000	
(Switzerland	4,500,000 bushels	4,500,000
		60,500,000
U.K. Flour	10/15,000,000 bushels	10/15,000,000
Total:		70/75,000,000 bushels
Surplus for export		100/110,000,000 bushels

40% absolutely sold.
30% will be signed in a month.
All European countries controlled by government;
none but U.K. and Germany want flour.
France and Belgium may take some.[19]

PARTICIPATION CERTIFICATES

By December, Stewart's sales effort had been largely accomplished and the prices he obtained enabled the board to make an interim payment of 30 cents per bushel on the participation certificates on July 9, 1920, and eventually a final payment of 18 cents on November 4 of that year, which brought the full redemption value of the certificates to 48 cents and the total net pooled return to $2.63, basis No. 1 Northern Fort William.

Because of their inexperience with participation certificates, many producers sold them early and at very low value. By hindsight, the government had erred in making the participation certificates transferable. To discourage their sale, Foster pleaded with producers not to dispose of them as he expounded at some length over the misconception that surrounded them. In the course of his speech (already quoted from) on second reading of the wheat board bill, Foster said:

There was a lot of misconception — I am not going to call it by a harsher name — I might say that it was misrepresentation — of the Government's position in reference to this matter. In the first place it was stated, and held to with the most wonderful tenacity that I ever experienced in this country, that the Government had fixed a price of $1.75 and that that was all they were going to pay or that was going to be allowed to be paid to the Canadian farmer. That all existed in the fertile, and not innocuous, imagination of some people who wanted that argument in order to use it to the detriment of somebody or of some Government. That is the only remark that I am going to

[19] *Foster Papers.*

make in regard to the matter. Neither by myself, by any member of the Government or by the Government as a whole, was there any decision or supposition or suggestion as to the fixing of a price of $1.75. Yet that has been made to do duty against the system which has been brought in by the Government, and to this day it is held more or less firmly by quite too many of the people of this country.

Then again, when the price was fixed, it was not a price fixed by the Government itself. It was a price which was fixed as the initial payment by the Canadian Wheat Board. I want to correct the misrepresentations which are abroad in reference to the relations between the Government and the old Board of Supervisors of last year and the preceding year and the present Canada Wheat Board. When the Government placed in the hands of the Board of Grain Supervisors in 1917 and 1918 the management of the marketing of the grain of Canada it left it with these gentlemen and it did not interfere with what they did. In the same way in relation to the Canada Wheat Board, the Government tried to get the best representative men that it could, and having got that board it leaves the matter in their hands and it does not interfere with what they do.

If representations are made to the Government, they will be submitted to the Canada Wheat Board, by whom they will be considered. The millers, the producers, the consumers and the varied interests are all represented on that board, and I do not think that its capacity or calibre has been adversely criticised with any success; nor indeed has it been largely criticised in any event. The board having once been appointed, comprised of practical men, the Government leaves them unhampered to do the work that has been entrusted to them and for the performance of which they are empowered. Now, the board took the situation into retrospective consideration, and they decided that the initial payment should be $2.15. But, as a matter of fact, this had to be approved by council, and council did approve of it immediately, as the recommendation of the board's mature consideration. In regard to the criticism that is made against that action, I think it is well that I should say something. The general trend of criticism is to this effect: "You have your $2.15, which is all you will get." I may mention just what the scheme is. The Board of Wheat Commissioners shall market the whole crop at the best possible advantage, shall pay the costs, and return shall be made, upon the basis of the quantity which each producer has sold, of any amount in excess of the $2.15 paid initially. The general trend of the criticism, as I say, is to induce the farmers to believe that they will get the $2.15, or the proportional amount wherever they have their grain, and no more. The contention is: "It will all be squandered and nothing will be left." There are participation certificates that every purchaser gets which entitle him to his proportionate return from the pool — his return proportionate to the quantity of grain that is sold. These certificates are negotiable and the farmer may sell them; and the whole force of such criticism, wherever it originates, tends to confirm in the farmer's mind the idea that he has all that he will get. Probably he lends a too-willing ear to the broker or the buyer who says to him: "You have your participation certificate for which you will never get much; but I am prepared to pay you a certain sum for it and will take my chances of loss". Now, it is but human nature that if that impression is forced upon the farmer, that he is not likely to get anything more, he will take what is offered to him by the broker or dealer and consequently part with his certificate. I would advise farmers to hold their participation certificates. Taking my view from the amount of grain that has already been marketed and the prospects for marketing all the rest of it, I would urge upon the farmer the importance of retaining the certificate and would counsel him not to part with it for a song. It will be a substantial advantage to him. No one can tell exactly how much the advantage will be, but looking at the matter in the light of present experience, the advantage will be considerable. I merely mention this as a sort of caution or warning in this respect; for undoubtedly I do not think that any man is doing the most good to the farmer in disseminating the idea that he is not going to derive any greater advantage than the initial payment of $2.15.[20]

In further discouragement of sale of participation certificates, the board announced on May 5, 1920, that the value of the certificates would be not less than 40 cents per bushel. Related to the undervaluation of the certificates was the sale by farmers adjacent to the border of their wheat to United States elevators, to which they were permitted to haul by the wagon load. The United States embargo was applicable only to rail and water shipment. By hauling their wheat across the border, Canadian farmers received prices which reflected premiums for wheat of high milling quality, and which were considerably above the spread of 11 cents between the Canadian initial advance and the American minimum-guaranteed price. Although the United States withdrew its embargo in December, 1919, it was not until May, 1920, that Canadian wheat moved through American ports.

CHAIRMAN'S REPORT

After the end of the 1919-1920 crop year, the Canadian Wheat Board remained in existence only long enough to wind up its affairs in respect of the handling of the 1919 wheat crop, whereupon Mr. Stewart returned to private business. Before doing so, he submitted a report on January 21, 1921 to Sir George Foster which described the board's operations. An interesting feature was that it was styled the "Chairman's Report" and bore Mr. Stewart's signature only.[21] Magill had set an example in this regard, but Stewart explained that although he consulted the other board members frequently on policy matters, several were active in the grain business for which reason he treated the day-to-day sales and pricing decisions as his confidential prerogative. For the same reason the concurrence in the report of the other board members, who had served in an advisory capacity, had not been sought.

The report gives a very concise summary of the circumstances leading up to the board's creation and it stresses the representative character of its membership. It gives a good account of the organizational period and states that in carrying out the government's instructions under the plan, the board had to blaze a new trail. Stewart attributed the concept of the plan to experiments being tried in Australia. No mention was made of his fellow board member, Mr. C. B. Watts, who had been the protagonist of the plan in Canada. Without mentioning Barnes as the source, Stewart reported that "some of the ablest men in the North American grain trade considered the plan as too 'communistic' and doomed to failure".

With regard to the board's sale policy, Mr. Stewart said that "the Chairman was entrusted with the responsibility of selling the crop, and his

---

[20] *House of Commons Debates,* October 9, 1919, pp. 914-915.

[21] The Canadian Wheat Board, *Chairman's Report,* Winnipeg, 1921. For ease of reference, the report is reproduced in Appendix 2.

relations with his fellow members were necessarily somewhat modified by the secrecy which had to be maintained in connection with the various transactions of the year's business."[22]

Because of the shortage of high-quality milling wheat in the United States, Stewart was able to obtain substantial premiums for the top grades of Canadian wheat in the European markets. In order to check on prices currently paid for premium wheats by the Minneapolis mills he kept one or two cars en route constantly to Minneapolis where their daily sales kept him informed on premiums actually paid. The volume was kept to a minimum lest it weaken the market. Stewart used the Minneapolis premiums in his negotiations with overseas buyers. This was one of the ways in which he sought to obtain the best prices available, and it contributed to the ultimate payment of 48 cents per bushel on the participation certificates.

The only financial statement provided at the end of the chairman's report was that of the board's assets and liabilities as of December 31, 1920, which disclosed a residual sum still payable on outstanding participation certificates. Neither in the text nor in the financial statement was there any indication of the amount of wheat purchased from producers and resold by the board or of other relevant detail.

Shortly after the chairman's report was submitted to Foster, the latter had it reproduced as a sessional paper entitled the *Report of the Canadian Wheat Board* which he tabled in the house on February 21, 1921.[23] Although the new title implied that it was the report of the full board, the text was that of the chairman's report with one notable addition, which was the inclusion on the last page of a statement of the board's much more revealing summary of its profit and loss account. Here it was shown that after deducting administrative expenses, the board realized a net profit of $65,552,700.30 on the 135,652,094 bushels it sold on behalf of producers. This yielded the 48 cent payment on the participation certificates, in addition to the $2.15 initial advance.

Following is the one-page statement as it appeared at the end of the report. The fact that this was just the summary of a longer and more detailed statement is evidenced by its references to preceding pages:

CANADIAN WHEAT BOARD[24]

PROFIT AND LOSS ACCOUNT
From Inception of Board to December 31, 1920.

By profit on wheat transactions, per page 4			$59,665,852.58
By profit on flour transactions, per page 5			6,277,048.80
By license fees			1,092.50
By interest received on investments and bank deposits			349,214.16
			$66,293,208.04
To bank exchange		$102,592.67	
To Administration costs —			
General Executive	$218,977.78		
Comptroller	119,316.30		
Registration	67,395.34		
Payment of certificates	174,433.88		
Assessments	37,708.70		
Carrying charges and statistics	20,083.07	637,915.07	740,507.74

[22] *Ibid.*, p. 6.
[23] *Report of the Canadian Wheat Board*, 11 George V, Sessional Paper No. 54, A 1921.
[24] *Ibid.*, p. 16.

Balance, being net profit on operations to December 31, 1920 .... 65,552,700.30
From which there has been appropriated under Regulations Nos.
119 and 127, 48 cents per bushel on 135,652,094 bushels,
12 lb.................... 65,113,005.22

December 31, 1920. Balance at credit Profit and Loss Account $439,695.08

WHEAT DEPARTMENT

TRADING AND PROFIT AND LOSS ACCOUNT

From Inception of Board to December 31, 1920.

	Bush.	Lb	
By sales..	71,706,856	22	$203,326,794.31
By Assessments collected......................	....	...	24,227,106.38
			$227,553,900.69
To purchases, including freight, storage, insurance, etc.............................	71,706,856	22	$164,014,834.97
To Carrying charges per regulations..			3,868,442.64
To Diversion charges...			96,348.72
			167,979,626.33
Trading profit...			$ 59,574,274.36
By interest on loans to Flour Department, less bank interest paid			$ 218,623.90
			$ 59,792,898.26
To Administration costs, including salaries, rentals, telegraph and telephones, travelling expense, postage, printing, stationery, etc			127,045.68
Net profit on wheat transactions..........................			$ 59,665,852.58

FLOUR DEPARTMENT

TRADING AND PROFIT AND LOSS ACCOUNT
From Inception of Board to December 31, 1920

By Sales (sacks, all sizes, 5,047,016)...	$47,419,991.43
By Export license fees..	105,863.52
	$47,525,854.95
To purchases, including freight, storage, insurance, etc. (sacks, all sizes, 5,047,016)........................	40,745,393.80
Trading profit	$6,780,461.15
To interest on loans from Bank and Wheat Department........................	$411,819.05
To Administration costs, including salaries, rentals, telegraphs and telephones, travelling expense, postage, printing, stationery, etc...................................	91,593.30
	503,412.35
Net profit on flour transactions................................	$6,277,048.80

Before the board's financial report had been completed, the leader of the opposition, Mr. W. L. Mackenzie King had drawn attention to the need for such an accounting when the wheat board legislation was introduced in the house a short time before parliament prorogued on June 30, 1920. Foster explained then that the financial operations of the board were being internally audited, and that they would be subsequently examined by a government auditor.[25] It is a matter of some surprise that such little publicity was given either by Stewart or Foster to the board's complete

[25]*House of Commons Debates,* June 24, 1920, pp. 4101, 4103.

financial statement. Stewart had omitted it from his report, and Foster released only the summary profit and loss statement. A more widespread distribution of the financial results would have helped to allay the misgivings of many producers that the marketing of their produce had been taken out of their hands to the benefit of parties other than themselves. The gap between prices available on either side of the border lent credence to their belief.

Mr. Robert Whiteside of Dunblane, Saskatchewan, articulated these misgivings in a lengthy exchange of correspondence with Sir George Foster extending over a period from January 19, 1920, to July 25, 1921. Whiteside declared that "every farmer in Western Canada is under the impression that our Federal Government premeditated and entered into an agreement to handle the wheat crop to make gains for themselves at our expense."[26] The charge was levelled at both the operations of the board of grain supervisors and the Canadian wheat board. Foster's earlier replies to Whiteside defended the two boards on principle, which failed to satisfy his correspondent. When Whiteside persisted with his questions, Foster give him short shrift, completely ignoring the opportunity to send him the financial facts.

The issue festered in Whiteside's mind for a good many years and he raised it again with the Honourable H. H. Stevens after the latter had become minister of trade and commerce in the Bennett administration. As a result, Stevens had the Whiteside charges referred to the house committee on agriculture and colonization in the spring of 1931. The whole of the Whiteside-Foster correspondence was referred to the committee, published in its proceedings, and Whiteside was called as a witness.[27]

During the course of the committee hearings, Stevens produced a great deal of material from departmental files including an unpublished auditor's statement of the receipts and expenditures of the board of grain supervisors, but even then the board's already published summary financial statement was not submitted. In the end, Whiteside was convinced that there had been no malfeasance and the committee reported its findings to the house as follows:

1. That the Board of Grain Supervisors and the Wheat Board discharged their respective duties in a highly commendable manner, and no criticism of their action is warranted.

2. That no evidence was adduced to substantiate the complaints and charges contained in the letters of Mr. Robert Whiteside (Returns Nos. 247 and 247A) referred to in the Order of Reference, or made to the Committee by him in person, appearing as a witness, and that the said complaints or charges were fully, and completely disproved by the evidence adduced.[28]

---

[26]House of Commons Select Standing Committee on Agriculture and Colonization, *Minutes of Proceedings and Evidence,* May 28, 1931, p. iv.

[27]*Ibid.,* pp. iv-xvi.

[28]*Ibid.,* June 23, 1931, p. 53.

8

END OF THE WHEAT BOARD

In the autumn of 1919 the government introduced two brief bills to provide specific legislative authority for the board of grain supervisors and the Canadian wheat board. Until then the two boards had existed by authority of the war measures act. The bill relating to the board of grain supervisors sought continuation of the orders in council under which it operated as long as necessary to wind up its affairs, including final disposition of the carrying charge fund. By that time, the Canadian wheat board was in full operation and the second bill sought legislative authority of limited duration for the powers which had been established initially by order in council. The two bills received royal assent on November 10, 1919.[1] It was on second reading of the wheat board bill that Foster made his great speech, already referred to, defending the government's policy. In that speech, Foster categorically declared that the board was a temporary expedient; in his opinion the board's operations would be completed within a year:

> But the question is asked: Is this to be a permanent system? My answer to that is an emphatic no. It is not a system that the Government coveted to have. A tremendous amount of difficulty, of criticism, and of bad feeling is inevitably aroused when a government takes hold of a thing of this kind and carries it through. No government courts a proceeding of that kind; and it was only the force of circumstances, and their conviction that nothing else could be done to save the situation well, that induced the Government to take the system of supervision and control this year. It is not the intention to make it permanent. We believe that this year is the last year during which the same system of government control will be carried out in the same way.[2]

CANADIAN WHEAT BOARD ACT, 1920

In 1920, when he was acting prime minister, Foster introduced a bill just two weeks before prorogation of parliament, to provide authority to the government to continue the board in operation, but only upon proclamation. The bill was intended to provide desirable latitude in event of an emergency. Once again, Foster emphasized that it was not the government's intention to proclaim the act unless the situation were to change in a way that would render its proclamation necessary. A terminal date of August 15, 1921, was specified in the act.

[1] *Statutes of Canada*, 10 George V, 1919, Chaps. 5 and 9.
[2] *House of Commons Debates*, October 9, 1919, p. 916.

Debate on the bill at the resolution stage and on second reading extended over the course of two days' sessions. Members who had strong feelings for or against the board and, in particular, against the socialistic implication of its prolonged continuation, broke party lines in expressing their convictions. For example, Mr. H. H. Stevens, a government supporter, said he would oppose the bill and he was supported by some of the eastern Conservatives. The leader of the opposition, Mr. King, did not oppose the resolution, but raised several housekeeping points for the government's consideration, including the issue of a report by the board. King was also the first member to query the constitutionality of the legislation, and suggested that the government look into it. It was a latent issue which would occupy centre stage in another two years. Mr. Meighen, who might have been expected to oppose the bill, had political motives attributed to his support. Mr. Crerar implied that the Conservative party was cultivating the farm vote it had lost on the tariff issue. It was left to Mr. Maharg to endorse the bill on behalf of the Canadian council of agriculture. Mr. Crerar was evidently not prepared to do this, because the council's official position was at variance with his own personal views. When needled by Meighen to declare his position, Crerar did so in dry humor, which left his own position unmistakably clear:

> Lest the very sensitive spirit of the Minister of the Interior (Mr. Meighen) be unduly exercised in regard to our attitude in this debate, I hasten to take some part. . . . I am of the opinion that no very great harm can be done through this measure. Rather let me state it this way; it may be a provision against conditions arising of which we have no inkling now, to leave this power in the hands of the Government for another year. Personally I am opposed entirely to any permanent policy that means the control of the marketing of grain in this country.[3]

One interesting facet of the debate was the explanation Meighen offered concerning the government's reimbursement of the trade for losses incurred as a result of the government's closure of the wheat futures market on July 29, 1919.[4] When actual losses were determined, the government had sought to have them paid out of the pooled funds of the board, and thereby paid by the producers. Meighen contended that the market had been closed in the interest of producers, and that costs related thereto were a fair charge on the producers' account. Stewart, however, had obtained legal opinion to the effect that the board had no authority to pay such costs, which were then met by the federal treasury. Meighen recommended that if the new act were proclaimed, it should be done before the market reopened and thereby no new losses incurred. Failing this, he had inserted a clause in the bill to provide for recovery of such losses from funds of the board.

Unquestionably, the government's most important disclosure during the debate was the Borden cable of July 14, 1919. Mr. James Robb had deduced from Magill's report to the exchange that the government had succeeded in making a bulk sale to the royal commission that July, from which he inferred that the government, having sold 50 to 75 million bushels short, had panicked over the price rise when futures trading was resumed and for

[3]*Ibid.*, June 24, 1920, pp. 4119-4120.
[4]*Ibid.*, June 28, 1920, pp. 4347.

that reason had ordered the market closed. To meet this allegation, Foster read into Hansard the prime minister's telegram and reported on the royal commission's desultory response.[5] The bill was then passed and received royal assent on July 1, 1920.[6]

Parliament prorogued July 1, and on July 10 the Honourable Arthur Meighen was sworn in as prime minister, replacing Sir Robert Borden, whose ill health had led to his resignation. In his new cabinet, Meighen retained Foster as minister of trade and commerce until the latter's appointment to the senate in 1921.

DECONTROL ANNOUNCEMENT

Because the house was prorogued, Foster issued a press release on July 16 announcing government policy respecting the 1920 crop. He reiterated the government's preference for a return to normal methods of marketing of grain; he noted that the factors which had prompted the government to close the market in 1919, namely, the concerted buying in Europe, the lack of credit facilities and the control of wheat marketing in the United States, "do not exist or are not in force to the same extent at the present time". Then he said:

> Under the circumstances above set forth, the Canadian government decided to take no steps at present to proclaim the enabling Act, which means the present Wheat Board will not function insofar as the wheat of the 1920 crop is concerned, and the marketing of this crop will revert to the usual and normal methods of prewar times.[7]

RESUMPTION OF PRIVATE TRADING

It is interesting to note that trading in wheat futures at Chicago had resumed on July 15, 1920, the day before the Canadian announcement. Congressional authority for grain corporation purchases of wheat and flour expired on June 1, 1920, whereupon the corporation wound up its operations. Following the Canadian announcement, the Winnipeg grain exchange prepared to resume wheat futures trading, which commenced on August 18, 1920, and continued until it was terminated, once again by government action, in 1943. Wheat futures trading at Chicago has been continuous since 1920. After the Winnipeg market opened, prices on the cash market ranged from $2.42½ to $2.45⅞ in August, 1920, and rose to a peak of $2.82½ in September of that year. Then a fairly steady erosion of prices set in to a low of $1.76⅞ in August, 1921, followed by another precipitous drop to a low of $1.11⅛ in December. Although there was some improvement in prices in the spring of 1922, prices ended the year with a December range of $1.08 to $1.11, and by December, 1923, they had fallen to 93¼¢.[8]

Throughout the price erosion, producers and their representatives urgently petitioned for reinstatement of the Canadian wheat board. For example, in 1920, the Saskatchewan association of rural municipalities had

[5]*Ibid.*, p. 4348.

[6]*The Canadian Wheat Board Act*, Statutes of Canada, 10-11 George V, Chap. 40, assented to 1st July, 1920.

[7]*Ottawa Citizen*, July 17, 1920.

[8]See Chart 8:1, end of this chapter.

each of its municipal organizations send a resolution to the minister of trade and commerce in the following form:

> Resolving that we do hereby petition the federal government to reinstate the Canada Wheat Board, with full powers as before, under the able chairmanship of James Stewart, Esq., with an advisory board.[9]

In the spring of 1920, before the board's operations were terminated, the royal commission actively bought wheat in order to build up a reserve against a coal strike which threatened to tie up transportation. Two years later, Crerar observed with perhaps more truth than charity:

> One fact that contributed more than anything else to the success of the Wheat Board in 1919, was the threatened coal strike in Great Britain in the summer of 1920, because it is a well known fact that the British Government at the time bought grain at every place which they could buy it, stored it in every warehouse in Great Britain and paid any price that was asked for it, in order that the United Kingdom might be provided with food reserves against a possible tie-up of transportation.[10]

But when futures trading was restored and Canadian export firms resumed their selling initiative, they found British buyers out of the market until after the close of navigation. As a proponent of the exchange, Magill dramatized this British absence from the market and also drew attention to the fact that in the transition from wheat board selling to the open market, no Canadian seller had authority to offer October futures and that thereby some markets were lost. He said:

> You remember when the market was open and when the British Commission was buying wheat enough to enable them to defy all exporting countries until Christmas, nobody in this country could offer them October wheat. The Wheat Board could not because it was tied by its law to the one year's crop, and our people could not because they were closed by law. The British Wheat Commission bought its supplies without us being able to give them a bit of October wheat. We opened the market and something struck us. There were people on this side who knew that the world's crops were not promising, but nobody knew how the British Government had bought to meet that situation, so far as I know. Whether our department or our Wheat Board knew it, we cannot tell. I do not think our authorities knew until it had been done. They had made themselves independent of our crop until Christmas, and something struck us. The people who bought our wheat were the United States, France and Italy, but our greatest purchaser, the United Kingdom, was not in our market, and did not come into our market for an appreciable volume of grain until after Christmas, just as they had stated. Cable after cable came across night after night to the effect that they were not interested in our offers. Our wheat began to go down immediately our mills were supplied, and you know the whole story.[11]

As Magill indicated, the Canadian trade uncovered an active demand for quality wheat by United States millers, and between September 1, 1920, and March 31, 1921, they sold over 42 million bushels of Canadian wheat to American mills. This heavy movement, in turn, drew protests from American farm interests. A 35-cent per bushel duty imposed by the Fordney

[9]*Trade and Commerce File 24181A.*
[10]*House of Commons Debates,* June 14, 1922, p. 2925.
[11]Select Standing Committee on Agriculture and Colonization, *Minutes of Proceedings and Evidence,* No. 7, April 25, 1922, p. 196.

emergency tariff act in May, 1921, put an effective end to that trade and depressed prices further. In the same year, the trade opened up another market in Japan, which had suffered a partial failure of its rice crop, and wheat was shipped through Vancouver to Japan for the first time. British European buyers were beginning to show interest also in west coast shipments via the Panama canal. Altogether, it was a good demonstration of the way in which the trade could operate to open up new markets.

CAMPAIGN TO REINSTATE THE WHEAT BOARD

Even before the price collapse, continuation of the wheat board's operations had won the preponderant support of farmers. On October 22, 1920, the Canadian council of agriculture passed a resolution urging reinstatement of the board. The council also established its own wheat markets committee to examine whether a co-operative wheat pool could be organized on a voluntary contract basis. Henry Wise Wood, president of the United farmers of Alberta, F. W. Riddell, general manager of the Saskatchewan Co-operative Elevator Company, who had served as assistant chairman of the Canadian wheat board, and J. R. Murray, assistant general manager of United Grain Growers Limited, (who served years later for a brief period as chief commissioner of the second wheat board), made up the committee.

While the wheat committee was getting its study under way, Premier W. M. Martin of Saskatchewan wrote to Messrs. Stewart and Riddell on March 19, 1921, submitting a list of eight exploratory questions on alternative methods for operating a wheat pool, on which he invited their view. On May 3, Stewart and Riddell replied by submitting a report which, because of its widespread interest, was given extensive circulation. Although Stewart and Riddell protested that they could only speculate on some of the hypothetical situations included in Premier Martin's eight questions, (which involved varying degrees of provincial participation and of voluntary or contractual participation by producers), they were prepared to speak with authority on the prospects of a national selling agency such as the wheat board, on which they had both served. They foresaw shortcomings in any provincial scheme which did not enjoy full monopoly control of all deliveries. They also considered that any contractual system would entail serious rigidities in administration. In their summary conclusion the authors stated:

> In the first place, we believe that the most perfect form of a centralized wheat marketing agency, at the present time, can be created only under the control of a national organization. And secondly, we believe that in considering any form of wheat marketing pool involving less than complete national control, one based upon voluntary cooperative effort on the part of producers is preferable to one bound by the provisions of legal contract.[12]

Notwithstanding this recommendation, the wheat markets committee drew up a pro forma wheat-marketing agreement which included a five-year contractual arrangement for the delivery of grain to a voluntary, co-operative and interprovincial pool functioning as the wheat board had done on the basis of initial advances, pooled sales returns, and participation

---

[12]James Stewart and F. W. Riddell, *Report to the Government of Saskatchewan on Wheat Marketing* (King's Printer, Regina, 1921), p. 20.

payments. Producers signing a contract would obligate themselves to deliver all their grain to the pool for the next five years. But any producer could choose whether to sign up, or remain out of the pool and, in that respect, the pool was voluntary. The plan was studied by producer organizations through the summer of 1921. By November, however, the committee reported little ground for hope of persuading 60 percent of producers to sign contracts, regarded as the minimum level of producer support required for successful operation. There was also some fear that producers who had signed up might be tempted to disregard their obligations if higher immediate cash returns were available elsewhere. More importantly, the venture required more working capital than was in sight to ensure adequate credit facilities from the banks. Thus the proposal stood in abeyance while the grain growers' organizations intensified their demand for reinstatement of the Canadian wheat board.

1921 ELECTION

During the election campaign of 1921, Prime Minister Meighen indicated that he was prepared to establish a government board to operate on a voluntary and non-contractual basis. His proposal had the identical features of one which had been submitted by the Canadian council of agriculture in 1918, and it would have afforded producers a choice between outright sale to the elevator companies at fluctuating prices or delivery to a pool offering an initial advance and a uniform final payment. The December 6 election returned 117 Liberals, 64 Progressives, 50 Conservatives, two Independent Labour, one Labour-Liberal and one Independent Liberal. The results left the Liberal party just short of a bare majority.

THE RIGHT HONOURABLE SIR GEORGE E. FOSTER, K.C.M.G.

When the 1921 election was called, the seventy-four year old Foster decided not to stand again, and he accepted an appointment from Meighen to the senate. At this point, an assessment of his role as a wheat policy maker seems appropriate. Born in New Brunswick in 1847, Foster began his career as a professor of classics at the University of New Brunswick. Then he was elected as a Conservative to the house of commons in 1882; appointed to Sir John A. Macdonald's cabinet in 1885, becoming minister of finance in 1888. He helped to bring the downfall of the Bowell cabinet in 1896 and, thereafter, except for one term, served in opposition as a financial critic of the Laurier administration. With the election of the Borden government in 1911, he was appointed minister of trade and commerce, proved to be an ourstanding member of the cabinet, and was eventually appointed to the senate in 1921. He served frequently as acting prime minister, as a cabinet representative on overseas missions, and as chairman of the Canadian delegation to the first league of nations assembly in 1920-21.

This review is concerned, of course, with Foster's career as minister of trade and commerce, which placed him in charge of the board of grain commissioners. But he had to fight an uphill battle in cabinet before he attained, against Borden's better judgment, the full responsibility for Canada's wheat marketing policy. As a policy-maker, Foster's capacity for decision emerged on numerous occasions from the time that, as incoming minister, he had accepted without change, the sponsorship of the Canada grain bill.[13] He was ready to commandeer wheat when he considered it necessary to honor sales commitments he had actively negotiated. His fault, if any, was his anxiety to get wheat sold under wartime conditions. His market judgment at times, and by hindsight, could easily have been criticized. In the wake to the market debacle in 1917 he moved with dispatch to seek representative advice, and then to appoint the board of grain supervisors. Two years later, when he would have been predisposed to return wheat marketing responsibilities to the private trade, he concluded that the overseas buying mechanism was not sufficiently restored to ensure a steady market for western wheat deliveries. Again he took representative advice and in the midst of a major debate between the trade and the producer organizations, he decided to recommend the creation of the first Canadian wheat board. Equally incisive was his decision to terminate the board after one year's operation, when the environment for decontrol presented greater assurance of success. In the process, Foster presided over the government's first intervention in wheat marketing in the midst of all the uncertainties of wartime conditions. He presided over the creation of the board of grain supervisors to meet the circumstances created by monopoly purchasing. That board, operating on a fixed-price basis was adequate so long as the buyer undertook to accept delivery of the entire Canadian wheat surplus. In July, 1919, when such assurance from the buyer no longer existed although purchasing still remained under centralized control, Foster decided upon the creation of the Canadian wheat board with its innovative system of initial payments, selling to best advantage, and producer participation in the results, which has since had a long usage in Canadian wheat marketing institutions. On these grounds, Sir George Foster deserves recognition as the first of Canada's outstanding wheat-policy makers.

CONTINUED PRESSURE TO REINSTATE THE BOARD

Before the new parliament opened in 1922, the Canadian council of agriculture passed another resolution favoring reinstatement of the Canadian wheat board for the handling of the 1922 crop, "not necessarily as a permanent institution, but as a temporary measure of relief". In so declaring, there was discernible accommodation between the views of the more dedicated advocates of a permanent board system and those which the leader of the Progressive party, Mr. Crerar, had expressed. The resolution was forwarded to the government together with a six-page memorandum supporting the need for reinstatement of the board. Included in the memorandum is a very early reference to the "orderly marketing" of wheat, which was shortly to become a slogan:

> The Wheat Board is necessary because it would mean a more orderly marketing of the wheat crop, thus enabling Canada to meet the changed conditions of the consuming foreign markets and of the domestic market as well. We need the machinery that will make possible a twelve-month system of marketing our wheat production instead of a three or four-month system as it is now under existing conditions. Immediately after the Canadian harvest

[13]See pp. 43-44.

almost every financial institute and collecting agent is employed to force the farmer to market his wheat. Accordingly, under pressuring financial conditions such as the country is feeling at the present time, the bulk of the farmers' wheat is thrown on the market between September and the close of navigation on the Great Lakes early in December. With the uncertainty of the export demand from abroad, and the well-directed operations of the representatives of foreign buyers on our exchange, the period of heavy receipts of farmers' wheat in the autumn months is bound to be characterized by needless declines in prices and consequent losses to the farmer and the numerous interests dependent upon him. Under the present uncontrolled marketing system, the bulk of western wheat leaves the farmers' hands during the first three or four months of the crop year.[14]

LIBERAL ADMINISTRATION STRATEGY

When Mackenzie King formed his first cabinet in December, 1921, he assigned the agriculture portfolio to the Honourable W. R. Motherwell, who homesteaded near Abernethy in 1882, became the first president of the Territorial grain growers' association in 1902, and served as minister of agriculture in Saskatchewan from the province's inception in 1905 until 1918. The trade and commerce portfolio was given to the Honourable James A. Robb, a flour miller with interests in Valleyfield (Quebec) and western Canada, who had been an active parliamentary critic of Foster's wheat and flour policies.

By the time the new King administration had settled into office and faced parliament for the first time in March, 1922, the prime minister had formulated a wheat strategy. This was to refer the council's memorandum to the select standing committee on agriculture and colonization for study and report. In his first speech in the house as prime minister, Mackenzie King announced that he would take this course, and that his motive for doing so was to have the committee explore the constitutionality of a compulsory wheat board. He had already raised the question with the former government during the course of the debate on the 1920 wheat board bill and, since that time, the Hyndman royal commission had stirred up the same issue in connection with the Canada grain act. If there was, in fact, a defect in the federal authority under the British North America act to administer the powers conferred upon the wheat board, this could provide a valid reason for the new government's failure to implement the council's resolution. As for policy, there was little doubt that the new Liberal government, encouraged by Crerar's opposition to any permanent form of government intervention in wheat marketing, was as much in favor as the previous government had been, of leaving the wheat marketing mechanism in the hands of the private trade.

What Mackenzie King actually said in the debate on the address was as follows:

> If I am correct, there are three main bodies of opinion as to the manner in which the marketing of wheat may best be carried on. The first may be described as the compulsory wheat board method, such as we had in Canada in 1919. The second is the voluntary wheat board method, such as my right

[14]Canadian Council of Agriculture, *Memorandum to the Dominion Government regarding the reestablishment of the Canadian Wheat Board,* March 15, 1922.

hon. friend advocated during the campaign. The third is the farmers' own co-operative method carried on by the co-operative companies, such as the United Grain Growers, of which the hon. member for Marquette is president, and the Saskatchewan Co-operative Company, they holding the view that these co-operative companies should handle the crop themselves. Here are three bodies of opinion each of which is entitled to consideration. The Government is anxious in this matter to do the best it can to serve the interests of Western Canada. Under the circumstances, is it possible to devise a better method of ascertaining what is likely to be of most sevice to those interests than that this question should, during the present session, be referred to the Select Standing Committee of Agriculture, with power to go carefully into the whole matter and report to the House as to which if any of the three methods it would recommend, or what course it thinks can be taken with most advantage? I may say that the Government has decided that that course will be adopted with respect to this important question. I hope that on that committee we shall have representatives from all groups in this House so that the policy ultimately adopted will be based upon the best information that can be obtained.[15]

The committee met, and its chairman, Mr. W. F. Kay, presented its second report to the house on April 4, as follows:

That without delaying investigation by this committee as to the advisability of the re-establishment of the Canada Wheat Board, the matter of the constitutionality of such re-establishment be referred to the Supreme Court of Canada and that every effort be made to secure decision at an early date.[16]

When the committee learned that there was a more expeditious way of clarifying the issue, Mr. Kay submitted a fourth report:

That the question of the constitutionality of the reconstruction of the Wheat Board, with the powers conferred thereon by the orders in council establishing or extending the same be referred to the law officers of the Crown for their reasoned opinion.[17]

The house concurred in the report and the law officers responded promptly with their opinion, which Mackenzie King tabled in the house on April 19, undoubtedly according to plan. The opinion, signed by Mr. E. L. Newcombe, extended over two pages of Hansard and was summarized in its concluding paragraph:

It is clear that so long as a subject matter of legislation finds place within the enumerations of provincial powers it does not belong to the Dominion under its general authority to make laws for the peace, order and good government of Canada. It is certain that the essential compulsory powers of the Wheat Board are prima facie included in the provincial enumeration of property and civil rights or local matters in the provinces. In my opinion these powers do not lie within the field which may be occupied by the execution of the Dominion power to regulate trade and commerce, as that power has been expounded in successive decisions by the ultimate tribunal of appeal; and I think it may be affirmed without uncertainty that the necessary reconstructive powers are not comprehended in any of the Dominion enumerations. While I do not suggest a doubt that conditions of export from the Dominion and foreign trade relations may be regulated by Parliament, I am impressed with the view that these powers cannot be made a cover for legislation which

[15]*House of Commons Debates,* March 13, 1922, p. 47.
[16]*Ibid.,* April 4, 1922, p. 657.
[17]*Ibid.,* April 11, 1922, p. 865.

denies the freedom of contract, capacity to buy and sell and the maintenance and exercise of proprietary rights which exist under the provincial laws. The powers of criminal legislation which belong exclusively to the Dominion are in their application to this case of an ancillary character and cannot as such be invoked to afford a sanction for measures in themselves ultra vires. Consequently it is my opinion that the reconstruction of the Wheat Board in the present circumstances with the powers conferred thereon by the Orders-in Council is a project constitutionally incompetent to the Parliament of Canada.[18]

This negative opinion was enough to absolve the government from creating a new compulsory board. But, in the meantime, the committee on agriculture proceeded to explore the economic merits of the varying proposals for a compulsory, voluntary or co-operative board, and they heard a number of witnesses, including H. W. Wood, president of the Canadian council of agriculture, J. A. Maharg and Cecil Rice-Jones, members of its executive, James Robinson, president of the Saskatchewan Co-operative Elevator Company, Dr. Robert Magill, secretary of the Winnipeg grain exchange, James A. Richardson, president of James Richardson & Sons, Limited, and James Stewart, former chairman of the wheat board. After these witnesses were heard, Motherwell who attended the hearings was concerned that the government should take positive action. As a Saskatchewan member of the cabinet, he shared the producer representatives' concern over market pressure resulting from heavy deliveries as soon as the 1922 crop was harvested. Accordingly, Motherwell sought to get some alternative marketing machinery into place before the new harvest commenced. He consulted the prime minister, cabinet, and Crerar, before the committee produced its fifth and final report which contained the following resolution:

1. That it is desirable in the National interests that the Government immediately create a National wheat marketing agency for the marketing of the wheat crop of 1922.

2. That this agency be given all the powers of the Wheat Board of 1919 as are within the jurisdiction of Parliament to grant except as they include the direct marketing of flour and other mill products.

3. That an act be passed based on this resolution, to become effective by Proclamation, as soon as two or more of the provinces have conferred upon this agency such powers possessed by the Wheat Board of 1919 as come within provincial jurisdiction.[19]

The report was noteworthy for the three qualifications attached to the committee's recommendation for the creation of a national wheat marketing agency. First, it proposed a temporary measure in deference to the opposition which had been voiced against the creation of a permanent board. Second, it recommended the exclusion of flour and other mill product sales from the jurisdiction of the proposed board. This was done at the request of the millers' associations which had advocated the creation of the Canadian wheat board in 1919. Third, the committee recommended that the new board be brought into operation if two of the three western provinces enacted complementary legislation. The point of this last proviso

[18]*Ibid.*, April 19, 1922, p. 942.
[19]*Ibid.*, June 13, 1922, p. 2915.

was that the premier of Manitoba had just called an election and the time element would have prevented the newly-elected Manitoba legislature from acting before the commencement of the 1922 harvest.

The agriculture committee's final report came as no surprise to the federal government. In the debate on concurrence, the prime minister stated that if the report were approved, the government would immediately introduce a bill (which it had already drafted), to create "a marketing agency endowed with such powers as it is within the jurisdiction of this Parliament to confer, with the further provision that as regards compulsory powers, these may be conferred on the board by provincial governments, which alone have jurisdiction in the matter of conferring such powers."[20]

CANADIAN WHEAT BOARD ACT, 1922

In keeping with this promise, the bill was introduced on June 19, and it received quick passage through its various stages. The new act retained the essential features of its 1920 predecessor in providing for initial advances, participation payments and selling to best advantage but it differed from the original act in several important respects. For one thing, it made the board a body corporate which made it liable to suit. It was intended that the board should function in those provinces which supported it by enacting the additional powers deemed necessary for its operation. Two provinces, at least, would have to confer such powers. As anticipated, the provisions of the new act were applicable to wheat, but not to flour, except insofar as the board was required to sell wheat to the mills for domestic flour consumption at prices in line with those of its prevailing export wheat sales.

Another significant departure was that under the new legislation the federal government accepted no responsibility for deficits which might occur from the operations of the board. Thus the risk involved in guaranteeing initial advances was to rest with the provinces, and the line of credit guaranteed to the banks to finance the board's operations became a matter of practical provincial concern. The 1922 act omitted control over transportation and the supply of box cars, which had been exercised by the 1919 board through the board of railway commissioners. The duration clause in the act permitted one full crop-year's operation by the board, with a possible extension for a second year. Otherwise the new act embodied some technical drafting improvements. For example, it set out the sales responsibility as a duty rather than a power of the board, by stating "it shall be the duty of the Board to use its best endeavours to sell and dispose of the wheat which it may acquire ... for the best price that may be obtainable therefor. ..." The bill was passed and received royal assent on June 28, 1922.[21]

PROVINCIAL RESPONSE

With time running out before the commencement of the 1922 harvest, Premiers Charles A. Dunning and H. Greenfield and their respective Attorneys-General, Colonel J. A. Cross and J. E. Brownlee conferred with

---

[20]*Ibid.*, June 14, 1922, p. 2922.
[21]*The Canadian Wheat Board Act, 1922,* Statutes of Canada, 12-13 George V, Chap. 14.

Messrs. James Stewart and F. W. Riddell on July 11. It was implicit in producers' minds that a new board would be operated by the successful heads of the old board. At that meeting, whatever reservations may have been expressed by Stewart and Riddell over the practicability of modifications introduced in the new federal legislation, Premier Dunning registered his concern to press ahead with the scheme. Because Mr. Henry Wise Wood had just called attention to problems connected with the nonparticipation of Manitoba, Premier Greenfield displayed some reluctance. Nevertheless, both premiers announced on July 18 that the provincial legislatures would be called into special session in Regina on July 21 and in Edmonton on July 24. July 18 also happened to be the day on which the Manitoba election was held. It resulted in a victory by the United farmers of Manitoba party over that of the incumbant Liberals and, on the following day, Mr. John Bracken was invited to head the new government.

The special sessions in Saskatchewan and Alberta dealt expeditiously with the wheat board legislation as the premiers conferred again with Stewart and Riddell on the line of credit the provinces would have to guarantee on behalf of the board. Of passing interest in the course of debate in the Saskatchewan legislature, the Honourable James G. Gardiner, minister of highways in Dunning's administration, declared his opposition to the underlying principle of compulsion, but he supported the bill on the understanding that the board would operate for only one crop year. By July 29, both legislatures had enacted the additional powers, and it became the federal government's turn to invite the Saskatchewan and Alberta premiers to nominate the personnel to fill executive positions of the board.

On August 2, 1922, the premiers nominated as chairman and vice-chairman James Stewart and F.W. Riddell and the nominations were accepted by the federal government. But when they were formally offered the appointments, Stewart and Riddell declined. Although no public explanation for their refusal was tendered, Mr. Riddell subsequently confirmed his concern for the satisfactory operation of the board under conditions which excluded control of export flour, transportation and even wheat marketed in Manitoba.[22]

The two premiers turned next to the producer organizations for personnel and they offered the top board positions to Messrs. H. W. Wood and C. Rice-Jones. This approach also proved abortive and after several days of quiet exploration, Premier Greenfield announced on August 13 that Mr. John I. McFarland, president of the Alberta Pacific Grain Company Limited and Mr. James R. Murray, assistant general manager of United Grain Growers Limited had been offered the positions. Messrs. McFarland and Murray contemplated the offer overnight and consulted some of their grain trade colleagues in the morning, whereupon they formally declined the appointments by letter of August 14 which they both signed and addressed to the two premiers:

> We regret that after most careful consideration, we are compelled to decline the offer you made to us of the positions of chairman and vice-chairman of the Canadian wheat board.
>
> We appreciate the honor very much, and desire to state our belief that

[22]H.S. Patton, *Grain Grower's Cooperation in Western Canada*, p. 204.

under the financial conditions now existing, the marketing of our crop in a steady and orderly manner is a matter of vital importance to all interests in Canada.

In our discussions with you during the past twenty-four hours it has been made clear to us that the Dominion and both provincial governments were prepared to give their fullest support to facilitate the operations of the board. We must, however, decline the positions for the reason that we believe that the board could only succeed in fulfilling the object for which you desire to create it provided that the sympathetic co-operation of the grain trade is assured. That is rendered even more vital by reason of the short time that would be available to us for organization purposes.

It is evident from the proceedings before the agricultural committee in Ottawa, and also statements made since then, that the majority of the grain trade is opposed to the operation of the proposed board. We are sure that without the use of the ordinary facilities of the trade we could not accomplish the objects of the legislation.

Our inquiries made since your proposals of yesterday convince us that the Board could not secure sympathetic co-operation in the use of all the necessary facilities.[23]

Upon receipt of this letter, Premiers Dunning and Greenfield notified the Honourable James Robb, minister of trade and commerce, that they were unable to recruit qualified and experienced personnel to head the wheat board and that they were abandoning the attempt to set up a board to handle the 1922 crop. In their formal statement of August 14, the two premiers said:

The governments of Saskatchewan and Alberta were asked by the federal government to name men suitable for appointment as chairman, vice-chairman and members of the Canadian wheat board.

The provincial governments first suggested James Stewart for chairman and F. W. Riddell for vice-chairman, believing these appointments would have the support and confidence of wheat producers.

These two men declined to act and every effort was made to get them to reconsider their decision, in which the federal government co-operated with us in joint assurances of full support by all three governments.

When it became certain that the services of these two men could not be secured, it became necessary for the provincial governments to endeavor to find two men with the necessary experience, ability and public confidence, willing to undertake the responsibility.

The other positions on the board have not caused any anxiety, as the governments concerned believed that having secured a suitable chairman and vice-chairman, there would be no difficulty in completing the personnel of the board.

We feel now after spending more than two weeks in the effort that we have canvassed the field fully for suitable men and have to state that men having the necessary ability and experience are unwilling to assume the great responsibility involved.

One of our greatest difficulties lay in the fact that most of the men best qualified for these positions belong to the ordinary grain trade and there is no doubt that the greatest majority of the men in the grain trade are opposed to the wheat board idea.

Those who believe the board to be a necessity this year, declined to take the

[23]*Manitoba Free Press*, August 15, 1922.

positions because of the opposition of the grain trade in general. In this connection they repeatedly pointed out to us that the use of facilities controlled by the various branches of the grain trade was absolutely necessary, especially in view of the short time available for organization.

For this reason, even those who felt personally favorable could not see their way to accept in face of a hostile trade, when sympathetic co-operation is an essential for success in such a huge undertaking.

After endeavoring for more than two weeks to secure suitable men, we have now concluded that we can go no further and have therefore wired the federal government to that effect.[24]

Despite the emphasis in the formal record on the difficulties of operating a board without co-operation of the grain trade, the modifications introduced into the 1922 legislation had also contributed to the failure to recruit competent administrative personnel. It is also of passing interest that Messrs. John I. McFarland and James R. Murray were recognized then as outstanding possibilities to co-operate in running a wheat board. Some thirteen years later the two found themselves in opposite camps, politically and in sales philosophy, as the one succeeded the other as head of the 1935 wheat board.

By December, 1922, Premier Dunning proposed an alternative plan by which the export subsidiaries of the Saskatchewan Co-operative Elevator Company and of the United Grain Growers Limited would be merged into a single export company which could accept deliveries on a voluntary basis from producers and sell wheat so delivered on the basis of initial payments and participation certificates. Dunning's proposal resembled that of the wheat markets committee except that his was not contractual. By utilizing the resources of the two farmer-owned companies, the Dunning proposal appeared to be viable, but the directors of the Saskatchewan co-operative regarded it as an unsatisfactory substitute for a government-operated board, which they still strove to obtain.

In Manitoba matters took another turn. In January, 1923, Premier Bracken announced that he would introduce a bill to permit a wheat board to operate in that province as a one-year proposition and on condition that the producer organizations and the provincial governments could agree on a policy of developing purely co-operative and non-compulsory measures to handle subsequent crops. His proposal was endorsed by Premiers Dunning and Greenfield. Even with this measure of support, Premier Bracken brought in his bill, nevertheless, as a non-party measure and it failed to carry by three votes.

The action of the Manitoba legislature effectively ended producers' hopes for reinstatement of the wheat board. The prospect for its revival had already been impaired by the inability of the other two provincial premiers to recruit competent personnel. In the result, the producer organizations abandoned their agitation for a government-operated board and turned their efforts toward creation of farmer-operated pools, which took form immediately afterwards. Meanwhile, in the years between the board's 1919-1920 operation and ultimate demise of hopes for its revival in 1923, another chapter in the history of the agrarian movement had been written in

[24]*Ibid.*

the rise and decline of the National Progressive party, which added a third dimension to events directly related to farmers' representations and to government response.

CHART 8:1

MONTHLY AVERAGE CASH PRICES OF NO. 1 NORTHERN WHEAT,

IN STORE FORT WILLIAM — PORT ARTHUR, BY CROP YEARS, 1908 - 09 TO 1929 - 30

(cents per bushel)

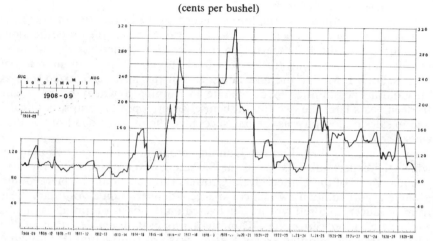

SOURCE: Statistics Canada. Prices for 1919-20 reflect the Canadian Wheat Board's sales prices. Prices to producers for the crop year were $2.63 including participation payments.

CHART 8:2

CANADIAN PRODUCTION, EXPORTS AND CARRYOVER OF WHEAT

BY CROP YEARS, 1908 - 09 TO 1929 - 30

(million bushels)

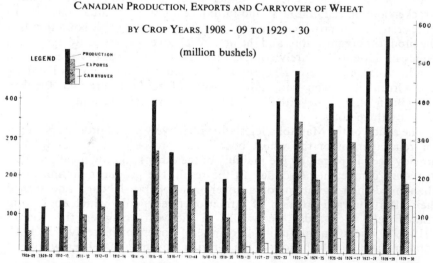

SOURCE: Statistics Canada. Exports include wheat and wheat flour equivalent. Crop year-end carryover estimates commenced with the crop year 1920-21.

9

POLITICS, ROYAL COMMISSIONS AND THE COURTS

The government's decision in July, 1920 to restore to the competitive trade the responsibility for marketing of wheat at home and abroad effectively terminated a five-year period in which the government had for the first time been directly involved in wheat marketing. It had been an innovative period and it culminated in the creation of the Canadian wheat board which, with only a year's operation, remained as a landmark institution.

For the next ten years however, the government's role in the grain industry was played in low key. In the precipitous price decline to 1923, the government went as far as it was politically pressed to go in making it possible to reinstate the board, with the legislative support of the provinces, and it was undoubtedly relieved when all of the requisite conditions were not fulfilled to render that reinstatement feasible.

When policy issues arose in the regulatory area of concern to the administration of the Canada grain act, the government adopted the royal commission technique which involved extensive hearings and the weighing of evidence before the commissions could report their recommendations on amendments to the act. With such precautionary measures taken in advance of any government decisions, and with the trade firmly in the saddle in the marketing area, the responsibilities devolving upon the successive ministers of trade and commerce over the next decade in grain policy matters were relatively light. For this reason the Honourable James A. Robb, the Honourable Thomas A. Low and the Honourable James Malcolm who successively held the portfolio were not in any substantive sense, successors to Foster as grain-policy makers.

What transpired of significance from the end of the war up to 1930 was the rise and fall of a farmers' political movement, and the development of co-operative marketing in competition with the open market. This chapter will describe the resort to politics and also, because they fit into the political narrative, the royal commissions of 1921 and 1923 and the resolution of the constitutional issue raised by the first of these commissions.

Before the war, there had been evidence of a desire at the local level for farm organizations to become involved in politics. The area of primary concern was the tariff issue; farmers rankled against the rejection of the reciprocity agreement and against the eastern political forces which had blocked it. The war had created a diversion during which the farmers' urge to engage in political action remained latent. As soon as hostilities ended however, the movement surfaced very quickly.

The Canadian council of agriculture, which had been struggling along with the support of the farmers' associations but without any permanent office or secretariat, considerably enlarged its scope and financial support in 1916 by admitting to its membership several of the co-operative companies. Thus to the original membership which included the Manitoba grain growers' association, the Saskatchewan grain growers' association, the United farmers of Alberta and the United farmers of Ontario there were now admitted their corporate offshoots including the Grain Growers' Grain Company, the Saskatchewan Co-operative Elevator Company, the Alberta Farmers' Elevator Company, the United Farmers Co-operative Company of Ontario and the *Grain Growers' Guide*. The presidents of these co-operative companies lent considerable prestige to the public image of the council. In addition to revising its constitution, the council engaged Mr. Roderick McKenzie, a vice-president of United Grain Growers Limited, as its first secretary. He was succeeded in 1918 by Mr. Norman P. Lambert, an associate editor of the *Grain Growers' Guide* and formerly the Winnipeg staff writer for the *Toronto Globe*. In the 1930's, Mr. Lambert became president of the National Liberal association and a member of the senate.

FARMERS' PLATFORM AND THE RECALL

Until 1916, the council had been concerned with providing non-partisan guidance to its member organizations and its representations to government were also of a non-partisan character. The council modified its policy in this respect however, in response to a growing restiveness among its own supporters for independent political action. The first evidence of the council's political involvement appeared in the publication of the farmers' platform on December 6, 1916, in which Mr. McKenzie had updated the original farmers' platform submitted during the siege of Ottawa in 1910, and had incorporated into it a number of resolutions more recently adopted by the council. The new platform fell short of recommending creation of a separate party, but it was designed as a vehicle to inform the existing parties about farm opinion on a number of issues. Although its main emphasis was upon tariff reform, the platform covered a wide spectrum as indicated in the following summary:

> The Farmers' Platform called for: a reduction of the British preferential schedule to a point where it would be fifty per cent of the general schedule, followed by a uniform lowering of rates until there would be free trade with Great Britain in five years; the acceptance by Canada of the reciprocity agreement of 1911; a placing on the free list of foodstuffs not included in the reciprocity agreement 1911, agricultural implements, farm machinery, fertilizers, coal, cement, lumber, vehicles, illuminating fuel and lubricating oils; a material reduction in the tariff rates on the necessaries of life; and an extention to Great Britain of all tariff concessions granted to other countries. As these changes were expected to cut down the government's revenue, it was urged that additional funds should be acquired by: a direct tax on

unimproved land values and natural resources; and by graduated taxes on income, inheritance, and excess profits. Besides the platform favoured: the nationalization of all railway, telegraph and express companies in Canada; short-term leasing of natural resources by public auction rather than their alienation from the Crown; the initiative, referendum and recall; abolition of the patronage system; provincial autonomy in liquor legislation; and the federal enfranchisement of women already accorded the franchise in any province.[1]

In the foregoing summary, only "the initiative, referendum and recall" require clarification. This referred to a political movement which had sprung up in the United States as early as 1898 from the belief that the two-party system had contributed to the concentration of political power in the hands of a privileged class and that such power should be restored to the people. The movement which had spilled over into Manitoba and Saskatchewan by 1910 rested upon three planks: (a) the initiative by which voters could propose laws by means of petition; (b) the referendum by which voters could demand that the government submit laws to the people for ratification, or by which the government could voluntarily do so; and (c) the recall by which voters could petition at any time that a sitting member resubmit himself to his constituency for reelection or dismissal.[2]

By so defining the responsibility of parliament and its members to the electorate, the movement inveighed against the party system. In Canada it was sponsored by the Direct legislation league and supported by several organizations including the Manitoba and Saskatchewan grain growers' associations. To enforce the recall, several Progressive party candidates had been required to sign, in advance, their resignations from parliament to be exercised at the discretion of their nominating committees. The practice became a political issue when Mr. Oliver R. Gould, who had successfully contested the Assiniboia by-election for the Progressive party in 1919, disclosed it during the course of an exchange in the house:

Mr. Edwards: Will my hon. friend now answer the question I asked him a few months ago about the recall?

Mr. Gould: The question is a very fair one. We have that, as recorded in our platform. We believe in the principle of direct legislation. We also believe that with the initiative and the referendum you may have the recall. That is one of the planks of our platform, it is one of the things we discussed in our local. An agreement does exist between my committee, whose names I have read, and myself. Forty per cent of the number of electors who voted at my election may, if I refuse to do what this committee asks me to do on the floor of this House — and that committee must meet very often and find out what public opinion is in the district of Assiniboia — if they advise me and I refuse to do that they can apply the recall, and ask me to go back. In going back I have the right of appearing before the people and giving an explanation of my attitude. The recall does not necessarily mean that they take the initiative away from me; in fact, it is both implied and actually written in my agreement with the committee that they do not wish to take the initiative away from me. I have given that agreement to my committee.

Mr. Edwards: How many are on that committee?

---

[1]L. A. Wood, *op.cit.*, p. 346. For the complete text of the 1916 Farmers' Platform, see W. L. Morton, *op.cit.*, Appendix B, pp. 300-301.

[2]*The Canadian Annual Review*, 1912, pp. 494-496.

Mr. Gould: It is a committee of fifteen that was appointed by a general gathering of the people from all over the electoral district. Everybody was welcome, and they got together and appointed that committee and told them to proceed.

Mr. Edwards: Did my hon. friend place his written resignation in the hands of that committee?

Mr. Gould: To call the document I have placed in the hands of the committee a resignation is a misnomer. I did not place my resignation in the hands of the committee. That would be a very difficult thing to do in practice. It is an idea that has gradually attached itself to the principle of the recall. It is not correct to say that you place your resignation in the hands of a committee. I have not been asked to do that. Some of the members of my committee did put it that way, but after an explanation they could all see the reason why such a thing could not exist.[3]

The principle of the recall was in such conflict with the party system's responsibility to caucus that a motion was introduced to amend the dominion franchise act in order to make the practice illegal, but the motion did not carry. Throughout the debate, members spoke knowledgeably about the "recall" the "pure recall" and the "radical recall" without shedding light on the distinctions.[4]

CRERAR, HENDERS AND THE 1919 BUDGET

Apropos of the recall, there were related, but separate, issues involved in the resignations of Crerar and Henders. The Honourable Thomas A. Crerar had been invited by Sir Robert Borden, prior to the general election of December 17, 1917, to join the cabinet as minister of agriculture. Crerar served in this capacity without resigning from the presidency of United Grain Growers Limited, but he fell out with the government in the spring of 1919 over the tariff issue when Sir Thomas White, minister of finance, was preparing his postwar budget. Mr. Crerar, as a cabinet member, was aware in advance of the budget proposals, and his demand for the adoption of a gradual reduction in tariff rates went unheeded. As a result, he tendered his resignation as minister of agriculture on June 14, 1919, and shortly thereafter led a group of western dissident members across the floor of the house to sit in opposition to the Union government. This group became the nucleus of the National progressive party in the house, and it added to its members as by-elections were held. By his personal stand on the tariff issue, Crerar created for himself a strong political backing in western Canada, and also in the rural areas of the east.

On the other hand, Mr. R. C. Henders, president of the Manitoba grain growers' association, who had been elected in 1917 to support the Union government, voted in favor of Sir Thomas White's budget. For this action he was called before the executive of the grain growers' association who demanded his resignation from the presidency, which he submitted. He retained his seat in parliament, however, and continued to support the Union government. He was reelected as a Conservative in the 1921 general election.

---

[3] *House of Commons Debates*, April 13, 1920, p. 1181.
[4] *Ibid.*, May 5, 1920, pp. 2023-2050.

FARMERS' DELEGATION

Among the issues which prompted producers' interest in independent political action was the conscription issue of 1918 in which exemptions granted to farmers' sons under the conscription act were cancelled in the midst of spring sowing operations. Ontario and Quebec farmers claimed that they could not meet production targets if family sources of farm labor were removed. The United farmers of Ontario took the initiative in organizing a monster delegation to Ottawa with the support of farm organizations in Quebec and smaller representations from the Maritimes and the west. Estimates of the size of the delegation ranged widely, but it was the largest such demonstration which had yet taken place in Ottawa. The delegates crowded into the Russell theatre on May 14, 1918, where Sir Robert Borden and members of his cabinet met with them for two and a half hours. The farm leaders made their representations and the prime minister defended the government's action in cancelling the exemptions and refused to alter his position.

In 1910, during the siege of Ottawa, Sir Wilfrid Laurier had suspended the house proceedings to admit the farm delegation to the floor of the house. On this occasion, however, Sir Robert Borden refused a similar request. When the delegation, nevertheless, marched on the house, its entrance was barred. Two leaders were admitted for a brief conference in the office of the prime minister who maintained the position he had taken in the morning, and the delegation moved off to the Ottawa arena to hold an indignation meeting. Foster's diary entry for May 15, 1918, recorded the event:

> The big thing this week is the farmers delegation more than a thousand strong which came to force exemption for farmers' sons. They were met firmly the situation explained their demands turned down. They were manipulated to a certain extent by Hawkes and other politicians (?) and blossomed out as constitutionalists and tried to force a hearing from the H of C, and protest against rule by Order in Council. One thing is significant that they received little sympathy from the west and did not command the support of the Eastern members.

The Ottawa rebuff and the ridicule of the delegation by some elements of the press had the effect, however, of arousing the demand for political action among the farm organizations. One of the results was a victory for the United farmers of Ontario in the October 20, 1919, provincial election, when E. C. Drury became premier of the province.

POLITICAL ACTION AT THE PROVINCIAL LEVEL

The United farmers of Alberta followed suit by organizing a political party in 1919, which lacked a titular head. However, Henry Wise Wood provided informal leadership and the farmers' party won the provincial election in 1921, whereupon Herbert Greenfield was invited to become the party leader and premier. Wood's first political intervention, on behalf of the United farmers of Alberta, occurred during a provincial by-election campaign in the Cochrane constituency when he spoke in support of a party nominee. On that occasion, Wood publicly propounded a unique political doctrine of representation by economic blocs in the place of political parties. This was a new theory of government which would function by abrasion and eventual resolution of conflicting economic interests effectively represented in parliament. Political organization on this basis must begin with individuals and local associations and could not be led from the top. In such respects, Wood's doctrine resembled the initiative, referendum and recall. It had evolved, however, from his concern that an attempt to organize a third political party to represent farmers would end in failure.[5] While political action in Alberta which led to the winning of the provincial campaign in 1921 was pursued on this basis of economic class organization, Wood's persistence in his political creed contributed in no small measure, on the contrary, to the early demise of the National progressive party which was struggling at the time to organize at the federal level.

Meanwhile, in Saskatchewan, the organization of a farmers' party failed to make effective headway primarily because the Liberal government under Premier W. M. Martin had taken several representatives of the Saskatchewan grain growers' association into the cabinet. However effectively the association organized for action at the federal level, it elected only a small number of farmers' candidates to the provincial legislature, and eventually withdrew from provincial politics. Moreover, representatives of the Saskatchewan association had repudiated at an early stage Wood's political philosophy of economic class representation.

In Manitoba, the United farmers' party contested the 1922 provincial election, won a majority and invited Mr. John Bracken to become premier. There were by now farm party governments in Ontario, Alberta and Manitoba, and farm organization representatives had been elected as minority groups in the legislatures of Saskatchewan, New Brunswick and Nova Scotia.

NEW NATIONAL POLICY

As political action in the provinces moved apace, the Canadian council of agriculture provided leadership on the national front by issuing a revised and very much enlarged farmers' platform in November, 1918. The platform was now described as the New National Policy, in contrast with the historic national policy which had been promulgated some forty years previously. Although still primarily preoccupied with the tariff issue, the new platform extended over a much wider range of issues, directed in general toward providing an economic climate in Canada favorable to the interests of the farmer, the wage earner and the returned soldier. Thus, the platform was designed to appeal to a much wider political base than the farm group. It was, in fact, a platform for a third political party. Following is a condensation of its ten paragraphs:[6]

1. A league of nations . . . to give permanence of the world's peace.

2. Further development of the British Empire should be sought along the lines of partnership between nations free and equal. . . . We are strongly opposed to any attempt to centralize Imperial control. Any attempt to set up an independent authority with power to bind the Dominion, whether this authority be termed Parliament, Council or Cabinet, would hamper the growth of responsible and informed democracy in the Dominions.

[5]L. A. Wood, *op.cit.*, p. 338; also W. L. Morton, *op. cit.*, pp. 86-95.
[6]For the full text of the platform see *The Canadian Annual Review* 1919, pp. 365-368. Also, W. L. Morton, *op.cit.*, Appendix C, pp. 302-305.

3. Whereas Canada's ... huge national war debt ... can be ... effectively reduced by development of our natural resources, chief of which is agricultural lands;

And whereas, ... an agricultural career should be made attractive to our returned soldiers ... and reduce to a minimum the cost of living and the cost of production;

And whereas (Great Britain demonstrated amazing financial strength during the war which resulted from her free trade policy);

And whereas the Protective Tariff has fostered combines, trusts and "gentlemen's agreements" in almost every line of Canadian industrial enterprise ... ; is the most wasteful and costly method ever designed;

And whereas the rural population is declining because of raising national revenue ... and is a chief corrupting influence in our national life ....

Therefore be it resolved that ... our tariff laws should be amended as follows:-

(a) By an immediate and substantial all-round reduction of the customs tariff.

(b) By reducing the customs duty on goods imported from Great Britain to one-half the rates charged under the general tariff, and that further gradual, uniform reductions be made in the remaining tariff on British imports that will ensure complete Free Trade between Great Britain and Canada in five years.

(c) That the Reciprocity Agreement of 1911, which still remains on the United States statute books, be accepted by the Parliament of Canada.

(d) That all food stuff not included in the Reciprocity Agreement be placed on the free list.

(e) That agricultural implements, farm machinery, vehicles, fertilizers, coal, lumber, cement, illuminating fuel and lubricating oils be placed on the free list ....

4. ... To provide the necessary additional revenue ... direct taxation be imposed in the following manner:-

(a) By direct tax on unimproved land values including all natural resources.

(b) By graduated personal income tax.

(c) By graduated inheritance tax on large estates.

(d) By graduated income tax on the profits of corporations.

(e) That ... the business profits tax be assessed upon the basis of the actual cash invested in the business and that no considerations be allowed for ... watered stock.

(f) That no more natural resources be alienated from the Crown, but ... only under short term leases ... granted only by public auction.

5. This paragraph contained a number of recommendations on demobilization, vocational training, and settlement on the land.

6. This paragraph recognized the very serious problem confronting labour on the cessation of war, and urged that every feasible means should be used by federal, provincial and municipal authorities to relieve unemployment in the cities and towns. It recommended, the principle of cooperation as a guide to future relations between capital and labour.

7. A land settlement scheme ... under which owners of idle areas should be obliged to file a selling price on their lands, that price also to be regarded as an assessable value for purposes of taxation.

8. Extension of cooperative agencies in agricuture to cover the whole field of marketing ... with a minimum of middlemen handling.

9. Public ownership and control of railway, water and aerial transportation, telephone, telegraph and express systems, all projects in the development of natural power, and of the coal-mining industry.

10. To bring about a greater measure of democracy in government, we recommend:-

(a) Immediate repeal of the War-Time Elections Act.

(b) The discontinuance of the practice of conferring titles upon citizens of Canada.

(c) The reform of the Federal Senate.

(d) An immediate check upon the growth of government by Order-in-Council, and increased responsibility of individual members of Parliament in all legislation.

(e) The complete abolition of patronage system.

(f) The publication of contributions and expenditures both before and after election campaigns.

(g) The removal of press censorship . . . and the immediate restoration of the rights of free speech.

(h) The setting forth by daily newspapers and periodical publications, of the facts of their ownership and control.

(i) Proportional representation.

(j) The establishment of measures of Direct Legislation through the initiative, referendum and recall.

(k) The opening of seats in Parliament to women on the same terms as men.

The new national policy thus proclaimed was declared to be "based upon the broad, national, economic interest of Canada without respect to class or occupation."[7] As Senator Lambert revealed years later, Dr. O. D. Skelton had collaborated with him in the drafting of the platform and was particularly concerned that Canada's constitutional objective be clearly stated, as was done in the second paragraph. He had written to Lambert: "Don't let anyone tone down the paragraph on imperial relations, and especially don't cut out the phase 'whether this authority be termed Parliament, Council or Cabinet.' " In December 1918, when the platform had been published, Dr. Skelton also wrote: "The platform is the most progressive and coherent ever put out in Canada, and it is apparent already that it is going to be a force."[8]

With the platform so clearly articulated, it now remained to organize a political party. On this latter point there developed two schools of thought, represented by the conflicting views of Henry Wise Wood and Thomas A. Crerar. Crerar had grown in stature as a public figure from the time that he assumed the presidency of the Grain Growers' Grain Company of 1907, and Wood came into public view when he became president of the United farmers of Alberta in 1915. Wood had arrived in Alberta with a very considerable background of experience in farmers' movements in the United States, which had left him with the firm conviction that the prospects for their successful political orientation were very remote. For the most part, Wood shunned public office and, in his opposition to the party system of government, he developed the novel political philosophy already

---

[7]Statement by the Canadian Council of Agriculture in L. A. Wood, *op.cit.,* p. 351.

[8]Senator Norman Lambert's review of W. L. Morton, *The Progressive Party in Canada,* in the *Winnipeg Free Press,* July 15, 1950.

mentioned that all parliamentary representation should be based upon economic class interest, and that accommodation and legislation would flow from a power struggle among economic groups. Farmers, he advocated, should organize politically through their local associations from which representative leadership would spring. By the same token, he decried any attempt to organize from the top.

Very shortly after Wood had become president of the United farmers of Alberta he was considered, together with Crerar, as a potential reinforcement in the federal cabinet. Sir Robert Borden discussed cabinet portfolios with both Wood and Crerar, but nothing developed so far as Wood was concerned when the prime minister appointed Crerar as minister of agriculture.

The two men, Crerar and Wood, were joined in a direct confrontation when the Canadian council of agriculture called a conference to determine what political organization should be created to promote the new national policy. The conference met in Winnipeg under Wood's chairmanship on January 6, 1920, when a vigorous debate ensued. Crerar sought a national party organization because he was convinced that the new national policy could be more effectively advanced by enlisting support from like-minded people outside the agrarian movement. The platform had been drafted, in fact, to attract labor and war veteran support. While this ran counter to Wood's philosophy of class representation, a majority of the delegates supported the following resolution:

> We ... do declare our intention of electing as many representatives as possible to the House of Commons at the next general election, who will endeavor to bring the farmers' platform into effect; and to this end invite the support and assistance of all citizens who believe in the principles enunciated in this platform.[9]

In deference to Wood, however, the conference stopped short of creating a third political party. By resolution, party organization was left in the hands of the existing provincial associations, and this denied Crerar a national organization. The cleavage between Crerar and Wood, exposed at this conference, was never repaired. It continued to divide the progressive movement over the next few years and to dissipate its force.

NATIONAL PROGRESSIVE PARTY

Having failed to launch a national party by decision and with the support of the Canadian council of agriculture, Crerar met next with the independent farm group which he led in the house. In caucus on February 26, 1920, the group of eleven decided to call themselves the "National Progressive Party". However small a group, and however much it lacked effective organization, the third party now existed and it provided a focal point around which to rally those demanding direct political action within the agrarian movement. The new party promoted the new national policy, and its intent was clear, however difficult it might be to assess the effective support it commanded within the divided agrarian movement.

Independent farm candidates had been successful in three federal by-elections in 1919, but failed to add to their numbers in 1920 when the

[9]L. A. Wood, *op.cit.,* p. 352.

seats opening up in eastern Canada went to candidates of the two older parties. There was no general election in the immediate offing however, for Sir Robert Borden did not retire until mid-1920, and his successor, the Right Honourable Arthur Meighen needed time to reorganize the Conservative party before calling the election which was eventually held in December, 1921.

HYNDMAN ROYAL GRAIN INQUIRY COMMISSION

During the throne speech debate at the beginning of the 1921 session Reverend R. C. Henders, who was now aligned with the Conservatives, made a dramatic speech on the rumors rife among producers about irregularities in grain handling. He attacked the exchange for predicting high prices under open market trading and then running the prices down through short sales. He attributed to a Saskatchewan government source the charge that grain was sold and shipped by country elevator companies which producers had delivered to them for storage. He also charged the companies with failure to rebate premiums to producers and with levying excessive carrying charges in their street prices. He recalled the report prepared by Price Waterhouse and Company on profits made by the public terminals on overages, and which had been the basis of an amendment to the Canada grain act in 1919 to limit such profits to one quarter of one percent. He charged the private terminal companies with making excessive profits by mixing grades. He carefully avoided naming individual companies but ended with a proposal that the government should make a thorough investigation into the handling of grain.[10] Other government supporters spoke in favor of an inquiry, so much so that Mr. J. A. Maharg, president of the Saskatchewan grain growers' association, and a member of the newly-named National Progressive group, wondered if all the solicitude from the government benches could have been inspired, and he added "if the statements that we hear as to the personnel of the commission have any foundation whatever, then I doubt very much whether the farmers of western Canada will be at all satisfied."[11] Other members pursued the point that if a commission were to be appointed, it should include members in whom producers had confidence.

The reason for Maharg's apprehension was that Mr. W. D. Staples, member of the board of grain commissioners and a friend of Meighen's, had proposed the royal commission. He had confided to Meighen that evidence could be adduced to embarrass United Grain Growers Limited and its president, Mr. Crerar, who now led the Progressive party. The choice of commissioners bore evidence of the conspiracy, and Foster's misgivings were recorded in his diary. Later he was to register his utter dismay over the commission's performance. The following entries are relevant:[12]

> February 24: Henders made a good speech. Criticised the elevators and Exchange.
>
> March 19: Decision of Premier as to Wheat Commission was made Hyndman Wood and Staples — a weak and unrepresentative commission in

---

[10] *House of Commons Debates,* February 24, 1921, pp. 277-278.
[11] *Ibid.,* March 3, 1921, p. 493.
[12] *Foster Diaries.*

my opinion. I wished 5 on Commission with Finance and the east represented but if only three then Stewart.

March 30: Arrived all right and was at work in office and Council all morning. Had long talk with Stewart over the Wheat Commission business. He is averse to going on mostly I believe because he does not want to be yoked up with Staples and partly from disinclination to investigate old associates. He returns to W. will interview Staples and let me know thereafter. If he does not go on I shall be very much disturbed at backing a Commission with Staples dominating it.

April 9: The Wheat Commission still drags. Bracken declines on account of Staples as I am convinced did Stewart. I suggested Goldie and Haslam was proposed for Sask. We shall see.

May 7: At the office early. Have conference with Judge Hyndman as to remuneration of Commission on Grain. He is a well-meaning man but not I should think very strong. On the whole I do not bank much on the Comm.

The prime minister's nominees as commissioners were Mr. Justice J.D. Hyndman, Henry Wise Wood and William D. Staples. In proposing Wood, Meighen was well aware of the controversy in which Crerar and Wood had been engaged, but Wood declined the appointment. Foster's diary reflects his concern over the calibre of the commission and that he approached James Stewart, and failing him, John Bracken. Eventually, Foster made a submission to cabinet which became P. C. 1270 of April 12, 1921, under authority of the provisions of Part I of the inquiries act, and which appointed Mr. Justice Hyndman, W. D. Staples, J. H. Haslam of Regina and Lincoln Goldie of Guelph as members. The commission was empowered to inquire into and report upon the handling and marketing of grain in Canada and in particular upon the following:

1. The grading and weighing of grain.
2. The handling of grain in and by country elevators and from country points.
3. The Grain Exchanges.
4. Financing of Grain.
5. The handling of grain at terminals and the charges therefor.
6. The operation of public and private elevators and Eastern public elevators.
7. Lake shipments.
8. The shipment of grain to the Atlantic and Pacific ports.[13]

At its first meeting in Winnipeg on April 26, the commission appointed Mr. Charles Birkett as secretary, Mr. R. A. Bonnar, K.C., as senior counsel, and proceeded to organize its work. A memorandum noted that "for the purpose of saving time and expense, the Commission decided to send questionnaires to all licensees of the Board of Grain Commissioners for Canada. These questionnaires were printed and distributed about May 15, but very few were returned, completed.[14]

The memorandum also indicated that arrangements were made to hold public sessions at the following points:

Winnipeg,	Man.	May 23rd.
Gretna,	Man.	May 25th.

[13] *Trade and Commerce File T-14-144.*

[14] *Memorandum on the work of the Commission,* forwarded by Hyndman to Foster by letter of July 12, 1921, Trade and Commerce File T-14-124.

Carnduff,	Sask.	May 27th.
North Portal,	Sask.	May 28th.
Weyburn,	Sask.	May 30th and 31st.
Assiniboia,	Sask.	June 1st.
Shaunavon,	Sask.	June 3rd.
Maple Creek,	Sask.	June 4th.
Fort William,	Ont.	June 4th.
Medicine Hat,	Alta.	June 6th.
Lethbridge,	Alta.	June 7th.
Macleod,	Alta.	June 8th.
Nanton,	Alta.	June 10th.
Calgary,	Alta.	June 13th.

The western papers carried front page stories on each of the sessions. Producers were invited to testify, and there were numerous complaints about prices and handling including the magnitude of the spreads taken to cover carrying charges. In Saskatchewan, the majority of witnesses advocated the reinstatement of the Canadian wheat board. In the list of public sessions provided, (as above), in the commission's memorandum, it will be noted that two meetings were held on June 4, one at Maple Creek, Saskatchewan, and the other at Fort William, Ontario. On that day the commission continued to take evidence from producers at Maple Creek. But the commission's secretary, Mr. Charles Birkett, had been appointed by the commission as a special commissioner to conduct a separate hearing at Fort William. No notice of the hearing was given but, accompanied by Mr. Bonnar, the senior counsel and one witness, Mr. R. V. Henderson, Mr. Birkett departed for Fort William to take evidence. Somehow, (unintentionally on the commission's part), Miss Cora Hind of the *Manitoba Free Press* heard of the plan and when she appeared, Birkett's first reaction was to exclude her by declaring that the meeting was private. Then he consulted Bonnar who reversed Birkett's ruling and accepted personal responsibility for failure to announce that a public meeting would be held. Counsel for United Grain Growers Limited had not been notified.

During the meeting, Henderson, the witness, stated that he had been employed by the Grain Growers' Grain Company in 1912 and 1913 as superintendent of their newly-leased terminal elevators at Fort William. He read into evidence a statutory declaration given by James Kittridge, an employee of the company, to the effect that in 1913 he had been ordered by a foreman (without Henderson's knowledge) to place false bottoms in certain bins. In addition to producing Kittridge's declaration, Henderson accused the Grain Growers' Grain Company of having failed to pay the Canadian Pacific Railway for forty thousand bushels of wheat in the elevator when the grain company took over. Henderson further alleged that the company had shipped out two million bushels of wheat for which the production of warehouse receipts had been very much delayed. Henderson claimed that he had made the same charges, two years earlier, at a semi-public meeting in the presence of Mr. J. R. Murray, assistant general manager of United Grain Growers Limited.[15]

[15] *Manitoba Free Press,* June 6, 1921.

As intended, the hearing at Fort William resulted in sensational headlines; Mr. Murray responded immediately to the effect that his company had been given no notice of the meeting, no opportunity to cross-examine the witness nor to defend itself. Murray charged that Staples had possession of the affidavit produced by Henderson and that it had been "in the knowledge of the Prime Minister of Canada for several months."[16] Crerar was in eastern Canada, but he returned immediately to Winnipeg and made a forceful rebuttal of Henderson's charges, and countercharged that the commission had been established for purely political purposes.[17]

Almost immediately thereafter United grain growers and the Northwest grain dealers' association took court action against the commission, as described in the commission's memorandum:

> On Monday, June 13th, the Northwest Grain Dealers' Association, along with, approximately, forty Line Elevator Companies and The United Grain Growers' Limited applied to the Court of King's Bench for a temporary injunction against the Commission. The Statement of Claim stated that the Commission and Order-in-Council, appointing the Royal Grain Inquiry Commission, and the Canada Grain Act were all ultra vires the Governor-in-Council and the Federal Parliament. Notice of the interim injunction was served on the Commissioners at Moose Jaw on June 15th., half an hour previous to the holding of a session in the City Hall at that point. The Chairman, on behalf of the Commission, immediately notified all interested parties by a statement in the press that, in deference to the Court, further meetings of the Commission would be suspended until the matter had been disposed of. The case came to trial on June 22nd, and by consent of the Plaintiffs and Defendants was turned into a motion for judgment. Argument proceeded on June 22, 23rd and 24th. Judgment was rendered on Monday, July 11th by Mr. Justice Curran to the effect that the Order-in-Council and Commission were ultra vires the Governor-in-Council and, therefore, the injunction was made permanent.[18]

In applying for an injunction, the plaintiffs had claimed that the order in council appointing the royal grain inquiry commission and the Canada grain act were ultra vires of the powers of the governor in council and the federal parliament. On these two points Mr. Justice Curran's judgment read:

> I find little difficulty in reaching a conclusion on the matters submitted to my decision in these two cases, save and except as to the question of the constitutionality of the Grain Act. This is too large and important a question to be dealt with in the time at my disposal for the determination of the Injunction proceedings, which ought not from the nature and importance of the matters involved to be delayed.
>
> The same cannot be said as to a determination of the validity of the Canada Grain Act, which has been in force in Canada, though not in its present form, for a period of twenty-one years without its constitutionality ever having been questioned. Besides this, I am not satisfied that the allegations in the respective statements of claim with reference to this Statute are of such a nature and disclose such allegations of fact as render it incumbent of this Court to pronounce upon the question of its validity.

[16]*Ibid.*, June 7, 1921.
[17]*Ibid.*, June 10, 1921.
[18]*Trade and Commerce File T-14-124.*

Foster's dismay over the developments was chronicled in his diary:

June 14: The injunction against the Grain Commission, by Judge Galt to be argued the 22nd sent us into consultation. The question raised is vital and if successful in the end would reduce grain legislation to confusion. The fight will be carried to the Privy Council by the protestants — so goodbye to the inquiry for this year.

June 16: Ballentyne goes next Tuesday to England, Guthrie too and at a most inappropriate time and the Grain Commission has certainly set the whole business interest agog and bitter opposition is aroused. I had no illusions as the composition of this Comm. with Staples and the lawyer as propelling agencies — but there you are.

June 17: All day Council — clearing up arrears — discussing Grain Commission injunction. Find it difficult to get any lawyer in W. to act. Biggar sent up — reports Wilson will act but only as to rights of Comm. to investigate but will not support acts of individual commissioners. They have acted oddly and unwisely in particulars.

July 14: The Curran decision on Grain Commission powers will be appealed and a long lengthy costly litigation looms up. What has been gained? The hostility of all the Exchange and grain interests, the reputation of having been actuated by party motives, the exhibition of the incapacity of the Commissioners and now a general confusion as to powers.

July 20: Passed the afternoon in office. Interviewed with Magill who in interest of Grain Exchange and trade seeks a way out without intensive litigation. Talk it over with Doherty. The Comm. had been inept and absurd. Haslam an impossible. Hyndman good but without backbone. Some of the proceedings and part of staff inadvisable. The whole Comm. is discredited and I think impossible of re-vivication. Meanwhile the legal proceedings must go on. My counsel to Magill was to avoid the Constitutionality of Grain Act — fight on constricture of Comm. as based on Inquiries Act.[19]

Foster's assessment was correct that the constitutionality of the Canada grain act, now left in limbo by the Curran judgment, was the most serious casualty in the whole incident. He immediately ordered the commission to discharge all staff, although Birkett was retained to wind up the commission's affairs. To clarify the status of the Canada grain act, the government decided that the injunction would have to be appealed. Foster confirmed this in his letter of July 16, 1921, to Judge Hyndman:

I have your letter of the 12th with information respecting the work of the Commission and the judgment given by Judge Curran, making permanent the injunction.

I have no idea as to the bulk of the files and material gathered during the work of the Commission, but do not suppose that they are very voluminous. Perhaps it would be better if these were sent to the Department here where they can be kept for future use, if and when required.

It is regrettable that the work of the Commission should have been interrupted, but that outcome was inevitable under the circumstances, and it would appear now that as the real question at issue is the validity of federal legislation in respect to grain matters, it will be carried to the highest court for ultimate authoritative decision. That renders the resumption of the work of the Commission altogether uncertain.

Allow me to thank you for your services so far and to hope that, without too much delay, it may be possible to resume the interrupted enquiry.[20]

[19] *Foster Diaries.*
[20] *Trade and Commerce File T-14-124.*

Foster's diary entry for July 20 noted that he had discussed with Magill the status of the grain act. This meeting prompted a letter from Magill which sheds light on the questionnaires the commission had circulated, undoubtedly in the hope of probing at random into the operations of United Grain Growers Limited. Magill addressed a personal letter to Foster on July 27, 1921:

Under separate cover I am sending you a number of the questionnaires issued by the Grain Inquiry Board. If you have other copies, it does not matter, and if you have not yet seen them it may interest you to glance through them. The set I send is not complete, but it includes all I have at the moment.

With this letter I enclose the Price-Waterhouse demand that the elevator companies produce all correspondence, wires, letters, etc., in connection with their elevator business. I understand that the Price-Waterhouse representative explained that he required all such correspondence, wires, letter., etc., from July last year, or, in other words, all the correspondence, wires, letters, etc., bearing on the handling of the last crop.

That is what I called the demand for the operating files of the elevator companies.

The companies refused to comply with this demand.

There was another demand made by the Price-Waterhouse representative which demanded still more than this. I have been unable so far to get a copy of their letter because the copies are in the hands of the lawyers, but I expect to be able to send you one in a short time.

This second demand of the Price-Waterhouse people was not made of all elevator companies. It was addressed only to a few, but it demanded everything in the shape of books and documents that the company possessed.

I enclose a copy of Mr. Justice Curran's judgment in the package.

In the questionnaire for producers at country points there is one question about banking and another about grain exchange methods. Mr. Pitblado advised us, after consultation with Mr. Hyndman, that Mr. Hyndman agreed with him as to the futility of asking such questions as 11 and 12, on the ground that farmers have hardly sufficient knowledge and experience to give evidence on such matters. Mr. Pitblado also stated that the questions would not be asked by the Board. They were, however, asked when Mr. Hyndman was absent.[21]

The government entered its appeal from the Curran decision in the court of appeal of Manitoba, and in November 1921, the judgment was reversed.[22] Although the commission was thereby free to resume its activities the new decision had come in the midst of the election campaign. Prime Minister Meighen immediately announced that the commission should resume its work, and Mr. Justice Hyndman made an attempt to comply. In his one appearance afterward as chairman of the commission in Winnipeg on November 29, Hyndman issued a press release which was not entirely unrelated to the federal election just a few days away. Meanwhile, as Crerar wound up his national campaign by touring his home province of Manitoba in November, he was confronted at each meeting by repetitions of Henderson's charges and he persistently refuted them. Earlier, in September, the Honourable H. H. Stevens had replaced Foster as minister

[21]*Ibid.*

[22]It was not until 1925, however, that the constitutionality of the Canada Grain Act was finally established. See below, pp. 207-210.

of trade and commerce, when the latter was appointed to the senate. When it appeared that the royal commission would be revived, Stevens obtained two governor-general's warrants for $10,000 each to defray the commission's continuing expenses. After the election, Mr. Hyndman awaited instructions from the new government which did not respond. On March 14, 1922, Mr. Meighen asked the new minister of trade and commerce, the Honourable James A. Robb, if it was the intention of the government to continue the work of the commission, to which Mr. Robb replied, "well, the (Commission) have apparently discontinued their own work. They have run out of supplies."[23]

INTERGOVERNMENTAL CO-OPERATION IN EXPORT CONTROL

One unexpected and unusual by-product of the Hyndman commission was the first recorded instance of an attempt to promote an intergovernmental conference of wheat exporting countries to consider the regulation of wheat exports in the interest of maintaining fair prices to producers. On the prime minister's instructions, Mr. Justice Hyndman had returned to Winnipeg on November 29, 1921, to reconvene the commission and he issued a press release which was assigned the main headline in the *Winnipeg Evening Tribune*:

> Judge Hyndman's official statement, issued after this morning's board meeting, follows:
>
> . . . Early in the work of the commission certain correspondence took place with the government of the United States and the various governments of Australia, with a view tentatively of arranging for a conference of some kind between the exporting countries of the world, to consider the whole problem of world marketing of grain. Replies have been received from all these governments in the meantime to the effect that they very sympathetically entertain the proposal. Only yesterday a cable was received from the prime minister of Australia to this effect. It was felt by the members of the commission that one of the results of such a conference might be the elimination of the violent fluctuations in price by a more evenly regulated movement of the crops, and at the same time ensure the farmers not only a steady price, but one that would at least give them a reasonable profit on the capital and labour expended, without working an injustice on the consumer.
>
> The commission intends to follow up this correspondence, and if considered advisable and possible recommend the invitations be extended by the proper authorities. . . .[24]

By way of follow-up, Mr. J. H. Haslem wrote to Mr. F. C. T. O'Hara, the deputy minister of trade and commerce on November 30, forwarding copies of the press release, the Australian prime minister's cable and a copy of his own letter of June 17, 1921, which, as a commissioner of the royal grain inquiry commission, he had addressed to the Honourable Walter Massey Greene, minister of state for trade and commerce in the commonwealth of Australia:

> In the year before the war I was chairman of a royal commission of the Province of Saskatchewan, investigating grain marketing in Europe, and also

[23] *House of Commons Debates,* March 14, 1922, p. 50.
[24] *Winnipeg Evening Tribune,* November 29, 1921.

chairman of a royal commission investigating rural credits. I was fortunate enough at that time to be attached to and practically a member of The American Commission, which travelled through Europe investigating these subjects.

During that time I had an opportunity of investigating the system of marketing wheat in Europe. I was in all the ports of Europe at which any considerable amount of grain is marketed and became reasonably familiar with the methods of handling it. I saw many of the principal grain merchants of Europe and had a long conference with Dreyfus & Company of Paris, the largest grain merchants in the world. I had a letter to Mr. Dreyfus from the governmental authorities of France and he discussed the matter with me with great frankness. I was particularly struck with his methods, which he went into with me very fully. I may say that I was struck, in all the different ports I visited in Southern and Central Europe, by the fact that most of the millers and grain merchants procured their supplies through Mr. Dreyfus who extended very liberal terms of credit. Mr. Dreyfus informed me that he contrived to feed the market as it was required and to have a continuous supply, rather under than over the requirements available. He also told me that the bulk of the Canadian crop was thrown on the British market during a few months of the year and had a very depressing effect on the price of our own grain and, incidentally, on the price of all grain. I may say that this Commission is asked by the Canadian Government to still further go into the subject of Marketing Grain. This Commission has had a lot of hearings through the country and there is almost an unanimous desire on the part of the producers of wheat to have a combined co-operative system of marketing our wheat under the auspices of the National Government and it looks as though this Commission would have to so report to the Government.

In the working out of a scheme of this kind, I feel that there should be some understanding with all the wheat exporting countries. In the United States there is being formed now amongst the farmers a wheat pool with the idea of combined cooperative marketing. When I was a member of the Saskatchewan Commission before the war, at the suggestion of the Russian authorities I entered into correspondence with the governments of different exporting countries with the view of having respresentatives of these governments assemble at either Washington or Ottawa to have a conference on this subject. The war interrupted the scheme. I have recently been in communication with the Secretary of Agriculture at Washington, asking him if he would issue an invitation, providing there was a reasonable prospect of its been accepted. I may say that it is not in the minds of anyone promoting these pools to fix a high price on wheat for that defeats its own object and would have the effect of eventually dissolving the pool. In the first place it would restrict the consumption of wheat and perhaps stimulate the production of wheat substitutes such as rye, but to fix a fair price not too high or too low because if the price is too low production is decreased and the law of supply and demand would mean abnormally high prices would follow as a result but the idea is to have a price that would be fair to the producers and give them, at least, some profit on their operations. The idea that is in our minds is to advertise our wheat extensively through Europe and to see that it is fed to the markets in continuous supply but not more in any month than in another month during the season.

Now what I wish to find out tentatively from you is, if you would entertain the proposal to be represented if an invitation was issued either from Washington or Ottawa.[25]

[25] *Trade and Commerce File T-14-124.*

Mr. O'Hara responded to Haslem in offended propriety on December 5, 1921:

> I have your letter of November 30th, enclosing a copy of a statement which you state was given to the press, and also a copy of a letter addressed to the Honourable W. M. Greene, Minister of State for Trade and Commerce of Australia, together with a copy of a reply received from the Prime Minister of Australia.
>
> The correspondence referred to will be placed before the attention of the Minister upon his return to Ottawa, though I may observe with all due respect, that I am of the opinion that the Commission has exceeded its authority in communicating with the Australian Government. Official communications between governments is usually the prerogative of the respective governments, such communications being sent through recognized official channels.
>
> It would, in my opinion, have been within the purview of the Grain Inquiry Commission to recommend to the Canadian Government, if they thought it desirable, that a conference be held with Australia or any other government. If, however, the Commission holds communications with Australia or any other government without the knowledge of the Canadian Government, an embarrassing situation might arise.
>
> I would be glad if you would bring this communication to the attention of Mr. Justice Hyndman.[26]

It would be a long road from that first informal approach to the ultimate negotiation of an international wheat agreement.

CABINET NEGOTIATIONS

Although the 1921 election had left the Liberal party short of a majority, it had captured the largest number of seats and Mackenzie King was invited to form a government. Coalition with the Progressives was one possibility but, after the wartime Union government experience, not very attractive to either party. From the outset Mackenzie King rejected coalition in favor of a policy of absorption of the Progressives into the Liberal party. His initial proposal to Crerar, conveyed by an intermediary, was in terms of taking three or four Progressives into the cabinet.[27] Mackenzie King also approached Premier E. C. Drury of Ontario. Crerar's and Drury's first reactions were favorable in the prospect that the number of protectionist Liberals in the cabinet could thereby be reduced, and they sought to obtain King's written undertaking to support the new national policy. While some of Crerar's advisers felt that coalition was essential to protect the Progressive party's interests, Crerar called a meeting of the western members-elect in Saskatoon, in the hope that they would support a less formal working arrangement between the parties, but one which would still permit his entry into the cabinet. In the main, Crerar found support except, notably, from the Alberta members-elect whose declared loyalties were exclusively to their local associations. Nevertheless, Crerar proceeded to meet with the Ontario members-elect who for various reasons were solidly opposed to the entry of any Progressives into the cabinet. Thus, with his

[26]*Ibid.*

[27]R. M. Dawson, *William Lyon Mackenzie King, 1874-1923,* (University of Toronto Press, 1958), pp. 357-371. Also W. L. Morton, *op. cit.,* pp. 130-145.

own party badly split on the issue, Crerar reluctantly informed Mackenzie King that in view of the opposition he had encountered he could not accept a portfolio. He promised that his party would support the government in the enactment of legislation which was consistent with Progressive policies and that, for this reason, his party did not wish to form the official opposition.[28] After the event, during the throne speech debate, King stated that he had invited Crerar to become a member of a Liberal administration, and Crerar replied that he had not understood he had been asked to enter the cabinet as a Liberal.[29]

PROGRESSIVE PARTY AND GRAIN POLICY

Because the agrarian movement had developed with such force and had returned the second largest party in the first election it faced, one is bound to look for its relevance to government grain policy. The surprising conclusion is that there was little direct connection. One searches in vain for a specific reference to grain regulation, handling or marketing in the farmers' platform. The main concern was the tariff which affected living and production costs, and it was on the tariff issue that the farmers' case against regional discrimination was based. Grain issues were not lacking, however, because the decline of wheat prices in the election year provided an incentive to farmers to agitate for the reinstatement of the wheat board. Carrying charges, which were no longer regulated, had increased and this was a sore point. But, except for government-created inequities such as the tariff, Crerar's economic and business philosophy was strongly laissez-faire, and his personal conviction lay against government interference in grain marketing. Although many of his followers in parliament took a strong stand in advocating reinstatement of the wheat board, Crerar limited himself to endorsement of the wheat board bill as an enabling measure to permit, on a trial basis, what farmers were evidently determined to try. This was the closest he could come to accommodation with the rank and file of his party members who gave their hearty support to the re-establishment of the board.

Some months later, after retirement from the party leadership, Crerar expressed his personal views on a permanent wheat board to the annual convention of the United farmers of Manitoba:

> One of these questions was the wheat board. He did not desire to give the convention a false lead on this or any other question, but this was one that must be viewed from all angles, and especially in the light of the principles of the association which he had mentioned. Moreover he spoke as an individual and the opinions he would express were his personally. The company of which he was the head was prepared to accept and to help to the utmost in any scheme of wheat marketing that might be adopted. He was not speaking for the United Grain Growers but for himself.
>
> He had, he said, no faith in government boards for the marketing of wheat. He recalled the efforts he had made in co-operation with others in the farmers' association for the establishment of government elevators in Manitoba. They got them and two years later the farmers would have held up both hands to get rid of them. Nothing, he said, can be done by government boards that cannot be achieved by co-operation.

[28] R. M. Dawson, *op.cit.,* p. 369.
[29] *House of Commons Debates,* 1922, pp. 48-51.

The wheat board, continued Mr. Crerar, would be compulsory. That was a violation of the principles of the association.[30]

The party could take little comfort from the 1922 budget debate. Under pressure from the protectionist element in the Liberal party, the government had introduced only token tariff amendments. Crerar was confronted by the dilemma of voting with the opposition to bring down the government and thus playing into Conservative hands, or of supporting the government to the resentment of many members of his party; he decided to vote with the government.

In the 1922 session, the Progressives were able to claim a legislative victory, however, in the restoration of the Crow's Nest Pass railway rates on grain and flour. The rates had been suspended in 1918 by authority of the war measures act, and a year later had been placed under the jurisdiction of the board of railway commissioners, but this legislation was about to expire. The Conservatives wanted this jurisdiction continued, and the Liberal party was widely split on the issue, whereas the Progressives wanted the Crow's Nest rates restored. In the end, Mackenzie King had to discipline his own caucus and, with Progressive party support, had a bill enacted to restore the Crow's Nest rates. This action was of immediate benefit to the depressed western economy. The rates fixed then have remained in effect since, despite the escalating cost of maintaining the service.

CRERAR'S RESIGNATION AND THE DECLINE OF THE PROGRESSIVE PARTY

The 1922 session had forcibly demonstrated to Crerar the problems of leading a political party whose members openly declared loyalties to their constituency associations instead of to their party leader. When cleavage developed within Liberal party ranks over enforcement of the Crow's Nest Pass rates, a suggestion was made that protectionist Liberals and Conservatives should make common cause. In this prospect, Crerar tried once again to enlist Progressive support for an alignment with the more progressive Liberals. In canvassing his party, he found little sympathy for the idea, and he wearied of trying to provide leadership. At a conference of Progressive members and farm leaders in Winnipeg on November 10, 1922, Crerar tendered his resignation as leader. In doing so, he identified the issue as one of organization rather than policy. He took direct aim at Wood's opposition to the party system and concluded:

> This view is further amplified in a recently published statement by a U.F.A. constituency executive officer in Alberta, in which it was seriously laid down that their federal member of parliament should be guided and directed in his work by the U.F.A. locals in his constituency ...(This) betrays a complete misunderstanding of the duties and responsibilities of a member ... (In this argument you) would have 235 members, each guided and directed by his constituents, some of whom were thousands of miles away, attempting to seriously carry on the work of government.[31]

Wood's response was just as vigorous. Among other things, he said of Crerar:

[30] *The Grain Growers' Guide*, January 17, 1923.
[31] W. L. Morton, *op. cit.*, p. 162.

He does not believe in organization of the people. His proposed organization is all at the top, none at the bottom. It is a political autocracy, as opposed to political democracy. If Mr. Crerar believes that the Farmers' movement can survive if they follow his advice, I sincerely believe he is mistaken.[32]

The convention elected Mr. Robert Forke, Progressive M.P. for Brandon to succeed Mr. Crerar as party leader. But it became increasingly inevitable that the party which had sprung from a genuine agrarian movement, whose policies had been well articulated in the farmers' platform, and whose exceptionally strong showing in the 1921 election left it holding the balance of power in parliament, should fail as a parliamentary force through inability to form a cohesive party organization. As Morton observed:

At the end of 1922, the Progressives had undergone outwardly only a change of leader. But an internal cleavage had developed in the movement, which had caused, and was to cause, differences over policy, tactics, and organization. These differences already threatened to destroy it as an independent third party. At the same time, the Manitoban Progressives had failed to develop, in the party as a whole, or among themselves, that discipline of organization and clearness of purpose which alone could accomplish their purpose of forcing a realignment of parties, with themselves as the nucleus of a popular party of reform. The Albertan Progressives, by their rigid insistence on constituency autonomy and occupational representation, the former fatal to the legislative caucus on which cabinet government rested, the latter contrary to the principle of general and territorial representation, were attempting to introduce into Canadian political practice procedures incompatible with its traditions and functioning. Each of the two wings of the party, pursuing conflicting aims, had failed to advance its own ends, and had thwarted and irritated the other. The disintegration of the movement was well begun.[33]

Under Forke's leadership, further dissension developed within the party in 1923. It was left isolated by both Liberals and Conservatives in the debate on the revision of the bank act, but could claim some satisfaction in the tariff reductions of the 1924 budget. When the Liberal party lost two by-elections to the Conservatives in 1923, it became even more dependent upon Progressive party support. In order to strengthen his position, Mackenzie King accepted the resignations of Sir Lomer Gouin, minister of justice, who had led the protectionist Liberal wing, and of the Right Honourable William S. Fielding, minister of finance. These changes facilitated the introduction of Mr. Robb's 1924 budget, which made significant reductions in the tariff rates on farm machinery and equipment.

In the 1925 general election only 24 Progressives were returned. The Liberals elected 102 and the Conservatives 116, but the Progressives held an effective balance of power. In the 1926 general election, while 118 Liberals and 91 Conservatives were elected, the Progressive representation was splintered into three groups, including 11 Liberal-Progressives, 11 United Farmers of Alberta and 9 Independent-Progressives. The Liberal-Progressives, mainly from Manitoba, had not been opposed by Liberal candidates in the constituencies they had won. They took their place on the

[32]*The Canadian Annual Review*, 1922, p. 323.
[33]W. L. Morton, *op. cit.*, p. 167.

government side of the house and this gave the Liberal government a working majority. The Honourable Robert Forke, former leader of the National Progressive party, entered the cabinet as minister of immigration and colonization. The other fragments of the party, including the United farmers of Alberta and the Independent-Progressives, sat with the opposition, but Mackenzie King's policy of rapprochement and absorption of the Progressives into the Liberal party was gradually being accomplished.

The decline and ultimate breakup of the National Progressive party brought to a disappointing end the promise of the farmers' political movement which had flourished in 1921. Neither had Wood succeeded in fulfilling his dream of a new political system wherein there was no leadership and every tub stood on its own bottom, nor could Crerar succeed in leading a party which had denied him a formal national organization and conventional party discipline. Nor did there appear to be much concern among the rank and file of farmers over the party's disintegration. Support for the Canadian council of agriculture was on the wane and there were some who wondered whether its political involvement had been a mistake. Disintegration of the council almost paralleled the decline of the progressive movement. The co-operative companies which had supported the council were by no means convinced that their company interests were best served by identification with a political party. Even United Grain Growers Limited recorded that the company's business had suffered from such identification.[34]

LIBERAL GOVERNMENT WHEAT POLICIES

The Liberal government's response to farm pressure to reinstate the Canadian wheat board has already been recounted in the previous chapter. As events transpired, Mackenzie King had been happily relieved of responsibility for intervention in wheat marketing operations. The farmers' preoccupation over such involvement was rapidly diverted by the rise and early success of the co-operative wheat pools. Thus, the federal government could revert to its prewar role in the regulatory field. This now became a residual responsibility of the successive ministers of trade and commerce.

Because of continuing complaints over the handling and purchasing of wheat, the speech from the throne at the opening of the 1923 session had promised a parliamentary inquiry into certain matters affecting the grain trade. During the throne speech debate, members advocated appointment of a royal commission to make a general investigation. The government referred the matter to a special committee of the house which reported, in turn, in favour of such a commission. In response to this demand, and on the recommendation of the Honourable James A. Robb, four commissioners were appointed by P. C. 774 of May 1, 1923, with very broad terms of reference:

> to inquire into and report upon the subject of handling and marketing of grain in Canada, and other questions incident to the buying, selling and transportation of grain; and in particular, but without restricting the generality of the foregoing terms, upon the following matters:-
> 1. The grading and weighing of grain;

[34]*The Grain Growers Record 1906 to 1943*, p. 26.

2. The handling of grain in and out by country elevators and from country points;
3. The operations of terminal, public and private elevators;
4. The mixing of grain; and
5. The disposition of screenings.[35]

In the light of the Hyndman commission debacle, the government exercised great care in selecting commissioners who could command the confidence of producers and of the trade. Hon. W. F. A. Turgeon, puisne judge of appeal court, Regina, was named chairman; Professor W. J. Rutherford, B.S.A., dean of the faculty of agriculture, University of Saskatchewan, Duncan Alexander MacGibbon, Ph.D., professor of economics, University of Alberta, and James Guthrie Scott, Quebec, commissioners; and Robert Deachman, Calgary, secretary.

ROYAL GRAIN INQUIRY COMMISSION, 1923-1925

The commission commenced public hearings in Winnipeg on June 25, 1923, which continued throughout the west. One of the commissioners, Dean Rutherford, was sent to the American east coast and to Britain to investigate the handling of Canadian wheat after it had left Canadian jurisdiction. The hearings gave producers ample opportunity to present their grievances, which the commission's report enumerated, described and analyzed in highly expository fashion so that no producer could fail to appreciate that his complaints had been adequately investigated. In like manner, the commission took evidence from the grain companies to their satisfaction.

In substance, the commission investigated street prices which were the most important source of dissatisfaction among producers and recommended that the board of grain commissioners revise the tariff charges allowed to country elevators to ensure the collection of proper charges from those who used the country elevators for storage purposes, thereby relieving wagonload sellers from bearing an unfair share of these unrelated costs. To speed up the movement from country elevators, thereby reducing the need for carrying charges, the commission recommended that country elevators be allowed to secure two cars at a time through the car-order book, in the place of one car in rotation as the law then provided. The commission investigated the grading, weighing, and cleaning of grain at the country elevators. It had no new recommendations to make on weighing methods, but on grading it recommended a more precise definition of the three statutory grades. It concluded that the cleaning of grain by the country elevators was too costly a method to recommend for general adoption, and urged that more cleaning be done on the farms. The commission reviewed the history of mixing grain in private terminal elevators. Although it concluded that the quality of the grades shipped from the private terminals was slightly lower than that of the average of the straight grades handled through public terminal elevators, the commission recommended that the Canada grain act recognize the status quo by licensing private terminal elevators as such, instead of having them operate under provisions that had originally been intended to apply to hospital elevators only.

[35]*Report of the Royal Grain Inquiry Commission,* (King's Printer, Ottawa, 1925), p. 5.

The commission made an extensive investigation of the Winnipeg grain exchange. Like the Millar royal commission in 1906, the Turgeon commission concluded that a futures market benefited producers in the prices they obtained. On this subject the commission's frequently quoted conclusions were as follows:

(1) That a futures market permits hedging and that hedging by dividing and eliminating risks in price variations reduces the spread between the prices paid to the farmer for his product and those obtained for it upon the ultimate market.

(2) That hedging facilitates the extension of credit and thereby reduces the cost of handling grain by making it possible for grain dealers to operate on less capital than would be the case otherwise.

(3) That for the same reason hedging makes a larger degree of competition possible in the grain trade, on a given amount of capital.

(4) That hedging is of advantage to exporters so that even in instances where grain is handled under a pooling organization where the initial risk is carried by the farmer himself, in order to handle successfully the export trade such organizations find it desirable to make use of the futures market.

(5) That a competent speculative element in the market ensures a continuous and searching study of all the conditions of supply and demand affecting market prices.

(6) That speculative transactions tend to keep prices as between the contract grades and as between present cash prices and cash prices in the future in proper adjustment to each other and to future conditions of supply and demand.

(7) That prices thereby tend to be stabilized and fluctuations reduced.

(8) That a speculative element is necessary in an exchange to ensure a continuous market so that when a crop is dumped upon the market in the fall the farmer will not suffer loss by a heavy drop through absence of demand for immediate use.

(9) That individuals who engage in speculative transactions without adequate knowledge or capital not only usually lose heavily but also are a disturbing element upon the market.

(10) That it does not seem possible to legislate effectively so as to eliminate such individuals without disturbing the general and genuine usefulness of the exchange; but that legislation should be directed towards preventing the incompetent from being lured into speculation.

(11) That Parliament should not at present enact restrictive legislation in the expectation of tempering fluctuations on the exchange, or of improving and stabilizing prices, but that time should first be taken to allow the new American law on this subject to demonstrate its efficacy.

(12) That the penalties and precautions against rigging the market, or dishonourable trading, seem calculated to make such practices rare and un-profitable.[36]

The report recommended appropriate amendments to the Canada grain act; these were incorporated in the 1925 revision of the act.[37] One of the important revisions, which requires separate explanation, established the constitutionality of the act. As a result, during the election campaign of 1926, Mackenzie King was able to claim that the revision of the Canada

[36] *Ibid.,* p. 139.

[37] *The Canada Grain Act,* Statutes of Canada, 15-16 George V, Chap. 33, assented to 27th June, 1925.

grain act had been one of the major accomplishments of his administration.

A somewhat different technique was adopted by the government four years later when complaints relating to the handling of grain were referred to the house committee on agriculture and colonization in 1929. On this occasion, the committee had available to it the report of the 1928 Saskatchewan royal grain inquiry commission. The committee's report became the basis for a major revision of the Canada grain act in 1930, in which form it stood subject only to minor amendments until its recent revision in 1970.[38] In the revisions of 1925 and 1930, the technique of referring such issues to a house committee and, if need be, to a royal commission with the time it borrowed and with the groundwork it laid for remedial legislative action was one which stood the Liberal administrations of the day in good stead, and it relieved the pressure upon ministerial capacity for decision. But the relatively few years from 1923 to 1930 marked the last period of respite which any federal administration enjoyed from preoccupation with wheat-marketing problems.

CONSTITUTIONALITY OF THE CANADA GRAIN ACT

The Curran judgment which granted an injunction against the Hyndman royal commission had raised, without answering, the question of the constitutionality of the Canada grain act, and the subsequent withdrawal of the injunction by the court of appeal was not directly related to the constitutional issue. Only a direct challenge of the board of grain commissioners' powers under the act could resolve the dilemma which had arisen over the act's validity. Such an opportunity came when the Eastern Terminal Elevator Company Limited refused to surrender overages to the board of grain commissioners in excess of one-quarter of one percent of the gross amount of grain it had handled in a recent crop year, as required by subsection 7 of section 95 of the Canada grain act.[39]

In due course, the minister of justice, the Honourable Ernest Lapointe, brought suit on behalf of the crown against the company in the exchequer court; the case was tried before the Honourable Mr. Justice A. K. Maclean at Fort William on April 15-16, 1924. Messrs. E. L. Taylor, K.C., and F. P. Varcoe appeared for the crown and Messrs. A. E. Hoskin, K.C., and E. W. Ireland for the defendant.[40]

The crown contended that several subsections of section 91 of the British North America act provided authority to the federal government for recovery of overages. The trade and commerce section was invoked because grain passing through terminal elevators was involved in interprovincial and export trade. Weights and measures were a federal responsibility. Section 95 setting out federal jurisdiction in agriculture was also invoked. But defence counsel contended that the operation of a terminal elevator

---

[38]*Ibid.*, 20-21 George V, Chap. 5, assented to 30th May, 1930, and 19 Elizabeth II, Chap. 7, assented to 18th December, 1970.

[39]The subsection in question had been introduced as an amendment to the act in 1919 (*Act to amend the Canada Grain Act,* Statutes of Canada, 9-10 George V, Chap. 40, assented to 7th July, 1919).

[40]Mr. Justice Maclean, formerly a member of the Union government, had been appointed to the bench. Mr. Varcoe subsequently became deputy-minister of justice.

involved a local work and that the recovery of overages concerned property and civil rights which rested within the exclusive jurisdiction of the provinces.

In his judgment delivered on June 24, Mr. Justice Maclean held that subsection 7 of section 95 of the Canada grain act "deals with a subject-matter falling within the powers exclusively assigned to the provincial legislatures by the B.N.A. Act, namely, property and civil rights, and is *ultra vires* of the Dominion Parliament".[41]

The tenor of Maclean's finding was that the establishment of federal jurisdiction over matters specifically assigned to the provinces by a liberal interpretation of federal powers under the BNA act "could completely abrogate any provincial power assigned specifically to the provinces under section 92". It was in this context that Maclean drew attention to the provisions of subsection 10 (a), (b), and (c), of section 92 of the act which except from provincial jurisdiction over local works:

(a) Lines of Steam or other Ships, Railways, Canals, Telegraphs, and other Works, and Undertakings connecting the Province with any other or others of the Provinces, or extending beyond the Limits of the Province:

(b) Lines of Steam Ships between the Province and any British or Foreign Country:

(c) Such Works as, although wholly situate within the Province, are before or after their Execution declared by the Parliament of Canada to be for the general Advantage of Canada or for the Advantage of Two or more of the Provinces.

Of these provisions, Maclean said:

Neither in my opinion can it be successfully urged, that because railways of the class defined in section 92 (a), (c) and which have been declared works for the general advantage of Canada, carry grain into and out of elevators, that therefore the legislation in question dealing with surpluses, can be upheld as coming within the legislative powers of Parliament. True, grain enters and departs from elevators, by transportation agencies, such as defined in section 92, No. 10 (a), (b), (c), but if Parliament can thus acquire jurisdiction to legislate in respect of what railways carry as freight, it would have little difficulty in absorbing much of the legislative field expressly assigned to the provincial legislatures. I cannot conclude that this contention is entitled to weight.[42]

Thus Maclean would have opposed any suggestion that elevators be declared by the parliament of Canada to be works for the general advantage of Canada, thereby bringing them under federal jurisdiction.

The Maclean decision which upset the validity of one provision of the Canada grain act invited challenge of other provisions. With federal regulatory authority over grain handling threatened, the government was bound to appeal the decision, in the first instance, to the supreme court of Canada and, if need be, to the privy council. The supreme court heard the appeal on March 9-10, 1925, judgment was handed down on May 5, which affirmed the judgment of the exchequer court. Justices Idington, Duff, Mignault and Rinfret supported the decision and the chief justice, the Right Honourable F. A. Anglin dissented. In a long written opinion, the chief

---

[41] *Canada Law Reports, Exchequer Court of Canada*, June 24, 1924, p. 167.
[42] *Ibid.*, p. 177.

justice argued the applicability of the federal powers within the BNA act and underlined the gravity of the situation if the federal government were left without regulatory authority over the handling of grain. In his written opinion supporting the court's decision, however, Mr. Justice Lyman Duff remarked; "There is one way in which the Dominion may acquire authority to regulate a local work such as an elevator; and that is, by a declaration properly framed under section 92 (10) of the B.N.A. Act. ..." thereby reopening the door to a valid declaration that elevators are works for the general advantage of Canada.[43]

The supreme court decision which upheld the judgment of the exchequer court impressed the house of commons select standing committee in session at the time on the revision of the Canada grain act. This impelled the committee to seek other legal recourse, and the chairman of the committee, Mr. W. F. Kay, presented the sixth report of the committee to the house on June 17, 1925 as follows:

> Your committee have had under consideration Bill No. 113, an Act respecting Grain, and have unanimously adopted the following resolution relating thereto, namely:
>
> That the Committee on Agriculture and Colonization strongly recommends to the government, that, in order that the provisions of Bill 113, An Act respecting Grain, may be made applicable to the whole Dominion of Canada without any possible doubt whatever, steps be taken by this government to approach the governments of the several provinces, and more particularly those provinces concerned with the growing of western grain, with the object of having necessary concurrent or enabling legislation passed by such provinces, to place beyond doubt, as far as is possible, the constitutionality of the said Act or any of the provisions thereof.[44]

As events transpired, however, there was no need to seek enabling provincial legislation. Although the department of justice had already given notice of appeal to the privy council from the supreme court's decision, it dropped the appeal after it took note of Mr. Justice Lyman Duff's suggestion. It drafted an amendment to bill 113 which the house approved without debate and incorporated in the declaratory sections 234 and 235 of the 1925 act:

> 234. All grain elevators and warehouses, of whatever variety or kind, mentioned in this Act, including public elevators, private elevators, eastern elevators, terminal elevators, mill elevators, manufacturing and country elevators, whether heretofore constructed or hereafter to be constructed are and each of them is hereby declared to be works or a work for the general advantage of Canada; and for greater certainty but not to so restrict the generality of the foregoing terms of this section it is hereby declared that each and every one of the grain elevators mentioned or described in the Second Schedule to this Act is a work for the general advantage of Canada.
>
> 235. If it is found that Parliament has exceeded its powers in the enactment of one or more of the provisions of this Act, none of the other or remaining provisions of the Act shall therefore be held to be inoperative or *ultra vires*, but the latter provisions shall stand as if they had been originally enacted as separate and independent enactments and as the only provisions of the Act;

---

[43]*Canada Law Reports, Supreme Court of Canada,* March 9, 10 and May 5, 1925, pp. 447-448.

[44]*House of Commons Debates,* June 17, 1925, p. 4361.

the intention of Parliament being to give independent effect to the extent of its powers to every enactment and provision in this Act contained.[45] Even justice department's lingering apprehension over the federal authority is reflected in the wording of section 235 and in the introduction of the second schedule to the act referred to in section 234. The schedule consisted of a seventy-one page list of all the existing grain elevators and warehouses described in section 234.

Since then a work declared to be for the general advantage of Canada under section 92 (10) (c) of the British North America act has almost continuously been relied upon to establish the federal government's regulatory power over the handling of grain. For the record, section 234 stood without amendment through a rather extensive revision of the act in 1929. However, in the major tidying up of the act which was completed in 1930, the Honourable James Malcolm, Mr. E. B. Ramsay and Colonel O. M. Biggar took credit for finding an alternative to sections 234 and 235, by forbidding any railway company or vessel from receiving or discharging grain from or into any unlicensed elevator. Thus the declaratory section was dropped from the 1930 act, and a new section 54 relating to the carriage of grain was introduced as follows:

54. (1) No railway company or vessel shall receive any western grain from any elevator or discharge any such grain into any elevator after the expiration of forty-eight hours from the time at which notice has been given to it by the Board that the manager of such elevator has not obtained a licence under this Act or that his licence thereunder has been revoked.

(2) . . .

(3) Any breach of the provisions of this section is punishable of indictment by a fine not exceeding five thousand dollars.[46]

Within a few years the department of justice had second thoughts on the 1930 alternative because, without abandoning it, the declaratory provision was reinstated in the act in 1939, together with a new schedule listing all the elevators in Canada.[47]

Ultimately, in 1950, the schedule was dropped and the declaratory section was amended to read:

173. All elevators in Canada heretofore or hereafter constructed are hereby declared to be works for the general advantage of Canada.[48]

A similar declaration is included in the 1970 Canada grain act and the Canadian wheat board act also relates its constitutional authority, in part, to the declaration in the Canada grain act.

---

[45]*The Canada Grain Act*, Statutes of Canada, 15-16 George V, Chap. 33, assented to 27th June, 1925.
[46]*Ibid.*, 20-21 George V, Chap. 5, assented to 30th May, 1930.
[47]New Section 173 and Schedule 4, *Act to amend the Canada Grain Act*, Statutes of Canada, 3 George VI, Chap. 36, assented to 3rd June, 1939.
[48]*Ibid.*, 14 George VI, Chap. 24, assented to 30th June, 1950.

10

RISE OF THE PROVINCIAL WHEAT POOLS

By early 1923 the farm organizations were reconciled to the fact that their campaign to revive the Canadian wheat board had failed. There had also been a perceptible decline in membership and support for the organizations, as disillusionment set in over the efficacy of independent political action. Crerar's comment at the beginning of the year that "nothing could be done by government boards which could not be achieved by co-operation" set the theme for reexamination of producer resources to determine whether they could do for themselves what they had been asking governments to do on their behalf. On an earlier occasion producers had agitated for public ownership of the elevator system and had ended by creating a farmer-owned system which operated competitively with that of the line companies. Now, after failure to obtain a government marketing board, it became a question whether producers could provide a competitive alternative to the futures marketing system. The wartime boards had replaced the futures market temporarily, and the concept of uniform advances and subsequent payments based on the average returns for the total crop had lingered in producers' minds. Moreover, it was difficult to persuade producers that the futures market functioned in their interest, especially in periods of declining prices. Therefore, it was understandable they should reexamine their own resources for the creation of a pooling system now that recourse to government had failed.

The search for a pooling system under farm auspices had actually begun in October 1920, when the Canadian council of agriculture set up its wheat markets committee to report on its feasibility. Premier Martin of Saskatchewan undoubtedly had a farmer-operated system in mind when he referred his series of questions to Messrs. Stewart and Riddell in 1921. Martin's successor, Premier Charles A. Dunning, had proposed in 1922 that the farmers' elevator companies operate a pool. Meanwhile, the *Grain Growers' Guide* published in 1920 and 1921 a series of articles on methods of operating commodity pools in the United States, which had been prepared by one of its editors, Mr. R. D. Colquette, on the basis of investigations he had made in that country.[1]

[1]Patton, *op. cit.*, p. 211. Colquette became editor of *The Country Guide*, successor to the *Grain Growers' Guide* and wrote *The First Fifty Years*, a history of United Grain Growers Limited.

Thus, when Premiers Greenfield and Dunning announced on June 22, 1923, their failure to recruit satisfactory personnel to operate a bi-provincial wheat board, the farm organizations already possessed a fair amount of background material on pooling systems. Within less than two weeks the council of agriculture held a meeting on July 4, 1923, at which Mr. Crerar, on behalf of United grain growers, proposed that the council organize an interprovincial wheat pool to be operated on a voluntary basis under contract terminable upon notice. Mr. Crerar offered the help of United grain growers and expressed the hope that the Saskatchewan Co-operative Elevator Company would co-operate in the same way. If the pool succeeded, it might even take over the existing farmer-owned elevator facilities. The organization of an interprovincial pool had much to commend it in respect of operational considerations and would have provided an organization of similar scope to that of the wheat board, except that participation in it would be voluntary. However, the provincial farm associations which comprised the western section of the Canadian council of agriculture were more strongly organized than the council itself, and the meeting decided to place organizational matters in the hands of the three provincial associations.

The United farmers of Alberta were also in session at the time of the council meeting, and they appointed a wheat pool committee to consult with a cabinet committee of the Alberta government (which had been elected by the United farmers of Alberta party) on the formation of a provincial pool based on a five-year contract.

In Saskatchewan, the situation was somewhat more complicated as a result of the formation of the Farmers' union of Canada whose initial support had sprung up in the northern part of the Saskatchewan. This organization grew out of discontent with conditions precipitated by the postwar depression, and as a revolt against the management of the existing farmers' associations, their overlapping directorates, and their entry into politics as members of parliament and of the provincial legislatures.[2] The new union was strongly opposed to the existing marketing structure and therefore in favor of a commodity pool. At its second annual conference at Saskatoon, July 2-4, 1923, the Farmers' union approved the immediate formation of a provincial pool and invited the co-operation of other bodies including the rival producer organizations. The Saskatchewan grain growers' association then met on July 17-18 and, in turn, announced its preparedness to operate a voluntary, non-contract pool for the 1923 crop. In the initial stages, the two organizations operated independently in forming pools under separate aegis.

The Farmers' union also invited Mr. Aaron Sapiro, a prominent American co-operative organizer, to address a meeting in Saskatoon. When this was announced, the *Calgary Herald* and the *Edmonton Journal* persuaded Mr. Sapiro to address meetings in Calgary and Edmonton before going to Saskatoon and thereafter, Regina. Mr. Sapiro was an orator of exceptional ability and his public addresses keynoted the commencement of the pools' organizational drives and membership campaigns. The press, the

[2]The Honourable J. A. Maharg, the Honourable George Langley and Mr. J. B. Musselman were typically associated with the interlocking directorates.

local boards of trade and the provincial governments gave their support. Apart from the mass meetings which he addressed, Mr. Sapiro also gave timely and effective advice on the need for organizational unity within each province. He also argued convincingly in favor of a five-year contract to be signed by producers as a means of joining the pools. Although his interventions in subsequent visits to western Canada were divisive because of his attempts to intervene in the management of the organization he had inspired, Mr. Sapiro's first representations were salutary in persuading the rival Farmers' union and Saskatchewan grain growers' association to support the formation of a single provincial pool.

ORGANIZATIONAL CAMPAIGNS OF THE WHEAT POOLS[3]

The immediate response to Mr. Sapiro's meetings in Alberta was the enlargement of the wheat pool committee already formed by the United farmers of Alberta, to include representatives of the provincial governments and of the banking, grain trade, commercial and newspaper interests. The committee mounted a campaign to sign up, by September 5, producers representing fifty percent of the provincial wheat acreage. In the short campaign this objective was almost reached, and by September 22, the committee decided to proceed with the pool. The contracts were the pool's assets, and the committee found ready support from the provincial government, United Grain Growers Limited, and the Canadian bankers' association, in providing the credit needed to cover the initial advance. The pool set its advance at 75 cents, under a guarantee from the provincial government to maintain, if necessary, a 15 percent margin between that level and the prevailing market price.

Both United Grain Growers Limited and the Alberta Pacific Grain Company Limited, followed by other grain companies, offered to enter into handling contracts with the pool as they had done with the Canadian wheat board. United grain growers also advanced funds for the purchase of a seat on the Winnipeg grain exchange and released two of their experienced staff to manage the Calgary and Winnipeg offices of the pool.

Thus the initial arrangements were completed and the pool, provisionally named Alberta Co-operative Wheat Producers Limited, commenced accepting deliveries from members as from October 29, 1923, although by that time much of the crop had already been marketed. In its first year of operation, the Alberta pool stood alone in pioneering the pooling system. Organizational procedures had prevented similar starts in Saskatchewan and Manitoba. But the experience the Alberta pool had gained in that first year was of considerable advantage to the organizers of the other pools as they planned on being ready for business by the beginning of the 1924 harvest.

As it turned out, the Alberta pool took delivery of 34 million bushels from the 1923 crop, or 26 percent of the total. Its sales averaged $1.016 per bushel and it paid out $1.01 in total on the deliveries made to it.

[3]The details of the organizational drives in the three provinces are well recorded by Booth and Patton in their respective works. Booth also cites as a reference, J. T. Hull in the *Grain Growers' Guide,* September 24 and October 1, 1924.

In Saskatchewan, the early organizational stages have been graphically described in the diary and letters of Alexander James McPhail, who had been appointed secretary and director of the Saskatchewan grain growers' association. As a director of that association he automatically became a member of the Canadian council of agriculture, through whose meetings McPhail discovered that the council was by no means wholly behind the council's official position of support for reinstatement of the wheat board. He suspected collusion among some of the members and the provincial governments upon whom implementation of the 1922 wheat board act depended. Especially implicated were the directors of the Saskatchewan Co-operative Elevator Company, who joined others in denying to James Stewart and the wheat board he might head, the right to dictate selling policy. If for no other reason, this attitude would have convinced Stewart to refuse chairmanship of the board.[4]

McPhail attended the meetings of the Canadian council of agriculture held at Winnipeg on July 4-6, 1923, and was nonplussed when the meeting did not pursue the United grain growers' memorandum presented by Mr. Crerar at the opening of the meeting. This was the proposal for an interprovincial pool which might combine the export departments of the Saskatchewan co-operative and United grain growers into one export department for the pool, and then take over the elevator systems of the two companies. In summarizing the discussions in a letter to Mrs. John McNaughton, a member of the Saskatchewan grain growers' board, McPhail commented;

> I am personally convinced that the Saskatchewan Co-op. men wanted a Wheat Board if they could have everything their own way, but not without, and the failure of the Wheat Board negotiations are due more to them than to any other cause or all causes put together. . . .
>
> At the conference this week they deliberately set out to block any progress, and it is quite apparent to me that they are determined above everything else to hold what they have. . . .
>
> Maharg, J. B. M. (Musselman), and Riddell have been together all the time and have been trying to hatch up ways and means of heading off interprovincial action. . . .
>
> I told him (Maharg) I was absolutely opposed to a provincial pool and had no use for provincialism in any shape or form.[5]

The letter also made clear that Maharg's intention was to form a non-contract provincial pool, with the help of the co-operative, the grain growers' association and the provincial government, as a means of heading off the pool which the Farmers' union proposed to organize.

It was in this state of counteractivity among farm organizations that Mr. Aaron Sapiro appeared. McPhail had advocated inviting Sapiro to speak, but had failed to get support, and the farmers' union intervened to extend the invitation. Sapiro's first impact both publicly and privately is graphically described by McPhail in the following paragraphs from his diary (with the third paragraph interposed by Innis):

August 6: We decided to ask the Farmers' Union to a conference next

[4]Harold A. Innis (ed.), *The Diary of Alexander James McPhail* (University of Toronto Press, 1940), p. 41.

[5]*Ibid.*, pp. 42-44.

morning. Robertson, Edwards, Wilson, and I hunted up the union men at the Labor Temple and arranged a meeting.

August 7: Wilson, Maharg, Edwards, Geo. Robertson, and I had an all morning conference with the Farmers' Union men at the Royal Hotel. Aaron Sapiro was present most of the time. We decided to scrap our S.G.G. pool and to join forces with the Farmers' Union and all other organizations to form a Saskatchewan Contract Wheat Pool for 1923. Mrs. McNaughton, Edwards, Geo. Robertson, and I went together to the Sapiro meeting. The Third Avenue Church was full and it was a wonderful meeting.

With the Hon. Chas. A. Dunning in the chair, Sapiro referred chiefly to experiments in co-operation in California and other states. He argued that "you have got to organize by the commodity and not by the locality," "you must organize on an absolutely non-profit basis, stick to your commodity and handle the commodity you are organized for," "Do not let anyone talk politics on a co-operative marketing association," "The contract must be a long-term contract," "You have got to make your contracts enforceable," "Stop dumping and start merchandising."

August 8: Arrived in Regina in the morning, and Geo. Edwards, Geo. Robertson, and I had breakfast with Sapiro. We talked over the formation of the Wheat Pool Committee. Sapiro insists I must head the real organization. Spent the morning at the office. Maharg, Edwards, and Geo. R. were in as well as Cushing. I left my office to Sapiro and Maharg. They had a conference of over two hours. Maharg was a transformed man when it was over. He appeared as if the worries of the world had been removed from his shoulders.[6]

The Saskatchewan campaign was now begun, but the canvass in so large a province was too much for its accomplishment in the few weeks before the deadline for commencement, set as September 2, 1923, in the contract offered to growers. By that date only two-thirds of the objective of 6,000,000 acres had been signed up, and the pool's directors decided that they should complete their campaign in readiness for the 1924 harvest. In Manitoba the wheat pool committee of the United farmers, which had no time to organize for that province's earlier harvest, planned to become operative in time for the 1924 harvest; this objective was readily met in that province, as well as in Saskatchewan. The three pools were incorporated, respectively, as the Alberta, Saskatchewan, and Manitoba Co-operative Wheat Producers Limited. The Alberta pool was headed by Henry Wise Wood, the Saskatchewan pool, by A. J. McPhail, with L. C. Brouillette of the Farmers' union as his vice-president, and the Manitoba pool, by C. H. Burnell.

COARSE GRAIN POOLS

Commencing with the 1925 crop, the Saskatchewan and Manitoba pools also organized pools requiring separate contracts for oats, barley, flax and rye, but the volume of coarse grains handled by the pools in relation to total marketings fell below that of wheat. Notwithstanding, the Saskatchewan pool signed up 28 percent of the coarse grains acreage in that province, and in Manitoba the coarse grains acreage signed up exceeded that of the provincial wheat acreage under contract.[7]

---

[6]*Ibid.*, pp. 48-49.
[7]Patton, *op. cit.*, pp. 224-226.

FORMATION OF ELEVATOR COMPANIES

Early in 1925 the Saskatchewan pool declared its intention of acquiring elevators at points where it would not compete with existing farmer-owned elevators, and it incorporated Saskatchewan Pool Elevators Limited on February 13, 1925. The Manitoba pool similarly incorporated Manitoba Pool Elevators Limited in the same year. The Saskatchewan pool proceeded to negotiate with the Saskatchewan Co-operative Elevator Company for the sale of all its physical elevator and marketing facilities, at a price to be determined by a board of arbitration. The elevator company named Mr. C. D. Howe, an engineer already noted as a terminal elevator designer, and the pool nominated Mr. W. G. Styles, National Trust Company, as arbitrators. The two chose as chairman, Mr. Justice W. F. A. Turgeon who had recently headed the royal grain inquiry commission. The assets were acquired and operated by Saskatchewan Pool Elevators, Limited, as from August 1, 1926, and the purchase was eventually completed in 1927 when the board placed a valuation of upwards of 11 million dollars on the assets of the Saskatchewan co-operative, which included 451 country elevators and two terminals at Port Arthur and a transfer elevator at Buffalo, plus a lease on the C.N.R. terminal at Fort William. At the time of acquisition a total of 575 country elevators had been acquired or built by Saskatchewan Pool Elevators Limited.

In Manitoba and Alberta, both pools incorporated subsidiary elevator companies for the purpose of acquiring elevator facilities. The Manitoba pool policy was to build, under joint arrangement between local associations and the pool elevator company. In Manitoba, pool elevators became competitive with United grain growers elevators, whereas the policy of the Alberta pool was to avoid such competition.

In 1926 each of the three pools approached United Grain Growers Limited independently regarding the sale or lease of its country elevators. These independent approaches were confirmed toward the end of the year when Canadian Co-operative Wheat Producers Limited, on behalf of the three pools, wrote to United grain growers indicating the interest of the three pools in purchasing its entire elevator system. This proposal was carefully weighed at the December 1, 1926, annual meeting of United Grain Growers Limited. As United grain growers were handling both pool and non-pool grain delivered to them, it was pointed out that a sale of their elevators to the pools would leave their non-pool customers with no alternative but to switch to elevators of investor-owned companies. Moreover, United grain growers were soundly entrenched with years of experience in the business, whereas the pools were still in an experimental stage. In the result, the annual meeting voted against the sale of its assets and United Grain Growers Limited has continued to operate as a farmer-owned company since. Even after this decision, United grain growers continued to co-operate with the pools by entering into agreements for the handling of pool wheat at country points where pool elevators were not yet established and by consulting on elevator construction plans in order to avoid overcapacity of farmer-owned facilities at any one point.[8]

---

[8]*Ibid.*, pp. 238-243.

Because of their inability to acquire the elevators of United grain growers, the Alberta and Manitoba organizations progressed more slowly in the development of country elevator systems. By 1926-27 crop year, the three pools had 42 elevators in Alberta, 40 in Manitoba, and 582 in Saskatchewan. After that the numbers rapidly increased and by the 1929-30 crop year, the totals had risen to 439 in Alberta, 155 in Manitoba, and 1,048 in Saskatchewan. In addition, the pools owned a total of 12 terminal elevators. These were located mainly at the lakehead, but the Alberta pool's terminal at Vancouver and its leasing of the government terminal at Prince Rupert lent impetus to export shipments from the west coast which had commenced in 1921 and had risen yearly until, in the record 1928-29 crop year, wheat exports via Pacific coast ports reached 98 million bushels, or 27.6 percent of the total wheat export volume.[9]

As the pools acquired terminal facilities they fought for reinstatement in the Canada grain act of a provision by which a producer delivering grain to a country elevator could have it shipped to the terminal of his choice. This was an important consideration when the pools were still accepting delivery through line elevators acting as pool agents at country points. In drafting the 1925 act, the Honourable Justice W. F. A. Turgeon had made this provision unequivocably clear, but an amendment introduced in the standing committee abrogated this right. On February 1, 1926, the house gave first reading to a private member's bill introduced by Mr. M. N. Campbell (Mackenzie), a Progressive, seeking its restoration. After the bill was referred to the standing committee and reported back favorably, the house debated it on June 10 and gave it third reading.[10] Because of the intervening election, royal assent was delayed until the following spring.[11] The amendment known as the Campbell amendment, assisted in directing the bulk of pool deliveries to the pool terminals.

PARALLEL DEVELOPMENT OF THE LINE ELEVATOR COMPANIES

The emergence and development of the pool elevator system in the late twenties to nearly 49 percent of the total country elevator capacity in western Canada was accompanied by a considerable expansion in capacity of the line elevator companies which, in number, had reached a peak at that time, and also by the consolidation of several companies to improve their competitive position against the pool system. MacGibbon has provided an excellent contemporary account of the position of line elevator companies, which need not be repeated here beyond mentioning the fact that firms such as Pioneer, prominent today, were actively consolidating their positions then, as were a number of others such as Federal, National, Bawlf, Searle, Reliance, Western, Canadian Consolidated, Alberta Pacific, British Empire, and Norris, which have since been absorbed by today's operating companies.[12]

---

[9]DBS, *Report on the Grain Trade of Canada*, 1929, p. 13.
[10]*House of Commons Debates*, June 10, 1926, pp. 4342-4360.
[11]*Act to amend the Canada Grain Act*, Statutes of Canada, 17 George V, Parts I-II, assented to 14th April, 1927.
[12]MacGibbon, *op. cit.*, Chap. XII.

These investor-owned companies, in their successive consolidations, continued to provide competition with the farmer-owned companies, through ancillary services to producers, and in other ways. The addition of the pool elevator system to that of the United Grain Growers Limited afforded farmers very effective freedom of choice of delivery as between farmer- and investor-owned companies.

POOL ELEVATOR AND COMMERCIAL RESERVE FUNDS

The five-year contracts which members signed with the three pools contained clauses authorizing deductions from payments to members, of not more than one percent of the gross selling price, for use as a commercial reserve and, in addition, a sum not exceeding two cents per bushel of wheat for use as an investment fund for the acquisition of elevators. Varying maximum amounts on deductions for the elevator reserve funds were also specified for coarse grains. The commercial reserves were employed in various ways, but mainly in financing the operations of the central selling agency. Patton has succinctly described the financial arrangements of the pools as follows:

> The capital financing of this, the world's largest elevator system, which was built up during a period of five years, was accomplished without any selling of securities and without any government loans. The funds were obtained entirely from the annual deductions from growers' returns, on elevator and commercial reserve accounts, which by 1929 had reached a cumulative total of nearly $29,000,000. Each member received certificates to the amount of his deductions, with interest, generally at 6 percent, paid or credited on his elevator reserve account. His individual equity in Pool capital assets was thus directly proportionate to the extent of his grain deliveries to the Pool. Operating under the double advantage of assured patronage and of centralized and integrated management, the Pool elevator subsidiaries were able, not only to reduce handling charges and street grain spreads, but also to realize excess earnings which permitted patronage distributions in cash or credits to members of over $6,000,000 between 1925 and 1929.[13]

The development of the Pool elevator system up to 1929 is summarized in Table 10:1

TABLE 10:1.
STATISTICS OF THE POOL ELEVATOR SYSTEM, 1925-1929

Pool	Elevator Reserves (Cumulative totals, 1925-29)	Commercial Reserves	No. of country elevators (1929)	No. of Terminal Elevators	Rebated excess elevator earnings (1925-29)
Manitoba	$ 1,897,333	$ 932,860	155	3	$ 427,977
Saskatchewan	12,195,488	6,572,706	1,048	6	4,268,934
Alberta	4,496,680	2,436,511	439	3	1,470,214
Three Pools	$18,589,501	$9,942,077	1,642	12	$6,167,125

SOURCE: *Canadian Wheat Pool Year Book, 1930.*

[13]H. S. Patton, "The Canadian Wheat Pool in Prosperity and Depression", *Economics, Sociology and the Modern World: Essays in honour of T. N. Carver* (Harvard University Press, Cambridge, 1935).

It is also interesting to note the various rates of the check-off from grain receipts which the pool members paid in order to build up these elevator and commercial reserves (see Table 10:2):

TABLE 10:2
POOL DEDUCTIONS FOR COMMERCIAL AND ELEVATOR RESERVES

Crop year	Variety of Grain	Alberta		Manitoba		Saskatchewan	
		Commercial reserve	Elevator reserve	Commercial reserve	Elevator reserve	Commercial reserve	Elevator reserve
		Cents	Cents	Cents	Cents	Cents	Cents
1923-24	Wheat	0.61	None				
1924-25	Wheat	.66	2	1.66	2.00	1.66	2.00
1925-26	Wheat	1.45	2	None	1.37	.73	2.00
	Oats			.48	1.00	.24	1.00
	Barley			.60	1.25	.30	1.50
	Flax			2.10	2.00	1.05	2.00
	Rye			.89	1.75	.44	1.50

SOURCE: J. F. Booth, *Cooperative Marketing of Grain in Western Canada*, USDA Technical Bulletin No. 63, 1928, p. 63.

CENTRAL SELLING AGENCY

From the outset the three pools recognized the desirability of creating a central selling agency to market wheat delivered to them, in order to avoid duplication and competition in their selling activities. On August 20, 1924, the pools entered into an agreement with Canadian Co-operative Wheat Producers Limited, which they incorporated under a federal charter to serve as their central selling agency. Mr. A. J. McPhail was elected president, Mr. H. W. Wood, vice-president and Mr. C. H. Burnell, secretary. Appointments included the Honourable J. E. Brownlee, attorney general of Alberta as general counsel; Mr. D. L. Smith, eastern sales manager, located at Winnipeg; and Mr. C. N. Elliott, western sales manager, located at Calgary. The latter two officials had been made available a year earlier to the Alberta pool by United Grain Growers Limited.

McPhail's diary recounts the effort made to recruit a general manager for the central selling agency. He first offered the position in September, 1924, to Norman P. Lambert at an annual salary of $15,000 and renewed the offer at $20,000 in February, 1925, but Mr. Lambert declined.[14] The offer was remarkable in the light of McPhail's objection to high salaries; he had set his own at $4,000. Several other persons were considered for the general manager's post, including J. R. Murray and Premier J. E. Brownlee, to whom an offer was made in May, 1925, but Brownlee declined. McPhail was left with the managerial responsibilities of the central selling agency in addition to those as president. Negotiations continued intermittently with Mr. Brownlee, but eventually Mr. E. B. Ramsay, who replaced Mr. Burnell as secretary, was appointed general manager. In November, 1926, Mr. George H. McIvor, then thirty-two years old, with grain sales experience in Winnipeg, Lethbridge and Calgary, was recruited as western sales manager.

[14]*The Diary of Alexander James McPhail*, p. 111.

Once again McPhail was troubled over salary levels, but agreed to McIvor's salary at $12,000.[15]

SALES POLICIES OF THE CENTRAL SELLING AGENCY

The Alberta pool, which was brought into operation toward the end of the 1923 harvest, conducted its first experiment in marketing unhedged wheat. The transition to direct selling was not a complete changeover from the hedging system, because the pool used the futures market when it appeared advantageous to sell futures for pricing purposes, and also to accommodate buyers who exchanged futures contracts against their wheat purchases in the ordinary way of doing business. For the seller, this type of transaction was commonly referred to as "taking in the options" against cash sales.

The selling policy of the Alberta pool is described in the report of the royal grain commission, 1925, where the evidence of Mr. H. T. Jaffray, chairman of the western subsection of the Canadian bankers' association and of Mr. C. E. Elliott, western sales manager of the Alberta pool, was cited:

> The Alberta Pool which had received a line of credit, Mr. Jaffray stated, was not required by the banks to hedge its grain because the farmer gets only a partial advance and carries all the risk himself. That is, the farmer retains such a substantial interest in the grain until it is ultimately disposed of that it is sufficient to protect the advance the bank makes against any loss. Loss, if it occurs will fall upon the pool members themselves. The witness believed that without hedging the farmer would be unable to dump his large crop on the market within three months of the harvest season without taking a smaller price for it. Evidence was later given by Chester Elliott, Western Sales Manager for the Alberta pool, that the Pool had sold wheat for future delivery "when prices looked attractive" and had also used the futures market in connection with the export business "to accommodate the buyer." Mr. Elliott, however, said they did not use the market to hedge grain of which control had been acquired in the country.
>
> The same general considerations apply to the hedging operations of private terminal elevators, exporters, foreign importers and millers, so that hedging in these instances need not be discussed in detail. It is important however, to note that in connection with the sale of grain the ability of the foreign importer to limit risks by the use of a future is of sufficient importance in itself to lead the Alberta Pool to enter the futures markets to meet the needs of importers even though, by reason of the farmer pool members carrying their own risk, it does not hedge the grain it actually acquires control of in the country.[16]

When the central selling agency commenced operations on behalf of the three pools in 1924, it adopted the sales practices initiated by the Alberta pool and actively sought out opportunities for direct selling, while still making some use of the futures market. By the end of its first year of operation the agency had disposed of 40 percent of the wheat it handled by direct sales to customers. In the next two crop years the proportion of direct sales stood at 75 percent.[17] To promote its method of direct selling the central selling agency established 28 agencies in 15 importing countries,

[15]*Ibid.*, p. 112.

[16]*Report of the Royal Grain Inquiry Commission, 1925*, p. 131.

[17]H. S. Patton, *Grain Growers' Cooperation in Western Canada*, p. 272.

including Britain, France, Germany, the Netherlands, Belgium, Sweden, Denmark, Switzerland, Italy, Greece, Portugal, Mexico, Brazil and China.[18] In Britain direct connections were established with some of the larger milling firms, including Joseph Rank and Sons, Limited.

In its first year of operation, the central agency's board debated whether the agency should take a market position in the hope of increasing returns to members. For example, if the pools hedged all their unsold wheat their method of operations would have paralleled that of the line elevator companies and their only opportunity to improve returns to members would have been limited to economies in service and handling costs. By making direct sales the agency could save commission charges and also enjoy some latitude in pricing. Still another possibility of increasing earnings existed, however speculative, if the central selling agency were to buy futures on market dips and sell when prices recovered. The issue was precipitated when Mr. D. L. Smith, the agency's general sales manager, visited London and cabled on January 24, 1925, that he foresaw much higher prices and advised a temporary reduction in sales. A sharp debate among the agency directors ensued, as McPhail recorded in his diary and letters:

January 30: Mr. Wood is insistent on getting long May and I am as insistent we shall not.

January 31: We had a very tense discussion on selling policy during the afternoon. Wood tried to force his theory of getting long May. I fought it and would have resigned if they had insisted on putting it into practice. I had to agree for the sake of harmony to sell no more May options, which I feel is bad policy in view of the present high speculation market. Wood withdrew the resolution.

On February 5 he wrote to Mr. Burnell:

I consider the decision of the Board at the last meeting in connection with the selling policy very unwise in view of the present high prices.

He wrote on February 23:

I have always taken the stand that a pooling organization should pursue a policy of trying to get an average price for the season. To the extent that it departs from a policy of that kind by trying to get more than an average price to that extent does it place itself in a position of getting something less. We must above everything else pursue a steady policy to eliminate the chances of speculation as much as possible in the marketing of our wheat.

March 6. The Alberta men were late getting into Winnipeg and it was 11.45 before we started our Board meeting. Discussed selling policy at length. 7. Had another discussion on selling policy in the afternoon. Wood would not sell a bu. of wheat under $2.00. It is $1.88 today. Absolute nonsense and exceedingly dangerous. Took the 10.45 train for Regina. Wood would like to buy options at these prices and make a profit when wheat goes up, as he is sure it will.

On March 9 he wrote again to Burnell:

I feel that we are in a very dangerous position having a section of the Board determined to pursue a selling policy with the definite opinion that prices are going to much higher levels. As I have said on many occasions if we do not consider present prices very attractive from the standpoint of the farmer and

18 *Ibid.*, pp. 272-273.

if we do not show that we consider them so by reasonably liberal selling if there should by any chance be a permanent drop in the market it would seriously affect the pool for many years to come.[19]

Meanwhile the central selling agency had to make a decision on an interim payment. With the initial payment set at one dollar and the current market price around $1.88, by late winter an interim payment was due. McPhail had explained to one of the pool districts in December that rather than make a payment before the main part of the crop had been sold, the pools should aim at an interim payment before seeding and a final payment before harvest, to help with these seasonal costs. If payments were to be made prematurely and prices later declined, the central selling agency might be forced to sell at a disadvantage in order to protect its margin with the banks. Consistently with the policy McPhail advocated, the three pools made interim payments of 35 cents in March, 1925, which raised the combined advance to $1.35. The interim payment had scarcely been announced when the slump in prices occurred. McPhail's diary relates the developments:

March 31, 1925. Arrived in Winnipeg at 8 A.M. I spent the greater part of the day at our office with Smith. Wheat prices went down to 1.41 this morning and closed at 1.48½. Smith and McIntyre are having a very anxious time. Smith wanted me to stay until this trouble is over. If the pool is smashed there is only one man to blame . . . Even now I cannot see with the knowledge I had, how I could have done more than I did to avert this near calamity. April 1. We did not get to selling policy. Wood did not say anything about the market. Gellie is quite frank in saying that I was right in my stand on selling policy throughout the season. . . . 2. We had a discussion on selling policy. There is now no difference of opinion on the Board regarding the necessity of making ourselves safe by selling as quickly as we can without further demoralizing the market. We are still in a strong position and the banks have not bothered us. Smith is greatly worried. 3. The market was very bad today. Went down to 1.36 and closed at 1.38. It is common gossip that certain interests are out to get the pool. The name of the Sask. Co-op Elevator Co., Fred Riddell, and Jim Stewart are freely used as being out to smash the market to put the pool out of business. They must be fiends if it is true. Read, Ramsay, and I had dinner with Fred Anderson of the British Empire Exchange Co. He is strongly of the opinion that there is no justification for the present market prices and that if any one strong enough would give a lead, it would turn the market upwards. If no one does, the bears may be able to put it where they want to. There is no confidence just now. Everyone is afraid, but everyone feels that wheat is too cheap now. Europe or the U.K. appears quite willing to buy our wheat all the way down, but it appears some interests on this side want to give it away cheaper.

4. I came to the Central Pool offices at 8 A.M. with Ramsay. We decided we would have to take drastic measures if wheat was to go lower. According to

---

[19]*Ibid.,* pp. 115-116. In the wake of the short crops at home and abroad in 1924, prices had risen above the $2.00 level in the period January 24 - February 4, 1925, dropped as low as $1.86 on February 11 and had risen again above $2.00 from February 26 to March 5. On March 6, cash wheat closed 11⅛ cents down and a further 3 cents down on March 7. From then the decline was almost continuous until April 3 when a bottom was reached at $1.38⅜. The ensuing recovery carried the price back to a peak of $1.98 on April 28. Thereafter prices fell with the oncoming improvement in crop conditions. The market behaviour in March lent credence to McPhail's allegation of a bear raid.

reports the market was likely to go down today.We simply cannot stand by
and let the present situation continue or grow worse without putting up some
kind of a fight. Read, Mahoney, Hutchinson, and I met Elevator Committee
at 10.30 to discuss with them security or margins on pool wheat in their
elevators. We must keep a 10 cent margin above the initial payment. This
morning we only had a 3 cent margin on 1 Northern on a basis of 1.35 and our
margin on lower grades has been wiped out several days ago. We assured
them we would give them security any time. Market closed at 1.44½. We took
steps (Innis noted that the pool purchased 3,435,000 bushels and sold it in
May and June at a profit of $386,000.) to help it today in the hopes it would
strengthen and enable us to sell wheat for export over the week-end. . . . 6.
May closed 1.46¾ or 2½ higher than Saturday's close. We bought 500,000 on
the Winnipeg market and sold it on Chicago. Chicago was higher by ¼ to ⅜
all morning. We are simply forced to take these measures to fight the bears on
the market. Apparently a few strong grain interests can bear down the market
if there is no bull resistance. All the bullish interests are afraid to buy for they
do not know when the pool may be forced to unload. The pool appears to be
the only organization that can go in and change the trend of the market and
to do it we must take steps which we would not under ordinary circumstances
take. But we must fight the devil with his own weapons. . . . I went to the
Legislature in the evening and met Burnell. We had a talk with Bracken, and
I talked to Brownlee at Edmonton on phone re the provincial Governments
coming out with an announcement that they will back the pool under all
circumstances. Very interesting and strenuous life. I am to call Brownlee
to-morrow. 7. Spent all day around office. . . . I talked with Smith re
Brownlee's suggestion of Western Governments coming out with announcement to back the pools. We decided the pool could stand on its own feet. We
would keep strictly away from Governments and politics. Market acted very
firm today and I think the worst is over. Talked to Bracken and also
Brownlee. Brouillette, Robertson, and I took the evening train to Regina.[20]

The thought of enlisting financial support from the provincial governments which had backed the pools in their organizational stage presaged an
occasion five years later when the help of the provinces would be required.
At this moment, however, the pools were able, and preferred, to get by on
their own resources. Nevertheless, the experience afforded a salutary lesson
on the gravity of the risk involved in taking a market position.

ORDERLY MARKETING

Quite apart from the issue which had been resolved in the first year of the
central selling agency, whether it should use the futures market specula-
tively, either in the expectation of a price rise or in support of the market,
the question remained as to what the agency's actual selling policy should
be. In the organizational campaigns conducted by the pools the term
"orderly marketing" had emerged as a campaign slogan, the meaning of
which was variously interpreted by its advocates. To some it meant the even
distribution of sales over the crop year and, to others, the equation of supply
with demand with a view to reducing the amplitude of short-term price
fluctuations. In either case, the slogan left a certain mystique surrounding
the precise sales policies which would accomplish either objective. Still
others identified "orderly marketing" as a synonym for co-operative

[20]*Ibid.,* pp. 117-119.

marketing which was incorporated as an object of the pools in their provincial charters. Since then orderly marketing has come to mean Canadian wheat board marketing and is referred to as such in the Canadian wheat board act. Moreover, the use of the expression has widened to denote any board or collective market system, as differentiated from the open or competitive market system.

Evidence that orderly marketing had been interpreted to mean the even distribution of sales over the crop year is to be found in the report of the central selling agency for the 1926-27 crop year which showed the monthly distribution of wheat delivered to it and of sales as follows:[21]

		Deliveries	Sales
Carryover 1926		10,319,764	
15/20	Sept. 1926	28,484,500	10,417,555
	Oct.	26,434,164	14,814,308
	Nov.	43,131,886	20,481,982
	Dec.	23,245,397	20,123,190
	Jan. 1927	17,154,266	17,319,700
	Feb.	9,695,512	13,714,785
	March	8,966,533	14,552,133
	April	7,386,050	15,662,517
	May	14,610,541	21,774,818
	June	5,322,172	14,290,607
	July	13,623,951	7,349,960
	Aug.	1,103,340	17,131,482
	Sept.	23,402	14,449,470
Carryover 1927		......	7,418,971
		209,501,478	209,501,478

This policy was explicitly expressed in McPhail's diary entry of February 23, 1925, already cited, to the effect that the pools should try to get an average price for the season.

The other interpretation that orderly marketing implied the regulation of sales to match market demand — selling on price rises and withholding on declines — is also reflected in McPhail's subsequent diary references to the fact that the agency had decided to slow down sales and at times even to withdraw offers entirely in the interest of supporting temporarily depressed markets. There was a tendency under this policy, however, toward the accumulation of residual stocks, as distinct from the deliberate build up of speculative long positions. This tendency became accentuated in the carryovers which accumulated with the onset of depression.

The agency's selling policy was rather severely tested in connection with the marketing of the 1928 crop which established a new record in production. Although the wheat crop of 545 million bushels in the prairie provinces was high in volume, late August frosts had seriously reduced the quality and a high proportion of the crop fell into lower grades. Because of the uncertainties surrounding the marketing of such a crop, the pools decided upon an initial payment of 85 cents. This was 15 cents less than the initial payment of one dollar maintained from 1924 through 1927. As it turned out, two additional payments were made on the 1928 crop, which brought the total payment to $1.18½, basis 1 Northern, Fort William, but not without considerable financial anxiety in the process.

The marketing of the 1928 crop, however, marked the last operation in which the pools avoided financial recourse to governments. In 1929 the

[21]Patton, *op. cit.*, p. 269.

initial payment was restored to one dollar at a time when the market price stood at $1.56 but the stock market collapse in October, 1929, signalled an erosion of commodity prices which continued through the next several years of depression. The wheat importing countries of continental Europe had already raised tariffs and placed other restrictions on wheat imports. When market prices fell below the level of the initial payment before the crop year ended, the pools were compelled to seek financial support to meet their obligations. That narrative, however belongs to subsequent parts of this review which deal with government grain policy in the ensuing chaotic decades. Until this time, however, the central selling agency had created an impressive record in developing the potential of voluntary pooling as an alternative to the futures market system. In volume, the pools had gained control of half of all the wheat deliveries, as shown in table 10:3:

TABLE 10:3
POOL DELIVERIES AND TOTAL WHEAT DELIVERIES 1924-25 TO 1929-30

Crop Year	Pool Deliveries	Total Deliveries in Western Inspection Division	Per Cent. Pool Deliveries
	Bushels	*Bushels*	
1924-25	81,668,348	219,241,130	37.3
1925-26	187,364,999	358,715,990	52.2
1926-27	179,993,435	338,936,053	53.1
1927-28	209,908,536	410,617,091	51.1
1928-29	243,929,491	475,711,628	51.3
1929-30	121,655,589	236,967,251	52.0

SOURCE: *Canadian Wheat Pool Year Book, 1930.*

The record of wheat pool payments is also of considerable interest. From the time that the final payment for the first pool year was announced, interest centred on whether on average pool patrons had fared better or worse than non-pool farmers whose wheat was sold through the futures market. Claims were advanced by both sides on the basis of disputable statistical evidence.[22] The actual record of pool payments stood as follows:

TABLE 10:4
WHEAT POOL PAYMENTS 1923-24 TO 1929-30.

	Initial Payment	1st Interim Payment	2nd Interim Payment	Final Payment[1]	Total
1923-24	$ .75	$ .10	$ --	$ .16	$1.01
1924-25	1.00	.35	.20	.11	1.66
1925-26	1.00	.20	.20	.05	1.45
1926-27	1.00	.15	.15	.12	1.42
1927-28	1.00	.15	.25	.02½	1.42¼
1928-29	.85	.12	.21½	--	1.18½
1929-30	1.00[2]	--	--	--	1.00

SOURCE: D. A. MacGibbon, *The Canadian Grain Trade* (MacMillan, Toronto, 1932), pp. 350-351.

([1]) Includes reserve fund deductions.
([2]) The initial payment was the only one made. This was reduced to 85 cents on wheat delivered from June 25 to August 31, 1930.

[22]For a detailed discussion of the price comparisons, see Patton, *op. cit.*, pp. 341-344, and Booth, *op. cit.*, pp. 61-62.

From their own standpoint, the most important accomplishment of the pools was the acquisition of country and terminal elevator systems purchased out of the elevator reserve deductions from deliveries. When the central selling agency eventually incurred a deficit in its unhedged operations, the pools had in their subsidiary elevator companies tangible assets which they could hypothecate against loans from the provincial governments. Except in Manitoba where the provincial loan was partially written off, the loans were repaid in full in Saskatchewan and Alberta, and the three pools regained unencumbered title to their elevator assets, which have since continued to grow.

11

RETROSPECT

Part I has sketched the formation of the western grain industry and its development to that state of maturity in 1930 in which most of the elements of the industry as it is known today had by then been fitted into place and competitive position. Migration and land settlement were essential elements, which could not properly flourish until the publicly-assisted private investment in railways and private investment in elevators had been made. An agrarian movement was spawned in opposition to the early monopoly created by the railways and elevator companies in grain handling facilities. Farmers pursued their interests along two fronts: first, in the quest for regulatory legislation; and second, in the formation of farmer-owned elevator companies until they had effective freedom of choice in their methods of grain marketing.

The route to farmer-owned facilities was not at all direct. Agitation for a publicly-owned system arose after the turn of the century, and the provinces escaped the pressure only after a public venture had been tried and failed. The federal government failed to escape all the pressure, but succeeded in confining its role to the construction of interior terminals, and to adding to terminal capacity at the lakehead, Vancouver, St. Lawrence and Maritime ports. Apart from this federal venture into terminal construction, the investor- and farmer-owned companies rivalled one another in the development of integrated elevator systems.

One of the more fascinating developments of this period was the farm movement's experiment with direct political action which succeeded in electing three provincial governments and substantial representation in Ottawa. With these results it is difficult, even now to understand why the Progressive party accomplished so little with its mandate. At the height of its success Crerar had sought a formal working agreement between his party and the Liberal administration, rather than assume responsibility as leader of the opposition. He resigned as party leader in disgust when he found himself, in fact, at the head of a party dedicated to lack of party discipline. Crerar remained as president of United grain growers until 1929 when he resigned to accept a cabinet post as a Liberal in the King administration, and was defeated and reelected, as was the Liberal party in the general elections of 1930 and 1935. While most Progressives were absorbed into the Liberal party, it remained for the Conservative party to adopt the Progressive party's name.

Although the Progressive party can be credited with a few legislative accomplishments in the matter of tariff policy and the restoration of the Crow's Nest Pass rates which helped the western economy, it made very little direct impact upon grain policy and legislation. The party was at its height at a time when the federal government was in the process of restoring grain marketing responsibilities to the trade and the farm organizations. Because the quest to improve the welfare of farmers by direct political action produced such mediocre results, it has deterred farm organizations since from seeking political identification. It was ironic, too, that the Canadian council of agriculture which had once been the recognized voice of the farmers, should follow the Progressive party into limbo by 1931.

Except for the period of the great war, the federal government was concerned primarily with regulatory legislation and adminstration. The evolution of the Canada grain act, from its early antecedents defining the weight of a bushel, to the complex legislation embodied in the 1930 act, would provide excellent material for an historical study of its own. The government, concerned at first with laying the ground rules between buyer and seller, became involved in protecting the rights of the seller, not only by ensuring proper grading and the elimination of abuses in weighing, dockage and mixing, but in providing freedom of choice to the producer in the method of his grain delivery. Then, as the farmer-owned elevator companies were reaching their full state of development, they sought amendments to the Canada grain act to protect their competitive position within the industry. In 1929 the act was again brought under review, and the pools and the line companies both offered extensive submissions. One by-product of this operation was that in 1929 the Honourable James Malcolm, minister of trade and commerce, hired away the general manager of the central selling agency, Mr. E. B. Ramsay, for appointment as chief commissioner of the board of grain commissioners for Canada, after Ramsay had very ably presented the pools' submission.

The constitutionality of the Canada grain act had been another moot issue, first raised in the injunction proceedings against the Hyndman commission, in 1921, when Mr. Justice Curran's judgment begged the question. It had directly affected the government's decision in 1922 to make the proclamation of the new wheat board act conditional upon enabling legislation by the provincial governments. This set up a chain of events on which the reinstatement of the wheat board foundered in 1923. Meanwhile, it had taken some time to get a test case on the Canada grain act before the courts and, in due course, Mr. Justice Lyman Duff suggested, in his written opinion, that the constitutionality of the act could be established if elevators were declared by the parliament of Canada to be works for the general advantage of Canada.

It is interesting, however irrelevent to the course of events, to speculate on the impact of Duff's opinion, had it been available three years earlier. In that case, the deputy minister of justice could not have advised the house committee on agriculture and colonization that the wheat board might be ultra vires of the parliament of Canada unless there was also enabling provincial legislation. With the necessary authority at hand the federal government would then have been clearly faced with a decision to terminate futures trading in wheat and to reinstate a compulsory wheat board. Alternatively, it could have adopted the Meighen proposal for a voluntary board. In either case, the federal government would have become re-involved in wheat marketing policy, and the need for producers to organize their own co-operative marketing system would have been removed. In the absence of such timing, events took a different course; producers demonstrated a capacity for organization in economic affairs which they had failed to do on the political front.

From the standpoint of government involvement in marketing policy, the period of transcendent interest was that of the great war when the country, still in colonial status, found its wheat supplies first in such limited demand and then of such strategic importance that not only did wheat marketing become a matter of government policy, but the government was drawn also into direct dealings with other governments on marketing issues. Under wartime conditions, abnormal pressure was placed upon the futures marketing system against which exchange members found themselves unable to cope, and they requested government intervention. The government, in turn, had to improvise a substitute marketing system which it did by creating the board of grain supervisors — in reality a marketing board. The board's method of fixing the basic price for a crop year at a time, proved to have limited applicability. Its subsequent replacement by the Canadian wheat board which, with futures trading still suspended, operated a compulsory pool and sold to best advantage briefly but beneficially, demonstrated for the first time a viable alternative to the futures market system — a mechanism capable of functioning in wartime or in peace.

The first Canadian wheat board stood as a landmark, therefore, and as the object of strong political representations for its reinstatement. When this course failed, farmers created their own voluntary pools whose operations were patterned upon those of the board. For a span of six years while the pools remained viable, the federal government enjoyed a respite from direct marketing responsibility. From 1930 forward, it was drawn back into the marketing field and has remained there since. In this renewed involvement, the antecedent wheat board would have a further role to play.

Another way of viewing this earlier period is in terms of the leadership it produced. From the standpoint of government grain policy, the outstanding performance of the period was that of Sir George Foster whose interest in the grain industry was a derived one and by no means his main interest. Although Foster enjoys a well-earned place in Canadian political history, the tendency has been to forget his role in the grain policy for which he deserves to be ranked as one of the great policy-makers. Sir John A. Macdonald is well remembered for his contribution to railway building and the opening up of the west, and Sir Clifford Sifton for his pursuit of a vigorous immigration policy, but neither had occasion to come directly to grips with grain policy in any semblance of its more recent ramifications. Several ministers of trade and commerce made their contributions to the redress of producer grievances and to the evolution of the Canada grain act, but none of them is identifiable with the resolution of such critical policy issues as Foster faced.

Apart from the policy-makers, there is also a lesser category of policy-advisers, among whom Mr. Charles C. Castle earned early recognition.

Castle served as a member of the first royal commission on grain, as a draftsman of the Manitoba grain act, and as the first warehouse commissioner to administer that act. But among policy-advisers, Dr. Robert Magill and Mr. James Stewart rank together as the outstanding examples of their time. Nor should Mr. Lloyd Harris be forgotten. He rendered excellent service in London and Paris in the negotiation of wheat contracts, and it was only toward the end of his overseas mission that he succumbed to the buyers' point of view, a hazard not uncommon in foreign service. Nor did Harris's unregenerate remarks in Hamilton endear him to his company's western customers.

If policy-advisers arose from within the industry as occasion demanded, they were notably non-existent among the ranks of the civil service. Deputy ministers of the day were undoubtedly familiar with the policy issues, but they observed much more strictly the boundary between ministerial responsibility and departmental administration. Ministers responsible for policy-making were inured to working without the assistance of support staff. The absence of any worthwhile advisory support has been poignantly, however inadvertently, recorded in a five-page memorandum which Mr. F. C. T. O'Hara, deputy minister of trade and commerce, prepared on May 31, 1931, for his minister, the Honourable H. H. Stevens, on the history of the board of grain supervisors. The concluding paragraph reads:

> As to the records of the Board of Grain Supervisors, these were turned over to the Wheat Board on its inception, and upon the conclusion of the Wheat Board's activities these records were lodged with the Board of Grain Commissioners in Winnipeg, and on January 17, 1929, according to the departmental records, 45 cases of Canadian Wheat Board records, including the more important records of the Board of Grain Supervisors, were sent to the Department of Public Works for storage at 8 Cliff Street and the basement of 389½ Wellington Street, Ottawa. These cases have never been opened since, as no member of the Department of Trade and Commerce was familiar with them. . . .[1]

Although it is beyond the scope of a government policy review to enumerate the many men who have risen to positions of leadership within the farm movement and the industry, a few deserve special mention. Among these, the Honourable Thomas A. Crerar comes first to mind. Not only was he president of the Grain Growers' Grain Company and its successor, United Grain Growers Limited, from 1907 to 1929, but he served as a cabinet minister and as leader of a political party. Undoubtedly his greatest contribution during this period was the way in which he drew to the attention of the rest of Canada the inequities of the tariff burden upon the western farmer. Crerar might have gained more success as a political leader, had he not been faced with the counteractivity of Henry Wise Wood. Alexander James McPhail also had his problems with Wood as a director of the central selling agency. While the earlier narrative in this review may seem to be biased against Wood, it is based upon available accounts of the events. Among the people who knew him and worked with him, Wood enjoyed warm admiration and respect. He held an impregnable position as

---

[1] *Trade and Commerce File T-14-144.* The present whereabouts, if any, of the 45 cases has not been researched, but the supreme court building stands now on the Cliff Street site, and the national library and public archives on that of 389½ Wellington Street.

the outstanding farm leader in Alberta, as president of the United farmers of Alberta, as a founder and president of the Alberta wheat pool, and as a power behind the provincial government. His confrontations with Crerar and McPhail are all the more interesting in that light.

Finally, a word should be said about Mr. Justice Hyndman. It seems unfortunate, in retrospect, that his name should be historically identified with the royal commission he headed but which, through the machinations of others, was drawn into disrepute. Mr. Hyndman deserves rather to be remembered for being the first Canadian to sponsor publicly the concept of international co-operation in wheat marketing. At the end of a long and distinguished legal and public career, he died in 1971, aged 97.

II
SEARCH FOR A POLICY

12

THE GREAT DEPRESSION

The tranquil note of retrospect on which Part I of this review ended was cruelly shattered by the disastrous chain of events which led to the stock market fiasco of 1929, the great depression of the thirties and a second recourse to war. The impact of these events struck the grain industry especially severely, and a corollary was the fresh impetus it imparted to the development of government grain policy. To understand this development, one needs also to understand the economic conditions which contributed to it, including the unbalanced state of the world economy after the first great war, the inflationary and speculative excesses which came to a climax in 1929, the deflation and its aggravation by mounting tariff and other trade barriers, by a competitive exchange devaluation as the gold standard disintegrated and, in more general terms, by the political and economic void which failed to provide an environment for lasting peace. Today it is easier to recall the spectacle of the stock market crash than it is to understand the complex of causes which contributed to the depression. Yet it was the economic malaise in post-war Europe, where Canada's principal wheat markets were prejudiced by the resort to policies of national self-sufficiency, which depressed the grain industry much more severely than did either the stock market crash, or any contributory factor within the industry itself.

Although economists of repute still commanded a measure of public respect through the depression years, a swell of resentment arose as the remedies they prescribed continued to produce negative results. Politicians who depended upon them for advice were prone to the same fate. The normal propensity to look backward and to rely upon experience persisted but, by now, it insured that the wrong solutions were endorsed. As an example, when the international gold standard collapsed, prominent economists predicted that there could be no permanent recovery until it had been restored. A few years would elapse before the revolutionary doctrine was proclaimed that deflationary forces could be countered by deficit financing. Meanwhile, economists, politicians, financiers and the afflicted public alike shared the conventional fiscal and monetary wisdom which prescribed just the reverse.

A general propensity to oversimplify the causes of the depression went hand in hand with failure to discover a way out of the morass. Experts within a particular industry were prone to identify endemic causes and, therefore, to seek internal solutions with equally disappointing results. This was especially true of the wheat industry. There were wide misconceptions over what had caused the wheat depression. Yet these assessments were the determinants of wheat policy. Therefore, in reviewing the prolific record of policy formulation through the depression years, one has constantly to distinguish between the actual and the attributed causes of the wheat depression, lest he fall into acceptance of the often repeated misconceptions, and fail to grasp why so many of the policy innovations devised in that time were stillborn.

One notable misconception was the theory that producers had failed to realize during the more prosperous years of the late twenties that European agricultural productivity was returning to normal, and that overseas exporting countries were by then overproducing for a naturally diminishing market. Therefore, once this thesis was accepted, it followed that the obvious remedy for the wheat problem was a reduction of production. Much time and energy was thereby expended by governments and their policy advisers on the organization of national and international campaigns for production control, while the evidence went unheeded that increased European production had been one response to a profound international malaise, which could not be relieved by a reduction in overseas wheat supplies. Instead, the production control campaign diverted attention from the need to recreate a political and economic climate in which international trade in wheat could flourish. What was really needed was a massive infusion of purchasing power in the hands of consumers and producers alike. However imprudent or impossible that seemed, any policy short of that could not hope to attain its objective.

The distinction between actual and attributed causes of the wheat depression is so fundamental to an understanding of the policy review for this period, that it is worthwhile to pause at the outset for an examination of what really caused the depression. Fortunately, there are good sources at hand to provide the necessary background. Among Canadian sources, one can hardly do better than to turn to the *Report of the Royal Commission on Dominion-Provincial Relations* for a highly competent account of the causes of the world-wide depression and its incidence upon the Canadian economy, including the wheat industry.[1] Two of the more familiar treatises on the subject are Professor Lionel Robbins's contemporary account of *The Great Depression,* published in 1934, and the more recent analysis of *The Great Crash 1929,* which Professor John Kenneth Galbraith wrote in 1955.[2] Robbins produced the earliest analytical account of cause and effect and, however much his recommendations are outdated, he left a durable record of what happened. Galbraith's work is more entertaining. Although he accounted for the contributory causes in Europe, Galbraith was mainly preoccupied with events in the United States, including the ineptitude of the federal reserve board and its non-interference with the inflationary money market which fed the climactic speculation. He concluded by wondering

[1]*Report of the Royal Commission on Dominion-Provincial Relations* (Ottawa, 1940), Book I, Chap. VI.

[2]Lionel Robbins, *The Great Depression,* (Macmillan, 1934), and J. K. Galbraith, *The Great Crash 1929,* (Houghton Mifflin, Boston, 1955).

when and how much of it could happen again. With such sources available, this introduction needs only to touch on the highlights to provide the necessary perspective for the continuing policy review.

INTERNATIONAL ORIGINS

In his analysis, Professor Robbins developed the sequence of international events which had precipitated the depression. In the chain, he emphasized:

1. The origin of the depression in the great war, through its wanton destruction of life and property, and a prolonged diversion of capital into non-productive use.

2. The Paris peace treaty, which demanded reparations from the vanquished countries inordinately beyond their economic capacity to provide. Professor John Maynard Keynes had drawn attention to this folly at the time, but he was an unheeded Cassandra, and the reparations issue militated against economic recovery in central Europe for years to come.[3]

3. The inflationary collapse of the Russian, German and Austrian currencies, which impoverished the middle classes in those countries, and which bogged down the German government in a budgetary morass.

4. Britain's return to the gold standard in 1925 at prewar parity for the pound which could not be supported by Britain's postwar economy.

5. The heads of the central banks in Britain, Germany and France, who appealed to the United States federal reserve board to pursue an easy money policy to keep interest rates low, in order to curb the flow of short-term funds to the United States. In response, the federal reserve banks bought securities heavily, thereby making cheap money available to the point of inflation and a speculative boom. Even when it was obvious that the boom had reached such proportions as to invite certain collapse, neither the United States government nor the federal reserve board took counter-action.

6. After the great crash, the typical reaction of governments in their resort to economic nationalism. The most prohibitive tariff legislation in United States history, in the making for more than a year, was enacted in 1930. France, Germany and Italy had already embarked upon policies of national self-sufficiency, to the detriment of Canadian exports. The United States had emerged from the war as a creditor country. Debtor countries found it even more difficult to service their debts when their exports were cut off by the Hawley-Smoot tariff. As Robbins observed, "Whenever a depression occurs — that is, a general contraction of trade — there is to be witnessed the odd spectacle of the nations of the world zealously endeavouring to bring about a further contraction by excluding each other's products."[4] Even the new Canadian prime minister followed suit as the Canadian economy suffered a direct blow from the tariffs on food and other primary products set under the Hawley-Smoot act.

7. The protraction of the deflationary process. Although deflation was the immediate and inevitable consequence of the collapse of the inflationary

---

[3]J. M. Keynes, *The Economic Consequences of the Peace* (Harcourt, Brace and Howe, New York, 1920).
[4]Lionel Robbins, *op. cit.,* pp. 65-66.

boom, the deflationary process need not have been so protracted, except that an effective remedy had not yet been discovered. Moreover, there were political overtones to the crisis in Europe where reparations and postwar boundaries remained live issues, and apprehension in other countries grew as Hitler flourished in the void by converting the disenchanted German middle class. This apprehension whetted policies of self-sufficiency which forced a contraction of world trade to one third of its former value.

8. The financial and exchange crisis of 1931. Before the deflationary process had run its course, it gained fresh impetus from the financial crisis which originated in a bank failure in Austria and several consequential bank failures in Berlin, where the government froze foreign deposits of short-term funds. This action threatened liquidity in London where a run on sterling began. By September 21, the Bank of England was forced to suspend gold payments, and the pound thus released from its gold parity declined in the next few months by 30 percent. Exchange devaluation had already been resorted to in primary producing countries such as Argentina and Australia. But the British action lent force to the trend by carrying the currencies of the sterling area countries with it, and the Canadian dollar fluctuated between sterling and dollar rates until the American dollar was devalued in 1933. The American action coincided with a banking moratorium declared by the new administration to halt the panic withdrawal of deposits after a series of bank failures.

PATENT PRESCRIPTIONS

One could embellish this summary of sorry events, as Galbraith has done, by describing the ineptitudes of the people identified with them. Although it affords more colorful reading, it also tends to gloss over the fact that men responsible for decisions, whether in government or in central banks, had almost worthless contemporary economic advice to guide them in counteracting the inflationary and deflationary forces which in turn had caused the depression. Classical economic theory had lost its relevance in the international crisis, and decisions had to be taken without benefit of competent advice. It took the economic fraternity some years to adjust to the new realities. As Galbraith observed:

> To regard the people of any time as particularly obtuse seems vaguely improper, and it also establishes a precedent which members of this generation might regret. Yet it seems certain that the economists and those who offered economic counsel in the late twenties and early thirties were almost uniquely perverse. In the months and years following the stock market crash, the burden of reputable economic advice was invariably on the side of measures that would make things worse.[5]

As the depression wore on through the exchange crisis and the gold standard abandonment, there was a notable upsurge of self-tutored monetary experts and pamphleteers who pressed their nostrums and, because of the hard times, their services on the governments of the day, whose files grew fat with such correspondence. As in biblical times, the world cried out for a Messiah, and the man who came closest to answering the call was John Maynard Keynes whose *General Theory of Employment*

[5] J. K. Galbraith, *op. cit.*, p. 164.

Interest and Money was published in 1936. Keynes addressed his *Theory* to his fellow economists, for it was quite unintelligible to the laymen, and a few years passed before Keynes's interpreters could persuade government leaders to abandon the notion that a balanced budget was a virtue in all circumstances. The depression of the thirties need not have become the great depression had fiscal and monetary policies operated to absorb excess purchasing power in the inflationary period prior to the crash and to create massive additions of it in the deflation which followed. In the 1930's, instead of putting a Keynsian multiplier to work, governments had contrived a divider which cumulatively shrank incomes, and notably farm incomes, almost to the vanishing point.

IMPACT OF SPECULATION ON WHEAT

Before turning to the incidence of these world events upon the Canadian economy, one might note in passing that, in respect of the more flamboyant features of the speculative boom and the stock market crash, there were counterparts peculiar to Canada which mirrored the more spectacular exposures and failures in the United States. Canadians through their brokerage facilities participated in the New York boom and, in its own right, Toronto had become a centre for speculation in new mining ventures. Moreover, interest had revived in trading in wheat futures. In 1929, when a short crop followed the record 1928 production, Canadian prices rose in comparison with those of Liverpool and Chicago as the pools, the line elevator companies and speculators alike seemed convinced that overseas buyers would soon have to pay considerably more for their wheat and that, therefore, Winnipeg futures were a good buy. A few months after the October crash, when several brokerage houses specializing in the promotion of mining securities were declared bankrupt, it was disclosed that they had also been substantially long in wheat. In fact, forced liquidation of their holdings had an unfortunate by-product in depressing the Winnipeg market to the point that margin calls on bank loans to the pools placed their credit in jeopardy and, for the first time, the pools were forced to turn to their provincial governments for support. Evidence of more speculative activity which had exerted pressure on prices at that time came to light a short time later when James Stewart, whose wartime record of service to the British and Canadian governments had established his reputation for market shrewdness, resigned from the top executive posts of the Maple Leaf Milling Company Limited, the Alberta Pacific Grain Company Limited and Federal Grain Limited, whose annual reports revealed substantial losses in trading accounts.[6] Although speculation in wheat was frowned upon, even by the participants when trades went the wrong way, it was not at all difficult for producers to persuade themselves that speculation by others was not in their own best interest, and their antipathy to the whole system of futures trading mounted as wheat prices declined. Yet the futures market was one of very few choices open to producers among marketing systems. The voluntary pools had provided a notable alternative until the depression struck, but from then on, it had to be either the open market with some

[6]*Manitoba Free Press,* August 18, 1930.

support from government, whether by entering the market or by operating a voluntary wheat board in competition with it. The only other alternative was the more drastic one of replacing the futures market with a monopoly board.

For the last four years of the Bennett administration the choice had been one of support to wheat prices in the futures market. Implementation of the policy, entrusted to Mr. John I. McFarland, brought into prominence a man whose association with the Alberta Pacific Grain Company afforded him an intimate knowledge of the utility of the futures market to the operation of an investor-owned line elevator company. McFarland had sold out his interest in that company in 1926 and had virtually retired to his non-grain interests in Calgary, but was still regarded as one of Canada's outstanding grain men when he became active again in 1930 by way of unsalaried public duty. Among many other attributes, McFarland enjoyed a reputation as a successful speculator, both on his own and on company account. He never traded in wheat futures for his own account, however, during the time that he served as general manager of Canadian Co-operative Wheat Producers Limited. On the other hand, Bennett acknowledged that when McFarland had taken on his new assignment he held long positions in oats and barley, which he eventually sold at a loss.[7]

No one was more acutely aware than McFarland of the role speculators normally play in providing liquidity to a market in which producers' deliveries must be hedged. But now that speculators had gone bankrupt or had voluntarily retired from the market, McFarland openly deplored their absence as he persuaded the government to authorize him to step into the breach and to buy the futures the elevator companies had to sell in order to hedge the cash wheat delivered to them by producers. He thereby became involved in a government-sponsored market position more easily built up than unwound. He warmly welcomed the establishment of branch offices in Winnipeg by American grain firms in the hope that they would revive speculative trading in the market. For almost two yeaars they were inactive, however, as McFarland continued to buy for government account. A brief speculative flurry developed in the early summer of 1933 but just as quickly subsided. When, to McFarland's outspoken chagrin, the speculators next returned to the market in the early autumn of 1934, they came in on the short side. Only one with a macabre sense of humor could have relished McFarland's plight. But he had already begun his metamorphosis from a champion of the futures system to an advocate of its abolition, for by now he was prepared to recommend the closing of the market and its replacement by a government grain board. Later, when he was retired as chairman of a new voluntary board, McFarland stirred up a political tempest by accusing his successor of being too friendly to the trade and of selling futures to accommodate the short interests.

The speculators who had been wooed were now reviled. In the process, two royal commissions, the Stamp commission of 1931 and the Turgeon commission of 1936 were requested to provide an objective resolution of the issue. Stamp endorsed the futures system, except under abnormal conditions, and Turgeon came essentially to the same conclusion as he

[7]*House of Commons Debates,* February 10, 1936, p. 46.

recommended continuation, for an indefinite period, of the Canadian board.

This digression into the subject of speculation has been made, not only because of its impact upon wheat prices at the onset of the depression, but because its prolonged absence and intermittent revival through the course of the depression had a bearing upon policy formulation as the continuing review will reveal.

THE DEPRESSION IN CANADA

But to come now to the incidence of the depression on the Canadian economy, one needs to recall that Canada had become a specialized producer of several staple products and that prosperity in these industries was dependent upon conditions in markets abroad. *The Report of the Royal Commisssion on Dominion-Provincial Relations* noted that, "in 1930 Canada supplied 32 per cent of the world's exports of wheat, 63 per cent of the world's exports of newsprint, 14 per cent of the world's exports of copper, 12 per cent of the world's exports of lead and zinc, and 31 per cent of the world's exports of aluminium."[8] To this list might be added our substantial exports of lumber and salt fish. With the contraction of newsprint consumption, the drop in demand for base metals, the Hawley-Smoot restrictions on lumber imports, the central European exclusion of wheat imports, and the Spanish, Portuguese, and Italian restrictions on salt fish imports, the impact upon prices for these raw materials was direct and very severe. On the other hand, production costs in these industries were included items more amenable to price maintenance so costs remained relatively very high. Thus Canada, and other raw-material producing countries such as Australia, New Zealand, and Argentina, found their economies more severely eroded than those of the larger, industrially diversified countries. Although the wheat industry in western Canada was a notable sufferer, it was not the only casualty. The newsprint industry, Canada's largest manufacturing enterprise, had been caught with excess capacity. Newsprint prices collapsed to the point that the companies were unable to cover their overhead costs. After attempting financial reorganization, several of the leading newsprint companies became bankrupt in 1931. Lumber prices collapsed when exports were cut off to the United States market. Decreased production in the automotive industry curtailed the market for base metals. The railways fell joint victims of the decline in the market for primary products, and were forced to seek government assistance. The plight of these other industries demonstrated that there was nothing unique about that of the wheat industry, and it refuted the contention that the latter had fallen a victim to its own contriving. All primary industries were acutely affected.

REACTION OF THE WHEAT ECONOMY

Although the Hawley-Smoot tariff act had been directed, among other things, at bothersome imports of Canadian agricultural and other primary products, it did not directly affect Canada's wheat trade because, back in

[8]Book I, p. 126.

1924, President Coolidge had raised the United States duty to 42 cents a bushel to the exclusion of Canadian wheat imports. So far as the market for Canadian wheat in the United States was concerned, the damage had already been done. But when similar policies of exclusion were adopted in France, Germany, and Italy, the loss to Canadian wheat exports was substantial. Before the era of high import tariffs on wheat, the futures market had wider scope in influencing not only the international pricing of wheat, but in affecting the production of wheat world-wide. Producers in every country moved in and out of the production of wheat according to the prevailing world price. But when import tariffs were imposed on wheat, the futures market was prevented from influencing acreage levels in the importing countries. For example, by 1930, the French government had placed an import duty of 85 cents per bushel on wheat, and it subsidized the export of French wheat by the differences between French and world prices. Germany's tariff had been successively raised to $1.62 per bushel on wheat. Italy also raised its tariff to $1.07.

As the depression progressed, the French government supplemented its import duties by setting import quotas, and by establishing milling regulations which limited the percentage of foreign wheat used in the production of flour. Germany also adopted restrictions on the use of foreign wheat in milling and these were supplemented by price-fixing and direct controls over the grain merchandising and milling industries. Italy followed the same pattern by placing compulsory limitations on the use of foreign wheat and by imposing a rationalization scheme on the milling industry. Until 1932, Britain maintained its long-standing policy of free trade in wheat. Under the commonwealth agreements concluded that year, the British government imposed a duty of six cents per bushel on non-empire wheat. It also passed a wheat act which guaranteed an annual average price to domestic producers. Mills were required to purchase the available supplies of domestic millable wheat. The two measures afforded moderate encouragement to domestic production. The Belgian, Netherlands, and Scandinavian governments were also relatively modest in their interventions. But the effect of the French, German, and Italian import restrictions on the volume of the world wheat trade was considerable, as is illustrated in table 12:1.

A comparison of the world wheat trade with the total volume of world trade during this period is particularly revealing. The physical volume of world trade declined in response to the quest for self-sufficiency which was reflected in the proliferation of retaliatory tariffs and other trade barriers, and world trade in wheat became a major casualty. Moreover, in dollar terms, the value of world trade declined much more steeply than the physical volume, because of the general decline in commodity prices. And again, the dollar value of the world wheat trade dropped still more drastically than the general values. These comparisons are shown in Chart 12:1.

Within the Canadian economy the results of imperfect competition in certain industries also showed up in stark contrast with those where competitive forces still operated. Where manufacturers could control supplies, they maintained prices at levels which would recover their unit

TABLE 12:1
WORLD NET EXPORTS OF WHEAT AND FLOUR
AND NET IMPORTS OF CERTAIN GROUPED COUNTRIES

Crops Years (Aug/July)	Net Exports		Net Imports	
	World	Britain Ireland	France Germany Italy	Rest of European Importing Countries	Ex-European Importing Countries
	(million bushels)				
1922/23	718	210	209	160	101
1923/24	835	240	169	184	163
1924/25	779	228	215	175	119
1925/26	702	208	150	170	146
1926/27	852	236	263	175	127
1927/28	827	232	220	198	139
1928/29	946	219	233	215	182
1929/30	613	224	96	188	140
1930/31	838	245	174	198	166
1931/32	802	261	135	215	184
1932/33	631	234	48	163	157
1933/34	555	238	26	133	126
1934/35	541	217	22	134	139
1935/36	523	220	13	118	114
1936/37	607	212	102	130	98
1937/38	546	208	59	138	98

SOURCE: C. F. Wilson, *An Appraisal of the World Wheat Situation,* Proceedings of the Conference on Markets for Western Farm Products (Winnipeg, 1938), p. 50.

costs, and they limited production to the reduced volume which could be sold at such prices. Such policies directly curtailed employment, and the unemployed in the cities bore the full brunt of the urban depression. On the other hand, wheat farmers remained employed, but grossly underpaid for their services. A chart which appeared in the *Report of the Royal Commission on Price Spreads* is reproduced in Chart 12:2 to illustrate the contrast. The royal commission was so concerned about the growth of imperfect competition in the economy that it recommended the creation of a federal trade and industry commission with wide authority to enforce competition, as it said:

> We have been forced by the evidence before us to conclude that the situation calls for a frank recognition of the necessity of more state intervention in business. . . . We propose the first steps to the goal (a Federal Trade and Industry Commission with wide authority to enforce competition) that has been well described as "the socialization of monopoly and the civilization of competition." Unless we can achieve this goal in the reasonably near future, there may well be forced upon us changes in our economic, social, and political organization beside which our proposals, important as we believe them to be, will pale into insignificance.[9]

Although the commission's terms of reference did not exclude investigation of wheat prices, its preponderant thrust was at the mass buying practices of the leading merchandising companies. Accordingly, the commission made no contribution toward recommending protection of the wheat producer from the effects of world-wide competition and regulatory

[9]*Report of the Royal Commission on Price Specials* (Ottawa, 1935), pp. 274-275.

CHART 12:1

INDEXES OF THE PHYSICAL VOLUME AND
GOLD DOLLAR VALUE OF WORLD TRADE, AND
OF WORLD NET EXPORTS OF WHEAT AND FLOUR.[1]

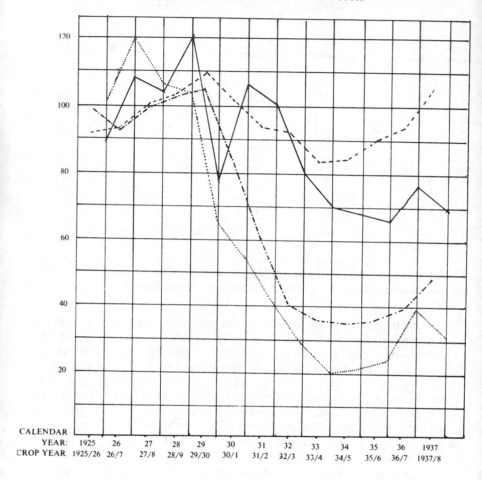

PHYSICAL VOLUME OF WORLD
TRADE, 1925/29 = 100 ————————

GOLD DOLLAR VALUE OF WORLD
TRADE, 1925/29 = 100 —.—.—.

PHYSICAL VOLUME OF WORLD NET EXPORTS OF WHEAT
AND FLOUR, 1925/26 - 29/30 = 100 ————————————

GOLD DOLLAR VALUE OF WORLD NET EXPORTS OF WHEAT
AN FLOUR, 1925/26 - 29/30 = 100 . . . .

SOURCE: C. F. Wilson, *An Appraisal of the World Wheat Situation,* Proceedings of the
Conference on Markets for Western Farm Products (Winnipeg, 1938).

[1]Indexes for physical volumes, Table 17, p. 56. The index of gold dollar value of
world trade is calculated from gold dollar value of world exports data in *League of
Nations Statistical Year Books,* 1930/31 - 1938/39. The index of gold dollar value of
wheat and flour is calculated by multiplying world net export data by crop year average
prices of British parcels as quoted in C. F. Wilson, *op, cit.,* Table 18, p. 56, and adjusted
to the gold value of the U.S. dollar. At the time, British parcels prices represented
average open market prices for wheat on a C.I.F. basis, and do not include any import
duties.

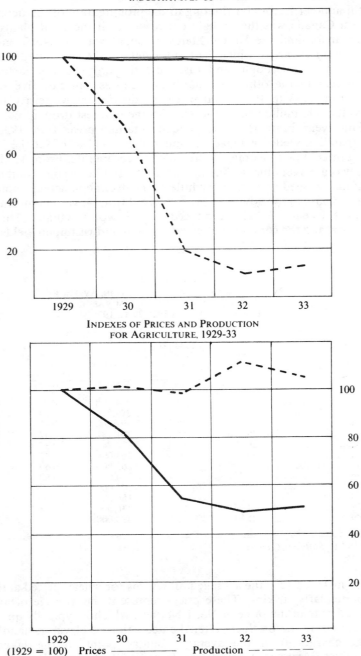

CHART 12:2
INDEXES OF PRICES AND PRODUCTION
FOR THE AGRICULTURAL IMPLEMENTS
INDUSTRY, 1929-33

INDEXES OF PRICES AND PRODUCTION
FOR AGRICULTURE, 1929-33

(1929 = 100)   Prices ——————   Production — — — — —
SOURCE: DBS data, published in the *Report of the Royal Commission on Price Spreads,* Ottawa, 1935, p. 9.

controls in other countries. That the commission recommended state control to enforce competition elsewhere in the Canadian economy was a daring as well as a controversial declaration at the time.

Still another factor contributing to the prolongation of the depression in western Canada was the drought cycle which hit the great plains areas of both Canada and the United States. Drought was the worst enemy, but crops in those areas which had sufficient rain encountered a different hazard in rust. Drought and rust were the only natural factors which contributed to the otherwise man-made depression. For five successive years from 1933 to 1937, total wheat production in western Canada fell below the 300 million bushel level, with the severest drought occurring in the latter year. Farmers had responded to falling prices from 1930 to 1933 by expanding seeded acreage. Although they tried to offset the impact of falling prices upon income, nature failed to co-operate. From 1933 to 1938, there was a perceptible decline in seeded acreage in response to the dry soil conditions at seeding time. Very little of the decline in acreage appeared to be in response to the advice farmers received from government sources that too much wheat was being produced to meet world demand. The acreage responses, and the combined effect of drought and rust upon yields per acre can be seen in table 12:2:

TABLE 12:2
WHEAT ACREAGE, YIELD, PRODUCTION, AVERAGE
FARM PRICE AND TOTAL FARM VALUE,
PRAIRIE PROVINCES 1928-29 TO 1939-40

Crop Year	Seeded Acreage	Average Yield per Seeded Acre	Production	Average Farm Price	Total Farm Value
	'000 acres	bu.	'000 bu.	$ per bu.	$'000
1928-29	23,158	23.5	544,598	0.78	424,039
1929-30	24,197	11.5	279,336	1.03	287,671
1930-31	23,960	16.6	397,300	0.47	187,279
1931-32	25,586	11.8	301,181	0.37	112,480
1932-33	26,395	16.0	422,947	0.34	144,333
1933-34	25,177	10.4	263,004	0.47	123,198
1934-35	23,296	11.3	263,800	0.60	159,027
1935-36	23,293	11.3	264,096	0.60	159,677
1936-37	24,838	8.1	202,000	0.92	185,580
1937-38	24,599	6.4	156,800	1.03	161,016
1938-39	24,946	13.5	336,000	0.58	196,380
1939-40	25,813	19.1	494,000	0.53	264,145

SOURCE: *Statistics Canada.*

Also in Table 12:2, the average unit returns for wheat, priced at the farm, are particularly striking. These prices represent the average of all grades sold, rather than the price of No. 1 Nothern which is typically quoted, and they are net to the producer after the deduction of elevator, handling and freight charges from the average country point to the lakehead or Vancouver. Average farm prices from 1930-31 through 1935-36 bore the full brunt of the depression.

Another yardstick which reveals the plight of western farmer; depression years is to be found in the computation of cash income ! sale of wheat and of all farm products in the prairie provinces as s.. Chart 12:3.

In recent years we have thought in round terms of two billion dollars as a breaking point in the level of farm cash income in the prairie provinces, below which some form of income supplementation becomes imperative. As costs have risen, this critical level has also risen. But under the prewar cost and price relations, government in the thirties might well have considered that in any year in which farm cash income dropped to 300 million dollars,

CHART 12:3
TOTAL CASH INCOME IN THE PRAIRIE PROVINCES FROM THE SALE
OF WHEAT AND OF ALL FARM PRODUCTS, CALENDAR YEARS 1926 - 1940

(million dollars)

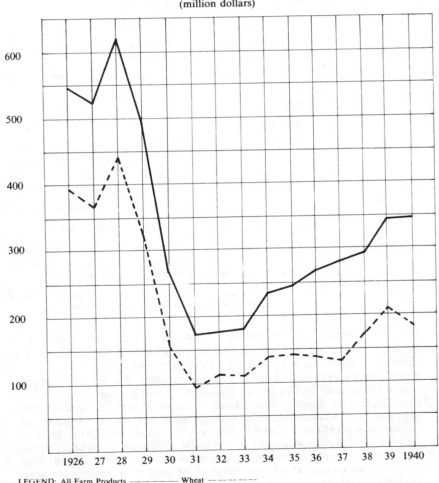

LEGEND: All Farm Products ——————— Wheat ————————

SOURCE: DBS *Handbook of Agricultural Statistics, Part II, Farm Incomes 1926-57* pp. 50-55.

government assistance would be necessary, whether through relief, debt moratoria, price supports, delivery bonuses, higher initial payments, or income maintenance by any other means. Although it seems almost ridiculous now to point back to a critical level that low, nevertheless, it underlines the fact that there were several years from 1930 through 1938 when such a low standard of necessity failed to be met.

The consequences of this failure upon the position of farm indebtness has been vividly portrayed by Professor E. C. Hope.[10] The larger spectrum of problems in municipal and provincial finance and the consequent breakdown in municipal services such as schools and hospitals, the need for direct relief in food and clothing and for federal assistance in taking over the financial burden of provincial relief administration are also well described in G.E. Britnell's study of the *The Wheat Economy* from which table 12:3, illustrative of the problem, is taken.

TABLE 12:3
CASH RETURNS PER ACRE OF WHEAT IN CROP-REPORTING
DISTRICTS OF SASKATCHEWAN, 1930-1938[1]

Districts	1930	1931	1932	1933	1934	1935	1936	1937	1938
South-eastern	$ 5.83	$1.29	$3.63	$ 3.29	$ 2.01	$1.40	$ 3.96	$2.73	$3.65
Regina-Weyburn	$ 4.56	$ .11	$3.32	$ 5.13	$ 2.01	$2.95	$ -7.39	Nil	$4.58
South-central	$ 3.25	$ .61	$2.37	$ 1.18	$ 1.28	$5.98	$ 2.82	Nil	$3.13
South-western	$ 5.74	$1.60	$4.96	$ 1.32	$ 1.60	$4.20	Nil	Nil	$4.35
Central	$ 4.28	$2.66	$3.53	$ 1.93	$ 3.98	$7.38	$ 7.93	Nil	$3.83
West-central	$ 8.65	$4.52	$5.39	$ 1.23	$ 4.33	$5.00	$ 3.34	Nil	$5.74
East-central	$ 6.82	$3.47	$5.49	$10.30	$10.12	$4.10	$14.26	$6.51	$7.65
North-eastern	$10.62	$7.79	$7.11	$ 7.10	$ 9.27	$9.32	$11.35	$9.55	$6.61
North-western	$13.07	$7.28	$6.65	$ 5.07	$10.12	$7.68	$ 5.81	$4.51	$4.06

SOURCE: G. E. Britnell, *The Wheat Economy* (University of Toronto Press, 1939), Table XXII, p. 78.
[1]Based on crop yields and farm prices as supplied by the Secretary of Statistics, Department of Agriculture, Regina. Italics indicate districts in which government assistance was necessary.

Britnell summed up the problems in the prairie provinces in his comments on the paper Professor Hope presented to the conference on markets for western farm products in 1938, when he said:

Yet in a period of depressed demand for export wheat, it is essential that the prairie wheat producers be put in a position where they can cut costs and carry on, but the maintenance of tariff schedules at high levels introduces rigidities into the cost structure of western agriculture and places the wheat growers in a peculiarly vulnerable position. The more inelastic the demand function for Canadian wheat, the more vicious will be the effects of inflexible elements in the cost structure of prairie wheat producers. Faced with dwindling markets, effectively prevented by the tariff from cutting costs, they are forced to sell their wheat crops at a heavy loss and live out of capital. The results of such a situation are seen in the exhaustion of reserves, a mounting

[10]E. C. Hope, *?Conference on Markets for Western Farm Products,* pp. 146-153.

burden of private and public debt and of governmental relief, abandoned farms and a steady depreciation of machinery, buildings and equipment, a sharp decline in the standard of living of the entire agricultural population, and all the other marks of a chronically depressed economic region.

Thus the wheat grower has found himself helpless in the grip of forces over which he can exercise no control and with a debt burden, private, municipal and provincial, increased to hopeless proportions. This mounting burden of private and governmental indebtedness in an area characterized by a highly variable net income, has thrown an increasing strain on economic and political institutions in the Prairie provinces with default and repudiation emerging as possible alternatives to further sacrifices. Such drastic policies ease the immediate pressure enormously, but have, obviously, undesirable social, political and economic repercussions. They can scarcely be regarded as offering a satisfactory solution of the problem. It should be possible for us, as Canadians, to work out a more orderly solution—a more equitable way of spreading the losses of prolonged depression and drought over the entire economy of Canada, and of cutting those losses in the future.

Materially higher prices appear in the light of the discussion of the past three days extremely unlikely. Therefore, lower costs are vital if the West is to survive. But lowered costs will not benefit the West alone. Wheat may not occupy, with the rise of mining, pulp and paper, and hydro-electric power in eastern Canada, as Professor Mackintosh has pointed out, as important or strategic a position in the Canadian economy as in the past, but a very large part of the economy of Canada—her railway systems and her manufacturing industries to mention only two instances—is geared to the production of between 300 and 400 million bushels of wheat a year on these western plains. If the continuance of that volume of production can be guaranteed by breaking down the rigid elements in the cost structure, the advantages to eastern Canada, in assistance in carrying the burden of the Candian railway structure, in increased western capacity to service a reduced debt, and in increased western purchasing power, must be obvious.[11]

INFERENCES FOR POLICY FORMULATION

This brief recollection of the facts of the great depression is an essential prelude to the understanding of events directly related to the evolution of government policy in that period. The contrast between the quiescent role of government in the grain industry from 1921 to 1930 and the increasing intervention since 1930 could hardly have been greater. Commencing with the drop in the level of farm cash income in 1930, the fundamental problem for government in relation to the grain industry has been the devising of measures which would insure a defensible level of farm income. The issue has not disappeared. The government's first approaches toward income maintenance were varied, tentative and grossly inadequate. But in examining the government record in the 1930's, one needs to recall that Canada's policy-makers had no more access to appropriate economic advice than had the responsible leaders in other countries. Our leaders were just as inhibited by the conventional wisdom of the day. As Galbraith observed in the United States context:

> The no-business meeting was an almost perfect instrument for the situation in which President Hoover found himself in the autumn of 1929. The modest tax cut apart, the President was clearly averse to any large-scale government

[11]*Conference on Markets for Western Farm Products,* p. 154.

action to counter the developing depression. Nor was it very certain, at the time, what could be done. Yet by 1929 popular faith in *laissez-faire* had been greatly weakened. No responsible political leader could safely proclaim a policy of keeping hands off. The no-business meetings at the White House were a practical expression of *laissez-faire*. No positive action resulted. At the same time they gave a sense of truly impressive action.[12]

There was a similar propensity to practice, if not to proclaim, laissez-faire policies in Canada. The two main political parties still espoused policies of nonintervention in business. If their critics complained, party leaders could invoke the civil and property rights provisions in the British North America act as a constitutional restraint upon federal government intervention. If this didn't suffice, the critics could be accused of advocating a socialistic solution. This attitude was exemplified by Dr. D. A. MacGibbon, who interpreted the resort to a wheat board in 1935 as a swing toward state socialism.[13]

MacGibbon served from time to time as a policy-adviser, and from his vantage point as a member of the board of grain commissioners for Canada he was intimately aware of conditions within the grain industry. His assessment of the problems, expressed in his writings, was wholly compatible with laissez-faire. He was not alone in this regard, but in good company instead with the political leaders of the day, of either party, who periodically detected and decried the entering wedge of state socialism. Nevertheless, demand for government intervention arose whenever one sector of the private economy failed to discharge its traditional responsibility to any other. MacGibbon's alternative to a wheat board would have been simply a substantial curtailment of wheat production in response to falling prices. He accepted the overproduction thesis at face value, and his remedy was to persuade producers voluntarily and without compensation to stop producing. In his summary of events from the great war to the great depression, MacGibbon said:

> The shift away from a free trading to a socialistic point of view with respect to marketing among the wheat growers had really begun with the slump in wheat prices that followed the First World War. Unable to secure a continuance of the Wheat Board of 1919 the wheat growers organized the Pools, and the success of these organizations for a time led them to believe that the pooling method of marketing wheat solved the problem of assuring to them at all times a reasonable average price. The disastrous collapse in prices of 1929 made it evident, however, that this position could not always be maintained. Thereafter the wheat growers looked to the federal Government to guarantee them a price for their product that would be satisfactory to them in the face of whatever fluctuations might occur in the international level of wheat values. That the unsatisfactory condition of the international wheat market was caused by the over-production of wheat did not come home to them clearly, but in shifting to a nationalistic viewpoint the Canadian wheat grower was in the broad current of the times. Over-production of wheat was a direct result of the general regime of nationalism and protection that developed in Europe after the First World War. With the onslaught of the depression in 1929, as protective tariffs rose and other restrictive devices

[12]J. K. Galbraith, *op. cit.*, p. 129.
[13]D. A. MacGibbon, *The Canadian Grain Trade 1931-1951*, (University of Toronto Press, 1952), pp. 46-47.

appeared in European countries, the situation became aggravated. Canadian wheat growers were only saved from complete disaster through the intervention of the federal Government. But having thus become beneficiaries of the Government's stabilizing policies, the Canadian wheat growers were no longer willing to face without protection the wide downward swings in price that from time to time were an unwelcome feature of unwise production practices. The Canadian Wheat Board became the chosen instrument to meet such a situation.[14]

Notwithstanding his detachment from producers' grievances during the depression and their redress, MacGibbon's second volume on *The Canadian Grain Trade* was an excellent attempt, and the first one to set forth a review of government grain policy in the 1931-1951 period. As with Robbins, his record of events is much more useful than the inferences he drew from them. Robbins, unlike MacGibbon, had deplored any artificial restrictions on production to cope with wheat surpluses as well as any similar attempts to lift prices above the market. But Robbins's recommendations would just as certainly have spelled political grief for the policy makers. His plea for the restoration of the international gold standard and its automatic strictures upon fiscal and monetary policy would have left any democratic government bereft of hope for re-election.

Here lay the tragedy of the Bennett years. With no useful economic advice available had he sought it, his own personal sense of financial integrity acquired in his highly successful business career just as effectively insured that the right measures would elude him. In his opinion financial responsibility whether personal, business or public demanded retrenchment in the face of a storm. It was his respect for financial rectitude in government as well as in personal affairs, more than anything else, that predestined Bennett's administration to failure.

In the special session Bennett convened just after the election, he asked for a vote of only 20 million dollars for unemployment relief. At the time many people, including farmers and their leaders, regarded this as an extraordinarily large sum. When Bennett brought down his first full budget nine months later, very little of this original amount had been spent. In his budget of June 1, 1931, when he was still doubling as minister of finance, Bennett estimated expenditures for the fiscal year 1931-32 at 430 million dollars and revenues at 325 million. After transferring the 20 million dollars tied up in public works projects to capital account, he proceeded to balance his budget by raising an additional 78 million through new import duties. To the Keynesian disciples (not yet on the scene), this was a fatal mistake. At the time, however Bennett was not criticized for lack of budgetary prescience. The leader of the opposition, Mr. Mackenzie King boasted instead of his administration's reduction in the national debt and that he had left a legacy by way of surplus in the 1929-30 accounts.[15] Even if Bennett had been inspired to prescribe deficit financing, not only would he have handed the opposition an issue but he would have had trouble borrowing in the badly buffeted money market from his friends who would have been shocked by such budgetary indiscretion.

[14]*Ibid.*, pp. 47-48.
[15]*House of Commons Debates,* June 1, 1931, pp. 2168-2169.

So it went with the later measures Bennett adopted to provide unemployment and farm relief. The combined dominion, provincial and municipal programs of direct relief in western Canada are part of the record of the total policies of the Bennett administration. Excellent accounts of the application of these measures can be found in Britnell's *The Wheat Economy* and Britnell's and Fowke's *Canadian Agriculture in War and Peace.* Too often, however, these measures typified spigots turned in the right direction, but all too timidly to replenish the purchasing power which, for other reasons, had been drained away.

SEARCH FOR A POLICY

Enough has been said now to demonstrate that, in the economic void, any policy Bennett pursued was foredoomed to failure unless, by accident in the process of trial and error, he happened to chance upon something that could succeed. In that context, it is all the more fascinating to observe the energy with which Bennett conducted his search for policy. Throughout the five years of his administration, one common thread bound together a long list of heterogeneous events — each represented an attempt to remedy the plight of the western farmer. All the failures of action he had charged against the government in the throne speech debate, February, 1930, Bennett strove vigorously to remedy after he became prime minister. But there was a very clear line of demarcation between the negotiations he pursued overseas to win concessions from other governments and the policies he reluctantly adopted, because of their treasury implications at home. In the long list of policy innovations he sponsored, the more memorable were his drive for an empire preferential tariff on wheat and the negotiation of an international wheat agreement. It was ironic to watch his more spectacular efforts come to naught as he fought a rearguard action at home against government involvement in the grain industry. One more factor added to the interest in his search. Despite the contemporary quips about his monolithic power—he held the external affairs portfolio throughout his administration and the finance portfolio for the first two years—Bennett also assigned to himself the unofficial portfolio of minister in charge of wheat policy. His ministers of trade and commerce, the Honourable H. H. Stevens and the Honourable R. B. Hanson were only nominally in charge. They presided over the administration of the Canada grain act; otherwise they were only interested observers as Bennett made the real policy decisions. Bennett was the first, and to now the only, prime minister who carried this particular responsibility.

SOURCES

The best published records of Bennett's search for a wheat policy are contained in the works already mentioned by MacGibbon, Britnell and Fowke. But more definitive material has now come to light in the *Bennett Papers* which Viscount Bennett bequeathed to the University of New Brunswick. The papers include all the incoming and outgoing correspondence of the prime minister's office. It is an enormous collection of material covering all the issues with which Bennett was concerned. The subject matter is filed alphabetically, and in between "Governor General" and

"Harbours" there are some 20,000 pages of correspondence on "Grain". To sift it out carefully would be the equivalent of reading a 400-page book every week for a year. An attempt was made to file the material chronologically by topic, but time and again the same subject recurs in some different place. Also, there is a certain amount of duplication because Bennett invited Mr. John I. McFarland to forward all his correspondence for incorporation with the Bennett papers. Thus it is possible to find both originals and carbon copies of all the Bennett-McFarland correspondence. It was Bennett's habit to write letters of one paragraph as he compressed much into little. But McFarland felt the need to be more expository as he elaborated by letter on his frequent telephone conversations with Bennett. From McFarland's letters it is possible to piece together an authentic account of the evolution of Bennett's wheat policies. McFarland had a habit of writing on two or three policy matters simultaneously, which emphasized their interrelation. To bring out the connection, the temptation is strong to present a chronological review of the whole, which would defy any comprehensible condensation. Yet it was how the events really happened. McFarland's other forte as a correspondent was that his description of situations and persons were refreshingly pithy. Lest one ponder the wisdom of some of the quotations, they are quoted because of their relation to policy. The more scathing of his personal comments have been omitted. The fact that Bennett took the trouble to obtain McFarland's files and to bequeath them as well as his to posterity is prima facie evidence that he hoped historians would some day interpret them. As a result, and because the telephone was not yet the exclusive means of communication, an accurate record can be pieced together. To some, the quotations may seem too long and too numerous. It would be a pity, however, to restrict the exposure of such prime source material.

13

TRANSITION

However unpredictable they were, events moved with inexorable force in 1930 to bring about a change in the federal administration and a change in control of the central selling agency's marketing policy. It was a year of transition both for the government and the pools. The King administration made way for the more dynamic leadership pledged by the Honourable Richard B. Bennett, and the pools became enmeshed in an exhausting controversy over their sales policy. Because of falling prices, the pools turned first to the provincial governments and then to the federal government to satisfy the banks, their creditors, with sufficient margin on their unhedged wheat stocks, with the end result that the federal government became once again, and this time permanently, involved in wheat marketing policy. What was at stake for the pools was the demise of the voluntary co-operative marketing system which producers had created as an alternative to the futures marketing system after the federal government had withdrawn its alternative in the form of a wheat board. By the end of 1930 this evolutionary process was reversed as the federal government began to retrace its steps, first, by employing the facilities of Canadian Co-operative Wheat Producers, Limited, for a price support operation in conjunction with the futures market and then in the course of time resorting to a voluntary, and eventually to a compulsory wheat board.

As the year began, Mr. A. J. McPhail, president of Canadian Co-operative Wheat Producers, Limited, which was informally referred to as the central selling agency or even more briefly as the agency, sailed to Britain at the invitation of the Right Honourable J. H. Thomas who had visited Canada in 1929 for the purpose of increasing two-way traffic for British shipping. Thomas had hoped to interest the pools in scheduling the shipping of a steady flow of wheat to Britain so that he could organize a similar return flow of British coal to Canada. While McPhail was in London, his lieutenants in the central selling agency were forced to turn to the provincial governments for help in guaranteeing the margins on the loans the pools had obtained from the banks.

A major controversy developed over the agency's sales policy as the federal parliament moved into its last session before a general election. The leader of the opposition, the Honourable R. B. Bennett mounted an aggressive campaign against the unemployment and tariff policies of the Liberal government and he also pressed home charges of ineptitude in the government's wheat policy. As soon as he assumed office, the new prime minister called a special session of parliament, raised tariffs and departed for London as head of the Canadian delegation to the imperial conference. There he pressed urgently for a system of imperial trade preferences, and took off for France and Ireland on a wheat selling mission. But in his absence the pools' position worsened. Even before he returned to Canada he was besieged with requests for federal government intervention. Since the pools' plight and Bennett's objectives at the imperial conference were separate issues, they will be reviewed in subsequent chapters, as we turn now to the 1930 election and the special session which followed.

1930 ELECTION

In February, as the King government prepared to meet a new session of parliament, it was in its fourth year of office and an election was in the offing. Late in 1929, the death of the Honourable James A. Robb had occasioned a cabinet reorganization. After brief terms in the trade and immigration portfolios, Mr. Robb had made his mark as minister of finance. Mr. King now appointed the Honourable Charles A. Dunning to the finance portfolio. Mr. Dunning had been one of the pioneer leaders of the Territorial grain growers' association, and he had organized the Saskatchewan Co-operative Elevator Company. He served in the provincial legislature and had become premier of Saskatchewan in 1922. In 1926 he entered the federal cabinet as minister of railways and canals. To succeed Dunning in that portfolio, Mr. King persuaded the Honourable T. A. Crerar to return to public life, and on this occasion Mr. Crerar resigned from the presidency of United Grain Growers Limited. As the new year began, Mr. John W. Dafoe, editor of the *Manitoba Free Press* and, indeed, the whole city of Winnipeg gave Mr. Crerar an accolade on his acceptance of the cabinet post. He was elected by acclamation in the Brandon constituency where the executive of the Conservative party graciously refrained from opposing him.

Quite apart from these cabinet changes, the death occurred January 15, 1930, of Dr. Robert Magill, who had been secretary of the Winnipeg grain exchange for years and also one of the pioneer grain-policy advisers. He was succeeded, temporarily, as secretary of the exchange by Mr. James R. Murray who had just left United Grain Growers Limited where as general manager he had been associated for years with Mr. Crerar. A few months later, Mr. Murray was appointed vice-president and general manager of the Alberta Pacific Grain Company Limited. He, too, was to emerge a few years later as a grain-policy adviser. As secretary of the exchange, Mr. Murray was succeeded by Mr. A. E. Darby who, until that time, had served as secretary of the Canadian council of agriculture.

By now a new policy-maker was standing in the wings in the person of the Honourable Richard B. Bennett. Because he was about to assume that role, Bennett's background is of interest. From relatively humble beginnings in New Brunswick, Bennett prospered in his law practice in Calgary and displayed an early interest in politics. The ventures which established

Bennett's first base of wealth were succinctly described by his lifelong friend, Lord Beaverbrook:

Bennett's first important financial venture outside of his law practice was launched as early as 1909. He borrowed $100,000, no doubt from his bank in Calgary, and invested the sum, with me, in financing the Canada Cement Company. I cannot recall his share of the profits, but since he took part in the original syndicate, the amount was substantial. With the proceeds of this successful investment Bennett was established as a man of small but real wealth.

Next year when I organised the Calgary Power Company, Bennett became the President and held office for ten years. When I sold my holdings to Killam, Bennett's shares were included and realised a large profit.

One day Bennett asked me to finance Mr. Cross's Calgary Brewing Company. I agreed. Mr. Cross was his intimate friend; an odd relationship, for Cross was after all in the drinking trade, of which Bennett strongly disapproved.

In 1912 Bennett joined me and Mr. Nicholas Bawlf of Winnipeg in buying and building grain elevators and a flour mill in Western Canada. By 1923, this business, known as the Alberta Pacific Grain Company, was sold to Spillers in Great Britain and Bennett's net gain amounted to just short of $1,350,000.[1]

Beaverbrook also related the remarkable story of Bennett's acquisition of the controlling interest in the E. B. Eddy Company, which greatly increased his fortune. Bennett was interested in the early Alberta oil development and he became a director of Imperial Oil Limited. He also acted as western counsel for the Canadian Pacific Railway. He confided to Beaverbrook afterward that his association with the Canadian Pacific Railway's affairs in the west had damaged and impaired his political appeal.[2]

Among Bennett's friends, Beaverbrook classed only five as intimate, Messrs. George Robinson and A. E. Cross of Calgary, Sir Edward Beatty, the Right Honourable Arthur Meighen and himself.[3] He barely mentioned Mr. John I. McFarland. Bennett's biographer, Ernest Watkins, who had access to the *Bennett Papers* a few years later paid surprisingly little more attention to McFarland, although Bennett had been closely associated with him in business and he became Bennett's intimate confidant and adviser on wheat policy, when the latter became prime minister.[4] McFarland was president of the Alberta Pacific Grain Company which Aitken and Bennett had formed, and McFarland and Bennett had been associated in the management of that company. It remained for Mr. R. K. Finlayson, Bennett's principal private secretary, to identify McFarland as one of Bennett's closest friends. Finlayson has written, "If I were to name R. B.'s four most genuine friends McFarland would be one of them and nearer to the top than the bottom of the list."[5]

From his two activities in the management of Alberta Pacific and as counsel for the CPR, Bennett had gained experience not only in the grain industry, but also in dealing with producers. When he was elected leader of

[1]Lord Beaverbrook, *Friends*, (Heineman, Toronto, 1959), pp. 44-55.
[2]*Ibid.*, pp. 106-107.
[3]*Ibid.*, pp. 83-84.
[4]Ernest Watkins, *R. B. Bennett*, (Secker and Warburg, London, 1963), p. 179.
[5]R. K. Finlayson, *Life with R. B.: That Man Bennett*, (unpublished manuscript edited by J. R. H. Wilbur, Public Archives of Canada). pp. 204-205.

the Conservative party in Winnipeg in 1927 in succession to Meighen, Bennett brought to the party and eventually to the prime ministership an expertise in grain unusual for the head of a political party. From his personal knowledge and experience, Bennett could debate on even terms with Dunning and Crerar as wheat experts and, in this respect, he outclassed Mackenzie King and Malcolm. Although Mr. King recruited many wheat experts to his cabinet, he reserved his most important wheat policy contributions to resolution of the issues in cabinet, when his colleagues were divided, and he usually delegated to the responsible ministers the announcement of policies and their defence.

In opening the debate on the speech from the throne on February 24, 1930, Bennett delivered a resounding attack on the government's laissez-faire attitude toward wheat policy, in which he displayed a remarkable grasp of current events:

But what has been done by this administration with respect to agriculture? During the last few months there has been propaganda carried on against Canada, falsely representing the position in the markets of the world with respect to the great wheat growing industry of the country. Some weeks ago I picked up a paper and I read statements that were allowed to go uncontradicted indicating that in Great Britain certain great purveyors placarded their waggons and drays with words indicating that they did not use Canadian wheat. I felt that was untrue; that no such propaganda was being carried on in Great Britain against this country's wheat, yet days went by and the days went into a week before any steps were taken by this administration to deal with that report. . . .

The first statement issued from Canada House was days late and in the meantime the provinces were endeavouring to grapple with the difficulty that confronted them. Why should not a statement have been made by the government of this country on behalf of the people of Canada stating just what the real situation was? . . .

Where was the Minister of Railways and Canals (Mr. Crerar), the past president of the United Grain Growers? Where was the Minister of Finance (Mr. Dunning), who formerly was interested in the grain trade? Where were they when the farmers of western Canada were faced with that situation? The situation required someone, speaking for this country as a whole, to make it clear that less than 55 per cent of the entire wheat production of western Canada was in the hands of the wheat pools and that the non-pool wheat constituted 45 per cent or more of the total production. On the grain exchange at Winnipeg we saw wheat selling at $1.45, $1.53, $1.60, and higher prices per bushel, and at that time the farmers were being advised over the radio, by men whom they thought, were responsible, to hold their wheat. Then the market broke, and the price of wheat fell to less than $1.20 a bushel. One of the primary causes was this: The pools have not sold wheat on the grain exchange this year. But there has never been a day in the last five months when you could not buy wheat from the pools at the market price on the Winnipeg grain exchange or for less than that price. Let that be told to the people of this and other countries. I say that the central government, having regard to the far-reaching consequences, was recreant to its duty when it did not make known to the world what the facts were. The Minister of Finance went out to Regina and said: You can trust the men in charge of the pools. Instead of simply saying that, the farmers should have received the support and assistance of the Canadian people because they were not selling wheat on the grain exchange, but only through their agents located throughout the world, and I repeat, there was no time during the last five months when wheat could not be bought from the pool at the same price or less than it was being sold in open competition on the Winnipeg grain exchange. I wonder how many members of this house realize that fact. I have found the gravest misunderstanding in this country with respect to the situation, and I would fail in my duty if I did not endeavour to clear up that misunderstanding without further delay.

When we talk about what the government has been doing, let me ask what the Minister of Trade and Commerce (Mr. Malcolm) was doing during the last year, and what the government of this country was doing to broaden the markets of the Canadian wheat grower? . . .

I am not unmindful of the fact that last year in June the Minister of Trade and Commerce stated from his place in the house:

"In so far as the sale of wheat is concerned, it is usually sold on contract, and I do not think a trade commissioner could be of very much assistance in that regard or in the sale of newsprint."

What a counsel of despair! It is not a question of helping the sale: it is a question of putting Canada's position right before the world and seeing to it that we are not discriminated against by trade treaties with France and Italy and Germany.[6]

By way of rejoinder, Mackenzie King took credit for the appointments of Dunning and Crerar, who did not participate in the debate. Neither did Malcolm offer a rebuttal. Malcolm had been heavily involved in the 1928 and 1930 revisions of the Canada grain act. He had announced before the house resumed that a more orderly draft of the act had been prepared, including a new means of establishing its constitutionality.[7] Malcolm circulated to members, including Mr. Bennett, Colonel O. M. Biggar's *Memorandum for the Minister of Trade and Commerce (on the) Revision of the Canada Grain Act,* of January 27, 1930, from which the following excerpts are quoted:

The chief technical difficulty with the Canada Grain Act as it stands is due to the arrangement and drafting of the provisions. They are arranged almost as if they had been thrown by chance out of a hat and many of them are extremely ill-expressed. Moreover, the same expressions are used in different sections to mean different things. The principal legal difficulty is the doubtful constitutionality of the Act as framed. It purports to regulate generally all dealings in grain, a course which can be supported only under the head of legislation "Regulation of Trade and Commerce" in section 91 of the B.N.A. Act. It is in the highest degree doubtful whether if the Act in its present form were seriously challenged, the Courts would not, on the authorities, be obliged to hold it to be beyond the competence of Parliament as being an unjustifiable interference with the jurisdiction of the provincial legislatures.

In the revised Bill an effort has been made to arrange the provisions in a logical and intelligible order so that provisions on any given subject may all be found together. . . .

The more fundamental, though not practically more serious even than was presented by the problem of arranging the provisions, was to discover a method by which the dealings in western grain might be regulated in such a way as to avoid raising any unnecessary doubt as to the constitutional validity of the legislation. It turned out to be practically possible so to draft the Bill as

[6] *House of Commons Debates,* February 24, 1930, pp. 19-20.
[7] *Manitoba Free Press,* February 14, 1930.

to base it on other heads of federal legislative jurisdiction besides the "Regulation of Trade and Commerce", and this course was accordingly taken.

The Canadian Parliament has exclusive legislative jurisdiction over "Navigation and Shipping" and also over certain lines of railway falling within a category which includes all the railway lines in Western Canada. Every bushel of such western grain as is intended to be affected by the legislation must begin its movement to the ultimate consumer over one of these railways, and the bulk of it must also move by vessel. Elevators are practically important only when they discharge grain directly into railway cars or vessels or receive it from them. Accordingly, a simple and entirely effective way of controlling elevators independently of any declaration that they are for the general advantage of Canada, is to forbid any railway company or vessel from receiving or discharging grain from or into any elevator which had not obtained a license from the Board of Grain Commissioners. The draft Bill contains such a prohibition, and moreover forbids railway companies and vessels to carry western grain within Western Canada unless either the grain has been inspected and graded under the Act, or the Board of Grain Commissioners authorizes the movement. It is in this way that the draft Bill proposes to solve the main constitutional problem . . .[8]

The revised bill was discussed in the standing committee on agriculture and colonization, which reported it favorably to the house and it was approved without debate.

As the session progressed, the polarity in personalities of the two party leaders became increasingly apparant. Mr. King was by now an urbane, cautious master of affairs and he commended his experience to the electorate. Mr. Bennett offered a dynamic personality in contrast. In a debate on the growing unemployment issue Mr. King, however, struck an unfortunate posture. He contended that unemployment was a provincial affair and that, on constitutional grounds, the federal government lacked authority to deal with it. On the question of federal financial assistance to the provincial governments in discharging their responsibilities in this field, Mr. King made one of his rarely incautious statements as he declared that he would not give a single cent to any Tory government, adding, for emphasis that he "would not give them a five-cent piece".[9] Although Mr. Bennett had not contributed to the unemployment debate he fell heir to a prime election issue.

At the time, the cabinet was preoccupied with the preparation of the budget under Mr. Dunning's new responsibilities as minister of finance. Canada's trade position required reassessment in the light of the Hawley-Smoot tariff legislation in the United States which was about to be signed into law. With the Hawley-Smoot tariff revisions aimed at cutting off imports from Canada of cattle, meats, maple sugar, cream, milk, potatoes, flax seed, hides, leather and shoes, lumber and a long list of industrial items, the King administration eyed Britain as Canada's second most important market, and as the most hopeful prospect at the moment for further trade development. The Dunning budget brought down on May 2 displayed a

---

[8]*Bennett Papers*, University of New Brunswick and Public Archives of Canada. See also Part I, pp. 209-210.

[9]*House of Commons Debates*, April 3, 1930.

desire to build up trade with countries, notably Britain, who wished to trade with Canada. Among other things, it was devised to open up markets for wheat, coarse grains, and other farm products. In its specific provisions, the Dunning budget unilaterally extended preferential tariff rates to a wide range of commodities imported from Empire sources, in the prospect that British buyers would become more favorably disposed toward Canadian products. The budget, momentarily, was widely acclaimed but Mr. Bennett developed an effective line of attack by ridiculing the government's bargaining stance. It had made a unilateral tariff reduction without exacting a quid pro quo from the beneficiaries. In the course of the budget debate Bennett dared King to call an election and King responded with exceptional haste by promising one forthwith. On May 30 parliament was dissoved and the election date was set for July 28.

Mr. Bennett opened his election campaign in Winnipeg on June 9, by reading a lengthy speech which Mr. W. D. Herridge had helped to prepare. Bennett pledged his party to a policy of protection for the natural resource, agricultural and manufacturing industries; the development of protection for consumers; the stabilization of economic conditions; a Canadian fuel policy; the development of foreign markets; improvements in transportation, expansion of empire trade on a basis of mutual advantage; and an old age pension scheme. Although the audience reaction to his prepared speech was less than enthusiastic, its message caught on. Bennett spoke next in Regina where a crowd of 8,000 awaited him, including a group of the unemployed, and his appearance in Calgary was triumphant. Both at Regina and Calgary, Bennett made a point of explaining that he had ceased to act as counsel for the CPR and that he did not own any shares. In his Calgary speech, Bennett repeated his criticism of the government's wheat policy that had remained unanswered in the throne speech debate, as he was reported to have said:

Again, the Conservative chieftain emphasized, there was the great problem of distribution of marketing and selling. He then put the question, "What has the government done? They have in effect said they could do nothing. They threw the responsibility on the wheat pool and blamed the co-operative marketers for the decline in agriculture. I deny that view, it is the duty of our trade commissioners to place our products before the world."

Fifty-three trade treaties had been entered into by the government, he proceeded. "Well," Mr. Bennett stated, "Italy has now raised the duty on Canadian wheat from 75 to 87 cents per bushel, France has raised it to 95 cents and Germany to 97 and a fraction. So we have these great countries placing prohibitive tariffs against Canada. In the meantime, the three nations were also exporting their surplus product.

Certain sections of the English Press had made an attack on the wheat pool, and had ridiculed the pool alleging that it was holding out for high prices. That attack should have been met by the Liberal government, Mr. Bennett asserted, and it was only after representation had been made by Mr. Greenfield, Alberta's representative in London, that action was taken.[10]

Bennett hammered away at the unemployment issue and he gained support as he promised to call a special session of parliament. Herridge was an able aide as a speechwriter and his language became heady at times as

[10]*Manitoba Free Press,* June 13, 1930.

Bennett promised to "blast his way into world markets". When King promised to call a conference on unemployment as soon as the election was over, Bennett replied:

I promise you action. He promises you consideration of unemployment. I promise to end unemployment. Which plan do you like.[11]

The two statements returned to haunt Bennett after the election.

In contrast, Mr. King had opened his election campaign in Brantford by declaring what he considered to be the issues. The first was the government's record which had lifted the country from depression to prosperity in the twenties. The second was the Dunning budget of 1930 which had opened up new avenues for the development of Canada's export trade. The third was the question of who should be entrusted to represent Canada at the imperial conference to be held in London in September of that year. He did not refer to unemployment in his opening speech, but he found it necessary to do so as the campaign wore on.

In the midst of the campaign Mr. Dunning defended his budget as a press account of his speech indicates:

Cobourg, Ontario, June 30. Attributing Canada's present unemployment problem primarily to the wheat situation, Honourable Charles A. Dunning, Minister of Finance in the King government, tonight upheld his budget of last May as presenting the country's one avenue to prosperity.

"No amount of Tory talk will make Canada eat all the wheat that the west grows," he told his audience amid cheers and laughter as he laid down his thesis that preference extended to Britain by Canada was the logical way to help the sale of Canadian grain in the Old Land and thereby boost prosperity here. . . .

Mr. Dunning said the Conservative party in Canada "would give no preference to British goods unless Great Britian consents to put a tax on food entering Great Britain in order to be able to give to Canada a lower rate of taxation than other countries."

This issue the speaker classified as "the greatest issue of the election campaign."[12]

Mr. Crerar was equally active. He appeared on behalf of Liberal candidates throughout the west and the substance of his advice was summed up in a press report:

Yorkton, Sask., July 3. Expressing the opinion that there was more unemployment in western Canada than in any other part of the Dominion and that this unemployment would disappear within eight months if Canada produced five hundred million bushels of wheat this fall, and could market this production, as he was of the opinion she could, Hon. T. A. Crerar, minister of railways, addressed an audience of about one thousand people in the local skating rink this evening.

The speaker pointed out to his audience that the cause of the serious unemployment situation in western Canada was the fact that during the fall of 1929 there was less than half as much grain produced in Canada as there was in the fall of 1928. Consequently not as many men were required to fill positions in grain elevators, railways, etc., as there were during the fall of 1928 and spring and summer of 1929.[13]

---

[11]*Ibid.*, July 11, 1930.
[12]*Ibid.*, July 1, 1930.
[13]*Ibid.*, July 4, 1930.

Mr. Crerar's campaign through western Canada was followed up by the Honourable H. H. Stevens, who played upon the inactivity of cabinet ministers on behalf of the wheat farmer. A press report indicated his repetition of the Bennett charges to which Stevens added a few of his own:

Regina, Sask., July 15. That Hon. Charles A. Dunning, minister of finance for Canada, was "laughing at the dilemma in which the wheat pool found itself last year," when its officials were in England meeting with the British government on the question of increased sales of Canadian wheat in Great Britain, was the charge made here tonight by Hon. Harry H. Stevens, member in the last parliament for Vancouver, when addressing a massed Conservative meeting in the interests of F. W. Turnbull, K. C., Conservative candidate for the Regina constituency.

Further, Hon. Mr. Stevens charged that "neither Dunning, Motherwell, Crerar, Malcolm or Stewart stirred a finger to help the western farmer, the pool, the private interests or the cooperative interests to sell an ounce of wheat."

"Mr. Dunning has never been sympathetic to the Pool," said Mr. Stevens. "He has always been opposed to it and unsympathetic. On the floor of parliament, he claimed to be a master salesman of wheat. And where was Mr. Crerar? Taking second place only to Mr. Dunning. He said he knew more about wheat than anyone else in parliament. Where were they? Not assisting the Pool. Where was Mr. Malcolm, the minister of trade and commerce? He told you frankly he was not interested in your affairs. He said: 'It is not my business.' The trade and commerce department is the one that controls the grain act and the administration of the wheat in the west. Where were they?

"Not one of them stirred a finger to help the western farmer, the pool or the private interests or the cooperative interests to sell an ounce of wheat. Neither Dunning, Crerar, Malcolm, Motherwell or Stewart turned a finger or made the slight(est) effort to assist the pool or the private operator to market a single ounce of your wheat."[14]

Just before the election Mr. King recognized the political necessity of committing the federal government to unemployment assistance; he promised to contribute dollar for dollar with the provincial governments and municipalities of Canada for the relief of unemployment, but his promise came too late.[15] On July 28 the Canadian electorate returned 139 Conservatives, 86 Liberals, 10 United Farmers, 2 Progressives, 3 Labour and 5 Independents to parliament. Mr. Bennett was sworn in as prime minister on August 7. In the west only one Liberal had been elected in Manitoba against eleven Conservatives, three Labour and two Independent

---

[14]*Ibid.*, July 16, 1930. Stevens had lifted Malcolm's observation that "it is not my business" out of its context in reference to domestic trade. On the other hand, Bennett had inveigled Malcolm into saying "In so far as the sale of wheat is concerned it is usually sold on contract, and I do not think a trade commissioner could be of very much assistance in that regard or in the sale of newsprint." (*House of Commons Debates,* June 5, 1929, p. 3436.) There is no corroborative evidence of Mr. Dunning's disenchantment with the pools. As premier of Saskatchewan he had assisted in their formation and advised McPhail on the purchase of the Saskatchewan Co-operative Elevator Company which he had formed. As his diary attests, McPhail regarded Dunning highly and could always turn to him for interested and helpful advice.

[15]*Ibid.*, July 16, 1930.

candidates. Mr. Crerar lost his seat in Brandon. In Saskatchewan, where eleven Liberals were elected, eight Conservatives and two Progressives, Mr. Dunning lost his seat while Mr. Motherwell retained his. Alberta elected three Liberals, four Conservatives and nine United Farmers.

SPECIAL SESSION, 1930

As promised during the election campaign, the new prime minister called a special session of parliament which met from September 8 to September 22, 1930, to deal with unemployment. Parliament was asked to deal with three pieces of legislation. The first was the appropriation of twenty million dollars from the consolidated revenue fund for purposes of unemployment relief, which has already been mentioned. The second was an amendment of the customs act to strengthen its anti-dumping provisions. The third measure was the most important Bennett introduced in that session, and it caught the country and its trading partners by surprise. This was the amendment to the schedules in the tariff act which provided for an upward revision in the rates of some 132 tariff items. The revision amounted to the highest boost in the Canadian tariff that had been made in the country's history. Bennett had pledged a policy of protection but no one expected him to take such extreme measures in advance of the imperial conference at which he had promised to bargain for reciprocal preferences. Evidently he felt the need of this bargaining stance as he led a large entourage to the conference. Before his return to Canada, he would be called upon to stem a rapidly deteriorating price situation by coming to the aid of the central selling agency.

14

CENTRAL SELLING AGENCY

At the beginning of 1930, the pools were at the pinnacle of their success. Mr. A. J. McPhail, president of Saskatchewan Co-operative Wheat Producers Limited, was also president of the Canadian Co-operative Wheat Producers Limited, created by the three provincial wheat pools to act as their central selling agency. This agency was governed by a board of nine directors, of whom three were nominated by each of the provincial pools. The agency's general manager, Mr. E. B. Ramsey, had resigned half a year earlier to fill, at the invitation of the Honourable James Malcolm, the vacant post of chief commissioner of the board of grain commissioners for Canada, which body represented the federal government's principal involvement in the grain industry. At the time, the government took credit for rejuvenating the board. But when Ramsey left the central selling agency, the pools found it very difficult to replace him, with the result that for a year and a half, and at a most critical stage, McPhail assumed the additional responsibilities of general manager.

With all his responsibilities, McPhail was a prominent figure on the Canadian scene. The British Labour government which was already facing an unemployment problem in 1929, sent the Right Honourable J. H. Thomas to Canada that September in search of a greater share of the Canadian market for coal and steel. An increasing flow of these commodities would produce greater tonnage for British shipping, but return cargo would also be needed. To explore the latter possibilities he met with McPhail. As a result of their preliminary talks, Thomas invited McPhail to pursue the discussions in London. In response McPhail departed in mid-January with two of his officials, Mr. D. R. McIntyre, eastern sales manager, and Mr. W. A. McLeod, director of education and publicity. En route from Winnipeg the party stopped off in Ottawa for a conference with the Honourable James Malcolm, minister of trade and commerce, although the Canadian government was not officially involved in the negotiations.

C. I. F. SALES

More specifically, Thomas had hoped he could interest the central selling agency in the building and operating of terminal elevators in Britain which could be supplied on a regular shipping schedule from Canada, and from which the agency could sell directly to British mills on a cost, insurance and freight basis which would leave to the seller full responsibility for the variable costs of movement until the wheat arrived at overseas ports. The notion was compatible with the agency's policy of direct selling which by this time accounted for half of its total volume of sales. This was the earliest known proposal for selling wheat on the c.i.f. basis in buyer's ports, but it fell on deaf ears. McPhail was well aware of the distress selling of Argentine cargoes when they got too close to buyers' ports after they had been put afloat unsold. But more importantly, McPhail had to take into account the fact that the commercial and elevator reserves of the three provincial pools had been expended upon the construction of country and terminal elevators in Canada, and that the pools could now ill afford the capital outlay required to enter the terminal elevator business in Britain. Thus Thomas's highly imaginative proposal came to naught.

During McPhail's stay in London, he was feted by the British government and by leading representatives of the trade and the British co-operative societies, as was due a leader in the Canadian grain industry. It was the last occasion, except for the imperial conference, in which he would go abroad in that capacity. While McPhail was in Britain, the central selling agency ran into its first serious predicament as the market performed rather badly.

PROVINCIAL GUARANTEES

As will be explained in more detail below in describing the controversy over selling policy, there were conflicting views on the course of the wheat market during the climactic autumn of 1929. The Canadian export movement had slowed down as an abnormally large Argentine crop, for which very little domestic storage space was available, was being forced onto the market. Canadian terminal elevators at the lakehead and in the east were clogged with unsold stocks from the 1928 crop. As both the pool and the line elevator companies counselled producers to withhold deliveries from the 1929 crop to ease congestion, they held out the prospect for higher prices as soon as the Argentine crop had moved. There was talk of two dollar wheat in the offing, and speculators were not slow to react. A little later, substantial holdings were uncovered as the market fell off in the other direction. Several Toronto brokerage houses were forced into liquidation of their speculative wheat holdings in January, 1930, as were certain of the milling and grain companies. In the price debacle of the last few days in January, McPhail suspected Mr. James Stewart of "bearing" the market when what actually transpired was that his companies' speculative holdings were being liquidated.[1]

The pools were vulnerable to such a price decline. On January 3, 1930, cash wheat closed at $1.39 ⅛. By January 31 the price was down to $1.20 ¾. The drop had been abrupt in the last three days of the month. The predicament of the pools stemmed from the fact that, unlike the line elevator companies, they carried their wheat unhedged. Both the pools and the line companies borrowed the money required to pay producers as they delivered wheat; the pools borrowed to make their initial payments, and the line companies to pay the current market price. By hedging the wheat

[1]*The Diary of Alexander James McPhail, p. 210.* See also *Manitoba Free Press,* October 28, 1930.

delivered to them—that is, by selling as many futures as they bought cash wheat—the line companies could freeze the value of their wheat inventories and borrow up to 100 percent of the value of the warehouse receipts they furnished to the banks as collateral. On that basis, the line companies and the banks suffered little risk from fluctuating wheat prices. However, it would have defeated the pool method of marketing, had the pools similarly hedged the wheat delivered to them. That would have required the pools to accept the market prices prevailing at the time the wheat was delivered, whereas their sales policy was one of "orderly marketing". This usually involved the spacing of sales over the whole marketing period, and of returning to their members through participation certificates the average price realized on all their sales. But their wheat inventories fluctuated in value as wheat prices rose and fell. Bank loans against such inventories involved considerable risk. For this reason the banks, by agreement with the pools, required the latter to maintain a 15 percent margin in the market value of their inventories in excess of the loans they advanced.

In 1929 the initial payment had been set at $1.00 and the pools had borrowed on that basis on the wheat delivered to them. As the price of wheat fell in January, 1930, the value of the pools' inventory was rapidly shrinking. Before it reached the point at which additional margin would be required, which was $1.15 on a cash basis, or $1.18 on the May futures basis, the central selling agency discussed the situation with a representative of the banks. In McPhail's absence, Mr. Paul F. Bredt, vice-president of the Manitoba pool and a director of the agency, accompanied by Messrs. George McIvor and Charles Folliott of the sales staff, met on January 29 with Mr. S. L. Cork, chairman of the lending banks' committee, to ascertain what course the banks might take if market prices were to penetrate the 15 percent margin. The agency's representatives were fearful lest the banks would require the pools to sell wheat in liquidation of their loans, thereby further depressing the market. Their fears were confirmed by Mr. Cork who could only anticipate that the banks would require the margins to be maintained, by liquidation of stocks if necessary, and the pool representatives interpreted his statement as an ultimatum. Mr. S. H. Logan, who represented the lending committee before the select standing committee on banking and commerce a few years later explained the position of the banks in the following terms:

> During the fall of 1929, generally speaking, there was a lack of export demand. Late in January, 1930, the market was acting very badly and on the 29th of that month when May wheat was $1.27 ⅜ and cash wheat $1.22 ⅜, the pool officials asked the chairman of the Lending Banks Committee what the attitude of the banks would be should wheat further decline to a point where the company would be unable to furnish the required margin of 15 per cent, which point was said to be $1.18 or $1.19 on a May basis. If the banks insisted on the margins being maintained, it would then become necessary either to reduce the initial payment or to sell grain in sufficient quantity to enable the margin percentage to be maintained, or both. The chairman told them that he could not give an answer without consulting the other banks but he felt that the banks would likely expect margins to be maintained even at the expense of some liquidation of grain holdings. Obviously, the pool officials then, and without awaiting any further intimation of the attitude of the banks,

approached the governments of the three Prairie Provinces for their guarantees, for at the next meeting which they had with the Lending Banks committee on 1st February they said that they were in a position to furnish such guarantees in place of margin.[2]

As indicated, the pool representatives turned to the premiers of the three prairie provinces to seek their financial support. The three provincial governments had helped to father the pools in their formative years. With more than half the wheat in western Canada being marketed through the pool system, the political welfare of the three governments was inextricably involved in the pools' present plight. The response of the three premiers to the agency's representations was immediate. Following their verbal assurances to the banks on February 1, the premiers of the three provinces, the Honourable John E. Brownlee of Alberta, the Honourable J. T. M. Anderson of Saskatchewan, and the Honourable John Bracken of Manitoba made simultaneous announcements on February 5 of the commitments they had made to the lending banks. The commitments guaranteeing the 15 percent margin of security required by the banks were expressed, as in Premier Bracken's letter of February 5, to the chairman of the lending committee:

> The Government of Manitoba, at the request of the Manitoba Wheat Pool board, is prepared to guarantee Manitoba's share of advances to the wheat pool to the extent of the 15 per cent, security over and above the advances made by the lending banks, which surplus it had been agreed upon between the banks and the pool, shall be maintained.[3]

In explanation of this action Premier Bracken made a statement in the Manitoba legislature. He justified the protection to producers and to the business stability of the west. He promised legislative action if it should be found necessary to provide a formal guarantee, as he said:

> Certain stock brokerage houses which had their funds seized by the government of Ontario were found to have had large holdings of grain on margin. As the price of wheat went down calls came for more margin, and with their funds tied up these calls could not be met. Through the efforts of the attorney-general, sufficient of these funds were released by the attorney-general of Ontario to protect these margins for the time being, thus preventing the dumping of this grain on the market.
>
> As the market went down during the last three or four weeks the lending banks demanded that the 15 per cent surplus security provided by the pools be maintained. This meant that if the prices went much lower the pool would be forced to sell on a falling market, and thus press it down still further.
>
> In addition to this it was current rumor that there was deliberate manipulation of the market in an effort to drive it down for the double purpose of embarrassing the financing of the pools and enabling speculators to buy at a low figure and profit by the ensuing rise.[4]

This statement was supported by Mr. George McIvor, general sales manager of the central selling agency, who said in the absence of Mr. McPhail:

> During the past few weeks the Canadian grain markets have been unduly

[2] *Select Standing Committee on Banking and Commerce,* Appendix to the Seventy-second Volume of the Journals of the House of Commons, Session 1934, p. 262.
[3] *Manitoba Free Press,* February 5, 1930.
[4] *Ibid.,* February 6, 1930.

depressed due to a loss of confidence on the part of the investing public, endangered by the uncertainties arising from the stock market crash and the present investigations of the transactions of certain brokerage houses. As a result of this condition grain in volume out of all proportion to the present actual demand has been offered on our commodity markets, which has naturally brought about a drastic reduction in prices not warranted by basic supply and demand conditions.

While the pools have fortunately been in a position to avoid liquidating any part of their holdings upon a market already embarrassed by extremely heavy selling orders, had the market been depressed to substantially lower levels, in order to meet the desire of the Canadian banks that the pools' margin of 15 per cent above their loans be maintained, we would have been forced to liquidate part of our holdings upon markets already unduly depressed, which, of course, would have had disastrous consequences not only to western farmers, but to the business structure of the entire country.[5]

The three premiers met shortly thereafter to discuss uniform legislation for implementing their guarantees to the lending banks. The meeting was held in Regina on Saturday, February 22, at the conclusion of which the premiers reported jointly:

We encountered no difficulty whatever in arranging uniform legislation covering the guarantee to be given the banks for their advances to the pool up to the present time, and to adequately finance the balance of the crop of 1929. The Central Selling Agency gave the governments the fullest information concerning their financial and sales position. The governments are perfectly satisfied with the results of the conference.

We found as we expected that the pool has been operating in conformity with the aims and objects of the organization. The legislation agreed upon will be introduced into the legislature at an early date.

In the meantime, the governments desire to make plain that this action is only in order to supplement the undertaking already arranged and not because of any impairment of the pool's margin with the banks, or because of any doubt of the pool's financial position, as the pools have at present on deposit with the banks collateral valued at current market prices at more than 15 per cent in excess of the total of the banks' loans to the pool.[6]

Thereafter, the premiers introduced bills in the three legislatures simultaneously on February 27 to formalize the guarantees. In explaining his legislation, Premier Bracken said that the government guarantees would make good to the seven lending banks any losses at the end of the crop year on advances made between August 1, 1929 and August 1, 1930. However, the unsold stocks would have to be sold at less than one dollar per bushel for the government to incur a loss. The pools had informed the three governments of their financial position and had undertaken to repay any losses sustained, either by cash or by pledging their physical assets.[7]

The action taken by the three premiers was an early example of the way they worked in unison, first with the pools, and later in their representations to the federal government. In fact they became the recognized spokesmen for producers in the void left by the decline and eventual disappearance of the Canadian council of agriculture. Whereas the pool leaders might

[5]*Ibid.*
[6]*Ibid.*, February 24, 1930.
[7]*Ibid.*, February 28, 1930.

themselves have filled this void, their influence was impaired by the financial plight of their organizations.

SALES POLICY DEBATE

McPhail returned to Winnipeg just as the legislation was being passed. On March 1, 1930, he gave a short press interview expressing optimism about wheat prices because British wheat stocks were at an abnormally low level. He had been extended a good reception everywhere. He was grateful for the confidence in the pools expressed by the three provincial premiers. He declined to comment on his discussions with Mr. Thomas until after the minister had spoken. In due course, Mr. Thomas reported to the British house on the failure of his proposal, and McPhail revealed in an address at Foam Lake that the talks had concerned a British request for the construction of pool terminal elevators in Britain, to which the pool representatives had been unable to accede.

But even while McPhail was still in London, a propaganda campaign was mounted against the sales policies of the pools. It almost seemed that the campaign had been timed to aggravate the pools' financial plight. The first salvo came in a statement by Mr. C. B. Watts, secretary of the Dominion Millers' Federation, that he had received reports of placards bearing the slogan "we do not use Canadian flour" appearing on hundreds of bread wagons and trucks and in the windows of the Lyons chain of restaurants in London. Although the management of Lyons Limited immediately denied the allegation, the fat was in the fire as the *Manitoba Free Press* editorialized on the alleged boycott in defence of the pools, and as politicians picked up the hue and cry. Bennett castigated the federal government for not coming immediately to the pools' defence, while Mr. W. Sanford Evans, now a Conservative member of the Manitoba legislature, elaborated on the charges against the pools, as he was reported to have said:

> There was no question but that Europe had taken a defensive position particularly against North America. Mr. Evans remarked that he had observed the world grain situation for years, particularly developments in Europe, and it was apparent that a factor of the present situation was due to the mistaken view in Europe that there has been or still is, an intention in other countries, to make Europe pay the maximum possible prices for foodstuffs. He did not care to discuss whether or not that belief was well founded.
>
> One of the first developments that had caused excitement in Europe over the food situation, Mr. Evans said, was a meeting called to organize an international wheat pool on the initiative of some leaders in the Canadian Wheat Pool at St. Paul in February, 1926. He read to the house an account of that conference, telling of hopes to raise the price of wheat 50 per cent.
>
> The doctrine of that conference was noted in Europe, and many comments made. It was the intention to form a pool of the three English-speaking countries, Canada, the United States and Australia.
>
> No very marked developments along the line suggested by the conference had taken place until a year ago last autumn when the United States government decided to introduce legislation heavily backed by public money to improve the price of agricultural staples for the farmers of the United States, and it was announced more than once that the views of representatives of the Canadian pool had considerable influence on the general idea. Then, a

little over a year ago in the belief that the farm relief legislation would have the desired effect the market in the United States started to rise, soaring upward last January and February, this increase of price taking place, according to Mr. Evans, in the face of the largest known surplus in history, and due solely to the belief that prices could be forced out of relationship to supply and demand.

It was about a year ago, Mr. Evans pointed out, that "Europe took to the trenches". For, Europe could not look at the action of the United States in any other way than this: the United States asked for payment of all sums loaned during the war, and at the same time was building up a tariff against all goods coming to the United States, making it still more difficult to pay the war debt in goods. . . .

Europe was in the position now of watching the wheat surplus accumulate in other countries. Every week her position was becoming stronger. . . .

"Today Great Britain is the hardest market in which to sell Canadian wheat, whereas a year ago it was the easiest and best. . . . The quantity of Canadian wheat used a year ago was from 40 to 50 per cent. Latest reports show that the millers have cut that proportion down to five per cent.

"The United Kingdom as has the rest of Europe, has taken a defensive position against the United States and against their conception of what is being done by the Canadian pool. . . . Not only among the trade, not only among the millers but circulated among the mass of the people this view is prevalent."

Mr. Evans read from a February number of a London publication condemning the attitude taken by the Canadian Wheat Pool in marketing its wheat and commented: "If this is not true it has got to be corrected. If this is true then we see something of the character of the problem before this country. . . .

"In my judgment the business policy which Canada adopts now, and which we can persuade Europe to accept, is the most important phase of this whole problem. The responsibility rests upon the government and upon the pools."[8]

The report of the Evans speech is quoted at length because it made a considerable impression on Bennett who used it, in turn, against McPhail on their first meeting after Bennett had become prime minister.

Mr. Aaron Sapiro joined in the refrain by accusing the pools of speculating instead of marketing wheat.[9] But Sapiro was hardly in a position to criticize for he could readily be quoted in contradiction of himself. The Right Honourable J. H. Thomas, in turn, was criticized for a remark he had made in the British house of commons and he cabled to McPhail:

My attention has been drawn to comment in Canada upon a statement made by me in the house of commons on the first of April. The suggestion that the statement was based upon any feeling that the pool had been attempting to hold up wheat is wholly baseless.

My statement was made in reply to an opposition supplementary question and was based on assurances given me by you at Winnipeg in September that the pool had been anxious to sell at prices substantially lower than those prevailing.

[8]*Ibid.,* March 5, 1930.
[9]*Ibid.,* April 2, 1930.

I fully accepted these assurances and welcomed them as evidence of a friendly attitude towards my plans for encouraging more regular interchange of goods between Canada and Great Britain.

I trust you will give full publicity to this explanation as you know I fully appreciate difficulties with which the pool has been confronted and I earnestly hope the situation may soon rectify itself to the advantage of both our countries. ....[10]

Throughout the spring of 1930, the *Grain Trade News,* published by Dawson-Richardson Publications Limited of which Mr. Sanford Evans was president, carried on a continuous editorial campaign in criticism of the pools. Even the Honourable Frank Oliver, who had been minister of the interior in the Laurier administration, went on a lecture tour throughout western Canada to disparage the pools. The campaign produced its heaviest broadside, however, in the autumn of 1930 when Mr. Sydney Gampell, a commodity statistician, delivered a lecture at the City of London College, on October 22, which consisted of a lengthy and inspired diatribe against the pools, their concept of orderly marketing and their exploitation of overseas consumers by refusing to compete with Argentine prices in 1929. The printed version of Mr. Gampell's lecture extended over 56 pages which would have taken at least four hours to deliver. In an equally remarkable feat for the surface mail, the lecture was reproduced in Winnipeg within eight days of its delivery in London. The presumption was strong that the material had originated on this side of the Atlantic, but this was never proven. It was immediately publicized in London, and the *Grain Trade News* reproduced it in Winnipeg with a foreword dated October 30. On the strength of the London publicity, John W. Dafoe ran an editorial on October 25:

> It seems impossible to achieve a reasonable discussion of the Canadian Wheat Pool, its aims, policies and achievements. No sooner is the name mentioned than prejudice and propaganda rear their heads to bedevil the argument, and the recent speech of Sydney S. Gampell, in London, England, is a fair sample of the kind of thing that is continually going on. It is a savage and unreasonable attack that bears little relation to the facts of the case, which are simple enough. It will be noticed also that most of the attacks upon the Pool are based not upon what Pool leaders themselves have said, but upon remarks made by "friends" of the Pool and by unfriendly observers.
>
> Some ground for these attacks is, of course, found in the mere size of the Pool. It became, during the last 18 months, the target at which all the shot was fired; but none of the English speech-makers have commented on the fact that the Pool selling policy was identical with that of all the other large units in the Canadian grain trade. On the other hand, the system of bulk selling introduced by the Pool was something new, and it was bitterly resented by the English grain trade who have also been opposed to the system of bulk buying introduced by the big British milling companies. New methods which tend to squeeze out older systems always incur hatred, and this has been a factor in the attacks upon the big co-operative organization.
>
> Responsible Pool leaders have never made loose statements such as those attributed to them by Mr. Gampell and others. They have undertaken the marketing of their members' grain, and by building up a big system of country and terminal elevators they have been in a position to hand back

[10]*Ibid.,* April 5, 1930.

former middle-man profits to the farmer members. If that is the way 140,000 western farmers choose to market their product no one has the right to interfere with them. Least of all a Mr. Gampell who has axes of his own to grind.[11]

Understandably, the Gampell lecture prompted two lengthy rebuttals by Saskatchewan Co-operative Wheat Producers Limited and the Alberta Wheat Pool, which slowly rallied to defend themselves against what had become a widespread and international attack, calculated to influence future events.

What appears to have emerged from the contretemps was that the grain trade had decided that the time was ripe for an open confrontation with the pools. Within the past six years the pools had captured half the western market in handling producers' grain. But for the fact that the total volume of grain deliveries was growing, this had been accomplished largely at the expense of the line elevator companies. Moreover, the central agency's policy of direct selling by which half of its total sales were being made constituted a threat to the survival of the futures trading system, as well as the grain brokers, exporters and import agents, whose services were being displaced. There was need to arrest the growing dominance of the pools if the private grain trade was to survive, and the pools' financial predicament signalled an opportunity to mount what was, in effect, an appeal over the heads of the pool leadership to the membership. It was not as though the basis of the charges had just arisen. The evidence adduced extended as far back as the origin of the pools, but the decision was now taken to marshall the charges, for anything that could destroy confidence in the pool leadership would play into the hands of the trade. A power struggle had been fairly joined between two competing marketing systems. With their survival at stake, the two sides embarked upon a bitter and prolonged confrontation in which the government was soon caught in the middle.

What, then, was the actual basis upon which the trade challenged pool policies? Four separate issues were thrown up in the debate, but they had a common theme in the alienation of the British mills which had sharply curtailed their purchases of Canadian wheat. These issues arose from (1) claims that the purpose of the pools was to raise the price of wheat; (2) that the policy of making direct sales was alienating the import trade; (3) that the central selling agency had occasionally supported the market by purchasing wheat futures; and that other times (4) the agency had pursued a withholding policy instead of selling wheat. Each charge merits examination.

Evidence on the first issue extended back to the origins of the pools. It had not been stated in their constitutions that the object of the pools was to raise the price of wheat, but it was not difficult to gather statements which lent credence to it as an undeclared objective. One example was to be found in a statement by Mr. Aaron Sapiro. Although he addressed his remarks to a wheat marketing conference in Indiana, Sapiro was identified with the organizational campaigns of the pools:

> When we go into co-operative marketing activities do we say we are simply going to try to get some little economy in the handling of wheat? No, because

[11]*Ibid.,* October 25, 1930.

you and I know that we can't handle wheat as far as the physical handling alone is concerned any more cheaply than the big elevator companies. . . . We don't say that the purpose of co-operative marketing is to introduce any economy in the physical handling of grain, because we think that particular point is absolutely too trifling to bother about. What are we trying to do? When we talk of co-operative marketing we say this: We are interested in raising the basic level of the price of wheat.[12]

The Honourable Mr. Justice W. F. A. Turgeon in his report of the royal grain inquiry commission, 1938, went into some detail in analyzing other remarks by Mr. D. L. Smith, sales manager of the central agency, Mr. W. G. A. Gourlay, a director of the Manitoba Pool, Mr. H. H. Wood, president of the Alberta pool, and Mr. J. H. Wesson, vice-president of the Saskatchewan pool, all to the effect that the object was a higher price for wheat. Three international wheat pool conferences had been convened in St. Paul, Minnesota, in 1926, at Kansas City, 1927, and at Regina in 1928. Wood's participation in the first of these conferences, attended by delegates from the United States, Canada, Australia, and the USSR, has been described by his biographer in the following terms:

Wood attended and took a prominent part in the discussion on pool selling policy. He asserted that if the four great wheat producing countries of the world would co-operate or even if Canada, Australia, and the United States would do so it would be possible to raise the world price of wheat. "If this wheat was sold intelligently, systematically and fed to the consumptive demand, just as that demand developed, we could maintain the price of our wheat on a level with the prices we have to pay, and we would not need any legislation to assist us in doing that either." He went on to declare that this method would remove the advantage that the wheat buyer enjoyed under the present system of marketing and that the "three great English speaking countries . . . can raise the price of wheat at least fifty per cent above the level of the price that has been maintained through the old system."[13]

At the Kansas City conference a year later, a resolution had been adopted:

As soon as practicable, the wheat producers of the chief exporting countries of the world should look towards co-ordination of their co-operative program. This must be preceded by thorough organization of the producers of wheat in each country on a permanent basis, and such organization must control a substantial percentage of the wheat grown in these countries. When these conditions are met, then international co-ordination will give the wheat growers the same control over the marketing of their crop already possessed by other industries and will materially assist in putting agriculture in its rightful place among the other industries of the world.[14]

Such statements appeared to smolder in the minds of overseas buyers for a few years, and then to catch fire in the crisis of 1930. As Dafoe had also observed in his editorial, the attacks on the pools had been based not so much upon what the pool leaders themselves had said but upon remarks made by friends as well as by unfriendly observers. An example of

---

[12]J. E. Boyle, *"The Farmers and the Grain Trade"*, Economic Journal, Vol. XXXV, 1925, p. 18, also quoted by Lionel Robbins, *op. cit.,* p. 137.
[13]William Kirby Rolph, *Henry Wise Wood of Alberta,* (University of Toronto Press, 1950), p. 165. Rolph's quotations were taken from the *Wheat Pool Conference, St. Paul, Proceedings, 1926,* pp. 65-70.
[14]*Report of the Royal Grain Inquiry Commission, 1938,* p. 85.

comments by friends appeared in Swanson and Armstrong's book on *Wheat*, published just at the height of the controversy:

> All these countries are already discussing pools, and in the United States and Australia at least a part of the crop is now pooled. Should this become general there would exist a very different situation from any known in the past. Pools representing three or four countries could, in the persons of their London Agents, meet any morning and come within reasonable distance of dictating the price of wheat in Britain, the price of flour, and the price of the people's staple food. Such conferences would be only sensible business and would inevitably occur.[15]

"Dictating the price" was quickly imputed to the pools, and Gampell pressed the charge to good effect. As Justice Turgeon observed in his report, the pools could not be faulted for having as an objective an improvement in the welfare of their members. He inferred, however, that the pool leaders had erred in talking about price improvement openly in the process of rallying support from their members, because such statements were readily turned by astute buyers to the pools' disadvantage. He commended a quiet, businesslike sales policy.[16]

The next issue arose over direct selling. It was obvious that in offering wheat directly to mills through its overseas offices, the central agency was bypassing some links in the merchandising chain and effecting some savings in commissions. The complaints of bypassed merchants would not have been so vocal, however, if the pools had been prepared to offer wheat through them at the same prices at which their direct sales were made. However, in the autumn of 1929, and in the face of heavy Argentine competition, Winnipeg market prices had risen out of line with those in Liverpool. During that period, the central selling agency had decided to weather the competition by waiting until the Argentine wheat was sold. The sales it did make, however, were done directly and at prices below the Winnipeg market. In these circumstances, there was no way that grain merchants having to pay market prices could compete with the central selling agency, and the complaints of the merchants on that score were justified.

A third issue had been made of the fact that the central agency had occasionally intervened to support the market. The first occasion was during a bear raid on April 4, 1925, when the agency purchased 3,435,000 bushels of futures and sold them in June at a profit. Again in May, 1929, under a similar situation, the agency purchased 6,153,000 bushels of futures and sold them in June at a profit. Then in November, 1929, the agency started buying again and the purchases were continued until April, 1930, with the knowledge of the provincial governments after they had given their guarantees. On this third occasion, the futures were disposed of at a sizable loss. The first two operations had netted the pools $1,023,000 and the third resulted in a loss of $2,014,000. The pool salesmen had gauged the market situation correctly in the first two instances. In the third situation they erred in underestimating the forced liquidation taking place. It was not just a bear market; a declining price trend had set in which would carry prices to

[15]W. W. Swanson and P. C. Armstrong, *Wheat* (MacMillan, Toronto, 1930), p. 226.
[16]*Report of the Royal Grain Inquiry Commission, 1938*, pp. 92-93.

disastrously low levels before its full course was run. Gampell contended that the effect of the central selling agency's intervention was to deny buyers the full benefit of the market declines. Both McPhail and Bredt defended the agency for taking a stand against "bear raids", but after reviewing these operations, Turgeon branded them as speculation.[17]

The fourth of the issues was the most serious, both from its consequences in the operation of the pools and from the inferences drawn by overseas buyers. This had to do with the holding policy adopted by the central agency in autumn of 1929. Turgeon heard a considerable amount of evidence on it and referred to it at length in his report.[18] In May, 1929, the central selling agency had bought futures for the second time to check a bear raid induced by Argentine competition, although it resumed selling in heavy volume on a rising market in June and sold 26,258,000 bushels in contrast with net purchases of 1,643,000 bushels in May. But, in July with the market still rising the agency sold only 13,561,000 bushels, which left it with an unsold carryover of 52 million bushels of wheat from the 1928 crop on July 31, 1929. At the time, Winnipeg prices were rising to unusually high premiums over the Liverpool market which reduced the volume of Canadian export sales. An excellent opportunity existed to sell futures, however, on the premium market in Winnipeg against which the agency could eventually have delivered cash wheat, but this course was not taken. The attitude of the agency appeared to be that it could afford in the main to withhold sales until after the Argentine crop had moved. Even a longshoremen's strike which had been called in the midst of the heavy Argentine movement was interpreted in Winnipeg as a bullish factor. The agency did, however, make direct offers through July, August and September at various discounts below the prevailing market price, but not sufficiently low to effect any large volume of sales.

The unreality of the Canadian position was highlighted in one of the Honourable James Malcolm's rare observations on the market situation as he wrote to his Kincardine friend and campaign manager, Mr. J. J. Hunter, on August 26, 1929:

> I had a very satisfactory trip to Fort William with Charlie Stewart. We installed our new Board of Grain Commissioners and I firmly believe they will handle the situation well. At the moment it is a difficult one. There is a complete blockade in the Canadian terminal elevators at Montreal, Port Colborne, the bay ports and Fort William, where 60 million bushels of wheat lie in storage.
>
> If you have been following the markets, you will notice that wheat is 16¢ higher in Canada than it is in U.S. and that American wheat is coming into Canada and paying the 12¢ duty in order to take advantage of the price being put on the Canadian wheat by the producers. As a result of this high price placed on our wheat by the owners, which includes the Pool, the European market has gone on a buyer's strike and so long as they can get wheat from United States and the Argentine, our terminal warehouses will not get relief.
>
> The situation for the British buyer is somewhat aggravated by the long shoremen's strike in the Argentine. If this strike continues, they will have to

[17] *Ibid.*, p. 71.
[18] *Ibid.*, pp. 74-81, 88-93.

break from starvation and pay the prices demanded by the Canadian owners. Should the strike be settled however we are in for a longer hold than ever and to this end the Pool and Grain Trade are making a big effort to hold this year's crop back in the country, both on the farms and the country elevators. It is a real financial battle, the Canadian grain trade and the British buyer, involving many tens of millions. My own opinion of it is that our holders of wheat are going to win and that we may have very dear wheat this fall.

The Canadian crop is short, but I think will run as high as 250 million bushels. At the moment, the quality is excellent in most districts although there are some spots where the wheat is a bit thin. If we pass the next two weeks successfully, without frosts and without excessive rains, I believe the crop will grade very high and that the areas which have not been affected will collect more dollars than in any other year. The great tragedy of the short crop however, is that the transportation companies are going to feel the loss of business very keenly and in some areas where the crop is a complete failure through drought, these farmers will be hard hit.

On the other hand, however, one must bear in mind that had we harvested a bumper crop and been affected as we were last year, with frost, or as in 1927-28 with too much moisture, causing the grain to grade tough and damp, our producers would have had to take a very low price for their commodity. So that taken all in all, we are liable to emerge from what appeared like a disaster, not too badly off. . . .[19]

Turgeon's contention was that even with the prospect of a smaller crop in 1929, the pool carryover of 52 million bushels merited an active selling policy in the July-September period. As it turned out, this was the last opportunity to sell at good price levels even at the cost of lowering the premium in order to make sales. Although the central agency did make direct offers at times at prices below the market, the sales policy had not been aggressive enough to move the normal volume of wheat into export for that time of year. It should be noted, of course, that the central selling agency controlled only roughly half of the total movement of Canadian wheat and that the grain trade responsible for the other half was not pursuing an aggressive sales policy either. Both the pools and the trade were caught up in the same market assessment that prices would rise later that autumn. Meanwhile, the pools had paid an interim payment of 21½ cents a bushel on July 31, 1929, on deliveries of all 1928 pool wheat, although there was a substantial remainder still unsold. Turgeon calculated that the interim payment had increased the central agency's borrowing from the banks by $40,000,000. The failure to dispose of the unsold carryover quickly thereafter had contributed to the pools' embarrassment as falling prices compelled the agency to seek guarantees from the provincial governments.[20] But the pricing of Canadian wheat out of line with the premium it normally enjoyed in overseas markets based on its actual quality differentials had built up sales resistance among buyers which was genuine, however difficult to evaluate. But it was not difficult for those who desired to do so to use the issue in the propaganda they circulated against the pools.

1930 INITIAL PAYMENT

After consulting the banks, the pools anounced on July 15, 1930, tentative initial payments for the various grains, including one of 70 cents for wheat.

[19] *Malcolm Papers*, Public Archives of Canada.
[20] *Report of the Royal Grain Inquiry Commission, 1938*, p. 77.

At the height of the election campaign, it had been difficult to ascertain whether the federal government would be party to the arrangement by way of a guarantee. Evidently both the pools and the banks assumed that the provincial governments would not renew their undertakings for the 1930 crop, as fairly sizable losses had already accrued under their existing guarantees. Shortly thereafter, a small contretemps developed between the banks and the pools over the date of expiry of the provincial guarantees. The banks claimed that, according to the undertakings given, the expiry date was July 31. The pools claimed that the guarantees applied to all deliveries from the 1929 crop. Although a cutoff had been made on 1929 crop deliveries at country elevators on July 15 as the new initial payments were announced, not all of that wheat could reach terminal elevators before July 31. But the banks did not accept the pools' contention and insisted upon written clarifications by the three governments. In response to the pools' request, Premier Bracken convened a meeting with Premiers Brownlee and Anderson in Winnipeg on August 1. In the morning the premiers met with the representatives of the agency, and in the afternoon with both those of the agency and of the banks. The banks agreed to make a temporary loan of two million dollars to tide the situation over until a meeting could be arranged with the heads of the lending banks in Toronto on August 5. At that meeting the banks agreed to finance the remaining deliveries from the 1929 crop, in exchange for new letters of guarantee which the premiers furnished on August 6.

The agency also discussed with the banks at the Toronto meeting the more important question of financing deliveries from the 1930 crop. The banks requested audited statements covering the operations of the three provincial pools and of the central selling agency, which required time to produce. The question remained open whether the newly elected federal government might provide a guarantee. The three premiers took up the cause on behalf of the agency and they were the first callers Prime Minister Bennett received after his government was sworn in. McPhail had been invited to attend, but he considered it prudent not to do so, while the premiers informed Bennett where matters stood with the banks. McPhail was satisfied with the outcome of the meeting in which the prime minister had undertaken to confer on the following Monday, with the interested parties including the banks. On August 11, Bennett met first with the bank representatives, and then with the provincial premiers and McPhail. On this first encounter between prime minster and pool leader, Bennett assumed something of a bullying attitude toward McPhail. He accused him of having failed to produce the audited statement McPhail had promised to the banks. Also, it will be recalled that in the house as leader of the opposition and through the election campaign Bennett had criticized the Liberal government for not answering immediately the allegations of a boycott against Canadian wheat. Now he accused McPhail of not answering the attack Mr. Sanford Evans had made on the pools. As McPhail observed in his diary:

> We discussed matters all afternoon. I was strongly impressed with the feeling that Bennett was a bankers' man and distinctly not a farmers' man. He is very prone to make ill-considered dogmatic statements which he cannot back up. He had to back down on one or two today.

Professor Innis commented in a footnote to this observation:

Mr. Bennett charged the pools with following a holding policy to secure $2.00 a bushel and that the speech of Mr. Sanford Evans at Winnipeg had not been answered.[21]

The meetings continued through the following week as the premiers stressed the economic importance to Canada of maintaining the 70 cent initial payment which had been tentatively announced. Although the new prime minister was prepared to use his good offices to bring the parties together, he made it clear that he would not involve the federal government in the arrangements, in the belief that the pools could move the 1930 crop with no more than the usual banking aid. The pools were not averse to managing their own affairs, and they made no request to the provincial governments to continue their guarantees for the 1930 crop. But when the banks realized that there would be no guarantees from any source, they insisted that the initial payment be lowered to 60 cents. As the Ottawa meetings adjourned inconclusively, but without federal aid, the pools and the banks pursued direct negotiations in Winnipeg. In addition to their insistence that the initial payment be 60 cents in the absence of a government guarantee, the banks also obtained a commitment for a 20 percent margin and an undertaking from the agency to divide sales evenly between old and new crop stocks. On August 26, the initial payment of 60 cents was announced. Only a few deliveries had been made at the preliminary 70 cent level.

Even the *Manitoba Free Press* did not fault Bennett for his refusal to intervene by way of a federal guarantee. But Dafoe reminded Bennett of his election promises to open up markets for Canadian wheat abroad, which he would shortly undertake at the imperial conference, and he also noted that Bennett had already taken a first step:

> He has had the Minister of Trade and Commerce cable all the Canadian trade Commissioners instructing them to stir about in their various communities imparting the information that Canada has wheat to sell and that it is very good wheat. This ought to start something.[22]

Bennett had already taken another step about which Dafoe and the public were unaware. On August 7, the day he had been sworn in as prime minister, Bennett had wired to Mr. John I. McFarland in Calgary, "May require you proceed to Europe re sale of wheat if requested you must not fail me."

To which McFarland replied immediately:

> Wire received. There are few things I would refuse do for you if within my power and while I do not now refuse in this instance yet from my limited knowledge of present situation I would consider it nonsense to go Europe make sales while there is Bull market in Winnipeg and Chicago pits and advantage should be taken of present speculative fever to reduce supplies which have been so burdensome and the best market in the world is now Winnipeg and Chicago kindest regards.[23]

In the week during which Bennett took office the market had spurted up by ten cents and was then just over the dollar level. It was the high point for prices in the 1930-31 crop year, which steadily eroded thereafter.

[21] *Diary of A. J. McPhail*, p. 217.
[22] *Manitoba Free Press*, August 14, 1930.
[23] *Bennett Papers*.

McFarland's response bore a remarkable resemblance to the unfortunate statement for which Bennett had so roundly criticized Malcolm, as he scoffed at the idea that wheat could be sold anywhere more effectively than in Winnipeg. But when Bennett's official party departed for the imperial conference in London, McFarland was one of its members. It was a large delegation of friends and government officials, but the presence of McFarland, McPhail, Dr. D. A. MacGibbon and Professor W. W. Swanson as wheat advisers drew public attention to Bennett's concern about honoring his commitment to open up wheat markets abroad.

FEDERAL GOVERNMENT GUARANTEE

After all the conferences and negotiations which had surrounded the setting of the initial payment at 60 cents on August 26, the situation remained fluid as prices continued to decline. The market had dropped from its peak of one dollar in the first week of August to 88⅝ cents when the 60 cent payment was announced. As prices continued to fall the banks agreed to reduce the margin requirement to 15 percent in the event that the market dropped below 75 cents. This happened early in October, and in response to the banks' request the initial payment was reduced on October 14 to 55 cents. On November 11, when the cash price had dropped to 65⅝ cents, the initial payment was reduced to 50 cents.

As the imperial conference (described in Chapter 14) ended inconclusively, Bennett departed for Paris and Dublin in pursuit of wheat sales. In Paris, he concluded a treaty for the sale of wheat. In London, the Honourable H. H. Stevens was host at a luncheon in honor of McPhail to which all the trade commissioners had been invited. But, during the conference, the wheat situation continued to deteriorate. McPhail returned to Canada before the conference concluded and found that with the declining prices the pools were again at the end of their credit with the banks; they must either liquidate their holdings with disastrous consequences to the market or make a fresh appeal to governments. McPhail had just arrived back in Winnipeg when the initial payment was lowered to 50 cents. Within the next two days, the three provincial premiers had gathered in Winnipeg to confer with the banks and the pools. As McPhail recorded in his diary on November 14 and 15:

14. Market fell today. We were two hours late in getting a cheque for $211,000 over to the clearing house as result of the reluctance of the banks to advance the money. As a result of the delay and the fear it inspired of our position, Frank Fowler notified us he would make a call Saturday morning for another 5 cents a bushel on 7,000,000 long. Premiers met banks in afternoon and again at 9 P.M. Everything is tottering. Bredt, Findlay, and I were called over near midnight and were in meeting until 1:30 with the banks and Premiers. Banks agreed to keep the long position margined until Monday morning, the 17th, on the Premiers signing a document that they would protect the banks against loss on the amounts put up. I also had to sign the same document agreeing to appoint a general manager suitable to the banks.

15. All day at the office. We had quite a time getting a cheque for $300,000 to put up in the clearing house. The banks last night agreed to put up margins until Monday. Spears told me this morning that the Royal Bank had backed out of putting up their share, and the Commerce and Montreal put it up. We

met the banks at 12. They had word from Toronto not to put up any more margins and we had to have $200,000 more up at 1:15. They finally agreed to stand by their agreement of last night. Otherwise the pool would be bust. The three Premiers and myself decided to go to Toronto on the evening train. I never went on a trip so reluctantly. I was tired to death.[24]

To persuade the banks to tide over the situation until Bennett's return to Canada, Premier J. T. M. Anderson on behalf of the three premiers sent an urgent telegram on November 14 to Mr. S. H. Logan for delivery to the Canadian bankers' association which met in Ottawa on the following day:

> On behalf Premiers of the Provinces of Manitoba, Saskatchewan and Alberta desire urge representations today jointly presented your Superintendents here. Firstly, we cannot too strongly state utter depression of agriculture throughout West, which is reflected in all branches of business. Secondly, the failure of wheat pool would strike final blow to hope of very great number farmers and business men, causing incalculable damage public morale, as well as a possible complete collapse market. Thirdly, present liquidation would leave Banks with wheat largely taken in at 60¢, while few weeks will result deliveries substantial quantities at 50¢ initial payments, so that Banks' ultimate risk of loss not increased by delay. Fourthly, demand for stabilization domestic prices at 70¢, without restricting export sales rapidly developing and supported by leaders all farmers' organizations. We propose to urge same before Premier immediately upon his return to the Dominion of Canada, believing farm industry cannot work through present crisis unassisted. Fifthly, Provincial Premiers desirous assisting in any way possible, but have already pledged credit provinces to limit. We urge, however, that in view of above, Banks carry present situation regardless price fluctuations until the Premier returns, when whole situation can be discussed with him, with view some action which will protect Banks and producers wheat. In the meantime we are discussing with wheat pool and superintendents here any question involving difference of opinion. It is our considered judgment that return confidence in wheat situation fundamental to purchasing power in West, and therefore recovery of general business conditions. We solicit your sympathetic consideration and cooperation.[25]

A copy of the telegram was also sent to Sir George Perley, the acting prime minister with a request for his consideration and assistance.

Representatives of the Canadian bankers' association met with the acting prime minister on November 15 to request a federal guarantee on any further extension of credit to the pool, as a result of which Perley exchanged cables with Bennett:

> Ottawa, Perley to Bennett, London, November 15, 1930, URGENT. Continued depression in wheat has endangered commercial position not only of wheat, but it is possible, so banks say, that panic may ensue. In this view, banks ask us to guarantee them up to ten million dollars. They expect this will not involve loss, but will enable them to make reassuring statement on Monday. Bankers are meeting us tomorrow two o'clock afternoon and we want your views. We intend to canvass further whole situation and if, in our judgment, it is necessary to accede to banks' request partially or wholly we want your authority. Will try telephone.
>
> London, Bennett to Perley, Ottawa, November 16, 1930, Western Premiers

[24] *Diary of A. J. McPhail*, pp. 227-228.
[25] *Bennett Papers*.

cabled me. Informed them investigations indicate surplus four hundred
million bushels wheat over requirements importing countries in addition last
year's carryovers. Fixing minimum price would increase difficulties and
improve opportunities competing countries. We cannot pay wheat subsidy.
McFarland will interview premiers on return first seeing you. Banks
directorate comprise greatest Canadian businessmen. They must realize and
accept responsibility as directors British banks are doing. We are powerless
give legal guarantee without parliamentary sanction. Banks should deal with
situation as they have in West Indies, Mexico and other places. Panic talk
ruinous. Reassuring statement necessary with courage and decisiveness. Any
event suggested proposals premature. Any government action must directly
benefit farmers. Now considering oriental possibilities. Unless banks demonstrate ability deal with situation certain agitation will result reconstruction
banking system.[26]

Up to that point, Bennett was determined not to become involved in the
wheat situation domestically. Bennett had asked McFarland to interview
the trade extensively in London and Liverpool and he gathered very
disquieting information about the wheat reserves in importing countries.
This strengthened Bennett's conviction that he should not yield to the
premiers' request for a minimum price of 70 cents, which they declared to
be essential for the economy, but at the risk of pricing Canadian wheat out
of the export market. There was one small ray of hope that a market might
open up in China. As for the banks, Bennett tried to bully them as he had
done with McPhail. On this occasion, he added a threat.

For the next several days matters remained at an impasse, with Bennett
daily in touch with Perley by telephone. After the banks had reluctantly put
up the money to meet the pools' clearing house call, the three premiers and
McPhail proceeded by train over the weekend to confer with the banks on
November 17 in Toronto. Following an unsatisfactory day there, the party
carried on to Ottawa where the premiers met with the acting prime minister
on the following day. Now that the pool leaders were no longer acceptable
to the federal government as intermediaries of producers' interests, the
provincial premiers became the recognized spokesmen for producers. After
their morning session with Perley on November 18, the three premiers
confirmed their representations by that same afternoon, stressing that it was
not so much a question of the wheat pools' remaining in business, as it was
of restoring some confidence to the market. To their letter they appended a
list of suggestions in order of preference, first a 70 cent floor, second a
guarantee of bank loans, or third a government stabilization board, but, in
any event, an investigation of short selling on the Winnipeg exchange:

1. That, without in any way interfering with the free movement of wheat by
grain companies and exporting agencies, the producers of wheat be assured of
a domestic price of not less than 70¢ Fort William. This suggestion is based on
the fact that producers of wheat today are passing through world conditions
not of their making and that they should not be singled out as one industry
that must work through these conditions unassisted by the state.

2. Failing this, that the Dominion Government, by guarantee or otherwise,
assure the banks against loss in carrying the Wheat Pool in an orderly way
under such direction as they care to arrange to satisfy themselves that
marketing is being properly carried out. This suggestion is based on the

conviction that uncertainty as to the Pool's financial position may be the most disturbing factor today. We also point out that the present initial payment was arranged with all the accumulated knowledge in Canada at the time as to world's conditions and in the belief that it was a safe payment.

3. Failing either of these, that the Government establish a Stabilization Board with the financial support to purchase wheat whenever the market falls below certain minimum levels. It is respectfully submitted that at present levels this action would involve a minimum of or no loss and would not be accompanied by any of the dangers which surrounded the American Wheat Board when it first began operation with wheat at more than double present prices.

4. Aside from the above, we suggested your Government might consider the advisability of instructing the Board of Grain Commissioners to inquire into short selling on the Winnipeg Grain Exchange with a view to proper action against offenders.[27]

In view of the gravity of the situation, Sir George Perley called in one of Bennett's closest friends, Mr. E. W. Beatty, president of the Canadian Pacific Railway, whose company was also gravely concerned over the impending breakdown in the western economy. Beatty had a long telephone conversation with Bennett who promised to call him back within a day. Finally, Bennett responded to the appeal in a fateful telegram to Perley which placed the federal government back in the wheat marketing business:

London, Bennett to Perley, Ottawa, November 20, 1930. Just talked with President Canadian Pacific will call upon you this morning. After finished French business only ship reaching Canadian port is Montclare sailing Twenty-ninth until Fourth December in which date expect sail reaching Canada about eleventh. Hope you can make satisfactory arrangements until then. Do not favour guaranteeing Ten million dollars but would be agreeable to advances being made to Provinces enable banks continue advances and maintain orderly marketing. Advised McFarland see you on arrival.[28]

Bennett's concession was minimal, and awkward to administer in its proposal to guarantee advances to the provinces instead of directly to the banks. His ministers were left to straighten out the details. From the time of Sir George Foster's announcement of July 16, 1920, which terminated the operations of the first wheat board and reverted the marketing of wheat "to the usual and normal methods of prewar times", the federal government had not been directly involved in wheat marketing. But at this point, with Bennett's commitment, the federal government resumed a long evolutionary course back toward complete involvement.

When Perley received Bennett's cable, he turned it over to Mr. Beatty who drafted a memorandum of understanding between the government and the banks. This was spelled out in detail in a letter which the Honourable E. B. Ryckman, acting minister of finance, addressed to Mr. Beaudry Leman, president of the Canadian bankers' association, on November 20:

After interviews culminating to-day in those between the Acting Prime Minister, yourself and myself, in relation to the present condition of the grain market which you and all interested regard as of most urgent public importance and extremely critical, the Executive of Government has agreed

[27] *Ibid.*
[28] *Ibid.*

in the interest of the Western farmers and of the continued orderly marketing of their grain as follows:

(a) Commencing 21st November, 1930, the Banks will continue grain credits in the usual way to permit orderly marketing and the Government will in the event of loss be responsible up to Five Million Dollars ($5,000,000.);

(b) This arrangement to remain in force until the return of the Prime Minister to Canada unless altered by agreement between the Government and the Banks;

(c) The Acting Minister of Finance is to be advised daily of the position of grain loans and to be notified promptly of any important change in the situation;

(d) The Banks are to be responsible for losses, if any incurred, in respect of advances or anything done prior to the 21st November, 1930;

(e) This arrangement, in the interest only of efficiacy, is to be kept wholly confidential, but the Banks are to make a definite reassuring statement that the situation will be taken care of;

(f) The government will make application to Parliament at its next Session to implement this arrangement by legislation so far as it may be necessary so to do.[29]

The limited, provisional guarantee which the banks received from the federal government fell far short of the full protection they had sought. A day earlier, while the issue was still in abeyance, the three premiers and McPhail met with the bankers in Montreal who were by then persuaded to liquidate the pools if no federal assurance was forthcoming. The bankers informed McPhail that several firms had already volunteered to sell the pool wheat, which would have terminated the voluntary pooling system. A few days later, on November 22, Mr. W. Sanford Evans wrote to Sir George Perley to deplore the excited behavior of the provincial premiers and to offer his opinion that a decision to liquidate the pool, under strong control, would strengthen the market.[30] However, at the meeting with the banks, McPhail argued persuasively that the banks would fare better with an orderly sales policy carried on by the pools under the direction of a general manager of their own choice, which McPhail had already conceded, in writing, to the banks. On this occasion, McPhail offered to seek the services of Mr. John I. McFarland who was en route home from Britain. Although McPhail would have preferred to obtain the services of Premier Brownlee, he recognized the bankers' preference for a grain man who was also well connected with Bennett.

On November 21, McPhail met McFarland in Montreal and asked him to become the agency's general manager. In the light of the crisis, which had become a national emergency, McFarland promised to consider it. He was evidently taken by surprise. McPhail still required the approval of his board, but no other option was open for the survival of co-operative marketing. As for the bankers, McPhail observed after talking to one of them in Toronto on November 22:

The bankers are not particularly interested in anything pool officials have to say. They are only interested just now in anything that will help to get the federal Government to protect them against loss. Hence the reason they are so

[29] *Ibid.*
[30] *Ibid.*

set on McFarland becoming general manager. They know he is one of, if not the most intimate friend of Bennett's, and that if he can be got into the pool it will probably do more than anything else to get the Dominion Government to do something.[31]

During the course of the next two days McPhail continued his talks with McFarland, who volunteered his services without salary, but made acceptance conditional upon having completely free hand in the agency's sales policy and upon the termination forthwith of direct selling. This entailed immediate closing of the agency's London, Paris, and Hamburg offices and ending of exclusive selling connections with firms in a number of countries. Fresh from contacts with the trade in Britain, McFarland considered this step essential in order to end the antagonism of the overseas trade. Having returned to Canada with the opposite assessment, McPhail was most upset over McFarland's insistence, but he recognized the necessity of McFarland's appointment and that the agency must temporarily forfeit its autonomy. McPhail counselled his Board accordingly and, at a meeting on November 26, the Board confirmed McFarland's appointment.

It is important to keep in mind that Canadian Co-operative Wheat Producers Limited engaged McFarland as its general manager; it was not a government appointment. The only question is whether Bennett was aware of the intention to appoint McFarland, and whether it was part of the package to which he had acceded when he authorized the federal advances. Sir George Perley was in daily touch with Bennett by telephone and McFarland's name was in play when Beatty phoned Bennett. It would be a plausible hypothesis that Bennett was not only party to the appointment, but that he made the federal commitment to the banks conditional upon it, or in the knowledge that it would be made. However, the prime minister persistently maintained that he had learned about McFarland's appointment only upon his return to Canada, and it was the statement of a man of unquestionable integrity. Years later, the following exchange took place in the house:

Mr. Crerar: . . . My hon. friend stated to-day that Mr. McFarland was asked by the pools to take the management of the cooperative wheat selling agency. I venture to suggest to the leader of the opposition that it was a condition stipulated by the federal government, of which Mr. Bennett was prime minister, when asked to give financial assistance, that Mr. McFarland should take charge of the selling operations.

Mr. Hanson (York-Sunbury): There is no evidence of that. The evidence was not given before the banking committee of 1934. My hon. friend was not here, and I was. That is only his inference. I say here and now that the pools suggested Mr. McFarland.

Mr. Crerar: I know the whole story.

Mr. Hanson (York-Sunbury): I do not think the hon. member does. He simply has some hearsay. . . .

Mr. Crerar: I did not get it second-hand, I got it first-hand. It was suggested to the pools that if they employed Mr. McFarland they would get a guarantee. My authority for that is a gentleman who was head of one of the pools.[32]

Apparently McFarland himself had little patience with such distinctions, or was unaware that they would become the subject of political debate,

[31]*Diary of A. J. McPhail*, p. 230.
[32]*House of Commons Debates*, August 1, 1940, pp. 2267-2268.

when he declared in his resume published in the Canadian Who's Who that he had been "apptd. by Premier R. B. Bennett, head of Central Selling Agency, Candn. Wheat Pools, Winnipeg Grain Exchange, 1930-35, . . ."[33] Even if McFarland had not become manager of the central agency, he would undoubtedly have continued to serve as Bennett's wheat adviser, as he had already undertaken to do by going to Britain. In the subsequent exercise of the federal guarantees, McFarland took his instructions from Bennett as the prime minister used the central selling agency as the instrument through which government wheat policy was implemented.

As soon as he was established in office, however, McFarland executed a policy decision of his own to terminate direct selling and to close the pools' overseas offices. His policy statement was issued on November 29:

> At a time when western agriculture, in common with that of the entire world, is confronted with formidable problems in marketing wheat and other grains at prices that will permit producers to live, it has become clear that growing responsibility for selling Canadian grain to the best possible advantage must be examined, as well as policies in the light of past experience, and of the market situation as it now actually exists. This responsibility rests upon all dealers in wheat and other grains, but it is peculiarly the duty of those in charge of the marketing policies of the western pools. These grain institutions have been built up on the labour and sacrifice, as well as on the unswerving loyalty of the many farmers of the prairie provinces. Their contribution to the economic life of the west has been substantial. The pools have played a part, and a great part, in deepening the faith of our people in agriculture, which is the most fundamental of all our industries. Even the keenest critics will admit that the pools have done much to sustain the farmers in their belief that agriculture should be elevated and kept in the first place in the economic structure of western Canada.
>
> The pools are living, growing institutions and should be ready to adapt themselves to changing conditions in a changing world. That must surely have always been the belief of the thousands of men and women who have built them and who have never faltered in giving the management their devoted support. If the pools, therefore, are to deal successfully with the present agricultural crisis, they must be ready to adapt themselves and take advantage of their past experience in the marketing problems that have arisen.
>
> Recently there was held at London, England, an Imperial Conference representative of all the nations of the British Commonwealth. One of the major matters discussed was the possibility of widening the market within the Empire for Empire products. Much attention was given to the marketing of wheat in the United Kingdom and elsewhere throughout the Empire, either as grain of flour. These discussions are to be resumed at Ottawa during the coming year.
>
> It is hoped that something definite and concrete will be accomplished at that time for the benefit of producers throughout the British dominions. In the meantime it is important to do all within our power to win the confidence and goodwill of British importers and millers, so that Canada may be in the strongest possible position to take advantage of any opportunity that may arise for consolidating its position in the markets of the United Kingdom and Ireland, as well as in Europe and elsewhere.
>
> To that end it has been considered advisable to withdraw our direct representatives from overseas. This should demonstrate beyond the possibility

[33]*The Canadian Who's Who*, Vol. II, 1936-37.

of doubt the truth, or otherwise, of the statements frequently made that the maintenance of direct representation overseas has militated against the sale of Canadian wheat.

It is my firm conviction that this change in policy will have immediate and favourable effects in strengthening the demand for Canadian wheat overseas, and that it will create a friendly feeling where there have been doubts and ill feeling concerning our selling policy in the past, that we shall be able to demonstrate beyond the possibility of doubt that our producers desire only fair and equitable treatment in the sale of their products.

This should make it easier for the pools to take advantage of the growing opinion in Great Britain and in the continent that agricultural living standards must be protected against the products of forced labour and ruthless and reckless competition. The management have complete confidence that the pools, by making adjustments to meet the existing conditions, will be able to render to their members a greater service than in the past, and that whatever changes will occur, it is certain that the farmers in the west will cooperate for the common good and will meet the common difficulties with the same loyalty that they have always shown in the past.

I do not hesitate in taking this action, as I am confident it is the duty of this great organization of farmers to take such action as will assist in removing from the minds of the grain and milling trades abroad, and in Canada as well, from the public mind, a prejudice which has unwittingly become prevalent that the pools' policy was designed to combat the world and plow a lone furrow to the detriment of the consumer abroad and to the grain and milling trade in general. There is no doubt that this sentiment prevails overseas.

I have spent my life in dealing with the farmer in the west, and no person knows better than I do his sterling qualities and that all he wants is a fair and equitable treatment; and I want the world to know that we are open to sell our wheat at a fair price as compared to that of other producing countries, and that we are ready and willing to use every established facility to that end and to transact business with whomsoever and wherever we can secure the best price and thus remove all prejudice, as I am firmly convinced that such a policy is the only policy by which these organizations can be successful and serve to the best advantage the best interests of our western farmers.

Trying times are with us and ahead of us, but by unselfish cooperation we shall pull through.[34]

Those who knew McFarland personally bear out his claim that he had, through his business interests, a remarkable personal contact with farmers, and the role of championing their problems came easily to him. But on this occasion, in what he considered to be their interest, he found himself in conflict with one of the cherished devices of the pool leaders, direct selling, and he was adamant that it should be ended.

At the same time, McFarland declared a second policy objective which extended beyond his own jurisdiction, but which he vigorously campaigned for until the autumn of 1934 when drought seriously reduced North American crops. This was his theory that overproduction had caused the wheat depression; he believed that the wheat problem could not be resolved until world wheat acreage was reduced, and the supply of wheat aligned with demand. A contrary thesis presented in Chapter 10 of this review is that the causes of the wheat depression were much more complex than any of the factors endemic to the industry. Support for this opposing thesis came

[34]*Manitoba Free Press,* December 9, 1930.

when the drought and rust of the mid-thirties sharply curtailed production, and the wheat problem remained unresolved. Yet McFarland was only one of many prominent exponents of the overproduction theory, and he was reported as saying on November 29, 1930, at the outset of his public career, "'Our Governments and farming organizations, should take every step to urge acreage reduction upon other countries, while insisting on similar measures at home. While this may be considered impossible, it must be done. . . .'"[35]

McFarland's change in selling policy required immediate notice to the pools' overseas offices and agents. A flood of cables passed back and forth, which reveal that Mr. David L. Smith, the London manager, wanted to return to Winnipeg immediately to discuss the change but was kept in London to handle the changeover. His office was instructed that it could no longer make direct offers to mills. The mills henceforth would buy on the basis of overnight market offers and acceptance. They could appoint their own agents within the trade for these transactions, or they could invite competitive offers. For the companies, especially on the continent, with which the pools had exclusive agency arrangements, their exclusive rights were withdrawn but they could still receive offers along with their competitors in the trade. The persons directly employed in pool offices on the continent were advised to set themselves up as traders, as the following telegrams were exchanged:

London, Smith to McPhail, Winnipeg, December 9, 1930. Confidential. No. 50. Step contemplated by McFarland such vital importance consider very unfair myself also feeling in any action taken without giving us full opportunity enter discussion. My experience Winnipeg London must be of value matter this kind. Appreciate your comments.

Winnipeg, McFarland to Smith, London, December 10, 1930. Please notify all exclusive agents that we are now cancelling exclusive feature of the agency but we will continue offering them wheat when desired at C.I.F. prices in the same manner as offered other exporters this side of Atlantic. Advise them we appreciate past cooperation and will cooperate closely in future in the manner outlined. No intention deal harshly with staff. Please advise what you recommend. Will write fully regarding yourself. Regarding Campbell, what do you recommend?

Winnipeg, McIvor to Pimpool, London, December 10, 1930. Please confer with Smith London as to future policy Italy.

Winnipeg, McIvor to Hoope, Poolstoff, Hamburg, December 10, 1930. Referring cable please confer Smith London who has had full instructions regarding new policy and will advise you. Regards.

Winnipeg, McIvor to Jardon, Paris, December 10, 1930. Referring cable French markets please confer Smith, London regarding future policy. Regards.

London, Smith to McFarland, Winnipeg, December 11, 1930. No. 64. Sorry but message not quite clear. Please advise if I correct understanding no offers be made direct to millers but will offer all reputable brokers, merchants, U.K. and continent on request. This be same procedure as followed prior London office except eliminating direct connections millers. However, shall be able to offer daily to selected firms. I want get this perfectly clear as evident you going continue export trade therefore important the few food grain houses left

---

[35] *Bennett Papers.*

ѹn the continent do not tie up exclusively with other shippers. Have advised Pim reference Italy. Jardon coming London tomorrow. Will notify all agents as soon as get your reply.

London, Smith to McFarland, Winnipeg, December 11, 1930. No. 65. Presume O.K. advise Co-op account changed policy. Unable make F.O.'s them direct. Hohley asking.

Winnipeg, McIvor to Smith, London, December 12, 1930. Jardon cabled re future Paris business. Suggest you advise him establish himself as grain merchant Paris, we give him offers same all other dealers. With his connections he should be able carry on. Have suggested this McFarland who concurs. Advise. Regards.

Winnipeg, McFarland to Smith, London, December 12, 1930. Answering cable No. 64, your understanding correct except it is necessary party inquiring must be financially responsible and must have definite inquiry for wheat. Please notify all agents accordingly also Hohley. Re staff and Campbell, will advise definitely tomorrow.

Winnipeg, McIvor to McFarland, Minneapolis, December 12, 1930. English Co-operative have office Montreal, Scottish Co-operative have office in Winnipeg. Both these people querying today about offers. Please wire if we should place these branch offices same footing as other dealers and submit offers to them or should we require they purchase through other dealers. Mailing statement requested tonight. Would like see some export business offering bring strength into this market as hear December wheat getting down to point where likely rushed into further stop-losses farmers cash wheat and options. Seemed to be some business late in day although don't think quantity sufficiently large to help market.

Ottawa, McFarland to McIvor, Winnipeg, December 15, 1930. Regarding British millers our policy work with them in same manner as rules and customs trade prescribe and would say we view business with their offices Montreal, New York or Winnipeg just same as Richardson or British Empire would. Difficult me advise but suggest you inquire from trade.[36]

After taking this action, McFarland wrote to his friend Sir Herbert Robson, one of the prominent British grain importers, who had served in New York during the great war as a member of the royal commission on wheat supplies. Robson had been one of the traders who had found it difficult to do business in Canadian wheat at market prices while the pools' overseas offices could quote directly at prices below the market in order to get the business. He had been a member of the committee that arranged for the series of grain lectures at the City of London College which had sponsored Gampell's tirade. He had obviously been one of those who complained about the agency's sales policy, and McFarland explained his new role, taking credit for the change of policy, in his letter of December 20 to Robson:

You will remember my visit to you when in London some time about the middle of October, when I went to see you in reference to getting your viewpoints regarding the various proposals discussed by your Government at the Imperial Conference with reference to wheat. At that time you enquired whether I was connected with the Canadian Pools and I informed you that I was not and that I was not connected with any grain company at that time. I am only writing now so as to confirm what I told you at the time of my visit to you, because it has occurred to me that probably you would be wondering

[36] *Ibid.*

how it happened that immediately after my return to Canada I was announced as the General Manager of the Sales Agency of the Pools. I wish to assure you that that announcement was as much of a surprise to me as anyone because at the time I was in London I had no thought of being in such a position. In the meantime we had discussed the Pool situation and I can recall that we were in agreement with reference to the Pools' sales policy; as a matter of fact, I had held that view for several years.

In assuming this position it was one of the stipulations that I should control the sales policy before I consented to the appointment, and conditions being what they were in Western Canada I accepted the appointment as a national duty, figuring that owing to the long years I had spent in Western Canada I owed the country something provided I could do anything for it. I can assure you now that anything I can do is a very small contribution and if I can only succeed in re-establishing confidence within the Grain Trade, itself, in regard to the handling of Canadian wheat, I shall have accomplished something probably worthwhile. It is evident that I cannot even accomplish this without the cooperation of such people as yourself and others holding influential positions in the U.K., by giving me your support in every way possible; what I mean by support is that you will do everything possible to influence the milling companies of the U.K., to increase their percentage of Canadian wheat in their gristing.

This country is a wheat producing country and it is of prime importance that buyers on your side of the Atlantic should have confidence that they will get their wheat at a fair market price at all times, and that is exactly the policy that I am endeavouring to carry out.

I will repeat to you what I have told others, namely: that our policy so far as sales for export is concerned, will be the policy of the Trade in general, namely: that any export business we may do will be done on the basis of Winnipeg values plus an export profit. There have been many complaints in the past that the old Pool policy resulted in the cutting of prices on your side of the Atlantic to the discomfiture of other dealers, and also to their loss. That is no longer the policy of this organization and I want you to feel confident that if you will turn your attention to the marketing of Canadian wheat you will not have any experiences such as have occurred in the past year or more.

I am well aware of your influence in the U.K. markets, and the object of this letter is to ask that you will do all you can to further the sales of Canadian wheat, no matter whether they are Pool or non-Pool holdings, but of course Pool by preference owing to my position at the present time.[37]

Sir Herbert's reply of January 2, 1931, is also of interest, and he became a regular correspondent of McFarland's thereafter:

Many thanks to your letter of the 20th December, which I have read with great interest.

I quite realize that when I saw you in London in October, you had no idea that you were likely to be called upon to come to the assistance of the Wheat Pool as their General Sales Manager. I have, I think, already assured you that the news of your appointment has been received on this side with great satisfaction.

I feel that I am entitled to say that you may rest assured that the grain traders of this country will do their utmost to assist Canada in marketing her wheat. For this there are now three reasons:

Firstly, the trade have been reassured that if they purchase Canadian wheat

[37] *Ibid.*

at a fair market price, they are no longer likely to be in danger of being undercut by the Pool selling agencies in London and elsewhere selling to large millers at artificially low prices.

Secondly, Canadian wheat being the finest red wheat in the world, the certificate under which it is sold being as good as Bank of England notes, there is always a large and free market for this wheat when it is competing in price with wheat from other parts of the world. In times past our millers have used as much as 60 per cent of Canadian wheat and will do so again so long as the price is suitable.

Thirdly, and this is not the least important point, for patriotic reasons, when Canadian wheat is in competition with other wheat, it gets the preference which in the trade is a matter of no small moment.

However, those who are responsible for the general management of the Canadian Pool ought not to forget that we in England dislike being threatened by a holdup by our brothers across the seas, as was the case some two years ago, almost as much as you in Canada would dislike any threat by organized English authority to raise the price of any commodity which Canada was taking freely from this country.

I hope the time is near at hand when we ourselves as a firm shall be able to do a large business with the Canadian Pool. You may rest assured that I will do my best to put business in your direction. Unfortunately, at the present time our ports are full of dumped Russian wheat and until this has been digested it will be difficult to do very much trade in your wheat, but the Russian shipments have fallen off considerably during the past three weeks, and Russia will not again ship freely until March or later. Before then, the stocks of Russian wheat in our ports will have been exhausted. Our millers will need Canadian wheat to mix with Australian and Argentine wheat, and there ought to be a revival in the demand before January is over.[38]

After his return from Britain, arrangements were soon made for the prime minister to confer with representatives of the banks. Following their meeting on December 22, Bennett handed the press a cryptic statement: "Arrangements have been concluded that ensure the orderly marketing of the 1930 wheat crop of western Canada."

Bennett declined to elaborate on his statement which was heralded in the press as a momentous declaration of policy. Banner headlines proclaimed Bennett's conference with the bank representatives and the assurance of orderly marketing which removed all possibility of a sudden liquidation of the crop. McFarland welcomed the announcement as restoring confidence and predicted that the market would soon advance. But the supporting news item could offer little more than the following:

The Hon. Mr. Bennett's statement that arrangements have been made to ensure the "orderly marketing" of the grain crop is taken in grain circles to mean that the dominion government will back the banks against loss of a falling market in the financing of the 1930 crop. This is the view generally held by the Winnipeg trade.[39]

Further clarification had to await the major policy speech which the prime minister planned to make in Regina on December 30. There, before an audience of eight thousand, Bennett delivered a lengthy address in which he reviewed the pledges he had made at the opening of his election campaign, as well as the programs he had implemented since the election.

[38]*Ibid.*
[39]*Manitoba Free Press,* December 23, 1930.

This included passage of the relief act which he claimed would help to relieve unemployment in the prairie provinces. Bennett also claimed that his emergency tariff had helped to arrest the decline in manufacturing production. Then he summed up the results of the imperial conference, and his sales mission to France. He reviewed the domestic situation, and defended the pool selling policy as he said:

... On the day after the session of Parliament ended, I sailed for England to attend the Imperial Conference. I left Canada determined to do my best to foster and support a plan for greater Empire trade based on mutual advantages. With that purpose in mind, I made a proposal to the Conference for closer Empire economic association based on mutually advantageous tariff preferences. I frankly stated my position. I said that the motive which governed my proposal was the interest of Canada first, and I said our primary concern at that time was to secure a more stable market in the United Kingdom for our wheat. How that market is to be secured to us as against a foreigner is naturally a matter to be determined by the government of the United Kingdom. For my part I expressed my entire willingness, having regard particularly to the Russian menace, to accept in lieu of a price preference a quantity preference (called the quota) which would guarantee us a minimum export of wheat to the United Kingdom. To say that this offer has been definitely declined is to unjustifiably anticipate the outcome of the continuing deliberations of the government of the United Kingdom.

For that market I offered to pay with favourable tariff preferences, realizing that for over thirty years a substantial preference had been enjoyed by the United Kingdom. My political opponents have criticized me for this frankness. Certainly if it is a fault, it is one of which they have never been guilty. But their criticism to me is praise, so long as I continue to promote the welfare of this country. The overseas dominions with unanimous voice endorsed the principle of my proposal. The government of the Mother country has not yet done so, but it has declared itself in favour of closer Empire economic association, and has joined in the resolution to which the overseas dominions gave assent, that the economic conference should adjourn to meet at Ottawa next year. That I may rightfully claim is an achievement which will mean much to Canada and to the Empire as a whole. ...

After the adjournment of the conference in London I waited on the government of France, whose duty on Canadian wheat is practically prohibitory and which has been raised several times since the trade treaty has been made, and informed it of the promise I had made and of my firm belief that the interest of Canada demanded its prompt and literal fulfillment. I have already had the pleasure of publicly acknowledging the courtesy and consideration with which I was received, and I may say now that the able statesmen with whom I conferred very readily appreciated the position I was compelled to take. Since the date of that conference the government has fallen, but despite the confusion incident to a period of inter regnum and the formation of a new ministry, the government of Canada is now in receipt of advices that France will guarantee the purchase of a minimum of nine and a half million bushels of our 1930 wheat crop. This is the first time in the history of France that such a guarantee has been given. The best information we are able to obtain indicates that the actual purchase of Canadian wheat by French millers during the current grain year may reach over twenty million bushels. That is good business for Canada. And it is the kind of business which carries with it the increased respect of the other party to the bargain. I do not hesitate to say that at no other time has the government of Canada stood higher in the esteem of France than it does today.

And so it will be with all the other countries whose treaties with us I am now reviewing. I will be fair with them and they must be fair with us. Business can never be conducted on any other basis. Canada, one of the great trading nations of the world, has the right and power to demand reciprocity of benefits in her international dealings. ...

During my absence in England I was in receipt of daily information regarding the wheat situation and of the careful survey the government was making preparatory to remedial action. We were thus able to announce on December 22nd that the government had concluded arrangements which would ensure the orderly marketing of the wheat crop of western Canada.

The government of the country, acting as trustee for all the people in the face of an admitted national emergency, has taken steps through the extension of credit facilities and by other means to prevent the forced and precipitate liquidation of the 1930 wheat crop. We have not fixed a price for wheat— the jurisdiction to fix such prices in peace time is under provincial jurisdiction, but apart from the legal difficulties it is clear that we cannot hope to absorb our surplus wheat by domestic consumption, either for food or otherwise, as is the case in the United States. To fix a price in excess of the world's price as determined by supply and demand would be unwise. ...

I repeat this is an emergency measure. Direct government aid to private enterprise cannot be justified on any other ground. Other producers in Canada are suffering from the present economic situation. They might equally claim the right to relief. ... I am aware that the marketing of our wheat will still leave many of our agriculturalists without a sufficient competence for the winter months, and will find them, when spring comes, without the seed for next year's crop. ... In this regard the suggestion made a few weeks ago by Mr. E. W. Beatty, the president of the Canadian Pacific Railway Company, is to be commended. A private organization having as shareholders the transportation companies, banks, industrial enterprises, insurance and mortgage corporations, with a reasonable capital used as a revolving loan fund, will meet the necessities of the situation. ...

When through such joint effort we shall have emerged from this unhappy state, there will yet remain the greatest problem of providing and maintaining broader markets for our products, both natural and fabricated. I have pledged ourselves to a policy of protection for Canadians in whatever legitimate role they may apply for it, and I have pledged ourselves to foster and develop our agricultural, livestock and dairy interests. I have told you that with a revision of many of the existing favoured nation treaties, I expect there will be open to us surer markets for our natural products. I have also told you that when the adjourned Economic Conference meets in Ottawa I believe an agreement will be reached which will mean broader Empire markets for our products. But even if the maximum benefits hoped for are secured, Canada will still have a wheat surplus to export. It therefore becomes our duty in the national interest, to find new markets and to aid in all proper ways our exporters to favourably compete in every market with the other wheat exporting countries of the world. ...

Our Minister to Japan, the Honourable H. H. Marler, is, I hope, at this very hour on his way to China to discuss with the government of that great country the purchase of millions of bushels of our wheat.

Nor will the government hesitate, if necessary, to assist by providing credit facilities and by any other means in its power the establishment of so incalculably valuable a channel of trade. ...

In passing may I say that I do not think it is quite fair to blame the wheat pools for not having disposed of last year's crop when the prices were high. . . .

The attitude of the pools was that taken by practically all the large private grain operators of Canada. I mention this because I find a tendency on the part of some Canadians to blame the western producer for existing conditions, alleging that he should have sold his 1929 crop before he did.[40]

Most importantly, Bennett had confirmed that the federal government would provide the financial guarantees required to forestall a forced liquidation of the pools' unsold wheat. His promise to implement Beatty's recommendation for a private lending corporation to assist farmers and of direct aid to the provinces in providing free food, clothing and seed grain to the needy, was well received. Bennett's negotiations with the French and the Chinese, and his undertaking to revise trade agreements as necessary to aid the sale of wheat were further indications of the revival of government interest in wheat marketing. He had reiterated his belief that government price fixing would be an impractical solution for wheat.

At the end of the year cash wheat fell as low as 53½ cents. It would be well into the new year before Bennett could meet with his caucus to secure party support for his policies and to obtain legislative authority for his undertaking to the banks. But there was widespread relief that the federal government had intervened. With the federal government now providing financial guarantees to the banks and McFarland in charge of the agency's sales policy, the federal government was once again involved in the marketing of wheat.

Considering the reluctance with which Bennett committed his government to this new responsibility, it is all the more remarkable that once he gave the undertaking, he gave it his personal and continuous attention and declined to delegate the responsibility to his minister of trade and commerce, the Honourable H. H. Stevens. As his private secretary, Mr. R. K. Finlayson observed:

> Government wheat merchandising was an undertaking that R.B. hadn't called for in his 1930 election campaign. But the problem having come to him, he faced it just as an enterprising lawyer greets a client; the bigger the client and the more serious his problem, the more eagerly Bennett accepted the challenge to get him out of trouble.[41]

FORMALIZATION OF THE BANK GUARANTEES

When the prime minister made his cryptic announcement on December 22, 1930, the government's undertaking to the banks was necessarily provisional. Reference has already been made to Ryckman's letter to Leman which tided matters over until Bennett's return to Canada but, even then, Bennett lacked any legislative authority to make such a guarantee. Moreover, he had to present his policy to cabinet and caucus who were less than happy with the guarantee as time wore on. Because it would be some time before the new session, the prime minister furnished a written confirmation of the provisional guarantee to the Canadian bankers' association and promised that appropriate legislation would be sought, as he wrote to Mr. Beaudry Leman on January 20, 1931:

The serious situation arising out of the falling prices for wheat and other grain

[40]*Ibid.*, December 31, 1930.
[41]R. K. Finlayson, *Life With R. B.: That Man Bennett*, p. 193.

has been engaging the attention of the Government practically ever since the crop for 1930 came upon the market. The Canadian Co-operative Wheat Producers Limited, hereinafter referred to as "The Wheat Pool" and Allied Companies, to wit:

Saskatchewan Co-operative Wheat Producers Limited
Alberta Co-operative Wheat Producers Limited
Manitoba Co-operative Wheat Producers Limited

hereinafter referred to as the Allied Companies and the subsidiaries of the Allied Companies have, we are informed been receiving advances in connection with their marketing operations from certain of the banks, known as the "Lending Banks" in order that the producers might receive a reasonable initial payment, and that the crop might be marketed in an orderly manner. We have been advised that a margin of 15 per cent was at all times to be maintained with the "Lending Banks" by the "Wheat Pool" and Allied Companies and subsidiaries, against prevailing market prices plus carrying and other charges. With the gradual decrease in prices that has taken place it is obvious that it has become difficult, in fact practically impossible, for the "Wheat Pool" and the Companies referred to to maintain that margin. The Government realize that if the "Wheat Pool" and these Companies were forced to suspend operations, the price of wheat in this country, now at a level unprecedently low in the history of the grain trade, will drastically decline, with great loss not only to the "Wheat Pool" and the other grain companies, but to the entire farming and business interests of Canada. Representations have been made to the Government to this effect, not only by the interests directly concerned, but by other important Canadian enterprises. We have canvassed the situation from all possible standpoints.

We are convinced, after mature consideration, that the Public Interest of Canada as a whole, is involved and that it is the duty of the Government to take such steps as will prevent what would be nothing short of a National disaster, if there was a forced liquidation of wheat and other grain in this country at this juncture. The Government, therefore undertakes with the Lending Banks to guarantee, and hereby, so far as it legally may, guarantees them against any loss they may ultimately sustain, through the making of advances to the Canadian Co-operative Wheat Producers Limited and Allied Companies and subsidiary companies including advances heretofore made, or to be made, and interest thereon, in connection with the marketing of the 1930 crop of wheat and other grains. Such legislation, if any, as may be required to implement this guarantee and undertaking will be introduced by the Government and pressed to enactment at the next ensuing session of the Parliament of Canada.[42]

It was not until August 3 that the 1931 unemployment and farm relief act received royal assent. It was this act which provided the governor in council authority to pay monies out of the consolidated revenue fund to relieve distress and provide employment. It was still later, on September 12, 1931, when the first two orders in council were passed under such authority to formalize the guarantees. P. C. 2238 provided a guarantee on bank loans made to Canadian Co-operative Wheat Producers Limited against 1930 crop deliveries to the pools. In the meantime, the federal government had agreed to furnish guarantees in order to permit the three provincial pools to operate small voluntary pools on grain delivered to them from the 1930 crop. P. C. 2239 of the same date provided these guarantees.

---

[42] *Bennett Papers.*

CHANGING ROLE OF THE CENTRAL SELLING AGENCY

Between the onset of its difficulties in February, 1930, and July of the following year, the central selling agency experienced a complete transformation. Until 1930, the agency had been master in its own house, with its selling policy under the control of its directors. The resort to the provincial governments for guarantees had marked the first departure from autonomy, because the governments acquired a stake in pool policy. Through most of the ensuing year, this fact did not materially alter the pools' management or that of their selling agency. But when the provincial governments were no longer equal to the burden, the pools paid a high price for federal government support in the surrender of their sales policy to their new general manager, Mr. John I. McFarland who, although reporting nominally to the agency's directorate, in fact, reported to the prime minister of Canada. When this surrender was made, the agency hopefully believed that its loss of autonomy would be temporary but, as the 1931 harvest approached, it was clear to all that some new arrangement would have to be made. Perhaps the least expected of solutions resulted, inasmuch as in the end the three provincial pools withdrew from the central selling agency and thereafter marketed their producer deliveries separately. From August 1, 1931, forward, each pool operated as a separate elevator company and either hedged the grain delivered to it, or pooled it on terms negotiated with the banks under federal guarantee. Canadian Co-operative Wheat Producers Limited remained in existence thereafter for two principal purposes: to dispose of the unsold balances of wheat, oats, barley, rye and flaxseed delivered to the pools from the 1930 crop, and to provide a corporate mechanism for the conduct of the federal government's market support operations. Both functions were entirely under the control of the federal government. The transition represented another step in the government's continuing search for a wheat policy.

100 PERCENT COMPULSORY POOL

During the course of this transition the issue over compulsory pooling came to a head. It was one possible avenue by which the pools might have extricated themselves from their difficulties but, for better or worse, it failed of support. For nearly two years the issue had been one of contention in the growing feud between the grain trade and that section of the farm movement which supported the proposal. The object of the proposal was to bring all non-pool farmers into the pool and thereby to free it of competition from the private trade. If it had succeeded, the line elevator companies would have been forced either to act as agents of the pools or to sell their facilities to them, and futures markets in grain would have ceased to function. The situation would have paralleled that of the first Canadian wheat board, except that the compulsory pool would have been producer-owned and operated. The idea had first been mooted in the late twenties by the United farmers of Canada (Saskatchewan section), whose leaders, Messrs. L. C. Brouillette and George H. Williams, were its active advocates. Mr. Brouillette was vice-president of Saskatchewan Co-operative Wheat Producers Limited, but its president, Mr. McPhail was just as actively opposed to it. Brouillette and Williams drew support from Sapiro, as relations between Sapiro and McPhail continued to deteriorate. Innis claimed that the high interim payment on the crop of 1928 which Turgeon had criticized, and that the high initial payment on the 1929 crop had been decided upon partly as a means of checking the spread of compulsory sentiment in Saskatchewan.[43]

In his public appearances and through correspondence, McPhail discouraged the idea as he wrote:

> I am certainly in favour of as great a control of wheat by the pool as it is possible to get up to 100 per cent, and there would undoubtedly be advantages through having 100 per cent control through our own marketing organization. I do believe, however, that the advantages of a 100 per cent control by one organization would be much more than offset by the disadvantages of the methods used to secure that control. For instance, I consider you would have a much stronger organization in any line of ten men who were free, voluntary, and enthusiastic members of the organization than if you increased that ten to fifteen by forcing the last five into the organization.[44]

To test the strength of support for compulsory pooling, the Saskatchewan wheat pool mailed out ballots to its 83,000 members on the question of whether the pool should request the provincial government to conduct a referendum among all producers on the issue. By the deadline on September 1, 1930, 48,545 members had returned ballots, of which 32,653 favored submission of the question to a referendum of all growers, and 12,991 were opposed. The remaining ballots were either unsigned or spoiled.

This appeared to be sufficient evidence of victory for the Brouillette-Williams team to prompt Premier Anderson, in the midst of negotiations on the setting of the 1930 initial payment, to invite his fellow premiers to Regina to discuss the proposal or, as an alternative, the re-establishment of the wheat board. But there had not been the same support for compulsory pooling in Manitoba and Alberta, and Premiers Bracken and Brownlee pleaded the pressure of other business in excusing themselves from the meeting. A director of the Manitoba pool, Mr. C. H. Burnell, said that the membership of his organization favored neither a compulsory pool nor a wheat board.[45] In 1931, Anderson put a bill through the Saskatchewan legislature to provide for a compulsory pool, but the constitutionality of the act was successfully challenged in the Saskatchewan court of appeal. An injunction was obtained against carrying an appeal from this decision to a higher court, and the 100 percent campaign petered out.

PROPOSAL FOR AN INTERPROVINCIAL COMPANY

Although the compulsory pool failed to materialize, it was one of the issues in play in the spring of 1931 when Bennett had to decide about the continuing role of the central selling agency and the federal government's involvement therein. Increasingly, in 1931, the provincial premiers took an interest in the activities of their respective provincial pools. Each pool had hypothecated its physical assets to its respective provincial government in return for the financial guarantees the three provincial governments had

[43] *Diary of A. J. McPhail*, p. 247.
[44] *Ibid.*, pp. 247-248.
[45] *Manitoba Free Press*, August 22-23, 1930.

given the banks on the marketing of 1929 pool deliveries. Understandably, each premier was interested in the capacity of the provincial pools to repay their indebtedness on past operations, but they were also just as much concerned that the federal government should make adequate financial arrangements for marketing of the 1931 crop. In the current state of affairs between the provinces and the pools, Brownlee, in particular, had begun to intervene in the management of the Alberta wheat pool, and Bennett went so far as to imply that the provincial governments were in fact the proprietors of the pools.[46]

At the same time the boards of the three pools as represented in the directorate of the central selling agency were trying to formulate their own solution for its future, and they found it increasingly difficult to agree upon a common role for the agency now that its sales policy was under the exclusive direction of the federal government as exercised through John I. McFarland. In the need to arrive at a decision for the handling of the oncoming 1931 crop, the three pool boards, three provincial premiers and Bennett were all involved in the problem.

At first the three premiers met in Saskatoon with representatives of the farm organizations, of the three pools, and of anti-100 percent pool organizations which had been formed. Their meeting of May 4, 1931, was inconclusive, but Premier Anderson forwarded a resolution approved by it to Bennett to the effect that if the international wheat conference to be held in London that year could agree on arrangements to eliminate competition among the exporting countries, the federal government should establish a wheat board or similar organization to discharge Canada's role in the undertaking. At the same time Premier Brownlee began to express his conviction that a wheat board would be necessary if low prices continued. The premiers requested a meeting with Bennett.[47] Of this first request nothing ensued but, as apprehension grew about what might happen to the market when deliveries from the 1931 crop commenced, Premier Anderson announced with relief that Bennett had agreed to a meeting on June 24 to discuss the marketing of the 1931 crop and the possibility of a federal export wheat board.

As arranged, Bennett and several of his cabinet members met on June 24 with Premiers Brownlee and Anderson and the Manitoba minister of education, Mr. R. A. Hoey, who represented Premier Bracken. Pool representatives included McPhail, H. W. Wood and R. D. Purdy, general manager of the Alberta pool. In his own notes jotted down during the course of the meeting, Bennett recorded that Brownlee, acting as spokesman for the premiers, expressed concern over the prospective lack of purchasing power in the west because the market would be unable to absorb hedges on country deliveries that autumn in the absence of speculative buyers. Since the pools could not operate on their own, he assessed the merits of (a) a financially assisted pool (b) a wheat export board which could coordinate its sales policy with that of a similar board in the United States, and (c) a federal wheat board. Brownlee recommended the third alternative with an initial payment of 50 or 55 cents in order to sustain buying power. It was

[46]See Bennett's letter, p. 302.
[47]Premier Anderson's letter of May 4, 1931 to Bennett, *Bennett Papers.*

known then that the 1931 crop had suffered considerable damage from drought. To Brownlee's proposal, possible objections were considered such as its monopoly implication, the closing of the futures market and consequent criticisms by overseas buyers. Anderson and Hoey supported Brownlee's wheat board proposal. Wood stated that he didn't believe in a wheat board but it appeared to be the only solution available in the absence of speculation, and growers needed protection. McPhail agreed.[48]

At that meeting the Honourable Hugh Guthrie recommended that an interprovincial company be incorporated to replace the central selling agency in marketing the 1931 crop and that the federal government should provide the new company with financial guarantees. Guthrie's proposal appealed to Bennett and to McPhail, but much less so to Brownlee who stood by his proposal for a federal wheat board. McFarland, when he heard of it, registered categoric opposition to the interprovincial company concept.

Bennett's record of the meeting was supplemented both by McPhail and Brownlee. McPhail's diary notation read:

> 24. Wood and Purdy arrived. We all met the Cabinet at 11 A.M. Brownlee presented the case for a Wheat Board. Anderson, Hoey, Wood, and I spoke briefly. Myself very briefly. We got a very good hearing. Bennett appeared sympathetic to doing something, but raised constitutional difficulties in the way of a national Board. I am sure they can be overcome by the Legislatures of the provinces conferring such powers as are necessary on a national Board. Guthrie suggested an inter-provincial Board, which I think is the best, but Brownlee does not seem to favour it. Bennett realizes the seriousness of conditions in the West.[49]

Brownlee recorded his representations in a letter he addressed from the Chateau Laurier to Bennett on June 27:

> Following is a summary of the representations made by me on behalf of the delegation from the three Prairie Provinces on Wednesday last the 24th instant.
>
> Subject to the uncertain factor of the effect of the present crop outlook, particularly in Saskatchewan, upon the wheat market in the next six weeks, two questions give us grave concern.
>
> 1) How the greatest possible amount of money can be brought into circulation this Fall from the 1931 crop? On the basis of the present level of prices we cannot see how any company can finance a larger advance per bushel to the farmer than say 40 cents basis one Northern (Fort) William. Deducting the usual freight rates this leaves very little after the payment of threshing costs. On this basis there must result a very small purchasing power in the three provinces with consequent greatly increased difficulties for business generally as well as for governments.
>
> 2) On the basis of present levels, we believe that a much larger percentage of farmers than usual will be obliged, through their necessity, to sell forthwith after delivery for whatever the market will bring. As there is practically no speculative element in the market, and as the large portion of the crop not hedged in recent years because of the operating of the Pool, will probably be handled on the open market this year, and will, therefore, add to the hedging pressure, it becomes a matter of serious doubt if present levels can be maintained.

[48]Bennett's undated memo, *Bennett Papers.*
[49]*Diary of A. J. MacPhail,* p. 244.

With the collapse in prices of all farm produce of the last eighteen months, ar.y further decline in prices would have rather disastrous consequences.

Having the above in mind the following alternative proposals have been considered:-

a) That through further financial support to a minimum advance, to be paid by the Wheat Pool, some stabilization might be effected. For reasons, known to you this proposal is hardly possible this year.

b) Acting alone, or in co-operation, with the Federal Government of the United States, to withhold from the market this Fall a substantial part of the then visible carry-over, thus leaving the market to absorb only the new crop.

c) The establishment of a Wheat Board clothed with the necessary authority by concurrent legislation of the Dominion and Provincial Governments.

For reasons outlined to you in our discussion we advocate this latter method of handling the crop this year.

The proposal that an inter-Provincial board be formed with the financial support of the Dominion Government is, in our judgment, simply another method of establishing a Wheat Board and could not be effected unless by appropriate legislation of both Dominion and Provincial Governments.

I desire to make it quite clear that these representations have not been made because of any anxiety over the operation of the Pool Elevator Systems, but solely because we believe some action is needed in view of the economic situation likely to be faced this year.

We will be glad to discuss any other proposal at any time and will be only too glad to co-operate in any way possible in respect to the difficult problem of marketing our wheat.[50]

Within a week of the June 24, 1931, meeting in Ottawa, Bennett brought McFarland from Winnipeg to review the alternatives, and he asked him to consider in particular the formation of an interprovincial company by the three provincial governments. While Bennett saw all the advantages of its organizational simplicity as an instrument through which the federal government could provide financial guarantees, McFarland thought in terms of the operational problems such a company would encounter. He undertook to consider the feasibility more carefully and shortly after his return to Winnipeg he addressed a lengthy letter to Bennett which identified the administrative flaws in the proposal and formulated an alternative price support scheme which Bennett eventually adopted. Accordingly, McFarland's letter of July 10 is quoted here, except for those portions which explained the difference between the pooling system about to be abandoned, and the hedging system which the provincial pools would now be required to adopt for their own protection. The point was that the pools handling roughly 50 percent of total crop deliveries had hitherto carried their share unhedged. In the arrangements now contemplated for the 1931 crop all deliveries would have to be hedged, thereby doubling the selling pressure on prices in the autumn months. The only extenuating factor was that the 1931 drought in the main wheat areas implied that the hedging pressure would not develop until crops from the north began to move. McFarland wrote:

Since leaving you I spent a day in Toronto seeing several bankers and arrived home here Wednesday.

[50] *Bennett Papers.*

I have been trying to figure out some definite conclusion regarding our conversation in respect of the problem which you had to decide in connection with the handling of the 1931 Western wheat crop, and I must confess the more I think of the proposal of the formation of an Interprovincial Company to handle the wheat from the three Provincial Lines of Elevators, with a proposed bank guarantee by your Government to the Interprovincial Company, the more I am convinced that this will not solve the marketing difficulties which may arise when the new crop starts to move. I think some other means must be thought out. You will recollect I expressed to you doubt of the workability of the scheme you mention, based along the lines above outlined. . . .

The three Provincial Governments, as above stated, are interested in a large way financially in lines of Country Elevators in the three Provinces. I do not imagine for a moment that these three Provincial Governments have any desire to operate a grain business in any manner by which any large losses could be sustained. In other words each of those three Provincial Lines of Country Elevators, by buying outright and paying cash to the farmer for his wheat, will have to sell such wheat every day in order to insure that their margin of profit has been secured and to accomplish that they will have to inaugurate a system under a management who will hedge their wheat immediately it is bought, and at no matter what the market price may be, otherwise the three Provincial Governments will be embarking upon a speculative method of handling grain and I do not think any one of the three Premiers intend that they will run a grain business of that type. What they want or should want will be some method which will be safe and which will be presumed to earn moderate profits each year so as to enable them over a period of years to recover the money which they now have invested as a result of their guarantee, and I have a very strong conviction that each one of those three Provincial Lines of Country Elevators should be operated independently and their selling done independently so that each of them will be responsible to see that their selling is done each day, either by sales of actual wheat or by hedging in the Futures Market. If an Interprovincial Company were organized to do the selling collectively for all three Provincial organizations, it would entail a very great deal of minute supervision and furthermore an Interprovincial Company could not sell the wheat or hedge the wheat at any better price than each of the three could do for themselves. Then if each of the three Provincial organizations are responsible for their own selling they will then be unable to blame some other organization if the results are not satisfactory. In other words they will be on their own bottom and it will be their own responsibility to look after their own stuff.

Now if an Interprovincial Company were organized and were receiving this grain from the three Provincial Organizations, then the Interprovincial Company would have to sell the wheat every day either by actual sales or by hedging in Futures and who would take the hedges from an Interprovincial company any more readily than they would from one of three Provincial organizations? And if for arguments sake your Government guaranteed the Interprovincial Company's account by becoming responsible for wheat at a certain price and if for argument's sake that price was 50 cents per bushel, and if again the open market price was 60 cents per bushel and the Provincial Country Elevators were buying wheat from farmers on a basis of the market price of 60 cents, there would only be one thing that an Interprovincial Company could do and that would be to sell the wheat every day it was bought by the Provincial Companies and in order to do that they would require to have wired advices as to quantities, all of which would be confusing and much more cumbersome than if each Provincial Company were looking after its own, and if the Interprovincial Company carrying out these daily sales depressed the prices down to say 55 cents per bushel, and did not feel inclined to press it further, then they would have to discontinue sales for the Provincial organizations, otherwise, presumably, they would knock the bottom out of the market. The whole thing is full of difficulties.

The method which should be employed is very clear to me but whether it could be done under the protection of a Democratic Government, I do no know, but it is as follows: Each of the three Provincial Lines of Country Elevators should be operated both as regards purchases and as regards sales policy by each Provincial Organization. There should be no Interprovincial Company whatsoever but the Dominion Government should create some sort of responsible body with authority to stabilize when necessary the futures market by purchases, thus creating at all times a hedging market, not only for the three Provincial Country Elevator organizations but also for all other organizations doing business in the west. Anything this stabilizing body might do from time to time would have to be done under cover and secretly. It would not be well that the world at large should know that any Dominion Government subsidized Company were buying wheat in order to sustain values. They might suspect that it was being done but it would only be suspicion on their part and it would have to be done so that it would not be advertised. In other words what we need in a Government subsidized guarantee body which will do enough buying to create a cushion under the market, when necessary at above a certain figure which would have to be agreed upon, and not higher than some other figure which would also have to be agreed upon, and I do not believe that any other method will prove satisfactory in taking care of any situation that may arise. I for one would certainly not wish to have anything to do with an Interprovincial Company in the handling of wheat of these Provincial organizations. It is up to them to handle their own. The wheat they handle will be their own, it will not belong to any pool of farmers but will be their own to be sold at a profit if they are to continue business, and not as in the past when it belonged to large numbers of farmers within a pool and only an initial payment made thereon. . . .

If the three Provincial organizations handling the three Provincial Lines of Country Elevators and buying wheat outright from the farmers and hedging it every day, then it will be a simple matter for these organizations to secure their credits from the banks because banks do not require large margins on any grain business which is run on straight hedging lines and if the Dominion Government creates a cushion to take those hedges, if it is found necessary to do so, I cannot see what more is required. . . .

P.S. Do not get mixed up in any interprovincial Comp. It cannot be operated. I would not touch it with a 40 foot pole.[51]

Unfortunately Bennett didn't wait to hear from McFarland. In the meantime he had discussed the matter in cabinet. On the assumption that the provincial governments were now in control of the physical assets of the pools, namely their country elevators, Bennett and his ministers decided that it would be possible for the governments to lease these facilities to a trading company incorporated by the three governments. With the trading corporation in control and McFarland in charge of the corporation, the cabinet believed that it would have an instrument which could cope with the marketing problem and which it could more confidently support by the

[51]*Ibid.*

provision of guarantees. Accordingly, Bennett wrote to the three premiers on July 11, with a copy of his letter to McFarland:

> The cabinet has carefully considered the proposals made by the three western provinces to the effect that a wheat board should be established by the federal government for the purpose of handling the crop of 1931.
>
> The government is of the opinion that under existing conditions the legal and other difficulties are such that no good purpose would be served by an endeavour being made by the government of Canada to enter into the business of marketing the grain crop of the year.
>
> The governments of the three central provinces control a very large number of elevators, and those facilities will be available for the handling of this year's crop.
>
> We suggest that representatives of the three provinces should meet together and undertake the formation of an ordinary trading corporation and that the elevator facilities, over which the provincial governments have control, direct and indirect, should be leased to the corporation so formed for this season at least.
>
> We further suggest that it is desirable, in view of the fact that the marketing of the wheat now owned by the pools in the three western provinces is under the direction of Mr. John I. McFarland, that he should be the general manager of the corporation. If this arrangement is satisfactory, the federal government will undertake to make the necessary financial arrangements to ensure the proper functioning of the corporation.[52]

Premier Anderson replied to the letter by telegram on July 14:

> Letter July 11 received. Saw McFarland in Winnipeg. He was unfavourable to scheme outlined your letter said he had written you expressing his opinion there will be an other proposition favourable your government. Please wire in time for interprovincial meeting Thursday.[53]

McFarland was dismayed when he saw Bennett's letter to the premiers. He wrote to Bennett again on July 15:

> I am in receipt of yours of the 11th enclosing copy of the letter which you wrote to he three provincial premiers on July 11th. In the meantime I wrote you on the 10th and regret now that I did not call you on the long distance. However, I do not think the three provincial bodies will look favourably on your proposition because there is no doubt in my mind that they want to control their own affairs and operate their own elevators. . . .
>
> When you suggest the formation of a trading corporation and that the elevator facilities should be leased to that trading corporation, I do not for a moment presume that you meant to suggest that the trading corporation should operate and control the business from the producer passing through those elevator facilities. I imagine you figured that the provincial bodies would operate their own facilities and that the trading corporation would simply take over from them the grain they purchased and look after the marketing of it, and in return for such services the trading corporation would pay the provincial companies on a rental or lease basis thus assuring the provincial organizations a certain earning from such rentals or leases based on the capital invested. If it were done in that way, then the provincial organizations would have a sure and certain income regardless of whether the trading corporation made or lost large sums of money. I cannot imagine that you would have suggested the other course of a trading corporation

[52] *Ibid.*
[53] *Ibid.*

controlling the operation of all those facilities. That would be a stupendous proposition which no sane person would think of undertaking.

In the meantime I have no expectations that the provincial organizations would accept the contents of your letter without further negotiation and for this reason I do not think your offer is likely to embarrass you.

The more I think of it the more convinced I am that the plan outlined in my letter of the 10th is the only feasible plan by which this proposition can be handled. It would put the responsibility upon the provincial organizations of making a success or failure of their management and that is exactly what should be accomplished without too much delay, because if the provincial governments are ever going to recover the monies which they have tied up in their guarantees, they must, without delay create an efficient management to carry on the business as any plan which will delay the creation of efficient organization must be inimical to the best interests of the provincial government. . . .[54]

Meanwhile, McPhail had been intrigued by the notion of an interprovincial company and he pursued it with the board of the central selling agency on July 2, 1931, where he won the support of the Saskatchewan and Manitoba representatives for an interprovincial company headed by Brownlee, but Wood and the other Alberta board members were opposed. On July 16-17 the three premiers met with representatives of the three pools in the council chamber of the Saskatchewan legislature to discuss Bennett's letter of July 11. After two days of meetings, the group reached a tentative agreement to be pursued in Winnipeg the following week. McFarland had not attended the meetings, but he had refused a second invitation from Premier Anderson to head the corporation when he wrote to Bennett on July 18:

I do not know what is happening at Regina except for the meagre reports in the press from day to day, but I would judge from those press reports that the conference in Regina has not accepted your proposition as outlined in your letter to the premiers on a basis of rental, because it would appear from the press reports that the three provincial pool organizations have agreed to go ahead and handle their provincial lines separately, which, in my opinion, is the correct thing to do.

On the other hand, however, it would seem that they are shifting their meeting from Regina and are coming to Winnipeg next Tuesday, and it would appear that they are still considering the matter of an interprovincial company to handle the wheat, with a guarantee from the Dominion government.

Mr. Anderson called me on the long-distance phone on Thursday afternoon and asked me if I had changed my mind since his conversation of last Sunday, and I told him most decidedly that I had not and could not think of doing so. The scheme is not workable and will only result in dissatisfaction for all concerned. The only thing that would save it would be an advancing market. . . .[55]

During the course of the Regina meeting, the three premiers wired Bennett on July 17:

Suggestions contained in your letter 11th instant considered by premiers and representatives of pools three western prairie provinces here today. All parties appreciate your offer help. Opinion of all is the proposal to lease provincial

[54]*Ibid.*
[55]*Ibid.*

elevator facilities to new trading corporation likely to be misunderstood by growers and interpreted as involving loss to them of elevator facilities they have constructed. Fear consequent reduction in volume of deliveries to these facilities thereby seriously reducing their earning power, to detriment of provincial governments securities. Suggest therefore that provincial elevator systems continue to function as separate units under present control but that they enter into an agreement with your proposed corporation to act as its agent to buy at open market prices and deliver their entire handling to such corporation for it to dispose of. Understand McFarland has refused to act. Would another general manager acceptable to you be satisfactory. Conference remaining in session pending your reply.[56]

Bennett replied on the same date:

Telegram received. Suggested corporation was to be created by provinces if they thought such action desirable. Being on ground your alternative probably preferable, involving as I understand it, separate provincial organizations functioning similar to private enterprise. We will assist you to do so. You can telephone up to two forty-five our time.[57]

By now McPhail's disenchantment with McFarland was complete, as he described the Winnipeg discussions in his diary entries for July 22-24:

22. Hutchinson, Plumer, Porter, and Purdy were here for Alberta. Brouillette, Read, and self for Saskatchewan and Bredt for Manitoba. We didn't make much progress. McFarland and Read were opposed to anything of an inter-provincial set-up. . . . We worked on a plan until after midnight as a committee of the conference which would make the provincial pools agents for a central organization. 23. We reported back to conference again, but J. I. McFarland was absolutely opposed to the plan. I had to tell ------- in as decent a way as I could to stop his opposition in the conference. We adjourned in the evening after appointing two committees to bring in two plans next evening at 7:30 P.M. 24. I was chairman of the principal committee Bredt, Hutchinson, and we had in McIntyre, Folliott, McIvor, Findlay, and Read. Each of these men agreed the plan we worked out providing a set-up to enable the three provincial organizations to hedge and sell their cash grain through one central was practical and feasible. When we met in Bracken's office and presented the plan, J. I. McFarland expressed strong disapproval. We decided that a committee would go to Ottawa to meet R. B. Bennett to see what arrangements he would make in the way of financial support to the provincial organizations. McFarland was to get in touch with the Prime Minister and representatives of the provincial Governments and pools would go.[58]

In the end, Mr. Wood had his way as the Alberta wheat pool withdrew from the central selling agency. In its place McPhail did his utmost to keep the interprovincial company substitute proposal alive and appeared to be holding his ground during the first day of meetings with the prime minister on August 4. The proposition appeared to have eluded him during the course of the second day's deliberations, however, as McPhail recorded his indignation over his exclusion from the discussions:

August 4. We met the Prime Minister at 11.15 to 1 P.M. We had a fairly satisfactory meeting. The Prime Minister agreed to guarantee the finances of the Elevator Co. on reasonable terms. We raised question of initial payment

[56]*Ibid.*
[57]*Ibid.*
[58]*Diary of A. J. MacPhail*, pp. 245-246.

on pool wheat. He evidenced willingness to support some payment. Brouillette and I met Weir at 3.45. We met the Prime Minister again at 4.45. He did not seem to want to support more than 35 cents of an initial payment. He spoke quite strongly against Brownlee coming into the pool on grounds that it would introduce a political element. . . . 5. All day Ottawa. Brownlee, McConnell, and McFarland met the Prime Minister with Wilson and White of the Bankers' Association. The only development was final agreement to a 35 cent pool initial payment. Bennett's attitude in leaving Bredt and me in his secretary's office while he discussed matters of vital concern to the pool with McFarland, is the greatest insult he could be guilty of so far as we are concerned. He showed his utter contempt for farmers in this act. I would not for one moment have tolerated it if I had not the organization to consider.[59]

As it turned out, Bennett was justified in excluding McPhail and Bredt from his discussion with McFarland. McFarland had already convinced Bennett of the necessity of market support operations which had just begun. Quite properly Bennett wanted to be informed by McFarland on what was taking place, but with the utmost secrecy. At the conclusion of the Ottawa meetings, the prime minister issued a press statement on August 7, 1931:

The wheat pools of the three western provinces, which own nearly sixteen hundred country elevators, as well as terminals, at Vancouver and Fort William, will operate this year in the same way as privately owned enterprises. They will have ample working capital, and the provinces will not be called upon to guarantee their obligations.

As a substantial number of producers desire to market their grain on the pool principle, the elevators operated by the pools in the several provinces will afford to such producers an opportunity to have their grain dealt with by the operation of a voluntary pool. The elevators will make to such producers an initial payment of thirty-five cents per bushel on the same basis as to quality and to point of delivery as in previous years.

The dominion government will take whatever action may be necessary to ensure the orderly marketing of the crop of the year. Panic conditions will not be permitted to control the prices obtainable for this year's western grain crop.[60]

The announcement indicated the direction which government policy would now take. Henceforth the three provincial pools operated as separate organizations under the management of their respective producer boards. They continued to manage their country and terminal elevator facilities, and the latter were now licensed as public terminals. They terminated their contracts with producers by which the latter had committed their deliveries to the pools. Producers now could either deliver to the pool elevators at street or carlot prices in which case the pools hedged their receipts of grain. Alternatively they could sell wheat to the pools on the basis of a 35 cent initial payment, but with their pressing need for cash, few producers could afford any longer to support the principle of the pooling system. The details of the financial arrangements between the pools and their provincial governments to liquidate their obligations have been described by Patton. As a result of the overpayment the pools made on their 1929 initial advances, the Manitoba pool owed $3,491,000, the Saskatchewan pool

[59]*Ibid.*, pp. 263-264.
[60]*Bennett Papers.*

$13,752,000 and the Alberta pool $5,649,000. By negotiation, the three governments issued interest-bearing bonds to the banks and they received interest-bearing bonds from the pools.[61] In due course the pool's indebtness was all repaid, with the exception of part written off in Manitoba and, in the end, the pools obtained unencumbered possession of their elevator facilities.

TRANSFORMATION OF THE CENTRAL SELLING AGENCY

From August 1, 1931, the three pool systems operated separately and, except for their token pools, similarly to the line elevator companies with whom they continued to compete for producer patronage. In doing so, the three provincial pools abandoned their central selling agency which dismissed most of its staff. Canadian Co-operative Wheat Producers Limited continued in existence after August 1, 1931, however, as the instrument through which the federal government held for disposal the unsold carryover of 1930 crop pool deliveries, and through which the government's market support operations were conducted. Mr. John I. McFarland continued as general manager, and he retained whatever central agency's sales and accounting staff were necessary to these operations. Notably, these included Mr. George H. McIvor as sales manager and Mr. R. C. Findlay as treasurer. As Patton observed, there was "a certain irony in the fact that the Pool Central Agency, which was created as an alternative to organized speculation, should have been destined to become the instrument of speculative support to the futures market, and in the further fact that what was established as a co-operative substitute for a government wheat board should continue to operate under the sponsorship of the federal government."[62]

Bennett and McFarland would not have thanked Patton for the reference to "speculative support". McFarland insisted throughout his support operations that his purchases of wheat futures were an unavoidable consequence of the necessity to provide hedges for producer deliveries in the absence of speculators. This phase of McFarland's activities is covered in a later chapter.

McPhail's effort to salvage the central selling agency or to replace it with an interprovincial company was his last service to the cause of the pool system. His had been an outstanding career in that service. A few months earlier his persuasiveness with the heads of the banks had helped to save the day when the pools were perilously close to liquidation. Now, due to overwork and overanxiety for the future of the interprovincial unity he had built and which now crumbled about him, McPhail fell ill. After an operation, he died on October 21, 1931, in his forty-eighth year. Mr. L. C. Brouillette succeeded him as president of Saskatchewan Co-operative Wheat Producers Limited.

At the end, McPhail was fortunately spared a final confrontation with Bennett. At Major H. G. L. Strange's instigation, Bennett addressed a petulant letter to McPhail on September 18, complaining about a speech one of McPhail's directors had made. If the remarks were substantiated,

---

[61]H. S. Patton: *The Canadian Wheat Pool in Prosperity and Depression, Essays in Honour of T. N. Carver,* (Harvard University Press, Cambridge, 1935), pp. 12-13.
[62]*Ibid.*

Bennett threatened to withdraw the federal guarantees to the banks. Mr. George W. Robertson, secretary of the Saskatchewan pool, replied in McPhail's absence, reporting his illness and reassuring Bennett that his board was appreciative of the assistance he had rendered.[63] Notwithstanding this last confrontation and his earlier harassment of McPhail over the production of audited statements on August 11, 1930, which were both characteristic of Bennett's occasionally brusque manner, Bennett had held McPhail in high regard. He had sought McPhail's advice and had included him in the delegation he had taken to the imperial conference in London in the autumn of 1930. It would be some time before Mr. L. C. Brouillette, McPhail's successor as president of Saskatchewan Co-operative Wheat Producers Limited, gained an equal place in Bennett's confidence.

[63]*Letter of H. G. L. Strange, September 15, 1931, Letter of R. B. Bennett, September 18, 1931, Letter of G. W. Robertson, October 6, 1931,* Bennett Papers.

15

OTHER DOMESTIC ISSUES

Apart from the major outstanding issue concerned with support for the price of wheat, there were also the Stamp commission and the five cent bonus which fit in with the chronology at this stage. In addition, there were a few miscellaneous items such as the Canadian wheat institute proposed by Mr. R. S. Law, president of United Grain Growers Limited, and McFarland's recommendations for reduced storage rates and for protein grading that arose later on, but which can be conveniently grouped among the other domestic issues.

STAMP COMMISSION

As already seen in the feud that had arisen between the pools and the line elevator companies during the sales policy debate, both parties were fighting for their own survival. The trade had mounted its offensive as the financial difficulties of the pools increased and, in due course, the pools fought back by demanding an investigation of the exchange. The three premiers were well aware of the growing farm support for such an investigation, and they drew this to the attention of Sir George Perley, the acting prime minister, in November, 1930, as they pressed for a minimum domestic price and a federal government guarantee.[1] McFarland also drew Bennett's attention to the farm agitation as he wrote on January 30, 1931:

> I presume you are aware that the farm leaders·are agitating for some legislation to control the Grain Exchange or supervise it, or something of that sort, their idea being to discourage speculation, believing that speculation is injurious; while I, on the other hand, hold just the opposite view, that speculation is what we need in the grain market. The broader the market the better it is when it comes to selling the product of the west. The whole trouble, as I see it at the present time, and this condition has existed now for some months, is that the speculators are either broke or discouraged, and one thing that discourages speculation on the grain markets of the North American continent is that the Federal Farm Board in the United States control the wheat of that country and have a large quantity of it in their ownership, while the pools of Canada hold a similar position on this side of the line, and all this wheat is hanging as a threat over the market, the public not knowing when it might be dumped or sold in large volume and cause them heavy losses. This keeps them out of the market. The only speculator of any importance left in Canada is the Wheat Pool. They are holding the wheat.[2]

[1]See pp. 281-282
[2]*Bennett Papers.*

About the same time, Canadian Co-operative Wheat Producers Limited submitted a memorandum to the minister of trade and commerce recommending supervision of the grain exchanges in Canada. The memorandum made extensive reference to the operations of the United States grain futures administration headed by Dr. J. W. T. Duvel and it concluded with the following recommendation: "It is urged, therefore, that legislation similar to the United States Grain Futures Act be introduced during the coming session of the Dominion Parliament and that this year, if possible, or in any event next year, enabling legislation be passed in the Legislatures of the several Provinces."[3]

Under pressure from the pools to enact supervisory legislation, and faced with the prospect that the federal government might have to continue guaranteeing pool operations on subsequent crops as it had done for the 1930 crop, Bennett sought a quick answer to the question of whether supervision of the grain futures markets was warranted. He was aware that Sir Josiah Stamp, an economist by training, chairman of one of the British railways, and a director of the Bank of England, had made a recent brilliant success of chairing two royal commissions in Britain. He, therefore, approached Stamp through the Canadian high commissioner in London, to invite him to conduct a brief, non-judicial inquiry into the grain futures market. Bennett cabled to the Canadian high commissioner in London on February 24, 1931: "Please ascertain if Sir Josiah Stamp would come to Canada to act as Chairman of Commission of three, the other two representing three western provinces and grain exchanges to determine whether or not selling of grain futures was injurious to agricultural interests or affected the actual selling price of wheat." Bennett followed this up by sending a cable on the following day directly to Stamp: "Hope you will accept matter about which our High Commissioner will call on you."[4]

A few days later, a speculative newspaper report alerted the trade that a royal commission was under consideration. The story appeared in the *Manitoba Free Press* on March 3, and McFarland wrote immediately to Bennett that the Honourable Robert Weir had just visited him and had explained that an investigation was necessary "to clear the air in the west". At that stage McFarland was concerned about the effect an investigating commission might have on confidence in the market at home and abroad, and he suggested that if there were to be a commission, it should be made to appear that it was being appointed at the request of the exchange. But his advice came too late; as the news story broke, Mr. A. P. White, president of the Winnipeg grain exchange, and Mr. A. E. Darby, secretary, despatched a long telegram to Bennett requesting that if there were to be an investigation of the exchange, it should also include the wheat and coarse grains pools, "to set at rest ideas in the public mind". At the time, the Manitoba government was conducting an inquiry into the operations of the Manitoba wheat pool in response to charges laid by Mr. J. R. Murray, vice-president and general manager of the Alberta Pacific Grain Company.

Bennett received a large number of letters from lawyers in Winnipeg, offering their services as counsel for the commission. He also received numerous letters from non-pool farmers, and from patrons of the Manitoba wheat pool, who echoed the exchange's request that the investigation should also cover the operations of the pools. McFarland pursued the same theme when he addressed a handwritten letter to Bennett on March 6:

> It is working out okay. Of course the Pool will not be anxious for it. They expected the Government might put through legislation controlling future trading without first finding out that such controlling legislation was necessary. Now what we need in the West is a probe into both systems of marketing. It's a case of the Pool system of marketing vs the established grain system, and that means the fallacies of this fool pool system will be given an airing. It will be welcomed by the Grain Trade the world over, and is considered constructive. I would say the big end of it will be the auditing by chartered accountants of the Grain Exchange Clearing House books, and an audit of the pool expenditures as well as an audit of their losses on over seas sales, which can be arrived at by comparing the price they received from their direct overseas sales as against the value of the same grade on the same date if it had been sold in store Fort William at the Grain Exchange values of that date. That's the big thing to show up.[5]

Despite all the urgings from the Exchange, from McFarland, and from an assortment of farmers, Bennett wanted no part of a long judicial inquiry into the operations of the exchange and the pools. Undoubtedly he recalled Meighen's unfortunate experience, for he had accepted the post of minister of justice in Meighen's reorganized cabinet in 1921 shortly after the Hyndman royal commission had backfired, and Bennett had no need of a similar experience. What he sought was an expeditious method of dealing with the pools' request for supervisory legislation. Moreover, he sought some justification for the futures market to continue. As Finlayson observed:

> There is little doubt, however, that (Bennett) still believed in the system of trading in wheat futures. He decided to appoint a Royal Commission to examine and report upon the advisability of permitting this system to continue. He took time out from the (Imperial) Conference deliberation to persuade Sir Josiah Stamp, a noted English economist, financier, and industrialist, to accept the Chairmanship of such a Commission.[6]

There was a natural tendency on the part of the public to read more into Bennett's motives in appointing the commission. As McPhail wrote on April 15:

> I tried to see the Prime Minister but did not make it today.... I had Weir to lunch. He is undoubtedly strongly behind co-operative marketing. He urged me again strongly to ask the Stamp Commission to investigate and report on the two methods of marketing — pool and grain trade. He suggests that, in his opinion, there would be only one report from a man like Stamp. If the report favoured the pool method it would clear up many doubts in many minds and pave the way for 100 per cent co-op. marketing in 12 months. I see his point but I doubt his conclusions. Then again one hears so many rumours and reports re the reason or original reason for the appointment of this commission. One thing we do know which tends to confirm suspicions is that the Government did not approach or consult the farmers in any way about the commission. They evidently did the grain trade.[7]

[5]*Ibid.*
[6]R. K. Finlayson, *That Man R. B.: Bennett,* p. 190.
[7]*The Diary of A. J. McPhail,* p. 241.

Gratton O'Leary made an almost opposite conjecture respecting Bennett's intentions. But he confirmed McPhail's evidence that one member, at least, of Bennett's cabinet had anticipated an investigation of the pool marketing system as well as the one offered by the grain exchange. Writing for a May issue of *Country Guide*, O'Leary said:

> Much more important and far-reaching is the Stamp Royal Commission. Its real object, in the first place, was not, as has been stated, a mere investigation of trading in wheat futures. What it sought to do, and what it was created to do, was to reveal the facts regarding the manner in which both the Grain Exchange and the Wheat Pools have been carrying on business. Those close to the government believe that from this commission will come revelations that will discredit the Pools, and that these will be of a sufficiently grave character to head off a 100 per cent. pool, thus enabling the government to resist any demand for a financial guarantee on the new crop. Official Ottawa may deny this, has already denied it by implication, but it is a fact nevertheless, one that will be borne out by developments of the next few weeks.[8]

As soon as Stamp accepted the invitation, Bennett proceeded to request nominations for the other two commissioners, respectively, from the exchange and the provincial premiers. He wired the three premiers and the exchange on March 31. In approaching the premiers, he tacitly recognized them as the only authentic representatives of the producers, but he did suggest the name of Mr. H. W. Wood, and Premier Brownlee ascertained that Wood was not available. The exchange promptly proposed Mr. W. Sanford Evans. A short time later the premiers nominated the Honourable J. T. Brown, chief justice, court of king's bench, Saskatchewan.

While these arrangements were under way, McFarland wrote in obvious regret to Bennett on April 1: "... I note your announcement re grain investigation which only applies to future trading on Grain Exchange and apparently the Pools are too sacred to be opened up to public inspection." Then on April 7 he wrote a remarkably prescient letter to Bennett, which questioned the wisdom of appointing Mr. Sanford Evans:

> ... Referring to the Commission headed by Josiah Stamp, I suggested to a couple of the prominent members of the Winnipeg Grain Exchange, prior to the time they made the appointment of Sanford-Evans, that they should not make their appointment until the Provincial Premiers had announced the name of their representative, at the same time telling them that if the Provincial Premiers picked out a representative who was not prejudiced and swayed by Communistic ideas, that in that case the Grain Exchange representative should be someone entirely outside the Grain Trade. However, they claimed that they had a wire from you and that they must act at once so they named Mr. Evans. Now, Mr. Evans is a very fine representative on any Commission, but unfortunately, in this instance, he had been known to have written many very scathing criticisms of the farmer movements and for that reason is not looked upon favourably by the farmers' organizations. Furthermore, I presume you are aware that Mr. Evans is very closely identified with the Grain Trade, and, in fact, his earnings are rather large from that source. I do not say that this connection would in any way close his mind to evidence that might be submitted before the Commission, but so far as the public are concerned they would always believe that Mr. Evans has his

[8]*Bennett Papers.*

mind made up before he starts. Then, let the Provincial Premiers appoint someone who is known to hold radical views, all that Commission will amount to would be an Arbitration Board, and I do not think that is what you would desire.

Since talking to Mr. Brownlee on Saturday night last, I have talked to some of the Grain officials and they intimate that you should appoint all three members of the Board. They are also quite willing, with your permission, to nominate someone else other than Mr. Evans. Such as an outstanding business man or a judge, provided the Provincial Premiers do likewise.[9]

But Bennett moving with customary expedition saw no reason for delaying matters at this stage, and P. C. 853 of April 10, 1931, appointed the commissioners and gave them a deliberately narrow remit: "to inquire into and report upon what effect, if any, the dealing in grain futures has upon the price received by the producer."[10]

On his arrival in Ottawa, Stamp was welcomed by the prime minister and feted at a country club luncheon on April 9, which was attended by members of the cabinet, heads of banks, and representatives of several provincial governments. Stamp entrained to Winnipeg, where he was met by the other two commissioners, and the hearings got under way.

To assist the commission, Bennett appointed Mr. Travers Sweatman, K.C., Winnipeg, as counsel. Mr. Sweatman was counsel for the board of grain commissioners and was involved at the time in the hearings before the Bracken government's commission chaired by Mr. E. K. Williams, K.C., on the charges that had been laid by Mr. J. R. Murray against the Manitoba wheat pool. Sweatman obtained a stay of these hearings in order to act for the Stamp commission. Mr. L. B. Pearson of the department of external affairs was named secretary of the commission. Bennett enjoined Sweatman to ensure that producers were given every opportunity to present their views.

The commission conducted hearings in Winnipeg April 13-16, Regina April 17, Calgary April 18, Winnipeg April 21-22, and held informal conversations in Minneapolis April 23 and in Chicago April 24-25. By April 29 in New York, Stamp had completed his draft report. It was the most expeditious of all royal grain inquiry commissions; except for the abortive Hyndman commission, there hadn't been a close runner.

At the public hearings in Canada, Stamp gained momentum by insisting that the inquiry was economic and not judicial. Accordingly, he disallowed cross-examination of witnesses by opposing counsel. He displayed a keen perception of the issues and a lively sense of humor which won him quick respect, confidence and a large attendance. He held as closely to the terms of the commission's remit as possible. As the hearings progressed, McFarland wrote to Bennett on April 14:

> Referring to the Stamp Commission which is now investigating the Futures Market. I have been pretty busy and have only been able to observe the proceedings for about an hour yesterday afternoon.
> It seems to me that you have picked out a very capable chairman. Everyone is unanimous in admiring his ability. Furthermore he is evidently a man with

an open mind. Unfortunately, however, some of the witnesses from the Grain Trade who have been giving evidence have not stacked up very well. The fact of the matter is, I believe Sir Josiah knows more about the workings of the Futures Market than some members of the Winnipeg Grain Exchange. I sincerely hope, however, that he is not going to find that the Futures Market should be abolished, because if you abolish the Futures Market, then there is only one thing left and that is Government Monopoly, and that would be too horrible to contemplate.[11]

At Regina, an issue flared up between the two Canadian commissioners when Mr. Justice Brown who had been nominated by the premiers requested that supervision of the exchange be explored. Mr. Evans claimed that Judge Brown's proposal lay outside the commission's remit, and it fell to Stamp to find an area of compromise. As a result, two American witnesses were heard in Winnipeg on April 21 when Dr. Alonzo E. Taylor of the Food Research Institute, Stanford University, California, gave evidence in support of the futures system, and Dr. J. W. T. Duvel, chief economist of the United States department of agriculture and administrator of the United States futures act reviewed his supervisory experience in the United States.

On April 22, the last day of hearings in Canada, Mr. A. J. McPhail and Mr. Andrew Cairns appeared on behalf of Canadian Co-operative Wheat Producers Limited. Stamp included the following excerpt from McPhail's statement in the body of the commission's report:

> The President of the Central Selling Agency of the Pool said that in the Saskatchewan Pool, of which he was also President, there were some 84,000 farmers the vast majority of whom would support him in declaring: "The organized farmers for many years, and as strongly today as at any time in the past, feel that the present system of futures trading does not work out in their best interests. They feel the price they receive for their wheat from day to day is largely influenced by the attitude of mind of the uninformed speculating public, and that such a method of determining or influencing the price level is too insecure and unstable a foundation upon which to build any industry. They feel that the effect of uncontrolled speculation results in much wider fluctuations in the market price than would otherwise be the case. A much more steady price level than now obtains would be of inestimable value to the producers . . . the majority of western farmers are equally of the opinion that the effect of futures trading on the price they receive is detrimental. They have no definite proof as they have not the facts on which to study the whole question."[12]

Between the conclusion of the commission's interviews in Chicago on April 25, and his departure from New York on April 29, Stamp wrote a report which ran to 65 printed pages, exclusive of appendices, and he obtained the concurrence of the other two commissioners in its text. The report was a lucid, orderly presentation of the commission's investigation, including a review of the historical background and economists' views on the question at issue, and a summary of the evidence he heard on either side. He did not evade the issue of supervision but, in a text calculated to appease his contending fellow commissioners, Stamp wrote:

> There is no doubt whatever that a feeling is prevalent amongst many farmers

[11]*Bennett Papers.*
[12]*Report of the Commission to Enquire into Trading in Grain Futures,* 1931, p. 57.

that someone is making money at their expense unfairly by inside knowledge, manipulation and undesirable practices. Nothing was given in evidence of a practical or satisfactory character as to what it actually is that is done or how it is done, and in that respect we share the experience of the Turgeon Commission.

But we cannot claim to have been able to satisfy ourselves conclusively as to the impossibility of such practices existing.

The fact that the Grain Exchange is self-governed without outside supervision or regulation in its futures trading and that, if complaints are made, the Exchange is the judge of its own cause, are sometimes used as arguments or proofs that its powers or practices can be abused. By its by-laws and regulations, however, it is clearly alive to the desirability of checking and abolishing every kind of undesirable practice likely to affect the interests of its members, and, through them, of its clients. We are given to understand that it does, in effect, without parade or publicity, uphold the standard of business conduct and correct any undesirable practices amongst its members. But, apparently, all this, happening behind closed doors, has not availed to improve public psychology and sentiment.

The feeling amongst farmers to which we have referred has persisted over a long period of years, and it has been particularly active at times when there has been a reaction from gambling and boom markets. If there is no substance, or small substance in actual fact, for the existence of that feeling, it seems a pity that no way can be found to remove it. We do not pretend that all farmers are positively antagonistic to the present system; we believe that, as usual, the dissatisfied element are the more conscious and articulate, and that a large number of farmers having no great feeling in the matter are not very active in giving expression to their moderation. The element that gives rise to the impression of the universality of the feeling consists of the active spirits who may genuinely believe there is a grievance, who draw the resolutions and speak at the meetings, and generally act in a representative capacity.

Any ameliorative action that might be taken, while perhaps not satisfying all sections, might at any rate affect the minds of a vast number and reduce the area of inflammatory feeling. It is essential that in any attempt to deal with this difficulty care should be taken to avoid ministering to merely idle curiosity on the part of individuals and introducing elements of individual publicity which would unfairly handicap this business as compared to others. In the same way it is essential that the day-to-day smooth conduct of the business should not suffer the bureaucratic touch of regulation and inquisitorial restriction. It might be well to introduce these when the moment for their necessity arises, but to put them in merely as a measure of assurance against mere suspicion seems inadvisable.[13]

Although the report continued by setting out the functions of a supervisor it tacitly assumed that the moment of necessity had not yet arrived, for it did not recommend that one be appointed.

Regarding the specific remit, Stamp distinguished between normal and abnormal times. In the former, he concluded that the effect of trading in futures was "to increase the average price received in the long run by the producer, to an indeterminate but appreciable extent". In abnormal times, no valid inferences could be drawn. Stamp then cited the conclusions the Turgeon royal grain inquiry commission had reached in 1925 on the complaint that "speculation either on the cash or futures market injuriously

[13]*Ibid.,* pp. 60-61.

affects the farmer and the community" and stated that his commission could agree with the Turgeon commission findings "as an alternative but less elaborated statement" of their own views. In his final summary, Stamp wrote:

> All the foregoing may seem very involved and elaborate to the man in the street who likes a plain "yes" or "no" to what seems to him a plain question.
>
> Unfortunately, however, no short statement on an economic matter is ever strictly and absolutely true, and this very natural desire for a plain answer can only be met by statements which are true generally, but leave room for times and cases where qualification is essential.
>
> However, in brief, our answer to the question submitted is that in addition to the benefits reflected to the producer in furnishing a system of insurance for the handling of his grain, and in providing an ever-ready and convenient means for marketing the same, futures trading, even with its disadvantages of numerous minor price fluctuations, is of distinct benefit to the producer in the price which he receives.[14]

At least Bennett had an answer to his question to the effect that there was no immediate need for supervision of the exchange, and the public once again were told that futures trading worked to the benefit of producers. Before his embarkation from New York on April 29, Stamp wrote to Bennett:

> We are signing the draft Futures Report this morning, subject to our definitive signatures of the final print proof in due course. Pearson will bring along two typed copies — one for you and one for printing and we are leaving him a pretty free hand to make any necessary revisions of a formal kind.
>
> I should be relieved if you will not allow your mind to be influenced by other peoples discussion — however well informed — as to what is in the Report before reading it yourself. It is the best we can do in three days — one for rough drafting, one for discussion (on the train) and one for second draft, but I do not think that many weeks more in evidence or in revision would materially change it. I only hope it may be of some use.
>
> Travers Sweatman and the other counsel sized up one point of view, and played the point on our lines splendidly. Pearson has been *most* useful and efficient, and Howe was an ideal private secretary.
>
> It has been an interesting experience for me, and has helped me to *know* Canada in a way that could never have been given me by any other experience.[15]

Bennett's reply expressed his considerable gratitude while the press editorialized on the conduct of the commission and its findings when the report was released. Then the bomb burst.

On the last day of the hearings in Winnipeg the commission had heard Mr. Andrew Cairns who appeared unexpectedly on behalf of the central selling agency to support Mr. A. J. McPhail's submission. Time had run out when Mr. Isaac Pitblado, counsel for the exchange, asked to enter several more exhibits on behalf of the exchange. He received permission to do so after the sitting adjourned, and Sir Josiah duly registered them including a piece of anti-pool propaganda which Sanford Evans had circulated earlier that year, and which now found its way into the report as Appendix XII, Chart 10. In New York, Stamp had looked at and approved several charts

[14]*Ibid., p. 72.*
[15]*Bennett Papers.*

for inclusion in the report's appendices and had turned them over to Pearson for inclusion in the printed report. Obviously, in his haste, Stamp had failed to scrutinize sufficiently this last particular chart, otherwise he would surely not have approved it.

When Pearson had time to look at it in Ottawa, he queried it with Sanford Evans who remained in Ottawa to assist with the publication of the report. When asked about Chart 10, Pearson recorded in a long memorandum he prepared for Mr. Bennett: "There was then raised the question of the wisdom or value of including Chart X, but Mr. Evans was of the opinion that, as the Chairman of the Commission had selected the material in New York for publication as statistical appendices, his duty was merely to edit and arrange such material and he had no authority to leave any of it out."[16] It was obvious from the memorandum that the prime minister had called Pearson to account. In a delightful passage in his memoirs years later Pearson confirmed that:

> The Prime Minister gave me some stormy minutes in our discussion on the matter and let me know in no uncertain terms that I had not only exceeded my authority but had acted stupidly or maliciously or both. When eventually I was allowed to get a word in, I was able to show that I was being most unfairly accused and that I was not responsible for the offending words and figures. Mr. Bennett at once apologized and directed his wrath elsewhere. His storms were rough, but they were usually of short duration and often cleared the air.[17]

As soon as he received his copy of the report Justice Brown protested. Bennett was queried about Appendix XII in the house on June 19, and he replied that he would have it suppressed. The chart had compared daily cash closing on Number 3 Northern wheat with the net prices received by pool patrons for the crop years in which the pools had been in operation. At the bottom of the chart, printed in red, was the following inference:

> The above chart represents 1990 market days, and during this time there are only 230 days on which a farmer could have sold his Three Northern wheat at a less price than the Pool net payment shown in the chart. Considering the years 1927-28, 1928-29, 1929-30 and 1930-31 to date, which represents a total of 1084 days, there are only 22 days on which a farmer could have sold his Three Northern wheat at a less price than the pool net payment.[18]

The pool demanded an immediate explanation as it issued the following statement:

> Without venturing to criticize the findings embodied in the text of the report of the royal commission inquiring into trading in grain futures, we feel compelled to protest and to draw the public attention to a regrettable feature of the appendix to the report. We refer to chart 10 given as Appendix 12, entitled "Open Market 3 Northern Cash Price vs Saskatchewan Pool 3 Northern Net Payment basis Fort William".
>
> This chart is an exact copy of one prepared for anti-pool propaganda purposes and distributed anonymously throughout western Canada early last spring. In contrast to the other charts and tables included in the appendix of the report, the identity of the party on whose behalf chart 10 was submitted is

[16]*Memorandum Re Appendix XII, Stamp Report, June 15, 1931*, Bennett Papers.
[17]*The Memoirs of the Right Honourable Lester B. Pearson, Volume I, 1897-1948* (University of Toronto Press, 1972), p. 74.
[18]*Manitoba Free Press*, June 20, 1931.

not disclosed. The chart has absolutely no bearing upon the subject of the inquiry; in fact, Sir Josiah Stamp consistently refused to regard any feature of the Pool and non-Pool price controversy as within the scope of the Commission's terms of reference. In view of these facts, we feel that Pool members and the general public are entitled to a full explanation of how and why chart 10 was included in the report. Furthermore, that the public is entitled to knowledge regarding the actual nature of the chart itself.[19]

Then it listed ten fallacies implicit in the comparison. Mr. Travers Sweatman and Mr. Sanford Evans absolved themselves from responsibility in the following statements to the *Free Press*:

Travers Sweatman, K.C., counsel for the commission, on being interviewed, said: "This chart was one of five filed by the Winnipeg Grain Exchange at the conclusion of the sittings of the commission in Winnipeg. So far as I can remember, it was never discussed in evidence. I am informed that it was one of a number of exhibits handed to Sir Josiah Stamp before sailing for the Old Country by L. B. Pearson, who acted as secretary of the commission, and in that way was included as one of the appendices to the report."

After perusing the pool's statement, W. Sanford Evans, a member of the Stamp Commission, said this morning: "As an individual member of the Stamp commission I would not enter into discussion of the point raised by the pool. The material referred to was filed with the commission by the Winnipeg grain exchange and accepted by the chairman just as was all other material and I took no individual initiative at any stage with respect to it."[20]

The fallacies in the comparison were listed by the pool but more succinctly described in a memorandum Pearson prepared after consulting Dr. T. W. Grindley, chief of the agricultural branch of the dominion bureau of statistics:

The Chart is defective in at least four respects:-

1. It compares a weighted with an unweighted average. The pool prices are weighted, the open market prices are unweighted and therefore the comparison has little meaning.

2. From 1928 the final payment of the pool has not been decided on. That payment may be higher or, more likely, it may be lower, but in any case it has not yet been established and therefore it cannot be compared with the open market as it is done in the Chart.

3. The Chart does refer to the pool payment as a *net* payment, but it should have been mentioned, to complete the picture, that the membership contract of the pool members authorised a deduction of two cents per bushel from the proceeds of the sale of members' grain for the purpose of providing country and terminal elevator facilities, from which investment the members receive six percent.

4. It might also have been mentioned that provision is made in the membership contract for the reduction of one percent of the gross sales price of grain to be used as commercial reserve. That would be one cent per bushel on dollar wheat and one-half cent on fifty-cent wheat.

No such deductions as in 3 and 4 are naturally made from the open market price, which makes the basis of comparison somewhat unsound.

Dr. Grindley was of the opinion that both prices were based on Fort William and that there was nothing in the contention that the comparison was unsound in this respect.

[19] *Ibid.*
[20] *Ibid.*

He also expressed the opinion that it would take years' work to make a really true statistical comparison of the open market and pool prices for the period.[21]

The affront to the pools was the subject of a lively debate on the evening of June 25 in the house. The house was in supply on trade and commerce estimates when Messrs. Motherwell, Mackenzie, Vallance and Garland mounted an attack on Stevens and the government over the insult to the pools. Five times during the course of the debate, Stevens attributed the responsibility for the chart to Evans, and said it had been inserted into the report without the knowledge of the other two commissioners. Because the prime minister was absent at the time, the opposition demanded that the item stand until he could speak to it.[22] On July 1st Bennett responded:

I have already indicated to the House the circumstances under which Sir Josiah Stamp was asked to become chairman of the commission. The grain trade selected Mr. Sanford Evans as its representative on the commission, and the Hon. Chief Justice Brown became the representative of the agrarian interests. As is indicated by the return filed to-day, Mr. Pearson of the Department of External Affairs was selected to act as secretary.

When the commission had concluded its labours Mr. Pearson returned to Ottawa and Mr. Sanford Evans also came here. Each of the commissioners had a copy of the evidence. The report had been drafted only, and it had been agreed that as Sir Josiah Stamp could stay in this country only a limited number of days, the typewriting of portions of the report that he had indicated, apart from what he had written, should be completed, and the report would be set up in type and mailed to him on the Mauretania, sailing on the succeeding Tuesday, so he might be able to revise and return the report to Canada. Mr. Pearson undertook the overseeing of that work. At the time among the appendices was the number 12 which had been put in evidence by Mr. Pitblado practically at the conclusion of the hearing, under the circumstances mentioned by him in his telegram.

I said the other day, and I now repeat in passing, that the real objection to that appendix was the red ink statement which drew inferences from the chart itself. I knew nothing of this, neither did anyone in the department so far as that is concerned. The report came back from London, approved by Sir Josiah Stamp. There were one or two typographical errors that he had corrected. But recall this, if you please, there were no appendices sent to Sir Josiah Stamp with the report.

When the report was returned, Mr. Pearson — a competent young man who has long been in the department and enjoys the confidence of his superiors — sent the draft to the printing office, had it printed, and included with the appendices the appendix in question. I am informed that this was done in the ordinary course, it being believed that this was one of the appendices that should be attached. I am informed by Mr. Pearson that some little conversation took place between him and Mr. Evans, Mr. Evans believing that the appendix should be included as part of the report, and Mr. Pearson, as secretary, concurring in the suggestion of the commissioner because the appendix had been put in evidence at the hearing. It is an elementary rule that any document put in in evidence may be printed as part of the report and the proceedings. This appendix was so included.

I tabled the report. I notice it is suggested that it was my duty to read the

---

[21]*Bennett Papers.*
[22]*House of Commons Debates,* June 25, 1931, pp. 3045-3061.

report. I think not. The report was made to me by the commission, and it was my duty to table the report as I received it, without making any comment on it in any way, shape or form; which I did. Some days later I was called up by telephone asking if I had observed that the Appendix had been included in the report to which exception had been taken by certain of the grain interests. I said the matter was entirely new to me because as a matter of fact I had not read the appendix. I immediately got the report and looked at the appendix. Then I went down to the office and inquired into the circumstances under which the appendix had been included in the report, with the results that I have just given to the committee.

I believe that the appendix would not have been received by a judge in a court of law if attention had been directed to the inferences drawn from it and which are printed in red. So far as the appendix itself is concerned, we would say that it could be put in evidence just for what it is worth. The inferences to be drawn would be left entirely to the commission itself rather than to the person who prepared the return. I understand the return was prepared by the statistical agency in Winnipeg of which Mr. Evans is the head. I am only told that; it does not appear so from the report.

There is nothing further that I can add. The copy of the evidence and the other documents were lodged in the department by Mr. Pearson in his capacity as secretary of the commission; they were not so lodged as a part of the files of the department. The documents are still in the department. I do not think the correspondence which took place is any part of the departmental correspondence, I not having written any communication then in respect to it. As I have said, the communications which took place between the chairman, the members of the commission and the unfortunate secretary are in no sense part of the records of the department over which I can in any sense have control, and I do not regard them as such. I regret more than I can say that these difficulties arose, but they would have arisen in spite of any supervision which might have been made, because Sir Josiah Stamp indicated when he came to Canada that it was absolutely necessary for him to leave on a certain date by a certain ship. The inclusion of the appendix as a part of the report is in no sense objectionable either as a matter of evidence or fair dealing or as a matter of good faith between the commission and the department from which the commission issued. But, as I stated when my attention was directed to it by the hon. member for Humboldt, in my opinion the red printing which drew inferences from the document should not have appeared.

I issued instructions that the appendix should be removed from all copies of the report in the department, and Mr. Pearson saw that the appendix was in fact removed. Those which have been circulated since that time have not contained that appendix. A certain number of copies, as indicated by the return filed today, have been issued to public libraries and to individuals who have asked for them; the Winnipeg Grain Exchange printed a certain number of copies of the evidence and obtained a number of copies of the report as well. From those copies of the report the appendix in question has been removed.[23]

It was typical of Bennett's misfortunes that the commission he so ably conceived, which Sir Josiah Stamp had so ably conducted and which would have commanded such public confidence, had the report been allowed to stand on its own merits, should have been so discredited.

[23]*Ibid.*, July 1, 1931, pp. 3291-3292.

With good intentions, however, Bennett accomplished his basic purpose in appointing the commission. Its report had referred to a supervisory body as probably having some merit, but without making any specific recommendations thereon. As a result, Bennett was relieved of the pressure to introduce regulatory legislation.

FIVE CENT BONUS

In contrast with the brilliant attack he had mounted against the wheat policies of the Mackenzie King administration during the course of the 1930 throne speech debate, Bennett made a surprisingly ill-considered speech as soon as he was placed on the defensive. In rebuttal of criticism of his own policies during the 1931 throne speech debate, Bennett referred to the state of the economy in western Canada and claimed that tens of thousands of farmers had deposits of money in the banks, that gross revenues from agriculture and industry in western Canada had attained record levels in recent years, that purchases of automobiles had been increasing, and that farmers had created some of their own problems by speculating in wheat.[24] The press in western Canada reacted predictably, and Bennett may have had his unfortunate assessment in mind when he included a measure of assistance to the western farmer in his June 1, 1931 budget. He had resisted pressures from the three provincial premiers to place a floor on the price of wheat and he would have been very hard put to claim that his principal innovations to date, unemployment relief and a high protective tariff, had been even indirectly of benefit to the prairie economy. Thus, after providing in his budget for increased federal contributions to old-age pensioners and for larger freight subventions on domestic coal, he said:

> The third matter to which attention might be directed is that touching the movement of wheat. There has been a succession of bad harvests in some parts of western Canada, and during the last few weeks lack of moisture—I speak subject to correction, I hope—has caused a loss of this year's prospective crop in a great deal of that area. My advices by telephone were that very few days would determine the fate of a considerable portion of the crop. In some parts of the country this is the third crop failure and the reserves of the people are entirely exhausted. Two things must happen: First, provision should be made to assist those who have a crop, because they have considerable obligations, taxes, etc., which must be discharged. Other methods will be taken to deal with the situation of the provinces which are not in a position to assist those who with their reserves exhausted and their crops a failure a third time are practically ruined. We therefore propose to provide that the freight rates shall be adjusted by this country absorbing five cents per bushel on all wheat that is exported of the crop of this year. That provision is effective this year. That amount is taken into consideration in the estimates I have given of the expenditures for the year.[25]

Evidently it was thought that the wheat bonus could be paid as a freight-rate subvention, as in the case of coal, and that it could be restricted to the amount of wheat exported. As soon as Bennett made the announcement, he received a flood of messages from interested parties. Messrs. C. H. G. Short, president of the Canadian national millers

[24]*Ibid.*, April 21, 1931, pp. 778-780.
[25]*Ibid.*, June 1, 1931, p. 2171.

association and C. B. Watts, secretary of the Dominion millers association urged that the bonus apply also to wheat flour. Mr. James A. Richardson wrote to the Honourable H. H. Stevens on June 4: "I think it will prove to be more satisfactory and practical if the Government should make the allowance of 5¢ a bushel to all wheat delivered in Western Canada rather than arrange to pay on the amount exported from the seaboard.[26]

The Northwest grain dealers' association made a similar suggestion and an offer of assistance by telegram of June 4, 1931, to Bennett:

> The announcement of your government's intended policy of assistance to western wheat producers while vaguely stated in the press has been very sympathetically received in agricultural and grain trade circles. If it is the intention of your government that this benefit accrue solely to the producer which we strongly recommend we suggest that payments upon export clearances will not accomplish this and we would therefore recommend that the payment be made at the time of delivery in the country. In order to insure the direct receipt by the producer of this assistance the members of this association will be pleased to place their facilities for making direct payment to the producer at the disposal of your government. We therefore respectfully suggest that in order to work out an effective and economical plan for distribution of the five cent per bushel the members of this organization would be pleased to cooperate with the Board of Grain Commissioners in an attempt to submit a plan of operation satisfactory to your government.[27]

McFarland's criticism of the proposed method of payment was more blunt as he urged payment in a manner that would reassure producers that they were, in fact, the beneficiaries. In a handwritten note of June 2 to Bennett, McFarland recommended the issuance of certificates at the point of delivery, which was the method eventually adopted:

> Re your 5¢ Bonus in wheat. Pardon a word of warning. The newspapers indicate this will be taken care of in some way on the freight and it is payable on wheat exported. Hope this is not correctly reported.
>
> 5¢ per Bus. will be good only provided the farmer actually gets it and knows he gets it. That cannot be if it is payable only on wheat exported. You must give it on wheat actually delivered and sold by each and every farmer. You could do this by having the grain Companies give each farmer a specified certificate which could probably be cashed by the Banks, or it could probably be done by the Government paying 5 cents per bushel of the freight rate from country points to Ft. William, Vancouver, Ft. Churchill and other interior Elevator and Milling points. Do not however apply it East of Ft. William or otherwise it will be lost in the shuffle and it could be proven that the Foreigner gets all or most of the benefit. You cannot get away with this thing and apply it on exports.
>
> Excuse my butting in, but these are my views, and you will find them correct.
>
> P.S. Crop conditions are tragic. What next? I wish I had authority to buy some futures and run the price up 5 to 10 cents.[28]

In his postscipt McFarland inferred that he could do farmers more good by supporting the market than the wheat bonus could possibly do. In less than two months, he received authority to commence support operations.

[26] *Bennett Papers.*
[27] *Ibid.*
[28] *Ibid.*

The board of grain commissioners were called upon to administer the payment and the board worked out a scheme of certificate distribution through the elevator agents of the country elevator companies. The law clerks had been put to work drafting legislation, but their first draft drawn up upon Bennett's instructions as "An Act Respecting the Export of Wheat" underwent two revisions before it appeared as "An Act Respecting Wheat". The legislation made provision for payment out of the consolidated revenue fund of a sum of five cents per bushel on wheat grown in the three prairie provinces in the year 1931, and delivered to any licensed elevator, commission merchant, track buyer, or grain dealer in the western inspection division.[29]

The act had left to the governor in council the responsibility for "determining the person to whom the said sum of five cents per bushel shall be paid." A question immediately arose over the interpretation of the word "producer"as used in the regulations, since it was a common practice for owners of farms to enter into owner-tenant agreements, and it was a valid question whether payment of the bonus should be divided accordingly. After considerable deliberation, the board of grain commissioners determined that the money in question should go "directly into the hands of the primary producer of wheat irrespective of the ownership of the same."[30] If the actual legislation required that decision, the principle was dubious, and the precedent was not followed in subsequent legislation.

Naturally, the method of subsidy in bonusing wheat deliveries was challenged on the basis of various inequities. During the autumn of 1931, the prime minister's office received numerous petitions from farm groups in areas that had been hailed out, and also from those that had suffered from drought. Both groups had an understandable grievance that they had been deprived of any benefit from the bonus. The wording of the standard petition underscored the inequity:

WHEREAS the farmers of the drought area in the West, besides not having a crop to market, can obviously get no benefit from the bonus of five cents a bushel on wheat and

WHEREAS the said farmers at seeding time showed as much faith in the world wheat prices as did the others, and, on the average, probably prepared their ground equally well, the fact they suffered a crop failure being due to circumstances beyond their control, and

WHEREAS by far the most of the wheat growers in the drought area are in dire want, and if it is necessary to help those farmers who have a crop to harvest, how much more do those who have no crop require a bonus, and

WHEREAS the burden of the bonus, as at present arranged, will be borne by the country at large, and therefore in this case the more fortunate are being helped at the expense of the less so, and

WHEREAS we feel sure the intent in passing the bonus measure of five cents a bushel was not to discriminate against any individuals or any particular locality, and we trust to your fairness to reconsider this matter,

THEREFORE we the undersigned citizens of CANADA respectfully request and urge a careful re-consideration of the terms of the bonus to the

[29]*Statutes of Canada,* 21-22 George V, Chap. 60, assented to August 3, 1931.
[30]*Annual Report of the Board of Grain Commissioners for Canada for the year 1932,* p. 9.

wheat growers for the above reasons, and suggest that the terms of the said bonus be so altered that the more needy ones may at least share equally in it, or in the event of the impossibility of making the change at this date, we would suggest that a special bonus be given to the wheat growers in the drought area on the basis of the number of acres seeded to wheat this year, and of an average fair crop of 20 bushels to the acre.[31]

Although there were no protests of discrimination against producers of coarse grains at the time, that basis of inequity also existed.

The 1931 bonus on wheat deliveries had been an exercise in remorse. Bennett had palpably misjudged the mood of the people in that part of the country he knew best. He reluctantly set about to pick up the tab, but thought he was doing so at half the amount the treasury ultimately paid out. Even at that the amount of $12,720,121.07 was woefully inadequate and the distribution was wrong. Yet it was a first and historic occasion upon which wheat growers received a direct subvention because it was recognized that within the national economy of which they were a vital part, they had not received a fair deal. After stumbling into making payment, Bennett retrieved himself as quickly as possible and avoided any repetition.

STORAGE RATES

With a relatively large crop of 423 million bushels coming up in 1932 on top of a carryover of 136 millions, the country and terminal elevator companies stood to earn increased revenues from storage, in addition to their earnings on the handling of wheat. Under the Canada grain act, the board of grain commissioners were empowered to fix maximum charges for each crop year, which they set after holding public hearings. In that manner, the maximum storage rate had stood at 1/30 cent per bushel per day for some years. Even with the changing conditions in 1932, no one had protested the rate. But because storage earnings appeared to be building up, as well as maintaining the level of the carrying charges the central selling agency had to pay, McFarland pleaded with Bennett for their reduction. He did not wish to be personally identified with his proposal because of his close business dealings with the elevator companies, but he contended that Bennett should act as a matter of political expediency before public criticism arose. He accused the provincial governments, accepted spokesmen for the producers, of neglecting their responsibilities in that regard because, as creditors of the pool elevator companies, they now had a direct interest in elevator earnings. It was not just the producer who held his grain in public storage whose interest was at stake. Pool members whose 1930 wheat was still unaccounted for had an interest in the level of carrying charges. The public treasury was also involved in respect of the government guarantee. Since the responsibility for action rested with the board of grain commissioners, McFarland recommended that Dr. MacGibbon be brought to Ottawa for consultations. If the board needed additional powers to set actual rates, McFarland hoped that these could be provided by order in council or by act of parliament. Altogether, McFarland wrote to Bennett three times on the subject. Following are excerpts from his first letter on October 4, 1932:

[31] *Bennett Papers.*

In the meantime elevator storage charges are just the same per bushel as they were when wheat was selling at $1.50 per bushel and when the quantities held in storage were very materially less than they are in these days of heavy stocks and carry-overs.

I am very aware that the storage rates are sanctioned each year by the Board of Grain Commissioners, but I believe the sanction is given on the basis of a maximum which does not mean that the rates are irrevocably fixed for the full year, and I do think, having regard to the large volumes of grain available for storage to elevator companies at country points as well as at terminal elevators, which grain is being held for long periods of time on account of the lack of demand, that the storage rates should be reduced, and I believe it is the duty of the Dominion Government to take the initiative in causing this reduction in the interests of the producers as well as in the interests of the Government itself. . . .

I am quite aware that it would be an unpopular thing to intimate a reduction in storage charges and will be met by the argument that the Elevator companies are having a hard struggle as it is, but the reply to that is that the elevator companies are not having nearly as hard a struggle as the farmer.

I prefer that you do not use my name in connection with this storage reduction movement, and I am writing this to you in strict confidence, and would suggest that if you are interested in it you should call Dr. MacGibbon of the Board of Grain Commissioners to Ottawa and put it up to him as to whether something should not be done.

The higher the storage charge the greater the carrying charge between the cash month and the futures. For instance today October Wheat, which is now cash wheat, is 49¼ cents, whereas May Wheat for delivery next May is 56¾ cents, which means 7½ cents a bushel of a cost for storage and interest from now until next May. You will, however, observe that the interest is a small item on 50 cent wheat so that the bulk of that difference is made up in storage which is earned by terminals. It increases the value of wheat for future delivery and makes it just that much more difficult to compete in foreign markets on future sales. Just what the storage rates should be I do not know, I should say that half a cent per bushel per month is not enough, on the other hand I would say that three quarters of a cent per bushel per month is ample, both at country elevators and at terminals.

If you do not take some action on this storage question you might find that the opposition will use it politically against you in the future, or indeed they might beat you to it and draw the attention of the country to the fact that these storage rates are too high in times like these when there are such huge volumes of all kinds of grain being held in storage because of the lack of markets for the stuff.

McFarland wrote a second time on October 18:

Re storage charges. I have heard nothing in regard to this subject since I was in Ottawa. I am so convinced that your government should do something in regard to this that I am constrained to write you further on the subject.

In my other letter today I mentioned that we have about 33 million bushels of December options. I deliberately purchased December because that is the nearest to cash wheat. December wheat today is 50 cents; May Wheat is 54¼ cents. The buying of December has resulted in the price of May wheat being lower than it otherwise would have been had we been purchasing May wheat instead of December wheat. The chances are May wheat would have been 6 or 6½ cents per bushel higher than December, whereas today it is 4¼ cents. It is only a short time since the spread was 5¼ cents. Of course, you realize the greater the premium of May wheat over December, the greater the profit the terminals are making in storage. They are looking for full carrying charges, which means a cent a bushel a month or the equivalent of five cents per bushel from December to May, which, plus interest would amount to between 6¼ and 6½ cents per bushel. That is where they would like to have it and even today they think that I will be stuck and have to pay the full carrying charge to carry this wheat from December to May, and as your Government is interested in carrying this wheat I just wish you to understand that it would make a difference of 2 cents per bushel to the Treasury if these storage charges are not reduced, because I will have no other option than to accept the dictation of the elevator companies as to what they will charge for carrying the wheat, and they will demand the full pound of flesh so as to give them the full maximum rate, which they are entitled to charge according to the Board of Grain Commissioners. You can figure for yourself what 2 cents per bushel would mean on the many millions which we alone are interested in and then add to that the millions which the farmers are holding in storage and you will get a picture of what the total might amount to. Besides if these so-called full carrying charges are permitted to become operative, it makes it just that much harder for Canadian Wheat to be sold in competition with our competitors, because it makes it that much higher.

Coupled with the above there is the undoubted fact that some of the informed public throughout the country are criticizing the heavy storage charges which grain companies are allowed to charge and it has been mentioned that even the Provincial Governments, because of the fact that the Pool Elevator Companies owe them a lot of money, are not taking any interest in reducing storage charges. There is no doubt in my mind that if the Prairie Governments were not interested in elevators they would be crying out loud for reductions, not only in storage charges but also in handling charges.

Now that I have found it necessary to start out on this campaign of reducing storage charges, I am going to go a step farther and suggest that the receiving fee at country elevators of 1¾ cents per bushel, which includes 15 days storage, is also extortionate under present economic conditions throughout this country and I believe in fairness to all parties concerned and in fairness to your Government, you should also reduce this fee.

I know that this is the duty of the Board of Grain Commissioners but they have taken no action. At the same time I feel that I would be delinquent in my duty if I did not bring these matters to your attention as well as to the attention of the Minister of Trade & Commerce. Furthermore, if it is within the powers of an Order-In-Council, I think these changes should be made by an Order-In-Council, and should be made without delay. The other method would be for the Board of Grain Commissioners to advertise for a public meeting to discuss these charges and Elevator Companies would be supposed to present figures and arguments against it. I say that the reasons for reduction are so obvious that no such meeting should be called but an arbitrary reduction should be made and should be made by an Order-In-Council if you have the power to do it in that way, which I believe you have.

There are enormous quantities of wheat and other grains in storage and if the full storage charges are permitted to obtain, then some of these line elevator companies are going to make such profits as will look like profiteering in times such as we are now living in.

The fact of the matter is these storage charges should have been reduced more than a year ago when it became evident that large stocks were going to be of necessity carried over for long periods of time owing to inadequate demand in world's markets.

Finally, McFarland wrote a third letter on October 29:

> ... It is stated in Grain Exchange circles that Dr. MacGibbon has been called to Ottawa and it is generally understood he has been called down in connection with the storage rates in Terminal Elevators. I can only add that the reduction should be made not only in Terminal Elevators at Fort William and Vancouver but also in all country and mill elevators. No doubt the grain trade would like to see the reduction applied to the Terminals only but it should take in more territory to really be effective, and do what it is intended to do, namely; reduce the carrying charges. Furthermore, I would suggest that you remain very firm in your demand that the rate should not exceed 1/45 of a cent per bushel per day. That means 2/3 of a cent per bushel per month and in my opinion is a fair rate, having regard to the huge volumes which are being stored and the low prices at which grain is selling.
>
> I was told yesterday that the exporting companies intend making an effort to have the Government reduce the rate in Terminal Elevators—Fort William and Eastern Ports—to a rate of 1/50 or even as low as 1/60 of a cent per day, and that it is intended that representations shall be made in connection therewith in time for the next crop. Of course, when this agitation was started I suppose they had no idea that we were already working on it and that you had the matter under consideration in regard to making it possible, by Act of Parliament.[32]

It was evident from this correspondence that Bennett had already acted by having the Honourable H. H. Stevens bring Dr. MacGibbon to Ottawa, and that the trade did not appear too upset by what was in the offing. While in Ottawa, MacGibbon advised Stevens that the Canada grain act, as presently worded, prevented the board from adjusting terminal charges during the course of a crop year after they had been initially established by the board. Section 134 of the act read: "Notwithstanding anything in this act, the tariff of charges made for cleaning, storage and handling of grain in any public or semi-public or terminal or eastern elevator shall not be subject to change during the crop year." Consequently MacGibbon recommended a simple amendment to the act by adding to section 134 the words: "except by order or regulation of the board".

A bill to effect this change received first reading in the house on November 4, 1932. On second reading, on November 7, Stevens observed:

> Hitherto, under section 134, such action by the board could be taken only once a year, and the fees having been fixed by the board could not make any change except subject to some other paragraphs in the act. The only object we have in view is this: During this time of stress the board is precluded from taking any action and we want to empower them to take action. I may say there is a very general willingness and desire, I am informed today, on the part of the elevator companies to conform to any reasonable action of the board. In fact it is possible they may take action even before this bill is passed. I am certain that there is a willingness and desire to meet this situation and all who are interested in lessening the burden of costs upon this commodity will welcome this privilege being given to the board of grain commissioners at this time.[33]

[32] *Ibid.*
[33] *House of Commons Debates,* November 7, 1932, p. 877.

In reply to a direct question from Malcolm, Stevens expressed his view on the reduction in prospect for the storage rate: "I have no objection to saying what is my view; I would say 1/45 instead of 1/30; I am not going to dictate to them, but since my hon. friend has asked me I will tell him what is my view."[34]

The bill was passed quickly by the house and senate, and the amending act was given royal assent on November 25. The board promptly conducted new tariff hearings, as a result of which storage rates for all elevators situated in the western inspection division were reduced to 1/45 per bushel per day. This action anticipated by a few days the historic low price for wheat basis in store Fort William.

CANADIAN WHEAT INSTITUTE

In 1933-34, United Grain Growers Limited took the initiative in proposing the formation of a Canadian wheat institute oriented toward getting the whole industry to take a more active interest in promotion of wheat sales and in advising the government on policy. Although the institute failed to get beyond the proposal stage, and was not sponsored by the government, its concept bore a remarkable resemblance to that of the Canada grains council established 1969. For that reason, note should be taken of this early attempt to form a trade association within the industry.

Mr. R. S. Law, president of United Grain Growers Limited, had a draft charter for a non-profit association drawn up. Its objects were:

(a) to promote the use of Canadian wheat and other grain grown in Canada, and the products thereof, throughout the world

(b) to collect, compile and publish information concerning conditions throughout the world affecting the marketing of grain grown in Canada for the purpose of making such information available to the public and private bodies.

The board of directors submitted the proposal to the November 1933 annual meeting of United Grain Growers Limited which endorsed it. A brochure was prepared to elaborate on the objects of the institute and was distributed widely within the industry while Mr. Law arranged an interview with the prime minister in the hope of securing Bennett's tacit or public approval.

The brochure was entitled *Proposals for the establishment of the Canadian Wheat Institute as a National Body to Conduct Work in the interests of Canadian Wheat*. Among proposed functions were the collation of information on economic and scientific research which bore upon the marketing of wheat, and assistance in formulating government wheat policy. Inasmuch as wheat had become a national problem and would likely remain so, the brochure contended: "it will be of great advantage if governments are able to turn to an impartial and well-equipped organization for opinion and advice, and the need in this direction is a continuing one."

In addition, it was proposed that the institute should supplement the work of the department of trade and commerce by sending technical missions to visit mills and the trade overseas, and by exploring the area of trade

[34]*Ibid.*, November 7, 1932, p. 879.

relations with wheat importing countries. It also contemplated direct advertising and merchandising campaigns on behalf of Canadian wheat and its products, as well as serving as a general information source.

In the main, these functions are embraced in the objects of the Canada grains council, and the differences between the council and the proposed institute are those of organization and emphasis. The Canada grains council is jointly sponsored and financed by the federal government and the industry, whereas the proposed institute was to have been a non-governmental organization, financed wholly by personal membership subscriptions and the sustaining memberships of the various industry organizations. Whereas the primary object of the council is coordination within the industry and of its advice to government, the proposed institute placed the primary emphasis upon assistance in the marketing of wheat. Thus the latter gave more explicit expression to functions such as overseas missions and advertising campaigns.

As a result of Mr. Law's interview with Bennett in February, 1934, he believed that he had received the prime minister's enthusiastic approval (sought as a matter of prestige, as no federal participation was involved). Bennett, however, took the precaution of asking Law to discuss the proposal with McFarland in Winnipeg. In a long session with Law, McFarland picked flaws in the scheme and reported adversely to Bennett. Although McFarland laid stress on the marketing competence of the export firms and the mills, it can be inferred that after closing the overseas offices of the central selling agency McFarland saw little virtue in resuming such activities in another guise. Moreover, as the person most directly responsible for the execution of wheat sales policy he undoubtedly foresaw problems with a supplementary sales force in the field under independent direction. But at least he took advantage of the opportunity to recruit Law to his campaign for a change in the Canadian grading system as he wrote to Bennett on March 1, 1934:

> Mr. Law, General Manager of the United Grain Growers, called to see me a few days ago and informed me that he had had one or two conferences with you in Ottawa regarding a scheme which he has in mind, and in which you appeared to show a very great interest, and also that you had suggested that he should come and see me.
>
> Now I heard Mr. Law's story in regard to his proposed wheat institute, which he explained he was starting out to organize by securing substantial subscriptions from some of the leading institutions and commercial companies throughout Canada, the object of the company being to further the sale of Canadian wheat and flour in foreign countries.
>
> I would not write you about this except that he mentioned your suggestion that he should come and see me, and all I want to say is that I think he has a very hazy idea of what he is setting out to accomplish. For instance, so far as wheat is concerned, his company operated an export company with offices in New York for quite a long number of years, and I enquired from him whether, in the operation of that company, it had ever been suspected there was any market for Canadian wheat which might be exploited and which were left undone. The only reply he made was that they had just recently closed up their export business. I also enquired about what prospects there might be of expanding the sale of flour and the only suggestion he had was there might be something done in some of the South American Republics or

in China; also a rather hazy plan to popularize high grade Canadian flour in the United Kingdom, but just how was another question which he was rather vague about.

After discussing the objects which he had in view, I informed him that I did not think there was a great field to be explored that had not already been explored by the big companies in flour, and the exporting companies in wheat, but I did think there were some things which might be done within the Dominion of Canada, which would help us to maintain the position which we have already established in foreign markets, namely; the matter of improving the quality of our wheat, and I told him that I had been writing the Minister of Trade & Commerce at Ottawa, urging upon him the desirability of amending the Inspection Act with that object in view, so as to eliminate Garnet and other inferior types of wheat from our grades of No. 1, 2 and 3 and probably No. 4 Manitoba Northern wheat, thus leaving Garnet and other inferior types to be sold on their merits, and probably in that way inducing farmers in the northern parts of these provinces to become less wheat-minded and more inclined to mixed farming, which would in a measure help us to solve our wheat problem to a greater extent than any other new-fangled undertaking. He seemed to think the suggestion was a good one and that he would be glad to incorporate that object along with the objects which he had in mind, and he asked me to send him a memorandum on it. . . .[35]

In the meantime Law had been soliciting support from the industry, and he wrote to Bennett on July 11, 1934:

We have made a good deal of progress with the Canadian Wheat Institute since your approval of the project was obtained, and from the interest it has aroused, we believe it will be possible for it to be successfully organized and adequately supported.

During the past few months we have withheld any definite announcement in this respect, awaiting the outcome of international discussions in wheat, but feel that the time has now arrived when progress can be made. The attached memorandum is accordingly being distributed to the various grain, transportation, steamship, financial and commercial organizations which it is thought will be interested. Any endorsation from you, of course, either privately or publicly, will be of great assistance and especially information as to your favourable attitude given to the railways, banks, or insurance companies. Anything, therefore, that you find occasion to do in this connection, will be highly valued.[36]

Because of McFarland's advice, Bennett evaded Law's appeal for moral support, as may be inferred from the carefully worded acknowledgment Bennett's private secretary, Mr. A. W. Merriam, addressed to Law on September 10:

The Prime Minister had hoped to find an opportunity to write you personally in reply to your letter of July 11, enclosing a memorandum with regard to the proposed Canadian Wheat Institute. However, owing to absence from the city, and his engagements with the different Provincial Governments he was unable to do so before his departure for the meetings of the Assembly of the League of Nations.

He asked me as he was leaving to acknowledge your letter and to express his thanks for the memorandum you were good enough to send.[37]

[35] *Bennett Papers.*
[36] *Ibid.*
[37] *Ibid.*

In the result, United Grain Growers Limited did not proceed with incorporation of the institute. Mr. Law referred to the proposal again when he testified before the Turgeon royal inquiry commission in 1937. By then the Canadian wheat board was in existence and Law acknowledged that the board was competent to perform the functions envisaged for the institute. In his report, Turgeon commended the proposal, and suggested that if the board were to be discontinued, other arrangements should be made to pursue such work.[38]

PROTEIN GRADING

Because of the drought in the southern plains which normally produce the highest protein wheat, a higher proportion of the 1933 crop had been drawn from the park belt where rainfall had been better, and this included the northern districts whose soil conditions normally yielded much less protein. This created new problems of inconsistency within the statutory grades, depending on whether the wheat was drawn from the southern or northern districts. Canadian and Buffalo mills which could draw their wheat straight from the south were prepared to pay premiums because of higher protein content. Terminal elevators which could segregate high protein wheat by separate binning within the same statutory grades could earn protein premiums which were not passed back to the producers. On the other hand, the high proportion of wheat moving from northern districts to Vancouver caused a serious deterioration in the value of No. 2 Northern wheat, especially, which sold at a discount of as much as 6 cents a bushel below the value of the same grade at Fort William. The problem was also aggravated by the fact that Garnet wheat had not yet been segregated from the other statutory grades.

McFarland took increasing notice of this problem as he undertook a campaign for protein grading which he pursued in a deluge of letters to the Honourable H. H. Stevens, minister of trade and commerce to whom the board of grain commissioners reported, and also to Bennett, who was concerned about the high premium for Canadian over Argentine wheat which he believed was impeding sales. McFarland explained to Stevens in a lengthy letter of February 6, 1934, that Canada was filling its full export quota at the premium and that , therefore, its reduction was unwarranted as he added:

> ... The fact of the matter is, the percentage of protein constitutes a very important element in the value of wheat, and the protein content in all countries varies from year to year, having regard to the climatic conditions of the various years in the various countries, and this brings me to another thought, and that is this, that it seems evident now that there is going to be a considerable reduction in the acreage sown to wheat throughout the southern areas of Saskatchewan, the Southeastern areas of Alberta and the Southwestern areas of Manitoba, and these southern areas have always been the parts of Western Canada which have produced the high protein content, whereas the more northern regions produce the lower content protein, together with Garnet wheat. It looks more and more as if the more fortunate farmers throughout the Northern districts, being more fortunate by securing better yields per acre, are to some extent riding on the backs of the poor devils who

[38]*Report of the Royal Grain Inquiry Commission, 1938,* pp. 190-191.

are located in the more southern districts where high protein wheat is grown, this, because of the fact that the wheat of the same grades both from north and south are graded almost regardless of their protein content, and mixed together at terminals, thus reducing, to the detriment of the southern farmer, the value of his average wheat, and to the benefit of the northern farmer for his poorer wheat.

I do not know whether the Inspection Department could really handle a crop under rules of inspection, based on the protein or gluten content, but if it could be done, I can conceive where it would be much more just to the more unfortunate farmers living in the southern areas than is the present system.

I would suggest to you that it might be worth your while to have a discussion on this with Mr. Ramsay of the Board of Grain Commissioners. I have not mentioned it to him but I believe it would be worthwhile your exploring it.[39]

McFarland wrote to Stevens again on February 13:

I received your letter regarding my suggestion about a revamping of the grades of wheat. Mr. Ramsay called to see me yesterday and he will be writing you fully. It is not an easy matter to handle, but I have great confidence in Mr. Ramsay's resourcefulness and abilities, and I know that he favours a change. The fact is, the more you think about it, the more desirable it is, having regard to the check which this country has received in wheat production and wheat markets. It now becomes all the more necessary that as great a percentage as possible of our wheat should be such as has been described "as the best wheat in the world", but I can assure you that a lot of the wheat being grown in the Northern districts in these three provinces cannot be so described, and if it is permitted to become mixed with the desirable wheat, or high protein wheat, at the terminals, it just means that we will not enjoy as wide a market in those countries where high protein is needed for mixing. Furthermore, we are endeavouring to readjust our agriculture, and if, for argument's sake, the southern portions of these provinces were entirely eliminated from wheat production, we could no longer claim ourselves producers of the best wheat in the world, and, therefore, our battle for a place in the sun would be that much more difficult throughout the present and future trying years which may be ahead of the wheat producers of the world. I feel that if the wheats grown in the northern territories had to be sold strictly on their milling quality merits, the prices of such wheats would not look so attractive to the farmers in the north, and would probably result in their voluntarily producing less wheat, and more of something else, which would, in a measure, assist in the solution of reducing acreage, and at the same time give the poor devil in the south a run for his money.

The northern farmer does not need any wheat assistance. It is a mixed farming country and it would be a good thing if it were forced to revert more to mixed farming. On the other hand, in recent years they have become wheat-minded.

If something really effective can be done in the matter of this wheat grading, now would be a good time to do it when the wheat problem is so prominent in the minds of so many people, not only in the west, but also in the east, and again, it rather fits in with the problem of reduction of acreage, because I really believe if northern farmers knew that their wheat—Garnet and some other inferior grades— had to be sold strictly on its intrinsic merit, they would not be so anxious to seed so many acres.[40]

[39] *Bennett Papers*
[40] *Ibid.*

McFarland wrote two much more pressing letters to Stevens on February 19 and 27 after Stevens had acknowledged "the Garnet wheat problem" but hoped he wouldn't have to amend the grain act that year. He also wrote a long letter to Bennett on February 22, Quoting from an address Mr. C. D. Howe had delivered to the Canadian Club in Winnipeg on the subject of improvement in Argentina's competitive position which he had observed in the course of his elevator construction in that country. Finally, Stevens yielded to McFarland's pressure, but in terms of Garnet wheat only, whereas McFarland was concerned about a much wider problem. In the process, Stevens complained about lack of support from the pools as he wrote to McFarland on March 3:

> I am in receipt of your further letter of the 27th, regarding grading Garnet wheat. I am glad to have your view on the subject. I tried to get this down as you know three years ago, but failed owing to bitter opposition by Motherwell and others.
>
> Another thing is this, the Pools will not state their views. I wish you could get the Pools to frankly state their views in favour of it. It is what the Pool really wishes to do apparently, but even when they know as leaders that it is a desirable thing to do, they are aware that a certain branch or section of the membership is dissatisfied, therefore they will not commit themselves, so that the Government can be blamed for the grief, and they take advantage of the help that may be given. This is an attitude that I do not appreciate. It is not courageous and it is unfair. I wish you could, therefore, induce the Pools to come out frankly in support of this. In the meantime I am placing the facts before the Prime Minister and I am quite willing myself to bring in an amendment to the Act.[41]

Meanwhile McFarland had lost no time in lining up support as he wrote twice to Stevens on March 5:

> I am in receipt of your letter of the 3rd. I note what you say about the grading of Garnet Wheat and that you are placing the facts before the Prime Minister, and that you are quite willing to bring in an amendment to the Act, but you would like the Pools to frankly state their views in favour of it.
>
> Mr. Brouillette was here from Regina on Saturday and I again took the matter up with him very fully. He is most emphatically in favour of it. One of his executive, namely; Mr. J. H. Wesson, from the northern part of Saskatchewan, is opposed to it, and very strongly opposed, but on purely selfish grounds. However, while Mr. Brouillette says it might take him a few days to work the thing out, yet he is so much in favour of it that he is going to press for a decision by the Board.
>
> I have been in touch with the Alberta Pool and they are unanimously in favour of it and if they carry out their promise to me, they will send you a wire within the next day or two, in fact they told me that they were already on record at Ottawa, so you may find something on your fyles dating back a year or two ago, which will indicate their decision.
>
> Mr. Sidney Smith tells me this morning that he has talked to quite a number of the Grain Trade over at the Grain Exchange and they also favour it, in fact to such an extent that he is going to bring the matter up at the regular Council Meeting of the Exchange on Wednesday and he hopes to be able to send you a telegram after that meeting.
>
> I understand that the flour millers are on record, dating back some year and a half or two years ago, and you have them on record in your fyles at Ottawa.

[41] *Ibid.*

However, Mr. Short will probably communicate with you in regard thereto. There is no doubt in my mind that now is the psychological time to make this change. It must come eventually and it is well that it should come before we take any further risks on the future. I dread to think that the next crop might be a fairly large crop of bushels, but a poor crop of grades, without much No. 1 Northern wheat, in which event all these hybrid varieties in the north would be mixed with the No. 2 Northern from the south, and it would very much complicate and probably reduce our sales abroad, which is not a pleasant prospect to look forward to with present world's conditions.[42]

McFarland's second letter of the same date complained about protein segregation in the terminal elevators. As a result of all this pressure, Mr. E. B. Ramsay, chief commissioner of the board of grain commissioners conferred frequently with McFarland, and also with the departmental officials on the drafting of an amendment to the act. In due course, Stevens introduced the amendment in the house on April 9. When bill 53 was printed, it revealed that Garnet wheat would be excluded from the existing statutory grades and separate statutory grades for No.'s 1 and 2 C. W. Garnet would be created with the changes to take effect on August 1, 1935. No reference was made to grading on the basis of protein content. The amendment was referred to the standing committee on agriculture and colonization and reported to the house on June 7. Royal assent for the amendment came on June 28. But still the question of protein grading had not been dealt with. McFarland continued to write to Stevens to press for action until, for quite other reasons, Stevens resigned as minister of trade and commerce on October 27. There the matter ended.

[42]*Ibid.*

16

SEARCH ABROAD

Bennett seldom enjoyed the luxury of coping with one wheat issue at a time. If he went abroad, invariably some problem cropped up at home. Because the issues were simultaneously in play it would be natural to deal with them chronologically, but some problems persisted longer than others and the endless cross references required to account for them render that approach almost impossible. It is much easier to deal with the issues topically, but at the cost of violating the chronology. Thus, now that the record of Bennett's domestic policy has been brought up to the point where he had the price support operation in place, it is appropriate to revert to the beginning of his administration and to outline his quest abroad for solutions to the wheat problem. Bennett's overseas efforts persisted through the first three years of his administration, including the two imperial conferences, the world monetary and economic conference, and the negotiation of the first international wheat agreement. After that account, the review will return to the implementation of the support operations and their evolution into a wheat board.

IMPERIAL CONFERENCE, 1930

Mackenzie King had already made a major contribution to the constitutional development of Canada through his participation in earlier imperial conferences. He was so widely regarded in the public mind as the best qualified Canadian representative to complete, at this upcoming conference, the arrangements culminating in the statute of Westminster that he had convinced himself of his entitlement to re-election in 1930. At the moment of truth, however, economic issues transcended constitutional aspirations on voting day and, in changed priorities, Bennett received the mandate to head the Canadian delegation to the conference. Even so, constitutional matters took precedence over economic issues, and it was only in the closing stages of the conference that economic affairs were discussed. This review is concerned only with the latter and to the extent that they had a bearing on wheat.

To understand Bennett's objective in economic affairs it is necessary to recall that from their youth both Max Aitken (by now Lord Beaverbrook) and he had been disciples of Joseph Chamberlain, whose crusade for a system of empire trade preferences had caught the imagination of many empire-minded supporters after the turn of the century. More specifically, Chamberlain had advocated (a) free trade in raw materials, (b) an import levy of two shillings a quarter (six cents a bushel) on non-empire wheat and a ten percent ad valorem tariff on non-empire manufactured goods. Chamberlain's proposals had been immediately countered by Liberal objections to the "taxation of food" and the "dear loaf". As he pressed his case, Chamberlain succeeded only in splitting the Conservative party, and the Unionist government of which he was a member was overwhelmingly defeated in 1906.

Even 25 years later, "no taxation on food" remained a political commandment which the British government could not afford to ignore. It was reminded of the issue, however, because Lord Beaverbrook had revived Chamberlain's crusade in the *Daily Express,* in 1929, and had turned the campaign into his own, busily lining up Conservative members in support of empire free trade and failing that, running United Empire party candidates of his own. With Beaverbrook's campaign gaining momentum in Britain and with Bennett's election in Canada on a platform of empire preferences, the prospects for the latter at the imperial conference were reasonably bright. With the power of empire rapidly eroding on the political front, this was the last real opportunity to turn it into an economic entity or, in effect, into an empire common market.

Bennett took a large entourage with him to London, including his sister, three cabinet ministers, Mr. W. D. Herridge and several senior civil servants, among them, Drs. O. D. Skelton and R. H. Coats. The importance of wheat in Bennett's mind was reflected in the appointment as technical advisers to the delegation of Mr. A. J. McPhail, Mr. John I. McFarland, Dr. D. A. MacGibbon, and Dr. W. W. Swanson. Of these the inclusion of Swanson arouses, at this distance, the most curiosity. A professed Liberal, he had been head of the department of economics at the University of Saskatchewan for some years, and the Saskatchewan government had used him to chair several committees of investigation into dairying, livestock, marketing, and immigration. The inference to be drawn from Swanson's inclusion is that Bennett had a considerable respect for economists as such. Swanson's book on *Wheat,* of which Mr. P. C. Armstrong was co-author, had just been published and this added to Swanson's stature as an authority. Swanson predicted that the growth of pools internationally would replace the Liverpool market, and he counselled the private trade in Canada to amalgamate in self-preservation into one company which should coordinate its activities with those of the pools.[1] Such recommended harmony was a far cry from the pitched battle the trade was waging at that time with the pools.

Aboard ship en route to England on September 29, McPhail recorded a group discussion with the Prime Minister:

> Swanson, MacGibbon, McFarland, and I were with Bennett from 10.30 to 1.30. We discussed extension of the Empire Marketing Board and agreed that we should have our own organization in Canada advertising and pushing Canadian production in U.K. markets and elsewhere. On bulk purchasing I took the attitude that we should be prepared to discuss any proposal that

[1]W. W. Swanson and P. C. Armstrong, *Wheat* (Macmillan, Toronto, 1930), pp. 130-136.

would give any promise however remote of helping to solve our marketing problems. The others were all inclined but MacGibbon to rule the question out of the discussion but I do not think Bennett will do so. On Bennett's proposal for a 10 per cent tariff preference within the Empire I approved, suggesting only that 10 per cent would probably not be enough to be effective. Bennett said 10 per cent was mentioned only as a talking point. He is very doubtful of any concrete results from this conference, but is going to make an effort to have an imperial economic conference in Ottawa next year which I think is a good idea. He thinks the Empire has reached a critical point in its career and whether or not it continues as a political entity depends on the ability of statesmen to work out some plan of tariff preferences that will result as much as possible in different parts of the Empire enjoying a market for their products in other parts.[2]

These notes were reasonably prophetic about the course of the conference itself. After items on the agenda concerning constitutional matters were disposed of, the conference turned to economic matters, and Bennett pressed, in ringing terms, his proposals for an exchange of tariff preferences. His speech was reported as follows:

London, October 8. Definitely and unequivocally, Premier R. B. Bennett of Canada today laid his plan for reciprocal empire trade preferences before the Imperial Conference. He spoke in words, the purport of which could not be doubted. The principle of empire preference, he declared, must be either approved or rejected.

"I put the question definitely to you," he explained, "and definitely it should be answered. There is no room here for compromise. There is no possibility of avoiding the issue. This is a time for plain speaking and I speak plainly when I say the day is now at hand when the peoples of the Empire must decide for once and all whether our welfare lies in close economic union or whether it does not. Delay is hazardous and further discussion of the principle is surely unnecessary. The time for action has come."

Premier Bennett was frank in saying the primary concern of Canada was to sell, profitably, her wheat. "This market" he declared, "we want and for it we are willing to pay by giving in the Canadian market preferences for British goods." He then stated his offer in these terms: "I offer to the Mother Country and to all other parts of the Empire a preference in the Canadian market in exchange for like preferences in theirs, based upon the addition of a 10 per cent increase in the prevailing general tariffs, or upon tariffs yet to be created. In the universal acceptance of this, and in like proposals and acceptances by all other parts of the Empire, we attain to the ideal of Empire preference." ...

"Empire free trade, in the opinion of the Canadian delegation, was neither desirable nor possible," Premier Bennett said. "It would defeat the very purpose we are striving to achieve." ...

The Canadian Prime Minister finally proposed that the Conference should reassemble in Ottawa early next year, as guests of the Canadian people, and in the interval an expert committee should study the plan and report.[3]

Bennett's claim that this was the moment for decision did not relate to any brand new issue. The empire crusade had been carried on for over 25 years. If, after that amount of time for consideration, empire preferences

---

[2]*Diary of A. J. MacPhail*, p. 220.
[3]*The Ottawa Journal*, October 9, 1930.

were not now adopted the dream of an empire integrated on economic lines might as well be forgotten.

The Canadian prime minister's enthusiasm for reciprocal tariff preferences was not shared by the MacDonald government in Britain, which had no reason to be pleased over Bennett's unilateral tariff hoist just before he left Canada. Now Bennett was proposing that reciprocal empire tariff preferences be created by increases in the general tariff rates, rather than by reduction in preferential rates. But there was reason for proposing an increase in general rates against non-empire countries. For foodstuffs on which Britain had no duties, this would be the means of placing, for example, a 10 percent duty rate against non-empire food and notably non-empire wheat. Such a tax proposal had defeated the Balfour-Chamberlain government in 1906, and Mr. MacDonald wanted no part of any such proposal now. His ministers placed an alternative proposal for import quotas before the conference, which appointed a committee to examine in detail the quota scheme.

While the issues remained under consideration, the Canadian delegation debated their pros and cons. The pool representative, McPhail, had already contended that any avenue offering help to the western farmer should be explored. Although McFarland did not commit his views to writing at the time, he counselled Bennett against quotas because their administration would be incompatible with the interests of the private trade. Later, he predicted the transfer of the Liverpool market to the continent, if a quota system were placed in operation.[4] Swanson prepared a long memorandum warning ministers against the risk, under a quota system, of adulteration of Canadian flour after its arrival in British ports. MacGibbon prepared a short memorandum for Stevens in which he concluded that a combined preferential tariff and quota might be the ideal arrangement. Stevens looked upon the quota as a more effective device for excluding Russian wheat from Britain and for reducing the heavy volume which had been coming in from Argentina. As a way out of the dilemma on the preference proposals he suggested establishment of continuing study committees in each of the Dominions to consider the empire wheat problem as a whole, and also the practical effect of preferences upon the trade of each empire country. The committees, in turn, would report to the next conference.[5]

Bennett made little use of the conflicting advice he received from his advisers. He appealed to the British people to support his proposal for reciprocal empire preferences in a radio broadcast on October 15, and maintained that position in the conference. Prime Minister Ramsay MacDonald responded at the opening of a new session of parliament on October 28 when, in Bennett's presence in the dominions gallery, he rejected the proposal for an import duty on non-empire wheat by declaring "we cannot do it". Bennett reacted by proposing that like-minded dominions should proceed with tariff negotiations among themselves in the absence of British participation. As the conference ended, he obtained agreement that an imperial economic conference be convened the following

---

[4]McFarland, *Memorandum Re Proposed Empire Wheat Quota*, January, 1932, Bennett Papers.
[5]*Stevens Papers*, Public Archives.

year to meet in Ottawa and that his tariff proposals, as well as the British proposals for import quotas, would remain on the agenda. Shortly afterward, in the British house of commons, the Right Honourable J. H. Thomas, now secretary of state for the Dominions, referred to Bennett's proposals as "humbug", to which Bennett understandably took umbrage.

Primarily because of the British election in 1931, the resumption of the imperial conference planned for that year was postponed until 1932. In the meantime, Britain's abandonment of the gold standard in September, 1931, had prompted the coalition of the three political parties in a national government headed by the Right Honourable Ramsay MacDonald, which was returned to office in the October election of that year.

IMPERIAL PREFERENCE ON WHEAT

In response to Bennett's 1930 invitation, the imperial economic conference was eventually convened in Ottawa, July 22-August 20, 1932. As prime minister of the host country, Bennett was elected chairman of the conference. He stood at the height of his power and influence, which lent force to the challenge he had issued to the commonwealth governments to unite economically under a system of tariff preferences. If ever there had been a moment, it was then that Joseph Chamberlain's empire crusade could be brought to fruition and an empire common market achieved. But from the opening day, the conference fell short of Bennett's aspirations of conducting the negotiations on a multilateral basis; instead, they broke down into a series of bilateral discussions. Difficulties were compounded in the British-Canadian talks when Bennett, after offering the British a concession on Canadian import tariffs on textiles, withdrew his offer at the insistence of the Honourable C. H. Cahan. More generally, the British were unhappy with Bennett's dual role as chairman of the conference and as principal Canadian negotiator. In the process, rather than fulfilling Joseph Chamberlain's dream, Bennett's relations with his son, the Right Honourable Neville Chamberlain, became permanently impaired.

In the long delay over the convening of the imperial economic conference, plenty of time had been afforded for the preparation of documents and negotiating briefs by the various delegations. In Canada this work was carried out by senior civil servants in consultation with the industries affected. As far as wheat was concerned, there remained the unresolved debate over the relative merits of a preferential tariff and a British import quota system. To assess the merits of the two alternatives, Bennett assigned the task to a general economic committee under the chairmanship of Dr. R. H. Coats which prepared a 175-page report on wheat and flour, drawn up after consideration of the briefs they invited and obtained from the major segments of the industry. In addition, Bennett had put McFarland to work on the problem. The latter submitted a memorandum in January, 1932, in which he made a long statistical presentation to demonstrate that the Commonwealth as a whole was a net exporter of wheat and that residual markets must still be found in foreign countries. Towards the end of his memo McFarland said:

> ... It is estimated that the United Kingdom, from their home-grown crop, uses approximately 40 million bushels for milling purposes so that her total

consumption is around 260 million annually. It has been suggested that the home-producer will be given a quota of 15% which would amount to about 39 million bushels. It has also been mentioned in Press Despatches that countries outside the Empire would be alloted somewhere between 15 and 30%.

If we assume other countries are alloted a quota of say 15%, then that would reduce the quantity from the Overseas Dominions by approximately 39 million bushels. Therefore, instead of the Overseas Dominions having an export surplus of 184 million bushels it would be increased to approximately 223 million bushels. In other words, the Overseas Dominions with their total exportable surplus of 404 million bushels and a quota percentage even as high as 70%, would be permitted to sell 182 million bushels in the United Kingdom, thus leaving them with 222 millions to dispose of in other countries outside the Empire.

Russia, Argentine and the United States, thus having a more limited market in the United Kingdom would be more anxious competitors on the continent of Europe and elsewhere, and the 222 million bushels from the Overseas Dominions would have to meet such competition. Russia, for arguments sake, would set the price on the Continent and Canadian wheat would have to be sold on the Continent in competition with their offerings, and it would be absurd to suppose that the English Miller would pay a greater price in the United Kingdom for Overseas Dominion Wheat than the price at which such wheat would be selling at in competition with other countries on the Continent.

It is well to bear in mind that the Overseas Dominions in the absence of crop failures, would have a greater quantity of wheat to sell outside the Empire than within the Empire and if by chance a calamity should happen to wheat crops in the Overseas Dominions so as to reduce their surplus to such proportions that the quota in the United Kingdom might absorb it all, then it is conceivable that speculation would unduly enhance the price and result in ill feeling and recriminations. On the other hand it is scarcely conceivable that the crops in any one year could so tragically fail as to reduce the quantity for export to a figure which would correspond with the quota.

Russia and the Argentine, during their shipping season, made a practice of loading large quantities and putting them afloat before they are sold, and these cargoes being shipped for orders, when they arrive at the order point, must find a buyer in order to avoid demurrage, and with their market restricted, it is not at all unlikely that those cargoes might exert such pressure on the Continental markets as to unduly depress prices, which in turn would fix the price for the Overseas Dominions under quota.

Liverpool is one of the leading cash grain markets of the world, if its business is disrupted by a quota system it is conceivable that its usefulness might be to a large extent eliminated and a broader and freer market might be established somewhere on the other side of the English Channel. Any fair-minded person must surely admit that a quota system is more disrupting to Trade than nominal tariffs, and in the opinion of the writer there is only one method whereby the British Government can give to the Overseas Dominions, something which might be of benefit to the wheat farmers in those Dominions, and that is the application of a preferential tariff within the Empire and the greatest value such a tariff would be to the Overseas Dominions would be that it might discourage wheat acreage in other countries, in view of the fact that other countries would have to pay that tariff in order to enter the largest wheat importing country in the world.[6]

[6] *Bennett Papers.*

Thus McFarland had not altered his opposition to a quota which he had expressed during the 1930 imperial conference, as he downplayed its only particular advantage that it could prevent massive incursions into the British market which Argentine and Russian exports had made in 1930-31. He regarded the preferential tariff as less disruptive to existing trade channels and he seemed unduly optimistic that a preferential tariff would discourage wheat acreage in non-empire countries. But he had become concerned over the unwarranted expectations the tariff proposals had generated in the country, as he wrote to Bennett again on May 27:

> Some months ago you asked me to prepare you a memorandum in connection with the quota on wheat, which I did. In that memorandum I expressed the opinion that the quota would be absolutely worthless to this country but I suggested that the application of a preference tariff within the Empire would be of greater value in that it might discourage wheat acreage in other countries. I, therefore, thought it might be well if I would write you something in regard to this preference.
>
> As you are doubtless aware the "Preference" has been receiving considerable discussion in the West. I think the general opinion is that the "Preference" would be more beneficial than the "Quota", but I have run up against this fact, namely; that the man in the street as well as some farmers throughout the country seem to have the idea that if, for arguments sake, a "Preference" was established of five cents a bushel, that would mean that every bushel of Canadian Wheat which might be imported into the United Kingdom would receive five cents per bushel more than the world's price, and the question is being asked "who is going to get that five cents?" Now, of course, the answer is that no one will get the five cents. The only people who will get the five cents per bushel will be the British Treasury and they will secure it on all the wheat that is imported from countries outside the Empire. I simply mention this to show you the confusion which exists in peoples minds. . . .[7]

At that time the only person who gave unqualified support to a preferential tariff was Mr. J. R. Murray who handed McFarland an undated memorandum. On later occasions McFarland complained bitterly to Bennett about Murray's political intrigues in the Liberal camp, but on this occasion Murray gave Bennett's objective his unqualified support as he wrote:

> It is ridiculous to suggest, as the Press despatches from Ottawa during the past few days indicate, that the entire Grain Trade of Canada and grain growers of the West consider that a preferential tariff in favor of Canadian Wheat in the British market would be of no advantage to Canada. Confidential briefs, indicating such a view, may have been submitted to the Dominion Government by the authorized spokesmen of various bodies, but it is absurd to assume there is no contrary opinion among those they purport to represent. The official representations made by Grain Trade spokesmen are not the view of all grain dealers anymore than the Wheat Pools and Provincial Governments express the view of all farmers in the West.
>
> Almost everyone can agree that a quota system would be cumbersome and useless, but a preferential tariff is a different matter. Personally, I believe the free entry of Canadian wheat into the British market, by far the biggest wheat importing market in the World, with a duty against non-Empire wheat, would be a distinct advantage in marketing our Canadian crop and over a period of

[7] *Ibid.*

years would assist in obtaining better prices for our Western grain growers. Considering the almost prohibitive tariffs against all wheat imports now in effect in all European countries, I believe there is much to be gained and nothing lost by such a preference.

It seems to me unfortunate, particularly at this time, when wheat growers in Western Canada need all the assistance and encouragement they can get that spokesmen, who at best supposedly represent less than half of the farmers of the West, should take the position that a preferential tariff in favor of our wheat in the British market is a matter of supreme indifference to them. Whatever the views of our Western farmers may have been on this matter fifteen or twenty years ago, I do not believe they are today indifferent to the advantages that would accrue to them from such a preference. I believe that if the Dominion Government can, in exchange for tariff concessions on British manufactures entering Canada, secure a preferential tariff in favor of Canadian wheat entering the British market, they will accomplish something of great benefit to the whole of Canada and will earn the thanks of the majority of farmers and business men in Western Canada.[8]

As Murray indicated, the industry had been filing briefs with the general economic committee, including submissions from the Winnipeg and Calgary grain exchanges, the Canadian national millers association, United Grain Growers Limited and a joint submission from the three provincial pools.

The brief from the grain exchanges predictably opposed import quotas. But it took almost as negative an attitude toward preferential tariffs, by claiming that the slightly higher price obtained in Britain would be offset by increased competition in foreign markets. It argued, as McFarland had done, that the Empire was a net exporter of wheat. Despite what Britain might do by way of improved access for Empire wheat, Canadian exports would have to face competition elsewhere. It was opposed to any restriction on the operations of the trade as militating against the real interests of producers. On the specific question of quotas, it said:

The adoption of quotas, by limiting the amount of Empire and foreign wheat admissable to the British market, might be expected to have grave effects upon both the Liverpool and Winnipeg grain markets. The former would cease to be a representative market, its function being performed elsewhere. The Winnipeg market would be liable to serious, and probably unwarranted, disturbances due to rumours and reports arising in connection with the proportion of the quota remaining unfilled at any moment. Hedging in these markets might therefore be rendered more difficult and less attractive. ...

It is generally admitted by both British and Canadian authorities that benefit in price to Canadian wheat producers under a quota system could result only if the whole Canadian crop were to be sold by a Central Agency or Wheat Board which could obtain the highest possible price in Great Britain and sell, or "dump", the balance of the crop in foreign markets are whatever price it would fetch.[9]

The memorandum submitted by United Grain Growers Limited agreed with that of the Winnipeg and Calgary grain exchanges in its distaste for either quotas or preferential tariffs, but its analysis and recommendations

[8]*Ibid.*
[9]*Memorandum on Wheat and Flour, Methods of Empire Preference with Special Reference to the Quota,* prepared by the General Economic Committee of the Preparatory Organization for the Imperial Economic Conference, 1932, Appendix III, pp. 3, 9-10.

were more specific, and it proposed a world rather than an empire approach to the problem. Its conclusions were as follows:

(a) That there would be no substantial advantage to the Western farmer in altering the present system of equal freedom of purchase of all wheat in the British market.

(b) That a system of wheat quotas in the British market would not only be of no benefit to farmers of Western Canada, but would be likely to injure their interests.

(c) That while a system of duties against wheat from outside the Empire would be less dangerous than a system of quotas, provided they were not applied in such a way as to seek exclusion of wheat from other countries, the possibilities of benefit are slight and the dangers are considerable.

(d) That in the interests of Canadian farmers a market for Canadian flour on equal terms with Canadian wheat should be maintained in the United Kingdom.

(e) that the governments of the countries of the Empire should together explore the possibilities of common negotiation with foreign countries, with a view to bringing about advantages to all concerned, and in particular to obtaining freer world wheat markets.[10]

Mr. C. H. G. Short, president of Lake of the Woods Milling Company, Limited, presented a brief on behalf of the Canadian national millers's association, and he shared Swanson's concern over the hazards to Canadian flour brands inherent in any system of quotas on preferential tariffs, as he admonished (in capitals):

IT MUST ALWAYS BE REMEMBERED THAT CANADIAN FLOUR, NOT CANADIAN WHEAT, FIXES THE STANDARD OF QUALITY OF BRITISH BREAD, AND THAT CANADIAN FLOURS ARE SINGLE WHEAT FLOURS WHICH HAVE BEEN SHIPPED BY CANADIAN MILLERS UNDER THEIR ESTABLISHED BRANDS FOR THE PAST FORTY YEARS. IT IS ESSENTIAL THAT CANADA SHALL NOT AGREE TO ANY PROPOSAL WHICH PREVENTS CANADIAN FLOUR REACHING THE BAKER CONSUMER IN THE ORIGINAL PACKAGES IN WHICH IT IS SHIPPED FROM CANADA BY CANADIAN MILLS: AND IT IS EQUALLY ESSENTIAL THAT TO MAINTAIN THE REGULAR FLOW OF CANADIAN FLOUR TO THE BRITISH MARKET, WHICH IS THE GREATEST ASSURANCE OF THE EMPLOYMENT OF CANADIAN WHEAT BY THE BRITISH MILLER AT A RESPECTABLE PRICE, THAT CANADIAN FLOUR SHALL BE PLACED IN NO DIFFERENT CATEGORY THAN IS CANADIAN WHEAT INASMUCH AS CANADI-AN FLOUR IS THE WHOLE BASIS OF THE CANADIAN GRAIN TRADE. IN CON-SEQUENCE, CANADA SHOULD, WE SUGGEST, STRENUOUSLY OPPOSE ANY MEA-SURE WHICH MILITATES IN ANY WAY AGAINST THE UNRESTRICTED IMPORT INTO GREAT BRITAIN OF CANADIAN FLOUR ON THE UNCHALLENGEABLE PREMISE THAT THE RESTRICTION OR ELIMINATION OF SUCH IMPORTS IS NEITHER IN THE INTERESTS OF THE CANADIAN MILLING INDUSTRY, OF THE CANADIAN WHEAT PRODUCER, NOR, AS A RESULT, IN THE INTERESTS OF THE DOMINION OF CANADA AS AN INTEGRAL WHOLE. TO ALLOW THE FREE ENTRANCE OF WHEAT, WITH A TAX UPON CANADIAN FLOUR, WOULD BE, AS WE HAVE POINTED OUT, A SEVERE BLOW TO THE INTERESTS OF THE CANADIAN WHEAT PRODUCER, AND IT SHOULD BE REMEMBERED THAT WHILE THE VOICE OF THE BRITISH MILLER IS LOUD IN ITS DEMANDS FOR THE EXCLUSION OF CANADIAN FLOUR OR FOR THE IMPOSITION OF HANDICAPS UPON THE IMPORT OF CANADIAN FLOUR INTO GREAT BRITAIN, THE BRITISH MILLER DOES NOT HAVE BEHIND HIM THE SUPPORT OF HIS COUNTRY AS A WHOLE. IT MUST ALSO BE

[10]*Ibid.,* Appendix IV, pp. 1-2.

ALWAYS REMEMBERED THAT THE BRITISH MILLER HAS ALREADY, AS DEMON-
STRATED, A VERY WIDE MARGIN OF PROTECTION AGAINST CANADIAN FLOUR,
AND THE OPPOSITION CREATED BY THE MILLING FRATERNITY TO ITS IMPORT
ARISES SOLELY FROM THE DESIRE TO REMOVE ITS QUALITY COMPETITION
WHICH WOULD HAVE THE FINAL RESULT OF PLACING THE EMPLOYMENT OF
CANADIAN WHEAT SOLELY AT HIS DICTATION AND DISCRETION.[11]

The joint submission from the three pools likewise emphasized the risk
involved, and failed to endorse either a quota or a preference. But it made
several other recommendations endorsing reciprocal trade with Britain as a
means of reducing farm production costs, an Empire currency to meet the
confused exchange situation, extended use of the empire marketing board to
promote not only trade within the empire, but also with other countries. It
also looked to a multilateral solution of trade problems through the
convening of a world economic conference in the following terms:

> Finally, we recommend that, if the spirit of goodwill and mutual give and take
> with which the representatives of the several countries of the Empire enter the
> coming conference is effective in promoting trade agreements that stimulate
> the movement of goods within the Empire, our delegates be requested to
> bring to the attention of the delegates from the United Kingdom and our
> sister Dominions the advisability of calling a world economic conference to
> bring about a general lowering of trade barriers and further consolidation of
> confidence, goodwill and co-operation between the nations of the world
> believing that such action will immediately stimulate the expansion of world
> trade in which we, as members of the British commonwealth, may share to the
> benefit of the great mass of our citizens.[12]

In preparing their brief the pools had invited comments from Dr.
Holbrook Working, chief economist of the Food Research Institute,
Stanford University, whose analysis predicted little benefit to Canada by
either preference or quota. Unlike McFarland, Working discounted the
possible influence on United States acreage.

While the exchange and pool briefs were under preparation, McFarland
wrote to Bennett on May 31:

> Representatives of the Western Wheat Pools met in Winnipeg last week to
> discuss the contents of the proposed brief which they intend forwarding in
> reply to your request under date of on/or about May 9th.
> I was requested to confer with them, which I did for a short time, and I
> have since received a copy of the conclusions they arrived at, also I have
> talked to one or two of the representatives and pointed out that their
> conclusions did not arrive anywhere in regard to the matter in which you are
> most interested in, namely; in regard to "quotas" and "preferences", as the
> case may be, on wheat. They said your communication did not mention
> anything at all about "quotas" or "preferences" and on looking up that
> communication I find that they are correct. I am, therefore, wondering
> whether it was an oversight by you that specific reference was not made to
> "quotas" or "preferences".
> I have talked to a couple of the leading members of the Winnipeg Grain
> Exchange and I understand they are preparing a statement, or have sent you a
> statement of their views. I might say that I am fairly well acquainted with
> what they are putting forward, or what they have already sent forward, and I
> do not think their submissions will be any more helpful to you than the

[11]*Ibid.*, Appendix V, pp. 15-16.
[12]*Ibid.*, Appendix VI, p. 4.

submissions which the Western Pool representatives have decided upon, in fact a person is inclined to reach the conclusion, in talking to these people, that a Preference on wheat is too dangerous a thing to put into effect for fear of reprisals which might be made by other groups of countries. Just why this sentiment should exist is beyond my understanding but I may be blind to the possible consequences of the future. However, I fail to see how there could be any motive which would prompt importing countries in Europe to link up with exporting countries like Argentine, the United States or Russia, in the way of forming a group with the object of reprisals against the Empire group because of a "preference" on wheat, when it is evident to anyone that the other importing countries in Europe may purchase from Canada the same grade of wheat at the same time and at the same price as the British Empire pays for it from day to day. What motive could there be for reprisals when that condition exists? Such reprisals surely could not be prompted by the suggested "preference" on wheat, it would have to come from other motives than that.

I believe there has been a sentiment in Western Canada also favouring a "preference" in the British market for bacon and other farm products of that nature. Now if, as is being represented in some quarters, a "preference" on wheat is of no value any more than a "quota" would be on wheat, and the "quota" is condemned as being worse than useless to us, then I say "if a 'preference' on wheat is of no value in the British market, then it follows that a 'preference' on any other product would be equally useless or valueless", so that following that line of thought it would appear to be gaining ground in the West that apparently no "preference" could be accorded to us in the British Market that would be of value, and having in mind these views it is difficult to keep from thinking that there must be some political manoeuvre at the bottom of the situation, and where it is coming from I do not know, neither do I know whether you take it seriously or not or whether these "preferences" on wheat and other farm products are viewed seriously by you in connection wth the outcome of the Conference. It does seem to me, however, that the principal quid pro quo which the British manufacturer can offer to Canada as a whole in return for more favourable tariffs on manufactured goods, must surely be related to farm produce. If there is nothing they can give us of value in the way of a market for farm produce, then just where can the economic conference arrive in reaching what would be considered a success.

I am placing these thoughts before you thinking that probably you may consider it advisable to convene a meeting of representatives of the many interested parties in the West, at Ottawa, rather than to depend on these submissions which you are going to receive from the various bodies out here to whom you addressed communications and requests.

P.S. Enquire and see if you have received a copy of the Wpg. Grain Exchange brief to Conference. Have just seen a copy. It seems to me a very poor document to come from such a body.[13]

With all these submissions at hand, Dr. Coats's committee summarized them and drew conclusions of their own:

An Empire quota in the United Kingdom would have a certain advantage to Canada in the event of a situation arising again, such as occurred in 1929 and 1930, when practically all exporting countries had surpluses to carry over. Under such conditions, where dumping and distress selling occurred on a very large scale with respect to Russian and Argentine wheat, it appears certain that a quota would have reduced somewhat the Canadian carry-over. Except

[13] *Bennett Papers.*

as a partial insurance against recurrence of such a situation, the potential effects of an Empire quota indicate an extremely doubtful balance, as between advantages and disadvantages.

While the immediate effects of a moderate tariff preference on wheat would be slight, such a preference would be of advantage to Empire producers in its long run effects, since it would tend to place the burden of reduction in acreage on non-Empire countries. It would be in accord with recognized international practice and would lend itself to permanency in policy to a degree that is difficult to associate with the use of the quota form of preference. Any tariff preference on wheat should carry with it a tariff adjustment in respect to flour which would preserve equality of treatment between the two commodities.

It would appear that Empire preferences on flour should serve to considerably increase Canadian exports of this product and that the only unfavourable reaction which can be foreseen is a possible loss of trade with Central Europe. This, however, should be amply compensated for by the increased exports to British markets.[14]

There is also an unsigned 31-page memorandum on file, over which the word "confidential" had been inscribed in the characteristic handwriting of Dr. O. D. Skelton. The memorandum was a final summation of the issues for Bennett's use as the conference began. It stressed that the conference was purely economic in character and it examined what might be gained through tariff negotiations and emphasized the need for increasing rather than diverting trade. It went into detail on the tariff concessions which might be sought by Canada, and reminded Bennett of the warning already received from the British that they would not even maintain the existing schedule of preferences, unless an adequate quid pro quo was forthcoming from Canada. On the question of a wheat preference, the memorandum stated:

Unless it is considered desirable as a political gesture, it doesn't appear desirable to use up any appreciable part of our limited bargaining power in demanding a preference or quota on wheat. (Why use our limited funds to buy a gold brick?) With the Empire production twice the United Kingdom imports, no price advantage and no appreciable advantage in an assured market can be assured. Australia, preferring other markets for much of her wheat, has definitely decided against asking for a preference on wheat. The prominence given wheat in discussions of imperial preference is a survival of the Chamberlain campaign of nearly 30 years ago; a preference then would have meant something when Canada's and Australia's total wheat crop was only 145,000,000 bushels and Empire exports were less than United Kingdom imports (Cf. special memorandum on Wheat Quota and Preference).[15]

Notwithstanding Skelton's admonition, Bennett headed the negotiation list he submitted to the British delegation with a guarantee on the continuation of existing preferences which was immediately followed by an empire preferential tariff of two shillings per quarter (six cents per bushel) on wheat. Although Bennett failed to get other preferences asked for, notably one on meats, the negotiations ended in agreement on the wheat preference.

[14]*Memorandum on Wheat and Flour, Methods of Empire Preference with Special Reference to the Quota*, pp. 51-52.
[15]*Bennett Papers.*

A huge effort had been mounted by Bennett in the convening in Ottawa of the 1932 imperial economic conference and in the preparations made therefor. At least he could be seen to be actively at work on behalf of the western wheat farmer, but the results of his efforts were predictably minimal, because Canadian prices to the British were no higher than to non-empire markets. Non-empire exporters were penalized by the preference.

MacGibbon, who had served on Dr. Coats's committee assigned a higher value to the preference, by claiming that it helped the volume of sales of lower-grade Canadian wheats in the British market, in competition with "filler" wheats imported from the United States and Argentina.[16] Quite unexpectedly, the ports of St. John and Halifax became rather substantial beneficiaries of the preference. British customs regulations required that proof of empire origin could be established only by direct transit from empire to British ports. The Canadian winter export movement of wheat which had hitherto been routed mainly through United States east coast ports now had to be shifted to Canadian Atlantic ports.

MONETARY AND ECONOMIC CONFERENCE, 1933

The monetary and economic conference was the last of three major conferences in which Bennett took an active and often leading part in his search abroad for solutions to the Canadian wheat problem. Unlike the first two which had been commonwealth gatherings, the 1933 conference was organized under the auspices of the League of Nations to convene that summer in London and it was world-wide in representation. In the wake of the 1931 exchange devaluations, the time had come to attempt a restoration of monetary order. After the conference was called, but before it had convened, United States devaluation in the spring of 1933 had set back the prospects for a new set of fixed exchange rates. The ablest monetary experts and economists had been recruited to work on a preparatory commission of experts for the conference. The consensus of the experts was that countries which had been forced to divorce their currencies from their gold backing should return to the international gold standard just as quickly as possible as a prerequisite for recovery. Although this was a sterile recommendation which would have required governments to abdicate control over monetary policy and revert to an automatic and arbitrary regulator, the economists also delved through a plethora of other proposals for economic recovery. One of the notions which gained support was that because of the cost-price imbalance among primary commodities, there was a universal need to restore the purchasing power of primary producers and that ways and means must be found to stimulate an increase in prices. Price recovery was placed on the agenda, and in their opening statements at the conference, the premiers of Britain and France, whose countries were notable consumers of raw materials and food products, spoke out in support of measures to raise the price level of primary products. This was a breakthrough in economic thinking, to the effect that self interest among importing countries was not always served by purchasing at the lowest possible prices. It opened the door for the first time to the possibility of concluding an agreement between

[16]D. A. MacGibbon, *The Canadian Grain Trade*, 1931-1951, pp. 22-25.

wheat exporting and importing countries which had as its object an increase in wheat prices. The recommendations of the preparatory commission of experts which produced this result were by no means unanimous as they placed on the conference agenda the subject of economic agreements in general, and more specifically the examination of a proposal for an intergovernmental wheat agreement:

> It is not for us to pronounce on the attitude which Governments may take up in regard to economic agreements. We consider that, generally speaking, international economic agreements have more of a chance of success if their formation is left to the initiative and free discussion of the producers concerned, for whom they represent an already advanced stage of industrial organisation.
>
> Some of us, however, think that the Governments might usefully take the opportunity of the coming Conference to discuss the attitude they should adopt in regard to these agreements. Such discussions might facilitate the conclusion of agreements, particularly in cases where the intervention of Governments is necessary to ensure the organisation of the production of, and trade in, certain staple products, especially in cases where the producers are not at present in a position themselves to regulate the production and distribution of their products.
>
> The desirability of inter-Governmental agreements in the case of wheat has been advocated on these grounds.
>
> The question of regulating the production and export of wheat by agreements between Governments has been the subject of international discussions for some time past. It has been investigated at Geneva, Paris, Rome and London, and, more recently, at Stresa.
>
> Of all the proposals which have been studied, those which were submitted in London have engaged our special attention. At that time, it was proposed to apply only a system of limitation of exports. Some still adhere to this proposal only, but others now consider that it might be combined with an agreed limitation on the areas sown. We had before us interesting suggestions from the Argentine Government relating to the reduction of the areas sown in the chief exporting countries and their limitation in importing countries, as a means of absorbing gradually the abnormal stocks which have accumulated through the failure of supply to adjust itself naturally to demand.
>
> Whatever practical difficulties may stand in the way of this proposal, the Conference might note it for careful examination, in view of the seriousness of the present situation, taking account of the lessons of past conferences and inviting the qualified technical organisations to collaborate with the Governments.[17]

The monetary and economic conference was convened in London on June 23, 1933. His Majesty King George V opened the conference which was presided over by Prime Minister Ramsay MacDonald. The conference reached a climax early in July when President Roosevelt refused to accede to proposals for stabilization of the United States dollar which had been floating downward since its devaluation commenced in April of that year. As no monetary agreement was possible, the conference was adjudged a failure. Yet for a period of two months the major wheat exporting countries used it as a front for their secret negotiations on wheat. By August 1933,

---

[17]*League of Nations, Monetary and Economic Conference, Draft Annotated Agenda submitted by the Preparatory Commission of Experts* (Geneva, January 20, 1933), pp.31-32.

when the exporting countries had reached a sufficient area of agreement among themselves that they were now ready to seek the much-needed co-operation of the importing countries, they reconstituted their meetings under the League of Nations monetary and economic conference auspices and Bennett's chairmanship at Canada House, where the first international wheat agreement was concluded. The history of these negotiations and of the conferences leading up to them merits a much more detailed review.

But at this stage, the world economic conference, as it was more popularly known, should be grouped with the 1930 and 1932 imperial conferences, and identified as the most important of the three forums through which Bennett pursued his search abroad for a resolution of the Canadian wheat problem. It may seem paradoxical to assert that the 1933 world conference marked the occasion of Bennett's greatest success abroad, when both the monetary and economic conference and the first international wheat agreement have been historically adjudged failures. The 1933 world conference was so regarded because it failed to produce order out of monetary chaos. That failure overshadowed the fact that the conference also marked a departure from well-entrenched concepts of national self-interest, and that the departure had made an intergovernmental approach to the wheat problem possible. Despite the fact that the first experiment in that direction failed to endure, it sustained producers' hopes that a more effective basis for international co-operation in wheat might be found.

17

PRELIMINARY WHEAT CONFERENCES

The notion that it might be possible to make an internationally coordinated approach to wheat marketing was almost as old as the Canadian wheat industry itself. In Part I of this review, reference was made to J.H. Haslam's letter of June 17, 1921, to the Australian minister of trade and commerce, proposing an international conference and referring to efforts he had made to bring about such a conference before the great war.[1] In 1920, the American farm bureau federation had made overtures to the Canadian council of agriculture regarding the coordination of wheat export policies, but nothing had come of their suggestion. After the formation of the wheat pools, conferences were held in St. Paul in 1926, in Kansas City in 1927, and in Regina in 1928, which were attended not only by representatives from the United States and Canada, but from Australia and the USSR as well. These conferences canvassed the possibilities of international co-operation in wheat marketing. Although they were held under pool auspices, and envisaged coordinated marketing policies among voluntary producers' pools, they were prototypes of international wheat conferences to follow. As Swanson mentioned, pools were already in partial operation in Australia and the United States, and were being contemplated in Argentina.[2]

In Rome, the international institute of agriculture, which had been founded by an American philanthropist just after the turn of the century, convened a world wheat conference in 1927, when the economic conditions which dominated subsequent conferences had not yet arisen. But with the onset of the depression, concern had mounted over the unprecedented sales by Argentina in 1929. In 1930, a blow was struck from a long-dormant quarter by the sudden revival of wheat exports from the USSR. Russia and the countries of the Danube basin had been major sources of wheat exports before the great war. The roller milling process had been invented in Hungary and that country, at one time, had set the flour quality standard for the world. Now, not only the USSR but Poland, Hungary, Yugoslavia, Romania and Bulgaria were trying to recover lost ground. In doing so, they looked askance at the inroads the wheat exporting countries of the new world had made into their former west European markets.

---

[1]*See*, pp. 198-199.
[2]W. W. Swanson and P. C. Armstrong, *Wheat*, p. 226.

PRELIMINARY CONFERENCES

The propensity to hold international discussions on wheat proliferated in 1930, and Professor Alonzo E. Taylor recorded the convening of sixteen conferences beginning in 1930 and culminating in the London wheat conference in May, 1931.[3] The first two of these, convened by the economic committee of the League of Nations, were largely orientation meetings on the growing depression and related agricultural problems. There followed a series of conferences in Bucharest, Sinaia and Warsaw, in which the East European wheat producing countries examined their regional problems. At the Warsaw meeting held on August 28-30, 1930, eight of the East European countries passed a series of resolutions, the most noteworthy of which embodied a request for preferential customs treatment by the grain-importing countries of Europe on cereals imported from their East European neighbors. The Warsaw resolutions were referred to the eleventh assembly of the League of Nations which met September 10-October 4, 1930. In a long debate in which the East European countries pressed their case, the Canadian and Australian delegates opposed the resolution on preferences as being inimical to their export interests, while the representatives of the European importing countries, in the main, drew attention to the conflict between the proposed preferences and the most-favoured-nation clauses in their commercial treaties with other countries. A departmental memorandum summarized the proceedings:

> The Warsaw resolutions were brought before the Assembly by the delegations of the eight states represented at the conference, for circulation to the members of the League and for consideration by the Second Committee. Speeches were made by the representatives of Rumania, Poland, etc. pointing out the necessity of such regional preferences and explaining that, as it would only supply a small percentage of the demand, their plan would not be detrimental to the great overseas-producing countries. . . .The Canadian delegate, while appreciating the value of certain of the resolutions, raised serious objections to the fourth, dealing with preferences for European-grown cereals in European markets and took the position that the Committee should merely take note of the resolution. Eventually a sub-committee was lined up in which the Canadian delegate drafted the following statement for insertion in the sub-committee's report to be incorporated in the report to the Assembly:
>
> "The delegations of Assyria, Canada, India, New Zealand, and the Union of South Africa, without pronouncing upon the substance of the Question, have expressed the opinion that the proposal contained in the Warsaw Resolution to accord preferential treatment on the European Markets to cereals produced in Europe is not a question on which the 11th Assembly of the League of Nations should express an opinion."[4]

In the end, the assembly adopted the sub-committee's report, and thereby merely took note of the Warsaw resolutions. Although the Canadian intervention at Geneva had at least delayed further action on a European preference system for wheat, it served as no deterrent to Bennett who almost

---

[3]Alonzo E. Taylor, *The International Wheat Conferences during 1930-31*, Wheat Studies of the Food Research Institute, Stanford University, California, Vol. VII, No. 9, (August, 1931), pp. 440-446.
[4]*Bennett Papers.*

immediately thereafter placed his proposal for an imperial preference on the same commodity before the imperial conference in London.

Meanwhile, three conferences were held in Bucharest, Warsaw and Belgrade at which the East European countries regrouped their forces. They met again at Geneva, November 17-28, 1930, where they resumed their quest for preferential treatment by the European importing countries. Still no agreement was reached, but some progress was made in proposing that regional cereal preferences be treated as temporary exceptions from most-favoured-nation commitments, and under conditions which safeguarded the rights of third parties.

Another full-fledged conference at which overseas exporting countries were represented, as well as the European exporting and importing countries, was convened by the economic committee of the League of Nations, January 12-14, 1931. The debate at that conference tended to repeat the one which had taken place at the assembly a few months earlier and no positive results ensued.

French political opinion, however, was already turning in favor of the East European bloc. Dr. W. A. Riddell, the Canadian advisory officer at the League of Nations, watched the developments very closely from Geneva. He reported that the French government had decided ro come to the assistance of the other agricultural countries of Europe, both by way of preferences and of an international loan to finance the storage of the surplus wheat until it could be absorbed by the importing countries. To reflect the change in the French attitude, Dr. Riddell forwarded copies of two speeches which Dr. Skelton drew to Bennett's attention. The first had been delivered by M. P. E. Flandin, French minister of finance, to a meeting of the national committee on social and economic questions, who said:

... Countries which regularly export cereals have requested importing countries to grant them a preference and have maintained that this was the first step towards a possible European organization. The plan appears to be easy and attractive because importing Europe consumes 100 million quintals of foreign cereals. Under these circumstances, it would seem that great opportunity is afforded to solve the acute agricultural crisis which weighs heavily on the life of Europe.

Objection may be raised against such a solution both on principle and on fact: first, the economic life of nations is based on the most-favoured-nation clause and this clause would be found of no effect if any kind of preference were instituted; second, countries receiving such surplus production have an agricultural industry, which they desire to protect and French Farmers, for instance, not too happily situated already, cannot be exposed to the competition of agricultural products selling at a lower price. ... Under these circumstances, what should be the solution as regards Europe? Such solution is found in collective action and several countries have understood its necessity. The Conference of Experts held at Belgrade has led to the constitution of a commission controlling exports; buyers and sellers have been organized collectively and the foundation has been laid for an organization which would function as follows: Cereal importing countries would reserve for the export countries of Eastern Europe twenty per cent of their average annual cereal imports and this process would be stabilized by a system of grain enabling them to carry over from year to year any surpluses resulting from excess production; harvesting would be financed by short term credits which, at the present time, are easily obtainable at moderate rates of interest; the security would be satisfactory because prices would to a certain extent be stabilized by the very fact that such a system is in operation. . . .

The stability obtainable by the method described above would be of advantage not only to Europe but to the world; to Canada, to the Argentine, to Australia, etc., in guaranteeing prices and markets for all producers.[5]

In an even more pointed speech on the same occasion, M. Jules Gauthier said:

. . . There is also a world wheat question resulting from the overproduction of overseas countries: Canada, Argentina, and Australia can increase their production indefinitely; if they do not restrain themselves and if they entertain the idea that Europe will change her historic agriculture in order to consume their production they are preparing themselves a grave disillusionment. It is up to them to seek other forms of production and not for Europe to transform her economy.[6]

The League of Nations now moved to convene two conferences in Paris under the auspices of its commission of enquiry for European union. The commission was presided over by M. A. Briand who had championed the union cause. Representation at the conference was restricted to that of European countries. The first conference, February 23-25, 1931, was called to consider the problem of disposing of the existing wheat surplus in Eastern Europe. In the resolution adopted at that conference, preferences were not specifically mentioned but, in substance, were given a formal blessing and commended to bilateral negotiation, including safeguards for third parties, as had earlier been discussed.

The second Paris conference, February 26-28, had been requested to consider the question of disposal of European wheat surpluses which might arise in the future. That conference recognized that the question involved not only European but world issues, and concluded that it could be considered more effectively at the second world wheat conference which the international institute of agriculture had scheduled for March 26 in Rome.

ROME CONFERENCE

Reports on all of the foregoing meetings were forwarded to the department of external affairs in Ottawa by Dr. Riddell. In turn, Dr. Skelton referred them to a young Rhodes scholar, Mr. Norman A. Robertson, whom he had recruited in 1929 into the department as a third secretary. Robertson assessed the information and prepared a memorandum which Skelton passed on with a covering note of his own to Bennett. It was the beginning of Bennett's and Robertson's mutual involvement in the negotiation of the first international wheat agreement. Over the course of the next four years, Robertson's numerous memos and reports to be found among the Bennett Papers, as well as on departmental files, constitute a prime Canadian source of information on that agreement. On this first occasion, Skelton's note of January 24, 1931, to Bennett read:

M. Briand's committee on "United States of Europe" is giving attention to schemes for continental preference and other strictly European economic

[5] *Ibid.*
[6] *Ibid.*

schemes. Attached is a telegram from Riddell and a memo prepared by Robertson; a full examination of the recent plans for special trade agreements between the western industrial states and the eastern agricultural states of Europe is being made.[7]

Robertson regarded the series of meetings as of vital interest to Canada. Although Canada could not be represented at the Paris meetings of the commission of enquiry for European union, Robertson felt that Canadian interests were nevertheless involved, which made it all the more important that Canada should be well represented at the Rome meeting. His undated memorandum on the international wheat situation and plans for "concerted action", which was the popular League of Nations expression for intergovernmental co-operation in those days, read as follows:

1. Pursuant to a Resolution of the Commission of Enquiry for European Union, authorized representatives of the grain-exporting countries of Central and Eastern Europe and European importing countries are meeting in Paris on the *23rd February* to make a common effort to find a means of *disposing of the grain surplus at present available in Europe*. This meeting has been called on the initiative of the President of the Commission, M. Briand, and his conclusions may be put into effect without further reference to the Commission of Enquiry.

2. Carrying out another resolution of the Commission of Enquiry a committee composed of eleven members, namely, the representatives of Austria, Belgium, Czechoslovakia, Estonia, France, Germany, Great Britain, Italy, Norway, Switzerland, Yugoslavia will meet in Paris on February 26, to study all measures, including tariff arrangements capable of solving the problems presented by the export of future European harvest surpluses. This committee will be assisted by the technical committees of the League of Nations and the International Institute of Agriculture; its conclusions will be submitted to the Commission of Enquiry for European Union.

3. The preparatory wheat conference will meet in Rome on March 26th to examine:

   (1) the international organization of agricultural production;
   (2) the organization of international agricultural credit for cereals' cultivation;
   (3) the organization of an international wheat market.

The two meetings to be held in Paris under the auspices of the Commission of Enquiry are to consider the immediate and anticipated problems of marketing the exportable cereals surplus of the European grain-exporting countries. The problems are continental and the committees considering them are drawn from the countries directly concerned. Canada is indirectly but vitally interested in their deliberations. Any real measure of relief granted the Danubian countries by the grain-importing nations of Western and Northern Europe must take the form of a guaranteed market for their grain exports. Whether this guarantee is given as a customs preference, governmental bulk purchases, or an assured quota of the importing countries' requirements, the result must be a certain contraction of the open world market in which Canada has to sell its grain. We cannot take part in the preliminary continental conferences in Paris, but we should be strongly represented at the World Conference next month in Rome when the international aspects of any decisions taken at Paris will come up for review. The United States will not be represented, but it must be emphasized that our position and our interests are

[7] *Ibid.*

not identical with theirs. They are, as a result of the holding policy of the Federal Farm Board, temporarily out of the wheat world market. Their ultimate objective is to get out of the world market altogether by restricting production of agricultural products to their domestic requirements. The recent trend in the United States farm production suggests that this objective may be realized in a very few years. Therefore, the United States run no great risks in refusing to cooperate in any concerted international action designed to stabilize and control the world wheat market.

But Canada's position is radically different. Our wheat question is not a domestic one—and saving a catastrophe it never will be. In our situation we cannot afford to adopt a policy of isolation and affect an indifference to matters that in fact closely concern us. The Argentine is to be represented at Rome, the U.S.S.R. probably will be there, strong Canadian representation in the circumstances seems most advisable.[8]

Shortly thereafter, Robertson produced another memorandum on what the conference at Rome might accomplish, which he began by saying that the situation could be summed up in two phrases: "over-production and consequent low prices", and "any remedial action must get behind the symptom, which is price, to the fundamental cause, which is the faulty adjustment of production to effective demand."

Thus like McFarland, Robertson fell prone to the plausible overproduction theory. As he proceeded, Robertson pointed out that France and the United States alone could afford to pursue domestic policies aloof from world conditions, but that Canada, Australia, Argentina, Soviet Russia, and the Danubian States were not so favored, and that effective remedial measures on their behalf needed to be pursued through international agreement. The remedy was to grow less wheat, but no conceivable cartel among farmers in western Canada could effect a concerted reduction in acreage. Implicitly he ruled out any governmental incentive plan in this regard, for that means was not suggested. But while he concluded that a direct limitation of production was impracticable, he proposed the exploration of another route to that end by seeking international agreement on a limitation of exports. To illustrate his point, Robertson described in some detail the operation of the Chadbourne agreement for the export control of sugar.

The idea caught Bennett's imagination, for he was still in the early stages of fulfilling the mandate he had sought and won to negotiate for markets abroad, and it was an inexpensive sort of external activity by which the government's interest on behalf of the Canadian wheat farmer could be demonstrated. Accordingly, Bennett proceeded to arrange top-drawer representation at the Rome conference. He telephoned the Canadian high commissioner in London, the Honourable Howard Ferguson, who was already committed to the farewell ceremonies for the Earl of Bessborough on his departure to take up his post as governor-general of Canada, and Ferguson's arrival in Rome was delayed on that account. As Bennett cabled to Ferguson on March 3, 1931:

International Institute Agriculture meeting at Rome on March 26. Practically every nation will be represented. President Michaelis very anxious Canada should be represented. Have asked Smith Wheat Pool call on you

[8]*Ibid.*

Wednesday. Riddell our permanent representative League of Nations will also attend. We are mailing you all available material. Am instructing Riddell to communicate with you. Conference promises to be of very great importance. Am afraid you should arrange to leave after reception on 24th and ask to be excused from other engagements. Stevens just out of hospital. Will cable tomorrow.[9]

As soon as it was announced that Canada would be officially represented at the conference by Ferguson and Riddell and the central selling agency's representative in London, Mr. David L. Smith, there developed a flurry of interest in unofficial representation for it was apparent that the conference was not restricted to government-accredited representatives. McFarland invited his British friend, Sir Herbert Robson, to look after his interests, as he wrote in some annoyance to Bennett on March 10:

> That agitator, namely, Geo. Williams, from somewhere around Saskatoon, has been appointed by the U. F. of C. as their representative to attend the conference in Rome. He is now on his way east. These farmers are the limit. I wonder where they get their money! . . .[10]

Mr. George H. Williams, immediate past president of the United farmers of Canada (Saskatchewan section) who, with Mr. L. C. Brouillette, had spearheaded the drive for a 100 percent compulsory wheat pool, announced that he had received an invitation to the conference to which he would proceed via New York in order to confer with Mr. Aaron Sapiro.[11]

Robertson's draftsmanship is apparent in the letter of instructions Bennett addressed to Ferguson on March 9, in which it was clear that Bennett had not supported Robertson's advocacy of a system of export quotas:

> With further reference to our conversations by cable and telephone on the subject of the Preparatory Wheat Conference at Rome, I am forwarding, under separate cover, by today's mail, copies of the correspondence exchanged with the International Institute of Agriculture regarding Canadian participation in the Wheat Conference together with memoranda dealing with certain aspects of the questions which will be discussed at Rome. For your information, I may outline briefly the steps leading up to the Rome Conference and the reasons which have impelled the Canadian Government to take part in it.
>
> The present Conference which will consider the international aspects of the wheat situation stems, more or less directly, from the preliminary negotiations undertaken early last summer by certain states in southeastern Europe which felt their economic prosperity menaced by the low prices prevailing for agricultural products. The first negotiations between Roumania and Yugoslavia were soon extended to include Hungary and, ultimately, the eight States which took part in the Warsaw Conference on the 25th August, 1930. These States, namely Roumania, Yugoslavia, Poland, Hungary, Bulgaria, Czechoslovakia, Latvia, and Estonia drew up an agreed program of concerted economic action which was embodied in a series of resolutions, copies of which are included in the material I am forwarding.
>
> The representatives of these States presented the Warsaw Resolutions for consideration by the League of Nations at the last Assembly where they were examined rather carefully in the Second Committee. Dr. Riddell, who was the

Canadian representative on that Committee and is thoroughly conversant with the history of these negotiations, was largely instrumental in preventing the Assembly from taking formal action on the propositions put forward by the agricultural states. The Assembly was content with taking notice of the Warsaw Resolutions and referring them to the second Session of the International Conference with a view to Concerted Economic Action which met in Geneva on November 17th to 28th, 1930. A Sub-Committee of this Conference examined, in particular, the proposal that a customs preference should be granted cereals exported from continental countries by the importing countries of Western Europe. The report of that Sub-Committee, defining the conditions which would limit any such preferential scheme, is contained in the Final Act of the Conference, a copy of which is enclosed in the packet.

While the agricultural countries of southeastern Europe were attempting to work out some scheme for the profitable disposition of their exportable surplus of farm products, the International Institute of Agriculture in Rome was preparing for the Second International Wheat Conference to be held sometime in 1931 or 1932 to study the international aspects of the wheat situation. It had planned to have two preparatory conferences, one for European countries to meet in Rome in December, 1930, the other for overseas wheat producing countries which it invited the Canadian Government to convene at a suitable time and place. Owing to the fact that the Conference for Concerted Economic Action had included the European agricultural situation on its agenda, the Institute first postponed the projected December conference to the 26th of March, and then generalized that conference by inviting all the wheat producing countries to take part in it.

In the meantime, the Commission for Enquiry into European Union which met in Geneva in January under the auspices of the League of Nations took note of the agricultural depression as a factor contributing to the general unsatisfactory economical and political situation on the continent, and expressed the hope that overseas wheat producing countries would participate in the Rome Conference in March. It instructed its chairman. M. Briand, to convene as quickly as possible conferences representing the states immediately affected to consider first, the problem of disposing of the surplus stock of grain at present held by the grain-exporting countries of Europe, and secondly, the problem of disposing of the recurring future surpluses in those countries.

At the first conference held in Paris on the 22nd of February to consider the disposal of this year's surplus, representatives of the importing nations expressed their readiness to reserve part of their imports of wheat, corn, and barley for European grain exports, and undertook to bring together shippers and importers to arrange for the marketing of European wheat and surpluses.

The second conference, which met in Paris later in the same week to examine the problem of disposing of future surpluses, came to the conclusion that this problem was not only a European but world one, and could be settled only by an agreement between all the parties concerned. It considered that the forthcoming Rome Conference on the international wheat situation offered a good opportunity for reaching such an agreement.

This, briefly, is the background for the Rome Conference. The European countries are obviously feeling their way towards some organisation of the world wheat market that will lead to the stabilization of wheat prices at a level substantially above that now prevailing. Some of the possible means towards this end, which have been under consideration in Warsaw, Geneva, and Paris, are obviously filled with danger for Canada, although it does not now appear probable that a continental customs preference for European wheat will materialize. The network of commercial treaties consolidating most European customs tariffs, makes it at present impossible for these countries to introduce preferential or discriminatory rates (which would violate the most-favoured-nation clause contained in modern trade treaties. This formal restriction is strengthened by considerations of interest as far as the grain-importing nations of Europe are concerned.

I feel we can safely leave the criticism of any proposals for a European customs preference that may be put forward at Rome to the representatives of Italy, the United Kingdom, and the low tariff countries of Northern Europe. We cannot formally oppose a preferential scheme on grounds of principle for we asked at London for what the Danubian states have been seeking at Paris and Geneva.

Similarly, I feel it would be unwise to get mixed up in a discussion of the theoretical benefits that might flow from the general adoption of a system, of import quotas, for the quota system, which was examined by the Imperial Conference as a substitute for customs preference, is still formally under consideration by the Governments of the Commonwealth. From a Canadian standpoint there are serious prima facie objections to any general introduction by European countries of import quotas for wheat. The allocation of such quotas would, undoubtedly, lead to a diplomatic scramble for concessions in which we are not prepared to engage, and would probably lead to demands for tariff reduction on our part which might prove difficult to meet.

On the whole, I feel that we are taking part in the Rome Conference, not with any lively expectation of benefits to come, but, frankly, because we dare not be absent when the nations of the world are considering a question of vital economic importance.

Apart altogether from the things that may be done or left undone at the Rome Conference, it will be a great satisfaction to the Government and to the people of Canada to know that you will be our representative there. At this juncture we cannot afford to leave any avenue unexplored that might lead to the relief of the agricultural situation.[12]

At the Rome conference which met from March 26 to April 2, the quality of the discussion left much to be desired, as the Robson and Coats letters cited below attest. Although the delegates read long formal statements, they were not the best informed of individuals on the wheat trade. Altogether 48 countries including eight dependent colonies were represented. A special committee of the conference was set up to deal with the East European proposal for European preferences, which was opposed by the Canadian, Australian and Argentine delegates as a derogation of their countries' most-favoured-nation rights, and on that occasion the East European bloc received no special encouragement from their European neighbors. The United States government did not send a delegate because it had earlier lost confidence in the competence of the host organization, the international institute of agriculture. In the end the Rome conference adopted a series of innocuous resolutions which recommended an increase in the consumption of bread; recognized that European countries could not give up the cultivation of wheat or allow it to be endangered; recommended a reduction in wheat acreage elsewhere by voluntary and educational means, and

[12] *Bennett Papers.*

considered that there should be an improved organization of the wheat market which would embrace the disposal of existing stocks.

It had proved impossible to make more progress in dealing with the substantive problems of price recovery, and of production and export control because the overseas wheat exporting countries had not yet made any attempt to reach an understanding among themselves on these questions. It was when this need became apparent that Ferguson proposed a separate meeting of the exporting countries, first in Ottawa and then for logistic reasons in London. The conference adopted the proposal for an exporters' meeting in London that May.

Robson's undated letter to McFarland betrayed the full disgust of a grain merchant over the performance of an indiscriminate and international collection of government officials:

> I have arrived back from the World Wheat Conference in Rome. I did not consider it necessary to cable you any report of the Conference, as short reports were appearing in the English papers, and I understood that they were being transmitted to Canada.
>
> This immense and most expensive Conference, which lasted for eight days, broke up without any really useful purpose having been served. The Conference consisted of some two hundred delegates from forty-nine different countries, including such important countries as Guatemala, Peru, Persia, Latvia, and many others of similar importance. Of the two hundred delegates, probably eight or ten had some knowledge of grain. The head of each delegation, and sometimes other members, had each of them arrived in Rome with a typed oration to be delivered at the assembly. The large majority of these orations were delivered, but when four days had been occupied by this means, unfortunately some of the delegates, including the delegate from Cyrenaica, were unable to give the assembly the benefit of their views, though on the morning of the fifth day the delegate from Turkey insisted on reading his oration. I sincerely hope that all the delegates were able to persuade the members of the Press to publish in their own countries the orations, whether they were delivered or not. . . .
>
> Mr. Howard Ferguson, High Commissioner for Canada in London, . . . was wise enough only to make a very short speech, in which he said that he could not agree to any compulsory limitation of acreage in Canada. After four and a half days spent upon the above mentioned orations, Mr. Howard Ferguson stated that, as no progress had been made, he proposed that there should be a meeting in May of delegates from the exporting countries, namely:
>
> Canada
> Australia
> Argentine
> Russia
> Hungary
> Jugo-Slavia
> Poland
> Bulgaria
>
> and that an invitation should be sent to the United States to send delegates to such a meeting, the object of this meeting to be to see if some means could be discovered to coordinate the production and shipment of wheat overseas. The assembly adopted this resolution, and a meeting will be held in London about the middle of May.

The delegates from Australia, the Argentine, and Russia were in agreement with Mr. Howard Ferguson, stating that they were radically opposed to the compulsory reduction in acreage in any of their countries.

The small Eastern European exporting countries such as Hungary, Poland, and Jugo-Slavia, pressed most strongly that they should be given preferential tariffs by those European countries which impose a tariff on imported wheat. These countries also were most anxious to secure from England large loans to enable them to set up organizations similar to the American Farm Board, whereby they could hold back their wheat after harvest. It is difficult for anyone such as myself, engaged in the grain trade, to understand why any poor country such as Hungary should wish to imitate the example of the United States, considering that the United States is rich and able to afford to pay for its mistakes, whereas Hungary is extremely poor, and ought not to consider the possibilty of gambling in wheat for a rise in price. . . .[13]

McFarland, in Winnipeg, was a very interested observer of the proceedings. He not only objected to the conference in principle but he continued to be concerned over the status of representatives as he forwarded Robson's letter to Bennett on April 23, with a handwritten note of his own:

I am enclosing you a copy of letter written by Sir Herbert Robson of London, Eng. on his return from the Rome conference. It will be of interest to you I am sure.

I am informed Dave Smith represented the Canadian Wheat Pools at the Conference whereas I thought he was going simply as Technical adviser to Ferguson. Now the Grain Trade feel Smith will represent the Pools at London on May 18th, and they feel in self protection they should have a representative there, otherwise it will appear as if the Pool is the only Grain interest in Canada. They may write you.

My personal opinion is this London Conference is a bunch of nonsense. It was fathered by the Regina Pool leaders. It is their idea. International control of wheat marketing discussions in such a conference can only prolong the agony, and probably delay the time when Importing countries will reduce their wheat tariffs and Milling regulations. If Europe were normal as regards wheat tariffs and Milling restrictions the world wheat situation would readily clear up. . . .

Pool leaders still think you are going to establish a government wheat Board to handle wht crop. This in spite of your recent utterances.[14]

Confirmation of Robson's assessment of the Rome conference is contained in Dr. R. H. Coats's letter of April 16 to Dr. Skelton:

You will no doubt receive a full report on the World Wheat Conference at Rome from Mr. Ferguson or Dr. Riddell. I am, however, enclosing herewith a file of the papers of the Conference—agenda, minutes, reports of committees, etc.,—in case you have not yet received them. I proceeded to Rome after receiving your cable, on March 27, and attended the Sessions from March 30 on in the capacity of "expert advisor" to the Canadian Delegation.

The outstanding and most constructive feature of the Conference was the proposal put forward by Mr. Ferguson that a separate meeting be convened forthwith (May 18) at London, between the wheat-exporting countries alone, acting on a basis entirely independent of the Rome conference. This was not accomplished without some objection and difficulty—first from the International Institute of Agriculture and second from some of the importing

[13]*Ibid.*
[14]*Ibid.*

countries—and our Delegation achieved a definite position of leadership in bringing it about. I might add privately that apart from this, most of the proceedings of the Conference, at least in plenary session, consisted of a more or less desultory setting out of the view-point of the respective countries, which while useful as enabling the situation to be envisaged as a whole did very little towards clearing it up. It is rather difficult to make up one's mind as to the final value of such a Conference. On the one hand, it seemed to constitute only another of the "talk-fests" in which the International Institute of Agriculture is, in the opinions of many, now dissipating its energies; on the other hand, without such a clearing of the decks it would have been difficult to bring about the London meeting, which at any rate holds out the prospect of "getting down to brass tacks" on the immediate problem. . . .

With regard to the line which the proposed London meeting should follow, I was not present at the private and informal discussions which took place between our delegation and the Russian, Argentine, and Australian and other delegations of exporting countries, but I do not think any clear-cut proposal was put forward. In general, it was felt that a meeting like that at Rome was too diffused in its interests and too unwieldy to get anywhere, and that the pressing problem was the disposition of existing and immediately pending wheat stocks. It seems to me personally that in preparing for the London meeting, we should clearly begin by weighing its possible implications and results. A conference *between governments* for the "orderly marketing" of wheat will almost certainly lead up to the conception of an international pool, with government control of exports and price-fixing as concomitants. It seems to me we should decide before we begin negotiating how far we are prepared to go in this direction. Perhaps the current developments in the world-marketing of sugar, copper and rubber may have suggestions for us. For the rest, it seems of first importance that we should go into the conference equipped with all the data we can possibly bring together on the world wheat situation and adjust our views thereby when we see what the other governments have in mind. . . .

A point on which we should use extreme care in calling the meeting is to avoid antagonizing the big consuming countries. The British delegation at Rome, though they did not oppose it, were not exactly friendly to the meeting. One of them said to me jokingly "Go ahead with your combine; there never was a wheat corner yet we didn't break". In open meeting they preserved silence. On the other hand the Germans were decidedly cordial. . . .[15]

Despite the Robson and Coats letters commending Ferguson for his initiative in moving the resolution for a meeting of the exporting countries in London, Bennett and Skelton reacted unfavorably as they learned of Ferguson's unauthorized action and Bennett asked Ferguson for an explanation. In reply Ferguson sent a telegram from London on April 17:

Private and Confidential. I have two objects in moving Resolution for London Conference. Firstly, there was evidence of strong tendency of Continental Countries reaching agreement between East and West which would be bad for us, and I felt necessity of introducing new factor to divert discussion; secondly, our Delegations were unanimous in opinion that we could not refuse to tackle marketing problems and make an effort to find improved methods. If Canada does her best she will at least be relieved from responsibility of failure to try. I believe it will be good thing if we do nothing more than show to the world the attitude of the various countries. Discussed matter fully with Ambassador Dawes and am writing him inviting United

[15]*Ibid.*

States to Conference. Doubt very much if they will attend. Russia promises to come. If no results come from Conference, responsibility can be placed on the United States for refusal to (cooperate). I believe it will be excellent if McFarland were sent here as delegate and could be here week in advance.[16]

To Ferguson's disappointment, McFarland was not available and, to his surprise, the United States government accepted his invitation.

LONDON CONFERENCE

The London conference, May 18-23, 1931, was convened at Ferguson's invitation on behalf of the Canadian government at Canada House, and Ferguson's staff provided secretarial facilities. The conference was attended by delegations from Argentina, Australia, Bulgaria, Canada, Hungary, India, Poland, Romania, USSR, United States and Yugoslavia. After the opening ceremonies on May 18, at which Ferguson as representative of the host government was elected permanent chairman, the meeting got down to business on the following day. The United States delegate Mr. Samuel R. McKelvie, member of the federal farm board, made a long opening statement in which he urged a world-wide persuasion toward reduction in wheat acreage, which had already been advocated by the federal farm board and by the secretary of agriculture in the United States. Admittedly, the problem was not readily adaptable to solution by legislation. Both Canada and Australia had constitutional problems therewith, because of provincial and state jurisdictions in the matter of production.

On the other key subject of the conference, the introduction of a system of export quotas, all but the American delegate fell in line with the proposal of the East European bloc that this remedy be explored. But while acceding to the principle, the USSR delegate served notice that his government would expect a quota related to the level of its prewar exports, which were far greater than the volume of wheat the USSR was currently exporting. The Russian stance, and the American refusal to consider an export quota under any circumstances, effectively blocked progress in that direction.

The Australian delegation under instructions received while the conference was under way, went so far as to propose that an international marketing organization be created by the wheat exporting countries to control all wheat exports and prices. A similar proposal by the Polish delegation which not only advocated an international marketing organization to administer quotas, but also to operate a wheat buffer stock.

In commenting upon the discussions which took place, Dr. Taylor observed that the position of the Canadian delegation "was then (and remains) inscrutable."[17] This was not surprising in view of the basic set of instructions Ferguson had received from Bennett for the Rome conference in which Bennett had suggested that the opposing views of the various delegations would render Canadian intervention unnecessary. What was more surprising was Ferguson's support of the proposal for export quotas in the light of Bennett's caution that this subject was still on the agenda of the postponed imperial conference discussions.

[16]*Ibid.*
[17]Alonzo E. Taylor, *op. cit.,* p. 453.

Because nothing more could be done at that stage, the delegations approved and signed a final act which had been drawn up on the basis of several committee reports. In it the conference attributed the cause of the wheat problem to the effects of the world economic depression as well as to the overproduction of wheat. In its substantive provisions, the final act went no further than to say:

> The Conference considers that, where possible, a reduction in the areas devoted to wheat should be undertaken in whatever way each country considers to be the most effective and practical.
>
> It was also felt to be especially desirable that there should be a careful exploration of all avenues for the greater utilisation of wheat, both for food and also for other purposes.
>
> The Conference further considered that current information regarding the supply, the demand, and the movements of wheat should be brought together in such a way as to assist the wheat exporting countries towards the orderly marketing of their surpluses.[18]

The final act then proceeded with its specific decision to create a clearing house of information for the wheat exporting countries, and a meeting was subsequently held to establish the international wheat information service, with a budget for the secretariat to be contributed by the signatory countries to the final act. Because the agreement embodied in the final act to create this new organization was not ratified by governments, the proposed information service was not established.

FURTHER EUROPEAN CONFERENCES

With no further action forthcoming from the overseas wheat exporting countries, the commission of inquiry for European union resumed its efforts on behalf of the East European bloc as it met in Geneva on June 25, 1931, and refined the conditions for a preferential system designed to minimize the objections of the third countries. France accepted the principle of European preferences and proposed that it be integrated into a federal organization of Europe, but this proposal was not pursued as countries proceeded to negotiate bilaterally on preferences. The first preferential agreement was signed by Germany and Romania on June 18, 1931. A second agreement was concluded shortly thereafter between Germany and Hungary. In the autumn of 1931 France concluded preferential agreements with Hungary, Yugoslavia and Romania. Austria followed suit by signing agreements with Hungary and Yugoslavia. In January, 1932, the British government conceded that assistance should be given to the Danubian countries, but argued that a genuine customs union should be formed instead of a system of bilateral preferences. This led to a further conference in London on April 6, 1932. But British and French views polarized around the alternative approaches, and no agreement was reached to proceed with the formation of a customs union.

Finally, in response to a resolution of the Lausanne conference on reparations, July 8, 1932, a committee of seventeen European countries met at Stresa on September 5, 1932. The committee drafted a convention under the terms of which the East European countries should receive either

---

[18]*Ibid.,* p.462. Also, *House of Commons Debates,* May 25, 1931, pp. 1927-1928.

preferences or direct financial assistance from their western neighbours, in return for which the eastern countries were expected to grant tariff concessions. The British, Belgian, Dutch, German and Czechoslovak delegations reserved their positions. Although the Stresa convention was endorsed by the twelfth assembly of the League of Nations and by the commission for European union, the convention did not operate because of the continued reservations of Britain, Belgium and the Netherlands.

This recital of preliminary conferences reveals how much political effort was expended upon the international wheat problem before the first successful negotiations got under way. It also underlines the fact that the strongest impetus for a regional arrangement, at least, on wheat originated from the depressed Danubian states. The four major wheat exporting countries had not yet found a common denominator for their own approach to the international wheat problem. But the importing countries had been activated at least into consideration of the problems of the countries whose welfare was tied up in the export of primary commodities. The first attempts to deal with wheat at an intergovernmental level through representation at the official level suffered perceptibly from lack of expertise in grain matters. Therefore, virtually from the outset, representatives of the grain trade decried the foundering efforts to intervene in grain matters internationally. The reactions of Sir Herbert Robson in Britain, and McFarland in Canada have already been noted. Professor Alonzo Taylor, an American, left the best contemporary legacy in a scholarly account of the actual proceedings. But he was motivated in doing so in order to deprecate their results.

18

NEGOTIATION OF THE INTERNATIONAL WHEAT AGREEMENT

By the end of 1932, an international approach to the world wheat problem appeared to have reached an impasse. The four major exporting countries had not attempted to get together since their 1931 conference in London had foundered, and the efforts of the East European bloc were only partially successful in securing regional preferential treatment. But at that moment, fresh initiatives arose both in Argentina and in the United States.

ARGENTINE AND AMERICAN INITIATIVES

The then minister of agriculture in Argentina, Sr. Antonio de Tomaso, became interested in the assignment which had been given to the preparatory commission for the forthcoming monetary and economic conference, and he wrote to Sr. Raoul Prebisch, the Argentine member of the preparatory commission, on October 25, 1932:

> It has been proposed to reduce the area sown. In my opinion it is evident that the United States, Canada, the Argentine and Australia must in any case examine this problem without delay. . . . Would it not be possible for these four countries to agree to apply a policy of rationalisation in respect of wheat for a few years, account being taken of their average production, their present surplus and their exports in recent years with a view to reducing the area under wheat (not) increasing it without good cause, in order to bring about a better equilibrium between production and consumption than exists at present.[1]

In response, Prebisch prepared a memorandum for the preparatory commission in which he recommended, without minimizing the difficulties, a restriction of production in the exporting countries, and an undertaking by importing countries not to extend their production while the exporting countries were reducing theirs. Such arrangements should also be accompanied by a restriction of exports and special measures to dispose of surplus stocks. As Prebisch drew these proposals to the attention of the preparatory commission, Dr. W. A. Riddell, the Canadian advisory officer in Geneva

---

[1] J. S. Davis, *Wheat and the AAA*, Brookings Institution, Washington, D.C., 1935, p. 309.

reported the developments to Ottawa, in his telegram of January 18, 1933:

No. 8. With further reference to my telegram No. 4 of the 16th January re Preparatory Commission of Experts.

The Argentine Government suggest that Economic Conference make enquiries as to the possibility of the four principal wheat exporting countries agreeing to policy of regulation in respect of their average production, their present surplus, and their exports in recent years, with a view to reducing area under wheat.

The Argentine experts on Preparatory Commission said that such regulations would involve:

(a) An undertaking by the main importing countries of Europe not to extend their production so long as plan is in operation;

(b) A combination, at any rate to some extent, of restrictions of area under wheat with a restriction of exports;

(c) The settlement of question as to what should be done with surplus production in countries which, as a result of very good harvest, have an export surplus in excess of fixed maximum in spite of a decrease in area under wheat;

(d) The assurance that each country shall adopt suitable measures for applying plan.

Leith Ross, the British economic adviser, today told me that the United States representatives were favourable to regulations for production of wheat, but in return would demand a reduction in European import barriers against overseas wheat.[2]

This Argentine initiative had been largely responsible for the recommendation in the preparatory commission's annotated agenda for the world economic conference that the possibility of an intergovernmental wheat agreement be explored.[3]

Meanwhile, the November 1932 election in the United States had given the incoming Roosevelt administration a decisive mandate for change. Although he would not assume office (under the constitution as it was then) until March 4, 1933, Roosevelt used the interregnum to deploy a shadow cabinet charged with policy revisions. In the agricultural portfolio, secretary-designate Henry A. Wallace recruited a new band of officials who were wedded to the theory of production control. A draft program of agricultural adjustment was drawn up; one of its key features was a substantial reduction in the United States area sown to wheat, which could only be price effective if the other exporting countries followed suit. Consequently, one of the president-elect's special representatives, Mr. Henry Morganthau, Jr., approached the Canadian government with a view to reconvening a conference of the major exporting countries. The new government was prepared to reverse the decision of the outgoing administration which had opposed the adoption of export quotas at the London conference of May, 1931, as a means of securing agreement on a multilateral restriction of wheat acreage. Two other matters raised at the Ottawa meeting concerned the venue for further discussions, and the extent of the interest among other exporting countries. It was known, of course, that the preparatory commission had commended the question to the

[2]*Bennett Papers.*
[3]See pp. 347-348 above.

consideration of the world economic conference to be held under League of Nations auspices in London. But the Ottawa group felt that greater progress could be made if a special conference were to be called in Washington, provided that the other exporting countries agreed. Bennett had arranged a luncheon for Morganthau which some of his colleagues and senior officials attended, including McFarland whom he had brought from Winnipeg for the discussions. McFarland found in Morganthau a man of like mind.

CANADIAN INITIATIVES

Immediately after the Ottawa meeting, Bennett cabled Ferguson that the United States was prepared to call a conference of the four largest wheat exporting countries in Washington as soon as possible after the inauguration of the new president. He added that one of the most important proposals would be that of lessening wheat production, with which he was very much in accord. He asked Ferguson to ascertain from the Right Honourable Stanley Bruce, former Australian prime minister and now Australian high commissioner in Britain and from the Argentine ambassador to that country what the attitudes of their governments might be, and also to consult the representatives of Hungary, Romania, and Bulgaria.[4]

Ferguson replied the following day that he had already been taking soundings. He had learned that the United States members of the preparatory commission advocated a policy of acreage restriction and had intimated that the Roosevelt administration-elect intended to initiate such a plan. He added that the Argentine delegate also favored the idea. On February 1, Ferguson also reported that the Bulgarian and Romanian representatives were strongly of the opinion that their governments would support a program of production control. The Hungarian ambassador who had left London a month earlier had been of the same view. He had also talked twice with Bruce who had not consulted his government, but who personally believed that Australia would go along with the decisions of other countries. Ferguson gathered that the representatives of the other exporting countries would favor a meeting in Washington.

This turn of events was very satisfactory to McFarland who continued to press his crusade against overproduction. He granted a press interview to the Calgary *Albertan* and mailed Bennett a copy of the report on February 13:

> Wheat acreage reduction as the only cure for the world's economic ills and the possibility of a reduced wheat carryover in Canada were suggested by John I. McFarland, general manager of the Central Selling Agency, in an interview Friday. He pointed out that bankruptcy might ultimately force wheat reduction in the west.
>
> He pointed out that owing to crop failures in Danubian countries and in Russia, Canada had a chance to market more wheat than would otherwise have been the case. Emphasizing the need for wheat acreage reduction, Mr. McFarland declared that it would be much better for a farmer to raise 2,000 bushels of wheat and sell them at 60 cents than to raise 6,000 bushels and sell them at 20 cents.
>
> He compared agriculture with industry, stating that manufacturers did not create a surplus, but ceased manufacturing when a certain point had been

4Cable of January 20, 1933, *Bennett Papers.*

reached and that agriculture should do the same. "It must be evident," he said, "that the principal cause of the present depression is the dislocation which resulted from the Great War."

"The disturbance to agriculture was pronounced owing to greatly reduced production of all kinds of foodstuffs in Europe during the progress of the war and after the war, and it required a number of years before normal production was obtained. Following this period large import demands from Europe with greatly stimulated prices, resulted in increased acreage being established in cereal crops, particularly wheat, as well as in hogs, sheep and cattle. These increases were not observed until surpluses of everything forced it upon public attention."

Mr. McFarland explained that the only sane thing left for Canada and other ex-European countries, now that Europe had almost re-established normal production of every kind in its borders, was to reduce production in an orderly and equitable manner by agreement with other surplus-reducing countries.

He pointed out that there could be no more than temporary improvement in values while the production areas were continued unabated. "The prime necessity," he concluded, "must be to re-establish an equilibrium between supply and demand."[5]

McFarland's campaign was by now receiving a sympathetic response from the three provincial premiers and the pools. The precise state of play between the pools, the provinces and the federal government was brought out in an exchange of correspondence dating back to October 11, 1932, when Mr. George W. Robertson, secretary of the Saskatchewan wheat pool reported to Bennett:

Following resolution approved by conference of representatives of western governments and western wheat pool organizations held today "Whereas for the past two years the prices for our principal agricultural product wheat have continued at levels disastrous to the ability of agriculture to carry on and equally disastrous to the industrial and community interests which depend upon the purchasing power of agriculture. And whereas we believe that an improvement in commodity prices is essential to economic recovery and further that wheat is the chief commodity to be considered in the matter of price. And whereas we believe much can be accomplished by a conference of the governments and producers of the chief wheat exporting countries. Now therefore we request the government of Canada to convene such a conference with a view to establishing such measures of international coordination as may be deemed necessary or advisable in the best interests of these countries."[6]

It will be noted that no reference was made in this telegram to restriction of acreage, and Bennett picked up the point in his acknowledgment of November 30:

I have not until today had an opportunity to send you an acknowledgment of your night letter of 11th October, indicating the terms of a resolution which you state was approved by a conference of representatives of the Western governments and the Western pool organizations on that date, regarding restriction of acreage.

Inasmuch as our Parliament has no jurisdiction over the control of acreage except insofar as export of the product is concerned, it follows we should not call a conference when we would not be in a position to implement its

[5] *Bennett Papers.*
[6] *Ibid.*

recommendations. The provinces must first indicate that they are willing to restrict the acreage before we would be in a position to call a conference.[7]

Premier Bracken pursued matters with a letter of his own to Bennett on January 10, 1933:

> During your absence in the Old Country the suggestion that the Federal Government call a conference of the governments and producers of the principal wheat exporting countries was again discussed by the three prairie premiers and was again endorsed. Since then I have attended a gathering of the leading rural economists of the United States in Cincinnati and found the sentiment there strongly favoured the holding of such a conference. As you know, serious consideration is being given in the United States to a Domestic Allotment plan which in principle is very similar to the Wheat Act in force in the United Kingdom, except that the Domestic Allotment plan aims at reducing instead of expanding the acreage under wheat.
>
> While there has been a good deal of discussion on the question of wheat acreage reduction in western Canada, I doubt very much whether it would be possible to bring about any substantial acreage reduction either by legislation or propaganda unless the Western farmers had some assurance that the effect on world markets of a reduction in acreage in this country would not be immediately nullified by an increase in the wheat acreage in one or more of the other principal wheat exporting countries. It is quite possible, of course, that no definite international agreement could be arrived at, but a full and frank discussion between governments and producers of what is to-day just as alarming a situation for the wheat farmers in the United States, Argentine, Australia and the Danubian countries, might have important bearings on the policies adopted by all these countries in adjusting their wheat industries to world conditions. Russia is apparently not going to be a serious factor as a wheat exporting country for at least another year, owing to difficulties encountered with their collective farm program and unfavourable climatic conditions.
>
> As it is the large surplus of wheat in the United States which is to a considerable extent responsible for the demoralization of world markets, the policy adopted by our neighbour to the South is of the greatest importance to the wheat producers of Canada, and I sincerely hope that your government, representing the world's greatest wheat exporter, will see your way clear to taking the initiative and calling the proposed conference.[8]

Bennett's reply of January 25 indicated that he was in favor of a conference called by some other wheat producing country as he wrote:

> I have your letter regarding the holding of a conference to deal with the restriction of wheat production.
>
> I may say that this matter has been engaging the careful attention of the Government for some time and I am hopeful that action may be taken within a reasonable time, but the unsettled condition of the United States arising out of their constitutional difficulties consequent upon the Presidential election, makes it very difficult to secure immediate action. My own view is that Canada should assist some other wheat producing country to call a conference, rather than call it herself.[9]

Because McFarland had found a new ally in Morganthau, he sent off a telegram and also a letter of congratulations upon Morganthau's appoint-

[7] *Ibid.*
[8] *Ibid.*
[9] *Ibid.*

ment as chairman of the federal farm board on March 3. In it he said, "... I was very glad at the opportunity of meeting you on your recent visit to Ottawa and the luncheon and discussion which took place at that time. I have been disappointed that no definite arrangements have as, so far as I am aware, been completed in regard to the conference which at that time it was thought might be arranged with different countries, although I am still hopeful that such a conference will yet be agreed upon by the different interested countries. ..."[10]

Morganthau acknowledged the letter on March 9:

... I remember with pleasure our meeting in Ottawa and I am still hopeful that something constructive may be accomplished in the way of an international agreement or understanding as to wheat exports.

The friendly and cooperative attitude shown by Premier Bennett and all the other participants in our informal talks in Ottawa was certainly most encouraging.[11]

McFarland kept alive the correspondence with Morganthau as he wrote again on March 14:

... I cannot disguise the fact that I am bitterly disappointed that nothing, so far, has been done in the way of an international agreement among the wheat producing export countries in regard to a reduction in acreage, and thus a reduction of production, and I fear that you have assumed your new office at too late a date to expect that very much can be accomplished no matter how willing you might be to encourage a conference, because of the fact that seed time for spring wheat in the Northern Hemisphere is drawing close, and besides seed time in the Southern Hemisphere is not very far away. I, therefore, fear that the world will have to depend upon natural causes to reduce production, for the time being. I am sure from our short conversation in Ottawa that you are convinced that it is overproduction that is causing our troubles and that you will be sympathetic in using your influence to get the different countries together. ...[12]

In the expectation that the Americans would call a special meeting of the exporters in Washington, Bennett and his officials were nonplussed and somewhat disconcerted when notification arrived that the economic committee of the League of Nations had invited the four major exporting countries to a conference in Geneva. As Ferguson cabled from London on May 3: "My fear is that with tendency of Geneva organizations to centralize all international action there, and their irrepressible desire to have part in and as far as possible direct international affairs they may manipulate the procedure so that they will dominate the handling of the wheat situation. The atmosphere there is so entirely European without understanding of our problems that they might create difficulties or at least embarrassment."[13]

Dr. Riddell reported from Geneva on May 8 that the League had called the meeting after receiving assurance from the United States that the other governments had been consulted and were prepared to attend. But the Canadians had not been approached about the change in venue. Bennett reluctantly accepted the invitation and instructed Riddell to maintain a watching brief. Ferguson was named as head of the Canadian delegation,

[10]*Ibid.*
[11]*Ibid.*
[12]*Ibid.*
[13]*Ibid.*

but he did not go to Geneva. Bennett was concerned that no proposal for wheat acreage reduction should emerge from the meeting, because he had yet no firm commitment of support from the provinces.

GENEVA CONFERENCE, MAY 10-17, 1933

Although Canada, Australia and Argentina were represented in low key by Riddell, Mr. F. L. McDougall, economic adviser to the Australian high commissioner in London and Sr. C. Brebbia, Argentine commercial counsellor in Rome, the United States sent a strong delegation headed by the 77-year old Henry Morganthau Sr., a retired diplomat (and father of the chairman of the federal farm board whom Roosevelt later appointed as secretary of the treasury). Morganthau was accompanied by Mr. Frederick E. Murphy, publisher of the *Minneapolis Tribune*, who was also a wheat producer and stock breeder, and by Mr. G. C. Haas of the federal farm board. Although the League provided a nominal chairman for the meetings, most of the discussion took place at informal sessions over which Morganthau presided. The latter pressed for an exporters' agreement which he was prepared to negotiate. Riddell and McDougall, lacking such instructions, recommended that Morganthau make a proposal, which could then be referred to governments. In the light of the *Preliminary Report on the Wheat Situation* which the conference prepared, including a recommendation for acreage restriction, Riddell was taken to task for exceeding his instructions. The report contained an embryonic outline for an international wheat agreement, and its contents were summarized in Robertson's memorandum on the London wheat agreement as follows:

> The first part of the Report discusses wheat and the world situation and indicates the nature of the problem to be solved in the light of prevailing conditions. It was recommended that the objective to be reached should include the restoration of the price of wheat to a level which, while not curtailing human consumption, would secure to the wheat growing industry a reasonable return. The report then suggested that to reach this objective, the governments of the four major wheat exporting countries should agree to act in concert. The Report then laid down tentative suggestions for such concerted action which might be considered by the governments concerned at the forthcoming World Economic Conference. The most important of these suggestions was that recommending restriction of acreage sown to wheat. Various suggestions were put forward as to the total acreage restriction to be aimed at and also as to the degree to which each of the four countries should contribute to the total reduction. The United States delegate suggested a 25% cut spread over two years. The Argentine and Australian delegates thought this too high, and urged that countries with large surplus stocks should bear a higher cut than those without such surpluses. The Canadian and American delegates objected to any differentiation. The Australian delegate tentatively suggested a 20% cut for the United States and 10% for the other three countries, but the United States delegate strongly objected to such discrimination. However, he agreed that the United States might be prepared to bear a larger share of the cut in the first year of the scheme, and tentatively suggested the following figures:

> United States   —   17½% the first year;
>
>   7½% the second year;

> The other countries   —   12½% each year.

It was finally decided that the question of actual figures of reduction should be left for determination at an adjourned meeting to be held in London on May 29th.

Other suggestions in the Report concerned export quotas; liquidation of stocks; the high tariff policies of European importing countries (in this connection the Report recommended that the European importing countries should be notified that the exporting countries could not undertake to continue any action beyond the first year unless there was some modification of their protective policy); the position of Russia and the Danubian countries, and the setting up of a Standing Advisory Committee.[14]

The conference was adjourned from May 17 until May 29 before resuming in London after governments had a brief period for consideration of the report.

CANADA - UNITED STATES CONSULTATIONS

Because of the mounting pressure through the Geneva conference for acreage restriction, Bennett authorized the Canadian legation in Washington to discuss the federal government's constitutional difficulty with the American authorities directly. Mr. Hume Wrong, secretary of the legation, met on May 26 with secretary of agriculture, Henry A. Wallace, and his advisers including Dr. Mordecai Ezekiel and Mr. G. C. Haas who had returned from Geneva. As Mr. Wrong reported:

The Secretary of Agriculture and Dr. Ezekiel both strongly advocated acreage reduction as the most effective means of dealing with the problem of surpluses. I asked them whether they thought that it would be possible for Canada to limit acreage by an allotment plan or leasing scheme similar to the methods included in the Farm Relief Act. I said that I had made a rough calculation that, to finance either scheme on the necessary scale by a processing tax on wheat milled for domestic consumption, this tax would have to be about eight times as high in Canada as in the United States, which would obviously be out of the question. Mr. Wallace readily agreed, but suggested that other means of securing acreage reduction might be found. Dr. Ezekiel stated that he had received information that sentiment in the Canadian West might favour the imposition of either an export tax on wheat or a levy of 10 or 15 cents on a bushel at the elevator, the proceeds in each case to be returned to the growers who had signed contracts to reduce acreage. I said that I was not in any position to discuss this; I felt sure that Canada, which had a larger relative interest in the world price of wheat than any other country, was prepared to examine any feasible method of increasing this price; but it was impossible to impose acreage reduction by fiat of the Government, and, in addition to the financial difficulties in the way of compensating farmers for reducing acreage, there were serious constitutional obstacles, since the matter primarily concerned the Provinces.

Mr. Wallace, who seemed ready to recognize the Canadian difficulties, then said that their problem might be solved by a Canadian limitation of exports combined with a limitation of acreage in the other three countries. He believed it very important that the four countries should agree; otherwise (and Mr. Haas strongly supported this) there was little hope that the importing countries would make any concessions at London. He preferred acreage reduction all round, and did not want an export quota for the United States. An agreement covering next year's crop only would be a considerable advance, though one extending to 1935 would be preferable. . . .

[14]*The London Wheat Agreement*, Bennett Papers.

I asked Mr. Haas whether he thought that Australia and the Argentine would really be prepared to consent to acreage reduction. He said that that was the opinion which he had formed at Geneva. The Conference had been adjourned to London at the instance of Mr. MacDougall of Australia after a telephone conversation with Mr. Bruce, on the ground that an agreement on reduction could probably be reached if an interval were left for consultation with governments. All the delegates recognized that each country would have to apply its own method of acreage reduction. The Argentine delegate had refused to consider export quotas, but seemed eager for reduction of acreage.

I asked Mr. Wallace if he would be ready to see that the instructions to Mr. Morganthau, Sr. for Monday's meeting in London were general enough in form not to exclude any feasible plan of co-operation. This he readily offered to do. It seems to me to be desirable, especially in view of the considerations mentioned in Paragraph 6 of this despatch, that the Canadian instructions should be such as to permit the question to be kept open, at any rate until the main London Conference is convened.[15]

Also included in Wrong's report was Secretary Wallace's threat that if no international agreement was reached, his department would maintain a high domestic price for wheat, and dispose of its surplus abroad for whatever price it might fetch.

In the light of Wrong's request for flexibility in the American instructions as well as in the Canadian instructions for the May 29 meeting in London, Bennett wired Ferguson on May 27 as follows:

Reference my telegram No. 67 of 25th May. Developments international situation — particulary stiffening of United States attitude indicate that it will not be possible to maintain indefinitely our noncommital position at resumed conference of wheat exporting countries. Information from Washington is to effect that United States will probably apply processing tax to wheat and abandon efforts for domestic acreage reduction if agreement on international acreage restriction is not reached. If United States should abandon effort at international solution of question, concentrate on maintaining high domestic price and dump surplus on world market — effect on Canadian export prices would be disastrous. In these circumstances, you should endeavor not to take up any fixed position but keep the question open for final disposition by interested countries at World Conference where broader considerations may prevail.

In statement to Committee if other representatives favour reduction, you should indicate that Canadian Government is not disposed to rule international acreage reduction out of consideration, and is studying ways and means by which proposals put forward in Geneva might be translated into domestic policy. Problem is accentuated in Canada by divided jurisdiction of Provinces and Dominion and solution along proposed lines would probably require concurrent legislation which could not be enacted on short notice. "Intentions to Plant" report of Dominion Bureau of Statistics on May 1st indicates that spring seeding of wheat is 6 per cent lower than 1932 — a reduction of 1,475,000 acres.

Government consider that effectiveness in raising price of wheat of concerted action to reduce acreage on part of export countries would be materially assisted by, and possibly should be conditional on, an undertaking by principal importing countries to enlarge world demand for wheat by lowering tariffs and relaxing quantitative restrictions on imports. Without

[15] *Bennett Papers.*

assurance of easier access to European markets and without some guarantee that Russia would not once more break world price of wheat, Government could not undertake to impose acreage restriction on its wheat growers. Committee might consider advisability of submitting this aspect of question to World Conference for examination.

Proceedings of Wheat Committee should continue to be secret and its recommendations should be made — ad referendum — for decision by interested Governments at or during World Conference.

Please keep us fully informed of developments.[16]

Ferguson had considerable difficulty in holding the line when Morganthau pressed for an immediate agreement which could be announced before the opening of the world economic conference. Ferguson reported on May 29:

Meeting of wheat delegates postponed until Wednesday 31st at Argentine request. Morganthau and two other American delegates spent an hour with me this morning, Monday. Their fixed purpose is to reach definite conclusions upon policy of reduction of acreage. In answer to my statement that policy was a matter for Governments, Morganthau informed me confidentially that he had received on Saturday full authority to make definite agreement on policy and basis of reduction. Their view is that agreement should be reached and policy settled before the opening of Economic Conference. He urges that a public announcement that such an arrangement had been completed by the four countries responsible for 90 per cent of wheat would have important helpful effect not only upon proceedings of Conference but upon world public opinion. He told me that he thought Argentine would agree, though reluctantly, to reduction of acreage if they had free markets. I enquired how America viewed Argentine position; he answered that his chief aim was to secure general policy of reduction and leave other features of situation to be worked out later. He says that if we are all committed to common policy of acreage restriction each country will have to find its own method of working it out. Have expressed sympathy with objects of Committee and our desire to co-operate in difficulties and urged that we could not accomplish ultimate object of improving wheat prices unless consuming countries were parties to such. Bruce tells me that they have not agreed to anything but would be disposed to fall in line on acreage reduction if Committee were unanimous. He agrees with the Americans that announcement of agreement in advance of Economic Conference would be good thing. I will listen on Wednesday and try to keep Committee going without committing us to anything and will report to you.[17]

At almost the same moment Bennett received the necessary assurance of support for acreage restriction from Premiers Brownlee and Bracken, and from the Honourable Murdo A. MacPherson, Saskatchewan provincial treasurer, acting for Anderson. Their telegram of May 29 to Bennett read:

The following resolution was passed at a meeting of the wheat problems committee representative of the governments of the three prairie provinces: That in the opinion of the committee an increase in commodity prices generally and wheat prices in particular is essentially a condition precedent to any sustained improvement in Canadian economic conditions. That in view of the present large world surplus of wheat and the present prospect of a further large Canadian crop, some plan of curtailment of wheat production in or exports from the four principal exporting countries is essential to any such

16*Ibid.*
17*Ibid.*

price increase. That we therefore strongly recommend to the government of Canada that it make every effort to secure for this question an early and prominent place in the discussion of the general economic conference and that the Governments of Manitoba, Saskatchewan, and Alberta, pledge the support of their respective provincial governments to the principle of such curtailment of wheat producton or control of exports and offer to co-operate with the Federal Government in formulating plans to carry this principle into operation in Canada. That any further discussion at the said economic conference should involve consideration of the possibility of any agreement arrived at between the said exporting countries becoming effective in the marketing of any crop handled after the first day of July nineteen thirty three.[18]

Supporting telegrams were forthcoming from each of the three pools as follows:

Winnipeg, Bredt to Bennett, Ottawa, May 30, 1933.

Manitoba Pool Elevators Limited strongly endorses stand of prairie provinces regarding the necessity of reducing world wheat production and adjusting exports to demands of importing countries. We respectfully urge that the proposals looking toward international agreements to secure this adjustment be supported by Canada at World Economic Conference.

Regina, Robertson to Bennett, Ottawa, May 30, 1933.

Executive Committee of the Saskatchewan Wheat Pool strongly recommends that Government of Canada should take leadership at World Economic Conference in securing early and urgent consideration of international wheat situation to the end that some plan of wheat control may be evolved which will tend to bring wheat exports and production into line with world consumption requirements. Also methods of dealing with existing world wheat surplus with a view to reduction.

Calgary, Wood to Bennett, Ottawa, June 1, 1933.

The directors of Alberta Wheat Pool are deeply concerned with the possibilities afforded by the forthcoming World Economic Conference of promoting a substantial measure of cooperation between the four chief wheat exporting countries and others similarly engaged to the end that the price-destroying factor of increasing wheat surplus may be diminished if not eliminated. We are firmly convinced that curtailment of production or export of wheat by such countries is essential to the permanent recovery of prices so vital to the happiness and prosperity of our people. We are further convinced that the wheat growers of the prairie provinces will gladly support such a policy provided they have assurance that similar reductions in equitable proportion will be effected by the other exporting countries. We therefore respectfully urge in the interest of Canada as a whole and her wheat growers in particular that you urge upon the nations represented thereat the utmost measure of international cooperation to the end therein referred to and we offer such assistance as we may be able to render in working out Canada's resultant internal problem.[19]

Even with these assurances of support, Bennett was concerned over the pace Morganthau was forcing at London, and he wired his brother-in-law, W. D. Herridge, the Canadian minister in Washington, on June 1, to persuade the Americans that matters should be held in abeyance until the economic conference delegates arrived in London:

Regarding Wheat Conference London. Ferguson telegraphs confirming fixed

[18]*Ibid.*
[19]*Ibid.*

purpose of the United States delegates to reach definite conclusions upon policy of reduction of acreage before World Economic Conference meets. Australia is definitely opposed at present to any scheme of restricting production though Bruce thinks Government might change view that difficulties might be increased if attempt was made to formulate and operate a plan without consulting European interests. The United States Representative from Berlin, Steere, agreed with his views and expressed opinion that suspicion would be aroused and perhaps opposition created by European block. Full telegrams being forwarded by mail.

I have sent Ferguson following telegram today. Quote. For your information Premiers of Prairie Provinces have advised me of their willingness to cooperate in carrying out any wheat restriction scheme. Unfortunately this offer was made public in Winnipeg and carried by Canadian Press so that our bargaining position in London will likely be impaired. I agree entirely with your approach to question in conversations with exporting countries and hope it will have effect of keeping question open and Committee in session until Conference opens. I am asking Herridge to point out to Washington the unwisdom of forcing pace in next ten days and to suggest that United States representatives be authorized to continue discussion of restriction scheme until our main delegations reach London.

I believe arguments for delay, which cannot in the circumstances be long are (1) necessity of ascertaining, informally or through diplomatic channel, the reaction of importing governments to restriction scheme; (2) desirability of securing assurance that Russia, even if standing outside acreage restriction, will not prejudice its success by expanding exports; (3) inter relations between any scheme for raising price of particular commodity and general programme of Conference — i.e. the higher general prices can be raised, the less stringent need be any restriction of wheat supply. End Quote.

You will please make representations indicated above.[20]

As a result of these representations, the Americans concurred, and matters were held in abeyance until the arrival of the delegations for the opening of the monetary and economic conference on June 16.

LONDON WHEAT CONFERENCE, JUNE-JULY, 1933

The separate talks among the four overseas wheat exporting countries coincided with the opening of the world economic conference. They were held in secret, and outside the framework of the world conference organization, but in the same building, the Geological Museum in South Kensington, at such times as the delegates could get together.

The delegation which accompanied Bennett was a far cry from the menage he had taken to the 1930 imperial conference. It included the Honourable E. N. Rhodes to whom Bennett had transferred the finance portfolio, and his deputy minister Dr. W. C. Clark; L. D. Wilgress, director of the commercial intelligence service, department of trade and commerce, N. A. Robertson of the external affairs department, and R. K. Finlayson, the prime minister's chief secretary. In London, the Honourable G. Howard Ferguson and the secretary of the high commissioner's office, Lt. Col. Georges P. Vanier, were added to the delegation. Ferguson and Robertson assisted Bennett in the wheat negotiations.

The main conference was opened on June 12 by King George V, and was presided over by Prime Minister Ramsay MacDonald. Representatives of

[20] *Ibid.*

66 countries attended. Among the opening speeches, Bennett's was typical in its generality of expression on the major issues of price, trade and exchange reforms, but he was quite specific in his advocacy of a wheat agreement as he said:

> ... In the case of wheat, the accumulated carryover of 350 million bushels can be effectively dealt with only by international agreement, involving a possible reduction of acreage cropped until the abnormal carryover which continues to depress the market has been disposed of. In this regard, the statement of the Chancellor of the Exchequer, that the world's greatest wheat importing country recognizes the necessity for such action, is most reassuring. It is a matter of record that with each fall in the price of wheat many of the principal wheat importing countries have raised their tariffs against this importation, strengthened their restrictive systems, and devised new defensive measures, which, by diminishing the effective demand for wheat, have first of all aggravated and then perpetuated a disastrous fall in price, which may, in the first instance, be attributed to the phenomenal harvest of the year 1928. And we would suggest that the importing countries should give their serious consideration to the feasibility of enlarging their demand for wheat *pari passu* with the producing countries' contraction of the available supply. In this way a new equilibrium could be reached more speedily and with less dislocation of established interests than if the process of adjustment were confined to the reduction of supply.[21]

When the wheat talks got under way on June 16, Canada was represented by Bennett and Ferguson; Australia by the Right Honourable S. M. Bruce, Australian high commissioner in London; Argentina by Sr. T. A. Le Breton, Argentine ambassador to Paris; and the United States by Mr. Henry Morganthau, Sr., and Mr. F. E. Murphy. All except the Americans were also delegates to the world economic conference.

On the technical and drafting committees of the wheat meetings, Canada was represented by Mr. Robertson; Australia by Mr. F. L. McDougall; Argentina by Sr. Carlos Brebbia, permanent representative in Rome to the international institute of agriculture; and the United States by Mr. L. W. Steere, American agriculture attache in Berlin, and by Mr. L. A. Wheeler, acting chief of the division of foreign markets in the department of agriculture. Mr. Andrew Cairns, formerly statistician to the central selling agency and at that time on the staff of the Empire Marketing Board in London, was seconded to the Australian and Canadian delegations and was of considerable help in preparing the statistical basis for the acreage and export-quota provisions and in the drafting of the agreement.

Robertson summarized the issues under negotiation and the attitude of the four governments in the two-week period prior to the initialling of the note of agreement of June 30, 1933:

> The initiative, in the early discussions, was assumed by the United States delegation whose leader, Mr. Morgenthau was asked to preside at the meetings. His instructions authorized him to conclude an agreement for the reduction of acreage or of exports. His Government was committed to the principle of reduction of production and believed that that policy could only be effective if applied by the other major producers as well. The United States did not expect any cooperation from importing countries, was not very much concerned whether Russia or the Danubian exporters accepted similar

[21]*Ibid.*

limitations, and thought that the four Overseas countries in their own interest should take steps to reduce production independently of any action by other exporters or by importing countries.

The Australian Government, which had made measurable progress in lowering its costs in producing wheat, had enjoyed a relatively favourable competitive position as a result of the depreciation of its exchange, and which was at that time finding English quantitive restrictions on the import of meat and butter, etc., rather galling, was not disposed to accept the principle of enforced restriction.

Argentina was prepared to accept any scheme of restriction on which the other exporting countries could agree.

The Canadian position, as set out by the Prime Minister in his speech in the Plenary session of the Economic Conference and in the meetings of the Wheat Committee, included:-

(1) Sympathetic reception of the United States proposals qualified by frank recognition that the methods of reduction contemplated by the United States could not, on financial and economic grounds, be applied in Canada;

(2) Insistence that any concerted effort by exporting countries to adjust world supply to effective demand by reducing production or exports should be met by simultaneous lowering of tariffs and relaxation of quantitive restrictions which now throttled effective demand for wheat on the part of normally importing countries; and

(3) Explanation of constitutional responsibility of provincial governments for any direct control or restriction of seeded acreage.

As the discussion proceeded during the last fortnight of June, these national positions were, to some extent, modified by events:-

(a) The progressive worsening of crop reports from the North American continent tended to moderate the American zeal for an immediate agreement and strengthened the hands of the economic nationalists in Washington who wished to abandon efforts for international agreement, and dump any subsequent surplus beyond domestic requirements on the world market.

(b) The Australian Government, under some pressure from the other exporting countries and possibly from the United Kingdom, withdrew its objections in principle to a restriction scheme and, though avoiding acreage reduction, agreed if unanimity were otherwise reached and the conditions outlined by Mr. Bennett fulfilled, that they would restrict exports within an international scheme.

(c) The crop estimates, as of the end of June, indicated a real possibility that one year's reduction of output by 15 per cent would liquidate the abnormal surplus overhanging the market and restore a new and satisfactory equilibrium between world supply and demand.

This prospect of clearing up in one year by concerted action a situation which had depressed prices to disastrous levels for nearly five years, was probably decisive in bringing the representatives into agreement in principle on the desirability of trying to adjust world supply in the crop year 1933-34. This agreement was worked out very hurriedly on the basis of estimates of world acreage, carryover, probable production, and import requirements in the confidential draft and which is generally referred to as the "Memorandum of June 30th, 1933" and which was subsequently initialled by representatives of the four Overseas countries as the basis of agreement upon which their further detailed negotiations rested.[22]

Although all the negotiations were held in camera and were kept outside the world conference orbit, the Canadian and American delegations kept

[22] *The London Wheat Agreement*, pp. 16-19, Bennett Papers.

the press reasonably informed on the developments, and some colorful reports were filed by The Canadian Press. By Thursday, June 22, Sr. Tomas Le Breton who chaired the informal meetings, reported that agreement on a 15 percent acreage reduction was reasonably close, with only the Australian delegation holding out. Henry Morganthau, Sr., had approached Maxim Litvinoff, the Soviet delegate to the conference, who promised that his country would not dump wheat on world markets if treated by those markets fairly. But over the following weekend, press reports from Australia indicated that all the state governments were opposed to the acreage restriction scheme, and on Monday, June 26, Bruce had to delay the meeting while he awaited instructions. By Wednesday, the crisis came to a head when Bruce reported that with the state governments all opposed, the Australian government could not join the agreement. Thereupon, Bennett and Morganthau importuned Bruce, as Morganthau threatened that the United States would dump its exportable surplus in the absence of an agreement. The prospect was serious enough that Bruce's altered instructions later that day included a request from his government for a definite restriction scheme which it could present to the state governments. The Australian government also requested that the European importing countries be approached and their co-operation assured. To that end it asked if Bennett and Murphy could be constituted as a committee to approach the governments of Germany, France, Italy, Belgium, the Netherlands, and Czechoslovakia.

On the same day, Wednesday, June 28, when the crisis was at its height, Prime Minister Ramsay MacDonald, chairman of the world conference, called in the representatives of the four exporting countries in the hope that the wheat talks could be now brought within the ambit of the world conference. He was told that the four exporters were close to an agreement in principle upon acreage reduction and export quotas, but that it would be premature to give the negotiations conference exposure in their present state. It was in this confused state of affairs that Bennett noted that an act of God in form of a "boom" in the market helped to ease matters. A draft basis for the operation of export quotas was initialled and referred to governments.[23]

OVERSEAS EXPORTERS' NOTE OF AGREEMENT, JUNE 30, 1933

The note of agreement was primarily a statistical calculation of the exportable surpluses for the four exporting countries in the crop years 1933-34 and 1934-35, which was used as a basis for assigning export quotas equated to the anticipated import demand. World import demand was predicted at 750 million bushels for 1933-34, although it was acknowledged that this figure might have to be revised. Although Canadian and United States production could be predicted in the light of current crop conditions, the Australian and Argentine crops were just being sown and their anticipated production had to be based on the latest three-year average acreage and ten-year average yield. United States production was estimated at 540 million bushels and domestic requirements at 610 million, which left a deficiency of 70 million in the 1933 crop. This was expected to reduce the

---

[23]A highly colorful and personal account of the negotiations at this stage is to be found in R. K. Finlayson, *That Man R. B.: Bennett,* pp. 194-199.

American surplus to 170 million and the Canadian surplus was placed at 140 million. Exports of new-crop wheat from Canada, Argentina, Australia and residual sources were estimated at 650 million. Of the 100 million remaining to equal the estimated import demand, the United States was given priority of 30 million for surplus reduction and the remaining 70 million was split evenly to reduce the surpluses of the United States and Canada. Thus the original formulation of the export quotas on June 30 could be tabulated as follows:

	Exports from New-Crop Wheat	Exports from Carryover	Total Export Quotas
	(million bushels)		
Canada	283	35	318
Argentina	150		150
Australia	142		142
United States		65	65
Other	75		75
Total (Export Quotas and Import Demand)	650	100	750[24]

Furthermore, if import demand were to fall below 750 million bushels, export quotas would be reduced to their share of the total, which would mean reductions for Canada of 47 percent, Argentina 22, Australia 21 and the United States of 10 percent respectively.

Because the Argentine and Australian exportable surpluses had been estimated in advance of the growing season in those countries, authority was proposed for the transfer of unused quotas of either one of these countries in 1933-34 to any exporting country having an export surplus larger than its quota. Any quota so surrendered should be restored to Argentina or Australia in 1934-35. This limited application of the principle of transferable quotas was very significant, inasmuch as the failure of a general application of the transferable principle contributed to the eventual breakdown of the agreement.

Then, in respect of the 1934-35 crop year, a categorical undertaking by each of the four exporting countries was given to reduce production by 15 percent. This undertaking prefaced the calculation of export quotas for that year. The elements of the calculation took into account the agreed 15 percent reduction in production in arriving at exportable surpluses of new-crop wheat in that crop year. This resulted in export quotas from new-crop wheat which would fall somewhat short of what was hoped to be an enlarged import demand of 800 million bushels. Any shortfall in new-crop supplies to meet world demand was to be allocated equally to Canada and the United States to assist the reduction of their surplus stocks, and a summary of the 1934-35 export quota position could be set out as follows:

	Exports from New-Crop Wheat	Exports from Carryover	Total Export Quotas
	(millions bushels)		
Canada	263	75.5	338.5
Argentina	114		114
Australia	113		113
United States	84	75.5	159.5
Other	75		75
Total (Export Quotas and Import Demand)	649	151	800

[24]*Draft*, Bennett Papers, and cf. Davis, *op. cit.*, p. 332.

The June 30 note of agreement was initialled by Bennett, Murphy, Le Breton and McDougall. That it was a tentative agreement, intended for revision when more accurate statistics were available and subject to reference to governments was more apparent from the immediately subsequent developments than it was from the actual wording of the text. Shortly thereafter, the whole agreement was recalculated statistically, but there remained embodied in the text of the June 30 initialled draft, a categorical commitment to reduce production by 15 percent in 1934, which was purposely omitted from subsequent texts. Nevertheless, a dispute arose whether the original undertaking remained valid. The precise words were a one-sentence paragraph in the document which read: "Each of the four countries agree to bring into effect a reduction of production of wheat to the extent of 15%."

PUBLIC REACTION TO ACREAGE RESTRICTION

Bennett immediately sought the concurrence of the three provincial premiers as he cabled to Sir George Perley, the acting prime minister on June 30:

> Just concluded meeting at which United States, Argentine and Australia have agreed to 15% reduction of wheat acreage crop year ending 31st July, 1935. Canadian acreage basis 26,300,000 which less 15% with average yield 17 and 24 hundredths bushels would make available crops about 380,000,000, in 1935. Based on average production, proposal will not entirely eliminate surplus carry-over but situation can be reviewed in the light of next year's experience.
>
> Please communicate above to Brownlee for immediate consideration so that on Monday next I can inform meeting whether or not Canada will agree to 15% acreage reduction.
>
> Proposed plans practicable with the co-operation of Federal Governments in the countries concerned.[25]

On July 4, Brownlee wired Perley:

> Have discussed wire thirtieth confidentially with other Provinces. All approve general principle crop reduction and prepared cooperate fully with Dominion Government and if necessary other countries in preparing plan. Fifteen per cent reduction not considered unreasonable. Believe assurance that other producing countries and European states will not take advantage agreement and increase production necessary to obtain consent western farmers. Our study leads to conclusion that simple provincial legislation calling for definite acreage reduction and subsequent police action not practicable but believe practical plan may be evolved by cooperation Federal Government and Provincial Governments. Strong feeling exists for limitation export as part any plan. As Provincial Governments reluctant obligate themselves to definite action without knowing plan can only express approval of principle. If more information as to proposals could be placed before joint meeting would be glad to arrange same on two days notice.[26]

Perley forwarded Brownlee's reply to Bennett, and sent a separate cable of his own on July 4 reporting that Bennett's cabinet colleagues were opposed to acreage restriction:

> Eight of us in meeting today wished me let you know that in light of information before us we are not favourable to restriction wheat acreage and

[25] *Bennett Papers*
[26] *Ibid.*

do not think it is practical. We discussed Brownlee's telegram of today and we think some clauses in it quite disturbing.[27]

Although the three premiers stood by their original commitment to Bennett on the principle of crop reduction, public opinion in Canada was rapidly turning away from that course of action. Perley had reported to Bennett on June 26 that, while Bracken and McFarland had issued statements favoring acreage restriction, the two Winnipeg papers, both Calgary papers, and the *Financial Post, Financial Times, Ottawa Journal, Toronto Star* and the *Montreal Standard* were either sceptical or adverse. The reason for the change in attitude toward acreage reduction has been succinctly described by Mr. R. K. Finlayson:

Since the governments of the prairie provinces by telegram had informed R. B. that they would accept the onus of providing for wheat acreage reduction, R. B. was fully armed to sign an acreage reduction agreement, as Bruce of Australia was not. After our arrival in London, I was receiving clippings almost daily from western Canadian newpapers. When the prairie governments dispatched the message, they were unaware that a crop failure was in prospect. After the meeting of the big four had proceeded for a couple of weeks, a crop failure in western Canada of near disaster proportions was known to be the immediate problem that both governments and wheat producers would have to deal with. The general tone of the newspaper clippings was that in face of a crop failure, a wheat acreage reduction agreement would be rejected with scorn by the people of western Canada.[28]

As early as June 23, Mr. J. H. Wesson, vice-president of the Saskatchewan wheat pool broke ranks from the position of support the executive committee of the pool had given as recently as May 30.[29] A press report from North Battleford on June 30 reported Mr. Wesson's views as follows:

Declaring his belief that restricted acreage is not the solution to the wheat problem, J. H. Wesson, vice-president of the Saskatchewan Wheat Pool, Thursday night told a city audience that he was opposed to any attempt to fit production with the present world chaos.

Mr. Wesson dealt in detail with the three-point policy of his organization — establishment of a national marketing board, agreement with other exporting countries for quota shipment and domestic price fixing for all wheat consumed in Canada $1.35 a bushel.

Mr. Wesson voiced opposition to restriction or reduction of wheat acreage, expressing the belief that it was neither practical nor enforceable in law, in any event was no solution to the wheat marketing or surplus problems.

Mr. Wesson urged agreement with the other exporting countries as to the amount of wheat or quota to be shipped from each country to fit supply and demand.

"By this method the so-called wheat surplus can be kept off the market." Restriction of acreage would not be acceptable to producers without guarantee of price, was the view put forward by Mr. Wesson, who declared that because of this attitude of mind of the producers it would require an army to enforce the necessary laws.[30]

[27] *Ibid.*
[28] R. K. Finlayson, *op. cit.*, p. 198.
[29] See p. 374
[30] *Winnipeg Free Press*, June 24, 1933.

On July 13, Mr. George W. Robertson secretary of the Saskatchewan wheat pool, who had signed the May 30 telegram on behalf of the executive committee, was reported from Wolseley as follows:

An international wheat export quota plan, rather than acreage reduction, is the means favored by the three western wheat pools to solve existing difficulties in marketing wheat, George W. Robertson, secretary of the Saskatchewan Pool, said Wednesday in an address to farmers.

This plan, he said, would remove the existing abnormal surplus, correlate supply with the effective demand at all times, and help the producer to get remunerative returns without penalizing the consumer.

Acreage reduction came in for severe criticism from Mr. Robertson. Legislation necessary to bring it into force would be difficult, if not impossible to enforce, he said, and the pools therefore had decided that bushelage, not acreage, is the best means of control.

A national wheat marketing board, he said, would greatly facilitate the successful carrying out of the plan.

The individual grower, Mr. Robertson declared, would be under no restriction whatever as to acreage or production, but the maximum amount of wheat he could market from any given crop would be fixed as the result of the quota agreement. How he treated the balance, he added, would be entirely in his own hands.

Mr. Robertson then proceeded to outline the general method of procedure:

"In establishing this quota, average deliveries over a period of possible ten years in each of the exporting countries should provide a reasonably satisfactory basis. Having determined world import requirements for the year, and having allocated to each of the principal wheat exporting countries its quota of the total requirements, each of these countries would then take such steps as might be deemed advisable, both to control the deliveries and also the marketing of the crop, within its own boundaries.

"So far as Canada is concerned, we are of opinion that the establishment of a national marketing board, with complete control over the marketing of wheat, would greatly facilitate the successful carrying out of this plan. We have suggested that after a quota has been established for the Dominion of Canada this should be allocated by the national organization to each of the wheat producing provinces and the responsibility should then be placed on the provinces for organized delivery of the provincial quota.

"Using the municipality as a basis it is not a difficult matter to determine deliveries to be accepted from each individual farmer on the basis of his average production over a period of years. This may sound somewhat complicated but, in carrying out the proposal, it is no more complex than the administration of any large-size business and, after all, the business of growing and marketing wheat in this province is of much greater importance than a combination of all other business interests within the province. . . ."[31]

The reaction from Australia was even more pronounced. On July 5, Bruce was reported to have repeated the adamant opposition of his government to an obligation to reduce wheat acreage, and to have offered instead to limit exports of wheat by 10 percent over a period of two years. Thus the erosion of the firm commitment to reduce production continued, and in the formal agreement eventually concluded, there was no direct

[31] *Ibid.*, July 13, 1933.

reference to such an obligation, which remained only by implication in the undertaking actually given to limit exports.

NEGOTIATIONS WITH OTHER EXPORTING COUNTRIES AND WITH THE IMPORTING COUNTRIES

Having reached a tentative agreement among themselves, however unstable, the delegations of the four exporting countries addressed themselves to the search for wider support for the agreement, including that of the Danubian states and the USSR as well as that of the importing countries whose participation was considered essential to the agreement's price-raising objective.

The Danubian countries were consulted on July 6, when the "big four" exporters proposed a global export figure of 40 million bushels for the group, based upon past performance, while the countries affected held out for 70 million bushels. In the end, they compromised at 50 million, with an upward tolerance of 4 million, if needed, to move their 1933 surplus. Negotiations were also opened with the USSR, but no progress was made.

By July 13, the chairman of the world conference, Prime Minister MacDonald, brought the representatives of the four exporting countries together with those of the smaller exporters and of the importing countries, to urge that they all get together within the aegis of the main conference for the prompt conclusion of an agreement that would coordinate wheat production and consumption and thereby raise the price. The representatives of the big four contended that the negotiations were proceeding satisfactorily outside the conference and that further progress was contingent upon that course. Their views were accepted, and the exporting countries proceeded to draft the form of commitment the importing countries might give, not to take advantage of the exporters' agreement by increasing their own production, and also to ease their import controls when wheat prices recovered to an agreed level. The importing countries examined the draft and proposed certain modifications. Meetings with the importing countries to consider the draft were held on July 20, and again on July 26, the day that the world economic conference adjourned. To allow time for reference of the importer undertakings to governments and for revision of the exporters' quota undertakings, it was agreed that a wheat conference should be convened at Canada House on August 21 and that, in order to clear up any misunderstandings about the way in which the negotiations had been conducted up to that point, the adjourned meeting should be called under League of Nations auspices.

As Bennett took off for a well-deserved holiday in England, Mr. F. E. Murphy responded to the Australian request that he tour the importing countries to enlist the support of their governments. Murphy visited Berlin, Prague, Rome and Paris for this purpose. On August 3, Ferguson addressed a formal request on behalf of the governments of the four exporting countries to M. Avanol, secretary-general of the monetary and economic conference, to issue invitations to an international conference of wheat exporting and importing countries to he held on August 21 at Canada House, London (offered as a meeting place by the Canadian government).

To his letter Ferguson attached three enclosures, the first being an outline of the draft agreement which had been reached by the major exporters, the second being the importers' undertakings as originally drafted by the representatives of the four exporting countries, and the third being the latter draft as amended by representatives of the importing countries. The enclosures served as an agenda for the conference.

LONDON WHEAT CONFERENCE, AUGUST 21-25, 1933

The importing countries which accepted the invitation to participate in the conference were Austria, Belgium, Britain, Czechoslovakia, Denmark, Estonia, Finland, France, Germany, Greece, Ireland, Italy, Lithuania, Netherlands, Spain, Sweden, Switzerland, and Turkey. The exporting countries in addition to the big four (Argentina, Australia, Canada and the United States) were Bulgaria, Hungary, Poland, Romania, USSR, and Yugoslavia.

Bennett headed the Canadian delegation and he was elected chairman of the conference. Bennett had asked the three premiers to name a representative to the Canadian delegation, and they proposed the Honourable M. A. MacPherson, provincial treasurer of Saskatchewan. Robertson and Finlayson served as advisers. Mr. Andrew Cairns assisted the conference secretariat.

So far as the exporting countries were concerned, the most important task of the conference was to reach agreement with the importing countries on a basis whereby the latter would not thwart the measures taken by the exporting countries to adjust production by increasing their own production but, on the other hand, would reduce their import controls and thereby expand consumption of overseas wheat as soon as an agreed measure of price recovery had taken place. Secondly, the big four exporters needed to formalize their agreement with the Danubian states and to bring the USSR into the agreement. Lastly, they had to revise the preliminary calculations of export quotas agreed among themselves on the basis of more up-to-date information on harvests and import demand, and to work out an exporters' commitment on production adjustment that would avoid any direct obligations to take specific internal measures of production control, thereby accommodating the preoccupations of the Australian, Argentine and Canadian governments against such obligations. That the conference came within reasonable striking distance of achieving such formidable objectives within a five-day span was a remarkable achievement. Much of the drive which accomplished the result was attributable to Bennett.

First, with respect to the importing countries, the original demands made upon them as they met with the exporting countries on July 20 had been

(a) not to encourage any extension of the area sown to wheat nor to take any governmental measures which would increase their domestic production;

(b) to adopt all possible measures to increase the consumption of wheat;

(c) to lower their customs tariffs as soon as the international price of wheat had been maintained at a specified level for a period of time, and

(d) to accompany any reduction in customs tariffs by a modification of the general regime of quantitative restriction of wheat imports.

Such provisions were incorporated into the final act of the conference, but only after the insertion of an important proviso, and the acceptance of several reservations which were made upon signature. The general proviso was inserted as follows:

> It is recognized that measures affecting the area of wheat grown and the degree of protection adopted are primarily dependent upon domestic conditions within each country, and that any change in these measures must often require the sanction of the legislature.
>
> The intention of this Agreement is nevertheless that the importing countries will not take advantage of a voluntary reduction of exports on the part of the exporting countries by developing their domestic policies in such a way as to frustrate the efforts which the exporting countries are making, in the common interest, to restore the price of wheat to a remunerative level.[32]

A committee of the conference was appointed to negotiate the price level and its duration at which the importers' obligation to lower customs tariffs would become operative. The exporting countries represented on the committee proposed a figure of 58 gold cents per bushel, and the importer representatives, notably of France, Italy and Switzerland proposed 68 gold cents, which would have materially lessened the likelihood that the tariff reduction provisions would become operative. A compromise was reached at 63 gold cents per bushel. Similarly, the exporters wanted the minimum period after this price was reached before the obligation became effective to be two months. The importers proposed a six-month period and compromised at four months.

The individual country reservations, incorporated in the minutes of the conference but not in the text of the agreement, had the effect of exempting from change the favorite systems each importing country had adopted for protection of its wheat growers, and thereby vitiating the commitments made in the agreement by those countries.[33] In the end this did not matter, however, because the gold price at which these obligations would have been brought into play had been placed sufficiently high that the general obligation to reduce tariffs and milling restrictions was never reached during the lifetime of the agreement.

In their negotiations with the Danubian states, the four major exporting countries were able to reach agreement on a global quota of 50 million bushels for those states, with a tolerance of an additional 4 million, if required for the movement of the 1933 crop. This provision was incorporated into article 3 of the final act. With the USSR export quota, the negotiations were less successful. The Russian representatives would give no undertaking regarding production in that country. As the export quota they demanded was so far out of line with their current export performance, the only agreement possible was that negotiation of the actual figure should be deferred to a later time. This was so provided in article 4 of the final act. As a matter of record, subsequent attempts at negotiation of the USSR export quota proved equally futile but, in actual practice, exports from the USSR

---

[32]*Conference of Wheat Exporting and Importing Countries, Final Act signed at London, August 25th, 1933,* Treaty Series, 1933, No. 11 (King's Printer, Ottawa), pp. 4-5.
[33]For details of the reservations see *The London Wheat Agreement,* Bennett Papers, pp. 31-36.

during the lifetime of the agreement created no embarrassment to the major exporting countries.

The problem which the four major exporting countries had to resolve among themselves was to find a method of avoiding any direct reference to an obligation to reduce production, in order to accommodate the positions of the Australian and Argentine governments. This was done by placing the onus of the obligation upon the observance of export quotas, which left to individual governments what methods they might adopt in order to adjust their total wheat supplies to their quota limitations. Since it was already too late to influence sowings for the 1933 crop, attention was directed toward the following year and export quotas for the 1934-35 crop year were set on the assumption that 15 percent less acreage would be sown for the 1934 harvest than on the average from 1931 to 1933. The specific provisions affecting the four major exporting countries were set out in articles 1 and 2 of the final act in the following terms:

Article 1

The Governments of Argentine, Australia, Canada and the United States of America agree that the exports of wheat from their several countries during the crop year August 1st, 1933, to July 31st, 1934, shall be adjusted, taking into consideration the exports of other countries, by the acceptance of export maxima on the assumption that world import demand for wheat will amount during this period to 560,000,000 bushels.

Article 2

They further agree to limit their exports to wheat during the crop year August 1st, 1934, to July 31st, 1935 to maximum figures 15 per cent less in the case of each country than the average outturn on the average acreage sown during the period 1931-1933 inclusive after deducting normal domestic requirements. The difference between the effective world demand for wheat in the crop year 1934-35 and the quantity of new wheat from the 1934 crop available for export will be shared between Canada and the United States of America as a supplementary export allocation with a view to the proportionate reduction of their respective carry-overs.[34]

Although the foregoing articles defined the formula by which quotas would be set in the two crop years, 1933-34 and 1934-35, the resultant calculations also had to be made. Since the first such calculation embodied in the note of agreement of June 30, 1933, better than expected yields had been realized in Europe and it became necessary to lower the estimate of total world import demand to 560 million bushels, as well as to make a more liberal allowance for the Danubian and USSR share thereof. The formula (agreed upon in June) for reducing quotas under such contingencies was now applied to exports for the 1933-34 crop year, and the quotas actually determined for that year were as follows, with the exemption of the United States figure which remained in dispute:

	bushels
Canada	200,000,000
Argentina	110,000,000
Australia	105,000,000
United States	45,000,000
Other	100,000,000
	560,000,000

[34]*Conference of Wheat Exporting and Importing Countries, Final Act,* loc. cit., p. 3.

In order to reach agreement on the figures for Argentina and Australia, the other exporting countries had to agree to higher export quotas for the Southern Hemisphere countries in the following year if their exportable surpluses in the 1933-34 crop year proved to be higher than were currently forecasted. These calculations were incorporated into a secret annex duly initialled and attached to the Memorandum of June 30 which also remained secret. Although agreement had been reached on the Argentine and Australian quotas, Bennett fell out with Murphy on the United States quota. The draft of the secret annex had provided a quota of 47 million bushels for the United States which Bennett considered to be unrealistically high in terms of the American export potential. He corrected the draft by crossing out the 47 million figure and replacing it with 45 millions which he initialled. Before Murphy would initial, however, he added a final paragraph to the document to the effect that it was initialled on the understanding that the United States quota was 47 million bushels. Although the note of agreement of June 30 and the annex of August 21 appended thereto were intended to be secret documents, the United States department of state, through a misunderstanding, published them as an appendix to the final act of the conference.[35] This caused a certain amount of consternation in Ottawa, but the damage had been done and some comfort was taken from the fact that the treaty information bulletin had very little circulation beyond a library list in the United States.[36] It remained the intention for almost a year that the quota difference for the United States be settled, a quota for the USSR established, and the amended documents published. But in practice, United States and USSR exports were so small that the final resolution of these issues was unnecessary.

Before the London wheat conference concluded, however, Mr. Murphy of the United States delegation tried to firm up the commitment given in the June 30 note, more commonly referred to as the "draft", by which each of the four countries had agreed to bring into effect the reduction of production to the extent of 15 percent in 1934-35. He was concerned about the Argentine and Australian retreat from any direct obligation to restrict acreage and he proposed that a statement be inserted in the annex which would commit Canada and the United States to reduce acreage by 15 percent, while Argentina and Australia would match this by accepting export quotas which would take into account a similar reduction, and by preventing the accumulation of stocks above normal by denaturing their surplus wheat, if necessary. In the light of the resistance which had developed in Canada to acreage restriction, the Canadian delegation objected to the inclusion of a provision in the annex which would bind Canada, and Mr. Cairns was credited with having persuaded Mr. Murphy to seek an interpretation of each country's obligations by an exchange of

---

[35]United States Department of State, *Treaty Information Bulletin No. 48,* September, 1933.

[36]For convenience of reference, the note of agreement of June 30, the annex of August 21 to the note of agreement and the final act of the conference of wheat exporting and wheat importing countries, August 25, 1933 are reproduced, respectively, in Appendices 3, 4 and 5.

letters. Consequently, Mr. Murphy addressed the following letter to the Argentine, Australian and Canadian delegations:

> With reference to the note of agreement between the overseas wheat exporting countries initialled today, I would deem it a great favour if you would confirm my understanding of the conversations in respect to the method whereby each country would give effect to the reduction of production, as mentioned on page 6 of the June draft.
>
> It is my understanding that the reduction of production to the extent of 15%, mentioned on page 6 of the draft in question, shall be given effect to in the case of Canada and the United States through the undertaking to reduce acreage by 15% from the 1931-33 average, and in the case of Australia and Argentina, by the acceptance of export quotas equivalent to such reduction (on basis of the years 1930-32 for Argentina), and by the undertaking not to accumulate stocks above normal.[37]

Although the Argentine delegation acknowledged and accepted this understanding, the Canadian delegation was not prepared to accept its undertaking expressed in this form. As a matter of fact, the proposal to reduce acreage by 15 percent was much more stringent than the undertaking written into the June 30 draft which was to reduce production by 15 percent. Canada and the United States at that time were in the midst of a cycle of low yields which were reducing production, quite apart from any acreage restriction. Shortly thereafter, the issue was pursued by Canadian and American officials by direct conversations in Washington.

[37] *The London Wheat Agreement*, Bennett Papers, p. 41.

19

OPERATION OF THE INTERNATIONAL WHEAT AGREEMENT

The final act of the London wheat conference provided for the creation of a wheat advisory committee "to watch over the working and application" of the agreement, on which exporting and importing countries should be equally represented. The office of the committee was to be located in London. At the first meeting of the committee on September 18-19, 1933, Argentina, Australia, Canada, the United States, and USSR were separately represented, whereas Hungary and Bulgaria were represented by one member, as were also Yugoslavia and Romania. Britain, France, Germany, Italy, Spain, and Switzerland also became members, but the seat offered to Sweden was declined. The head of the United States delegation, Ambassador R. W. Bingham was elected chairman, and Mr. A. W. Cairns was appointed secretary. Much of the first meeting was devoted to organizational matters. Because of the uncertainty of exchange rates at the time, the budget was calculated in terms of gold francs and assessed among the member countries on the basis of their relative production or exports.

On substantive matters, the Russian member of the committee reported that negotiations were still being pursued with the other exporting countries on the USSR export quota, but that nothing had been agreed. The division of the Danubian global quota among the individual countries was also considered, and French and German wheat policies were discussed.

SUBSIDIZED WHEAT EXPORTS AND MINIMUM PRICE PROPOSALS

French wheat policy was the most important item on the agenda of the advisory committee's first meeting. Earlier that year French flour had been moving under subsidy in substantial quantities to Britain. At the London wheat conference, Bennett had secured the agreement of the French minister of agriculture to temporary suspension of their subsidies, pending further discussions between the two governments on a limitation of the volume.

At the first session of the wheat advisory committee, the French delegate, M. Devinat, reviewed his country's wheat position. France, normally an importing country, had produced a surplus in 1933 of nearly 48 million bushels of which as much as 11 million might have to be exported, and the balance disposed of by lowering the milling extraction rate and by use as livestock feed.

At the same time, M. Devinat requested that the Canadian government send a representative to Paris immediately for the negotiation of an agreed limitation of exports because his government was under criticism due to the temporary suspension. As a basis of negotiation, M. Devinat suggested that France limit exports to Britain during the coming year to 1,850,000 bushels.

When these developments were reported to Bennett he proposed that Mr. Andrew Cairns, who had participated in the discussions with the French at the London wheat conference, should undertake negotiations on Canada's behalf. The instructions sent to Cairns made it clear that he was not to negotiate an agreement for the sale of French wheat in Britain, but rather to seek ways and means by which the French exports could be contained. Cairns arrived in Paris during the first week of October where he met with M. T. Queuille, the French minister of agriculture who was being pressed to lift his prohibition on wheat exports to Britain. Despite the corresponding ban on subsidized flour exports, French flour was still being exported under the temporary admission system whereby if a miller imported wheat, he could export an equivalent amount of domestic flour. In this latter connection, M. Queuille promised that such exports of flour would not exceed France's total imports of Canadian wheat. M. Queuille claimed that the government assistance Germany and Italy extended to flour millers under their temporary admission systems was much more damaging to Canadian interests than was the French method. Quite apart from these import-compensated exports, he stood by the French offer to restrict exports to Britain to 1,850,000 bushels, but on condition that the wheat be sold at not less than an agreed minimum price which the German government should be asked to observe in its export arrangements.

When Cairns reported this information to Ottawa, Bennett regarded the French proposals as reasonable. Because they were contingent, however, upon negotiation of minimum prices with Germany, Bennett asked for a delay in their acceptance to which the French agreed while the negotiations proceeded.

Before he went to Berlin, Cairns consulted the chairman of the advisory committee who, with the approval of the Canadian government, authorized him to continue the negotiations in his capacity as secretary of the wheat advisory committee. By acquiescing in this apparent improvement in his status, however, the Canadian government lost effective control over Cairns as a negotiator. The point was of some significance, because the Canadian government was anxious to prevent the minimum price proposals from obscuring the real issue, which was the containment of French wheat exports. On the other hand Cairns, as secretary of the wheat advisory committee, was more interested in adding a minimum price arrangement to the international wheat agreement.

On his arrival in Berlin, Cairns learned that the minimum price proposal was the only aspect of the French situation in which the German government was interested. He discovered also that the Germans interpreted the French suggestion for minimum prices as being applicable not just to

France and Germany but to all signatories of the international wheat agreement, exporting and importing countries alike. When he returned to Paris, Cairns confirmed that this was actually what the French had originally intended because the plan, if adopted on an international basis, would make it easier for the French government to secure its domestic acceptance.

By now, Bennett and his officials were considerably disturbed by the turn of events. What had begun as a discussion on how to minimize France's subsidized flour exports had spiralled into a proposal for an international price cartel. Bennett tried, unsuccessfully, to redirect attention to the original issue when the wheat advisory committee met a second time on November 25. Just prior to the meeting, Ferguson discussed the situation with Cairns who defended the position of the French and German governments. He claimed that the French stood by their offer to place a ceiling on French exports, and that the German government intended to import as much wheat as was exported in flour equivalent. Cairns believed that both governments were adamant in their insistence on an international minimum price scheme. Cairns also contended that British millers would not oppose such a scheme, but Ferguson maintained that their consent must be obtained lest they charge the exporting countries with creation of a world wheat-price cartel. All of this was revealed in an exchange of cables between Bennett and Ferguson. In Bennett's cable of November 26, he renewed his effort to separate the issues and to play down the minimum price proposal:

> Your telegram No. 165 of the 24th November regarding wheat exports. Cairns' report of French and German attitude indicates attempt to evade issue which was and is simply situation created of subsidized wheat or flour by France and Germany to United Kingdom market. Previous French offer to limit amount they ship and fix minimum price acceptable. New proposal making agreement contingent on all exporting countries fixing export prices has no bearing on situation of which we complained. As regards latter proposal in itself, while of course any increase in wheat prices is desirable, Cairns will recognize necessity of utmost caution. If any idea of universal price-fixing gets into mind of British miller whole existing attempt to work out international wheat regulation would be jeopardized. Better bring discussion back to French and German shipments to United Kingdom.[1]

Ferguson's telegram of November 27 recited the views Cairns had expressed and reported that the French and German delegates, with United States support, would press the minimum price proposal. The telegram reveals how skilfully Cairns manoeuvered to gain support for the scheme:

> Your telegram No. 155, November 26th. Cairns feels that French not attempting to evade issue as their offer to restrict exports to the United Kingdom to one half million quintals still stands unconditional. Devinat, however, repeats that to fix minimum export prices is contingent on all exporting countries fixing similar prices. Germany definitely repeats that she will import as much as she exports, therefore, question of quantitative restriction does not arise as her wheat exports are similar to France's flour exports which results from temporary admission which flour exports are not covered by 500,000 quintal limitation. France has exported practically no

[1] *Bennett Papers.*

wheat to the United Kingdom since Canada House Wheat Conference. Cairns informs me that France and Germany will press tomorrow request for minimum export prices; that Danubian countries will probably support it; that the United States gives it very sympathetic consideration; that McDougall describes his official attitude as "hesitant interest"; that British will likely listen sympathetically to the views expressed by the leading exporters and refer the matter to Government. Cairns appreciates the need for caution but is apprehensive of repercussions on overseas farmers if the leading exporters entirely non-committal when proposal pressed by France and Germany and others. Cairns does not consider that wheat agreement jeopardized if British millers hear of proposed minimum export prices as British Millers' Association and Bakers' Association have recently been negotiating minimum prices for flour and bread. Committee today considered tentatively the effect of subsidized exports of wheat and flour and adjourned discussion on this point until tomorrow. . . .[2]

Another telegram from Ferguson on November 29 showed that the Canadian and Australian delegations had tried, unsuccessfully, to restrict the application of the minimum price proposal to subsidized exports only:

... In preliminary discussions regarding effect of subsidized exports, Canadian and Australian points of view supported by Switzerland and the United Kingdom, both of whom proposed that if minimum export prices for all countries found impracticable might be applied to only subsidized exports, but latter proposal not acceptable to France and Germany. French and German proposal regarding minimum export prices formally supported by the United States and Hungary.

Committee fully aware of necessity for caution regarding minimum export prices proposal and unanimously agreed to avoid any publicity and to call first sub-Committee "sub-Committee on market conditions."[3]

In order to examine the minimum price proposal further, the committee appointed a sub-committee on markets, referred to in that telegram, which met in mid-December to prepare a report considered by the wheat advisory committee at its third session on January 29, 1934. The Canadian delegation was instructed, once again, to keep the question of subsidized exports and of minimum prices separate, if possible, and to stress the harmful effects of direct export subsidies in the hope that the latter might be abandoned. But Bennett was aware that there was little hope of suppressing the price issue, when he sent the following instructions to the delegation:

We are, of course, strongly in favour of any practical proposal to raise wheat prices. We doubt, however, whether minimum price scheme proposed would satisfactorily achieve this purpose, having in mind grave administrative difficulties that would arise; also, as report of Sub-Committee states, minimum prices are not a solution for the main problems of the wheat situation. There are certain points that would need careful examination, some general and some applying especially to this country, e.g. —

(a) Scheme such as outlined in Appendix to Sub-Committee's report would necessitate drastic changes in our present methods of marketing in order to give government power to control prices.

(b) Administration of minimum price schemes much easier in countries where governments already controlling or supervising exports.

[2]*Ibid.*
[3]*Ibid.*

(c) There would be constitutional difficulties in Canada regarding provincial jurisdiction which would require careful consideration.

(d) Question of effect of minimum price schemes on existing surplus stocks and current domestic sales would need examination. The dealer should not be allowed to receive benefits intended for producer.

(e) There is difficulty of satisfactorily establishing spreads between categories. Page 26 of Sub-Committee report shows that Canadian wheat would be subject to highest minimum price and margin over lower priced wheat could not be reduced even if circumstances necessitated it thereby making more difficult our competitive position. In this connection, in lieu of scheme of minimum prices for separate grades, suggest you might sound out Committee as to single minimum price below which no kind of wheat would be sold.[4]

In the end, the minimum price proposal was held over for final consideration by the fourth meeting of the wheat advisory committee which had accepted an invition to meet in Rome in April. The Argentine harvest had been much larger than expected, and the government of that country was urgently seeking to renegotiate the Argentine 110 million bushel export quota for the 1933-34 crop year. Because of the importance of the issues on the agenda for the Rome meeting, Bennett asked McFarland to represent Canada with the assistance of Lt. Col. Georges P. Vanier who had participated in the negotiation of the agreement and had attended the earlier meetings of the advisory committee in London. But in his trusted adviser, McFarland, Bennett fared no better in staving off the minimum price proposals than he had done with Cairns. Although McFarland had not participated in the wheat agreement negotiations, he had been sceptical from the outset of the efficacy of an export quota system in raising prices; he supported the price-raising objective of the agreement and was an ardent supporter of the acreage restriction feature as a means therto; similarly he was predisposed toward an international price agreement if it could have any effect in influencing prices upward. McFarland had not persuaded Bennett to his point of view before proceeding to Rome, but he cabled Bennett from the meeting on April 11:

Secret. No. 2. Discussion on minimum price indicates that Committee may be prepared to recommend, probably unanimously, to Governments for consideration and approval proposals envisaging very slight initial increase in price approximately 5% with slight progressive increases at future times when warranted. Outline of type of Agreement attached as Appendices to draft report of Technical sub-Committee not accepted by the Committee as drafted. Suggested system is of elastic character based on minimum price under the supervision of Central Committee of Experts, London, which will revise differentials or spreads when necessary so as to control or attract equitable proportion of exports of wheat based on quotas of each country. Conversations proceeding in splendid cooperative spirit on lines which indicate that system will work satisfactorily.[5]

Bennett was utterly unconvinced; he replied to McFarland on the same day:

Your telegram number 2 April 11. You are fully aware of my view as to undesirability of government price fixing of wheat. Cannot accept minimum

[4]*The London Wheat Agreement,* Bennett Papers, p. 74.
[5]*Bennett Papers.*

price proposal without further information and presentation of valid grounds for belief that system will work satisfactorily. What is the attitude of the United Kingdom to scheme, also of other exporters including Russia? Has position of France, Germany and other occasional exporters under any minimum price system been carefully considered? Are other exporting nations prepared to set up machinery that will be necessary to enforce minimum prices, and has the effect of establishing such prices on efforts to reduce production which is main objective of original Wheat Agreement been considered? Has any agreement been reached to deal with depressing effects of subsidies , dumping, etc. We understand grant of additional subsidy of 20 million bushels to Argentine is conditional on control of dumping by that country, and if this condition is accepted, is not one of strongest arguments for minimum price system removed, as Argentine export policy largely to blame for present position. To upset existing marketing arrangements and institute such elaborate and difficult machinery controlled by a board in London seems hardly warranted in order to secure an immediate price increase of three cents a bushel. Please advise further on above points.[6]

McFarland's response did not come until April 14 when he answered Bennett's questions, and reported in a message signed by Vanier and himself that he had already concurred in the decision:

Secret. No. 4. Your telegram reference minimum price proposal received April 12, not possible to obtain all information required until today. McFarland believes system will work satisfactorily subject to Governments implementing proposal. United Kingdom delegation accepted report and all exporting keen about scheme except Argentina which however does not dissent. Position in regard to France and Germany, and other occasional exporters has been safeguarded by requiring from countries which grant export subsidies an undertaking that amount of such subsidies will not exceed the difference by which internal price of wheat exceeds corresponding export price minimum and that such subsidies will be granted only under conditions (which will?) prevent export of wheat at prices under specified minimum or of flour at prices below equivalent of wheat export price minimum. If other exporting countries do not implement by perfecting necessary machinery agreement will not operate. Increase in prices if any would be so slight as not to encourage production. Position as regards depressing effect of subsidies and dumping has been safeguarded as indicated above. Discussion proceeded rapidly on proposal and end came unexpectedly today when no representatives expressed dissent on report. In the circumstances believe it inadvisable abstain pending further instructions from you particularly as report is only recommendation to Governments for their approval. Eight pages of report will be forwarded first available ship unless you desire cabled version.[7]

Just how completely McFarland endorsed the minimum price agreement may be judged from the statement he made toward the end of the Rome meeting:

As we have now agreed upon a plan to establish minimum price control, based on the London Wheat Agreement, ... I want to record a few comments.

This plan envisages the control of Export movement and distribution by what may be termed

A. Managed price differentials.

B. Maintenance of internal prices in export countries by Governments.

[6] *Ibid.*
[7] *Ibid.*

Price or cost has always been the controlling factor in the movement and distribution of goods, and this system or plan does not attempt any revolution in respect thereto.

The interplay of differentials or spreads between the different grades or qualities of wheats, from various countries, have always governed the volume of the flow from time to time, and in normal times has regulated trading in the international wheat market.

Prior to the great depression resulting from overproduction and over-expansion, and when trade was normal, it always happened, if for a time, an unusually large business was done in wheat of some particular quality or grade, or from any particular country, it would soon be observed that the price of such wheat would advance, or the price of other wheats would decline relative thereto, thus making attractive those sorts which had been neglected. Thus the widening or narrowing of price differentials acted as the regulator of volume from every export country. That is the principle upon which this plan has been based. The plan may be described as "Control of prices" and it is so intended. It is, however, just as certainly "Regulation by price influence", of "the movement of the quotas from each country", and by the proven method of changing spreads between prices of the various wheats.

Providing the Governments of the various countries carry out the very necessary control of values within each country, this plan cannot fail to work. It will assure to each country some reasonable recompense for that portion of their wheat for which there is a market demand. It will assist in tiding over a difficult period by giving the various countries time to adjust their production to effective demand. . . .

The mere act of dividing up 560 millions out of a total 1,100 millions did not constitute any grounds for confidence in prices. Nor would it have been more effective had only 535 million been divided.

Furthermore the only thing which prevented a very much lower world's price disaster in the past several months was the fact that two countries who were parties to the Agreement, were preventing their surplus from being dumped upon a world's market which could not absorb it. I refer to the United States as one of these countries, which in one form or another, prevented the great bulk of their surplus from being dumped in large quantities. The other country was Canada where under Government guarantees, prices were supported, and the policy followed in Canada was no doubt effective in steadying and in fact supporting the whole world export price structure from complete collapse.

This plan if adopted by Governments will serve to bring all countries into co-operation to support prices, and aid each other in time to reduce production nearer to world's demand. It will prevent unwanted excess supplies from destroying the value of that portion which the world really requires. It will not create a scarcity of wheat in any part of the world where wheat is wanted. It will not destroy the grain trade, but will leave them to carry on distribution as usual. Nor will it prevent the speculator or investor from returning to his former occupation, at any time his confidence returns, and again carry on his one time service, which he abandoned some time ago, because of the over-produced world's situation.[8]

Despite all this apparent agreement, Argentina had not concurred. The minimum price scheme became a pawn in the negotiations for an enlarged quota for that country, as described later in this chapter, and it fell through with the failure of the quota negotiations. Historically, it is unfortunate that

[8] *Ibid.*

the experiment was not made. It had been intended that a technical committee in London would supervise and adjust the necessary quality and basing-point differentials to keep them in line with their relative values established by market demand, and to keep the exports from each country moving in accordance with the established quotas. The representatives attending the advisory committee meetings were apparently convinced that a technical committee could function in this manner to coordinate a minimum-pricing with a market-sharing scheme. Whether a technical committee with adequate intergovernmental support could have succeeded under the conditions of that time is a question that could only have been answered by the experiment. Much more recently the international grains arrangement broke down because the governments principally involved were not prepared to cede to a technical committee the authority to administer and enforce the minimum price provisions of a price agreement.

ACREAGE AND PRODUCTION RESTRICTION

The bold commitment "to bring into effect a reduction of production of wheat to the extent of 15%" in the June 30 draft had been made, for Canada's part, by Bennett who reconfirmed that he had the approval of the three provincial premiers in doing so. The pools had also given their prior endorsement to the undertaking in their concern to reach an international agreement, but even they could not anticipate the misgivings that developed within Canada after the June 30 note had been initialled. A possible retreat from the obligation opened up when the Argentine and Australian governments opted for quota restrictions as defined in articles 1 and 2 of the final act in lieu of a direct obligation to reduce production. In the process, the United States government which had already made a policy decision on its own domestic acreage allotment plan whereby acreage reduction in the United States would be subsidized from a flour milling equalization tax, now found itself being isolated in its endeavor to justify its domestic program on the basis of an international undertaking to do so. Consequently, the American representatives in London held on tenaciously to whatever might be salvaged from the June 30 agreement to reduce production. For this reason Murphy had addressed the letter to the other delegations in which Canada was tied to the United States in observing a 15 percent acreage restriction. As already noted, the acreage formulation therein proposed was more onerous than the production commitment actually given. When the London conference concluded, the Canadian-American issue was deferred for joint consultations in Washington. A resume of these talks was recorded by Robertson who participated in them:

> One of the early difficulties in connection with the Exporters' Agreement was, as we have seen, the tendency of the United States to read into it a definite promise on the part of Canada to reduce wheat acreage 15%. Statements emanating from Washington after the London Conference and which assume an obligation for acreage reduction on the part of this country, made it necessary to remove any wrong impressions which might be created thereby. This was attempted by conversations which were held in Washington in September between Mr. Herridge, Mr. Wrong, and Mr. Robertson on the one side, and Mr. Wallace, Mr. Feis of the State Department; Dr. Ezekiel of the Department of Agriculture on the other. The Canadian representatives

explained the difference between the Canadian and the United States situation which made identical wheat reduction programmes impracticable. Canada had accepted the obligations of the Wheat Agreement but must determine itself how these could best be carried out. Such determination was for each of the signatory states a matter of domestic policy. It was emphasized that the signatories should not, therefore, embarrass each other by premature and misleading statements—outlining methods which might be interpreted as applying to all the signatory states, when in fact they only apply to one country.

The Americans agreed that methods would have to vary and that financial and economic conditions in Canada would not permit anything like the land leasing and domestic allottment schemes in force in the United States. Mr. Wallace suggested that for Canada a tax on wheat exports might be imposed, the proceeds of which might be paid as a bonus to farmers for wheat reduction. He stated that the American Government was anxious to do anything that might assist in the advancement of the Canadian agricultural programme and would co-operate in any way we suggested. It was pointed out that for the time being the most helpful thing they could do would be to concentrate on working out their own acreage reduction plan, leaving Canada to work out ways and means of meeting its own obligations under the Wheat Agreement.

At these conversations, the American officials seemed to agree that wheat acreage reduction, as such, was not feasible in respect to Canada, and the impression was gained that no more would be heard from Washington of a request for an explicit Canadian undertaking to reduce acreage by 15% in 1934-35.[9]

The thought, however repugnant, at least must have occurred to Bennett that acreage reduction in Canada might be paid by the public treasury, if the result was in the national interest, in order to compensate producers for the loss of vitally needed income in the process of compliance. But in Mr. Wrong's intervention with Secretary Wallace in May of that year, and now again in September, the Canadian officials stressed that this was beyond the financial competence of Canada.

This did not deter the federal and provincial governments, however, from mounting a campaign of persuasion for voluntary acreage reduction which was pursued by an organized speaking campaign and the distribution of literature, to which McFarland contributed his enthusiastic support. As soon as the Honourable M. A. MacPherson, the Saskatchewan provincial treasurer, returned from the London wheat conference he stopped in Ottawa to consult with Mr. R. K. Finlayson, Bennett's principal secretary, on the preparation of a pamphlet which could be used in the publicity campaign. For this purpose, the two were assisted by Mr. Clive B. Davidson, grain statistician at the dominion bureau of statistics, who did much of the writing and organization of the background material for the pamphlet entitled *The World Wheat Problem and the London Agreement*, which was distributed directly to producers. Davidson had done such a good job in preparing the pamphlet that McFarland obtained his secondment from the bureau, and for the next six months until the 1934 crop was seeded, Davidson remained in western Canada at the disposal of the provincial governments which pursued the campaign.

[9]*The London Wheat Agreement, loc. cit.*, pp. 52-53.

The other aspect of these developments was the need of provision for enforcement, if necessary, of the Canadian export quota of 200 million bushels. The arrangements made in that connection are reviewed later in this chapter. Apart from Canada, the United States had introduced its wheat acreage allotment program. In doing so, Secretary Wallace declared that the program was in fulfillment of the United States obligation under the international wheat agreement to reduce acreage by 15 percent. The program provided bonus payments to producers who signed contracts for reduction compliance; by December, 1933, the agricultural adjustment administration had paid out $135,000,000 to producers who co-operated in the scheme. In speeches made by American officials promoting the acreage reduction campaign, the statement was repeated that both Canada and the United States were committed under the international agreement to the reduction of acreage by 15 percent. This caused the Canadian officials some concern as Robertson recorded:

> There is one feature of Canada's position under the agreement which should be emphasized. We have never admitted that our obligations under the wheat agreement constitute a specific promise to reduce our acreage by 15 percent. When the United States desired to insert an Annex to the Exporters' Agreement by which Canada would undertake this specific obligation we objected. We also attempted to make it clear in September last to the authorities in Washington, in view of statements emanating from United States officials, that Canada had definitely promised to reduce acreage, that we had made no such promise. During these conversations the American officials seemed to agree that wheat acreage reduction as such was not feasible in respect to Canada but since that time more than one statement has emanated from official sources in Washington reiterating that, while Australia and Argentina had agreed to reduce exports, Canada and the United States had agreed to reduce acreage. In any public statement made by the Canadian Government or in any publication of the Exporters' Agreement this point should be cleared up.
>
> It should be emphasized that the single positive undertaking assumed by the four overseas countries is that they will severally regulate their exports of wheat during the duration of the agreement, in accordance with the figures agreed upon. The operative undertaking is to restrict exports. Implicit in this is the necessity of reducing production but it is important to distinguish between the formal obligation acknowledged in the International Agreement and the collateral measures of domestic policy which may have to be taken as a consequence of implementing that Agreement.[10]

In Argentina and Australia, whose governments had clearly established that they had assumed no direct commitment to reduce acreage, there was some reduction nevertheless. In Canada, because of the constitutional problem, the federal and the three Provincial governments jointly watched the 1934 crop situation and planned a survey of acreage intentions but, in the end, no direct action regarding acreage became necessary. The campaign of persuasion, and other disincentives to plant wheat such as drought and grasshoppers were sufficient to keep the Canadian position in line. As Professor Davis calculated, sown acreage for the 1934 harvests was

[10]*Ibid.*, pp. 86-87.

reduced from the base average of 1931-33 by 8.2 percent in the United States, 9.4 percent in Canada, 5.0 percent in Argentina and 14.5 percent in Australia. Consistently with the formula upon which the calculations were made in the June 30 draft, base production for each country was calculated on the average 1931-33 acreage times the ten-year average yield for each country. From each base, 1934 production showed a reduction of 39 percent in the United States and Canada, 1 percent in Argentina and 29 percent in Australia.[11] Thus, for the assumption in article 2 of the agreement that production would be reduced, there was ample compliance in Australia, Canada and the United States. Unlike the crops in these countries, the Argentine crop yielded well in 1934 and there had been less of a campaign to reduce acreage. Much of the difficulty with Argentina for the life of the agreement lay in the fact that the Argentine minister of agriculture, Sr. Antonio de Tomaso, who had taken the early initiative in commending an international wheat agreement to the preparatory commission of the world economic conference, died in August, 1933, and his successor, Ing. Luis Duhau, represented a group in Argentina which was not in sympathy with the objectives of the agreement.[12] Moreover, because of limited storage capacity of their elevators, the Argentine government had no effective means of enforcing compliance with the limitation imposed by its export quota commitment.

Although, with the exception of Argentina, the reduction in 1934 production was more than ample for compliance with the export quota commitments under the agreement, the tragedy was that the emphasis upon reduction of production had been misplaced. One needs only to glance at Chart 19:1 to see the extent to which production fell below normal in Canada in the years 1933 to 1937 and how quickly drought and rust eliminated the burdensome Canadian and world carryovers of wheat over which McFarland had been so concerned. By August, 1934, when a second drought-stricken crop was about to be harvested, McFarland acknowledged that concern about overproduction was no longer necessary. What was vitally needed was an improvement in farm income and the restriction of production, whether naturally or artifically contrived, did not contribute toward that end.[13]

In the United States, the position became even more salutary. In reflection of the acreage reduction campaign and the drought in that country, production fell below the amount necessary to cover domestic requirements. For two crop-years, 1934-35 and 1935-36, the United States wheat position was on a net import basis. Although there was some apprehension over the marketing of the higher yielding 1938 crop, the question of overproduction did not seriously arise again until Canada was cut off from its export markets in continental Europe during the second world war.

[11]J. S Davis, *Wheat and the AAA*, p. 335.

[12]*Ibid.,* p. 319.

[13]Normally the dramatic decline in production would have caused some upward pressure on prices. The slump in wheat prices during that same period (see chart 19:2) reflected the overriding effect of worldwide depression in incomes and, consequently, demand.

CHART 19:1
CANADIAN PRODUCTION, EXPORTS AND CARRYOVER OF WHEAT BY CROP YEARS, 1928-29 TO 1949-50
(Million bushels)

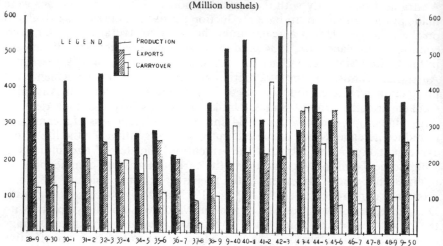

SOURCE: *Statistics Canada and Annual Reports of the Canadian Wheat Board.* Exports include wheat and wheat flour equivalent.

CHART 19:2
MONTHLY AVERAGE CASH PRICES OF NO. 1 NORTHERN WHEAT, IN STORE FORT WILLIAM - PORT ARTHUR, BY CROP YEARS, 1928-29 TO 1949-50
(Canadian cents per bushel)

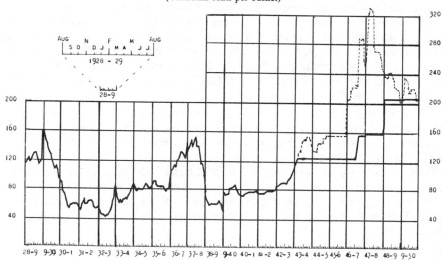

SOURCE: *Statistics Canada* and *Annual Reports of the Canadian Wheat Board.* The solid line represents domestic and all export prices up to September 1943, when wheat futures trading was terminated. Thereafter the solid line represents domestic prices. The dotted line denotes the Canadian Wheat Board's Class II prices at which wheat was sold for export, with the following exceptions: (A) Wheat delivered to Allied Governments as mutual aid, (B) Wheat sold to Britain under the terms of the Canadian-United Kingdom Agreement, 1946/47 - 1949/50, and (C) Wheat sold to countries under terms of the International Wheat Agreement in 1949/50.

CANADIAN IMPLEMENTATION OF THE EXPORT QUOTA

The Canadian undertaking was to export not more than 200 million bushels of wheat in the 1933-34 crop year. When he made this commitment, Bennett was uncertain about the constitutional means of implementation, and after he returned to Ottawa he referred the question to his law officers. They advised that there should be sufficient authority within the proposed natural products marketing act for the federal government to license wheat exports, which would obviate the need for separate legislation. The Australian government had already enacted an export licensing system. The matter was further eased for the federal government, however, at the dominion-provincial conference held in January, 1934, which Bennett called to consider the legal aspects of implementing the Canadian commitments under the wheat agreement. The provincial premiers had already shied away from the contemplation of legislation which would enforce compulsory restriction of acreage, but they found an acceptable alternative in proposed legislation which would authorize the provincial governments, if necessary, to place a limitation upon the amounts of wheat individual producers could deliver from farms. The proposed legislation for the restriction of deliveries to a rate consistent with the Canadian export quota would serve also as an indirect deterrent to production. Agreement was reached to proceed on this basis and in March, 1934, each of the three provincial governments enacted standby farm quota delivery legislation. As it turned out, the legislation did not have to be invoked because in the one year in which export quotas were operative, the anticipated shipments fell within the quota limit.

PRICE IMPLICATIONS OF THE EXPORT QUOTA SYSTEM

It was a matter of considerable disappointment to the negotiators of the first international wheat agreement that the operation of the export quota system failed to make any discernible contribution to the price-raising objectives of the agreement. In fact, prices eased in the early autumn of 1933. The conventional theory of an export quota system is that the matching of competing export offers with actual import demand eliminates the price-depressing effect of excessive competition which would otherwise have pressed an imbalanced surplus upon available demand. But there was no sign of price improvement and McFarland, who opposed the import quota system sponsored by the British at the imperial conference in 1930, was one of the first experts to detect the fallacy of a quota system, operating in isolation, as a price-raising force. As McFarland watched the market behavior during the first several weeks of the agreement, he was approached by Mr. L. C. Brouillette, president of the Saskatchewan wheat pool and also of the central selling agency, who was seeking support for the creation of a wheat board in Canada to administer the Canadian undertakings under the agreement. At the time, McFarland was firmly opposed to the creation of a board, but he recognized that the quota mechanism would have to be bolstered in order to become effective, and he pondered the possibility of wheat boards in all four of the major exporting countries which could work in collaboration to support prices. In this vein, he wrote to Mr. Andrew Cairns, the newly-appointed secretary of the wheat advisory committee, on October 30, 1933:

... I do not know what you think of the London Agreement, although I have no doubt that you must be satisfied with it or you would not be on the Advisory Board, but I would say that so far as I am concerned, while it may (not) be a perfect arrangement, yet in my opinion an arrangement or any agreement that will result in reducing production, is justifiable, and if on no other grounds than the matter of securing a reduction of acreage and production of wheat, the Prime Minister of this country was certainly amply justified in forcing the Agreement through. ...

Watching the International market since the London Agreement, I fail to see how present open marketing system is going to result in any benefit to any of the exporting countries working under their quotas, namely; the Argentine, Australia, Russia, the Balkans, Canada and the United States of America. It is quite evident that if our market goes down five cents per bushel, other countries reduce their prices immediately to the same extent, and if we go up, they generally follow; in fact, some of the prices in some of these countries, at times, drop further than they do in this market, all of which would indicate that all these countries are competing against each other just as keenly as if there (were) no quota agreements whatsoever. Now so long as it works this way, I fail to see how these countries are going to benefit in any way by having agreed upon quotas. If the quotas were considered to be of any value, all these countries would expect to benefit to some extent by a better price, and each of them would be willing to withhold their wheat from the market until their competitors had got through forcing their quota upon unwilling buyers. Now what I am trying to lead up to is that I would like an opinion from you as to whether you think any of these countries are going to reap any benefit by having entered into quota agreements unless these same countries organize Government Wheat Boards so that the Boards of all these countries will be able to work together and in some measure, at least, cut out competition on their product.

There is an agitation in influential quarters in this country for the establishment of a Government Wheat Board. From my viewpoint I cannot see how a Government Wheat Board in Canada would result in any benefit to the country in the matter of price, unless this Canadian Board had a similar organization in the other countries with whom they could co-operate and work together. For instance, what chance would a Government Board in Canada have in reaching an understanding with the International exporting firms who handle the Argentine crop, and the same thing would apply to Australia and the United States. Have you thought of this matter and what conclusion have you arrived at? I would imagine it would be very discouraging to the Argentine farmer, after limiting his exports to 110 millions, if he finds at the end of the year that all these various wheats are competing with each other in the world's markets, and each one trying to see which can sell the cheapest, so that they can get the business, in just the same manner as they would if there was no quota whatsoever, and yet that is exactly what is being done.

I have been adverse to Government Wheat Boards, as you are probably aware, and I still am adverse to a Government Wheat Board in Canada, but since this London Agreement has given an allotment for export to each of these various countries, and since the basis of this Agreement is that it is desirous to raise the price, and importing countries have also subscribed to that desire, then surely it is up to the exporting countries to try to work out some plan whereby this object would have some chance of being accomplished, and while, as I have already stated, I have been adverse to a Wheat Board in Canada, yet I would be 100% in favor of it if the other countries agreed to adopt the same method, simply because I believe that is the only manner in which this country or any of the other countries can secure for themselves any benefit under the London Agreement.[14]

To McFarland's amazement, some months elapsed before Cairns replied to his pointed query. In the meantime, Cairns was preoccupied with his errands to Paris and Berlin, and with the prospects for negotiating a minimum price agreement which would have answered McFarland's price concern. McFarland was anxious to convince Bennett of the inadequacy of the quota provisions operating in isolation, and he sent him a copy of his letter to Cairns. On another occasion, when the minimum price proposals had become known, and after being interviewed by the Australian trade commissioner in Ottawa who was returning to Canberra, McFarland wrote to Bennett on December 12, 1933:

... I explained to him that in all probability the world export (price) level would be largely dictated by the importing miller in Europe and the importing miller in Europe is never satisfied unless he is buying wheat a little cheaper all the time, and that as buyers are so few as compared with the sellers of these times, it is a buyers market and the buyer is in the enviable position of having the sellers competing to see who can make the most attractive price in order to get the business. I explained to him that this system might be all okay in normal times, or it might be a reasonable procedure even in these times if there were not an agreement existing whereby the different countries have divided up the world's import requirements into quotas among the different exporters, of which his quota in Australia is 105,000,000 bushels, but in making this division among the different exporters, the members of the London Conference had found that there was more wheat, in fact, there was much more wheat available for export than 560 millions, and it was presumed that all or part of the different exporting countries might have more for export than was represented by the quota, in which event each country that did have more, would have what might be described as an unsaleable surplus, which they would have to get rid of in some manner. I described this unsaleable portion as a "corpse" and told him that so long as all these different exporting countries are strenuously competing from day to day for the available import orders in the market, it simply meant that the "corpse" would make the price for that portion of each country's supplies which were saleable abroad under the quota agreement, and that, therefore, the arrangement made by his Government, binding the exporter to purchase from the farmers in Australia at the world's export price, meant nothing more than the selling of such wheat on a basis of what the "corpse" might be worth. ...

It is clear to my mind that so long as the surplus countries have surpluses, and maintain surpluses by overproduction, each country is going to have a surplus problem on their hands, over and above the requirements of importing countries, for which no export sale can be effected, and unless the twenty-two countries who have signed the agreement in London can get together and agree that it is in the interests of all to place minimum prices from time to time on the quota from each country, then just so long will people like Jimmy Rank and other less powerful millers in the United Kingdom and Europe fix the price at which wheat will be worth. There can be no other outcome, and if we, for arguments sake, are going to produce more

[14]*Bennett Papers.*

wheat than our fair share of the export demand calls for, then so long are we going to have a problem of disposing of the unwanted surplus within our own borders, presumably at bankrupt prices, and until there is some international agreement, this unwanted left-over wheat is going to exert a very undue influence upon the price we secure for that portion of our production which is wanted abroad, and which is covered by our quota.

I hope I have made myself clear. I am not advocating a Government Wheat Board because I know the present system for the balance of this crop, can be adapted to the carrying out of any such arrangement that might be made with the other twenty-one countries. In the meantime, a real Wheat Board is in the lap of the Gods and the necessity or non-necessity depends upon the kind of weather which Providence distributes in the Crop Year 1934.[15]

Thereafter McFarland, as already mentioned, became an advocate of a minimum price system, however much he failed to persuade Bennett of its wisdom. Nevertheless, he continued to drive home his conviction about the inadequacy of export quotas in operation by themselves as he lectured the wheat advisory committee which met in Rome in April, 1934:

The founders of the London Wheat Agreement last August arrived at what appeared at that time a conservative estimate of import requirements, when they divided 560 millions between the various countries. As a matter of fact it was a reasonably close estimate.

The world's requirements were fixed at 560 millions, and from that limited supply the importers were presumed to have to draw their full requirements for the following 12 month period. Theoretically that was a close adjustment of supply to demand, and some people thought such a close adjustment would result in the maintenance of prices or possibly an advance. It did not, however, create an atmosphere of price confidence in the minds of the public, the merchants or the millers. It did not work as some people expected, and for the very good reason there was over 500 millions more wheat in excess of the quotas, and everyone was well aware of its existence. If that 560 millions had in reality been all the wheat available in the world for importers' requirements, there would most certainly have occurred a substantial advance.

The feature which was overlooked was the fact that everyone knew perfectly well there was nearly twice as much available as was distributed under the quota agreements. Everyone knew or suspected there would be no close adjustment or scarcity while there was an additional reserve of upwards of 500 millions, and of that extra quantity a very large percentage was uncontrolled by any government.[16]

RENEGOTIATION OF THE QUOTAS

It was noted earlier that the issue between Canada and the United States over the American quota, whether 45 or 47 million bushels, remained unsettled and, eventually, was not relevant. Similarly, the USSR quota was never established, although several attempts were made to reach an understanding. At the London conference, the other exporting countries had proposed a figure of 37 million bushels, to which the Russian delegate countered by insisting upon 75 millions. It was in this impasse that the decision was taken at the conference to leave the USSR quota open for further negotiation by the wheat advisory committee. At its first meeting on

[15]*Ibid.*
[16]*Ibid.*

September 16, 1933, the committee renewed the attempt. The American delegation stood by the 37 million bushel figure, but suggested that if world demand should exceed 560 million bushels, the USSR might share the excess with Canada and the United States by way of a supplementary quota up to a maximum of eight million bushels. The Canadian delegation, on instructions from Ottawa, took exception to this proposal on the ground that the major purpose of the agreement was to liquidate the abnormal surplus in North America, and offered as an alternative a supplementary quota to the USSR based on any deficiency of actual exports below the Australian and Danubian quotas. This was of no avail to the Russians, who stood by their figure of 75 million. Subsequently, two further attempts were made to reach agreement. In the latter one, on November 30, the American delegate proposed a figure of 45 million bushels, on the understanding that the last 8 million bushels would not be exported until after July 31, 1934, unless world demand exceeded the 560 million bushel estimate. By the end of 1933, the Russians had lowered their asking figure to 60 million bushels, but the remaining gap was never closed. USSR actual exports, however, created no embarrassment to the other exporters in that crop year.

The main issue, and the one which proved crucial to the life of the agreement, arose over the Argentine quota of 110 million bushels for the 1933-34 crop year. By January, 1934, an above-average crop came on the market, and it was painfully apparent that the Argentine government was taking no action to contain the movement within its quota. As already noted, the Argentine minister now responsible was out of sympathy with the philosophy of the agreement and thereafter the Argentine approach to the agreement was one of negotiation with the other exporting countries on an adjustment of its quota to a size within which it could operate without restraint. The Argentine government's first move in that regard was to apply to the wheat advisory committee for an increase of 40 million bushels in its 1933-34 quota, which would have allowed it to move the expected additional surplus from its January 1934 crop. Because of the problem with the Argentine quota, Bennett had despatched McFarland to attend the Rome meeting of the advisory committee. A series of telegrams, which McFarland exchanged with Bennett from Rome, recorded the attempt at renegotiation and the attitudes of the various governments thereto. After McFarland's first report on April 9, 1934, from Rome, Bennett cabled McFarland on April 10:

> Your telegram April 9th. Much perturbed by Argentina's demands for additional quota, which amount to attempt to capitalize her own failure to carry out agreement having adopted export policy inconsistent with quota agreed upon and broken market by selling at any price. If, however, you are convinced that new arrangement will improve situation and cause Argentina to cooperate loyally in carrying out agreement, we would concur in proposal to add 20 million bushels if it is surrounded by strict conditions as outlined in your telegram, as follows: (1) Argentina must accept Russian quota as agreed upon by other three exporters; (2) minimum price to prevent dumping; and (3) assurance that measures would be taken in regard to production. . . .[17]

McFarland's reply of April 14 reflected the dissatisfaction of the

[17] *Ibid.*

Argentine government with the agreement and, equally, the determination of the United States and Australian delegates to effect a compromise:

> Secret. No. 3. My telegram of the 9th of April and your reply, reference Argentine demands additional quota. Lebreton informs us that his Government cabled stating conditions . . . they would require additional quota not less than 40 million, adding that Government had lost faith in efficacy of Wheat Agreement which has not reduced stocks or raised prices. Although Argentine attitude uncompromising, United States, Australia and we agree that every effort should be made to effect compromise. United States and Australia cabling their Governments as to possibility of jointly negotiating on the following basis with Argentine.
>
> Increase of quota by 30 million, plus 10 million to be denatured but not counted in quota. 30 million to be repaid in one of two following ways:
>
> (a) Total of 30 million to be deducted from next year's quota supposing no extension of Wheat Agreement;
>
> (b) 15 million deducted next year's quota and 15 million the following year supposing one year extension.
>
> These 30 million to be found as follows, United States and Australia 12 million each, Canada 6 million. Following conditions to be attached to concessions. Acceptance of Russia quota and assurance that;
>
> (a) Measures will be taken to reduce production in conformity with undertaking governing exports quota;
>
> (b) Carry over July, 1935, will not be beyond normal;
>
> (c) Argentine will cooperate in general endeavour to stabilise prices; and
>
> (d) Argentine will not maintain internal prices so far above world level as to encouage expansion in production.
>
> Argentine fear that minimum agreement might raise prices to such an extent as to stimulate production. Situation appears serious but possible that Argentine may be seeking bargain. Please telegraph instructions.[18]

Bennett was critical of the performance of the other governments and was barely in a compromising mood as he instructed McFarland (on April 15) to use his best judgment:

> Your telegram No. 3, April 14, reference Argentina additional quota. These demands present much more difficult problem for Canada than for other exporting countries. Australia's present quota is excessive and postponement of 12 million bushels involves no sacrifice and may well be advantageous. I assume result of United States restriction policy in increasing winter wheat production by 140 million bushels leads Murphy to assume more sympathetic and benevolent attitude to Argentina.[19] Canada has been more injuriously affected than any other exporter in both price and quantity by Argentine failure to implement existing Agreement. Your knowledge of market conditions and consumption demand should enable you to conclude definitely whether we can afford to reduce quota by 6 million bushels. If conditions agreed to by Argentina are in your opinion of sufficient value to warrant reduction of our export quota for this year and of course if United States and Australia also agree, you should not hesitate to complete arrangement.[20]

---

[18]*Ibid.*

[19]Winter wheat production in the United States showed a small increase in 1934, offset by a larger decrease in spring wheat production.

[20]*Bennett Papers.*

McFarland reported again, on April 17 on the defensive position taken by the Argentine government, as the other delegates countered with a proposal for diplomatic representations:

Secret. No. 5. My telegram 14th April, No. 3. Cairns has informed the United Kingdom, Australian and Canadian delegates that Beyro asked to have a talk with him obviously to communicate to us afterwards substance of conversation. With telegram before him received by Le Breton from the Minister of Agriculture, Argentine, Beyro stated *inter alia,*

(a) Argentine Government fully prepared to accept full consequences of determination export additional 40 million;

(b) United States and Canada have not carried out 15% acreage reduction and Argentina signed Wheat Agreement on this understanding;

(c) United States should cease uneconomical growing of wheat;

(d) Argentina does not want any further commitments in the way of international wheat agreement;

(e) Argentine Government cannot restrict exports, their public opinion being against it.

Obvious from above Argentina is seeking excuse to withdraw from Agreement. On the other hand Murphy states that in personal talk with Le Breton latter seemed hopeful of softening his Government's attitude. McDougall and we believe diplomatic intervention Buenos Aires by British and United States Ambassadors more likely to produce results than through Le Breton and Minister of Agriculture's medium. Your telegram of the 15th April received in reply to our telegram No. 3. Will report developments.[21]

Bennett replied on the same date, and strove to put the Canadian record in the clear:

... On the whole, reports indicate that there will be very substantial reduction of acreage through natural causes and control by government of financial assistance. Bureau of Statistics has evidence that there will also be planned reduction as a result of propaganda which is having effect. Total wheat acreage reduction will be large and 15% objective may be exceeded. While above details are for your own information, I feel that Committee, especially Argentine, should be made aware extent of reduction, with emphasis being placed on the steps our governments have taken and on fact that, with conditions being as indicated above, further governmental steps not necessary thus far though full power available for supplementary action if needed. We are carrying out the obligations of the Wheat Agreement in respect to reduction of production, though never at any time did we accept a specific commitment to reduce acreage by any stated percentage. We cannot, therefore, permit Argentine to contend that their failure to live up to Agreement is justified by the fact that Canada has not carried out a 15% acreage reduction. No one can say yet that 15% acreage reduction will not be, in fact, achieved. These facts should be made clear to Argentine delegates and others. ...[22]

The Rome conference adjourned on April 17, 1934, and the quota negotiations were pursued thereafter in London. McFarland cabled on April 26:

No. 87. Secret. After conferring at Canada House, McDougall, Australia, has sent the following telegram to his Prime Minister, Begins:

Have had preliminary discussions about Argentine with United Kingdom officials and with the High Commissioner for Canada, McFarland and

[21]*Ibid.*
[22]*Ibid.*

Vanier. United Kingdom Government appears to take serious view of threatened Argentine action but in order to place the matter on proper basis suggest you should cable to United Kingdom Government stressing disastrous effect of Argentine breach of Wheat Agreement on prices and on the whole idea of international collaboration and asking whether the United Kingdom Government prepared to instruct the British Ambassador at Buenos Aires to make joint representations on behalf of the United Kingdom, Canada and Australian Governments. Your telegram might also suggest that if such representations were made in collaboration with the United States of America effect would be markedly increased. Your telegram might further mention desirability of discussions of situation between the United Kingdom, United States, Canada and Australia before overseas exporting countries renew discussions with Argentine about 4th May. High Commissioner for Canada cabling on similar lines to Ottawa. Ends.

High Commissioner for Canada entirely concurs in our view that action along the lines suggested might be extemely helpful. Please advise. McFarland sailing "Empress of Australia", Saturday.[23]

The upshot was an intervention by the British government through foreign office instruction to the British ambassador in Argentina, which was then the only official channel for Canada and Australia with the Argentine government. On this occasion, the British ambassador made the representations on behalf of his own government as well. On May 12, 1934, the British secretary of state for dominion affairs communicated the Argentine government's reply:

Confidential. My telegram of the 3rd May, No. 30. Attitude of Argentine to International Wheat Agreement. Following reply has been received from His Majesty's representative at Buenos Aires, Begins:

Argentine Government's reply gives detailed reasons for their attitude in regard to Agreement of 1933 and their objection to world minimum price pact.

As regards first, Argentine Government maintains that neither the United States nor Canada have fulfilled their undertakings in connection with reduction of acreage. The United States' and Canada's conditions for agreeing to Argentine Government's request for an increase in her quota for this year would moreover entail a probable reduction by 41 per cent of her forthcoming sowing which would constitute an overwhelming sacrifice.

Argentine Government strongly object to minimum price pact but state they are prepared to make every effort to achieve a reduction of ten to fifteen per cent in forthcoming wheat sowing by encouraging maize and linseed cultivation and reducing fixed prices given for wheat.

Note ends with an expression of Argentine Government's determination to contribute as far as possible to a satisfactory agreement in London. Ends.[24]

Bennett wired his reaction to Ferguson on May 12:

Your telegram 105. Suggest statement to United Kingdom representatives in answer to Argentine reply should be, so far as Canada is concerned, along following lines.

Sole formal undertaking of four wheat exporting countries as embodied in London Wheat Agreement is to regulate exports within accepted quotas. Canada's export figures show she is living up to this undertaking. We agree, however, that the acceptance of a wheat production figure for 1934-35 of 385 million bushels made up of export quota of 268 million plus domestic consumption 117 million, which is based upon a 15% reduction of production, necessitates efforts by this country to reduce acreage to keep production within that figure. Effective steps toward this end have already been taken. Our estimates of wheat acreage for current season show a reduction over average for base period of 2,753,743 acres, or 10.4%, which reduction will in all probability be increased on basis of later returns. Latest report of crop conditions indicates an average yield which will be low enough to bring our total production figure well below 385 million bushels. In case crop conditions improve, however, and it appears that production may be above that figure, recourse will be had to legislation passed by the governments of the three Prairie Provinces which give them ample power to do all such acts as may be necessary and requisite to bring production of wheat into proper alignment with quota applicable to this country under Wheat Agreement. We feel, therefore, that this country has most amply and satisfactorily carried out its obligations under the Wheat Agreement itself and under the Note of Agreement of the overseas exporters by which we promised to reduce production 15%. This stands out in sharp contrast to Argentine attitude towards her obligations under the Agreement. We are at a loss to understand Argentine insistence on 40 million bushel additional quota. Our information is that Argentine could not sell that amount during current year even under present conditions, to say nothing of conditions which would exist if her policy broke the Wheat Agreement and forced Canada into competitive selling. We appreciate impossibility of Argentine reducing acreage by anything like 41%, but feel that if she is sincere in her determination to contribute to a satisfactory agreement she should accept as a generous concession a 30 million additional quota on the following conditions:

(a) Reduction of 10 to 15% in wheat acreage; (b) Acceptance of Russian quota; (c) Abandonment or reduction of fixed prices on wheat; (d) An undertaking to market the additional quota in such a way as to not unduly depress prices; (e) The question of 1934-35 export quotas to be decided at June meeting of Wheat Advisory Committee. You will note these conditions are less stringent than those outlined in Canadian telegram No. 3, April 14, from Rome.

If Argentine refuses above conditions, difficult to prevent Wheat Agreement from collapsing with disastrous results for all exporting countries including Argentine. Responsibility for this would be placed squarely on her shoulders.[25]

Bennett's instructions were sufficient authority to Ferguson to proceed in support of his American and Australian colleagues with further negotiations with the Argentine representative. As a result, Mr. R. W. Bingham, American ambassador to Britain and the Australian and Canadian high commissioners met with Dr. Tomas Le Breton, the Argentine ambassador in London. The representations made orally at this May meeting were repeated in a letter the United States minister to Latvia handed to Le Breton on May 15. Mr. J. V. A. McMurray was Mr. Bingham's alternate as chairman of the wheat advisory committee. Although conciliatory in tone, the letter repeated that the additional quota of 40 million bushels Argentina was seeking was beyond her export capability in the remainder of the 1933-34 crop season. In its place the other representatives proposed a transfer of 30 millions for the current crop year, but repayable from the

[25] *Ibid.*

Argentine quota in the following crop year, although the wheat advisory committee was prepared to reconsider the repayable amount if that figure placed too great a burden on the Argentine capacity to reduce acreage for the next harvest consistently with the adjusted quota. When these representations drew no positive response, Bennett's apprehension grew that the agreement was worthless. On May 21, 1934, he wrote to McFarland who was by now back in Winnipeg:

... In the cable which I sent Friday, I stressed the necessity for some improvement in Argentine prices, but I suspect that may be very difficult, if not impossible. The real truth is that the Wheat Agreement is of no value at all so long as Argentine pursues her present course of selling wheat at ruinous prices. Do you think it makes any difference whether the Agreement lasts or not, under existing conditions? Giving up some of our quota might do some good for the moment but it will do no good unless we have a decent price structure. We will probably know something further about the matter during the next few days.[26]

McFarland concurred in Bennett's view as he replied on May 26:

Referring to yours of the 21st re Argentine. I also have copies of cablegrams, under separate cover, which I will destroy as per your instructions. I am glad to have these to look over.

It seems quite evident, having regard to all the pressure which has been brought to bear on the Government of that country, that there must be something in their political situation which is overwhelming them. I presume ... that the Government simply cannot pursue the policy which they might themselves consider best for the country, and fortunately, or unfortunately, crop deterioration in other parts of the world are contriving to make it possible for the Argentine to force an extra quantity of wheat on to the market by selling at slaughter prices. If it had occurred that crop prospects were normally good in the Northern Hemisphere at this time, then I would say, without fear of contradiction, that the Argentine could not have sold the extra 40 millions of wheat except at a give-away price. Furthermore, even with the bad prospects which have developed in the last few weeks, I also feel quite sure that if they go ahead and force their 30 million bushels on importing countries in the next ten weeks, they will take relatively ruinous prices for their product.

There can be no doubt that their action is injuring Canada, and other exporting countries at the present time. Just how much they have injured this country would be impossible to even estimate, but there is no doubt if their wheat was selling at some reasonable price, our wheat would have been meeting with a good demand right along for the past ten days, whereas the demand has been what you would call "very indifferent". ...

You asked me a question, namely; "Whether I think it makes any difference if the Agreement lasts or not under existing conditions?" My candid opinion is that unless the Argentine give some positive assurance that they are not going to flood the importing markets with a lot of unwanted wheat at sacrifice prices, and unless they can give reasonable assurances that they are going to hold the price of their wheat up to a reasonable figure during the next few months when they are disposing of their surplus, then I would say, in the absence of these assurances, you might just as well let the Agreement go by the boards, and probably the sooner that is done, the sooner would the Argentine be back asking to have the Agreement renewed.

[26] *Ibid.*

I would not favour disbanding the Advisory Committee—I think they should continue in existence, but their members should be allowed to pursue their own sweet will until such time as the South American roughrider comes back into the fold, if ever. Personally I think it would be just mockery to pretend that the Agreement was working unless the Argentine are doing something reasonable in the matter of controlling their sales and prices. If everyone knows the Agreement is suspended until further notice, then each country will have a chance to do whatever they think is best in their own interests. . . .

It is certain that Australia and Argentine made the best deal of any of the countries when they got their quotas fixed definitely for the two year period. If world's crops had been good, then Canada and the United States would have found themselves in a very difficult situation for the season 1934-35. For these reasons I should not be particular if the Agreement were suspended; in fact I should think it should be suspended unless the Argentine bind themselves to carry out the provisions as outlined in the cables between London and Ottawa recently.

PS

Wheat agreement would be better suspended. If and when Argentine comes back we might get a better deal for 1934-35. The quota in 1933-34 was fair, but 1934-35 did not look very good.[27]

While the representatives of the three exporting countries still awaited a reply to their representations from the Argentine ambassador, the Americans and Canadians turned to bilateral consultations on the North American side. McFarland wrote to Bennett on May 29:

I acknowledge my conversations with you this morning. There is no doubt the Department of Agriculture at Washington has reason to adopt a very liberal-minded attitude towards the requests of the Argentine for enlargement in their quota this year, and probably to some extent for next year. This, because of the fact that their wheat problem, so far as it is humanly possible to judge it, has been solved by the most disastrous drouth and heat wave in the history of the North American Continent. I therefore ventured to suggest to you, that having regard to that position in the United States, it would be reasonable to suggest to them that they should renounce any quota for export from the United States of America in 1934-35. If they did that then this country would have a perfectly justifiable economic and political reason for assuming a very liberal attitude towards Argentine, and thus maintain the integrity of the London Agreement. . . .[28]

McFarland's hopes for agreement were revived when a report reached Bennett from London that the Argentine government had responded to McMurray's letter of May 15. McFarland wrote Bennett on June 9, 1934:

I confirm our telephone conversation this morning, from which I understand that the Argentine have virtually agreed to all the conditions suggested by the Committee, except that they want a total increase in their two year quota of 36 million bushels but, in consideration of that, I infer from our conversation that they will undertake to reduce their acreage this year, 1934, by 15%, and to adjust their carryover as at August 1st, 1935. Now I consider this is very good news indeed. The other countries can far far better afford now to give them 36 million bushels increase than we could have thought of giving them a million bushel increase six or eight weeks ago, and while it is undoubtedly unfair to the rest of us that they should demand this increase, yet in view of the fact

[27] *Ibid.*
[28] *Ibid.*

that there has been a great change in the prospective possible exports from various countries in the last six weeks, should make it much easier for all the countries to accede to their demand.[29]

But the apparent agreement was ephemeral, as McFarland wrote again to Bennett on June 25:

> I had a long distance call today from Dr. Ezekiel of the Agricultural Department of the Washington Government. ... It was a little difficult to catch all his words over the telephone. However, I inferred from the conversation that they are making one last effort to hold Argentine in the Agreement. He was anxious to know whether I thought Canada was at all likely to export the full amount of 200 million bushels. I told him just as I mentioned to you last week over the 'phone, that I did not believe there was any likelihood of it and that so far as I could see, the giving of 9 million bushels to Argentine from our quota this year would make no difference. I might say that he seemed rather dubious about Argentine agreeing to anything at the present moment, but he thought it was probably worthwhile to let them go with a free hand if they wanted to until a meeting of the Advisory Committee in London in August. He asked me what I thought about entering into a price war in the event of Argentine not agreeing to some compromise at the present time. I told him I could see no advantage to any country to start in with a price war at this time. He was in perfect accord with that sentiment. ... [30]

Bennett agreed that a price war made nonsense. In July, McFarland and Dr. H. C. Grant, a University of Manitoba professor of economics who had worked on the acreage reduction campaign, made a trip to Minneapolis to confer with a group which included Mr. Frederick E. Murphy and Dr. Mordecai Ezekiel. McFarland reported to Bennett by letter on July 21:

> I returned from Minneapolis on Thursday. We had quite an interesting and I would say, satisfactory conference. One thing which impresses me with our American friends is their desire to work with Canada and to understand our Canadian problem as it affects wheat. Of course, as you are aware, the Agricultural Department at Washington and all its officials could realize quite fully that the short crops this year throughout the Northern Hemisphere, together with the prospective poor crop in Australia, has completely changed the immediate world's picture for the next twelve months. On the other hand they still believe, and I think we all believe, that the one feature which we must continue to work upon is the matter of seeded acreage in the various countries, because none of us are prepared to admit that this great American plain is going to go back to the desert. We feel that the moisture conditions will change, and when they do change production on our present acreages will again re-create our old problem, so that the one feature which was stressed in Minneapolis was the one of acreage control, and that will be the chief issue at the London meeting in August.
>
> Let me say, however, that they do not expect Canada to reduce her acreage more than 15%, but they do think it is important that we should continue to maintain that 15% reduction for the coming year. On the other hand they have a problem of their own as to what they should do owing to the policy which has been pursued by the Argentine. They almost feel inclined to drop the plan of reducing their winter wheat acreage this fall, and let the farmers go ahead and use their own judgment as to what they should seed. Dr. Grant and I urged them that it would be fatal for them not to pursue their policy into the

[29] *Ibid.*
[30] *Ibid.*

next year, and I do not believe there is any doubt but that they will pursue it providing any satisfactory results are attained at the conference in London in August. However, the difficulty with them is that their winter wheat seeding must start late in August and throughout September, and their policy cannot be unduly delayed on account of waiting for the results of the London meeting in August. . . .

The following suggestions were put forth to be considered at the London meeting:

1. To continue the Wheat Advisory Committee in its present form, but to abandon all commitments with respect to export quotas and acreage reduction for the crop year 1935-36.

2. To extend the wheat agreement for one or more additional years beginning August 1, 1935, with a definite obligation on the part of Argentina either to

(a) reduce its acreage by 15% for the crop year of 1935-36, or

(b) in the event it has actually achieved a reduction of 15% or more for 1934-35 to maintain the acreage at the achieved level for 1935-36.

3. To abandon all commitments with respect to acreage reduction and to substitute therefor a more flexible system of export quotas, possibly on a quarterly basis.

4. In combination with either number 2 or 3 above to secure from Argentina a commitment with respect to minimum export prices.

I may say that I took the view that if the London Conference should decide upon establishing quotas for the coming crop year the quotas might be based in such a manner as would give Canada and Argentina a fair break in cleaning up their surplus stocks: That is to say, that it being admitted that the normal Canadian carryover is, say, 50 million bushels at August 1st, and the normal Australian carryover 40 million, and the normal American carryover 125 million, and the normal Argentine carryover 50 to 60 million, then the quotas should be so arranged as to not permit any of these surplus producing countries to reduce their stocks lower than their normal carryovers, until such time as Canada and the Argentine had got their carryovers down to normal. I made the statement that any quota arrangements for the coming year be so based in such a way as to prevent other surplus producing countries shipping out their last bushel of wheat while Canada and the Argentina, and Canada in particular, had not succeeded in reducing theirs to normal, would be manifestly unfair, and I would prefer to have no quotas whatsoever, because I felt that Providence, having so reduced the world's production, it was only fair that all countries should be permitted as nearly as possible to reduce their surplus stocks to normal proportions as at August 1st, 1935, thus giving each country a chance to start from scratch and then if any country got into trouble from there on by over-production it would be their responsibility. I may say that they all agreed with this view. They thought it was absolutely fair to view quotas from that angle.

The view was also taken that if it were at all possible to continue the Wheat Advisory Committee it should be done, in the belief that it will be needed at a future time, although as far as the next crop year is concerned I do not believe it is needed at all, because I think the crop disaster is such that everybody will be able to clean up their surplus stocks without any agreement. Besides, if we can get the Argentina educated to co-operate with other countries, it would be all to the good. . . .

Dr. Ezekiel does not intend going to the London meeting as he thinks he can be of more service at the end of the cable in Washington, and the Americans will be represented by Mr. MacMurray, Mr. Bingham and Mr.

Steere. I may say that the Washington representatives still have hopes that the Argentina will eventually line up in some manner. They admit that we may have to give way to them to the extent of only asking them to reduce their acreage 10% instead of 15%, and after all is said and done we must remember that Australia and Canada were the great offenders in the matter of acreage extension and the Argentina were only minor offenders, so that they have some grounds for their stubborn attitude in that respect at least, although we cannot forgive them for their policy of ruining the world's price structure by slaughtering their wheat and continuing to do so even up to the present time. That, however, may be to their detriment only, because of the crop failures throughout the world. . . .[31]

Because the quota negotiations were crucial to a continuation of the agreement, Bennett insisted that McFarland attend the August 14, 1934, meeting of the wheat advisory committee in London. Although that meeting extended over several days, no progress could be made on the revision of export quotas for 1934-35. As no agreement had been reached on the supplementary quota for Argentina in the 1933-34 crop year just ended, that country was technically in breach of its quota commitment. All that the August meeting of the advisory committee could accomplish was to agree upon a quota holiday for the 1934-35 crop year, in the light of the North American crop disaster, and pending the next session of the committee which was invited to meet in Budapest that November. By now, Bennett was so disillusioned over the agreement that he questioned the need to have a Canadian representative attend. But McFarland persuaded Bennett to send Mr. C. B. Davidson, who had done an outstanding job on behalf of the provincial governments in the campaign for voluntary acreage reduction. The agreement was slowly grinding to a halt, and Davis summarized the terminal proceedings:

When the advisory committee assembled in Budapest late in November, however, world wheat prices had slumped instead of continuing to advance. . . . Crops of importing countries were estimated higher than during the summer; and with large carry-overs in continental Europe, the prospects were that her imports in 1934-35 would not much exceed the very low imports on 1933-34. All recognized that a material reduction in world surplus carry-over, not its elimination, was the most that could reasonably be hoped for, as the committee's secretariat had forecast in August. Hence earnest efforts were made to reach not only export quotas for 1934-35, but also agreement on restricting acreage for 1935 to the level of 1934, perfecting the export arrangement in important details so as to make it more flexible and workable, and extending the agreement for two more years. Substantial progress toward general agreement was reached, but again Argentina held back. Her representatives refused to accept the draft proposal for 1935 acreage limitation, on the ground that the basis suggested was unfair to his country, and rejected the proposed export quotas on the ground that acreage reduction had failed in 1934. Consequently, decisions on other points had to be deferred. Compromises had not been worked out when the session ended on December 1.

When representatives of the four overseas exporting countries next met, in London on March 6, 1935, Argentina's position was unchanged. Thus the agreement remains virtually inoperative in 1934-35 and prospects for extending the present agreement are negligible. The wheat advisory committee and its secretariat are, however, being continued.[32]

When the end came, McFarland confided that he never had been in favor of export quotas. But Bennett had every reason for disappointment in the demise of his last major effort to negotiate abroad on behalf of the western wheat producer. As the agreement broke down, Canadian and United States authorities inevitably turned toward introspection on who shared the blame. Inevitably, Argentina was identified as the main culprit, but Canada's share of the responsibility did not escape question in Davis's summarization:

> Since Argentina faced the dilemma of exceeding her quota unless other countries conceded her a larger one, her refusal to accede to various proposals seemed to put on her the onus of failure to reach agreement. But Canada, with huge stocks to dispose of, was reluctant to make the full concessions that Argentine representatives demanded, especially in view of Argentina's unwillingness to give assurances of "realistic" co-operation. Effectual adoption of each fresh proposal required substantial unanimity among representatives of several countries, each of whom was compelled to consider not only its special interests but public sentiment at home. While a close approach to unanimity was reached repeatedly, the obstacles proved too great to be surmounted.[33]

Now that the documentary evidence is available, there is ample support to be found in the Canadian messages already quoted that Bennett was very alert to the Canadian interests which were affected by Argentina's abnormal quota demands. Bennett also was sharply critical at times of American and Australian compliance with their obligations under the agreement. But in none of the correspondence is there evidence that Bennett obstructed negotiations with Argentina; instead he persistently kept the door open with concessions and related conditions in the hope that Argentina would come into line. Bennett regarded the agreement primarily as a device for the liquidation of the North American surpluses, and any accommodation to other countries which countered that accomplishment appeared to him to be defeating the main object of the agreement. When he became painfully aware that this objective was not being achieved, he lost interest.

Although Cairns worked valiantly in the advisory committee meetings held in the early months of 1935 to salvage an operating agreement, the confidence of the major participants in reaching a workable arrangement had, by then, been thoroughly eroded. In the end, the only agreement attainable was to continue the wheat advisory committee as a body for consultation among member goverments, and for the dissemination of wheat information. It was through the initiative of that committee that further attempts to negotiate an international agreement were revived in 1939 and again in 1947.

---

[32] J. S. Davis, *op. cit.*, pp. 342-343.
[33] *Ibid.*

20

SEARCH AT HOME: PRICE SUPPORT

Throughout the period in which the prime minister had pursued his quest for a wheat policy abroad, he was simultaneously preoccupied, however reluctantly, by his search for a policy at home. On the domestic side, Bennett's two most important policy decisions in the earlier years of his administration were his guarantee, on behalf of the federal government, of the bank loans on the 1930 pool account and subsequent authorization to the banks to finance McFarland's purchases of futures to support the price of wheat. In fact, what started out as an undertaking to insure the orderly marketing of wheat delivered to the 1930 pool gradually evolved into a total price-support operation. The federal government's guarantee in respect of the 1930 pool account had been given not merely as a gesture to salvage the pools, but to forestall the complete collapse of the western economy. This latter necessity was stressed in the representations the three premiers made to the federal government in November, 1930, and it prompted the government's market support operations over the next four and a half years. For a clear understanding of the total support operations it is useful, however, to identify the central selling agency's separate accounts relating to the unsold balances of deliveries from the 1928, 1929 and 1930 crops and to the special option account which represented the purchase and holding of wheat futures unrelated to the disposition of the unsold stocks from those crops.

1930 POOL ACCOUNT

Although, in February, 1930, the provincial governments had guaranteed the bank loans on the unsold balances in the 1928 and 1929 pool accounts, it will be recalled that the initial arrangements for handling the 1930 crop had been made between the central selling agency and the banks without any government guarantee. That autumn the banks not only dictated the level of the pools' initial payments but they took a direct interest in the progress of their wheat sales. For one thing, the central selling agency was required to apportion sales among the 1928, 1929 and 1930 accounts, because the provincial governments had a financial stake in the liquidation of the 1928 and 1929 accounts, whereas the banks and pools alone were interested in the disposal of the 1930 account. Quite apart from this distinction, the central selling agency had to contend with a declining market, whichever crop they tried to sell.

To appreciate the agency's dilemma, one needs to understand the hedging system normally employed by the trade when the wheat futures market operated. As already mentioned, the line elevator companies and United Grain Growers Limited kept all their stocks of cash wheat protected against price changes by the sale of an equal quantity of wheat futures. The banks required the borrowing companies to take this precaution. On the other hand, the shippers, exporters and mills were selling wheat and flour to importers or for domestic consumption. Whenever they made sales to their customers, they also hedged their transactions by making offsetting purchases of wheat futures. As these companies bought cash wheat to fill their sales contracts, they paid for it by giving futures in exchange. In trade parlance, the elevator companies "took back the options" in exchange for cash wheat. In turn, the line elevator companies surrendered their "long" futures to the exchange clearing association to cancel out their holdings of "short" contracts which had been covering the cash wheat they had just sold.

The central selling agency's position was different by virtue of the fact that the pools did not hedge the wheat delivered to them by producers. But to conform with the customary practice of "taking back the options" from the exporters and mills as they sold cash wheat, the agency acquired a temporary "long" position in wheat futures which they could and normally did dispose of by selling the futures to buyers in the pit.

In the autumn of 1930, however, there were almost no speculators to provide liquidity to the market, and the central selling agency found that in selling futures to complete its cash sales transactions, it was simply forcing down futures prices. The agency thereupon arranged with the banks to finance the temporary holding of its futures until such time as the market could absorb them, hopefully, without lowering the price. By mid-November, the agency had acquired a long position of 15 million bushels in futures. It should be noted, in passing, that this was an embryonic price-support operation of the type McFarland adopted as soon as he took charge of the agency's selling policy. But in mid-November, it was the banks' immediate anxiety over the agency's accumulation of wheat futures which prompted their representations to the federal government. As they awaited the appointment of a general manager acceptable to them and a decision on the guarantee, the banks insisted that the agency's position in futures be liquidated. Accordingly, the 15 millions of futures were sold by the end of November, despite the consequent price decline.

As of November 30, the day after McFarland's appointment, the central agency had on hand cash wheat stocks of 21, 229,902 bushels from the 1928 and 1929 crops, and 42,047,836 bushels from the 1930 crop. The provincial governments had guaranteed the bank loans on the stocks of 1928 and 1929 crop wheat which were segregated in various elevator positions and their ultimate disposal depended upon the opportunity for sale from those positions. By July 31, 1931, these stocks had all been disposed of, and the ultimate liability of the provincial governments to the banks was thereby determined. At that stage, the federal government's liability was confined to the wheat and coarse grains delivered to the ports from the 1930 crop. The unsold balance of 42,047,836 bushels as McFarland took charge had grown by July 31, 1931, to 76,738,000 bushels. From that date forward, the federal government also guaranteed the loans on the small wheat and coarse grain pools which continued to be operated. In the main, however, commencing in 1931, the three provincial pools bought grain outright from producers in the same fashion as the line companies and United grain growers and they also hedged their purchases.

As just mentioned, the federal government started off in December, 1930, with an unsold balance from the 1930 crop which grew to 76,738,000 bushels by July 31, 1931. More than four years later, on December 2, 1935, when the Canadian wheat board took over the cash wheat futures held by Canadian Co-operative Wheat Producers Limited, the unsold balance of 1930 crop wheat still remained at 74,778,000 bushels. In the interim, McFarland's failure to liquidate these stocks was deliberate, and their retention was one aspect of his price support operations. Although the 1930 crop account was kept separately for accounting purposes, McFarland converted the cash wheat stocks into futures and merged them with his direct purchases of futures into a combined market support operation, which he conducted for four and a half years.

Since carrying charges were involved in holding unsold stocks, whether in the form of cash wheat or futures, McFarland chose the less costly way of carrying them, which he did by moving the cash wheat into export or milling and "taking back the options" without selling them, just as the central agency had done for a time in the previous autumn. McFarland estimated the annual carrying charges involved in holding wheat futures, and switching them as need be from one delivery month to another, at an average cost of 10 cents per bushel per year. Average storage charges on wheat held in country or terminal elevators would have cost 15½ to 16 cents per bushel per year.

ORIGIN OF THE SPECIAL OPTION ACCOUNT

McFarland had scarcely begun his service as general manager of the central selling agency when the question arose over the need for market support. As McFarland later explained, prices were pressed down to toward the 50 cent level at the end of December, 1930, when he received two separate representations. The first came from the pools to lower the initial payment to 40 cents. McFarland could not agree, because he believed buyers would interpret the action as an indication that the government expected prices to drop to that level. The other representation came from the heads of line elevator companies who foresaw the loss of their customers if the market price were to drop below the 50 cent initial payment available to pool customers.

As Bennett passed through Winnipeg on his return from Regina after delivering his first major wheat policy speech since assuming office, McFarland had an opportunity to acquaint him with the problem. McFarland confirmed the understanding they reached in his handwritten note of January 23, 1931, as he tried to reassure Bennett:

> I have not bought a bushel of wheat to sustain the market, and will not buy any, unless the price gets down to where it is necessary in order to prevent the price from going under the 50 cent basis, or say 50½ cents, to save non-pool

farmers from being forced out at less than pool farmers' initial payment price, as agreed and understood between us when you were here. I do hope I will not have to buy any wheat to sustain price. . . .[1]

McFarland ascribed the need for purchasing wheat futures to the absence of speculators from the market. He made his point succinctly in his letter of January 30,1931, to Bennett:

> I presume you are aware that the farm leaders are agitating for some legislation to control the Grain Exchange or supervise it, or something of that sort, their idea being to discourage speculation, believing that speculation is injurious; while I, on the other hand, hold just the opposite view, that speculation is what we need in the grain market. The broader the market the better it is when it comes to selling the product of the west. The whole trouble, as I see it at the present time, and this condition has existed now for some months, is that the speculators are either broke or discouraged, and one thing that discourages speculation on the grain markets of the North American continent is that the Federal Farm Board in the United States control the wheat of that country and have a large quantity of it in their ownership, while the pool of Canada hold a similar position on this side of the line, and all this wheat is hanging as a threat over the market, the public not knowing when it might be dumped or sold in large volume and cause them heavy losses. This keeps them out of the market. The only speculator of any importance left in Canada is the Wheat Pool. They are holding the wheat.[2]

After McFarland had been in charge of the central selling agency for a few months and had not made any discernible progress in selling the 1930 crop, the lending banks which received weekly statements on the agency's position expressed apprehension. McFarland discussed his position with Mr. E. E. Henderson, chairman of the lending banks' committee, and confirmed his explanation by letter on April 1:

> Referring to our conversation of today regarding various matters in connection with the handling of the Pool grain, and complying with your request, I will try to outline as briefly as possible the situation confronting us.
>
> You will recall about the end of December last, wheat prices were gradually dropping and approaching very close to 50 cents per bushel in store Fort William for cash No. 1 Northern. The Pool initial payment price, you will also recall, was 50 cents per bushel delivered Fort William for No. 1 Northern wheat. The banks who were handling the Pool account were extremely nervous owing to the fact that there was a lack of demand to take care of a sufficient volume in order to reduce the stocks held for the Pool account, and the whole West was in a panicky condition as to how much lower the price of wheat was going to fall. About the same time two of the Provincial Pools were clamouring to reduce the initial payment price to 40 cents per bushel for No. 1 Northern wheat in store Fort William. I took the view at that time, that as Manager of the Central Selling Agency I would not give my consent to reduce that price to 40 cents unless and until the Lending Banks and the Premier of the Dominion of Canada authorized or insisted that it should be done, my view being that had the Pools reduced their initial price to 40 cents it would have been construed as a very bearish action by other exporting countries as well as importing countries and the chances were all in favour that confidence would be so disturbed that prices would probably decline to 40 cents in just

[1] *Bennett Papers.*
[2] *Ibid.*

the same manner as they did decline to 50 cents after the Pool had reduced their initial payment to 50 cents.

In the meantime, while this condition existed, the matter was being considered by our Prime Minister, the Rt. Hon. R. B. Bennett, as to whether the Dominion Government would in some manner guarantee the banks from loss, and he had announced that he would address a public meeting in Regina on, I think, January 2nd, at which meeting he would outline his policy regarding wheat.

Prior to the end of the year the market was very weak and the price in the neighborhood of 50 cents for No. 1 Northern cash wheat in store Fort William. The organised Grain Elevator Trade, handling non-Pool Farmers' wheat, approached me a few days before the end of the year intimating that the price of cash wheat was practically down to 50 cents per bushel and that in some instances their list prices in the country for wagon loads at their elevators was even less than the Pool list prices which was based on the 50 cent initial payment, and they submitted to me that if the Pool price was going to be maintained at 50 cents it would be manifestly unfair to the non-Pool Farmer and to themselves if they were forced by market circumstances to reduce their price in the country to lower than the Pool price. I admitted that it would be unfair but that it would only be a few days until Mr. Bennett would make his announcement in Regina and that regardless of how low the price might go for those few days the Grain Trade should not reduce their price to less than 50 cents in store Fort William and I am pleased to say that the Grain Trade agreed, and sent notices out accordingly.

I took the matter up with the Prime Minister and discussed with him the fact that one or two of the Western Pools had wished to reduce their price to 40 cents basis Fort William for No. 1 Northern Wheat and that I had refused to consent to it until such time as such procedure had been authorized by himself and the Lending Banks. He confirmed my action and stated that wheat should not be permitted to go under the 50 cent mark at Fort William. I explained to him that in order to avoid this happening it might be necessary for me, on behalf of the Pool, to purchase options in the Winnipeg Market. I may say that he did not relish the idea but as it was the only means of combatting a drop in prices, to the detriment of the non-Pool farmer and the general business interests of the West, I had his authority to use my discretion.

If you look up the records you will find that cash wheat in Fort William touched the 50 cent mark and May wheat touched 52½ cents, but fortunately we did not have to purchase anything as the market turned at these points and has not since been so low.

In the meantime I estimated that if May wheat goes to a price around 54 cents, it would endanger the non-pool farmers who have been holding car load lots since January 1st and whose carrying charges would have increased such advances to a point where they would be closed out. It has, therefore, been necessary that I should keep in mind the fact that 54 cents is a point where purchases would have to be made in order to maintain the non-Pool farmers' position and I think you will agree with me that throughout these three months there have been few days when the price was far enough away from that figure to make it feel safe to sell any large quantity of wheat. As a matter of fact that market was only getting into a position of taking fairly good quantities of May Option at the time when the American Farm Board decided to offer some of their wheat for export, about the last week in February. Since that time the buying power has been very weak indeed and as a consequence our holdings of Options have increased to a greater extent than I hoped for.

In the meantime I estimate roughly that we will have to sell our wheat at around an average of 60 cents for May delivery in order to break even on the prices advanced by the banks to the various Pools. For that reason it is only natural that I should be reluctant to sell wheat under 60 cents. There is, however, another reason why I am reluctant to press sales under 60 cents and that is that the market is a very unwilling market and is easily depressed and if we depress the price by our selling it only means that in order to protect the 50 cent basis at the 1st of the year, we would have to enter the pit and buy wheat and this I am most anxious to avoid. We have not bought a bushel of wheat and we do not want to have to purchase any because of the fact that if we start manipulating in the pit it will very quickly disturb confidence throughout the world and be injurious. There is no doubt millions of bushels of wheat could be sold in the pit if we did not mind to what extent the price might decline, but should we do that it would be contrary to the statements emanating from Ottawa to the effect that the Government's action has stabilized the market and I would submit to you that while the policy pursued since January 2nd has not advanced the price, yet it has maintained the price, which otherwise might very easily have gone to 40 cents per bushel. Had this occurred it is easy to visualize the conditions in Western Canada would have been immeasurebly worse than they have been. . . .[3]

The balance of McFarland's long explanation was concerned mostly with technical matters, such as the exchange of options for cash wheat which failed to improve the agency's sales position but at least moved the actual wheat into consumption and export. In this practice of "taking back the options", the banks would have required any commercial firm to sell the futures immediately thereby completing the sale. But as the agency had done just before he took over, McFarland refrained from selling the futures in order to reduce the pressure on the market. Although he was moving the actual wheat into consumption, he was simultaneously acquiring a long position in futures, as the agency's net sales position remained unchanged. McFarland observed in his January 23, 1931, note to Bennett, which illustrated his use of the 1930 pool account in a market support operation: "Canada is actually clearing around 5,000,000 per week, which is all right for this season of the year, and so long as Canada's wheat is going out that is the vital factor in the end, even we "the pool" do have to take back May option against cash sales, in order to hold wheat from going under 50¢ for cash wheat in store Fort William, which is the pool initial payment."[4]

As the central agency accumulated futures, the need arose for switching from nearby to more distant contracts as the delivery months approached. That spring McFarland was unable to spread all of his May futures over to October and, to satisfy the banks, he had to obtain Bennett's authorization to take delivery of about 15 million bushels of wheat in store, tendered on May contracts. He made light of the fact that non-pool wheat was being tendered because he could exchange the cash wheat for futures whenever the export demand might catch up.

At the end of May the house of commons requested its select standing committee on agriculture and colonization to undertake an investigation

[3] *Bennett Papers.*
[4] *Ibid.*

into methods of handling and marketing agricultural products. In due course the committee took up the question of wheat marketing and invited representatives from the Winnipeg grain exchange and the pools to give evidence. Messrs. James A. Richardson, Sidney T. Smith and A. E. Darby appeared for the exchange and Andrew Cairns represented the pools. Mr. Richardson's evidence was the most frequently quoted. He opposed the establishment of a wheat board, but suggested a milder and more economical form of intervention, if necessary, and for a brief period, as he said:

> I am satisfied that the wheat board would be resented by the buyer abroad. It sets up an artificial resistance. I do not say that he will not buy our stuff, but we will not have the preference; everybody else will have the preference. Now, the way I feel to-day, with economic conditions the way they are, is that one has to be careful in being too emphatic in what he says. I would not want to guarantee what the wheat price will be, although I did go on record last November in a very emphatic way in saying that our One Northern was worth sixty cents a bushel, and I could not see that there was any risk in carrying it. I thought . . . that we would sell probably just as much wheat at sixty cents as at several cents a bushel below sixty cents. The way I feel to-day is that none of the channels of trade should be destroyed or should be out of joint, and that if the government, in their wisdom, feel that a temporary economic situation is resulting in wheat selling for the time being below what it should sell for, and that that would right itself in six weeks or two months time — if they want to do that — if they want to put a little muscle into the market — inject a crutch under it for a little while — if they think it is wise to do that, whilst operating through the ordinary channels of trade where you can step in, it has cost you nothing if you are right. If you are wrong, you have taken a limited loss and you are out; but you have not disturbed or destroyed any of the existing machinery which I believe to be highly efficient. . . . Mr. McFarland is operating for the general manger of the Wheat Pools, and it might be possible that his services and facilities would be utilized. . . . Let Mr. McFarland, or whoever is in charge of the job, step into the market and, say, buy ten million bushels of wheat to take care of this crop. There is ten million bushels of sixty cent wheat. How much would you lose on it? You might lose ten cents a bushel.[5]

Thus, just a few weeks before its inception, Mr. Richardson had presented the case publicly for a temporary and modest price-support operation. Although prices held for some months above the 50 cent level Bennett had authorized McFarland to maintain, it was not long after Richardson's statement when the inevitable happened and McFarland wired Bennett on July 27:

> Expect to go Ottawa middle week. But this market needs some support right now as farmers consigned cars being closed out and if it goes any lower will be a lot more. Panicky conditions exist. Have I your authority to purchase around fifty-five. It won't require much. Crop conditions much worse owing extreme heat past few days.[6]

It will be recalled how much Bennett had initially resisted committing his government financially before making his momentous one-sentence policy

[5]Select Standing Committee on Agriculture and Colonization, *Minutes of Proceedings and Evidence*, July 9, 1931, pp. 151-152.
[6]*Bennett Papers.*

announcement on December 22, 1930. This time he responded immediately, but even more cryptically: "Yes, but most limited quantities possible."

McFarland's purpose in going to Ottawa was to attend the conference Bennett had called with the premiers, the pools and the banks. He described the meeting in a memorandum he prepared some time later for Bennett's use:

> This was the picture as at *August 1st, 1931,* when a meeting of representatives of Western governments, and farmer organizations met representatives of banks, in the Minister of Finance's Office, and when it was strongly represented that the situation was such that when the crop started to move there would be a price debacle unless some support was put into the market to absorb hedges against farmers' sales. I was authorized to give such support so as to prevent prices dropping below 50 cents at Fort William, if that could be accomplished without putting our values out of line for export, relative to the world's market.
>
> As a result of these operations during the Cereal Year 1931-32, prices were maintained at about 50 cents Fort William and the maximum quantity purchased during the year was 23,602,000 bushels. These purchases, which were made for stabilization purposes, were sold prior to the movement of the new 1932 crop, and showed a profit of $17,211.00. None of the 76,330,000 bushels of Pool wheat carried forward from the 1st of August, 1931, were disposed of, nor could they have been sold without crashing prices.[7]

The particular meeting at which the prime minister had discussed with McFarland privately the arrangements for supporting the price level at 50 cents took place during the day of August 5, 1931, to which McPhail had taken umbrage because Bredt and he were excluded.[8] Undoubtedly Bennett considered that the issue of supporting the market was outside the direct concern of the pools, and he was anxious to preserve as much secrecy as possible. During the course of the same day, Bennett also met with Messrs. Brownlee, McConnell, Wilson and White, with McPhail and Bredt present.

[7]*Memorandum, December, 1932,* Bennett Papers, p. 5. This was a seven-page defence of his support operations, which McFarland prepared in response to press criticism that he had not sold the 1930 crop pool wheat by July 31, 1931. It was a very competent, but technical, account which Bennett had difficulty in understanding, although McFarland claimed that Stevens understood it. Nevertheless, McFarland revised the memo and resubmitted it to Bennett on February 22, 1933, in response to a letter from the latter describing the wheat debate in the House on February 13. In his covering letter McFarland wrote:
". . . I can imagine you were somewhat annoyed at what you had been through in having to listen to Motherwell and having to reply to him, and you thought you would pass some of the annoyance on to me. That is alright, but really I have already answered the same question and sent you a memorandum thereon, which I fear you did not read, or if you did, you did not understand it. Therefore, I am enclosing you another copy which I sincerely commend to your perusal. If this memorandum fails to answer the question, then I am licked, and much as I would love to do so I cannot command words to make it any clearer. . . ."
"I fear you do not fully understand the intricacies of the grain business in relation to its hedges and what is commonly called "futures". While we were in the A. P. Grain Company we should have discussed such perplexities more than we did, but then who could have foreseen the present necessity? Mr. Stevens seems to have made a very careful study of the different phases of the grain business (probably in his time he may have had some deals in "futures", but I do not believe you ever did any investing in grain "futures") and he apparently understands the present dilemma. Why not discuss it fully with him and probably he can explain more clearly what I have failed to accomplish. . . ."
[8]See pp. 304-305.

To record McFarland's purchases which were made expressly to support the market, the central agency maintained a "special" option account. It was intended that these purchases remain secret, and precise information concerning them was only disclosed some four years later to a special committee of the house. It then became known that McFarland's first purchases had been made during the last few trading days of July, 1931, and that he had bought 3,178,000 bushels of futures to support prices at that time.[9] Although information on the transactions was consistently denied to the house, it was inevitable from the nature of the operations that they were fairly accurately known by the trade and were precisely known to the staffs of the chartered banks who carefully watched the limits of the authorization the federal government extended from time to time on this special account.

DETAILS OF OPERATIONS IN THE SPECIAL OPTION ACCOUNT

At this stage it would be helpful to understand the full details of the operations in the special option account. The information on all the trades up to May 31, 1935, which was furnished to the special committee on bill 98, is reproduced in Chart 20:1. In graphic form, it is easy to visualize the three major operations which McFarland undertook to provide hedges for producer deliveries from the three crops of 1932, 1933 and 1934. Heavy purchases in the autumn months were followed by less successful attempts to reduce holdings in the latter months of each year. There was only one other major operation and that was in connection with the speculative boom and collapse in the summer of 1933.

Apart from that extraordinary operation, McFarland's purchases were confined to provision of an adequate hedging market for producers, and of consequent price support in their interest. He began in a modest way in the 1931-32 crop year, before the end of which he had more than completely sold out what he bought in the special option account, although his temporary short position in that account was more than covered by his holdings in the 1930 crop account. McFarland's first major market support operation took place in October, 1932, when he bought a phenomenal quantity of 63.6 million bushels to steady the market during the heavy deliveries from that year's large crop. He bought an additional 14.6 millions in November but, for reasons explained below, his authority to purchase ran out and the market broke sharply in December to its historic low of 38 cents. Except in the spring of 1932, McFarland never succeeded in disposing of his autumn purchases in the following spring.

In the early summer of 1933, an opportunity presented itself for McFarland to dispose of his holdings as speculation inspired by drought drove up the price of wheat. But he refrained from selling in the belief that it would injure the market for producers still delivering wheat from the 1932 crop. By mid-July he had managed to sell about 20 million bushels, but he promptly bought it back as soon as the boom collapsed, and the size of the special option account grew as he resorted to further purchases that autumn.

[9]Special Committee on Bill 98, Canadian Grain Board Act, *Minutes of Proceedings and Evidence, Exhibit "G"*, June 27, 1935, p. 333.

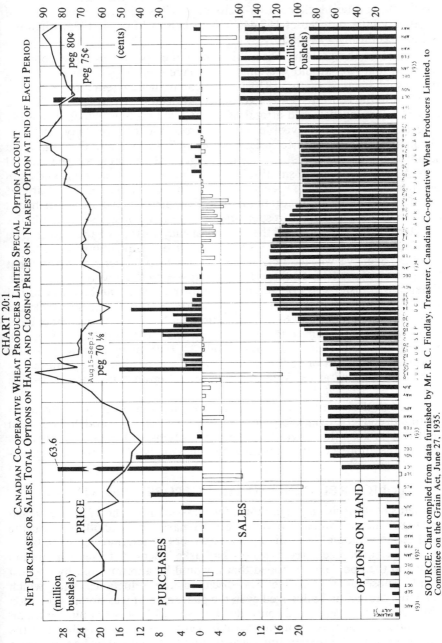

CHART 20:1

Canadian Co-operative Wheat Producers Limited Special Option Account

Net Purchases or Sales, Total Options on Hand, and Closing Prices on Nearest Option at End of Each Period

SOURCE: Chart compiled from data furnished by Mr. R. C. Findlay, Treasurer, Canadian Co-operative Wheat Producers Limited, to Committee on the Grain Act, June 27, 1935.

By December, 1933, the long position in the special account had risen to 133.4 million bushels. Although McFarland succeeded in reducing his inventory to 95 million bushels in May, 1934, he had pushed it up again to 158.8 million after his September-October purchases in that year. This total stood very little reduced at 152,446,000 bushels at May 31, 1935, when the public accounting was made.

Because of the growing accumulation in the special option account, it followed that McFarland was unable to make any progress in liquidating the unsold balance of the 1930 pool account, which remained almost a constant in the central agency's accounts. Altogether, by May 31, 1935, the central selling agency held a total of 228,562,000 bushels, which ostensibly exceeded the country's visible supply. From the end of May, 1935, to October of that year, McFarland continued to operate the combined stabilization account in his capacity as general manager of the central selling agency. He made small sales from the 1930 pool account and both purchased and sold in the special account. On August 14, 1935, McFarland was also appointed chief commissioner of the new Canadian wheat board and he discharged his two responsibilities simultaneously, as he gradually transferred the sales staff of the central agency to that of the board. The Canadian wheat board act, 1935, provided for the acquisition by the board of all the agency's wheat stocks in respect of which the federal government had given a guarantee, on terms to be approved by the governor in council. When this transfer was effected on December 2, 1935, the board acquired 205,186,980 bushels of wheat and wheat contracts from the agency.[10] On the same date, the McFarland board was retired and the new board, under chief commissioner Mr. James R. Murray and his successor Mr. George H. McIvor, disposed of these holdings by July 31, 1938, at which date the board reported a net profit of $8,953,343.07 on the sale of all wheat acquired by Canadian Co-operative Wheat Producers Limited in the 1930-1935 period.[11]

Although these were the bare facts of the support operations, Bennett's continual concern over the extent of the financial risk and his constant endeavor to keep the magnitude of the operations within bounds provides one of the more colorful passages in the annals of government grain-policy.

POLICY RELATING TO THE SUPPORT OPERATIONS

Bennett's basic decision to guarantee the bank loans on the 1930 pool wheat and to use the guarantee also to support the market around 50 cents was the most economical and least disruptive of the policy alternatives available to him at the time. The three premiers had asked Bennett to set a minimum price and the pool leaders hoped that it would be administered by a wheat board. Subsequent evidence has disclosed the reluctance with which Bennett's cabinet had approved even the guarantee. It was not an operation which could be covered and controlled by a specific vote of public funds; on the contrary, prudence required that it be kept as secret as possible. For the time being, no public expenditure was required, for the public liability was a

[10]*Report of the Canadian Wheat Board,* Crop Year 1935-1936, p. 8.
[11]*Ibid.,* Crop Year 1937-1938, p. 2.

contingent one depending upon what the ultimate disposition of the wheat carried might realize. Thus, at no given time, could the liability under the government's guarantee be measured. One could take the current market price and apply it to the quantity of the unsold balance but, as everyone realized, there was no market for the whole of the unsold stocks and most assuredly not at the day's market price. Therefore one could only wait to see what the gradual liquidation of the stocks might bring. These were the considerations Bennett had in mind when he authorized McFarland to make purchases in support of the market in the "most limited quantities possible". For almost a year, however, the problem was contained as prices remained above the 50 cent level, and purchases for the special option account remained minimal.

A small contretemps blew up in the House on April 15, 1932, when western members E. J. Young, John Vallance, and Dr. Thomas F. Donnelly queried the Honourable H. H. Stevens about the operations. By their questions, they appeared to be reasonably well informed. In his concern to maintain the government's intended secrecy, Stevens replied that the government had done nothing beyond guaranteeing the banks against loss on the pools' initial payment to producers. Vallance argued that this action had steadied the market, as he said:

> The Prime Minister while acting as Minister of Finance last year claimed that because of the guarantee given by the government to the banks, they maintained the price for wheat. I contended at the time that to argue that way was to claim credit for steadying the world's market; for he spoke not only of the Canadian market but of steadying the world's market. At least he said that those in the grain trade acknowledged that his actions had brought about that result. There is a strong suspicion throughout western Canada that there is a large volume of grain being held, and I would ask the minister to find out if that is true. If it is not true it should be stated accordingly, because it is strongly rumoured that John I. McFarland is to-day holding large volumes of wheat, speculating in futures, with the Canadian people's money.[12]

To extricate himself, Stevens drew an ill-considered inference:

> Mr. John McFarland, of course, is independent of parliament and of the government. He is a gentleman of means, a gentleman with knowledge of the wheat business, and if he had bought wheat on his own account that is his own business. In regard to the pool, Mr. McFarland had served the pool, so I am informed, without salary, as a matter of public service, and I am advised by those who are in a position to know, that it has been a service that is highly appreciated by all. I think we should pay a tribute to Mr. McFarland for the service that he has rendered in that respect.[13]

The *Free Press* quoted Hansard, with predictable repercussions from McFarland to Bennett as he wrote on April 22:

> It is really a pity that a portion of Hansard should have found its way into the public press. This sort of thing does not help out the world's situation nor Canada's situation, in fact it can only be detrimental because it arouses suspicion and disturbs confidence. However, I presume there is no way of throttling these politicians so that their utterances could be controlled, and they will go on ruining democracy until they have it blotted out.

[12]*House of Commons Debates,* April 15, 1932, p. 2082.
[13]*Ibid.,* p. 2083.

There is one feature about this publication which rather annoys me and that is that it leaves the impression that I may be doing some personal speculation in wheat. Of course, you are well aware that I am not. I did not promise anybody but myself that I would not but such are the facts and the Grain Trade here are certainly well aware of it, and from what I can gather it is rather remarkable the revulsion of feeling, throughout the Grain Trade and financial circles, against this publication by the Free Press. . . .[14]

McFarland maintained a steady flow of correspondence with Bennett on his handling of the special option account. For example, by the spring of 1932, the time had come for him to try to reduce the agency's holdings. In one of his more interesting letters, he described the results to Bennett on June 6:

As you are aware, I have maintained for many months that the only thing which has sustained the values of our wheat has been the long line which we have been holding, and that while Canada has been doing a fair export business the supplies of wheat to take care of that business have been coming from the producer in sufficient volume to even up the supplies necessary to take care of the weekly exports. In other words, there was no investment or speculative interest in wheat and the only substantial support from day to day was the export business which was being done, which make it impossible for us to dispose of our holdings without crashing the price.

While I have been claiming that the above was a fact, yet it had never been proven. Many people probably did not believe it. I, therefore decided a few days ago to test it out and while July Option was standing around 62 cents, and in fact it has been hovering around that figure for a good many weeks, we decided to do some selling and do it in a very carefully concealed manner. In three days' time the market absorbed 3,300,000 bushels which were fed into it up until Saturday morning at prices ranging from 61⅞ cents down to 59¾ cents. From there on the bottom dropped out of it and this morning it completely collapsed without any selling whatsoever on our part. It fell rapidly from 57 to 53 cents and in order to avert a panic we placed orders and it required 2,750,000 bushels of buying by us to stem the tide and what would have happened if we had not stemmed the tide, it is very hard to say. Remember we did no selling from 59¾ cents down to 53 and then we had to support the market or otherwise there was no knowing how much longer it would have dropped. There was a complete break of 6¾ cents while we did nothing. . . .[15]

On July 14, McFarland elaborated further on his attempted sales and the need to buy in again, which had brought the special option account up to 20,000,000 bushels. He decried the liquidation of holdings by the United States federal farm board, and declared that Bennett would be threatened with the prospect of a wheat board in Canada if he were to let prices fall:

When I wrote you last I told you of having tested out the Future Market by endeavouring to sell some wheat. . . . Since that time there have been various occasions when we have had to step in and prevent panic and chaos. The past few days have been the worst, however. You, of course, receive the statements from the banks, and you see the situation from time to time as contained in those statements. I may tell you, however, that the highest peak on our stabilization operations this year, prior to June 1st, was 8,360,000 bushels. It is now 20 million bushels. I know you will be apprehensive in regard to this,

[14]*Bennett Papers.*
[15]*Ibid.*

probably more apprehensive than I am, but you cannot be any more regretful than I am that conditions have been such as to make it, in my opinion, a necessity to support the market to this extent.

In the past we have referred to stock exchanges and grain exchanges as being "markets". They used to be markets, and these institutions have the machinery and had the ability to perform the functions of markets, but those days are in the past and you will probably agree with me when I state that for a good many months past stock exchanges such as New York, Montreal, and grain exchanges such as Winnipeg and Chicago, are no longer "markets" and do not fulfill the functions that formerly were supposed to be the functions of "markets" — they are now nothing more than "slaughter houses", as has been amply demonstrated by the stock exchanges above referred to, where gilt-edged securities have been ruthlessly thrown upon a market in which there were no buyers except at prices far below their intrinsic worth, and I would state without fear of any serious contradiction that the Winnipeg Grain Exchange during the last year and longer would have been nothing more than a "slaughter-house" except for the support given by the line of Futures which we are holding owing to the assistance of the Dominion Government guarantee, and now that we are approaching another crop bearish features predominate, particularly throughout North America and except with our support, wheat would be down, not in the forties but in the thirties. . . .

There are rumours that the Farm Board are forcing their wheat into the Chicago pit. Now just imagine that institution starting out stabilizing wheat at $1.20 — again stabilizing it at 83 cents, and then liquidating it at around 45 cents in Chicago, a price which would give the farmers in Kansas around 20 to 23 cents per bushel. If it were not a tragedy it would be farcical, but unfortunately it is a tragedy for many farmers in the United States as well as business people. . . .

I might also probably explain to you that if we do not hold our wheat at around 53 cents for July delivery, and we let the market go, it would result in every farmer, who is holding cash wheat expecting higher prices, and who has taken an advance on it from the Elevator Companies, being closed out on stop-loss orders as well as all those who may be holding some options in a small way, looking for higher prices, and I submit to you that if we let it go we would have to buy twice as much lower down in order to stop its downward flight, and on top of that we would have the condemnation of everyone in the West who would be cleaned out on the drop. . . .

There is another angle to this which I want you to have in mind and that is that just so sure as we permitted our wheat to go down into the forties, there would be such a demand made upon the Government, not only from Western Canada but from Eastern Canada, that would compel the Government, probably against its will, to create a Government Monopoly, put in a Wheat Board, and go into the wheat business. I do not know whether your ideas of a Wheat Board have changed in the last eighteen months — it may be that you favour a Wheat Board. If you do I certainly would not try to persuade you otherwise, but as for me, my views in that respect have not altered. . . .[16]

Before deliveries commenced from the large 1932 crop, Bennett held another meeting with representatives of the provincial governments and banks, together with McFarland, to determine what action might be required. McFarland described the meeting in the same memorandum as he had referred to a similar conference held a year earlier:[17]

[16]*Ibid.*
[17]See p. 423.

In August 1932 a meeting of Western representatives again met the Government at Ottawa, together with bankers, in order to discuss what should be done to provide purchasing power to take the hedges when this year's large crop commenced moving from the farms. It was realized that a crop then estimated at 467 million bushels created a serious situation. (It has since been estimated at 431 million bushels.) It was decided that an effort should be made to sustain a price of 50 cents Fort William so long as world's prices and export demand would warrant.

McFarland failed to mention, however, that at that meeting Bennett had authorized him to purchase up to 50 million bushels, if need be, to support the price. This was actually the first of several ceilings Bennett imposed upon McFarland's operations, and even then he hadn't authorized the banks specifically to provide the necessary credit under federal guarantee. This oversight Mr. J. W. Spears, chairman of the lending banks' committee, drew to McFarland's attention in his letter of September 9:

> Referring to our conversation after your return from the conference in Ottawa, at which Wheat Pool matters were discussed by the Prime Minister with representatives of the Provincial Governments, Banks, Provincial Wheat Pools and yourself, I understand that the Prime Minister wishes the price of wheat kept from falling below a certain price between now and 31st December next at which time the future stabilization policy will be reviewed.
> While it would appear that the Prime Minister evidently expects the banks to stand behind the Government, he made no request for assistance and the banks came under no commitment to finance market stabilization operations. If it should transpire therefore that additional funds for margins will be required, I would ask that you make application through myself as Chairman of the Lending Banks' Committee so that the position may be reviewed and taken up with the other banks. . . . [18]

While the tidying up of the financial arrangements with the banks proceeded, and even before McFarland embarked on his support purchases that autumn, Bennett expressed apprehension over the magnitude of the risk on the guarantee at that stage as he wrote to McFarland on September 22:

> I confess the financial report makes me very depressed for I do not know how I can face Parliament with any such loss as that indicated. I know you are doing your best, and we are all endeavouring to do the same, but the results are hardly in keeping with the effort and patience we have all shown under such trying circumstances. [19]

It was understandable, too, that the banks sought a precise authorization from Bennett for the resumption of purchases in the special option account. Overriding authority was already available in P. C. 1576 of July 11, 1932, which had renewed the government's guarantee under the provisions of the unemployment and farm relief act of 1932. The order in council imposed no limit on the "purchases of wheat or other grains already made or to be made", but with all the uncertainty over the extent to which McFarland might need to support the market with deliveries from the large 1932 crop about to commence, the banks requested precise written authority from the government in respect of the ceilings. Spears made such a request in his letter of September 30 to McFarland:

Referring to my letter of 9th September and my conversation with you yesterday afternoon when you intimated that it might be necessary for you to purchase some wheat on stabilization account, I advised each of the other banks what might happen and I have no doubt that they have been in touch with their General Managers. In the meantime my General Manager is of opinion that it would be advisable for you to apply to the lending banks for a stated amount for future stabilization purposes and that you should arrange for the Prime Minister to write the banks a letter asking them to meet your request. In the meantime we would be prepared to join with the other banks in making additional advances on stabilization account protected by the Dominion Government guarantee but we desire that a definite amount be arranged in the form of a credit. You can understand that it is undesirable to authorize credits with no limitations.[20]

Thereafter, Spears corresponded directly with Bennett and his letters showed, first, a request for a special credit of $5 million which, at a 20 cent margin, permitted the purchase of 25 million bushels. Another request doubled the amount to $10 million or to the full limit of 50 million bushels Bennett had already verbally approved. But during the course of the unprecedented purchases made in October, 1932, McFarland had overshot his limit and was up to 58 million bushels when Spears telephoned Bennett on October 26 and obtained his consent for a new ceiling not exceeding 75 million bushels. This was later confirmed by letter.

It was in the midst of this great flurry of activity in respect of the special option account that McFarland became exercised over the prevailing level of elevator storage charges. With his increasing holdings, McFarland was concerned over the rate of carrying charges accumulating against them. His effort to get these reduced has already been described.[21] At the special session of parliament called in the autumn of 1932, Bennett made his first public disclosure of the support operations in his statement of policy, but without disclosing the actual details:

The purchases of futures, as it is called in this hedging operation, has heretofore in this country been carried on by two classes, speaking broadly: (a) the investor; and (b) the speculator. In the first class were the milling companies or the purchasers abroad, what we will call those engaged in the grain business, who purchase wheat as a commodity in their line of business and deal with it as an investment for the purposes of their business. These operations continue to some extent, of course, curtailed naturally by the recent diminution in trade throughout the world. The second class, the speculator, had practically disappeared. There has been some speculation in Canada in wheat during the last six to eight months, the buying having been in Chicago; but I think I am correct in saying that, broadly, the speculator is no longer in evidence as a purchaser of wheat. Therefore, so far as hedging operations are concerned, you have the disappearance of the speculator, who thereby played a very important part, as Sir Josiah Stamp pointed out in his report, in connection with the marketing of wheat; and you have left the investor, with his ability to purchase curtailed by reason of the general trade depression.

Under these circumstances, Canadian Co-operative Wheat Producers Limited, to which I have referred, became the only available hedging organization left in western Canada, and the government is faced at the

[20]*Ibid.*
[21]See pp. 323-327.

moment with the issue as to whether or not, under these circumstances, it would give its support as provided by the Relief Act passed in 1931 and 1932 as well — this being a product of the field and farm — by guaranteeing to the banks such sums as might be necessary to enable these operations to be carried on by this organization. But before that was done the government had to consider whether or not the interest of Canada as a whole would be best served by continuing the bonus which we granted last year or by taking the steps I have just indicated for the purpose of protecting the general situation in connection with the marketing of wheat.

I need hardly say to the house that it gave us very great anxiety and concern, but it was quite apparent from the reports we received from every person interested in the trade that unless hedging operations could be carried on there could be no marketing of this year's crop. The result would be that the price of wheat would fall back to less than forty cents per bushel. Therefore, not pegging the price and not interfering in any sense with the operations of the law of supply and demand but to secure the orderly and regulated disposition of the crop, the steps I have indicated were taken and the Canadian Cooperative Wheat Pools, Limited became the hedging agency in order to enable, with the assistance of the government, sales to take place and the crop to be marketed. . . .

I hasten to assure the house that on a balance of financial benefits it is clear that in respect of any obligations which might be incurred — it is not possible that any heavy obligations will be incurred unless something very unforeseen happens — the amount involved will be less than would be involved by the payment of the bonus requested. Weighing the situation as a whole, the probabilities pro and con, the effect upon the dominion, the business which would be secured and the chaos which would result from the absolute failure to sell wheat except as a distress commodity, the steps which I have indicated were taken.

If I might say so, I do not think any good purpose would be served by going into the details of the operations which we have entrusted to the organizations I have mentioned under the management of Mr. McFarland. However, the closest supervision has been exercised and we believe and we have had no reason to change our minds at the present moment, that the steps taken will be more beneficial to the dominion as a whole and will secure for the country as a whole greater advantages than if we paid the producer the bonus which was paid last year and which we are pressed to continue this year.[22]

Western opposition members returned to the attack during the debate on unemployment and farm relief which took place as the emergency session ended on November 25. Their protests were climaxed by Dr. T. F. Donnelly's first-hand description of famine conditions among the farmers of his constitutency. No references were made at that stage by the opposition to eastern press criticism that Bennett had been speculating in wheat, but the debate had hurt Bennett as he confided to McFarland in his letter of November 26:

There is no doubt but that there is an antipathy to the pools in Eastern Canada because they are very properly blamed for the mess they made in 1929 and possibly '30. On the other hand, it is only fair to say that the Eastern farmer is just as badly off as the Western farmer, and he cannot understand why the West should be picked out for favoured treatment while he receives nothing except a chance to contribute by taxation the money that is expended

[22]*House of Commons Debates,* November 14, 1932, pp. 1093-1094.

in other parts of the country. The feeling grows, and is intensified by the conviction brought about by Darby's statement that we have been speculating in wheat; and Donnelly in the House of Commons last night made the attack in such a way as to greatly embarrass us.[23]

One of the Toronto papers had interviewed Mr. A. E. Darby, secretary of the Winnipeg grain exchange, by telephone and Darby made the statement which he quickly regretted. As his policies fell under increasing criticism by the press, Bennett displayed his discomfiture over the size of McFarland's holdings as he wrote to him on November 21:

> I note that the total of your account and stabilization account combined has reached a tremendously large figure, especially when you add to it the short options carried as accommodation for the three provincial pool elevator companies. I know you fully realize the gravity of the situation and will use every possible means to minimize the difficulties. . . .[24]

Bennett's letter alarmed McFarland, and he felt that he should forewarn Bennett of the probability that the need for support would increase. He wrote on November 28:

> I note from press reports you are preparing to go overseas the end of this week.
>
> Before you go probably it would be well for you to advise me what the programme is to be after we reach 75,000,000 options which you advised is the maximum we are to take? We are now up close to 70 million. I am in hopes we won't need more, but you can never tell in times such as these. One Northern Wheat is now 45¢ Ft. Wm. Canadian dollars are around 16½% discount which on a gold parity means 37½¢. . . .[25]

Bennett remained adamant as he replied on November 30:

> I have just received your letter.
>
> I was unable to get away today. I may possibly get off at the end of the week. I do not know.
>
> We cannot take any wheat more than 75 million bushels. I do not think you have any appreciation of just how Members of the Government feel and how fearful they are that this is going to wreck the Government. It is a terrible thing. When you contemplate what we have in the way of options, I think you will agree that it is a terrible situation and whatever may happen we might as well make up our minds that there is a limit to what a country can do and if the situation becomes as acute as I believe it may, the blame will have to be attributed to those responsible, namely, the politicians.[26]

Even with Bennett's refusal so firmly expressed, McFarland insisted that it was a wrong decision. He called Bennett, to no avail, and wired him the next morning, on December 3:

> After due consideration since talking to you last night I am impelled to advise that your decision in present circumstance which might have such far reaching effects is ill-advised. If ever there was an occasion for courage and action it is certainly now. This is no time to waver or show indecision and I hope before you sail you will reconsider and wire me. I showed Stevens copy of that recent statement I sent you and he understands it perfectly and was delighted with it and is confident such facts will overcome all honest

[23]*Bennett Papers.*
[24]*Ibid.*
[25]*Ibid.*
[26]*Ibid.*

criticism.[27] If you suggest my going East immediately I will gladly go and deliberate and confer with any party or parties you designate.[28]

Bennett was unmoved by this last appeal as he sailed from Halifax for London on December 5, primarily "to get a little rest". Earlier that autumn, the market had penetrated the original support level of 50 cents and McFarland had succeeded in holding it through October and November around the mid-forties. But, in the week commencing Monday, December 12, McFarland had exhausted his ceiling and prices declined daily. He telephoned Bennett in London and obtained his consent to purchase just an additional 3,624,000 bushels. But by the time he relayed Bennett's approval through the acting prime minister, Sir George Perley and the finance minister, the Honourable Edgar N. Rhodes, to the Bank of Montreal, the market session of December 16 had closed, during which the historic low sales of December wheat at 38 cents per bushel (No. 1 Northern, in store, Fort William), had been recorded. Rhodes's letter of December 16 to Mr. W. R. Creighton, manager of the main branch of the Bank of Montreal in Ottawa conveyed the required authority:

> I have your letter of December 15th and have wired John McFarland as follows:
>
> "Have received telegram from J. W. Spears, Assistant General Manager of the Bank of Montreal, Winnipeg, through the Bank of Montreal here requesting authority to increase long futures position. Have written letter and am delivering it to W. R. Creighton, Manager of the Bank of Montreal here, granting authority for you to make purchases to the extent of three million, six hundred and twenty-four thousand bushels. It being clearly understood that this authorization is to be limited to this amount."
>
> Mr. Spears' telegram, which is quoted in your letter, makes reference to a request for authorization to increase the long futures position to 155 million bushels if necessary.
>
> It is not clear how this amount is reached in view of the succeeding request that an arrangement be made with the banks to finance operations increasing the stabilization amount totalling 78,624,000 bushels, or 3,624,000 bushels over the authorization of the 26th of October. However, I desire it to be made very clear to you that this authorization has reference only to the purchase of an additional amount not to exceed 3,624,000 bushels.[29]

If Rhodes was confused over the arithmetic, it was because he had not been given the complete information that the agency held 76,376,000 bushels of futures representing the unsold balance of the 1930 pool wheat as well as 75,000,000 bushels in the special option account. The otherwise undefined additional authority for 3,642,000 bushels in the latter account had simply rounded McFarland's total authority to 155 million bushels.

Bennett returned to Ottawa before the end of December, and McFarland's letter of January 3, 1933, briefed him on the climax the market had reached on December 16:

> I confirm my long distance telephone conversations with you while you were in London. In the meantime the authority to assume additional purchases in order to prevent declines in the market could not be arranged on this side of the Atlantic as readily as you anticipated when you spoke to me on the

---

[27]See McFarland's *Memorandum*, December, 1932, Bennett Papers.
[28]*Bennett Papers.*
[29]*Ibid.*

telephone and as a result of delays we had no authority and the Bank of Montreal would not consent to give their authority for an enlargement of the volume until everything was fixed up satisfactorily by the Government at Ottawa.

During the time this was being attended to the market broke four cents per bushel in one day, December wheat going down to 38 cents. This was on December 16th. The break caused very wide-spread consternation throughout the country. The mere thought of wheat going down into the thirties seemed to be looked upon as impossible, not only in the East but also in the West. As a result, some of the Provincial Premiers in the West and the heads of the farmers organizations got suspicious that speculators in the Winnipeg Grain Exchange were responsible for the drastic decline and the Western Premiers talked about closing up the Winnipeg Grain Exchange and other such rot as that. It was intimated that large quantities of farmers stored wheat had been closed out that day on stop-loss orders because the farmers' equity had been dissipated by the decline. There were also rumours that huge quantities had been liquidated. As a result the Grain Exchange officials got busy and investigated and every elevator company had to show just how much farmers' wheat was forced on the market that day. I may say that I had the opinion that there might have been as much as four million bushels, which I did not consider would be a large amount, but I thought it might aggregate that quantity. However, just today they have shown me the result of their investigations and instead of being anything like what was talked about, it is found to have only amounted to the moderate quantity of 2,150,000 Bushels, which, of course, would be a mere bagatelle in normal times and would not cause a ripple, and the only thing that four cent break really demonstrated to me was the pitiful lack of investment or speculation. There were lots of days last Fall when the crop was moving, when farmers sold several times that quantity voluntarily, and nothing was said about it. Of course, there would have been a lot said about it if we had not been given support to maintain the price structure.

The following day the credit was arranged with the banks and we had permission to purchase the moderate quantity which you mentioned over the long distance 'phone, but as the market did not appear to require any substantial support after that big break, we have not seen fit to use more than 700,000 Bushels of the extra quantity which we were permitted to use. There may come a time later on when it will be necessary, but with farmers' deliveries very small and every prospect of their being very small on the balance of this crop, and with a certain amount of export business being done and the further fact of the total of 275 million bushels delivered from this crop by farmers it is estimated that not more than 25 millions remain unsold, it is, therefore, unlikely that there will be any great pressure from farmers' marketings until another crop is grown.[30]

McFarland's report of the action taken by the council of the Winnipeg grain exchange to police the trades that day understates the concern of its members that the market should not be depressed further. Mr. M. O. Thomas, president, Louis Dreyfus Canada, Limited, informed the writer that he was a floor trader at the time and that he had sold at the historically low price. At the opening on December 16 he had received a substantial selling order to work off, and when the price dropped to 38 cents, his principal intervened and instructed him to stop selling. Another person who

[30] *Ibid.*

vividly recalls that occasion is Mr. George McIvor who was McFarland's principal assistant. Mr. McIvor wrote some 41 years later:

My recollection of that situation is that Mr. McFarland was in Ottawa and Mr. Bennett in London. . . . I knew that our limits authorized by the Prime Minister were very close to being run out. Mr. McFarland telephoned me from Ottawa. He seemed more concerned than I had ever sensed during our association. As I recall he said to me, "What do you think we should do?" I had concluded in my own mind that by carrying on buying of futures day after day in the Winnipeg market we were just trying to make water run uphill, and that something had to happen so that a bottom could be found in the market. In other words, the world at that time simply took the Canadian government purchases for granted, and we were not effective in stimulating others to join us in buying wheat even at these low prices. I suggested to Mr. McFarland that I should watch the Chicago market which had been breaking badly, and if it continued to break we should pull out. To me we had no other alternative. He agreed. I did not cancel any orders, but suddenly as was described to me by some traders in the pit, there was a vacuum; the government was out of the market and the market in a matter of seconds, broke . . . to 38¢. Then on its own steam over the following days it started to come back and it seemed to find its feet gradually working up without further government buying. I liken these operations on December 16 to similar conditions which arise from time to time in the international money market where it seems to have to find its feet before a turn for the better. My main point is that I think December 16th was the turning point, not only in price, but also that a new feeling came into the market when it was realized that there was a bottom as bad as it was.[31]

As McFarland and McIvor indicated, the market encountered little additional pressure for the balance of the crop year and prices mounted a slow recovery during the remaining winter months. Then the price rise accelerated as the American dollar was devalued and evidence emerged of North America's worst drought disaster yet experienced. Paricularly because the United States crop appeared to be falling short of domestic requirements, Winnipeg prices had risen to 70 cents by the end of June. Up to that time, McFarland had decided to stand aside lest he depress the market while producers were still delivering wheat but, in the process, he forewent a good opportunity to liquidate his own holdings. By then it was evident that speculators had returned to the Chicago market in force, and that their spreading operations had spilled over into the Winnipeg market.[32]

The activities of the large operators had also reattracted the small speculators. During the first half of July the price rise was spectacular, and culminated in a high of 95¾ cents at Winnipeg on July 15. Bennett was in

[31]Mr. George McIvor's letter of November 6, 1973, to the author.

[32]McIvor's letter of November 6, 1973 observed: "The 1933 market in Chicago was generally described as the Crawford Bull Market, and it was named as such because of the fact that a Dr. Crawford decided to enter the market on a big scale and he was encouraged by reports of heavy damage to the American wheat crop due to drought. I have never been able to determine in my own mind why Mr. McFarland did not take more advantage of this relatively strong market. I think, however, it was due to the fact that he still had as an objective the prospect of cleaning up the Pools' old debts which they had paid off to the provinces. He never expressed this view to me, but this is just my feeling."

the midst of the international wheat agreement negotiations in London as he sent off an immediate cable to Perley on July 4:

> Following for McFarland. Begins: Winnipeg wheat prices apparently reflecting Chicago situation out of line with export prices which is sending business to the Argentine and Australia. Imperative that you should sell wheat at every possible opportunity. Might it not be desirable to fix a price level on which you could freely make offerings? Have you disposed of any of your holdings? And how many bushels do you now carry? In view of reported market shortage and Canadian indication, is restriction Canadian acreage possible? Ends.[33]

Perley had made a marginal note on the telegram: "Telephoned him at one o'clock. Arranged with him to call up the Prime Minister in London and talk with him on the telephone." An account of that telephone conversation has been recorded by R. K. Finlayson:

> When Roosevelt cheapened the American dollar in terms of gold there was, for a time at least, a corresponding rise in North American wheat prices. It then occurred to Canadians in London that McFarland should be instructed to sell some wheat. With this in mind, R.B. put in a call to McFarland in Winnipeg. McFarland was on the telephone at eight o'clock in the evening which corresponded to two a.m. London time. Transatlantic telephone communications were then so unsatisfactory that conversations would be turned into shouting matches. My bedroom being close to R.B.'s sitting room I was able to hear the voices of both.
>
> These two old friends were literally shouting at each other in a way that would cause a stranger to believe that they would never again be on speaking terms. The conversation ran somewhat as follows:
> "How about selling some wheat, John?
> No, I don't think so.
> Why?
> Well, those people over there have been skinning us alive for three years; now the shoe is on the other foot and we are going to make the ———— pay.
> John, I think you should sell."
> I could hear the voices, McFarland's as well as R.B.'s:
> "No,I will not sell.
> I order you to sell.
> All right, I'll resign.
> John, I do not want you to do that, but you must sell."
> Eventually, McFarland agreed to sell some wheat. As soon as the conversation was over, R.B., wearing bedroom slippers and pyjamas, walked into my room in one of his friendliest and most jovial moods to recall old times in Calgary. He and John had made a lot of money speculating on the wheat market, nearly always on the long side. R.B. told me that on one occasion, when they owed the bank a million dollars, they held on to come out in the end with a substantial profit. Later, having made some enquiries, we found out that John had sold a little wheat and bought considerably more.[34]

Bennett's concern that McFarland should be selling remained undiminished as he cabled again on July 10:

---

[33] *Bennett Papers.*
[34] R. K. Finlayson, *That Man R. B.: Bennett*, pp. 203-204.

Send following message to McFarland—I am receiving by cable and otherwise, strongest representations as to necessity of your reducing wheat stocks every available opportunity, especially in view of effect on public borrowing this Fall. It is possible that the speculative mania in United States will collapse with disastrous consequences. I urge that every possible effort be made even by price reduction. You might telephone when convenient, first advising hour.[35]

Perley reported back to Bennett on July 17:

Referring our conversation Friday evening telephoned our Winnipeg friend as promised and urged him take advantage present opportunity dispose of holdings. He tells me that in the past week he has reduced quantity by nearly twenty millions and that he will continue dispose further quantities quickly as possible on orderly basis. He further tells me that he has travelled around a good deal lately and finds conditions crop growing steadily worse. This helps him in handling our business but must unfortunately make things very difficult for people there.[36]

On July 17, the day he had reported to Perley, McFarland sold another 6.3 million bushels, bringing his total sales since July 1 to 27 million bushels before the market broke. Mr. George McIvor stood in for McFarland, during the latter's illness some two years later, to testify before the special committee on bill 98. In his evidence, McIvor provided a vivid description of the events of the next several days:

On July 19th a disastrous situation developed on markets in the United States and wheat prices at Chicago crashed from $1.14⅞ to $1.05 for the July future, and substantial sales were made in our market. The net result was that the Winnipeg market declined 6¾ cents a bushel without either sales or purchases by Mr. McFarland.

On July 20th a complete debacle was witnessed in United States grain markets when wheat prices at Chicago fell 15 cents per bushel, making a total break of 25 cents per bushel in two days' trading.

On the same day selling orders flooded the Winnipeg market and prices broke 9 cents a bushel. Feeling that developments of the past two days in the United States were due to factors wholly unrelated to the basic wheat situation and with due regard to the fact that the new Canadian wheat crop (a small one) was about to be harvested, Mr. McFarland felt that it was his duty to exercise all the control he could over a situation which might have proved disastrous to Canadian producers.

On July 20th, we purchased a total of 4,150,000 bushels and in spite of this support prices showed a net loss of 9 cents a bushel for the day. I would like to ask you a simple question. What would have happened to prices at Winnipeg if we had not supported the market to the extent we did, with Chicago breaking to the extent of 15 cents a bushel. It was apparent that the situation had got out of control in the United States and the Chicago Board of Trade decided to close their market until such time as they felt the trade could cope with the situation. Winnipeg, therefore, was the only North American market of consequence remaining open on July 21st.

In the four years of stabilization operations, and through all the difficulties which Mr. McFarland was confronted with from time to time, and I assure you that probably there has not been a day in his whole four years of operations that he has not been required to make decisions of great

[35] *Bennett Papers.*
[36] *Ibid.*

importance to the country as a whole, one day probably stands out more vividly in his memory than any other days, i.e., July 21st, 1933. Remember the Chicago market was closed. A feeling of panic existed every place, and when the Winnipeg market opened on the 21st July, it became apparent that only by a courageous stand could a complete breakdown in the price structure be averted. The Winnipeg Free Press of July 21st makes the following comment:-

The market advanced two cents on the opening. This advance was short-lived as Chicago traders began to sell wheat in a big way causing prices to slump 3 to 4 cents.

On this day it was necessary for Mr. McFarland to purchase 15,705,000 bushels of wheat. I wonder if it is realized what the results would have been had this action not been taken. Remember the price structure, due to the changed crop conditions in North America was gradually being worked back to a basis where the producer could obtain a more liveable price for his wheat, and had this huge quantity of wheat been thrown on the market without support surely one does not need to stretch the imagination to realize what a condition of chaos would have developed.

On July 22nd, in spite of the tremendous purchases of the previous day the further purchases of July 22nd by Mr. McFarland of 3,303,000 bushels, the market broke 4¾ cents. Remember Chicago market was still closed, but was re-opened again on July 24th, and a minimum price was established.[37]

Although the setting of a minimum price by the Chicago board of trade on July 31 helped to relieve the pressure on the Winnipeg market, McFarland purchased another 12.8 million bushels in the period up to August 12 at which point he reached his limit of 155 million bushels. He appealed by phone and by letter on August 3 to Perley to raise the limit, but Perley responded on August 10:

... The facts and arguments which you put forward have not altered our views as I expressed them to you on the telephone last week. Whether you are right or wrong in thinking that wheat will go higher, we want you to reduce your holdings as quickly as you can without unduly depressing the market. As you know, the only object of the operations that you have been carrying on was to steady the market and enable the farmers to dispose of their crop in an orderly way. Now, as I told you on the telephone, we wish to have the whole transaction closed up as soon as it can reasonably be done.[38]

McFarland replied in a long letter to Perley on August 12 to explain his position and to justify his request that the government enlarge his authority. Meanwhile, as he remained powerless to take any further action, McFarland turned to the council of the Winnipeg grain exchange which welcomed his suggestion that minimum prices be enforced for a temporary period. On August 15 the exchange announced that minimum prices would remain in effect until further notice, at levels of the previous day's close. On this basis, cash wheat was pegged at 70⅛ cents and, for a short period, minimum prices were in effect both in Chicago and Winnipeg. In the latter market, minimum prices remained in force until September 14, and trading remained active at prices a little above the peg.

Just as the peg had been placed in force however, Perley sent off a long cable to Bennett which reviewed the government's policy with regard to the

[37]Special Committee on Bill 98, Canadian Grain Board Act, *Proceedings and Evidence*, June 28, 1935, pp. 367-368.
[38]*Bennett Papers.*

limit, and disclosed some disagreement over the issue. His cable of August 17 read:

> I reported to you in my cable of July seventeenth that McFarland had reduced amount by nearly twenty millions and that he would continue dispose further quantities on orderly basis. Was much surprised and disappointed to learn that during slump shortly afterwards he bought back nearly all he had sold. Spoke to him again twice on telephone and told him we did not think he should buy any more but sell whenever opportunity offered. He has written me two letters explaining definitely his opinion that wheat cannot help being higher in price later but some of our colleagues disagree with this view. McFarland stated that Canadian carry-over this year is two hundred millions and they had expected crop of four hundred and fifty millions. On account bad weather conditions he now estimates this year's crop at about two hundred and twenty-five millions. In other words crop and carry-over will not be more than they had estimated for this year's crop. As price during next few weeks may be affected through pressing sales new crop by farmers needing money McFarland urges that market should be supported during that time and of course farmers would feel sore if price dropped much just now. Last week's reports showed him as within four or five million bushels of his limit of one hundred and fifty-eight millions and although we would naturally regret very much if farmers should be disappointed in price of new crop nearly all Ministers now in Ottawa unwilling authorize any further increase.[39] Minister National Revenue was in Winnipeg Monday and at our request discussed situation with McFarland. Minister National Revenue feels very strongly that we should give at this time support to our chosen expert who is so convinced in his forward view and Minister National Revenue thinks any alternative means heavy crash in the market which at this time with the new wheat offering would mean return to deep depression through the West and all Canada. Almost all the rest of us are unwilling to authorize further purchases in your absence but at the same time we appreciate McFarland's ability and willingness to carry on this rather unpleasant task without any remuneration. We are particularly disinclined to further commit Government in view of fact that you definitely refused before leaving here to increase his authorization and you have during last few weeks instructed him reduce holdings and asked me place same views strongly before him. Personally feel that you should be the one to decide.[40]

On the following day, Perley sent another cable upon hearing from McFarland:

> I have another letter from McFarland this morning. Optimistic regarding long future but cautious regarding present situation. Among other things he says QUOTE In view of fact, as you are aware, the balance of purchases for stabilization account, which can be made by me are down to a very small amount and not sufficient to take care of the situation such as was developing I therefore suggested to the officers of the Winnipeg Grain Exchange that it would be no discredit to the Exchange if they put a minimum price here for a short period. UNQUOTE
>
> QUOTE Of course it is inconceivable that this restriction can be kept there indefinitely if there are no buyers at that figure. UNQUOTE QUOTE This, however, will be a breathing spell which will give your Government time to decide whether any further increase will be made in the way of stabilization

---

[39]Perley later corrected the 158 million figure to 155 million. McFarland had already reached his limit by then.

[40]*Bennett Papers.*

operations UNQUOTE QUOTE I think it must be admitted by all that in the face of such wide-spread crop failures on the North American Continent the price of seventy cents at Fort William for No. One NorthernWheat is a very meagre return on the bushels raised and is a very low price to expect from world markets. UNQUOTE Most of us here fear that he is basing his opinions too much on Canadian conditions and forgetting that many other countries are growing wheat. Also that his views may tend to precipitate controversy with European buyers similar that with Western pools in nineteen twenty-nine which in our opinion would be disastrous. Pegged price at Winnipeg is seventy and one eighth cent. Price on Winnipeg exchange has been higher than that almost continuously since pegging. MacPherson is well acquainted with Western conditions and should be in London now. McFarland is anxious that you should talk this question over fully with him.[41]

When he learned that his instructions had been flouted, Bennett's reaction was explosive as he replied on August 21:

Am amazed at your information and greatly resent McFarland's failure to follow instructions and unload upon American speculators large quantities of wheat which under present European conditions will not substantially increase in price. If majority of Council think that we should make further attempt am content, but personally think that we should not authorize purchase of another bushel.[42]

Perley's memorandum of August 24 recorded the substance of his telephone call that day to Bennett:

I telephoned the Prime Minister at half past one today, and told him that pressure was coming from various directions, asking that stabilization be continued. The main reason, at the moment, is the fact that farmers are now beginning to deliver the new wheat and some of our colleagues feel that it would be disastrous if the price went down at this juncture.

The Prime Minister said that he would not approve of giving any further authority to McFarland to buy wheat pending his own return to Canada next week.

I further explained to him that I had received a telegram from McFarland today, saying that some are actively pressing the exchange to remove the present minimum or peg. "All right", said the Prime Minister, "let them do it". However, I explained to him that we thought it might be better if the peg remained on until his own return from England, when he could see McFarland and talk it over. He agreed with that idea and asked me to arrange with McFarland to be here a week from next Saturday.[43]

McFarland met Bennett on his arrival in Ottawa and the two discussed the uppermost issues of the moment which were the implementation of Canada's obligation under the international wheat agreement just conclud-ed and the question of McFarland's limit. McFarland succeeded in marrying the two issues by contending that it would be difficult to operate a system of export quotas in conjunction with the existing open-market system, unless government-financed operations were available to support export prices in keeping with the objects of the agreement. This conviction that the signatory exporting governments would require such agencies was reflected in the letter, already referred to, which McFarland addressed to Andrew Cairns. In the optimism generated by the successful negotiation of

[41] *Ibid.*
[42] *Ibid.*
[43] *Ibid.*

the international wheat agreement, Bennett now appeared to be more tractable to McFarland's representations. He agreed to raise the ceiling and they called in Mr. J. W. Spears, chairman of the lending banks' committee, to complete arrangements. Just what were the immediate provisions is not clear, but McFarland resumed hedging purchases almost immediately. His purchases of 8.3 millions in the week ending September 9 and 11.7 millions in the following week put him that much in excess of the old ceiling of 155 million bushels.

Spears was succeeded as chairman of the lending committee by Mr. S. L. Cork. By October 28, 1933, McFarland recorded that the ceiling had by then been raised to 205 million bushels and that Bennett had already given verbal assurance to Mr. Cork on another 5 million. This last amount had to be confirmed in writing and, when this was done, McFarland's limit had reached 210 million by the end of October. All autumn McFarland kept Bennett informed by daily wire on the total of his purchases. In addition to wiring him on December 12 he also sent off a handwritten note, as his exasperation with the market situation mounted:

> You will note our long line reached 210,000,000 today. That is our limit. It has been hovering around between 209,500,000 and 209,750,000 for quite some time. Chicago was inclined to drop today and I thought we might just as well complete the limit, and hope for a revival of business to hold it from now on. Export interest is very slow but should improve soon as no worthwhile volume has been taken for 2 weeks or more. The Grain Exchange Pit is dead as is also the Chicago Pit.The Public are out of the game everywhere. Out of Canada's total visible supply of 242,000,000 we have 210,000,000 and no doubt farmers own 10 to 15,000,000 of the 242,000,000, so that the great so called Public, plus the grain Trade are owners of not more than 17 to 22,000,000 Bus. That's how close we are to a "Government Wheat Board."[44]

McFarland's contention that the government owned virtually all the visible supply was not altogether valid as Mr. R. W. Milner, president of the Winnipeg grain exchange, later took some pains to point out.[45] In the later stages of support operations, McFarland could readily have cornered the market by insisting on delivery against all his futures, but he would have been the last person to indulge in such irresponsibility. Nevertheless, he continued to claim that the agency held title to all the wheat in Canada.

McFarland passed through Ottawa en route to the meeting of the wheat advisory committee in Rome when, unexpectedly, he was called to appear before the select standing committee of the house of commons on banking and commerce. The main issue before the committee was Canada's need for a central bank, and the chartered banks' performance including the financing of the wheat operations was brought under review. McFarland appeared as a witness on the afternoon and evening of March 22, 1934. After a brief oral statement, he was followed by Mr. Charles E. Bothwell (Swift Current) who reviewed the history of the provincial governments' guarantees to the pools on the marketing of the 1928 and 1929 crops before leading into the implementation of the federal government's

[44]*Ibid.*
[45]Special Committee on Bill 98, Canadian Grain Act, *Minutes of Proceedings and Evidence,* June 20, 1935, p. 27.

guarantee on the 1930 crop. Thereafter, McFarland was cross-examined by the Liberal members of the committee, including Mr. William Duff (Antigonish-Guysborough), the Honourable James L. Ralston (Shelburne-Yarmouth) and Major Charles G. (Chubby) Power (Quebec South). They elicited statements to the effect that the 1928 and 1929 crops had been cleaned up; that the unsold balance of the 1930 crop had been converted into futures to reduce carrying costs, and that the carrying of the unsold balance of the 1930 crop in itself represented a support operation on behalf of producers. McFarland also acknowledged he had been authorized to buy futures in the same cause. All attempts made by the committee members at that stage to ascertain either the limits of McFarland's credit authorization, the amount of futures held at any time or the government's contingent liability in respect of the operations were frustrated by majority votes of the committee on grounds that such disclosure would not be in the public interest. Mr. S. H. Logan of the Canadian Bank of Commerce followed McFarland and presented a useful summary of the commitments actually given by the provincial and federal governments, in turn, respecting the 1928, 1929 and 1930 crops.[46] Full disclosure of the support operations came more than a year later.[47]

To revert to the question of the limit, the 210 million bushel figure remained in effect until purchases, to provide hedges against deliveries, were once again required in the autumn of 1934. Bennett had gone again to London, and while he was there both McFarland and Perley had cabled him about a fresh crisis. Bennett agreed to another extension of 15 millions which brought the new limit to 225 million bushels. The circumstances were described in Perley's exchange of cables with Bennett on October 2, 1934:

Rush. Urgent. McFarland telephones that outside short sales have been so large today that in the rush he overran your figure about five million bushels without intending. He asks for instructions about future but we think you should decide that. Only few members in council but they do not see how you can stop now. McFarland says under this unfair pressure prices may break badly and urges that he be authorized further fifteen or twenty million which he states would in his opinion be sufficient to defeat this scheme to break market. He thinks only alternative is to take steps to close Exchange. Told him all I could do is cable you. Please answer in time for opening market Tuesday.[48]

To which Bennett replied:

McFarland also cabled, apparently gigantic combine has been organised here to break Canadian market, particulars just published in the press. As brokers are selling wheat they do not own and cannot secure except from McFarland, please authorize him to extend his operations to additional 15 million, also advise him that under circumstances his open cable may be helpful for its contents are probably known by this time.[49]

While these latest events were shaping up, fresh evidence of cabinet dissension over policy on the support operations was contained in a letter

[46] *Proceedings of the Select Standing Committee of the House of Commons on Banking and Commerce, March 22, 1934*, pp. 210-273.

[47] Special Committee on Bill 98, Canadian Grain Board Act, *Minutes of Proceedings and Evidence*, June 27-28, 1935, pp. 285-418.

[48] *Bennett Papers.*

[49] *Ibid.*

which the Honourable H. H. Stevens wrote to McFarland on October 5, 1934:

> Your very complete letter of the 1st instant is just received this morning. I do not quite know why it should have been so long in coming forward. It is a very excellent recital and I find myself in very complete sympathy with the view that you hold. Your letter is private and confidential, therefore I cannot show it to Sir George Perley, much as I would like to do so, because I think there is nothing there but what he could, and perhaps should, see.
>
> I have endeavoured as faithfully as I can to represent your views to him and I can assure you that I have already defended your position. You know yourself that he has not agreed with our policy. Other members of the Cabinet took the same stand; indeed, they take the stand that as Bennett started this off his own bat, the responsibility is his. I have taken the view however, very strongly, that as we have for the last three and a half years endorsed what has been going on, we owe it to our own self-respect to see it through, and that it would be sheer folly and madness for us to do otherwise at the present time.
>
> Furthermore, while it is quite true that the Prime Minister initiated this policy, I am convinced after three and a half years that it was the wisest thing we could possibly have done. I believe it has proven to be, under the circumstances, a better method than had we adopted a *Wheat Board,* and while I fully appreciate the great strain that has been put upon you and the very grave responsibility, I cannot but feel that you have handled the whole situation with exceptional skill and ability. . . .[50]

Although it is not documented in the correspondence among the Bennett papers, another and final increase of 10 million bushels must have been approved later that month. By October 31, 1934, McFarland's purchases in the special option account stood at their all-time peak of 158,806,000 bushels, and his balance of upwards of 76 million bushels in the 1930 crop account would have brought his total holdings to 235 million. Bennett had gone from London to head the Canadian delegation at the general assembly of the League of Nations in Geneva, and he arrived back in Ottawa on October 21. It is probable that the last extension of the limit to 235 million was approved by Bennett just after his return.

Other wheat issues were also pending at the time. Out of his indignation over speculative short-selling in the Winnipeg market, McFarland recommended that some means of restricting such trades should be adopted, the details of which are discussed in the next chapter. Much as McFarland had decried the absence of speculative buying in the depression years, he was not prepared now to see his support measures thwarted by speculation on the short side. To combat this and, at the same time, to relieve the necessity for further purchases, McFarland made a second and more prolonged resort to a price peg. The first minimum price order had been amicably arranged between McFarland and the council of the exchange on August 15, 1933. On this occasion however, just after having publicly criticized the performance of the futures market, McFarland sought Bennett's approval and support as he wired him on October 31:

> Heavy selling continues from outside sources. There can be no doubt this market is being made a target from Chicago and elsewhere October wheat closed today seventy four and quarter and three northern sixty nine cents and

[50]*Ibid.*

as most remaining wheat will be number three and lower which gives the farmer only about fifty cents for number three which is certainly cheap wheat. If you agree would recommend that you order Grain Exchange forbid trading until further notice at under today's close and this action can be justified on the grounds that it takes time until plans and regulations can be formulated and put into effect to control and restrict short selling. If such action meets with your approval please call me on long distance.[51]

McFarland followed up with another telegram to Bennett on the same day: "Have arranged as per our conversation and the change becomes effective morning."[52] McFarland's representations to the council had succeeded, for the following notice was posted by the secretary before opening of trading on November 1:

> On and after November 1 the minimum prices on futures contracts for wheat for December delivery shall be 75 cents per bushel, and for May delivery 80 cents per bushel, and until further notice no trades in these contracts shall be made below these minimum prices.
>
> By order of council passed October 31, 1934.[53]

McFarland reported to Bennett immediately upon the reaction as he wrote on November 1:

> I confirm having wired you yesterday in regard to the matter of fixing a minimum price on the Winnipeg market. I need not enter into the details as I gave them to you in the telegram.
>
> I confess to you I sent the telegram with considerable misgiving. I felt positive it was the right course to pursue and at the same time I know that these are very difficult times and I was fearful of doing anything that might react against you in any way if it went wrong. However, something had to be done so I placed the matter before you and I was delighted with the promptness with which you came back and okayed the suggestion—it was certainly a very cheering incident.
>
> It caused quite a commotion outside, as well as locally in the Exchange, but it has been well received in many quarters, even importers in Rotterdam and Antwerp have wired their connections here complimenting the action taken. Of course, it will not be at all popular in Chicago because those people down there are already restricted, and resentful of their local restrictions, and they will now be more resentful because Canada has seen fit to even talk about putting on restrictions, and particularly so at having put on a minimum price. . . .[54]

Bennett was by no means as cheered as McFarland over the decision, because it entailed an extension of the government's liability in a manner he had resisted when he refused to set a floor price back in December, 1930. He replied to McFarland on November 5:

> You realize, of course, that I am greatly concerned about the situation arising out of the pegging the price at Winnipeg. You know my views on that subject. As long as the price is better than seventy-five and eighty for December and May, no difficulty arises, but if the price drops below that we are faced with the situation which developed in the United States, which may mean a great loss. I think we must get restrictions in operation without delay.[55]

[51] *Ibid.*
[52] *Ibid.*
[53] *Ibid.*
[54] *Ibid.*
[55] *Ibid.*

McFarland only confirmed Bennett's apprehension when he wrote on November 8 to explain the government's responsibility if prices dropped to the minimum levels of 75 cents for December or 80 cents for May futures:

> I am in receipt of yours of the 5th at which time I note you were greatly concerned about the situation arising out of the pegging of prices at Winnipeg. In the meantime I had a word with you on the telephone last evening and I think you have an understanding of just how this stands. However, I will repeat, if the price drops to 80 cents for May and 75 cents for December, then we stand committed to take hedges on the grain sold each day by farmers to the elevator companies, unless the elevator companies can dispose of it to exporters or others in the trade, but until the price goes down to 80 cents and becomes water-logged at that level, we do not have to take any hedges. . . .[56]

In fact, as the minimum prices went into effect, McFarland's purchases dried up. By then, deliveries from the 1934 crop had been 75 percent completed and export demand, even from the United States feed-short markets, helped to sustain prices. Although McFarland had bought an additional 53.4 million bushels through September and October, this was his last major operation in the stabilization account. Small sales and purchases continued, however, until the day after the election, which took place on October 14, 1935. Prices held in the mid-eighties for the life of the May contract upon which the 80 cent floor had been placed. At no time was McFarland required to purchase at the floor, which remained in force for the life of the December and May contracts. But, McFarland soon became concerned about another threat to the price stability just achieved as he sought to head off the opening of trading in the new-crop October future whose price relation to old-crop futures could not be readily gauged at that time nor a minimum price set. Moreover, with a change in the government's marketing policy already in the wind there were substantial reasons it would have been awkward to have trading commitments built up in the October future at that time. These concerns, however, would have to be read into McFarland's letter of December 17, 1934, and the prime minister's reply:

> Early in January the Winnipeg Grain Exchange have always opened the October futures market for trading purposes. This you will note is a new crop month for wheat which will not be seeded for another four months or more. I have always held the view that it does not look right that short selling and gambling should be permitted in a future month, against a product which the farmer has not yet seeded, and yet speculators start playing ball with the farmers' product these long months in advance of harvest.
>
> Having regard to our operations and the fact that we will take delivery of wheat in the month of May, I feel that we should not permit the Exchange to open operations in the October future for a good while to come. In fact I would say we will not be doing anybody any harm if we forbid the opening of October options until the month of June at the earliest. In the meantime what I want from you is an expression of opinion that will back me up if I take the initiative in advising the President of the Grain Exchange that trading must not be started in that option until further notice. You can either delegate me to give that order or if you wish you can write to R. W. Milner, President of

the Winnipeg Grain Exchange. This should be done at an early date because they are almost sure to open it up early in January. My own view is that it is a menace at this time to permit operations for such a distant future delivery.[57]

After talking the matter over with McFarland, Bennett wrote back on December 20: "This is to confirm my telephone conversation with you indicating that it is the wish of the Government that you make known to the Winnipeg Grain Exchange that we are opposed to their dealing in October options until such time as the Government may approve. The reasons for this action are obvious."[58]

It was not until some months later that trading was opened in the July future, and then in an unusual August contract, before trading in the October future was approved.

Full disclosure of the transactions involved in the support operations and the liability to the banks in connection therewith awaited the special committee on bill 98. In response to Col. Ralston's motion, Bennett agreed to supply the information the select committee on banking and commerce had withheld a year earlier. On June 22, 1935, Mr. R. C. Findlay provided the details and, in the absence of Mr. McFarland, Mr. George McIvor defended the government's policy. Even at that time, no one called for information on the limits imposed by the government on McFarland's purchases and that information was not provided.

When one considers the long record of Bennett's concern and genuine anxiety over the financial risk and its political implications and McFarland's personal concern that his judgment be vindicated it seems almost incredible that their fears were not realized. Because the government changed hands in 1935, neither Bennett nor McFarland was involved in carrying the government's liability through to its ultimate resolution. But, in October, 1935, as chairman of the new Canadian wheat board, McFarland began negotiations with Mr. L. C. Brouillette, president of Canadian Co-operative Wheat Producers Limited for the board's take-over of the agency's holdings including the unsold balance of the 1930 pool stocks. The take-over was effected on December 2, 1935, on the same day that Mr. J. R. Murray was appointed chief commissioner of the board, in replacement of Mr. McFarland. As will be described later, a settlement was effected with Canadian Co-operative Wheat Producers Limited on the 1930 pool wheat account by act of parliament in 1936, sponsored by the successor King government, which authorized a sum of not more than $6,600,000 to be paid out of the consolidated revenue fund as a total final payment on that account. The actual amount claimed was $6,509,269.03 in order to bring the total wheat payment up to 60 cents a bushel, basis One Northern Fort William, for producers who had delivered at lower initial payments in that crop year. Tha act also authorized the payment to producers of the net credit balances showing in the coarse grains pool accounts of Canadian Co-operative Wheat Producers Limited at the time of transfer of its wheat account to the Canadian wheat board. Final payments on the coarse grains accounts totalled $350,684.65.

[57] *Ibid.*
[58] *Ibid.*

By July 31, 1939, when they had all been disposed of, the Canadian wheat board realized a net profit of $8,953,343.07 on the 205,287,000 bushels of wheat and wheat contracts which the board had taken over from Canadian Co-operative Wheat Producers Limited on December 2, 1935. This amount was paid by the board into the consolidated revenue fund. Although the federal treasury had already paid the arbitrary settlement of $6,509,269.03 on the 1930 pool wheat account, it still ended up with a small surplus, after deducting this payment, of $2,414,074.04 on the prolonged price support operation.

But after accounting for the financial results of these operations, the question remains as to what price-benefit producers actually received in the four crop years from August 1, 1931 to July 31, 1935, as a result of the market price support. Toward the end of that period, McFarland began to place a value on this contribution and, during his illness, Mr. George McIvor testified to the special committee on bill 98 that, in his own opinion, the support operations had added 15 cents a bushel to producers' income. Although the prices producers actually received were known there was no way, of course, to determine objectively what prices would have been in the absence of support operations. McIvor cautioned that his figure was nothing more than an intelligent guess. In the election campaign in 1935, however, the Honourable Earl Lawson, without Bennett's knowledge, had prepared a campaign advertisement which appeared on billboards throughout western Canada and read: "Stand by Canada. McFarland saved the wheat grower. Bennett gave the grain growers $150,000,000 and a wheat board. Stand by Bennett's grain board, for higher wheat prices. Vote Bennett."[59]

If McIvor's estimate of 15 cents were applied to all the wheat delivered from farms from 1931 to 1935 the total of $150 million would not have been far off the mark, but the figure was only as good as McIvor's guess. There could be no doubt, however, that the support operations had yielded tangible price benefits.

[59]*House of Commons Debates*, February 1, 1936, pp. 80, 118.

21

FROM CENTRAL SELLING AGENCY TO WHEAT BOARD

When John I. MacFarland accepted the general managership of Canadian Co-operative Wheat Producers Limited, he had many years of experience behind him as president of a line elevator company which made daily use of the futures market as he built the company up from the initial investment of Max Aitken and R. B. Bennett into a prosperous enterprise. As head of an investor-owned company, he had no reason to be enamoured of the pools which had been organized to provide an alternative marketing system. This is not to say that he lacked a lively and warm sense of the producers' interests, which he developed over the years of direct dealings with them.

When the central agency's sales policy came under criticism and financial difficulties arose, McFarland's prejudice against the pools, as such, was expressed in his derisive personal references to them and his insistence upon closing the agency's overseas offices. Of the various alternatives open to Bennett as McFarland took charge, one would have been to entrust the marketing of the entire crop to the open futures market system, but the point had already been reached beyond which Bennett could not survive politically by pursuing a policy of nonintervention. At the other end of the spectrum, however, his government was being asked to assume the risk of establishing a floor price. He had seen this policy fail at great cost to the federal farm board in the United States. At this stage, Bennett was determined to have nothing to do with price-fixing or a government marketing board, and in this conviction he was amply supported by McFarland. Thus Bennett adopted a middle course, vaguely defined as "ensuring the orderly marketing of the 1930 crop" but secretly acquiescing when McFarland advised him of the need to support the market at 50 cents. Although that figure became the initial target of the government's price support, the level varied from time to time and the policy which McFarland carried out is best described as a price support operation which was flexible in the sense that the market was supported at various levels as time wore on. This policy was distinct from that of a price stabilization operation which would have required the maintenance of a fixed minimum price to producers irrespective of world market prices and at considerable financial risk to the government. Yet for convenience' sake, the McFarland price support operations were contemporarily referred to as "stabilization" operations.

McFarland's method of price support for which he conveniently used the facilities of the central selling agency, first by withholding sales of the 1930 pool account and then by the direct purchase of futures, was undoubtedly the most economical, and the least disruptive to the existing trade mechanism, which any governmental intervention at that time could have devised.

In the process of pursuing the price support operations, however, Bennett's and McFarland's disenchantment grew with the marketing system they were trying to protect; the purpose of this chapter is to trace the course by which they passed through a metamorphosis in their attitudes until they emerged as champions of the replacement of the Winnipeg grain futures market by a compulsory grain board.

EARLY ANTIPATHY TO A BOARD

It will be recalled from the early stages of Bennett's exposure to the domestic wheat problem, that the influence of the pool leaders as policy-advisers waned as soon as the financial difficulties of the pools required federal action. Although Bennett held McPhail and the Albertan farm leader, Henry Wise Wood, personally in high regard, he was frequently critical of the pool performance collectively and, as an institution, he regarded it as a company in receivership. On the other hand, Bennett considered that the policy he had adopted to keep the futures market intact would command the appreciation of the private grain trade. It was only when, to his surprise and obvious annoyance, criticism of his policy emanated from trade sources that Bennett began to think in terms of a wheat board, not as a proposal he had ever favored, but as a punitive measure. At the beginning of his administration, however, Bennett turned back every recommendation which came to him in favor of a government-operated wheat board.

It will be recalled that in the autumn of 1930, the pools and provincial premiers pressed strongly for a government-supported floor price of 70 cents. While Bennett was still abroad at the imperial conference, the three premiers met with Sir George Perley in Ottawa on November 18. As a third preference among their suggestions, they had advocated a national stabilization board. As the movement for a 100 percent compulsory pool receded, the pools passed a series of resolutions advocating the establishment of a national marketing board. Early in 1933, Mr. George W. Robertson, secretary of Saskatchewan Co-operative Wheat Producers Limited, mounted a gigantic campaign with the object of securing one hundred thousand signatures to petitions to that end. Numerous petitions with thousands of signatures found their way into the prime minister's files. But McFarland had sent Bennett an early copy of the form of petition which the latter acknowledged on February 11, 1933:

> I have your letter with enclosure regarding the formation of a marketing board.
> These people are incapable of appreciating anything. You know what injury they did the country on one occasion and I suppose they are endeavouring to see if they can't do it again.[1]

[1] *Bennett Papers.*

While this campaign was under way, Mr. C. R. McIntosh (North Battleford) repeatedly asked Bennett if the government was giving consideration to the establishment of a board. On February 13, 1933, Bennett replied:

No consideration has been given to this matter at this particular time or any other time. It will be within the memory of Hon. members that in 1930, and I think in the previous year or years, efforts were made to induce the government to establish a national wheat board. These efforts did not succeed, they have not yet succeeded.[2]

After the pool leaders presented their request formally to Bennett at the end of that month, he replied to another question from McIntosh on March 6: "I have advised the representatives of the pools that the government has no intention of setting up a national wheat marketing board at this session."[3]

CHANGING ATTITUDES

The first incident to jar Bennett's complacency regarding the Winnipeg grain exchange had been its secretary's spontaneous, but ill-guarded observation that the government had been speculating in wheat. Bennett's first letter of November 26, 1932, to McFarland regarding Mr. A. E. Darby's statement has already been quoted. That Bennett resented the implication strongly was reflected in the fact that he wrote twice to McFarland on the same day and issue, and in his second letter of November 26 he broached the wheat board proposal as a retaliatory move:

Motherwell, Vallance, and Donnelly tried to make life a burden for me last night in connection with the wheat situation. The matter will have to be thrashed out on the floor of the House after adjournment.

It is a very embarrassing position and I may say to you that it is no use for Darby to deny a statement. He gave it by telephone and it has caused us in the East a tremendous amount of trouble because it was his statement that "I speculated and lost" that the subsequent criticisms have been based. . . . He has done me great harm and caused me much trouble; and I suppose the proper thing now to do is to create a wheat board, take over the crop, close up the Exchange, and see what we can do, without having to worry with the unfair and unjust criticism of those we have endeavoured to protect from destruction.[4]

McFarland did his best to mollify Bennett as he replied on November 29:

. . . Of course, when a thing gets mixed up in politics people are liable to lose their perspective as well as their judgement and notwithstanding this it is my firm belief that this whole operation will stand for the fullest discussion in every detail, and I believe you should take the offensive instead of being on the defensive and from past experience I know your abilities on the offensive are much more effective than in trying to defend.

The sinister part is that there is an element who are trying to force the Government into a Government Wheat Board Monopoly policy. You may have to submit in the end, although I firmly believe that had you established a Wheat Board two years ago your difficulties today would be much greater

---

[2]*House of Commons Debates,* February 13, 1933, p. 2019.
[3]*Ibid.,* March 6, 1933, p. 2716.
[4]*Bennett Papers.*

than they are, because under a Government Monopoly or by the system which has been used for the last two years, the government in any event would be held responsible, not only for the low prices but also for the monetary losses, which might ensue. It must be remembered that Canada's experience with a Wheat Board in the past was during a period when supplies of wheat as well as crops of wheat were very small and when it was not a matter of trying to find customers but simply a matter of seeing how little the customer could get along with. That is a vastly different condition than has been existing for the last several years and a Wheat Board, no matter how constituted, and operated, would by this time have been utterly discredited, besides having cost the country lots of money.. . .

PS You mention closing the Grain Exchange and forming a wheat Board. Don't jump too hastily.[5]

But the real blow came during the course of the budget debate when, on March 24, 1933, the Honourable J. L. Ralston accused the Bennett government of gambling in wheat, as he said:

They have also entered into a guarantee with regard to the marketing of the 1930 wheat crop. I do not intend to spend much time on that subject this afternoon, but it is being discussed in the public press of the country. While I am prepared to admit that the Prime Minister did not deliberately mean to mislead the house, he certainly left an impression which was different from the facts with regard to the marketing of the 1930 wheat crop and the guarantee that was given. He left on the house the impression that the operations which were being conducted by Mr. McFarland were in connection with the wheat which was being taken over from the farmers. Instead of that, what was done, as I am informed, was this: they took the wheat purchased from the farmer and converted it into "futures" from time to time. This may or may not have been a good policy, because it was betting against the future, but it had this in its favour, that the "futures" represented wheat actually purchased from the farmer, and it might be legitimately a matter which the government might, to save carrying charges, turn over and over in the hope that a loss might eventually be saved. But I say it is absolutely wrong for the government to guarantee that marketing operation and permit it not simply to deal in wheat purchased from the farmer but to speculate in futures which have nothing to do with the wheat purchased from the farmer originally, and to do this in order to accomplish two objects: first to bolster up the market, that is, Mr. McFarland or his agency, having attempted to sell find the market low, and adopt the simple expedient of themselves buying "futures" in order to create a demand. That is the way they bolster up the market. Secondly, faced with a situation where there is a drop in the "futures" which they hold, they go into the market, but not simply to handle the same quantity of wheat they had before, but to speculate and to cover their loss by making a bet in July for instance that the price of wheat in October, say, will have gone up by that time, and they buy more wheat in the form of futures. While my right hon. friend (Mr. Bennett) calls it hedging, it is no more hedging than it is for me, if I am in the market holding Montreal Light, Heat and Power and find it going down, to go and buy Consolidated Gas to endeavour to recover my losses. That is not hedging at all. It is just plain, ordinary speculation, or what is more properly called gambling in the wheat market.[6]

[5]*Ibid.*
[6]*House of Commons Debates,* March 24, 1933, pp. 3367-3368.

Years later, Mr. George McIvor recalled the fact that the public then had come to regard wheat as the major Canadian political problem which would not have loomed so large had the government simply invested in cash wheat instead of buying futures. McIvor has written:

I am sure that you will recall the fact that wheat became really the number one consideration in the Canadian political scene in the period 1933/35. It was felt by a great many that these operations in the futures market was simply a big gamble. To-day, of course, the carrying of 220 million bushels of wheat would not even create a stir or make the front page because we are used to that sort of thing. I think, however, one of the reasons for public interest in the years referred to above, is the fact that the government agency was dealing in futures. I do not think that if the government agency had been carrying actual wheat that there would have been such a stir, but a lot of people were suspicious of futures, although the purchase of a future is simply a contract to take delivery of wheat at a certain period, or sale of a future is the reverse of that, and I think the thing that most people overlooked was the fact that through the use of the futures market Mr. McFarland was able to save millions and millions and millions of dollars in carrying charges. The use of the futures market enabled him to carry wheat at a much more reasonable cost than it would have been had he carried actual wheat at the current rate of storage.[7]

Strangely enough, Bennett left it to Stevens to reply to the Ralston charge which he did, to little effect, by reading from a prepared statement which recounted the reasons for the support operations.[8] Nevertheless, Bennett was much upset by the charge, made first by Darby, repeated in the press, and made now in the house of commons by Ralston. He frequently referred to Ralston's attack, in injured tones, in subsequent debates. For Colonel Ralston, his speech launched him as a critic of the government's wheat policy and he developed that role over the next two years.

Although Ralston pursued the accusation, Bennett did not permit himself to be carried away by his reprisal notion, and in the spring of 1933 he acknowledged in the house that he had rejected the wheat pools' petition for a board.

In the absence of a board, however, the lending banks' committee was developing certain misgivings, not of a personal nature, but over the concentration of responsibility in one person for the day-to-day decisions on the support operations. Mr. J. W. Spears, who was about to retire as chairman of the lending banks' committee, sent a telegram to his president, Mr. Jackson Dodds, which Mr. W. R. Creighton, Ottawa manager of the Bank of Montreal, transmitted by letter on September 1, 1933, to Bennett:

Mr. Dodds has asked me to send you the following telegram which he has received from Mr. J. W. Spears, Assistant General Manager of the Bank in Winnipeg.

"Strictly confidential. Canadian Co-operative Wheat Producers Limited. Having in mind Dominion Government will be in grain business for long time and at the same time undesirability form wheat board I suggest consideration be given to advisability there being in charge of Government operations committee of three headed by J. I. McFarland in place of latter having whole

[7]See Mr. George McIvor's letter of November 6, 1973, appendix 7.
[8]*House of Commons Debates,* March 28, 1933, pp. 3467-3468.

say. Appointment of small committee should be in interest of J. I. McFarland himself, Canada as a whole, Dominion Government, Banks, grain trade and Western Canada. Canada having agreed to export quotas means future will be different from past and one should not be asked to bear whole responsibility of buying and selling. McFarland disposed to lean too far one way or other on occasions and in everyone's interest seems he should have benefit of two others of mature judgment and experience. Such men should be available. There have been occasions when our market was held above export basis all with the best intentions and I believe grain trade as a whole would say that although that has been the case Canada would notwithstanding have had a very large carry-over this year there are those who feel that temperamentally McFarland finds it difficult to let wheat go also he may be motivated on occasions by desire make large profits and so vindicate past policies. I have been considering this question in last day or two and you will recall that last Autumn McFarland discussed with me advisability form small committee but in telegraphing you now I was prompted by long interview with J. R. Murray yesterday afternoon. Murray strongly favours formation of committee although in doing so he is not criticizing McFarland who he believes could not in the main have done very much different in past two or three years. Murray has also discussed situation with S. T. Smith, President of Exchange, but with no other. Smith favours small committee and agreed Murray should discuss with me. I am telegraphing these views in case Prime Minister discusses grain situation with you before arrival McFarland Saturday morning."[9]

Nothing came of the proposal for a three-man board, particularly since it was sponsored by a well-known Liberal, Mr. J. R. Murray, who had long been associated with the Honourable Thomas A. Crerar in United Grain Growers Limited. Mr. Murray was now managing Bennett's and McFarland's former company, the Alberta Pacific Grain Company Limited.

The next incident which directed Bennett's thinking in terms of a wheat board arose from an attempt by McFarland to get endorsement from the council of the Winnipeg grain exchange for the production control aspects of the international wheat agreement. In the autumn of 1933, the federal and provincial governments were in the midst of their campaign to elicit support for acreage reduction when McFarland asked the exchange to endorse the campaign. After considerable deliberation the council of the exchange issued the following statement on October 28, 1933:

The impression is abroad that the Winnipeg Grain Exchange is opposed to plans recently adopted with a view to improving the wheat situation. The council of the exchange feels that this impression should be removed. No statement has previously been made or authorized by the council in connection with the international wheat agreement. Individual members may have expressed opinions but these cannot be taken as representing the views of the exchange as a whole.

The only function of the Winnipeg Grain Exchange is to provide a market place and trading facilities for all those interested in the producing, handling and marketing of our crops. These facilities are continuous and they will be utilized under whatever conditions may from time to time prevail. Under these circumstances it is obvious that the Exchange, as such, cannot undertake to formulate any statement which could reflect the unanimous views of the members.

[9] *Bennett Papers.*

Without entering into any discussion of the causes which have produced the Canadian wheat surplus, it is the fact that its existence has led to support being given by the government to wheat prices. Many members of the Exchange have regarded this policy as beneficial to the producers and as in the national interest, and any reasonable measures which may be taken by the Canadian government to reduce or dispose of the surplus will meet with the co-operation of the members of the Grain Exchange insofar as such co-operation is within their power.

Actions have been taken by importing countries which have led to the use of lands for wheat growing which are more suitable for the production of other commodities, in the course of time, with restoration of more normal trade conditions, these lands will revert to more advantageous uses. When this development occurs the markets for Canadian grain will again expand. In the meantime, however, government measures which assist in maintaining a free world market for our grain will receive every possible co-operation from the members of the exchange.

The maintenance of the free market system which has functioned continuously and, on the whole, smoothly, under the abnormal strains of the past three or four years is essential. It is necessary to the retention of the goodwill of importers in the existing markets abroad, and it is only through the development of this goodwill that Canada can maintain or increase her share of the available world markets.[10]

McFarland was incensed, not only because the council of the exchange had failed to agree upon an endorsement of the acreage reduction campaign, but particularly by the inference in the last paragraph of the release to the effect that the free market system had functioned smoothly, on the whole, in the past three or four years of abnormal strains. This was too much for McFarland, as he wrote to Bennett on October 30:

I am enclosing for your information, clipping from the Free Press Evening Bulletin, showing a copy of the Resolution issued by the Council of the Winnipeg Grain Exchange. I had no knowledge of what was going to be in this Resolution until I saw it in the newspaper Saturday night. I may be entirely prejudiced and wrong in my views, but my reaction to this Resolution is that it is just a bunch of dishwater and does not contain a single constructive suggestion. On the other hand, however, the last paragraph is just the kind of stuff which will make the enemies of the Grain Exchange all the more determined to have a Government Wheat Board.

This Resolution, you will note, was put out by the elected council of the Exchange, consisting of some nine or ten members. I do not know whether it was unanimous with them or not, but I do know that Mr. Smith had intended something much more constructive and definite than this Resolution contains.

In the meantime, I do not think the Council represents the body of the Exchange and there may be a counter-Resolution from the Exchange as a whole before they get through with the squabble.

It seems that the Elevator Companies pretty well dominate the Winnipeg Grain Exchange and from the motives of selfishness they are not likely to agree that production should be decreased, because they are so short-sighted that they cannot see that eventually it will be detrimental to them and that there will be something more than large bushelage or tonnage of importance, not only to themselves, but to the country.

[10]*Free Press Evening Bulletin*, Winnipeg, October 28, 1933.

The Resolution points out that their Institution has functioned continuously and smoothly under abnormal strains of the past three or four years. This, of course, is untrue. It has neither functioned continuously nor smoothly. The only way it functions smoothly is when it is going down. Most things run pretty well downhill, and it is one of them, and the only thing that has kept it from going out of existence has been the fact that the Government operations have taken care of the farmers' hedges, but these men who operate this Exchange, are either blind, or determined not to admit anything, although I do think that our friend Sidney Smith will come out with a blast in the other direction. He is past-president of the Exchange and a councillor for this year.[11]

Bennett's reaction was even more explosive as he replied to McFarland on November 2, 1933:

I have your letter enclosing copy of the resolution passed by the Winnipeg Grain Exchange.

It is incredible that men should pass such a resolution. I am sending a letter to Mr. Smith, copy of which I enclose herewith. If they are unwilling to be of any assistance at this time, I think it is quite clear that we will have to create a wheat board and close the Grain Exchange. If their idea of running smoothly is to have the Government support the grain business to the extent we are now doing, then all I can say is that, so far as I am able to control it, it will not run smoothly any longer than I can help.[12]

The letter of which Bennett had enclosed a copy had been addressed on the same date to Mr. Sidney T. Smith:

My attention has been directed to the resolution recently passed by your Council, and I should like to know just what is meant by indicating that, on the whole, the market system has functioned smoothly. The resolution in question is an insult to the intelligence of those who read it and I find it incredible that men charged with serious responsibilities should have passed it. I must say that it is the strongest argument that has yet been presented to me for the creation of a wheat board at the earliest possible moment. I feel quite certain, Mr. Smith, from what I know of you, that you will agree that you never have read such an aggregation of unmeaning words, put forth by business men as a contribution towards the solution of the problem of our surplus wheat, as that contained in the so-called resolution.

I hope you will pardon me for taking up your time in connection with this matter.

P.S. I have instructed the Law Officers to prepare me a memorandum as to just what we can do in the way of a wheat board.[13]

It befell Mr. Smith to make personal amends; this he did very gracefully in his letter of November 6 to Bennett:

Your letter of November 2nd received and I am not surprised at your opinion of the resolution that was issued by the Council of the Grain Exchange. I thoroughly agree with every word you say about it being an aggregation of meaningless words. Personally I disapproved of it entirely and drew up a short statement which I felt would have met the situation positively and clearly in loyal support of you and your policies in connection with the wheat business, but a number of men, including Mr. J. R. Murray, who has some influence in the Exchange, were in favour of the modified statement which they put out.

[11] *Bennett Papers.*
[12] *Ibid.*
[13] *Ibid.*

I would like very much indeed to have shown your letter to some of these men, but owing to the fact that it was personal, I could not, of course, take that liberty without consulting you.

As you are aware, I have always given the fullest support in any public statements I have made and in every other way I could to you and your policies in connection with the grain business, and I shall continue to do so, as I feel certain that what you have done has been in the interest of the producers and in the national interest, and that the operations in the market have been carried on in the best possible way and at a minimal of cost to the country.

I regret that you feel constrained to consider the advisability of the establishment of a Wheat Board as I do not think a Wheat Board can possibly accomplish any thing more than has been accomplished in the interests of the producers, and of course it is a very expensive thing to carry out.

If at any time you feel there is any matter in which I can give assistance to you, you have but to call upon me and you will receive my full co-operation. I think of you often and the heavy responsibilities you are carrying in these strenuous times, and all that you have done for the grain trade, and am therefore doubly sorry that such a poor statement should have been issued.[14]

Bennett returned his acknowledgment on November 8:

It was very kind of you to write to me as you did on the 6th instant.

The speech made by Mr. Bracken is one that commends itself to most people and, candidly, I was amazed that he made so clear-cut and definite a statement.

I have heard of Mr. Murray's activities. He is the one man who should have supported us in our efforts to improve prices. That he has not done so indicates, in my judgment, faulty appreciation of the situation. I dislike a Wheat Board more than you do but if the Grain Exchange is working against us in our endeavour to reduce inventories, we will have to provide some other means to deal with the situation; and the jumble of words that was sent by the Grain Exchange has made many people wonder if the Exchange is composed of businessmen or some other class that need not be described. If the Grain Exchange desired to oppose our action it would be perfectly within its rights to do so; but to produce a mass of meaningless words and send them out to the world has reflected greatly upon the business capacity and the intelligence of the members of the Grain Exchange. I tell you this very frankly because it has been impressed upon me very strongly.[15]

Although he had been directly responsible for inflaming Bennett's wrath, McFarland made a very modest attempt to put out the fire as he wrote on November 6, 1933:

I am in receipt of yours of the 2nd, also copy of letter enclosed to Mr. Smith. Your estimate of the value of that Resolution is just about right, and I am glad that you wrote Mr. Smith in those terms.

In the meantime, to be fair with Sidney, I will say that I do know that that Resolution did not contain the ideas which he wished to embody in it, but he was over-ruled by a clique led by our friend J. R. Murray. . . .

Mr. Smith has been over to see me and read me your letter and he is very much worried for fear that you may think that this Resolution represents his sentiments. As a matter of fact he addressed the Kiwanis Club some ten days ago and he was very outspoken as to his attitude, and I understand from him

[14]*Ibid.*
[15]*Ibid.*

that he is making another address before one of the other Clubs at an early date and his address in this instance will be published in full and he is going to make a full statement.

Now, referring to the matter of the formation of a Canadian Wheat Board. You, of course, are well aware that I have been adverse to a Wheat Board just as much as you have been, and if there was any possible way of avoiding a Wheat Board I would still be adverse to it, but nothing short of a miracle between now and the next crop, in my opinion, can avoid the necessity of the formation of such a Board to take charge of the whole operation of the Grain Trade. I can see that some things can yet happen which would render it unnecessary, but they are not yet apparent.

I always held the view that if and when different countries should agree upon an export quota, it would be at least very difficult if not impossible to get along without a Wheat Board in this country as well as Wheat Boards in other countries. It is quite clear in my mind that a Wheat Board in Canada could not operate satisfactorily unless there were similar Boards in other countries, charged with the responsibility of at least handling the export business of those countries, and I refer particularly to Argentine, Australia and the United States. So far as Russia is concerned they have a Wheat Board now and a very complete one, and all that is necessary there is to have an agreement upon the quota. The Balkan countries are of minor importance, but, of course, it would be smoother sailing if they were also governed by a Board in the matter of their exports. I included the United States in the above list because I am not yet prepared to believe that the United States will be out of the export business next year unless they have another crop failure in wheat such as this year. For that reason it is necessary to include them in any plan. I can imagine it would not be difficult for Australia to arrange a Wheat Board, but I do not know how difficult it might be in the Argentine. . . .

A week ago I wrote to Andy Cairns, and I am enclosing you a copy of my letter. When I wrote him I had in mind the, to me, apparent fact that this open marketing system, under the quota agreements, will not deliver the goods. On the other hand I am obsessed with the belief that a Wheat Board in Canada only, without Wheat Boards in the other countries to co-ordinate and co-operate with a Board in this country, would be largely futile. . . .[16]

Bennett maintained his attack on the exchange when he met Mr. James A. Richardson in Toronto on November 29. The tenor of their conversation can be gauged from the letter Richardson wrote to Bennett on the following day:

I have been turning over in my mind the general remarks you made to me in Toronto yesterday with reference to the grain trade.

It is possible that in a conversation I might be able to remove from your mind some apprehensions you have in regard to the grain trade as a whole. There are, though, in the business in which I am primarily engaged, as in every other business, all kinds of people. We are not a unanimous body in regard to the problems surrounding the grain trade; much less are we a unanimous body in regard to problems outside of it. . . .

I early believed that we were justified in giving the farmer some support during this trying period. I did, however, expect at that time that the price factor would soon have an effect on production. High tariff policies in importing countries, on the one hand, and depreciated currencies in exporting countries, on the other, intervened and as I saw the decline in the peso and the Australian pound I saw the acreage in these countries increase. Therefore it

[16] *Ibid.*

seemed to me that if we were, in this country, going to maintain sound money and not abandon our wheat production in favor of the Southern Hemisphere, it was necessary for us to protect our farmer some other way.

It bore my judgment that the policy of supporting the markets in the way it has been done, rather than through a Wheat Board, was desirable and necessary. It seemed to me that it offered all the advantages that a Wheat Board could possibly offer, without the many disadvantages attached to it; in fact I advocated a similar plan before the Committee on Agriculture at Ottawa. It was considerable time before Mr. McFarland took office. My views on this subject are well-known to the members of the Winnipeg Grain Exchange.

I am sorry indeed if you feel that you have not had my best co-operation in these difficult times. However, whether you think so or not you have had it and I would welcome an opportunity of answering any other point of view that might be presented by anyone.

I hardly feel it is necessary for me to write this letter, but I only do it to clear up any possible misunderstanding you might have. I understand from our talk in Toronto, that consideration is being given to changes of a rather momentous character, affecting the whole grain business of Canada, and before anything of this character should be consummated I would welcome an opportunity of learning something of what is in your mind, which would give me an opportunity of giving some thought to the proposals and giving you my judgment, as a grain merchant, for whatever my judgment might be worth. I am quite capable of taking a disinterested viewpoint on these matters. I have never yet advocated a policy that I thought was against the best public interest and I have no intention of doing so. Whether my views would agree with those you now hold I do not know, but my best opinion and judgment is yours to command at all times, whenever you feel it might possibly be worth while to have it.[17]

In addition to his own letter to Bennett, Mr. Sidney Smith brought a delegation from the council of the exchange to Ottawa early in December to intercede with Bennett. Upon their return to Winnipeg the delegation reported to McFarland that they had a very satisfactory and pleasant visit. There matters rested for a while on the wheat board issue.

CAPITULATION

If, in earlier days, McFarland had derided the pool philosophy he became even more articulate now in his condemnation of the attitude of exchange members who upheld the virtue of the futures mechanism while doing little to assist him in the load the government was carrying. Some years earlier Dr. Robert A. Magill, while he was chairman of the board of grain supervisors, had recognized and acknowledged that the futures market had not been designed to function under wartime controls. Sir Josiah Stamp, in turn, had grappled with the notion that there could be abnormal conditions in peacetime when it would have difficulty in functioning. It was undoubtedly the failure of his contemporaries to acknowledge the current difficulties that roused McFarland's ire. But he had become despondent when, by the spring of 1934, he found no opportunity of reducing his holdings without breaking the market and he realized, moreover, that there could be no return to a normal market as long as the government holdings were the dominant factor in it. It was when he gave up hope of solution by the continuation of his own operations that he sent a handwritten note to Bennett on June 2, 1934:

> I have labored diligently and so far as I can see unselfishly since Dec 1930 on this wheat problem. You have given me wonderful co-operation and sympathy, and we have both had in mind the saving of the present existing open market system. I have been adverse to the demands for a Government Wheat Board monopoly, because I have considered it in the best interests of Canada to avoid destroying the old system and hoped the supply situation might get back to normal in some reasonable time, and then we could look back and feel we had done the right and as well the decent thing. There can be no doubt the open market system cannot survive in a period of surplus such as the world has had, and in a time when farmers in all other countries have been protected by Tariffs, quotas and Bonuses. The only factor which has saved the system thus far, has been our support. I am now coming to the conclusion that we are near the end of the road. The wheat we hold creates the price so long as we hold it. The Public and also many otherwise practical men of affairs see the price advance on the blackboards, and they think we could sell out if we so desired, whereas the fact is the opposite. It gives the public a false impression. The fact is the quoted price is a false measuring rod, and we are measured by that yard stick. I am therefore putting it up to you as to the advisability of seriously considering a national wheat control board. Brouillette and his followers want it and will not rest until they succeed. Indeed I am not sure they may be right. The Pit operations are a sham, and have been for several years. The registered price represents only the value of that portion of the supplies which we do not own, and as you fully realize that has been but a small percentage of the available supplies.
>
> I am depressed and discouraged more than usual the past couple of days because when we tried to sell a good lot yesterday the price fell away. Stop loss orders were uncovered and the public holdings, which were really not large, were thrown overboard.
>
> I am sure you think I am against a Board, and it is true I have been, but from here on I have no argument against it. I have no regrets for what I so ardently hoped to accomplish, and to which I so diligently applied myself. There is no doubt 1934-35 cereal year is more promising than any of the previous five years. That however is no assurance that the present system of open marketing will operate thereafter, unaided. It might however be a good time to turn the whole thing over to Government monopoly. I put this up to you for your consideration.
>
> Remember I am not quitting so long as you want to carry on as at present, but I do want to go on record in stating that a National Board may be the better policy. It would relieve you and your government of direct responsibility.[18]

From this confession of his change of view, McFarland never turned back. Although he would continue to advise Bennett not to move with too great haste, these were political considerations which did not reflect any change of heart. Confirmation that McFarland continued to recommend a board can be found in a letter he received from the Honourable H. H. Stevens just a few weeks before the latter's resignation from the cabinet. Stevens wrote on October 5, 1934:

> . . . I note that you say the time perhaps has come when the whole question of the establishment of a Wheat Board should be considered. If I were to tell this

---

[18]*Ibid.*

to our friend, Sir George Perley, he would probably die of apoplexy forthwith because if there is one thing that is anathema to him it is a Wheat Board. Yet to any person acquainted with the general world situation it must be obvious that where the whole of the buying market is under control, most of it under a quota system, and where the exporting countries, at least Argentine and Australia, are substantially in a condition of Government direction and control, and the United States is on a domestic basis, surely it is not common sense for Canada to expect that it can function in the old-fashioned way with an open futures market. As a matter of fact, of course, we have not been so functioning because had you not been there, Canada's market would have collapsed three years ago, and wheat probably would have been today, and for the last two or three years, around 25 cents. So why kid ourselves that there is going to be a restoration of normal trade?

I will cull out of your letter some observations and pass them on to Sir George as suggestions, more particularly the question of the investigation, which I have already talked over with him and he is not very warm in regard to it. In fact, I am certain he will do nothing, but it might be well to have it placed before him in some official way. In the meantime I will keep your letter confidential.[19]

SUPERVISION OF THE EXCHANGE

The reference to "the question of the investigation" in Stevens' letter referred to the action McFarland had recommended following the bear raid which had begun in late September, 1934. For years McFarland had deplored the absence of speculators from the market and for that reason had welcomed the purchase of seats on the Winnipeg exchange by Chicago traders. But under depression conditions, and in the light of the size of the holdings in the 1930 pool and special option accounts which, although under government control, nevertheless overhung the market, speculators found nothing attractive about helping to relieve McFarland's burden by buying futures; on the contrary, they saw more opportunity for profit by taking a short position. Thus, on this occasion, when speculators did return to the market, they came in on the wrong side and embarrassed McFarland's operations to the point that he had to request a further increase in his limit.[20] On October 1, 1934, the day before he had wired Sir George Perley and cabled Bennett overseas about the increase, McFarland had given a press interview in Winnipeg in which he recommended an investigation of selling in the Winnipeg, Buenos Aires and Liverpool futures markets, and he also prepared a fifteen-page memorandum in which he elaborated his recommendation on the need for legislation to provide for the investigation of trading on the Winnipeg exchange and if need be, to prohibit certain types of trading. McFarland was well informed on the operations of the grain futures administration in the United States which permitted a government agency to investigate the trades of individual operators. Although McFarland started out by preparing a memorandum for Bennett's benefit, he was convinced that the time had come to make a public statement criticizing the way in which the open futures market was

[19]*Ibid.* The first portion of this letter which disclosed cabinet dissension over the McFarland operations was cited on p. 444.
[20]See p. 443.

being used in an unconstructive manner; he forwarded the memorandum to Bennett with his covering letter of October 16, 1934:

I understand you will be back in Ottawa by Sunday. I presume you will be too busy to want to have me go to Ottawa at the present time, although I can quite realize that you probably would like to talk over what has occurred in the wheat situation since you went to Geneva, and I will be glad to go down whenever you feel that you have time to talk the matter over.

I have prepared the enclosed statement. At the moment it may be regarded as a memorandum which I have made out for your perusal, although, as a matter of fact, I had in mind when preparing it that it might receive greater publicity. My personal feeling is that such a statement as this, coming from myself, is probably overdue. I think I owe it to the public of this country to do some plain talking through the press. There is no further object to be gained by temporizing with the Grain Exchanges. There is only one thing to do and that is to take the bull by the horns and control such institutions, and the sooner it is done, the better. I think you will find the enclosed article is free from venom, prejudice or spite — it is a plain statement of facts which I do not believe anyone can dispute or refute. I will not publish it until I hear from you or until I have an opportunity of talking the matter over with you.[21]

At the conclusion of his statement, McFarland warned of the need for government supervision of trading; he claimed that his support operations had saved producers $200 million, and that the futures system could not have been relied upon without intervention, as he wrote:

It is evident that the merchant dealing in actual grain cannot afford the risk involved in this large investment without protection. It is equally evident that this protection is under the present system, in some measure, provided by a large body of non-members of Grain Exchanges, who are uninformed as to the operations of the large speculator who is in a position to manipulate the market for his own profit. If the Futures Marketing System is the best system which can be devised to finance and distribute the crop, then there is a moral responsibility on the Governments of this country to take such steps as will protect the operation of this system in some measure at least against unwarranted operations by large speculators.

It is impossible to compute the price benefit received by the people of this Dominion during the past four years, as a result of the support of the price structure under the guarantee, by the Bennett Government. Unprejudiced observers of world market conditions, of production figures, and of the enormously reduced constructive speculative factors, have estimated such benefits at upwards of 200 millions of dollars. It is now quite evident that without government support in these years, the Futures System would have failed in its essential function.[22]

McFarland's estimate of the value of his support operations to producers was considerably more sanguine than McIvor's. But Bennett liked the statement and approved its publication which the papers carried on October 29. In the meantime, McFarland visited officials of the grain futures administration in Chicago, as well as writing to Dr. J. W. T. Duvel, chief of the administration in Washington, before reporting by letter to Bennett on the same day as his statement was released:

I visited Mr. Fitz who is the head Government official in Chicago of the Futures Administration Act. I told him what we had in mind in Canada and

[21]*Bennett Papers.*
[22]*Ibid.*

he remarked that it has been a great surprise to him that we have succeeded in avoidance of such rules and regulations so long as we have and that it was no surprise to him to learn that such a step was contemplated in Canada.

I mailed Mr. Finlayson a copy of the Act under which they are working and no doubt he will take the matter up with you. Mr. Fitz explained that their present act really does not give them dictatorial powers in regard to limiting the operations of any individual trader, but it does give them authority to demand and receive all the information they might desire from every member of the Chicago Board of Trade, and unless the members of the Board of Trade live up to the requirements, they have authority to cancel the license and close the Exchange. Now the way in which they limit the operations is by working in conjunction with a Committee of the Board of Trade, known as the "Business Conduct Committee" and this Business Conduct Committee co-operates with the Government Department in giving any assistance they can give at any time that the Government Official feels that any individual operator is going beyond the bounds of reason. He freely admits that if any individual trader has already established a long or short line in excess of what would be reasonable, they have no authority to compel that trader to liquidate, but they have authority to prevent any further trades for that operator's account, and he can bring such pressure to bear on the "Business Conduct Committee" as to virtually force any trader to do as they direct.

Mr. Fitz tells me that the Department at Washington are contemplating further legislation so that the officer in charge can dictate direct to any member. He freely admits and most emphatically states that the Chicago Futures market is no longer an open futures market such as we have here in Winnipeg at present. At the same time I must admit that I would gather from his conversation that they are permitting some of the larger operators to go short or go long to a greater extent than I would consider it advisable.

My statement was in both of the afternoon papers today and had front page prominence. On towards the end of the daily session, reports started coming in to this Grain Exchange from Chicago, to the effect that the statement was then being received over the tape from Ottawa or Toronto, and even before they had time to get the statement and read it, they had already sent out advice that the statement was bearish and they immediately started to knock down the price in Chicago and also in Winnipeg. There is not a doubt that there are powerful factors who are determined, if at all possible, to discredit the operations of any Government in the grain business. These same operators hold up as a model example, the manner in which the Argentine is handling their wheat business. On the other hand they bitterly denounce the controlling influences on the Chicago market, as well as the operations here in Canada, and you may be sure these interests will do all they can to discredit, not only the writer but also yourself. . . .

I understand the statement published today has been rather a shock to the leaders in the Winnipeg Grain Exchange. The President called me up and suggested that probably the only action they would take would be to request that you should give them an opportunity to appear and assist in working out the restriction programme. I believe they are going to wire you to this effect. I told them I could see no reason why their wish should not be granted.[23]

McFarland also sent Bennett copies of the United States legislation with proposed amendments for study by the Ottawa law officers. Very shortly, attention was diverted to the market in flax. Because of a violent price drop, Bennett instructed McFarland to have the exchange close the flax futures

[23] *Ibid.*

market. But McFarland offered an alternative solution by way of placing daily limits on the price fluctuations, as he wrote to Bennett on November 8:

> Yours of the 5th to hand. I fear you will not be at all pleased with the way I have carried out your instructions with regard to flax. The fact is I could not convince myself that it would be good business, either for you or the country at large, to take such drastic action as to absolutely close the flax market, but I do admit there is some grounds for your alarm and no doubt you have had some representations made to you because of one striking incident which occurred, I believe, about the 1st of October when the price of flax dropped precipitately over 20 cents per bushel, and I do not think there was 5,000 bushels sold all the way down, and the price again recovered before the close nearly as much as it had declined without very much in the way of transactions. Of course, that was a most unusual happening, but in a time like this when there is such a lack of speculation, it is always liable to occur, and, in fact, would occur in wheat in a similar manner if it were not for our stabilization operations. However, just to give you time to think the matter over, I have arranged with the Grain Exchange that they will limit the daily fluctuations so that the price may not fluctuate more than five cents per bushel from the previous close. I think you will find this action will take care of the situation and you will probably hear no further complaints about these violent fluctuations in flax.[24]

Bennett accepted this alternative in his reply on November 12: "I have your letter regarding flax. Probably what you have done is entirely satisfactory for the moment but the operations in October last were of such a character as to induce observers to believe that they were the result of manipulation."[25]

In response to McFarland's public demand for legislation to provide for supervision of trading, the council of the Winnipeg grain exchange reacted in good faith. First the council consulted the exchange members, including those representing international firms which had been accused of organizing a bear raid, and it obtained their consent to disclosure of their individual trading records, either directly to Mr. McFarland, or to a government-appointed supervisor such as had been considered by the Stamp commission. Then the council issued a statement on November 2, 1934:

> On October 1st Winnipeg newspapers carried an interview with Mr. John I. McFarland, who is in charge of the government's wheat operations, in which he stated that he would recommend to the government at Ottawa that an investigation be made into the selling of wheat on the Winnipeg market and would urge the government to make representations to the governments of Argentine and the United Kingdom that they take similar action in regard to the futures markets in Buenos Aires and Liverpool. About October 6th a mischievous despatch purporting to be the inside story of an organized bear raid on the Winnipeg grain market during the two previous weeks appeared in many of the leading newspapers throughout Canada. This despatch originated apparently from some newspaper service in Winnipeg. It made free use of Mr. McFarland's name and its contents would lead many people to believe that figures and supposed facts given in it must have originated from Mr. McFarland's organization. The article is inaccurate and misleading; there

[24]*Ibid.*
[25]*Ibid.*

was no condition existing in the trading on the Winnipeg Grain Exchange that would justify such a story. It reads like fiction, and to the best of our knowledge that is just what it is. There is no evidence in the figures showing the market position of grain firms as at September 17th and October 1st, secured by the Council of the Exchange from the Clearing House, and which have been disclosed to Mr. McFarland, that any bear raid was attempted. Mr. McFarland has also been advised by the Council that the international firms whose names have been mentioned in this connection were ready to authorize the Clearing House to make the figures showing their trading available to him.

The international investigation suggested by Mr. McFarland on October 1st should, in our opinion, not be lost sight of. There can be no argument about the fact that our greatest need is to export more Canadian wheat, and if there is any hope that an independent international investigation into the situation in the Canadian, Argentine and English markets will disclose anything in the actions of government agencies or individuals that is making it difficult for us to market our wheat abroad, it should be undertaken at once. It would obviously be in the interest of the whole country as well as of our wheat producers. It would, we are sure, be welcomed by the grain trade of Canada.

The Council of the Exchange is prepared to afford facilities for investigation of the trading operations of all its members, without exception by competent and impartial persons, if such an investigation is deemed to be in the public interest, and has previously advised Mr. McFarland that the Exchange would, in addition, lend all possible assistance to a government supervisor of the kind recommended by the Stamp Commission should the government see fit to appoint one.

The action of the Winnipeg Grain Exchange in setting minimum prices for December and May wheat of 75¢ and 80¢ per bushel respectively was taken at the instance of the Dominion government and in pursuance of the policy the Exchange has consistently pursued of co-operating with the Dominion government, and government wheat agency.[26]

In the wake of the council's offer, it is strange that neither McFarland nor Bennett accepted it. Probably the explanation lay in the fact that McFarland had forwarded his memorandum to Bennett, together with the relevant United States legislation, and the matter awaited legislative action in the 1935 session. But by the time that session got under way, more portentous legislation was under preparation for a monopoly grain board which would replace the Winnipeg futures market and thus render its supervision unnecessary. For a year however, short selling was alleged and publicly decried, although no corrective government action was taken as events moved swiftly toward the creation of a government board.

WHEAT BOARD DECISION

Because of the defeat of the Conservative provincial governments in Ontario and Saskatchewan in 1934, and because of his soundings on Conservative party prospects federally, Bennett had foregone an appeal to the country in his fourth year of office. In 1935, it became mandatory that he hold an election. He began the year by a series of radio addresses and, after that, McFarland's communications with him were less objective. To

---

[26] *Minutes of the Council of the Winnipeg Grain Exchange.*

compound Bennett's difficulties, he took ill that winter and then McFarland took ill in the spring; both men fell victim to the strain of their responsibilities. These facts should be recalled as McFarland became more of a political adviser, and also a public speaker in the undeclared election campaign. On January 19, 1935, McFarland wrote:

Enclosed find Free Press Editorial of 18th. It is generally thought this is inspired from the East. Crerar, Hudson and Jim Murray were down East and are said to have conferred with King. It would sound as if the Liberals may announce a fixed price to farmers, and advocate slaughtering present stocks. What a damned fool idea? How Jimmy Rank would love such a policy? Of course a fixed price can only be carried out under a National Wheat Board Policy. Probably they may yet announce a "Wheat Board". Your opposition are in a mess on this wheat question. Even (if) they do announce a Wheat Board Policy, you can still combat that, I presume, by saying we have one and have had the effect of one for nearly four years, and as we hold all the wheat on May delivery, we may decide to establish a Board to take the wheat over in May, unless the demand greatly increases so as to clear out our stocks. In any event, put it anyway you like, but at an early date I do think you should let it be known that your Government will not hesitate to establish a National Board at once if and when it is necessary from a National standpoint, as you have protected the wheat farmer through four years, and will not forsake him so long as International conditions continue as they are now and as they have been the past four years.[27]

He wrote again on January 30:

Sid was in to see me. I feel certain he has cut loose from his liberal friends and is now at variance with fellows such as Jim Murray.

This for your information only, and I believe it is true, namely Jim Murray, Tom Crerar and Hudson (probably some others) went East about the time I was down there. They visited the Financial Post at Toronto, and had planned seeing Mackenzie King to discuss a Wheat Policy for the Liberal Campaign. King refused to see them to discuss it. They (had) seen Ralston, and his reaction was that McFarland had been doing all that could be done. They had an unsatisfactory visit.

It would seem now as if Jim Murray would favor a Wheat Board as a liberal Policy, always provided it is directed by proper directors and officials. He would probably be willing to head the board. He seems to think the Elevator companies would have satisfactory margins of profit, and they could not be much worse off under a board, than they are now.

Passing this on to you in confidence, as it would seem as if King has no attractive ideas on wheat for elections, and you may not have to fear him announcing a Wheat Board as his policy in the west. If this gossip is true it means you need not go off the deep end for a Board, until you are forced later.[28]

McFarland was uncannily fascinated by Murray's movements, and some of his surmises were prescient. When Bennett announced his intention of bringing in grain board legislation, McFarland continued to question the timing, as he wrote to Bennett on February 28:

The bombshell fell today in the Grain Exchange, in the form of your announced intentions of bringing in a measure to provide for the organization of a wheat or grain board. It caused considerable consternation for a time.

[27] *Bennett Papers.*
[28] *Ibid.*

Naturally, I got a lot of telephone calls and I took the liberty of expressing the view that there was no immediate intention of the formation of any wheat board, and in fact, there could not be anything of that nature attempted until the new crop next August. But that in view of the possibility of the necessity of some such board, it was obvious that you were providing for the emergency if it should arise.

I can see where the necessity for a wheat board might not materialize, provided the drought is not broken on this continent. On the other hand, if the drought should break and a good crop is in prospect in North America, I can readily convince myself at least, that such a board may be a national necessity. In the meantime, very bad reports are coming in from large areas of the winter belt of the United States. It is also recognized that there is no moisture in the spring wheat territory except a light snow covering, and the prospect for the coming year is far from being promising. If these conditions continue for a time, and it becomes evident that there is not going to be a normal crop in North America, then I can agree that you will see a very big revival in the world's wheat market. It could be such a revival as would result in our cleaning up our carryover to such an extent as to make the necessity of a wheat board appear very much minimized. The whole thing is in the lap of the gods. . . .[29]

After that the correspondence tapered off through the period of Bennett's and McFarland's illnesses.

DRAFT LEGISLATION

The Canadian grain board bill (as prepared for the first reading it received on June 10, 1935) had been modelled on the Canadian wheat board act, 1922, which had not been proclaimed. As that act had done, the board was made the sole agency to which producers could deliver their wheat and a compulsory board was again envisaged except that, in this case, it was intended that the board should take delivery of all grains. Thus the first draft provided for a complete government grain monopoly; trading in futures contracts of all grains on the Winnipeg grain exchange would have been terminated. On second reading, Bennett made an introductory statement in which he justified the legislation; he referred again to the short selling which McFarland had alleged the previous autumn. To facilitate passage of the bill, Bennett volunteered its reference to a special committee of the house for study. Bennett proposed a small committee of nine members which, at its first sitting, elected him as chairman. It was an unusual procedure for a prime minister to chair a house committee, but Bennett had to call an election very soon, and this was one of the vital pieces of legislation he needed to pilot through the house before dissolution. His performance as committee chairman was in character, however, with the role he had played of wheat-policy maker and he needed, now, to implement his most important wheat-policy decision.

Because of their direct interest in the implications of the bill, both the pools and the grain exchange had already sent delegations to Ottawa to protect their interests. The pools were represented by Messrs. George Bennett, L. C. Brouillette, and Paul F. Bredt, and the exchange was represented by a committee comprised of Messrs. Roy W. Milner, president,

[29] *Ibid.*

R. T. Evans, James A. Richardson, Sidney T. Smith, L. W. Brockington, counsel for the North-west grain dealers' association, Isaac Pitblado, counsel for the exchange and A. E. Darby, secretary. When the latter committee heard Bennett repeat the charge of a bear raid they consulted with the council of the exchange in Winnipeg, which released the following statement:

> On Friday afternoon the Prime Minister in a speech in the House of Commons reiterated the allegation originally made by Mr. John I. McFarland last October that foreign grain firms were engaged in a bear raid in the Winnipeg market. This allegation was investigated by the Council of the Winnipeg Grain Exchange and was fully answered in a statement issued and published in the press November 2, 1934.[30] . . . Following the issuance of this statement, R. W. Milner, the President, with the authority of the Council, advised Mr. McFarland that the Winnipeg Grain Exchange would welcome the appointment by the Dominion Government, to the position of Grain Exchange supervisor, of George McIvor, who has been assistant to Mr. McFarland since December 1930, and who previously to that was General Sales Manager of the Canadian Co-operative Wheat Producers Limited (the Pool Central Selling Agency). The offer of the Council that it was prepared to afford facilities for investigation of the trading operations of all its members, without exception, and as to the appointment of a Grain Exchange supervisor, as suggested by the Stamp Commission, has never been withdrawn. Representatives of the Winnipeg Grain Exchange now in Ottawa are prepared and anxious to appear before the special committee of the House of Commons, which has just been appointed, to meet the allegations which have been made with reference to the bear raid and the supposed present short position, and to supply any information which the committee may require.[31]

SPECIAL COMMITTEE ON BILL 98

Interest in bill 98 was evidenced by the array of witnesses which appeared to give evidence before the committee hearings, June 20 - 29. The committee reported the bill with amendments on July 2. Witnesses included Mr. Roy W. Milner, president of the Winnipeg grain exchange; Mr. Robert McKee, Vancouver grain exchange; Mr. R. S. Law, president of United Grain Growers Limited; Messrs. James A. Richardson and Sidney T. Smith, representing their companies; and Messrs. George Bennett, L. C. Brouillette and Paul F. Bredt representing the Alberta, Saskatchewan and Manitoba wheat pools. Messrs. R. C. Findlay and George McIvor appeared for the central selling agency.

As president of the Winnipeg grain exchange, Mr. Milner presented a carefully prepared statement in the drawing up of which he had the help of the committee which accompanied him to Ottawa. Mr. J. R. Murray had also come to Ottawa primarily to meet with his contacts in the Liberal party but, as a member of the exchange, he also worked with its committee. Mr Milner's statement covered the organizational set-up of the exchange and also the contribution which its hedging facilities made to minimization of risk in the handling of grain with benefit in prices received by producers. He

---

[30]The statement then repeated the release already quoted on pp. 464-465.
[31]*Minutes of the Council of the Winnipeg Grain Exchange.*

replied to the charge Bennett had just made in the house that there was a short interest in the Winnipeg market. Bennett had established his point by showing that McFarland's holdings exceeded the visible supply of wheat in Canada, and claimed that the difference showed the extent of the short interest. Under ordinary market conditions, if there are substantial speculative positions on both sides of the market there is no reason that the open interest—that is, the total volume of futures contracts outstanding—should not greatly exceed the actual physical stocks of the commodity. But Mr. Milner could not claim at that moment a large speculative interest on both sides. As the only substantial holder on the long side, McFarland was in a technical position to have forced a complete corner, but Mr. Milner acknowledged that MacFarland would not have taken advantage of his position. Therefore, he was left with the task of demonstrating that more wheat was hedged in Winnipeg than appeared in the visible supply. There was some wheat inside and outside the country which required hedges, but which the visible supply did not include. Mr. Milner also recorded that the exchange itself had investigated the charges of a bear raid the previous October. He offered on behalf of the exchange to permit investigation of the trading operations of any of its members by competent and impartial persons. Unquestionably, supervision was preferable to termination of the futures market which the bill threatened. On the charge that the exchange had failed to provide adequate hedging facilities, he said:

> From the time that wheat prices in Winnipeg began to be sustained above the natural level of prices in the markets of the world the ability of the futures market to absorb hedging transactions began to decline. In face of the uncertainty as to the course which might from time to time be pursued by the Government Wheat Agency, and the artificial level of prices on the Winnipeg Grain Exchange established by its operations, the futures market has become increasingly less able to cope with hedging requirements. In other words, the alleged break-down of the Winnipeg market has been the natural accompaniment of the government's operations, and its failure to take the hedges, to the extent that there has been a failure, is a result of the co-operation of the Exchange in the policy of the government.[32]

Mr. Milner concluded his statement as follows:

> We hold the sincere and honest opinion that to resort to compulsion and centralized control, with the consequent destruction of the established methods of marketing is not reasonable or justified by the conditions, and therefore register our objections to the proposals embodied in this bill.
>
> The Winnipeg Grain Exchange realizes the gravity of the present situation but feels that the sooner a policy is adopted of selling our grain crop in the open market at prices that will find purchasers in the markets in competition with the grain of other countries the sooner will the present difficulties disappear. In the meantime it may be necessary to subsidize the producers either by some system of price support, or by other means, and in that case the Winnipeg Grain Exchange will continue to co-operate with the government.[33]

[32]Special Committee on Bill 98, Canadian Grain Board Act, *Minutes of Proceedings and Evidence*, June 20, 1935, p. 25.
[33]*Ibid.*, p. 26.

In his evidence, Mr. R. S. Law on behalf of United grain growers endorsed appointment of a board to provide producer protection but he was strongly opposed to the compulsory feature of the legislation which would be provided by giving the board authority over the operation of elevators. He feared that the marketing of annual crops could no longer be completed in time to make participation payments practicable and he was one of the first to suggest exclusion of coarse grains from the provisions of the act. He summarized his recommendations:

(1) We believe a commission should be appointed through which the government would directly assume responsibility for the disposal of present government wheat holdings, and through which it would take such further steps as may be required to protect producers from a disastrously low price.

(2) The losses, if any, which may ultimately occur in the disposal of the surplus wheat accumulated on government account should be a continuing responsibility of the government and should not be made a charge against the proceeds to farmers of the 1935 or any subsequent crop.

(3) The provisions for the operation and control of elevators covered by clause 7 (d) and clause 8, 9 and 10 of the bill should be deleted.

(4) A system involving partial payments to farmers for their wheat and the issuance of participation certificates is not practicable under present conditions.

(5) There should be no interference with the present system of marketing of coarse grains.

(6) Special regulation of short selling in the futures market should be introduced by the Winnipeg Grain Exchange, and in connection therewith a government market supervisor should be appointed.

(7) That aggressive work should be undertaken to enlarge the market for Canadian wheat.[34]

Mr. Law's last recommendation was a renewal of his proposal for a Canadian wheat institute, to which reference was made in an earlier chapter. On this present occasion he explained:

We also desire to call attention to the need for aggressive work towards enlarging the market for Canadian wheat, not only through trade agreements with various countries, but also in endeavouring to increase the number of wheat consumers in the world, both human and animal, and in promoting the demand for wheat of high quality, such as is produced by Canada, instead of simply leaving wheat to find a market through sheer weight of supplies. Some time ago this company put forward suggestions for means of conducting such work through establishment of a Canadian Wheat Institute. While circumstances recently prevailing have prevented progress towards this organization, the need for such work as proposed is, we believe, apparent to all who study the matter.[35]

Mr. James Richardson, the next witness, spoke from his experience as an exporter and defended the open market system. He summarized his position in the following terms:

I appear before this committee because I feel that I must make the most vigorous protest of which I am capable against the establishment in this country of a compulsory wheat board.

I believe my experience as a merchant entitles me to speak on this question and I have no hesitation in saying that I believe the establishment of a

34*Ibid.,* p. 84.
35*Ibid.,* p. 84.

compulsory wheat board in Canada would result in greatly delaying the restoration of more satisfactory conditions to our wheat producers, and would also seriously endanger the financial resources of this country.

I make no apology for appearing before this committee. Part of the bill under discussion proposes the practical confiscation of the grain elevators of Canada, in which an enormous amount of private money has been invested. It is maintained in justification of this confiscation of private property that the legislation is in the interests of the Dominion of Canada.

I maintain that on no sound grounds can it be said that this legislation is in the general interests of Canada. I am opposed to all compulsory clauses of the bill. I maintain that, quite aside from the matter of confiscation of private property and all that this must ultimately lead to, it is against the best interests of Canada that it should lose the benefit of the highly trained personnel of the Canadian grain trade, and that it is impossible to satisfactorily and intelligently market the grain crop of Canada without the benefit of a barometer such as the open market provides. . . .[36]

At the end of his statement, however, Richardson made a suggestion which was eventually incorporated in an amendment of the bill to create a voluntary rather than a compulsory board, as he said:

As long as the government owns a large quantity of wheat they must naturally appoint a guardian to look after it, either in the shape of some board or commission. The carry-over should not be allowed to entirely undermine the price structure of our new crop of wheat, but it should be disposed of over quite a considerable period of time, or as fast as reasonably satisfactory markets can be found.

If our government wants to give our farmers financial assistance under existing conditions (and I would certainly like to see them do it) then there are several ways that this can be done. I consider it is possible to assure our producer a guaranteed fixed price, but still to permit an open market, so that if our market declined below the fixed price the farmer would get a certificate from the elevator company entitling him to collect the difference between the fixed price and what his wheat actually realized. The farmer might, on the other hand, if thought advisable be paid a direct subsidy. It is a government problem as to how this matter may best be met, but it must be accepted as a fact that the foreign buyer will continue to buy wherever he can buy the most with his money, and that he will take full advantage of depreciated currencies in certain parts of the world, and it is quite futile to try and induce him to subsidize citizens of other countries.[37]

As was to be expected, Messrs. George Bennett, Brouillette and Bredt stressed the need for the legislation. Mr. Brouillette had earlier championed the cause of a 100 percent producers' compulsory pool and he now favored the same system under government auspices and risk.

After Mr. Findlay had accounted for the purchases and sales of futures in the special account, it was left to Mr. McIvor to defend McFarland's operations and to rebut some of the claims made in the exchange brief. Mr. McIvor regretted the fact that, because of illness, McFarland was unable to be present to give his own report on the support operations, but he offered a spirited account of McFarland's performance during the most critical of the market sessions. He discounted Mr. Milner's evidence to the effect that all the selling in the market could be accounted for by hedges, as he concluded:

[36] *Ibid.*, pp. 85-86.
[37] *Ibid.*, pp. 89-90.

"My view, after analyzing the figures of the Canadian visible and having in mind the amount of wheat which is on hand for stabilization purposes, is that there is no question of doubt that there is a large short interest in the Winnipeg market and the figures which I have quoted absolutely prove this fact."[38]

Among opposition members of the committee, the main burden of cross-examination fell to the Honourable James L. Ralston and the Honourable Charles Stewart. Ralston had demanded for more than a year the disclosure of the support operations, and he was one of the principal architects, if not the key one, of a voluntary—as opposed to a compulsory—board.

Mr. Finlayson has also provided a personal account of the original drafting of bill 98 and of the metamorphosis of its provisions from a compulsory to a voluntary board during the special committee hearings:

> By 1935, the need for the government's exercise of emergency powers was believed to have ended and a decision was consequently made to establish a wheat board under normal legislative authority vested in the Dominion government. R.B.'s idea in the first instance was to make provision for McFarland to continue his stabilization operations as he had been authorized to do under the Unemployment and Farm Relief Act and to merge his personal authority with that of two other members of the wheat board, of which he would be chairman. I carried the P.M.'s instructions to Fred Varcoe, an important one of which was that he should draft a bill that would not founder on the rocks of divided Dominion-Provincial jurisdiction, as was the fate of the earlier Wheat Board Act of 1922. Varcoe came up with the idea of declaring all Canadian line elevators to be works for the general advantage of Canada. This would enable McFarland and his associates to lay down a selling policy to which he could compel the line elevator companies to conform. The measure was not intended in any way as one of confiscation, but leading grain men claimed that this was just what it was; and when the bill came up for study before a committee of the House of Commons of which R.B. was the Chairman, a quiet, impressive type of grain merchant from Vancouver condemned the bill on that score. R.B. turned to me and whispered: "That bill must be changed". After listening to arguments of a Liberal member of the committee, Colonel J. L. Ralston, it was altered into a different measure altogether. By the newly drafted bill the line elevator system was left undisturbed; it empowered the board to take over the McFarland contracts, act as a purchaser of grain and sell for future delivery on the open market.[39]

CANADIAN WHEAT BOARD ACT, 1935

The special committee concluded public hearings on the evening of June 29. But over the Dominion Day weekend, the interested parties were all feverishly at work on the drafting and acceptance of amendments that would make it possible to get the legislation through the house. The Conservative members of the committee led by Bennett had the support of the pool representatives, but by now Bennett had been convinced that he should come to terms with the Liberal forces led by Ralston or face a delay in the house which he could not afford. In McFarland's absence, Bennett

[38]*Ibid.*, p. 362.
[39]R. K. Finlayson, *That Man R. B.: Bennett*, pp. 202-203.

kept McIvor in Ottawa throughout this period to act as an adviser. The large and determined delegation from the exchange were primarily concerned to fend off the clauses in the legislation which threatened the futures market. The delegation interviewed both political groups, but worked primarily with the Liberal opposition who were more sympathetic to a voluntary board.

The offending clauses in the draft bill were sections 9, 10, and 11 which would have required every elevator to be operated on behalf of the board and which would have prevented any railway company from receiving or delivering wheat to an elevator operating in contravention of the act. Nor could a grade or weight certificate be issued on grain held in such an elevator. With these clauses in force, no elevator could handle wheat except as an agent of the board. Therein lay the compulsory feature of the act. Without these clauses, elevator companies would be free to operate both as agents of a voluntary board and on their own account outside the board's jurisdiction. Secondly, since the support operations had been conducted only for wheat, it was a moot point whether the act needed to apply to coarse grains.

In the inevitable compromise which was struck in camera in the special committee, Bennett conceded that sections 9, 10 and 11 as well as the section on coarse grains should take effect only upon proclamation, whereas the rest of the act would come into force upon royal assent. With these changes, Col. Ralston could claim a victory in the creation of a voluntary board, and the Liberal party took credit for the amended bill as their act. It was a victory, in fact, for the exchange.

Other important features of the original bill remained unchanged. A board of three members was created to take charge of what recently had been a one-man responsibility. Murray and the banks had proposed such a change two years earlier, and McFarland's illness had convinced Bennett that the responsibility had grown beyond the capacity of one man. The act also authorized the appointment of an advisory committee to the board of not more than seven members, four of whom were to be representatives of producers. The board was to function as the 1919 Canadian wheat board had done by recommending, subject to approval by the governor in council, an initial payment. Producer participation in profits was provided for; net losses, if any, were to be for government account.[40] In view of Bennett's traditional objection to a federal support price because of its treasury implications and the deterrent effect it might have on marketing, his

---

[40]In Part I, pp. 162-164, reference is made to the 1919 participation certificates which were transferable. On November 27, 1972, Mr. George McIvor wrote: "... you refer to the fact that participation certificates were sold early at very low value. My recollection was that some of these were sold for as little as .05¢ a bushel. There was a considerable amount of delay before the payment was made and unscrupulous people went around the country and bought these certificates at low values. You may be interested in knowing that in the summer of 1935, when the second Wheat Board Act was written, the late Errick Willis and the writer, assisted Mr. Bennett in the drafting of this Act. The first draft states that these certificates were transferable — this was copied from the first Wheat Board Act. I pointed out to Mr. Bennett the tragic effect of the payment in 1920 and he took his pen and wrote the word 'non' in front of transferable. I think, what seemed to be a very simple action by Mr. Bennett, saved the farmers millions and millions of dollars."

acceptance of a guaranteed initial payment represented a major policy reversal.

Apart from providing for orderly marketing of the 1935 and subsequent crops, the act also provided for acquisition from Canadian Co-operative Wheat Producers Limited, on terms approved by the governor in council, of all wheat or wheat contracts in respect of which the government had given a guarantee. This included the outstanding 1930 pool and the special accounts. The board's duty was to sell wheat delivered to it by producers "for such price as it may consider reasonable, with the object of promoting the sale and use of Canadian wheat in world markets" and to sell and dispose of the central agency stocks "as may be reasonably possible, having regard to economic and other conditions". Clearly, it was the intent that the sale of current crop wheat was the prior consideration. In respect of its obligation to undertake the disposal of the central agency stocks, the board was a logical projection of the government support measures which had commenced in 1931. As Dr. T. W. Grindley observed a few years later: ". . . It seems fair to conclude that the Canadian Wheat Board Act, 1935, was not a radical or new move in marketing method but merely a natural development from the past, of which the stabilization measures were a transition phase."[41]

Lastly, the board was enjoined, at its discretion, to utilize and employ without discrimination all the facilities of the trade, but with the significant proviso that if existing agencies were not operating satisfactorily the board could use other marketing agencies or establish its own. To this clause was added a section that gave the board the authority of a commissioner under the inquiries act to investigate at any time the operations of the Winnipeg and Vancouver grain exchanges and the Winnipeg grain and produce clearing association. While this provision satisfied Bennett's and McFarland's concern for supervisory powers, this authority was never exercised. On the other hand, as long as the wheat futures market remained open, the board made full use of it in making wheat sales.

The special committee submitted its report on July 2; the house passed the amended bill on July 4, and the senate did likewise on the day of prorogation, July 5, 1935, when the bill received royal assent.[42] When he moved the resolution on the original bill in the house, Bennett made a lengthly, exhaustive speech on the wheat situation in which he reviewed the whole evolution of his wheat policy, and defended the need for a compulsory grain board. But, on July 4, fresh from the proceedings of the special committee, Bennett made a brilliant defense of the bill as it now stood. It was his last substantive speech in the house as prime minister. Mr. Mackenzie King congratulated him on his performance, and only quarreled with his failure to give both parties credit for the revisions that had been made by the special committee. During the course of the election campaign that autumn, both political parties claimed credit for the wheat board act.

[41]*The Canadian Wheat Board 1935-46*, (reprinted from the Canada Year Book [1939 and 1947 editions] King's Printer, 1947), p. 6.
[42]*The Canadian Wheat Board Act, 1935*, Statutes of Canada, 25-26 George V, Chap. 53.

SELF-SUPERVISION OF THE EXCHANGE

As Milner and his colleagues returned to Winnipeg, the members of the Winnipeg grain exchange had good reason for satisfaction that the proposal for a monopoly board had been fended off, but the formal proceedings of the first regular general meeting of the exchange held on July 16, 1935, simply recorded "that a note of thanks to the President and all the members who recently represented the Exchange at Ottawa" was moved, and that "in this motion the members enthusiastically concurred". The business before that meeting, however, was the president's report on his mission to Ottawa from which a case could be made for self-discipline by the exchange. Milner drew attention to the fact that the existing floor on futures trading of 80 cents maintained at government request had priced Canadian wheat out of line with competing supplies, and that when the new board determined a trading price, the prospects were that it would have to be lower than 80 cents. This situation created an invitation to short selling which Milner sought to avoid. He addressed the members as follows:

Your representatives at Ottawa discussed the grain situation with a great many people — members of Parliament, newspaper men, business men and others. I think that without exception the question of short selling came up in each discussion. Those of us who have read Hansard will recall the great prominence given to the question of short selling. It was, in fact, the one complaint against this Exchange that our facilities have been used to permit of short selling to the detriment of the price paid to the producer. Let me assure you that I believe that every member of your Council is of the opinion that short selling is a benefit to our market under normal conditions. You will, I think, agree that conditions are not normal. It has been generally stated that the minimum price of 80¢ which has been maintained in this market is higher than the price at which importing countries are prepared to make purchases of our wheat in volume. I suppose that one of the first considerations of the Wheat Board, when appointed, will be to determine the minimum price to be paid to the producer. It would seem reasonable, in view of all the conditions surrounding the grain situation, that this minimum price will be less than 80¢. When the minimum price has been announced, no doubt the 80¢ minimum restriction on trading will be removed. The price will, I suppose, then move to a level where international trading in this market will commence. It is for the period of time necessary for the readjustment of values from the 80¢ level to the level at which trading will commence that I suggest it may be advisable to restrict short selling or, if necessary, to prohibit it.

Your representatives have maintained that there has never existed in this market a condition which necessitated the restriction of short selling in any manner. We have answered the charges that were made and have proven that a supposed short interest did not exist.

One of the powers of the Wheat Board, with the approval of the Governor in Council, is to examine the trading records of all members of the Exchange. We have up to the present time a clear record of trading. I would not like to see an investigation made which would disclose heavy short selling during the period required for this market to reach an export level. It would simply give added color to the incorrect statements made in the past regarding short selling. I believe that normally the correcting influence of short selling, putting our market on an export basis, should be given an opportunity to operate, but the market is not now in a normal condition.

We are all in agreement that the market must be free of restrictions to be of the greatest assistance in the marketing of our crops and in providing the highest price to the producer. I want to emphasize that any regulation restricting short selling should be only for the period to which the Council's recommendation refers and must not be in effect after the market has reached a trading level.

The question of the appointment of a market supervisor does not require any comment on my part; it was recommended by the Stamp Commission and is an appointment which I think should be made.[43]

In response to the president's statement it was moved "that the Council be authorized and empowered to appoint a Market Supervisor and that during the period July 16, 1935, to January 1, 1936, the Council be authorized and empowered to put into effect such rules and regulations governing trading in grain futures as may be deemed necessary."[44] Both motions carried, and by August 7, 1935, the secretary posted a notice that the following addition had been made to the exchange's bylaws:

Whenever, in the opinion of the Council, there has been any manipulation of the futures market or any undue concentration of futures contracts in the possession of any member or group of members of the Exchange such as might impede the marketing of any grain through the normal commercial channels, every member of the Exchange shall supply such information and produce as the Council may direct all such books, letters, accounts, papers and other documents as the Council may in its discretion require. The neglect or refusal on the part of any member, or on the part of any registered firm or corporation, to give the information or produce the books, letters, accounts, papers and other documents referred to in this section shall, without the necessity of any formal charge being entered and without further investigation, render such member liable to be fined, suspended for such period as the Council may determine, or expelled from the Association, and in the case of a firm or corporation, shall render such firm or corporation liable to have its certificate of registration cancelled.[45]

As Milner had pointed out, speculative short selling is desirable in a futures market system under normal conditions. But now that the government had acquired a direct and dominant position in the market, the situation was not normal, and the exchange acknowledged that its members should not trade upon the probable course of government decisions.

FIRST 1935 BOARD

With the act in force as parliament was dissolved, Bennett's next task was to appoint a board. Bennett was genuinely concerned over the state of McFarland's health, and whether it would be wise to ask him to take on the responsibility for the new board. He sent his principal secretary, Mr. R. K. Finlayson to check up on McFarland's condition, and to canvass other names for the board. On July 31, Finlayson reported to Bennett:

... McFarland is looking pretty well and gaining strength quickly. He will have to have some rest, but I have no doubt he expects to be made Chairman of the Board. In fact, if he isn't, I think it will be more detrimental to his health than if he is.

[43] *Minutes of the Council of the Winnipeg Grain Exchange.*
[44] *Ibid.*
[45] *Ibid.*

McFarland wants Clauses 9, 10 and 11 proclaimed as soon as the Board is appointed. He feels that you cannot adequately deal with the elevator companies without them. He thinks that the Futures Market should be closed and a great moral issue made out of it. Brouillette shares his view as to proclaiming the three clauses, but Bredt does not. . . .[46]

It is interesting that McFarland continued to counsel Bennett for a compulsory grain board, even after Bennett had struck a compromise with the opposition in the amended bill. McFarland's attitude reflected his continuing dissatisfaction with the performance of the grain trade.

In other corresopondence, Mr. E. B. Ramsay's name was prominently mentioned along with that of Mr. David L. Smith, who formerly represented the central selling agency in London and then had gone into business as a grain merchant. Mr. R. D. Purdy, general manager of the Alberta wheat pool was also approached. In Mr. Finlayson's conversations with McFarland he inquired about Mr. Paul Bredt, but McFarland was opposed to having representatives, as such, of either producers or the exchange on the board. McFarland mentioned his principal assistant, George McIvor, but for reasons that would shortly unfold, it is fortunate that McIvor was not more seriously considered. In the end, P. C. 2497 of August 14, 1935, appointed Mr. John I. McFarland as chief commissioner, Mr. David L. Smith as assistant chief commissioner and Dr. Henry C. Grant, commissioner. Dr. Grant was a professor of economics at the University of Manitoba who had collaborated with McFarland during the acreage reduction campaign. On the same date, P. C. 2518 appointed as members of the board's advisory committee, Messrs. C. H. G. Short, Sidney T. Smith, Robert McKee, L. C. Brouillette, P. F. Bredt, Lew Hutchison and Brooks Catton, (the first three representative, respectively, of the mills, elevator companies and exporters, and the last four, the required number of producer representatives, of the three pools and United Grain Growers Limited).

In respect of the appointment of the board members, Mr. McIvor has written:

Regarding consideration for me in respect to the naming of the Wheat Board in 1935, Mr. Bennett was very frank in telling me that I would not be appointed to the Board, and candidly I did not make any attempt to argue with him because his point was well taken. He thought that the public reaction would be that with Mr. McFarland and myself on the Board, the public would feel it was just the same old deal. He therefore decided in his wisdom to appoint Dave Smith and Dr. Grant. Dave Smith was a very experienced, capable grain man, and Dr. Grant a professor from the University of Manitoba. Mr. Bennett thought that it would be of great assistance to the Board to have an economist as a member. I had no hard feelings about the matter at all, although I alone accepted the responsibility during the summer of 1935, having overnight been put in charge of all operations by Mr. McFarland. I made it a point to consult Mr. McFarland whenever I could, although he was very ill at times, and I tried not to worry him too much about the grain situation which was, to put it mildly, extraordinarily difficult.[47]

[46]*Bennett Papers.*
[47]McIvor's letter of November 6, 1973, appendix 7.

INITIAL PAYMENT

The first task which faced the new board and its advisory committee was to recommend the initial payment for deliveries from the 1935 crop. By late August, rust and frost had taken their toll of the crop, and it would have been difficult for anyone close to the conditions to disregard the farmers' need for special consideration in the light of their continuing hardships. But the act offered no guidance on criteria the board should consider in arriving at its recommendation. As it turned out, Bennett expected the board to be concerned exclusively with market considerations, and this caught both the board and its advisory committee off guard as they ventured to take into account the farmers' plight. Although not required to do so under the provisions of the act, the board invited the advisory committee to consider the initial payment, as well as formulating its own recommendation. It was a questionable procedure, at best, to involve the advisory committee because of the direct interest of the producer members in a matter affecting the public treasury. Nevertheless, if the committee arrived at a figure acceptable to the government, Bennett could say that the initial payment had been set in accordance with the committee's advice; but this was not to be. Bennett was entitled to expect from his board, however, a recommendation reflecting a realistic assessment of market prospects as the committee and the board addressed themselves to the task.

The advisory committee met for three days, August 27-29, and were unable to find a compromise between the 80 cents Mr. Robert McKee proposed in the light of market considerations, and the 95 cents Mr. Paul F. Bredt proposed on behalf of producers. On August 29, the board informed the advisory committee of its own decision to recommend a payment of 90 cents. The minutes of the advisory committee discussions which incorporated the board's recommendation were transmitted to the minister of trade and commerce, who was now officially responsible for the new wheat board.

Throughout these developments, McFarland kept Bennett informed daily by telephone and by letter. His letter of August 27 reflected his concern that Bennett appeared to regard the initial payment as a peg, or a floor price upon the market. But his reassurance that wheat would be sold below the initial payment, if need be, was no comfort to Bennett. McFarland's concern about the small returns producers were facing on their low-grade wheat was reflected in the formal minute of the board's decision on August 29, which McFarland immediately reported to Bennett:

> The Board has unanimously agreed that the fixed price should be 90 cents a bushel for No. 1 Northern Fort William basis. This price should not be considered as having anything to do with the concept of an average cost of production. Neither is it based on what might have been conceived as a subsidy price under crop conditions which existed during the passage of the Act. We have quite frankly ignored those conditions and have rather based the price, which is a minimum price to producers, on present and potential market conditions and from the producers' angle we could not ignore the implications involved in the low quality of wheat which in effect means a far lower price on the average to producers than that implied in our fixed price of 90 cents for No. 1 Northern.[48]

[48] *Bennett Papers.*

The board's recommendation of 90 cents was 6 cents above the cash market which closed at 84 cents on August 29, and which dropped in the next two days to 81¾ cents. On August 31, Bennett protested by wire to McFarland:

> So far as we can ascertain no wheat has been sold for as high as ninety cents in Canada this crop year. There is no authority under the Act to fix a price so out of line with market quotations as suggested by the Board. We will await the receipt of a formal recommendation and thereupon take immediate action, but the Act is neither a relief or bonus measure and its terms do not contemplate such action as that indicated by your telephone message.[49]

Bennett also received the advisory committee minutes on August 31, and he wrote to McFarland:

> I have received your letter of August 27th, and I understand that the Board has recommended to the Government a price of 90¢ for No. 1 Northern at Fort William.
>
> How can you justify any such Price? I read the report of the Advisory Committee and I am simply "stunned". I wonder if we have lost all sense of proportion. The farmers will receive for this year's crop not a bonus but the price at which it can be sold. It was for that reason we provided that, if it is sold at an increased price beyond what is paid for it, the produce will share in the profit. I confess that, when I hear people talking about a dollar and ninety-five cents and such figures, I do not know what is meant, because the Statute does not contemplate any such action being taken by the Board as that involved in the fixing of a 90 cent price.[50]

Mr. Paul F. Bredt joined McFarland to press the case for a higher minimum to which Bennett replied by wire on September 5:

> Great regard for your judgment but we cannot permit any consideration to deter us from acting in accordance with the purpose of the legislation and in the national interest. Figure mentioned is far beyond what is generally regarded as proper but will be done to meet the very conditions to which you refer. If expectations are realized producers will benefit from sharing in results. If not taxpayers must carry the burdon. On that state of facts we are doing our very best and regardless of consequences to ourselves must abide the result.[51]

Bennett followed this up by a slightly more expository letter on September 9:

> I have your telegram to which I promptly replied.
>
> I do not think you appreciate the fact that the fixing of the price of wheat is not only a matter affecting a commodity; it also affects the credit of this country both in London and New York. You would be surprised to know the extent of the interest in the fixing of the price, and had we set a price that went out of the eighties I can hardly picture to you what the result would be. The whole Canadian situation would have been subject to fierce criticism both in the United States and Great Britain. . . .
>
> I attach great importance to your judgement, and should like to feel that your opinion is that the price fixed was reasonable under all the circumstances.[52]

In the meantime, the board had revised its recommendation by

[49]*Ibid.*
[50]*Ibid.*
[51]*Ibid.*
[52]*Ibid.*

September 6 when it discovered some fresh evidence for being a little more accommodating to Bennett's views. Mr. Clive B. Davidson, who had been appointed secretary to the board, wrote a letter to the prime minister which explained:

The Canadian Wheat Board has instructed me to officially advise you that its recommendation in respect to the fixed minimum price has been changed from 90 cents per bushel to 87½ cents per bushel basis in store Fort William.

In arriving at its final decision in respect to the fixed minimum price the Board gave further consideration to the question of the fixed minimum price resulting from

(1) The decision of F. M. Burbidge, K.C. in respect to settlement by grades.

(2) A further survey of the crop situation conducted jointly by the board and the Federal Government.

The Board considered the fixing of the minimum price in the light of the following opinion of Counsel:

The words "surplus if any" in 7-E and the provisions for participation certificates in that section and in section 13 contained clearly indicate that the Act contemplates both deficits and surpluses as a result of the operations of the Board. Then, as to the inquiry as to whether a surplus realized in the marketing of one grade of wheat can be distributed not only amongst the producers of that grade but also the producers of another grade on which the Board has sustained a loss, I am of opinion that the distribution must be confined to the producers whose wheat realized the surplus. Otherwise the producers who had received, to the extent of the deficit, too much for the grade of wheat produced by them would share with the producers who had, to the extent of the surplus, received too little.

The above decision meant that the Board had to account for each grade separately, and the volume of low grade wheat available in Western Canada during 1935-36 will be such as to present a serious marketing problem for the Board and for other agencies handling this product.

The Board gave further consideration to the crop situation in Western Canada resulting from the joint survey made by the Board and the Federal Government. This survey revealed a much larger quantity of low grade wheat than had been anticipated a week ago. The facts placed before the Board indicated that the Board's responsibility to the farmer lay in the direction of giving maximum assistance to lower grades of wheat, it being apparent that the scarcity of wheat graded No. 3 Northern or better guaranteed a relatively higher price for such grades. In order to be in a financial position to offer greater assistance to the large proportion of farmers who have produced small yields of low grade wheat in the frosted and rusted areas, the Board agreed that some adjustment should be made in its original recommendation in respect to No. 1 Northern. The Board further considered the fact that in all probability there would not be a market within the next twelve months for the quantities of feed wheat from rusted areas which would be delivered to the Board and that provision would have to be made for the carrying of a portion of feed wheat produced in 1935 into the succeeding crop year.

On the basis of consideration of the above points, the Board agreed to change its recommendation with respect to the minimum price for No. 1 Northern wheat basis in store Fort William from 90 cents to 87½ cents per bushel.[53]

[53] *Ibid.*

The governor in council approved this second recommendation and the initial payment of 87½ cents per bushel, basis No. 1 Northern in store Fort William, was announced on September 6. Prices for other grades were announced on September 22, and the board commenced accepting deliveries from producers on September 25. Very little wheat was delivered to the board, however, until market prices dropped to the level of the initial payment on October 26, and then eased down below that level until the following July. Out of total country-deliveries of 216,300,000 bushels of wheat in the 1935-36 crop year, 150,700,000 bushels were delivered to the board.

With reference to the fixing of the initial payment at 87½ cents, Mr. R. K. Finlayson provided a more elliptic and somewhat different account:

> If McFarland was a bull on the market, and he certainly was before he was aware of the crop disaster, Herridge and I reasoned that he would be a still more determined bull after his wheat surplus problem had become much less acute. That the price to be approved by the Governor in Council was to be political rather than economic was made plain by Mackenzie King in opening his 1935 election campaign in western Canada where he claimed full credit for the fixed price provided by the act. By long distance telephone calls that went on for two days, Herridge and I urged McFarland to hold out for a price of 90 cents. R. B. knew that we were intriguing with McFarland, but realizing that we had his political interests at heart, did not complain. The Governor of the Bank of Canada warned, "Mr. Bennett, if you fix that wheat price at 90 cents, you will bankrupt the country." R. B., paying lip service to the Governor's warning agreed upon a price of 87½ cents. When the Governor of the Bank and the Deputy Minister of Finance departed, he observed: "Those fellows know something about banking but they do not know anything about marketing wheat."[54]

BOARD TAKE-OVER OF THE CCWP STOCKS

As soon as the board completed the urgently needed arrangements for accepting deliveries from the 1935 crop, it turned its attention to the acquisition of the wheat stocks from Canadian Co-operative Wheat Producers Limited in respect of which the government had given a guarantee. This was not a simple undertaking in view of the fact that the guarantee had applied to all the agency's undertakings in 1930-31 including the separate wheat, oats, barley, rye and flaxseed pools as well as to McFarland's wheat purchases in the course of the support operations. Now that authority existed in the new act for the board's acquisition, on terms to be approved by the governor in council; of all the wheat and wheat contracts held by the central agency under government guarantee, a separate accounting of all these operations became essential. A bargain had to be struck between the central selling agency and the board on the terms of acquisition which would be acceptable to the government as well as to the directors of the central selling agency who were the custodians of the producers' interests. The issue was further complicated by the fact that while the agency maintained separate records of each of the foregoing accounts, their funding had been lumped into one line of credit with the banks which the government had guaranteed, and also by the fact that for

[54]R. K. Finlayson, *op. cit.*, p. 205.

the past five years attention had been concentrated upon the state of this outstanding single indebtedness rather than upon the timely accounting to producers of the disposition of 1930 pool wheat, oats, barley, rye, and flaxseed accounts.

Evidence of this apparent disregard for the producers' interest in the result is to be found in the actual handling of the coarse grain accounts. As shown in the report of the royal grain inquiry commission, 1938, the position of the coarse grains pools was as follows:

	Delivered to Pool by members from the 1930 crop	Balance remaining unsold at Aug. 31, 1931
	(thousand bushels)	
Oats	5,317	1,285
Barley	6,356	1,752
Rye	2,257	758
Flaxseed	1,431	405

In contrast with the 76,376,000 bushels of wheat remaining unsold at that time, the disposition of these small unsold balances of coarse grains should not have been too difficult, nor too prolonged. When questioned sometime later on the point by Mr. Justice Turgeon, McFarland testified that he had not conducted support operations in coarse grains, as he had done for wheat, but that he had simply held the unsold stocks for a price rise in the hope of realizing enough to equalize the differences in the initial payments which had been successively lowered during the autumn of 1930. A good opportunity to close out all the coarse grain accounts had occurred during the bull market in 1933, when the sale of rye and flaxseed was completed. But when asked why he had not disposed of oats and barley as well, McFarland replied that at the time he had been too preoccupied with wheat.[55] Elsewhere it was established that the barley account had been closed out in October, 1935, and the oats account a month later. In the end, only the oats account had realized a loss. The small surpluses in the rye and flaxseed accounts could have been paid out to producers in the autumn of 1933.

Of much greater moment, however, was the handling of the 1930 pool wheat account. After he had embarked on his support operations in the summer of 1931, McFarland left the unsold balance of 76,376,000 bushels in the 1930 account intact, as he commenced buying futures in order to support the market for producers delivering wheat from the 1931 and subsequent crops. The unsold balance of 1930 pool wheat was still on the agency's books in 1935. Technically, producers should have awaited ultimate disposition before demanding an accounting of the 1930 crop. In the result, it would have paid them to wait, but because the unsold balance had been arbitrarily segregated and withheld from the market for a period of five years, it was small wonder that producers were prepared to strike a bargain on its disposition to the wheat board, as Bennett faced the polls and tried to demonstrate some tangible results from his wheat policy.

In arriving at a basis for the bargain, the pool directors looked back to the selling methods employed by the central agency after McFarland took

[55] *Report of the Royal Grain Inquiry Commission*, 1938, pp. 103-106.

charge. In the simplest terms, McFarland had kept wheat moving to the mills and for export by exchanging cash wheat for futures options held by the buyers. To complete his sales transactions McFarland only needed to sell the futures so acquired but, for reasons well known, he had refrained from selling them. Nevertheless, as the cash wheat had been priced to the buyers, and at current market differentials on the grades delivered, the pool directors could establish that by February 29, 1932, 76 million bushels of wheat had been moved into consumption at identifiable prices, and that producers had a reasonable claim for compensation on that basis. The results of such a calculation showed that an average of 60½ cents per bushel, basis No. 1 Northern in store Fort William-Port Arthur had been realized. The wheat had been delivered to the 1930 pool at initial payments of 70, 60, 55, and 50 cents respectively. Very few members had delivered at the 70 cent level before the 60 cent initial payment had been announced, so that the object of the proposed settlement was to equalize the returns to all other pool members at a level of 60 cents. Since the prices actually realized, by grades, were somewhat better than the grade differentials reflected in the initial payments, there were some sums due to those who had delivered on the basis of 60 cents as well as to those who had delivered at the 55 and 50 cent levels.

Therein lay the basis of a bargain to be struck between the pool directors and the board. When the talks reached that stage, McFarland sought to involve Bennett in the negotiations since government approval was necessary. He wired Bennett on September 10: "Could you arrange a meeting on your private car on way west from Winnipeg with representatives of Canadian Co-op Wheat Producers Company relative to discussion of terms on which the producers' Company will turn over their holdings to the Wheat Board."[56]

The pool directors were encouraged by the outcome of that meeting and proceeded to verify their claim. This required a hurried report from the auditors based on records they had already prepared on an arbitrary basis under instruction from the central selling agency. The auditor's report was submitted on October 5.

The report showed the successive initial payments for each of the grains but, in its accounting for the coarse grains, instead of recording the results on the basis of cash prices realized on sales, it showed an arbitrary schedule of "revised" prices which would have been necessary to permit the equalization of coarse grain payments at the level of the highest initial payments set at the beginning of the 1930-31 crop year. The various payments set through the course of that crop year were as follows:

Oats 2 C.W.	30 cents
	25 cents
Barley 3 C.W.	25 cents
	20 cents
Flax 1 C.W.	$1.25
	1.00
	.75
Rye 2 C.W.	35 cents
	30 cents
	25 cents

[56]*Bennett Papers.*

In the case of coarse grains, therefore, the auditor's report simply showed the amounts necessary to equalize payments at 30 cents for oats, 25 cents for barley, $1.25 for flax and 35 cents for rye. It had been an objective of McFarland's sales policy to produce this result, but he failed. Nevertheless, the auditor's calculation of these arbitrary amounts was used as the basis of the pool's proposal for settlement on the various pool accounts as follows:[57]

	Initial prices	Revised prices (thousand dollars)	Difference
Wheat	$66,123	$72,450	$6,327
add net overpayments on wheat delivered at 70 cents			182
			6,509
Oats	1,107	1,378	270
Barley	1,520	1,611	91
Flax	1,357	1,781	424
Rye	669	774	105
	4,653	5,544	891
Total, all grains			$7,400

To this total the pools added $862,000 to cover their operating expenses in the 1930-31 crop year, which raised their total claim to $8,262,000. While McFarland worked with Brouillette in Winnipeg, Bredt had come to Ottawa to work with Bennett's principal secretary Mr. R. K. Finlayson and departmental officials. An exchange of letters between Canadian Co-operative Wheat Producers Limited and the Canadian wheat board had to be drafted to the satisfaction of the government, and supported by order in council. Time was rapidly running out, with the election just a few days away. On October 8, the agency and the board exchanged the following letters signed by Brouillette and McFarland:

Under the provisions of the Canadian Wheat Board Act, 1935, it is provided by section 7 (f) that your board shall have the power to acquire all wheat and contracts to purchase wheat from the Canadian Cooperative Wheat Producers Limited upon terms to be approved by the governor in council.

On behalf of the Canadian Cooperative Wheat Producers Limited I hereby offer to sell and transfer to your board all wheat or contracts to purchase or take delivery of wheat in respect of which the government of Canada has given a guarantee, such sale or transfer to be upon the following terms:

(a) The Canadian Wheat Board assumes all liabilities of the Canadian Cooperative Wheat Producers Limited in respect of the said wheat and the said contracts, for advances made connection with the acquisition and holding thereof by the following banks:

Bank of Montreal
Royal Bank of Canada
Canadian Bank of Commerce
Dominion Bank
Imperial Bank of Canada
Bank of Nova Scotia
Bank of Toronto

(b) The Canadian Wheat Board will pay to the Canadian Cooperative Wheat Producers Limited the sum of $8,262,415.37 being the sum total of balances due to the primary producers, and expenses and other charges in connection with the holding and handling of the wheat.

[57] *House of Commons Debates,* March 31, 1936, pp. 1644-1645.

And McFarland replied:

I beg to acknowledge receipt of your letter of even date from the president of Canadian Co-operative Wheat Producers Limited, offering to sell and transfer all wheat or contracts to purchase or take delivery of wheat in respect of which the Government of Canada has given a guarantee upon terms therein set out. I beg to inform you that the Canadian Wheat Board is prepared to acquire the said wheat and contracts on the terms mentioned in your letter and I am directed to accept your offer accordingly.[58]

These letters had been prepared under the guidance of finance and justice department officials, and their texts were conveyed by telephone to Winnipeg on October 8, the date of their signature, as the justice department proceeded to draft an order in council after their texts had been approved by Bennett. The draft submission to council approved the terms of the acquisition but there were not enough ministers in Ottawa for a meeting of council, so it was necessary for the Honourable E. N. Rhodes to circulate the draft to the Honourable Earl Lawson in Ottawa, and by messenger to the Honourable Messrs. Cahan and Gendron in Montreal and to Bennett in Toronto to get the required five signatures. After the other ministers had signed, Bennett added to the draft submission the words "subject to the amount ... being verified by auditors' certificates" and it was initialled by the governor general with that addition. The procedure of amending a draft order by one minister after the others had signed, was subsequently challenged, but all it provoked was a heated debate. At the time, there was evidence that despite all the haste, finance department officials had developed serious misgivings over the basis of the payment they had helped to draft, and that the departmental officer who took the draft order to Bennett in Toronto had been instructed to persuade him to add the proviso which entailed a considerable delay in final approval of the payment, certainly until well after the election.

Nevertheless, the passage of P. C. 3199 made possible the announcement of the terms of the settlement, including the payments to be made on coarse grains, on October 10, just four days before voting took place. Mr. L. C. Brouillette, president of Canadian Co-operative Wheat Producers Limited issued a press release:

L. C. Brouillette, president of the central board of the Canadian Co-operative Wheat Producers, Limited, stated to-day that negotiations have been completed for the taking over of all wheat and contracts from Canadian Co-operative Wheat Producers, Limited, by the Canadian wheat board as provided in section 7 of the act. It has been made possible at last to provide for the adjustment of payments to the members of the 1930 pools who received for their wheat an initial payment of less than 60 cents a bushel delivered basis No. 1 Northern Fort William and to members of the coarse grain pools who received less than the highest initial prices.

"For over four years pool members have been hoping that such an equitable adjustment could be made," said Mr. Brouillette. "If the 1930 pool carry-over had been thrown on the market it would have been impossible to have carried on the stabilization operation carried on by John I. McFarland, general manager of the Canadian Co-operative Wheat Producers, Limited, at the request of producers and prominent Canadian citizens, and with the financial backing of the federal government for his operations. For over two

[58]*P.C. 3199*, October 10, 1935.

years of these operations the 1930 pool carry-over composed nearly 100 per cent of the holdings which were used in the stabilization operations.

It is impossible to make any accurate estimate of how much these stabilization operations have meant to all producers of wheat from the time they were undertaken until the stocks and contracts have now been taken over by the Canadian wheat board. It is admitted by all competent authorities that the increased price received by wheat producers as a result of these operations amounted to many cents per bushel.

And the total benefits to growers have been estimated between $150,000,000 and $200,000,000 as the operations covered the marketing by Canada of close to 1,750,000,000 of bushels.[59]

Other press statements inferred that cheques would be mailed to producers by the following Monday, the day of the election, which prompted Mackenzie King to observe that producers would resent the attempt to bribe them with their own money. The press statements, however, had failed to take into account Bennett's addition to the submission to council which entailed a considerable delay in the payments while a proper audit was being obtained. Nor did it occur to anyone at the moment that P. C. 3199 had been based on the authority of the Canadian wheat board act which applied to the acquisition of wheat, but not of coarse grains, by the board from Canadian Co-operative Wheat Producers Limited.

Notwithstanding, the announcement that payments would be forthcoming on the participation certificates of the 1930 wheat and coarse grains pools had established a value for the certificates. Because they were assignable, producers proceeded to assign them in large numbers to the banks, the grocers and the implement dealers who had extended credit to them.

Bennett's wheat policy was also brought into the election campaign by the advertisement, already referred to, that Bennett had given the grain growers 150 million dollars and a wheat board.

OCTOBER 14, 1935, ELECTION

Parliament was dissolved by proclamation on August 15 and the election date set for Monday, October 14. The results were a landslide for the Liberal party. Of chief interest to this review, Colonel J. L. Ralson did not stand for re-election but returned to his private law practice. The Honourable Thomas A. Crerar was elected in the Manitoba riding of Churchill. Although Messrs. Honourable Charles A. Dunning and James G. Gardiner did not stand for election, Mr. King invited them to join his cabinet and seats were opened up for them in Queens, P.E.I., and Assiniboia, Saskatchewan, respectively. Mr. Dunning resumed the finance portfolio he had held at the end of the previous King administration. Mr. Gardiner, who had already enjoyed a long career in Saskatchewan politics, and was presently premier of that province, now became the federal minister of agriculture. The Conservatives had elected one candidate in each of the three prairie provinces, The Right Honourable R. B. Bennett (Calgary West), Mr. E. E. Perley (Qu'Appelle) and Mr. D. W. Beaubier

[59]*House of Commons Debates,* March 27, 1936, pp. 1549-1550.

(Brandon). The results of the 1935 election in comparison with those of 1930 were as follows:

	Manitoba		Saskatchewan		Alberta		All Canada	
	1935	1930	1935	1930	1935	1930	1935	1930
Conservatives	1	11	1	8	1	4	39	138
Ind. Conservatives							1	
Liberals	12	1	16	11	1	3	171	87
Ind. Liberals							5	
Lib. Progressives	2	3					2	3
Progressives				2				2
C.C.F.	2		2				7	
Labour		2						3
Social Credit			2		15		17	
U.F.A.						9		9
Other							3	3
	17	17	21	21	17	16	245	245

McFarland's handwritten note of October 16 expressing his personal condolence to Bennett was poignant:

My Dear R. B.

We are all in mourning here. The boys around our office are distressed beyond words. The Grain Exchange is in large degree jubilant. Paul Bredt is heart broken, and cannot understand how it could have been as disastrous. You (have) done a wonderful five years of service and wound up with a wonderful campaign. I did so want to see you successful and it is a bitter disappointment to me. In these five years of grim struggle I have had only one object in view, namely to do a beneficial job for the country and do it so as to bring credit to you and your Government. In the meantime the defeat of Gov't candidates would almost indicate such services are not appreciated. The fact is however I do not believe wheat caused the election of Liberals, except to the extent that Liberals claimed credit for the Wheat Board. It's a sorry outcome at best, but I am not ashamed of what I have done, and I shall always treasure the memory of serving under you during your term of office which is about to terminate. If nature again returns world normal crop yields, your successors in office will then gain some appreciation of what you and I have had to contend with on wheat.[60]

---

[60]*Bennett Papers.*

22

AN APPRAISAL

It is difficult to make any clean cutoff in the transition between the second and third parts of this review. In terms of policy, Part II could logically be terminated with the passage of the Canadian wheat board act. In terms of operations, it would be just as logical to make the cut off at the transfer of the Canadian Co-operative Wheat Producers Limited holdings to the Canadian wheat board as the personnel of board changed on December 2, 1935. But Part II has been concerned with the evolution of wheat policy in the Bennett era which ended with the October 14 election. Thus, it is appropriate to stop at that point for an appraisal of Bennett's contribution while such unresolved matters as changes in board personnel and sales policy, the transfer of the central selling agency's holdings and the settlement made with producers on the 1930 pool wheat account are deferred to Part III.

Part II has described the plight of government and producers alike in an extraordinarily difficult period for which no proven remedies were available. However persistent the government's search, its quest for solutions was essentially random, and the results were too frequently minimal. Yet out of the search came the decision, by 1935, to create a voluntary wheat board which provided a federally guaranteed floor price to producers despite the fact that, in the October 14 election, they repudiated its sponsoring government. The return of a Liberal administration brought an end to a remarkable five-year period in which a prime minister had assumed exclusive charge of wheat policy, a responsibility which would shortly be transferred to a cabinet wheat committee of four ministers who believed just as McFarland had in 1930, that reform in Canada's wheat selling policy was overdue. In 1930, the pools had been made the "scapegoat", and now it was McFarland's turn.

At the outset of Part II the thesis was developed that fiscal and monetary policies were needed of a type and magnitude which had not yet been devised, and that in their absence whatever policies Bennett contrived were predestined to failure. This overriding observation is necessary in fairness to a prime minister who exerted an amazing amount of energy and contrived innovation upon innovation in fruitless search in so many other directions for the right policy. Although most of his energy was expended upon transitory concerns, two institutions were products of his regime — the international wheat agreement and the Canadian wheat board — which have since become landmarks of government wheat-policy, and if he earned no contemporary political credit thereby, Bennett deserves historical credit for his sponsorship of them, and a high rank among the grain-policy makers.

It was characteristic of Bennett that he declined to delegate responsibility for important economic matters to members of his cabinet. For more than a year after he became prime minister, he held the finance portfolio before turning it over to the Honourable E. N. Rhodes. As Mackenzie King had done, he retained the portfolio of external affairs. Although he had one of his ablest ministers, the Honourable H. H. Stevens, in the trade and commerce portfolio and allowed him responsibility for the board of grain commissioners, he never delegated the responsibility for wheat policy. This was partly because he considered he had been more directly in touch with the wheat situation than any of his ministers. But he had also vigorously attacked the Liberal wheat policies during the 1930 election campaign, and he took a direct interest in proving that what the Liberals had failed to do was capable of achievement.

Moreover, at that time, wheat was regarded as the most important of Canada's economic problems and it was by no means illogical that a prime minister should be directly concerned about Canada's leading industry. Now that Canadian industry has diversified and matured, it is less probable that any of his successors will repeat Bennett's decision to reserve to himself responsibility for wheat policy.

Specifically, the measures Bennett adopted included the activation of the trade commissioner service in exploring potential wheat markets, and the negotiation of trade treaties involving the sale of wheat. Bennett succeeded in such negotiations with France and Greece, but the Honourable Herbert Marler's mission to China foundered on the Chinese need for credit. Bennett's main thrust was in the direction of an imperial conference in London in 1930, he brought the whole show to Ottawa in 1932, presided over it and in the end won a series of preferential concessions. Hackles were raised in the process. The British ministers resented Bennett's backing away, at the behest of the Honourable C. H. Cahan, from a promise he had already made for a reduction in preferential rates on textiles. Bennett heeded Cahan again at the time of his estrangement with Stevens. Cahan had taken strong exception to Stevens's conduct of the inquiry into price spreads and mass buying. But the winning of the imperial preference on wheat only demonstrated that the wheat problem extended far beyond the remedy of tariff adjustment.

Bennett's next international venture was to head the Canadian delegation to the world monetary and economic conference in 1933. Although the conference foundered on President Roosevelt's refusal to participate in a currency stabilization accord at the time, the preparatory committee of the conference had drawn up a useful agenda which drew attention, among other things, to the need for a rise in the level of international commodity prices. It was the British acceptance of this thesis which paved the way for negotiation of a wheat agreement in which importing countries as well as exporting countries would participate, and Bennett used the presence of representatives of the large number of governments to press ahead with the negotiation of the first international wheat agreement which he chaired, after placing the facilities of Canada House at the disposal of the wheat conference. Bennett's personal magnetism and forcefulness undoubtedly had much to do with the success of the negotiations. But this first agreement foundered in administration and Bennett derived little credit from his contribution. As early as 1933, Mr. J. H. Wesson, vice-president of Saskatchewan Co-operative Wheat Producers Limited who later succeeded Mr. L. C. Brouillette as president of that organization had formulated the three objectives of pool policy: the establishment of a national marketing board, agreement with other exporting countries on export quotas, and a fixed domestic price on wheat consumed in Canada. It seemed almost ironic therefore that Bennett helped the pools, in whose business capacity he had little confidence, to attain two of their three policy objectives.

On the domestic side, Bennett had started out with no predetermined policy such as he had declared in advance of his overseas missions. He soon found himself coping with pressing financial issues, and he relied for advice primarily upon Mr. John I. McFarland and Premiers Brownlee, Anderson and Bracken. The period was noteworthy for the comparative absence of strong representation by producers. The Canadian council of agriculture had folded in the first year of the Bennett administration. The pool leaders were still there, but Bennett was unable to dissociate their function as spokesmen for a large body of producers from the fact that their organizations had encountered financial difficulties. Although McPhail died early in the Bennett administration and Bennett never lost his high personal regard for Henry Wise Wood, he turned, nevertheless, to the three premiers, the Honourable John Bracken, the Honourable J. T. M Anderson and the Honourable J. E. Brownlee as the elected and thereby qualified spokesmen for producers. He seemed to rely upon Brownlee, as a fellow Albertan, more than the others, but this may also have been due to the fact that Brownlee acted as the premiers' spokesman. Certainly, the performance of these three premiers until Anderson's defeat in 1934 was one of outstanding co-operation and of persistent representation to the federal government on policy matters relating to wheat. The premiers had given the first guarantees of bank credit to the pools, and they jointly pressed the federal government to assume this responsibility. They worked closely with the prime minister on all matters pertaining to relief. They co-operated in passing enabling provincial legislation to implement the expert quota provisions of the international wheat agreement, and they co-operated in the educational campaign for the wheat acreage reduction program.

Another aspect of this remarkable period was that so little direct demand came from producers or their representatives for heavier government expenditures. Producers were realists of the old school of economics too. They needed help desperately, but they were loath to accept relief, even when income from any source was their vital need. Remarkably too, the pool leaders and the three premiers refrained from demanding direct subventions, except through the provisions of the unemployment and farm relief acts.

Bennett was also very much in need of a personal wheat-adviser who could undertake specific assignments. He had his candidate clearly in mind, but neither Bennett nor McFarland could forsee the major role in store for him as Bennett insisted that he join the delegation to the imperial conference. As the conference concluded Bennett sent McFarland back to Ottawa as his special emissary on wheat matters with instructions on what he should convey to Sir George Perley and the three premiers. McFarland would have continued as Bennett's principal wheat-adviser, in any event, but even Bennett appeared to be surprised that his lieutenant had been co-opted into the general managership of Canadian Co-operative Wheat Producers Limited. McFarland had looked upon the situation as a national crisis, and he offered his services without salary in such an emergency.

According to McFarland, under the abnormal circumstances, the Winnipeg market was not broad enough to cope with the hedges required on grain delivered by producers. There was little doubt that such was the case but, in peacetime, the council of the grain exchange was not prepared to admit, as the former secretary of the exchange Dr. Robert Magill had done in wartime, that there could be abnormal situations in which the futures market could not function adequately. When McFarland began his career as general manager of Canadian Co-operative Wheat Producers Limited, in 1930, he was strongly opposed to the central selling agency's sales policies. He forthwith reversed the pool policy of direct selling, and he presided over the termination of the pooling of deliveries under producer auspices, except for the very small pools which continued thereafter, and in his private communications to Bennett, he made light of the pools. But if his own business background allied him with the private trade, McFarland broke ranks as he realized that he was getting little substantive support from the trade in the pit, and as he became more and more deeply involved in support operations. Although McFarland started off with the objective of keeping the market above 50 cents, the support levels varied as McFarland exhausted his successive credit limits and as new situations arose. Without doubt, McFarland's massive purchases of futures provided support to the market at the time they were made. Later on, as McFarland failed to reduce his holdings at opportune times by any major extent, it became a moot point how much those holdings by themselves served to depress prices. This was the basis of the only valid criticism levelled against the McFarland support operations that he seemed reluctant to reduce holdings when opportunity offered. In his defense, McFarland had proved what could happen if he tried to sell in a fragile market, but there were times, such as during the speculative boom of 1933, when he could have sold more aggressively than he did. Hence, the mounting accumulation in his special account.

Except for the one bonus payment and the relief measures, producers received no other direct income support from the federal government. Even the special account operations were not a current charge on the treasury. There was no budgetary provision connected with the guarantee of bank credit, but rather a contingent liability that if McFarland could not sell his futures for what he had paid for them plus carrying costs, eventually the government would have to make up the difference. At a time of most urgent need for income supplementation by one means or another, this was all that

Bennett's domestic policy offered. He worried about the government's liability enormously, as his correspondence showed, and as he tried hopefully, but unsuccessfully, to hold a rein on McFarland's purchases. As it turned out, the support operations had infused some additional purchasing power into the west. Although it defied objective calculation, a 150 million dollar benefit was claimed. Also, as it turned out, the operation was conducted without cost to the treasury. But lest one be impressed by the success of the support program in terms of cost-benefit analysis, the contingent liability had been considerable, and the accumulated stocks were eventually liquidated without loss primarily because of the unprecedented drought.

On policy matters other than his support operations, McFarland was always ready with advice. Bennett unquestionably enjoyed McFarland's long communications. As an adviser, McFarland tended to oversimplify the causes of the wheat depression. His long personal campaign for Canadian and world reduction in acreage was a case in point. In the end, he convinced many key people, and his efforts were abetted by the new deal administration in the United States. Secretary Henry A. Wallace, under the provisions of the agricultural adjustment act, levied a processing tax on the domestic milling of wheat to pay farmers for compliance with his wheat acreage reduction program. But no Canadian official, and certainly not McFarland, believed that the Canadian treasury could afford to pay a bonus to wheat farmers who, producing primarily for export, responded to the government's campaign for acreage reduction. The United States experiment, undertaken just prior to the worst drought in the history of the mid-west, had placed the United States in a precarious wheat supply position. Her imports from Canada for consumption in 1934-35 and 1935-36 amounted to 53 million bushels. It was also ironic that if Canadian wheat acreage had been reduced to the full extent recommended, its impact upon farm income would have been slight. As it turned out, drought reduced Canadian production far more drastically than the recommended acreage reduction had sought to achieve. But the price benefits accruing from the reduced production were not nearly sufficient to offset the loss of income on the reduced volume. It was income, in which the western producer stood in dire need. Empty store windows and implement lots bespoke the effect of that lack on the rest of the Canadian economy.

As McFarland lost patience with the trade because of the intractability of the market, he reached the point where the hitherto abhorrent thought of a wheat board no longer seemed worse than that of a futures market in endless need of support. At that point he confided to Bennett that he was resigned to the creation of a board. But Bennett had already been aroused when he read the statement of the council of the grain exchange which evaded support for the government's acreage reduction program. In a characteristic outburst, Bennett threatened the exchange with closure. Although its members sent a deputation to Bennett who was mollified for a time, the issue was revived when short selling was inspired by the size of McFarland's holdings. Eventually, faced with an election, Bennett opted for legislation which would replace the futures market by a compulsory grain board.

Over the years as McFarland's operations developed, he had a prescient feeling of distrust in respect of one of his colleagues in the trade, Mr. J. R. Murray. His increasing references to Murray's activities reflected a substantial foreboding. Both McFarland and Murray were able and successful grain men; both were political partisans. McFarland had a long business association with Bennett in earlier years; over the same period Murray had been associated with the Honourable T. A. Crerar in United Grain Growers Limited. In the personality clash, McFarland and Murray mostly avoided direct confrontation, but each stalked the other's movements. In the end, Murray considerably influenced the Liberal party group that won from Bennett the major concessions which led to a voluntary instead of a compulsory board and allowed the futures market to survive.

McFarland did not quarrel with the outcome of the legislation, although he would have preferred to see the market completely closed. Appointed chief commissioner of the new board, he was more concerned than ever to preside over its affairs of which he considered himself the rightful heir. But he had just come through a serious illness, brought on without question by the strain of his responsibilities, and there was a reservation in Bennett's mind whether he should be asked to carry on. But McFarland wanted to do so, at a time when he could have broken off, with a record of outstanding accomplishment. His attempt to carry on, and his contribution to the political debate over his successor board, proved to be less fortunate.

Little account would have been available on the day-to-day operations by McFarland, had it not been that the McFarland-Bennett correspondence was included in the collection of papers Bennett bequeathed to the University of New Brunswick. Correspondence between these two men, written in a personal manner on the business of the day, does more than anything else could have done to preserve an authentic portrait of the two men. What comes to light about Bennett was his indefatigable interest and personal attention to the wheat problem throughout the years in which he was prime minister.

Because McFarland carried on for a brief period after Bennett's resignation as prime minister, the further assessment of his contribution as a policy-adviser is deferred to Part III. As for Bennett, his career after defeat in 1935 was rather tragic. For two years, Bennett carried on with the same capacity for work he had displayed as prime minister, but now as leader of the opposition. Increasingly he developed the feeling that he was unwanted by the Canadian public and, in 1938, he retired to England where he took up residence alongside his friend of earlier years, Lord Beaverbrook. In 1941, he was raised to the peerage and became Viscount Bennett of Mickleham, Calgary and Hopewell, which honored the names of his English village, his home base in Canada, and his birthplace in New Brunswick. During the war he served in a civilian capacity as far as his health would permit, and he died in 1947.

III
FROM VOLUNTARY TO
COMPULSORY BOARD

23

WHEAT BOARD IN POLITICS

Part III requires little introduction. From 1935 to 1943 there were numerous divergent and related policy developments—divergent in the sense that they sprang from background conditions as different as the 1937 drought was from the outbreak of war—but nevetheless related in a broader sense that wheat marketing policy was examined and tested, and the questions were ultimately resolved whether the wheat board could be terminated after the liquidation of the agency stocks or whether there was a permanent place in the marketing system for a board and, if so, whether on a voluntary or exclusive basis. Thus, a number of seemingly unrelated events occurred which all fitted into the permanent record, and they all tied in, in one way or another, with the principal issue at stake — the form the marketing system should take.

From here on the review covers a lengthy list of main events. These include the liquidation of the agency stocks, the relatively inactive period for the board in the wake of the 1937 drought, the 1938 report of the Turgeon royal grain inquiry commission, the unsuccessful attempt to terminate the board in the light of the commission's recommendation that wheat marketing should revert to the private trade and co-operative marketing agencies, a similar attempt to revive the international wheat agreement in 1939, the commencement of bulk selling with the outbreak of war, the depression of wheat prices and the storage congestion which resulted from the European blockade, the 1941-42 negotiations on the Washington memoradum of agreement and the draft wheat convention, the issue which arose over wheat prices in conjunction with the general price ceiling policy and the eventual resumption of demand for wheat arising out of the American feed grain shortage which sent prices soaring, relatively speaking, and thereby prompting the closing of the market and its replacement by a monopoly wheat board. This was the broad evolution of policy in the period encompassed by Part III and it illustrates why that period can be described as a transition from voluntary to compulsory board.

There is no break, however, in the narrative between Part II and Part III. Part II ended with the October 1935 election, as it had begun with the July 1930 election to describe the Bennett administration as a distinct era in the history of government wheat policy. The marketing policy which Bennett had ultimately compromised upon in the 1935 Canadian wheat board act was already in operation and it had to be continued by one government or the other. For a period, however, the operations of the new board were engulfed in political controversy. Because this had not been a continuing situation, it is worthwhile to look back upon its initial stages when the board operated, in a manner of speaking, in a glass bowl.

THE WHEAT COMMITTEE OF THE CABINET

One of the first decisions of Mackenzie King after his government was sworn in was the assignment of cabinet responsibility for wheat policy. King and his colleagues had felt strongly about the hazards of the support program under a one-man operation, and they were just as convinced that wheat policy should not be a one-man ministerial responsibility as it had been with Bennett. Fortunately, King's new cabinet included several ministers whose careers had been identified with the western agrarian movement. To utilize their experience, King formed a cabinet wheat committee. The committee was formalized by P. C. 3455 of October 31, 1935, which named its members and defined its responsibilities in the following terms:

> The committee (of the Privy Council), therefore, on the recommendation of the Right Honourable the Prime Minister and the President of the Privy Council, advise that the Minister of Trade and Commerce, the Minister of Agriculture, the Minister of the Interior and the Minister of Finance be hereby constituted a sub-committee of the Privy Council for the purpose of coordinating governmental policy and advising in respect to the performance of such duties and the exercise of such powers as are imposed or conferred by the Canadian Wheat Board Act, 1935.

Of the four ministers named, only the Honourable W. D. Euler was an easterner, but because responsibility for grain handling and marketing policy had been assigned to the minister of trade and commerce in previous administrations (except Bennett's), the newly-appointed minister of that department acted as chairman of the cabinet wheat committee. Euler had been elected to parliament in 1917 in the midst of controversy and harassment over his German ancestry, and he had served as minister of national revenue from 1926 to 1930. His wide experience as a business executive was an asset, but his outlook was inherently eastern, and it provided a counterbalance to that of his western colleagues, notably the Honourable J. G. Gardiner, who had most at stake in the committee's decisions. Gardiner had been in provincial politics for the whole of his career, defeated the Anderson goverment in 1934, had been premier of Saskatchewan for more than a year, and was at the height of his political power in that province when King invited him to join the federal cabinet as minister of agriculture. Gardiner later claimed he had accepted the appointment on the understanding that he would be a member of the cabinet wheat committee. The Honourable T. A. Crerar had won a seat in Churchill in the recent election and he joined the cabinet as minister of the interior. His earlier career was featured in Part I of this review. The Honourable Charles A. Dunning had first risen to prominence as a director of the Saskatchewan grain growers' association. He had organized the

Saskatchewan Co-operative Elevator Company Limited in 1911, and had been general manager of that company until 1916 when he became provincial treasurer of Saskatchewan and later premier of that province. He had joined the King government as minister of finance in 1929. When he formed his new cabinet in 1935, Mr. King invited Mr. Dunning to return to that portfolio. By now, Crerar and Dunning had achieved the rank of elder statesmen, in contrast with Gardiner who was still in his political prime. Both Crerar and Dunning, however, were invaluable advisers at critical times.

Thus a four-man committee replaced Bennett in the role of wheat-policy maker. Under Mr. Euler's tenure as minister of trade and commerce, the committee functioned without official secretarial or support staff. Although it consulted regularly with members of the wheat board and brought them to Ottawa for that purpose, no formal record of the committee's decisions exists, and the account must be pieced together from various announcements, press reports, Hansard, and from the W. L. Mackenzie King papers and correspondence, and also his diary. When the Honourable W. D. Euler resigned as minister of trade and commerce upon his appointment to the Senate in 1940, he ordered that his files be destroyed, so that source of material was lost.

LIBERAL GOVERNMENT WHEAT POLICIES

In order to follow the course of events after the appointment of the cabinet wheat committee, it is helpful to understand the general policy attitudes of the incoming administration which motivated the changes. In respect of wheat policy it would be a considerable oversimplification to say that whatever the Bennett administration was for, the succeeding King administration was against; nevertheless, such a conclusion is not completely wide of the mark. It had been the Liberal party's responsibility in opposition to criticize the measures Bennett introduced, which lent a negative cast to some of the Liberal policies. Examples of this had been Colonel Ralston's characterization of the support operations as gambling in the wheat market, and also his opposition to legislation extending the life of the wheat board beyond one year's duration. Mackenzie King had criticized Bennett's signature of the international wheat agreement without seeking approval of parliament, and also the agreement's orientation toward acreage restriction. In broader terms, the Liberal opposition condemned Bennett's high-tariff policies, as they commended a liberalization of trade channels to open up wheat markets.

In more positive terms, Liberal wheat policies at the time of the election could be summed up as follows:

1. An orderly liquidation of the wheat surplus.
2. Retention of the wheat board, for the duration of the crisis only.
3. Restoration of the status quo prior to the depression, whereby the government would extricate itself from direct wheat marketing responsibility and return it to the private trade and the pools.
4. Ancillary sales support through advertising campaigns, reassurances to customers of governmental nonintervention, and negotiation of expansionary trade agreements.

It would scarcely be an oversimplification to say that these policies were essentially laissez-faire. There was a strong element of faith among the Liberal party leadership and followers that such policies could result in a nostalgic return to the prosperity of the late twenties. Direct government intervention in any industry must be eschewed, lest it become the entering wedge of state socialism. Members of the Liberal administration, from King down, sought to avoid the adoption of policies which might open the door to state socialism; hence their concern over the existence of a government wheat board. Among the four ministers King appointed to the cabinet wheat committee—Euler, Crerar, Dunning, Gardiner—there was none whose business or political background would have suggested any other stance.

Direct evidence of the Liberal party's platform during the 1935 election campaign was offered by the Honourable J. G. Gardiner during the course of a wheat debate in the house a year and a half later when he read from a party pamphlet circulated throughout western Canada during the campaign, which stated:

> The pegging of domestic wheat prices, a year ago, in the interests of the farmers was endorsed by the Liberals. But after the domestic price was pegged the federal government should have made every effort to dispose of the Canadian wheat stocks which were piling up and depressing the market. And any financial losses which such a course might have involved should have been borne by the country as a whole. . . .
> The Bennett wheat policy is:
> 1. Close the channels of trade so no one can buy Canadian wheat, and pile up surpluses which impoverish the farmer and burden the national treasury.
> 2. Place the burden of this disastrous policy on the farmer.
> 3. Protect the manufacturer of farm implements and household needs, so living costs can be kept at a level beyond the farmer's needs.
> The King wheat policy is:
> 1. Guarantee a satisfactory minimum price to the farmer during the crisis.
> 2. Sell our wheat in the world's markets at world prices, and distribute any resultant loss equitably.
> 3. Open the channels of trade to enable other countries to exchange their goods for our wheat, thus increasing demand and price of Canadian wheat.
> 4. Lower the tariff on the implements of production and household needs, thus bringing close to parity the farmer's income and expenses.[1]

As Gardiner continued, he declared:

> Many members of this house have been attempting to imply that during the last election the Liberal party stood for certain things and that it had not carried out its policy. I wish to state to the house what the policy of the Liberal party was, particularly with reference to western Canada. This was the policy announced, not only by the candidates speaking in western Canada, but by our leader himself when he was there. This policy can best be expressed in these words: That a wheat board should be maintained in existence until the surplus accumulated by the McFarland stabilization activities had been so far liquidated as to remove their lowering influence upon the price which could be obtained in the world market. The Liberal

[1]*House of Commons Debates,* March 9, 1937, p. 1636.

party maintained that our wheat should be exchanged in an orderly manner for goods we require in this country, thus restoring prosperity and removing unemployment. This was the policy of the party.[2] As Gardiner emphasized, in reading from the pamphlet and in his own summation, the Liberals had endorsed a wheat board for the duration of the crisis but not for all time.

Dr. John W. Dafoe, editor of the *Winnipeg Free Press,* shrewdly drew attention to the nuances which differentiated Conservative and Liberal policies in his editorial of November 4, 1935, on the future of the wheat industry:

> For three or four years there has been much discussion in that part of Canada about the future of western agriculture and particularly of wheat-growing. There was ground for uncertainty. Up to about 1930, or until the depression started, it was usually assumed that Western Canada's market for wheat in Britain and Europe was permanent. These plains grew the best wheat in the world and could count on selling it freely as long as farmers here wanted to grow it. That was the optimistic theory of the pre-1930 period. But two years ago the Canadian prime minister put his name to an agreement pledging this country to limit exports, and by inference production, of wheat. That event made many people ask if Western Canada's day as a wheat country was coming to an end.
>
> The defeatist theory was encouraged by men in authority. Farmers were told they had grown too much wheat in the past and would have to submit to restrictions imposed by government officials, Western Canada would have to accept a permanent cut in its volume of foreign wheat sales, its share of the world trade, and consequently its income. Furthermore, a Government Board would have to be set up to control the outward flow of wheat, possibly to limit farmers' deliveries and so, by indirection, to check wheat-growing. That was a view of the West's future which became, with official backing, fairly current a year or two ago.
>
> The change of Government at Ottawa is an occasion for reviewing the question. the Liberal party took no stock in the idea that the West was through as the leading producer of wheat for export. Liberals opposed putting restrictions on wheat-growing. They opposed the wheat agreement so far as they could, which was not very effectively, because that bargain was never submitted to Parliament for approval. One may say, then, that the Liberal victory in the West on October 14 was a rejection of the pessimistic view of Western Canada's future as a wheat country. The voters accepted the Liberal opinion that markets are recoverable, that bumper crops will be a blessing, not a misfortune, if Canada goes the right way about getting business, and that there is no need to impose limits in the farmers' output. These views were endorsed by the public. The question now is how they are to be given practical effect.
>
> To begin with, it may be said with assurance that the new Government has no intention of dumping the existing wheat surplus or of leaving the farmers unprotected against the price drop which even cautious selling of the surplus might entail. The Liberals, though they have favored aggressive selling, have recognized the present carryover as an accomplished fact. They supported and helped to draft the legislation creating the present Wheat Board. they admit the necessity of going carefully in disposing of the wheat piled up by the holding policy. It may be taken for granted that the new Government does not mean to risk breaking the market by selling the wheat in a hurry. Mr.

[2]*Ibid.*

Euler, of the cabinet committee in charge of wheat policy, gave an assurance to that effect last week when he denied rumors that the sale of the wheat at sacrifice prices had been ordered.

But it may also be assumed that the policy of holding, needed temporarily to get over a difficulty created by mistakes in the past, will be dropped as soon as possible. Sitting on the wheat crop and waiting for buyers or for crop failures in other countries is definitely not the Liberal idea of a national wheat policy for Canada. The present Government may be expected to begin at an early date a systematic effort to recapture lost markets for wheat and to find new ones. There is not the least doubt it can be done—if Canada goes half-way and offers trading concessions in return for the chance to sell wheat. The West looks to the Government to start action along that line as quickly as it can.

On the other side of the picture Liberal policy, if it is consistent with the Liberal economic philosophy the voters have endorsed, will mean the greatest possible individual freedom for the wheat grower. United Farmers of Manitoba, at their convention last week, discussed limitation of wheat acreage and the idea found favor. Next spring, quite possibly, many farmers may think it good business to sow barley or oats on what has hitherto been wheat land. That will be obviously in order. It has never been the Liberal idea to urge or coerce farmers to grow all the wheat they can. The Liberal view is that farmers should be at liberty to use their own judgment on the subject, free entirely of government restriction. It may be safely assumed the present Dominion Government will never be found attempting to limit either a farmer's acreage or his deliveries to the elevator.

It will take time for the results to flow from the wheat policy to which the new Government is committed, especially as that policy cannot be applied to the full extent at once. But results will appear in due course. Nothing is more certain than that Canada can improve its position in the wheat trade by going after markets and loosening up the restrictions which have hampered commerce in the past five years.[3]

CABINET WHEAT COMMITTEE RELATIONS WITH THE McFARLAND BOARD

As soon as the wheat committee of the cabinet was formed McFarland made the first overture from the board to the committee by wiring to Euler on October 28, 1935. McFarland had received several inquiries by cable regarding the board's sales policy under the new government and rumors were rife that sales would be pressed at sacrifice prices. Accordingly, he pointed up the need for a statement and for an early meeting of the board with the new cabinet committee:

> Wheat buyers here and abroad are awaiting for some statement of the selling policy of the Canadian Wheat Board. The Board does not feel that they can appropriately make statement at this time without your advice and are anxious to confer with your Cabinet Committee on Wheat as soon as possible. Uncertainty of policy seriously affecting sales of Canadian Wheat.[4]

McFarland's telegram awaited the cabinet wheat committee's attention at its first meeting on the day of its formal appointment, October 31, 1935. Even before it could begin to consider ways and means to implement its

[3] *Winnipeg Free Press,* November 4, 1935. In making the assumption at the end of his penultimate paragraph, Dafoe could not have been expected to anticipate what happened after the invasion of Norway and France in World War II.

[4] *Bennett Papers.*

own policies, the committee decided that it must put the trade rumors at rest so Euler issued an immediate statement:

There are rumors abroad the government intends to direct that the western wheat now held by the wheat board be sold, even at sacrifice prices. The rumors are entirely without foundation. Under the law the board headed by John I. McFarland has full authority with regard to the selling policy.[5]

McFarland wrote to Euler to compliment him on the effectiveness of his statement which was well received overseas but which, in fact, barely steadied the market. However, the question of an early meeting between the board and the cabinet committee raised a more complex issue. McFarland had carefully evaded the question of whether the present board had the confidence of the incoming government and whether it should carry on or resign. The implication in his wire was that the board, in fact, was carrying on and that it wanted to get down to business quickly with the new government. Even before the cabinet wheat committee held its first meeting, Euler had wired back to McFarland on October 28, to say that McFarland's request would be held for the committee's attention, but also to ask McFarland to forward a full statement on the board's selling policy. Obviously, the members of the cabinet wheat committee wanted to consider this key issue before establishing working relations with the existing board. McFarland replied to Euler's request by letter on October 29. In it, McFarland continued to stress the need for a government declaration of policy and admitted that with the market price below the initial payment of 87½ cents he was "taking back the options" without selling futures, thereby acquiring a long futures position for the wheat board account:

With respect to the sales of 1935 wheat, we have attempted to follow the instructions outlined in the Statute which governs our operations. (See Sec. 8 (b) & (c) of the Act).

So instructed we have sold wheat at times and in quantities which the market could absorb. There is, of course, no way of knowing what the market can absorb other than what is registered by the offers and bids in the open market. You will observe from our statements that during the period of rising prices shortly after the Board's fixed price was announced, that the Board was a free seller of wheat. Deliveries to the Board during this period of rising prices were in a smaller proportion than they have been since prices started to decline. During the early days of our operation, information with respect to what our deliveries actually were, was by the nature of things not readily available and the probable deliveries were, of course, unknown. Up until ten or twelve days ago, the Board has been able to operate on the open market fairly satisfactorily. Since that time, the open market has not registered anything of meaning simply because gossip with respect to the Canadian wheat policy has frightened buyers from the market and opened the way for short selling to further depress prices.

As far as we know, the Board has received about 40% of the wheat delivered to date (Oct. 25th). This would indicate that the larger proportion of deliveries which are in the hands of the Trade, have already been hedged. In other words, the open market price is being pressed down without actual wheat being offered. All that we can say, therefore, is that we have attempted to meet any demand which existed, but at present the open market does not register any real demand for our wheat.

[5] *Winnipeg Free Press*, November 1, 1935.

As you will realize, if buyers believe that we are going to force sales, they will stay out of the market. We are enclosing you a statement prepared by our Mr. McAnsh, which indicates that Canadian Wheat has been at an attractive price level for many weeks. The only reason why there has not been a more active demand recently, is that buyers are afraid that there may be an announcement of a change in selling policy. Until this uncertainty is removed by competent authority, buying will be restricted and short selling will be encouraged.

According to the Act, our selling must be confined to existing trade channels which, means selling entirely through the Winnipeg futures market, as all purchases made by the Trade, of cash wheat, are on the basis of options. In other words, if we sell 100,000 bus. No. 1 Northern, we have to take back options against the sale. To complete the sale we must sell the options on the futures market. This operated successfully so long as the market was over the Board's fixed price and there existed a steady demand from abroad; but now when the futures market moves well under our fixed price and there is practically no business in Canadian wheat emanating from any source, we would place ourselves in the position, if we continued selling futures, of causing a regular debacle in prices. This is quite apparent as the futures market, without pressure of hedging from the Trade or any selling by this Board, has declined from 86⅞¢ on October 26th to 84¼¢ at noon on October 29th; in other words, a break of 2⅝¢ on purely speculative selling.[6]

After he received this report, Euler continued to press McFarland for a more complete statement of the past sales policy of the board. Confirmation of the slow-selling policy the McFarland board was pursuing arrived in the weekly statements the board was required to furnish to the minister of trade and commerce. The results for that autumn were summed up two and a half years later when Mr. Justice Turgeon reported:

Mr. McFarland started his operations under the new Act on September 12 by making sales on the futures market. In the four month period August to November, country deliveries amounted to 167,475,000 bushels, of which the board received 102,766,855 bushels (Exhibit 428). Net sales during the same period amounted to only 12,577,668 bushels. While considerable quantities of cash grain were sold (34,960,668 bushels), futures were acquired in exchange to the extent of 34,778,000 bushels. It has been pointed out earlier in this chapter that market prices for cash wheat remained above the initial payment of the Board until late October. With such prices prevailing and having in mind heavy deliveries to the Board, it is hard to conclude that the intentions of the Act (particularly Section 8)), were carried out.[7]

Thus, although Euler's first public statement had been in support of the board, the wheat committee members were by now validly concerned whether McFarland and his board colleagues could be depended upon to market the 1935 crop during the course of the crop year, not to mention the accumulated holdings from the earlier support operations. It clearly had been the intention of the act to terminate the support measures by the establishment of a government-guaranteed initial payment. McFarland's attitude in allowing the board to accumulate futures when the market behaved badly demonstrated that he still was more in a support—than in a sales—frame of mind.

[6]*Bennett Papers.*
[7]*Report of the Royal Grain Inquiry Commission,* 1938, p. 103.

It was over this policy dilemma that the wheat committee of the cabinet held a long session on November 13 and reviewed the position. Although Euler reiterated at the end of the meeting that there was no intention of forcing Canadian wheat on the market at sacrifice prices, and there was some press speculation that McFarland would continue as chairman of the board, the cabinet committee had, in fact, decided that a change in the personnel of the board was necessary, and they awaited a discussion with Mr. J. R. Murray. Meanwhile, McFarland had endeavoured to improve relations between the committee and the board, by inviting the wheat committee to send a representative with a general knowledge of the trade to Winnipeg, to observe the operations of the board and to attend the meeting of its advisory committee scheduled for November 12. Euler agreed to send Dr. T. W. Grindley, chief of the agricultural branch of the dominion bureau of statistics, who was the only wheat-marketing expert on staff in Ottawa at that time.

Another matter of some urgency was the acquisition by the wheat board of the wheat and wheat contracts from Canadian Co-operative Wheat Producers Limited on which the government of Canada had given a guarantee. Action was initiated by Dr. W. C. Clark, deputy minister of finance, who wrote to McFarland on October 29 to point out that the auditors' statements originally furnished did not give the information required to implement P. C. 3199, and to ask that the responsible officer of Price Waterhouse and Company, the central agency's auditing firm, come to Ottawa immediately for consultation. Mr. K. Drennan responded and at the conclusion of his discussions with the department, the Honourable Charles A. Dunning set out the area of the government's concern in his letter of November 5 to Price Waterhouse and Company, Winnipeg:

> I have received from the Chairman of the Canadian Wheat Board your Report on "Equalization Payments" in connection with the 1930 Wheat Pool. This Report was submitted to us as your certificate required under the concluding paragraph of Order-in-Council P.C. 3199, dated October 10, 1935.
>
> I am attaching a copy of this Order-in-Council. You will note that the Order authorized the Canadian Wheat Board to take over wheat and contracts to purchase or take delivery of wheat from the Co-operative Wheat Producers, Ltd., and to pay the sum of $8,262,415.37 "being the sum total of balances due to the primary producers, and expenses and other charges in connection with the holding and handling of the wheat," subject to this amount being "verified by auditors' certificates."
>
> It is obvious that your Report on the "Equalization Payments" does not in any sense meet the requirements of this Order-in-Council. It does not purport to show the sum total of balances due primary producers and it includes payments to be made for coarse grains, whereas the Order-in-Council refers only to the sale to the Board of wheat and contracts to purchase or take delivery of wheat. However, we understand, from discussion with your representative, Mr. K. Drennan, that your Report was prepared before the Order-in-Council was passed and was obviously not intended by you to carry out the terms of the Order-in-Council, a copy of which you had not at that time seen.
>
> As it is not possible for us to approve the implementing of the Order-in-Council without much more information than is now available either in the Departmental files or in the auditors' reports which have been

submitted, I desire you on behalf of the Department of Finance to make to us a complete report on the operations of the Canadian Co-operative Wheat Producers Limited in connection with the 1930 Pool, with a view to giving us the facts necessary to determine "the amount due to primary producers" as required under the terms of the Order-in-Council.

Your report should include, in particular, the following:

(1) General review in report form of the operations of the 1930 Pool from its commencement until October 31, 1935.

(2) Operating statements of the grain and contracts held for the 1930 Pool, following through what happened to the grain originally taken over.

(3) Operating statements of the stabilizing operations carried on by Canadian Co-operative Wheat Producers under Dominion Government guarantee, explaining what relation, if any, these operations had to the 1930 Pool account.

(4) Detailed reports on the charges for carrying the grain and contracts, with explanatory comments as to each item, as to the allocation of costs between the 1930 Pool account and the Stabilization account and the justification of the procedure followed.

In brief, this Department desires to have from you a full report with necessary supporting data relative to the situation arising from the operations of Canadian Co-operative Wheat Producers Ltd., with special reference to what further payment, if any, is due to the primary producer as a result of those operations.

As you know, the Board has also submitted to us reports from the auditors of the three Provincial Pools regarding certain expenses and charges of the provincial Pools in connection with the 1930 crop. I wish you to consider and report upon what justification there may be for the payment of all or any part of these items by the Board, or whether, on the contrary, such expenses should not be deducted from any payment that might otherwise be due to primary producers.

I would appreciate it if you would immediately undertake this investigation and submit your report at the earliest possible date.

I am quite sure that the Pool authorities will afford you every facility on presentation of this letter.[8]

Now that the essential information required from the auditors had been clarified, Euler pressed McFarland for a prompt consummation of the acquisition as he wrote on November 12:

The Committee of the Cabinet appointed to deal with the wheat situation, regards it as desirable that the acquisition from the Canadian Co-operative Wheat Producers Limited, upon terms to be approved by the Governor-in-Council of "All wheat or contracts to purchase or take delivery of wheat in respect of which the Government of Canada has given a guarantee" be consummated immediately.

The Order-in-Council P.C. 3199, provides that the sum to be paid shall be verified by auditors' certificate. I enclose herewith copy of the Order-in-Council dated October 10, 1935.

The Committee desires that the transfer take place at once in order to consolidate the whole situation, the amount to be paid to the Canadian Co-operative Wheat Producers Limited to be subject to the report of the auditors, which will be made at an early date.

Will you kindly proceed immediately with the matter.[9]

[8] *Bennett Papers.*
[9] *Ibid.*

RETIREMENT OF THE McFARLAND BOARD

McFarland did his best to expedite the audit before his first meeting with the wheat committee which was scheduled for November 29. But Mr. James R. Murray preceded him to Ottawa, and he obviously convinced the committee that a more aggressive sales policy was feasible because the committee discussed with him the conditions under which he would seek a leave of absence from his present position in order to replace McFarland on the board. Thus, when McFarland arrived, he met only with Euler and, in their first encounter, it was Euler's painful duty to invite all three members of the board to tender their resignations. McFarland offered to do so, if Euler would declare that the resignations had been requested "for political purposes". This Euler declined to do, as he wrote to McFarland immediately after their meeting and furnished a different reason for his request:

> During the last month the problem of the Canadian wheat surplus has been engaging the earnest consideration of the Government. The seriousness of this problem requires no emphasis here.
>
> In the opinion of the Government a definite and persistent sales resistance has existed, and does now exist, in world markets, which is based on antagonism to the present Board. For this reason the Government feels that in the public interest the retirement of the present Board is advisable.
>
> In our conversation this morning you met my suggestion in this regard by declining to retire except on formal request. Please, therefore, accept this letter as such request, made for the reason given.
>
> May I express to you my appreciation of your efforts in the service of the Government. Kindly let me have an early reply.[10]

Instead of tendering his resignation as requested, McFarland reacted by challenging the statement that a sales resistance existed, based on antagonism to the present board, and he proceeded to gather evidence to the contrary. However, he responded to Euler's letter in a joint telegram of December 2 signed by Smith, Grant and himself which re-offered their resignations provided that three conditions were met: the government would acknowledge its desire to have a board of its own choice; would withdraw the accusation of sales resistance against the retiring board; and would pay its members an honorarium in lieu of salary they otherwise would have earned.

As McFarland continued to marshall his evidence regarding sales resistance, the cabinet wheat committee settled the issue by order in council. P.C. 3756 retired the existing board and appointed another board in its place. The preamble of the order reiterated the allegation made in Euler's letter of November 29, in the following terms:

> ... The Minister further states that his opinion, concurred in by the other members of the aforesaid Sub-Committee, is that a definite and persistent resistance against the sale of Canadian wheat has existed and now exists in the world markets, which resistance is based on antagonism to the members of the present Canadian Wheat Board.
>
> The Minster is of opinion that it is inimical to the best interests of Canada in the circumstances that the present members of the Canadian Wheat Board should continue in office and, therefore, recommends that the said members,

[10] *Ibid.*

namely, John Irwin McFarland, Esquire, chief commissioner, David Livingston Smith, Esquire, Assistant Chief Commissioner, and Henry Clark Grant, Esquire, member of the Board, be retired, the said retirements to take effect on the 3rd day of December, 1935.

The Minister further recommends that the following persons be appointed members of the Canadian Wheat Board in place of those retired, namely, James R. Murray, Esquire, George McIvor, Esquire, and Alexander Malcolm Shaw, Esquire, and that James R. Murray be appointed Chief Commissioner, and George McIvor be appointed Assistant Chief Commissioner of the said Board, the appointments aforesaid to take effect as of the said 3rd day of December, 1935.[11]

McFarland was cruelly hurt by the assertion in the order in council that his service had been "inimical to the best interests of Canada". In subsequent correspondence with McFarland, Euler addressed a formal letter and also a personel letter on December 12 to offer an honorarium to the retiring board members. In the personal communication he wrote:

Your letter of December 10th is here, as also the joint letter signed by yourself and your former colleagues of the Wheat Board.

When you and I had the conversation in my office I believe you appreciated my attitude in the matter, and that the manner of providing for the discontinuance of your services was personally distasteful to me. However, the change had been decided upon as a matter of policy and I regretted that you could not accept my suggestion, that your resignation be submitted, as the best way out. You, of course acted as you felt you must, and I have no fault to find with that. The circumstances were unfortunate but definitely unavoidable as I believe you appreciate.

You ask that your retirement be made in such a manner as will remove from the public mind any possibility of stigma. Certainly, neither my letter to you, nor my wires to the other members reflected in any way upon your integrity and honesty of purpose and, most emphatically was not intended so to do. I do not know just what action could be taken now to ease your mind. Anything I can properly do I will do gladly. So far as the press is concerned, it has in no way given the impression you fear, and I do not intend to initiate anything here that will give publicity to the matter.

As you know, the newspapers inferred that you resigned and I let it pass, leaving it for you to correct if you desired to do so. Unless the matter is brought up in the House I am quite prepared to let it rest, and I leave it to you whether that is not the best course to follow.

I am sorry about Dr. Grant as, indeed, I regret any disagreeable incidents in connection with the whole matter. Again, his retirement was unavoidable as it was felt that a complete change would be advisable.

Frankly, I realize the situation constitutes a hardship for all of you, financially and otherwise. It was always my intention to suggest that some provision be made in due course. I intend to mention it to my colleagues and, in the meantime, I am writing to yourself and Messrs. Smith and Grant, making the same suggestion in a more formal way.[12]

In the end, honoraria were paid to the three commissioners, but McFarland returned his because the stigma of antagonism toward the board had not been withdrawn.

[11]*P. C. 3756,* December 3, 1935.
[12]*Bennett Papers.*

AN APPRECIATION OF JOHN I. McFARLAND

Most of the following comments upon the contribution of Mr. John I. McFarland as a wheat-policy adviser belong more properly to Part II of this review in which he was associated with the Right Honourable R. B. Bennett. But, because McFarland held an official position as chief commissioner of the Canadian wheat board for a brief span under the Liberal administration, his record extends into the beginning of Part III, where his deeply-felt personal hurt and resentment over the manner of his dismissal stand in sharp contrast to the brilliant contribution he made as Bennett's confidant and adviser, and as the man who was alone responsible for the day-to-day decisions on the support operations over a period of five years. His record of accomplishment in that respect was chronicled and summarized in Part II. As general manager of Canadian Co-operative Wheat Producers Limited, McFarland's initial expectation was that he would be able to surmount the crisis within a year. As the situation worsened for reasons beyond his control, McFarland persisted in his attempt to make the futures system work, not for its own sake, (though he had believed in and supported it previously), but out of his deeply ingrained respect for the plight of producers. The object of his personal endeavor was to recover for producers the money they had lost through the price decline in 1930 and, at the height of his support operations, he continued to endeavor to bring them to a conclusion in a way which would recompense the producers and justify Bennett's confidence in him. But the responsibility eventually became too much of a strain on his physical capacity, with the result that in the fifth year he suffered a serious and prolonged illness. Either at the time of his illness or at the time of his appointment to the Canadian wheat board, McFarland would have been well counselled to retire from his responsibilities, but he believed that he could not do so while government holdings remained at a peak. It became a matter of personal pride that he, himself, should try to bring the operation to a successful conclusion. He was crestfallen when the election results proved that Bennett had lost the support of the western provinces, but even then it did not occur to him that a personal adviser so closely associated and identified with Bennett should resign and let the incoming government (with its overwhelming mandate) assume full responsibility for the situation. Even when his resignation was requested, McFarland refused to tender it except on conditions the government was not prepared to meet. In the process, Euler's letter of request and the ensuing order in council retiring the members of the board were so worded that they caused McFarland grievous personal offence. McFarland had every reason to expect that the country should honor him for his selfless contribution, rather than castigate him in that way. On the other hand, the incoming administration had every right to appoint an administrative board in which it had confidence.

The action the wheat committee took was not intended to call in question McFarland's personal integrity. No one can read McFarland's voluminous correspondence with Bennett without being impressed by the ability, the utter sincerity and integrity of the man. There is also the evidence of those who knew McFarland at first hand and worked with him intimately throughout the period of his public service. Mr George McIvor has written recently:

The writer had the priviledge of serving Mr. McFarland for five years. In no way could I have had a finer association. Mr. McFarland at the outset was very confident that the wheat situation could be cleaned up far quicker than was ultimately the case. In fact he said to me when we made our arrangement, "I think we can clean this whole thing up in one year". He took over the job, I would say, with almost 100% support by the press. I recall an editorial that Dr. Dafoe wrote in which he spoke of this man who would plough a lone furrow for the benefit of the producer and so on. As time went on, of course, he experienced many disappointments. Rightly or wrongly, he felt that the grain trade, who at the outset he had considered his friends, had turned against him, and the Pools, who at the outset were cool to him, I think with one exception Henry Wise Wood who was always a great admirer of Mr. McFarland. In the last several years he felt the Pools were his friends and many in the grain trade were his enemies. I am not sure that he judged the situation correctly in this regard as I know for a fact that he had many admirers in the grain trade. Whatever comment that might be made about McFarland, I think it can be summed up in what I term sincerity of purpose. No one tried harder than he did, and time after time he was up against great disappointments which eventually injured his health. I think one thing that worried him was the fact that he had been used to having his own way when he operated Alberta Pacific Grain Company so successfully and he never quite understood the pull and tug of day to day politics. I think it should be said that the Pool leaders in the 1935 period admired Mr. McFarland tremendously. . . .

Mr. McFarland sincerely believed in acreage reduction as the only solution to the wheat depresson. We know by experience now that this type of policy at times does not work. I often wondered why Mr. McFarland accepted the responsibility which meant five years of worry and eventually the loss of his health, and I have come to the conclusion that first of all he was deeply concerned about the financial position of the producers, and he told me one time that he hoped to come out of the stabilization operations with a sufficient surplus that could be paid out to the producers' organisations (the Pools) to offset the loss which they experienced in the 1929 debacle.

The second consideration I think was his very deep regard for the Prime Minister, Mr. Bennett, and the hope that his operations would reflect favourably for Mr. Bennett on the political scene. On both of these objectives, of course, he realised a great disappointment. The third consideration I think was the fact that he felt that he perhaps was the only one who could set the grain business right, not from the standpoint of arrogance or conceit, but he thought his vast experience made him more suitable for the job than anyone else, and I think perhaps in the tough going of the five years, when really there was no solution in sight, it took a man of Mr. McFarland's dogged perseverance to do the job. He worried a good deal about criticism a lot of which he thought was unfair. I used to tell him that these people were not criticising him personally, but were simply not in accord with his policy, but I don't think it was easy for him to get away from the feeling that he was experiencing personal attacks. . . .

I often think that it is very regrettable that Mr. McFarland was not in the state of health that would have enabled him to appear before the Special Committee of the House of Commons in June 1935. Mr. Findlay and myself tried our best to deal with the situation, but we were handicapped by the fact that after all there were many occasions when Mr. McFarland instructed me with regard to wheat purchases without at the same time telling me what was in his mind. At other times he went to great lengths to tell me why he was doing certain things, but we have to keep in mind that it was a one man operation and I was simply his chief of staff carrying out his orders. Had he been able to attend the Committee and give his own reasons I think it would have made a much better impression on the Committee, although I do not think the outcome would have been changed and the findings of the Committee would have been the same. I think, however, that Mr. McFarland's own position would have been much improved, and the proof of this is that when he eventually appeared before the Turgeon Commission, his evidence was very well received. . . .

The results of the election, which were so disastrous for the Conservative party, were a great disappointment to Mr. McFarland. I think he had assumed that his operations would result in the government of the day maintaining their position in Western Canada. As you know they experienced a disastrous defeat all along the line. Although one would conclude that this election was a denial by the producers of their faith in Mr. McFarland, I don't think this would be a fair assessment as the producers gave him a huge dinner in Calgary which was a tribute of appreciation for his work on their behalf.

I suppose, looking back, there could be some criticism of some of the things Mr. McFarland did or did not do, but I often enliken his operations to the efforts of President Hoover who endeavoured to maintain the economic health of the United States in a world crisis and failed. In other words, there were so many factors that affected Mr. McFarland's operations over which he had no control whatsoever, that his position at times was just impossible.[13]

Elsewhere, Mr. McIvor mentioned that Mr. McFarland had suffered rather seriously financially, as well as in health, through his neglect of personal affairs in his five years of service. Little needs to be added to Mr. McIvor's tribute. Suffice it to say, for purposes of this review, that McFarland earned a unique position among the ranks of the grain-policy advisers.

APPOINTMENT OF THE MURRAY BOARD

The same order in council, P. C. 3756 of December 3, 1935, which retired the McFarland board, appointed the Murray board. The three new members were James R. Murray, George McIvor and A. M. Shaw. Murray was named chief commissioner, and McIvor, assistant chief commissioner. Crerar and Murray were former business associates in United Grain Growers Limited. Murray had advised the Liberal party, including Crerar, during the passage of the wheat board legislation. Although Euler and Murray met for the first time that November, Crerar was influential in Murray's selection as McFarland's successor. Similarly, the Honourable J. G. Gardiner sponsored the appointment of Mr. A. M. Shaw, dean of agriculture at the University of Saskatchewan. McIvor's appointment as assistant chief commissioner was a fortunate one. With a long background as general sales manager of the central selling agency and as McFarland's principal assistant, McIvor had kept aloof from political alignment and, because of his experience, Murray urged upon the government McIvor's inclusion among the new appointees. Although taken by surprise, McIvor made a point of consulting McFarland who encouraged him to accept the appointment.[14]

---

[13]Mr. George McIvor's letter of November 6, 1973 (see Appendix 7).
[14]See Mr. McIvor's comments, Appendix 7.

Two other orders in council were also passed on December 3. P. C. 3757 established the salary rates for the new commissioners, and P. C. 3758 rescinded P. C. 2518 of August 13, 1935, which had appointed the advisory committee of the board. Although P. C. 3758 did not declare any reason for abolishing the advisory committee, Mr. Euler's statement announcing the new board mentioned that because the cabinet wheat committee had been established for the purpose of advising the board on policy, the advisory committee was no longer deemed necessary. As subsequently revealed, however, the immediate reason for the disbanding of the advisory committee was that Murray had made it a condition of accepting the post of chief commissioner. Murray was prepared to conform with the policies laid down by the wheat committee, but he foresaw areas of conflict if he was also to be guided by an independent advisory group.

Of much greater consequence was Mr. Euler's declaration of the government's concern to have wheat holdings reduced and to seek the co-operation of the trade to that end, as he said:

> The concentration of surplus stocks of wheat in Canada during the past few years has created an abnormal situation in the world wheat trade.
>
> Last June this situation was recognized by parliament as not being in the best interests of Canada or her wheat producers, and the Dominion Government desires to have our surplus restored on a normal basis. To accomplish this the wheat board will seek the goodwill and co-operation of the grain and milling trades in all importing countries.
>
> It is not necessary to have and there will not be any "fire sale" of Canadian wheat, but it will be for sale at competitive values and will not be held at exorbitant premiums over other wheats.[15]

MURRAY BOARD IN ACTION

Without question, the wheat committee's most crucial early decision was the appointment of a board whose members believed that a positive effort could be made to liquidate the wheat surplus. When the new board was announced on December 3, 1935, only Murray was on hand in Ottawa to consult with the committee. McIvor was in charge of the board office in Winnipeg, and Dean Shaw was still in Saskatoon. Nevertheless, the wheat committee discussed the sales problem in great detail with Murray and decided that everything should be done to regain the confidence of local exporters and the overseas trade in Canada's selling agency. There had been criticism that autumn that Canadian prices were being maintained at unrealistic premiums over competing wheats. For almost the same reasons that McFarland had sought the co-operation of the trade in December, 1930, to overcome hostility against the sales policy of the central selling agency, the wheat committee now encouraged Murray to mend fences with the domestic and overseas trade over the uncertainty surrounding the sales policy of the McFarland board. The committee and Murray made a realistic survey of sales prospects. They were conscious of the fact that in the 1935-36 crop year, 17 of the best selling weeks in the 52 had already elapsed, and that to reduce the carryover to a normal figure by the end of the crop year would require average weekly sales almost equivalent to the total of the weekly world import demand. One factor favoring Canadian sales was that neither the United States nor Argentina had exportable surpluses that year. In fact, the United States was temporarily an importer of Canadian wheat. The only real competition would come from the new Australian crop that winter, and Canadian wheat would have to be offered at realistic premium in order to meet it. It was decided that Canadian wheat should be kept on offer continuously without regard to possible world crop developments in the next season, and that the support of the trade should be enlisted and cultivated. This implied the use of all the facilities of the trade, as the act envisaged. Murray undertook to consult the trade in Winnipeg immediately and to send someone overseas to make direct contact with the millers and the trade in Britain and Europe. Murray also predicted that the new sales policy would be fraught with political controversy, as it was.

Another important decision taken at that meeting of the cabinet wheat committee was to authorize the transfer of the wheat and wheat contracts held by Canadian Co-operative Wheat Producers Limited in respect of which the government had given a guarantee. Altogether, 205,186,980 bushels were involved in the transfer, and this amount included the 74,778,000 bushels still held in the 1930 pool wheat account. Although negotiations on the settlement of that account still remained to be completed with Canadian Co-operative Wheat Producers Limited, (the custodians of the producers' interest therein), the actual wheat and wheat contracts were now taken over by the board. For accounting purposes, the total stocks of 205,186,980 bushels were valued at the market price of December 2, which resulted in a "book loss" of $15,856,645.43. This amount was paid by the government as an advance to the board, but it was ultimately recouped out of profits realized when the stocks were sold. Bennett protested the arbitrary valuation of the stocks and the determination of an apparent loss, as of December 2, 1935, as the profit or loss could not finally be ascertained until the sale of the stocks had been actually completed.

After his meeting with the committee, Murray returned immediately to Winnipeg. The new board, consisting of Murray, McIvor and Shaw, met on December 9, 1935. The minutes of its first meeting were read into the record of a special committee of the house the next spring at Bennett's request. This was a dubious procedure, to say the least, if the board was to function without public exposure of every decision, but the political atmosphere remained turbulent, especially in the area of wheat policy.

The executive of Canadian Co-operative Wheat Producers Limited called on the board on its first day in office. The executive sought to enlist the board's support in its negotiations with the wheat committee over the settlement to be made on the agency holdings, but Murray contended that this was an issue between the agency and the government, and not one for the board. A minute of the meeting recorded that:

> The executive of Canadian Co-operative Wheat Producers Limited, consisting of Mr. L. C. Brouillette, Mr. P. F. Bredt, Mr. George Bennett, along with Mr. Marsh Porter, Counsel, met with the Board to discuss the basis upon which the holdings of Canadian Co-operative Wheat Producers Limited are to be taken over by the Board. During the discussion the delegation was advised that the basis upon which the Board takes over the holdings of Canadian Co-operative Wheat Producers Limited, is a matter entirely

between Canadian Co-operative Wheat Producers Limited and the Federal Government. The delegation agreed that the Board had taken a satisfactory position.[16]

On the next day, December 10, the board established for its memberships on the Winnipeg grain exchange and the Winnipeg grain and produce exchange clearing association by purchasing the memberships which had been held by Canadian Co-operative Wheat Producers Limited.

To implement the wheat committee's and the new board's policy of rapprochement with the trade, the board met, December 11, with a committee representing the shippers and exporters. The committee, consisting of Messrs. R. C. Reece, S. T. Smith, H. Gauer and George Mathieson, submitted a memorandum covering six points of concern, some of them technical, but the sense of the more important ones can be inferred from the board's first memorandum which set out the board's response:

1. The Board agree with the exporters that it is desirable that a proper parity be maintained between Canadian wheat and other competing wheats, in order that Canadian wheat may secure the maximum percentage that can reasonably be expected of the International wheat trade.

2. The Board are willing to agree to the second suggestion made by the exporters committee; namely, that the Board will make wheat available to exporters in sufficient quantity to cover their overnight acceptances during the first ten minutes after the opening of the market, at not more than ¼c. over the previous day's close, provided that exporters will agree that the Board should have the right at any time they so desire, to have an independent auditor's check-up to insure that no unfair advantage has been taken of the Board in connection with this matter. . . .

6. The Board are prepared, in so far as possible, not to compete unfairly in business with the exporters' own stocks of wheat that they now have east of the lakes. The Board consider it would assist in the working out of this problem if each shipper with stocks of wheat in the east, would furnish for the confidential use of the Board, the amount and position of their stocks and the shipper's asking price.[17]

The board's undertaking to offer wheat at realistic premiums did as much as anything could to insure the continuous sale of wheat. The second point covered one of protection to exporters on their overnight offers. At the close each day it was the practice of the exporters to cable offers to their overseas connections which, if accepted, necessitated covering their sales by purchasing futures the next morning. At the time, the exchange had in force a three-cent limit upon the daily price change in either direction from the previous close. If the market were to open sharply higher as the exporters were covering their sales they were faced with substantial losses. It was to protect them against such loss, and to encourage their offering more freely, that the board agreed to fill their export orders at not more than ¼ cent per bushel over the previous close. An audit was imposed to insure that the wheat so priced represented legitimate exports and excluded speculative transactions. This undertaking remained effective until December 22, when the board assured the exporters that it would have wheat continuously on offer at the opening each day in sufficient quantities to take care of export sales, and the ¼ cent limit was withdrawn.

On December 11, the board also met with Mr. Cecil Lamont who undertook to depart immediately for Britain and the continent for personal interviews with the millers and the trade. The board incorporated Mr. Lamont's instructions in a memorandum of that date, which appears in evidence later submitted to a special committee of the house, but the purpose of Mr. Lamont's trip is more succinctly recorded in Mr. Murray's letter of January 17, 1936, which he addressed to a complete list of mills in Britain to explain the board's sales policy:

> The Canadian Wheat Board and the government of Canada are anxious to obtain the goodwill of millers and importers abroad, and especially those in the United Kingdom, with a view to increasing the use of Canadian wheat in the flour blends of overseas mills.
>
> With this in mind, the board dispatched a special representative to England shortly before Christmas, in the person of Cecil Lamont, with instructions to visit British millers or their representatives and discuss with them the new Canadian wheat policy and seek their co-operation in carrying it out.
>
> You will appreciate that to visit every flour miller in the United Kingdom would require more time than the board's representative has at his disposal, and for that reason the board is sending this letter to you, outlining briefly the wheat policy of Canada.
>
> Canadian wheat will no longer be held at exorbitant premiums over other world wheats, and it is the intention of this board to offer wheat consistently at competitive values. It is desired to assure millers and importers that in the event of their increasing the percentage of Manitobas in their flour blend, Canadian wheat will be made available to them at competitive values and in quantities sufficient to meet their requirements.
>
> In the sale of its wheat, the board will utilize existing channels of trade, and the board invites millers to feel free to communicate their views to the board at any time concerning matters relative to the use of Canadian wheat.
>
> If there is any feeling of antagonism toward Canada and her wheat because of past policies the board is anxious that millers dismiss the past and work with it in the future on the basis of mutual profit and goodwill. The board believes it to be in the best interests of Canada to cultivate increased trade with the mother country and hopes for the sake of empire ties and other good reasons, that British millers will feel it to be in their interest to cultivate similar relations with Canada.
>
> It is the desire of the board to regain permanently for Canadian wheat, a full share of the import requirements of wheat in the British Isles. In this, it seeks your co-operation and goodwill.
>
> The board has much pleasure in forwarding a detailed report of the milling and baking quality and other characteristics of western Canada's 1935 wheat crop, for your information and guidance in the use of Canadian wheat.
>
> The board's representative, Mr. Lamont, can be reached through the Canadian High Commissioner's office, in Canada House, London, in case you have any particular matter to discuss with him in the immediate future.[18]

On his arrival in London before Christmas, Lamont called on the Honourable Vincent Massey (who had replaced the Honourable Howard

---

[18]*Ibid.*, April 24, 1936, pp. 143-144.

Ferguson as high commissioner) to acquaint him, and through him the British government, with the purpose of his mission.

The board dealt with a third matter on December 11, having to do with the division of sales between the current crop deliveries and the agency stocks it had acquired. The board minutes read: "The Board agreed that for the present two-thirds of current sales of wheat would be credited to the holdings taken over from Canadian Co-operative Wheat Producers, Limited, and one-third to wheat delivered to the Board by producers. The foregoing division of sales is to be effective from December 10."[19] As Murray explained, that represented the ratio between what they had taken over and what had come in from the 1935 crop.

Then on December 13, the unexpected happened. McIvor got the news first and called Murray at his home early that morning to inform him that the Argentine government had announced an increase of twenty cents in the price paid to its producers. The board met at 8:30 a.m. to decide upon its sales program for the day in the light of the bullish news from Argentina, and it agreed that it should take full advantage of the windfall opportunity to make sales. On that one day the Board sold 11,684,000 bushels of May futures in the pit, at 89⅞ cents a bushel which represented the three-cent limit over the previous day's close. In addition, it sold 861,445 bushels of cash wheat at a related price. It also sold 7,782,000 bushels to wheat exporters and 901,000 bushels to mills to cover the exceptionally heavy volume of acceptances of overnight export offers which had been prompted by the Argentine news. These export transactions were covered at 87⅛ cents or ¼ cent over the previous day's close in accordance with the agreement the board had made with the trade on December 11. Altogether the board's sales on December 13 totalled a record 22,025,445 bushels. For the next week the board's sales ranged between 2 and 3 million bushels per day. From December 9 (when the new board commenced to operate), to the end of that month, the board sales had amounted to 49,471,713 bushels. In the month of January, sales totalled 26,458,092 bushels. In the result, the sales policy approved by the new government was being very effectively implemented.

CHARGES AGAINST THE BOARD

The 11,684,000 bushels sold in the pit on December 13, 1935, created an issue raised first by Mr. John I. McFarland. As he prepared to leave Winnipeg to return to private business in Calgary on December 19, McFarland alleged in a press interview that:

> Among other things the big speculators and manipulators who had effected enormous short sales in the Winnipeg futures market awaiting a smash in prices because of the vicious propaganda carried on in this country and abroad were caught napping and stood to lose millions of dollars. The public are wondering, and they have a right to know, whether these destructive short sellers were rescued from their predicament by the reports of the enormous sales made by the Canadian Wheat Board.[20]

In his reference to the "vicious propaganda carried on in this country and abroad", McFarland was apparently referring to the interpretation in the

[19]*Ibid.*, May 1, 1936, p. 262.
[20]*Ibid.*, April 28, 1936, p. 155.

market of the sales policy which had been announced by Mr. Euler, and he implied that the board had bailed out the shorts on December 13. Just as soon as Bennett had an opportunity to do so in the debate on the speech from the throne as the new parliament assembled in February, 1936, he repeated McFarland's charge, and Mr. E. E. Perley (Qu'Appelle) pursued the attack.

Bennett was particularly incensed over the manner in which the McFarland board had been retired, and went to great statistical lengths to challenge the theory that there had been sales resistance against Canadian wheat. He claimed that McFarland and his colleagues would have offered their resignations if Euler had based his request on political grounds. In addition to his charge that the Murray board had accommodated the shorts, Bennett branded McFarland's successor as "Grain exchange Murray" who for years had been closely identified with the operation of the grain exchange, and who represented "opposition, violent, unquestioning, to what is known as the pool interests in western Canada". Bennett alleged that Lamont had been sent to Britain to reassure the trade that the pools would never function again, and he attributed the source of his information to an unnamed minister of the crown. To support his charge of an exchange-dominated board, Bennett referred to the overnight cover the board had extended to exporters, on terms that involved the country in a financial loss, and he asked:

Is it done for the purpose of casting disrepute upon a former administration? Is it done for the purpose of casting disrepute upon the pools? Is it for the purpose of trying once and for all to finish cooperative selling in western Canada? Is that the reason? Men are asking everywhere: is that the reason? I simply mention the boast that was made by the grain exchange and the members of it before the last election, a boast which was known to me, of course, as to what they would do in western Canada. They were going to see to it that Liberals were returned in those constituencies, and they saw to it wherever they could. And I would like to know if this is the price we have to pay for it, that is what I want to know.[21]

Mr. Euler had an opportunity to reply two days later. He blamed the Bennett government's holding policy for the present plight, and he cited other statistics to show that there had been sales resistance. He criticized Bennett's defamation of Murray as a tool of the grain exchange, and of its members for voting Liberal along with a great many other Canadians. Euler identified Bennett's allegation of protection to the shorts as his most serious charge, and he invited him to request an investigation by a parliamentary committee, which Bennett did. Then to answer Bennett's claim that there had been no trade antagonism toward McFarland, Euler cited two articles from *Broomhall's Corn Trade News* in support of the government's contention.[22]

In connection with the existing surplus, Euler restated the government's sales policy in the following terms:

As a matter of fact, the surplus of 127 million bushels in 1930, when (McFarland) took charge, has been increased, as I said before, to nearly 300 million bushels in the last year. Suppose we have this year, as it is almost time we should have, a large crop in this country, and there are also large crops in

[21] *House of Commons Debates*, February 10, 1936, p. 53.
[22] *Ibid.*, February 12, 1936, p. 137.

the other wheat producing countries, how in the world can we hope to reduce this surplus of between 200 and 300 million bushels and to sell the wheat that we may produce, unless we deliberately offer our wheat in the world markets at competitive prices and give the people a real opportunity to buy it? This government believes in the policy of offering wheat at competitive prices and in clearing the bins as far as possible at fair prices — not at fire sale prices, as they have sometimes been described — before a new crop comes in. It seems to me that that is just ordinary business common sense; it is the practice any man in business would follow. It applies particularly in the case of wheat, because the longer you keep wheat the more it costs you to store it. Your storage charges are mounting at the rate of two-thirds of a cent per bushel per month.[23]

A short time later, Euler referred the Bennett charges and more generally the question of grain marketing policy to a special committee of the house. As matters stood, Bennett's line of attack was to identify the Liberal party and the Murray board as strong supporters of the grain exchange and the futures market system, and thereby to appeal for the support of the pool membership. In this he had some competition from the C.C.F. party, because Mr. M. J. Coldwell also claimed that the Liberals were oriented toward the exchange, which he regarded as the traditional enemy of the pools. Bennett made his charge of wrongdoing in rescuing the shorts as evidence of an exchange-dominated board. In rebuttal, Euler criticized the former government as a reluctant seller of wheat turning the wheat surplus into a national problem. He justified the change in the board personnel as necessary to carry out the new policy of offering wheat at competitive prices, eliminating the surplus, and getting back to the sale of crops on a year-to-year basis. But, as the new parliament opened, the throne speech debate demonstrated that any discussion of wheat policy that year could be depended upon to be a politically explosive affair.

In passing, it might be noted that Mr. E. E. Perley introduced a motion to have the provisions of the Canadian wheat board act made applicable to oats, barley, rye and flax. The Saskatchewan wheat pool had passed a resolution at its annual meeting to that end. The pool delegates had also sought the proclamation of the compulsory clauses in the act to channel deliveries of all grain through the board and the continuation of its operations for at least five years. Although no limit on the duration of the wheat board had been incorporated in the act, Colonel Ralston had advocated one and understandably the pools were looking for some reassurance that the wheat board would be continued, now that a Liberal government was in office.

Nevertheless, Perley's motion embraced only the application of the act to coarse grains. It was the least the Conservatives could do in support of the pool resolution, particularly when they were accusing the Liberals of supporting the exchange. Perley's motion was talked out when it came up for debate on March 9, 1936. When it came up the next time on the order paper, Perley simply asked that his motion be withdrawn.[24]

---

[23]*Ibid.*, pp. 135-136.
[24]*Ibid.*, March 9, 1936, pp. 809-904, and June 7, 1936, p. 3447.

EQUALIZATION PAYMENTS — 1930 POOL WHEAT AND COARSE GRAINS

Before it proceeded with the special committee to weigh the McFarland-Bennett-Perley charges that the board had protected the shorts, the government dealt with the fairly urgent matter of completing settlement on the 1930 pool wheat and coarse grains accounts. It will be recalled from Part II of this review that the issue remained in abeyance after Bennett's last-minute attempt to effect a settlement before the election. Although the incoming government had arranged the take-over of all the central agency's stocks of wheat and wheat futures on December 3, 1935, and had made an advance to the new board on the basis of an arbitrary valuation, the settlement of the central selling agency's claim to compensation on the 1930 pool accounts still remained for negotiation. The executive of the central agency, Messrs. L. C. Brouillette, P. F. Bredt, and George Bennett, together with Mr. Marsh Porter, counsel, had sought to have the Murray board intercede in the negotiations as McFarland earlier had done but, as already noted, Murray took the position that this was a matter for direct negotiation between the agency and the government.

Accordingly the executive proceeded to Ottawa, and they brought with them the revised auditors' statement which had been requested in November by Dunning. The basic items in the agency's claim, which Bennett had already approved, "subject to auditors' certificates" were as follows:

Wheat	$6,509,269.36
Coarse grains	890,658.44
1930-31 expenses of the provincial pools	862,487.57
	$8,262,415.37

It will also be recalled that the central selling agency had kept accurate records of cash wheat sales by grades and that by February 29, 1932, it had moved into consumption and export the equivalent of the 76,376,000 bushels of wheat futures immobilized for stabilization purposes in the 1930 account. Had this movement been written off against the account, an average of 60½ cents per bushel, basis one Northern, would have been realized by that time. As the executive committee of the agency now represented to the cabinet wheat committee, the reason distribution to producers was not made in 1932 was because the government had incorporated the 1930 pool account into its total support operation. Additionally, such proceeds would have permitted the pools to equalize the payments to producers, by way of bringing those who had delivered at initial payments of 55 and 50 cents, respectively, up to the 60 cent level. Such a settlement could also have compensated for differences between the grade differentials as arbitrarily set in the initial payments and as determined by actual sales. Bennett had recognized this claim respecting wheat, and the wheat committee, upon review, acknowledged it as valid.

But when it came to coarse grains, as the original auditors' report had pointed out, the amount claimed by the agency had been based not upon sales records, as in the case of wheat, but rather upon the amounts required to equalize payments at the highest initial payments set for each grain to producers who had delivered at lower initial payments in the 1930-31 crop year. As the second auditors' report pointed out, there had been no stabilization operations in coarse grains, and the wheat committee decided, for that reason, that the coarse grains producers were not entitled to the arbitrary compensation claimed by the agency and which, on the eve of the election, Mr. L. C. Brouillette had announced as being paid. On the other hand, despite the undue delay in the completion of sales of the 1930 coarse grains accounts, there stood in the books of the agency, now taken over by the wheat board, some small surpluses in the barley, flax and rye accounts. Oats had been ultimately disposed of at a loss. The auditors' report showed surpluses in the other accounts as follows:

Barley	$ 15,482.58
Flax	210,926.05
Rye	124,276.02
	$350,684.65

The wheat committee approved the distribution of these surpluses which fell far short of the $890,658.44 required to equalize initial payments on all the coarse grains.

The third item in the agency's claim of $862,487.57 for the 1930-31 operating expenses of the three provincial pools was based on the fact that such expenses had been customarily deducted from the proceeds realised on the sales of pool grain before interim or final payments were made. Since no such payments had been possible on the 1930 operations, the pools had not been able to recover their expenses. Nevertheless, the wheat committee disallowed this claim because, as Mr. Gardiner subsequently explained to the house, the pools had deducted two cents per bushel from interim or final payments in previous years from which a reserve of $6,500,000 had been accumulated, and against which the wheat committee believed the 1930-31 operating expenses were a reasonable charge.[25]

In summary, the wheat committee approved the amount of $6,509,269.36 in order to make equalization payments on the 1930 pool wheat account, but for which the government would have to obtain legislative authority to make payment from the consolidated revenue fund. Additionally, the legislation authorized payment of $350,684.65 on coarse grains from surpluses properly due on barley, flax and rye, but which had been carried in the accounts transferred by the agency to the board in the general take-over on December 3, 1935.

On March 20, 1936, the Honourable J. G. Gardiner introduced a resolution in the house to provide for the payment. It was curious that Gardiner was selected to pilot the legislation through the House. Euler, as chairman of the wheat committee, would have been the logical minister, or alternatively Dunning, as minister of finance. The main substance of the bill was not controversial, because both governments had endorsed the proposed payment on wheat. But, as already noted, wheat policy was a particularly sensitive issue that year, and it was anticipated that a debate would ensue for which Euler, by temperament, had no particular relish, whereas it was Gardiner's first appearance in the federal house, after he had

[25]*Ibid.*, March 27, 1936, p. 1546.

accomplished the rout of the Anderson government in Saskatchewan in 1934. He was now ready for a direct confrontation with Bennett, and the debate was Gardiner's first tour de force in the span of his twenty-one year tenure as minister of agriculture. The debate on the resolution began on March 25. What might have been disposed of in an hour extended over two sittings. When Bennett put the traditional opposition question of why there had been so much delay in introducing the measure, Gardiner read P. C. 3199 of October 10, 1935, into the record with dramatic effect to identify Bennett's addition of the words "subject to the amount . . . being verified by auditors' certificates" as the culprit in the delay. Bennett took umbrage and prolonged the debate for two days. The manner of preparing and signing the submission and its role on the eve of the election were fully aired. Even Mackenzie King joined in by questioning the propriety of a submission which was altered after most of the signatures had been obtained.

On his motion for second reading on March 27, Mr. Gardiner spoke for two and a half hours in which he presented an historical review of the wheat pools and the 1930 crisis which had led to McFarland's appointment as general manager of the agency, and to the evolution of the support operations and the financial guarantees related thereto. On the subject of coarse grains, Gardiner drove home the point that settlement on the rye and flax accounts should have been made in 1932 or 1933, before he cited the basis for the current settlement on coarse grains, and made the most out of Brouillette's announcement of October 10 which had engendered greater expectations. He presented the wheat committee's case for nonpayment of the 1930-31 operating expenses of the pools, and then explained the wheat committee's position on the wheat payment in the following terms:

On July 31, 1931, there were 76,375,000 bushels of 1930 pool wheat in the hands of Mr. McFarland; that was at the time the change was made that I said was a cut off on July 31, 1931. Now what was done with that wheat? Well, the auditor's report shows that that quantity of 76,000,000 bushels was dealt with in accordance with the policy laid down by the then Prime Minister and Mr. McFarland. It was actually taken off the market, put into an account by itself, retained in that account in order to stabilize the price to other people who were producing wheat throughout the length and breadth of Canada, and it is because these 76,000,000 bushels were taken off the market and kept off the market from 1931 to 1935 that the wheat pools have been claiming that they should have payment in connection with that wheat. The government is inclined to think their claim is well founded and that some payment should be made as a result of the fact that this wheat was taken and kept off the market, for the purpose, as the leader of the opposition would admit, whether it accomplished the purpose or not, of raising the price to other people, the same people who produced grain in other years. There is really no other ground for the claim than that.[26]

Bennett summed up Gardiner's performance in one sentence:

Mr. Speaker, for two hours and a half the chamber has listened to the most violent political speech that I have heard in it for many years about a matter that affects the welfare of every province in the Dominion of Canada, and which was made purely as a vindictive pronouncement against those who had

[26]*Ibid.*, March 27, 1936, p. 1549.

endeavoured to stabilize the price of wheat and prevent disaster from coming to the farmers of western Canada.[27]

Thereupon, Bennett obtained an adjournment of the debate until March 30 when he likewise took two and a half hours to give his version of the same historical events, and it took two sittings to get the bill through committee on second reading. Third reading was given on April 1, and after minor amendments in the senate, the 1930 wheat crop equalization payments act obtained royal assent on April 8, 1936.[28] In its preamble, the act declared that the stabilization operations had resulted in a loss, but that primary producers who had accepted initial payments on a basis of 60 or 55 cents were justified in expecting those payments to be equalized on a basis of 60 cents, with the spreads between the various grades determined on the basis of actual transactions. To accomplish this, the act authorized payment of not more than $6,000,000 from the consolidated revenue fund.

SPECIAL COMMITTEE OF THE HOUSE, 1936

Meanwhile on March 18, 1936, the house appointed a special committee to investigate and report upon the marketing of wheat and other grains under guarantees by the Dominion government. The committee held an organizational meeting on March 24 and commenced public hearings on April 21, under the chairmanship of Mr. Euler. The chairman explained that after the March meeting he had appointed a steering committee consisting of Messrs. Bennett, Crerar, Donnelly, Ross and Coldwell which had met and recommended an investigation of certain references made in the house with regard to the operations of the present wheat board and, more importantly, to make a thorough survey of the whole wheat situation and how it might best be dealt with. These two items served as the agenda for the committee, and witnesses were called to Ottawa to give evidence. Since the references in the house concerned the relief of the speculative shorts, the committee endeavoured to get at the facts by examining Mr. A. E. Darby, secretary of the exchange, Mr. Frank O. Fowler, manager of the Winnipeg grain and produce clearing association, and Mr. J. R. Murray, the chief commissioner of the board. On April 21, Darby delivered a masterly essay on the functions and operations of the exchange. Any one desiring a better understanding of the futures marketing system would do well to read that account. Fowler also reported on the services provided by the clearing association which he had organized in 1903, and of which he had since been manager. Murray took the stand on April 22 and his cross-examination lasted until April 30. Aware that he would be under attack, he characteristically came out fighting. Murray's opening statement contained enough barbs to arouse Bennett's resentment, but the latter was quite capable of replying in kind. At one stage, when Murray acknowledged that one of his failings was to express strong opinions and that, at times, he was very difficult to work with, Bennett greeted Murray's confession with glee. In the course of his lengthy cross-examination of Murray, Bennett endeavored to develop the theme of an exchange-dominated board. He cited the interventions Murray had made to the committee of the grain

---

[27] *Ibid.*, March 27, 1936, p. 1553.
[28] *Statutes of Canada,* 1 Edward VIII, Chap. 12.

exchange which had met in Ottawa to prepare the brief Mr. Milner presented to the special committee on Bill 98 a year earlier. Mr. Coldwell pursued the same theme in his cross-examination of Murray.

At one stage, Bennett caught Murray off guard in a statement to the effect that in selling cash wheat the Board normally "bought" back futures. Bennett alleged that this was a contravention of the act which limited board purchases to wheat delivered by producers. Murray altered his phrase to the "exchange" of futures against cash sales. He explained that this exchange (distinct from purchasing in the pit which was prohibited) was the normal method of selling wheat used by the predecessor board and that the procedure was embraced in the injunction to use the facilities of the trade. If this were not the case, Murray claimed that the act had been villainously drawn. Later, his Winnipeg staff sent him a legal opinion McFarland had obtained in August that such exchange of futures was consistent with the terms of the act.

Bennett's and Perley's main purpose, however, was to demonstrate that the board had accommodated the shorts. As Euler defined the issue: "What the committee is concerned with at the moment is not whether this Wheat Board used good judgment in making that big sale back in December, but whether they showed undue favor to certain persons, whether they did something that is sinister."[29]

In reply to the charge, Murray made a long statement, the key parts of which ran as follows:

> It should be borne in mind that we started to work on December 9 and that four days afterwards this situation arose, and that very shortly thereafter — December 19 was the first date — statements were made reflecting on the actions of our Board.
>
> Now, as to what happened to shorts, large shorts or small shorts, international shorts or domestic shorts, on December 13, our Board has no knowledge. The Committee can through other sources, if they desire, get that information. . . .

He then recited McFarland's charge of December 19 and Coldwell's article to the effect that the new board was dominated by the farmers' old enemy the grain exchange. He reviewed McFarland's record in dealing with the shorts. He quoted from McFarland's statement of October 1, 1934, respecting the bear raid at that time and that it was McFarland's intention to place the matter before the proper authorities in Ottawa. Also he referred to McFarland's lengthier statement of October 31, 1934, in which he had said that there was a moral responsibility on the government of the country to offer protection against the unwarranted operations of large speculators. Then Murray continued:

> That was at the beginning of November, 1934. During the following months, and particularly coming down to May, 1935, there were numerous reports in trade circles that the shorts were going to be squeezed in the month of May when the time for delivery of the May option came along, but nothing happened. May wheat closed at the end of the month at 81¾ cents, and July wheat at 82⅞ cents, on the last day of May. Mr. McFarland switched hedges from May to July with the trade at 1⅜ cents per bushel difference just the

[29]Special Committee on the Marketing of Wheat and Other Grains, *Proceedings and Evidence*, April 30, 1936, p. 245.

same as our Board have done this year. In June, 1935, Mr. Bennett made a speech in the House of Commons in which he dealt with this matter of shorts at some length. It was discussed then in some detail before the Special Committee of parliament which sat here last June, and on July 4, after it had been discussed, the committee reported the Canadian Wheat Board Act to the House of Commons and parliament passed that Act, after all the discussion there had been over a period of nine months about the bear raids and about the shorts. And I would ask you gentlemen to note that the Act passed for the purpose of providing machinery that in the judgment of the Committee, and I presume in the judgment of parliament, was thought the best machinery to use for the handling of the problem that confronted the government of this country through the ownership of over 200,000,000 bushels of wheat, and also for the purpose of providing what, in the judgment of the committee and in the judgment of parliament was the best means of handling the 1935 crop for the farmers, set out certain duties for the Board to which in due course we became subject. There is I think nowhere in that Act a word which says that our duty is to distinguish between bulls or bears, or longs or shorts, or exporters or importers, or any other kind of people that there may be who do business in the grain trade of Canada. We were told, in short, in the Act, to sell wheat.[30]

Murray's claim was irrefutable that the previous government had taken no action to correct the situation, nor was there any injunction in the act against the sale of futures to any buyer. Still Bennett and Perley pursued the charge by calling for the clearing house statements on December 13, in the hope of revealing the persons or firms to whom board wheat had been sold. Murray produced a list of exporters whose overnight acceptances the board had covered, but the clearing association records showed only the names of brokers to whom the board had sold over 11 million bushels in the pit. When both Murray and Mr. Frank Fowler confirmed that the only way to pursue the hunt would be to subpoena all the pit brokers, Bennett and Perley abandoned the chase. But Perley insisted that the charge stand because the committee had failed to make a complete investigation. As a result, the charge was referred to the Turgeon royal grain inquiry commission whose report in May, 1938, eventually exonerated the board.

While all this discussion dragged on in the committee, Euler had to decide upon the substance of the committee's report. The committee had conducted the investigation as far as it could in respect of the first half of its terms of reference, but the more important question of the best marketing system in present circumstances was clearly beyond the capacity of a politically-motivated committee to resolve. Murray had been advocating privately for almost a year that such a question should be assigned to a royal commission, and in his discussions with the cabinet wheat committee, he had now persuaded the government that this was the best means of resolving the issue. With the wheat committee's blessing, he made a statement to the special committee on April 30, and Mr. Euler effectively backed the proposal from the chair. The special committee accepted the proposal and embodied it in its final report on June 11, 1936, to the house, part of which read:

After a full examination of Mr. Murray and the records placed by him at the disposal of the committee, we are of the opinion that the course taken by the

[30]*Ibid.,* April 28, 1936, pp. 155-159.

board in the marketing of wheat was consistent with the intention of parliament in enacting the Wheat Board Act of 1935, and with the policy of the government to reduce the wheat surplus to reasonable proportions.

While there was a short interest in the Winnipeg wheat market in December of 1935, no evidence was produced that would warrant the conclusion that speculative short interests were protected by the board in that month. As the committee finds it impracticable to obtain conclusive evidence on this point, we recommend that this matter be referred for further investigation to the Royal Commission, the appointment of which is recommended in this report.

The committee further gave general consideration to the whole problem of the production and marketing of Canadian wheat and other facts pertaining to the wheat problem. Because of the gravity of this problem, and because your committee has neither the time nor the facilities to make a comprehensive survey of the situation, we recommend the appointment by the government of a Royal Commission to make a complete survey of the production, grading and distribution of Canadian grain, including the methods of marketing by, —

(a) the producers themselves through co-operative and stabilizing effort;

(b) the agency of a government wheat board and the powers such a board should possess;

(c) the open market or competitive method;

and, further, to inquire into the general effect of mixing, if any, and of selection for protein content by millers and exporters. This would involve not only a full examination into the methods referred to above, but also into the conditions which obtain in world markets; what effect, if any, these methods have had upon European purchasers, and, generally, what measures should be taken to retain and enlarge markets for Canadian wheat, and products of wheat and other grains, throughout the world.[31]

APPOINTMENT OF THE TURGEON ROYAL GRAIN INQUIRY COMMISSION

The house adopted the committee's report without dissent on June 17, 1936, and the acting minister of trade and commerce made a submission to council on behalf of the wheat committee of the cabinet almost immediately. The wheat committee had persuaded the Honourable W. F. A. Turgeon, judge of the Court of Appeal of Saskatchewan, to act as sole commissioner of a royal commission. Thirteen years earlier Turgeon had been appointed as chairman of the royal grain inquiry commission which had reported in 1925. Although he was now adjured to report as speedily as possible, the government had already appointed him to head an inquiry into conditions in the textile industry so that Turgeon's time on the grain commission over the next two years had to be shared with his responsibility for the textile commission. P. C. 1577 of June 27, 1936, appointing Turgeon as commissioner also set out the terms of reference for the commission. The remit picked up the recommendations of the special committee of the house with its emphasis upon an investigation into the alternative methods of marketing wheat as the main issue, but including the specific issues of protecting the speculative short interests in December, 1935, and the handling of grain for relief and seeding purposes in the prairie provinces, so far as the stabilization operations were concerned. It also referred to the

[31]*Ibid.*, June 11, 1936, pp. 331-332.

question of mixing and of grading for protein content, and it called upon the commissioner to investigate the causes of the decrease in Canadian grain exports in recent years and to recommend measures which should be taken to retain and extend Canada's grain markets. Mr. Justice Turgeon, in turn, recruited the Honourable J. L. Ralston as senior counsel. Mr. Ralston had opted to return to his law practice in 1935 instead of standing for re-election. His involvement in the formation of the Canadian wheat board particularly qualified him for this task. Mr. James E. Coyne was recruited as junior counsel,[32] and Dr. T. W. Grindley, chief of the agricultural branch of the dominion bureau of statistics, was seconded as secretary. The commission's hearings did not get under way because of the commissioner's other involvements until December, 1936, and for the next year were held in western Canada, Britain, the Low Countries and Chicago. Findings of the report (submitted on May 6, 1938), are covered in a subsequent chapter.

One immediate result of the commission's appointment, however, was the diffusion of the political atmosphere which had surrounded the wheat board's activities as it commenced operation. This cooling-off process appeared to be deliberate policy of the wheat committee of cabinet, once it had appointed its own board with a clearly defined policy of orderly liquidation of the stabilization holdings together with the prompt marketing of the current crop. At its inception, the Canadian wheat board had been fraught with controversy, as recriminations passed back and forth between McFarland and Murray. McFarland had criticized his successor board, and Murray defended himself in kind. Bennett and E. E. Perley had picked up McFarland's contentions and Euler, as head of the new group of four policy-makers, was determined to have the charges against his government's board thoroughly aired. As chairman of the special committee, Euler performed effectively, if almost silently, in stark contrast with Bennett's performance as chairman of a similar committee a year earlier. Although Murray lent color to the situation by his temperamental instinct never to back away from a fight, a man of that personality was needed to weather the political storm. How much he brought upon himself and how much was inflicted upon him is debatable, but in the midst of all the controversy Murray never deviated from the new government's policy of liquidating the accumulated stocks.

INITIAL PAYMENT FOR THE 1936 CROP

The first initial payment had been approved by order in council by the Bennett government at 87½ cents for the 1935-36 crop year. Although not specifically directed by the act in its original form in 1935 to establish the initial payment on a crop-year basis, this was evidently the intention and the order in council defined the period for which the initial payment had been approved. Thus, in order to have an initial payment in operation for the 1936-37 crop year, the wheat board would have to "fix" a price, and the governor in council approve it. This exercise gave Euler grave concern as he prepared to take off for London in June on the first round of talks on a new trade agreement. He expected to be away for the next two months, and

---

[32]This was one of Mr. Coyne's early assignments after admission to the bar. Later he was recruited by the Bank of Canada and succeeded Mr. Graham Towers as governor.

Gardiner was also going overseas in search of farm markets. Thus, the cabinet wheat committee would be scattered at the end of the crop year when the board's initial payment for the new crop year needed to be determined. The extent of Euler's concern was expressed in a personal letter addressed on June 25, 1936, from his home in Kitchener to King:

As the wheat policy for the coming year will be decided before I return, I desire to place my views before you and Council.

In my opinion, if the government is ever going out of the wheat business, this is the time to do it. If it is delayed, it will become increasingly difficult as the time for an election approaches. I never approved of Mr. Bennett's policy and we should end it as soon as possible. It can be excused only as an emergency measure at the best, for it is not only class legislation of the worst kind, but is confined to one class in one particular section of the country. The loss on wheat today is probably in the neighborhood of $40,000,000 is a heavy burden on the general taxpayers of Canada. In my opinion there should be no fixed price for the coming year, and some arrangement should be made by which the stock now held should be disposed of by a continuing Wheat Board without detriment to the sale of the coming crop, perhaps by a quota allotment each month.

I am sure that such a course will be justified ultimately. If we continue the policy, the demands of the wheat producers for higher prices (fixed) will be augmented. Moreover, with the principle established, the government will probably be forced to yield to a similar policy with regard to coarse grains and then to products of all kinds. That would constitute a very definite advance towards socialism. If the situation is still to be regarded as an emergency, I would favour the lesser evil of granting a bonus, which could be terminated more easily.

Should the government decide on fixing a price for wheat for the coming crop, it should be not higher than 60 cents a bushel, so that possible loss will be definitely limited.[33]

Because of the scattered state of the wheat committee, Euler's letter was placed on the cabinet agenda where it remained until the policy for the 1936 crop was eventually decided. Quite apart from Euler's view of the discriminatory elements in the wheat board legislation, even the western ministers shared his opinion that it should be repealed as soon as the emergency ended. Even if that point had been reached, however, parliament had already prorogued and repeal was out of the question. Meanwhile, the executive of the central selling agency, L. C. Brouillette, P. F. Bredt and George Bennett met in Ottawa on July 6 with Gardiner, Crerar and the Honourable J. L. Ilsley, minister of national revenue and acting minister of trade and commerce, to urge that the 1936 initial payment be fixed at a "cost of production" level. By now the pool representatives were once again in the ascendancy as spokesmen for producers, as the working arrangement in that area among the three provincial premiers fell apart. The premiers were by now more actively concerned with negotiations on the federal-provincial sharing of relief costs. A Social Credit government had been elected in Alberta, and a Liberal government was already in office in Saskatchewan. Of the three premiers who actively represented producers during the Bennett regime, only Premier Bracken had survived, being barely sustained in office by the Manitoba election in 1936. When, by late

[33] *W. L. M. King Papers,* Public Archives of Canada.

August, the government still had not announced the 1936 initial payment, the pool executive wired the government to recommend that the minimum price should be set not lower than the market level which at that time was just below one dollar.

But Euler's recommendation was still before the cabinet as it came to grips with the issue in August. The question, in simplest terms, was how to avoid a repetition of the 1935-36 crop year experience on which the wheat board's deficit was heading toward 12 million dollars. In the end, King and his colleagues came up with an ingenious solution. By putting the justice department law clerks to work on the problem, they learned that the act did not bind the governor in council to approve the initial payment recommended by the board. Murray was also drawn into the consultations and met with the cabinet on August 26-27 when the decision was taken. In the result, the government had the board make a formal recommendation that the payment be "fixed" again at 87½ cents, which the governor in council disapproved, except in the event that the closing market price dropped below 90 cents.

Obviously, some difficulty was experienced in drafting the explanatory section of the submission. It was decided that justification for the change in policy should be attributed to the royal grain inquiry commission, and one draft of the submission declared that: "the undersigned is of the opinion that pending the report of the said Commission, it is inadvisable that any step be taken which might be considered as pre-judging the Report of the Commission as respects the methods of marketing to be employed."[34] This explanation seemed too specific, and the following was substituted in P. C. 2202 of August 28, 1936, which gave effect to the decision. After reciting that the board had fixed a price of 87½ cents, the order continued:

> That the Honourable William Ferdinand Alphonse Turgeon, of Regina, Sask., a Judge of the Court of Appeal of Saskatchewan, was appointed a Commissioner under Part I of The Enquiries Act, being Chapter 99 of the Revised Statutes of Canada, 1927, to enquire into and to report upon the subject of the production, buying, selling, holding, storing, transporting and exporting of Canadian Grains and Grain Products, and other questions incident to such matters, and in particular, but without restricting the generality of the foregoing terms, to enquire into and to report upon:
>
> The methods now or heretofore employed in marketing Canadian grains abroad, including Government Grain Boards, co-operative or pool market-ing, price stabilization measures and the open market or competitive method; and the effect of these various methods upon markets;
>
> The measures which should be taken to retain and to extend the marketing throughout the world of Canadian Wheat and other grains and their prod-ucts.
>
> The Minister, therefore, recommends that the recommendation of the Canadian Wheat Board be not approved unconditionally but that approval be given only in the event of the closing market price for wheat dropping below ninety cents per bushel for wheat graded as No. 1 Northern at Fort William, in which event a price of 87½¢ per bushel as recommended by the Board shall be approved, and this Order in Council be regarded as approving the same.

[34] *Ibid.*

The totally unexpected nature of the decision which King announced after cabinet rose on August 27 was greeted in the west by surprise, if not outright shock. In his press interview, King alluded to the necessity of not prejudging the report of the royal commission on marketing methods. The reaction of the executive of the central agency of the pools was immediate, and it issued a statement which read in part:

> ... At the moment, two points stand out clearly. One, that the western grain grower has been denied the right given him by parliament in the Wheat Board act to deliver his grain to the board, unless the price declines below 90 cents (basis one northern, Fort William).
>
> Two, the efforts of organized agriculture to place their industry on a footing of economic equality has sustained a major reverse. It is not the first time; there have been others since the farmers began fighting for centralized marketing 16 years ago. Nor would it be correct to say that we are back where we were in 1920 when the old Canada wheat board was disbanded. A guarantee against market collapse is of course a stride forward. But as matters now stand the speculative system which we have fought so persistently remains in possession of the field.
>
> Through the decision announced from Ottawa, the alternative system of controlled grain marketing in the interest of producer and consumer alike, had been forced to pause. ...[35]

Matters were not left there, however, because the pool leaders made another trip to Ottawa where they met with Messrs. Euler, Crerar and Gardiner on September 10. Their representations were of no avail, however, in persuading the government to reverse its decision; the delegation commented on the results:

> We believe that this restriction on the operations of the board is contrary to the spirit and intent of the Canada Wheat Board act and to all intents and purposes may be regarded as repealing the wheat board legislation by making it entirely ineffective, except in the contingency of wheat prices dropping to such a level. With producers denied the right to deliver the wheat to the board, it must inevitably go out of business. If such should be the deliberate intention of the government, the policy will be received with alarm and dismay not only by wheat producers but by western Canada generally. ...
>
> Even after the recent announcement by the government of the setting of the minimum price, we hoped that its decision might be reconsidered and modified. While fully realizing the difficulties our federal government has to deal with and the grave problem of relief in the areas again devastated by drought in the prairie provinces, we regret that this 11th hour attempt has been without result.[36]

In light of the government's decision, the pools had to reexamine their own policy. At a meeting of the central executive on September 5, 1936, a resolution confirmed the executive's decision not to attempt the resumption of provincial pools. Although this decision was later reviewed (after the royal commission's report when the government invited the pools to resume their own pooling operations by enacting enabling legislation), it was not altered. From 1936 forward, the policy of the pools was predominantly one of pressing for compulsory deliveries to a government-operated board. Little, if any, enthusiasm was displayed for a return to producer-operated

---

[35] *Winnipeg Free Press*, August 29, 1936.
[36] *Ibid.*, September 10, 1936.

pools. Hence the immediate concern of the pools to retain a voluntary government board in full operation as a step toward their ultimate objective. Such concern was given explicit expression as Mr. George W. Robertson, secretary of the Saskatchewan wheat pool, organized another of his protest campaigns in which the pool local organizations and the rural municipalities passed resolutions regretting that producers had been denied the opportunity of delivering through the board.

The pools were not alone in their concern over the government's decision. Western Liberal backbenchers were confronted by the reaction of their constituents. A rift began to develop between the Honourable W. R. Motherwell and King, which led to Motherwell's open attack later. Motherwell had been King's minister of agriculture up to 1930, and in his eighties he still sat as a private member. From his home in Abernethy on August 31, 1936, Motherwell addressed a letter to King which he marked "Confidential except to your colleagues":

> Your press statement, at least as attributed to you, under date of August 28 that the Wheat Board will not begin to function until the open market price fell to 90 cents Fort William basis 1°, came as a stunner to Sask. farmers even though it had been preceded by many seemingly semi-inspired despatches for weeks past, indicating that the Fed. gov't. were preparing to glide gracefully out of the wheat merchandizing picture.
>
> These rumours and reports while quite disturbing to many I took little stock in, as I knew the gov. could not by Executive Order repeal the Wheat Board Act or indeed any other act, as that is the prorogative of Parliament as you have so frequently demonstrated. . . .

After referring to King's statement that any other action at the present time might prejudice the findings of the commission headed by Mr. Justice W. F. A. Turgeon, Motherwell continued:

> Surely this reason for the government's recent alleged action pending Mr. Justice Turgeon's Report, upon which he has not even begun to take evidence in Canada yet, would constitute a stronger and sounder argument for *non-action* on such a vital matter, than *action,* in advance of the anticipated report. . . .
>
> If I may make a suggestion at this distance, and with so little evidence at my disposal upon which the gov. has based its reported conclusions, it would be that one or more of the four members of the subcom. of the gov. especially charged with the administration of the Wheat Board problems, would come west forthwith and explain first-hand what has really been done and why. This would doubtless substantially allay the many misgivings and fears aroused during recent days and weeks. . . .[37]

King acted upon Motherwell's recommendation by despatching Gardiner and Crerar on speaking tours to defend the government's policy. The two ministers stressed the priority placed by the government on the sale of wheat which was visibly helping to improve future marketing prospects. As prices continued to rise, it became increasingly apparent that very little wheat would have been delivered to the board had it accepted wheat at 87½ cents. Nevertheless, Motherwell kept up his correspondence with King on the issue, and he also upbraided the Honourable Ernest Lapointe for permitting his law officers to give the government such advice.

[37] *King Papers.*

The issue over the government's marketing policy for the 1936 crop was bound to come up as soon as parliament reassembled. In the debate on the address from the throne, Bennett asked what power the governor in council had to change a statute, and he continued:

The statute passed by this parliament was not repealed although an attempt was made when we were in committee to have it provided that the statute should die after a certain period of time. We took the view then, as we are doing now, that as the statute was for the well-being of the western farmer and the whole class of wheat producers, it should only cease being in effect when repealed. It has not been repealed to this day. During the season just ended the farmer has had no opportunity to sell his wheat to the board unless the price dropped below 90 cents. That was not the purpose of the statute. The purpose was exactly the opposite; it was to afford the farmer an opportunity to sell.[38]

Mackenzie King responded almost immediately in defence of his policy, saying:

What about wheat? My right hon. friend's policy with respect to wheat was to hold wheat and not sell it. As a result this country was getting such a quantity of wheat in storage that the surplus was creating a problem of itself. This government entered upon a policy of selling wheat, and as a result of that policy a great burden of contractual obligation has been lifted off the shoulders of the nation and the farmers of western Canada have profited immensely in ways they previously had but little reason to expect. . . .

My right hon. friend has also referred this afternoon to the government's action with respect to the sale to wheat, and he has asked by what authority we took the step we did. May I say to him that before taking action in the matter we conferred with the chairman of the wheat board, and we also took counsel with the law officers of the crown, and the law officers of the crown assured us that in taking the step we eventually did we would be entirely within the law which governs in this matter. I am not going to enter into a legal argument with my right hon. friend at this moment, but I am giving him the facts with respect to the government's action as taken at the time it was.

The government carried out its statutory obligation, which was to approve or disapprove the recommendation of the board with respect to fixing a price. The duty of the board was to fix a price, and the government's to give such approval as it saw fit. It was quite within the province of the government to attach a provision if it so desired. The machinery of the act has been preserved and is ready to function in the event of emergency conditions returning. The main purpose of the act, if I mistake not, was to help solve the existing wheat problem.

Now what are the facts, for after all the merit of any course of action is best judged by the results. During my right hon. friend's term of office it was found necessary fo fix a minimum price of 87½ cents for wheat. Since the present administration took the action to which my right hon. friend now takes exception, wheat has never dropped below 94 cents, and it has gone up as high as 128 cents. I think the farmers of this country will view the actions of the respective administrations by the prices which they have been able to get for their grain as being perhaps the most effective of all indices.[39]

[38]*House of Commons Debates*, January 18, 1937, pp. 30-31.
[39]*Ibid.*, pp. 46-47.

Although Mr. Coldwell spoke in support of the pools' position that an initial payment of at least one dollar should have been made, the debate was a far cry from the stormy exchanges which had taken place a year earlier. Wheat policy came up for discussion during the course of the budget debate as Bennett and Mr. E. E. Perley pursued the issue of the producer's right to deliver to the board. Mr. T. C. Douglas twitted the western Liberal members about their position on the resolutions which had poured in from local organizations to members as well as to the government. It was at this stage that Gardiner declared the government's policy in respect of the wheat board, as recited at the beginning of this chapter.[40] This was the clearest indication offered that it was the government's intention to terminate the board after the McFarland surplus had been liquidated. In support of his statement, Gardiner placed on record the Liberal party pamphlet already cited which supported a guaranteed minimum price "during the crisis".

The Conservative opposition was able to exploit the discomfort of the Liberal back-benchers by forcing a vote. This was done on Mr. Dunning's motion that the house go into committee of ways and means. Mr. Perley promptly moved an amendment that: "this house regrets that the government rendered the Canadian Wheat Board Act, 1935, inoperative in its application to the 1936 wheat crop."[41] In doing so, Perley challenged the western Liberal members by name to support the amendment. Bennett attacked the legality of the government's decision again, and Gardiner stressed that even if the government had approved the 87½ cent initial payment unconditionally, producers would not have delivered wheat to the board. Several Liberal members spoke on the amendment. Dr. Thomas F. Donnelly (Wood Mountain) explained that he would be absent for the vote, otherwise he would have felt obliged to support the amendment. The Honourable W. R. Motherwell was ill, and not in the house. Mr. Harry Leader (Portage la Prairie) declared his intention to vote for the amendment. Mr. J. Gordon Ross (Moose Jaw) defended the government's policy, and Messrs. W. A. Tucker (Rosthern) and W. G. Weir (Macdonald), while critical of the decision, declared that they would vote confidence in the government.

A unique defence of the government's decision was offered by the Honourable Charles A. Dunning, in which he admitted that the government had sought to avoid cluttering up the disposal of the McFarland holdings by allowing the board to handle the 1936 crop, but he claimed that the government had championed the cause of producers' co-operative marketing, as he said:

> What faced the government of Canada last fall was that it was in the wheat business to a greater extent than any other organization in the world had been. Joseph in Egypt was a piker compared with the government of Canada. We had a very great volume of wheat, and who owned it? The people of Canada. They had taken delivery of it. They had paid a price for it, a price which was greater than the price which up to that time they had been able to obtain in the markets of the world when they went to sell it. The people of Canada were holding the bag for the farmers of western Canada. I am not

---

[40]See pp. 499-501.
[41]*House of Commons Debates,* March 17, 1937, p. 1866.

quarrelling with the policy in that regard. In a national crisis such as was involved in relation to the wheat business it was necessary for this nation to take some action with regard to a national asset of such tremendous importance. But the people owned that wheat — nearly 300,000,000 bushels of it, as the hon. member for Qu'Appelle indicated. . . .

The government had this enormous liability. It had another problem — which brings me to my second point. Another crop was coming along in western Canada, a crop which at that time and until its disposal was owned by the individual farmer producing it. It was in the highest national interest that the individual farmer who owned the growing crop of 1936 should be put in a position to get the best possible price for it. Who was the greatest competitor with that growing crop? The government of Canada, owning the vast quantity of wheat to which I have made reference. In the light of those circumstances what was the best policy to follow? To make provision for further increasing the load of wheat carried by the government, or so to handle that load as to give the farmers of western Canada the maximum possible opportunity of disposing of their new crop? The course the government took involved two or three major advantages of a national character, and some considerable advantages to the farmers of western Canada. I will deal with the latter first.

What was the advantage to the farmer of western Canada? First, the announcement of the government policy rendered utterly impossible bear raiding during the process of rush marketing. There was no possibility of organized bear speculation forcing down the price of wheat for the farmer's new crop. Why? Because the world had notice that the government of Canada was prepared to take delivery at any time the price was forced down to ninety cents. That was a degree of protection which the farmers of western Canada have never enjoyed during all the period of their marketing — never in the world. In consequence, for the first time during a period of free marketing, there was no attempt at a bear raid during the time of rush marketing of the 1936 crop. That was one advantage reaped by the farmers of western Canada. As the Minister of Agriculture (Mr. Gardiner) reminds me, the development of bear raiding was already apparent before we took action. It was plain to be seen.

What was the second point? The greatest competitor of the farmer of western Canada in the marketing of his 1936 crop was the wheat board holding these hundreds of millions of bushels of old wheat. Always in the past the size of the carry-over from the preceding crop has had a bearish price influence upon the new crop — always. The larger the carry-over of old wheat the more likelihood is there of successful bear raids on the price of new wheat. What happened? By the development of the government's policy, for the first time in the history of open market wheat trading, there was from the farmer's point of view no carry-over in competition with the marketing of his new wheat. Why was that? It was because the wheat board did not sell any old wheat in competition with the rush marketing by the farmer of wheat of the new crop. The government continued to hold back, as it had been holding back for years; it kept out of the farmer's way and left him a free rein to sell his 1936 crop without the bearish influence of any carry-over from the old year. . . .

In addition, we performed, by reason of this policy, a further great service to the farmers of western Canada, and without injuring the national well-being in so doing. The hon. member for Rosthern touched on it. For the first time in the history of marketing in western Canada cooperative marketing on the pool plan was made possible, insured against any loss on the part of the pools. Think what that means. We are all aware of the great disaster which overtook the pool marketing organizations in consequence of having made during one year a larger initial payment than they were afterwards able to realize from the wheat. We know that the provinces concerned, which undertook a part of the load resulting from that occurrence, became financially embarrassed. We know that subsequently the former government of Canada had to come to the rescue, and we know that because of that the tremendous load of wheat developed.

Now in 1936 for the first time the wheat pool could have said to all farmers, "Deliver your wheat to the pool; you will get 87½ cents as an initial payment and whatever else we may make out of the wheat as a result of its disposal in due course." I am not criticizing the pools for not taking that step; that is their business. Nor am I foolish enough to overlook the fact that they are one of the greatest business organizations in Canada, one of the most powerful in point of size of assets and control of volume of commodity — because it has been said repeatedly that the wheat pools control normally forty-seven per cent of the wheat. See what an opportunity was given by the government of Canada to the cooperative organization controlling forty-seven per cent of the wheat to operate a pool and make an initial payment without any fear of loss in so doing, because the government would come in and take delivery of the wheat at 87½ cents. Why that was not done remains a matter of policy with the pools themselves; they had a perfect right to make a decision. But I have a perfect right to point out that the policy of the government would have enabled the wheat pools to give to all of their customers all of the advantage, if any, which has come about by the increased price of wheat since that time and without any risk of loss to the pools, for the first time in the history of cooperative marketing in the west.

Mr. Perley (Qu'Appelle): When was that offer made to the pools on the part of the government?

Mr. Dunning: No offer was made; the order in council itself constituted the offer.

Mr. Perley (Qu'Appelle): What was the date of it?

Mr. Dunning: August 28, I believe. But it does not matter what the date was, the effect is just the same. Prior to that date every farmer marketing his wheat had a right to market with the board at 87½ cents initial payment. The extent to which he did so prior to that date was indicated by the Minister of Agriculture. There were 38,000,000 marketed and 600,000 delivered to the wheat board. Those figures constitute in my opinion the main reason why the pool organization decided not to continue, not to go ahead as a pooling organization on the same basis. I am not questioning their wisdom; that is an internal matter for themselves; but I do point out that they are very powerful organizations. . . .

I think there is nothing further I wish to say, except that, as one who believes in cooperative marketing and not state socialism, I believe that the government of Canada on behalf of the people of Canada should extend to wheat growers or anyone else the maximum assistance in the way of promoting self-help on the part of those directly interested. I believe that the order in council of last August was truly cooperative in the spirit of what I have just said. It represented a degree of cooperation on the part of the people of the whole of Canada with those who are joined together in an effort to market a commodity, and I doubt very much if we whose hearts are in the life of western Canada shall make any progress by attempting to follow the line of state socialism, by attempting to dragoon the whole of Canada into applying the principles of state socialism to the marketing of our chief product; because quite obviously if we insist on support for that we must be content to move in the direction of state socialism in the marketing of many other commodities as well as wheat. I believe that governmental assistance in the marketing of all these commodities can best be given by helping those who are engaged in the cooperative marketing of their own products to help themselves.[42]

In replying to Perley's question, Dunning indicated that the government had not made a direct proposition to the pool representatives on the resumption of co-operative pooling, but that the offer of support in doing so had been implicit in the order in council. Dunning's explanation was elliptic in the sense that P. C. 2202 of itself was not sufficient authority for the pools to offer producers co-operative pooling without risk of loss. Under the wheat board act the 87½ cent price would have been available only to producers delivering to the board. A similar price offered by the pools afforded the latter no protection against loss. An amendment to the act would have been required to authorize the board to accept the redelivery of wheat from the pools at 87½ cents plus carrying charges and other pool operating expenses, or to reimburse the pools directly on losses, without taking delivery, in order to ensure the pools against loss.

Undoubtedly, what Dunning intended to imply was that if the pools had been prepared in August, 1936, to negotiate with the government along those lines, the government would have been willing to accommodate them. Even now, Dunning's statement constituted an open invitation to the pools to resume co-operative marketing, but the latter had already decided not to do so. Under present circumstances they were convinced that it would be difficult for them to demonstrate a competitive marketing advantage against the trade, even if guaranteed against loss, and that their members would fare better in the hands of a government board.

Reverting to Perley's amendment, only Mr. Leader broke party ranks when the vote was taken; other Liberals present voted against the amendment, which was defeated. The debate marked the end, however, of the period of the wheat board in politics. It had taken a stormy session in 1936, a special committee of the house, the appointment of a royal commission, and the somewhat less tempestuous session of 1937 to phase out the political limelight on the board.

[42]*Ibid.*, March 18, 1937, pp. 1901-1904.

24

OPERATIONS OF THE WHEAT BOARD UNDER MURRAY AND McIVOR

Mr. Murray's tenure as chief commissioner of the Canadian wheat board lasted from his appointment on December 3, 1935, until he resigned on July 20, 1937. By that time the board had completed the sale of the "stabilization" stocks, except for a small quantity of 6.9 million bushels which the government had asked to be held in order to ensure an adequate supply of seed wheat for the spring of 1938. All wheat delivered to the board from the 1935 crop had been sold by July 31, 1936.

Records covering the period of Murray's tenure reveal how assiduously the board had carried out its instructions. Table 24:1 illustrates the paralysis which had developed in the McFarland sales operations, both in respect of the stocks accumulated by Canadian Co-operative Wheat Producers Limited and of the deliveries from the 1935 crop. The record justified the change in sales policy, if not in sales personnel as well, as the new cabinet wheat committee replaced the McFarland board.

1935-36 OPERATIONS

From the inception of the Murray board (which included Messrs. George McIvor and A. M. Shaw), a series of innovations was introduced to dispose of wheat in a crop year which recorded a new low in the total volume of world wheat trade. Out of a total of world net exports of 514 million bushels, Canada shipped 253 million bushels or nearly 50 percent. To accomplish this, the Murray board set weekly sales targets during the remaining winter months and at higher levels after the opening of navigation. Its sales task was increased by the small volume which had been moved in the preceding autumn months of normally heavy sales. To sell Canadian wheat in competition with Australian supplies, the board offered Canadian wheat at more competitive quality differentials. To back up this tangible gesture toward the restoration of sales, the board had dispatched Mr. Cecil Lamont to Britain (as already mentioned), in an effort to restore goodwill on the part of British mills and the trade. Murray's circular letter to millers had helped to strengthen Lamont's direct representations.

Mr. Lamont's trip to Britain was followed by a mission in May headed by Mr. George McIvor, the assistant chief commissioner. The mission included Mr. H. Cockfield of the Montreal advertising firm of Cockfield, Brown and

TABLE 24:1

CANADIAN WHEAT BOARD DISPOSITION OF THE 1935 CROP AND "STABILIZATION" WHEAT

1935	Deliveries to Board from 1935 crop	Board Sales of 1935 Crop	Board Sales of Old Wheat	Balance of 1935 Wheat	Balance of Old Wheat
		(million bushels)			
SEP	3.0	3.0	—	—	207.1[1]
OCT	60.7	4.7	—	55.9	205.3[1]
NOV	38.9	4.7	—	90.1	205.1[1]
DEC	14.8	28.1	22.0	76.9	183.0
1936					
JAN	3.8	17.2	9.2	63.4	173.8
FEB	2.4	10.8	12.4	55.0	161.3
MAR	6.7	16.4	11.7	45.3	149.6
APR	4.7	16.7	12.7	33.2	136.8
MAY	4.8	16.0	.3	22.1	136.5
JUN	8.9	20.7	1.4	10.3	135.1
JUL	1.5	9.8	52.4	2.0[2]	82.6
AUG			4.5		78.1
SEP			—		78.1
OCT			3.2		74.8
NOV			11.2		63.6
DEC			9.1		54.4
1937					
JAN			7.7		46.7
FEB			7.0		39.7
MAR			8.3		31.3
APR			12.3		19.0
MAY			6.1		12.9
JUN			5.9		6.9
JUL			—		6.9

SOURCE: *Canadian Wheat Board Reports, Crop Years 1935-36 and 1936-37.*
[1] Central selling agency stocks not yet taken over by the wheat board.
[2] Sale of the 1935 crop wheat was completed by November 21, 1936.

Company, Limited, and Dr. W. F. Geddes, chemist in charge of the board of grain commissioners' research laboratory. The mission laid the groundwork for an advertising campaign in Britain, which was implemented that autumn, and assiduously pursued until the outbreak of war.

The Murray board also worked on the trade at home. Its initial gesture in inviting the trade to consult on their problems, and in protecting exporters on their overnight offers was of considerable help. Within a few weeks, the board was able to persuade exporters that formal protection was no longer necessary because of the board's policy of keeping wheat continuously on offer. By restoring all export transactions to the market, the board improved the market's liquidity which had been somewhat impaired by the direct cover arrangement. Shortly thereafter, Murray took another step to broaden the market. Up to that time the elevator companies could rely upon the board to switch the companies' futures from one delivery month to another, and Murray put them on notice that the board could reach a point where it would no longer be able to accommodate them, and that the companies should plan to make their switches in the pit.

Also, as mentioned earlier, the government had placed an arbitrary valuation on the 205,186,980 bushels of wheat and wheat futures taken over from the central selling agency which, on the basis of December 2, 1935, market prices, had shown a paper loss of $15,856,645.35. The government then sought parliamentary approval by submitting an estimate for an advance of that amount to be paid to the board. The item did not come up for debate until June 22, 1936, a day before parliament was prorogued. It was Bennett's first opportunity to protest; he did in the most vigorous of terms, but to no avail, against such means of imputing a loss on the McFarland support operations, when the actual profit or loss could not be determined until final disposition of the stocks.

During the course of the 1935-36 crop year, prices dropped through the 87½ cent initial payment level on October 26, 1935, and they kept easing down gradually for the several months until a low of 73⅝ cents was reached on May 26, 1936. Then in response to adverse weather conditions, prices rose above the 87½ cent level in early July, and above the dollar level by the end of that month. Because most of the 1935 crop had already been sold at prices below the level of the initial payment, the board realized a loss of $11,858,104.18 on the disposition of that crop. Although it might not have seemed so at the time, this was a very small amount, considering that the initial payment had been set at the beginning of the crop year without guiding criteria, nor did the act permit its reduction during the course of the year. Had McFarland's reluctant-selling policy been permitted to continue, the unit prices would undoubtedly have been higher, but the crop would not have been sold, and carrying charges would have accrued. In the absence of power to foresee the crop disasters of 1936 and 1937, there can be little question that the direction the wheat committee had given to the Murray board on its sales policy was the proper one in the circumstances. The result was that the sale of the 1935 crop had been completed by the end of the crop year, with the exception of 2½ million bushels held back for shipment via Churchill when navigation opened in August. Moreover, the old stocks which stood at 205,187,000 bushels when the Murray board took over had been reduced to 82,667,891 bushels by July 31, 1936.

To insure that sales of "old" wheat would not interfere with the prompt disposition of the 1935 crop, the board gave priority to the disposition of the latter with a view to completing its sale by July 31, 1936. Table 23:1 illustrates the attainment of that objective in the spring and early summer months of 1936. But as soon as the 1935 crop was out of the way, the board made huge sales of 52,456,000 bushels from the old account in July, 1936, before the new crop was ready to move.

1936-37 OPERATIONS

Board operations in the 1936-37 crop year were materially curtailed in the wake of the decision to prohibit board acceptance of deliveries so long as the trade offered an alternative market at 90 cents or above. Prices rose almost steadily during the remainder of the crop year so the board had no wheat delivered to it after the August 27 announcement. Prior to that decision, the board had accepted a small quantity of 617,655 bushels of new-crop wheat which was then either returned to producers or accepted at the open-market price. With no current receipts for disposition, the board concentrated on the sale of the remaining balance of the stabilization account. At his meeting with the cabinet on August 26-27, Murray obtained ministerial approval to ease up on sales from the old account, while primary receipts from the new crop were at their peak and had to be hedged. Table

24:1 shows that very light sales of old wheat were made in the August-October period. Then in November, sales of old wheat recommenced and continued until their disposition had been completed in July 1937 except for the 6,964,000 bushels which was eventually sold to the Saskatchewan government for seed distribution.

In the autumn of 1936, Mr. George McIvor returned to Britain to supervise the advertising campaign he had recommended at the end of his first visit that spring to stimulate the use of Canadian wheat. During McIvor's autumn visit, Mr. R. V. Biddulph was appointed as European commisioner of the board with headquarters in London. Biddulph's first assignment was concerned with the advertising compaign which was pursued through the press and the distribution of films. Later on, during the war, he performed an invaluable liaison service between the Canadian wheat board and the imported cereals division of the British ministry of food.

TRANSITION FROM THE MURRAY TO THE McIVOR BOARD

Upon the successful completion of their objective in disposing of the stabilization stocks, Messrs. Murray and McIvor notified Mr. Euler of their intention to resign from the board. This reopened the issue of the termination of the board, which Mr. Euler had raised a year earlier. It was impossible at the moment to convene a meeting of the full cabinet wheat committtee because Prime Minister Mackenzie King and several of his ministers were in London. In their absence, Euler discussed the matter with Gardiner and reported by cable to the prime minister on June 10, 1937:

> After discussion yesterday, Gardiner and I agree that it is advisable pending the receipt of the Turgeon report that the Wheat Board should continue for coming year. Discussion as to policy including wheat prices not necessary until after return of colleagues to Canada. Mr. Gardiner in letter to you arriving by Queen Mary outlines various proposals which you might consider. Murray and McIvor have definitely decided to resign.[1]

Euler's message evoked the prime minister's reply of June 11:

> Colleagues here concur in view of Gardiner and yourself respecting continuation of the Wheat Board. Matters of policy and action with respect to resignations can be determined after our return. Gardiner's communication not yet received.[2]

In the meantime, McIvor had gone to England again in connection with the board's advertising campaign. As he left Winnipeg the newly sown crop was deteriorating, but it was still too early to predict a disaster of major proportions.

While McIvor was absent, it was confirmed that western Canada had experienced the worst crop failure in its history, and Euler cabled McIvor to return urgently via Ottawa where he persuaded him to take over, for the time being, as head of the board.[3]

The cabinet dilemma over its desire to terminate the board and the need for a government program to protect seed supplies was complicated by the

[1] *King Papers.*
[2] *Ibid.*
[3] See Appendix 7.

fact that the Turgeon Commission was still in the midst of its hearings. Hopefully, the commission report when submitted would recommend the termination of the board but, in the immediate circumstances, the government could not act in anticipation of the report. The dilemma was resolved by cabinet on July 14, 1937, when King took with him into the meeting Euler's cable of June 11 on which King had pencilled his immediate reaction to the effect that the government should get out of the wheat business while ensuring that enough wheat was held back for domestic requirements.[4]

Following the cabinet discussion, Mr. E. A. Pickering, an assistant private secretary, made a note of its decision:

> Decided to continue skeleton board. Murray's resignation to be accepted. McIvor to be Chairman; and vacancy to be filled by nominal appointment, without salary, perhaps by civil servant. Arrangements of last year to be continued, price 87½¢ per bushel. Wheat to be taken only when price below 90¢. Intention of Council to abolish Board altogether when Turgeon report submitted, if report so recommends. Euler to draft statement setting forth decision of Council, and available for giving to Press after Council Wednesday. General opinion of government against continuing Wheat Board. Reason for continuing temporarily to enable government to get wheat enough for distribution for seed grain purposes, also to have Board in existence, pending Turgeon report. Ralston and other legal opinion, that nothing compulsory in legislation.[5]

In the result, Murray's resignation was accepted, and McIvor was appointed to replace him as chief commissioner, by P. C. 1771 of July 23, 1937. A fuller account of those developments, as far as McIvor himself was involved, is to be found in Appendix 7. Instead of recruiting a civil servant to fill the board vacancy, as contemplated in cabinet, Mr. McIvor recommended that Mr. R. C. Findlay, comptroller of the board, be appointed as assistant chief commissioner. Dean Shaw continued as a member of the board although he spent most of his time during the following crop year in Ottawa in connection with his new duties in the department of agriculture.

1937-38 OPERATIONS

In 1937, western Canada and notably Saskatchewan suffered its worst drought disaster. Because there was so little wheat for export, prices rose above $1.50 in October and again in January, 1938. The government stood by its decision in the previous year not to allow the wheat board to accept deliveries unless the market were to fall below 90 cents, and repeated the formality of having the board recommend an initial payment of 87½ cents for the 1937-38 crop year, and deciding in turn by P. C. 1770 of July 27, 1937, that the recommendation of the board be not approved unconditionally, but only in the event that the market price dropped below 90 cents. Although the Turgeon commission was still sitting, no reference was made to it in P. C. 1770. The board, therefore, became inoperative in that crop year in respect of wheat sales. Its annual report described the final results of the stabilization account, and it described in detail the advertising campaign

[4]*King Papers.*
[5]*Ibid.*

carried on in Britain throughout that crop year. Even some aspects of the campaign required adjustment in the light of Canada's small wheat export supplies. Moreover, as already mentioned, the board exchanged the balance of its futures against the acquisition and distribution of relief seed supplies on behalf of the government of Saskatchewan to ensure enough seed for the 1938 crop. The need for that operation, and its details, are graphically described by Mr. McIvor in Appendix 7.

25

ROYAL GRAIN INQUIRY COMMISSION, 1938

The Turgeon grain inquiry commission had been appointed in 1936 to abate the feud waged by the Conservative opposition against the wheat policy of the new administration. In its selection of commissioner and counsel, the government was accused of taking ample precautions to protect itself from any untoward findings. Mr. Justice Turgeon had been active in his earlier years in the Liberal party; he commanded wide public respect for his impartiality, and his own views on wheat marketing had already been developed in the report of the royal grain inquiry commission, 1925, which he headed. In addition, the government appointed the Honourable J. L. Ralston as commission counsel. Colonel Ralston had been the liberal opposition's wheat critic while Bennett was in office; he had opposed Bennett's compulsory draft legislation, and although he proposed the voluntary board as an alternative, he had tried to limit its duration to one year. He did not stand for reelection in order to devote full time to his private law practice. Mr. James E. Coyne (a Manitoba Rhodes scholar) recently appointed to the bar, was made assistant commission counsel. Despite the imputations laid against the commissioner and counsel, the commission commanded public respect for its nonpartisan conduct of the hearings.

TERMS OF REFERENCE

The commission's terms of reference (recommended by the report of the special committee of the house) were set out in P.C. 1577 of June 27, 1936, which included all issues left unresolved by the committee, including the extent, if any, to which the board had protected the speculative short interests in December, 1935; the central selling agency's handling of oats transactions for relief and seed purposes on behalf of the province of Saskatchewan; and the effect of the practice of mixing and of the selection of grain for protein content by millers and exporters.

The more general, and by far the more important, questions remitted to the commission were those of the alternative marketing systems and their appropriateness for Canada: voluntary or compulsory pooling by the producers themselves, a voluntary or compulsory government wheat board, or the open market system. To these were added the identification of causes of the decrease in Canadian grain exports in recent years, and the recommendation of measures to retain and to extend world markets for Canadian grain and their products.

Among these, the question of alternative marketing methods remained very much a live, contemporary issue. As Gardiner placed on record, the Liberal party's wheat platform in the 1935 election had been a minimum price guarantee to the farmer during the crisis, but not for all time. This gave as good a clue as any to the government's hope that the commission might find that the crisis was over, and that grain marketing could revert to the open-market system without need of a federal guarantee. Moreover, the government's action in rendering the wheat board inoperative unless the market fell below 90 cents signified a wishful step in that direction. This was by no means a negative wheat policy. Along with the free rein to the open-market system was added the government's support for an advertising campaign aimed at increasing the percentage of Canadian wheat used in millers' grists abroad. The government had also embarked upon a series of trade agreement negotiations aimed at opening up the channels of trade in a way that would encourage the increased sale of wheat.

OPENING OF THE INQUIRY

Before the commission hearings opened, a great deal of planning and organization was necessary to obtain witnesses who could provide information on which the commission's recommendations could be based. Each subject referred to the commission was examined in this respect by Turgeon, Ralston, Coyne and Grindley, and prospective witnesses were notified well in advance of the subject matter that should be covered in the briefs. By September, 1936, the decision had been taken to proceed first with the examination of Canada's lost markets, not for the sake of embarrassing the Conservatives, but simply to get a mass of factual material on the record at the outset which would help to avoid repetition in evidence and yet be of use in framing the commission's report.

Several statisticians and economists lined up to give evidence on Canada's lost markets. James McAnsh who had resigned as market editor of the *Winnipeg Free Press* to accept an appointment from McFarland as statistician of the wheat board was the first witness on December 1, and he was followed by Davidson, the board's secretary. McAnsh presented a complete statistical record of wheat production and trade (by countries around the world) and Davidson presented a case for bilateral trade arrangements if Canada hoped to regain lost wheat markets. For the remainder of the week, the commission heard evidence on a trilogy of papers prepared by three University of Manitoba economics professors, Robert McQueen, John Stuart Mill Allely, and H. C. Grant. McQueen dealt with the present state of international trade theory, and Allely with the anticipated effect of monetary changes on world trade. On December 7, Dr. H. C. Grant, a member of the McFarland board, now back at the University of Manitoba, presented a paper on agricultural protection in Europe. He traced the historical trend toward self-sufficiency, branded it as self-defeating, and contended that the only hope for an increase in the export of Canadian wheat lay in the increased prosperity of the European countries.

Understandably, he refrained from joining the chorus in favor of trade liberalization.

Then followed Dr. C. F. Wilson, newly-appointed grain statistician in the dominion bureau of statistics[1], * and Dr. W. F. Geddes, chief chemist of the board of grain commissioners who had accompanied McIvor and Mr. H. Cockfield on the board's mission to Europe in May, 1936. Dr. D. A. McGibbon, commissioner of the board of grain commissioners, also gave a paper on the marketing systems of the four major exporting countries. On December 10, the commission moved to Regina.

The Winnipeg papers gave full coverage in their news columns to the briefs presented. At the end of the first week of hearings, the *Free Press* carried a lead editorial written by J. B. McGeachy who covered the hearings and whose daily "Wheat and Chaff" column provided a humorous but shrewd interpretation of proceedings:

> The Turgeon inquiry into the grain trade began its second week yesterday. Colonel J. L. Ralston, K.C., once a leader of the Liberal party in the House of Commons, is still in charge of the proceedings. All the witnesses who have testified up till now have been called by him. There is still no drama, no contention, no excitement to report. Wheat pool spokesmen attending the inquiry wonder when they will have a chance to put an oar in. In accordance with the injunction of Cromwell, they are trusting in the Lord and keeping their powder dry.
>
> A leading member of the Winnipeg bar who has observed the inquiry to date, commenting on the briefs so far submitted to Mr. Justice Turgeon, quoted G. K. Chesterton: "If a thing is worth doing, it is worth doing badly." The case presented up till now has been, as propaganda for the Liberal side in Canadian politics, almost too good to be true. The argument for lowering the Canadian tariff, especially of textiles, is irresistable if the evidence now on the books is accepted without challenge. Yet it cannot be said that the statistics have been handpicked by the witnesses. All the figures have been filed. It may be arguable that the statisticians and other experts have drawn conclusions which fit a party programme. But there is no point in saying that they have presented a put-up case. Anybody is free to take the stand and confute them.
>
> Speaking of statistics, there will be a considerable waste of the Commission's time if the learned counsel attending the inquiry do not pay attention to the evidence put on record. Yesterday, C. F. Wilson, a diffident statistician from Ottawa, was asked to give the figures for wheat production, imports and exports of several European countries, information not included in the formal brief he had prepared. All statistics demanded from him were filed a week ago by James McAnsh and are contained in exhibits which have been duly embalmed or otherwise preserved in accordance with the custom of Royal Commissions. The memory of expert observers ought not to be so short. If they want to know the wheat acreage of Czechoslovakia since the war, the

---

[1] *the author*

* Editor's note: When McFarland recruited C.B. Davidson as secretary of the wheat board, Davidson resigned from his temporary position as grain statistician in D.B.S. Dr. T.W. Grindley, chief of the agricultural branch in the bureau, succeeded in having a permanent position created and he invited Wilson to apply for the position. Wilson had just completed his doctoral thesis at Harvard on "Agricultural Adjustment in Canada"; in the thesis he had paid particular attention (but without benefit of the Bennett Papers) to the McFarland support operations and the negotiation of the international wheat agreement. He had also groped for a plan to supplement farm income.

wheat imports of France or any kindred fact, they have only to consult the records of this inquiry. The purpose of bringing on Mr. McAnsh and other statisticians at the start was to avoid repetition. Yesterday several figures were laboriously produced, at probably astronomical expense to the interested clients, which have been on the table since last Tuesday. Mr. Wilson presented a brief describing the measures taken by European and other countries to the control of selling of wheat. the picture he gave was astonishing. It appears that there is no free market for wheat anywhere on the earth outside Canada, meaning a market where buyers and sellers agree on a price and do business without any kind of state interference. The wheat business, it seems from Mr. Wilson's evidence, has been taken in hand by the government everywhere from Greece to Argentina. European countries which commonly import wheat, not growing their own, have set up public boards which decide where their supplies shall originate. They give preference to countries which will take payment in goods, Canada being conspicuously absent from the list since 1930. Their common practice is to impose a prohibitive duty on wheat—their rates running as high as $3.83 a bushel—and then to allow duty-free importations under license.

Mr. Wilson's evidence introduced a new point. It has been established that continental Europe is the place where Canada has lost business in the last six years. Mr. Wilson suggested the division of the recalcitrant customers into two groups. There are countries—chiefly Germany, France and Italy—which have almost stopped importing wheat from anywhere. There is another group of countries, not growers of wheat, which still supply their needs from outside but have diverted their business from Canada because the Dominion imposes high customs duties on their goods. These countries, taken one by one, buy very little wheat. In the aggregate their business is important. The point which sticks out in the evidence is that in every country, exporter or importer, the wheat trade is regulated by the state. This seems to mean that salesmanship is not enough. Canada must somehow strike a trading bargain with overseas governments if the market for the western wheat surplus is to be regained. This appears to be the main conclusion from Mr. Wilson's evidence. . . .[2]

PROGRESS OF THE INQUIRY

Through the first half of 1937, the commission conducted hearings intermittently as Mr. Justice Turgeon divided his time between his two commissions on grain and textiles. In January, 1937, the commission resumed in Winnipeg and heard a number of witnesses who presented the trade point of view, including Dr. W. Sanford Evans, Mr. W. J. Dowler, president of the Winnipeg grain exchange, Mr. A. E. Darby, secretary, Mr. Frank Fowler, manager of the Winnipeg grain exchange and produce clearing association and Messrs. Sidney T. Smith, Charles E. Hayles and Henry Gauer. Under the guidance of Mr. Isaac Pitblado, counsel for the exchange, and the cross-examination of Messrs. E. K. Williams, R. H. Milliken and M. M. Porter, counsel for the pools, the case for retention of the open-market system was effectively maintained, although the trade representatives were prepared to concede supervision of the futures market, if desired. Dr. Harald S. Patton, now a professor of economics at Michigan State College, presented a brief in support of co-operative pooling, backed by a government-guaranteed initial payment.

[2] *Winnipeg Free Press*, December 8, 1936.

In April, the commission took evidence in Vancouver, Edmonton and Calgary. Mr. Paul Bredt appeared in Calgary on behalf of the pools. During the course of Bredt's evidence, the commission received word of Mr. L. C. Brouillette's untimely death, at the age of 51. Mr. Bredt presented a brief on the history of the pools and was cross-examined at length, particularly by the commissioner, for reasons that later became apparent in Turgeon's recommendation that co-operative pooling be revived. Bredt was a forthright witness on all the shortcomings of pool management in the past, but maintained that this was irrelevant in the sense that the pools had resolved not to resume pooling operations, but rather to press for a permanent government grain board. In this change of pool policy, the key issue was the guarantee by the federal treasury of minimum prices. As the *Winnipeg Free Press* reported:

Calgary May 1.—Government insurance of a reasonable return to farmers for their wheat production was advocated by Paul Bredt, president of Manitoba Pool Elevators, limited, before the Turgeon royal grain commission Friday.

"We should have a marketing system that will take care of the producers," Mr. Bredt declared during his examination by Hon. J. L. Ralston, K.C., Montreal, commission counsel.

"Doesn't it all come down to state insurance?" asked Mr. Justice Turgeon, conducting the inquiry. "It is not a question of whether there is a board or not a board. You want a system whereby the producer is assured a certain return for his wheat each year by the government?"

"That is what it finally comes down to," answered Mr. Bredt. It should give a more definite return to the Producer to enable him to carry out a form of insurance, Mr. Bredt added.

The government should purchase the wheat supplies in years of surplus production, he added. It would be up to the government organization to decide whether the surplus supplies were sold on the world market or carried over as a reserve.

Any loss, however, should not be passed on to the producer. The state should be ready to assist the producer at all times, even though the assistance might never be necessary. . . .

Present unrest in the west, said Mr. Bredt, when questioned by Col. Ralston, was "due to ruinously low prices for farm products, particularly wheat."[3]

Mr. John I. McFarland, the next major witness, presented a full review of his stabilization operations; an earlier opportunity had been denied him because of illness during the special committee hearings in 1935. His presentation was well received. Commissioner and counsel alike treated McFarland with deference. His brief is available in the Bennett Papers. An unexpected turn came at the end of McFarland's testimony when he was asked to recommend a policy for the future. To everyone's surprise, particularly that of the pools, McFarland declared against a compulsory grain board and the closing of the futures market, which he recommended in 1935. He now recommended a voluntary wheat board with a minimum price and the continuation of the open market under regulation, which would provide farmers a choice of selling through either medium.

Mr. J. H. Wesson, vice-president of Saskatchewan Co-operative Wheat Producers Limited, about to succeed the late Mr. Brouillette as head of that

[3] *Ibid.*, May 1, 1937.

organization, followed Mr. McFarland, as the commission moved to Regina. Mr. Wesson claimed that the pools would not have sought an initial payment as high as 95 cents or a dollar, if a compulsory board had been established. He also declared that the pools would be willing to have the board accept an export quota if an international wheat agreement was possible among the exporting countries. As reported on May 20, Mr. Wesson said:

> His plan, the Pool plan, is a wheat board selling all the wheat every year. This board would pay a basic minimum price each fall. If the average realized price were higher, the growers would get the surplus pro rata. If the average realized price were lower, the taxpayers would pay the shot. In years of glut and poor prices, Mr. Wesson says, wheat should be held and the crown of the scheme is a world agreement by exporting nations to keep wheat off the market in such years.[4]

Under cross-examination by Col. Ralston, Wesson admitted that it was not necessary to have a compulsory board and the elimination of the exchange system in order to obtain a subsidy for producers when prices were low. He also conceded that the 1933 international wheat agreement had been a failure.

Mr. J. R. Murray was the next witness. Murray believed that producers should form their own contract pool. He was opposed to a voluntary government wheat board of the type he headed, because a voluntary system offered no assurance of the supplies that would be delivered to it. A compulsory board might fare better in the absence of any real yardstick that it was securing the best prices obtainable, but he also believed that a compulsory board would collapse if it had to operate in a falling market. In his support for the open-market system, Murray endorsed supervision, and also a processing tax on wheat consumed domestically, which had also been proposed by Wesson.

By the end of May, the commission concluded its hearings in Regina. In addition to its key witnesses, the commission also heard a great deal of evidence from producers in Edmonton, Calgary, Saskatoon and Regina. The producers fell into two groups, those for and against the open-market system.

J. B. McGeachy continued to cover the proceedings, and after the principal Canadian witnesses had been heard, he summed up the progress in a series of "Wheat and Chaff" columns on the editorial page of his paper, from which the following excerpts are taken:

> Six months have passed since Mr. Justice Turgeon's inquiry into the grain business began. The first witness took the oath and kissed the Bible on the first of December last. Since that date 2,250,000 words have been embalmed in the record, including such conversational gems as "Beg pardon, I didn't catch that last remark." Everything said was taken down in shorthand, typed, mimeographed and bound, not omitting bon mots, quotations from Scripture and cross-purpose arguments. The evidence is in 71 volumes, each half the size of a novel. A complete set can be acquired for around $350.
>
> Many of the witnesses were old hands at the game. They could quote, and they did, the evidence they gave to Sir Josiah Stamp when he studied futures trading in 1931 and the evidence they gave to Judge Turgeon in 1923. A few

[4]*Ibid.*, May 20, 1937.

have an unbroken record as witnesses at every public inquiry since A.D. 1900. These habitual testifiers, a group as well defined as bird-lovers or writers of letters to the editor, are obviously in favor of Royal Commissions, welcome each new one with prayers of thankfulness. So, perhaps, do the eminent barristers who are briefed by interested parties.

The rest of the public look upon Royal Commissions with a jaundiced eye. No discernment is needed to find that the average citizen is cynical about this latest scrutiny of the grain trade. He complains that it must cost a lot of money, that it probably had a partisan purpose, that it won't find out anything, and that in any event the report will be shelved in a dusty pigeon-hole. Speaking from observation of the Commission in action in six western towns, we suggest that this popular opinion is inaccurate. . . .

Altogether ten high-powered lawyers have practised in Mr. Justice Turgeon's court in the last six months. Only two of them get their fees from the taxpayers. The score in barristers was: Wheat Pool, 4; Grain Exchange, 1; Northwest Grain Dealers (which means line elevator companies), 1; U.G.G., 2; the taxpaying public, 2. From which it may be gathered that the greater part of the shot is being paid by the poolers and the grain trade. As the pools rank among Western Canada's richest corporations and some members of the Exchange are reputed to be doing fairly well, lamentations about the cost of this inquiry are inappropriate. The expense is mainly a private splurge, by people who can well afford it. . . .

The theory that the inquiry has a purely partisan object has been exploded by events. It was suggested by cynical observers at the start of Judge Turgeon's labors that the main purpose the Dominion Government had in view was to discredit the wheat policy of Messrs. Bennett and McFarland. As it turned out. Mr. McFarland was a voluntary witness and was gently treated by all lawyers who questioned him. Mr. Ralston, K.C., the Commission counsel, was perhaps a little tougher in examining Mr. J. R. Murray, who carried out the Liberal policy of selling the wheat surplus, than he was in examining John I. McFarland, exponent of the Bennett policy of holding for a rise. . . .

The inquiry, in fact, has been a free-for-all debate and in six months' time, by the democratic process of letting everyone speak his mind, it has arrived at some truths about the grain trade and about rural opinion. Probably no one will ever read all of the 71-volume record of evidence—which may be doubled in size before the inquiry stops—but the final report will not be put in the archives to gather dust. This Commission, farmers and taxpayers may rest assured, will produce results.

The principal questions argued at Judge Turgeon's grain inquiry so far are how—how, not where—future wheat crops should be sold, and whether the Dominion treasury should guarantee a price to the producers. Should the wheat be sold, as it is now, by merchants and exporters of the Winnipeg Grain Exchange? Should a Dominion board take over that job and operate a Canadian wheat monopoly? Or should there be a compromise plan giving farmers the choice of pooling or selling to the trade? Above all—this is most important—should wheat-growers be bonused by the taxpayers of the nation? If so, when, on what terms, and in what amount? These are the points the farmers pondered as they ploughed the land this spring.

In ten years the West has seen three wheat-marketing schemes in action. Contract pools, started in 1924, lasted six years and blew up in the crash of prices. Then came the period of one-man control. John I. McFarland took over the pool wheat, augmented his stock in the name of "stabilization," and at his dizziest peak held more wheat and options than the Canadian visible supply. James R. Murray, inheriting his post in 1935, did a brisk selling job. Now the wheat board, which he heads, has hardly any wheat left and is not in the market as a buyer. So that the pendulum has swung full around and the open traders have a free field again with no pool, board or stabilizer to give them nightmares. The point of this sketchy history is that nearly every western farmer knows now by direct experience how the various systems work. He knows what to expect from a pool, from a board and from the Winnipeg market because in a decade he has sold wheat to all three. . . .

Free market or 100 per cent wheat board—one or the other—gets the vote of practically every farmer. The remarkable thing about the evidence was that the third possible plan—revival of the voluntary contract pools—got hardly any support. Witnesses who would like to see the pools back again generally said they would not join but thought their neighbors might. The present leaders of the pools (called "pools" for convenience only because they are now really elevator companies) are vigorously opposed to resurrection of the contract pool idea. Paul Bredt and J. H. Wesson, who lead the Manitoba and Saskatchewan pools, both admitted eagerly that the 1924-30 pool failed and would fail again. Mr. Ralston, K.C., suggested that the pool crash didn't prove pooling was unsound because, after all, lots of business ventures went up in smoke in 1929-30. But Messrs. Bredt and Wesson weren't having any of that line of argument. "Never again" is their motto.

The reasons why the poolers shy away from a new pool are pretty clear. To begin with, they don't think enough farmers would sign contracts to make a pool of respectable size. And they don't believe a pool, supposing it did get substantial support at the start, could satisfy its clients and stay solvent. The leading poolers have thrown overboard the theory, preached in the halcyon days of 1923 and 1924, that a pool—either by holding up supplies or by shrewd guessing of the market—can get a better price than the open market pays. They know that a pool has to be cleverly managed to get even the market average, that it would lose its clients if it paid less, and that it would go broke if it paid more. A contract pool would have to take the same risks as other business enterprises, and its members might have to suffer the anguish of seeing a competitor do better. One farmer blandly told Judge Turgeon, in support of an argument for a wheat board, that when he belonged to the pool it used to upset him to see his neighbors getting more for their wheat than the pool price. He doesn't want to be upset like that again. And Messrs. Bredt and Wesson don't want to have to listen to his complaints.

All this explains why they and their followers are against a wheat pool—they won't sponsor an enterprise which would have to compete for business and would go under if not adroitly managed. But it still doesn't explain why they want a board. (We leave out of account personal ambition to figure as Napoleons of the grain trade, and academic attachment to the theory of economic planning.) If a wheat pool can't jack up the price, how can a wheat board do it? This is getting close to the heart of the matter. A wheat board could boost the price—to the farmers—because it could run at a loss, having the Dominion treasury as a backer. A wheat board is wanted by the poolers (if this reading of the evidence is correct) not because it could exact a higher price from buyers, not because it would destroy the Grain Exchange, but because the poolers see the board as the dispenser of a subsidy. Every vote for a board was coupled with a demand for a guaranteed minimum price. . . .

A majority of farmers who testified at the Turgeon grain inquiry, as recorded in the last of these pieces, want freedom to sell their wheat as they please and a chance to guess the market. They are against the proposition that a Dominion board—which in practice means Mr. McFarland or Mr. Murray or some other solo performer—should corral the crop, sell it and pay every grower the same price.

The weight of evidence was tilted further against a wheat monopoly by the two citizens who have lately run a wheat monopoly in this country. Messrs. Murray and McFarland. Not considering the wear and tear on their own nerves, which was considerable, they agree that the experiment should not be tried again. Mr. McFarland's remarks on this point were a volte-face. He began by denouncing the futures market, wound up by saying it should be allowed to live. Mr. Murray was positive from the start that a monopolistic wheat board is bound to fail. . . .

The Grain Exchange, though more popular than it once was on the plains, still excites a lot of rural indignation. It has been underlined at this inquiry, in patient questioning by counsel, that the Exchange is not a conspiracy but a geographical expression. It doesn't buy, sell or set prices. It is a place, a point on the map, at which buyers and sellers of grain habitually meet. But the suspicion lingers in some minds that the members of the Exchange are in league to beat the farmers and smart enough to do it annually. This dark view is not nearly so common as it used to be. The Exchange got compliments from farmers which the most complacent broker would hesitate to quote. But the hostile opinions are still worth noting. . . .

The grain trade, in this correspondent's opinion, came out of the argument with a whole skin. . . .

In spite of all this, the Grain Exchange may be in for a spell of regulation. The open market system will survive but a Dominion "supervisor" may be installed in the Exchange to keep tab on the bulls and the bears. Many witnesses friendly to the grain trade suggested this appointment. Even though nobody ever does attempt either a corner or a bear raid in the Grain Exchange, the argument is that either is theoretically possible. The proposed supervisor would be only a fact-finder at first. If he uncovers price manipulation by long or short traders, then and not sooner will he be given power to discipline offending speculators. That is the plan suggested to Judge Turgeon—with no objection, but some support, from the trade. . . .

There are two possible ways (short of a 100 per cent wheat board which is demanded by the poolers but isn't going to happen) to meet the demands of these citizens. One is a "voluntary" board, meaning a permanent wheat board which would accept and sell all wheat delivered to it—making an interim payment at once and a final settlement later. The other possibility is a contract wheat pool.

Mr. Murray, chief of the present board, says the first of these plans won't work. A "voluntary" board couldn't frame a coherent selling policy and it couldn't make firm contracts for future delivery, because it would never know how much wheat, if any, it was going to receive. Conceivably the board might not get a bushel if it offered (playing absolutely safe with the taxpayers' money) 85 cents as an initial payment with the market at $1.25. Then there would be nothing for the board to do but play golf. Mr. Murray doesn't think any really bright grain man could be found to take the job.

A revived contract pool is the alternative if there are enough farmers who are poolers by temperament to make a go of it. Messrs. Bredt and Wesson are as sure a pool won't work as Mr. Murray is sure a board (100 per cent or voluntary) won't work, but their argument is not so convincing as his. A contract pool, unlike a 100 per cent board, coerces nobody. Unlike a voluntary board, it has a known volume of support and can plan accordingly. So that the problems a pool runs into are those which bother every business enterprise, how to stay solvent and how to satisfy the customers. Messrs. Bredt and Wesson say it can't be done. Even so, if this inquiry yields any aid or comfort to farmers who want to pool their grain, it will likely be a suggestion that they get together and try again (using the wisdom of experience) the experiment launched in 1924.[5]

In his good-humored critique of the competing marketing systems, McGeachy had shrewdly gauged where the commission findings were heading. In July, the commission broke off this phase of its investigation as it went overseas to look into the question of expanding markets; later it visited Chicago to look into American methods of supervising commodity exchanges, and returned to complete its hearings in Winnipeg in the autumn of 1937.

REPORT OF THE COMMISSION

Mr. Justice Turgeon submitted his report to the Honourable W. D. Euler on May 4, 1938. The report proper ran 185 pages, and with appendices to 264 pages. Such minor issues as the protecting of the shorts and the handling of oats for the Saskatchewan government were relegated to the latter. The main report began with an historical review of the development and importance of the grain industry in western Canada and with the evolution of the different systems of marketing. Appropriate attention was paid to the contribution made by the Winnipeg grain exchange and the Winnipeg grain and produce clearing association which had made possible the commencement of trading in futures in 1904. Brief reference was made to the operations of the board of grain supervisors and of the 1919-20 Canadian wheat board, the organization and operation of the pools, the McFarland price-support measures, and the Canadian wheat board operations since 1935. Then, for the next several chapters, the report went into a detailed analysis of futures trading and the role of speculation, the operations of the wheat pools and the source of their financial difficulties, and McFarland's price-support activities. Most of the ground covered on the open-market system had already been traversed by previous royal commissions, but Turgeon's exhaustive interrogation of Mr. Paul F. Bredt resulted in a detailed exposure of the mistakes. in the light of hindsight, committed by the pool management. The purpose of his interrogation emerged later. Turgeon continued with a critical examination of McFarland's price stabilization measures.

As McGeachy had predicted, the open-market system survived the examination "with a whole skin". Turgeon took as his point of departure the opinion expressed by the three provincial pool organizations in their brief:

> We are satisfied that the futures market does cause fluctuations not justified by the supply and demand for wheat, and this fluctuating price does not necessarily reflect world value. Indeed, it would appear to be true to say that the futures market is not a system of intelligent merchandising; it is merely an example of irresponsible mob blundering. This tendency toward instability in price, which many farmers are convinced is aggravated by speculation, is one of the most serious indictments numerous farmers level against the futures market.[6]

[5] J. B. McGeachy, *Judge Turgeon Looks at the Grain Trade,* reprinted from editorial pages of the Winnipeg Free Press, June, 1937.

[6] *Report of the Royal Grain Inquiry Commission,* 1938, p. 39.

After examining the hedging process and the role of the speculator to which Turgeon attached importance, and the submissions thereon made by Mr. W. J. Dowler, president of the Winnipeg grain exchange and Mr. A. E. Darby, the exchange secretary, as well as by Dr. J. W. T. Duvel, chief of the grain futures administration in the United States department of agriculture and Dr. Alonzo Taylor, director emeritus of the Food Research Institute, Turgeon concluded:

I said at the beginning that no positive demonstration as to the incidence of the cost of futures trading including speculation, has yet been found; all we have on the question being opinions based upon certain calculations. However, I must say that I have no difficulty in agreeing with these opinions. I can quite understand that those who are in the market as hedging traders add the cost of their operations to the commodity they handle, because they are actual dealers in physical wheat. They pass it on, backwards or forwards. On the other hand it seems to me that those (speculators) who never handle wheat, who neither buy nor sell it as an actual commodity, but who stand by, study conditions, watch market movements, and then go in and out merely as makers of contracts which they never execute except by set-off, are in a different position. In addition to their costs, such as brokerage charges, these people have actual losses or actual profits. Those profits they take out of the market; the losses, they pay in. The only other people in the futures market are the hedgers. Profits taken out by speculators must make business more expensive for the hedgers and consequently, by reason of the "passing on," for those with whom they deal,—producers and consumers. But, on the other side of the case, speculators' losses remaining in the market lessen the hedgers' expenses, and this benefit is again "passed on" to the producer and consumer, by reason partly, at least, of the competition of hedging traders among themselves. Experience seems to show that in the long run speculators, as a body, lose. This final result of speculative loss helps to make business easier for the hedging trader and is consequently, of benefit to the producer and the consumer. The trader who hedges takes advantage, according to his means and ability, of all the incidents of the market and he must compete with others to get his share of the business. . . .

In my opinion, the result of this inquiry into speculation and hedging is to show by reasonable inference: (1) that speculators' costs are paid by themselves, while hedgers' costs are charged against the grain; (2) that in the aggregate the speculators are losers and therefore make a money contribution to the market where the only other operators are the hedgers; (3) that whatever benefit the market receives through speculators' losses is passed on to the producers and consumers mainly as a result of the competition among themselves of the hedgers as traders.[7]

After finding in favor of continuing the open-market system, Turgeon carefully invited a resumption of voluntary pooling. He gave his reasons for his exhaustive examination of the management of the pools together with his conclusions:

I have dealt with the work of the pools at some length and have made an attempt to pass lightly over such defects in the system or in its operation as have been made known to me by the evidence. In doing this, I have had in mind the thought that the co-operative marketing of wheat is something essentially sound and that it it contains possibilities for the future. It is all the more necessary then that this important experience in co-operation should be

[7]*Ibid.,* pp. 59-61.

recorded and analyzed with care. If the idea was to be considered as intrinsically false and now definitely abandoned, the wise thing to do would be to say little about it. I have not followed this course. My examination of pooling as carried on in western Canada for a number of years has been as searching and as critical as I have been able to make it because I think that the history of those years is of value, now, and will continue to be of value in the working out of future problems.

To sum up as briefly as possible, I may say that, in my opinion, the wheat pooling system was beneficial in several respects: (1) it relieved its members of their principal market worries, which are considerable, and procured them a uniform price within each year; (2) on the whole, the price obtained was a fair and satisfactory price; (3) it continued and expanded an integrated farmer-owned grain-handling system; (4) it provided a "service at cost" basis of operations; (5) in so far as its own members are concerned, it relieved them of whatever evil effects may attend heavy hedging pressure in the fall. . . .

But there is another side to the story. I think (1) that the policy of the Pool not to deal through grain merchants in the United Kingdom was injurious both to the United Kingdom traders and to the selling of Canadian wheat; (2) that Canadian traders also suffered to some extent and permanently; (3) that a feeling of alarm was engendered in importing countries by some of the declarations made at the international conferences at St. Paul in 1926 and Kansas City in 1927 which were attended by Canadian Pool representatives; (4) that the statements made with great publicity in the fall of 1929 by Pool officials and organs, coupled with the non-selling policy pursued, were detrimental to our market interests.

On the whole, it seems to me, in regard to (3) and (4), that too much talk and agitation were mixed with business. All these announcements took the form of indirect promises to the Pool farmers, and made a change of selling policy all the more difficult to adopt, even if those who made the announcements became convinced subsequently that a change was imperative. In my opinion, Mr. Bredt's evidence reveals this situation. Then again, human nature has its exigencies, and those making such announcements could not help feeling an inward reluctance to go back on them. Finally, the challenging nature of some of these declarations must have had a bad effect among buyers.

Those who buy our wheat are shrewd business men interested in getting a good product at a price measured in relation to their necessities and to the value of competing products. They do their buying quietly and on considerations which they have reduced to a science. It seems to me that selling also should be conducted without undue publicity, on business principles, by men who keep themselves free to shape and reshape their policy from day to day, if necessary, to meet shifting conditions. There is no reason why a pool should not be operated on such lines.[8]

As for the stabilization operations, Turgeon acknowledged that McFarland had a heavy burden thrown upon him by the misfortunes of the pools and the world-wide depression, with no guide available from past experience. If such circumstances were to recur, Turgeon recommended some other form of intervention. He had been impressed by the information he gathered overseas from millers and merchants that the system had been injurious to the sale of Canadian wheat. Turgeon was critical of the fact that McFarland had continued his stabilization operations as general manager

[8]*Ibid.*, pp. 91-93.

of the central selling agency for a short period after the Canadian wheat board commenced operations. He was strongly critical of the failure to close out and make a settlement on the coarse grains pools which were not involved in the stabilization operations.

One of the tasks assigned to the commission had been to examine the effect of the practice of mixing and of the selection of grain for protein content by millers and exporters. Although considerable evidence was heard, Turgeon concluded that selection for protein content within grade was a legal practice within the terms of the Canada grain act, and that the problems arising therefrom were not of great significance in normal years. The non-mixing provision among the top grades introduced by amendment to the Canada grain act in 1929 met with Turgeon's approval. He simply admonished constant vigilance against violation of the regulations.

On the question of lost markets, Turgeon reviewed in detail protective measures introduced in European and other importing countries and also government interventions on behalf of wheat producers in the four major exporting countries. He summed up his findings as follows:

Looking then at a reduced overseas market and at a reduction in our share of that market during most of the depression period, I find certain factors in the situation which we ourselves have contributed.

In the first place we have had a succession of short crops with a relatively small exportable surplus. . . . This is one of the causes of our decresed share in international wheat exports, and is one which is usually overlooked when the question is under discussion. For this misfortune no blame can be attributed to anybody. . . .

In the second place we have Canada's tariff policy which, inevitably, came up for some discussion on an inquiry of this nature. I do not think that it is within my remit or within my competence, to deal with the Canadian tariff question in all its bearings on our national life. There is however no doubt, in my opinion, that the customs laws of other countries, including Canada, played some part in the adoption of policies that led to a shrinkage of wheat imports into the following countries: Switzerland, Italy, Belgium, Holland, and in a less degree, Germany and France. Whether or not disadvantages in respect to wheat may, within Canada, have been offset in whole or in part, or may have been totally overborne, by advantages in other directions, is not for me to attempt to say. . . .

However, speaking only of our wheat, I agree with what was said in evidence by Mr. J. R. Murray, former Chief Commissioner of the Canadian Wheat Board, that tariff or other arrangements which will result in each case in disposing annually of even only small quantities of wheat, such as say 5 million bushels, are worth while striving for. The sure disposal of these additional quantities, here and there, will count in the aggregate and will tend to prevent the accumulation of surpluses from year to year. . . .

In the third place, I think some contribution to the narrowing of the export market was made by the announcements of policy tending towards an international selling monopoly and high prices, made on such occasions already referred to as the conferences held at St. Paul and Kansas City in 1926 and 1927 and in which representatives of our Wheat Pools took part.

Fourthly, we have the incidents attending our 1929-30 crop year and which have been dealt with at length in discussing the Wheat Pools, including the unfortunate pronouncements which accompanied the withholding of our wheat supplies.

And finally we have the effect of our stabilization measures, particularly in 1934-35. In that year there was a maintenance of out-of-line prices and a consequent accumulation of unexported supplies which undoubtedly had a bad effect on our overseas customers. Our farmers who sold at these prices received the immediate benefit of the policy; but our export market suffered.

Speaking of these last two incidents, I must say that I am also satisfied, on the evidence I received overseas, that their unfavourable effect has now disappeared, having been removed by the policy of continuous offering carried on by the Board under the provisions of the Canadian Wheat Board Act, 1935, and which resulted in the liquidation of our accumulated surplus. From now on, with a reasonable selling policy, there is no reason why we should not receive, from year to year, the share of the overseas market which the quality of our wheat deserves.[9]

In turning to a consideration of expanding markets, Turgeon stressed quality and price. Under the latter heading he had heard much evidence, especially in Britain about the dependence millers and merchants placed on the Winnipeg futures market, which they hoped would continue in operation and without government intervention.

With regard to future marketing policy and under the assumption of normal marketing conditions, Turgeon recommended the continuation of the Winnipeg futures market and the building up of producers' co-operative marketing associations along the lines adopted by the Australian pools which operated on a voluntary basis and hedged many of their transactions through the Winnipeg market. He was categorically opposed to the creation of a compulsory wheat board to which all wheat would be delivered, not only on grounds of overseas opposition, but on the testimony of both McFarland and Murray who, for somewhat different reasons, opposed the idea. McFarland believed a compulsory board might be needed if conditions such as existed in 1932-34 were to return. Turgeon recommended the supervision of the Winnipeg grain exchange by the board of grain commissioners. He also saw merit in the proposal of United Grain Growers Limited for the creation of a Canadian wheat institute, although as long as the Canadian wheat board remained in existence the board could perform the functions contemplated for the institute.

Finally, Turgeon took a look at the near future and he was disturbed by the market prospects shaping up for the 1938 crop. Although he believed the wheat board could be dispensed with under normal conditions, he felt bound to oppose its immediate dissolution as he concluded:

I have expressed my opinion upon the question of the method which should be pursued under normal conditions, and in the interest of the wheat producers, as well as in that of the country as a whole, the return of such conditions is eagerly hoped for. But upon the facts before me today, I must say that such return is not immediately in sight. I think that there are several factors in the present situation which cannot be ignored and which call for special action. For instance, I am disappointed in one important respect: world wheat exports for the year 1936-37 were 622 million bushels, but in this present year, 1937-38, they have fallen off considerably and are now estimated, by the Secretariat of the Wheat Advisory Committee not to exceed 520 million bushels. This estimate is confirmed by that of other competent

[9]*Ibid.*, pp. 140-142.

observers. On the other hand, the United States 1938 crop promises to reach 900 million bushels, with a considerable carryover likely to be added to it. The Secretariat above referred to estimates that the area sown for harvest in 1938 in European countries is substantially larger than last year, and, that, with normal weather until harvest time, the world yield in 1938 will be considerably higher than in any year since 1933. I note that in Winnipeg the May future closed to-day (April 30) at $1.20¼b. and the October future at 88⅞ cents. In another aspect of the situation ther are certain world factors of uncertainty which cannot be ignored.

For all these reasons (and notwithstanding the adverse considerations to which I have referred in relation to government Boards) I do not feel that I can suggest the immediate dissolution of the Canadian Wheat Board. There is a strong possibility that conditions may develop which will require a measure of assistance in the marketing of the coming crop, and I do not know, of course, how long these conditions may continue after the final chapter of this report is written. In the meantime I can think of nothing better to suggest than that the Board be maintained to meet any situation which may arise.

While the Board is in existence it can continue, and, if deemed advisable, extend the work recommended for the proposed Canadian Wheat Institute.[10]

In the first appendix, Turgeon put the issue of protection to the speculative shorts finally to rest. He had cross-examined the three commissioners and invited any interested parties to testify. In the absence of other evidence, Turgeon concluded:

I find, on the whole of the evidence that the members of the Board cannot be said to have protected speculative short interests in the Winnipeg wheat market in December 1935. The Board, in the exercise of its legitimate discretion, decided that it was advisable to sell. They sold without, of course, knowing what proportion of their sales would fall to speculators and what proportion to others: and I cannot see how a knowledge that short speculators were buying should have deterred them from selling, if they had such knowledge.[11]

In a second appendix, Turgeon disposed of the Saskatchewan oats question. From his treatment of the issue it was apparent that Turgeon believed what had been referred to him was a tempest in a teapot. In these, and in all other respects, the cabinet wheat committee had reason to be grateful for such a report. The report confirmed that in the matter of policy direction, the wheat committee had been on the right course.

[10]*Ibid.*, pp. 194-195.
[11]*Ibid.*, p. 206.

26

SHADOW OF RECURRING SURPLUSES

Turgeon's warning that current crop developments in North America and Europe and the low volume of world export trade were creating a situation which warranted retention of the Canadian wheat board was increasingly substantiated as the 1938 season progressed. Prices for wheat from the record low harvest of 1937 were fairly well maintained up to mid-April in 1938. During the winter they had occasionally risen above the $1.50 level, but after Easter they began a steady and dramatic decline to 60 cents by September.

One of the earliest predictions of disaster came from the wheat advisory committee in London on January 20, 1938. In a working paper prepared for the committee, Mr. Andrew Cairns, its secretary, had estimated (on the basis of average yields) that world wheat acreage (maintained at existing levels) would produce a world carryover of wheat on August 1, 1940, of 1,370,000,000 bushels. By making such a projection, Cairns hoped to stimulate interest in the negotiation of another international wheat agreement, but the reliability of his long-term forecast based on assumed acreages and average yields was heavily discounted by Mr. George McIvor, chief commissioner of the wheat board, and by Mr. Henry Gauer, president of the Winnipeg grain exchange.[1] As a matter of record, Cairns's projection eventually proved to be accurate.

More gloomy news emanated from London after the wheat advisory committee met. A Canadian Press despatch reported:

Four reasons are advanced by the secretariat of the wheat advisory committee for its prediction world wheat production in 1938 will be higher than for any year since 1933, and will top the record year of 1928.

The prediction is contained in a report entitled, The International Wheat Situation, issued by the secretariat. It is based on the assumption that weather conditions will be normal until harvest time.

The report summarized the four reasons thus:

1. Soil in the spring wheat belts of both Canada and the United States now contains much more moisture.

2. Condition of the United States winter crop Dec. 1, 1937, was estimated officially at 76 per cent compared with 75.8 per cent a year ago.

3. The new crop in European exporting countries has a good snow cover.

[1] *Winnipeg Free Press,* January 20, 1938.

4. Present conditions of winter wheat in most European exporting countries is good to excellent.

In several large wheat-producing countries, France among them, there are definite prospects of much higher yields.

The report foresees accumulation during the next few years of another huge wheat surplus such as that which existed after the record production of 3,989,000,000 bushels in 1928.

"There is no doubt," says the report, "consumption of wheat would have been far higher in the past decade in many European and exEuropean countries if the population of those countries had enjoyed free access to duty-free imported wheat."

World total stocks of old wheat next Aug. 1 will be 685,000,000 bushels, the secretariat estimates. The figure last Aug. 1 was 568,000,000. Average world stocks between 1932 and 1936 — during the glut — were 1,013,000,000 bushels.[2]

Wheat prices only started downward, however, as the condition of the maturing United States winter wheat crop confirmed predictions of the best yields since 1932, and as spring conditions in western Canada raised hopes for the first good crop in as many years.

It was in the wake of the rapidly improving crop conditions that the government received the Turgeon commission report and, along with it, representations from western members that the wheat board be reactivated. The government responded through Euler's announcement in the house on May 19, only ten days after the report had been tabled, that the wheat board would be continued for the 1938-39 crop year. He added, however, that the question of the level of the initial payment would not be decided until the situation became clearer, but he promised an announcement well in advance of the new crop year.

Until the eve of prorogation, the 1938 parliamentary session had been one of the quietest in years in respect of wheat controversy. Nothing in the throne speech or the budget had impinged on wheat and the subject was not debated until June 30 when an item in trade and commerce estimates to cover the balance of expenses of the Turgeon commission provided an opportunity. Mr. E. E. Perley seized the occasion to make a spirited and, at times, vicious personal attack on Murray. This was rather pointless since almost a year had elapsed after Murray had completed the disposal of the McFarland surplus and had resigned from the board. Perley also attacked the bona fides of the Turgeon commission, claiming that Turgeon had only superficially examined the issues referred to him, particularly protection of the shorts.

He was followed by the Honourable W. R. Motherwell, formerly minister of agriculture and now a private member, who had been ill a year earlier when the Perley amendment was defeated. After his correspondence with King, Motherwell had accused the government of "sterilizing" the wheat board, and he would undoubtedly have joined Harry Leader in voting against the government, had he been in the house. In a move now calculated to delay prorogation, Motherwell repeated his charge. Opposition members acknowledged his courage in denouncing his own party's policy, and they

[2]*Ibid.*, February 3, 1938.

paid tribute to his devotion over the years to the cause of co-operative wheat marketing.

Both the prime minister and Euler heard the two speakers out in restrained silence, except when King intervened after Perley accused the government of making a private commitment to the western Liberal members to reactivate the wheat board. King denied that any such commitment had been made. Euler added that his May 19 announcement on the continuation of the board had been made in the house and that any private commitment to the western Liberals would have been superfluous. Messrs. Coldwell and Douglas then proceeded to press Euler to declare that the wheat board would accept deliveries from producers regardless of the market price level, but Euler contended that it was unreasonable to ask the government to elaborate on details before it could make its basic price decision, and the debate ended there.[3]

That evening, King committed to his diary his reflections on Mother-well's attack and on the manner in which the wheat board legislation had worked out in practice, as he wrote:

> Mr. Motherwell made a very bitter and vindictive speech. He had cherished resentment against the Government for two years for the fixing of price to which wheat should fall before wheat could be taken by the Board at the price at which it was fixed. He quite evidently wanted a policy which would make the Government stand all losses while the farmers would get all gains in addition to being protected by way of a minimum rate. I do not believe nor do I think the members of Parliament believe that, when the Bill was passed, anything of the kind was ever intended.[4]

King had put his finger on a weakness in the voluntary wheat board system created by the 1935 act, upon which Gardiner subsequently enlarged as he urged upon the pools, and the house, the need for changing from an emergency to a permanent wheat policy.

POLICY FOR THE 1938 CROP

While the government pondered the elements of the changed wheat situation, the directorate of the three pools worked on the coordination of their recommendations on policy. Although Bredt and Wesson had categorically declared in their evidence before the Turgeon commission that the pools would fail if they undertook co-operative marketing again, Mr. Lew Hutchinson, now chairman of the Alberta pool, disclosed that the issue was not altogether dead. He made it clear, however, that resumption of co-operative marketing would be considered only if the government refused to reactivate the board. A Canadian Press despatch from Calgary reported:

> Lew Hutchinson, chairman of the Alberta Wheat Pool, said today executive officials of the Saskatchewan and Alberta wheat pools were considering a return to a system of selling their grain through a pool unless the Dominion Government establishes a wheat board that will purchase wheat regardless of the price and sell it on a participation basis. The present board will purchase wheat at 87½ cents a bushel basis No. 1 Northern Fort William if the open market price declines to 90 cents.

[3] *House of Commons Debates,* June 30, 1938, pp. 4435-4475.
[4] *King Diary,* June 30, 1938.

The Alberta pool, with its 42,000 members, had not decided whether to call a conference of delegates to discuss the subject, Hutchinson said, but executive officials were sounding out members on what actually would be advisable if the dominion maintains the present wheat board system.

The pool executive said definite decisions on pooling of grain probably would not be reached until mid-summer.[5]

Mr. J. H. Wesson pointed out that the pools could not afford to set up co-operative marketing machinery again unless the government would guarantee their initial payments. He was reported as follows:

J. H. Wesson, president of the Saskatchewan wheat pool and vice-president of the central board of the three western pools, said today officials of the pool organizations will consult the Dominion government regarding marketing of the 1938-39 wheat crop.

"Pool officials and federal ministers will meet in Ottawa about the middle of July," Wesson said, "when the pools hope the government will decide whether the wheat board this year will be active or passive."

Mr. Wesson mentioned several factors having a bearing of the situation:

"There is a possible billion-bushel crop in the United States this year. At this time the crop prospects in western Canada are the best in several years. Further, world imports are sitll comparatively low. A potential emergency faces the western farmer. If this develops, the pools believe the futures market would not absorb the selling pressure which would develop next fall as a consequence, without price collapse."

Wesson said the pool organizations were formed to develop co-operative marketing. "They ceased this function only because world wheat prices completely collapsed, making impossible an initial payment high enough to enable farmers to do fall financing," he said.

"In view of the experiences in 1929 and 1930, the pool organizations feel they cannot further jeopardize their present assets without some reasonable protection should another condition of surplus arise."

This meant, he said, the pools would be most reluctant to undertake the setting up of co-operative marketing machinery again unless their initial payment was protected by a minimum guaranteed price by the government.[6]

There could be little doubt that the Turgeon commission recommendation on the resumption of voluntary pools prompted these acknowledgments by the pool leaders of their preparedness to reconsider their attitude against a resumption of pooling, although under necessary and specific modifications. Nevertheless, when they met with the wheat committee of the cabinet in July, the main thrust of their representation was that the government should reactivate the wheat board by permitting it to accept deliveries irrespective of the market price, and that the initial payment should be not lower than the prevailing market level which was still above 90 cents.

Another matter arising out of the Turgeon report was that of providing for supervision of the exchange. The cabinet wheat committee called representatives of the board of grain commissioners and of the wheat board to Ottawa for consultation, and the Canadian press reported:

The government has decided to drop its plans for revision of the Canada Grain Act this session, but is giving serious consideration, it was learned

[5] *Winnipeg Free Press,* May 30, 1938.
[6] *Ibid.,* June 2, 1938.

Monday, to introducing legislation which would place trading on the Winnipeg Grain Exchange under the supervision of a government agency.

In his report following his royal commission inquiry into wheat trading, Mr. Justice W. F. A. Turgeon recommended that the board of grain commissioners should be made responsible for supervising futures trading in the Winnipeg pit. It is understood the board members do not want the job. They suggested it should be handed over to the Canadian Wheat Board.

Members of both boards are in Ottawa and have said to be arguing it out with Hon. W. D. Euler, minister of trade. Grain commissioners here are E. B. Ramsay, Dr. D. A. MacGibbon, and C. M. Hamilton. George McIvor, chairman of the wheat board, is in Ottawa.

The commissioners are urging, it is stated, that they form an administrative body regulating grades, elevators, and transportation of grain and regulating the speculators in the wheat pit would be out of their line.

On the other hand, the wheat board officials say they may have to buy a portion of next season's crop if wheat goes below the price the government decides upon as a minimum and then might have to sell the wheat through the exchange. It would place the board in a position of regulating the facilities it was itself using.[7]

With neither board happy about taking on the assignment, and because parliament was so close to prorogation, the cabinet wheat committee withheld action on the supervision issue until the 1939 session.

But the question of wheat board policy for the 1938 crop still had to be faced. Newspaper reporters speculated about a sharp division in cabinet over the issue. Gardiner and Crerar were reported as favoring an initial payment at the current market level, reasoning that if it were set any lower, traders would interpret it as indicating how much the government expected the market price to fall. Farmers would rush to sell their wheat and overseas buyers would delay their purchases in the expectation of lower prices. On the other hand, the outlook was not helped by current forecasts of world supplies, and the analysis in the *Monthly Review of the Wheat Situation* (together with Secretary Wallace's announcement of intention to subsidize the export of 100 million bushels of American wheat) was cited in confirmation of the bearish situation.

Mackenzie King took note of the developing situation. Following a cabinet meeting on July 5, 1938, at which wheat policy was discussed, the prime minister announced to the press that it was the government's intention to reactivate the wheat board in the 1938-39 crop year. As King recorded in his diary on that date:

> I called in the Press . . . I also announced the intention of the Government to resume the Wheat Board for this year. I had left this to Euler but felt he might neglect doing it before the Conservatives themselves might embody it in their platform. (Thought) we should take no chances but get the statement out at once.[8]

In light of this decision, Euler requested that the board make a recommendation on the level of the initial payment for 1938. Mr. McIvor has described in detail the difficult problem created by the declining level of export prices and the board's understanding of its act which required a recommendation in line with market expectations. For these reasons,

[7]*Ibid.*, June 21, 1938.
[8]*King Diary*, July 5, 1938.

McIvor wrote to Mr. Euler on behalf of the board and recommended an initial payment of 60 cents.[9]

The board's recommendation rendered the government's consideration and action all the more difficult and significant. To revert to a depressed level of wheat prices in the crop year immediately following the worst drought disaster in western Canada could only aggravate the producers' lack of income. Nevertheless, King was confronted by a sharp cleavage of opinion within his own cabinet which reflected eastern resentment against any special treatment for the west. Dunning, his finance minister and a member of the cabiner wheat committee, was ailing at the time but King made a point of consulting him as he recorded in his diary:

> I then went to see Dunning who was lying on a sofa on the verandah of his house. . . . He advised strongly to fix an .80 rate for wheat, saying that anything between .70 and .80 would hardly prove adequate to meet conditions likely to grow out of the enormous world crop of this year. We would be saving relief in the end by giving State help to the producers.[10]

When cabinet came to grips with the issue on July 26, Mr. Chester Bloom reported:

> Evidence of the severe internal struggle going on at the federal cabinet over the fixing of a 1938 wheat price was clear Tuesday night in the fact that the cabinet sat from 2 p.m. to 7 p.m. without arriving at a decision.
>
> Prime Minister W. L. Mackenzie King told pressmen after the meeting that the decision would probably not be made until another cabinet meeting on Thursday of next week. The prime minister, in reply to cabinet on what the price should be. Mr. King however, admitted the subject had been discussed at length.[11]

Information on what really transpired at that cabinet session is provided by the King diary which confirmed the east-west cleavage among ministers over the price recommendation. It revealed Dunning, but more importantly King himself, as the author of the 80-cent initial payment proposal which was eventually adopted. It also revealed the Liberal government's determination to replace the wheat board by returning to the pools the responsibility for wheat marketing backed by pool initial payments guaranteed by the government. As King wrote on July 26, 1938:

> Shortly before two, left for a meeting of Council. Present in Cabinet from a quarter to three till half past six. Many routine Orders. Long discussion on fixation on price of wheat. Euler wanted .70; said he thought that that was what the Board would recommend. Gardiner pointed out that the present Board was a make-shift, and not truly representative, nor supported by an Advisory Committee, as the original board had been. Euler's argument was that a higher rate would mean taxing the rest of the country to help the wheat growers of the West make their profits — which is correct. Gardiner was for the old rate of 87½c. Ilsley supported Euler quite strongly, and Lapointe, Cardin and Rinfret were inclined to favour the lower rate. Mackenzie thought something higher should be granted. Rogers was not too definite, but inclined towards the lower rate.
>
> I took the position that farmers had had a very difficult time in the West, for some years past; that this year, when their hopes had been raised, they

[9]See Appendix 7.
[10]*King Diary,* July 19, 1938.
[11]*Winnipeg Free Press,* July 27, 1938.

were again being dashed because of the size of the crop, but more particularly, the world's total yield which is the largest in the country's history. It was better to give money to producers than distribute relief. Said the situation throughout the world was dangerous politically; that unrest in the West, coupled by unrest in the cities, might be very serious. That it was better to try to avert this. That the business of Government was to avert disaster, even more than to accomplish things. We all did the greatest good by what was prevented rather than by what we did. I said I thought, in the circumstances, a rate of 80c. would be fair. Previously, I had cited my conversation with Dunning who took strongly the view that 80c. should be the rate; that anything lower would not give satisfaction; that 70c. would produce bad feelings. Gardiner came down to the 80c. rate, saying he thought that we could meet the situation with that. Lapointe supported me after further consideration, and members of Council generally seemed to take that as the conclusion which would eventually be the one reached. It was agreed that Euler would talk with the Board about the necessity of their presenting a report for consideration at the next meeting of Council. He is to let members know, meanwhile, how the Cabinet were inclined to view the matter.

Rogers said, Ilsley too, that we should be prepared to go into a planning scheme for primary products, particularly fisheries, at a subsequent session. Gardiner pointed out that prices of other agricultural commodities were fairly good. It was agreed that Gardiner should seek to have the pools ask the Government to legislate respecting the grain exchange, and to peg the price of wheat, each year, leaving the sales to the pools instead of to a Government Board. He believed he can get them to do this, and that the Government should get out of the grain business before another year, in this way.[12]

Euler now had no alternative but to request the wheat board to recommend the fixing of an 80-cent initial payment. When this was done, cabinet approved the recommendation on August 4, 1938, at a time when cash wheat was selling at 86⅛ cents and the October future traded at 76⅛ cents. As King recorded: "Had a very busy afternoon in Council. . . . Set the price for the West at eighty cents, which, I think, everything considered, was the best compromise possible."[13]

When King announced the decision, the *Winnipeg Free Press* headline read: "Wheat Price Fixed, Set at Minimum of 80 Cents: To be No Hoarding by Board" and Chester Bloom's report followed:

Outstanding in the government announcement Thursday night, of a minimum price of 80 cents a bushel for No. 1 wheat, was the emphasis laid by Prime Minister W. L. Mackenzie King on the fact that there will be no hoarding — the prime minister's own phrase — of wheat by the Canadian wheat board. It will be sold as fast as delivered, with no restrictions, declared Mr. King, in competition on the world's markets.

This announcement had been particularly desired by Hon. W. D. Euler, minister of trade and commerce, said the prime minister. He quoted from the text of an order drafted by Mr. Euler, which read:

"The milling and grain traders of the world are advised that, notwithstanding the internal initial price of 80 cents per bushel, the Canadian wheat board will continue its work of encouraging the use of Canadian wheat, which will at all times be competitive on the world's markets."

[12]*King Diary,* July 26, 1938.
[13]*Ibid.,* August 4, 1938.

Mr. King said this statement had been formulated at the request of Mr. Euler as it appeared the grain people were anxious that there should be no thought of hoarding the wheat by the government board.

Asked whether this meant that the wheat would be moved to market as rapidly as the board got it, the prime minister said:

"Yes, that's the idea." He added there would be no restriction on the board taking wheat at any time.

To a question what he thought of eastern newspaper stories that this price meant subsidizing western farmers to the extent of some $20,000,000 from the federal treasury, the prime minister passed the query over by simply saying: "the wheat board recommended the price the government approved it."

The prime minister was besought to say a few words dealing with the reason why the board chose 80 cents as the price which should be fixed.

"You had better ask the Wheat Board which made the recommendation," said Mr. King. However, he added a moment later: "All circumstances were taken into account — the condition of the west in recent years, the condition of the world today."

"The entire position was weighed as well as the relation of the east to the west."

The price fixed Thursday is lower than the 87½ cents which had been fixed during the three previous years the wheat board has been in existence. It is higher than the prevailing price for the October future which closed at 76⅞ cents on the Winnipeg Grain Exchange Thursday. The October future price is the market's estimate of what wheat will bring when the new crop is harvested and threshed.[14]

In the wake of the decision, a courageous one in the face of certain loss to the treasury, there was little western criticism that the initial payment had been lowered from the 87½ cent level which had been set in 1935. Mr. Lew Hutchinson, chairman of the Alberta pool, observed that "the government feels 80 cents is the best it can do and we must abide by that". Mr. Norman V. Priestley, vice-president of the United Farmers of Alberta said that he was very disappointed. Reverse criticism in the east exposed the east-west conflict over the issue as the Honourable P. M. Dewan, Ontario minister of agriculture informed the press that he had telephoned Prime Minister Mackenzie King to protest the discrimination against Ontario farmers by setting a minimum price for western wheat. Premier Hepburn was quick to follow up, and he was reported by The Canadian Press as follows:

Premier Hepburn of Ontario . . . termed "absolutely asinine" Sunday night the Dominion government's action in setting a minimum price for wheat.

"It will cause irreparable damage," the premier said. "Trying to interfere with the laws of supply and demand is absolutely asinine."

Told the prime minister had advised Mr. Dewan the Dominion government had no power under existing legislation to extend the operations of the Canadian wheat board to Ontario, the premier then said:

"I would expect that. Mr. King never did like Ontario."

Asked if he agreed with the action of Agricultural Minister P. M. Dewan who requested the federal government Aug. 3 to set a minimum price for Ontario wheat, on the grounds farmers in this province were being "discriminated" against, Premier Hepburn said:

"Certainly. If we're going to be crazy let us be crazy all over the country."[15]

[14] *Winnipeg Free Press*, August 5, 1938.

[15] *Ibid.*, August 8, 1938.

If Hepburn's explosion did nothing more, it put western farm leaders on notice that they must justify their claims for income protection, both in the eyes of the public and in those of the federal cabinet whose commitment on western-wheat policy did not extend beyond the current 1938-39 crop year.

As for the actual handling operations on the 1938 crop, early estimates of the loss ranged from 20 to 40 million dollars. In the end, the wheat board realized a loss of $61,525,691 which was covered by the public treasury. Because of the level of the initial, and only, payment in relation to market prices, producers delivered all of their wheat to the board. Deliveries amounted to 292,360,030 bushels of which 86,539,554 bushels remained unsold at the end of the crop year. Sales had to be apportioned between the 1938 and 1939 crops until the disposition of the 1938 crop was completed on May 31, 1940.

Another problem which faced the cabinet wheat committee at the moment was an administrative one. Because of the relative inactivity of the wheat board, its personnel had almost disintegrated. McIvor had indicated his desire to resign, and Shaw had already left. If the board was to handle the 1938 crop, competent new personnel had to be recruited. Euler, Gardiner and Crerar explored possibilities and on a trip west, Gardiner discussed both policy and personnel problems with Murray. Murray recommended that the cabinet committee should persuade McIvor to remain as chief commissioner, because he was "in every way competent to handle the position". Findlay was also very useful, too, but Shaw was so committed in Ottawa that he could not possibly give full time to the work of a reactivated wheat board. For tactical reasons, Murray thought that Shaw's replacement should be named and participate in the board's price recommendation before the payment was announced. To strengthen the board, there appeared to be two possibilities, one involving Mr. E. B. Ramsay and the other the appointment of a prominent Saskatchewan farmer. Gardiner rejected the first alternative because Ramsay could not retire from a permanent position to accept what was tantamount to a one-year appointment on the wheat board, nor could he act simultaneously in the regulatory and marketing fields. Accordingly, Gardiner wrote to Euler to recommend his second alternative of appointing a farmer, but Euler opposed any such appointment, and did not concur in Murray's view that announcement of the payment should be withheld until Shaw was replaced. It was, therefore, only after the announcement that Euler, Gardiner and Crerar undertook to persuade McIvor to remain as head of the board. Euler telephoned McIvor from Ottawa on August 11, 1938. On the same day, Gardiner telephoned him from Calgary. Crerar was in The Pas. Euler hoped that both Gardiner and Crerar would go to Winnipeg to settle the matter with McIvor, as King and Gardiner exchanged wires. In the result, McIvor agreed to remain. He also recommended Mr. W. Charles Folliott as Shaw's replacement, and that appointment was confirmed by P. C. 2153 of August 31, 1938. Mr. Folliott had joined the staff of the Saskatchewan wheat pool at its inception and had been associated with McIvor for years on the sales staff of the central selling agency. The policy of recruiting experienced traders rather than public figures as members of the board, which was reflected in Folliott's selection, not only contributed to efficiency in the board's operations, but also helped to diminish the image of the board as a political entity.

CANADIAN-AMERICAN CONSULTATIONS AND THE WHEAT ADVISORY COMMITTEE

As North American crop prospects improved, and world markets offered no haven for the surplus, United States department of agriculture officials tried to resolve their own wheat problem and, in doing so, sought to enlist the co-operation of the Canadian authorities in a common approach to the world problem. In the latter respect, their first move was to solicit Canadian support for continuation of the wheat advisory committee which would go out of existence on July 31, 1938, unless its extension were approved. Dr. Skelton's memorandum of April 20, 1938, to Mackenzie King summarized the case the American officials had made for the extension, based on the deteriorating statistical position. In particular, the Americans wanted to have an international agency in existence which could explore possibilities of international collaboration on the production and marketing of wheat. The question would have to be decided at the July meeting of the wheat advisory committee.

On the home front, President Roosevelt undertook to referee an issue developing between the agriculture and state departments on the use of export subsidies. On June 11, he convened a White House conference at which he directed the two departments to survey foreign market possibilities with a view to pricing surplus wheat into export markets. The state department had objected in principle to export subsidies, but the agriculture department regarded their temporary use as justified in an emergency. While the survey proceeded, Secretary Wallace announced on July 15 that his department would make nonrecourse loans on wheat from the 1938 crop at rates averaging between 59 and 60 cents a bushel at the farm to producers who desired to hold supplies for better prices. At the same time, he announced that United States wheat farmers would be asked to reduce plantings for the 1939 crop by 32 percent to avoid further surplus accumulation.

With the United States once again in a surplus dilemma, Wallace sent Dr. Edwin Black to London to enlist support for the exploration of an agreement on export quotas at the ninth session of the wheat advisory committee which met in London, July 14-15, 1938. It was an ambitious assignment in view of the 1933 international agreement's frustrating record of performance. Moreover, the Canadian government, now in office, had openly opposed the policy of restriction embodied in the agreement and had criticized the predecessor government for failure to submit the agreement to parliament for approval. In fact, since taking office, King and his ministers had barely tolerated the existence of the wheat advisory committee and insisted that its activities be circumscribed. Canadian policy in that regard had first been expressed at a meeting of the wheat advisory committee held in July, 1936. Prior to the meeting, Vincent Massey had cabled to the department of external affairs for instructions and advice on representation, and had received a somewhat petulant reply that as three members of the cabinet wheat committee were present in London, he might arrange for representation and instructions locally. Mr. Norman Robertson was also in London and he consulted Gardiner and Dunning. Judge Turgeon was there too, and it was decided that Robertson should represent Canada and that Turgeon should accompany him as an observer. The ministers agreed that Canada should concur in the wheat advisory committee's extension for two years but, as Robertson disclosed at the meeting, they objected to analyses of the wheat situation emanating from the secretariat and to attempts to revive the international wheat agreement. Robertson's statement read:

> ... I should make it clear that the Canadian Government is not disposed to accept the diagnosis or the prognosis of the Secretariat, nor the judgments which have been expressed at this meeting, and would have to reserve its position with regard to the possibility or desirability of further international efforts to restrict and control production and exports. That is a reservation for the future, and does not limit the Government's acceptance of the continuation of the Committee's work. ... .the Canadian Government at the present stage would view with some considerable doubt the wisdom of the preparation of reports dealing with definite forms of international collaboration with regard either to the control of production or of exports.[16]

But to move on to 1938, Cairns had not endeared himself to the members of the cabinet wheat committee in January of that year when he heralded the return to surplus conditions in his three-year projection. As the July 14 meeting of the wheat advisory committee approached, Paul F. Bredt had obtained Mackenzie King's permission to attend as an observer. Massey cabled on July 12: "Would appreciate knowing what arrangement has been made for Canadian representation at meeting of Wheat Advisory Committee July 14 apart from attendance of Bredt observer."[17]

After consulting Euler, King replied on July 13:

> Would be grateful if arrangements could be made to have Pearson attend meeting of Wheat Advisory Committee July 14. He should support United States proposal to continue Committee until August 1, 1940. It is not desired to take an active part in discussions on other questions. Pearson might cable brief summary of discussions and should not commit Government to do anything without first asking for further instructions.[18]

With such a rigid assignment, Pearson stoutly resisted the considerable pressure placed upon him by Black, and by United States Ambassador Joseph P. Kennedy who presided over the meeting, to support a resolution recommending to member governments that a conference be called in a renewed attempt to reach an international wheat agreement. Pearson's stonewalling performance is best described in his own words as he reported to Skelton on July 18, 1938:

> Confirming my telegrams Nos. 156 and 157, it might be well if I sent you a short report on the recent meeting of the Wheat Advisory Committee.
>
> Four sittings in all were held, morning and afternoon of Thursday, July 14th and morning and afternoon of Friday, July 15th. All the member states of the Committee were represented, ... including the United States (Dr. Black, Chief of the Agriculture Economics Branch at Washington, Dr. Taylor

---

[16] *King Papers.*
[17] *Ibid.*
[18] *Ibid.*

and Mr. Steere); United Kingdom, (Carlill, Board of Trade, and Enfield, Board of Agriculture); Australia, (MacDougall) and France (Devinat). Mr. Kennedy, the United States Ambassador, was in the Chair. The International Institute of Agriculture was there in the person of Dr. Capone, while there was an observer from the Economic Section of the League.

At the first session Dr. Capone made quite an extensive survey of the wheat situation in which he expressed his agreement with the facts and figures of the Secretariat Report, though he thought that possibly they might prove to be somewhat conservative in the light of more recent information. He stated that the European wheat crop would be better than anybody could have expected two months ago while there would be a huge exportable surplus from North America. He painted a gloomy picture of a stock position arising soon which would be comparable to 1933-34.

Dr. Black then commented on the Secretariat Report accepting its figures for the United States. It was obvious from this first speech that the Americans were anxious to force the Committee into a resolution which would declare for some new attempt at international wheat control. Black talked a good deal about the normal and traditional position of the United States as a wheat exporter and their determination to secure their share of the world market. It was a sort of "we've got the men, we've got the wheat and we've got the machinery too" refrain and he was very definite that they would use their machinery (which he explained at some length) to assist export sales if necessary. At the same time, he said that his Government were most anxious to solve this approaching problem by international co-operation and he hoped that this Committee would declare itself strongly in favour of such co-operation, the details of which could be worked out at the next session. . . .

Then MacDougall (Australia) expressed his agreement with the Secretariat's Report, which, he thought, was probably a little too conservative. Cairns was visibly pleased by this criticism and explained that he was so anxious to remove all excuses for criticism that he had decided to err on the side of caution in his estimates and conclusions! Enfield for the United Kingdom then accepted the conclusions of the Report, made a plea for international co-operation and explained British wheat policy. The Chairman concluded Thursday's session by a vigorous plea for action; "We must do something, we must face the facts, a crisis approaches, deeds not words, etc., etc."

I did not say anything on Thursday, but, after the session, had some conversation with the Chairman and the Secretary in which I explained to them very definitely that I was not in a position to agree to any resolution which, gave approval to a report which my Government had not yet seen, or which favoured any particular solution for a crisis which might or might not arise. I suggested that they had better take this point of view of the Canadian delegation into consideration before any resolution was submitted to the Committee next day.

On Friday morning the Committee . . . moved on to Item 5. Though I had no instructions on the subject I felt quite certain that the Canadian Government would not wish to authorize the Secretary to repeat his performance of last January and issue periodically public statements on the wheat situation in order to "enlighten" public opinion.

One or two delegates thought that it might be useful if the Secretary could do this with purely factual statements. The view was expressed, in which I concurred, that if the statements were factual only, there were other agencies issuing public reports of this kind, and if they were more than factual they should be for Governments only. The Chairman then suggested that the whole question be postponed until the next meeting of the Committee. I agreed to this on the understanding that, meanwhile, the Secretary should not issue any public statements of any kind. This was accepted.

We then got back to Item 4, on which the United States hoped to discuss their "strong resolution" referred to above. There was no objection to the proposal that the Committee should be continued for two years, though in my acceptance of the proposal I added the words "on its present basis." . . .

The Chairman then suggested that a resolution be put to the Committee approving the Secretariat Report and making proposals for action at the next meeting. I was then forced to state to the Committee that I was unable to express any opinion on the Secretariat Report, approving or otherwise. There was a lengthy, desultory discussion in which I seemed to be more or less in a minority of one and during which it was pointed out that some report to Governments had to be made. It was ultimately agreed just before lunch that a sub-committee should be set up to draft such a report. This sub-committee consisted of Carlill, Ceccato (Italy), myself and the Secretary. We met Cairns at three o'clock and he submitted to us a draft which is attached to this letter as Annex I. I said I could not possibly accept any such draft and though the Italian representative seemed to think it was all right and Carlill was non-committal, I managed to get it altered so that when it was presented to the Committee at 4.30 it was in the form of Annex II of this despatch.

The Chairman seemed to think our revised draft was satisfactory but Dr. Black, Steere, MacDougall and others pleaded for a more positive declaration and a resolution of some kind. Black made quite a long harangue in which he argued that the report should at least urge the governments, in the light of the critical situation outlined in the Secretariat Report, to formulate plans for international control which could be considered at the next meeting of the Committee. He felt that the report should make a plea for stability for wheat prices both in the interests of producers and consumers; should urge a fair allocation of markets among produceres by international agreement and approve the principle of "an international, ever-normal granary". He added that the report should also definitely support the holding of a full-dress wheat conference in the Autumn to consider the above and other matters. The Chairman was inclined to agree with him, whereupon the Americans proposed certain specific amendments to strengthen the "almost meaningless statements" of the Report. I was, I think, about the only person who spoke against these amendments. The others approved, were non-committal or were silent. I was categorical, however, that if the amendments were included in the report I would not be able to accept it.

Carlill then put forward a proposal that the following words should be added to the last paragraph before the last sentence. "At that meeting the Committee will consider what action it should recommend to the constituent governments." As this seemed more or less meaningless I accepted it after some argument. . . .

Friday was a most exhausting day. I was nearly always fighting a lone battle and was subjected to a certain amount of verbal battering by my American friends. I was even in a minority of one among my compatriots. Cairns views on these matters are well-known, while Mr. Bredt, who sat beside me as an observer, made no secret of his disapproval of my objections and hesitations.

From the United States' attitude at this session of the Committee, I think it likely that their representatives will press hard for some new wheat agreement at the next session. It is also I think likely that prior to the next meeting the

United States authorities may make overtures to the Canadian Government and other Governments, direct, in order to ascertain their attitude towards such a development. Towards the end of the recent meeting, Mr. Kennedy hinted once or twice that such a procedure might be adopted.[19]

Although the next session of the wheat advisory committee was proposed for October, the meeting was postponed until January 10, 1939.

At their interprovincial conference on July 22, 1938, the western wheat pools took cognizance of the wheat advisory committee proceedings which seemed to indicate that a new wheat agreement was in the wind, and The Canadian Press reported:

> Artificial restriction of wheat acreage is not favored by directors of the prairie wheat pools.
>
> At an inter-provincial conference of the Manitoba, Saskatchewan and Alberta pools here Friday it was declared a prescribed quota of wheat for each individual farmer to sell would be preferable in Canada to artificial restrictions of acreage.
>
> Under the quota system a farmer could put in whatever acreage desired, but he would be allowed to sell only his "quota rights."
>
> Acreage was considered, it was announced, during a discussion on the marketing policy at the afternoon session. . . .[20]

The pools' quota position reflected the attitude they had taken against legislative restriction of acreage after the first international wheat agreement had been signed in 1933, and during the enactment of quota legislation by the three provincial parliaments in March, 1934. The predilection of the pools for marketing quotas over acreage control had actually predated by seven years the delivery quota system inaugurated in 1941.

The chief bargaining weapon the American government possessed was the threat of an export subsidy. After the rebuff administered by the Canadian government in London, the Americans tried a direct approach to Ottawa. At his press conference on August 18, 1938, Secretary Wallace announced that his department was studying an export subsidy program to move 100 million bushels of wheat which he regarded as the United States' fair share of the world wheat market. However, before placing a subsidy program in operation, Wallace said that his officials would consult with Canadians to see if the two countries could coordinate their export programs in the interests of both countries. In short, where the multilateral approach had failed, Wallace now sought a bilateral market-sharing program.

The presidents of the three pools, Bredt, Wesson and Hutchinson reacted immediately by wiring the prime minister in support of the American proposal. When an official of the American legation called on Dr. O. D. Skelton, undersecretary of state for external affairs, on Saturday, August 20, to make a formal request for a meeting of officials, to be held early in the following week, Skelton replied that he "was sure the Canadian government was completely in sympathy in general with the idea of discussing such question" but a practical difficulty lay in the fact that three of the four members of the cabinet wheat committee were absent from Ottawa and that

[19]*Ibid.*
[20]*Winnipeg Free Press,* July 23, 1938.

the current whereabouts of the key officials was unknown. King raised the matter in council on Wednesday, August 24, and the Canadian officials were named with instructions to conduct informal conversations with the Americans and to avoid commitments. How thoroughly the Canadian officials obeyed their instructions was recorded in Mr. J. Scott Macdonald's minutes of the meeting held on Thursday, August 25:

At the request of the United States Government a meeting was held this afternoon in the Conference Room of the Department of External Affairs between officials of the Canadian and the United States Governments for the purpose of discussing the respective wheat export policies of the two countries.

The Canadian officials present were Dr. W. C. Clark, Deputy Minister of Finance, who acted as Chairman; Mr. George H. McIvor, Chief Commissioner, and Dr. T. W. Grindley, Secretary, Canadian Wheat Board; Dr. A. M. Shaw, Director of Marketing Service, Department of Agriculture; and Mr. J. S. Macdonald, of the Department of External Affairs, who acted as Secretary.

The United States officials were Mr. M. L. Wilson, Assistant Secretary of Agriculture; Mr. Leslie A. Wheeler, and Mr. Christie also of the United States Department of Agriculture; Mr. J. F. Simmons, Charge d'Affaires, and Mr. Robert English of the United States Legation in Ottawa.

Emphasizing the informal character of the meeting Dr. Clark invited the United States officials to give their views on the wheat marketing situation and to outline any proposals they might have in mind.

Mr. Wilson proceeded to set forth the views of his Department on the present and prospective wheat situation and the position of the United States, basing his remarks on the attached memorandum which he read and distributed to the meeting. He then outlined the wheat marketing arrangements now being worked out in Washington. The Federal Surplus Commodities Corporation will purchase wheat in the market and will also, if prices continue downward, acquire title to large quantities of wheat under the Agricultural Adjustment Act. Some of the wheat will be de-natured, and some of it made into flour for distribution in relief projects. It is expected, however, that it will be necessary to export approximately 100,000,000 bushels, having in mind the maximum carry-over which they would want to show at the end of the current crop year. In selling wheat abroad, the Corporation would, of course, make every effort to avoid demoralizing prices. It would, from time to time, invite bids from private firms in the grain trade for the purchase of wheat to be sold abroad. If the Corporation feels that the prices offered are too low, they will defer selling, but if prices offered are regarded as satisfactory in the circumstances, wheat will be released for export. The Corporation will, of course, have to bear any loss which would result from export prices being lower than the price at which the wheat was bought in the United States market or acquired under the Wheat Loan System.

Dr. Clark raised the question as to whether there was any feeling in the minds of the United States officials that our guaranteed price of 80¢ for No. 1 Northern at Fort William was out of line with their lending rates, and they replied that they realized perfectly well that our 80¢ figure was not to be compared with their 59¢ figure but with a series of lending rates which they established running up to 81¢ in the case of No. 1 Dark Northern at Minneapolis, and that in comparing the two sets of figures one had to take into account adjustments in price for different grades, differences in export freight rates from the various base points and the normal premiums which world markets have given Canadian hard wheat.

At the suggestion of the Chairman, Mr. McIvor outlined conditions in the Canadian wheat areas, and explained in detail the working of the Canadian wheat marketing system. He pointed out that in his view the system of guaranteed minimum prices was not an export subsidy though at present market levels it might be regarded as including a bonus to the producer. He emphasized that in its marketing arrangements the Board did not follow a hoarding or holding or dumping policy but continued to sell wheat through the regular trade channels at competitive prices. He argued that by sound merchandising methods Canada and the United States could do far more to maintain reasonable prices than could be accomplished by subsidizing exports.

Mr. Christie of the United States delegation was inclined to argue that the Canadian system would, in fact, amount to paying an export subsidy or rather that it was as much a subsidy as the system contemplated for marketing United States wheat. He and Mr. Wheeler were inclined to consider some credit due the United States for the fact that, whereas Canada would probably sell 200 million bushels abroad out of an export surplus of 250 million bushels, the United States would be content with selling 100 million bushels out of a surplus of at least 300 million bushels, and also for the fact that the United States, to a large extent, had stayed out of the export market for three or four years. The Canadian officials pointed out that while the United States needed for home consumption 650 to 700 million bushels of wheat, or over ⅔ of their total crop, Canada's position was entirely different. We would require for domestic use only about 20% of our total wheat crop. It was therefore essential for us to maintain our export market unimpaired.

The American officials were quite willing to admit that it was a mistake to have let the impression get abroad that an export subsidy was contemplated and to have stated that 100 million bushels of American wheat would have to be sold abroad in the coming months. As, however, it had already got into the press nothing could now be done about it. Considering the long term view they were inclined to think that the world demand has sunk to a point where there will continue to be an annual surplus of wheat which will have to be disposed of. A World Wheat Agreement would be the only permanent solution. The United States Government would continue the policy of reducing acreage as the best method of controlling the situation within their power. All that, however, had to do with a long term programme with which they were not concerned at present.

After the discussion had developed to the point when the United States officials stated that they agreed with the Canadian policy as expressed at the Conference, and that the policy which they were contemplating was, in substance, identical with it, they said that the only concrete suggestion they now had to make was that, as both Governments are in the wheat export business and equally desirous of preventing any demoralization of prices, it would be to their mutual advantage to provide for an exchange of information as to what each side is doing — what merchandising policy is being followed from time to time. The present delegation was, of course, not familiar with the details of the wheat marketing operations but they hoped it would be possible for arrangements to be made between two Governments, under which the officials actually in charge of the selling operations on each side might get together from time to time and keep each other informed of their operations.

Mr. McIvor, in reply, pointed out that while he personally saw advantages in exchange of information on these lines he could not, as an official, make any commitments on the proposals. He would, however, see that it was brought to the attention of the Wheat Committee of the Cabinet and their views could later on be communicated to Washington.

Mr. Clark pointed out that, in view of the publicity which had already gone out regarding the visit of the officials from Washington, and the undesirability of the impression getting abroad that Canadian and United States officials were planning concerted marketing action, possibly by way of dumping, it might be desirable to give the press a short statement on the nature of the meeting. The attached statement was agreed upon and given to the press, not as a joint communique but rather as a short statement of what transpired at the meeting.

In closing, the Chairman expressed the pleasure of the Canadian group at the visit of the United States Officials and for the opportunity of having a frank discussion of an important problem that was common to both of them. Mr. Wilson, in reply, thanked the Canadian Officials for the trouble they had taken in describing the operation of the Canadian wheat marketing system and the opportunity which had been afforded for a frank exchange of views.[21]

The press statement approved by the group read as follows:

Taking advantage of their presence in Canada to attend the Conference of Agricultural Economists being held this week at MacDonald College, a group of United States officials, headed by Mr. M. L. Wilson, Under Secretary of Agriculture, came to Ottawa today and discussed with Canadian officials interested in the wheat marketing policies being followed by the two countries. Mr. Wilson outlined the crop situation in the United States and market prospects having regard to the world wheat situation. In reply to his enquiry the Canadian officials outlined conditions in the Canadian wheat areas, and explained in detail the working of the Canadian marketing system, involving guaranteed minimum prices and an export policy based on normal merchandising of wheat at competitive prices through the regular trade channels. The United States programme which is now being formulated contemplates, it was pointed out, a similar policy with respect to the sale of wheat through the regular channels at competitive prices in response to the demands of the market. The United States party left for Washington late this afternoon.[22]

Thus, far from coordinating their export programs, the two sides had informed each other of their intention to sell competitively and that, so far as the Canadians were concerned, they would exchange information from time to time, subject to the approval of the cabinet wheat committee. The position actually taken by the Canadian delegation had been consistent with the wheat board's sales objective of selling 250 million bushels in export markets on a strictly competitive basis, which had been approved by the cabinet wheat committee and reflected King's announcement in connection with the 80-cent initial payment, that Canadian wheat would be offered continuously and freely. Such a policy left no room for a bilateral export arrangement which might inhibit it. Macdonald's report of the meeting was reviewed by cabinet on August 30, and a minute recorded the action taken:

---

[21]*King Papers.*
[22]*Ibid.*

It was agreed that the Chairman of the Wheat Board might meet officials of the American Department of Agriculture without publicity, but it was stipulated that before any information was exchanged with the American officials, its nature should be communicated to the Wheat Committee of the Cabinet. Mr. McIvor to be so informed by the Acting Minister of Trade and Commerce, Mr. Howe.[23]

The meeting in Ottawa coincided with the fifth international conference of agricultural economists which was in session at Ste. Anne de Bellevue, Quebec, where both Wallace and his undersecretary, Mr. M. L. Wilson, were scheduled to speak. In his address on August 27, Wallace defended the American export subsidy program as necessary to secure a fair share in world trade for the United States, but that they would co-operate with Canada fully in the process, by way of exchanging information. He regarded long-term and large-scale export subsidies as a type of economic warfare which harmed the user more than anyone else, but he believed that in certain emergencies, export subsidies could be used for limited and temporary purposes, as was now the case. In his distinction between permanent and temporary policy, Wallace had found a means of reconciling the conflicting state and agriculture departmental views. For the longer term, he appealed for international co-operation in agriculture and proposed an international conference of ministers of agriculture to formulate general principles. More specifically, Wallace urged the creation of an international ever-normal granary which would extend the United States program internationally, by setting up wheat reserves, protecting farmers against price collapse, and stabilizing each exporting country's share of the world market in the bountiful years, while assuring consumers of supplies in the bad.

With implementation of the American subsidy program along with the Canadian policy of selling freely below the 80-cent floor price (to producers), market prices had fallen almost to the 60-cent level by August 31. On September 7, Mr. Grant Dexter, London representative of the *Free Press,* filed a speculative report on the efforts that had been made by the American representatives through the wheat advisory committee to mount another world wheat conference for the purpose of negotiating a new international wheat agreement which had been thwarted by Canadian unwillingness to adopt "rationed exports and regulative production." Dexter wrote:

> The slump in wheat prices is attributed here to competition between the United States and Canada. Financial editors who were referring to cut throat competition, and the News-Chronicle feels the Canadian government's fixed prices, plus disposal on the British market at the prevailing prices, constitutes an aggravated case of dumping.
>
> The United States is known keenly to desire a world conference to deal with the wheat situation, with the purpose of negotiating a new wheat agreement rationing the export market and regulating production within exporting countries. Careful inquiry reveals that nobody, including the United States experts, knows if a new conference would succeed any better than the 1933 conference and an agreement today admittedly would be more difficult to obtain than it was then. But the United States seems determined to

[23]*Ibid.*

make an attempt and Canada, rightly or wrongly, is held to be the chief obstacle in the path.

While its proceedings and report are strictly confidential, it is widely believed that the wheat committee, at its meeting in August, failed to support the United States viewpoint because Canada was unable to approve a policy of rationed exports and regulated production. The United States delegates are unwilling to accept an inconclusive decision and it is learned the committee adjourned until October or November instead of for a year. The United States delegates seemed to think that Canada would modify its views before the meeting was resumed. There was much talk by the United States delegates about dumping of wheat on the market in the meantime. Whether this is being done is not clear, although the impression here is that the United States is selling heavily.[24]

Confirmation that the United States authorities were still pressing for a new international agreement came in Secretary Wallace's press conference of October 12, 1938. Wallace expressed confidence that exporting countries could agree on a method of combating surpluses and he expected that an international conference would be convened during the winter. The exportable surplus of the four major exporting countries ranged between 800 and 900 million bushels, but the import markets required only 550 million, which accounted for the low level of wheat prices. If the conference was called, the United States delegation would propose an international ever-normal granary for the regulation of production and exports. Under his proposal, export quotas would obviate the need for export subsidies. Moreover, each exporting country would be obligated to store surpluses in bumper years for domestic and export use in years of short crops. Wallace had been informed recently that the Argentine government was prepared to participate in such a conference, which enhanced its prospects of success. Wallace's statement was followed up a month later by Mr. F. R. Wilcox, vice-president of the surplus commodities corporation, who visited London to promote the convening of the conference. He regarded an accord as absolutely essential for the wheat producing nations.[25]

END OF THE EMPIRE WHEAT PREFERENCE

In 1938, the Canadian government actively engaged in the three-way negotiation of trade agreements with Britain and the United States for the purpose of concluding more moderate tariff arrangements among the three countries than the high levels which had been legislated, particularly in North America, with the onset of the depression. The negotiations brought together Canada's famous official team of L. Dana Wilgress, trade and commerce, Hector B. McKinnon, tariff board, and Norman A. Robertson, external affairs. In the midst of the negotiations, a speculative news report emanated from London to the effect that Britain might give up the six-cent imperial preference on wheat. It was known that the United States state department attached particular importance in principle to the abandonment of this discriminatory tariff which penalized the entry of United States wheat into Britain.

---

[24]*Winnipeg Free Press*, September 8, 1938.
[25]*Ibid.*, October 14 and November 15, 1938.

A Canadian Press reporter covering the conference of agricultural economists at Ste. Anne de Bellevue questioned Dr. C. F. Wilson on the subject. He was reported as follows:

> Possibility that the Dominion might give up the preference to pave the way for an Anglo-American agreement was admitted by Dr. Charles F. Wilson, chief wheat statistician at Ottawa. But he thought any relinquishment of this advantage would not bear heavily on the Canadian wheat grower.
>
> Dr. Wilson considered what advantage Canada had gained through the preference had been only "slight." Any decrease in the export trade to the British through the yielding up of the favorable tariff, he held, would be correspondingly small.[26]*

A similar opinion was expressed by J. H. Wesson and appeared in another Canadian Press dispatch:

> J. H. Wesson, president of the Saskatchewan Wheat Pool, did not appear greatly concerned over reports of the removal of Canada's wheat preference. When Canada obtained a preference in the British market under the 1932 trade agreements it did not mean any more money for the Canadian producer, he stated today.[27]

On November 17, 1938, the new British-Canadian, British-American and Canadian-American trade agreements were signed, and termination of the British wheat preference was confirmed. The ultimate assessment of the value of that preference would have to take into account whatever tariff concessions our Canadian negotiators extracted from their United States counterparts in exchange for ceding the preference.

CONFERENCE ON MARKETS FOR WESTERN FARM PRODUCTS

As Messrs. Lew Hutchinson, J. H. Wesson and Paul Bredt moved into ascendency as western spokesmen for producers, they were not only reoccupying the position attained by the pool leaders prior to 1930 but they were also filling the void left by the team of provincial premiers which had served as spokesmen for producers from 1930 to 1934. Of the original team, only Premier John Bracken of Manitoba remained in office, (and only barely so, with the support of five Social Credit members). It was only natural that, in the developing wheat crisis in 1938, Bracken would try to reestablish his position as a spokesman for western farm interests, and in this he received unexpected assistance from Premier Mitchell Hepburn who had sharply criticized the attitude of the western provinces toward federal assistance as reflected in their briefs submitted to the royal commission on dominion-provincial relations. When it came Hepburn's turn to present Ontario's case to the commission, he was reported by The Canadian Press as follows:

---

[26]*Ibid.*, August 25, 1938.

* Editor's note: Dr. Wilson later recalled this incident, describing it as the "worst gaffe of my early career". No less a person than the prime minister had instructed that Wilson be reminded that his remarks unwittingly undermined the value of the preference as a Canadian bargaining counter in the tariff negotiations.

[27]*Winnipeg Free Press*, August 26, 1938. At a later date, Gardiner also stated in the House: "So far as we have been able to make out during the period this agreement has been in existence, the six-cent preference has not benefited the wheat growers of the western or any other part of Canada." *House of Commons Debates*, January 19, 1940, p. 140.

The balance of economic advantage resulting from Confederation lies with the prairies, despite the west's repeated charge that the east has benefited most, Premier Mitchell F. Hepburn asserted today before the Rowell commision.

If the west had suffered more than the east there were several explanations, apart from any federal policy, he contended. The claims of the prairie provinces for compensation "at our expense" rested on the fallen fortunes of the wheat growers.

"While wheat is still important, it is not the life and soul of the west," the Ontario premier said.

"I have every sympathy for those 90,000 farmers whose main source of revenue (wheat) has declined, but really I do not see that it is necessary to upset confederation on their behalf . . ."

As far as the wheat situation was concerned a committee of the League of Nations had concluded that over-production of wheat was responsible for the agricultural crisis and that Canada, in this instance, western Canada, was responsible for the greatest absolute and relative over-production of the world's wheat supply.

"Then the prairie provinces are the makers of their own, and other people's misfortunes," Premier Hepburn said. . . .[28]

Shortly afterward, the Honourable Leopold Macauley, Conservative house leader in the Ontario legislature supported Hepburn's outburst on the 80-cent initial payment when he spoke in Toronto on October 17:

Sometimes I don't like Premier Hepburn's methods or the violent phrasing of his statements, but I think he is completely justified in his protests against the wheat bonus. I can't blame the administration for feeling that Ontario is being made the milch cow for Canada when western farmers get 85 cents a bushel for wheat and the Ontario farmer can get only 50 cents.[29]

Bracken replied to Hepburn's charges against the west in the final brief he presented on behalf of the Manitoba government to the royal commission on dominion-provincial relations on November 29. The Canadian Press reported Bracken's statement as follows:

Premier John Bracken of Manitoba today called for a definite national policy regarding the increasingly grave world wheat situation.

"Factors outside our own control have reduced from 760,000,000 to 540,000,000 bushels the world demand in the last eight or 10 years, and the world is producing as much as in the past." he said. "What is to be the national policy under these conditions? If we had known 30 years ago of this situation, we would not have developed more than half the acreage we have. If the situation we actually have can't be saved, let us start to back up. Let the railway deficit become greater, and a quarter of a million farmers go on relief."

"If the world won't take the wheat that is being grown, the one thing left is to try to set a planned arrangement between the Argentine, Australia, the United States and Canada, to limit production. The alternative is to go on fighting each other for the little market there is."

Premier Bracken said a conference had been called for Winnipeg for the middle of next month to try to bring together all the pertinent facts regarding Canada's relation to the world wheat problems, all the facts regarding this cloud seen on the horizon by the west.

[28] *Winnipeg Free Press,* May 3, 1938.
[29] *Ibid.,* October 18, 1938.

"For ourselves, we want to know what the prospects are for getting markets and what are the prospects of keeping the prairie provinces from complete bankruptcy. If not, we want to know if we have to start a new era of economy. We have to decide, if we have 40 cent wheat, whether we can continue to meet $700,000,000 debt charges (provincial and municipal). If we are not going to have markets, whose acreage are we going to reduce?"

Establishment of fixed prices for western wheat this year saved the prairies from "an economic disaster of unprecedented proportions" Mr. Bracken said.[30]

The conference Bracken referred to in his brief had been announced in October and it was scheduled for December 12-15 in Winnipeg. He had been planning the conference for almost a year, for the purposes he mentioned in the brief, but also to refute eastern criticism of the west, to back up the federal government's policy respecting the 80-cent initial payment and to press for its continuation. The detailed organization of the conference, attended by 200 representatives of the grain industry in western Canada, was placed in the hands of Mr. C. B. Davidson, formerly secretary of the wheat board, whom Bracken had engaged a year earlier to chair a provincial economic survey board. To mount the conference, Davidson recruited a large panel of experts who delivered some 29 papers on all aspects of western agriculture, including grains and their products, livestock, dairy, poultry, honey and fishery products, as well as land use.

As the conference opened, two ministers of the King government, the Honourable C. D. Howe and the Honourable Norman M. Rogers charged elsewhere that a Hepburn-Duplessis plot had been laid to oust King as leader of the Liberal party, and the breach between the federal and Ontario Liberals was openly acknowledged.

To open the conference, Dr. W. A. Mackintosh of Queen's University presented an historical summary of western development in relation to the national policy. He was one of the first persons to declare that wheat was about to lose the dominant position it had held for years in the total Canadian economy, because of the ascendency of other industries. Professors E. C. Hope and G. E. Britnell developed the theme of western farm indebtedness. Hope's declaration that on the basis of 80-cent wheat, western growers could not meet their debt obligations made a considerable impression.

On the grain side, Dr. C. F. Wilson led off with an appraisal of the world wheat situation which took an hour and a half to deliver with the help of charts illustrated on a screen. At a time when the volume of world wheat trade had fallen to an historically low level, the message conveyed was unavoidably depressing. He was joined by Mr. H. L. Griffin and Dr. W. Sanford Evans who also dealt with Canadian and world situations, and by Paul F. Bredt and Dr. D. A. MacGibbon who spoke on the Australian and Argentine wheat industries.

Dr. L. A. Wheeler, chief of the foreign agricultural service in the United States department of agriculture, and Mr. R. M. Evans, administrator of the agricultural adjustment administration, presented papers on European wheat requirements and policies, and on the wheat problem in the United

[30]*Ibid.*, November 30, 1938.

States. So it went for four days as all alternatives for more diversified production were explored.

At the end of the conference, Premier Bracken announced that he would name a western committee on markets and agricultural readjustment to follow up on the findings of the conference, which he condensed into a national radio broadcast on December 18, as follows:

... The price of wheat in Canada has dropped in recent months to less than half of what it was a year ago. As a result this year's Canadian crop, which was more than twice as large as that of last year, would bring on the open market some 30 million dollars less than that of a year ago. The economic consequences of such a disastrous fall in prices was early recognized by the Dominion government. It therefore guaranteed a minimum price of 80 cents per bushel for wheat delivered at the lake port of Fort William. This meant that after freight and other charges are deducted, the price actually received by the western farmer for average grades is about 55 cents per bushel.

The consequence upon the West, and upon all Canada, of any continuation of such low prices was considered to be very serious. For that reason a conference of all the national interests affected was called in an effort to throw more light on the problem. . . .

Answers to certain basic questions were sought and obtained from those in a position to speak with authority. For example, it was shown that western Canada produces more than three times the needs of all Canada for wheat, and that consequently markets for more than two-thirds, or some 250 million bushels per year, must be obtained in other countries.

Then the question was asked, "Has there been a shrinkage in the world demand for wheat?" The answer was, "Yes." Within the last seven or eight years there was shown to be a shrinkage of about 200 million bushels per year in the demand from importing countries. This was considered to be the chief basic cause of the present problem.

Another question was, "Is the annual production of wheat in the world being maintained?" The answer was, "Yes." In 1938 the crop was the largest known in the history of the world. With the world import demand down, and the world export supply up, a third question scarcely needed an answer. That question was, "Has the price of wheat declined in Canada?" The answer was of course "Yes." The average price a year ago at Fort William was $1.31 — today it is about 60 cents on the open market. The guaranteed price of 80 cents means about 55 cents per bushel to the grower for average grades. If farmers in the Prairie provinces were receiving the open market price instead of the guaranteed price, they would be getting but little more than 40 cents a bushel. . . .

It was then asked, "Is this low price in the West likely to continue?" The analysis of demand and supply as presented to the conference indicated that the demand continues to be down; that unless something is done to lessen production the supply is likely to remain high; that a large increase in carry-over at the end of the year is probable, and that consequently low prices are again in prospect. We were told that at the end of July next, there would be 1,100 million bushels of a world carry-over of wheat, whereas the normal carry-over is around 600 million bushels. Such an increase in surplus stocks inevitably spells low prices.

It was the view of the conference that the situation which I have just described represented the result of broad international trends; trends of interference with world trade; trends which were bearing heavily and unfavourably upon the wheat industry in Canada. It was the unanimous view also that the Prairie provinces alone could not withstand the effects of this impact; it was felt that the nation must continue to deal with this extraordinary situation, with measures fitted to the urgency of the case at least until such time as the international trade picture has changed, or until such time as other adjustments can be made by which the wheat industry of Canada can be put on a better basis.

Still other questions followed. One was, "Can we solve the problem by international agreement to reduce wheat acreage or wheat exports?" This method of reducing production or export was tried under the International Wheat Agreement of 1933, and it failed. Some say it may yet be made to work, but others are strongly of the opposite view.

Another question was, "If the price is low can we reduce our costs to offset it?" It was pointed out that as compared with Australia and Argentina our competitors, the Prairie provinces find themselves in a high cost producing area. The costs are high here, not because of any disadvantages in soil or climate, but because of geographical position and unfavourable tariff policies.

Still another question was, "Can we bring about a reduction of the wheat acreage of western Canada?" It was agreed that some shifts in land-use could be made, but it was made clear, also, that fundamentally the Prairie part of the region must remain a grain growing area, and that other farm enterprises must fit themselves into that general type of production. In this connection the conference was warned that any important swing in western Canada towards the production of livestock and dairy products would have very unfavourable repercussions upon agriculture in other parts of Canada. It was shown that if the wheat surplus problem were to be solved by shifting to other types of farming, that it would but transfer the problem to other agricultural products and to agriculture in other parts of Canada. In this connection it is interesting here to note that the Canadian Chamber of Agriculture, just last night, issued a call for a similar conference in Ontario on the same subject.

While the Winnipeg conference was primarily concerned with securing a complete statement of the facts which lie behind these distressed conditions with respect to wheat and other grains, there was a unanimous desire to approach the whole problem of markets in a constructive way. While it was clearly understood that the problem of outside markets was a problem for the national government, it was fully realized that there were many matters pertaining to western agriculture which could only be satisfactorily dealt with by local effort. With this fact in mind the conference considered carefully the question of the adaptability of different western agricultural zones to various other types of farming, and it discussed thoroughly the question of the possibility of new avenues of production replacing wheat. . . .

At the conclusion of the conference it was agreed that a representative committee on "Markets and Agricultural Readjustment" should be named to carry on from the point where the conference left off.

Some of the matters arising out of the conference that will come under the survey of the committee might be mentioned. The first is the necessity of more aggressive action in solving the basic problems of this particular region, viz., export markets and reduced costs of production. It was felt that there could be no desire, in any part of Canada, to see any region in this country forced into becoming a permanently distressed area. It was felt that the trade policies of the Dominion should, therefore, be further developed along the lines of regaining lost markets, and of finding new markets, and of lessening the cost of production. Likewise it was felt that Canadian monetary policy in the future should take proper cognizance of the importance of maintaining a sounder relationship between debtor an creditor classes, and between the income of farmers in any part of Canada, who sell their products at the low prices of world export markets, and other classes in the community. In the recent depression years the monetary policy followed in Canada failed to correct the maladjustment between farm income and the income of other economic groups to an extent that was possible, and which would, in our opinion, have been in the general public interest.

It was clearly understood and accepted that in facing the problem the Prairie provinces are not without a major responsibility. It was felt that we must give consideration to a greater diversity in our agricultural production; that we must energetically pursue research work in connection with the many related problems, and that we must vigorously press for new uses for the products of the soil. ... The delegates realized that western Canada particularly was facing an extremely difficult position. But they realized more than that; they realized that depressed conditions in the Prairies will not be without serious economic consequences to other parts of Canada, and they realized that if we shift to other types of agriculture the welfare of large numbers of farmers elsewhere in Canada will be adversely affected. Throughout the conference there was a unanimous desire not only that the problems of western agriculture should be dealt with, but that they should be dealt with in such a way as to promote the welfare of Canada as a whole, and in a manner that would promote the utmost of national unity.[31]

On January 21, 1939, Bracken announced the membership of his committee which included the Honourable J. G. Taggart, minister of agriculture in Saskatchewan, and the Honourable D. B. Mullen, minister of agriculture in Alberta. J. H. Wesson, Lew Hutchinson and Paul Bredt were named for the pools, and George Bickerton, J. K. Sutherland, Paul Farnalls, and J. S. Wood other farm organizations. D. G. McKenzie, vice-president of United Grain Growers Limited, representatives of the Saskatoon, Regina, Calgary and Edmonton boards of trade, W. McG. Rait, general manager of the Pioneer Grain Company Limited, L. W. Brockington, K.C., counsel, Northwest Grain Dealers' Association, E. K. Williams, K.C., and Dr. J. S. Thomson, president, University of Saskatchewan, completed the committee.

The committee moved with considerable dispatch to prepare a submission to the federal government. Because its representations concerned primarily the government's policy for the 1939 crop and the legislation relating thereto, the committee's activities are covered in the next chapter. What had been most notable during 1938 was the rapid transition from shortage to a renewed surplus situation. The financial burden of the surplus, as reflected in the wheat board loss on its operations, had forced a reconsideration of wheat policy. External pressures were renewed for international action. Bracken's initiative had joined the issue on eastern charges of discrimination. Turgeon's report had recommended two different courses for fair weather and foul. As it entered its fourth year of office, the Liberal administration was still involved in the search for a permanent wheat policy which could be defended across Canada, despite all the market uncertainties of surpluses and impending war.

---

[31] *Proceedings of the Conference on Markets for Western Farm Products,* Winnipeg, December 12-15, 1938, pp. 325-328.

27

1939 LEGISLATIVE PROGRAM

So far, the wheat policy of the Liberal government elected in 1935 had been consistently one of disposal of the inherited wheat surplus and restoral of wheat marketing to the pools and the trade on a basis that would permit the termination of the wheat board. In its 1935 election platform, the Liberal party had promised to continue the wheat board only for the duration of the emergency. Euler believed that emergency had passed when he recommended to King on June 25, 1936, that the time had come for the government to get out of the wheat business. Instead, the board had been permitted to continue on a restricted basis, which prevented it from accepting deliveries from the 1937 and 1938 crops. The government's policy in respect of the board had been reviewed again in 1937 when it was decided to keep the board in existence, on a skeleton basis, pending receipt of the Turgeon report.

In the meantime, the Turgeon commission had heard exhaustive evidence on the merits and weaknesses of alternative wheat marketing systems and had reported conclusions (very much to the liking of the government) that, under normal conditions, marketing should be left to the open market and co-operative marketing systems. But, at the end of his report, Turgeon acknowledged the return of world surplus conditions in 1938, and for that reason he found himself unable to recommend an immediate dissolution of the board.

As the government faced its critical policy decision about the level of the initial payment for the 1938 crop, King had rued in his diary that the government could only lose money as it implemented the provisions of the existing act. In the crucial cabinet session of July 26, 1938, Gardiner had responded to the Dunning and King support for an 80-cent initial payment by offering to persuade the pools to revert to co-operative marketing under government guarantee, in the hope that it would obviate the need for a wheat board beyond the handling of the 1938 crop.[1] At the August 4, 1938, meeting of council when the 80-cent payment was accepted, Gardiner was authorized to proceed with discussions with the pools in the hope of persuading them to revert to their original function of operating producers' pools.

[1]See pp. 562-563.

GARDINER'S DISCUSSIONS WITH THE POOLS

Gardiner proceeded almost at once to Regina where he met on August 9, 1938, with representatives of the boards of the three pools. From his subsequent correspondence, it is evident that Gardiner candidly informed the pool directors of the government's dissatisfaction with the way in which the wheat board legislation had worked out, and of its awareness that alternative machinery needed to be explored in the search for a permanent policy. After explaining the reasons for the government's dissatisfaction, Gardiner proposed new legislation under which any organization, pool or trade could enter into an agreement with the government to operate a pooled system of producer deliveries, with initial payments at levels approved by the government, which would guarantee the organization against loss thereon. On September 10, 1938, Gardiner reported the results of his discussions in a confidential letter to King:

You will recall, that at the last meeting of Council before I left for the West, I was authorized to meet the western Wheat Pools and discuss possible future policy in relation to wheat marketing.

I met the Board of the Saskatchewan Pool, together with representatives of the Boards of the Manitoba and Alberta Pools, in Regina, at the Pool office, at 10 o'clock on August 9th.

From the discussions, I gathered that the Wheat Pools would prefer a Wheat Board handling 100% of the wheat under International Agreements with regard to quotas made between importing and exporting countries. Discussion, however, brought out the difficulties in the way of having any such plan worked out satisfactorily. Most of the prominent members of the Boards were quite candid in acknowledging the almost unsurmountable difficulties in the way of establishing any such system.

After this view was fairly well established, the position which would arise as a result of a Wheat Board operating under the present legislation, taking enormous losses, was fully discussed and I think it was pretty generally agreed that no Government could maintain a Wheat Board in operation as a permanent method of handling wheat if such losses were always a possibility. The dangers both to Canada's financial position and to the possibility of establishing a permanent system of grain marketing on that basis were, I think, fully realized.

It seemed to me to be the general opinion, at the end of the discussion, that if their first suggestion is impracticable the Wheat Pools would prefer a system based upon the principles which I outlined to Council, namely, that we should have legislation licensing Pools and establishing an initial payment guaranteed by the Government, provided the Pool did not pay a higher initial price than that set out in the legislation.

Mr. Wesson, President of the Saskatchewan Pool, has written me giving the results of a discussion which the Saskatchewan Pool had at a later date, of the proposals made on August 9th. You will note the views reached at that gathering conform very closely to the impressions which I gathered during my discussions with the representatives of the three Boards.

Information which I received personally from Mr. Wesson and others is to the effect that the other two Pools will follow the Saskatchewan Pool.

You will note that the one condition which they suggest is that the present legislation providing for a Wheat Board should be left on the statute books to provide for dealing with emergencies which may arise in future as a result of conditions similar to those existing at present.

While they suggest they would favour a 70¢ payment I, personally, think that is too high, and am of opinion that there would be no considerable objection to it being set at 60¢. As a matter of fact, very strong arguments in favour of a 60¢ price can be made both to the Pools and to the farmers themselves.

It appears to me that it would be much sounder for the financing of Canadian western farmers to be based upon a 60¢ initial payment, with prospects of receiving any additional monies spread over the year, than to have it set at any higher rate. The whole financial structure of western Canada would eventually be based upon the fact that a certain amount is going to be paid at the end of the threshing season when wheat is delivered, and that further payments are going to be spread over the year. Personally, I am of opinion that a 50¢ initial payment would be more in the interests of the future welfare of farmers in western Canada than even a 60¢ rate, and I would be very strongly opposed to going beyond 60¢.

If the international situation does not become more complicated, I think it would be wise to have this matter further discussed in Council and a position reached upon any further action at as early a date as possible.

I am sure that the earlier we can start the advocacy of a sound marketing policy for wheat, the better it will be for all concerned politically and otherwise.

I am enclosing a copy of Mr. Wesson's letter for your personal information.[2]

Wesson's personal letter of September 7, 1938, to Gardiner confirmed the latter's understanding of the discussions:

Following our very short conversation in Winnipeg and on my return to Regina discussing Mr. Milliken's conversation with you, I thought it might be advisable to write a confidential letter for your own information, pointing out generally the attitude of our Board on the future of wheat marketing.

It was only natural, under the present wheat debacle in the world with ever-lowering prices and surpluses looming in the future, that our Board should have what might be called a surplus psychology. For that reason it was the opinion of the Board that in view of world conditions and in view of a substantial additional surplus at the end of this year, it will be almost necessary for the Wheat Board to function.

At the time our discussion took place in the Board Room, you will remember the United States, through Secretary Wallace, was making press statements dealing with the necessity of the United States exporting a minimum of one hundred million bushels and of the possibility of some kind of co-operation between our own country and theirs, with a view to maintaining price levels. Our Board believed that this suggestion was a very good one and might lead up to a working agreement with Australia and Argentine later on when their crops started to move on to the world's market.

While discussing this international situation our Board was unanimously of the opinion that you, as Minister of Agriculture, should attend the next meeting of the International Wheat Advisory Committee in London so that you might have first-hand contact with the international wheat problem as well as getting the viewpoint of both importing and exporting countries. In this regard you will remember that the Prime Minister authorized our Mr. Bredt to sit in on the last meeting in London as an observer. In telling us confidentially of his impressions, Mr. Bredt said the outstanding feature of

[2] *King Papers.*

the meeting was the attitude of the importing countries which did not want cheap wheat dumped into their own countries, which means a lower price level for their own producers and they could not understand why it was not possible for the exporting countries to get together to ship every bushel of wheat required at a reasonable price level and not allow unwanted surpluses to depress the price of the whole. However, dealing with the possibility of your attending, that can be taken up later on the basis of your suggestion.

Following this discussion on the whole wheat question, our Board then gave attention to your plan and agreed, almost unanimously, that in the event of the surplus not being particularly burdensome at the end of the present year and following a decision of the Government that the Wheat Board would not function, the Pool would be prepared to operate under a scheme suggested by yourself two weeks previously, the understanding of the Board being that legislation would be provided to guarantee an initial payment made by the Pools, such guarantee to be sufficiently wide to protect the organization against loss in the event of a drastic decline in market prices.

While no decision was made regarding what the initial payment, guaranteed under the legislation, ought to be, in the discussion seventy cents seemed to be the figure that would provide a sound basis for pooling and that the Government of Canada should recognise that that figure is an extremely low price for our producers to get by with on account of all our crop hazards.

The Board also agreed that the Wheat Board legislation now in the statute books should remain there to take care of any emergency which may arise.

The Board at this time, with this surplus bogey in front of them could not believe that this proposal for pooling would be the solution of the wheat marketing problem, but view it from the angle that it is the best method by which this organization could make available to its members adequate machinery for pooling for those who wanted to use it to secure the average price for the year, whatever it might be, and without risk of loss to the organization itself.

You remember, Mr. Gardiner, in your discussion in the Board Room, you raised the question of a number of pools, pools that might be organized by groups of people and take out licenses under the legislation. Our Board are unanimously of the opinion that this legislation should only be used by producer organizations marketing grain for their own members, that it should involve some form of a grower's contract to give at least an approximate idea of what grain would be delivered during the season and that only one pool in each province should be entitled to operate with a license under Dominion legislation.

This, I believe, gives a general picture of our discussion in the Board Room. In the final analysis it means that in the event of production and consumption being normal and with normal carryover in the world our Board will be prepared to give serious consideration to a sound basis of pooling under federal legislation, providing a guarantee of an initial payment is mutually agreed upon between the Government and the Pools.[3]

King was appreciative of Gardiner's efforts and he responded to Gardiner's sense of urgency in his acknowledgment of September 15:

I thank you for your letter of September the 10th re marketing of wheat. I agree with you that the earlier we can start the advocacy of a sound marketing policy for wheat, the better it will be for all concerned politically and

[3]*Ibid.*

otherwise. For this reason, I should welcome the matter being discussed in Council, at the earliest possible date. . . .[4]

Council duly approved Gardiner's action and authorized him to pursue the co-operative marketing proposal with the delegates to the annual meeting of Saskatchewan Co-operative Wheat Producers Limited, on November 3, 1938. Gardiner prepared a formal presentation of his ideas which he read to the meeting. At first he reviewed the government's policy and experience with respect to the handling of the 1935, 1936 and 1937 crops under the wheat board act, and then used the 1938 experience to illustrate the need for a more satisfactory policy, as he said:

When the 1938 crop was coming on the market the world conditions were different from those of either 1936 or 1937. It became evident that the unsettled situation in Europe, together with the enormous world production, would result in a low world price.

It was also evident that if war resulted in Europe in the fall of 1938 wheat would rise rapidly in price. It was therefore considered that an emergency existed which, together with the difficulties experienced by the wheat producers in the years immediately preceding, necessitated the establishment of a minimum price which would in all probability pay a bonus to the wheat producing farmer.

The price was set at 80 cents a bushel which has resulted to date in paying the producer what amounts to a bonus of from 15 cents to 20 cents a bushel. I think a bonus of even that amount can be justified for this year under all the circumstances. It can be justified as the legislation has been justified from the beginning, namely, that it is dealing with an emergency condition. With the world price below the set price the Board naturally gets all the wheat.

The question arises as to whether legislation which admittedly deals effectively with certain emergencies can be the basis of a permanent and continuous system for the marketing of wheat.

There are difficulties in the way. Some of them are:-

1. The maintenance of an organization which does not get wheat in a normal year.

2. The paying of a considerable bonus to those with a good crop in a year like the present while those with a poor crop must exist on relief.

3. The opposition which comes from other parts of Canada to the paying of a considerable bonus even in a year like the present would be greatly increased if it were paid in a normal year.

4. There are international difficulties which do not exist at present but would if the emergencies were to pass.

It therefore occurs to me that at a time when we are still enjoying the advantages of emergent legislation we should be considering a permanent policy which might come into effect when the present emergency passes.

Personally I have always been a strong advocate of the pooling method of marketing and have seen no reason to change my mind. My reasons for this are that the pooling method provides for:-

1. The farmer carrying his own risks thus removing the influence of the speculative element from price setting.

2. The producers of the wheat growing areas who desire to do so can handle their own product thus eliminating the criticism and influence of those outside the wheat growing areas who have no direct interest.

3. The pooling method applied to the marketing of our wheat involving an initial payment which would be reasonably assured, interim payments and a

[4]*Ibid.*

final payment could be made over a period of years the regulator of the whole economy of the wheat growing area.

The first two reasons have been obvious and are the particular interest of the wheat producers.

The whole of Canada should be interested in the last for the reason that our railway system and the whole credit system of the country is involved.

Because of this latter fact I think a Dominion Government, no matter what its political alignment, would be prepared to maintain and support a pooling system of marketing once established, thus rendering it permanent. There is in the recommendation of the Turgeon Commission the basis for a possible system under which those farmers still desiring to use the open market system and those desiring to use the co-operative pooling system could demonstrate the strength of each system by competing to give service. . . .

It would be necessary to the setting up of such a (co-operative pooling) system that the government of Canada encourage financially the maintenance of the pooling system by guaranteeing an initial price and checking the financial activities of the pool sufficiently to guarantee efficient management.

In my opinion wheat can be successfullly marketed by a producers organization controlled by producers. The Government, through the initial payment, should come into the picture in emergencies such as 1932 and this year to render permanent a system essential to the welfare of the producer, the transportation companies, and our credit facilities. I think all of this could be arranged for in legislation which could be drafted to suit both the Dominion Government and the producers. . . .[5]

In Gardiner's statement, it was implicit that the government was seeking to terminate the board, and he presented cogent reasons for change in the existing policy as he made out his case for the resumption of co-operative marketing by the pools, under the protection of a government guarantee. The pool directors and delegates, however, reacted to Gardiner's advice by accepting it conditionally on the understanding that the existing wheat board legislation be left on the statute books, in order that resort to it could be made in the event of an emergency. The *Regina Leader Post* reported on November 9, 1938, that:

In view of the still unresolved problem of recurring large world wheat surpluses with consequent depressed prices to producers, the Saskatchewan wheat pool delegates decided here Tuesday that their organization should seek to secure the continued operation of the Canadian wheat board with a guaranteed minimum price to the grower at the time of delivery.

Taking a long view, the delegates favored legislation that would place grain marketing in the hands of the producers themselves when a specified majority had approved such action.

Both these proposals were contained in the board of directors' report, which continued: "We believe, however, that even the passage of such legislation will not relieve the Dominion government from responsibility in the matter of grain prices so long as Canada's fiscal policy remains unchanged. In addition, your board will support all legitimate efforts which may be made looking toward the greatest possible measure of practical international co-operation and co-ordination in the interests of western grain growers."

Referring to the possibility of an international agreement, in which several of the leading wheat exporting countries recently have shown definite signs of being interested, the board's report observed that it would be difficult if not

[5]*Ibid.*

impossible for Canada to give effect to an agreement unless control of the marketing of Canadian grain were vested in the wheat board or some other similar body.

"Your board is of the opinion," the report went on, "that any plan calling for reduction in seeded acreage will not be practical in western Canada, in view of the wide variations in production. We believe, however, that it would be possible to evolve a plan which would control deliveries and prevent the dumping of large quantities of grain at primary markets out of all proportion to requirements. Such a plan would almost inevitably provide a practical plan of crop assurance as a result of the creation of reserve supplies of grain held in store on the farms for domestic use and which would be available for export in short crop years."

The pool delegates also went on record in favor of a domestic price for wheat in Canada. It was pointed out that similar legislation is now pending in Australia, as part of a wide scheme for the stabilization of the Australian wheat industry.

Future policy has been under consideration by the annual meeting of delegates for most of the past two days.

Gardiner duly reported the latest developments to King. He recommended that the government proceed with co-operative marketing legislation and also that he should be the minister responsible for it. His reference to King's statement on the division of authority between the departments of agriculture and of trade and commerce recalled Euler's open confrontation with Gardiner over the Shaw report which had questioned the competence of Euler's department in promoting exports of farm products. Gardiner addressed a personal letter to King on November 15:

Attached is a copy of the manuscript which I read to delegates of the Saskatchewan Wheat Pool on November 3rd, 1938, setting forth the present position in relation to wheat, and suggesting that certain changes be embodied in new legislation. After this memorandum was read many questions were asked by individual delegates but no discussion took place on the matter while I was present. My understanding was that they would communicate to me later their views regarding the whole matter. I have not yet received an intimation as to what the results of the discussion were other than what appeared in the Press. I am enclosing a clipping from the newspaper, which indicates the desire to have the Board and set price continued during the period of surplus production.

I would point out that the whole wheat question was discussed fully in the Manitoba by-election. I am enclosing a copy of a statement which I had published and which was read by Mr. Rogers at his Brandon meeting, indicating the position taken when the price was set at eighty cents. Perley and Coldwell on the other hand attacked very strongly the position taken by the Government. Judging from press reports of speeches delivered by Mr. Crerar in the last week of the Campaign, I would say that we were not at any time committed to continue the present policy in relation to wheat as a result of any discussions which took place there.

I think this fairly well clears the way for the establishment of a permanent wheat policy along the lines suggested. While I do not wish to press the matter unduly, I am inclined to think the matter could be much more satisfactorily handled if this legislation were being prepared in the Agriculture Department where the production as well as the marketing of wheat is thoroughly understood and where the Minister happens to be the only one representing a section of the Country where wheat is the outstanding product, and where wheat is our whole political background.

So many things inadvertently happen which have an important political bearing in the West when wheat is handled outside the Department of Agriculture, that it is almost impossible to keep things right in that section of Canada. If we had full control over the matter and were free to go ahead and prepare legislation which would be complimentary to legislation provided for the handling of livestock and dairy products, I am certain we could settle much of the controversy which goes on from time to time with regard to the marketing of farm products without transgressing any of the principles of liberalism. When livestock and dairy products are being handled in one Department and wheat in another it is almost impossible to keep feeling right among agriculturists in the different parts of Canada.

I would respectfully suggest that the statement which you made last Session to the House on a division of authority as between the two Departments, indicates that all matters having to do with the handling of wheat while it is in this country should rest with the Department of Agriculture.

Again I would state that I do not wish to press the matter but would point out that we are now in a position to proceed to establish a permanent policy in relation to the handling of wheat which I think could be put over with the producers of Western Canada.[6]

ACREAGE PAYMENTS

As soon as he had his co-operative wheat marketing ligislation on the way toward approval, Gardiner began to search for a solution to the problem he had pointed up that any subsidy element in the initial payment rewarded those producers having good crops while leaving others with poor crops on relief. This had been Bennett's problem with the 5 cent bonus. It was obvious that if the same subsidy monies were distributed on some other basis greater equity in the distribution might be achieved. Even while Premier Bracken was winding up his conference on markets for western farm products with a concerted plea for the retention of 80-cent price guarantee, Gardiner was devising a system of acreage payments graduated by the degree of crop failure and also by the prevailing level of wheat prices. As Mr. Chester Bloom, Ottawa correspondent of the *Winnipeg Free Press* reported:

Faced with the payment this year of possibly $40,000,000 or more bonus to prairie wheat growers — a difference between the world market price of wheat and the government's guarantee of 80 cents a bushel to producers — ministers most interested in solving Canada's greatest economic problem are considering alternative methods of dealing with the question next year.

Two new proposals are under scrutiny. Briefly, one envisages putting the wheat pools back on the job of co-operative marketing of wheat, plus a government guarantee of a minimum price at a reasonably average world market level. The other, much more complicated, would be based on two factors: A sliding scale of government guaranteed payments increasing as the world price of wheat fell below a fixed level but paid on a percentage of normally cultivated acreage instead of seeded land. Both proposals will be discussed in more detail in a later article.

Each of the still somewhat nebulous schemes, however, would tend to put bonusing of wheat production upon a basis more equitable than mere quantity output. Perhaps more important still they would operate in time

---
[6]*Ibid.*

gradually to separate the bonusing of wheat production from the problem of agriculture relief with which it is now inextricably tangled. . . .[7]

Bloom followed up this report by another on February 3, 1939, to the effect that:

As described last December in the Winnipeg Free Press, a new plan for aiding prairie wheat growers instead of fixing a guaranteed price is under consideration by the cabinet council. The main objectives are two: First, to avoid encouraging acreage increase by bonusing and, second, to provide aid for the small farmer who loses his crop and can receive no benefit from any fixed marketing price. . . .[8]

PRELUDE TO THE LEGISLATION

In the speech from the throne on January 12, 1939, grain legislation was referred to in a very limited way: "Bills will be introduced to regulate grain exchanges along the lines laid down in the report of the royal commission on grain marketing, to revise the Canada Grain Act, and to assist further in the marketing of farm products."[9]

But, as Gardiner continued to press his proposals in cabinet, Mackenzie King observed:

A little time was taken later with considering agricultural policy. While I do not altogether like Gardiner's proposals which head rather far in the direction of State control and guarantee, I nevertheless feel that some bending below the storm is necessary to let us hold our own in these times. That the trend to more in the way of Government control is inevitable; to resist what seems reasonable in the light of conditions as they have developed in other parts of the world would mean that we would simply lose power to some extreme party in a manner which, in the long run, would prove disastrous to the country.[10]

Two days later, after another cabinet session, King wrote:

Attended Council. Got agreement on agricultural policy as outlined in statement by Gardiner, Council accepting my view as, oddly enough, I had dictated it before going — with reference to wisdom of bowing somewhat before the storm of Government control and guarantee. Besides I have a good deal of faith in Gardiner's judgment though money in public policies is not as much a consideration to him as it should be. Dunning is seeking to safeguard that side.[11]

The cabinet decision on February 15, 1939, paved the way for Gardiner's major policy statement on the following day in the house, in response to opposition queries about the government's 1939 wheat policy. In his statement, Gardiner reviewed the 1935-37 experience almost word for word as he had done before the Saskatchewan pool delegates and the reasons for setting the 1938 payment. Then he digressed into the incidence of the subsidy element in the payment. He produced tables of the number of municipalities in which producers would receive little or no benefit from the bonus because of crop failure. Out of a total payment from the treasury

[7] *Winnipeg Free Press,* December 22, 1938.
[8] *Ibid.,* February 3, 1939.
[9] *House of Commons Debates,* January 12, 1939, p. 4.
[10] *King Diary,* February 13, 1939.
[11] *Ibid.,* February 15, 1939.

which he estimated then at $48,000,000 he calculated that Saskatchewan producers would receive only $18,000,000 in comparison with those in Alberta (with its smaller wheat acreage) who would receive $22,800,000. Then Gardiner continued:

Three years ago when we came into office a wheat board had been set up under the Wheat Board Act of 1935. The government was of the opinion that this legislation only provided a means for dealing with an emergency created through the methods followed during previous years in attempting to market Canadian wheat under existing world conditions. It was therefore decided to appoint a royal commission to hold sittings throughout Canada and elsewhere and to report upon past and present methods of marketing wheat as well as make recommendations of policy for the future. The commission has reported and recommended the continuance of the open market system, regulation of the grain exchange and encouragement of the pool system of marketing as an alternative to the open market which might be utilized by producers.

Between 1935 and now we have had a continuation of crop failures which has necessitated government assistance. It is now evident that marketing legislation alone will not solve the problems of the wheat growing areas. It is evident that an area which produced the wealth of the period from 1922 to 1928 must be utilized to the fullest possible extent in the effort to develop a nation of home builders. . . .

The objective of this government has been and will continue to be to set up as many homes as can possibly be maintained on farms in the prairie section of western Canada. We believe that to do so will assist in solving our labour problem, our railway problem and every other national problem. . . .

Three years of experience with the Wheat Board Act of 1935 has shown that it is legislation which can only be helpful to deal with a marketing emergency, and could not form the basis for a permanent system of marketing. The present year has shown that it does not provide an equitable method of dealing with the emergency created through drought and grasshoppers. The minimum price per bushel results in those having most receiving most and those having no crop receiving nothing.

Realizing that the present legislation does not offer a solution for our marketing problems and does not provide a means of dealing equitably with the difficulties which stand in the way of home building on the prairies, we intend to introduce legislation which will carry out as far as possible the recommendations of the Turgeon commission, which were:

First, that the government should remain out of the grain trade and our wheat should be marketed by means of the futures market system.

Second, that the grain exchange should be placed under proper supervision.

Third, that encouragement be given to the creation of cooperative marketing associations or pools.

May I repeat that it is our intention to bring down legislation which we hope will make effective all of those recommendations. In addition, we intend to deal by legislation with another phase of the subject which has not been dealt with particularly by the Turgeon commission. We intend to introduce a bill to deal with emergencies, which legislation we hope will make home building on the prairies more secure. This bill will be drafted on the principle that assistance will be given in proportion to need, calculated on an acreage basis, and so adjusted as to encourage home building and maintenance rather then increased wheat production. . . .[12]

[12]*House of Commons Debates*, February 16, 1939, pp. 1036-1037.

Gardiner's statement touched off a massive protest by resolution and petition in the west against the demise of the wheat board, as the cabinet wheat committee awaited the presentation of the Bracken brief. Bracken's western committee on markets and agricultural readjustment had met in Regina, January 31, February 1, 1939, and in Saskatoon, February 14, to prepare its submission to the federal cabinet. Although the issues were of primary concern to the cabinet wheat committee, Euler was anxious that as many ministers as possible should receive the delegation, and the prime minister arranged for the meeting to take place on March 1 in his east block office with ten ministers present, including himself. All the members of Bracken's committee attended, and Mr. L. W. Brockington read the committee's submission. In essence, it recommended in connection with the 1939-40 crop year (a) continuation of the wheat board, (b) a guarantee initial payment of at least 80 cents, (c) subsidiary assistance to coarse grain producers, and (d) assistance through crop insurance or other income support to producers adversely affected by crop failure.[13]

The favorable impression which the western committee's representations had made upon the prime minister was reflected in Mackenzie King's diary notation:

Was at the office at 10.30, and along with colleagues, received a delegation from Western Canada headed by Premier Bracken and composed of representatives of organizations having to do with grain production in Western Canada.

Brockington read the statement of the Committee which was the one that along with Bracken, considered Western grain growing problems at Regina and Saskatoon, some months ago. It was as fine a delegation as I have ever listened to. The material was admirably prepared and splendidly presented. I think every Minister was deeply impressed by the presentation which was most helpful. Was delighted to see the farmers getting themselves into the position where they could hold themselves against industrialists of large cities. I felt in the main they were right in their presentations.

When I spoke at the end, I stressed the necessity of viewing present day problems in the light of the fact that the world is going through a period of transition; that we must distinguish between the normal and the abnormal; the immediate situation and the long range policy. What is for relief, and what is for agricultural adjustment. These points were all stressed in statements made. One of the delegates said to me, as they went away, that they had seen they had been understood in their presentation.

It was an intellectual treat to listen to what was said, and one felt one was getting a really splendid picture of the whole situation in relation of Western Canada to the rest of Canada. One felt the strength of self government where men could present a case of the kind to a Ministry and help a Ministry formulate policies in the light of best available experience.

I felt proud and pleased with the way in which they all spoke of what the Government had done, and how we had really saved a terrible situation in Western Canada by our action. Instead of talking of lack of leadership, the country would have done well to hear the kind of things that were being said by this delegation today. I let the delegates go and had the Ministers remain till one o'clock.[14]

---

[13]For the text of the Western Committee's first submission, see *House of Commons Debates*, May 10, 1939, pp. 3845-3848.

[14]*King Diary*, March 1, 1939.

Mackenzie King also recorded that on March 3, 1939, he received a delegation from the Winnipeg grain exchange "who seemed more favorable to Gardiner's legislation than to the views expressed by the Bracken delegation".

Meanwhile, Gardiner continued to take his own soundings among pool officials, the Patterson government in Regina which Gardiner had previously led, and western Liberal members in the house. On March 10, 1939, he addressed a letter to King in which he acknowledged the pressure that had built up over his February 16 statement and how little support he had marshalled for his project of co-operative wheat marketing. He was now prepared to recommend the continuation of the wheat board, but with the subsidy element in the initial payment diverted into an acreage bonus. This was why he recommended an initial payment at 60 cents, as he wrote:

> I have just gone over my correspondence as well as the press comment, and I am satisfied that the time has come to act on our wheat policy.
>
> The present position is that the Saskatchewan Government is definitely of the opinion that the policy will win the support of our people. I have letters from our most reliable supporters who are on the ground to the same effect.
>
> The Free Press has an editorial in its issue of Wednesday, March 8th, which I think summarizes the position very well. Their suggestions are completely covered by our proposed legislation.
>
> Our Members become restless under this continuous lobby going on, but will line up almost, if not solidly, immediately the legislation can be discussed openly.
>
> Dr. Motherwell is our chief difficulty, and his concern is still that of departmental control over agriculture with authority to mark out policies.
>
> My present recommendation is that we enact the Bill to encourage the Co-operative Marketing of Wheat to be brought in on proclamation. This will place clearly before the farmers that we are prepared to assist their co-operative organizations if they are prepared to function. It will remove from us the charge that we are not friendly to co-operation. I do not think we would be called upon to put it into effect for a year of two, but it would act as a guide to discussion of permanent policy.
>
> We should enact and put into effect immediately the Act to Assist Prairie Agriculture. This is based upon the acreage bonus and will give better returns to more than half the farmers than they got last year. Those who would receive less are those with good crops which paid for their production without Government assistance. This Act gives us absolute control over expenditure for any year following 1939-40 and states exactly the outside limit of that assistance for 1939-40.
>
> I am recommending that we repeal the present Wheat Board Act, and enact a new one. The new one should leave out all unnecessary parts of the present one. There is a draft of this Bill before you. I think that in addition to what has been left out the section providing for coarse grain should be left out. The initial payment should be stated in the Act at sixty cents. This, together with the acreage assistance, would provide a living allowance for every farmer because our grant on an acreage bonus would be unattachable.
>
> The second and third Acts would form the basis of our immediate emergency policy, and the first and second an invitation to follow a permanent policy under the control of the producers.

I think this meets every legitimate request of the Bracken committee and gives the required leadership from here.

I am certain that further delay will make it more difficult to formulate policies suitable to other parts of Canada, in relation to the marketing of farm products.[15]

The editorial to which Gardiner referred read as follows:

So far as they are now known the latest plans for a revised wheat policy at Ottawa call for the retention of the pooling idea, e.g. the handling of all wheat through co-operatives, either the old pools or pools formed by elevator companies, but also for the retention of the Wheat Board which is to be a kind of central selling agency for the pools. The Wheat Board would take over all the wheat from the pools as soon as the market fell below the guaranteed initial price. As that price is likely to be as high as 70 cents instead of the 55 or 60 cents first mentioned, there is every possibility that it will be above world levels from the very beginning. The Wheat Board therefore would again handle the crop.

This brings us back to one of our original objections to the proposals made by Mr. Gardiner. Why must all farmers be forced into co-operatives in order to get the benefit of the government fixed price? If that price is to be available at all, it must be available to every farmer in Western Canada whether he joins a pool or not. This is simple justice, and removes the discrimination that would exist otherwise.

But apart from that important consideration it is worth asking why, if the Wheat Board is to be the effective operating organization, is there any need to insist upon the formation of a whole new series of pools? Is the Government insistent upon forcing compulsory pooling upon the western farmers? If so, why? What value is there in that idea? Above all, under conditions as they are envisaged this year, why should an extra piece of machinery be inserted between the Wheat Board and the producer? The farmers, apparently, are not to sell direct to the Board. They are to be made to deliver to pools. The pools will get the initial price from the Board and pay it over, the Board assuming all expenses and storage charges, etc., just as it did this year. It seems curious that, under these conditions, there remains this insistence on the creation of pools when they would only be agents of the Wheat Board, without any scope of independent action on their own.

Apart from these two apparent features of the new plan, there is something to be said for the idea of combining a lower initial price with some form of acreage subsidy. After the Saskatoon meeting of the Western Wheat Committee, the Free Press expressed some disappointment that its recommendations involved maintenance of the 80-cent fixed price, plus a crop insurance scheme. The reason for that disappointment was that this newspaper believes that (world conditions being as difficult as they are) the 80-cent fixed price was too high to be either politically or economically defensible. Politically, we believe that eastern protests will eventually destroy it. It is too vulnerable.

Economically, we believe it follows far too closely the principle that "to him that hath shall be given." The farmer who gets a crop gets 80 cents a bushel (minus the usual freight and grade deductions of course). The farmer without a crop gets nothing. The fixed price, therefore, works all to the benefit of the farmer who has something to sell, and does nothing for the man who has seeded his acreage and cultivated it well, only to suffer a complete loss from one of the hazards of agriculture, drought, pests, rust, and so on.

[15] *King Papers.*

This was the reason which inclined a large body of western opinion to support some form of acreage bonus, which would spread the amount spent in federal aid to a distressed industry more equitably than it was being distributed by means of the 80-cent fixed price. And for this reason it may be that there is soundness in some revision of policy which would combine a lower fixed price (or initial price, if the unnecessary pooling feature is retained) with a scheme of acreage subsidy.

A good argument can be built up for the abandonment of the fixed price altogether and its substitution solely by a scheme based on acreage. But it may be that there are considerations political in nature which would make this undesirable, apart from the excellent simplicity of the 80-cent fixed price scheme, a simplicity which undoubtedly lessens the chance of administrative abuse even though economically it is subject to criticism.

In any event, it is apparent that no final decision has yet been reached. The re-drafted legislation has not yet been presented to Parliament. The problem remains in the discussion stage, and there is a great deal to be said for holding it there as long as possible, in order that select committees can study the plan and possible alternatives thoroughly.[16]

Gardiner's proposals came before cabinet again on March 16; some progress was made without settling the issue. Mackenzie King's diary notation for that day revealed principally the issue which had arisen over Gardiner's demand, with Motherwell's support, that he take over the responsibility for the administration of the Canada grain act. As King observed: "at Council, discussed at some length Gardiner's bills and made some headway with them. . . . He was ready to go out West at Easter to get his policies through. I am determined to make Euler give in to him on the administration of the Grain Act, which I think will do more to help him personally and all of us politically than anything else."[17]

While the legislative program remained to be decided, King also noted a discussion which had taken place in the Liberal caucus:

Johnson and Tucker were urging that if we could not get 70¢ wheat in the West, and additional allowances for poor crops, the West would forget all we had done for them, and we could not hope to carry any seats there. As I listened to them, I was wondering how much we could count on any quarter at this time, and whether the statement I had made this afternoon while helping in one direction, might not cost us heavily in others. I said to them all one could do in a situation such as the present, was what one believed to be right in the light of existing conditions as one knows them. Personally, I fear more and more that doing anything for the sake of winning at the polls is the utmost folly unless what is being done is, in itself, the right and the proper course to take regardless of political consequences.[18]

The extent to which the council members, notably the members of the cabinet wheat committee, were divided on the issue of the legislative program was revealed in King's diary notation of March 21:

At Council, the time was taken up mostly with considering Gardiner's Bill for assistance to farmers—a measure on which it was quite impossible to get unanimity in the Cabinet. Crerar, decidedly of one view. Dunning, of another. Gardiner, of yet another. Euler opposed to all three. Ilsley unable to agree to any of the three. I frankly confess that while I thought I had

[16] *Winnipeg Free Press*, March 8, 1939.
[17] *King Diary*, March 16, 1939.
[18] *Ibid.*, March 20, 1939.

understood the problem at one time, I had now become so confused as to not be able to say what the consensus of view was, or to give any decision that seemed to be at all representative. Dunning finally suggested that Gardiner should be given a chance to see what he could do with his Bill and probably the Senate would defeat it, in which event we would be justified possibly in continuing the Wheat Board. The understanding in the Cabinet was that he would be given this opportunity on condition that he did not ask a guaranteed price for wheat, above 60¢, to be spoken of in discussion of his further supplementary measures.

This afternoon, I called in Mr. Motherwell to talk about his differences of view with Gardiner. Found him very strong for a Wheat Board and more concerned about that than turning over administration of Grain Act to Gardiner which he was so strong on formerly. . . .

I had Euler come in to discuss the transfer of the Grain Act. He tried to link it up with appointment to the Senate. Was agreeable to my making the transfer after the Session. Did not like it while the Session was on because of reflection on himself. . . .

Had Gardiner come in to go over my conversations with Motherwell and Euler, and suggested a reconsideration by him of continuing the Wheat Board. I agreed that having given the farmers 80¢ guarantee, to cut that down to 60 while the election is on, would mean a pretty certain loss of seats. Gardiner, however, seemed to feel that he was right in his own judgment. He is not only Minister of Agriculture but a former Premier in a Western province, and I think he knows the West as well as anyone. I feel, in such a situation, there is nothing left to do but to accept his advice and let him proceed.[19]

Although no immediate action ensued on the transfer of the Canada grain act to the department of agriculture, the issue remained alive as the cabinet gave approval to the 1939 legislative program, including a 60-cent initial payment for the 1939 crop and an acreage subsidy in areas of low yield. On March 24, 1939, the legislative process commenced in the house when Euler introduced a resolution for the supervision and regulation of trading in grain futures by a supervisor to be appointed under the jurisdiction of the board of grain commissioners. Gardiner also introduced two resolutions, the first to provide for a levy on all grain marketed and to make other sums available to be used in making acreage payments in emergent conditions, and the second to encourage co-operative marketing by guaranteeing the initial payments of co-operative associations and elevator companies. On March 27, 1939, Euler moved first reading of a bill covering an extensive revision of the Canada grain act, and also first reading of a bill amending the Canadian wheat board act to provide for a statutory 60-cent initial payment in lieu of one set by the board with the approval of the governor in council. Both Gardiner and Euler made it clear that with the exception of the periodic revision of the Canada grain act which was currently being undertaken, all of the other proposed legislation was interrelated in the formulation of a permanent wheat policy, as distinct from the temporary emergency character of the 1935 Canadian wheat board act. Another related bill to encourage the co-operative marketing of coarse grains and farm products, other than wheat, was introduced by Gardiner on April 6. This was the companion piece to his bill respecting the co-operative

[19]*Ibid.,* March 21, 1939.

marketing of wheat and it gave expression to Gardiner's endeavour to have the marketing of all farm products placed on the same footing. The interrelation of these bills within a comprehensive marketing program should be kept in mind as the several pieces of legislation are examined in turn.

ACT TO AMEND THE CANADIAN WHEAT BOARD ACT, 1935

At first reading, the bill made statutory provision for an initial payment of 60 cents for the 1939-40 crop year, and the principle of paying out any surplus to producers through participation certificates was retained. By specifying the initial payment in the bill the government sought parliamentary approval for this amount, thereby allaying the criticism in eastern Canada which arose the previous year when the amount had been determined by the governor in council. Sixty cents was in line with market prices prevailing at the time. This amount had been put into the bill on Gardiner's recommendation, and it took into account a diversion of federal funds from support of the initial payment into the acreage bonus being legislated into the prairie farm assistance program.

The reaction to the announcement of the 60-cent payment on March 27 was as pronounced as that which greeted Gardiner's first policy statement on February 16. The Saskatchewan wheat pool circulated petitions at a time when seasonal road conditions were at their worst, and succeeded in obtaining the signatures of 155,000 producers urging retention of the 80-cent payment. As reports of western dissatisfaction poured in, the debate over the legislative program flared up again in cabinet. King's reaction was that the issue should be resolved in the cabinet wheat committee, or else abandoned, as he noted in his diary: "At Council, some of Gardiner's legislation was again discussed without much unanimity. I informed the Committee to get agreement on it before bringing it back to Council, and told that failing reasonable agreement, the legislation would have to be dropped."[20]

But the argument was pursued in cabinet two days later when Mackenzie King observed:

Attended Council. Some discussion on Wheat policy. I am far from sure that Gardiner is right in believing that we can get Western Canada to accept favourably legislation which will reduce price to be guaranteed farmers for wheat from 80¢ as it is now under the Wheat Board, to 60¢. I am afraid this legislation if it carries will cost us many seats in Western Canada. It is right enough in itself but having regard to the circumstances that brought the legislation into being in the first instance, it will be, I fear, a sort of suicide to proceed with it. My own feeling at the moment is that changes will come in the course of discussion in Parliament, possibly through action of the Senate respecting part of our legislation.

Both Crerar and Dunning think Gardiner's judgment is wholly wrong and most of the members seem to share this view. Bracken, I think, has a clearer view of the situation.[21]

Because of the differences of opinion, Gardiner, Crerar and the western members took advantage of the upcoming Easter weekend to visit their

---

[20]*Ibid.*, April 3, 1939.
[21]*Ibid.*, April 5, 1939.

constituencies and other contacts in the west to take soundings. Crerar returned to Ottawa with a pessimistic report which he submitted in his personal and confidential letter of April 13, 1939, to King:

The Bills relating to legislation on wheat will be before Council within the next few days. If the measures, in their present form, are carried through the House, there is no doubt whatever in my mind of the political results that will follow. On the basis of the present proposals I think it certain that we would lose at least from eight to ten seats in Manitoba. I spent last Saturday and Sunday in Winnipeg and talked there with several people whose judgment I value in matters political. One of these had just returned a few days previously from Alberta and Saskatchewan. The price matter is not one in which alone the farmers are interested, but the whole business community as well. The seats we would lose in Manitoba would go, in my opinion, with possibly a few exceptions, to the C.C.F.

I do not profess to speak for Saskatchewan. There, the acreage bonus plan makes an appeal in the southern part of the province, where they have had repeated crop failures: in the northern part of the province I imagine the feeling would be much the same as it is in Manitoba. The agitation which has developed all over the Prairies, in the last month particularly, cannot wholly be overcome unless the price were fixed at the same level as last year.

We should fix the price to the Wheat Board at not less than Seventy Cents a bushel. There might be some modification of the acreage bonus plan lessening the liability on the Treasury. I think we could add that any wheat which was taken in at Seventy Cents would be for the account of the Board; that is to say, if the Board realized on the average a price higher than Seventy Cents it would retain the surplus thus created.

This Seventy Cents would be on the basis of One Northern grade. In ordinary years, the average of the grades is somewhere between Two and Three Northern, at a discount of probably Five or Six Cents a bushel. If we take the average freight rate of Fourteen Cents a bushel, plus the One Cent a bushel commission charge for handling, plus Two Cents a bushel for elevator charges and weighing and inspection fees, the average net price to the farmer, after all these deductions and the allowance for the average of the grades have been considered, would be around Forty-Eight Cents a bushel.

I propose to mention in Council the matter of a processing tax on flour consumed in Canada. This flour consumption represents approximately forty million bushels of wheat. If flour prices were fixed to the Canadian consumer on the basis of Dollar wheat with, say, a price level of Sixty Cents at Fort William, this would provide approximately Sixteen Million Dollars as an offset to any loss the Treasury would sustain. This appears to me to be a reasonable basis for the price of flour in Canada.

If the wheat price is left at Sixty Cents, as suggested now, there will be—

(1) The political repercussions.

(2) The inability of farmers to pay their operating expenses, exclusive of interest on mortgage debts — an important matter to Life Insurance Companies —

(3) The effect produced on manufacturing and distributing businesses of the Dominion.

There is one other point. If Europe should again be thrown into a general war of several years' duration, the question of food supplies would sooner or later become serious. As in the last war, this is one place where Canada could help. Is there not, then, some justification for maintaining our wheat economy on this ground alone, if for no other?

Generally speaking, our wheat producers are in this plight because of world forces over which Canada has no control. There is scarcely another country in the world that is not, directly or indirectly, aiding its wheat producers. Much as I dislike Government intervention in these matters and much as I dislike anything in the nature of Government subsidies or bonuses, I don't think we can afford to ignore the realities of the situation facing our wheat producers.[22]

On the following day, Mackenzie King noted some progress, and that the cabinet was moving closer to agreement on an upward revision of the initial payment, as he wrote: "Attended Council from 12 to 1.30. Much time taken in discussing agricultural policy, members of Government drawing a little closer together. Looks like agreement on a 70¢ rate for wheat in the West."[23]

His dilemma over the problem was reflected in King's diary entry of April 20:

Covered a few letters before attending Council. Discussion largely upon budget matters and, in part, on agricultural programme, trying to find some means to overcome price fixing in connection with outlays by way of relief to Western farmers — an extremely difficult matter. The Party is getting much divided, both in Council and in the House, and I fear also in the country over this business of fixing minimum prices for wheat, dairy products, fish, etc., etc. It seems necessary in times like the present, and is perhaps better than doling out relief in other ways. It is, however, a bad precedent and something which it will be hard to get rid of.[24]

Bracken's committee also took up the cause and prepared a second submission to the government which it presented on April 24 in the prime minister's office with ten members of the cabinet in attendance. On the question of the level of the initial payment, the committee said:

We submitted to you our considered conclusion that the continuance of a guarantee of not less than 80 cents for No. 1 Northern Wheat is the fairest and most feasible method available for the 1939 crop by which western agriculture can be partially saved from the national and particularly from the international conditions which those who depend upon wheat-growing had obviously not created and were powerless to control.

In support of our case we advanced arguments which can very briefly be summarized as follows:

(a) The west, the expansion and development of which made possible the growth of modern Canada, has made a tremendous contribution by way of purchase of goods and the payment of tariffs to the prosperity of Eastern Canada and is justified in asking, as a partial return, for national support in its own special emergency as a reciprocal national contribution.

(b) This request is particularly reasonable and its granting particularly essential at the present time, because of the ever present necessity of selling some two-thirds of our output in international markets where we receive no protection for our product.

(c) The assistance actually rendered to the wheat industry over a period of years has been infinitesmal in relation to its contribution to the production of national wealth.

[22]*King Papers.*
[23]*King Diary,* April 14, 1939.
[24]*Ibid.,* April 20, 1939.

(d) The same economic disaster which threatened our wheat growers in 1938 is still as near in 1939 unless the government is prepared to continue the same measure of justified support.

(e) An 80 cent wheat price which means an estimated average price of 57 cents on the western farm does not bring prosperity, but in the main only a restricted level of almost bare subsistence. It is no more than equivalent to the unsupported domestic price obtained by eastern farmers for similar grains.

(f) A determined national effort to meet the western emergency is also necessary to maintain a satisfactory national credit position which would be seriously jeopardized by a breakdown in the financial structure of Western Canada inevitably resultant from an abandonment of western agriculture to the prevailing disastrously low wheat prices.

(g) The wheat industry should not be expected to bear the impossible simultaneous double burden of high tariff and other costs and low wheat prices.

(h) Any disturbance of the balance of western agriculture with its natural concentration upon wheat growing must be also a devastating disturbance of eastern agriculture. It is in the national interest to prevent a disorderly retreat from wheat.

(i) The wheat board plan coupled with adequate price protection, in spite of some inequalities which are at least no less inevitable in any alternative plan, is the simplest and most effective method of tiding over in a period of emergency a temporarily depressed industry.[25]

The brief then continued with comments on other aspects (referred to later) of the total legislative package. Messrs. D. G. McKenzie, Howard Wright, Paul Farnalls, G. Bickerton, J. H. Wesson and the Honourable J. G. Taggart spoke on behalf of the delegation, following which Mr. Wesson presented the petition signed by 155,000 farmers for the retention of the 80-cent payment. Messrs. Gardiner and Dunning responded for the wheat committee, before Mackenzie King addressed the meeting. One of the committee members had made a remark to which King took umbrage and it prompted him to make an eloquent and quite different statement in substance from the one he had delivered at the conclusion of the previous meeting with the Bracken committee, as King recorded:

. . . Then to my office to meet with delegation from Western Canada headed by Premier Bracken regarding agricultural policy. A large delegation. Had most of the Cabinet present.

After listening to brief read by Brockington, and further representations, and having one or two of the ministers ask questions, I then told the delegation very plainly that they had stated their problem and that I wanted them now to see mine and the problem of our Government. I spoke first of one reference made by a member of the delegation, to what our legislation amounted to for the locality he represented — that it was like holding of an empty bag with a hole at each end. I asked if that was all the thanks and appreciation the Government got for efforts to help Western Canada. He was quick to reply that was just a reference as to how the people felt in one small community. I mentioned that as regards delegation such as this one, of which he was a member, he should not then put forward that kind of an argument to the Cabinet. I then pointed out he had spoken of the two problems — the position of industry and relief as being separate, and said I wholly agreed with

[25]*Second Submission of the Western Committee on Markets and Agricultural Readjustment,* April 24, 1939.

that. I pointed out how we were trying to meet both. I then asked a question of the delegation, whether if this were not an emergency year, they would favour our programme as outlined. Brockington came back and indicated approval of certain features but made no reference to the price of wheat, thereby leaving an implication they would still want. 80¢.

I drew attention to that at once. Pointed out how unfair it was to take the part of the programme that was acceptable, and leave the other part which it was necessary to keep in order to get approval of the whole from other parts of Canada. I then launched out that the delegation, in their demands, represented those only of two or three provinces, pointing out that to get anything through in the H. of C., I had to consider what would be supported by our own following, and by the Opposition, from each of the other provinces. I turned to my own Ministers and pointed out that I could not compel them to accept the views of Western Canada and ignore the views of the provinces they represented. I spoke very strongly against the attempt to bring pressure on the Cabinet by the signing of petitions as had been done and sent to members. I told them if that was starting in one province, it would start equally in the others, and we would begin to have this country divided east against west. I then pointed out to my folder and told them if they could see some of the despatches that were within its covers, they would realize we would be fortunate if we escaped an appalling world situation within the next few weeks or months or, at very best, within a year.

I pointed out too the record of our Government in the past in meeting the Western situation; they knew Mr. Gardiner and of his desire to further the West, and had reason to believe I was anxious to show my appreciation, being a member of a western constituency. This should be sufficient guarantee of our desire to meet the West without seeking to drive us into an impossible position.

My colleagues told me after the meeting that it was the best speech I had ever made, and members of the delegation came up and shook hands. I was told by some that it had been worth while for the delegation to come to Ottawa a second time to hear what I had to say. I felt the moment had come to launch out and get an understanding of our agricultural policy.[26]

On the following day in cabinet, Gardiner and Ilsley came into head on collision, and it took Crerar as well as King to break up the conflict. But before the cabinet meeting, King met with Premier Bracken, as his diary entry recorded:

I left early for the office to talk with Bracken, of Manitoba. I felt, as he was talking, that while anxious to have it appear that he was most friendly to myself and the Government, in reality, what he said was so phrased so as to prepare the way for him, if need be, to go out on his own in agricultural policies which would appeal to western Manitoba. . . .

We had another difficult meeting of the Cabinet, dealing for the last time with agricultural policy. Members discussed the situation for an hour very calmly, but with Gardiner very definitely set in his own way, and Euler and Ilsley equally so in theirs. Finally, I said it was clear to me there were only one or two courses: one was to drop some of the proposed legislation and simply let the Wheat Board act stand, applying it in July next, probably at 80 cent minimum, or taking the proposed legislation, making the minimum 70 cents, and agreeing upon some acreage payments for the relief part, extending the legislation to cover Ontario and Quebec and fixing a penalty which would prevent persons receiving guaranteed rate from making beyond a certain sum

[26]*King Diary*, April 24, 1939.

out of the public treasury. Gardiner said if the first course were adopted there was only one thing he could do. I asked him what it was, and he said to resign. That caused Ilsley to flare up, and say he would have to consider very seriously if he would not have to take that course if the other alternative were adopted. He did not like trying to compromise at the expense of public treasury, etc. I said we had allowed Gardiner to go to the West and put over his policy, and I thought we would have to stand by him, but that he would have to be reasonable himself. To Ilsley I said that I felt sure once he saw what was back of the whole discussion, namely, a desire to support western industry in the teeth of changed world conditions as affecting western Canada through markets closing and population being practically engaged in the one industry, that he would see the reasonableness of meeting the situation this year in a way that would tide over the worst. Finally, at Crerar's quiet suggestion, referred the matter to the four members of the Wheat Board: Euler, Ilsley, Gardiner, and Crerar, and Howe to be added, to see if Gardiner's Bill could not be framed on the lines I had indicated, with the understanding that the relief would be fixed not on the 15 year basis, as he suggested, or on the five, as previously suggested, but on 12. I had suggested 10, but other members of Council thought it made little difference as between 10 and 12. The matter was left in this way.[27]

In the end, cabinet decided to accept Crerar's recommendation of 70 cents, which entailed a compensating reduction in the scale of Gardiner's proposed acreage payments. It rejected Crerar's suggestion that the participation certificates be dropped, which would have brewed another political storm, and it added two other features to make the 70-cent payment acceptable across Canada. One was to place a limitation on deliveries to the board to avoid criticism that the payment benefited large-scale producers unduly, and the other was to extend the provisions of the wheat board act to producers in eastern Canada. To get these amendments into the bill, Euler obtained the consent of the house on May 2, for a reprinting of the bill. When it came up for second reading on May 10, the debate on the prairie farm assistance bill had already taken place, and Euler said:

I shall content myself, therefore, with stating very briefly the provisions of the bill. It speaks for itself and is perfectly clear, whether hon. members agree with it or not. The most important part of the bill deals with the removal of the power of the government, upon the recommendation of the wheat board, to fix an advanced payment, usually at the beginning of the crop season. That clause is replaced with one by which the bill itself fixes the advance price definitely at 70 cents a bushel, basis No. 1 northern Fort William. In other respects the bill is practically as it was originally. That is to say, the provisions are practically the same as they were before, with, of course, the participation clause remaining.

There are, however, two other clauses, one of which might be said to limit the application of the present wheat board act, and the other to broaden or extend it. The first one limits to 5,000 the number of bushels which may be sold by any one producer to the wheat board. The other provides for the extension of the application of the provisions of the bill to what is known as the eastern provinces.[28]

[27]*Ibid.*, April 25, 1939.
[28]*House of Commons Debates*, May 10, 1939, p. 3842.

The debate continued over the next four sittings. When the vote was taken on second reading on May 11, five western Liberals, Dr. H. R. Fleming, Harry Leader, J. A. MacMillan, the Honourable W. R. Motherwell, and W. J. Ward voted against the government, which otherwise had no difficulty in mustering an affirmative vote. Third reading was given and the bill passed on May 15. Royal assent was obtained on June 3.[29] Essential features incorporated in the act were:

1. A statutory initial payment, or "sum certain", of 70 cents, plus the issuance of nontransferable participation certificates. To give Alberta and western Saskatchewan producers the benefit of lower freight costs to Vancouver, the initial payment was based on Vancouver as well as on Fort William-Port Arthur.

2. A limitation of 5,000 bushels upon deliveries to the board by any one producer, beyond which no producer had access to the board's initial payment, with violations subject to prescribed penalties.

3. Extension of the provisions of the wheat board act to wheat produced in the eastern division. This clause replaced one which had given the governor in council authority to extend the provisions of the act to oats, barley, rye and flaxseed, and which was now repealed.

By removing from the government the responsibility of approving the initial payment, King had transferred to parliament (and more broadly to the people of Canada) that responsibility. In the light of the criticism the government had generated in the east over the fixing of the 1938 payment, this represented a shrewd political response in the cause on national unity. By extending the benefits of the act to Ontario wheat growers, the government removed the basis for the charges of discrimination which had been made. Also, by limiting the application of the act to deliveries of not more than 5,000 bushels by any one producer, or combination of producers operating a farm or group of farms as a unit, the government sought to allay criticism that the benefit accrued unduly, at taxpayers' expense, to large operators. Because of the difficulties encountered in the administration of the 5,000 bushel limitation, this provision was dropped, by amendment to the act, a year later.

PRAIRIE FARM ASSISTANCE ACT, 1939

Gardiner had persistently pointed out that the Canadian wheat board act by itself was defective for the purposes of implementing a permanent wheat policy. A voluntary board, without having producers under contract to deliver to it was bound to be inactive when prices were good, uncertain of the quantities of wheat that would be delivered to it if the initial payment was close to the market and bound to incur losses when prices were weak. In addition to these general criticisms, the 1938 experience had demonstrated the inequitable distribution of benefits among farmers who had good crops and those who had none. Thus, if some of the subsidy paid out through the initial payment on a bushel basis were to be paid out on an acreage basis in areas of partial or total crop failure, the total distribution could be made more equitably. Nevertheless, the definition of the conditions under which acreage subsidies would be paid was necessarily arbitrary and flexible, and

[29]*3 George VI*, Chap. 39.

a long debate ensued on the equity of the terms proposed by the government. All four parties, Liberals, Conservatives, C.C.F., and Social Credit took positions in the debate. Much concern was expressed whether the new legislation would produce as much additional farm income as was taken away by lowering the board's initial payment from 80 to 70 cents. Moreover, the bill's proposed levy of one percent on all grain deliveries to contribute toward the acreage payments was contested. Gardiner was confident that the total subsidy provided by the combined legislation would not be reduced. As it worked out, when the board's initial payment was raised from 60 to 70 cents, 50 cents per acre had to be taken off the acreage subsidies. In its final form, the act took into account both economic and crop emergencies as it provided two different bases for relief:

1. National Emergency. Declaration by the governor in council of any crop year in which the average price is less than 80 cents as an emergency year. The 1939-40 crop year was declared by statute to be one. In an emergency year, on up to half the cultivated acreage or not more than 200 acres per farm, the minister could make the following payments, based on township average yields per acre:

Bushels per acre	Payments per acre
8 - 12	10¢ for each cent or fraction thereof not exceeding 10, by which the average price is less than 80¢.
4 - 8	$1.50
0 - 4	$2.00

2. Crop failure assistance. In any year that the average yield of wheat is 5 bushels per acre or less in 135 townships in Saskatchewan or 100 townships in Manitoba or Alberta, such areas may be designated as crop failure areas, in which case a minimum of $200 and up to a maximum of $500 per farm may be paid, depending upon the size of the cultivated acreage.

3. A levy of one percent to be made from the net purchase price of all grain primary marketings. Proceeds of the levy are to be used for the acreage payments, with the balance of funds required for that purpose to be paid out of the consolidated revenue fund.

Thereafter (subject to amendment and improvement from time to time) the prairie farm assistance act provided a much needed supplementary western farm income support which helped to reduce the variability in income resulting from fluctuations in yields.

WHEAT CO-OPERATIVE MARKETING ACT, 1939

The second of Gardiner's projects was government encouragement for restoration of co-operative marketing which, in time, might obviate the need for the wheat board. The idea was first mooted by Dunning in his 1937 speech and, it will be recalled, it was one of the key recommendations of the Turgeon report. What Dunning had overlooked by way of enabling legislation, the government now offered through a bill which would authorize it to guarantee the initial payment and operating expenses of any co-operative marketing association or line elevator company prepared to set up a producers' pool. Over the objections of the existing pools whose directors contended that the application of the act should be confined to producers' associations, the government maintained that its offer should be extended to line elevator companies providing similar facilities as a matter of non-discrimination. Gardiner was careful to point out that Turgeon had recommended encouragement to pools, rather than to a single pool. At the same time, the existing pools had not pressed the government for such legislation. As already mentioned, their preference was for continuation of the wheat board on an active basis. Only in the event of the board's termination were they seriously interested in reviving pooling as a means of providing an alternative choice to the open-market system. By the time the bill was introduced, Gardiner was under no illusion about the pools' lukewarm support, and Bracken's committee on which the three pools were represented was constrained to advise:

> With reference to this Bill, the Committee wishes to say that it is its unanimous opinion that under existing conditions the method proposed is impracticable and no organization could undertake to operate successfully such a selling agency as contemplated in the face of present marketing uncertainties. Individual members of our Committee will probably seek an opportunity to discuss the Bill with the Minister.[30]

In essence, the act provided that the government could enter into agreements with selling agencies established by producer co-operative associations or by line elevator companies or associations thereof owning one hundred or more country elevators, under which the government could guarantee a total of 60 cents a bushel, basis No. 1 Northern, Fort William. In turn, the central selling agencies could set initial payments below that level. In the event of loss, the agencies could recover their initial payments plus storage, carrying and transportation charges and operating expenses up to a maximum total of 60 cents a bushel. In the event of a surplus the agencies could pay, with the approval of the governor in council, the net proceeds to producers through participation certificates. The bill had a relatively easy passage and King George VI, who was in Canada on tour, gave his assent to the act on May 19, 1939.[31]

Professor G. E. Britnell has provided a convenient summary of the first year's operations under the act:

> The only reason that there was any organization under the Wheat Co-operative Marketing Act during the current crop year was the limitation on deliveries to the Board which left the larger farmers without price protection on any surplus over 5,000 bushels. At the beginning of the year when the open market price was well below seventy cents the Saskatchewan and Alberta Wheat Pools and Manitoba Pool Elevators each entered into an agreement with the Government under which an initial payment of fifty-six cents for No. 1 Northern, basis Fort William, would be made to the grower.[6] A group of companies from the North West Line Elevator Association formed the Grain Sales Agency Limited and entered into a similar agreement with the Government, as did also several other individual elevator companies.

[30] *Second Submission of the Western Committee on Markets and Agricultural Readjustment,* April 24, 1939.
[31] *3 George VI,* Chap. 34.

Thus, the wheat grower has the choice, this season, of three methods of marketing his wheat: the Wheat Board with a guaranteed advance of seventy cents a bushel for No. 1 Northern, basis Fort William, up to a maximum of 5,000 bushels; the co-operative or pooling method with a guaranteed advance of fifty-six cents,[7] No. 1 Northern, Fort William, with no limit on the amount; and the open market. The proportion of wheat sold under the various marketing methods has varied from time to time depending largely on the level of open market prices. When, as at the beginning of the season, open market prices were below Wheat Board minima practically all deliveries (up to the 5,000 bushel limit) went to the Board. On the other hand, when open market prices have been high relative to Board prices, farmers have tended to sell their wheat outright. The proportion of the total crop marketed through sales agencies organized under the Co-operative Act would have been small in any circumstances, and, since open market prices for No. 1 Northern were only below fifty-six cents for a short period at the beginning of the season, there has been little inducement, even for farmers with very large crops, to market through such agencies. It is estimated that of total deliveries this season amounting to 382,000,000 bushels (as at April 5) from seventy to seventy-five per cent has gone to the Wheat Board, not more than one per cent to sales agencies operating under the Co-operative Act, with the remainder sold on the open market.[32]

With the removal in 1940 of the 5,000 bushel limitation, this incentive for delivery to the co-operative pools was eliminated. Thereafter, these pools became dormant, and the whole experiment was terminated in 1943 when the futures market was closed.

In the demise of the co-operative system as applied to wheat marketing, it would be interesting to speculate on the course of events had the government of Canada presciently offered the facilities of the wheat co-operative marketing act before the pools ceased to accept deliveries of pooled grain in 1931 when, several years before the Canadian wheat board was reestablished, they were virtually left with no alternative but to terminate their contracts with produces and withdraw from the central selling agency. Under the prevailing conditions in 1931, undoubtedly, the pool executives would have warmly welcomed a government guarantee of pool initial payments and they might have prolonged co-operative marketing indefinitely.

AGRICULTURAL PRODUCTS CO-OPERATIVE MARKETING ACT, 1939

This was the companion legislation to the co-operative wheat marketing act, providing the same type of co-operative marketing support to all agricultural products other than wheat. For other products there was no price benchmark such as that provided in the wheat board act; therefore, to

---

[32]G. E. Britnell, "Dominion Legislation Affecting Western Agriculture, 1939", *The Canadian Journal of Economics and Political Science,* Volume 6, Number 2, May 1940, pp. 276-277. Britnell's footnotes:

[6]Manitoba Pool Elevators have not operated a pool although some Manitoba farmers have pooled wheat through the Saskatchewan Pool organization.

[7]On April 1, 1940, Grain Sales Agency announced an interim payment of fourteen cents a bushel to growers on all deliveries under the Act, bringing total payments up to the Wheat Board price.

establish reference prices below which initial payments might be set, the act specified the average wholesale price for each commodity over the three years preceding the year of production as the basis upon which the government could guarantee up to 80 percent. While this was the first co-operative marketing legislation applicable to all agricultural products other than wheat, the interest here was in its relevance to coarse grains. Bracken's committee had recommended that something be done for coarse grains and the government could point to this legislation as fulfilling that request. This act also received the King's assent on May 19, 1939.[33]

Although the pools and others negotiated with the government for some months over the establishment of coarse grains pools under this legislation, the requirements for the initial payments to be established resulted in figures so low that no agreements were signed.

GRAIN FUTURES ACT, 1939

Apart from the extensive periodic revision of the Canada grain act which was also undertaken in 1939, but which was otherwise unrelated to the grain marketing legislative package, Euler's two concerns were with the wheat board bill and a bill to provide for the supervision and regulation of trading in grain futures. The issue had hung over the futures market and policy-makers ever since the Stamp commission had discussed the problem but had made no clear-cut recommendation. It was revived by McFarland's complaints over short selling and by the special committee of the house which investigated Murray's alleged accommodation of the shorts. More recently, supervision had been endorsed by the Turgeon report and the government had approached the reluctant grain commissioners and wheat boards to take on the assignment. Eventually it was decided that the board of grain commissioners as a regulatory body was the logical choice and drafting of legislation proceeded on that basis. The law officers had the benefit of drawing on the experience of the grain futures administration in the United States. The bill enabled the board of grain commissioners to:

(a) obtain records and information from the Winnipeg grain exchange, the Winnipeg grain and produce exchange clearing association and their members on trading in grain,

(b) employ a supervisor to watch trading and to report upon conditions "prejudicial to the public interest arising from trading in grain futures",

(c) regulate margins, to fix the maximum futures commitments of any one trader, to suspend his trading privileges and to order amendments or revocation of exchange bylaws, all subject to appropriate appeals and penalties.

The act, subject to proclamation, had wide public approval and an easy passage. It also received the King's assent on May 19, and was proclaimed on August 1, 1939.[34]

But the legislation came when it was no longer really needed. Because the wheat board had accepted delivery of the entire 1938 crop it was the predominant seller in the market. Very soon war would be declared and render the legislation even less necessary. For a time there were rumors

---

[33] *3 George VI,* Chap. 28.
[34] *3 George VI,* Chap. 31.

concerning the appointment of a supervisor. Dr. T. W. Grindley's name was mentioned in a speculative news report, but no appointment was made and the act remained dormant.

SUMMARY

Altogether, the 1939 legislative program had been substantial. Although it failed in its initial objective of replacing emergency provisions with permanent legislation intended to take the government out of the wheat marketing business, the wheat board was continued with less subsidy element in its initial payment and a reasonably equitable distribution of the total government subsidy through the provisions of the prairie farm assistance act. The King administration would shortly face an election. With four years of experience under a voluntary wheat board and with benefit of a comprehensive marketing analysis by the Turgeon commission, the government had deliberately undertaken a search for a more adequate and permanent wheat marketing policy. It used the consultative process as Gardiner tested out his personal theories on the pools and on the Saskatchewan government, and as the federal government received sympathetically the representations of the Bracken committee and also took aboard features that would make its new wheat policy acceptable to all parts of Canada. In arriving at its decisions, the government was inhibited by the current financial constraints. Gardiner was justified in drawing attention to the shortcomings of the wheat board legislation as it stood, which he did in order to enlist support for his co-operative marketing and prairie farm assistance schemes. The government admittedly would have preferred to replace the wheat board with a co-operative marketing system, which still involved a government guarantee of initial payments. The timing of the transition, sooner or later, was dependent upon producer acceptance. The co-operative system seemed to offer a sounder alternative to compete with the open market than the wheat board system had so far proven. But on each occasion that the government pressed the pools to revert to their earlier role, even with the protection of a government guarantee against loss, the pools shied away. They adhered to the policy they had formulated at the time of the 1935 wheat board legislation that the government should undertake the marketing responsibilty with the guarantee of a minimum price to producers, while the pools restricted their activities to the operation of their elevator facilities and to their role as advisers to the government. Although Gardiner had done his best to persuade the pools otherwise, he confided to King in the end that the revival of co-operative marketing had failed to be accepted. In its place he recommended that a statute related thereto be enacted as a reminder to the pools of the government's preparedness to assist such a revival. Thereupon, he turned his attention to the terms upon which the wheat board legislation should be continued in conjunction with his acreage bonus scheme. In doing so, Gardiner also misjudged western sentiment by recommending too low an initial payment, in order to divert more funds into acreage payments. Consequently, the government was embarrassed by having to raise the initial payment it had originally announced. Although the government yielded to public pressure in doing so, it made a compensating reduction in the amount of the acreage bonus. Essentially, it was an issue of balancing the conflicting interests of producers in high and low yielding areas. Gardiner's intimate knowledge of conditions in southern Saskatchewan and his concern about controlling the administration of the prairie farm assistance act had influenced his initial recommendation on the transfer of funds. Crerar's soundings in Manitoba and the insurrection among western Liberals had demonstrated the extent of the error.

Two measures in the legislative package came to naught. The grain futures act remained dormant and the wheat co-operative marketing act fell into disuse, after an impressive trial period, within the next few years. On the other hand, the revised wheat board and prairie farm assistance acts represented substantial progress in search of a defensible, continuing policy. In combination, they also served the immediate purpose of assisting western agriculture equitably in a period of recognized need.

28

1939 WHEAT ADVISORY COMMITTEE MEETINGS

It will be recalled from Chapter 24 how stubbornly the cabinet wheat committee resisted involvement in the American effort to revive the international wheat agreement negotiations. Pearson's performance in blocking progress at the July 1938 meeting of the wheat advisory committee (in keeping with instructions), was instrumental in the postponement of the autumn session of the committee which the other delegations had approved. Argentina had not been represented at the July, 1938, meeting but the Americans, through diplomatic channels, had obtained the Argentine government's agreement to resumption of negotiations. Mr. F. R. Wilcox of the United States commodity credit corporation spent some time in London that autumn promoting a revival in the wheat advisory committee's activities. Matters got under way when Ambassador Joseph P. Kennedy sent notices to representatives of the 21 member governments on December 5, 1938, to the effect that the governments of Australia, Britain, France, and the United States had requested a meeting of the committee to consider the prospects for reaching agreement in principle on an international scheme. An annotated agenda and other related documents were circulated which contained the elements of an agreement on minimum prices, export quotas, surplus disposal and production control. The meeting was set for January 10, 1939. Although the department of external affairs circulated copies of the invitation and related documents to the four members of the wheat committee the ministers made no response, to the considerable exasperation of Norman Robertson who wrote the following personal memorandum to Skelton on December 30, 1938:

> In a telegram of December 5th the High Commissioner advised that a meeting of the Wheat Advisory Committee would be held in London on January 10th. In telegrams of the 6th and 7th December he cabled the agenda and a summary prepared by the Secretariat of the proposals that would be submitted for consideration. In a despatch of December 12th he forwarded copies of the United States Ambassador's communication convoking the meeting and of the official agenda.
>
> All these communications were immediately brought to the attention of the Ministers of Trade and Commerce, Finance, Agriculture, and Mines and Resources who make up the Cabinet Committee on Wheat Policy. None of

them have expressed any opinions as to who should be nominated to represent Canada at this meeting or as to what instructions should be given him. At the moment Messrs. Euler and Crerar are somewhere in the South and Mr. Gardiner is in Saskatchewan.

It is understood that the Prime Minister has been receiving representations from the Prairie Governments and from the farmers' organizations in Western Canada that a member of the Cabinet should represent Canada at this meeting. If time had allowed it the Minister of Agriculture would have been the best man to send. As matters stand the only alternative to relying on the London staff for representation would appear to be to ask McIvor, the Chairman of the Wheat Board to attend. Whether his arrangments and the sailing list at this time of year would permit him to get from Winnipeg to London by January 10th is doubtful.

More important than representation are the questions of policy arising out of the Committee's agenda — or, more accurately — out of the facts of the wheat situation. They will have to be faced and some indication of the Government's attitude toward them given our representatives. This is where the existing machinery breaks down. The Department, or group of departments, feels responsible for following the development of the international wheat situation and, consequently, none is in a position to submit recommendations regarding policy for consideration by Council. Every six months or so this situation recurs — evasive instructions are improvised — usually in this Department. Our representatives are cautioned to act as "observers", avoid all commitments but maintain a front of Canadian participation in a work that some parts of this country take very seriously (cf. the Winnipeg Conference on Wheat Marketing held this month).

It is submitted that responsibility for watching the development of the international wheat situation as a whole should be definitely fixed on some department or group of departments who could supply some kind of secretariat for the Cabinet Wheat Committee, keep them continuously advised of shifting developments that react on Government policies, and help to introduce some elements of continuity and responsibility into our handling of what is probably the most serious single economic problem confronting this country.[1]

Robertson had no way of telling that it would be more than four years before the cabinet wheat committee had a secretary, let alone an interdepartmental staff to keep it informed of developments. The first reaction to his memo came within 24 hours when a cable went off to Massey naming him head of the delegation to the January 10 meeting with L. B. Pearson, Dr. William Allen (recently appointed at Gardiner's request as Canadian agricultural commissioner at Canada House) and R. V. Biddulph as advisers.

JANUARY MEETING OF THE ADVISORY COMMITTEE

Although the delegation had been decided upon, instructions were not forthcoming until January 10, 1939, when the London meeting began. As Robertson had indicated, the wheat committee was scattered. On January 9, Mr. A. D. P. Heeney succeeded in reaching Euler who recommended that the Canadian representatives be instructed to confine themselves to the role of observers. This had been the policy in the past. But Heeney asked Robertson to have a memo ready for cabinet the following day. Robertson

[1] *King Papers.*

took the initiative by telephoning Mr. George McIvor and Dr. T. W. Grindley. The three put together a draft telegram of instructions which was not so utterly negative as Euler had proposed. Cabinet approved the draft which categorically opposed acreage limitation and price fixing but added that; "at the same time we are prepared to consider any proposals that may be put forward and suggest you communicate with us regarding any other concrete proposals on which Government view is desired."[2]

Then the telegram raised a series of detailed questions on the practicality of the proposals included in the December 5 annotated agenda. Massey furnished daily reports on the meetings which Mackenzie King read and initialled.

In the secretary's report, circulated to the meeting, Cairns had once again predicted that the world wheat carryover as of July 31, 1940, would exceed 1,300 million bushels. He deplored competitive export subsidies as neutralizing one another in the absence of coordinated international policies. Upon receipt of his instructions, Massey declared that the solution of the wheat problem must be sought by each producing country in the light of its own circumstances. His government was not convinced that acreage reduction was a practical solution. He reserved his position on the convening of a negotiating conference for the time being. On the other hand, Mr. L. W. Steere warned that the United States government would not modify its export subsidy program unless an accord was reached on concerted international action. He regarded export quotas as essential to any successful agreement, and he believed it was feasible to operate a minimum price scheme. He urged the early convening of a negotiating conference, and he was supported by the Australian, Belgian, British, French, German, Netherlands, and Swiss delegates. Carlill of the British delegation proposed to Massey privately that the four major exporting countries get together for preliminary negotiations, as they had done in 1933. In view of the overwhelming support for a wheat conference, Massey agreed in principle and indicated Canadian preparedness to participate ad referendum. McDougall proposed that a preparatory committee be established to plan the conference and to give preliminary consideration to the proposals to be submitted to it. Against some objection, Massey persuaded the others that the preparatory committee should ascertain if there was sufficient agreement to make a full conference desirable. As he reassured King by personal letter on January 13: "We, of course, will be a member of that sub-committee, and if its deliberations reveal the fact that no useful purpose will be served by a Conference, the sub-committee will have in its power to postpone action leading to the summoning of the Conference sine die."[3]

JANUARY—FEBRUARY PREPARATORY COMMITTEE MEETINGS

At the concluding meeting of the tenth session of the wheat advisory committee on January 13, 1939, the committee referred Cairns's statistical report to the preparatory committee, deleting at Massey's request Cairns's

[2]*Ibid.*
[3]*Ibid.*

observations, and over the protest of the American delegation which wanted a more positive resolution. It made the calling of a conference dependent upon the recommendation of the preparatory committee supported by a further meeting of the wheat advisory committee. The main committee referred to its preparatory committee the further consideration of the proposals on an international agreement of five years' duration with minimum prices and export quotas, plus commitments by the importing countries, such as they had given in the 1933 agreement, to lift import restrictions if prices rose. The membership of the preparatory committee included the four major exporting countries, two Danubian countries, Britain, France, Germany, and the USSR. After an organizational meeting on January 14, the preparatory committee met again on January 31. By that time, Cairns had prepared a draft heads of agreement, with explanatory notes. Members of the preparatory committee agreed to speak in their personal capacities without committing their governments but, as Massey observed, several delegates were already authorized to express their governments' views. It was agreed that the committee should hear economists J. M. Keynes and Sir William Beveridge, officials of other commodity control schemes, and representatives of the wheat and milling trades. The Canadians referred to the impracticable features they discerned in the draft heads of agreement, such as the minimum price and quota reserve proposals, but it was generally agreed that there must be provision for export quotas. Representatives of importing countries appeared to be shying away from commitments such as their governments had made in the 1933 agreement. Massey drew the government's attention to a significant draft article which would impose on exporting countries the obligation to adopt appropriate measures to prevent wheat production from exceeding quantities required for domestic consumption, export quotas and the maintenance of agreed stocks of old wheat. This was a more clearly articulated draft of the indirect production control commitment contained in the 1933 agreement, inasmuch as it was now proposed that an agreed limitation upon the amount of carryover stocks held in each exporting country must be observed, in addition to the export quota limitations.

Massey summed up the other proposals in his telegram of February 3, 1939:

Following are main proposals on which detailed views would be of great assistance:

(1) Export countries agree not to permit sale for export for 5 year period of agreement below equivalent of a basic minimum price — such equivalent to be set up by Committee of a proposed Wheat Council.

(2) Export quotas to be set for overseas countries in terms of percentage of world demand as estimated by Council less a fixed amount to be divided among other exporters.

(3) Overseas exporters' quotas to be increased by Wheat Council when United Kingdom prices remain for six weeks a certain amount above set minimum.

(4) Quarterly quotas within annual quotas.

(5) Unusable portion of quota to be surrendered into a quota reserve, or if necessary commandeered by Council for that reserve which will be allocated as Council thinks desirable.

(6) Contribution by overseas exporters to a fund for increasing wheat consumption and for relief purposes.

(7) Importers not to encourage extension of wheat areas by governmental action; to remove the measures tending to lower the quotas on bread stuffs; to initiate the reduction of tariffs and relax quantitative restrictions on imports when price not less than minimum for period of not less than 16 weeks; not to export without prior consultation with Council and not below price equivalent as set by Committee above. Importers also to agree to modify regulations governing temporary admission so that this trade will no longer enjoy any form of subsidy.

(8) Overseas exporters, in view of minimum price which makes unnecessary the payment of direct or indirect subsidies on exports, to agree not to fix domestic prices above export minimum. Temporary exporters not to subsidize exports in such a way as to encourage production beyond domestic requirements.

(9) Importers agree to consider and so far as their law permits to apply recommendations of Council against signatories which have broken agreement.[4]

On February 2, the preparatory committee met with Mr. J. M. Keynes and Sir William Beveridge who had been asked to relate papers they had recently delivered to a meeting of the British Association for the Advancement of Science to the negotiation of a wheat agreement. Keynes elaborated his buffer stocks proposal for commodities whose supplies fluctuated widely and recommended the expansion of storage facilities in the overseas exporting countries and in Britain. A central authority could be established by the participating governments to purchase stocks at a minimum price and to sell from stocks at a maximum price. Sir William Beveridge presented a trade-cycle study he had directed at Oxford in which he established a causal relation between agricultural depressions in overseas countries and resulting unemployment in Britain. His principal assistant in the study was Mr. Harold Wilson, research fellow at University College at that time.[5]

Then, on February 15, Dr. C. Brebbia, the Argentine ambassador, caused some consternation, according to Massey's report sent the following day:

At what was expected to be last meeting yesterday, Brebbia, Argentine, made two important reservations to final draft of Heads of Agreement as follows:

(1) Though feeling Agreement should be signed as soon as possible its price production and quota provisions could not become operative for Argentine before January 1st, 1941.

(2) Though Agreement should be for 5 years there must be provision for withdrawal at the end of two.

As to (1) Committee felt Agreement must go into operation at the same time for all signatories, and has asked Brebbia whether he can agree date suggested for this purpose should be August 1st, 1940.

As to (2) Committee felt that any withdrawal of clause should be qualified in such a way that no signatory should be permitted to withdraw merely because its own policy or lack of policy had made Agreement unworkable. Some restrictions on withdrawal similar to those of Sugar Agreement should be included and formula along those lines now being sought.[6]

[4]*Ibid.*
[5]*Wheat Advisory Committee Documents*, P. C. 4 and P. C. 5, 2nd February, 1939.
[6]*King Papers.*

To make progress on the negotiation of export quotas and minimum prices, the preparatory committee decided to convene a meeting of the four major exporting countries who were most directly concerned. The date of the meeting was set for April 13 and, because of the undertaking to participate which Massey had given, the cabinet wheat committee was now compelled to give something more than cursory consideration to its next move.

PREPARATIONS FOR THE APRIL MEETING

Since Euler had become minister, he had been accumulating the documents issued by the wheat advisory committee. In preparation for the April meeting in London, Euler's private secretary, Mr. Finlay Sim, asked Dr. C. F. Wilson to prepare a summary of those documents, including the recent draft heads of agreement, for Mr. Euler's information. It did not occur to Wilson, nor apparently to Sim, that the minister or the department must have a file of the communications passing between Vincent Massey (Canadian High Commissioner in London) and the department of external affairs. Wilson proceeded with the documentation, which he supplemented from Professor Joseph Davis's account, and his own doctoral dissertation, to provide a summary of the 1933 agreement and of the concepts therein which were once again coming up for negotiation.

Late in March, a meeting of the cabinet wheat committee was called. The four ministers (Euler, Dunning, Crerar and Gardiner) were present as well as C. F. Wilson and J. R. Murray, long since retired from the wheat board but who still served informally as the cabinet wheat committee's closest and most respected policy-adviser. The ministers had brought Murray to Ottawa in the hope they could persuade him to be their delegate to the April 13 meeting in London. Murray insisted that he could not spare time from his business and he recommended George McIvor.

As for the substance of the negotiations, the proposals now before the preparatory committee appeared to the ministers to be ludicrous, and therefore improbable of negotiation or operation. But in view of the current deterioration in the wheat position the ministers were constrained to treat the proposals seriously. They were hopeful that the negotiations would break down, without discredit to Canada. Gardiner, in particular, had taken umbrage at Cairn's bearish predictions, and saw no reason they should help to perpetuate a job for Andrew Cairns in London. As leader of the opposition in the Saskatchewan legislative assembly, Gardiner had also criticized the wheat acreage reduction legislation introduced by the Anderson government in support of the 1933 international wheat agreement.

As the meeting drew to an end, Gardiner said that he would like Dean Shaw to accompany McIvor, Crerar suggested Wilson. Euler asked Wilson to see that Massey was informed.

Wilson's effort to carry out Euler's instruction ended up unwittingly in causing Massey considerable consternation. As he left the minister's office, Wilson enlisted Finlay Sim's help in drafting a cable which Sim forwarded (after obtaining the signature of Major J. G. Parmalee, deputy minister of trade and commerce) to Dr. O. D. Skelton, undersecretary of state for external affairs, for transmission to the high commissioner. Somehow it got by both heads of department unheeded and on March 31, 1939, it went out as follows: "Canadian delegation at forthcoming meeting of the Preparatory Committee of the Wheat Advisory Committee will consist of G. H. McIvor, Chief Commissioner, Canadian Wheat Board, C. F. Wilson, Dominion Bureau of Statistics, and A. M. Shaw, Director, Marketing Service, Department of Agriculture. McIvor will head delegation."[7]

Unfortunately this message conflicted with Dr. O. D. Skelton's letter of March 22, 1939, to Massey, which had been prepared by Norman Robertson and cleared with the cabinet wheat committee. That letter contained a detailed statement of instructions which indicated that the Canadian government was not prepared to accept any form of acreage reduction or to maintain carryover stocks within a minimum-maximum range. The ministers were prepared to negotiate on export quotas, provided that the Canadian quota amounted to 200 million bushels out of a total world import requirement of 560 million bushels, and also provided that the agreement would result in a basic minimum price of 33.6d per 480 lb. quarter for No. 3 Northern c.i.f. London (equivalent to 80½ cents per bushel for No. 3 Northern at Fort William). The ministers regarded such a minimum price as of potential benefit to Canada; without it the quota commitment would not be worthwhile. In conclusion, the message read:

> The foregoing paragraphs represent our basic viewpoint on the substantive provisions of the draft agreement. Negotiations on the more detailed provisions of the agreement should be undertaken by you, consistently with the major considerations we have outlined. For your further assistance in the April meetings of the Preparatory Committee we propose to send additional delegates to be appointed later. It is expressly understood, of course, that negotiations in the Preparatory Committee do not represent final commitments, the latter to be reserved for a formal conference.[8]

The paragraph just quoted clearly implied that Massey would continue to head the Canadian delegation, assisted by his staff and by delegates from Canada to be appointed later. Because the message had gone off prior to the appointment of the latter, Major Parmalee, deputy minister of trade and commerce, had simply filed his copy of the Skelton message. Nor did he draw it from the file again to refer it to McIvor, Shaw or Wilson, after the wheat committee had decided to send them to London. Consequently, they were unaware of the existence of these instructions until they called on Massey in London. Also, it was only then that they learned from Massey that he had headed the delegation in January, and had taken a keen interest in the proceedings and in reporting on them. He had every reason to be upset at being replaced as head of the delegation, without explanation from Ottawa. Massey was nevertheless discreet enough to draw Wilson aside after the meeting to complain that the messages from Ottawa had been "rather untidy". The fault, of course, lay in the departments of external affairs and trade and commerce, and it was an extraordinary example of lack of liaison between and within departments in those days.

APRIL-MAY PREPARATORY COMMITTEE MEETINGS

Among the major exporting countries represented on the preparatory committee, the United States was the only country, other than Canada,

[7] *Ibid.*
[8] *Department of Trade and Commerce File 26204-14.*

which sent a special delegation to the proceedings. Although Ambassador Joseph P. Kennedy was chairman of the wheat advisory committee, the United States provided a career diplomat to chair the current meetings, the Honourable Ray Atherton, a minister of the American embassy in Paris (who was shortly appointed as American minister to Denmark and, during the war, as American minister to Canada).[9] The American delegation was headed by Dr. Edwin Black and included Mr. Lloyd V. Steere, Dr.Clifford C. Taylor and Mr. Robert Post. Australia was represented by the Australian high commissioner in London, the Right Honourable Stanley Bruce, formerly an Australian prime minister, and by Mr. F. L. McDougall, who became one of the founding fathers of the United Nations Food and Agriculture Organization. The Argentine delegation was headed by the Argentine ambassador, Dr. C. Brebbia, at one time a minister of agriculture in Argentina, and by Dr. Anselmo Viacava, the Argentine commercial counsellor.

With the full preparatory committee in attendance on April 13, work began on a revision of the heads of agreement which culminated in the April 24 draft of an international wheat agreement. This was as far as the attempt was carried that year to provide the text for a new agreement, and it formally terminated the work of the preparatory committee as a whole. Thereafter, negotiations on quotas were pursued by the preparatory committee's subcommittee comprised of the four major exporting countries.

In its essentials, the April 24, 1939, draft was an export-quota or market-sharing type of agreement patterned for the most part on the 1933 agreement, which included undertakings by importing countries not to increase domestic production or import restrictions so as to thwart the agreement's objectives. But a minimum price clause which had been mooted after the signing of the 1933 agreement was incorporated now in the new draft. Whereas, in the 1933 agreement, production control had been tacitly included in the observance of export quotas, the April 24 draft went further by requiring each exporting country to maintain its carryover stocks within an agreed minimum-maximum range, in addition to the quota limitation on exports. This allowed each country freedom to determine its own method of production control, compatible with its legislative or constitutional requirements, to conform with its agreed minimum-maximum stock range. In more detail, the preamble of the draft agreement recognized that:

> International trade in wheat forms so important a part of the commerce between nations that the maintenance of satisfactory wheat prices might be expected to have beneficial effects on the general economy of the world, the signatory governments have agreed that relatively stable wheat prices, at levels remunerative to producers and fair to consumers of wheat, will prove to be in the best interests of wheat exporting and wheat importing countries alike.[10]

[9]Mr. Atherton was appointed Minister to Canada on August 3, 1943. On November 19 of the same year, he became the first American Ambassador to Canada and served in that capacity until August 31, 1948.

[10]*Draft of International Wheat Agreement,* Wheat Advisory Committee Document P. C. 22, 24th April, 1939.

Article I of the draft summarized the essence of the draft agreement in the following terms:

1. The signatory governments recognize that the provisions of the Agreement for export quotas and the maintenance of prices related to a basic minimum price will not be permanently effective unless steps are taken by governments to adjust their total wheat production to cover only their domestic requirements, export demand and the maintenance of adequate reserve stocks.

2. Owing to differences in the constitutional and legal framework of their respective countries, the signatory governments have considered it impracticable to set forth, by uniform methods of procedure, the precise obligations of governments regarding the adjustment of production, the necessity of which is emphasized in the preceding paragraph. The Governments of the normal exporting countries, . . . nevertheless undertake to adopt all possible measures . . . aimed at preventing wheat production from exceeding the quantity required to provide for adequate domestic consumption, to fulfill export quotas and to maintain reserve stocks. . . .

3. The Governments of the normal importing countries, . . . recognising the importance to their own consumers of supplies from the wheat exporting countries, agree to operate their domestic wheat policies so as to assist the efforts which the normal wheat exporting countries . . . are making in the common interest to adjust the available supply of wheat to effective demand and thereby to restore its price to a remunerative level. They agree not to encourage any extension of the area sown to wheat and not to take any governmental measures, the effect of which would be to increase the domestic production of wheat. They also agree to initiate a reduction of customs tariffs and to relax quantitative restrictions on imported wheat, when the United Kingdom average price of parcels of imported wheat . . . is for a period of sixteen weeks not less than (a specified formula).[11]

The rest of the draft agreement was an extension in detail of the principles laid down in the first article. Export quotas as a percentage of estimated world demand remained to be negotiated, as did also the range of minimum-maximum carryover stocks. In his explanatory notes to the original draft, Cairns had suggested figures of 75-150 million bushels for Argentina, 60-120 million for Australia, 100-200 million for Canada and 200-400 million bushels for the United States. The minimum figures were based on 1922-1928 average of carryover stocks in each country, and the maximum figures were based on double that amount. Their consideration was set aside pending the outcome of the quota negotiations, and they did not come up for review again in 1939.

The basic minimum price and its equivalents the exporting countries would undertake to maintain was originally proposed by Cairns in his first draft at 33/6 per 480 lb. quarter c.i.f. London, England computed as follows:

	Canadian cents per bushel
Price of No. 3 Manitoba Northern, basis in store Fort William......................................	80½
Lake freight from Fort William to Montreal..	7
Handling charges, insurance, etc. to f.o.b. ocean steamer	2½

[11]*Ibid.*

Ocean freight from Montreal to
London (fixed minimum) 8½

Total (equated to 33/6 per
quarter c.i.f. London) 98½

As Cairns pointed out, the price of 80½ cents for No. 3 Northern Fort William was 6½ cents more than the current wheat board initial advance for that grade but in line with the 87½ cent price for No. 1 Northern which had been guaranteed by the Canadian government in the three previous crop years.[12] In discussions, the representatives of other exporting countries were not prepared to accept a minimum price so clearly identified with the Canadian domestic support price of 80 cents in 1938. Accordingly, Cairns devised a scheme by which the minimum price would be set at a negotiated percentage of the following formula:

say (75 percent) of $\dfrac{a \times b}{c}$

a = the 1909-14 United Kingdom average market price
   (35.5 shillings per quarter),
b = the Board of Trade's latest monthly index of wholesale prices of all commodities converted to a 1913 base,
c = the Board of Trade's 1913 index (100) of the wholesale prices of 200 commodities.

This formula introduced another weakness in its exclusive reliance upon British wholesales prices, but the problem was not resolved at that time.

It was intended that the agreement operate for five years from August 1, 1940 to July 31, 1945, but the Argentine delegation stood on its instructions not to accept export quotas or minimum prices prior to 1941. The Canadian delegation reported through Massey to Ottawa on April 18:

Argentine delegate at Preparatory Comittee today stated that his government remains unprepared to undertake quota or minimum price limitation prior to January 1941. Other delegates were of the opinion that minimum prices and quotas were not practical before August 1941 in view of the Argentine attitude. Previous discussions were concerned with minimum prices. Australian Government favours minimum prices and desires a level higher than suggested in draft agreement W. 7 E. United States Government also suggest a higher level. Statement by head of Canadian delegation given that minimum prices are an important part of the agreement. Today Argentine delegate stated that suggested minimum price level in draft agreement would lead to increased acreage in Argentina and would disturb measures being presently undertaken to eliminate wheat production on marginal land.

Head of Argentine delegation stated decree signed today eliminating guaranteed prices on marginal land wheat production. United Kingdom Government attitude impartial but indicated suggested minimum price too high. Americans exceedingly anxious to continue the discussion on the 1941 agreement, coupled with the exploration of the possibility of arriving at some agreement exclusive of Argentina covering interim period to 1941. Failing ability to obtain agreement of producers pressure in the United Kingdom will continue for subsidizing exports on basic commodities plus high domestic

[12]*Memorandum for the Preparatory Committee for the International Wheat Conference and Draft of International Wheat Agreement,* Wheat Advisory Committee Document, P. C. 1 and P. C. 2, 28th January, 1929.

prices, and relaxation of acreage restriction. in view of circumstances mentioned we are continuing to discuss detailed draft agreement W. 7 E. subject to reservation of Argentina.[13]

Again on April 26 the delegation reported:

Preparatory Committee meeting adjourned today, reconvening May 3rd. This to enable Danubian countries, Russia and the others to endeavour to arrive at quota figures. Four major exporting countries meeting as Sub-Committee Thursday to attempt to arrive at suitable quota figures for each country. Sub-Committee will also try to bridge the present cleavage minimum price views. Widely divergent views making progress difficult.[14]

On April 28, following the initial meeting of the exporters' sub-committee, McIvor presented a proposal for export quotas which had been carefully studied by the delegation. Wilson's statistical experience was of help; they took the longest continuous period of years for which the comparative wheat export figures were undistorted by war conditions. They were able to show that over the 16-year period from 1922-23 to 1937-38 Canadian wheat and flour exports had averaged 41.02 percent, Argentina 23.29, Australia 17.12 and the United States 18.57 percent of the total exports of the big four. These percentages were related to a world import demand figure of 560 million bushels of which 108 millions were set aside for other exporters. In bushels, this gave Canada a crop-year quota of 186 million bushels.

The Argentine delegate made the next proposal, based on the most recent 10-year average which favoured his country at the expense of the United States which had been out of the export market in recent years. Dr. Black's first counter was to suggest that the best consecutive 10-year period be selected for each country, which gave startlingly different results. On May 10, he withdrew his first proposal and recommended taking a twelve-year period 1922-23 to 1933-34 then skipping the next three years in which the United States had withdrawn from the export market but adding the 1937-38 crop year. Comparison of the four proposals stood as follows:

	Canadian Proposal	Argentine Proposal	First American Proposal	Second American Proposal
	1922-23 to 1937-38	1928-29 to 1937-38	Best consecutive 10 years	1922-23 to 1933-34 and 1937-38
			(percentages)	
Argentina	23.29	25.58	22.07	22.07
Australia	17.12	21.00	18.05	16.14
Canada	41.02	40.38	37.08	40.25
United States	18.57	13.04	22.80	21.54

During all this time, the Australian delegation had not been able to submit a proposal because a change of government had rendered any decision difficult, but as the various formulae were bandied about the debate was pursued primarily by the Argentine, Australian and United States delegations. Canada found itself in almost an impregnable position because its formula had taken into account the whole of the ups and downs of the post-war period to date, whereas the others were attempting to make opportunistic selections within that period to improve their percentages.

On May 6, the Canadian delegation reported to Ottawa as the prospects for an agreement waned:

[13]*King Papers.*
[14]*Ibid.*

In an endeavour to bring the Conference to some practical basis after two weeks indefinite discussion, we suggested that formula of 16 crop year period 1922-1923 to 1937-1938 exports be discussed at Preparatory Committee as being the most equitable basis upon which agreement on export quotas might be reached. This suggestion entirely subject to your final approval and subject to a satisfactory minimum price basis. Based on estimated annual import requirements of 560 million bushels, and assuming global quotas of 107 million bushels for exporting countries (other than the four major exporting countries,) the suggested formula would provide Canada a percentage of the remaining 453 million bushels of 41 per cent or 186 million bushels, Argentine 23 per cent or 106 million bushels, United States 19 per cent or 84 million bushels, and Australia 17 per cent or 77 million bushels. This period was suggested as being the only equitable period that would embrace all kinds of market and crop conditions.

United States up to this point were demanding quotas on basis of 10 best crop years exports for each country, thus escaping their 5 light crop years. On their formula Canada's quota would be only 37½ per cent or 168 million bushels.

Argentine, Australia and United States delegations agreed to consult their Governments re our formula but proceedings this week indicate very little hope of agreement. Argentine demanding fixed quota of 135 million bushels. Australia demanding higher quota than the United States but Australian delegate without definite instructions apparently due to change in Government. United States withholding quota figures until Australia declares. United States delegates present attitude seems not to indicate that they consider our suggested formula a reasonable compromise, but Conference now developed into considerable argument between Argentine, Australia, and United States. Ourselves, Australia and the United States definitely reject Argentine request for quota as being decidedly too high and object to fixed quota rather than percentage quota of estimated world demand for any of four leading exporters. Our opinion 107 million bushels suggested for countries other than big four a liberal quota, but will not likely be acceptable by those countries. Hungary declaring figures 10,000,000 bushels more than her named share confirms this view. No declaration from Russia yet. General impression Roumanian delegation will demand excessive quota. Yugoslavia states uninterested in agreement due bilateral arrangements. Looks as if Committee will terminate eventually in arguments between United States, Argentine and Australia on quotas, plus impossible quotas for Danubian countries. Meetings now recessed until some time next week pending more definite figures from Australia and Danubian countries.[15]

The final report on May 17 read:

Preparatory Committee of Wheat Advisory Committee today adjourned until July 7th. Reason for adjournment Bruce, High Commissioner for Australia, was in attendance yesterday and stated that due to home political uncertainties Australia unable to put forward their views at least until above date, when they will make every effort to state their position. Controversial questions, Argentine quota, minimum price and prospective agreement date as outlined in our memorandum of May 8th, still unsettled.

Full Canadian delegation sailing "Duchess of Richmond" May 19th.[16]

---

[15]*Ibid.*
[16]*Ibid.* The memorandum referred to was a mailed report which does not appear to have found its way into the King Papers. The telegrams were read and initialled by Mackenzie King and circulated to the members of the wheat committee.

JULY-AUGUST PREPARATORY COMMITTEE MEETINGS

The prospects for an agreement were so remote that no good purpose would have been served by the return of McIvor, Shaw or Wilson to London in July. Thenceforth, Massey, Pearson and Biddulph took over again as the Canadian representatives. By now, the war was much closer at hand and the need for an international wheat agreement seemed remote. Moreover, Mackenzie King was preoccupied over a much more serious problem. He had already sounded out his ministers on the party's prospects in an election and, after four years in office, he was encouraged enough by reports to want to call it that autumn. But he was also determined that if Canada entered the war it should be by vote of parliament. Thus he was confronted by the prospect of having no parliament to resort to if war broke out in Europe after he had dissolved the house and before a new parliament was elected. In the midst of such uncertainties that July, the Government's concern over the fate of the wheat negotiations paled into insignificance.

In London, the exporters' subcommittee of the preparatory committee resumed on July 7 under the chairmanship of Mr. Ray Atherton. The main problem was to reduce the percentage quota demands of the four countries to 100 percent. But harvest time was now approaching in North America, and it permitted a closer approximation to what the exportable supply position would be for each country in 1939-40. The United States pressed for a quota agreement for the crop year immediately ahead which would permit Australia and the United States to relinquish some quota for that year in return for more favorable consideration on the basic long-term quotas. The Argentine government appeared also to be relaxing the firm stand it had taken earlier against any quota commitment in that year.

By now, Cairns took the initiative in preparing for Atherton a series of compromise proposals which involved both the basic percentage and adjustments in the nearby crop year. Atherton's first compromise proposal was broached on July 14, and it was simply an average of the Canadian proposal based on the 16-year period 1922-23 to 1937-38 and of the first American proposal based on each country's share of toal exports in the best 10 of the 16 crop years for each country. In the wake of the chairman's proposal, Massey reported the state of negotiations on July 20, as follows:

> Argentine considers Chairman's quota percentages allowed her too low, suggests somewhat higher desirable but no percentage indicated. This is caused by request that consideration must be given for first and second years and asks United States and Australia what they are prepared to relinquish.
>
> Australia advise no reply has been received relative to Chairman's report but convinced Commonwealth sympathetic situation toward Canada and Argentine and cabling tonight what contribution they are prepared to make from basic quota this year.
>
> United States report are prepared to export 50 million bushels this year providing basic percentages of Chairman's report substantially agreed to and acreage reduction plan considered they reserve decision for second year until situation more clarified.
>
> Chairman suggested that as United States makes a substantial surrender and Australia may follow suit that both Canadian and Argentine representatives communicate with their Governments requesting guidance re allocation of surrendered quotas.

Would appreciate early advice and suggest instructions on percentage basis. Next meeting on July 24th.[17]

The wheat committee could not be brought together until July 26, when it approved the following instructions:

Considering improved Canadian crop prospects since May and in relation to a 1939 rather than a 1941 agreement we are presently faced with a prospective 1939 crop of 400 million bushels plus carryover of 100 million which, less domestic requirements, leaves us 1939 export surplus of 390 million bushels. Under these circumstances for the 1939-40 crop year we are unable to contemplate an export quota of less than 200 million bushels which would still leave a yearend carryover of 190 million bushels. Our prospective stock position in worse situation than in Argentina. Accordingly we ask Preparatory Committee to consider 1939-40 quota of 200 million bushels for Canada and this with minimum prices provision in draft agreement. Will consider adherence to percentage quotas for five year period following 1939-40 with minimum price provision and based on sixteen year average as proposed in Canadian memorandum of April 28, if Preparatory Committee gives favourable consideration to 1939-40 Canadian quota of 200 million bushels.[18]

The telegram inferred that the government was standing firm on its basic export quota of 41.02 percent, and the delegation reported on July 27:

Canadian report presented and considered very reasonable by United States in view of stock position, but it was hoped that Canada would not adopt a position too rigid for further negotiations in terms of percentage as it was felt this would be somewhat high.

Argentine representative indisposed. Australian Cabinet special meeting July 28th, full report expected Monday July 31st.

Next meeting Wheat Advisory Committee Monday. Chairman stressing importance of speeding up negotiations strongly supported by United States delegation.[19]

Meanwhile, the Australian delegation reported that the Australian government was having extreme difficulty in obtaining the co-operation of the State governments for a quota of less than 90 million bushels or 21 percent, which was quite out of line with Australia's previous export performance. On August 1, the Chairman submitted a further compromise proposal on quotas in his memorandum summing up the state of the negotiations. The Canadian delegation reported:

The following Chairman's statement is being cabled to Australia, United States, and Argentine, this afternoon, Begins:

In response to their request at this morning's meeting, the Chairman of the Preparatory Committee for the proposed International Wheat Conference submits to the representatives of Argentine, Australia, Canada and the United States, the following memorandum:

1. The replies of the four Governments to the formula suggested in the Chairman's memorandum of July 14th may be summarised thus:

Argentine Government considers the suggested basic export quota of 22.86% too low, but are prepared favourably to consider a somewhat higher percentage in the light of their probable 1939/40 quota.

[17]*Ibid.*
[18]*Ibid.*
[19]*Ibid.*

The Commonwealth Government considers the suggested basic export quota of 17.57% unacceptable and have requested a percentage which would indicate a probable average quota of 90 million bushels for the duration of the proposed agreement.

The Canadian Government considers 41.02% their appropriate basic export quota and have renewed their offer to accept that figure (i.e. the 16 year average) subject to acceptance of the suggested basic minimum price, providing favourable consideration is given to their request for a 1939/40 export quota of 200 million bushels.

The United States Government have agreed to accept as a basis for discussion the suggested basic export quota of 19.83% and have offered to relinquish in 1939/40 the difference between their quota and 50 million bushels.

2. The Chairman is convinced that any considerable departure from the formula suggested in his July 14th memorandum would make an agreement impossible. In his considered opinion the maximum limit of such an (word omitted) are: Argentine plus 050%, Australia plus 050%, Canada minus 050%, United States minus 050%. As prerequisite of an agreement he therefore submitted for consideration of the Governments concerned the following:

(i) Acceptance of the basic minimum price formula . . .

(ii) Relinquishment by Australia of difference between her 1939/40 quota and 70 million bushels.

(iii) Acceptance by Argentine and Canada of downward adjustments of their basic export quotas necessary to increase Australia's basic export quota to a maximum of 18.50%.

(iv) Allocation of one half to Argentine and one half to Canada of the total 1939/40 relinquishments of basic export quotas by Australia and the United States, and

(v) Subject to acceptance of (i) to (iv) inclusive, agreement upon the following basic export quotas . . . Argentine 23.15%, Australia 18.50%, Canada 39.02%, United States 19.33%.

3. Whatever the aggregate demands for wheat from four countries, the 1939/40 quotas for Australia and United States would be fixed at 70 and 50 million bushels respectively. If the aggregate demand for wheat from the four countries is only 435 million bushels, the 1939/40 quotas for the Argentine and Canada would be 123.0 and 192.0 million bushels respectively. But if the aggregate demand for wheat from four countries is 450 million bushels, the 1939/40 quotas Argentine and Canada would be 129.3 and 200.7 million bushels respectively. In view of the possible relinquishment of part of their 1939/40 quotas . . . by the countries other than Australia and the United States, it appears reasonable to anticipate that the aggregate demand for wheat from the four overseas countries will be nearer to 450 than to 435 million bushels.

4. At this morning's meeting representatives of the four countries undertook to emphasize to their Governments the urgency of the matter and to request instructions which will permit of a decision being reached at the next meeting (11 a.m. Friday, August 4th) whether the basis of an agreement does or does not exist.

5. When this memorandum was presented for elucidation at this afternoon's meeting, it was agreed that the following sentence should be added to the end of paragraph 3 of the memorandum.

"Should aggregate 1939/40 demand for wheat from the four countries exceed 470 million bushels, the 1939/40 export quotas shall be increased pro rata in accordance with the basic export percentage of quotas in sub-paragraph (v) of paragraph 2".

6. The Australian representative declared before joining the representatives of the other three countries in agreeing to transmit the text of the Chairman's memorandum to their Governments that the figure of 75 should be substituted for 70 in the text of sub-paragraph (ii) of paragraph 2 if there was to be any hope of his Government finding it possible to accept the Chairman's memorandum as a basis for discussion. Ends.

Please instruct us by Thursday, August 3rd, if possible.[20]

This report was studied by the cabinet wheat committee, and Norman Robertson telephoned Massey on August 4 the committee's decision:

Because of the decline in Canadian crop prospects from ten days ago we would accept quota for nineteen thirty nine-forty of one hundred and ninety two million bushels if aggregate demand from four countries is four hundred and thirty five million bushels and two hundred point seven million bushels if aggregate demand is four hundred and fifty million bushels. Respecting continuing quota for Canada beyond nineteen thirty nine-forty we definitely remain of opinion that basic percentage export quota of forty one point nought two percent for Canada derived from sixteen year average as suggested by us is fairest possible and most consistent basis for effecting an agreement. These proposals subject of course to satisfactory basic minimum price agreement as in telegram two seven nine paragraph two clause one. Meanwhile we would appreciate having greater clarification other countries response as result of chairman's statement.[21]

Massey reported the several reactions to the chairman's memorandum of August 1 in his telegram of August 4:

This morning United States prepared to discuss on the basis of the Chairman's second memorandum. Australians prepared to urge their states to agree to 75 million maximum for 1939 season and 18.5 of Chairman's second formula, adding that in order to make this acceptable to various states Prime Minister must speak to them personally and meeting is arranged August 10th. Prime Minister fully anticipates that agreement will be obtained but suggests that there should be written into draft agreement some arrangement of low fixed prices for markets of low purchasing Powers such as Far East. Argentine states quantities at the end of first year put them in worse position than now, even if coming crop is poor, if they considered 120 to 123 million bushels as their quota. Point out that they doubted from the beginning the advisability of joining prior to 1941 and suggested a free hand until then. They regret but it looks as if they must still hold to that reservation. 120 to 123 million bushels quite acceptable. They reiterate that at the end of this calendar year they would still have 4,700,000 tons or say 172.5 million bushels. They considered their Government's statements as being agreement on minimum price. They have no definite suggestion as to their idea of quota but referred again to the 172.5 million bushels.

Canada presented telephoned statement. Discussion general with criticism of 41.02% quota following the initial year. Strong united comments upon Argentine's lack of definition of quota and first year demand. Argentine cabling regarding this. Mr. Black returns to United States August 11th, announced cabling his Government tonight to go ahead with wheat subsidy programme. This implies his opinion as to reaching agreement unlikely. Next meeting of Committee Monday, August 14th, when Chairman sums up situation in case Governments have any modifications of previous instructions prior to calling general Committee meeting.[22]

By August 15 Dr. Brebbia, head of the Argentine delegation, reported that the Argentine government had agreed to a first-year quota of 150 million bushels unless the big four exports exceeded 470 million bushels, beyond which the four countries would share proportionately. Then his government proposed 24 percent as the Argentine quota for the following four years which Brebbia regarded as Argentine's final position. Massey reported again on the state of play and the opinion of his delegation that the Canadian government was being backed into a position where it must make the agreement by further concessions or accept responsibility for its breakdown as he cabled that same day:

> Preparatory Wheat Committee meeting this afternoon. Chairman remarked that he was positive Argentine had said last word and only accepted by Argentine Government on account of Brebbia's five year standing as Agricultural Minister. Chairman also confidentially remarked that unless all Governments were willing to study position promptly he felt the other unwilling sections in Argentine would sabotage present suggestions and would undoubtedly force withdrawal of Brebbia's proposals especially absolute agreement to five year contract at minimum price with no escape clause. The Chairman stressed this particularly. The United States agreed with Chairman's remarks and believed here was a hopeful basis and immediately offered further sacrifice of five million bushels for first year providing percentages were basis 39 Canada 24 Argentina 18 Australia 19 per cent United States. Therefore their first year quota export being 45 million bushels. Australia agreed with Chairman regarding Argentine's last word and possibility of withdrawal unless quick action likely, but reiterated last cable report and felt that although would cable urging further reduction thought that below first year quota of 75 million bushels would be most difficult for Prime Minister to obtain agreement with the various States Ministers, but hoped for a five million reduction, and with regard to basic quotas thought 18% would also be difficult unless presented to Australian people as being reduction shared by United States and Australia toward Argentine's quota, namely, in shape of 18.1 for Australia and 18.90 for United States. It was generally pointed out that although Canadian position looks like a sacrifice of 22 million bushels basis of 435 million for first year and 2.02% for subsequent years, that considering that world position by virtue of less European crop would easily result in over 450 million being big four proportion that therefore everything over 435 million would automatically come to Canada alone up to 470 million bushels, and in the opinion of United States and Australia it gave Canada sufficient compensation for her loss of subsequent quotas allowing for general sacrifice all around. Canadian delegate pointed out magnitude of sacrifices demanded of them and declined making any statement until instructed by Ottawa. The Canadian delegates feel that probably the last word has been said by both Australian and United States and certainly Argentine, and if agreement is to materialise further concessions are required of us. Next meeting Thursday morning August 17th for consideration of instructions from Governments.[23]

The cabinet wheat committee sent back the following message on August 16:

[22] *Ibid.*
[23] *Ibid.*

With all figures million bushels, we understand present suggestion for 1939-40 is that Canada should accept 170 actual and all excess over 435 and up to 470, compared with 150 Argentina, 70 Australia, 45 United States all actual. If this correct interpretation it means Canada will have carry-over August 1st next of about 220 on basis 435 and 205 on basis 450. Telegram No. 279 August 1st, proposed Canada's 1939-40 quota be 192 if 435, and 200.7 if 450. We agreed to accept in our cable August 4th. Against Argentina's stated exportable stock position January 1st, 1940, of 172 Canada will have about 312. Evidently no consideration given our stock position, being 140 over Argentina's when we are granted only 20 higher actual export quota 1939-40 and speculative possibility if 435 exceeded. We suggest distinction necessary between countries that made admittedly reasonable proposition from the outset and the making of concessions now from unreasonably high first offer. Canada will accept actual quota of 185 for 1939-40 and share proportionately excess over 435 with others making further concessions necessary to give Canada 185. We repeat Canada's 41% continuing quota was based on broadest practical period of past events and this further supported by our prospective stock position at August 1st, 1940.[24]

In turn, the delegation reported on the August 18 proceedings as Cairns submitted the last compromise proposal in a memorandum of his own. Massey's telegram was dated August 21:

Big Four section of Preparatory Wheat Committee in session Friday, August 18th.

Argentine delegate Brebbia prepared to recommend 150 million bushels basis 450 with percentage adjustment of 33.33 above or below. Nothing further reported from others. General opinion that agreement relatively near but three others feel that progress unlikely without Canda reconsidering 41 per cent basic quota. To clarify position Secretary was entrusted to prepare statement summarizing general opinion which showed 2.5 per cent over basic quotas and 16 million excess basis 450 first year. Extracts from this memorandum follow:

(1) Danger was expressed that fixed quotas first year would prove unworkable but converted to percentage figures might avoid difficulties;

(2) All Governments to be cabled suggesting that if an agreement is to result it must be somewhere around the following basis, namely, first year percentages, Argentine 33.33, Australia 16.21, Canada 40.69, United States 9.77, giving on basis 450 respectively 150, 72.9, 183.1, and 44. These same percentages will govern first year regardless of total Big Four world trade whether 470 or 435. Basic quota following four years percentages respectively, 24, 17.84, 39.5, 18.66. This means spreading over five years respectively 25.87, 17.51. 39.74. 16.88. United States and Australian delegates thought their Governments might be favourable to above suggestions which were being cabled. Argentine also concurred. Canada advised they were reporting.

Other exporting members of Preparatory Committee insist on early meeting which Chairman is arranging for this week. Chairman desires to return to Washington as soon as possible to receive instructions regarding new appointment as Minister to Denmark.

In view of above developments, Canadian delegates are of opinion that, assuming possible acceptance of above points by other Governments, some type limited discretion expressed in terms of percentage would be very helpful to us.[25]

[24]*Ibid.*
[25]*Ibid.*

On August 25, Euler administered the coup de grace as he cabled Massey:

Considering present International situation would suggest advisability of recessing Preparatory Committee meetings to be resumed at call of Chairman if and when political situation improves.[26]

Massey replied by a despatch of the same date:

I have the honour to refer to your telegram No. 255 of August 25th, regarding the advisability of recessing the Preparatory Committee of the proposed International Wheat Conference.

2. Representatives of the four overseas countries on this Committee met this morning, August 25th. Because of the difficult international situation it was decided to discontinue these sessions for the time being, but as soon as possible further meetings would be held subject to the call of the Chairman.[27]

To compare the basic quota compromise proposals advanced in July-August and the government responses to them, they are shown in tabular form:

	Chairman's Proposal July 14	Government Responses	Chairman's Proposal August 1	Government Responses	Secretary's Proposal August 18	Government Responses
			(percentages)			
Argentina	22.86	too low	23.15	24.00	24.00	Yes
Australia	17.57	too low	18.50	18.50	17.84	Nil
Canada	39.74	41.02	39.02	41.00	39.50	Nil
United States	19.83	19.83	19.33	19.00	18.66	Yes
	100.00		100.00	102.50	100.00	

While Massey and his aides in London would have preferred to close the gap, even at Canada's expense, in order to reach agreement, the feeling at home was that such sacrifice was not in the Canadian interest, in view of the claims of Argentina and Australia unsupported by their long-term performance but demanded by their governments' inflexible positions. As Secretary Henry A. Wallace declared later, the negotiations were very close to agreement when they were broken off. In the narrow sense, the negotiations were very close to a breakdown with the Argentine, Australian and Canadian governments digging in over the last 2.5 percent. On the eve of war, it is surprising that the efforts to reach agreement lasted that long. Had the threat of war not been present, the future the agreement was designed to provide for would more nearly have approximated reality, and a greater willingness to compromise might have been present. In the process, the Canadians gained an invaluable lesson in the negotiating prowess of their competitors, which stood them in good stead when the issue came up again. For Cairns, the breakdown was a cruel disappointment. Even after August 25, he tried to keep the meetings going informally, and the documentation continued to pour out. Soon he would recommend intergovernmentally controlled buying and selling under wartime conditions. He was personally convinced that the days of the open market system were numbered and that the wheat trade of the future would be placed in charge of an international agency.

[26] *Ibid.*
[27] *Ibid.*

29

INITIAL IMPACT OF WORLD WAR II

The developing war situation had set aside Mackenzie King's hopes for an autumn election. In response to the British and French declarations of war against Germany on September 3, King summoned parliament which approved the Canadian declaration of war on September 10.

Prior to the outbreak of war, the British government had made fairly elaborate and detailed plans on what it would have to do to place its administration on a war footing. To protect its food supply, the government established a food (defence plans) department which became the ministry of food when the war began. In that department a cereals control board was established, initially headed by Sir Alan Anderson who, during the first world war, was a member of the royal commission on wheat supplies and represented that purchasing body in New York (Sir Alan had been instrumental in the creation of the board of grain supervisors for Canada after the Winnipeg grain exchange ceased trading in wheat futures in 1917). Messrs James Rank, Alfred Hooker, Norman Vernon and J. H. Pillman were recruited from the trade to serve as a cereals purchasing committee, which later became variously known as the cereals import branch or the imported cereals division of the ministry of food, and operated as a unit separately from the cereals control board.

BRITISH FOOD CONTROL PLANS

As early as January, 1938, the British government had addressed a secret memorandum to the Canadian government on the subject of British food control plans in the event of war which set out in detail their proposed courses of action. After describing the departmental organization of the ministry of food, it outlined the proposed procedures for that ministry in the purchase of imported food supplies, and the methods of internal food distribution. With respect to imported supplies, the memorandum stated:

> The directors of the various Supply Organizations, with the assistance of expert Committees, would then proceed to make the necessary arrangements for the purchasee of oversea supplies. Different methods would be adopted according to conditions in each producing country. In certain cases negotiations would probably take place for the bulk purchase of cereals, meat, sugar, dairy produce and other foodstuffs on long term contracts. Where

necessary, agencies would be appointed in oversea countries for supervising delivery and shipments. Where bulk contracts were not possible or desirable, purchases in the country of origin might be made by private firms operating on account of the Food Controller in the United Kingdom. Whichever method were adopted, existing importers would continue to handle imports on arrival as Government agents. By prohibition of imports on private account and concentration of buying and shipment in the hands of a single organization, speculative trading would be eliminated and prices would, it is hoped, be stabilised at a level satisfactory to producers and consumers.

Then on the subject of import purchases from Canada, the memorandum continued:

(a) *Wheat and other cereals.* The most important foodstuffs which the Food Controller would in all probability wish to purchase from Canada in the event of war, are wheat, flour, barley and oats; butter and cheese, bacon and hams; canned salmon and apples. In regard to wheat and other cereals it is contemplated that if complete control were to be established on the outbreak of war, the Liverpool Futures market would be closed and the Food Controller would take over all wheat belonging to British subjects resident in the United Kingdom. Purchases by private importers and millers would cease and the Food Controller would become the sole buyer of wheat and other cereals. In these circumstances the question arises whether it is possible that private trading on the Winnipeg Grain Exchange might also be suspended and that some central authority, such as the Canadian Wheat Board, might have to intervene to undertake the sale of wheat to the United Kingdom and negotiate prices and deliveries. His Majesty's Government in the United Kingdom would be glad to be informed of the views of His Majesty's Government in Canada on this question and in particular to learn whether the Canadian Wheat Board is formulating any plans for dealing with such an emergency and if so what is the nature of such plans.

(b) *Other Commodities.* With regard to the other commodities, special importance would probably be attached to supplies of bacon and hams and also of butter in view of the possible interruption of supplies from European sources. In the absence of any central agency in Canada for controlling export sales, the Food Controller would presumably negotiate direct with Canadian exporting interests and place contracts for delivery of increased supplies for some months ahead. Advice as to the best procedure to follow in placing these contracts would be much appreciated.[1]

It appears that the wheat committee of cabinet failed to give the British memorandum any serious attention for more than a year, because in May, 1939, while George McIvor was still in London for the wheat advisory committee's preparatory committee meetings, Mr. James Rank and his colleagues on the cereals purchasing committee called him in for secret consultations. Rank gave McIvor a copy of the memorandum just quoted and asked quite pointedly if it was the intention of the Canadian government to close the Winnipeg wheat futures market in coordination with the proposed closing of the Liverpool futures market in the event of war. McIvor could only take this question back to Canada, and upon his return to Winnipeg he prepared a ten-page memorandum to his minister, the Honourable W. D. Euler, which referred to the British plans if war broke out and traced the history of British purchasing methods in the last war, of the closing of the Winnipeg wheat futures market in 1917, and of the

[1] *United Kingdom Food Control Plans in the Event of War,* Canadian Wheat Board files.

operations of the board of grain supervisors and of the first Canadian wheat board. Then, on the subject of the Canadian position in the event of war, McIvor said:

It will be noted that the first secret memorandum attached enquires regarding the procedure to be followed in Canada in the event of war. The procedure to be adopted in Canada would depend in some respects upon the measures adopted in the competing exporting countries.

There are two main alternatives open. In the first place, the Winnipeg Futures Market could be allowed to continue in operation. In this event, deliveries to the Canadian Wheat Board as at present constituted and operating under a fixed initial price of 70¢ per bushel for No. 1 Northern at Fort William or Vancouver would be doubtful, depending on the level of the Market. With advancing markets, the bulk of the wheat would go to the private grain trade. With speculation uncontrolled, there would be a possibility of erratic and higher prices and in that event, the further possibility that the British authorities might turn to other countries for their supplies.

If the Futures Market were left open the British Cereal Purchasing Committee or any Allied Government agency would deal direct with the Canadian grain trade by cable or, alternatively, would begin the purchase operation by buying futures at Winnipeg. The continued operation of the Futures Market at Winnipeg might prove satisfactory under some supply conditions. As a matter of fact, the Futures Market operated fairly satisfactorily for the first year or two after the last war started, although there was continuous criticism from the United Kingdom regarding the fluctuations of prices. Much would depend on the attitude of the Canadian grain trade as to whether offers could be freely made abroad under a widely fluctuating market. The danger would be that speculation or holding might divert demand to other countries and that Canadian trade would suffer. During the last war the short, poor quality crop of 1916 really set the stage for the difficulties of the Futures Market that followed.

The second alternative would be to close the Winnipeg Futures Market and then take various steps to establish the Canadian Wheat Board as a monopoly controlling the entire movement of Canadian wheat.

Then after reviewing in more detail the course of events in 1917, McIvor continued:

In 1917 when trading in wheat futures was suspended on the Winnipeg Grain Exchange, the new powers given to the Board of Grain Supervisors were conferred upon it by Orders in Council under the War Measures Act. The following steps would appear to be necessary if trading in grain futures is discontinued once more:

1. Settlement with the trade would require to be made by the Government Board on the basis of the prices registered at the immediately previous close. The hedges in the futures market would then be cancelled out and the Government Board would take over the actual Canadian wheat stocks at negotiated spreads compared with the level of futures prices.

2. The Canadian Wheat Board, then becoming a monopoly body, it might be considered desirable to add to its members by giving representation to such groups as farmers, consumers, flour millers, elevator operators and shippers in the grain trade.

3. The Board would take over the control of lake shipping and after negotiation fix the lake freight rates and undertake the allocation of cargoes equitably among the various shipping companies. In this connection the Board would probably work with a chartering committee, the companies retaining the management of their vessels.

4. The Canadian Wheat Board would have to be granted more control over the rates and movement of wheat in and out of elevators than it has at present.

5. The Board would have to exercise full control over the mills and have power to set maximum prices of wheat flour and offal.

6. Provisions for public meetings would have to be included if a monopoly board were established.

7. Provisions for control by license or otherwise of the export and sale of wheat and flour outside Canada would have to be established.

8. It would also be necessary to make provision for taking delivery of wheat at such time and place as the Board may direct by regulation.

9. Provision would be made to use the services and facilities of the grain trade as far as possible. This would follow the practice of the Board of Grain Supervisors and the Canadian Wheat Board of 1919-20 and correspond with the United Kingdom plans.[2]

RETENTION OF THE OPEN MARKET IN WINNIPEG

Even McIvor's memorandum provoked no decision by the wheat committee of cabinet to close the Winnipeg wheat futures market in the event of war. Such action ran counter to the government's policy of eventually terminating its direct involvement in wheat marketing. McIvor's enumeration of the measures consequent upon the closing of the market could also have accounted for the wheat committee's inaction. The current situation was not the exact parallel of that which had existed under the first wheat board in 1919. For one thing, the present board was a voluntary board, and it was prevented from accepting deliveries of more than 5,000 bushels from any one farm unit. Moreover, whether the board would receive any wheat from each farm was dependent entirely upon the course of prices. If open-market prices rose above the board's statutory 70-cent initial payment, the board would have very little wheat delivered to it, and producers would be all the more dependent upon the open market as a mechanism for the disposal of their wheat. In addition, since private trade channels remained open to a number of neutral countries, buyers in such countries were likewise dependent upon the futures system to facilitate their purchases. At the beginning of the 1939-40 crop year, the board had an unsold carryover of 86.5 million bushels on hand, and it could work on the disposal of those stocks. But, in the course of the first crop year during the war, although prices did fluctuate above and below the 70-cent level, the board had delivered to it 342 million bushels of 1939 crop wheat out of total primary marketings of 416 million bushels.

As war was declared however, Mr. James Rank cabled to ask McIvor again about the Canadian government's intentions regarding the closing of the Winnipeg futures market, as the ministry of food acted promptly to terminate futures trading in Liverpool. McIvor and Grindley had, in fact, spent the last week of August, 1939, in Ottawa conferring with the cabinet wheat committee on that subject. The two returned to Winnipeg for the weekend and came back to Ottawa for another meeting with the wheat committee on September 5. At the conclusion of that meeting, McIvor

[2]*Memorandum re Measures to Control the Prices and Movement of Wheat in the United Kingdom and Canada in Time of War,* Canadian Wheat Board files.

abled to Rank the government's decision not to close the market for the
present, as Euler told the press that the cabinet wheat committee had
discussed the situation but contemplated no immediate action. On
September 7, Euler offered a fuller statement in the following release:

The Honourable W. D. Euler, M.P., Minister of Trade and Commerce,
announced today the Government's decision that, for the present, the
Winnipeg Wheat Market would not be closed. It was felt that it would not be
in the producers' interest, nor in the national interest, to close the market now.
He emphasized that the producers who so desired could to the extent of 5,000
bushels deliver their wheat to The Canadian Wheat Board, at the fixed
minimum price of seventy cents for No. 1 Northern, Fort William-Port
Arthur or Vancouver, and secure participation certificates entitling them to
share in any additional price secured upon the sale of wheat delivered to the
Board. He pointed out further that any gains made by the Wheat Board on
the 1939 crop could not and would not be used to offset losses on the 1938
crop. In addition to this, producers could deliver their wheat in excess of 5,000
bushels to pools operating under the Wheat Co-operative Marketing Act,
obtain an initial payment of fifty-six cents for No. 1 Northern, Fort
William-Port Arthur, and share in any additional price obtained by these
pools. Another alternative is that the producer can sell his wheat on the open
market.

In Ontario, the farmer has the alternative of selling his wheat on the
market, or delivering it to The Canadian Wheat Board and securing an initial
price and participation certificates, the same as in the West.[3]

The inference to be drawn from the reference to the producers' and
national interests is that the ministers were acutely aware of the depressed
state of wheat prices which, if frozen by government intervention, would
jeopardize farm incomes and the balance of payments and discourage
farmers from contributing to the war effort through the production of
wheat. Several practical difficulties also stood in the way. In the absence of
a market barometer, the Canadian and British governments would have to
negotiate the price directly for each transaction. Such negotiated prices
might look foolish by hindsight in comparison with prices on the Chicago
market which remained open. Canada's other customers in neutral
countries depended upon the open-market mechanism to facilitate their
purchases and, in the absence of a market, the board would have problems
in pricing such sales. But even more importantly, the wheat board was not
the exclusive marketing agency. Because of the 5,000-bushel limitation
written into the act, the board could not accept all deliveries, even if the
price were to fall below 70 cents, and this left non-board deliveries
dependent upon the hedging facilities of the open market, or upon the
co-operative marketing machinery. Notwithstanding these problems which
weighed in the government's decision, the news was received coldly in
London, and the cereals control board responded by making no purchases
of Canadian wheat.

In the midst of this dilemma, the cabinet wheat committee received a
delegation from the pools on October 12, 1939. In their representations, the
pool directors declared that the statutory initial payment of 70 cents was too
low in peacetime and much too low in wartime when food might again

[3] *Report of the Canadian Wheat Board, Crop Year 1939-1940*, pp. 4-5.

become a major factor in winning the war. They noted the absence of British buying and the exclusion of Canadian wheat from the British grist, as they recommended the closing of the Winnipeg futures market and the negotiation with the British of a parity price in their summary:

1. That the Government should negotiate direct with the British Government, and endeavour to arrange price levels for wheat which would bear a fair relation to the cost of other commodities;

2. That these prices should be as near as possible to parity (based on 1926 levels) with all commodities the farmer has to buy;

3. That in view of the performance of the futures market since the outbreak of war, with continuing controlled purchasing in Great Britain, the Government should reconsider closing the futures market and that the Wheat Board be given complete control of Canadian wheat supplies.[4]

EARLY SALES PROBLEMS

The cereals purchasing committee had already commenced buying Canadian wheat in advance of the outbreak of war. On August 24, it completed negotiations on a direct purchase from the wheat board of 5 million bushels, basis the close of the December future at 62½ cents, and on August 29 it purchased directly from the board another 5 millions based on the cash close of 56 cents for No. 1 Northern. These purchases were intended as a security reserve to be held for British account in Canada but, with the outbreak of war, they were shipped to Britain that autumn.

As the month of September wore on, the board became painfully aware that no British inquiries were being made for Canadian wheat as the cereals purchasing committee diverted its purchases to Argentina. The situation was aggravated by a trade report that British mills had been directed not to use more than 10 percent of Canadian wheat in their mix. Later, a Broomhall cable reported that the milling rate for Canadian wheat had been raised to 20 percent. Either rate spelled disaster for export sales of Canadian wheat so long as such restrictions remained in effect. During this period of withholding purchases, exchange problems were very much to the fore and extended to the whole area of Britain's wartime procurement in Canada. Although McIvor invited the control board to purchase on the open market in Canada, the British authorities failed to respond. It has been subsequently confirmed by British official sources that the abstention from purchases was deliberate in the belief that Canadian quotations were too high. Britnell and Fowke have quoted the following statement:

A large contract for Canadian wheat, settled on the eve of the war at the market price, enabled the Government to abstain from buying any Canadian wheat at all for some weeks after the outbreak of war, when it considered the new Canadian quotations were too high. Not until the summer of 1940, when the market was weaker, did the Government enter into the first of a series of bulk contracts at a price well below that suggested by the Canadian Government in the autumn.[5]

---

[4]*Memorandum from the three Canadian Wheat Pools to the Members of the Wheat Committee of the Federal Government,* October 12, 1939.

[5]W. K. Hancock and M. M. Gowing, *British War Economy,* (History of the Second World War, U.K. Civil Series, 1947), pp. 154-155, as quoted in G. E. Britnell and V. C. Fowke, *Canadian Agriculture in War and Peace, 1935-50,* p. 222.

McIvor drew the situation to his minister's attention by letter which Euler took up in council and referred to the newly-formed advisory committee on economic policy.[6] Dr. W. C. Clark, chairman of the committee, reported as follows to the prime minister on September 29, 1939:

> Hon. W. D. Euler handed me yesterday afternoon a letter addressed to him by the Chief Commissioner of the Canadian Wheat Board, outlining the situation in the wheat market resulting from the lack of sales to the United Kingdom during the recent past. Mr. Euler stated that it was the desire of Council that the questions raised by this letter should be considered by the Economic Advisory Committtee and, if possible, that a cable to be sent to the United Kingdom should be drafted by the Committee.
>
> The Committee considered the question of wheat this morning and desires to make an initial report as follows:
>
> 1. We feel that we cannot over-emphasize the seriousness of the problems which result from the apparent unwillingness of the British Cereals Control Board to buy Canadian wheat since the commencement of the war, and the urgency of endeavouring to negotiate a sale to the United Kingdom of a substantial volume of our wheat (say, at least 50 to 60 million bushels) before the season of navigation closes.
>
> We feel, also, that our own position is fundamentally vulnerable.
>
> 2. We believe that, as a first step, a cable should be sent immediately to the United Kingdom, explaining our point of view in regard to the seriousness of the present situation and the untoward consequences which may result to the Canadian economy and the prosecution of our full war effort, if the present impasse is allowed to continue. Draft cable is attached hereto.
>
> As it would appear that the Canadian Wheat Board has done as much as it could possibly do in endeavouring to negotiate with the British Cereals Control Board, we believe that it is necessary to introduce considerations of high policy into the negotiations and we therefore recommend that the cable should be sent from the Prime Minister of Canada to the Prime Minister of the United Kingdom.
>
> 3. If Council so desires, the Committee would be glad to give further consideration during the next two or three days to some of the general and technical aspects of the problem with a view to getting additional data and summarizing it with a view to enabling Council to reach definitive decisions. These aspects of the problem which we have in mind include the following:
>
> (1) The position of the Winnipeg Grain Exchange and the futures market;
>
> (2) The technique of carrying out a $50 to $60 million sale of wheat to the British authorities and the possible effects of various alternative techniques;
>
> (3) Reviewing the British purchases of Argentine wheat with a view to discovering whether the United Kingdom is absorbing the additional costs of

[6]The Advisory Committee on Economic Policy was appointed by P. C. 2698 of September 14, 1939, and its membership (which was added to from time to time) initially included:

W. C. Clark, deputy minister of finance (chairman)
G. F. Towers, governor of the bank of Canada
H. D. Scully, commissioner of customs
H. B. McKinnon, chairman of wartime prices and trade board
G. S. H. Barton, deputy minister of agriculture
Charles Camsell, deputy minister of mines and resources
L. D. Wilgress, director of commercial intelligence service
R. H. Coats, dominion statistician
Lt-Col Henri Desrosiers, associate deputy minister of national defence
N. A. Robertson, external affairs
R. B. Bryce, department of finance (secretary)

freight and insurance and what the real costs of such Argentine wheat to Great Britain are as compared with real costs of similar purchases in Canada.

(4) The utilization of our wheat in the United Kingdom and the relation between the fixed price of bread in United Kingdom and the price of Canadian wheat.

These are, of course, technical questions, and it would seem to be desirable if Mr. McIvor and Mr. Grindley could come to Ottawa for a discussion on, say, Monday next.[7]

The draft cable was approved with little amendment by council and was sent on September 30:

Following for Prime Minister from my Prime Minister, Begins:

1. My colleagues and I are seriously concerned by the situation which is developing between Canada and the United Kingdom in respect of wheat.

2. No purchases have been made on United Kingdom Government account since commencement of the war. We understand that United Kingdom mills have been instructed greatly to reduce their use of Canadian wheat and the surface indications all point to efforts to secure or utilize other varieties with the probable result that Canadian shipments during the present season of navigation on the St. Lawrence may be seriously curtailed. If this should be the case, the bulk of our crop will remain in storage at points distant from the seaboard, and the later movement overseas would involve not only a greater expense for carriage but also some dislocation of our rail transport arrangements, with resultant prejudice of movements of other war materials and munitions.

3. It may be that the United Kingdom authority dealing with wheat purchases has misunderstood our attitude in respect of continuance of the open market in Winnipeg, and has the impression that this implies merely a desire to obtain higher prices. Whether or not the British Cereals Control Board has this impression, the fact remains that the policy being pursued has all the aspects of a commercial struggle between opposing interests. Our people in the West are already commencing to sense this situation.

4. I cannot over emphasize the painful impression that would be produced in this country if it is thought that our relationships with the United Kingdom are developing on the basis referred to above. Unity of purpose and consequently successful prosecution of our war effort would be seriously prejudiced.

5. The present impasse threatens to produce a situation which, both from an economic and psychological point of view will weaken our ability to render assistance. As time is of the essence, very early consideration would be appreciated. Ends.[8]

Prime Minister Chamberlain replied on October 6:

Following from Prime Minister for your Prime Minister, Begins:

I have given, in conjunction with my colleagues directly concerned, the most careful consideration to your representations regarding wheat situation and am glad to have this opportunity of removing any misunderstanding which may exist in the minds of the Canadian Government as to our attitude on this question.

We fully appreciate position of your Government as explained in your message and I should like to assure you at once that we are anxious to cooperate to the fullest extent in our power in removing or lessening

[7] *King Papers.*
[8] *Ibid.*

difficulties which you feel. The Ministry of Food desires, if finance can be arranged, to buy wheat, flour, maize and barley from Canada. But the extent of the purchases which will be possible depends on dollar resources available to us. Final decision had, therefore, to be deferred until financial position has been discussed with Osborne. In the meantime everything possible has been done to establish contacts in relation to wheat in particular. Earlier this year the Food Ministry had most valuable discussions in London with McIvor, Chairman of Canadian Wheat Board, full details of which were doubtless made available by him to the Canadian authorities.

Our understanding of position, as left by these conversations, was that McIvor would communicate further with United Kingdom authorities after consultation with Canadian Ministers as to coordinated plan for sales of wheat in the event of war. Food Ministry had understood from him that the Canadian Government would probably close Winnipeg Grain Exchange in time of war and establish one single organization for negotiating sales. Impression here is that present unsettled condition of Canadian market has to some extent resulted from absence of some such arrangement.

The whole question has, I understand, been the subject of recent informal discussions between officials of the Ministry of Food and Exporting Countries Sub-Committee of Wheat Advisory Committee in London, and Canadian representative will no doubt have reported to his Department the desire expressed by Ministry of Food that matter should be dealt with on basis of coordinated arrangements rather than of deals on a purely commercial basis between various importing and exporting countries.

It would be of great assistance to ministry of Food in the circumstances if it were possible for McIvor to return to this country at an early date in order to continue discussions with a view to concluding long-term contract for wheat as soon as position in regard to finance is clearer. I very much hope this can be arranged. Ends.[9]

After a careful study of Chamberlain's reply by the officials immediately concerned, and by cabinet, Mackenzie King was constrained to send a rejoinder on October 10, in the following terms:

Following from Prime Minister to your Prime Minister:

1. My colleagues and I appreciate the consideration you have given our representations in regard to wheat and share your anxiety to remove all difficulties standing in the way of full cooperation. We also appreciate the willingness of your Government to purchase wheat, flour, barley and other cereal products from Canada to the extent of the dollar resources available to you.

2. Since Mr. Osborne's arrival we have had the opportunity of discussing with him the whole range of problems connected with financing purchases of your Government in this country. We have acquainted him with the plans we have in mind for the immediate future. We are advised that he has communicated these plans to the Treasury and we believe that your Government should now understand that exchange or financial factors should not now constitute a barrier to immediate and substantial purchases here.

3. At the same time we have explained to Mr. Osborne our objections to arrangements suggested by various United Kingom agencies for purchase of various Canadian products on a basis which would involve our producers accepting either the risk of fluctuations in sterling or a part of their sales proceeds in the form of blocked sterling. We believe that our objections to

[9] *Ibid.*

such arrangements are based on cogent arguments and we trust that now that they have been communicated through Mr. Osborne your Treasury will see and accept their validity.

4. We are aware of the conversations which took place between the Food Ministry and Mr. McIvor last summer but would point out that on September fifth the Cereals Control Board was informed by Mr. McIvor of the Canadian Government's decision to keep the Winnipeg Grain Exchange open for the time being at least. For your information we still believe that there is virtue, from the point of view of your Government as well as our own, in keeping the Exchange open for some further period in order that price may be determined by the open market without placing the onus on *both* Governments for such price determination. The Cereals Control Board has apparently been impressed with the difficulty of buying a substantial quantity of wheat in open market but Mr. McIvor has previously and again today cabled suggestions as to methods by which such purchases could in our opinion be effected at a fair and reasonable price to the United Kingdom.

5. May I be permitted to emphasize again the painful impression that may be created in this country and the adverse effect on our national unity and our war effort by the present policy which has all the aspects of a commercial struggle between two opposing interests. Indeed there is already evidence that our fears in this respect are justified as the public begins to understand that the British Control authorities have purchased no wheat from Canada since the outbreak of war although substantial purchases are continually being made from neutral countries. Unsettlement in Canadian market to which you refer is due primarilly to absence of any buying by the United Kingdom.

6. In this connection we cannot see the justification for or the practicability of the suggestions referred to in your second last paragraph made at the recent informal conferences between officials of the Food Ministry and Exporting Countries Sub-Committee of the Wheat Advisory Committee in London. With due deference we regard such proposals as overlooking the realities of the situation resulting from the fact that the Empire is at war and we suggest that the obligations which the Dominions are assuming warrant some preferential treatment in purchases of wheat and the acceptance of a high fixed percentage of Empire wheat in the United Kingdom grist during the continuance of the war.

7. In regard to your last suggestion, my Government would be glad to send Mr. McIvor to London if this were felt necessary to a complete meeting of minds on this difficult question. However the Canadian Wheat Board has already a European Commissioner in London, Mr. R. V. Biddulph, who has been acting as liaison officer with Cereals Control Board. In view of this fact, we had hoped that it would not be necessary to send over Mr. McIvor who is much needed here at this time.[10]

There was an interesting reference in the reply Chamberlain had sent to King on October 6 to informal discussions between the ministry of food and the exporters' subcommittee of the wheat advisory committee. Mr. E. M. H. Lloyd of the ministry of food had drawn Andrew Cairns into ministry discussions on a plan to coordinate all wheat buying from the four major exporting countries. Prices were to bear some relation to the minimum price which had been discussed in the draft international agreement. The proposal was of obvious interest to Cairns, who saw in it an opportunity to bring the export allocation and price provisions of the prosposed international agreement into operation under wartime conditions. Massey

[10]*Ibid.*

had duly reported on the informal discussions which had taken place between the ministry of food and representatives of the four major exporting countries in his telegram of September 29, 1939:

> There have recently been informal discussions here between Ministry of Food and representatives of the Argentine, Australia, Canada, and the United States on the subject of long-term bulk purchases of wheat. In these discussions Lloyd, Assistant Director in the Ministry and Sir Alan Anderson, Chairman of the Cereal Control Board, outlined the Ministry's desire as follows:
>
> (a) to maintain contact with and in so far as possible negotiate with representatives of overseas countries collectively, as well as individually, so as to avoid any suspicion of one country playing off against another;
>
> (b) to purchase at fixed prices reasonable to buyers and sellers alike the annual wheat and food grain requirements of the United Kingdom, and to co-operate with France, Ireland and certain European neutrals in the purchase of their requirements;
>
> (c) to examine in their mutual interest every possibility of over-coming the difficult problem of obtaining necessary dollars and other foreign exchange;
>
> (d) to furnish at periodic intervals information about the exigencies of shipping, etc.;
>
> (e) to avoid using the Ministry's monopoly powers to the disadvantage of any suppliers;
>
> (f) to postpone action on the question of prohibiting the use of wheat for animal feeding and on the suggested increase of milling extraction ratio.
>
> The Ministry also express the hope that pending negotiation of long term bulk purchase contracts envisaged there would be no temporary holding back of supplies in any position.
>
> In connection with points (a) and (b) above, would appreciate authorization or otherwise to participate in suggested discussions on a reasonable price for wheat purchases. If so authorized, would appreciate your views as to what constitutes reasonable price. Understand Ministry's views are that a price somewhere between immediate pre-war price and that accepted by overseas exporters in their August discussions would be acceptable. Argentine and United States representatives at meeting indicated their readiness to carry on discussions but Australia and Canada merely stated they would ask for instructions.[11]

Cairns' drafting is discernible in the ministry's proposals, which held out some promise for everybody but which, if implemented, would have transferred from governments to an international agency the vital questions of price determination and market sharing. For the reasons mentioned earlier, the Canadian government had decided to keep the Winnipeg market open. This course was incompatible with the type of coordination Cairns envisaged, and the cabinet wheat committee refused to authorize Massey to participate in the ministry discussions. Pearson's report of October 11 revealed a cleavage of opinion between Lloyd and Cairns on the one hand, and the grain men on the control board on the other, as to the need for such an export coordinating and price-determining body, as he wrote:

> I am enclosing herewith copies of correspondence exchanged between myself and Mr. Eden regarding the Canadian wheat situation. . . .

[11]*Ibid.*

2. In Mr. Chamberlain's telegram No. 86 of October 6th, to which Mr. Eden refers, there is a paragraph, the second from the last, which refers to the desire of the Ministry of Food that wheat matters should be dealt with on a "basis of co-ordinated arrangements rather than of details on a purely commercial basis between various importing and exporting countries". This apparently is a reference to the request to which we have as yet had no reply, contained in our telegram No. 439 of September 29th, that there should be collective as well as individual discussions.

3. I have been informed that the paragraph in Mr. Chamberlain's telegram under reference was inserted without the knowledge of Mr. Rank and the Wheat Commission and there is some suspicion that its inclusion was due to the efforts of certain officials of the Ministry of Food, possibly Mr. Lloyd and Mr. Cairns, who seem anxious to have collective discussions on this matter in London. Mr. Biddulph, my informant in this particular instance, ventures the opinion that there is some division of opinion among United Kingdom authorities in this regard and feels that the desire for collective discussions is not as strong or widespread as the memorandum from the Secretariat of the Wheat Advisory Committee, which was enclosed in my despatch No. 630 of October 3rd, would suggest.

4. In this connection, I should add that Mr. Cairns 'phoned Mr. Pearson of this Office today to the effect that the Argentine and Australia had authorized their representatives on the Wheat Advisory Committee to participate in price discussions. Similar authorization was received by Mr. Steere of the United States Government on the understanding that these discussions would be purely informal in character. Mr. Cairns enquired if there is a possibility of an early reply from the Canadian Government in this matter. I did not, however, think the matter required a cabled reminder, but I am venturing to bring it to your attention in this way.[12]

Meanwhile, the economic advisory committee in Ottawa returned to its consideration of the wheat problem, as it met with McIvor and Grindley on October 3 to determine a method whereby substantial sales could be made to the cereals purchasing committee. After the meeting, Dr. Clark reported to the prime minister:

The committee gave further consideration to the question of wheat and particularly the problem of finding ways and means of assuring the making of immediate arrangements with the British authorities for the sale of a substantial volume (say, at least 60,000,000 bushels) of Canadian wheat for shipment to the United Kingdom before the close of navigation on the St. Lawrence.

Mr. McIvor and Mr. Grindley of the Canadian Wheat Board were present at the meeting and were of great assistance to the Committee in answering technical questions and discussing the pros and cons of the various alternative proposals.

As it is understood that a meeting of the Wheat Committee of the Cabinet was held this morning with Mr. McIvor and Mr. Grindley present, it is perhaps not necessary in this report to do anything more than outline the main suggestion which the Committee desires to make as a result of its discussion.

The Committee assumes that as a result of the cable sent last Friday night by the Prime Minister of Canada to the Prime Minister of the United Kingdom, instructions may be issued by the War Cabinet to the Cereals Control Board to make a serious effort to work out a satisfactory arrangement

[12]*Ibid.*

for the purchase of a substantial volume of Canadian Wheat immediately. On that assumption the Canadian authorities should be ready to make a constructive proposal to the Cereals Control Board. We believe that, if it is the Government's decision to leave the Winnipeg futures market open for some additional period, the most practical proposal that could be made would be as follows.

1. An offer to facilitate the purchase by the Cereals Control Board of at least 60,000,000 bushels of Canadian wheat in the open market.

2. To assure the British authorities that this could be done without too rapid a run up in prices, the Canadian Wheat Board should agree to give exporters overnight protection against half of the sales made each day by the Cereals Control Board. This would mean that our Wheat Board would be providing half of the wheat necessary to fill the British order and that the other half would be supplied by the trade, particularly by farmers who have wheat to sell over and above what they may have delivered to the Wheat Board. The advantage of this arrangement is believed to be that the Wheat Board would be sharing with others the responsibility for the determination of the prices at which British purchases were made. If such a scheme were not worked out there would be criticism of the Board for selling a substantial quantity of wheat, which it holds, so to speak, "in trust" for Western farmers, at prices which might turn out to be lower than prices that may be obtained by farmers holding off the sale of their wheat until a later period.

3. In addition to the above it will probably be necessary to give the British authorities some assurance that they will be able to purchase the 60,000,000 bushels of wheat at an average price not in excess of some reasonable figure, say, 75 cents per bushel. Consequently the Canadian Wheat Board may have to agree that, if necessary, it will intervene at a later stage during the course of the operation to a greater extent than is proposed under No. 2, above, in order to prevent the market from getting out of hand.

After discussion with Mr. McIvor and Mr. Grindley the Committee believes that the above represents the only practicable basis upon which the British could be induced to, and could satisfactorily carry out, a purchase of Canadian wheat on a large scale before the close of navigation. The only alternative seems to be to close the futures market at once and to arrange a deal directly between the two control organizations. This alternative would probably be preferred by the British Cereals Control Board, but it would throw on the two Governments, and particularly upon the Canadian Government, a heavy onus for establishing a price which Western farmers would probably believe to be unduly low. On the whole we believe that both Governments have much to gain by preserving the anonymity of the price-making process by keeping the Grain Exchange open. On the other hand we are just as strongly convinced that unless some such program as we have outlined above can be devised in order to make sure of a substantial volume of immediate sales to the United Kingdom, it is unwise not to close the Grain Exchange. It appears to be essential that sales should be made immediately and in substantial volume.

Whether rightly or wrongly, there still appears to be some misunderstanding on the part of the British authorities in regard to the possibility of getting Canadian dollars to finance their purchases in Canada. Repeatedly the Cereal Control Board has apparently used the difficulty of obtaining dollar exchange as an alibi for their failure to purchase Canadian wheat. If there ever was any ground for this attitude we do not think that such ground exists today in view of the cables that have been despatched to London during the last ten days and also in view of the discussions which we have had with Sir James Rae and Mr. Osborne representing the British treasury.[13]

For the next two weeks, cables passed back and forth between McIvor and Biddulph as the wheat board tried to get the cereals control board to commence purchasing through the open market, in accordance with the terms proposed by the wheat advisory committee. Messrs. McIvor, Folliott and Grindley remained in Ottawa throughout this period. Because the wheat board recognized its responsibility to the sellers of non-board wheat not to preempt the market for board account, it persisted in trying to facilitate cereals control board purchases through the open market in which the board would take a good part, but not all of the business. it seemed a complicated and unnecessary process to the control board which asked why it could not buy directly from the wheat board as it had done for the 10 million bushels it had purchased in August. But the wheat board cabled through Biddulph explaining carefully why it considered it had to use the market especially for larger quantities, as it proposed schemes by which the British could buy without running up prices. At first cereals proposed a purchase of 20 million bushels but in accordance with the economic advisory committee's recommendation, the wheat board pressed for a purchase of 60 million bushels, or as much as could be moved out of the St. Lawrence before the close of navigation. The German submarine campaign had begun at the outbreak of war and merchant ships had to be convoyed. A first convoy of 25 ships had arrived in Montreal on September 30. Prime Minister Chamberlain cabled King on October 10 that another 28 ships were on the way, but these were insufficient and shipping problems continued to plague the movement of wheat throughout that autumn.

To get the cereals control board to purchase through the open market, the wheat board acted upon the recommendation of the economic advisory committee by offering to protect exporters on one half of their overnight sales, and to average prices on an agreed basis of what would be "fair and reasonable". The price averaging would be undertaken by board sales of futures through the market in quantities sufficient to offset the price-raising influence of the British control board's purchases. In the absence of an assurance that the British would take a firm commitment of 60 million bushels before the close of navigation, the wheat board obtained a promise that the control board would try to increase the use of Canadian wheat to above 50 percent of the mill grist. The notion of what a "fair and reasonable price" would be had to be straightened out. The wheat board rejected a formula based on Argentine and Australian prices which seemed to have originated with Cairns, because Canadian quality differentials and Chicago market prices appeared to be ignored.

Because of the difficulties over purchasing and shipping, the cereals control board had purchased only 7 million bushels of Canadian wheat by November 1 through the open market and there were not enough ships to move this quantity, plus the 10 million bushels purchased in August, out of St. Lawrence ports before the close of navigation. The small export movement left lakehead elevators badly congested, and wheat stored in St. Lawrence ports had to be diverted by rail to Atlantic ports for winter shipment.

[13] *Ibid.*

CRERAR MISSION

As the wheat board and cereals control board resolved details of the purchasing arrangements, an exchange of cables at the prime minister level took place on an even broader issue, and this time at the initiative of Prime Minister Chamberlain. The whole question of military coordination and supply plus the purchase of essential commodities needed to be discussed at a ministerial level, and Chamberlain invited King to send a minister and officials to London for this purpose. With cabinet approval, King responded promptly to Chamberlain's request by sending the Honourable T. A. Crerar, accompanied by Brigadier H. D. Crerar, Air Commodore L. S. Breadner, L. D. Wilgress, A. M. Shaw, C. W. Jackson (mines and resources) and George McIvor. Although Mackenzie King had intimated earlier that McIvor could not be spared for a trip to London, the decision to send him now prompted a change in the membership of the board as, on October 26, 1939, Mr. C. Gordon Smith was appointed assistant chief commissioner, in the place of Mr. R. C. Findlay who remained as comptroller of the board. Mr. W. C. Folliott continued as the third member of the board. Mr. Smith was an experienced grain merchant in the firm headed by his father, Mr. Sidney T. Smith.

Mr. Crerar's mission remained overseas for six weeks and accomplished a great deal by way of establishing a compatible working basis between the two governments, in the light of their separate interests, and it is only necessary to describe here the results of his intercession on wheat.

On November 2 and 14, 1939, meetings took place on shipping at which Mr. Anthony Eden, secretary of state for dominion affairs, presided. With officials of the two governments in attendance, Crerar took up the problem of the grain congestion in St. Lawrence ports. There was an absolute shortage of tonnage, however, which had arisen from the need for refitting merchant ships with arms and from the delays in convoy formations. McIvor made a detailed presentation of the St. Lawrence grain position but, in the end, it was impossible for the British ministry of shipping to supply tonnage to lift all of the 17 million bushels of wheat already purchased and, as already mentioned, a winter rail diversion to Atlantic ports was made.

As Crerar cabled to Euler on the shipping situation he also reported on talks he had with the minister of food regarding a bulk contract for Canadian wheat. His cable of November 6 read:

> Regarding wheat, from information received here shipping situation very serious and difficult. Neutral tonnage available confined to Greece and Norway. They are timid and asking rate 3 to 4 times pre-war which Shipping Control here reluctant to pay. Moreover convoy systems slows up effective carrying power of ships. Further difficulty arises from extraordinary demand due war conditions. At meeting Thursday with Shipping and Food Administrations pressed for shipment of wheat owned by Cereal Board, St. Lawrence ports and Lake ports some 13 million bushels. Says will do their best. Another meeting Tuesday to see what progress made. Main difficulty here is that various controls tend to work independently of each other. Cereal Board wants to move wheat but cannot get anywhere with Shipping Committee. Approval of Treasury necessary before commitment can be (word omitted). They estimate their total import requirements all sources about 18 million bushels of wheat and flour per month. Everything indicates

inevitably will have to get large part of this from us. Sources superior to Rank's Purchasing Committee have suggested that present open market methods be discontinued and bulk contract for year's supply be entered into with Canadian Wheat Board, and under such conditions unofficially suggested price of 10 to 15 cents above present level. What would be the view of Wheat Committee if such proposal made? Doubt in my mind arises from fear Chicago May wheat owing to extremely serious condition of United States winter wheat may sell considerably higher than present level, and price suggested above for bulk deal might be criticized by Pools and farmers generally six months hence as being wholly inadequate. On the other hand having in mind our stocks, with heavy carry-over next August and another crop on our hands, think we should seriously consider such a proposal should it be made.[14]

Crerar's cable was given prompt consideration by the cabinet wheat committee which consulted the wheat board commissioners in Winnipeg and also Mr. J. R. Murray whose advice the ministers continued to seek. On November 8, Euler replied to Crerar:

If British Government would agree to take say 75 percent of their requirements between now and July 31st at say ninety cents, they to pay carrying charges, we would be disposed to view proposal favourably.

Wheat Committee would prefer alternative proposal to sell say 60 per cent of British requirements to May thirty-first at not less than 80 cents and should be 85 cents all subject to views of yourself and McIvor. Members of Wheat Board at Winnipeg and Murray favour first proposal, but not inclined close market, one reason being difficulty fixing price for neutral country purchases.[15]

Toward the end of his mission Crerar explored the possibilities of a much larger bulk contract with senior members of the British cabinet. On December 2, he cabled to the prime minister:

The Minister of Food some days ago brought up the question of long term contract for wheat. After considering and discussing the matter here I later informed him that I would be prepared to recommend that the Canadian Government, who had as yet no knowledge of this proposal, should undertake through Wheat Board the sale of between 250 and 300 million bushels of wheat and/or flour at a price of one dollar per bushel, basis number 1 northern in store Fort William, delivery of which is to be taken between now and July 31st, 1941; other grades to apply at price equivalents mutually agreed upon. Canadian Wheat Board will undertake that the wheat and the flour would be forwarded to such positions as required for loading at sea board, costs of such forwarding and all other charges involved to be for United Kingdom account. Interest, insurance and storage charges on wheat and flour in North America to be borne by Canada on condition that three twentieths of total amount of wheat and flour purchases shall be shipped in each three month period and in event of any stocks of that proportion not being cleared within the three month period additional to cost of carrying of such balance until shipped shall be for account of United Kingdom Government.

2. As alternative proposal to above I would be prepared to recommend to the Canadian Government sale of 150 to 180 million bushels covering the twelve months supply commencing on December 1st, 1939, at a price of 93½ cents per bushel basis number 1 northern in store Fort William and on the

[14]*Ibid.*
[15]*Ibid.*

other terms and conditions mentioned in proposal above for longer period with the understanding that one fourth of total quantity would be shipped each three months.

3. My alternative proposal given above was discussed at some length at meeting today mentioned in telegram No. 731. Discussion centred round contention of British Ministers that price was much too high in view of

(i) prevailing market price and volume of visible supplies, and

(ii) effect on cost of living in the United Kingdom.

The Chancellor of the Exchequer and the Minister of Food emphasized particularly the political and economic difficulties resulting from purchases at suggested price and involving rise in price of bread. I pointed out

(1) current prices were abnormally low and substantial increase was not unlikely;

(2) no effective world price existed, and

(3) long term contract at prevailing prices was politically and economically impossible on our side.

I added that the Winnipeg market might have to close in any event and control of selling centralized in Canada in which case some bargain would have to be struck between solely Canadian seller and solely United Kingdom buyer. (In this connection I may say Rank is now one of strongest supporters of keeping the Grain Exchange open). I explained that price suggested was based on minimum fair return to farmers without Government subsidy. Towers pointed out that current rise in cost of living here was caused mainly by domestic factors particularly depreciation of sterling and freight rates which should not be charged against Canadian wheat growers.

4. Meeting ended without any visible approach to agreement, with the Chancellor of the Exchequer saying that he felt conversations had been enlightening but difficulties at his end remained unsolved. I expect further meeting to take place early next week. I should be glad to learn by then whether the Government approve my proposal in paragraphs one and two above. In my judgment this would mean closing of Winnipeg market but in view of attitude of pools this may in any case have to be considered. The chairman of the Wheat Board approves proposals but wishes matter to be referred to his colleagues for their opinions. It is very important to keep it entirely secret. Any cables signed by his colleagues Winnipeg should be directed through you at Ottawa.[16]

This cable prompted the cabinet wheat committee to bring the new assistant chief commissioner, C. Gordon Smith, and James R. Murray, to Ottawa. After they met with the ministers, Euler cabled to Crerar on December 5, 1939:

At meeting here today attended by Ralston, Gardiner, Howe, Euler, Smith and Murray opinion unanimous that both proposals your cable number 732 December 2nd unsatisfactory. Folliott agreeing. Proposal Number one would net less than ninety cents for one northern in store Fort William after we pay carrying charges. It would be a grave mistake to sell nearly two years supply at this price. Any sale at such a price covering a period during which two new crops grow and mature in North America is too much of a gamble. Proposal number two would net only an average of about eighty-seven and one half cents one northern in store Fort William after we pay carrying charges.The period covered is objectionable but to a lesser degree than number one because it attempts to discount the future too far ahead in another crop year. The price would be all right for a proportionate quantity for the period up to

16*Ibid.*

July 31st, 1940. The only really attractive feature of both proposals is the quantity suggested, because it equals about seventy-five percent of British import requirements. We feel strongly all offers should be withdrawn as they are also obviously unacceptable to British. We are curious to know whether my cable to you through High Commissioner Number 517 of November eighth was received by you and suggestions made to British as you have never commented on same. We feel that further efforts should be concentrated on securing commitment that not less than seventy-five percent British imports be Canadian. Suggest initiative on further negotiations should come from British.[17]

Euler's cable closed off any further negotiations on a bulk contract at that time, and Crerar returned shortly thereafter to Ottawa. In the light of subsequent developments a bulk contract at that time within the range of prices discussed would have been fortuitous.[18]

As a result of Crerar's and McIvor's representations in London, the earlier differences which arose over purchasing methods were resolved. Thereafter, British buying was done by the purchase of Winnipeg futures and their exchange as needed for cash wheat. Because the cereals control board had to obtain treasury authorization for each purchase, this requirement was conducive to intermittent rather than continuous purchasing. As time wore on, the British came into the market less and less frequently, but for larger quantities when it bought. Examples were a 25 million bushel purchase of futures on January 10, 1940, and another 27 million bushels in April.

1940 GENERAL ELECTION

When parliament reconvened for a day in January 25, 1940, Prime Minister Mackenzie King announced its dissolution. He had postponed doing so in the crisis preceding the declaration of war, but by now he had the choice of calling an election or of seeking legislation to extend the life of parliament as had been done during the previous war. His preference was strongly in favor of an election, and he was handed a ready issue on January 18 when the Ontario legislature, led by Premier Hepburn, approved a motion censuring the federal government for making such little effort to implement Canada's participation in the war. Because the war issue transcended economic concerns, such as the government's wheat policy in western Canada, the March 26 election results failed to reflect the deep concern about the government's wheat policy which the Honourable T. A. Crerar had expressed to King a year earlier. Liberal members in western Canada had little difficulty in retaining their seats as Liberal representation increased in Manitoba and Alberta, while yielding only slightly to the C.C.F. party in Saskatchewan. Party standings in the 1940 election were as follows:

	Mani-toba	Saskat-chewan	Alber-ta	All Canada
Liberals	14	12	7	178
Liberal-Progressives	1			3
Independent-Liberals				3
Conservatives	1	2		39
Independent-Conservatives				1

[17] *Ibid.*
[18] See Mr. McIvor's comments, Appendix 7.

New Democracy (Social Credit)			10	10
C.C.F.	1	5		8
Independent				1
Unity		1		1
Unity Reform		1		1
Total	17	21	17	245

When Mackenzie King reorganized his cabinet prior to meeting the new parliament on May 16, the Honourable W. D. Euler who had chaired the cabinet wheat committee since it was formed on October 31, 1935, was appointed to the senate on May 9, 1940. The Honourable James A. MacKinnon (Edmonton West) who had been minister without portfolio since January 23, 1939, replaced Mr. Euler as minister of trade and commerce and as chairman of the wheat committee on May 10, 1940. Within the next two months, further changes were made in the membership of the wheat committee of the cabinet. As early as the previous September, the Honourable J. L. Ralston, who returned to public life on the outbreak of war, had been sworn in as minister of finance in the place of the Honourable Charles A. Dunning who was in failing health. Ralston served for less than a year on the cabinet wheat committee when the tragic death in an air accident on June 10, 1940, of the Honourable Norman Mcleod Rogers, minister of national defence, required a replacement in that portfolio. On June 13, the prime minister announced that Ralston would assume that responsibility as soon as he had presented his budget as minister of finance. On July 8, in the course of announcing several cabinet changes to the house, the prime minister indicated that the Honourable J. L. Ilsley, minister of national revenue, who had frequently served as acting minister of finance, would be transferred to the finance portfolio. At the same time, Mackenzie King announced the appointment of the Honourable James G. Gardiner as minister of national war services. In doing so, he explained that Gardiner would shortly vacate the agriculture portfolio in order to devote his undivided energies and time to the new portfolio. King had discussed with Gardiner at length the implications of his new assignment and it was clearly their understanding at the time that Gardiner would give up agriculture. But if this was the intention, it never materialized because Gardiner held the two portfolios for a period of two years and then gave up national war services. Crerar and he were now the two remaining charter members of the cabinet wheat committee, with MacKinnon and Ilsley the new members. This composition of the committee, with MacKinnon as chairman, remained unchanged for the duration of the war.

IMPACT OF THE GERMAN INVASION

In the interval between the election and the opening of the new parliament, the German invasion of Norway, Denmark, Belgium and the Netherlands took place which culminated in the evacuation of British troops from Dunkerque and the fall of France. Quite apart from its serious military implications, the German occupation cut off Canadian access to wheat markets on the continent, and the Winnipeg futures market reflected the sharply altered position. Prices which ruled around the 90-cent level in late April and early May dropped by 20 cents between May 10 and May 17 and the full limit of 10 cents on May 18 when a low of 60⅜ cents for the May future was registered. The wheat board urgently consulted the cabinet wheat committee and, with its approval, requested the Winnipeg grain exchange to peg wheat futures at the closing prices of Friday, May 17. Those prices were May 70⅜, July 71⅜ and October 73⅝ cents. The exchange authorities responded immediately, as MacKinnon explained to the house:

> Last Saturday morning May 18, after consultations between the wheat committee of the cabinet and the Canadian wheat board, the Canadian wheat board addressed the following communication to the Winnipeg grain exchange:
>
> "We have been asked to advise you that the government requests that the Winnipeg grain exchange peg the wheat futures market as at the close of Friday, May 17. This action is taken as a temporary measure, pending full discussion with the government."
>
> Upon receipt of this communication the Winnipeg grain exchange promptly issued the following statement:
>
> "At the request of the government the council has decided that the prices in wheat futures will be pegged as a minimum at the prices ruling at the close of the market on Friday, May 17, 1940, namely: May 70⅜, July 71⅜, October 73⅝, to become effective at the close of trading to-day and to continue until further notice. This action is taken as a temporary measure pending a full discussion with the government."
>
> This action means that until further notice it is not permissible to trade in the Winnipeg futures market at less than the prices mentioned, namely, May 70⅜, July 71⅜, October 73⅝. It should be made clear that trading may proceed normally at or above these prices. . . .[19]

In late May and early June trading took place slightly above the pegged levels but, with a bumper crop looming up and export markets drastically curtailed, trading became dormant in late June and through July as futures prices rested upon their pegged levels. Except for domestic demand, there was now no other means of providing hedges on deliveries of old-crop wheat. After the invasion, the cereals import branch confined its buying to bulk purchases of futures direct from the wheat board, and bought 50 million bushels on May 31. During July, negotiations proceeded on a sale of 100 million bushels of wheat futures which was completed on August 8. It was a record wheat transaction for Canada, and it had equalled a similar transaction the British had entered into with the United States during the first world war. But by midsummer, 1940, the Canadian wheat situation had settled into an acute surplus position for which additional storage facilities were needed. These were the circumstances, as the government once again undertook to revise its wheat legislation.

[19]*House of Commons Debates,* May 20, 1940, pp. 19-20.

30

WARTIME WHEAT SURPLUS AND GOVERNMENT RESPONSE

As the cabinet wheat committee faced the new wartime situation, it did so against a statistical background of hard facts. The 1939 wheat crop of 414 million bushels was the second largest produced in the prairie provinces to that time, and a carryover of 300 millions loomed up in the midsummer of 1940. Total exports of wheat and flour in 1939-1940 were only 192.6 million bushels, and export prospects were now diminished by the invasion. Moreover, in expectation that the war would create an increased demand, producers had sown a record 27,750,000 acres in 1940, and the crop prospects on that area appeared to be exceptionally good. When harvested, the 1940 crop displaced that of 1939 as the second largest on record; at 513.8 million bushels it fell short of the historically high yield in 1928 by only 30 million bushels. Although exports rose modestly to 231 millions in the 1940-1941 crop year, the carryover at the end of that season amounted to 480 million bushels, which more than doubled the carryovers the Bennett administration had contended with during the depression.

After the chairmanship of the cabinet wheat committee passed from Euler to MacKinnon, Gardiner continued in his ascendency as de facto wheat-policy maker. One of Euler's preoccupations as minister of trade and commerce had been to contain Gardiner's ambition to take over responsibility for wheat marketing as well as the export sale of all farm products. Mackenzie King had been compelled to arbitrate the ministerial dispute and he had spelled out in the house a demarcation of responsibilities between the two departments. Gardiner's correspondence and his public statements respected the official jurisdictions. Nevertheless, as he pressed his claim to responsibility for wheat policy, Gardiner stressed the fact that he represented Canada's largest wheat producing province. King envisaged for Gardiner, in his new assignment as minister of national war services, a coordinating function among the several departmental responsibilities in the interest of prosecuting the war effort; in turn, Gardiner discerned that such coordination could be extended to wheat, as he described his new assignment to the house:

> The leader of the opposition this afternoon said that the Minister of Agriculture was running away from wheat. It is rather a surprise to hear him make that statement, because the leader of the opposition at one time was

Minister of Trade and Commerce; and if he knew the duties of that office he must have known that ever since the Department of Trade and Commerce was set up, or, in other words, ever since we had a Canada Grain Act, wheat has been under the Department of Trade and Commerce and not under the Department of Agriculture. Never since I have been in this house or been Minister of Agriculture have I had anything whatsoever to do in my administrative capacity as Minister of Agriculture with the marketing of wheat.

Wheat has always been under the Department of Trade and Commerce. Wheat is still under that department. If I have shown any interest in wheat during the time I have been here it has not been because I have been Minister of Agriculture, but because I come from the very centre of the district in which wheat is grown in western Canada. . . .

Therefore my speaking from time to time in this house and in the country with regard to the marketing of wheat has not been because I am Minister of Agriculture. Nor have I had any authority to speak on it because of the fact that I am Minister of Agriculture. That authority has always been with the Minister of Trade and Commerce. I would rather think that the new position I have been asked to assume places me in a position of greater responsibility because, as was stated by the Prime Minister (Mr. Mackenzie King) in introducing the measure which created the new department, that department was to be concerned with the mobilization of the human and material resources of this country. If there is in Canada one material resource that is of greater importance than any other, in order that this war might be prosecuted to a successful conclusion, surely it is wheat. Wheat is the outstanding Canadian product which will play a very important part in the prosecution of the war, and in taking care of the people when the war is over. Therefore, in so far as the new department is concerned, my interests in wheat have in fact increased, rather than diminished, and my responsibility in relation to wheat has increased rather than diminished.[1]

GARDINER'S POLICY PROPOSALS

As the war situation changed, Gardiner set out in a letter to Mackenzie King a list of policy changes which the new conditions warranted, including a recommendation on wheat. In his letter of June 17, 1940, Gardiner wrote:

We might close the Winnipeg Grain Exchange immediately and take possession of all wheat at 70¢ paid last year plus the costs of carrying.

1. Set a price to the farmer for the wheat of 1940.

2. Arrange a price with Britain for 1939 and 1940 wheat which would as near as possible cover a price to the farmer.

3. The 1939 plus the 1940 wheat would cost the government not more than 85¢ a bushel, if we paid 90 cents for 1940 wheat basis Ft. Wm. If we could get 85¢ plus carrying charges from the British Government for it all this would not cost the government anything on the two year crop. If we could not get enough to cover the price offered the farmer the additional amount would again come from the treasury.[2]

As soon as he had been sworn in as minister of national war services, Gardiner spelled out his wheat policy recommendations more explicitly in his memorandum of July 14 to the prime minister:

[1] *House of Commons Debates,* August 1, 1940, pp. 2308-2309.
[2] *King Papers.*

... I come now, however, to the matter which I shall deal with particularly. I think it goes without saying that one product in Canada which is going to be more useful than any other in feeding Britain and her armies during the war, and taking care of populations when the war is over, is wheat. I think I can say as well, that up to date the marketing of wheat has been more affected by the war than any other farm product.

We have in Canada at present at least 250,000,000 bushels of last year's wheat. We have 70,000,000 bushels of last year's wheat which has already been sold to Britain but is still in storage in Canada. We have another crop coming on which in all probability, will amout to 400,000,000 bushels and will be available for storage during the month of September. At least 500,000,000 bushels of this wheat will be consumed, if consumed at all, outside of Canada, and so long as the military position is what it is today, any of it which is consumed will have to be consumed in Britain. It is obvious, therefore, that we have at least three times as much wheat in sight in Canada as we can dispose of in any one year while the war lasts, and while the military situation has resulted in a condition where we cannot market the wheat anywhere but in Britain.

I merely state these few facts in order to indicate that this is the biggest problem which is on our doorstep at the moment, and the solution of it will have a greater effect one way or another upon our war effort than probably anything else. Our economic position and the morale of our people is probably dependent upon the proper handling of the wheat question, more so than upon anything else.

Another point worth making is that this question must be dealt with inside the next two weeks. Farmers must know what we are intending to do.

There is not sufficient storage in Canada to store the wheat that is in sight now. I think we should encourage farmers to store this wheat on their own farms. A simple method of doing that would be to give a cent a bushel a month less for the wheat in August than in September and as the months go by increase it a cent month by month. This would have the effect of paying the farmer a cent a bushel a month to store his wheat on the farm, and if the Government is going to take it anyway, we would have to pay at least two-thirds of a cent a bushel per month for carrying charges of all kinds in the elevators. During the past year we have paid one cent.

I do not think that we can get away from paying the farmer a reasonable amount for his wheat this year. I think the Government is going to be compelled to take all of the wheat and make some payment on it. This being the case there is no reason why the Grain Exchange should operate. As a matter of fact it has not been operating for the greater part of the time since we pegged the price. The Exchange is only operating when it is providing ways and means of hedging. It has not been doing that. There has been no bidding on the market. The price has remained at the peg, and therefore the Exchange has not been operating at all. It can never operate as it does in peace time so long as there is only one buyer outside of Canada, namely, Britain.

My first suggestion, therefore, would be that the Grain Exchange should be closed. We should then proceed to make an arrangement under which those who are in the grain trade still continue to perform the things during the war which they performed before the war and may be required to perform when the war is over, and that they should be paid reasonable commissions for doing so. This would necessitate contacting the trade which is associated with the Grain Exchange and have a satisfactory arrangement made which would bring us the co-operation of all necessary parties of the trade. I think we then should go to Britain and make an arrangement similar to that which Australia has made with regard to wool.

I doubt if we could get Britain to take all her wheat from us, but I think we could get her to take a very considerable portion of it from us under a guarantee that she would pay a certain minimum price until one year after the end of the war for all that she was able to take. We could then proceed to set a price to our farmers based upon the undertaking which we have from Britain. In my opinion, we cannot get a sufficiently high guarantee of price from Britain to make it possible for us to handle the coming crop without putting up more than the British guarantee would amount to.

I do not see how, under all the circumstances, we can ask the farmer of Western Canada to accept less than 90¢ basis Ft. William for his wheat this fall. I think we should definitely undertake to do so even if we lose 10¢ a bushel on it in the end, but if we undertake to do that I think we should balance any losses which we may have on the 1940 crop against any profits which we may make on the 1939 crop, before paying any further returns to the farmer on either crop. I am certain that a satisfactory arrangement should be made on that basis and that changes which could be made would be accepted by our farmers.

I do not think we should lose any time in getting along with a policy for handling the coming crop.

To summarize I would say we should close the Grain Exchange at once; we should negotiate with Britain for a minimum price for the portion of the wheat which she would take, with the provision that changed conditions would warrant our asking for more; we should establish a price to the farmer on this year's crop on a basis which would give him encouragement to store as much as possible upon the farm.

If it is the desire of the Government that this policy should be pushed forward by the new Department, I am prepared to do it in either one of two ways; either through taking charge of the matter as one concerning a number of Departments, or to have it done as a co-operative effort with the Department of Trade and Commerce, which now administers the Wheat Board Act; but however it is done, something ought to be done immediately and no time lost in making an announcement to that effect. Either the Minister of Trade and Commerce or I should give direction to a policy immediately.[3]

Meanwhile, Gardiner had been making a more direct bid to take over from trade and commerce the responsibility for the Canadian wheat board. Council referred the issue to the advisory committee on economic policy with request for a recommendation. The committee considered Gardiner's proposal that both the wheat board and the agricultural supplies board be transferred from trade and commerce and agriculture, respectively, to national war services which would have given Gardiner the authority he sought over the marketing of all agricultural products. Had he achieved that objective, Gardiner would have given up the agriculture portfolio. But the economic committee, whose membership embraced the deputy ministers of agriculture, trade and commerce and finance recommended otherwise, and the transfer of responsibilities was not made. And on the policy for the 1940 crop, the cabinet wheat committee received certain outside recommendations.

3 *Ibid.*

RECOMMENDATIONS OF THE POOL CENTRAL EXECUTIVE

At the outbreak of war, the central executive of Canadian Co-operative Wheat Producers Limited had recommended to the government that the Winnipeg futures market be closed; that the government should purchase the 1939-40 crop; that the 70-cent price was too low, and that the government should negotiate a price with Britain which "bore a fair relation to the cost of other commodities". Now that the government approached a policy decision on the handling of the 1940 crop, the central executive renewed their representations. MacKinnon described them to the house:

> Representatives of the three western pools, Alberta being represented by Mr. Hutchinson; Manitoba, by Mr. Bredt, and Saskatchewan, by Mr. Sproule, the vice-president, in place of Mr. Wesson, who was unable to attend, and also Mr. W. A. MacLeod, the public relations officer of the wheat pools, met me and asked, . . . that a price of at least 70 cents be paid. . . . These men did not state that they were satisfied with the price of 70 cents. They did ask, though, that a minimum of 70 cents be paid, intimating to me that although they would have liked to see a much larger price, they were satisfied at this time, being actuated by a sense of fairness and feelings of patriotism, that probably 70 cents a bushel was all that this parliament could and should provide.[4]

According to their annual report, the central executive also recommended that: "the Wheat Board should take delivery of all wheat; that provision be made for the making of advances on farm stored wheat and that such advances be, on the farm, approximately 55 percent. to 60 percent. of the Wheat Board initial payment; that a quota system of deliveries be put into effect; that a domestic price be set for wheat consumed in Canada."[5]

RECOMMENDATIONS OF THE WESTERN UNION OF MUNICIPALITIES

At their convention in Edmonton, the western union of municipalities discussed wheat policy and telegraphed to MacKinnon on July 16, 1940:

> Western Union of Municipalities representing municipalities of three prairie provinces meeting in Edmonton to-day are greatly concerned with urgent problems relating to handling 1940 crop feeling that unless adequate measures taken immediately great hardships will result to farmers and stability of western economy will be undermined. We recommend that Canadian Wheat Board Act be maintained for handling entire 1940 crop with initial payment not less than seventy cents per bushel Fort William. That to encourage farm storage wheat board should arrange to pay farmer for farm storage on reasonable basis comparable to storage paid by board to elevator companies. That we favour principle of quota system of delivery to ensure equality of treatment to all growers. That where necessary advances be made to farmer on security of grain stored on farm preferably through grain trade financed by Canadian wheat board.[6]

After the convention, the officers of the union, Mr. Paul Farnalls (Alberta), Mr. James G. Knox (Saskatchewan) and Mr. J. A. Ross, member for Souris (representing Manitoba), called upon the wheat committee to present these recommendations.

[4] *House of Commons Debates*, August 2, 1940, p. 2359.
[5] *Canadian Co-operative Wheat Producers Limited, Directors' Report 1939-1940*, included in *Saskatchewan Co-operative Wheat Producers Limited Sixteenth Annual Report*, 1940, p. 64.
[6] *House of Commons Debates*, August 2, 1940, p. 2359.

CABINET WHEAT COMMITTEE POLICY REVIEW

The Honourable James A. MacKinnon had only been in the trade and commerce portfolio for a period of two months when, as chairman of the cabinet wheat committee, he presided over his first important wheat-policy review. The new minister was a good businessman but had no direct involvement in the wheat industry, nor did he pretend any intimate knowledge. Soon after MacKinnon took over from Euler, his private secretary (on the advice of Finlay Sim) started referring a goodly portion of the minister's wheat correspondence to C. F. Wilson for draft reply. After MacKinnon called the wheat board to Ottawa in July, 1940, for a prolonged stay Wilson also helped with the communications to the cereals import branch in London. Just at that time, the board was in the midst of negotiations on the first large bulk sale of futures amounting to 100 million bushels, and the telegrams passed back and forth through external affairs to the board's London representative, Mr. R. V. Biddulph, who was the liaison with Messrs. Rank and Hooker. By mid-July, when the wheat committee were ready to submit their proposals to council, MacKinnon was faced with the responsibility of making his first major cabinet presentation. Hitherto Euler had done this on his own without the assistance of briefs. But in this case MacKinnon wished to have a brief prepared for his use and Clive Davidson (now back on the board staff) undertook the assignment. It was a remarkable early "submission to cabinet" and its key proposals which MacKinnon read to council on July 18, 1940, were as follows:

> There are numerous problems with regard to wheat and the handling of the 1940 crop, all more or less related, that require the attention of the government at this time.
>
> 1. **Initial Payment For Ontario Wheat Crop**
> In the first place, there is the question of an initial payment for the Ontario winter wheat crop. This is urgent because the harvesting of that crop will be under way at the first of next week. The Canadian Wheat Board, in conformance with its duties under the Canadian Wheat Board Act as amended 1939, has fixed an initial price of 70 cents per bushel, basis Montreal for the top grades of Ontario winter wheat, subject to the approval of the Governor-in-Council, and provided the government plans to continue the present statutory price of 70 cents for No. 1 Northern at Fort William.
>
> I have two recommendations to Council in this regard. The first approves a price of 70 cents, as fixed by the Board. The second approves the form and content of the 1940 producers' certificates for the handling of the Ontario crop. . . .
>
> 2. **Initial Payment For Western Wheat Crop**
> As I have pointed out in connection with the fixing of the Ontario initial payment at 70 cents per bushel basis Montreal, this is conditioned upon the acceptance of a similar figure for No. 1 Northern western wheat at Fort William.
>
> Considering everything and provided the Canadian Wheat Board can make a satisfactory price arrangement with the Cereals Imports Committee of the Ministry of Food of the United Kingdom Government for their requirements and further provided that a domestic wheat price can be arranged, it would seem safe and desirable that the 70 cent initial payment be continued for 1940-41 as already provided in the statute by the amendments of the 1939 session.

3. Upward Scaling Of Initial Payment To Encourage Farm Storing

I am recommending an upward scaling of the initial price with the season to encourage the farm storage of wheat and to at least partially reward those farmers who are unable to deliver their wheat at the primary markets due to elevator congestion.

There will be a record carry-over of wheat in Canada at July 31, 1940, amounting to about 270 million bushels, with a further 20 or 25 millions in United States positions. Canadian elevators, after allowance of 10 per cent for working space, have a capacity of about 400 million bushels. With the outward movement limited by the loss of markets overseas, it is apparent that there will not be sufficient space in elevators for handling a big fall rush of wheat from the new crop, which is currently estimated around 375 million bushels for the three provinces.

Certain provisions must be made for the handling of the new crop so that the western farmers may be treated equitably and so that all may market enough wheat to get money to pay their urgent and current bills. The problem will probably be worked out by a number of provisions and developments.

1) The elevator companies will probably build annexes to their country elevators which will add to the 20 million bushels extra space provided for the 1939 crop.

2) Some space can possibly be secured in U.S. elevators.

3) At the close of navigation additional space for around 20 million bushels will be available in lake vessels for winter storage.

4) There is considerable farm bin space and this will be increased where farmers can obtain credit for new building, or can improvise some storage space.

5) A quota system of primary deliveries to the Board will make purchases from farmers more equitable.

6) Those producers who hold and store wheat on their farms will be compensated by an advance in the Board price as the season progresses . . .

If and when consideration is given to a further payment on the producers' certificates, each farmer will be treated as if he had delivered his wheat to the Board on the basis of 70 cents.

4. Quota On Deliveries

Since there is only a limited space available in elevators for new deliveries, it is very necessary that the privilege of making these deliveries should be distributed somewhat proportionately among the western producers.

To this end, it is proposed that each producer with a farm or group of farms operated as a unit should be issued a permit book in which all deliveries will be listed. This permit book will be obtained from the municipal office (or from a Justice of the Peace in unorganized districts) and the producer shall make a statutory declaration regarding the amount of wheat he has threshed. At the outset or for the first quarter of the crop year each producer will be permitted to market a certain proportion of his crop to a maximum of say 1,000 to 2,000 bushels. As space becomes available, the quota will be increased by the Board and further deliveries permitted on an equitable basis. The details of this plan can be worked out by the Board in consultation with the Board of Grain Commissioners and other bodies, but I would like at this time to secure the approval of the government for the principle of the scheme.

Consideration has been given to the possibility of controlling also the primary movement of the other grains. It is felt that no direct control will be necessary and that an appeal for co-operation from the farmers on a matter of such public importance will suffice.

5. Summary Of The Opinions Of The Cereals Import Committee Of The Ministry Of Food Of The United Kingdom

Various proposals have been put forward, pro and con, for the closing of the Winnipeg Wheat Futures Market. The Canadian Wheat Board has recommended to the Wheat Committee of the Cabinet that the market be closed.

At the end of May 1940, the Board made a sale of 50,000,000 bushels of October futures to the Cereals Import Committee of the Ministry of Food. This purchase was made by the Cereals Committee with the understanding that the Winnipeg Wheat Futures Market would be kept open until August 15, 1940, at least.

The attitude of the Cereals Committee has been again stated informally to the European Commissioner of the Canadian Wheat Board, Mr. R. V. Biddulph, who conveyed their opinions to the Canadian Wheat Board here in a cable dated July 13. They continue to dislike the thought of closing the market and are convinced that Canada is bound to suffer under a closed market. They believe that the present 60% Canadian wheat in their grist might be reduced to 40%. They also state that they can pay more with the market open than they can with the market closed.

If the decision is to leave the market open, then the Board will proceed along the lines given in the immediately following section.

6. Mechanics Of Operations As Planned For 1940-41 If Market Left Open

(a) It will be necessary to continue the peg on the Winnipeg Futures Market for 1940-41. My recommendation is that the pegs should be at a level that might give the futures market a chance to function and trade above the pegs. Therefore, I would suggest the following prices:-

Aug. Sept. & Oct. wheats basis 70   cents
Dec. wheats basis 71½ cents
May wheats basis 75¼ cents
July wheats basis 76¾ cents

(b) Spreads between the various future months are on the basis of ¾ of 1 cent per month. It would be necessary to do this, as under this idea millers, exporters, etc., would continue to carry their present stocks, together with any new stocks they might acquire. Therefore, they should have some reasonable carrying charge with which to work.

(c) The Board would agree with millers, exporters, etc., to guarantee their spreads on the above basis, or the Board could permit them to go into the pit if millers, exporters, so desired.

(d) Present owners of cash wheat in Fort William - Port Arthur and Western positions would ship to Fort William - Port Arthur and deliver against their present hedge, or the Board would agree to give them spreads as in the case of millers, etc., in 6 (c)

(e) Present owners of speculative long wheat would be obliged either to hold same until purchasers were found to take actual delivery of the wheat, or to spread into some deferred future. There should be no real hardship under these arrangements.

(f) The Board would continue to sell to millers, shippers, etc., cash wheat in store Fort William - Port Arthur as in the past. The Board would not do any eastern shipping unless it was found that millers, exporters, etc., were not doing the necessary shipping in order that all the available storage space would be utilized, as well as to ensure that wheat would always be available for the Cereals Committee.

(g) The Board would have an arrangement with the Cereals Committee agreeing to give them offers of futures in large amounts either at an outright price, to be decided each three months' period, or at a stated premium over the Winnipeg futures that might be required by the Cereals Committee.

(h) For example we could sell them fifty million futures at say 80 cents, as was the method in our last sale to them.

(i) If we agreed to a stated premium (which we think more satisfactory) of say 8½ cents per bushel, this would mean that the Cereals Committee would pay the following, they taking the positions most satisfactory to them:

	Cereals Price
Oct. peg price 70 + 8½ ———	78½
Dec. peg price 71½ + 8½ ———	80
May peg price 75¼ + 8½ ———	83¾
July peg price 76¾ + 8½ ———	85¼

(j) If the market should function the Cereals Committee would agree, providing futures prices were above the prices shown in 6 (i), to negotiate with the Board on a price. In this case the Board would agree to forego the premium mentioned in 6 (i), but would negotiate on the then market price. This would mean that the Cereals Committee would never be able to buy under the prices quoted in 6 (i), but would pay the market price, if futures market should function above these 6 (i) levels.

(k) In view of our agreeing to have the Winnipeg Futures Market open, the Cereals Committee would be asked to agree to buy all futures from the Board. These would cover all wheat and flour purchases from Canada. Their futures would then be turned over to millers, exporters, etc., as we are now doing on the 50 million sale. (In handling the Cereals Committee last May, the procedure is as follows:- When Cereals buy cash wheat from the exporter at the seaboard, the exporter is then short his hedge in the Winnipeg Futures Market. Cereals instruct him to get his futures from the Board and this is deducted from the 50 million bushel sale. The futures are cleared between the Board and the exporter at the market price and since this has been below the sale basis, Cereals cables the difference in price for each purchase direct to the Board.)

(l) All facilities of the Winnipeg Grain Exchange would be utilized, as is now the case.

(If this plan were found unworkable, the market could still be closed. In this case the Board would likely have most of the 1940 deliveries and it would be quite a simple procedure to take over the millers' and exporters' stock of wheat. If the decision is to close the market then an Order-in-Council along the lines of that passed under the War Measures Act in 1917, when the Board of Grain Supervisors was appointed, would be put into force in Canada. I might say that I have a draft Order-in-Council already prepared for such an eventuality.)

7. Ninety Cent Domestic Price For Wheat

Because of existing circumstances under which our wheat brings a low price on the export market, I do not believe that the same circumstances should govern the price paid for wheat by millers supplying our domestic flour requirements. Whether wheat at Fort William is available to millers at 70 cents or 90 cents has made, and should make, no appreciable difference in the retail price to the consumer for bread. Bread costs vary about ½ cent a pound loaf with each 30 cent a bushel change in the price of wheat.) I recommend, therefore, that if the market remains open, the millers, grist millers, and other processors of wheat for domestic consumption be subjected to a tax on wheat purchased which will equate their buying price to 90 cents per bushel, basis No. 1. Northern in store, Fort William, or No. 1 of the Eastern grades in store, Montreal. The proceeds of the tax accruing to the Board will become part of the Board's revenue from the sale of the western and eastern crops respectively. If the market is closed, the Board would then sell directly to millers at 90 cents, basis as above, the wheat required for domestic flour manufacture. In any event, the 90 cent price would rule for home-consumed wheat, regardless of any lower price which may be ruling for exported wheat.

An alternative proposal that would be more easily administered and perhaps more satisfactory to the millers would be to have the millers pay a sum of 20 to 25 cents to the Board on every bushel of wheat milled for domestic consumption.

It will also be necessary to prohibit imports of wheat and wheat flour into Canada.

8. **Amendments To The Wheat Board Act**

I have for your consideration a proposed amendment to the Canadian Wheat Board Act to provide for an interim payment if and when such can be made without loss to the government under its guarantees respecting any one crop. While this is worded as an amendment to the Act, there are some considerations which suggest that it might better be done by Order-in-Council.

Depending on our decisions on other points there may also be other amendments to be made to the Act. For example:

1) If the principle of scaling the initial price upward as the season advances is adopted, then the Act must be revised in this respect. At present, the Act provides that the Board must pay the same price to each farmer for the same grade of wheat.

2) The present Act provided that the Board must pay the same initial price on the basis of Vancouver as of Fort William. Under war conditions and a shortage of shipping space, there is a very limited market for wheat out of Vancouver and it is not logical to pay for the Alberta crop on the basis of Vancouver freights. If there is a profit on the whole crop, the increased freight differentials on wheat shipped east from the Vancouver freight shed will be shared by the producers of Saskatchewan and Manitoba. This should be remedied.

3) The 5,000 bushel limitation will have to be removed from the Act in order to give the Board control of the wheat and to permit the Board to regulate deliveries at country points.

4) Section 8 (j) of the Act requiring the Board to offer "continuously wheat for sale in the markets of the world" will have to be repealed.

5) The Act will need a new section providing the power to establish a domestic price.[7]

MacKinnon obtained cabinet concurrence as he read the memo, paragraph by paragraph. Thus the 70-cent initial advance, applicable to Ontario and the 1940 producers' certificates in connection with deliveries of Ontario wheat were approved. The proposal for payment of farm storage by gradual increases in the initial payments was approved in principle, with the rates left for later decision. The delivery quota system was also accepted in principle, and the consensus was that the market should be left open. All proposed amendments to the wheat board act were approved.

[7]*Memorandum Re the Handling of the 1940-41 Wheat Crop, with the Futures Market Open,* Canadian Wheat Board files.

1940-41 INITIAL PAYMENT

Although Gardiner recognized the need for a higher wheat price in western Canada and had recommended an initial payment of 90 cents, he had not received sufficient support from the central executive of the pools nor from the western union of municipalities to warrant pressing his case. Both organizations had failed to come out categorically in support of a higher payment. Instead, they acknowledged that they would go along, however reluctantly, with the continuation of the initial payment at 70 cents. Their positions relieved pressure upon Mr. Ilsley who would have been very much concerned if the additional 20 cents, recommended by Gardiner, had to be met by the Canadian treasury. In fairness to Mr. Gardiner, however, he had suggested that the additional price, or most of it, could be obtained from the British. The wheat board had confirmed that they might be able to realize from 8½ to 15¼ cents on British sales. In the circumstances, cabinet decided against amending the act to increase the amount of the statutory initial payment of 70 cents; on the other hand, cabinet approved a clause in the amending bill to authorize an interim payment to producers from any board surplus, provided that the amount of the interim payment could not possibly result in a loss to the treasury.

REVIEW OF THE DECISION TO RETAIN THE FUTURES MARKET

Although, in recent years, the pools had consistently recommended the closing of the futures market and the delivery of all grain through a government board, their position was strengthened when the Liverpool market was closed and the cereals import branch emerged as the principal buyer of Canadian wheat. A precedent existed in the closing of the Winnipeg wheat futures market during the first world war. On the other hand, Gardiner regarded the issue, not as one of principle, but rather of practicality. When futures trading came to rest on the pegs it was difficult, if not impossible, for the market to discharge its primary function of providing hedging facilities for the trade and for producers trying to sell through the open market. Gardiner recognized the advantages now of having a single seller to negotiate with a single buyer, and it seemed logical that the market should close. The wheat board had arrived at the same conclusion. However, the wheat committee decided, as a stop gap measure, to keep the futures market open at least until the end of the crop year. In response to questions in the house, MacKinnon announced that the market would remain open for that period at least. When the wheat committee consulted the board, McIvor reviewed the pros and cons set out in the submission which went to cabinet. But before any disclosure was made to the house of the government's decision to keep the market open, Biddulph was asked to get on record the views of the cereals import division. This he did by obtaining the following message from Hooker:

> Please transmit to government following message dated twenty-third July from cereal imports branch ministry food: "This branch of the ministry food is desirous that the Winnipeg futures market be kept open to enable the free movement of grain through normal trade channels. It feels it is only by this method this country can secure shipment of the maximum quantity of Canadian grain and under present conditions hesitates to experiment with the

delicate trade mechanism. Signed on behalf of the committee. A. Hooker, deputy director cereal imports."[8]

Moreover, at that time, McIvor was negotiating with the cereals import branch the sale of 100 million bushels of wheat futures to be applied against British cash wheat requirements over the next several months. Therefore, it was practical to keep the futures machinery in operation for the time being.

STORAGE CAPACITY

In respect of the storage problem which Gardiner described, there was need not only for additional capacity within the existing elevator system but also for new capacity for the storage of wheat on farms. When the farm storage problem loomed up that spring, Dr. Wilson made a trip to Washington to obtain from United States commodity credit corporation officials detailed information on American government assistance to grain growers in the purchase of commercially-produced steel storage bins. These, however, turned out to be an expensive luxury by Canadian standards and the cabinet wheat committee preferred Gardiner's proposal to scale up the initial payment during the course of the crop year by the equivalent of what would be paid in elevator storage charges, had the wheat not remained on farms. In the board's handling agreement with the elevator companies negotiated for the 1940-41 crop year the country elevator storage rate had been fixed at 1/45 of a cent per bushel per day. Under authority of a consequential amendment to the act, and with the approval of council, the board worked out a schedule whereby, commencing on November 1, the initial payment was raised to 70½ cents and ½ cent thereafter every three weeks until, by the following July, a maximum storage increment of 6 cents per bushel was paid. It was calculated that the maximum storage payment, if earned, would cover the cost of the lumber required by producers for construction of wooden bins. These farm storage payments totalled $6,147,524 in the 1940-41 crop year. Although they were continued in 1941-42, payments were smaller because market prices ruled above the level of the board's initial payment for much of that crop year. Thereafter farm storage payments were discontinued.

To encourage the elevator companies to build temporary annexes, the government allowed accelerated depreciation by which the companies could write off in two years the capital outlay on such construction. Good progress was made in the building of annexes at congested points. To the existing country elevator capacity of 212 million bushels, 97 million bushels was added in temporary structures during the course of the crop year. Then on January 23, 1941, representatives of the three pools, of United grain growers, and of the north-west line elevators association met in Ottawa with the cabinet wheat committee, members of the wheat board and of the board of grain commissioners to present proposals for construction of temporary storage at the lakehead. As a result, the government entered into an agreement with the companies on February 19, 1941, for construction of 50 million bushels temporary storage space at the lakehead, 3 millions at Sarnia, and 3 million also at Three Rivers. This additional storage space helped the wheat board considerably in accepting delivery of wheat from farms.

[8]*House of Commons Debates,* August 2, 1940, p. 2360.

DELIVERY QUOTAS

Experience with the handling of the 1939 crop had shown that producers whose crop matured earliest were filling up local storage space to the disadvantage of other producers who, by the time they could deliver, found the elevators congested. The problem prompted both the central executive of the pools and the western union of municipalities to recommend a delivery quota system. The proposal was not a new concept; it will be recalled that in 1934 the pools had reacted against the notion of enforcing acreage reduction by legislation and had advocated a delivery quota system, instead. Although the three provincial governments had provided legislative authority, the quota system was not implemented at that time. Also, during the course of the 1939 international wheat agreement negotiations the central executive of the pools had reminded the government that, if required to implement a new international agreement, the pools favored a system of delivery quotas to regulate the supply of wheat to markets. Now, the question was not one of limiting supply, but rather of sharing available storage space equitably.

Accordingly, cabinet approved an amendment to the act which authorized the board to regulate deliveries not only of wheat, but also of oats and barley. To administer the system the board for the first time issued delivery permit books in which each producer was required to make a sworn declaration of his seeded acreage of wheat, oats and barley. On August 7, 1940, the board announced its initial delivery quota of five bushels per seeded acre of the three grains, but quotas were not transferable among those grains. In announcing the new quota system the board explained:

> The extreme difficulties of the situation will be apparent when it is pointed out that at July 31, 1940 the carry-over of old wheat in Canada was about 270,000,000 bushels, with a further 20,000,000 or 25,000,000 bushels of Canadian wheat in the United States. The new wheat crop in the West is estimated at well over 400,000,000 bushels and there will be about 22,000,000 bushels more produced in Ontario. Our present elevator storage capacity is 424,000,000 but a deduction from this figure is necessary to provide working space. After allowance for temporary elevator annexes, and some additional storage in the United States, it is calculated that the net available storage capacity for the new crop will be 150,000,000 to 160,000,000 bushels.
>
> The first quotas are patterned to fill this space and to enable every producer to deliver a portion of his crop at the outset. As additional storage space becomes available through exports or consumption, the quotas will be extended.[9]

Because the delivery quota system was a completely new departure, the details (by which equal delivery access to limited elevator space were worked out) became the responsibility of Mr. McIvor and Dr. T. W. Grindley. The system required re-patterning of boxcar distribution so that all points would have equal opportunity to deliver up to quota, in replacement of the traditional distribution to the shortest-hauling delivery points first. In Appendix 7, Mr. McIvor has described how the system was structured and how it was accepted by producers whose deliveries were delayed in the equalization process.

[9] *Report of the Canadian Wheat Board, Crop Year 1940-1941*, p. 5.

Apart from special exemptions to cover family gristing and the delivery of seed grains and malting barley, the general quotas were raised as soon as elevator space became available. Quotas on barley and oats were soon removed, and by September 14, the general quota on wheat was raised from 5 to 8 bushels per seeded acre. Quotas continued to be raised as space became available at local delivery points. By November 22, MacKinnon was able to assure the house that all the marketable surplus from the 1940 crop would be delivered by the end of the crop year.

PROCESSING LEVY

One of the three planks in the policy platform of the pools, from the trough of the depression onward, had been a domestic price for wheat unrelated to the market-dictated export price. Now, the two-price proposal came to the fore after export prices had dropped from the 90- to the 70- cent level in the wake of the invasion. In MacKinnon's submission to cabinet, he recommended that the price to producers should be restored to 90 cents for wheat used for domestic flour milling. Cabinet reduced the recommended increase to 15 cents which it authorized as a levy to be paid by processors on the domestic use of wheat in milling and other products. The wheat board was designated as the collecting agent and the proceeds were to be used as revenue of the board to supplement participation payments, if any, to producers. Authority for the levy was included in Part II of the board's amending act, and the board's regulations in connection therewith were approved by orders in council P. C. 3888 of August 13 and P. C. 4387 of September 3, 1940.[10] This was the first instance in which the government introduced a two-price system for wheat, by which Canadian consumers paid a higher price for wheat than could be realized in the export market. However, the levy was collected only in the 1940-41 crop year P. C. 5844 of July 31, 1941, under the authority of the War Measures Act, repealed the section in the Canadian wheat board act authorizing the levy. This action was taken in response to the overall 1941-42 program (described later in this chapter) which introduced other income supplements. In the 1941-42 crop year in which the processing levy was assessed, it added $5,859,068 to producer's revenues.

WHEAT BOARD ADVISORY COMMITTEE

Included in the annual representations of the central executive of the pools to the government was a recommendation that the advisory committee to the wheat board be reestablished. In their campaign speeches prior to the 1940 election, both Gardiner and Euler had promised that an advisory committee would be appointed. In the amending act, two changes were made in respect of the clause concerning the advisory committee. One was to increase the membership to eleven with not less than six producer representatives. The other was to direct the committee to "assist" instead of to "advise" the board. The nuance was more important than the literal distinction. Much of the concern by the board (particularly that expressed by Murray) was whether the advisory committee had authority to supervise or direct the board's sales activities. If so, this would have created a conflict

[10]*Ibid.* pp. 10-11 and Appendix B to the Report.

n authority which would have resulted in an unworkable management. So ong as the advisory committee was without such authority, the board could ccept or reject the advisory committee's advice, and it was thought that the tatus of the committee was rendered clearer by the description of its unction as "assisting" the board. After the act was amended, the government appointed by P. C. 4214 of August 27, 1940, the following members of the committee:

D. A. Campbell, Toronto, Ont. (representing milling interests)
Fred H. Clendenning, Vancouver, B.C. (Pacific Coast shipping interests)
Paul Farnalls, Halkirk, Alta. (Alberta producers)
Lew Hutchinson, Duhamel, Alta. (Alberta producers)
I. A. McCowan, Summerberry, Sask. (Saskatchewan producers)
D. G. McKenzie, Winnipeg, Man. (Manitoba producers)
Rosario Messier, Contrecoeur, Que. (Quebec consumers)
Fred Pettypiece, Auld, Ont. (Ontario producers)
R. C. Reece, Winnipeg, Man. (exporters)
A. C. Reid, Winnipeg, Man. (line elevator companies)
J. H. Wesson, Regina, Sask. (Saskatchewan producers)

As can be seen from the list of appointments, the cabinet wheat committee maintained a balance between the representation of pool and non-pool producers in the western provinces, and also a balance between the pools and the private trade. Apart from offering advice on operating matters when requested to do so by the board, the advisory committee's principal contribution was made through its consideration and recommendations on wheat policy requirements to meet the everchanging wartime conditions.

LOANS AGAINST FARM-STORED WHEAT

Both the executive committee of the pool directors and the western union of municipalities had recommended the provision of cash advances against farm-stored grain. With delivery quotas in operation, a good case could be made on the need for such advances. In response to questions in the house, MacKinnon replied that the government was giving serious consideration to the proposal, but in his policy statement on July 24, he made no reference to it. As a matter of fact, however, the wheat committee had seriously considered making such advances. The committee's advisers pointed out the considerable administrative difficulties under government operation. Adequate farm storage of a type which could be sealed was deemed necessary, and it was believed that a bureaucracy of inspectors would be required to seal the wheat used as collateral against loans to ensure that it would not disappear into livestock feeding after the advances had been made. Notwithstanding, the ministers approached the banks and the elevator companies to enlist their supervisory capacity in a joint-risk operation, but found they were disinclined to assume such a risk. MacKinnon summarized the situation in the house, as he explained:

> With regard to loans against farm-stored wheat, the government approached the banks and elevator companies to act as principals in a loan programme. Because of the lack of adequate safe storage on the farms no private agency would assume the risk in making loans. These agencies, the banks and

elevator companies, were in a better position to discriminate between good and bad risks than was the government, had the latter attempted to direct a lending programme. The very fact that private agencies would not interest themselves in this business suggested that a loan programme under the conditions of open storage on farms might be subject to wide abuse if undertaken by the government. The government had no alternative except to make as extensive provision as possible for deliveries from the farms and, as I have pointed out, this has to my mind been successfully accomplished.[11]

END OF CONTINUOUS OFFERINGS

The Canadian wheat board act, 1935, required the board "to offer continuously wheat for sale on the markets of the world through established channels". The word "continuously" had been inserted to ensure against the practice which had developed during the support operations to withhold sales when prices were weak. Now, because of the cereal imports branch's method of purchasing in bulk quantities at infrequent intervals, it was no longer technically feasible for the board to offer wheat for sale continuously, and this requirement was deleted from the act. In fact, in the 1940-41 crop year, the cereals import branch made only two purchases including the first large contract of 100 million bushels on August 8, 1940, and a second and record-breaking quantity of 120 million bushels on May 13, 1941.

1940 AMENDING LEGISLATION

Following the cabinet wheat committee deliberations, which extended over three weeks, council gave its final approval to the 1940 amendments to the Canadian wheat board act. Other decisions had already been taken on administrative amendments to the prairie farm assistance and the wheat co-operative marketing acts. As he moved the resolution on the Canadian wheat board act amending bill on July 24, 1940, MacKinnon read a statement to the house, prepared by Clive Davidson, which brought the new situation and the legislative response to it into perspective:

> On several occasions during the present session members of the house have asked questions relating to the government's wheat policy. The matter which has apparently given greatest concern is in respect to the handling of the 1940 crop in light of a prospective lack of storage space. The matter has engaged the constant attention of the government and its advisers, the Canadian wheat board and the board of grain commissioners. The situation has been sufficiently clarified that I can now indicate some of the lines of action we propose to undertake to meet the situation we shall probably face in the next few months.
>
> Briefly the situation will be this. As at the end of July there will be a total carry-over of between 290,000,000 and 295,000,000 bushels, of which 270,000,000 bushels are actually in Canada. The 1940 crop in the western provinces is currently estimated at from 350,000,000 to 400,000,000 bushels. Our present elevator storage capacity is 424,000,000 bushels, which gives a net capacity of 382,000,000 bushels after deducting a ten per cent allowance for working space. Temporary elevator annexes already available and to be built this year will provide additional storage space for probably 30,000,000 bushels. Approximately 20,000,000 bushels can, in addition, be stored in

[11]*House of Commons Debates,* November 22, 1940, p. 341.

United States terminal lake elevators. This brings the total storage space, at the commencement of the new crop year, to approximately 432,000,000 bushels. With wheat and coarse grains, actually in elevators in Canada at July 31, amounting to about 275,000,000 bushels, the net available storage capacity will be 150,000,000 to 160,000,000 bushels.

During the autumn months considerable additional storage space will become available as wheat is exported or consumed, and finally, wheat can be stored in the holds of lake vessels for winter storage afloat. Despite these provisions, however, it remains apparent that a larger amount of wheat than usual will need to be held on farms beyond the customary early period of heavy marketings.

In dealing with this situation the government recommends that a plan be followed which is designed to permit the equitable use of available storage space by all the producers. The plan to be followed will require an amendment to the Canadian Wheat Board Act. This plan will enable every producer to deliver a portion of his crop at the outset. The amount to be delivered will be based on the total available supplies of wheat and the available storage space. As the season progresses, this quota will be advanced as exports and other outlets ease the storage situation. In brief, the plan is to use all storage space, country and terminal, east and west to the best advantage of all producers.

For that portion of the crop which cannot be accepted during the fall months the government recommends that an allowance be made to the producer to compensate him for the storing of wheat on his own farm. This allowance will vary in accordance with the length of time the grain is held, and will be in addition to the board's initial payment for wheat. The basis of the allowance will be announced very shortly — as soon as possible.

Regarding the initial payment to the producer basis No. 1 northern in store Fort William, Port Arthur and Vancouver, this price will remain at 70 cents as fixed by statute in the Canadian Wheat Board Act as amended last year.

On June 1 last, Mr. Chairman, I informed hon. members of the house that pending further developments the Winnipeg wheat futures market would remain open at least to the end of the crop year. At the present time the government has decided not to request closure of this market. This decision was made after consultation with the cereals import committee of the United Kingdom Ministry of Food who strongly recommend that the market be left open. The present cash wheat and futures pegged prices will be continued at or about the present levels.

Because of our recommendation that the grain futures market be left open at pegged levels, we also recommend the repeal of that portion of section 7(b) of the Canadian Wheat Board Act, which limits deliveries from any one producer to 5,000 bushels, as well as repeal of section 7(2), which deals with the penalties for the violation of the 5,000 bushel limitation. The removal of this limitation will enable every producer to deliver all of his wheat crop to the Canadian wheat board if he so desires.

The personnel of an advisory committee to assist the Canadian wheat board will be announced shortly. Provision is also being made to authorize an interim payment on producers' participation certificates, at a time when such payment cannot possibly result in a loss to the board.

The government also recommends that a processing levy be made against all wheat utilized for the manufacture of wheat flour and other wheat products entering domestic human consumption. The levy will be effective as of midnight July 23, 1940, and will be at the rate of 15 cents a bushel on the wheat utilized in the manufacture of wheat products. The levy will be collected against delivery of the wheat product by the processor to the purchaser thereof. A clause in the amendment to the wheat board act will authorize the collection of the levy on all existing contracts for future delivery of flour and other wheat products. Millers offering flour through merchants on consignment will pay the levy on flour not actually delivered to the purchaser by July 23, 1940. The detailed provisions will enable the levy to be applied equitably as far as all purchasers of flour and other wheat products are concerned, and will avoid any hurried buying on the part of the latter by way of anticipating the levy. The levy will not apply to deliveries of flour and other wheat products for export.

The proceeds of the levy will be payable to the Canadian wheat board by the processors on a certain day of each month, at which time appropriate statements on the deliveries made by the processors during the preceding month will be filed. The Canadian wheat board will use the proceeds of the levy as part of its regular revenue from the sale of the crop. The equity of this levy on domestically consumed wheat will be apparent to all parties concerned. Because of existing circumstances, under which our wheat brings a low price on the export market, we do not feel that the same circumstances should govern the price paid for wheat by millers supplying our domestic flour requirements. Based on the experience of past relationships between the price of wheat and the retail prices of bread throughout Canada, the rate of levy we are recommending should not require any change in the retail price of bread. Hon. members will recall that from January to May of this year Fort William wheat prices were around 90 cents per bushel; since May they have been in the neighbourhood of 70 cents. The effect of the processing levy will be partly to restore this Fort William price so far as the domestic human consumption of wheat is concerned. Some other necessary amendments to bring the act into line with present conditions will also be introduced.

May I add, Mr. Chairman, that the events of the last several months in Europe have had a serious effect on the market outlook for Canadian wheat. One by one the countries which were formerly outlets for our exports of wheat have been invaded and have disappeared temporarily as customers for our wheat. Denmark and Norway, ordinarily excellent markets for our wheat, were the first to go. These were followed by the low countries, Belgium and Holland, both substantial buyers under ordinary conditions. The entry of Italy into the war, the capitulation of France and the consequent inaccessibility of Switzerland have also removed present and prospective markets. The result has been that the only export markets now available are those of the United Kingdom and Eire; a limited market, chiefly for flour, in the islands of the West Indies and Newfoundland, and a very limited market in the orient and in South America. These factors are primarily responsible for the storage problem in this country. The value of Canada's wheat in the war effort can be known only in the light of future events. But it can be definitely said now that it is essential in the prosecution of this war that ample food supplies, particularly wheat, be available to Britain from the closest possible point, which is Canada. Therefore the government appeals to all the producers and other interests in this country to cooperate to the full extent of their ability in the plans being undertaken to meet this difficult situation. This cooperation can take practical form on the part of producers, who should start now to make the best provision within their means to provide for adequate grain bins or other storage facilities on their own farms.[12]

As MacKinnon's bill moved through the legislative process, cabinet continued to discuss and revise the details; Mackenzie King observed:

[12]*Ibid.*

At six o'clock, attended meeting of Cabinet in Room 401, H. of C., which lasted till nearly 8. Discussed the wheat matter at some length. Got certain modifications of the Bill which I think will help to gain for it more acceptance by our members in the House. The problem is very intricate and involved. What I feel to be most serious of all is that western Canada is shut out of markets on account of war and policy concerned with war, which, combined, makes England about the only market for our wheat, while costs are going up for the farmer on materials and labour and his sons are going into the army. In the industrial east, industry is so prosperous that orders are greater than can possibly be filled. Markets have come to the doors of manufacturers and of business community. It is a dangerous thing to get two sides of a country which are separated become so widely diverse in their economic fortunes. Certainly, the government is justified in guaranteeing a price which will hold the wheat and give the farmers a subsistence until the day of famine follows that of war and Canada may come to be the saviour of a famished Europe.[13]

By third reading, MacKinnon could claim from his press surveys that the policy innovations had received wide public acceptance and support. The amending act received royal assent on August 7, and the orders in council concerning the quota deliveries, the processing levy and the advisory committee were promptly approved.[14]

GARDINER'S MISSION TO LONDON

As a member of the cabinet wheat committee Gardiner shared with three other ministers the responsibility for wheat policy but, without any administrative jurisdiction over the wheat board which was vested in the minister of trade and commerce, he went to considerable lengths with King, his cabinet colleagues, in correspondence, and in the house to establish his special responsibility for wheat policy. His appointment as minister of national war services had provided a fillip in this regard and, as soon as the appointment was made, he planned to head a mission to London in the belief that it would consolidate his position in relation to wheat. It will be recalled that Gardiner had recommended the closing of the futures market and the fixing of a 90-cent initial payment, backed up by a sales agreement with Britain. Crerar had already discussed such an agreement during his mission to Britain, but had failed to win the support of his cabinet colleagues on its terms. On September 16, 1940, Gardiner took the initiative in promoting his own mission, as he wrote to King:

I have been giving considerable thought to the discussion which we had at the time I took over the Department of War Services. I am more convinced now than I was then that I should go to England as soon as possible.

The Agreement which we have with Britain with regard to pork products was to have been reconsidered in August. We are making very little headway with the reconsideration of it.

The Agreement on cheese must be reconsidered by November.

Britain is taking no tobacco and no apples this year up to date. Certain arrangements must be made with regard to the disposal of our fibre flax and flax seed.

In addition to this there is the wheat problem which I cannot escape some responsibility for no matter what Department I may be administering, in view

[13]*King Diary,* July 30, 1940.
[14]*Statutes of Canada,* 4 George VI, Chap. 25.

of the fact that I represent the largest wheat producing Province in Canada.

It seems to me that if we are going to be able to keep agriculture moving along in a manner which will be helpful toward the winning of the war, there must be definite understandings with the British Government with regard to at least the products I have mentioned. My officials here, as well as I, are convinced that there is only one way of having these matters properly settled and without too great delay, and that is by a mission to England. If it meets with your approval I am prepared to head it, and believe, under all the circumstances, I ought to. If it is your desire to have any other Minister go with me that is quite satisfactory. A number of officials should, of course, go along. . . .[15]

When King broached MacKinnon with Gardiner's proposal, the latter appeared willing to accompany Gardiner who also wanted Messrs. George McIvor and L. D. Wilgress to join the official party. But, when Gardiner's mandate on wheat was considered in cabinet, he was not empowered to negotiate a long-term contract. The British had just completed the purchase of 100 million bushels of wheat futures which would cover their requirements until the following spring. As a result, Gardiner was authorized to discuss only Britain's longer-term purchasing intentions and, in the event, neither MacKinnon nor McIvor accompanied him. In his wheat discussions, Gardiner was assisted by Mr. R. V. Biddulph, the wheat board's liaison officer with the cereals import branch.

Although Gardiner made progress in his discussions on bacon, cheese and tobacco for which he had direct marketing responsibility, he concluded from the British reaction that the Canadians had been pressing their case for wheat sales far too strenuously, as he reported in a postscript to his letter of October 9, 1940 from London to King:

We had a very satisfactory conference yesterday with Lord Cranborne, Sir Kingsley-Wood and Lord Woolton and staffs. The exchange matter seems the only obstacle to agreements which would satisfactorily deal with our present agricultural problems in all but wheat. I am hopeful that adjustments as among commodities can be arranged which will work out satisfactorily. Wheat is another matter but I am satisfied since coming here that we have been pressing quantity further than conditions here warrant or our own long time policy requires to the detriment of other farm products and the long time returns from wheat.[16]

Gardiner pursued his wheat talks, however, with the British authorities on a statistical basis as he indicated in a subsequent report to the house. In doing so, he made an almost incredible five-year projection of a type for which he had earlier roundly criticized Andrew Cairns. The difference was, however, that Cairns had projected a world surplus situation in support of international action. In contrast, the thrust of Gardiner's projection was to demonstrate that within five years Canadian wheat supplies could be in balance, as he explained on November 14, to the house:

I did not go to Britain with authority to make an agreement on wheat. The duty of selling wheat has been entrusted by this house to a wheat board. It is not the duty of any minister to market wheat, but that of the wheat board which under the act reports to the Minister of Trade and Commerce.

---

[15]*King Papers.*
[16]*Ibid.*

Both the Minister of Trade and Commerce and the chairman of the wheat board asked me to discuss wheat and instructed their representatives in Britain to facilitate the discussions in every way possible. I wish here to state that I and those with me appreciated the assistance received from the very competent staffs of the Department of Trade and Commerce and the Department of External Affairs, including the high commissioner. In so far as wheat was concerned the assistance of Mr. Biddulph was indispensable. No official could know his job better or carry it out with greater courtesy and efficiency.

To illustrate Canada's wheat position to Britain I used certain figures, as follows:

	Million bushels
Wheat carried forward from previous years into 1940-41 and now in storage	282
Canada's crop in the year 1939-40	561
Stocks in sight to dispose of at August 1st, 1940	843
Canada will probably consume in 1940-41	130
Canada therefore has for sale	713
In the 14 years before the war, Canada sold to the United Kingdom an annual average of	90
Canada exported to the United Kingdom in calendar year 1939	132
Canada exported last year to all countries, except the United Kingdom which it is now open to her to sell	25
Canada exported before the war to countries now blockaded, an annual average of	35

The wheat carried forward from previous years covers the amount in the elevators of Canada at August 1, 1940, because I was dealing with the storage situation.

The United Kingdom imported 230 million bushels of wheat in the year 1938-39. It appeared, therefore, that Canada could meet the entire demands of the United Kingdom for wheat for the next three years out of her present stocks of 843 million bushels. Canada realized, of course—these were the representations made—that the United Kingdom would want to buy wheat also from countries other than Canada. But it appeared that in recent months about seventy per cent of the United Kingdom purchases had been of Canadian origin, and I suggested that the United Kingdom might think it desirable to maintain this percentage. On this basis it appeared that the United Kingdom would want to take about 160 million bushels of wheat a year from Canada.

With regard to the future, I examined the prospects first on the demand and then on the supply side. On the demand side, assuming that the blockade would not be lifted for two more years, Canada expected to be able to dispose of 160 million bushels a year to the United Kingdom, and to raise the consumption within Canada for food and feed from 130 million to 160 million bushels a year. During this two year period it would thus be possible for Canada to dispose of 640 million bushels at home and to the United Kingdom. In addition, Canada expected that after the blockade was lifted it would be possible for her to dispose of 160 million bushels a year to countries now blockaded, or say 480 million bushels a year over a three year period. Thus during the next five years, assuming two years of blockade and three years of offensive warfare or peace, it should be possible for Canada to dispose of the following quantities of wheat:

	Million bushels
To the United Kingdom:	
5 years at 160 million bushels a year	800
By internal consumption:	
5 years at 160 million bushels a year	800
To countries now blockaded:	
3 years at 160 million bushels a year	480
Total........................	2,080

On the supply side, Canada could expect to produce on an average 380 million bushels of wheat a year. That is her average for the last fourteen years and more than her average for the last five years, including the last two crops. Her total production in five years thus would amount to 1,900 million bushels. To this should be added the 280 million bushels carried over into 1940-41 from previous years, making a total quantity of 2,180 million bushels which it would be necessary for Canada to dispose of in the five year period.

It appeared, therefore, according to the above figures that Canada would have 2,180 million bushels of wheat to sell in the five year period, and that during the same period she probably would be able to market 2,080 million bushels, leaving a carry-over at the end of that time of only 100 million bushels. Moreover, if Canada continued to be able to sell 30 million bushels a year to those countries outside Europe which were not being blockaded, instead of there being a surplus of 100 million bushels at the end of the five year period the demand for Canadian wheat would be 50 million bushels greater than the supply.

I did not consider, therefore, that Canadian wheat producers need be pessimistic, but may I say again that there is nothing in these figures which should induce Canadian wheat growers to increase their acreage this year. As a matter of fact there is very much in them upon which to ask farmers at least to go back to the acreage they had in the year previous to last year, which was 2,000,000 acres lower than the land sowed to grain last year.

Canada could supply Britain's needs and did not anticipate that unsold stocks would grow to excessive amounts. The difficulty, however, was that of financing the quantities of wheat which would have to be carried. About 800 million bushels of wheat would need to be financed, of which roughly half would be financed for two years at a cost of about 80 cents a bushel and the other half for one year at a cost of some 75 cents a bushel, if the present arrangement is continued. This would mean that the Canadian government would require to put out about $320 million on the two year arrangement and about $300 million on the one year arrangement, making a total of $620 million. The dominion government is obliged to pay the farmer any additional amounts received for the wheat. It is generally admitted that 70 cents advance at Fort William, which nets the farmer about 50 cents a bushel, does not cover his total costs of production and therefore does not maintain him as a contented producer. If he is to receive more money, it must come from the sale price of wheat, or from the taxpayers of Canada, or from both.

Those were the representations made. We made it plain to the British government that we were there not to discuss an agreement but to get their opinions with regard to the wheat situation. I have received those opinions as a result of the representations made through officials of the department concerned, and I have presented them to the Minister of Trade and Commerce (Mr. MacKinnon) to be given consideration under his direction by the government of Canada. When he is in a position to make the pronouncement he desires to make with regard to the policy to be followed as a result of them, he will make the announcement to the house.[17]

Made at a time when others could see no end to the burdensome surplus, Gardiner's forecast appeared to be wishful ministerial thinking but, as a long-term forecaster, Gardiner turned out to be not too bad. In January, 1938, Cairns had projected the world carryover of wheat as of August 1, 1940, with almost unerring accuracy. Gardiner's projection of a zero carryover for Canadian wheat within five years came reasonably close. By July, 31, 1945, the Canadian figure stood at 258 million bushels; by July 31, 1946, it had been reduced to 73.6 millions, which was hardly enough for working stocks.

WHEAT PROGRAM FOR 1941-42

With the increased storage space, the wheat board made a notable effort through the 1940-41 crop year to raise delivery quotas as elevator space opened up at the country elevators. In doing so, the wheat board had the co-operation of the board of grain commissioners and its car allocation committee in the distribution of cars to areas of heaviest congestion. As early as November 22, 1940, MacKinnon was able to announce in the house that arrangements were being made so that all of the wheat deliverable to the board could be accepted prior to the end of the crop year. At the same time, it was evident that the storage problem would be intensified if another crop such as those harvested in 1939 and in 1940 were to be produced in 1941. As the advisory committee on economic policy observed in its review of developments during the first year of the war:

The wheat situation, of course, now overshadows almost everything else in the farm picture. With much the highest carry-over in our history, about 300 million bushels, the new crop is estimated to be about 560 million bushels—only about 1% less than the bumper harvest of 1928 and its quality high. Unless the war ends this year, it is difficult to foresee exports of more than 200 million bushels. (They were 192 million in 1939-40). The supply of feed grains is high. Consequently, it would seem probable that we must expect a carry-over of more than 500 million bushels next August. The storage situation is, of course, already proving difficult, and it seems that next August there must remain some 50 to 100 million bushels on the farms, with the elevators full, when the new crop arrives. This indicates that barring unexpected developments some action will have to be taken either to restrict very substantially next year's crop, or to dispose of a large quantity of our wheat, or to increase greatly the storage capacity somewhere or other. In addition, of course, the financing of the accumulation presents a real problem at this time when there are so many urgent calls upon public funds. We now have this major economic problem superimposed upon the war and the gravity of this situation does not yet appear to be publicly realized.[18]

[17]*House of Commons Debates*, November 14, 1940, pp. 101-102.
[18]*King Papers.*

To face up to this situation, the government invited both the economic committee and the advisory committee to the wheat board to make recommendations on wheat policy for the 1941-42 crop year. The wheat committee of cabinet, and especially Gardiner, were aware that the executive directors of the wheat pools whether directly or through the Canadian federation of agriculture would also be making recommendations. Lest the Liberal party presence in Saskatchewan conclude that it was being left out of the picture, Gardiner also met with the party organization in Regina and assisted it in formulating recommendations. He also mounted a conference in Saskatoon, at which the senior officials of the department of agriculture presented a symposium on the current state of markets for all western farm products. Thus a major policy review was launched in several directions, with a view to having as many inputs as possible into the cabinet wheat committee's and eventually council's determination of policy. Although many of the meetings were carried on simultaneously, they are described separately for a better understanding of the contribution made by each group.

ECONOMIC ADVISORY COMMITTEE REPORT ON WHEAT

The economic committee met several times in the preparation of its report which was submitted to cabinet in January, 1941. After stating the facts of the situation, the committee made a notable contribution by defining for the first time a defensible level of prairie farm income. Wilson was involved in the preparation of the $300,000,000 figure set out in that report. Although he was not a member of the committee, Dr. R. H. Coats had asked him to prepare the study based on cash receipts from the sale of farm products in the prairie provinces; his data showed that in the previous twelve years, whenever the total fell below $300,000,000 the federal government had been involved in one form of relief or another. The committee then gave consideration to the best means of assuring that western farm income would not drop below that level in 1941-1942. In the process, it advanced an ingenious scheme, not adopted, for producers to sell a portion of their delivery quotas to the government at a price which would maintain income as they reduced wheat acreage. The committee also commented on other possible forms of income maintenance, such as an increase in the initial payment, the setting aside of the 1941 carryover in order to give the 1941 crop the right of way in sales, and thereby to realize something on the participation certificates; it also referred to the proposal emanating from other groups for an increase in the processing levy. A summary of the report presented to cabinet follows:

Prospective Markets
   Markets in 1941-42 will be found for 284,000,000 bushels, based on present expectations. This allows for exports of 160,000,000 bushels, and domestic use of 125 million bushels. For the Prairie Provinces, after allowing for seed and feed, the above markets would take care of commercial deliveries of 207,000,000 bushels.

   Limitation of Wheat Deliveries
   The case for limitation of wheat deliveries rests not on lack of storage space (which could be expanded) but on lack of markets, and the cost of carrying further quantities of unsaleable wheat. The Committee favours a maximum

delivery quota of 205—225,000,000 bushels. The method of allocation suggested is a uniform yield per acre of the 1940 individually sworn acreages, with a Board of Review to adjust obvious inequalities. Generally, this basis would induce relatively heavy reductions of wheat acreage in the park belt where alternative opportunities are greater, and would require only small adjustments in the grass plains area where alternative opportunities are less.

Storage Situation

With total storage space of 582,000,000 bushels in sight to house the 575,000,000 bushel carry-over expected at the end of July, no further provision for storage space appears necessary if the 1941-42 deliveries are taken as the wheat moves into domestic use and export.

Maintenance of Prairie Farm Income

The Committee regards $300,000,000 or more as a defensible Prairie farm income. In only two years since 1929 has it exceeded this amount (1929 - $484,000,000; 1939 - $337,000,000; 1940 - $327,000,000). Because of heavy sales of 1940 wheat prior to July 31 next, the 1941 calendar year income is forecast at $328,000,000, and no supplementary aid is needed. But for the 1941-42 crop year, maximum wheat deliveries of 225,000,000 bushels would realize $117,000,000. With income from the sale of other farm products estimated at $163,000,000, the total 1941-42 receipts would be $280,000,000, indicating need for at least $20,000,000 of supplementary income.

To provide this supplementary income the Committee evaluated the following proposals, in descending order of merit:

(a) **Saleable Quotas** - Instead of placing the maximum deliveries at 225,000,000 bushels, they could be placed at 330,000,000 bushels representing normal deliveries from acreage at the 1940 level. Before seeding, the Government would offer to purchase farmers' rights to deliver 105,000,000 bushels at 20 cents per bushel, providing $21,000,000 additional income, and reducing the total deliveries to 225,000,000 bushels. The offer would have to be contingent on the sale to the Government of the full 105,000,000 bushels of quotas. But if some farms sold more than their pro-rata share and others less, this would permit some flexibility in individual farm adjustments. (It might be hard to administer in the short time available.)

(b) **Initial Price** - Advance the initial price by five or ten cents, and deny the farmer any participating rights in the proceeds of the sale. An increased price doesn't help to encourage reduced production.

(c) **Participation Rights** - Set aside the 1941 carry-over of 575,000,000 bushels, and allocate the receipts from all 1941-42 sales to 1941-42 deliveries. This relief from accumulated carrying charges might realize something on the participation certificates. This would seriously restrict the Government in making any disposition of the accumulated carry-over.

(d) **Fifty Cent Processing Tax** - Applied to domestic millings would provide $25,000,000 or 11 cents per bushel extra income on the 225,000,000 bushels deliverable. The form of the tax increase has definite objections, and is contrary to the general tax policy. A less objectionable alternative would be to provide the sum out of general taxation.

Educational Program

The Committee attaches the greatest importance to a broad educational program to place the factual wheat situation before western farmers.[19]

[19]*Ibid.*

WHEAT BOARD ADVISORY COMMITTEE
RECOMMENDATIONS

The new advisory committee to the wheat board which was formally appointed on August 27, 1940, had held only two sessions on August 26-27, and on September 30 - October 1 when it was plunged into a review of wheat policy on November 18-19, for which Mr. C. B. Davidson prepared a position paper. Davidson's paper pointed up the need for wheat acreage reduction and for a substantial increase in barley acreage to meet expanding wartime feed requirements. Although the Bracken conference on markets for western farm products had examined with rather discouraging results the prospects of converting wheat policy into a more comprehensive grain policy, this was the first occasion since that a shift in emphasis away from wheat seemed warranted. To expedite matters, the advisory committee named five of its members to draft concrete recommendations, which were reported back to the January 13-15, 1941, meeting of the main committee. By the conclusion of that meeting, the committee had approved a list of ten recommendations in respect of 1941-42 wheat policy for transmission to the cabinet wheat committee. In the preamble of its report, the advisory committee reviewed developments leading up to the record wheat acreage level in 1940, including the early sentiment that the war would increase the demand for wheat, that production had been built up as an offset to low prices throughout the past decade, and that governmental assistance to the wheat industry had been clearly defined, in contrast to the more indirect assitance offered to other branches of farm production. However, identification of the causes of the increase was not so important as the need for a sounder diversification of crops. The committee was opposed to compulsory reduction of acreage because of the practical problems of equity and administration. Instead, it recommended a limitation on the volume of wheat which could be marketed, coupled with appropriate economies in production practices and with an educational program on the need for adjustment. The committee's specific recommendations were as follows:

1. The Advisory Committee recommends that stocks of wheat owned by The Canadian Wheat Board as at July 31st, 1941 (and which will amount to approximately 500 million bushels) be viewed as a war-time reserve.

2. That the Dominion Government continue a price guarantee for 1941-42 but that this guarantee be limited to the volume of wheat which can be marketed within the 1941-42 crop year. Marketable quantities are estimated as follows:

Domestic Consumption...............	50 Million Bushels
Sold for Export..........................	180 Million Bushels
Total	230 Million Bushels

The Advisory Committee recommends that such a fixed price for 1941-42 be established by the Dominion Government as it may deem advisable, having in mind the restricted deliveries, and that it is in the national interest to maintain an adequate farm income.

3. That the fixing of minimum prices for wheat futures on the Winnipeg Grain Exchange be continued during the crop year 1941-42.

4. That the powers of The Canadian Wheat Board be enlarged to enable the board to control all sales of wheat by producers and others, having in

mind that any excess production in 1941 must, of necessity, be retained on farms for an indefinite period.

5. That the Processing Levy now in effect be increased as from July 31st, 1941 or sooner, to such an amount as when added to the minimum prices above mentioned, shall equal a figure deemed to give the producer a remunerative return on that portion of his production as is:

(a) Consumed as flour in Canada for any purpose whatsoever;

(b) Utilized in all other wheat products used in Canada for any purpose whatsoever, except for the feeding of livestock and poultry.

6. That the net proceeds of the increased Processing Levy be paid to producers in the form of a 'domestic premium' on a per bushel basis on deliveries of 230 million bushels in 1941-42. The 'domestic premium' will be in addition to the fixed price provided for under The Canadian Wheat Board Act.

7. That quotas be established upon the equitable distribution among producers of the amount of wheat which will be sold in the domestic and export markets during 1941-42.

8. That agriculture join with all other industries in Canada in effecting "savings" wherever possible as a war-time measure. In the case of agriculture, this can best be done by diversifying production and making the farm home as self-supporting as possible in respect to such commodities as eggs, milk, butter, vegetables, etc.

9. That the Dominion Government be requested to enlarge its research facilities in respect to finding edible and inedible uses for wheat and other farm products.

10. That an effort be made by the Dominion Government and the Provincial Departments of Agriculture, to fully explain the facts of the present wheat situation to the farmers of the prairie provinces.[20]

The recommendations were promptly forwarded to the cabinet wheat committee on January 15, 1941, following which the latter committee brought the wheat board to Ottawa for consultation, and the advisory committee's recommendations were considered both by the wheat committee and in council. The chief commissioner of the wheat board reported back to the advisory committee on February 17, 1941, that their recommendations had been carefully reviewed by the cabinet wheat committee and by the full council. The government had concurred in the 230 million bushel overall delivery limitation and in the retention of the initial payment at 70 cents. But neither the wheat committee nor the cabinet could agree with the advisory committee's recommendation that the processing levy on domestic human consumption be raised to 50 cents. MacKinnon had asked on behalf of the cabinet that this latter recommendation be referred back to the advisory committee for reconsideration.

The advisory committee met in Winnipeg, February 17-19. The issue over the amount of the processing levy was essentially one of balancing the need for supplementing western farm income, in the light of the proposed curtailment of deliveries, against the extra burden entailed on the price of bread. The opinion of the economic advisory committee in Ottawa was reported[21] that $300,000,000 or more was the rock-bottom level to which western cash income from the sale of farm products could go without

---

[20]*Minutes of the Advisory Committee,* Canadian Wheat Board files.
[21]By the author who had been invited to attend.

necessitating the provision of direct relief. The advisory committee, in turn, took note of the $300,000,000 "or more" and they raised the figure to $325,000,000. On February 19, 1941, the advisory committee reported back to the government in the following terms:

Inasmuch as the Government has asked the Advisory Committee to reconsider its recommendations of January 16, 1941, the Committee has given further careful thought to the situation and is firmly convinced that during the crop year 1941-42 the least farm income necessary from the sale of all farm products to sustain the Western economy is a total of approximately $325,000,000.

The Committee wishes also to re-affirm its belief in the processing levy.

In the original submission to the Government entitled "Recommendations of the Advisory Committee in Respect to 1941-42 Wheat Policy", the reasons for the Advisory Committee's endorsement of the processing levy were set out in detail. These might be summarized as follows:

1. The processing levy is the most efficient and equitable means of compensating the Western wheat producer, in part, for the handicap under which he operates in that most of his wheat is sold on the basis of world competition, whereas his farm implements and other necessities are generally purchased in a protected market.

2. The wheat producer is entitled to a fair price for the amount of his production that is utilized in Canada.

3. The wheat producer has been adversely affected by the loss of markets due to war and blockade, while the other consumers of wheat in Canada and especially many groups of wage-earners are either unaffected or assisted in a monetary way by the war. The processing levy tends to narrow such disparities in the effects of war.

As a means of raising a part of the additional revenue necessary to reach the total of $325,000,000, it is recommended that a processing levy of fifty cents per bushel be placed on all wheat utilized for human consumption in Canada and further that the proceeds (estimated at $24,000,000) should be made available to the wheat producer if possible on the first deliverable proportion of his wheat crop, and that payment of same be made by means of a cash certificate or warrant for the sum per bushel fixed for the processing levy.[22]

SASKATCHEWAN LIBERAL COUNCIL RESOLUTIONS

At a meeting of the Saskatchewan Liberal Council held in Regina, December 12, 1940, Gardiner discussed a series of resolutions, notable because they had Gardiner's endorsation of the type of policy for which he wanted the party to take credit. As reported in the press, the resolutions called for:

(1) Federal government advances to farmers to enable them to build storage for the 1940 crop.

(2) Grain to be taken over by the government, or grain-purchasing institution either set up, or approved by, the government, while stored on the farm.

(3) A greater minimum price for a fixed maximum number of bushels produced by each farmer, in other words, minimum wage protection.

(4) Announcement of a definite agricultural policy by the federal government as early as possible, but not later than March 1, 1941.

[22]*Minutes of the Advisory Committee,* February 17-19, 1941, pp. 13-14, Canadian Wheat Board files.

Another resolution approved in principle, the quota system as applied to 1940 crop. . . .

The first resolution, dealing with government advances to build storage for the balance of the 1940 crop and subsequent crops, is based upon the general plan that with provision now made for the payment of storage on farm-stored grain, the government could make an advance to the farmer to permit him to build a granary and at the end of a period of months the storage-earning capacity of the new granary would equal the amount of the loan and the farmer in disposing of his grain would then receive the amount due, less the amount of the advance made.

The second resolution aims at some of the features of the ever-normal granary policy of the A.A.A. in the United States. It would permit of the utilization of off-sight storage so that the farmer could actually sell his grain while it was still in the granary, the government or the grain-purchasing institution taking delivery of it at the farm granary and padlocking it to guarantee its ultimate delivery. This resolution is broad enough in its scope to permit the wheat board to be the grain-purchasing institution, or such powers could be delegated by the government to line elevator companies or to the wheat pools.

The council approved in principle the wheat quota system as operated during the present crop year and commended the government for the system as applied to this year's crop during difficult circumstances, but called for the adoption of an increase in the maximum price for a fixed minimum number of bushels produced by each farmer as a guarantee of a reasonable return to the farmer to ensure him a livelihood, after which the regular prices as fixed under existing legislation would apply sofar as the marketing of any balances was concerned.[23]

In the process, the Liberal council had made one of the best articulated statements of a proposal for advances against farm-stored grain, pointing out the need for announcement of 1941-42 policy by March 1, 1941, well in advance of seeding, rather than having policy announced in late July as it had been done for the current crop year.

The resolutions of the Saskatchewan Liberal council were followed up in the Saskatchewan legislature. On February 28, 1941, Premier W. J. Patterson sponsored a motion which incorporated all of the recommendations of the council and made a notable addition by specifically proposing that the initial payment be increased to 85 cents.

CANADIAN FEDERATION OF AGRICULTURE RESOLUTIONS

While Gardiner was in Regina for the meeting with the Saskatchewan Liberal Council he also attended the December 11-12, 1940, meetings of the western agricultural conference, the western arm of the newly-organized Canadian federation of agriculture. The federation which had been organized on provincial and federal lines in 1940 was an association of producer organizations, of which the three pools, among other organizations, became members. The executive directors of the pools had taken the initiative in presenting a series of draft resolutions for consideration of the conference. In addressing the meeting, Gardiner welcomed their intiative as he reported on his recent trip to London and on the general prospects for marketing Canadian farm products in Britain. He also called a meeting of

[23] *The Leader-Post*, December 13, 1940.

his own the following week in Saskatoon at which the key officials of his department spoke on marketing prospects in 1941. The western agricultural conference, however, drew up a seven-point resolution on the wheat situation and submitted it to the annual meeting of the Canadian federation of agriculture which was held in Toronto, January 21-24, 1941. The resolutions were not unlike those drafted by the Saskatchewan Liberal council and by the advisory committee to the wheat board. In the latter case, Messrs. J. H. Wesson and Lew Hutchinson were members of that body as well as representatives of the pools in the western agricultural conference. Thus, the federation's recommendations included opposition to compulsory acreage reduction, support for a maximum delivery quota system, an increase in the processing tax to 50 cents to supplement the board's initial payment, an unspecified increase in the initial payment itself, the setting aside of the existing surplus to meet postwar requirements, financial assistance for the construction of farm-storage facilities, and the continuation of farm-storage payments featured the recommendations, to which was added a proposal for advances on farm-stored grain.

On January 27, 1941, the federation presented its recommendations to the cabinet with Mackenzie King presiding. It was the first of such meetings between the federation and the cabinet. Surrounded by his colleagues, King cordially received the delegation in his office. The federation's brief covered the agricultural situation across Canada, but its recommendations on wheat were those proposed by the western agricultural conference. The delegation of 23 members was headed by Mr. Herbert H. Hannam, president of the Canadian federation of agriculture. Western members included Mr. Lew Hutchinson, chairman of the Alberta wheat pool, Mr. George W. Robertson, secretary of the Saskatchewan wheat pool, Mr. W. A. McLeod, publicity director of the Canadian Co-operative Wheat Producers Limited and William J. Parker, president of Manitoba Pool Elevators Limited. Mr. Parker had been elected president of the latter organization following the death of Mr. Paul F. Bredt.

DECISION ON WHEAT ACREAGE REDUCTION PAYMENTS

Even with the benefit of all the foregoing advice, much of it in unison on what the 1941-42 policy should be, the wheat committee and cabinet experienced rather prolonged difficulty in reaching a decision. The ministers were confronted with a wartime wheat surplus situation of far greater magnitude than the Right Honourable R. B. Bennett had to cope with in the depression. As already noted, the wheat committee had brought the wheat board to Ottawa for consideration of its advisory committee recommendations which the wheat board had endorsed. At that stage, the wheat committee and cabinet accepted the continuation of the 70 cent advance on total deliveries in all Canada of 230 million bushels in 1941-42 (222 millions in the prairie provinces) but had rejected for reasons of the extra incidence on domestic bread consumers the advisory committee's and the several other recommendations for an increase in the processing levy to 50 cents. When McIvor reported that rejection to the advisory committee, it responded with a recommendation which said in effect that although the committee continued to endorse the increase in the processing levy, the main consideration should be to assure prairie farm income at $325,000,000 which, if not done through the processing levy, should be done by some other means.

As the wheat committee continued its policy review, it devoted a day to a review of the recommendations of the advisory committee on economic policy. The wheat committee noted that the economic committee had recommended maintenance of prairie farm income at $300,000,000 or more but it eliminated in turn the various means by which the economic committee had proposed that this be done by dismissing in turn the proposal for salable quotas, an increase in the initial payment and the 50 cent processing tax. This left only the economic committee's recommendation on participation rights which would have given effect to the recommendation from all sources that the July 31, 1941, carryover of 575,000,000 bushels be set aside as a wartime reserve, and that all 1941-42 sales should be allocated to 1941-42 deliveries so that producers would receive participation payments on their restricted deliveries.

At that point however, Gardiner and Ilsley engaged in another of their several confrontations. As Gardiner reckoned, he could still salvage $325,000,000 in western farm income if the 1941 accumulation in the carryover were to be set aside, so that participation in 1941-42 sales could accrue to producers. Gardiner's balance sheet ran as follows:

Based on the initial payment set at 70¢ Ft. William
the net return at the farm was 52 cents on 222,000,000

bushels	$ 115,440,000
Cash farm income from sales other than wheat	148,000,000
	263,440,000
Leaving	61,560,000
to bring the total up to	$ 325,000,000

The economic committee's calculations had been considerably at variance. That committee had added a price increase factor into the $148,000,000 earned through sales other than wheat which it had placed at $15,000,000 and which raised the total to $163,000,000. Gardiner challenged the $15,000,000 figure by claiming that there had been no price increases to warrant such an adjustment. Ilsley also wanted to include the payments made under prairie farm assistance, but Gardiner claimed that these were crop deficiency payments which were a part of the income reckoned on the basis of sales of 222,000,000 bushels.

When Gardiner and Ilsley took their differences to cabinet and reported their disagreement, there was a long discussion in council during which the principle of maintaining western farm income at $325,000,000 was accepted, and Gardiner was authorized to work out a plan to achieve that objective, while holding the initial payment at 70 cents and total deliveries at not more than 230 millions for all of Canada.

The cabinet deliberations were not easy. They ran over three days, until on March 7, 1941, the session ran from midnight until 2:40 a.m., as King's diary entries attested:

> Was at Council from noon until nearly 2.30. Mostly discussion of the agricultural situation in western Canada—problem of over-supply of wheat and need to limit wheat acreage—one of the most difficult problems thus far

considered. Many different views held in Council re trying to meet the farmers difficulties by more payments out of the Treasury.

Spent two hours in the Cabinet, again considering agricultural policy, the Western situation, and I think helped to bring the right view to prevail out of the general concensus. Gardiner is so set in his own way that he is almost without a supporter in the Cabinet, but is terribly tenacious. There are of course two sides to every question. Gardiner never sees the side that saves the treasury. He is all for using public money to help numbers of people—a kind of socialistic instinct. At the bottom I think he is governed very largely by a political motive. Reads everything in terms of how things will go in time of an election.

Tonight from 12 till 20 to 3; most of the time discussion on wheat policy.[24]

Gardiner's first attempt to draft a plan included a proposal to make an additional 6 cent per bushel payment at the end of each crop year. His arithmetic went a little astray as he applied the 76 cents, less freight and handling charges to Fort William, or a net of 58 cents to the whole of the 1941-42 deliveries of 230 million bushels, instead of the 222 million bushel western portion thereof. As he calculated, this would bring the western farmers (230,000,000 x 58 cents) $133,400,000. At this point, however, he introduced a wheat acreage reduction payment plan whereby, if 6,000,000 acres diverted to summerfallow were reimbursed at $5.00 per acre, and 2,000,000 acres returned to permanent grass at $1.50 per acre, the additional payments of $30,000,000 and $3,000,000, respectively, would be added as follows:

230 million bushels at 58 cents	$133,400,000
6,000,000 acres of summerfallow at $5.00	30,000,000
2,000,000 acres of grass at $1.50	3,000,000
From other crops	148,000,000
Total	$314,400,000

Although this total fell short of the objective of $325,000,000, Gardiner reckoned that the balance of $10,600,000 could be realized out of participation payments if the 1941 carryover was treated as a reserve, that is, carried with carrying charges accruing to the treasury, and all sales in 1941-42 credited to the 1941-42 crop account.

When Gardiner brought this proposal back to council, the principle of adding a carrying charge figure of 6 cents per bushel to the initial payment at the end of each year was rejected. Gardiner was then asked to rework his plan and to present it to the cabinet wheat committee for consideration for which purpose the Honourable C. D. Howe was added to the committee. In the wheat committee, Gardiner presented a revised statement as follows:

222,000,000 bushels with an advance of 70 cents which would average the producer 52 cents, or approximately	$115,000,000
1940 returns on non-wheat products	148,000,000
Payments on areas taken out of wheat	36,000,000
Participation payments based upon wheat sales net to the Wheat Board at 82 cents, which was what the	

[24]*King Diary*, March 5-7, 1941.

wheat was already practically sold for, it would add
(222 million bushels x 12 cents) <u>26,640,000</u>
and bring the total to $325,640,000

By way of breakdown on the payments to be made for the areas taken out of wheat, a revised basis was submitted involving $4.00 per acre for wheat land diverted to summerfallow, $2.00 per acre for diversion to coarse grains, and $2.00 per acre for land diverted into grass, clover or rye.

This last revision in the proposal was referred back to council, and approved. The cabinet wheat committee met again on the morning of March 12, 1941, to reconcile the policy statements to be made by Messrs. MacKinnon and Gardiner on the retention of the 70-cent initial advance, the maximum limitation on deliveries and the wheat acreage reduction payments related thereto. In the course of that meeting, however, Ilsley objected to any reference in MacKinnon's statement to the holding of the 575,000,000 bushel 1941 carryover as a wartime reserve. Gardiner later recorded Ilsley's objection in his letter of March 29, 1941, to Ilsley:

> You will recall that on March 12th when we were considering the announcement of the wheat policy which was to be made by Mr. MacKinnon and myself that afternoon, and just before the final endorsation was given to the policy announced, you raised the question of the effect of placing the accumulated wheat in a reserve. If I remember your words correctly they were in effect: —
> "No one else seems to take this matter seriously excepting myself. My officials tell me that we are providing now for an income of more than the 325 million dollars agreed to and that if we set this stored wheat up in reserve and pay an advance of 70 cents on 230,000,000 bushels of wheat, and are still responsible for paying participation, we will be paying far more out of the Treasury than we should".
> My reply to that was that the effect of the present Wheat Board legislation is that the 70 cents plus participation would be payable on the 230,000,000 bushels, and that the only question involved so far as I could see was as to whether the practice followed up to date of pro rating the sales between new crop and old crop was to be followed. I stated further that I did not agree with your officials that more than 325,000,000 dollars is assured the farmers under the proposed plan, but in view of the fact that this needed further discussion the announcement should not be made so definite as to preclude further discussion.
> It was because of this understanding that I brought the matter up before further consideration took place in the House on my estimates.
> I would like, therefore, to review the consideration which has been given to the matter by the Wheat Committee, and upon which the definite recommendation was made to Council. I am enclosing a memorandum in which that is done.
> I am sorry that I have not found time to discuss it fully with you, and thought the best way would be to review the whole matter.[25]

Attached to that letter was Gardiner's 11-page memorandum in which he traced the whole course of the cabinet wheat committee and council review of the 1941-42 policy, commencing with the review of the wheat board advisory committee's and the economic committee's recommendations and ending with the approval by cabinet of Gardiner's latest package of wheat

[25] *King Papers.*

acreage reduction and participation payments. But, because of Ilsley's last minute objection to the wartime reserve proposal on the assumption that it would overcompensate producers in relation to the $325,000,000 objective, there was no reference in the two statements of policy made on March 12, 1941 to the creation of the 1941 carryover as a wartime reserve. Along with that deletion went the notion of allocating all sales to the 1941 crop in order to create an early participation payment on that crop. Gardiner then forwarded to King on March 31, 1941, an explanatory letter in which he enclosed a copy of his letter of March 29 to Ilsley with the accompanying memorandum. Gardiner wrote to King:

> Enclosed is a copy of a letter which I have addressed to Mr. Ilsley, and a memorandum which was attached dealing with the question of a wheat advance of 70 cents and participation.
>
> This memorandum was the subject of discussion in your absence today but I understand it was agreed that the price to be paid is a 70 cent advance plus participation, as provided for in the Wheat Board Act.
>
> The question as to how the amount of participation is to be arrived at is still under discussion.
>
> The method followed since 1936 has been to allow the Wheat Board to establish a proportion which will be applied to the carried over wheat as compared with the new crop in all sales made during the year.
>
> That method might be considered reasonably fair when farmers are permitted to grow and market all the wheat they can. When we state that the amount to be accepted is not more than 230 million bushels, then I think the 1941 wheat should be pooled by itself particularly because we have arrived at the 230 million bushels as the amount which we can sell in 1941-42. It was agreed that if more than 230 million bushels is sold in 1941-42 it is to be taken out of the reserve. In view of this fact it is my contention that the 230 million bushels is set up as a separate pool and that all the money received for wheat between August 1st, 1941 and July 31st 1942 should go to the farmers who grew the first 230 million sold and that all other wheat sold this year should be taken from the carryover from previous years, and whatever is received for it should be credited to that account.
>
> To proceed otherwise would be to tax the farmers who produce the 230 million bushels to pay themselves for reducing their acreage.[26]

Gardiner was unsuccessful in his pursuit of the issue, in which Ilsley could claim that the matter was a fait accompli, with the policy announcements that were made on March 12. The matter did not rest there because Gardiner continued to press the issue with the treasury. His long memorandum had recorded in detail the lengthy preoccupation of cabinet and its wheat committee over 1941-42 policy. It listed Gardiners' recommendations for a wartime wheat reserve and for a 50 cent processing levy, both of which he had supported at the Saskatchewan Liberal council meeting in the previous December. It explained why these provisions had been dropped from the government's 1941-42 policy, and why the processing levy proposal had been replaced by the wheat acreage reduction program.

Long after the policy announcements were made, Gardiner pursued the wartime reserve and separate 1941-42 crop year pool issues with King. In

[26] *Ibid.*

his letter of July 28, 1941 to the prime minister, Gardiner added an enclosure on wheat:

> I desire to recommend we declare the year 1941 an emergency year and at once announce the decision to so declare it at once and proceed to make our check accordingly.
>
> I also desire to suggest that under the Wheat Board Act we declare that the delivery of wheat from the 1941 crop be on a basis of 65% of the 1940 acreage and that no one be allowed to deliver from any higher acreage. When the deliveries from that acreage are completed at the highest quota allowed, the total delivery should not exceed 230,000,000 bushels.
>
> I suggest that all wheat exported on and after October 1, 1941, should be charged to the crop of 1941, and that when the quota delivered by farmers not to exceed 230,000,000 bushels is reached, the pool for 1941 wheat should be closed out and settlement made for the 1941 crop by paying the farmers the full amount received less costs on the 1941 crop alone.
>
> If any additional sales are made, I suggest they be taken from the carryover from previous years.[27]

While Gardiner's first two recommendations on the declaration of 1941 as an emergency year under the prairie farm assistance act and the delivery rights on 65 percent of 1940 acreage were adopted, his key recommendation to build up the amount of participation payments by giving priority to the sale of 1941 crop wheat failed to dissipate Ilsley's opposition.

1941-42 WHEAT POLICY ANNOUNCEMENTS

Deprived of their intention to announce the wartime reserve by Ilsley's last-minute objection, MacKinnon and Gardiner jointly announced the 1941-42 program in the house on the afternoon of March 12, 1941, in the course of which, after an explanatory preamble, MacKinnon said:

> ... I shall now outline the plans the government proposes to make effective this year in connection with the 1941 crop.
>
> (1) To take such action as will ensure as nearly as possible that the visible supply of Canadian wheat on July 31, 1942, shall be no larger than on July 31, 1941. In other words we feel that we have reached the limit of the volume of wheat reserves which should be carried.
>
> (2) To accomplish this a definite limit will be set on the amount of wheat which it will be possible to deliver either to the board, on the open market or otherwise, during the crop year 1941-42. The limit will be 230 million bushels — for the whole of Canada, an amount which it hopes can be sold in the domestic and export markets in 1941-42.
>
> (3) The Canadian wheat board and the government have given the most careful consideration to an equitable plan by which deliveries of the 230 million bushels will be distributed among wheat producers. The quota system so successful this year will be maintained and these quotas will be based on the production from 65 per cent of the 1940 acreage. The first quota will be a general one and will allow the delivery of the same amount of wheat per acre from every farmer. The second and following quotas will be certain proportions of the 1941 yield for the farmer's shipping point; that is a high yield point in 1941 will have a higher quota per acre than a low yield point. I cannot at the moment give further details of the delivery plan but I can say that the plan will be equitable as between farmers and as between areas in the prairie provinces. This plan of quotas will operate only if total production

[27] *Ibid.*

provides a marketable surplus of wheat in excess of 230 million bushels. In the event of the crop being smaller than this the system of quotas will require to be varied to meet this condition.

(4) The dominion government through the Canadian wheat board will continue to guarantee an initial payment of 70 cents a bushel basis one Northern on wheat delivered during the crop year 1941-42.

(5) The Canadian wheat board will continue to pay storage to the producers on the same basis as in 1940-41, but only on the undelivered portion of the 230 million bushels.

(6) No change will be made in the amount or incidence of the processing levy as at present established.[28]

MacKinnon's reference to the continuation of payment of storage to producers referred to the increase in the initial payment by one-half cent every three weeks to compensate producers for farm storage. This is not to be confused with Gardiner's recommendation that an additional six cents be added to the initial payment at the end of each crop year, which was rejected by cabinet. Gardiner immediately followed MacKinnon's announcement by making a statement relating to his own departmental administration:

... It is considered by the government that only 230 million bushels of wheat can be delivered to the board on the open market or otherwise. In view of all the uncertain circumstances, the government is of the opinion that the advance upon the amount delivered should not be increased. The outstanding reason for that conclusion is the opinion that production of wheat should be decreased.

The figure arrived at will suggest that farmers keep before them an objective of not more than 65 per cent of last year's acreage. It has also been pointed out that a certain farm income is necessary to the maintenance of western economy. It is generally agreed that this should be not less than 325 million dollars.

If this income is going to be realized it will be necessary for the farmer to obtain from the lands which were in wheat last year a net return at least equal to that of 1940.

The government has therefore attempted to set up a plan under which that may be accomplished, while at the same time securing a reduction of the acreage in wheat to an area which is not likely to produce more than 230 million bushels.

It is not our intention to pay farmers for not growing wheat or to compel them to reduce acreage. It is our intention to pay them to do something other than grow wheat, which we believe in the long run will improve western agriculture.

We intend to do this in a manner in which, if the happenings of the war or the after-war period require it, reasonable quantities of wheat may be produced.

But, most important for the time being, we will attempt to do it in a manner which will give the farmer a net cash return comparable with what he would have had if he had followed his pre-war methods of agriculture and could have disposed of his products in the usual way.

It is our intention, therefore, to make payments of certain sums per acre on all reductions made in wheat sowings in the prairie provinces in 1941 as compared with 1940, provided the farmer does certain specified things with the land.

[28]*House of Commons Debates,* March 12, 1941, p. 1464.

1. If he summer-fallows the reduced wheat acreage or part of it, the government will pay him $4 an acre for the reduced wheat acreage which is black July 1, 1941; payments to be made as soon as possible after July 1, 1941.

2. If he sows the reduced wheat acreage or part of it to coarse grains in the spring or, in the case of rye, in the fall of 1941 on lands not summer-fallowed, the government will pay him $2 an acre in 1941 as soon as possible after proof of sowing is established.

3. If he sows the reduced wheat acreage or part of it to grass or clover during 1941 provided the land has not also been sown to coarse grain or summer-fallowed, the government will pay him $2 an acre as soon as possible after proof of sowing has been established and an additional $2 an acre if the same land is still seeded down to grass on July 1, 1942.

4. If he sows reduced wheat acreage or part of it which is also sown to coarse grain, or which is summer-fallowed in 1941, to grass or/and clover or to rye in 1941, the government will pay $2 an acre as soon as possible after July 1, 1942, provided the same land is in grass or/and clover, or rye, on that date.

The above payments are considered to be liberal allowances for the work necessary to utilize the lands for the different purposes outlined. The methods by which the money can be earned are intended to be varied enough to permit of the farmer adopting the one most suited to his farming conditions in order to obtain revenue which he has been denied because he is unable to deliver the amount of wheat he has been accustomed to market.

An estimate of the amount of money which can be earned is possible. If the entire 9,000,000 acres were removed from wheat as summer-fallow, the amount distributed would be $36,000,000. If 6,000,000 acres were utilized as summer-fallow and 3,000,000 for coarse grains and grass, the amount distributed in 1941 would be $24,000,000 for summer-fallow and $6,000,000 for coarse grains or grass, or both, whereas the farmer would have additional returns from the increased coarse grains in this latter case, and in 1942 could collect additional amounts if the grass and rye lands are still out of wheat. Any other combination can be estimated similarly.[29]

WHEAT ACREAGE REDUCTION IN OPERATION

Authority for the first year of operation of the wheat acreage reduction program was provided by order in council. P. C. 3047 of April 30, 1941, established the regulations for that program, and P. C. 3849 of May 30, 1941, established the regulations for the maximum delivery quota limitation. A year later, Gardiner introduced a bill in parliament to authorize continuation of the wheat acreage reduction program but, in the first year, there had not been sufficient time to introduce and enact legislation in advance of seeding, when producers needed to know what the policy would be. Gardiner undertook to have his draft regulations debated in committee of the whole of his supply estimates, in which a $35,000,000 item had been included for wheat acreage reduction. He had trouble in getting the item passed before the easter recess and the debate continued in May after the regulations had been approved by the governor in council.[30]

---

[29]*Ibid.*, pp. 1464-1465.
[30]For the text of P. C. 3047 see *House of Commons Debates*, May 2, 1941, pp. 2523-2525.

During the easter recess, Gardiner returned to Saskatchewan to explain the policy by holding some 12 meetings with farmers. Other western members did likewise. The publicity campaign which Clive Davidson had advocated took two forms: the first, a Canadian wheat board pamphlet entitled *Canada's Wheat Problem* which was distributed to producers and placed on Hansard by MacKinnon;[31] the second, a pamphlet entitled *A Plan to Reduce Wheat Acreage and Make More Money Available for Necessary War Supplies,* distributed to producers by the department of agriculture.

When acreage estimates for 1941 were released, the wheat area in the Prairie Provinces was shown reduced by 24 percent to 21,140,000 acres from the 1940 peak of 27,750,000 acres.[32] Yields also were lighter; production of 296 million bushels contrasted with the 514 million produced in 1940, a reduction of 42 percent. In the result, the wheat available for delivery from the 1941 crop could not exceed the maximum of 222 million bushels set. During the course of the crop year, the board was able to raise its delivery quotas until it placed the whole crop on open quota. Total deliveries to country elevators in the 1941-42 crop year amounted to 222 million bushels, and total primary marketings including deliveries over platforms and at interior and mill elevators amounted to 227.9 millions. Of this total 99.5 millions, or 44 percent, were delivered by producers to the board. Open-market prices ruled just enough above the board's initial payment to attract sales to the private trade. In ordinary circumstances, the open-market sales would have reduced the board's capacity to enter into bulk commitments with the imported cereals division, but the backlog of stocks in board hands permitted the board to function competently in this regard. During the course of the crop year, the board made two sales of 120 million bushels of Winnipeg wheat futures to Britain in November, 1941, and in May, 1942.

In summary, the mounting domestic wheat surplus in the wake of the German invasion had produced two major government responses. The first was the approval of the delivery quota system designed for the equitable sharing of available commercial storage space and it was operated for the first time in connection with the delivery of the 1940 crop. Then, in order to ward off a further increase in the size of the surplus in 1941, maximum delivery quotas were similarly adopted for the first time and announced in advance of seeding, to permit producers to adjust production plans accordingly. This maximum quota restriction upon wheat deliveries was combined with acreage payment incentives offered for diversion of wheat acreage into summerfallow and into coarse grains. The combination had a salutary result in wheat acreage reduction. It was also the first occasion on which the government had placed a priority on the production of feed

---

[31] *House of Commons Debates,* May 2, 1941, pp. 2526-2527.

[32] The official figure of 27,500,000 acres for 1940 was later called in question by the Canadian Wheat Board whose permit book acreage declarations indicated a 1940 wheat area of about 29,000,000 acres. Some error had undoubtedly crept into the official estimates, based upon annual sample acreage surveys which, by 1940, were four years beyond their most recent 1936 census base. On the other hand, the 1940 acreages declared in the permit books were probably biased on the high side.

grains over that of wheat. Nor should it be lost sight of that the delivery quota system and the maximum delivery quota limitation enjoyed the support of organized producers. The system had first been mooted by the central board of the pools as an alternative to compulsory wheat acreage reduction which the board had viewed with growing alarm as a means of compliance with the terms of the first international wheat agreement. The United States had successfully operated a voluntary acreage reduction program with the provision of financial incentives for compliance. At the same time, its officials urged the adoption of a similar "ever normal granary" operation in the other exporting countries. In 1934, no one in Canada had seriously thought that the country could afford to offer financial assistance to compensate for wheat acreage reduction. In 1941, such assistance was forthcoming, but in connection with a delivery control system which was a Canadian alternative to the American method of acreage control.

31

WASHINGTON WHEAT MEETING, 1941-1942

The first inkling the Canadian government received of British-American interest in the revival of international discussions on wheat, even under wartime conditions, came in a note which Mr. W. C. Hankinson, acting British high commissioner, addressed to Mr. Norman Robertson on February 3, 1941. The note began by explaining that the British (whose dependent territories had a seller's interest in a number of primary commodities) had taken the initiative the previous autumn to elicit American support for the consideration of commodity surplus problems generally. The Americans, in turn, had countered that a collective consideration of commodity problems was impracticable, and that an individual commodity approach was necessary. An attempt had already been made to consider the wheat problem internationally and, if the British were in earnest, the Americans suggested that they should seek Canadian support for reopening the international wheat discussions. Should the British and Canadian governments so propose, the American government would invite the wheat advisory committee to reconvene in Washington. Then the note continued:

> Indications are that the United States Government may be making a test case of wheat, and that the response of the United Kingdom Government to their suggestions will be an important factor in determining their attitude towards co-operation on the surplus problem as a whole. The United Kingdom Government had reason to believe that, rightly or wrongly, the United States Government feels that neither the United Kingdom nor Canada have ever been in earnest in coming to grips with the problem of wheat and ascribe to United Kingdom and Canadian hesitations the poor progress made as a result of various initiatives which they themselves have taken during the past seven years. The United Kingdom Government are anxious therefore to take full advantage of the suggestion which the United States authorities have now made. . . .
>
> The United Kingdom Government feel bound to do everything in their power to secure the co-operation of the United States in agreed arrangements on the one hand for preventing the accumulation of surpluses of primary products to an extent which will be ruinous to all producers, and on the other hand for organizing supplies to be made available to the countries of Europe as and when they are liberated. The first aspect involves consideration of the amount of stocks that can be stored without unduly affecting the market and of the possibility of regulating production within that limit. The second aspect

involves consideration of financial and other arrangements for the orderly marketing of these stocks after the war. On both aspects co-operation with the United States will be essential, and the United Kingdom government feel that they cannot afford to decline the suggestion now put forward which the United States evidently regard as the first step to a general discussion on the subject of surpluses, storage and supply to Europe.

In these circumstances the United Kingdom government attach utmost importance to returning a prompt and favourable reply to the United States suggestion, and they earnestly hope that they may count on the Canadian Government to join them in returning such a reply. . . .[1]

The note reached Robertson just after the sudden and tragic death of Dr. O. D. Skelton, on January 28, 1941, whom Robertson would shortly succeed as undersecretary of state for external affairs. Robertson sent a copy of the note, requesting the consideration of the wheat committee of the cabinet, to L. Dana Wilgress, who had been appointed deputy minister of trade and commerce on October 1, 1940. Wilgress, in turn, referred the British note with a covering memorandum of his own to his minister, the chairman of the cabinet wheat committee. In his note, Wilgress observed that the British government had already gone a long way toward accepting the American proposal, and that the Canadian government could not very well decline to take part, as long as the discussions were confined to the postwar situation, and prevented from intervening in current affairs. Then, he said:

> I am informed by Mr. Hume Wrong who has just returned from London where he acted as Special Economic Advisor to the High Commissioner, that he had a discussion on this subject with Sir Frederick Leith-Ross, the permanent head of the Ministry of Economic Warfare, who has also been made Chairman of the Inter-Departmental Committee to consider the question of surplus commodities. Sir Frederick referred to wheat and intimated that he had been approached by the United States Agricultural Attache in London regarding the holding of a meeting of the Wheat Advisory Committee, but he had taken the view that such a meeting could only be held if Canada were prepared to co-operate.
>
> In this connection it may be mentioned that Mr. Andrew Cairns, Secretary of the Wheat Advisory Committee, is now on the staff of the Ministry of Economic Warfare, so that possibly he has had something to do with furthering the proposal for a meeting of the major countries concerned with the wheat problem. . . .[2]

Whether it was Wilgress's inference that Andrew Cairns had fathered the project or otherwise, the cabinet wheat committee made no response. To its members, the resumption of international wheat discussions at that stage of the war seemed futile and irrelevant. More than six weeks elapsed before Wilgress reminded MacKinnon that external affairs had requested guidance on the attitude of the Canadian government, but even the reminder evoked no reply. In his frustration, Robertson raised the matter with Mackenzie King from whom he drew a prompt reaction as he indicated by letter, April 12, 1941, to Wilgress:

> I have brought to the Prime Minister's attention the letters from the Office of the United Kingdom High Commissioner of February 3rd and March 28th regarding the possibility of holding a meeting in Washington of the Wheat

[1]*Trade and Commerce file 26204:14.*
[2]*Ibid.*

Advisory Committee to consider the world wheat surplus problem. Mr. King has noted the importance which the United Kingdom Government attach to returning a prompt and favourable reply to the United States suggestion that such a meeting should be held and their hope that the Canadian Government would join them in returning such a reply. The Prime Minister does not feel that there is anything to be lost while there may possibly be something to be gained in taking up the American suggestion of a joint discussion of the wheat problem. He has asked me to bring his views to the attention of your Minister and the members of the Wheat Committee to ascertain whether they would be agreeable to sending an affirmative reply to the United Kingdom enquiries immediately.[3]

Wilgress passed on the prime minister's reaction to MacKinnon in Edmonton. MacKinnon spoke to Gardiner, and Wilgress also wrote to Crerar. Now that Mackenzie King had given a lead, the three ministers fell into line, and on April 21, 1941, Robertson informed the Right Honourable Malcolm MacDonald, the newly-arrived British high commissioner, on April 21, of the Canadian government's concurrence.

In anticipation that a meeting would be called, Wilgress proceeded to arrange for Canadian representation. He consulted George McIvor and Dr. Charles Wilson; McIvor proposed bringing Biddulph over from London. Later on, Dr. G. S. H. Barton, deputy minister of agriculture, suggested that Dean Shaw represent the department of agriculture, and the department of external affairs named Mr. James E. Coyne, who was financial attache of the Canadian legation in Washington, as the legation's representative.

On May 14, several American officials came to Ottawa for formal consultations prior to the imposition of an American wheat import quota on Canadian wheat, made necessary because, with domestic wheat prices in the United States rising in response to new support legislation, Canadian wheat could move into the United States over its 42 cent protective tariff. Wilson was asked to have a preliminary conversation with Leslie A. Wheeler, a member of the official party, about the probable course of the Washington discussions. As a result, Wilson was able to allay Wilgress's concern over becoming involved in any American or other encroachment on our current trade with Britain; he also pointed out the need for instructions to the delegation on the resumption of negotiations (broken off in 1939 in London) in a letter to Wilgress on May 23, 1941:

> I had intended seeing you this week, but this memorandum will convey what I learned about the anticipated agenda of the Washington wheat discussions from the United States officials who were here May 14. Dr. Wheeler and I had a chat about the matter, and he said they realized that not much could be done about the present export position beyond recognizing a de facto situation, but that they hoped some agreement might be reached now to prevent a chaotic export competition in the immediate post-war period. Dr. Wheeler surmised it might take about a week in Washington to determine if any real basis exists, among the governments represented, for an agreement on future export quotas. I asked if the Argentine and Australian governments had yet intimated that they would take part in the discussions, but he had not yet heard one way or the other.
>
> In the light of the intended agenda, it would seem to be important that the Wheat Committee of the Cabinet give consideration beforehand to the matter

---

[3] *Ibid.*

of quotas and price. In this connection you will recall that in the 1939 discussions, our Government was prepared to accept a fairly-based quota, if the latter were to be accompanied by a minimum-price undertaking on the part of the importing countries. The price in mind at that time was the equivalent of 87½ cents per bushel, basis Fort William-Port Arthur. The 1939 discussions were entirely absorbed in reaching a mutually acceptable quota basis. The four exporting countries were on the verge of agreement when the war altered the whole position. Up to the end of those discussions, the United Kingdom Government had not yet been drawn into a serious discussion on price.

Insofar as the United Kingdom Government has sponsored the forthcoming discussions, it would follow that they are, or should be, now prepared to take an amenable position on price. Herein lies the main interest, so far as we are concerned. Any quota position to which we might agree, could only be made acceptable to our public if the price returns warranted. Therefore, I think our Government should consider beforehand the price that would be acceptable to us. If we aren't prepared to move in this direction, the Canadian delegation will be placed in a negative role in the discussions.

I have talked these matters over with George McIvor, who adds that we have much to gain by cultivating within reason the good will of the United States Department of Agriculture. If the latter choose to disregard our interests, they could request the United Kingdom Government to take, say, 100 million bushels under the lease-lend provisions, a request that would be awkward to refuse.[4]

The apprehension, which George McIvor had expressed over the possibility that the Americans might extend their lend-lease provisions to wheat, was quite genuine at that time, and it was allayed only as the Washington discussions progressed.

To get their instructions, George McIvor and Wilson met with the cabinet wheat committee early in June. The ministers took the attitude that they must go along with the untimely negotiation out of recognition of higher political considerations as the United States government, still technically neutral, moved closer to becoming an outright ally. They expected that little substance would emerge from the talks, but were concerned that the onus for any breakdown should not rest upon Canada, and they gave the instructions needed to proceed with the quota and price negotiations.

JULY-AUGUST SESSIONS, 1941

To help allay concern among the countries not represented in the discussions, the American government officially described the gathering as a meeting, a designation less formal than that of a conference. Hence the references to the Washington wheat meeting which convened with only two breaks in the period from July 10, 1941 to April 22, 1942. The first session extended from July 10 to August 3, 1941. When the meeting convened in Washington on July 10, it was learned that Argentina, Australia and Britain had sent single representatives: Anselmo Viacava, commercial counsellor of the Argentine embassy, London; F. L. McDougall, economic adviser to the Australian high commissioner, London; and H. F. Carlill, of the British board of trade who was now chairman of the wheat advisory committee in London. The three had been associated with the 1933 agreement

[4]*Ibid.*

negotiations, and since then with the affairs of the wheat advisory committee. At first glance, it appeared that the Canadian government had over-responded. But the Canadian delegation was more than matched in numbers by the large and somewhat flexible delegation headed by Leslie A. Wheeler, director of the office of foreign agricultural relations in the department of agriculture, who had also attended the 1933 meetings. Wheeler continued to play a leading role in the continuing negotiations until the 1949 agreement came into operation. The American delegation included prominent officials such as R. M. Evans, head of the agricultural adjustment administration; L. V. Steere, agricultural attache who had been transferred from Berlin to London; Carl Farrington, vice-president of the commodity credit corporation and Harry C. Hawkins, chief of the division of commercial treaties and agreements in the department of state. Mr. N. E. Dodd, assistant secretary of agriculture, took part intermittently. Other officials included Messrs George Kublin, Clyde Marquis, Gordon Boals and Robert Post.

The meeting was formally opened in the state department on the morning of July 10. Mr. Sumner Welles, acting secretary of state, welcomed the delegations as he said:

... All of us today are faced with grave and difficult problems. Our preoccupation with the most immediate of these problems, however, should not blind us to the necessity of keeping longer-term objectives clearly in mind. Neither should the problems of war prevent us from working towards solutions which will enable us to deal with the questions of peace. Many of our current problems can be solved only on the basis of assurances as to the plans and programs of other countries in dealing with similar problems now and after the war. I do not think it is an overstatement to say that the shape of the post-war world will be determined in no small measure by the actions which we take during the war.

In calling the present meeting to discuss the international wheat situation, the Government of the United States has had in mind the fact that all of us who are wheat producers are faced at present with problems of a somewhat similar character, although of varying degrees of intensity. All of us are faced with growing surpluses of wheat. I am informed that the prospect is that in another year, these surpluses will probably total a billion and a half bushels, a quantity which may well hang over the international wheat markets for years. As producers and holders of these surpluses, we have a common interest in the possibilities which may exist of providing for their orderly liquidation. We have a common interest in the conditions which will prevail in the international wheat market when the war is over. We have a common interest in the restoration of the prosperity of our purchasers of wheat and in the need for relief in devastated areas immediately after the war. ....[5]

In the afternoon, the meeting assembled in the department of agriculture and Carlill was invited to take the chair. A simple agenda had been prepared which included:

1. A country by country review of the current and prospective situation.

2. A review of the 1939 negotiations.

[5] *Washington Wheat Meeting Minutes 1/41, July 10, 1941*, Trade and Commerce File 26204:14.

3. A discussion on the scope of a new agreement.

4. Drafting of a new agreement.

The first item afforded the heads of delegations an opportunity to review the developments in each country. McIvor gave a first-rate summary of the measures already taken in Canada to reduce wheat acreage by bonusing the areas devoted to summerfallow and other crops, and by the delivery quota system which had just been introduced. R. M. Evans similarly reviewed the acreage allotment system in the United States. Viacava and McDougall had arrived unprepared to make any statements.

The review of the 1939 negotiations was provided in resumes prepared by the United States department of agriculture and by Cairns. As the cabinet wheat committee had learned to their considerable apprehension, Cairns had already been in Washington for some time working on preparations for the meeting in conjunction with the American officials. He produced a carefully prepared list of items for inclusion in a new wheat agreement, and the chairman invited him to open the discussion. It was Cairns at his best and also at his worst. In his unflagging enthusiasm for his cause, Cairns headed the list with a declaration of common purpose to limit high-cost production and to encourage efficient production in the overseas exporting countries. The list continued with the need for production control in all countries, export quotas, minimum and maximum prices linked to the operation of the quotas, the maintenance of reserve stocks within minimum-maximum ranges, "sanctions" by wheat importing countries to ensure enforcement of quotas among exporting countries and to control the exports of non-signatory exporting countries, the reduction of tariff and quantitative restrictions on the importation of wheat, measures to increase the consumption of wheat; all to be embodied in an agreement of five years' duration commencing, in the first instance, from the end of the war. To that point he had drawn upon the heads of agreement discussed in 1939. Then he introduced the use of surplus stocks for relief purposes after the war for which, except for the proposed method of handling, there was strong support. His last recommendation, however, took everyone except the Americans by surprise as he proposed that an international wheat pool be created for the purposes of administering the agreement. He had revived the idea which had originated in the international wheat pool conference held in Kansas City, Missouri, in 1927, which he had attended, except that in the place of an international producers' pool, governments would now become the sponsors of an international agency to which member exporting countries would sell the equivalent of their crop-year quotas at prices to be fixed by agreement each year, and from which the member importing countries would purchase their import requirements, plus storage, transportation and handling charges. Cairns enumerated a number of administrative advantages of the scheme as follows:

(a) It would ease the task of agreeing upon the estimated demand for imported wheat and avoid competition if that estimate proved to be too high.

(b) It would greatly simplify the operation of the price clauses of the proposed agreement and do away with the need for constant discussion of equitable price differentials.

(c) It would facilitate the differentiation between commercial and relief demand.

(d) It would remove the necessity for adhering countries to adopt "sanctions".

(e) It would make possible an allocation of purchases immediately after the war in accordance with the agreed export quotas, even if the lifting of the full crop-year quotas of the more distant countries had to be postponed until shipping facilities were increased.

(f) It would give a guaranteed price for a known volume of wheat to each overseas country and thus ease their problem of financing surplus stocks.

(g) It would facilitate the earmarking, financing and distribution of part of the surplus stocks for the post-war relief of European and non-European countries.[6]

The proposal for an international wheat pool, or wheat union as it came to be called, was referred to a committee under the chairmanship of George McIvor. In his committee, McIvor had to deal with the Americans, McDougall and Cairns, all of whom strongly supported the proposal McIvor was acutely conscious of its implications in superseding the open market and the private trade. The committee's first report exposed differences of opinion as McIvor recorded his own views that an international pool was too radical a step to contemplate in the absence of any operating experience. However, the committee report reached a compromise by recommending that the union commence operations with the handling of surplus wheat for relief purposes. After it gained experience in that capacity, the signatory governments could then judge whether the union had acquired sufficient expertise to handle commercial wheat. The proposal was then incorporated into the provisional draft of a wheat agreement which, on August 3, 1941, was referred to governments for instructions.

McIvor's committee also recommended that the proposed agreement take into account three periods: wartime, transitional and normal, in which different phases of the agreement should come into operation. Even in wartime, it was proposed to make maximum reserve stocks provision operative, together with such production control measures as would implement the stocks agreement. The current wheat trade would carry on as at present, and consultations would take place on commercial exports until export quotas could come into operation. In the intermediate period the production control and maximum stocks provisions would be continued, and the union would be established to handle relief wheat. Finally in the normal period, a full export agreement, including export quotas, would come into operation.

The discussions continued on the basis that export quotas among the "big four" must be agreed upon forthwith, and not left to negotiation after the war. To further the quota negotiations, private conversations took place outside the meetings in which McIvor agreed, ad referendum, with the Americans that they would each retreat one percent, so that the quotas could balance at Argentina 24, Australia 18, Canada 40, and the United States 18 percent.

---

[6] *Washington Wheat Meeting Minutes 3/41, July 11, 1941*, loc. cit.

This was where matters stood when McIvor had to leave Washington for Winnipeg on July 19. Dean Shaw had already returned to Ottawa, Biddulph, Coyne and Wilson continued to attend the meetings. As he left Washington, McIvor telephoned Oliver Master, the acting deputy minister of trade and commerce, who reported in turn to Wilgress:

... Contrary to what the Canadian delegation had been inclined to expect—there has been no evidence of a desire on the part of the United States to attempt to edge in on Canada's present trade. On the contrary, there appeared to be pretty clear recognition that this trade does, and should, belong to Canada. At any rate, Mr. McIvor intimated that he was decidedly relieved at the failure of any fears on this score to materialize. ...[7]

As George McIvor left Washington, consideration was being given draft articles covering the obligations of importing countries with respect to production and to the policing of export quotas. It was not difficult for the representatives of the exporting countries (in the absence of the importing countries, save Britain) to formulate obligations for the importers which would roll back high-cost production in Europe and create a relatively free market for overseas wheat. The most sanguine expression of hope in this direction appeared in a draft submitted by Wheeler:

The governments of the normal wheat importing countries, recognizing the importance to their consumers of supplies of high quality wheat from the wheat exporting countries, declare it to be their purpose to operate their respective domestic wheat policies in harmony with the terms and spirit of this agreement and specifically agree:

1. To eliminate all regulations requiring the use of stated percentages of domestic wheat by domestic mills.

2. To eliminate all regulations requiring the admixture of products other than wheat to wheat flour for the manufacture of bread.

3. To reduce their customs tariffs on imported wheat to a level not exceeding 20 per cent of the cost of imported wheat as landed in their respective ports.

4. To confine any subsidies to domestic wheat producers to a total production of wheat not exceeding the average production in their respective countries during the period 1925-1929.

5. To encourage by such means as may be available in the individual countries the production of livestock products for domestic consumption as an alternative to the production of wheat, and

6. To purchase their full national requirements of imported wheat and imported flour from the World Wheat Pool.[8]

Carlill demurred at only those points which cut across British policy, notably the roll back of production to a 1925-29 base when British acreage was at its lowest point, and also the sanctions against purchases from non-signatory exporters. A more forceful protest by Carlill could have saved much subsequent time, but in his position as chairman he seemed reluctant to intervene in the debate. More probably, the reason for Carlill's reticence was that his instructions were not inconsistent with what was being proposed. Before leaving for Washington, Cairns had presided over a group of British officials which had prepared the instructions, and these had been

---

[7] *Trade and Commerce file 26204:14.*
[8] *Washington Wheat Meeting Minutes,* July 17, 1941, loc. cit.

approved without having been sufficiently considered.[9] In the result, Wheeler's draft was very little watered down in a production control paragraph that would require importing countries to roll back production to a 1922-29 base, a paragraph in the export control article which required the importing countries to police the export sales of the signatory exporting countries, a second paragraph in the same article to refrain from purchases from non-signatory exporters beyond the export allowances set for them by the council, an undertaking elsewhere to reduce domestic prices for wheat to not more than one-third above the basic price established by the council, and the abolition of mixing regulations. The inclusion of these proposals in the provisional draft agreement circulated to governments early in August, made the subsequent negotiations considerably more difficult.

In McIvor's absence, Wilson had the responsibility for presenting the Canadian position on minimum and maximum reserve stocks. The initial proposal in the draft agreement circulated on July 21 in million bushels had been:

	Argentina	Australia	Canada	United States
Minimum:	60	32	108	200
Maximum:	120	64	216	400

When these figures came under discussion next day, Mr. Dodd was the first to point out that the United States range was inconsistent with its national legislation. Wilson calculated that the Canadian range allowed for an annual departure of 3 bushels per acre from the Canadian average yield whereas the standard deviation from the mean was 7 bushels. The foregoing ranges had also been related to July 1 and it was agreed that the relation of each country's stocks to its respective crop year end would be more meaningful. The negotiations on the stock range occupied two days. In the end, Steere produced statistical evidence to support Wilson's contention that the amplitude of yield variations had to be taken into account, and by July 24 the following figures were agreed upon:

	Argentina	Australia	Canada	United States
Minimum:	45	25	80	150
Maximum	125	80	325	400

The importance of the carryover stock limits lay in the fact the agreed figures were the explicit obligations imposed upon the four exporting countries, to which implicit obligations regarding production control were related. The clause covering the latter obligations required the exporting countries to adopt "positive measures" to ensure that after meeting domestic consumption and export quota requirements, carryover stocks were maintained within the minimum-maximum range. This begged the issue of what would happen if the actual carryover in any country exceeded its maximum agreed figure. Cairns proposed that any excess should be donated by the offending country to the international wheat council for use in relief or other disposal.

There still remained the question of price control, and the meeting adopted Cairns' proposal that the average market price of all parcels of wheat imported into Britain in the August 1922 - July 1939 period (38/6

[9]R. J. Hammond, *Food, Volume I: The Growth of Policy,* (History of the Second World War U.K. Civil Series, 1951), p. 352.

shillings per quarter of 480 pounds) be adjusted by the latest available index of British wholesale prices in relation to the 1922-39 base period of 100. This was referred to as the standard price. Adjustments were to be made to compensate for major changes in exchange and freight rates. It did not go unnoticed, however, that the British board of trade index of wholesale prices had climbed by almost 50 percent since the outbreak of war.

This completed preparation of the provisional draft agreement, which was circulated on August 3, 1941, to the participating governments for their consideration. The meeting adjourned on that date in the expectation that a short break would suffice for fresh instructions, but it was not until October 14 that the meeting reconvened.

BRITISH REACTION

A succinct and lively description of the shock which the provisional draft agreement transmitted to the British was provided by a ministry of food historian after the end of the war:

> The explosive reaction that these proposals aroused in Whitehall must have bewildered the United Kingdom delegation. Mr. Keynes described the draft terms as a 'fantastic piece of chicanery'; the Minister of Agriculture found in them good reason for pressing his technical objection to acreage restriction, and asked where was the *quid pro quo*; all agreed that the price proposals were unreasonably high, calculated as they were to mean a shilling quartern loaf once the Treasury subsidy were removed. The objections of the Cereals Division of the Ministry of Food were more fundamental; the price and quota provisions, it said, would make it impossible for the United Kingdom to revert to private importation of grain during the life of the Agreement. If, as was proposed, the Agreement were to last five years, this would probably extinguish the grain trade for good. Hence the article providing for the regulation of export quotas by reference to a freely determined United Kingdom import price could not operate, since there would be no such price. Moreover, the Division questioned whether acreage limitation in this country could be enforced if the c.i.f. price of wheat rose, as it would under the Agreement, to 55s. 6d. a quarter.
>
> These criticisms went to the root, not merely of the specific proposals now under debate, but of the principles that had been hawked around Whitehall at intervals during two years without arousing suspicion or protest. The price and quota provisions of the 1939 agreement had been scarcely less drastic than these in their implications for private trade in grain and the working of the futures market. What was in question was not the livelihood of a few speculators, but the existence of a sensitive and effective mechanism that not only procured supplies at the lowest possible cost, but contributed to invisible exports both directly and indirectly through the shipping and insurance business that went with it. This was now threatened, not as a result of a high-level decision taken after due deliberation, but through sheer inadvertence. Worse, the United Kingdom was more than half committed to an agreement likely to have such far-reaching effects at a meeting of its own seeking.[10]

Several weeks elapsed before the first intimation of the British reaction was communicated to Canada. Norman Robertson was in London during the first week in September when he met Sir Frederick Leith-Ross who had initially solicited the support of the Canadian government in getting the

[10]*Ibid.*

Washington discussions started. Sir Frederick handed Robertson a note which indicated the views the British delegation would express when the meetings resumed:

The draft Wheat Agreement only reached us three weeks ago and the proposals made in it are of such importance that they require careful study. But our preliminary views are :-

(1) We are entirely in favour of the general objectives of the Wheat Committee and we sincerely hope that an agreement may be reached which will lay the foundations for a more stable market for wheat;

(2) The first essential for this purpose is to find means of adjusting the supply position to potential demand by a regulation of wheat production and exports by the exporting countries, and on all the main provisions of the Agreement on this point we have no questions to raise, though we suggest that the Wheat Committee should give further consideration to the effect of their proposals on the international grain trade and to the advisability of maintaining buffer stocks. It should also be borne in mind that the implementation of the quota arrangements by the importing countries will in the long run depend on their foreign exchange possibilities.

(3) The proposal to fix a standard export price seems to us much more questionable. This has never been attempted in any other commodity agreement and is immensely difficult in the case of a commodity like wheat. The actual formula proposed seems to us both unsound in principle and unworkable in practice. It would have the effect of raising the price of wheat to a quite unreasonable figure, and therefore conflicts with the first principle of the Agreement. We fully agree that when the supply position has been adjusted, the Wheat Council should aim at maintaining the price of wheat at a reasonable level, fair to producers and consumers alike, but the methods by which this aim can be achieved need very careful consideration, and it appears to us that the price of wheat cannot be fixed except in relation to other cereals.

(4) We are ready to join with other importing countries in "policing" the agreement but we are not clear that the Wheat Committee have given adequate consideration to the difficulties involved. We can arrange to police the export quotas if necessary, though this will involve the retention of an import licensing system after the war. The policing of imports from non-signatory countries involves measures of discrimination contrary to the m.f.n. principle in our commercial treaties. There would be political as well as economic objections to limiting imports, e.g., from Russia to a figure fixed without her consent and the adherence of Russia to the Agreement seems to us almost essential. To police the price at which imports are purchased would be still more difficult, and could not be done effectively unless all the principal importing countries adopted a system of Government monopoly, which would be incompatible with the maintenance of a free grain market. Our difficulties would be largely met if the voting provisions were so altered as to ensure that no obligation affecting importers is imposed without our concurrence. But, in fact, any policing by the U.K. alone could not be effective and the utility of these provisions ultimately depends on the general acceptance of the Agreement by other importing countries.

(5) The definite limitation of wheat acreage in the U.K. on the lines proposed raises important political issues, which are under consideration. But, in fact, we have no intention of maintaining our wartime wheat acreage and our imports of wheat (which are not subject to any tariff restrictions) have been remarkably constant. We are doing our best to see whether a proposal

can be framed to assure the wheat exporting countries that our policy will conform with their objectives.

(6) The U.K. wheat production however is, in itself, far less important than that of the European countries. We are entirely in favour of securing a reduction of the excessive agrarian protectionism adopted in these countries and, so far as we are concerned, we have no objection to the proposals in the Agreement relating to domestic price control and milling regulations. But we would suggest that these articles are far too rigid and that few, if any, of the European countries could accept them in their present form. These articles could easily be represented to imply that the aim of the Agreement was to destroy the livelihood of the farming populations of Europe and thus give a very dangerous handle to German propaganda. In our view, the reduction of agrarian protectionism is more likely to be secured by a gradual process of consultation between the Wheat Council and the countries of Europe, accompanied by measures to restore international trade generally. The provisions of the draft Agreement on this hand appear to us to need redrafting so as to define the reasonable objective aimed at and provide for further discussions as to how it can be achieved.

(7) We welcome wholeheartedly the proposals for the creation of a Relief Pool and though our position is substantially different from that of the wheat exporting countries, we are ready to offer an appropriate contribution. The relations between the Wheat Union and the organization of Relief to Europe generally appear to us to require further study.

(8) To sum up, we welcome the proposals in the draft Agreement for the regulation of production in the exporting countries which must be the foundation of any commodity control. We will do our best to collaborate from the importing end but the adherence of other importing countries has to be secured, and the proposals in the draft Agreement about their obligations, as well as about export prices, seem to us much more rigid than the circumstances justify. We hope to make some constructive suggestions which will help during the transition period.[11]

On September 17, 1941, following his return to Ottawa, Robertson sent a copy of the note to Oliver Master, acting deputy minister of trade and commerce, who passed it on to Wilson with the request that he send comments to the Honourable T, A. Crerar, acting chairman of the wheat committee. Wilson's memo of September 20 to Mr. Crerar was sharply critical of the position the British had taken on prices and he said that, without an effective price clause, the agreement would be useless to Canada:

Mr. Master sent a copy of the above memorandum to you yesterday, and has suggested that I comment briefly on it, since Mr. Robertson, the Under-Secretary of State for External Affairs regards the views expressed as those that are likely to be presented by the United Kingdom delegation in Washington.

1. The approval expressed over the general objectives of the wheat agreement, and the willingness to help "police" the agreement up to a point, were only to be expected in light of representations made to our Government by the United Kingdom Government last February. The essence of these representations was that, as a matter of improving economic relations with the United States, consideration should be given to international control of a number of commodities with wheat as the proving ground for this sort of collaboration. For this reason, the United Kingdom Government suggested

[11]*Trade and Commerce file* 26204:14.

that the Canadian Government take a more serious view of the possibilities of an international wheat agreement than had been done in the past. Any retreat by the United Kingdom from the position they took last February would leave the door open for us as well.

2. Apart from the objection raised in the Leith-Ross memorandum to the attempt to maintain a standard price, the most serious reservation is the apparent unwillingness to refuse imports from non-signatory exporters who exceed their quota allocations. Although such sanctions would undoubtedly call for some modification of existing commercial treaties embracing the most-favoured-nation principle, the importing countries must be made to realize that the four exporters cannot be expected to accept limited production and export quotas only to have non-signatory exporters seize a larger share of the market by unrestricted selling at lower prices. For this reason, the United Kingdom should be pressed to extend its "policing" function to imports from non-signatory exporters in one way or another.

3. The difficulty in getting the continental European countries to accept a reduction of production, and removal of import and milling restrictions was fully realized at Washington. Relief considerations and a genuine willingness to encourage exports of manufactures from Europe were regarded as necessary avenues of approach to this end.

4. Paragraph (3) of the Leith-Ross memorandum is overly pessimistic on the practicability of maintaining a standard wheat price, and is not correct in contending that "it would have the effect of raising the price of wheat to quite an unreasonable level." The parity price as it would have worked out in 1938-39 at 35/3 per quarter, c.i.f. London could only be unreasonably high if it were agreed that a "distress" price is the only proper price during conditions of oversupply. The same logic justifies a "scarcity" price during periods of shortage. Apart from assuring importing countries continuous supplies, the whole purpose of regulating production, thereby keeping supplies within a minimum-maximum range, is to avoid the occurrence of both scarcity and distress prices. By this means, the interests of consumers and producers are both served. The practicability of maintaining a standard price is largely tied up in the appointment of personnel with trade experience to the Price-equivalents Committee. One of the first considerations of this Committee would be to relate the necessary degree of price latitude to permit the grain trade to function, with the maintenance of an over-all average of British parcels prices close to the parity level.

5. Unless the United Kingdom is prepared to support some form of minimum price control, there is no practical interest in the agreement for Canada. Our only interest in regulating production and accepting export quotas is to stabilize the price. If assurance of price stability is to be denied by the United Kingdom, then there isn't much point in our accepting a long-time commitment on production control and quotas.[12]

This was preliminary to a meeting McIvor and Wilson had with the cabinet wheat committee on September 22 in which the ministers reviewed their position and concluded that the provisional agreement was so untimely in the midst of the war that the Canadian delegation should seek support of the other delegations for an adjournment of the discussions pending a more appropriate occasion. But not wishing to accept the onus for ending the talks against the wishes of other governments, and in particular that of the United States, the ministers made it clear that they should be informed if the Canadians found themselves in a minority, and in need of

12*Ibid.*

further instructions. Mr. Crerar, as acting minister of trade and commerce, made a submission to cabinet along these lines, which was referred to the cabinet war committee on October 9, 1941. A minute of that committee's decision was prepared by Mr. Arnold Heeney, which he forwarded to Crerar and to Oliver Master on October 11:

> International Wheat Conference, Washington. The Committee agreed that the memorandum which you submitted should form the basis of the government's instructions to the Canadian delegation, subject to further consideration of the question by the Cabinet Wheat Committee and their advisers.[13]

The next communication from the British government was addressed by its secretary of state for dominion affairs directly to the prime minister on October 28, 1941, some two weeks after the Washington meetings had resumed. The message reported on an exchange of views between Prime Minister Churchill and President Roosevelt as it read:

> 1. We have followed with close interest discussions in Washington of Preparatory Committee of Wheat Advisory Committee and have studied with care preliminary draft agreement drawn up by the Committee for each of the five participating Governments. From the moment when the United States Government first suggested that the Preparatory Committee should be summoned to consider wheat problem in its broadest aspects, we have been most anxious to do what we could to promote successful sketching out of an international agreement, both in general interests of economic co-operation with the United States, and also because of the intrinsic importance of wheat as foremost staple commodity and the great part which it is bound to play in plans for relief of occupied countries in the immediate post war period. The fact that Canada and Australia are as vitally interested as the United States in an equitable distribution of wheat markets of the world has naturally increased our desire to assist the Committee to arrive at a common understanding on future policy.

> 2. There are, however, certain features of the draft agreement as it at present stands which have caused us some concern in view of their possible repercussions on the war situation at this stage. In particular the draft gives the impression that it is contemplated to force on wheat importing countries of Europe, as a condition of immediate post war relief, a series of obligations, including a drastic restriction of their wheat production, which would vitally affect their agricultural systems. Any agreement capable of this construction would, in our view, be most inopportune and indeed dangerous in the extreme. It would supply Nazi propaganda in Europe with a most potent weapon, and would be bound to arouse suspicion as to the use which the British Commonwealth and the United States intend to make of their power when the war has been won. We regard it as essential at this stage therefore to remove from the draft agreement all provisions implying interference by the British Commonwealth and the United States in European agriculture policy.

> 3. A further point is the position of Russia in relation to proposals outlined in the draft. Russia was still a neutral country when arrangements for meeting of Preparatory Committee were made. But as things are now it appears to us virtually out of the question either to conclude an agreement which may seriously affect her interests without consulting her, or to approach her on such a matter at a time when she is engaged in a life and death struggle, and when her richest wheat fields are being overrun by the enemy.

[13]*Ibid.*

4. We have endeavoured to devise means of overcoming these special difficulties, but have reached the conclusion that it is almost impossible to do so while leaving intact the present framework of the draft agreement. In these circumstances we have been considering whether it might not be the wisest course for the Preparatory Committee to deal first with immediate practical issues, such as the establishment of a pool for post war relief, provision for an "ever-normal" granary, and other features of present draft which could not be regarded as prejudicing in any way the interests of unrepresented countries. The other issues of policy would, no doubt, be discussed by the Committee, and there might be great advantage in this, but conclusions upon them might be deferred until a later date.

5. Tentative suggestions on these lines were recently made by the Prime Minister in a private and personal message to President Roosevelt which drew special attention to considerations mentioned in paragraphs 4 and 5 above. The Prime Minister has now received a message from President Roosevelt in reply, the substance of which is as follows:

(1) The President fully agrees as to the importance of avoiding any impression as in paragraph 2 above, and sees no objection to our delegation stressing this consideration in discussions.

(2) The President also agrees as to the importance of considering interests of Russia, but he suggests it should be feasible to arrive at a framework which would leave the way open for Russian adherence later.

(3) President states that the United States Government have not looked upon these discussions as a conference in any formal sense, but rather as an exchange of ideas between experts in a position to reflect the views of their Governments.

(4) He is pleased at the progress made in July and August but holds no brief for precise form or working of draft agreement. Much of the draft will no doubt require revision, but he hopes that it will be possible to find a large area of agreement. He adds that special importance is attached by the United States Government at this juncture to plans for equitable sharing of post war markets and to our co-operation as largest importer.

6. We have instructed our delegates in the light of this exchange of messages with the President, and we hope that after a full exchange of views on draft agreement in its present form some means for overcoming difficulties which we foresee may be found. We have informed them that in exploring possibilities with their colleagues they should stress considerations mentioned in the Prime Minister's message to the President, particularly those in paragraphs 2 and 3 above, and should refer home for further instructions if discussions should develop in such a way as to prejudice any of the main points which, as explained above, we consider it essential in the present circumstances to safeguard.[14]

OCTOBER-FEBRUARY SESSIONS, 1941-42

Visible evidence of British apprehension over the provisional draft of August 3 appeared in the substantially strengthened delegation which attended the resumption of the meetings on October 14, 1941. The Right Honourable Sir Arthur Salter, parliamentary secretary for the ministry of war transport, who had been posted to Washington as head of the British shipping mission there, now headed the British delegation. Sir Arthur was accompanied by Carlill, Mr. R. R. Enfield of the ministry of agriculture and fisheries, Mr. E. H. M. Lloyd of the ministry of food, and Mr. R. A. Furness

[14]*Ibid.*

of the imported cereals branch. Salter's assignment of vitiating, clause by clause, the importing countries' obligations in the provisional agreement, became apparent as the days wore on.

Because of Salter's presence, the Americans named the under secretary of agriculture, Mr. Paul Appleby, to head their delegation, and Appleby replaced Carlill as chairman. The Canadian delegation remained unchanged as George McIvor returned to Washington with fresh instructions.

During the recess, Viacava had returned to Buenos Aires and he had come back to Washington with a complete briefing. The Australians, apparently at British prompting, had strengthened their delegation. McDougall was replaced by Mr. Edwin McCarthy (later Sir Edwin), the Australian assistant secretary of commerce. This was McCarthy's first exposure to the negotiations (later, while he was deputy Australian high commissioner in London, he participated in the postwar negotiations and served for several years as vice-chairman of the international wheat council). McCarthy had brought with him to Washington an assistant from his department, Mr. J. Richardson. He arrived without firm instructions, however, for the Australian government had just changed hands. A new set of ministers was in charge and they had to consult the agricultural council, on which the commonwealth and state governments were represented.

On October 17, Appleby, the new chairman, invited in alphabetical order the delegations to report on the instructions they had received. Viacava led off by reporting that the Argentine government had become friendlier to the concept of an international wheat agreement and that it had accepted the provisional draft in principle, but with several specific reservations. First, that country's experience with production control had recently produced limited results, beyond which the government was not prepared to go. On the other hand, Viacava reported that the price objective in the agreement, if achieved, would react as a powerful incentive to production in Argentina. Although his government was prepared to adopt legislative and administrative measures to regulate production, it held out no prospect for reducing acreage below the level prevailing in recent years. Argentina's minimum reserve stock figure of 45 million bushels was much too high because storage capacity in that country was only 20 million bushels. Its basic export quota of 24 percent was considered too low. That figure, accepted in London, had been coupled with the granting of a supplementary quota. The Argentine government also recommended a reduction in the standard price, because of the production incentive it implied for that country.

Since McCarthy's instructions were not yet at hand, McIvor spoke next. He read a statement which had been approved by the cabinet war committee to the effect that the Canadian government had looked at the phasing of the proposals, commencing with relief needs, a transitional period when shipping would still dictate the sources of wheat supply, and the third phase when reasonably normal conditions once again would prevail. The Canadian government was prepared to join with other countries in making relief contributions on the basis of their export quotas but considered that relief wheat was only one aspect of a general distribution of food under a relief plan, and that consultation would be required on the timing of the distribution through agencies which could most effectively handle the undertaking. In the transitional period, shipping and exchange rates would still be seriously dislocated, and it was important in that period, food supplies would have to be obtained from the most accessible sources. This, incidentally, was one of the major Canadian policy concerns that Canada should not be called upon to surrender any advantage which the shortage of shipping conferred upon it as a source of supply before that shortage was relieved. Nevertheless, when shipping and exchange conditions did revert to normal, the Canadian government agreed that a wheat agreement would be needed, although it was seriously concerned over the timing of an announcement of the conclusion of an agreement in advance of the free participation in the negotiations of a number of the European countries. At present, with many of the key importing countries ranged against each other, any such announcement apparently affecting their agricultural policies by the five signatory governments would be seized upon by the propaganda agencies of the axis powers. Accordingly, the Canadian government proposed:

> that the Conference agree that an international wheat agreement will be entered into when the danger of adverse propaganda is removed, and when the importing countries can freely participate in working out the precise terms of such an agreement. The Canadian Government commend these views to the Conference. If, however, the rest of the Governments continue to favour proceeding with the formulation of a post-war agreement now, the Canadian Government are prepared to reconsider their position in the light of the views expressed by other Governments.[15]

Sir Arthur Salter spoke next and, because of the position his government had taken, his task was to make a strategic retreat from the offending provisions affecting the importing countries. He had just been given an opportunity to support the Canadian recommendation for a postponement of negotiations but, at the moment, this perhaps exceeded his instructions, as Salter proceeded to argue instead for a modified agreement. He began by describing the provisional draft as the exploratory work of experts in advance of the calling of a negotiating conference, and that the experts had not been empowered to commit their governments. Two things had happened during the recess: the proclamation of the Atlantic Charter and the entry of the USSR into the war as an active belligerent. The first implied that there would be many trade agreements negotiated of which wheat would form a part. The Russian participation in the war outlined the need for consulting that government in respect of any wheat agreement. His government shared the Canadian government's concern over nazi propaganda, if the details of an agreement were to be disclosed now. Nevertheless, his government welcomed the relief proposals, and he assured the meeting they were not opposed to a wheat agreement in principle. The British government was not interested in benefiting from distress commodity prices. Although Britain was a wheat importing country, there were many commodities "in which the United Kingdom, or its colonial non-governing empire, was on the other side of the table". He was prepared, therefore, to continue the discussions.

[15] *Washington Wheat Meeting Minutes,* 26/41, October 17, 1941, Trade and Commerce File 26204:14.

Mr. Wheeler spoke next on behalf of the United States. The Americans were convinced that too much wheat was being produced, as evidenced by the growth in carryover stocks. As governments in the exporting countries were becoming more involved in the management of surpluses the United States government considered that the interests of the importing countries were also involved. They attached importance to the participation of the United Kingdom in the present instance and that other importing countries should be represented when possible. While they did not stand by the letter of the draft agreement, it represented the most workable scheme advanced over the past eight years of negotiations. In particular they supported the basic points which would estimate world demand as a basis for allocating quotas to the exporting countries, and which would assure a fair share of the market to each exporting country. They attached considerable importance to the reserve stocks provisions as an extension of the United States' "ever normal granary" principle to the international sphere. They looked for a more precise formulation of the price objective. They supported the principle of establishing a relief pool of wheat, and agreed that it should be incorporated into other relief operations after the war. They also supported the establishment of a wheat union or international pool to handle relief wheat at first, and then commercial wheat after the war, which would facilitate the administration of the wheat agreement. Above all else, they attached importance to the principle of market sharing by the exporting countries and to co-operation with the importing countries as a fresh approach to general economic collaboration in the postwar world.

There followed a brief discussion on procedure and the order in which the several proposals might be discussed. McIvor pointed out that he had been given authority to discuss the relief proposal only, until after he had reported back the views of other governments on the Canadian proposal to postpone further negotiations. Both the chairman and Sir Arthur Salter said that questions of timing could not be considered until after it had been determined what proposals could be agreed upon. At Salter's suggestion, McIvor agreed to participate in further discussions, while reserving the position of his government.

In the sessions which followed, the relief pool was considered first as the opening statements of delegations had indicated general support. McIvor endorsed contributions by the exporting countries on the basis of their percentage export quotas. Britain expected to contribute its share in shipping. A relief pool of 250 million bushels was agreed in principle, but related questions of administration and dovetailing with other relief operations were referred to a committee for further consideration.

On the subject of production control it was agreed that each country should be left to devise its own methods, and each delegation reviewed domestic practices already in operation. Wheeler contended that the immediate need for production control argued in favor of bringing an agreement into operation forthwith. McIvor drew attention to the severity of the stipulation that any excess over the maximum reserve stock limits should be either disposed of immediately within the country or placed at the disposal of the council. His objection produced an easement which allowed each country twelve months' grace in which to adjust its stock position.

When export quotas came up for discussion, Viacava requested a supplementary quota of 250,000 tons for shipment to neighboring countries, in addition to Argentina's basic quota price of 24 percent. McCarthy expressed the opinion that 18 percent would not be acceptable to Australia in terms of a total basic market for the "big four" of 450 million bushels, but did not suggest an alternative percentage. McIvor and Wheeler reported that Canada and the United States had now agreed between themselves on figures of 40 and 18 percent respectively. The other representatives rejected Viacava's proposal for supplementary quotas to cover privileged markets. But, because no immediate headway could be made in resolving the basic quota figures for Argentina and Australia, this question was reserved for direct discussion among the heads of delegation.

The next item to be considered was the proposed obligation on the importing countries to police export quotas. This implied two types of action: one, to stop buying from signatory exporters as they completed their quotas, and the other to refrain from purchases from non-signatory exporters. McIvor expressed the Canadian government's view that the participation of a large number of importing countries was essential; otherwise the production restraints imposed upon signatory exporting countries would be offset by increased production in the importing countries and in the non-signatory exporting countries.

Sir Arthur Salter intervened by saying that the policing by the importing countries of the exporters' quotas involved exchange considerations. At the moment, it mattered a great deal to Britain whether they purchased wheat from dollar or sterling countries. Britain had most-favored nation treaties with non-signatory exporting countries, under which a refusal to purchase wheat would be a violation.

Moreover, his government were not prepared to recommend such a course to other importing countries in the absence of their free consent. Therefore, he rejected the suggestion that signatory importing countries should prohibit imports from non-signatory exporting countries. His position in that regard would be modified only if nearly all of the exporting countries were to adhere to the agreement. Lest his attitude seem too negative, he was prepared to agree to policing the exporting quotas of the signatory exporters. This could be done now under Britain's wartime powers, but licensing legislation would have to be enacted after the war.

Mr. Wheeler referred to the coffee agreement which established limits in the amount of coffee signatory importing countries could import from non-signatory exporters. Mr. McIvor repeated his government's concern over the confrontation of importing countries, not now represented, by a prepared case. This raised a question about the timing of entering into an agreement, over which his government had expressed concern. An additional consideration was that non-signatory countries should not be permitted to undermine the agreement.

On the question of reserve stocks, there was general acceptance of the figures circulated, with the exception of Argentina's minimum figure which exceeded her permanent storage capacity. At a later stage of the negotiations, the Canadian maximum reserve stock figure was reduced from 325 to 275 million bushels, with its consent.

When the obligations of the importing countries came under discussion, representatives of the exporting countries, notably Wheeler and McIvor, expressed doubt that an agreement could be operated successfully in the absence of co-operation by the importing countries. At the same time, McIvor acknowledged the weakness in formulating specific provisions affecting the importing countries in their absence. Sir Arthur Salter repeated his concern over the propaganda implications generally, as he entered his objection to the specific provision that wheat acreage in the importing countries be reduced to a 1922-1929 base. He pointed out that, in many cases, this would require importing countries at the end of the war to reduce acreage to one-third and even to one-fifth of their current levels. More generally, there were balance of payments implications in the proposal which would entail compensatory concessions by exporting countries in other areas of trade. As a compromise, he was prepared to support a policy of acreage reduction, provided that its specific provisions were to remain for negotiation at a later time when all importing countries could participate.

The proposal for a wheat union was also discussed. The Argentine government had accepted the scheme in principle. Salter drew attention to the socialistic implications in the implied abolition of the international wheat trade, not to mention its impact on the trade in other cereals. Appleby contended that the question was not one of ideology but rather whether the mechanism proposed was a good step in itself. He acknowledged that replacement of the existing marketing mechanism was involved. Wheeler referred to the administrative advantages of a union in making the wheat agreement work. Prices and price equivalents would be easier to determine and enforce if turned over to one governing body. Its principal disadvantage, he considered, would be its effect upon the grain trade, although Steere believed the personnel in the trade could continue to operate as agents of the union rather than as principals in buying and selling wheat.

In the end, it was left to McIvor to shatter Cairns's dream of a wheat union. McIvor distinguished between two systems, one an exporter's agreement in which each country would observe the quota and price provisions, and the other a union or trust which would take over the complete merchandising function. Under the former, as long as there was some flexibility in the price provisions, the grain trade could carry on. If prices were rigid, agreed allowances would be necessary to permit the trade to carry on with some opportunity for profit in buying and selling. Under a union the trade would be put out of business, and if for any reason the union subsequently broke down, there would be difficulty in reestablishing the trade. He accused the advocates of the union of attempting to run before they had learned to walk, and recommended instead that an exporters' agreement be tried first. There were several reasons why a union might not work. The complete co-operation of exporting and importing countries would be required in committing supplies and purchases to a body in which confidence was essential. In Canada, under the central selling agency, the three provincial pools had entered into an agreement in which each pool was equally represented on a board. Notwithstanding, differences of opinion arose, despite excellent leadership. He believed that friction would be more apt to arise if the parties were separate nations. A wheat union might also place the Canadian government in a position where it would have to purchase the elevator system from private owners if the latter could not operate effectively under the new system. McIvor's intervention was effective in rejecting the wheat union proposal.

Finally, the price provisions remained to be resolved. The provisional draft had proposed a "standard" price, based on the average price of parcels c.i.f. Liverpool over the period from August, 1922 to July, 1939. For current application, this standard price of 38/6 shillings per quarter of 480 pounds was to be adjusted by the current British board of trade wholesale price index calculated in relation to the 1922-29 base of 100. The aspect of the formula which had upset the British government more than anything else was that the British index of wholesale prices by July, 1941, had risen by 56.4 percent since the outbreak of war. Apart from the British concern, both Viacava and McCarthy considered that the standard price, adjusted for changes in the general price level, would stimulate world wheat production unduly and thereby defeat the purpose of the agreement. More flexibility in the price level was proposed, and McIvor suggested a miminum-maximum range of prices with adjustments in export quotas related thereto. It was also suggested that instead of using, as an adjustment factor, the British index of wholesale prices which had climbed the sharpest, a composite index of wholesale prices in the four exporting countries, which had risen much less steeply, should be used.

Acting upon these suggestions, the prices committee produced a report which recommended a basic minimum-maximum range of prices for each country, with a minimum of 79 cents and a maximum of 94 cents per bushel for No. 3 Northern, in store Fort William. The range was subject to an upward adjustment of 22 percent as indicated by the weighted composite index of wholesale prices which had occurred since 1939. In speaking to the proposed price formula, McIvor referred to the 80-cent price his government had paid producers in 1938 when they were selling the wheat at 60 cents. He defied anyone to say that 80 cents then was not a fair price. R. M. Evans commented on the demand Saskatchewan farmers had recently made for dollar wheat, adding wryly that he was glad he had disposed of his interest in a Saskatchewan farm. Sir Arthur also objected to the standard price formula and considered that he had the support of three of the four exporting countries in doing so. He criticized the existing proposal to support a fixed price which permitted the exporting countries to enlarge their quotas if prices rose, but required importing countries to police the quotas if prices fell. He contended that the same mechanism of reducing quotas should be used if prices fell. He was prepared to discuss a buffer stock scheme. Wheeler pointed out that price enforcement would have been greatly simplified had the idea of a wheat union been accepted.

Salter reserved his most categoric opposition to a price clause for private discussion with the other heads of delegations. When he spoke to McIvor, Salter informed him that the British government were prepared to consider a buffer stocks scheme for wheat such as J. M. Keynes had most recently proposed, or a system of bulk contracts such as Britain was then negotiating with Canada, as alternatives to the price clause to which they had taken exception. As the Canadian delegation needed guidance on the response to be made to the British alternatives, Wilson prepared a memorandum on

November 22, 1941, to Mr. MacKinnon, which George McIvor took with him from Washington to Ottawa:

The Canadian delegates attended an opening meeting on October the 17th at which Mr. McIvor read a statement from the Canadian Government to the effect that our Government were in favour of a wheat agreement, but that they questioned the wisdom of entering into such an agreement at the present time because of the adverse propaganda use which might be made of it in the importing countries under German domination, and which might lessen the opportunity of concluding a satisfactory agreement after the end of the war. The United States delegation replied that it would be impossible to appraise the propaganda aspects until the terms which might be arrived at in an agreement were fully explored. The United Kingdom delegation drew attention to the propaganda possibilities insofar as they might affect the course of the war, but they supported the United States delegation rather than our own, in saying that this issue could not be judged until the terms of an agreement could be further explored.

Since that meeting the Canadian delegates have proceeded with the others in discussion of revised terms of an agreement which have included the contribution of wheat for relief, the abandonment of earlier proposals for a Wheat Union, the percentage export quotas for each of the four exporting countries, and an agreement on prices.

Throughout these discussions the United Kingdom delegation have increasingly disclosed their reluctance to agree upon any specific terms. They were in agreement with the relief proposals, but it was quite evident that they tacitly hoped the exporting countries would not be able to agree among themselves upon the basis for export quotas or upon a common level of prices. When the four exporting countries did come to an arrangement satisfactory to themselves upon both these items the United Kingdom delegation declared that they could not enter into an agreement which designated a basis for wheat price levels now which would prevail during the life of an agreement operating after the war.

On the other hand, the British delegation proposed that prices be left to negotiation within the Wheat Council, at the time the agreement would come into operation, and in this regard it would be quite possible for a majority of importing countries over the exporting countries represented to dominate the price negotiations within the Council.

Prior to the latest meeting in Washington, Sir Arthur Salter, the Head of the British delegation, called in Mr. McIvor for a private discussion of the position. Mr. McIvor pointed out that leaving the price to negotiation within the Council would be unsatisfactory to our Government. Sir Arthur Salter, on the other hand, stated that his Government could not agree to specific prices now. As an alternative proposal he suggested that the meeting should discuss an agreement to cover the unsettled period immediately after the war, in which the United Kingdom would enter into bulk contracts with the four exporting countries on the basis of their percentage export quotas. Any countries unable to obtain shipping to move their quotas to the United Kingdom would obtain credits from other countries making the necessary shipments, so as to permit them to ship in excess of their quotas in a later year when shipping would be available. Mr. McIvor replied that this would necessitate Canada's sacrifice of any advantage through geographic position, which she might have after the Armistice, as a result of any continuation of the tight shipping position, and indicated that such a proposal would not be acceptable to our Government.

In the full meeting held on Wednesday, November 19, Sir Arthur Salter put forward the above proposal for bulk contracts, which he had discussed with with Mr. McIvor privately. He asked that any possibilities along these lines be explored, after having refused to refer to his Government the basis of price levels which had been agreed upon by the delegations of the four exporting countries as a reasonable basis, and which would have provided for a range of prices for No. 3 Northern at Fort William, with a minimum of 79 cents and a maximum of 94 cents per bushel including any special adjustments required because of changed general levels of prices, or because of changed exchange rates.

The British proposal for bulk contracts at the end of the war remains to be discussed in Washington. It is quite possible that if the British delegation continue to oppose an agreement of any specific nature on satisfactory lines to the exporting countries, the United States Government may press for an agreement to be entered into by the four exporting countries only. The Canadian delegation, therefore, wish to seek instruction from Council upon the two main issues of the British proposal for bulk contracts at the end of the war, and secondly the attitudes to be taken toward any move for an agreement among the exporting countries only.

Bulk Contracts

The issue is as follows: The United Kingdom would enter into contracts with the four exporting countries for her annual wheat requirements of 160 to 200 million bushels on the basis of all the percentage export quotas. Assuming 200 millions, involved, Canada would get a contract for 40 percent or 80 million bushels, Australia would get a contract for 18.5 per cent or 37 million bushels. If in the first year after the war Australia cannot get shipping for more than 10 million bushels to the United Kingdom, the remaining 27 millions would have to be shipped by Canada or possibly the United States. Australia would ask, however, that for the 27 millions she failed to ship in the first year, she would be allowed to ship that much in excess of her 37 millions during the second or third years. During those years Canada's shipments would be correspondingly reduced from our annual quota of 80 millions. The proposal simply involves Canada's forfeiting her favoured geographic position immediately at the end of the war, rather than at the time when shipping will be restored to normal. The Canadian delegation are against this proposal.

Agreement among The Exporting Countries

This proposal differs from the sort of wheat agreement which has been contemplated, insofar as importing countries would be free to buy wheat in any quantities and at the lowest possible prices from countries other than the Big Four. An exporters' agreement would require the Big Four to control production, to keep within export quotas and to maintain prices. All of these terms would have the effect of holding up an umbrella over the smaller exporting countries which could obviously profit most by remaining outside the agreement and expanding their production at lower price levels in competition against the Big Four. This proposal could only have a restrictive effect upon the wheat position in the signatory countries. It would fail to keep production in check in competing exporting countries and it would fail to bind the European importing countries to the principle to a reduction in the European wheat acreage after the war. The Canadian delegation do not regard this as a satisfactory proposal.[16]

[16]*Trade and Commerce file 26204:14.*

Evidence that the British were working outside the sessions to undermine the negotiations came from an unexpected source. Mr. E. M. H. Lloyd, a senior official in the British ministry of food and a member of the British delegation, had come in contact with Mr. Graham Towers, governor of the Bank of Canada, to whom he presented a scathing account of what the exporting countries were attempting to do; so much so in fact that Towers on his return to Ottawa telephoned Wilgress to acquaint him with the representations made and to ask that he be informed on the terms of the agreement under negotiation and, in particular, the price clause. Wilgress sent Towers the provisional draft and the memorandum just quoted which McIvor had given MacKinnon for the latter's presentation to cabinet, and he also asked Wilson to forward from Washington the latest proposals on the price formula. After studying the documents, Towers remained convinced that the British had a case, and he wrote to Wilgress on January 29, 1942, setting out his own very forthright and critical assessment of the negotiations:

I am much obliged for the information contained in your letters of December 6th and December 23rd on the subject of the proposed Wheat Agreement. The Canadian attitude towards the Agreement is, of course, a matter of high policy. For what an individual opinion may be worth, my appraisal of the proposals in as follows:-

1. The Agreement sets out to establish now the basis on which prices will be determined at some future date under conditions which are unknown. It is recognized that the price formula may produce results which would be somewhat ridiculous. I refer to the proviso that inflation in one or more of the exporting countries might cause the Council to reconsider the price clauses. Alterations in exchange rates might also have the same effect. The agreement in respect to prices could really be written in these terms:

"We, the exporting countries, have decided to obtain a price which will be satisfactory from our point of view. If the formula which we have adopted produces a price figure which is impossibly high, we will pick one which we think is more likely to work. We do not think that the formula is likely to produce a price which is too low from our point of view, so that possibility is not referred to in the Agreement."

2. The character of any realistic agreement will necessarily depend upon the kind of political and economic set-up which emerges in Europe after the war, and the extent to which the United States will support an international order.

The present draft agreement is appropriate to the conditions of undeclared, economic war which prevailed during the thirties. It would appear to assume that importing countries will not be interested in taking more than a bare minimum of imports and, for this amount, will use all the weapons of autarchy to force a sacrifice price upon the exporter. This may, in fact, be the situation which the Big Four will have to face, but there is no point in openly indicating such a belief while attainment of a better alternative remains a possibility. Announcement of the present draft agreement would do much to encourage the autarchic tendencies which now exist, and to make the less desirable alternative inevitable.

3. Even if the agreement were a good one, there does not appear to be much that it could do in a positive way while the war is on. It is difficult to see how an agreement could, in practice, limit production any more effectively than it is now being limited by the physical amount of storage capacity which it is practicable to supply. In view of the uncertainty as to relief needs after the

war, and the possible need of allies during the war, it would probably be undesirable to attempt greater restriction in any case.

4. Needless to say, I realize the vital importance, from a Canadian point of view, of good markets and satisfactory prices for wheat. But we would not want to participate in an arrangement which was likely to break down, having in mind that the after-effects of such a break-down would undoubtedly be very bad.

In the initial draft of the Agreement, there was some recognition of the fact that a combine which did not include a number of the major importing countries, and certain of the exporting countries was not a very practical affair. The earlier proposals, therefore, carried the thought that major importers would be forced to participate, and a form of coercing minor exporters could then be evolved. These ideas have been dropped. Is it not likely that a combine of the four large exporters, and one large importer, would not have a chance of imposing its terms on the rest of the world, except possibly for a very short time? Too large a proportion of wheat consuming capacity, and actual and potential wheat producing capacity, remains outside the orbit of such a combine. If the one large importer does not enter the combine, the thing becomes doubly ridiculous.

5. I should think that early announcement of a concrete scheme for post-war relief would be a good thing. But I doubt the advisability of attaching too many conditions to gifts of this character. After the gifts have been made, terms which are regarded as unfair are usually unenforceable.[17]

Wilgress drafted a very disarming reply, which more accurately reflected the outcome of the negotiations, as he wrote to Towers on February 4, 1942:

I have received your secret letter of January 29, replying to my letters of December 6 and 23, on the subject of the proposed Wheat Agreement.

I carefully note your comments on the proposals which have been discussed in Washington and, needless to say, I share your views to a very considerable degree. It is necessary, however, to bear in mind the history of these wheat discussions.

A year ago we received telegrams from London regarding United States proposals for a meeting to discuss an International Wheat Agreement, and the United Kingdom Government went out of its way to urge that Canada agree to participate in this meeting. This led to the first meeting, which was held last summer and which resulted in a Draft Agreement. The meeting was resumed in October and at the first meeting our representatives, according to instructions, pointed out the danger of confronting the importing countries in Europe with a fait accompli in the shape of a wheat agreement concluded without their having the opportunity of making their views known. The United Kingdom representatives took the initiative in pointing out that it could only be determined what effect an agreement was likely to have on the importing countries when it was seen what kind of agreement was coming out of the discussions. In this they were naturally supported by the United States representatives, who had all along held to this view. The important point is that we gave the   United Kingdom representatives the opportunity at the outset of the discussions, which commenced last October, to oppose the conclusion of an agreement for more or less the reasons indicated in your letter, but they preferred at that time to play along with the United States. It was only during the course of the discussions, when the price clauses began to take shape, that the United Kingdom reversed their policy, and from that time on they began to do everything they could to prevent the conclusion of an agreement. If we had then supported the United Kingdom we would have incurred the disfavor of the United States and our representatives felt that they were carrying out the instructions of the Government in doing everything to cooperate with the other countries, once they had registered their basic objections to the conclusion of the wheat agreement.

The way things have developed will mean an agreement which is free of nearly all the objections to which you refer in your letter. The United Kingdom have advised that they cannot accept an agreement with the price provision. Accordingly, the United States are now proposing that the question of price should be left for determination by the Wheat Council after the war, and an "escape" clause is to be drafted which will enable the United Kingdom to withdraw from the agreement if the price determined upon by the Wheat Council is not satisfactory. Secondly, other countries, such as Russia, Belgium and the Netherlands, are to have an opportunity after the war of becoming parties to the agreement, but if they are unable to accept the agreement as it now stands there will be a clause in the agreement providing for a revision of the whole agreement in order to conform to the wishes of the other countries.

This means, in effect, that a harmless but ineffective agreement is to be concluded, but it will enable the United States to show that they have secured some measure of agreement among the countries who are now free to discuss the question of wheat. We will have come out of these discussions with a clear record and without having shown the United States that we are not willing to cooperate, and also without having incurred the disfavour of the United Kingdom although Lloyd and others may think that we should have taken a more active part in supporting the efforts of the United Kingdom when it became clear that they were endeavouring to undermine the discussions.

I am passing this information on to you because I know that you will be relieved to hear that the final agreement which is likely to take shape will be free of most of the objections which you have raised, and also to let you know that there is another side to the story than that given by certain of the United Kingdom representatives who have taken part in the discussions.[18]

Meanwhile, the United States delegation had taken the initiative in trying to hold the negotiations together. To meet the British objection to prior agreement upon a price range to take effect on the cessation of hostilities, the Americans proposed that the five governments agree upon a relatively simple memorandum of agreement now, to which the provisional agreement would be attached as a draft convention, the only purpose of which would be to serve as a guide to a negotiating conference to be convened at the end of hostilities when all interested governments could take part in the negotiations. Nevertheless, in order to prevent a price collapse which was feared in the absence of an agreement when hostilities ceased, the Americans pressed for inclusion of a simple price clause in the memorandum of agreement. What they proposed was that wheat should continue to trade on the basis of the last price negotiated by the British for a bulk purchase prior to the cessation of hostilities. They proposed that this price commitment remain in effect for at least a year after the armistice to allow sufficient time for negotiation of a replacement clause in the new agreement. In order that the British might be further reassured, the Americans also agreed to insert a veto provision in the arrangements for

[18]*Ibid.*

negotiating the ongoing price clause, so that if the British were dissatisfied with the price terms therein, they were under no obligation to adhere to the postwar agreement. British acceptance of these terms appeared certain as the protracted sessions and committee meetings which had begun on October 14, 1941, drew to a close.

The other important issue remaining to be resolved was the amount of the export quotas. The Canadians and Americans had made their peace the previous autumn by accepting quotas of 40 and 18 percent, while proposing that the Argentine and Australian quotas be 24 and 18 per cent of the estimated world demand from the four exporting countries combined. Subsequently, the Americans conceded another percentage point, and the quota proposal stood at Canada 40, United States 17, Argentina 24.5 and Australia 18.5, which the latter countries still did not accept. The latter figures were rejected by the two governments concerned. The reconciliation of the export quotas was still outstanding when the draft memorandum of agreement was completed and circulated on February 28, 1942. Consequently, the quota figures had to be bracketed to indicate that they still remained to be reconciled. In that state, however, the draft memorandum of agreement and the considerably revised draft convention were circulated to governments for approval. In a letter from Wilson to Norman Robertson, March 17, 1942 the new terms were summarized:

I am enclosing herewith five copies of the draft documents relating to the Washingon Wheat Agreement which are being circulated for final consideration by the five participating Governments.

The present drafts represent a wide departure from the provisional draft of the International Wheat Agreement circulated last August. In the first place, for the purpose of avoiding offense to non-represented countries, the principal document embodying the present agreement is an informally worded "Memorandum of Agreement" which recognizes that an international wheat agreement requires a conference of all the nations having a substantial interest in wheat, and which provides for the calling of such a conference as soon as the time becomes suitable.

Since the conference may not be called and conclude its deliberations until some time after a general armistice, interim measures are regarded as necessary to prevent competitive disorganization of the international wheat trade in the period between the end of the war and the conclusion of a new agreement. These measures are provided for in the "Memorandum of Agreement" and include:

(a) provisions for relief wheat distribution and for the machinery connected therewith to be set up now.

(b) an undertaking to regulate production during the war so as to prevent the accumulation of excessive stocks.

(c) at the end of the war, or at such earlier agreed date to bring into operation the production control, reserve stocks and export quota provisions as set out in the "Draft Convention".

(d) to maintain during the interim period wheat prices properly related to the price paid by the United Kingdom for the last bulk purchase from the principal country of supply prior to the end of hostilities. Provision is made for alteration in the light of substantial changes in freight and exchange rates. If any interested country is dissatisfied with these prices, resort will be had to the price arrangements in the "Draft Convention" which provide for a price range to be negotiated, subject to the concurrence of the United Kingdom.

(e) The "Memorandum of Agreement" is to be superseded by the agreement arising from the larger conference. Failing such new agreement, the "Memorandum of Agreement" is to terminate in any event within two years.

The "Draft Convention" is a considerably revised version of the provisional draft circulated last August, which was intended as a five year wheat agreement. Its present purpose is two-fold. It is related to the "Memorandum of Agreement" through the "Minutes of the Final Session of the Washington Meeting" which places in operation the necessary portions of the "Draft Convention" in order to carry out the provisions of the "Memorandum of Agreement". Its other purpose is to place before the new wheat conference a draft agreement as a basis for negotiations within that conference.

Within the Draft Convention, the percentage export quotas remain within one per cent of final agreement with Australia asking 19, Argentina 25, Canada 40, and the United States 17 per cent of the total exports for the four countries, and the quota negotiations are still continuing. Approval is sought from the Canadian Government for the new maximum stock figure of 275 million bushels for Canada in relation to the revised stocks article.

As indicated in the attached letter from Mr. Carlill, the British Delegation has proposed that the three documents be initialled by the delegates for each country at the final meeting. The United States State Department would then send certified copies of the document to the diplomatic representatives of the other four countries and would invite each government to signify their willingness to adopt and give effect to the "Memorandum of Agreement" and its interpretation in the Final Minutes. When the State Department receives the assent of each government the interim arrangements regarding relief and production control during the war would be deemed to have come into effect.[19]

FINAL REVISIONS

When McIvor and Wilson discussed the new drafts with the cabinet wheat committee, Gardiner expressed considerable apprehension over the price clause in the memorandum of agreement. He feared that if the price of the last bulk purchase prior to the armistice were to prevail for a year afterward, the British would try to bargain too aggressively toward the end of the war. McIvor undertook to see if he could get the period of this bridge foreshortened when he and Wilson returned to Washington toward the end of March to sort out the final instructions from governments. On April 1, 1942, McIvor telephoned the results of these last negotiations to Wilgress who summarized them in a memorandum to MacKinnon:

Mr. George McIvor, Chief Commissioner of the Canadian Wheat Board, has telephoned from Washington giving a preliminary report on the International Wheat Discussions which have been taking place in that city.

He advises he has been successful in maintaining Canada's share of exports from the four principal countries at 40 per cent. Nothing further has been heard of the proposal of Mr. McCarthy, the Australian delegate, that the four exporting countries should sign a declaration as to their understanding of the prices which should be approved by the Wheat Council, after it is formed.

A great deal of the time during the past three days has been occupied in discussions regarding paragraph six of the proposed "Memorandum of Agreement". You will recall that this paragraph concerns the arrangements for maintaining the price of wheat until the Draft Convention comes into operation. This paragraph has now been redrafted to read as follows:

[19] *Ibid.*

"The five countries will, as from the cessation of hostilities or from such earlier date as they may agree, determine the prices of wheat in accordance with the arrangements described in the attached Draft Convention, except that the determination will be by unanimous agreement. Pending such determination, the five countries will, for a period not exceeding six months, maintain as the export price of wheat the last price negotiated by the United Kingdom for the bulk purchase of wheat from the principal country of supply; equivalent f.o.b. prices will be calculated for wheats of the other exporting countries and will be adjusted from time to time to meet substantial changes in freight and exchange rates."

Mr. McIvor strongly recommends that Canada should agree to the above revised proposal. You will note that the most significant change is that the price of the last bulk sale to the United Kingdom will be maintained for a period not exceeding **six months**.

Mr. McIvor points out that this safeguards our position, in that during the six months the wheat which will be imported into the United Kingdom will be the wheat negotiated under the last bulk purchase, which is certain to cover requirements for a fairly long period. The limitation to the six months' period also removes the political objection raised by Mr. Gardiner, in that as the price will only be in force for a period of six months there would not be any great inducement for the United Kingdom to depress the price for the last bulk purchase.

Mr. McIvor reports that the United States very much wanted the period to be a year instead of six months, but they finally agreed to the six months' period as a means of meeting Canada. The United States attach the greatest importance to having this provision in about prices during the interim period and our refusal to agree to the revised formula will be certain to create difficulties with the United States.

Finally, Mr. McIvor points out that in another part of the memorandum Canada is defined as the principal country of supply for wheat imported into the United Kingdom. This is clearly of value as bringing about an official recognition of our position in relation to the supply of wheat to the United Kingdom and obviates any arguments being put forward by the United States in favour of the supply of wheat to the United Kingdom under lend-lease.

Dr. C. F. Wilson will be returning to Ottawa at the end of the week, when he will be in a position to report fully. The revised draft of paragraph six is being referred to the other Governments and it is expected that the International Wheat Discussions will have to be resumed in about ten days to two weeks, when it is hoped to reach finality and to initial the various documents. In the meantime, Mr. McIvor thought that you would like to have this preliminary report of what has transpired in Washington in case you may have the opportunity of discussing the whole question with the Hon. Mr. Gardiner and the other members of the Wheat Committee of Council. Mr. McIvor most strongly urges our acceptance of the revised draft of paragraph six, in view of the considerations referred to above.[20]

In the meeting which took place at the end of March, the export quota figures were finally resolved. In a gesture of concession, the Americans agreed to reduce their percentage to 16, in order that Argentina might have 25 and Australia 19, while the Canadian percentage remained at 40. Neither the Argentine nor Australian figure was justified by average export performance, but the Americans were under no immediate pressure to find

[20]*Ibid.*

export markets, and they were determined that the international agreement they had been seeking since 1938 should not elude them now.

MEMORANDUM OF AGREEMENT

With these last outstanding issues approved by the cabinet wheat committee, the way was cleared for the conclusion of the agreement. The memorandum of agreement was prepared in final form, and a meeting set for April 22, 1942, for the initialling of the agreement. In the meantime, McIvor had returned to Winnipeg, and Wilson to Ottawa. McIvor was the logical person as head of the Canadian delegation to return to Washington for the concluding ceremony, but he telephoned Wilgress that he was too involved in Winnipeg to make another trip and they agreed that Wilson should be authorized to initial the agreement in his stead. The text of the memorandum of agreement read as follows:

1. Officials of Argentina, Australia, Canada and the United States, wheat exporting countries, and the United Kingdom, a wheat importing country, met in Washington on July 10, 1941 to resume the wheat discussions which were interrupted in London by the outbreak of war in September 1939 and to consider what steps might be taken toward a solution of the international wheat problem.

2. The discussions at Washington, which extended over a period of many months, have made it clear that a satisfactory solution of the problem requires an international wheat agreement and that such an agreement requires a conference of the nations willing to participate which have a substantial interest in international trade in wheat. It was also recognized that pending the holding of such a conference the situation should not be allowed to deteriorate. The Washington Wheat Meeting has recorded the results of its deliberations in the attached Draft Convention in order to facilitate further international consideration of the subject at such time as may be possible and to provide a basis for such interim measures as may be found necessary.

3. The Washington Wheat Meeting has recognized that it is impracticable to convene at the present time the international wheat conference referred to above. Accordingly, the five countries present at that Meeting have agreed that the United States, so soon as after consultation with other countries it deems the time propitious, should convene a wheat conference of the nations having a substantial interest in international trade in wheat which are willing to participate, and that the Draft Convention above mentioned should be submitted to that conference for consideration.

4. In the meantime there should be no delay in the provision of wheat for relief in war-stricken and other necessitous areas so soon as in the view of the five countries circumstances permit. Likewise it is imperative that the absence of control measures over the accumulation of stocks in the four countries now producing large quantities of wheat for markets no longer available should not create insoluble problems for a future conference. Accordingly, the five countries have agreed to regard as in effect among themselves, pending the conclusions of the conference referred to above, those arrangements described in the attached Draft Convention which are necessary to the administration and distribution of the relief pool of wheat and to the control of production of wheat other than those involving the control of exports.

5. If the conference contemplated above shall have met and concluded an agreement prior to the cessation of hostilities, no further action will be needed by the countries represented at the Washington Meeting. However, if this is not the case, it will be necessary, in order to prevent disorganization and

confusion in international trade in wheat, to institute temporary controls pending the conclusions of the conference. Accordingly the five countries agree that in the period following the cessation of hostilities and pending the conclusion of a wheat agreement at the conference referred to the arrangements described in the attached Draft Convention which relate to the control of production, stocks and exports of wheat and to the administration thereof will be brought into effect among themselves. Those arrangements will come into effect on such date as may be unanimously agreed. Announcement of that date will be made within six months after the cessation of hostilities.

6. Pending the conclusions of the conference contemplated above, the five countries, on the cessation of hostilities or such earlier date as they may agree, will regard as in effect among themselves the arrangements described in the attached Draft Convention for the control of the prices of wheat. The determination of prices required to be made in accordance with those arrangements will be made by unanimous consent. If no determination of prices has been made on the cessation of hostilities, the five countries will, pending such determination but for a period not exceeding six months, maintain as the export price of wheat the last price negotiated by the United Kingdom for a bulk purchase of wheat from the principal country of supply; equivalent f.o.b. prices will be calculated for wheats of the other exporting countries and will be adjusted from time to time to meet substantial changes in freight and exchange rates.

7. In taking any decisions under this Memorandum and the arrangements of the Draft Convention which it brings into operation each of the five countries will have one vote and a two-thirds majority will be required for decision except as otherwise provided herein.

8. The provisions of this Memorandum will be superseded by any agreement reached at the proposed wheat conference or by any arrangements which the five countries and other interested countries may make to deal with the period pending such a conference. In any event they are to terminate two years from the cessation of hostilities.[21]

Before the Canadian government notified the United States Secretary of State of its formal acceptance of the agreement, the cabinet wheat committee desired that the agreement be submitted to council for approval, and MacKinnon asked Wilson to prepare an explanatory submission for the purpose. His memorandum of April 30 spelled out in detail the implications of the provisions in the memorandum of agreement and highlighted the limitations on our Canadian commitments.

Because of MacKinnon's temporary illness, Crerar used Wilson's memorandum to secure cabinet approval of the agreement on May 5, 1942. By June 27, 1942, the United States Secretary of State notified the other governments that all had approved the memorandum of agreement which was now deemed to have come into effect.

---

[21] *Canada: Treaty Series 1942, No. 11*, pp. 3-5. The text of the Draft Convention is reproduced in the same source, pp. 5-17, also, Minutes of the Final Session of the Washington Wheat Meeting are to be found on pp. 16-17.

32

DOMESTIC ISSUES IN THE MIDST OF WAR

Although the international negotiations recorded in the preceding chapter preoccupied the members of the cabinet wheat committee on numerous occasions, domestic issues dominated their attention throughout that period. The primary features of the government's wheat policy at the outbreak of war had been the wheat board's guaranteed initial payment of 70 cents, plus acreage payments in circumstances as defined in the prairie farm assistance act. This policy had been supplemented by the delivery quota system introduced in 1940 which, in turn, had been converted into a maximum delivery quota system with compensatory wheat acreage reduction payments in 1941. In addition, the wheat board had collected since August, 1940, a processing levy of 15 cents on wheat used for domestic human consumption, with the proceeds accruing to the board for producers' account. On the whole, these wartime measures had operated very effectively as instruments of government policy but, as far as prairie farm income was concerned, the two supplemental acreage payments through prairie farm assistance and wheat acreage reduction had failed to compensate for the maximum delivery quota of 222 million bushels to which the 70-cent initial payment applied. The combined program fell considerably short of helping western wheat producers to keep in step with the rest of the economy, or even of helping to maintain their income at the level of the previous year.

WAGE AND PRICE CONTROL POLICY

Although the wartime prices and trade board had been appointed in September, 1939, to monitor price increases, the situation had begun to get out of hand by midsummer of 1941 as the wholesale price index moved up by 27 percent since 1939, while the cost of living index rose by 13 percent. Such indications of inflation were sufficiently alarming to induce the cabinet to consider extraordinary measures. The most effective device appeared to be an absolute freeze on salaries, wages and prices. Profits were already under control through the excess profits tax. But the imposition of a price freeze was bound to create inequities in the degree of hardship experienced by different industries and also, in some cases, to discourage the production of adequate supplies. Among all others the wheat industry stood out as the one most depressed in 1941. Before reaching a decision on general price controls, Mackenzie King consulted Gardiner about their impact on agricultural production and Gardiner replied to King in his memorandum of October 13, 1941:

It has been suggested that Price Control be applied to all products including food, and that this control be administered by the Wartime Prices and Trade Board. The position of the farmer is somewhat different from that of other producers, unless it be fishermen, in that he is still an individualist. Even the raw materials of the forest and the mines are largely under the control of corporations limited in numbers. Each farmer is his own manager and therefore experiences some difficulty in making his wishes known.

I think, therefore, that the wartime Argicultural Supplies Board should continue to arrange to support minima prices for farm products which would as far as possible cover costs of production on economically operated farms. This could be accomplished by continuing . . . to enter into agreements with Britain for the sale of food products needed in the war, such as pork products, and cheese, and eggs, and arranging to take surpluses off the market where we could not agree with Britain to ship a definite quantity as is now arranged in connection with butter. The Wartime Prices and Trade Board would then be in a position to set a maximum price for these products which must not be exceeded on the Canadian market, although it is possible the price would always be above the minimum and below the maximum because of competition.

It would appear to me to be dangerous to try at present to control beef and cattle prices. Our whole surplus of cattle must go to the United States. We cannot, therefore, close the American boundary to cattle as we have to hogs, nor can we bargain to send the surplus to Britain. If the price of beef is set too low it will result in cattle being purchased at a comparatively low level on the Canadian market and sold to the United States on a much higher market. I think it would be wise to set the maximum price at which beef can be sold so high as not to interfere or better leave beef and cattle alone for the time being.

Grain

If coarse grains are to be dealt with then I think either the highest price at which they have sold during the present grain year or certain definite prices of not less than 50 cents for oats, 65 cents for barley, 65 cents for rye, and (—) cents for corn should be established. Neither price level would bring prices up to the average level from 1926-29, but if the plan suggested for wheat is followed any difference would be partially taken care of in those areas from which surplus coarse grains come.

Wheat

I would suggest that if the intention is to distribute income without encouraging wheat production the distribution of assistance should be made on an acreage basis without reference to wheat. We have already the machinery and regulations which would make such a distribution possible. The Prairie Farm Assistance Act provides for making payments on one half of the cultivated acreage with a limitation of 200 acres. This would mean that not more than $200 could be paid to any one person if $1.00 an acre were the amount suggested, and the total amount paid out would be approximately $25,000,000.

The Northwest Grain Dealers Association have already passed a resolution asking that this be done, and it has received the support of a number of rural municipal councils.

It is claimed by the Saskatchewan Pools that in our policy of last spring we estimated the western farmers' income from the advance on wheat at $111,500,000 and that it will not exceed $90,000,000 because of the poor crop. The above proposal would place the amount back where we estimated it.

I think it would be a mistake so far as wheat is concerned to try to deal with it on a calendar year basis. It would be much better to associate the assistance with the crop year which opens August 1st.

Freight on Feed

The Eastern Canadian position, where livestock is being fed, could be equalized with the western where surplus grain is produced by paying a greater part or all of the freight rates on feed from Fort William east. (The same plan should be applied to British Columbia). I would suggest the total freight should be paid. This would cost the government approximately $6,000,000.[1]

Although Gardiner had lost his argument with Ilsley over the creation of a 1941 wartime wheat reserve which would have ensured producers of a higher return on their participation certificates, he now noted that income from the initial payment was running $21,500,000 below earlier expectations, and that this shortfall could be made up if an additional sum were to be paid out on an acreage basis. He also recommended some compensation for eastern feeders, in the form of freight assistance on feed grains moving to eastern Canada and to British Columbia to an amount of $6,000,000. Both of Gardiner's proposals were accepted by cabinet before the general price freeze was announced. The decision was to pay an additional acreage bonus in the amount of $20,000,000 to compensate for the shortfall in income which Gardiner had identified, and also to pay feed freight assistance. This was the inception of the latter program which has been continued over the years. In his announcement of Saturday, October 18, 1941, of the general wage and price control program based upon the highest prices received in the September 15 - October 11 base period, Mackenzie King referred to agricultural products, including wheat, in the following terms:

In undertaking to control the cost of living, particular attention has been given by the government to the effect of its policy on the position of agriculture. The policy touches the farmer in two ways.

The principle of the price ceiling will be applied to agricultural prices, while, at the same time, total agricultural income will be supported where necessary, by government action. In other words, while wages and the prices of farm products will be stabilized, the income of both labor and agriculture will be safeguarded.

Agricultural prices, with a few conspicuous exceptions, especially wheat, are higher today than they have been at any time during the past 10 years. In cases where agricultural prices have not kept pace with increases in costs of production, measures are being taken to bring about a more satisfactory relationship without significantly affecting the general level of retail prices to the consumer.

The major problem of maintaining incomes in western Canada, where grain growing is the largest source of income, is closely related to the problem in eastern Canada where feed supplies are not sufficient to enable farmers to produce the bacon and dairy products required for Britain and ourselves. Both these situations need adjustment.

[1] *King Papers.*

It is therefore the intention of the government to make supplementary payments to farmers in the spring wheat area, on the basis of their cultivated acreage as defined under the Prairie Farm Assistance act. For farmers in eastern Canada, the government will provide the transportation costs on feed grain and other feed from Fort William or Port Arthur to points in eastern Canada.

In determining the price of farm products, it is obvious that the maximum price cannot be based upon the individual selling prices of individual farmers, which is the method applied to factories and stores. Instead, the wartime prices and trade board will determine maximum prices for certain farm products on the basis of maximum market prices during the four-week period ending on Oct. 11 last.

Other special adaptations may be found necessary. Thus, in the case of farm products whose prices rise and fall seasonally, the setting of maximum prices may also require the setting of minimum prices, or action to remove temporary surpluses from the market.

In most cases, however, the demand for food products, especially the export demand, is so great as to assure that prices will not fall much, if at all, below the maximum. For example, in the cases of bacon and cheese, reasonably stable prices will be assured under large scale agreements with the United Kingdom.

The wartime prices and trade board will, before Nov. 17, take the necessary action, or advise the government as to the steps which should be taken, to achieve these objectives without violating the basic principles of the general price ceiling.[2]

By coupling the announcement of the first freight assistance on feed grains moving to eastern Canada with that of the additional acreage bonus on western wheat, King was mindful of the continuing need for justifying in the east any additional assistance to the west. The freight assistance amounted to some 12 cents a bushel to feeders in central Ontario with correspondingly higher rates farther east. In the west, however, the press quickly calculated that the additional acreage bonus of $2,000,000, if calculated on a bushel basis, had the effect of raising the initial payment to a dollar. By estimating deliveries from the 1941 crop at 200,000,000 bushels, wheat acreage reduction payments as originally announced at $30,000,000, prairie farm assistance payments at $10,000,000 and the new acreage bonus, calculated on half a producer's cultivated acreage up to 200 acres at $20,000,000, the total of acreage payments was brought to $60,000,000 or 30 cents a bushel on deliveries of 200,000,000. The 30 cents added to the initial payment of 70 cents justified the reference to dollar wheat. Notwithstanding, the real purpose of the $20,000,000 supplementary payment had been to bring western wheat income up to its initially announced target of $325,000,000.

The prime minister's announcement was followed by issuance of the maximum prices regulations approved by P. C. 8527 of November 1, 1941. These regulations were universal in their application, although they empowered the wartime prices and trade board in its discretion to exempt any commodity from the provisions of the regulations. The initial order in council was amended by P. C. 8818 of November 11, which postponed the effective date of the regulations from November 17 to December 1, 1941. To

2 *Winnipeg Free Press,* October 20, 1941.

facilitate determination of ceilings for grains, the wartime prices and trade board enlisted the help of the Canadian wheat board in acting as administrator on its behalf in respect of grain prices. The wheat board promptly began its identification of the maximum prices at which grain had been traded in the base period, and by November 8, 1941, it had summarized its investigation in a long explanatory memorandum to the prices board in which the ceiling prices had been determined for the various grains as follows:

Cents per bushel		basis
wheat	82¾	No, 1 Northern, in store Ft. William
oats	51½	No. 2 CW in store Ft. William
barley	64¾	No. 2 CW 2 Row in store Ft. William
flax	164	No. 1 CW in store Ft. William
rye	66⅝	No. 1 CW in store Ft. William
corn	104	delivered Montreal
wheat	126	No. 1 CE delivered Montreal

In the case of wheat, 82¾ cents was the highest price at which wheat futures were traded in the base period. The transaction took place in the May future on October 4. According to correspondence between Mr. W. C. Folliott, commissioner of the wheat board and Professor K. W. Taylor, secretary of the prices board, it was the intention to make all the ceiling prices on grain effective as from December 1, 1941. This would have conformed with the provisions of the maximum prices regulations. On December 2, however, Folliott wired to Taylor that, as administrator on behalf of the prices board, the wheat board had announced prices of $1.26 on Ontario wheat and 64¾ cents on malting barley. Then Folliott's telegram continued: "Considering question of announcing all maximum grain prices but we feel obliged to refer matter of wheat ceiling to wheat committee of cabinet for reasons mentioned to you in our meeting of November twenty first. We will do this at once and advise you."[3]

Obviously, the cabinet wheat committee, because of representations being made to them and out of their own concern for the situation, were in a quandary whether western wheat should be exempted from the regulations. As representations continued to come, the ceiling on western wheat never was formally announced. Yet the issue remained active and it came to a head two months later.

REPRESENTATION BY THE NORTH-WEST LINE ELEVATORS ASSOCIATION

Representations to Ottawa were made on behalf of producers by several trade sources. The James Richardson & Sons Limited *Weekly Review* recommended on November 18, 1941, "that the ceiling for wheat prices, which comes into effect on December 1 should be fixed not at the maximum during the period September 15 to October 11, but at some higher level" (It is interesting that this was written by Mr. Mitchell W. Sharp who edited the *Weekly Review* at that time). Also, on November 21, 1941, the north-west line elevators association made a direct representation to the cabinet wheat

[3] *Wartime Prices and Trade Board Grain file*, Public Archives of Canada.

committee and to the chairman of the wartime prices and trade board in the following terms:

Since 1930 low prices for wheat have been the cause of much distress amongst wheat producers in Canada. In announcing the Government's price control policy on October 18th to the people of Canada, the Prime Minister mentioned the exceptional and unsatisfactory position occupied by wheat. In view of the fact that wheat was selling at depressed prices in the base period chosen by the Government for fixing of price ceilings, we would urge strongly that special consideration be given to this commodity in fixing a price ceiling.

It is our understanding that 82¢ per bushel for One Northern, Fort William, would be about the price ceiling under the terms of the recent Order-in-Council. Our organization proposes for your most earnest consideration, that the price ceiling for wheat should be at least not less than $1.02 per bushel, basis One Northern, Fort William. This figure represents the average of the high monthly price recorded for One Northern wheat in store Fort William, for the period January 1, 1926 to December 16, 1940. Under the recent Order-in Council the ceiling for labor (consumer) wages is based on the highest rate in effect during either of two periods, namely, 1926-29 or 1926-40. Strong argument can be advanced that no ceiling should be set for producer commodities at a figure lower than that which would put the producer in this respect on a parity with the consumer. In the case of wheat the average of the daily closing price for One Northern at Fort William during the 1926-29 crop years was $1.35¼, which is substantially higher than the average of the high monthly price of the 1926-40 period.

The following price table shows that while the ceiling prices of coarse grains will be relatively close to the average 1926-40 prices, the ceiling price for wheat is unduly low:

	Average high monthly price - Jan. 1/26 to December, 1940	Indicated Ceiling Price under provisions of Order-in-Council
Wheat	$1.02¾	$ .82¾
Oats	.46	.50¼
Barley	.54¼	.62¾
Flax	1.66⅛	1.64
Rye	.70⅜	.66⅝

The need for maintaining substantial reserves of wheat as an essential requirement of war and the subsequent peace negotiations is recognized by the Governments of Canada and the United Kingdom. It is only three years since having carried a burdensome surplus of wheat for some years, Canada's wheat bins were scraped bare following the poor crops of 1936 and 1937. Recurrence of such a situation would be most serious. It is our belief that nothing could be more destructive to the morale of the western wheat farmer than to use a depressed price period as the basis for the ceiling price. Fixing a ceiling upon such a basis would destroy his last hope for putting his farming operations on a profitable basis. We urge that it is not in the public interest to fix a ceiling price for wheat based on such depressed values as have recently existed.

We recognize the necessity of, and we support the price controls being established by the Government. The sudden and drastic drop in wheat prices in May 1940, when markets in neutral European countries were suddenly cut off, proves very definitely that wheat is a war casualty. The price control

Order-in-Council provides for exceptions being made where the facts justify the same. We believe that all the facts justify a price ceiling standard other than the maximum price existing between September 15, 1941, and October 11, 1941, being used for this commodity and also justify reconsideration being given annually to any ceiling that may be established.[4]

The memorandum pointed up the very considerable anomaly that, for purposes of the general freeze, wage ceilings were to be based upon the highest rates in effect during either of two periods, 1926-29 or 1926-40. This wage provision inspired the concept that ceiling prices for agricultural products should be based on either one of those "parities." The north-west line elevators association memorandum set out the results for the 1926-40 period. Much higher results for grain prices could have been obtained by using the 1926-29 period, as in the case of $1.417 per bushel for wheat, which the pools adopted as "parity."

The memorandum of the north-west line elevators association arrived in Ottawa just as the government announced a change in the composition of the wartime prices and trade board. Mr. Donald Gordon, deputy governor of the Bank of Canada, who had actively assisted in the formulation of the general freeze, was appointed chairman of the board on November 20, 1941, in the place of Mr. Hector B. McKinnon who became chairman of the commodity prices stabilization corporation, a subsidiary of the board, which administered subventions to industries in need of help in maintaining output. Some new members were also added to the prices board, including Mr. L. D. Wilgress, deputy minister of trade and commerce, Dr. Bryce M. Stewart, deputy minister of labour, Dr. J. G. Bouchard, assistant deputy minister of agriculture and Mr. Walter L. Gordon, who at that time was serving as special assistant to the deputy minister of finance. Upon his appointment, Mr. Donald Gordon issued a firm warning that the price controls would be strictly enforced. Gordon's personality, enthusiasm and utter integrity contributed to the outstanding success of those wartime measures. Another unrelated appointment might be noted in passing. Mr. D. G. McKenzie, vice-president of United Grain Growers Limited succeeded Mr. E. B. Ramsay as chief commissioner of the board of grain commissioners, following Ramsay's resignation, due to ill health, on October 22, 1941. Following his appointment, Mr. McKenzie resigned as chairman of the wheat board advisory committee.

SASKATCHEWAN WHEAT POOL COMPAIGN

Meanwhile, the directors of Saskatchewan Co-operative Wheat Producers Limited became convinced that a major move must be made to persuade the government that western wheat prices should not be locked into the general price freeze. Accordingly, Mr. J. H. Wesson and his directors prepared a resolution which was submitted for approval to the annual meeting of Saskatchewan Co-operative Wheat Producers Limited that November. The resolution as finally drafted, read:

> Whereas the government has now instituted a program of price control to include agricultural products, the effect of which may be to limit prices to

[4]*Minutes of the Advisory Committee, Canadian Wheat Board,* December 8-9, 1941, Canadian Wheat Board files. The indicated ceilings for grains other than wheat as shown in this quotation are somewhat at variance with those actually determined by the wheat board.

those prevailing during the four-week period 15th   September to 11th October, 1941; and

Whereas the government has recognized that the wheat prices prevailing during this period are inadequate to maintain reasonable living conditions in western farm homes, and has undertaken to make supplementary payments to farmers in the spring wheat area on an acreage basis as defined by the Prairie Farm Assistance Act; and

Whereas we believe that a different method of dealing with farm income is required as between those growers who have produced a satisfactory crop and those who have suffered crop failure; and

Whereas we believe that the government's agricultural policy has resulted in serious discrimination against those engaged in farming when compared with the government's policy for labour and industry;

We would therefore urge that it is in the national interest that consideration be given to the following changes in the existing agricultural policy in order that this discrimination may be removed.

1. That the government recognize and accept the principle of parity prices for all agricultural products.

2. That no price ceiling should be established on agricultural commodities below parity levels which may be established by the Dominion Bureau of Statistics.

3. That equitable delivery quotas on wheat should be established and continued as long as required.

4. That the initial payment on all wheat delivered to the Wheat Board should be not less than $1.00 per bushel, basis 1 Northern in store Fort William, and that the final settlement should be made on the basis of parity prices above referred to.

5. That the carryover of wheat as at 31st July, 1941, should be regarded as a national emergency war reserve, and that all sales made by the Wheat Board after 31st July, 1941, should be credited to the current season's deliveries.

6. That suitable amendments should be introduced to the Prairie Farm Assistance Act so that an adequate and practical crop insurance scheme may be established irrespective of market prices prevailing or the number of townships suffering crop failure.

7. That since the future of our agricultural industry depends largely on our ability:

(a) to conserve the fertility of our soil;

(b) to establish production and marketing methods which while maintaining continuity of supplies will also prevent avoiding surpluses, and since these objectives may involve an increasing degree of control and regulations, including international agreement, such changes should be made in our agricultural policy as may be necessary to achieve these objectives.[5]

The annual meeting also decided that the resolution should be the subject of a mass petition to be signed by farmers throughout Saskatchewan and presented to the government in Ottawa by a delegation made up of producers and western businessmen. Although the campaign was initiated by the Saskatchewan pool its impact spilled over into Alberta and Manitoba. In the campaign for signatures, the organizing skill of Mr. George W. Robertson, secretary of the Saskatchewan pool, was clearly discernible. Robertson had previously initiated petitions to Ottawa which usually took the form of resolutions adopted and forwarded by pool district

[5]Saskatchewan Co-operative Wheat Producers Limited, *Eighteenth Annual Report*, Regina, 1942, pp. 25-26.

organizations and by rural municipalities. But, as in 1939, this petition called for individual signatures which had to be obtained by province-wide canvas under winter conditions. Each person who signed the petition made a contribution of 25 cents to help cover the cost of sending a delegation to Ottawa. In all, 185,000 signatures were obtained, and a delegation of 400 representatives of producers and businessmen was selected to make the trip.

OTHER RECOMMENDATIONS ON POLICY

The issues at stake in the determination of grain policy for the 1942-43 crop year were so important that practically every responsible body sought to offer advice. One issue had been precipitated by the wages and price ceiling policy which begged the question whether wheat prices should be frozen at a depressed level. The official recognition of a parity for wage levels on the 1926-29 or 1926-40 base precipitated a demand for similar parities for the prices of agricultural products. The wheat issue was complicated by the fact that the necessity for income maintenance dictated the need for a higher wheat price at a time when the exigencies of wartime food requirements had shifted the emphasis from wheat to coarse grain production, and the problem was how to prevent an increased price from acting as an encouragement to wheat production. There was also a conflicting interest in the method of paying government subsidies, whether on a bushel or acreage basis. While it was realized that the wheat acreage reduction payments must be of a temporary nature, the prairie farm assistance payments could be justified pending a better form of direct crop insurance. Whatever form assistance to western agriculture might take, it had to be justified in the east.

In response to these issues, the recommendations of the north-west line elevators association and of the Saskatchewan wheat pool have already been noted. Other bodies which concerned themselves with policy recommendations included United grain growers, the Canadian federation of agriculture, an Ottawa interdepartmental committee, the Canadian wheat board and its advisory committee.

Following the Saskatchewan pool resolution of November, 1941, the next recommendations on policy for the 1942-43 crop year came in a statement issued by the board of directors of United Grain Growers Limited on January 8, 1942. After urging the need for an official statement on policy well in advance of seeding time, the board recommended a guarantee of prevailing prices for livestock and livestock products for a period of two years and also a guarantee of feed grain supplies which could be supplemented out of wheat reserves if necessary. As for grain production, the statement pointed to the need for guaranteeing a minimum price for barley at 60 cents and a minimum price for flaxseed at $2.25 or $2.50. If a guaranteed market for livestock products was offered, the board felt that the production of oats would be sufficiently encouraged without a price guarantee. As for wheat, the board recommended maintenance of acreage at the reduced 1941 level, with delivery quotas restricted to what could be sold in 1942-43 for export, domestic milling and feed.

Regarding price, the United grain growers statement drew attention to the fact that Canada had reached the point where, instead of selling war supplies to Britain, it had begun to furnish these at its own cost in the common war effort, and that the price paid to farmers for wheat was no longer of concern to other governments, but rather a matter for settlement between the Canadian government and the farmers concerned. Although the price ceiling policy assured a definite price to domestic millers, this need not be the price paid to farmers. Accordingly, United Grain Growers Limited recommended a price of not less than $1.00 per bushel on a quantity based on actual disappearance, on the assumption that the special forms of acreage bonus paid in 1941-42 would be discontinued in 1942-43, thereby making imperative an increase in price.

After drawing attention to the growing shortages of farm labor and of machinery supplies, the statement concluded with a reference to the government's post-war reconstruction committee already appointed, and suggested that the committee give immediate attention to a recommendation that the government prepare, with the assistance of the department of external affairs, an international wheat convention "designed to make wheat a free trade commodity throughout the world." Such a step, the board of directors believed, would do more than any other to solve the agricultural problems of Canada. The seven-page statement was later endorsed by the Canadian federation of agriculture and presented as an appendix to the latter's submission to the prime minister on February 2, 1942.

Early in the new year, the cabinet wheat committee referred the question of 1942-43 wheat policy to an interdepartmental committee in Ottawa, as it had earlier done to the Canadian wheat board and its advisory committee. Among these bodies the Canadian wheat board was the first to report on January 17, 1942. The board identified three objectives, namely the holding of wheat acreage at very little more than the 1941 level, increasing farm income from wheat without unduly expanding wheat acreage, and encouraging feed grain and livestock production in the west. The board recommended specifically:

1. That limitation of marketings and optional limitation of acreage be continued for 1942-43.

2. That the basic acreage for delivery purposes in 1942-43 be increased by 10 percent, or from about 20,000,000 acres to 22,000,000 acres.

3. That marketing in the prairie provinces and British Columbia, including wheat for gristing, be restricted to the equivalent of domestic and export demand for wheat in 1942-43, and not to be in excess of 290 million bushels.

4. That direct acreage reduction payments be abandoned in 1942-43 in favour of a conditional increase in price.

5. That the fixed price of wheat remain at 70 cents per bushel basis in store Ft. William or Vancouver, but that an additional payment of 20 cents per bushel on marketable wheat be made to producers who limit their 1942 wheat acreage to the proposed basic acreage for 1942, namely, the 1941 basic acreage plus 10 percent.

6. That the payment of farm storage be discontinued on July 31, 1942.

7. That the government's policy in respect to wheat be made part of a broad agricultural program for western Canada, designed to meet wartime conditions.[6]

[6]*Recommendations of the Canadian Wheat Board re 1942-43 Wheat Policy,* January 17, 1942. Canadian Wheat board files.

Of these recommendations, the most unusual one was the idea that a 20-cent increase in the initial payment should be made conditional upon compliance with wheat acreage reduction. It was the board's solution to the problem of how to increase the basic price to the producer without encouraging an expansion in wheat acreage. The control device, however, had a precedent in the United States wheat program.

Now it was the wheat board advisory committee's turn to submit a report. When the committee met on December 8-9, 1941, George McIvor conveyed to it the cabinet wheat committee's request that the advisory committee should examine the situation and make recommendations on wheat policy for the 1942-43 crop year. At that time McIvor indicated that the board would be submitting its recommendations separately, rather than jointly with the advisory committee as had been done a year earlier. Nevertheless, McIvor indicated that Clive Davidson would be available to assist the committee in its separate deliberations. The fact that Davidson participated in, and prepared position papers for both the board and its advisory committee, and also was in liaison with the interdepartmental committee in Ottawa, lent a common denominator to the deliberations of all three bodies, as did the participation of Messrs. Hutchinson, Wesson and Parker for the three pools and Mr. R. C. Brown for United grain growers in those of the wheat board advisory committee and of the Canadian federation of agriculture. Davidson had prepared a working paper for the wheat board advisory committee, during the discussion of which Mr. J. H. Wesson proposed that the committee should recommend the four-year period 1926-29 as "parity" upon which the ceiling prices for grain should be based, namely, wheat $1.41, oats 60 cents, barley 73 cents, rye $1.00 and flax $2.07. However Wesson's proposal lacked general support. Although the dropping of wheat acreage reduction payments was considered in exchange for an increase in the initial payment, Mr. Lew Hutchinson, from previous experience, was wary lest the treasury-saving proposal be accepted, and the increase in the initial payment be refused. However, the committee's views ran in favor of a higher initial payment without the acreage bonus; it arrived at a series of tentative conclusions which it reserved for further considera-tion at its next meeting, held on January 12-14, 1942, when its recommendations were finalized. At this meeting, the members of the advisory committee were divided only on the issue of the level of the initial payment to be recommended. The five producer members supported $1.00 and the four trade members 90 cents. Otherwise, their recommendations were unanimous, and ran as follows:

1. That the Dominion Government continue a price guarantee for 1942-43 but that this guarantee be limited to the volume of wheat which can be disposed of within the 1942-43 crop year. These quantities are estimated as follows:

For Domestic Consumption	50 Million bushels
For Export Sales	240 Million bushels
Total	290

2. That the initial price to be paid producers on the deliverable quantity of 290 million bushels be raised from 70¢ per bushel to $1.00 per bushel, basis in store Fort William/Port Arthur or Vancouver.

3. That all bonuses and allowances given under the Wheat Acreage Reduction Plan and supplementary Order-in Council be discontinued.

4. That the Prairie Farm Assistance Act be continued but that it be amended to provide a more comprehensive scheme of crop insurance without limitation either as to the prevailing price required for an emergency year or the number of townships required in a crop failure area.

5. That the present powers of The Canadian Wheat Board be continued, enabling the Board to control all disposition of wheat by producers or other, having in mind that any excess production in 1942 must, of necessity, be retained on farms for an indefinite period.

6. That there be no obligation whatsoever on the Government to accept a greater quantity of wheat than may be necessary to comply with the conditions set out in recommendation No. 1, and that any farmer producing in excess of his quota must retain such excess wheat on his farm for his own use.

7. That the price at which wheat is sold for domestic consumption in Canada should be more closely and equitably related to the prices of other goods and services.[7]

The interdepartmental committee on wheat policy reported next on February 11, 1942. The composition of this committee is obscure, but it evidently included officials from the departments of agriculture, finance, trade and commerce and the wartime prices and trade board, as well as a representative from the Canadian wheat board. In its premises the committee recognized the need for an increase in farm income for those producers who were particularly dependent upon wheat, but that an increase in the guaranteed price and also in the deliverable quantities ran the risk of encouraging an expansion in wheat acreage, whereas needed increases in the production of coarse grains and flaxseed should take up the high proportion of land which had been summerfallowed in 1941. The committee endorsed the policy objectives set out in the Canadian wheat board recommendations, as it in turn recommended an immediate and comprehensive educational campaign setting out the national requirements for farm products in the coming crop year. It drew attention to the possibilities for the sale of feed grain in the United States, after Canadian requirements had been met.

The committee was so divided over the need for acreage payments and the alternative forms in which they might have to be made that its conclusions in that regard were of little value. In their disagreement, the officials were undoubtedly protecting their respective departmental positions.

However, the committee recommended a fixed price of $2.50 for flaxseed, if the wartime prices and trade board verified the need for increased production. The committee also asked for an easement in the ceiling price on malting grades of barley. In recognition of the need for increased income for those producers dependent upon wheat, the committee was divided among those recommending an initial payment of 90 cents and authorized marketings of 290,000,000 bushels, and those who held that the authorized marketings should be restricted to 275,000,000 bushels if there were to be a 90 cent payment. Other recommendations included the termination of farm

[7] *Trade and Commerce file 1-17-187.*

storage payments in view of the price increase, and a clarification of the ceiling price issue on wheat. The committee concluded by recommending continuance of prairie farm assistance payments until a contributory system of crop insurance could be established.[8]

Finally, the Canadian federation of agriculture requested in advance the opportunity to interview the prime minister and members of his cabinet on the morning of February 2, 1942, when the farmers' delegation from Saskatchewan had arrived in Ottawa. King agreed to a meeting with the federation delegation that morning, which several of his colleagues attended. Mr. Hannam presented a submission in which the federation claimed an affiliated membership of more than 350,000 farmers which entitled it to speak for a substantial proportion of the farm population of Canada. The submission reviewed the war effort in terms of agriculture and asked that the industry be assigned wartime priorities in keeping with the treatment of other industries, and that what was done now should be consistent with the development of a long-term agricultural policy. It made a special plea for support of its earlier recommendation on adoption of the principle of parity prices for agricultural products, and asked that the dominion bureau of statistics determine price levels for agricultural products which would correspond to the purchasing power of those products in some earlier period. On an earlier occasion a 1926 base had been suggested. Then the submission drew attention to the fact that all the western Canadian member bodies of the federation were already on record to the effect that the initial payment for wheat should be not less than $1.00 as it continued with the following specific recommendations:

1. That in order to assure the necessary volume of production of live stock and live stock products, required as a result of war conditions, the Government should announce that presently prevailing prices for live stock and live stock products will be guaranteed to farmers for a definite period, preferably two years.

2. That there should be guaranteed to farmers purchasing feed grains an adequate supply at prices consistent with the level of live stock prices, to implement which, if necessary, Government wheat stocks could be made available, while the present freight assistance policy should be continued.

3. That a basic price for feed barley at Lakehead or Seaboard terminals of sixty cents per bushel should be guaranteed; the production of oats we believe, will be sufficiently encouraged by a live stock programme such as recommended.

4. That the Government should vigorously promote a programme of soil conservation and continue to encourage the seeding of land to grass and clover.

5. That to secure the production of flax-seed to the extent required on account of the present scarcity of fats and oils, a guaranteed price of from $2.25 to $2.50 per bushel should be assured to the producers.

6. That the present carryover of wheat be regarded as a necessary war-time reserve, the carrying of which should not reduce the returns to producers from current crops.[9]

---

[8]*Report of the Inter-Departmental Committee on Wheat Policy,* Ottawa, February 11, 1942, Canadian Wheat Board files.

[9]*Canadian Federation of Agriculture Submission to the Prime Minister of Canada and Members of the Government,* Ottawa, February 2nd, 1942, Canadian Wheat Board files.

FARMERS' DELEGATION

The farmers' delegation which had been thoroughly organized by the Saskatchewan pool directors and officials got under way on January 30, 1942, when two special trains left Regina and Saskatoon and arrived in Ottawa, Sunday, February 1, 1942. The descent upon Ottawa was reminiscent of the siege of 1910, and of the farmers' delegation in 1918. Because there was insufficient hotel accomodation, the 403 delegates slept on their trains which were placed on sidings at the union station. The government had planned to receive the delegation in the centre block but, with parliament in session, this was out of the question since the house of commons chamber was the only room large enough to accommodate it. Alternatively, the organizers booked the convention hall at the Chateau Laurier which the delegation used for the next several days.

After the delegation held an organizational meeting on the day of its arrival, formal proceedings got underway at noon, Monday, February 2, 1942, when the prime minister and the majority of his cabinet heard ten speakers (led by Mr. J. H. Wesson and the Honourable W. R. Motherwell) present the substance of their petition. After the speakers concluded and presented the petition containing the 185,000 signatures (a pile of pages which reached breast high from the floor) Mackenzie King acknowledged the representations by saying that they were "convincing in many respects" and that the government was prepared to give "renewed, helpful and, I believe, fruitful consideration to the representations of the prairie wheat growers". In return, Mr. Wesson expressed the appreciation of the delegation for the courteous reception they had received from the prime minister and the nine members of his cabinet, while he stressed that the recommendations had not been submitted on a "trading" basis but represented "the minimum requirements to meet the economic needs of the west."[10]

At four o'clock that afternoon, the cabinet wheat committee returned from the house of commons to the meeting for a general discussion. Although the other members of the committee, MacKinnon, Crerar, and Ilsley took part in a minor way, Gardiner acted as the main spokesman for the committee. In this, he was in his element. Gardiner was thoroughly at home in addressing farm meetings; he had the capacity to hold his audience spellbound. At the outset of the meeting, the ministers assured the delegates that the difficulties of the wheat farmers were recognized and that the government was prepared to give full consideration to them. Then Gardiner proceeded to discuss the seven points of the resolution embodied in the farmers' petition in detail.[11]

On the first point which recommended parity prices for wheat, Gardiner asked the delegation for its definition of parity and referred at the same time to the 1926-1929 concept. Mr. Wesson replied that the delegation would accept whatever the dominion bureau of statistics would calculate as parity, but the government did not transmit this request to the bureau.[12]

---

[10]*Ibid.*, p. 29.

[11]For the text of the resolution, see pp. 725-726.

[12]Had it done so, the author would have had to ask it to select the base period, because the results of any such comparison of prices received and of prices paid by farmers varied

Gardiner accepted the 1926-29 average prices of farm products as parity, which was defensible in the light of the treatment accorded to wage ceilings. It also happened to be the most favorable period for agricultural prices in Canada in the interwar period, and it was useful as a bench mark for comparison with the prices Gardiner had been able to establish in wartime for cattle, hogs, cheese, butter and eggs, mostly through contracts negotiated with the British ministry of food. In several cases, the wartime agricultural prices compared favorably with their 1926-29 averages, but wheat was a notable exception. The 1926-29 average for wheat, basis No. 1 Northern, Fort William was $1.417, against which the wheat board's wartime initial payment stood in sharp contrast. Whereas the government had succeeded in providing "parity" prices in some other instances, Gardiner admitted that it would take time and the reopening of markets lost during the war to achieve parity for wheat. Nevertheless, Gardiner declared that to be the government's long-term objective.

On the second point that price ceilings should not be imposed on agricultural commodities below parity levels established by the dominion bureau of statistics, Gardiner confirmed that no price ceilings had been established for wheat, cattle and hogs. The price ceilings which were in force pertained to prices of bread, beef and pork.

The third point relating to equitable delivery quotas for as long as needed had been the policy of the government.

The fourth point recommended an initial payment of not less than $1.00 with final settlement to be made on the basis of parity. The delegation confirmed that these recommendations referred to the 1942 crop. Gardiner reiterated that parity for wheat remained the government's objective. On the treatment of the wheat carryover of 1941 as a wartime reserve, Gardiner claimed that this proposal had been initiated by the western Liberal members. Although the proposal remained under consideration, farmers had been selling wheat outright to the trade, so that the question of protecting participation rights was no longer a practical issue.

On the sixth point, that suitable amendments be introduced to the prairie farm assistance act to free it of its market-price restrictions and to convert it into a crop insurance program, Gardiner favored the first suggestion, but explained that acreage subventions had been made in the place of crop insurance because the latter fell within provincial jurisdiction under the terms of the British North America act. On the seventh and last point of soil conservation, Gardiner was able to point out that the measures adopted in the wheat acreage reduction program were consistent with this recommendation. He also referred to the continuation of operations under the provisions of the prairie farm rehabilitation act.

The Tuesday morning session was devoted to a discussion of the presentations made by Dean A. M. Shaw, chairman of the agricultural supplies board, and by the Honourable J. G. Taggart, minister of agriculture in Saskatchewan. At Gardiner's request Premier W. J. Patterson

accordingly. The United States department of agriculture, for example, had been the first to employ the parity concept. In doing so, it had selected 1909-1913 as the base period, when prices received offered the most favorable comparison of any period with prices paid out in production costs.

had agreed to Taggart's secondment to Ottawa where he became chairman of the bacon board and also, just recently, food administrator of the wartime prices and trade board. Taggart dealt with the ticklish question of wheat prices in relation to the maximum prices regulations. All he could do was to reiterate that price ceilings for western wheat had not yet been announced. Before the farm delegation had arrived in Ottawa, Gardiner had asked that Donald Gordon address the meeting. In his note of January 20, 1942, to Gardiner, Mr. Walter Turnbull said: ". . . I have also passed on to Mr. King your suggestion that Donald Gordon, and others who are working out the various economic controls, be asked to speak to these men while they are here."[13]

Notwithstanding this request, for some reason, Gordon had Taggart speak for him. This proved to be an unfortunate decision in the light of subsequent events.

At the concluding session on Tuesday afternoon, February 3, the members of the cabinet wheat committee and officials, including George McIvor were again in attendance. The flavor of that meeting was caught in a Canadian Press report:

> With members of the cabinet wheat committee present at an afternoon session, the delegation provided speaker after speaker who dwelt on economic hardships faced by the wheat producer.
>
> Mr. Gardiner gave the delegates assurance that the Prairie Farm Assistance act, praised by various speakers, would continue in operation this year and, as a policy in which he had much pride, would continue to be supported thereafter as far as he is concerned.
>
> "I consider it my responsibility to go before the wheat committee of the (cabinet) council and the council and submit your views as I understand them," Mr. Gardiner said.
>
> Every member of the government recognized the decline in the wheat farmers' income.
>
> "Don't go away with the understanding I have promised you that you'll get all you have made representations for," Mr. Gardiner said. "These representations have to be considered."
>
> The minister said he understood the delegation was asking for an advance in the initial payment for wheat to $1 a bushel for the 1942 crop, compared with the present 70 cents. Beyond that, he assumed they wanted further payments made during the crop year 1942-43 to bring the total payment to a parity price of $1.41.
>
> Some farmers had not signed the petition carrying 185,000 names and supported by the delegation, Mr. Gardiner said. Some who had not signed the petition had drawn the government's attention to cases like those of districts where the payments by way of bonuses for acreage reduction, prairie farm income assistance had totalled more, or nearly as much, as the amounts actually received from wheat in low production areas.
>
> Mr. Gardiner said the attitude of farmers in such areas was that while they did not oppose an increase in the initial wheat price they were anxious about the effects of such an increase on other payments now made by the government.
>
> "The government must consider that," said Mr. Gardiner.
>
> He said there seemed to be a slight difference of opinion in the delegation as to whether the parity price of $1.41 a bushel for wheat was being asked for

[13] *King Papers.*

payment next year, or whether only the $1 initial payment was being request-
ed.

The meeting shouted its approval when Mr. Gardiner said he believed the
delegates were prepared to leave it to someone to establish what the parity
price for wheat should be and to go home asking that the payment for the
season be on that basis.

"If once we get this parity price I hope we can hold it," Mr. Gardiner
said.

The minister said he felt the delegation had been modest in suggesting
wheat deliveries to be accepted by the Wheat board in 1942-43 should be
between 280,000,000 and 300,000,000 bushels compared with the 230,000,000
bushels accepted in 1941-42.

"You should have made it at least 300,000,000," Mr. Gardiner said.[14]

There was still one important question outstanding, however, and that
was the continuation of wheat acreage reduction payments, even if on a
reduced scale. The petition presented by the farmers' delegation had made
no reference to this, but other bodies, including the wheat board advisory
committee, had recommended discontinuance if the initial payment were to
be raised. On this issue there was a conflict of interest among wheat growers
in the more dependable producing areas who were more concerned about
the price of wheat than about acreage payments, and those in the
less-certain producing areas. But, Gardiner also had a departmental interest
in the continuation of the wheat acreage reduction payments which were
under his administration. Consequently, he made a point of securing from
the delegation a strong affirmation that they favored continuation of the
latter. Gardiner continued by saying: "You have presented your case in a
reasonable way, and I am sure you have left a good impression on everyone."[15]

But in the same way as he had cautioned the delegation, Gardiner also
informed the house that the government had not committed itself to meet all
demands, citing:

> I am pleased that at your first meeting yesterday you had the opportunity of
> meeting nearly all the members of the government and that in the afternoon
> you met all the members of the wheat committee of council, and, this
> afternoon, three of those members. For I consider it my responsibility to go
> before the wheat committee of council and also to go before the full council
> and submit your views presented on this occasion as I have understood them.
> And I may say I intend to do that. But let me repeat what I said yesterday. Do
> not go away from the meeting understanding because I have promised to
> submit your views you are going to get all that you have asked for. Your
> representations will be made to the whole government and will be considered
> by the whole government. Legislation will be necessary to effect whatever we
> decide to do. Any legislative bill introduced into council as a result of
> discussions in the wheat committee relating to the price of wheat must of
> necessity be introduced by the Minister of Trade and Commerce, but it will be
> considered and passed on by the members of the government, and it will be
> the decision of the whole government which will finally rule in the mat-
> ter.[16]

---

[14]*Winnipeg Free Press*, February 4, 1942.

[15]Saskatchewan Co-operative Wheat Producers Limited, *Eighteenth Annual Report*, Regina,
1942, p. 29.

[16]*House of Commons Debates*, March 10, 1942, p. 1202.

On Monday night, February 2, all 21 Saskatchewan members of parliament, including Mackenzie King, entertained the delegation at a dinner in the parliamentary restaurant. Next evening the delegation returned the hospitality at a dinner for the members at the Chateau Laurier. The delegation had achieved its objective of presenting the wheat growers' case in an objective and impressive manner. The whole exercise commanded great attention and support among the rank and file of farmers in the west. But the man who unquestionably dominated the scene was the Honourable J. G. Gardiner.

CEILING PRICE ISSUE

Ilsley, as minister of finance, was a member of the cabinet wheat committee; he was also the minister responsible for the wartime prices and trade board. As soon as the wheat committee took under consideration the numerous recommendations for an increase in the initial payment, Ilsley brought his wartime prices and trade board officials, notably Donald Gordon, into the discussions. At meetings of the wheat committee held over the weekend of February 21-22, 1942, the most difficult problem the committee faced was reconciliation of an increased initial payment with the general price freeze. Gordon took the position that there must be no breach of the maximum prices regulations; otherwise it would be impossible to hold the line on other commodities. At first, a compromise was advanced whereby the initial payment would be raised to 75 cents, but still below the undeclared ceiling. On that basis, Ilsley was prepared to approve a 15 cent bonus payable by the treasury in order to raise the initial payment to 90 cents.

This compromise stood for a few days until the wheat committee heard from the western Liberal members and from Premier W. J. Patterson who had flown from Regina to spearhead the opposition to a price ceiling on wheat. During the first week of March, Patterson met with the western Liberal caucus, with the cabinet wheat committee and also with Mackenzie King.

By the time the wheat committee reconvened, Gardiner and Gordon were embarked upon a collision course. Gardiner was acutely aware of the political repercussions in the west if the ceiling entrenched a depressed price for wheat, and Gordon was determined that his responsibility to enforce the general price ceiling should not be impaired by exemption for any commodity, no matter of how much importance, even wheat. Unfortunately, the argument embroiled the two personalities as Gardiner upbraided Gordon for not having faced the farm delegation at the beginning of the month.

Eventually, the issue was resolved in a manner that placated both parties. The wheat committee recommended, and cabinet decided, that because western wheat was primarily an export commodity, no ceiling needed to be placed on it so long as domestic consumers were protected against price increases. Accordingly, the initial payment was increased to 90 cents, and domestic consumers were assured that when the new initial payment came into effect on August 1, 1942, they would be protected. Thus Gardiner had his way on the increased initial payment, and Donald Gordon his on the maintenance of domestic price ceilings. When the policy was announced on March 9, 1942, MacKinnon implied that the Canadian wheat board would continue to sell wheat to millers at prices within the maximum price regulations.[17] But even this solution did not wash, because it required producers to bear the brunt of consumer price protection. Nevertheless, the way had been momentarily cleared for an immediate policy announcement.

1942-43 WHEAT POLICY ANNOUNCEMENTS

On March 9, 1942, by agreement among the house party leaders, MacKinnon moved both an amended resolution and also second reading of a bill to amend the Canadian wheat board act, and Gardiner followed by moving second reading of a bill to make statutory provision for the wheat acreage reduction payments. The two bills ensued from related parts of the same policy announcement, and were debated together. For MacKinnon's use, Clive Davidson had prepared a long expository statement which underlined the thoroughness of the government's policy review.

While recognizing the necessity of an increased initial payment, the statement placed a low priority on wheat production as it stressed the need for more coarse grains to support other food programs. MacKinnon said:

... Wheat production in 1942 cannot be regarded as an extremely urgent matter. This cannot be said, however, in respect to practically all other farm products produced in the prairie provinces. We urgently need more hogs; we urgently need more feed grains; we urgently need more milk, butter and cheese. If the government were to establish priorities in respect to the production of farm products in 1942, it would be necessary to place wheat well down on the list, topped in point of urgency by feed grains, live stock and live stock products. My colleague, the Minister of Agriculture, will be dealing with the coarse grain situation but the situation is a most vital one and had to be considered along with our wheat policy. I stress this point deliberately in order to make it clear that an undue expansion in wheat acreage and wheat production in 1942 is not advisable, and at the same time to strongly urge every producer in the prairie provinces to make certain that the government's wheat policy does not influence him one iota to cease, or in any way interfere with his efforts to increase feed grain and live stock production to the limit of his resources.

When the full grain programme for 1942 is before the house it will be seen that the government has made provision for encouraging farm production along the lines most urgently required, and provision will be made whereby wheat producers may benefit from the 1942-43 wheat programme without unduly expanding wheat acreage. ...

It is my responsibility to announce the government's decision in respect to the price which will be paid to the farmers for wheat in 1942-43, the volume of wheat which we propose to accept in that crop year and decisions which have been made in regard to price of certain coarse grains and flaxseed.

The government proposes that the fixed initial price for wheat delivered in 1942-43 under authorized delivery quotas shall be 90 cents per bushel, basis No. 1 northern wheat in store Fort William/Port Arthur or Vancouver.

In reaching its decision in regard to the fixed price per bushel of wheat, the government has taken into account the position of producers who, by virtue of geographical location, and established farm practice, must depend mainly upon wheat production in their farm operations. Producers in this position have not been able to take as much advantage as producers in other areas of remunerative markets which have existed for live stock and live stock

[17] *House of Commons Debates*, March 9, 1942, pp. 1123.

products. With due regard to the percentage of total wheat acreage in the prairie provinces which is normally seeded to wheat in these areas, the government feels that an increase in the per bushel price is an effective way of assisting those who need assistance most.

It is not the intention of the government that domestic buyers of wheat and wheat products shall be deprived of the protection of the price control policy.

Accordingly, the Canadian wheat board will continue to sell wheat to domestic buyers for flour or other use at a price which conforms to the spirit and intention of the maximum prices regulations and is an appropriate price in relation to the domestic selling prices of goods made from wheat or in the production of which wheat is used.

The wartime prices and trade board, in the discharge of its responsibilities under the maximum prices regulations and the wartime prices and trade regulations, will have the duty of determining the price at which wheat will be sold to domestic buyers in accordance with these principles.

The wartime prices and trade board will discharge this duty from time to time after consultation with the Canadian wheat board. . . .

In addition to increasing the fixed price per bushel of wheat, the government proposes to substantially increase authorized deliveries of wheat in the prairie provinces and British Columbia during 1942-43 to a total of 280 million bushels. . . .

In the main, the government's proposal to permit marketing of 280 million bushels in the prairie provinces and British Columbia during 1942-43 was designed to limit such marketings to about the quantity which will go into export trade or domestic consumption in Canada. As a result, the government does not anticipate much change in year-end stocks on July 31, 1943, as compared with stocks which will be carried on July 31, 1942.

Delivery Quotas — As long as maximum authorized deliveries are established for the prairie provinces, it will be necessary to provide for the limitation of farm deliveries. This is the only way in which total deliveries may be regulated. . . .

So far I have dealt mainly with that phase of the government's grain programme which deals primarily with the desire of the government to increase farm income and add greater security to the position of the wheat producer. I now wish to submit three additional and important proposals for the particular purpose of securing increased production of three farm products which are necessary to our national war effort.

These proposals are:

1. That a minimum price level for barley be established. This minimum price level will be 60c. per bushel basis in store Fort William/Port Arthur for Winnipeg barley futures as well as for all cash barley, basis No. 2 C.W. 6 row at 60 cents. The Canadian wheat board will be empowered to carry out this policy and regulations will be prepared in due course.

2. That a minimum price level for oats be established. This minimum price level will be 45 cents per bushel basis in store Fort William/Port Arthur for Winnipeg oats futures as well as for all cash oats, basis No. 2 C.W. at 45 cents. As in the case of barley the Canadian wheat board will be empowered to administer this policy and regulations will be issued in due course.

3. That the price of flaxseed be fixed at $2.25 per bushel basis No. 1 C.W., flaxseed in store Fort William/Port Arthur. The dominion government will empower the Canadian wheat board to purchase and handle all flaxseed delivered by producers in Canada in 1942-43. Trading in futures and cash flax will be stopped on all Canadian markets at some date to be determined. An

order in council has been passed which prohibits any person under very heavy penalty from moving flaxseed from any licensed or unlicensed elevator or mill from utilizing flaxseed without the written authority of the Canadian wheat board. Needless to say there will be no interference with the processing of flaxseed in Canada. In the near future regulations will be issued for the handling of flaxseed under the new plan.[18]

Gardiner followed MacKinnon, giving a more elaborate explanation of the need for raising income through the increase in the initial payment; he outlined the relation between current prices for agricultural products, their 1926-29 averages, and the ceilings which had been announced. He also traced his policy of developing floor prices for agricultural products, notably for hogs, butter, cheese and eggs, and now floor prices for oats and barley, with a fixed price for flaxseed. He described the effect of the combined measures on the level of farm income and stressed the need for the production of animal fats and vegetable oils in the face of shortages created by the Japanese conquest of Asian vegetable oil sources, as he said:

... The average annual return for wheat in 1926-29 was $405 million, whereas the return in 1941, including all acreage payments, was only $210 million. That is, the return for wheat in 1941 was just a little more than half the average return in 1926-29. The average annual return for all farm products other than wheat during the 1926-29 period was $561 million, whereas the return in 1941 was $711 million. On the one hand, you have one product produced by the farmers of Canada, the income from which dropped from $405 million to $210 million. On the other hand, you have another set of products produced by the farmers of Canada, the income from which in the same period increased from $561 to $711 million. The annual return per farm in the first period was $795, whereas in 1941 it was $961. These figures leave wheat out of the picture. In other words, the return from products outside wheat in 1941 was better than the return in 1926-29, whereas the return from wheat in 1941 was only a little better than fifty per cent of the return in 1926-29. I should like hon. members to keep this fact in mind when we are dealing with the assistance that is to be given to wheat growers by means of the increase in the advance mentioned a few moments ago by the Minister of Trade and Commerce, and also under the provisions of the two bills to which before I sit down I am going to ask the house to give second reading.

It is to improve the position of the farmer who depends largely upon wheat that the advance on wheat has been increased from 70 to 90 cents. This, however, will only improve the position of the wheat farmer, on 280 million bushels of wheat, being the maximum of which we will receive delivery under the advance of 20 cents per bushel, by an increase in revenue of a maximum of $56 million, which will still leave the wheat farmer at least $176 million below the 1926-29 level. If we add the $20 million which he will receive under wheat acreage reduction and the estimated $10 million under prairie farm assistance, he will still be $146 million below the 1926-29 level.

As I say, that part of the farmer's operations which is related to wheat will be down by about $176 million. We are going to try to improve this position by taking two steps. We are going to pay $2 an acre for wheat acreage reduction, which on the basis of our 1941 experience will bring $20 million. You will naturally ask me how that improves the position of the wheat farmer. Well, it would not if the government were prepared to take all the

---

[18]*Ibid.*, pp. 1122-1126.

wheat the farmer could grow. But we are saying to him: No matter how good your crop is, we are going to take only 280 million bushels of wheat this year. It is quite a common thing in western Canada to produce on the average 15 bushels to the acre, and an average of 15 bushels to the acre on 20 million acres will produce 300 million bushels of wheat. It is possible therefore that if the farmers seeded 29 million acres in wheat, as some estimate they did in 1940, and grew even less than 15 bushels to the acre, they might have a very considerable amount of wheat which during this year they would not be able to market. So that the government is saying to the farmer, "we are prepared to pay $2 an acre for a reduction in wheat acreage, which may net you less income than the wheat would". . . .

Last year we paid $4 an acre when the acreage taken out of wheat was put into summer-fallow, and this year we are paying only $2 an acre. Last year we paid $2 an acre on all coarse grains including flax. This year we are paying $2 on all coarse grains excluding flax. In other words we are paying $2 on the rye which was mentioned while the Minister of Trade and Commerce was speaking, but we are not paying $2 on flax because the government is prepared to guarantee a price of $2.25 a bushel for flax which it is hoped will induce the production of all the flax that is required.

It might be asked why we are anxious to have an increase in the production of flax and an increase in the production of coarse grains this year. The reason is found in what has been happening in the war in recent months. We had lengthy discussions last year as to the amount of coarse grains that would be required, and whether we could get rid of all our coarse grain if grown in the quantities per acre in which they are sometimes grown. We also had lengthy discussions on the question whether we should increase the production of flax. I think I am correct when I say that the flax which we did produce last year was more than twice the amount required to keep the crushers which we have in Canada running, so that if nothing had happened which we did not expect at that time probably those who were then arguing on the other side would have turned out to be right. But many things have happened. Japan has taken possession of by far the greater part of the areas from which vegetable oils come, and immediately Japan took possession of those areas vegetable oils were not available to the allies. Those allies included all the democracies fighting on our side in this war. The United States will suffer from a shortage of oil, Canada will suffer from a shortage of oil. Great Britian will suffer from a shortage of oil, and so will all the other countries fighting on our side. The appeal is made to us to produce animal fats in the northern part of this continent, where it is very difficult to produce vegetable oils. We can produce more flax and soya beans. We can produce sunflowers from which oil can be taken. But we can produce more animal fats through increasing our hogs and dairy products and even through the production of beef. So we are making an appeal to our people this year, by putting a floor under the price of oats and barley; offering $2 an acre on land converted from wheat to coarse grains in order that we may produce animal fats to take the place of the vegetable oils which for the time being we are not going to be able to get. We are asking for more flax to increase vegetable oils. That is the reason for our action in that regard. It will be realized at once that the proposal does cut down somewhat on the return which the wheat farmer will get from the production of wheat. We are asking him to transfer from the production of wheat into the production of coarse grains and flax and hope he will make up by that means some, if not all of the $146 million he is still below the average 1926-29 level.[19]

[19]*Ibid.*, pp. 1130-1132.

In their statements, the two ministers had expressed the concern of the government that the increased initial payment on wheat was an income support consideration, and that it should not serve as a stimulus to increased wheat acreage. On the contrary, because of the wartime requirements for other foods, notably bacon, animal fats and vegetable oils, the government clearly placed the emphasis upon the production of coarse grains and flaxseed. Oats and barley were assigned minimum support prices of 45 and 60 cents respectively, as production incentives; flaxseed was dealt with more dramatically by the closing of the flaxseed futures market, government acquisition of existing stocks through the agency of the wheat board, and by the offer of a fixed price of $2.25 per bushel for deliveries from the 1942 crop. The shift of emphasis away from wheat in favor of coarse grain production was duly noted and well received by the press. Even Mr. Donald Gordon, in a Winnipeg address, emphasized the need for the shift as he called for wheat acreage reduction.

In the process, the wartime responsibilities of the Canadian wheat board were multiplying. Apart from the board's primary responsibility for wheat sales which had evolved into the bulk selling of futures to Britain, the board had undertaken to administer the processing levy. Then at the request of the wartime prices and trade board, the wheat board had become the administrator of the maximum price provisions on grains. Now, as agent of the government, it would also undertake to assure minimum prices on deliveries of oats and barley as from August 1, 1942. Further, it became immediately engaged in the takeover for government account of existing flaxseed stocks and thereafter acted as the sole buyer of flaxseed. This was done under the authority of P. C. 1800, of March 9, 1942, which was brought into effect on March 19. The order also provided for the suspension of trading in flaxseed futures. Prior to commencement of the 1942-43 crop year, the board was also empowered to buy soybeans at $1.95 per bushel for No. 2 Yellow, basis Toronto, for the account of the wartime prices and trade board.

Prior to MacKinnon's announcement of March 9, 1942, of the increase in the wheat initial payment from 70 to 90 cents, a resolution had appeared on the order paper on March 5 which indicated an increase in the payment. Because of the possibility that speculative profits could be made in the open market on the basis of the government's indication of an increased level in wheat prices, the wheat board issued a press statement on March 6, prior to the opening of the market, to the effect that "all open wheat futures would be adjusted to the new level of wheat prices on or before July 31, 1942, and that all open wheat futures will be cleared on or before this date at the closing prices of Thursday, March 5th, that is May wheat futures at 79¼ cents and/or July wheat futures at 80⅜ cents."[20] From this operation, the wheat board recovered $1,990,310 due to the difference in prices, which was paid to the federal treasury.

Still further, because of the increase in the initial payment, it was no longer considered necessary to continue the farm-storage payments by which the initial payment had been scaled up during the course of the 1941-42 crop season. Accordingly, with the commencement of the new

[20]*Report of the Canadian Wheat Board, Crop Year 1941-42*, p. 10.

crop season, these farm-storage payments were dropped. No announcement of the decision was made at the time, but MacKinnon offered an explanation of the action to the house on January 29, 1943.[21]

DOMESTIC WHEAT PRICE POLICY

When the Honourable James A. MacKinnon made his wheat policy statement on March 9, 1942, the issue of the price at which wheat would be made available to millers and feeders, and at whose expense, was still unresolved. MacKinnon announced the principle which had been agreed upon in the resolution of the Gardiner-Gordon dispute, namely of making wheat available to domestic users within the ceiling price regulations. In his statement, MacKinnon revealed that the wartime prices and trade board would determine the "appropriate price in relation to the domestic selling prices of goods made from wheat or in the production of which wheat is used". Thereupon the wartime prices and trade board proceeded with its determination. Its investigation showed a somewhat chaotic condition in eastern Canadian flour markets in the base period ending October 11, 1941, with several different maxima for flour prices determined for the competing mills which had offered flour on the basis of the varying day to day prices they had paid for wheat. In the end, the prices board named 77⅜ cents, basis No. 1 Northern at Fort William, as the single "appropriate" price at which the wheat board should make wheat available to all domestic users. This led to several meetings between the two boards which found themselves in disagreement, both as to the price named and as to the manner of its administration. Although the wheat board challenged the basis on which the price had been determined, it failed to persuade the prices board. Donald Gordon recommended that the wheat board sell directly to mills and to feeders at that price, and took the position that any question whether this should be done at producers' expense or otherwise, was a matter between the wheat board and the government.

Although the domestic pricing basis would not come into operation until August 1, 1942, when the wheat board's initial payment would be raised to 90 cents, the board raised the issue with the cabinet wheat committee twice and forwarded to it the correspondence which had taken place between the two boards. This was where matters stood when the wheat board met with the wheat committee for a second time, in July, and presented a thirteen-page submission in support of its position. The first question the board raised was the effect upon the open market if domestic users bought directly from the board instead of through the market. The board's method of making bulk sales of futures directly to the British had already taken the British requirements out of the market. If domestic sales of anywhere from 50 to 75 million bushels were also removed, this would leave only the export business to neutral countries of some 30 to 35 million bushels annually to be transacted in the open market. With that small volume the market could hardly be expected to operate efficiently. If the board were forced to carry cash wheat instead of futures, its costs of operation would rise substantially. An alternative would be to have the mills and feeders buy on the open market and receive a drawback to adjust their prices to the 77⅜ cent basis.

[21]*House of Commons Debates*, January 29, 1943, pp. 11-12.

This, in turn, raised the question of whether the wheat board or the commodity prices stabilization corporation or some other treasury source should bear the cost of the subsidy. If it were to be for board account, the cost might easily outweigh the profits on export sales; the producers would be denied any participation, and the government would have to make up the deficit.

The whole issue begged the question of the board's responsibilities under the provisions of its act which stipulated the duty of the board to sell "for such prices as it considers reasonable". That obligation placed the board in the position of a trustee for producers delivering to it, and toward whom the board was responsible for selling their wheat to best advantage. Any derogation of that obligation could only militate against the successful operation of the board and destroy the producers' confidence in it. The board enjoined the ministers to consider carefully the implications of a low domestic price for wheat in relation to the basic principles of its act and "the producers's understanding that all board wheat shall be sold to the best advantage and any surplus returned to him on the basis of his participation certificates". After pointing out that the wartime prices and trade board had the power under its order in council "to exempt any goods or services or any transaction, wholly or in part, from the provisions" and that recourse to that power was warranted in respect of wheat, the board's submission concluded with the simple recommendation that domestic users continue to purchase on the open market on the basis of approximately 90 cents, and that no ceiling price on wheat be established or announced.

In the process, the board had presented two compelling arguments that direct sales by it at the price named by the wartime prices and trade board would threaten the viability of the open market and violate the principle underlying the Canadian wheat board act. On the other hand, its recommendation that there be no domestic ceiling on the price of wheat threatened to topple the government's overall price ceiling policy. In the end, the wheat committee and the cabinet had to reconcile these conflicting issues, in the only way possible, by subsidizing the difference between open-market prices paid by domestic users and the 77⅜ cent price determined by the wartime prices and trade board. The Canadian wheat board now became the wartime prices and trade board's agent for the administration of the drawback, which bridged the difference between the prevailing market prices in the producer's interest and the lower fixed price for the benefit of consumers. The wartime prices and trade board announced the arrangement on August 22, 1942, effective on the first day of that month. The wheat board paid the drawback against sales contracts for flour from funds provided by the federal treasury.

33

WARTIME AGENCIES AND OPERATIONS

Because of the many emergency problems which arose under wartime conditions with the sale any movement of grain, the tendency was to appoint new agencies to deal with such matters as transportation, labor priorities, the finacing of Britain's wartime requirements, the coordination of Canadian and American agricultural policies, the interdepartmental coordination of Canadian food requirements and supplies, British-American food supply arrangements and the Canadian interest therein. As the Canadian industrial war effort grew, the strain on rail transportation facilities became severe; similarly in the United States the loss of Canadian boxcars to the American railway system was a matter of considerable concern. As recruitment for the armed forces grew, labor shortages emerged not only on farms, but in the flour mills and terminal elevators. In the early stages of the war, Britain financed her purchases in Canada and the United States primarily by liquidation of British investments in those countries, and by the accumulation of sterling balances by her creditors. But there was a limit to Britains's overseas resources, and new ways of financing her purchases had to be found. The loss of Chinese vegetable oil supplies presented United States and Canadian agriculture with a new challenge to overcome the shortfall. In this and in other respects, the need arose for tripartite coordination of British, American and Canadian food policies.

In addition to the maintenance of an increased wartime flow of foodstuffs to Britain, Canada by mid-war exported susbstantial quantities of feed grains, including wheat, to the United States. A listing of the wartime agencies, and the problems they dealt with in achieving such coordination, is therefore in order.

CANADA-UNITED STATES JOINT ECONOMIC COMMITTEE

One of the early coordinating committees between Canada and the United States was the Canada-United States joint economic committee formed in 1941, even before the United States was formally at war. Among other things this committee was enjoined to explore the scope for coordinating the agricultural efforts of the two countries. Dr. W. A. Mackintosh, who had undertaken a wartime assignment as special adviser in the department of finance, became the Canadian co-chairman of the committee, and he was assisted by Mr. John Deutsch. Dr. C. F. Wilson was asked to produce a working paper for the committee; he recommended the coordination of the agricultural policies of the two countries on the basis of comparative advantage in production, having wheat particularly in mind. In the light of the well-entrenched American wheat support policies, this was a futile exercise. Nevertheless, Mackintosh and Deutsch injected some realism into the Canadian contribution to the committee. By mid-April, 1942, the joint economic committee recommended the pooling of farm labor and machinery resources which resulted in the free movement across the border in either direction of harvesting crews and their equipment. Because of the earlier harvesting season on the American side of the border, Canadian crews could move south for the United States harvest and American crews could move north for Canada's. Secondly, the committee recommended that the United States switch some of its coarse grain production into vegetable oil seeds. Because the Canadian climate was not conducive to that production, Canada could grow some of the American feed grain requirements and increase its own production of animal fats.

Thereafter, the committee became inactive on the agricultural front, as a ministerial committee of the two governments and later the combined food board superseded its function, and the two governments became involved in the direct movement of Canadian feed grains into the United States.

WHEAT AND GRAIN DIVISION

C. F. Wilson was settling down again at the Dominion bureau of statistics at the end of April, 1942, following the conclusion of the Washington wheat meeting when Mr. MacKinnon asked if he could arrange to spend mornings in the west block attending to his wheat correspondence and afternoons at the bureau. This arrangement lasted for a short time until it became evident that the west block assignment was a full-time job. However, Wilson remained on informal loan from the bureau for more than a year while a new position was being created in the department of trade and commerce. At that time, the whole department occupied one floor of the west block. MacKinnon's move to recruit Wilson had the support of Dana Wilgress, his deputy minister, but the transfer was not completed until after Wilgress had been posted to Moscow as Canadian minister and Oliver Master, who served for the next three years as acting deputy minister, took over. Both Wilgress and Master recognized the need for Wilson to have direct access to the minister. As the 1942-43 wheat policy was being implemented, the administrative as well as policy load on the minister's office in connection with grain policy had reached a new peak.

The wheat and grain division of the department was established, and Wilson beame its first director. The appointment was completed in 1943. For the first time, the department of trade and commerce had formally recognized the need for direct support staff for its minister who, in the role of chairman of the cabinet wheat committee, was responsible for wheat policy. The name of the new division was carefully considered. It would have been simpler to designate it as the grain division as was done later. But, despite the fact that wheat had just been dethroned as the number one production priority in western Canada, it still towered in importance and was specially recognized in the naming of the "wheat and grain" division. As the department filled the void, in this seemingly long-overdue fashion, it did so with the utmost economy. As director, Wilson was the sole officer of the division, assisted by two secretaries, until after the end of the war.

Wilson's duties, as director, were manifold; commencing in October, 1942, he attended meetings of the cabinet wheat committee as secretary, arranged its agenda, meetings, and oversaw the implementation of its decisions. When the mutual aid administration was established, the expenditures on wheat and flour became his responsibility. He served as departmental liaison officer to the Canadian wheat board and as departmental representative on a number of related committees.

MUTUAL AID

Canadian mutual aid to Britain and other allied countries arose out of the magnitude of the British war effort whereby expenditures on munitions equipment and food supplies had greatly outstripped Britain's capacity to provide the required foreign exchange. The United States had recognized this problem by the passage of its lend-lease legislation in 1941, in advance of its actual entry into the war. In the early stages of the war, Britain had undertaken to meet her abnormal requirements for Canadian dollars by arrangement with Canada to redeem her government holdings of Canadian government and Canadian National Railway bonds which the Canadian government repaid in advance of their due dates. When this source of Canadian dollars was exhausted in 1941, the Canadian government accumulated some $700 million dollars in sterling exchange which it converted into an interest-free loan for the duration of the war. In 1942, the Canadian government made an outright gift of one billion dollars which the British used to meet its own Canadian dollar requirements and those of other sterling area countries such as Australia and New Zealand as well as providing assistance to the USSR.

Early in 1943, Mr. Ilsley announced to the house the government's intention to introduce legislation to provide for the continuing provision of war supplies, including farm products and raw materials, to the "United Nations" in the common war effort. The legislation was intended to provide the allies with all their Canadian requirements for essential war purposes, to avoid the creation of war debts that would upset the balance of payments following the war, to explore the possibilities of (but not to demand) reciprocal aid, and to deal directly rather than through the British with other countries, such as the dominions and the USSR. The legislation provided initially for the provision out of war appropriations of a billion dollars for expenditures in Canada on goods, the title of which would be transferred to the allied governments concerned.[1]

The bill, of which Mr. Ilsley moved first reading on May 6, 1943, completed the parliamentary process and received royal assent on May 20, 1943, under the title of The War Appropriation (United Nations Mutual Aid) Act, 1943. Under the act a mutual aid board was created, which was comprised of the minister of munitions and supply (the Honourable C. D. Howe) as chairman, and four other cabinet ministers. A small secretariat

[1] *House of Commons Debates,* May 6, 1943, pp. 2436-2446.

was also appointed, but the main work of mutual aid procurement was parceled out to the existing agencies. The procurement of wheat, flour and other cereals under mutual aid commenced very shortly under the new mutual aid provisions. To employ existing machinery, the board appointed the British ministry of food as purchasing agent for British requirements, and the department of trade and commerce as the disbursing agent for all wheat and flour shipped to Britain. This was a temporary arrangement intended to last only until the ministry of food's holdings of Canadian wheat futures were used up. Thereafter, the department became, technically, the purchasing agent, although the purchasing decisions were made directly between the imported cereals division of the British ministry of food and the Canadian wheat board. For other allied governments, the department of trade and commerce also became the purchasing agent. These trade and commerce responsibilities were delegated, in turn, to the newly created wheat and grain division. The arrangements were fairly simple but, because of the sums of money involved, the payments had to be expeditious. The price paid for wheat cargoes was predetermined by the wheat board's price on wheat for British account, plus costs from the lakehead to seaboard, and the cost of superintendence. Ocean freight costs remained a British responsibility. The original bills of lading were turned over directly, without charge, by the forwarding agents to the imported cereals division. The exporting firms' invoices and copies of the bills of lading were forwarded to the latter's banks in Ottawa, whose messengers brought them to Wilson's office in the west block. It was his responsibility to certify the accuracy of the invoices and to turn them over to the departmental treasury officer for payment. Within an hour's time, the bank messengers returned for the treasury cheques. The average payment for a 10,000-ton cargo ran to $335,000. Although the payments tended to bunch with the arrival and departure of convoys, the payments averaged three cargoes or $1,000,000 per day. The Canadian flour mills, large and small, all had contracts for the production of a standardized brand of flour, known as G. R. flour, for Britain. These payments presented no problem, because the flour had a standard price, based upon the wheat board's price for the wheat.

By April, 1943, the USSR government applied for wheat and flour under mutual aid for shipment via Vancouver to Vladivostock. The Russians used American liberty ships acquired under lend-lease, and the latter were usually in need of minor repairs in the Vancouver dry docks after the Pacific crossing. This was the only sure means of knowing when wheat was required for loading. Otherwise, the Russians gave no prior notice of their ship arrivals for security reasons.

Unlike the first world war when the British set up their own purchasing company in Winnipeg, the imported cereals division dealt directly with the Canadian wheat board and used the forwarding firm of Thomson and Earle, Limited, Montreal, of which Mr. Charles Gowans was president. Mr. Gowans performed indefatigably and anonymously throughout the war in that capacity. Wilson was in touch with him daily and had a complete picture of the export movement over which Gowans presided as he received notice of the arrival of British ships.

Apart from the wheat and flour purchases for the USSR, there were also a few products shipped under mutual aid such as linseed oil and rolled oats for which the purchases had to be made by the department. This was done by tender, but despite encouragement for competitive offers, the effort was futile. As the supplying companies were all under excess-profits tax which afforded them no additional earnings, they offered at uniform prices, and the business had to be rotated.

Immediately after VJ Day, mutual aid was terminated to Britain and to the USSR. Nevertheless, Canadian procurement for the United Nations Relief and Rehabilitation Administration continued through the mutual aid facilities. By the time that the UNRRA operations were completed, Wilson had processed payments of one billion dollars for mutual aid and UNRRA grain and grain product shipments. The whole operation ran without delay in payments, except for one slip. On one occasion, much to his personal embarrassment, the treasury officer issued two cheques against the same invoice. The grain exporting firm promptly returned the second cheque and there the matter ended.

LABOR PRIORITIES COMMITTEE

Because of recruitment for the armed services and increased industrial employment, labor shortages had become acute by mid-war. The department of labor established a labor priorities committee for the purpose of guiding the national selective service offices on the priorities to be assigned to the supply of available labor to the various industries. Dr. Wilson served as departmental representative on this committee, primarily because of the shortage of labor in the terminal elevators and mills. By 1943 the labor shortage at the lakehead terminals was so acute that an embargo had to be placed upon the consignment of cars to the lakehead. This, in turn, had caused a widening in the spreads between terminal grain prices and the street prices in the country. The situation was so serious that the cabinet wheat committee made direct representations to the minister of labor, the Honourable Humphrey Mitchell, who ordered the Winnipeg national selective service office to despatch 150 men to the terminals. Even with an A labor priority, the Winnipeg office was unable to recruit more than 30 men. Grain shovelling was dusty and onerous in the days before automatic car dumps were in general use in the elevators, and workers avoided this type of employment if they had any option. Later in the war, the department of labor appointed a labor commissioner at the lakehead, Mr. A. A. Heaps, a former member of parliament, who worked with the unions in an attempt to maintain the labor supply and a satisfactory rate of car unloadings. Wilson obtained an A priority for the supply of labor to the large flour mills, but could get only a B priority for the small mills which were also fully booked for the production of G. R. flour. Even the A priority for the large mills was withdrawn from time to time, and pressure was required to bring its reinstatement.

SUNFLOWER SEED AND RAPESEED

Reference has already been made to the wartime shortage of vegetable oils and that because of climate, Canada was at a disadvantage in the production of the latter. A principal source of vegetable oil was the Chinese soybean which could be produced under American climatic conditions and in a small portion of southern Ontario. The wartime impetus given to the development of soybean production in the United States midwest helped to establish a new industry in that area which has since grown to bonanza proportions. It was noted, however, that the Mennonites in Manitoba were producing sunflower seed which yielded an excellent edible oil, and it was decided that this industry should be encouraged. The main reponsibility for the encouragement of vegetable oil production in Canada rested upon Mrs. Phyliss Turner, an economist in the tariff board, whom Mr. Hector McKinnon had recruited to the staff of the wartime prices and trade board as fats and oils administrator. Another oilseed which the British authorities brought to Mrs. Turner's attention was rapeseed which produced an inedible oil at that time, but which had a specialized use as a marine-engine lubricant. Thus, it was a navy as well as a marine requirement. Just how Mrs. Turner arranged for a supply of the seed, whose production appeared to be nonexistent in Canada, is unknown to the author, but she had the resources of the department of agriculture at her disposal. To provide an incentive price for the production of sunflower seed and rapeseed, Mrs. Turner had the approval of the wartime prices and trade board, but if farmers were to produce these seeds they needed a ready and continuous market. Mrs. Turner's object was to have the prices and delivery terms announced well in advance of seeding time in 1943.

Accordingly, the fats and oils administrator approached the Canadian wheat board to act as agent of the prices board in accepting delivery of these crops. The board members, George McIvor and Gordon Smith particularly, regarded with little favor the prospect of adding to their proliferating responsibilities the handling of two new commodities which were bound to be a nuisance in preempting much needed elevator space because of their small quantities. On one of George McIvor's visits to Ottawa, Mrs. Turner convinced him that wheat board involvement was a necessity. But Gordon Smith who remained behind in Winnipeg vetoed the project. On his next visit to Ottawa McIvor brought Smith with him and, on the pretext of another engagement, sent Smith to face Mrs. Turner who gained his support for the project.

P. C. 2894 of April 9, 1943, authorized the board to buy sunflower seed and rapeseed from producers at 5 and 6 cents a pound, respectively, for the top grades at shipping points designated by the board. A few years later the sunflower seed price was also raised to 6 cents. The rapeseed price worked out to $3.00 per bushel of 50 pounds. At 6 cents a pound, the sunflower seed price worked out to $1.80 per bushel of 30 pounds. The board assumed the carrying charges but all costs were reimbursed by the federal treasury. The board's authority to make purchases of these seeds was continued by order in council for each of the crop years from 1943-44 to 1948-49. Deliveries to the board over this period as shown by the board's annual reports were as follows:

	Sunflower seed	Rapeseed
	(bushels)	
1943-44	151,815	19,630
1944-45	149,542	69,717
1945-46	105,969	132,085
1946-47	360,712	147,143
1947-48	451,958	345,102
1948-49	—	1,048,230

The figures illustrate how amply the fledgling rapeseed industry flourished under government encouragement. By 1948-49, the market price for sunflower seed exceeded the government's fixed price and no deliveries were made to the board. But there was no market demand for rapeseed which still produced an inedible oil, and the government discontinued its support of the industry after the heavy deliveries it received in 1948-49. Thereafter, the production of rapeseed waned until scientists succeeded in homogenizing the oil and in rendering it edible. Thereafter, the rapeseed industry was sponsored and encouraged by the private trade until the Winnipeg grain exchange established a futures market for it. Since then rapeseed has meant to prairie production what soybeans have meant to the American midwest. The circumstances of the inception of the rapeseed industry have been almost forgotton, however, and the industry owes a debt of considerable gratitude to Mrs. Turner for her initiative in getting it established.[2]

COMBINED FOOD BOARD

The origin of the combined food board created by the British and American governments in the wake of Pearl Harbor to deal with threatening food shortages and the most effective use of available resources, as well as the exclusion of Canadian membership on that board for more than a year, has been well documented.[3] The announcement of the board's establishment by the British and American governments was made on June 9, 1942. Because the terms of reference for the new board intimately concerned the Canadian food effort on behalf of Britain and implied that food scarcities would call for equal sacrifice by all the allied governments, King was questioned in the house regarding Canadian membership and made formal application for such to the two other governments on July 15, 1942. Opposition came mainly from the British government on grounds that the admission of Canada would invite applications from the other dominions and dilute the effectiveness of the board. As an alternative, the two major powers offered Canadian participation in committee activities, and consultation with the Canadian government (but not on a membership basis) when issues directly involved Canada. In doing so, they promised a priority on the movement of Canadian supplies. Nevertheless, the Canadian government continued to press its case for membership until it was ultimately agreed on October 25, 1943.

[2]Mrs. Turner, after the war, married the Honourable Frank Ross who became lieutenent governor of British Columbia.

[3]G. E. Britnell and V. C. Fowke, *Canadian Agriculture in War and Peace 1935-50*, pp. 138-143.

Eric Roll, *The Combined Food Board*, (Stanford University Press, 1956), pp. 63-67, 93-97.

Meanwhile, the combined food board invited Canadian membership on its proposed committees and, in the spring of 1943, Mr. M. I. Hutton conveyed, through the Canadian legation in Washington, an invitation for Canadian membership on a proposed cereals committee, whose function was then described as recommending allocations of flour supplies. The invitation was transmitted to the food requirements committee which referred it, in turn, to the cabinet wheat committee.[4] When the item was reached during the June 4 meeting of that committee, Gardiner took the line that Canada did not need membership on the combined food board as long as it was assured of first consideration in the movement of our supplies. As for the proposed cereals committee, there was some apprehension that it might be a device for giving the British a strong voice in the allocation of Canadian flour supplies and the reaction of the cabinet wheat committee was to decline the invitation. Accordingly, the cereals committee was formed in 1943 without Canadian membership, and its first task was to undertake a survey of flour milling capacity in anticipation of relief needs. But as the American demand for feed grains including wheat pyramided in 1943, questions were raised whether British requirements from North America could be restricted, which offered limited possibilities unless the British could import more from Argentina and Australia in the light of available shipping. As the cereals committee broadened its scope to the consideration of allocations of wheat and feed grains, more serious attention was paid to its activities. On this basis, the Canadian government changed its position regarding Canadian membership in the committee. Early in January, 1944, Mr. George McIvor was named to the committee which elected him chairman. McIvor attended the committee meetings which were held almost monthly, and C. F. Wilson usually accompanied him for the purpose of keeping the cabinet wheat committee and the food requirements committee informed.

Because of the grain transportation problem common to both Canada and the United States which had developed in the winter of 1942-43, the need for more frequent liaison with the American grain and transportation authorities had become obvious in the spring of 1943. In response to this need, the wheat board transferred to Washington in June, 1943, Mr. William C. McNamara, who had served as the board's supervisor of transportation for the past year. In addition to his transportation assignment in Washington, McNamara also served as McIvor's alternate on the cereals committee, and participated in its day-to-day activities, after McIvor had become its chairman.

JOINT AGRICULTURAL COMMITTEE OF CANADA AND THE UNITED STATES

While Canadian membership on the combined food board remained in abeyance, Gardiner met with the Honourable Claude R. Wickard, United States secretary of agriculture, in January, 1943, on the coordination of Canadian and American production goals. The upshot was the creation of a

---

[4]For the food requirements committee, see p. 752.

joint agricultural committee headed by Gardiner and Wickard. This committee had a very brief existence, and it ceased functioning as soon as Gardiner became the Canadian member of the combined food board. The joint agricultural committee recommended increased Canadian production of feed grains, oilseeds, peas and beans in Canada which was similar to the recommendation of the joint economic committee of the two countries a year earlier.[5] But the joint agricultural committee took note of the American plans to increase wheat acreage in 1944 from 54 to 68 million acres.[6] Although he was unable to persuade the Americans differently, Gardiner regarded the American step with keen personal disfavor in the light of the wheat surplus in Canada which the Americans could have drawn upon instead of expanding their own acreage. Obviously, Gardiner shared Wilson's views on the merits of comparative advantage as a criterion for assigning production priorities between the two countries. But, regarded in the light of their own needs and of the growing requirements for wheat toward the war's end, the Americans had good reason for relaxing their strict controls on wheat acreage in connection with which they had been pressing until then for similar "positive measures" in the other wheat exporting countries.

FOOD REQUIREMENTS COMMITTEE

Canadian departments had begun naming representatives to commodity committees of the combined food board in 1942, and this gave rise to the need for an interdepartmental committee to study Canadian food requirements in relation to wartime export commitments, and to coordinate Canadian participation in the activities of the combined food board committees. In October, 1942, by P. C. 9692, cabinet created the food requirements committee which was comprised of the deputy ministers, or their alternates, of the departments concerned. Dr. H. G. S. Barton, deputy minister of agriculture, was appointed chairman of the committee, and Dr. C. F. Wilson was asked to serve as secretary. Members of the committee included Dr. Donald B. Finn, deputy minister of fisheries, Dr. L. B. Pett, nutritionist in the department of pensions and national health, the Honourable J. G. Taggart, food coordinator of the wartime prices and trade board, Oliver Master, acting deputy minister of trade and commerce, and various representatives of finance and external affairs. Mr. George Paterson, agricultural counsellor of the Canadian legation in Washington, who served as liaison officer with the combined food board, also reported to the food requirements committee. While the committee recommended such food rationing as took place in Canada, and coordinated these measures with similar action undertaken in the United States, its main function was that of coordinating Canadian participation in the activities of the combined food board. In 1944, when the food requirements committee was given the additional assignment of coordinating Canadian contributions for relief and rehabilitation, Dr. Wilson asked to be relieved as secretary because of other responsibilities.

---

[5] See pp. 744-745.
[6] G. E. Britnell and V. C. Fowke, *Canadian Agriculture in War and Peace, 1935-50, p. 142.*

EMERGENCY GRAIN TRANSPORTATION COMMITTEE

Because of the high yields in 1942 of both wheat and coarse grains, and because of the sharply higher requirements for feed grains both in eastern Canada and in the traditionally deficit feed grains areas of the United States, the wheat board encountered its most serious transportation difficulties to date during the war. On October 15, 1942, the board took over from the railways the responsibility for allocation of grain cars under the provisions of the Canada grain act, as the board undertook to allocate cars for the loading of wheat and coarse grains at country elevators. The car allocation was placed under the immediate responsibility of Mr. W. C. McNamara, who had been seconded by Saskatchewan pool elevators to the board. To meet the feed grain demand the board allocated more cars to the oats and barley movement through the autumn of 1942 than it did to wheat. Even so, the current demand for feed grains plus a reserve for winter requirements in eastern Canada was barely met. Then at mid-December the weather turned severely cold, which lowered the efficiency of locomotive power, and the winter movement to replenish empty bins at the lakehead fell seriously behind. The representations which the wheat board made to the railways, to the transport controller, to the cabinet wheat committee, and to American transportation officials are set out in the next chapter.[7] But when the Americans began to schedule an emergency movement of feed grains (including wheat) from Canada as a result of a small domestic harvest in the summer of 1943, the Canadian transport controller realized that the time had come for regular consultations between the Canadian railways, the wheat board, the Canadian shipping board, and himself on the movement of grain.

Thus Mr. T. C. Lockwood, Canadian transport controller, set up a committee informally in June, 1943, to which he invited the membership of the Canadian wheat board, the general transportation superintendents of the two railways, the Canadian shipping board, the feeds administrator, and C. F. Wilson as a means of keeping the cabinet wheat committee informed. When Mr. Lockwood reported to the cabinet wheat committee on September 21, 1943, that the committee had been formed, the ministers expressed their appreciation, and Mr. MacKinnon announced the appointment of the committee, subsequently confirmed by order in council. By bringing together on a regular basis the railways and the wheat board, car loading projections were made, debated and adopted at each meeting, the wheat board's shipping program benefited materially from co-operation of the railways. The committee continued to function through the remainder of the war and in the critical transportation period immediately thereafter. In the absence of any overriding priority for the grain movement compared to that of other commodities equally essential for the war effort, the committee got results and exploited every opportunity on behalf of grain, due in large measure to Mr. Lockwood's personality and coordinating skill. The effort of the railway officials was magnificent, considering the labor and equipment shortages with which they had to cope in the face of all the extraordinary wartime demands for rail transportation.

[7]See pp. 762-766.

34

REAPPEARANCE OF DEMAND AND THE CLOSING OF THE MARKET

After all the elaborate consideration and study that went into the formulation of the 1942-43 crop year grain policy, the prairie provinces were blessed with a year of high yields. The wheat crop was just under the historic yield in 1929 in the prairie provinces, and the yields of all other grains were correspondingly high. Acreages sown to the various grains generally reflected the priorities the government had placed on them in advance of seeding, and the combined effects of acreage and yield are illustrated in the following figures:[1]

	1942	1941	1942	1941	1942	1941
	('000 acres)		(yield per acre)		('000 bushels)	
Wheat	20,653	21,216	25.6	14.0	529,000	296,000
Oats	9,528	8,204	51.7	21.9	492,700	179,600
Barley	6,365	4,779	37.6	20.0	239,200	95,500
Rye	1,227	844	18.4	11.5	22,632	10,346
Flax	1,510	1,030	10.1	6.4	15,180	6,643

Because of poor harvesting weather, the prevailing grades of wheat were No. 3 and 4 Northern. The government was committed to the acceptance of only 280 million bushels of wheat but, in view of the undertakings given on the support prices for oats and barley and the fixed price on flaxseed, it was bound to move these grains to every market that offered. Although the harvest was late, a survey conducted in late September showed only 205 million bushels of available elevator space. The high yields had resulted in extra harvesting costs but, in view of the limited elevator space, the wheat board could establish an initial delivery quota of only 5 bushels per basic acre, and this restricted current income at a time when its need had increased. Because of these difficulties, the executive directors of the pools made fresh representations to the cabinet wheat committee.

POOL REPRESENTATION OF OCTOBER 9, 1942

On October 9, 1942, Messrs. George Bennett (Alberta), J. H. Wesson, G. W. Robertson and A. D. Young, (Saskatchewan), W. J. Parker, (Manitoba) and

[1]*Statistics Canada.*

W. A. McLeod (central agency) called on Messrs. Crerar, Gardiner and Ilsley, in the absence of Mr. MacKinnon, and presented a submission which drew attention to the high harvesting costs and to the relative lack of delivery opportunities. They renewed the recommendation they had made over the past two years for a system of advances against farm-stored grain. The pool representatives proposed an advance of 40 cents a bushel on wheat and corresponding advances on coarse grains, to be administered by the wheat board with the elevator companies acting as agents. Additionally, they asked for a continuation of the scaled-up initial payments to cover the cost of farm storage, which had been dropped when the initial payment was increased to 90 cents. No minimum price had been established for rye, which they now proposed, and they also asked for fixed prices for oats and barley at levels at least midway between the existing support prices and the ceilings which had been established by the wartime prices and trade board.

In the discussion which followed the presentation of the submission, Mr. Wesson suggested that with all wheat deliveries under permit and tied to single delivery points, the risk factor involved in loans on farm-stored grain would be negligible. This prompted Mr. Gardiner to inquire why the elevator companies themselves should not accept responsibility for the advances. Mr. Wesson replied to the effect that the companies lacked the necessary capital and were unable to obtain credit from the banks for this purpose. Mr. Ilsley inquired rather petulantly why, in such times, people wanted to lay every problem on the government's doorstep, when there was much they could do for themselves, particularly in the light of the claim of low risk. Mr. Crerar recalled that past experience had shown that when the federal government undertook risks of this sort losses usually resulted. He believed that the municipalities and provincial governments could do a better job of administration. Mr. Wesson contended that no new obligation of the federal government would be involved, if the wheat board were to borrow from the banks to make the advances. The government had undertaken to accept deliveries of 280 million bushels of wheat, and it was simply a question of whether partial advances could be made ahead of actual deliveries up to the total commitment. At the end of the discussion, Mr. Parker asked if the government would consider helping to make credit available to the elevator companies, if the risk factor were to deter the government from making advances through the wheat board. Although the ministers gave no assurances, they followed up this latter suggestion over the course of the next several months by having the finance department explore the feasibility of the plan with the banks and the elevator companies.

The pool representations on renewal of payments for farm storage ran into the arguments that the initial payment had been raised, which obviated their need, and that the scaled-up payments would induce farmers to hold back deliveries and congest the elevators by the following July. Mr. Ilsley observed that there was no basis for asking more than 90 cents for wheat when so much of the present excess of supplies over current needs was about as useless to the war effort as gold. A different case existed for commodities such as bacon and cheese which were badly needed. With respect to rye, Mr.

Gardiner pointed out that there were no market prospects in sight, such as existed for oats and barley, when minimum prices on the latter grains were set.

In recommending fixed prices for oats and barley, Mr. Wesson observed that the handling companies were experiencing losses on the spreading of October barley and oats into December, with the latter futures ruling below October, which resulted in a negative payment for the carrying of the grain. The wheat board's responsibility was to buy oats and barley futures only at the minimum guaranteed levels, and this tended to attract prices to the minimum. Nothing came of this recommendation however, as the open market began to reflect the United States demand. Because Mr. MacKinnon was unable to be present, the other ministers invited C. F. Wilson to attend in order to keep MacKinnon informed. In such unpremeditated fashion, Wilson embarked on his duties as secretary of the cabinet wheat committee. Shortly thereafter, MacKinnon asked him to attend the meetings regularly, to arrange them, to circulate their agendas and minutes and to see that decisions were implemented.

1943-44 GRAIN POLICY

Because of the basic decisions taken with respect to the marketing of the 1942 grain crops, including the increase in the initial payment for wheat to 90 cents, the maximum delivery quota, the floor prices for oats and barley, the fixed price for flaxseed and the continuation of the wheat acreage reduction payments, all of which had worked out reasonably satisfactorily as a composite grain policy, the government and its advisory agencies were not under the same pressure to review grain policy for the 1943 crop as they had done so exhaustively in 1942. In fact, early in January, 1943, the cabinet wheat committee proceeded with the determination of 1943 policy with the intention of having it announced at the opening of parliament later that month. The committee called the wheat board to Ottawa for a meeting on January 10 and got its review under way before it had received recommendations from such obvious sources as the wheat board advisory committee and the Canadian federation of agriculture. Although Mr. Gardiner was absent, the three other ministers, MacKinnon, Ilsley and Crerar met with George McIvor and Gordon Smith of the wheat board who brought with them their supervisor of transportation, W. C. McNamara. Mr. Ilsley brought two of his advisers with him, Dr. W. A. Mackintosh and Mr. Mitchell W. Sharp. Sharp had just been lent by James A. Richardson & Sons Limited to the department of finance after that department realized that it, too, needed the services of a grain marketing specialist. From then on, Sharp accompanied Ilsley to the meetings of the cabinet wheat committee and, with Ilsley's encouragement, acted as the latter's spokesman on the items under review. At that meeting, the ministers undertook a preliminary review of policy as they discussed the level of the maximum delivery quota for 1943-44.

MacKinnon asked if deliveries could be maintained at the 280 million bushel level set for 1942-43. McIvor had in mind a figure of 260 to 280 million bushels, and mentioned that if the figure were to be placed at less than 280 millions, it would invite renewed demands for a higher initial payment. At the current rate of disappearance in 1942-43, he expected that only 250 million bushels would be moved commercially. December export clearances had been at the lowest rate yet, but the flour mills were now fully booked to the end of April, and some wheat had been shipped all rail to Mexico. Mitchell Sharp doubted that there would be sufficient elevator space in 1943-44 to handle 280 millions, and he thought that any undertaking to accept that figure would have to be made conditional upon availability of elevator space.

As for the level of the initial payment on wheat, both McIvor and Crerar expressed the belief that there was now little concern in the country about the level of the initial payment, and it was agreed that it should be maintained at 90 cents. After McIvor reported on the board's coarse grains operations, it was agreed to continue the 45-cent support price for oats and the 60-cent level for barley. McIvor mentioned that in the current crop year to date, the board had taken less than half the total deliveries of barley and oats, and that the price of the latter was within a cent of the ceiling. The United States demand for oats had been much greater than expected, and the demand for feed barley was increasing. With regard to the flaxseed price, Dr. Mackintosh cited Mr. Taggart's view that the farmers in flax growing areas had so much wheat on hand to deliver against their 1943-44 quotas, they would sow flaxseed considerably beyond the market's needs. There was also considerable uncertainty, at the time, over how much flaxseed the United States would import under the coordinated program on oilseeds. It was agreed that the flaxseed price should remain at $2.25, on the understanding that no announcement would be made regarding priority on flaxseed deliveries in 1943-44, and that this would act as some deterrent on flaxseed acreage.

Mr. MacKinnon raised the question of payments for farm storage and advances on farm-stored grain. He was personally in favor of a restoration of farm-storage payments and the introduction of advances, but McIvor maintained that the payment of farm storage would encourage elevator congestion at the end of the crop year, and Ilsley indicated that this payment had been made as a price supplement which was no longer necessary with the price at 90 cents. On the question of advances, McIvor thought that interest had diminished in them when delivery quotas were raised. Crerar also believed that the interest had waned.

Mr. Ilsley asked what would happen if the wheat acreage reduction payments were withdrawn. He believed that wheat acreage would be reduced in 1943 for reasons other than the payments, but he did not press the issue.

After this preliminary discussion, the wheat board members returned to Winnipeg for the scheduled meeting of the advisory committee to the board on January 14-15. At that meeting, the advisory committee decided to support the existing program on maximum delivery quotas, but added that it would assist the maintenance of wheat acreage reduction in 1943 if producers could deliver any undeliverable surpluses under the maximum quota provisions from the 1942 crop against their 1943 quotas. Producers having such surpluses could then afford to divert even more of their 1943 wheat acreage into other crops. The advisory committee also recommended the retention of the floor prices on oats and barley and the removal of the ceilings on those grains. It also reiterated its position that wheat should not be sold domestically at less than the 1926-29 parity but that, in any case, it should not be sold in Canada below the board's initial payment of 90 cents. With respect to flaxseed, the advisory committee had been informed that the extent of the market was uncertain for that crop in 1943-44, and the committee recommended specifically as follows:

> That the present minimum price for flaxseed be continued in 1943-44 and that the movement of flaxseed from farms in 1943-44 be not subject to delivery quotas; provided, however, that if the Government desires an increase in flaxseed production in 1943-44 the guaranteed price be increased. The Committee further recommends that the Dominion Government promptly (issue) a complete statement on the flaxseed position, in order to remove the present uncertainty in regard to requirements for 1943-44.[2]

As for the key question of the level of the initial payment for 1943-44, the advisory committee made no specific reference to it, but its endorsement of the 90-cent level could be inferred from its recommendation "that the general principles involved in the 1942-43 grain policy be continued, and that adjustments be made where necessary for 1943-44."

When the wheat committee reconvened on January 20, the ministers had these recommendations before them. They decided to proceed with the 90-cent initial payment, the maximum delivery quota at the same level as last year, and with the right to deliver old-crop wheat against 1943-44 quotas as the advisory committee had recommended, but retained the ceilings on oats and barley because of Ilsley's concern with the general price-ceiling policy and Gardiner's concern for the maintenance of livestock production. After submitting the 1943-44 program to council, MacKinnon made the following policy statement to the house on January 29, 1943, the day after parliament reopened:

> ... My purpose in making a statement on this subject at this early date—so far in advance of the actual commencement of the next crop year—is to assist producers, as far as possible, to plan their 1943 crops. The government has arrived at its 1943-44 grain programme after very careful consideration on its own part; after full discussion with the Canadian wheat board; after having received the recommendations of the advisory committee to the Canadian wheat board; after a conference between federal agricultural officials and provincial agricultural officials and the Canadian federation of agriculture; and after consultations between the United States and Canadian agricultural authorities.
>
> The 1943-44 programme involved some important adjustments as compared with the 1942-43 programme, but retains the same general objectives. The marketing policy is definitely related to the general farm production programme announced by the Department of Agriculture.
>
> 1. The fixed initial price of wheat under the Canadian Wheat Board Act will remain at 90 cents a bushel for No. 1 northern wheat basis in store Fort William-Port Arthur or Vancouver.
>
> 2. Marketings of wheat in western Canada in 1943-44 will be restricted to 14 bushels per authorized acre. The limitation of marketings to 14 bushels per authorized acre, instead of using a total marketable quantity, will greatly

---

[2]*Minutes of the Canadian Wheat Board Advisory Committee*, January 14-15, 1943.

simplify administration and each producer will know exactly how much wheat he can market.

3. The most important change in policy is in connection with wheat deliverable in 1943-44. Under the present regulations only wheat grown in 1942 may be delivered against the 1942-43 quota of 280 million bushels. Under the new programme any wheat which the farmer has on hand produced in 1943 or in any previous year will be deliverable within the quotas fixed for the crop year 1943-44. The government feels that this feature of its 1943-44 policy will result in a further reduction in wheat acreage and will enable producers to devote more of their land to the production of other crops which are required. Most producers in the west will have wheat on their farms at the end of the crop year, and consequently will be able to further reduce their wheat acreage in 1943 and still fill their 1943-44 delivery quota. The general farm production programme contemplates a reduction of at least three million acres in the area sown to wheat in 1943 as compared with 1942.

4. Minimum prices for oats and barley in 1943-44 will be continued at 45 cents a bushel for No. 2 C.W. oats, basis in store Fort William-Port Arthur, and 60 cents a bushel for Nos. 1 and 2 C.W. barley, basis in store Fort William-Port Arthur, with lower grades in their proper relationship. Old crop as well as 1943 production of oats and barley may be delivered during the coming crop year.

5. The fixed price for flaxseed in 1943-44 will be continued at $2.25 a bushel basis in store Fort William-Port Arthur.

6. In connection with its policies in respect to delivery quotas, the use of available storage space and shipping facilities, the Canadian wheat board will give first consideration to the movement of those grains or grades of grain which are most in demand in 1943-44.

May I now turn to those aspects of the grain policy for 1943-44, which relate primarily to production and in regard to which, on behalf of my colleague the Minister of Agriculture, I wish to state the main decisions that have been reached.

The agricultural programmes for 1943 announced following the conference held in Ottawa on December 8 and 9, 1942, required that there be an increased production of hog, cattle and poultry products in 1943 which should be continued into 1944.

The considered opinion of those best informed in the United States and Canada is that if we are to reach our objectives in live stock production in 1943 and 1944 there must be an increased acreage of coarse grains in Canada in 1943.

We are asking a 12 per cent increase in oat acreage and an 11 per cent increase in barley acreage. This is being encouraged by guaranteed minimum prices on barley and oats as last year.

In order to make provision for the required acreage we are asking farmers to reduce their wheat acreage by not less than 3,000,000 acres. To encourage this, the Minister of Agriculture will submit amendments to the Wheat Acreage Reduction Act, 1942, to provide payment of $2 an acre on each acre by which land seeded to wheat in 1943 is less than land seeded to wheat in 1940 based on the same acreage. If there is new breaking involved, 80 per cent of it will be counted as wheat and 20 percent as coarse grains. No payment will be made in respect of abandoned land.

There is no assurance that flaxseed from an additional acreage can be disposed of in 1943. We are, therefore, not asking farmers to increase flax acreage over 1942. If there is a change in the requirements of flaxseed, farmers will be notified later.

Some difficulty is experienced in disposing of rye. We are, therefore, suggesting that rye acreage be reduced by 31 per cent. . . .[3]

MacKinnon concluded with an explanation of why farm-storage payments had been discontinued in the 1942-43 crop year (This had not been done when the payments were terminated on July 31, 1942). The uncertainty over flaxseed marketing prospects which MacKinnon reflected in his statement and which had also confused the wheat board advisory committee, arose from the fact that Canada was dependent on a market for its surplus in the United States. Two separate agencies of the American government had made diametrically-opposed assessments of immediate requirements and in the confusion, Canadian officials were afraid that producers would increase their flaxseed acreage, even without the assurance of a market, simply because of the overall limitation upon wheat deliveries. After McIvor and Wilson had sought to clarify the situation in Washington, Secretary Wickard wrote a reassuring letter to Gardiner on February 17, 1943:

> Mr. George McIvor of the Canadian Wheat Board and Dr. Charles Wilson of the Canadian Department of Trade and Commerce have recently had several conferences with members of this Department during which the problem of the production and disposition of Canadian flaxseed during the coming year was discussed.
>
> These conferences have resulted in an understanding whereby we are happy to assure you that Canada shall have a market for the exportable surplus of the coming year's flaxseed production. The specific mechanics of handling the matter will be developed in the course of time.
>
> It is hoped that this assurance will serve to encourage the planting of not less than 2½ million acres of flaxseed in Canada during the coming planting season.[4]

Lastly, Mr. MacKinnon's reference to the Canadian federation of agriculture at the opening of his policy statement was rather misleading inasmuch as the federation had not yet made formal recommendations on 1943-44 policy. The federation was represented at the dominion-provincial agricultural conference in December, 1942, and appeared to concur in the findings of that conference, but it had become the annual custom of the federation to submit its agricultural recommendations, including grain, directly to the prime minister and his cabinet. In fact, the federation was in session drawing up its recommendations when, to its surprise and consternation, the policy decisions were announced in the house.

Nevertheless, the federation completed its task and presented its formal recommendations to Mackenzie King and his colleagues on March 5, 1943. In respect of grains, it went on record as endorsing an initial payment of not less than one dollar; that all wheat sold for domestic consumption should return not less than $1.35 per bushel to producers; that the maximum delivery quota of 280 million bushels should not be reduced, and that wheat of any crop year should be deliverable. The federation regretted that farm-storage payments had been discontinued, and recommended an increase in the flaxseed price from $2.25 to $2.50. Regrets were also expressed over the failure to provide a system of advances against

---

[3]*House of Commons Debates,* January 29, 1943, pp. 10-11.
[4]*Trade and Commerce file 20-141-11.*

deliverable grain stored on farms. The submission stressed the importance of the developing export market for oats and barley, and protested the application of the ceiling prices on export sales. It recommended that the wheat board should handle oats and barley on the same basis as wheat, and that until such time as that was done, the ceilings on oats and barley should be lifted so that producers could have access to the higher prices ruling in United States markets.[5]

EQUALIZATION FEES ON OATS AND BARLEY

Although the Canadian federation of agriculture had drawn attention to the anomaly of selling feed grains into the higher-priced American markets at the Canadian ceiling prices for oats and barley, the Canadian wheat board had already raised this issue with the cabinet wheat committee at its meeting of February 18, 1943. McIvor explained that United States prices had risen to the point where Canadian prices were held at their ceilings. In the prospect that the former would rise further, the question arose of securing for Canadian producers a share of the United States prices. The board had been able to give only preliminary thought to the problem, but two alternatives appeared to be the handling of coarse grains by the board with initial payments and participation, as in the case of wheat, or removing the ceilings on coarse grains and subsidizing their domestic use, as was also now being done for wheat. Because the board was not yet ready to make a specific recommendation, the ministers agreed in principle that any profits on the export of feed grains should be captured for the benefit of producers, and they referred the question of the most suitable method to a subcommittee on feed grains comprised of representatives of the wheat board, the wartime prices and trade board, finance, agriculture and trade and commerce. When the subcommittee met, the wheat board proposed that the oats and barley ceilings be maintained by subsidy, with the Winnipeg market permitted to find its own level. This suggestion was opposed by the wartime prices and finance officials, as the subcommittee set out four alternative methods including (a) a levy on the issuance of export permits, (b) a wheat board monopoly on the export business, (c) wheat board purchase of all feed grains at ceiling prices, domestic sale at ceiling prices, and sale for export on the open market which would be free to reflect export demand, (d) same as (c) except with the oats and barley futures markets closed, and with board sales for export at the best prices obtainable.[6] After weighing the pros and cons of the five alternatives, including that of the initial wheat board proposal, the subcommittee concluded that a levy on export permits was the most defensible alternative, because it held out the prospect for recapturing export profits for the benefit of producers with least disruption to the existing marketing system. The subcommittee's alternatives (b) (c) and (d) each implied the adoption of new marketing methods from which it would be difficult to retreat. Acting upon this advice, the cabinet wheat committee and council approved, and MacKinnon announced to the house on April 6, 1943, that:

[5]Canadian Federation of Agriculture, *Submission to the Prime Minister of Canada and Members of the Government*, March 5, 1943, pp. 4-6.
[6]*Recommendations of the Sub-Committee Re Feed Grains*, p. 4. Trade and Commerce File 20-141-11.

... The government are instructing the Canadian wheat board to charge an equalization fee on the issuance of export permits to exporters of Canadian oats and barley. The equalization fee will, as nearly as possible, represent the difference between Canadian prices and United States prices, less transportation costs, United States import duty and forwarding costs, and with allowance for exchange. The equalization fee will not be fixed but will vary in accordance with the United States prices as compared with Canadian prices.

The Canadian wheat board will set up two special funds into which equalization fees for oats and barley, respectively, will be paid. These funds, in turn, will be distributed at the end of the crop year on a pro rata basis to the growers who have delivered these grains since March 31. Naturally, the amount in either of these funds for distribution to farmers will depend upon the future margin between Canadian and United States prices and upon the volume of exports.

By the method I have just outlined, the growers who sell their coarse grains will receive, in effect, a combined price, which reflects the ceiling price on that portion of their sales which has been disposed of in the domestic market, and the export price on that portion which had been disposed of in the export market.[7]

MacKinnon also explained the necessity for retention of ceiling prices on domestic prices of oats and barley, not only to conform with the national price control policy but to hold production costs in line for the bacon, beef, dairy and poultry products sold in the domestic market and committed under contract to Britain. At the same time, MacKinnon announced on behalf of Ilsley the withdrawal of the ceiling on rye. With only about one million bushels of rye sold commercially, it was not considered that open-market prices for that commodity would affect the wartime economy.

As a result of the maximum delivery quota regulations announced for the 1943-44 crop year, producers sowed only 16 million acres to wheat in 1943. This was a reduction of 22 percent from the previous year, and the smallest area sown to wheat since the first world war.

TRANSPORTATION PROBLEM

The resurgence of grain demand in the winter of 1942-43 coincided with a particularly severe spell of cold weather during which the operating efficiency of the railways was reduced by 50 per cent, and the locomotives could only haul shorter trains. Added to this was a shortage of railway boxcars and a growing shortage of experienced train crews. By now, in addition to the wheat export movement, there was an increased demand for western feed grains in eastern Canada, in the traditionally deficit-feeding areas of the northeastern United States, and even in the midwestern states. For years the philosophy of the United States department of agriculture, under the Roosevelt administration, had been to place emphasis upon price support associated with production control but, by now, production was failing to keep pace with the growing wartime demands for meat and dairy products which required an expanded use of feed grains. In the case of oats, processors for human consumption preferred the relatively heavy Canadian

[7] *House of Commons Debates,* April 6, 1943, p. 1883.

oats. The United States department of agriculture officials were well aware, however, of the reserves of grain being carried in Canada, and that wheat could be fed, if necessary, in addition to coarse grains. It had been recommended by both the joint economic and the joint agricultural committees that Canada should supply a part of United States requirements for feed grains.

The United States demand for Canadian feed grains rose during the winter-feeding season of 1942-43, and this coincided with the transportation problem which was aggravated by the cold weather. The Canadian wheat board approached the railways directly in early January, 1943, as a result of which the board undertook to expedite the turnaround of grain cars arriving at the lakehead on the understanding that these cars would be returned to the west to relieve congestion in the country elevators. Because of the urgent demand for feed grain in eastern Canada, however, the railways used the cars to supply that market instead, and the country elevators in the west went unrelieved. The wheat board then prevailed upon the cabinet wheat committee to call a meeting with the vice-presidents of the two railways and their officials in the hope of obtaining a priority for the movement of grain. The meeting was held in Ottawa on February 10, 1943, with all members of the wheat committee present, George McIvor, Gordon Smith and Clive Davidson representing the wheat board, Messrs. W. D. Neal and G. Main, representing the Canadian Pacific Railway, Messrs. N. B. Walton and Kirkpatrick the Canadian National Railways, and Mr. Henry Borden, special assistant to the Honourable C. D. Howe.

McIvor presented the board's case that the current rate of carloadings had been running at half the requirement to implement the government's undertaking to accept delivery of 280 million bushels of wheat, and that export business in coarse grains was having to be declined for the lack of car supply. There followed a long discussion over priorities, in which it was brought out that the railways, although reluctant to see priorities introduced, had already examined what commodities might be given less emphasis, but in every case the commodity in question, such as lumber, was serving some need in the war production effort. Coal, at the moment, deserved a high priority, because of the extraordinary winter conditions. The vice-presidents asked rather pointedly if the government would direct them on priorities, which the ministers declined to do. Mr. Gardiner commended the railways for responding to the feed grain demand in eastern Canada, and Mr. Crerar recommended that consultations be held with the American authorities in the hope of obtaining assistance from the American railroads in supplying boxcars for the grain movement to the United States. The railway representatives cautioned that while the Canadian lines tended to lose boxcars to the United States lines, the reverse was true of flat cars and hoppers which the American railways wanted returned to them. Apart from recognizing the wheat board's and the government's transportation problem, the railway executives could only offer to do their utmost, bearing in mind the other demands made upon them, and McIvor concluded that, with no solution to the grain transportation problem in sight, it remained for the board and the government to find an answer.[8]

[8]*Minutes of the Wheat Committee of the Cabinet,* February 10, 1943.

To emphasize the grain transportation problem facing the government, McIvor prepared a memorandum which he left with Mr. MacKinnon after the meeting. The memorandum noted the impasse which had been reached in the cabinet wheat committee discussions with the railway representatives, and continued:

... With the whole problem at this stage the Board feels that it is its duty to submit to the Government a clear picture of the transportation problem in connection with grain and to inform the Government of the position in which it is being placed through lack of transportation facilities.

To keep the market supplied with feed grains, flax and small quantities of rye, and to move enough wheat to permit the marketing of 280,000,000 bushels of wheat in 1942-43 and to create 85,000,000 bushels of available storage space in country elevators by July 31, 1943 would involve the movement of the following quantities of grain between February 1, 1943 and July 31, 1943.

Wheat	—	196,000,000 bu. --	122,500 cars
Oats	—	59,000,000 bu. --	29,500 cars
Barley	—	27,000,000 bu. --	16,300 cars
Flax	—	300,000 bu. --	200 cars
Rye	—	1,000,000 bu. --	520 cars
			169,120 cars

The above table shows that for the remaining twenty-six weeks of the present crop year daily loadings of 1180 cars will be required as compared with a recent average of approximately 400 cars per day. On December 10, 1942 the same results could have been obtained by a daily loading of slightly over 1000 cars. If present curtailed loadings continue until March 31, 1943 daily loadings of over 1500 cars per day will be required from April 1 to July 31 to accomplish the shipping program set out above. It is doubtful whether daily loadings of 1500 cars would be physically possible during the last four months of the crop year with due regard to storage and other factors.

The Board stresses the point that every week's delay in coming to grips with the grain transportation problem increases the extent of the remaining problem. In other words if the problem is to be dealt with it should be dealt with now as it becomes increasingly severe as each week passes.

It may be stated that the Board is asking too much in seeking to provide for 85,000,000 bushels of storage space for 1943-44 deliveries. The problem, however, can be examined from the standpoint of implementing the 1942-43 grain program and accepting the risk of congested country elevators by August 1, 1943.

On this restricted basis to implement only the 1942-43 grain program and to move the necessary quantities of feed grains, flax and rye will require 115,000 cars from February 1, 1943 to July 31, 1943. This means daily loadings of slightly over 800 cars per day for the balance of the crop year. At the present time, therefore, car loadings are about one-half the volume required to implement this year's wheat program without making any space for 1943-44 deliveries and to provide market requirements of coarse grains. If car loadings continue at the present rate until March 31, 1943 daily loadings of about 1000 cars will be required to implement this year's program. This fact again stresses the importance of early action because of the accumulative nature of grain shipping problems.

It may be useful at this point to indicate how the car supply will effect the implementing of the Government's 1942-43 program on the basis of specific daily car loadings. In the following table no provision is made for country elevator space on August 1, 1943 (country elevators filled).

Daily Loadings	Weekly Loadings (5½ day week)	Total Loadings Feb. 1 to July 31	Total Required	Short	Approximate Bushelage of Car Shortage
400	2,200	57,200	115,000	57,800	104,040,000
500	2,750	71,500	115,000	43,500	78,300,000
600	3,300	85,800	115,000	29,200	52,560,000
700	3,850	100,100	115,000	14,900	26,820,000
800	4,400	114,400	115,000	600	720,000

The above table indicates in round figures the year end position which will result from daily loadings of from 400 to 800 cars per day for the balance of the crop year. For example, if car loadings average 500 cars per day from February 1 to July 31 the Board will be short 78,300,000 bushels of implementing the 1942-43 grain program, assuming a moderate obligation in respect to the movement of feed grains. As previously pointed out daily car loadings of 800 cars from February 1 to July 31 will largely implement the 1942-43 grain program but will leave severe congestion in country elevators on August 1, 1943.[9]

Immediately after the meeting, McIvor and Wilson left for Washington, as Crerar had suggested, to acquaint Mr. L. A. Wheeler in the United States department of agriculture with the Canadian transportation difficulties. Because of the American concern over a continuing supply of feed grains, Wheeler set up a meeting with representatives of the commodity cre-lit corporation and of the transportation division of the war production board. On the strength of the deapartment of agriculture's endorsement of the need, the head of the transportation division approved the use of American boxcars in moving feed grain from country points in western Canada to American midwest points although he rejected, because of the long haul from the lakehead, similar use of American cars to meet the feed grain requirements of the northeastern states. With the approval of the office of defence transportation following that of the war production board, McIvor was told to have the Canadian railways undertake direct negotiations with the association of American railroads for the supply of cars. On behalf of the department of agriculture, Mr. Wheeler expressed a great deal of interest in the longer-run transportation problem, and in the need for a lake and rail movement of feed grains into the northeastern states. McIvor reported the results of the Washington interviews to the cabinet wheat committee, to the Honourable C. D. Howe and Mr. T. C. Lockwood, the Canadian transport controller.

As a result of the wheat board's representations on transportation and of the effort made by the railways to cope with it, the board had almost completed, by the end of the crop year, the program of taking delivery of 280 million bushels of wheat in addition to supplying the feed grain markets, but without providing a margin of storage space in the country elevators for the handling of the 1943 crop. In a report which the board made to the cabinet wheat committee on July 26, 1943, the board drew attention to the fact that the request it had made for 85 million bushels of space in country elevators by the end of July (in addition to the completion of the wheat delivery program) had not been met, and that as a consequence 1700 out of 2100 delivery points in the country were plugged. Available

[9]*Canadian Wheat Board Memorandum Re Transportation of Grains,* February, 1943.

storage space existed at the lakehead and in the east, but there was only 20 million bushels of available space in the country. This meant that only a three-bushel quota could be established initially for 1943 wheat deliveries, with the prospect of a five-bushel quota by November. The implications of this situation were that there would be renewed pressure for the provision of advances on farm-stored grain. In response, the ministers agreed that the announcement of the three-bushel quota should be accompanied by a statement of government policy respecting advances on farm-stored grain. They were aware that the pools had offered to bear the risk, if the government would guarantee their loans from the banks. However, such arrangements remained to be completed with the pools, and also with the line elevator companies which had not yet been consulted. For this purpose, the wheat board, (with the assistance of Mitchell Sharp representing the department of finance), was assigned to approach the pools and the other companies.[10]

ISSUE OVER ADVANCES ON FARM-STORED WHEAT

With the country elevators plugged, and the new crop coming on, the wheat board and Sharp pursued their mission with the elevator companies through the month of August and Sharp brought back to the wheat committee on September 6, 1943, an account of the mixed reception to the government's farm-storage proposals. In brief, the Alberta pool and United grain growers declined to participate; the Manitoba and Saskatchewan pools submitted a draft scheme, and the north-west line elevator association suggested some alterations which might make their participation possible. By correspondence, the Alberta pool had indicated to the government that it was prepared to meet the problems of its members, but asked rather pointedly about surpluses in the wheat board's 1940 and 1941 crop accounts which might be paid out now. United grain growers emphasized the administrative difficulties created if that organization operated its own scheme, but offered to co-operate if the wheat board operated one. Mr. R. S. Law also recommended the closing out of the 1940 and 1941 crop accounts and an interim payment on the 1942 account. Relief of the labor shortage at the lakehead would also help.

Even with this partial indication of participation, the cabinet wheat committee proceeded to approve the details of a system of advances. Rates of interest which the companies would charge producers and which they would pay the banks under government guarantee were decided upon. On wheat, the advances would be 50 cents per bushel, without respect to grade, on two-thirds of each producer's annual delivery quota. Loans and repayments would be recorded in the delivery permit books. A service fee of one-half of one percent was approved to cover administrative expenses. The companies were to bear 50 percent of the risk, and the federal government the other 50 percent, to be paid after two years out of the consolidated revenue fund. The commitment was to be given by order in council under the war measures act.[11]

The scheme was not implemented, however, because of an abrupt change in the marketing outlook.

[10]*Minutes of the Wheat Committee of Cabinet,* July 26, 1943.
[11]*Ibid.,* September 6, 1943.

UNITED STATES DEMAND FOR WHEAT AS FEED

The United States demand for Canadian feed grains arose out of the recommendations of the joint economic and joint agricultural committees as a means of coordinating the wartime production policies of the two governments. It emerged next in the transportation problem reviewed earlier in this chapter, in the course of which the American authorities had expressed, as early as January, 1943, a keen interest in expediting the movement. Because the weather conditions had not been propitious for the winter-wheat crop sown in the autumn of 1942, it was already known that 1943 wheat production in the United States would be light. Although feed grain production sown in the spring could not be predicted that far ahead, the American officials were already anticipating that an abnormal importation of grain for feed would be required that year. By March, 1943, the commodity credit corporation of the United States department of agriculture had begun to place orders through the private trade for the purchase of Canadian wheat, regardless of grade, for distribution to American feed manufacturers, as distinct from milling for human consumption, and for this purpose had waived the duty and the quota restriction of 800,000 bushels which applied to imports of millable grades of wheat. In that month, the American trade had purchased 45 million bushels of wheat futures in Winnipeg which the wheat board had supplied through the pit. The board applied the sales to the closing out of the 1939 producers' crop account which ended in a deficit at treasury expense, so that no participation was paid.

When McIvor reported these developments to the cabinet wheat committee on April 7, 1943, he believed that American import demand for all grains would reach as much as 170 million bushels in the 1943-44 crop year. Mr. Leslie A. Wheeler of the office of foreign agricultural relations had requested McIvor and the Canadian transport authorities, Messrs. T. C. Lockwood and A. W. MacCallum (lake shipping), to meet the American grain and transportation officials in Washington on April 12, with a view to scheduling a continuous grain movement to the United States. Accordingly, the cabinet wheat committee authorized McIvor to negotiate a price at which wheat would be sold to the commodity credit corporation, provided that the negotiated price would realize not less than one dollar per bushel for a quantity up to 50 million bushels. At the Washington meeting there was no price negotiation, however, as the Americans scheduled a shipping program and continued to buy through the trade. In so doing, the commodity credit corporation bought indirectly from the board as well as wheat offered by the Canadian trade.

The emergence of the American demand considerably reduced the remaining stocks of wheat in the hands of the board. This was reflected in the board's negotiations in June, 1943, for a bulk sale of futures to the imported cereals division in Britain. The last bulk contract had been concluded by May, 1942, for a quantity of 120 million bushels of futures which, by now, had been used almost completely. In June, 1943, the board could offer only 40 million bushels because, with the rise in prices, producers were selling at open-market prices rather than delivering their wheat to the board. In view of the market rise the board raised its offering price to the British to one dollar, which provoked a complaint from the British treasury to the Canadian department of finance.

The Canadian and American grain and transportation authorities met in Washington again on September 17, 1943, and McIvor, Lockwood and MacCallum reported to the cabinet wheat committee on September 21 that American requirements for wheat alone would amount to 150 million bushels over the next nine months, and that the Americans had firmed up a shipping program for 74.5 million bushels from September to January inclusive. The program required the American railways to provide an average of 235 cars per day at Canadian border points for loading at country elevator points and direct return to United States lines. In this way, additional pressure on the lakehead facilities was avoided. Part of this program involved delivery to Seattle for barge shipment to Californian feeding areas. The main movement, however, was to the American midwest. Later on, some grain had to be moved through the lakehead to supply the northeastern states.

When (as will be presently described) the wheat futures market was closed in Winnipeg, the commodity credit corporation continued to make its Canadian wheat purchases through the American grain firms which dealt with the Canadian shippers and exporters operating now as agents of the wheat board. It was the responsibility of the wheat board to determine the prices at which the wheat would be sold from the 1943 crop account in which producers had a participating interest. Under its act, the board had to sell at prices it considered "reasonable" in the interest of producers, and it did so by using United States market prices for comparable grades and delivery bases as a guide. Because such prices in the United States represented the value of milling wheats which commanded a considerable premium over feed grains, the commodity credit corporation had to subsidize the imported wheat into feed channels. Thus, the commodity credit corporation had a very direct interest in the level of prices charged by the board, and it was well aware that wheat was being sold at Canadian government direction from its crown account for mutual aid and for domestic use at $1.25 which was below the level of prices charged by the board on commercial sales from the 1943 crop account to the United States and to neutral countries.

As the American government was also committed to supply pork and other meat products to Britain under lend lease, and as the imported Canadian wheat was helping to fulfil that commitment, the Americans advanced a proposition that they, too, should be able to buy from the crown account at $1.25. Representations along these lines were made by the American legation in Ottawa to the department of external affairs on October 30, 1943, when a request was placed before the Canadian government to make a price offer on a quantity of wheat ranging from 100 to 150 million bushels. The request was not referred to the cabinet wheat committee, but dealt with in council because ministers already held firm views on the issue. As will be presently shown, the crown account had been created to meet the government's obligations under mutual aid and the domestic subsidy, where the price was of direct concern to the treasury and at variance with producers' participating interest. The ministers were very conscious of the fact Canada enjoyed no price protection on imports from the United States; Canadian buyers had to pay the prevailing American prices. Accordingly, on November 23, 1943, the department of external affairs informed the American legation (which had just been raised to embassy status) that: "it was the view of the Government of Canada that under present conditions it should not instruct the Wheat Board to offer a bulk quantity at an agreed price." Had it done otherwise, the government risked instructing the board to contravene the provisions of its act.

Nevertheless, the Americans renewed their representations both to the Canadian embassy in Washington on December 16, 1943, and also through the American embassy to the department of external affairs on the following day, to which no formal reply was made.[12] Instead, McIvor was instructed to explain to the American officials concerned why it was that neither the government nor the board could respond to the American proposal. At a meeting in Washington in mid-January, McIvor dwelt upon the following considerations as he reported later to the cabinet wheat committee:

(1) The Canadian Mutual Aid price to the United Kingdom was in reality a bookkeeping proposition for the Canadian Government;

(2) The Canadian Government's action in closing futures market had relieved the Americans from the necessity of buying on an open market in competition with the British purchases;

(3) Since the market was closed, the Board's price policy on sales to the C.C.C. had been to follow the advance in United States markets. The Board's price at present to the C.C.C. was $1.46. The Chicago ceiling is at $1.71 U.S., but the C.C.C. in turn resell the Canadian wheat at around $1.10 to $1.20 for feed use.[13]

As a result of his discussions in Washington, McIvor reported that the American officials were content to proceed without a bulk contract, so long as they were assured of supplies. The question of supply assurance, which the wheat board was very willing to make up to the limits of available transportation, was now referred to the cereals committee of the combined food board.

In their interest to maximize their imports, the American officials asked the British to keep their wheat imports to a minimum. A similar request had been made under comparable circumstances during World War I. On the other hand, the wheat board had to reckon now not only with British and American import requirements, but also with the heavy demand for feed grains in eastern Canada. For this reason, the board took the position that any reduction in British imports would have to accrue to Canadian livestock feeders.

As these problems were sorted out in the cereals committee of the combined food board, the American authorities requested a firm allocation of supply from Canada. They did so after McIvor had intimated that he could not obtain the co-operation of the Canadian transportation authorities in a shipping program unless he had a firm commitment from the

---

[12]*Canadian Embassy Teletype WA - 6280,* December 16, 1943, and *Memorandum of Conversation,* December 17, 1943, Trade and Commerce file 20-141-11.

[13]*Minutes of the Wheat Committee of the Cabinet,* January 26, 1944.

United States. For this reason, the wheat allocation to the United States for the 1943-44 crop year was agreed at 170 million bushels.

By the spring of 1944, domestic crop prospects had materially improved and the Americans sought a reduction in their allocation. This was done by transfer and postponement of shipment. First an amount of 15 million bushels was transferred from the American allocation to meet the requirements of neutral countries. Then in the summer of 1944 a shipping holiday was agreed because of congestion in American elevators. Shipments under the allocation were completed in the 1944-45 crop year. Altogether the Americans had imported 160 million bushels of wheat from Canada in the 1943-44 crop year, and 42 millions in 1944-45. Although the Canadian wheat board was concerned to see shipment of the allocation completed, it must also be remembered that the board, with the approval of the government, had rejected an earlier American proposal that a firm contract be negotiated on both quantity and price.

DECISION TO CLOSE THE MARKET

Although the decision to close the wheat futures market was the culmination of a series of almost daily cabinet wheat committee meetings through the month of September, 1943, the issue had arisen as early as July 26 of that year when McIvor drew the attention of the cabinet wheat committee to the need for considering the open market situation. The question arose in connection with a recommendation which had come from the pools to raise the board's initial payment from 90 cents to one dollar. McIvor pointed to the danger in raising the board's initial payment with each increase in the open market price, because of the subsequent difficulty in following the market down. He drew the committee's attention to the board's position in making sales on a rising market with no replacement wheat being delivered to it. Open market prices were such that the wheat was being sold outright instead. The cereals import division had just inquired about another bulk purchase of 40 million bushels of futures, which McIvor considered the board was not in a position to offer. The alternative for cereals was to buy its futures on the open market, which would introduce new upward pressure. The result would be that the Canadian government would have to pay much higher prices for wheat to cover mutual aid and relief purchases, as well as a higher subsidy on domestic consumption. For such reasons, the cabinet wheat committee agreed to keep the open market situation under constant review.[14]

On August 28, 1943, Mr. Gardiner attended a meeting in Regina with the directors of the three pools. At the conclusion of the meeting, the directors summarized their recommendations as follows:

1. All grain to be marketed through the Canadian Wheat Board;
    2. An initial payment of $1.00 per bushel on wheat;
    3. Cut-off on the 1940 and 1941 crop accounts;
    4. Initial payments on oats and barley to be made at the ceilings of 51½ cents and 64¾ cents;
    5. Profits on the export sales of flaxseed to be returned to its growers on participation certificates;

[14]*Minutes of the Meeting of the Wheat Committee of Cabinet,* July 26, 1943.

6. Consideration be given to rye growers who are finding it exceedingly difficult to get acceptance of deliveries at the elevators;

7. The Government to facilitate the supply of lumber for the building of granaries.[15]

In reporting these recommendations to the cabinet wheat committee on September 6, Gardiner explained that the pools had placed their main emphasis on the creation of a monopoly grain board. When he asked if they were advocating closing of the futures market, the pools had been noncommittal, but they assumed that if all grains were deliverable to the board, the exchange would have to make its own decision regarding the continuation of futures trading. The wheat committee then discussed the implications of closing out the 1940 and 1941 accounts. The pools had not specified whether the balances in those accounts should be transferred at current market prices to the 1942 crop account, or whether all board sales should now be allocated to the 1940 and 1941 accounts until the latter were closed out. The matter was left in abeyance, pending further advice from the pools and the board.

When the cabinet wheat committee met again on September 11, all three board members were in attendance; George McIvor, Gordon Smith and D. A. Kane (formerly general manager of Manitoba Pool Elevators, Limited), who had been appointed to the board in June in the place of the late Mr. W. Charles Folliott whose untimely death had occurred on March 13, 1943. Dr. W. A. Mackintosh and Mitchell Sharp accompanied Mr. Ilsley. Sharp reported that the draft order in council on advances against farm-stored wheat was ready for consideration by the elevator companies. The arrangements for the mutual aid purchase of wheat (as already described in Chapter 31) were approved. The ministers pressed the board to close out the 1940 crop account in order that a final payment could be made. A lengthy discussion followed on coarse grains policy because of growing producer dissatisfaction with the ceiling prices. The board was disturbed because it was directing the sale of most coarse grains to the domestic market, whereas better prices could be realized in the United States. The rates of its equalization fees on oats and barley were misleading to producers because such a small proportion of the current movement was going for export. Reference was made to the recommendations of the Canadian federation of agriculture and the pools that the board should handle oats and barley on the same basis as wheat, but such a policy did nothing of itself to resolve the issue of the price ceilings in force on these grains, and it was also related to the issue of closing the wheat futures market, which by now had become the paramount issue. Because of the labor shortages at the lakehead, street spreads had widened out to the producers' disadvantage and, as already mentioned, the board's ability to make bulk sales of futures to Britain was jeopardized by the deliveries to the private trade. This, in turn, raised the question of what effect British bidding for futures would have on prices in an open market. In the bullish prospect, it was apparent that Canada's mutual aid costs would be raised. This contingency, plus the existing threat to the maintenance of the price ceiling on coarse grains, was of major concern to Ilsley who also foresaw public criticism if speculators took

[15]*Ibid.*, September 6, 1943.

advantage of the rising wheat market. Once again, while no immediate decisions were taken, the ministers were apprised of the gravity of the situation.

Meanwhile, the ministers addressed themselves to the growing dissatisfaction among producers over the prices of oats, barley and flaxseed. With market prices more firm because of the extraordinary United States feed demand, the cabinet wheat committee decided to make advance payments from the equalization funds on oats and barley, to be paid to producers as they delivered their coarse grains to country elevators. They also decided that the fixed price for flaxseed should be raised by 25 cents. With parliament prorogued, Mr. MacKinnon announced the decisions by press release on September 17:

> At time of delivery Prairie farmers will receive payments of 10 cents per bushel on oats and 15 cents per bushel on barley in addition to market prices, according to an announcement made by Trade Minister MacKinnon today. He also announced that the fixed price to farmers for flaxseed had been raised to $2.50 per bushel, basis 1 CW flaxseed in store Fort William. These arrangements cover oats, barley, and flaxseed marketed during the crop year 1943-44, which began on August 1.
>
> The additional payments on oats and barley represent a guaranteed initial advance against equalization fees being collected by the Wheat Board on exports of these grains to the United States. No change has been made in ceiling prices on oats and barley which remain at 51½ cents for oats and 64¾ cents for barley, basis Fort William.
>
> The increase of 25 cents in the price of flaxseed bringing the fixed and overall price to the farmer up to $2.50 per bushel, also represents an adjustment by reason of expected profits on export sales to the United States. Provided United States demand for flaxseed continues active and prices remain close to present levels, the Wheat Board is likely to realize an average of approximately $2.50 per bushel on sales in Canada for export flaxseed acquired from farmers during the present crop year. Crushers and other domestic users of flaxseed will continue to be protected by ceiling prices on their purchases. There is an equalization fee on exports of oats and barley to the United States. Under arrangements now in effect the proceeds from these fees, which are collected on the portion of grain exported, are paid into separate accounts for distribution to farmers on the basis of all oats and barley delivered by them either for sale on the domestic market or for export during the current crop year. In this way the farmer receives the full benefit of the export price on oats and barley shipped to the United States.
>
> Given a continuation of present United States demand and prices, it is expected that the Wheat Board will recover at least enough by way of equalization fees on oats to justify the initial advance of 10 cents per bushel.
>
> Because of serious damage to crops in Eastern Canada, that area will require greatly increased quantities of western feed grains. In order to protect the vital livestock feeding programme of Eastern Canadian farmers it may be necessary to retain in Canada larger quantities of western feeds, particularly barley. By guaranteeing an additional 15 cents per bushel on barley at time of delivery, the Dominion Government is, in effect, assuring the farmer that any resulting curtailment of exports will not be permitted to reduce the additional return he might reasonably have expected to receive at the end of the crop year.

The surplus, if any, in the equalization funds in excess of 10 cents on oats and 15 cents on barley will be distributed to farmers after July 31, 1944.[16]

When the cabinet wheat committe met again on September 21 to consider the specific question of the pools' recommendation to increase the initial payment to one dollar, that issue became inseparably entwined with the question of closing the market. That question, in turn, involved the related questions of closing out the old crop accounts, of the price to be paid to producers for the unsold wheat remaining in those accounts, and of settling the terms under which the 1943 crop would be delivered to the board. The urgency of such issues was underlined by the fact that because of the subsidy on domestic consumption and the mutual aid purchases for Britain and the USSR, every cent of increase in the open market price for wheat was costing the federal treasury $2,500,000. Under the circumstances, Mr. Ilsley would have been satisfied with a fixed price for wheat, and an instruction to the board to sell wheat for the domestic market and mutual aid at that price. He specifically recommended $1.25 as the fixed price. McIvor drew attention to the implications of such a policy, which contravened the provisions of the Canadian wheat board act, including the onus upon the board to act as a steward of producers' interests in selling wheat to best advantage and of the producers' rights of participation. Here the issue became fairly joined between the treasury interest in fixing the wheat price in order to limit the cost of mutual aid and of the domestic wheat subsidy and the producer interest in having wheat sold at the best prices the board could realize.

Mitchell Sharp reverted to Ilsley's question of whether the government should, at any point, take a stand on the price of wheat. Either a ceiling on wheat must be set at some level, or the whole price ceiling policy would go. Secondly, the market price affected the treasury on all sales of wheat, except those to the United States. Mr. Ilsley confirmed that his primary concern was over the price ceiling, in order to avoid criticism that the government was favoring one economic group. His secondary concern was that of saving money. Mr. Sharp thought it was a question either of closing the market and fixing the price of wheat now, or announcing a ceiling later.

In opposing Ilsley's proposal, Gardiner reverted to the pools' recommendation for an initial payment of one dollar, which he was prepared to support, provided that there would be continuing participation, and no ceiling, on the grounds that wheat prices had been held at uneconomically low levels until then, and that farmers should be allowed to benefit from the rising market now. Crerar referred to a promise the pool leaders had made to mount a campaign in support of the one dollar initial payment, but he was very sceptical that it would succeed. Mr. Sharp claimed that Gardiner's proposal would be a negation of the price ceiling policy, to which Gardiner responded that he would not object to a price ceiling provided that it was high enough and also that it was coupled with a commitment to provide price floor supports after the war. He referred to the stand he had taken when the price ceiling prolicy was introduced, that prices of all farm commodities should have been placed in fair relation to the prices of other products. This revived the consideration of the 1926-29 "parity" price of

[16]*Trade and Commerce file 20-141-11.*

$1.41 for wheat as a possible ceiling. Gardiner said that he would be prepared to close the market now with the settlement on producer accounts to be made at $1.41, provided that the parity principle was extended to all farm products, and that floor prices would be assured after the war. Both Crerar and Ilsley expressed misgivings about entering into commitments now on postwar floors.

The discussion then shifted to the basis upon which the market could be closed. McIvor explained the procedure, including the suspension of futures trading, and the cancelling out of long and short futures positions at the previous day's close. But the question remained of whether the 191 million bushels of producers' wheat still in board hands should be closed out at those prices or at the initial price to be set for current deliveries. Mr. Sharp volunteered two alternatives: if the initial price were to be set at $1.25, he would recommend closing out the old-crop accounts at that price with immediate payment on participation certificates; if the initial payment were to be set at $1.41, however, he would recommend that the old accounts be left open, which would entail carrying charges at producers' expense until the old stocks were sold. With immediate settlement on the $1.25 basis, carrying charges on the old wheat would be for government account. Mr. Gardiner's reaction was that if the war were to last for two more years, farmers would fare better on Sharp's $1.41 alternative.

After the meeting had run into the late evening of September 21, it was adjourned until the following morning at 12 noon, which gave Mr. Ilsley an opportunity to review his position with his officials, and Mackintosh and Sharp returned with him to the meeting on September 22. In his opening statement, Ilsley disclosed that he could accede to the $1.41 proposal as a fixed price, which he considered to be necessary in order to relieve the board from having to bargain in all cases for the highest price. As the discussion developed, Mackintosh disclosed Ilsley's main concern that the price for British requirements under mutual aid should be fixed. Unless that could be done he did not see how it would be possible for the Canadian government to continue providing wheat to Britain under mutual aid. McIvor, in turn, deplored the prospect of having to sell wheat at two or three different prices, even if one of the prices were set by government directive. In any event, as long as the participation feature remained in the wheat board act, the board could not accept a directive on its selling prices. The alternative would force the board to resign. Gardiner supported McIvor by claiming that not even parliament could order wheat sold for prices less than those available in the highest market, if the participation feature remained. Sharp observed that if mutual aid sales had to be made at United States prices, the market might as well remain open.

Gardiner continued to stand on his recommendation of an initial payment of one dollar with no ceiling, and participation remaining. Under a closed market, Ilsley believed that Gardiner's recommendation would cause the least difficulty for the general price ceiling policy. Sharp, on the other hand, saw little prospect for acceptance of one dollar as an initial payment by the producers. Mackintosh asked if, under the Gardiner proposal, the board could make a bulk contract with Britain for a twelve-month supply. McIvor replied that this would have to be a decision of the board. However, in his personal view and under present market conditions, he would not favor a sale covering such a long period.

The meeting was adjourned again until the following morning, September 24, 1943, when Gardiner withdrew his proposal for an initial payment of $1.00, because producers' meetings had just been held in which the latter had raised their demand to $1.25. Under the circumstances, no fixed prices for wheat could be considered at a level under $1.50. Both Crerar and Ilsley were concerned about the dissent such a price would create while other price controls remained. Ilsley intimated that the price controls would go, and he along with them. As it was impossible to meet Gardiner's demand, they must find another approach; he suggested an initial payment of $1.20 plus participation payments. Gardiner agreed, provided that all sales were made on the same price basis. If mutual aid sales were to be separately priced, the initial payment would have to be higher.

At that stage, Ilsley advanced a proposal which proved to be the eventual solution. He suggested that existing stocks of wheat, including the old-crop accounts and the unsold stocks of wheat in trade hands be taken over by the government at market prices and held in a special account from which domestic and mutual aid sales could be made. The mutual aid price could be negotiated with the British who had already asked if the Canadian government was prepared to negotiate a minimum-maximum range of prices within the framework of the 1942 memorandum of agreement. The cabinet wheat committee had earlier decided that it would be impossible to reach agreement on the limits of the range, under rising market conditions, and had rejected the British request. Ilsley believed that with a special government stock available in which the producers' interests had already been closed out at the market, the government would then be in a position to negotiate the mutual aid price. Such negotiation might still be required, because current British dollar receipts were being used in addition to Canadian mutual aid funds for British purchases. Producer deliveries from the 1943 crop could be accepted by the board on the basis of an initial payment and participation in commercial export sales to best advantage. By this means, Ilsley met Gardiner's resolute stand on behalf of producers by offering to buy all existing stocks at the current market price, which was defensible. After they had been bought by the government, the latter could dispose of the stocks it now owned at whatever prices it determined. Thus the treasury could protect itself on price, and save the price ceiling on wheat entering domestic consumption. Apart from that special account, the board could continue to accept current deliveries from producers and sell them to best advantage in commercial export markets. Gardiner found this to be an acceptable solution and volunteered that he could obtain the support of the pools for an initial advance and the price to the British at the same level, with producer participation in sales to the rest of the world. With that understanding, the wheat committee agreed to refer the proposal to council that same afternoon.

Because of the rise in market prices, increasing public attention had begun to focus upon the issue. The council of the Winnipeg grain exchange sensed that the interests of the exchange were at stake. On September 23, the president of the exchange, Mr. Alex Christie wired MacKinnon as follows:

> The Executive and members of the Winnipeg Grain Exchange have done all in their power at all times to co-operate with the Government and Government agencies in the efficient handling of Canada's grain and grain products and are greatly concerned at reports emanating from Ottawa that Government considering closing Exchange. Members are receiving numerous inquiries from outside connections as the report has received wide publicity in Canada and the United States. Would greatly appreciate enlightenment on any proposed change in government policy and respectfully urge that if any such serious and drastic action is contemplated the Exchange be given an opportunity to present their views.[17]

With no positive response from this request, the council of the exchange decided to send its president, Mr. Alex Christie, Mr. George Mathieson and Mr. K. A. Powell to Ottawa to place the exchange's position before the cabinet wheat committee and members of the wheat board. They arrived on the morning of September 27, but were unsuccessful in reaching any of the ministers or board members. In fact, elaborate precautions were taken that day to screen the principals involved from delegations and the press. Instead of using Mr. MacKinnon's office that afternoon, Wilson transferred the meeting of the wheat committee to a suite in the Chateau Laurier, after council had approved the closing of the market in principle and had left it to the wheat committee to work out the details. The steadily rising futures market lent considerable urgency to the action. If the market were to remain open another day it risked costing the treasury that many more million dollars. The meeting at the Chateau had been scheduled for 3 p.m. Ilsley was manifestly upset when Gardiner failed to appear. Gardiner arrived half an hour late, which was unusual for him. From then until midnight the committee worked away with their advisers on the details.

During the course of the meeting, the terms of the take-over were settled. The balances of unsold wheat in the 1940, 1941 and 1942 crop accounts, and all unsold wheat in commercial hands, would be taken over by the government at $1.23¼ per bushel, basis No. 1 Northern which was the cash closing price on September 27, 1943. These stocks would be held in a separate crown account administered by the board under government direction, and from which mutual aid and domestic wheat sales would be made. The take-over made possible the closing out of the three producer accounts, and it enabled participation payments on those accounts to be paid. It was also decided to set the initial payment for the 1943 and 1944 crop accounts at $1.25 per bushel, basis No. 1 Northern, Fort William or Vancouver, which the wheat board would sell at prices it deemed reasonable. The declared intention was that all the facilities of the trade would continue to be used, with as little disruption as possible arising from the termination of wheat futures trading.

In anticipation that the decision would be taken that night, McIvor requested that his other board members, C. Gordon Smith and D. A. Kane return to Winnipeg overnight to be on hand to deal with the situation on the floor of the exchange when the announcement was made. In Appendix 7

---

[17] *Minutes of Special Meeting of the Council of the Winnipeg Grain Exchange*, September 28, 1943.

Mr. McIvor has paid tribute to his colleagues for the manner in which they handled the take-over of contracts outstanding in connection with non-board wheat which was necessitated by termination of trading.

By midnight on September 27, 1943, MacKinnon addressed the following telegram to the Winnipeg grain exchange:

> You are hereby advised that the Government is ordering the discontinuance of wheat trading on the Winnipeg Grain Exchange as of September 27, 1943, with the exception that open trades may be closed out at the closing prices registered on the Winnipeg Grain Exchange Monday, September 27th.
>
> Since it will take some time to arrange the final clearing of all the outstanding futures contracts and for the Board to take over all the unsold cash wheat, the final closing out of these contracts will be deferred for several days.
>
> In the meantime, all futures prices and all cash wheat prices are fixed at the closing prices for Monday, September 27th. No purchases or sales may be made at other than these prices. In particular, it must be emphasized that no export sales may be made until further notice.
>
> Another order affects the buying of wheat from producers and it should be drawn to the attention of your members concerned that all purchasing of wheat from producers on an open market basis will also be discontinued as from Monday, September 27th.
>
> For any further clarification of these orders please get in touch with the Canadian Wheat Board.[18]

In the small hours of the morning, McIvor informed the exchange delegation (Messrs. Christie, Mathieson and Powell) of the government's decision and of the telegram which had been sent directly to the exchange. The delegation had a long session with Crerar later that morning, but Crerar could only report on the reasons for the government's action. Vice-president W. J. Dowler read the minister's telegram to the exchange before the opening of Tuesday morning, as the council of the exchange met and resolved to comply with the government's order.[19]

MacKinnon also issued a press release explaining the action:

> Trade Minister MacKinnon tonight announced the discontinuance of wheat trading on the Winnipeg Grain Exchange; the payment to producers of an initial advance of $1.25 per bushel, basis One Northern, in store Fort William, with participation for the crop years 1943-44 and 1944-45; together with the early distribution of payments on participation certificates outstanding in the hands of producers in connection with the 1940, 1941 and 1942 crops.
>
> The Dominion Government has decided to order the discontinuance of wheat trading on the Winnipeg Grain Exchange. The Canadian Wheat Board will take over at the closing prices of September 27 all stocks of cash wheat. Until the Wheat Board has completed the necessary arrangements, the closing out of futures contracts will be permitted at Monday's closing prices on the Exchange.
>
> The Canadian Wheat Board's initial payment to producers on authorized deliveries, beginning Tuesday, September 28, and for the remainder of the crop year 1943-44 and for the full crop year 1944-45, will be $1.25 per bushel, basis No. 1 Northern wheat, basis in store Fort William-Port Arthur, or Vancouver, Participation certificates will be issued.

---

[18]*Trade and Commerce file 20-141-11.*
[19]See Mr. McIvor's comments, Appendix 7.

The Canadian Wheat Board will be empowered to purchase for Government account all unsold wheat stocks in commercial positions in Canada, including wheat held in the 1940-41, 1941-42 and 1942-43 Canadian Wheat Board crop accounts, at the closing prices as registered for each grade of wheat on the Winnipeg Grain Exchange, Monday, September 27.

Since it will take some time to make the necessary arrangements for the final clearing of all outstanding futures contracts and to take over all the unsold cash wheat, the final closing out of these contracts will be deferred for several days. In the meantime, all futures prices and all cash wheat prices of all grades are fixed at the closing prices for Monday, September 27. No purchases or sales may be made at other than these prices and no export sales may be made until further notice.

As at Tuesday, September 28, all purchasing of wheat from producers on an open market basis will be discontinued. The Canadian Wheat Board will provide the elevator companies with price lists for country purchases as soon as possible. Meanwhile, wheat may be received into country elevators under established quotas, and pending the establishment of definite initial prices for all grades of wheat on the new basis, advances may be given by the elevator companies.

The action in closing out the 1940-41, 1941-42 and 1942-43 Wheat Board crop accounts at Monday's closing prices will mean that instead of the producer having to wait until the balances of these crops are sold, he will receive a final payment on his deliveries to the Board as soon as the accounting has been completed and the cheques can be issued.

The immediate result of the new initial payments on 1943-44 and 1944-45 deliveries will be a materially higher price to the producer at country elevators. This results both from the increased price, basis in store Fort William-Port Arthur, or Vancouver, and from the reduction of the buying margin at country points.

As a result of this action, the Canadian Government, through the Canadian Wheat Board, will own all unsold stocks of western Canadian wheat, except wheat held by producers on farms. Any losses resulting from the sale of this wheat will be absorbed by the Government. Participation certificates will be issued entitling producers to share in profits, if any, realized on the sale of wheat acquired by the Board from producers during the 1943-44 and 1944-45 crop years.

Mr. MacKinnon explained that the change in wheat policy is necessary because of the unusual circumstances surrounding the marketing of Canadian wheat at the present time. By placing control of the purchase and sale of Canadian wheat in the hands of the Wheat Board, it will be possible to deal with current and future marketing problems on a basis more suitable to war conditions.

Transportation difficulties have interfered with the normal functioning of the Winnipeg wheat market, Mr. MacKinnon pointed out, and farmers have not been able to benefit fully from rising prices. Under this new arrangement, the Government intends to meet requirements under the Mutual Aid plan and to provide wheat to subsidized domestic purchasers out of the Government owned wheat, rather than out of wheat in which the farmer has a participation interest. The Government will thus be able to avoid the position of being both the farmers' agent and, in effect, the ultimate buyer of the wheat. Other export sales, including sales to the United States, will be made out of wheat delivered to the Board during the 1943-44 and 1944-45 crop years, in which producers have a participating interest.[20]

[20]*Trade and Commerce file 20-141-11.*

Because of the intricate detail involved in the take-over regulations, it required Mr. Henry Monk, now serving as counsel to the wheat board, to work out with the justice department law officers the wording of the order in council giving effect to the decision, which was passed on October 12, 1943. While not replacing the wheat board act, particularly in respect of the board's responsibility to sell deliveries from the 1943 and 1944 crops to best advantage, the order had to provide for the acquisition by the crown of producers' wheat remaining in the 1940, 1941 and 1942 accounts and all unsold commercial stocks. It had to provide authority for the termination of trading in wheat futures, and for the delivery of all producers' wheat thenceforth to the board, and it had to fix the initial payment at $1.25 for the 1943 and 1944 crops. The order contained an expiry date of August 1, 1945. But the most interesting part of the order was its preamble, which set out the government's reasons for closing the market. The preamble read:

Whereas by reason of wartime developments it is deemed necessary that the Government of Canada should exercise greater control over the marketing of Canadian wheat so that supplies of wheat and wheat flour may be made available at appropriate prices, as required for domestic use and for shipment abroad to countries in receipt of Mutual Aid;

And whereas under existing financial arrangements with Canadian flour millers and with countries in receipt of Mutual Aid, the Government of Canada has been, in effect, the ultimate buyer of large quantities of wheat and at the same time has been acting through the Canadian Wheat Board as the farmers' selling agent, thus placing dual and opposing responsibilities upon the Government which it is desirable to avoid;

And whereas transportation difficulties and other unusual circumstances have interfered with the normal operation of existing market machinery;

And whereas it is desirable to afford greater certainty to farmers as to prices during the remainder of the crop year 1943-44 and during the full crop year 1944-45 and to reduce the abnormal buying margins at country points that have prevailed on the open market;

And whereas it is therefore considered necessary to make provisions for:-

(1) the discontinuance of wheat trading on the Winnipeg Grain Exchange;

(2) the empowering of The Canadian Wheat Board to acquire for Government account all wheat in commercial positions in Canada in respect of which no contract of sale or agreement for sale of actual wheat or wheat products is outstanding, including wheat held in the 1940-41, 1941-42 and 1942-43 Wheat Board crop accounts on the basis of the closing prices for each grade of wheat on the Winnipeg Grain Exchange on Monday, September 27th, 1943;

(3) the fixing of prices at the closing levels registered on the Winnipeg Grain Exchange on September 27th, 1943, for the closing out of the outstanding open futures contracts in the period before the final clearance thereof;

(4) the discontinuance of export sales of wheat until further notice;

(5) the discontinuance of the purchase of wheat from producers on an open market basis;

(6) the payment to producers delivering wheat to the Board of an initial advance of one dollar and twenty-five cents per bushel basis No. One Manitoba Northern wheat in store Fort William/Port Arthur or Vancouver for the remainder of the crop year 1943-44 from September 28th and for the

full crop year 1944-45, and for the issuance to producers of participation certificates in respect thereof;

(7) the distribution of payments on participation certificates outstanding in the hands of producers in connection with the 1940-41, 1941-42 and 1942-43 crop accounts of the Canadian Wheat Board.

And whereas by reason of the unusual conditions prevailing in the wheat trade and the necessity of avoiding serious disturbance of normal trading therein prior to provision for the foregoing matters being made, it was deemed to be essential in the public interest to issue instructions that immediate steps be taken to carry the foregoing into effect and instructions were so issued on September 28th, 1943; and pursuant thereto such steps were taken. . . .[21]

After providing for the curb on futures trading, the regulations created the crown account made up of the board's unsold stocks and the commercial stocks which were taken over at the closing prices on September 27. The board was required to make crown wheat available, at prices fixed from time to time by the governor in council, to fill domestic and mutual aid requirements in priority over all other wheat held by the board. Carrying charges and the portion of the board's operating expenses attributable to crown account wheat were payable by the account. Eventually any profit or loss on the operation of the account was for the treasury. The producers' interest therein had been closed out by the crown purchase, at September 27 closing prices, of the residual stocks.

Another section of the regulations covered producers' deliveries to the board as from August 1, 1943. The board was required to purchase all such wheat, thereby establishing it as a monopoly board. The initial payment was fixed at $1.25 and the board was instructed to sell all such wheat and for such prices as it considered reasonable. The board was also directed to utilize existing marketing agencies to the extent that they were useful. In practice, all the facilities of the trade continued to be employed, except those of the futures brokers whose services became redundant. In due course representations were made on their behalf to the government to keep the group intact through the emergency, but in the end most or all of the individuals concerned were absorbed into other branches of the trade.

As a footnote to the order in council embodying the government's decision to close the market and to create a monopoly wheat board, the council of the Winnipeg grain exchange took exception to some implications in the preamble of the order which appeared to reflect on the conduct of the exchange in recent months. On the recent price rise, the exchange had performed unquestionably to the producers' benefit. The fact that transportation shortages and labor shortages at the lakehead terminals had interfered with the movement of grain from country elevators to the terminals, thereby prompting the elevator companies to widen their spreads between street and terminal prices, could not be attributed to the exchange. Sensing that the government's decision on futures trading might be an historic one, the council of the exchange enlisted the help of its counsel, Mr. Isaac Pitblado, to draft a letter from the president of the exchange to MacKinnon in the following terms:

Since receipt of Order-in-Council P.C. 7942, a copy of which you kindly forwarded to me on the 15th ultimo, the Council of the Exchange has

[21]*P. C. 7942*, October 12, 1943.

carefully considered the matters therein set forth.

It appears to us that as this Order-in-Council is an historical document which in later years may be referred to before Royal Commissions, Parliamentary Committees, or the Houses of Parliament, or elsewhere, and as it may also be referred to in plans for post-war return to open wheat marketing, it is desirable that there should appear a true picture of conditions existing at the time of its enactment, as well as the full reasons for the Government's action.

We therefore deem it necessary that the following considerations be placed before you and the Government as a matter of record:

(1) In our opinion the preamble does not contain an adequate outline of the reasons by which it is sought to justify such drastic action on the part of the Government. The preamble appears to suggest that the system of marketing, of which the Winnipeg Grain Exchange is the focal point, was not functioning normally. This assumption is entirely wrong.

The market machinery provided by the Winnipeg Grain Exchange was as efficient as it always had been. The failure of transportation and other factors to bring grain steadily to market was certainly no reflection on the marketing machinery.

(2) We protest any idea that the marketing system was responsible for "abnormal buying margins at country points". The system merely reflected abnormal conditions caused by other factors. The difference between the price of grain actually in store at Fort William and the street price available to producers at country points has apparently been interpreted as an "abnormal" buying margin. The fact of the matter is that competition among elevator operators, Pools included, has always assured the farmer being paid at the country point the highest possible price in relation to the price at which the grain so purchased could be shipped to market and sold. The inability of any farmer to realize the full terminal market prices was not the fault of the market or of the market machinery but must be placed squarely on those responsible for transportation difficulties. Because of these transportation difficulties there was no likelihood that wheat purchased at country points in September or October last could be moved to the Head of the Lakes much before the opening of navigation next spring. Moreover, the serious shortage of manpower required for the operation of the terminal elevators at Fort William-Port Arthur (of which no mention is made in the preamble) was a further abnormal condition. These conditions made carrying charges for several months unavoidable. But responsibility therefor cannot be charged to the market machinery or to the marketing system.

(3) Again it is to be regretted that in the preamble it is not clearly stated that one of the main problems of the Government centered on the conflict between (on one hand) that of paying the farmer a price representing the true value of his wheat after several years of low income, and (on the other) of protecting the taxpayer from demands on the Treasury arising out of the drawback to the mills and the Mutual Aid Pact.

(4) In connection with paragraph three of the preamble, we respectfully suggest that the inability of the railroads and the lake carriers to move grain in timely and sufficient volume and the serious shortage of manpower at the elevators (while all due to abnormal causes) cast no reflection whatever on the existing marketing machinery, which was in no way responsible for these abnormal conditions.

(5) Moreover, it is an obvious deduction that one important reason for the Government's action was the threat of inflation—the danger that possible higher prices of wheat would threaten the whole price stabilization plan of the

Government. To make the record complete we feel that this should have been frankly stated in the preamble.

(6) As far as the "open market" is concerned, the fact is that practically all wheat being delivered at the time of the Government's order was not being delivered to the Canadian Wheat Board but was being sold on the open market; which would indicate that the producer was convinced (as we are) that his returns by actual sale under the open market system were the best then available from any source.

These are the considered views of our Council and in submitting them we hope for some action on your part which will be the means of placing on official record a more complete and accurate appraisal of the situation than is at present contained in the preamble to the Order-in-Council.

We would at the same time assure you that insofar as members of the Exchange are concerned the full measure of co-operation which members have given the Government during this war period will continue without interruption, believing as we do that after the war the "open market" system and facilities of the Winnipeg Grain Exchange will be essential to the most efficient marketing of our grain crops.[22]

Unquestionably, the government's basic reason for the creation of a monopoly wheat board was concern over possible inflation in one sector of the economy which threatened the tenure of its wartime price controls. Secondly, the government had been placed on the horns of a dilemma in acting as seller and also as ultimate buyer of most of the producers' wheat. The creation of the crown account, at the expense of closing the market, and the closing out any further producer interest in the balance of the 1940, 1941 and 1942 accounts, had afforded a solution to both problems. Had no action been taken, the board would shortly have been unable to make further offers to the British. Either the latter or the Canadian government on their behalf would have had to make their purchases on the open market. Meanwhile, transportation and labor shortages had interfered with the shipment of wheat to the lakehead, resulting in abnormal spreads between street and terminal prices.

The creation of a monopoly wheat board was a consequence of, but only incidental to, the resolution of these problems. Thus it happened that the pools secured a windfall victory in the government's decision to close the market and to replace it with a monopoly board. The reasons for the decision were unrelated to the pools' advocacy over the years of that type of marketing system.

It was ironic, too, that the Liberal government had come full circle on the wheat marketing policy it had originally embarked upon to get the government out of the wheat marketing business and to terminate the wheat board. Instead of doing so, the government had now gone to the opposite extreme of creating a monopoly board. But this was not because the government had concluded that a monopoly board was the best alternative among marketing systems. Instead, it adopted this policy as a temporary, wartime expedient to resolve the extraordinary issues with which it was immediately confronted.

---

[22]*Minutes of the Council of the Winnipeg Grain Exchange,* November 3, 1943.

35

RECAPITULATION

Looking back upon the span of eight years during which the Liberal administration completed the transition from voluntary to compulsory board in direct opposition to its avowed plans for a permanent wheat policy, one can readily identify the broad phases of that evolution. *Firstly*, there was the liquidation of the government holdings which was an essential prerequisite to getting out of the grain business; *secondly*, came the relapse into prewar surplus conditions when the government decided it was, on balance, in the best interests of the country as a whole to support western farm income as a means of quelling unrest in that part of the country. At the same time, the government tried, unsuccessfully, to revive interest in co-operative marketing as an alternative to the continuation of the wheat board. In the process, however, the government introduced a more equitable method of distributing subsidies by basing payments upon acreage sown as well as upon deliveries. *Thirdly*, after a brief wartime flurry, the wheat surplus position became so aggravated that extraordinary steps had to be taken to curtail production and at the same time to support western farm income. What began with the introduction of delivery permit books and the delivery quota system for the equitable sharing of available storage space was extended to a maximum limitation upon deliveries as a means of curtailing wheat production. Although such a limitation upon deliveries was applied for three crop years only, and was lifted whenever elevator space permitted, delivery quotas became a permanent feature of the marketing system. In providing for income support, the government eventually established a level at which income must be maintained. In doing so, it experimented with various measures including the processing levy, wheat acreage reduction payments and special acreage bonuses. Of all the measures so devised, the one which endured was also one of the earliest, namely, the prairie farm assistance payments on an annual basis in areas where yields were low. Although the maintenance of farm income at a minimum essential level was adopted in principle in 1938 when the 80-cent initial payment was set, it was not until 1941 that a target of $325 million was accepted and sufficient subsidies devised for its maintenance. Although the figure initially set was incredibly low compared with today's income levels, it remains of historical significance that the principle was adopted at that time of supporting western farm income when necessary as a requisite to the welfare of the total Canadian economy. The *fourth* phase in the transition from a voluntary to a compulsory board came with the resurgence of wartime demand for wheat in 1943 resulting in the circumstances (recounted in the last chapter) which prompted the closing of the wheat futures market. In the result, those circumstances combined to leave the government little option but to create a compulsory wheat board in contravention of its earlier intentions to do just the opposite. Within the broad transition, just outlined, there is also a wealth of interesting detail.

While the Canadian wheat board act, 1935, was still in the legislative process, the Liberal opposition and the Winnipeg grain exchange had both exerted sufficient pressure on the outgoing Conservative administration to dissuade it from its original intention of creating a monopoly grain board. The alternative form of voluntary wheat board adopted had enabled the futures marketing system to continue and the trade to offer a market outlet for producers' wheat in competition with the board. After the Liberals were returned to office and appointed the board headed by J. R. Murray, that board used the futures market to good advantage in liquidating the government stocks of wheat. Not only was Murray convinced that the futures system afforded the best marketing alternative, but the Liberal government shared that view and regarded the voluntary wheat board as a temporary institution required for the emergency only. Euler's proposal that the board be liquidated in 1936 revealed how firmly Liberal ministers held that view. Gardiner's determined effort some two years later, with cabinet approval, to persuade the pools to resume co-operative marketing in lieu of a wheat board afforded further corroboration. Until the outbreak of war, the experience gained from the operation of a voluntary board had demonstrated that producers would use it only when open market prices were at or below the level of the board's initial payment; there was no contract between producers and government by which producers obligated themselves to deliver to the board, as they had done with the provincial pools. Therefore, the board was given no opportunity to break even, let alone show a profit for producers on its operating results. The board had wheat delivered to it only when prices were low, and marketing opportunities were limited. Mackenzie King's and Gardiner's conclusion that a voluntary board could operate only at a loss justified its rejection, in principle, as a permanent institution.

But the quest for a permanent marketing policy, which bore a striking resemblance to the status quo prior to the depression, foundered upon the ultimate conviction of the pool leaders first, that they would have difficulty in persuading a majority of producers to enter again into contractual delivery commitments with the pools; second, they were uncertain that as marketers of wheat, they could outperform the futures market and, third, they were now engaged in a profitable elevator operation the financial success of which they were not prepared to jeopardize by resuming the marketing function. Gardiner misjudged the strength of their resistance as he tried to convince the pools in the autumn of 1938 that they should reenter the marketing field. Had Gardiner succeeded in his persuasion, the government could have repealed the wheat board act as it legislated its promised guarantee of the initial payment in a co-operative marketing system. Gardiner also misjudged the mood in the west, particularly in Alberta and Manitoba when, on behalf of Saskatchewan producers prone to low crop yields, he recommended an initial payment as low as 60 cents in combination with acreage payments. The upshot was that the voluntary wheat board was continued in 1939 with a statutory initial payment of 70 cents, plus a system of acreage payments in areas of low yield, and legislation which sought to revive co-operative marketing.

Concurrently with these developments in domestic marketing policy, the United States administration continued to exert pressure upon the Canadian government to cope with the problem of restricted overseas markets on an international basis. This raised the question of market sharing either on a bilateral basis, such as the Americans proposed in 1938, or on an international basis as pursued in the negotiations of 1939 and of 1941-42. Prior to 1939, the Liberal administration had displayed an almost completely negative stance toward the wheat advisory committee which was the legatee of the international wheat agreement Bennett had negotiated in 1933. Although the Canadian government formally supported the continuation of the advisory committee, it did so on condition that it make no findings or forecasts. During the 1939 and 1941-42 meetings the government attitude shifted from opposition to sufferance because it was not prepared to resist the pressures of the British and United States governments, and also because it expected that the talks would break down, without undue reflection upon Canada. On the other hand, if an international agreement were to be reached, it could serve a useful purpose by providing for international price maintenance.

The outbreak of hostilities in 1939 justified the contention of the pools that the wheat board was still required in the continuing emergency, and it also raised anew the question of the closing of the futures market. Although this had long been an object of pool policy, it was incompatible with the Liberal objective of government withdrawal from the wheat marketing field. Thus, against the desire expressed in the British war plans that the Winnipeg futures market be closed simultaneously with that of the Liverpool market on the outbreak of war, the Canadian government resisted that step, which would have entailed creation of a monopoly grain board, as well as direct price negotiations between the two governments. Although the decision not to close the Winnipeg market was greeted with initial dissatisfaction by the British purchasing authorities, which they indicated by withholding purchases in the early autumn of 1939, Crerar and McIvor succeeded in convincing Rank that use of the Winnipeg market was in the best interests of both governments, and the system of bulk purchases of futures evolved. This sufficed until, by 1943, the British had exhausted their loans, the board's stocks were approaching depletion, and a fundamental change in the demand for wheat occurred. Notwithstanding, between 1939 and 1943, the pools continuously recommended the closing of the market, and it remained a contingency step which members of the cabinet wheat committee frequently contemplated through that period.

In the interval between the fall of France and the revival of demand in 1943, the wheat movement experienced one of the most congested periods in Canadian grain handling annals. Loss of access to many markets and a succession of high yields taxed the elevator facilities. These circumstances compelled a series of remarkable innovations in grain policy, including the introduction of the delivery quota system, maximum quotas and wheat acreage reduction payments designed to divert wheat acreage into summerfallow and into the production of more needed coarse grains. This was the first occasion on which the government placed a higher priority on the production of oats and barley than it did on wheat. In adopting the policy innovations, the government displayed an active concern over the level of farm income as wheat remained in an abnormally depressed position in relation to other sectors of the economy. This contrast was highlighted when the general price ceiling policy was introduced. At the time of its announcement, Mackenzie King acknowledged the inequity of the policy in relation to wheat producers and he tried to meet the situation by an increase in subsidies. But, when faced with the issue, the government avoided the political consequences of imposing a price ceiling on western wheat for a period of two years after ceilings were placed upon other commodities. Eventually, the wheat price ceiling issue became entwined with that of closing the market.

Despite Gardiner's optimistic prediction as early as 1940 that the whole of the Canadian wheat surplus would disappear in five years, there appeared to be little realism in his forecast until the wheat position took a fundamental turn in 1943. This was occasioned by the American feed grain shortage in relation to the expanding meat production in that country. The feed grain demand spilled over into wheat for feed use when the United States harvested mediocre crops that year and the agricultural administration called for an expansion of 16 million acres in wheat for the 1944 harvest. By July 1943, the American officials confided to the wheat board that they would need as much as 150,000,000 bushels of Canadian wheat in the crop year just beginning, and they proceeded to organize a transportation program for its movement. While this estimate was both raised and lowered as shipments progressed, the basic shift in demand for Canadian wheat was enough to stimulate Chicago and Winnipeg futures prices to an extent not experienced for many years. The market rise from around 90 cents in March to $1.20 in September, 1943, was enough to place the Canadian anti-inflationary policy in jeopardy, with direct consequences to the treasury which was subsidizing the domestic consumption of wheat in Canada and paying under mutual aid for the wheat requirements of Britain and the USSR. The government's response to its dilemma was to close the market, and the readily identifiable reasons for its action were the preservation of the government's overall price stabilization policy, the implications of mutual aid purchases and the domestic wheat subsidy at direct cost to the Canadian treasury on a rising market, the question of board supplies for mutual aid and domestic sales with no more wheat being delivered to it on a rising market and the transportation and labor shortages.

The position of the wheat pools with respect to the closing of the market was particularly interesting. Mr. J. H. Wesson had expressed the three basic principles of pool policy as early as 1933, to wit: the establishment of a national marketing board, agreement with other exporting countries on export quotas and a fixed price (above the market) on wheat consumed in Canada. The history of the government's participation in the attempts to bring about an international wheat agreement have been documented in detail in this review. The nucleus of a two-price policy for domestic and export wheat was formed in the adoption of the 15-cent processing levy imposed in 1940-41. This first experiment with the system lasted only one crop year. Thereafter consumers got a break when domestic prices were subsidized to the level of the 77⅜ cent price ceiling. But the closing of the futures market and the creation of a compulsory wheat board came as a windfall to the pools, for quite extraneous reasons unrelated to their repeated resolutions that a national board should handle all grains. These resolutions had been unanimously approved by the executive directors of the pools up to 1943, when the Manitoba and Alberta directors broke ranks with those of their Saskatchewan colleagues. In the summer of 1943, Mr. Wesson continued to recommend a national grain board but the Manitoba and Alberta boards demurred at the closing of the market just at that juncture when, for the first time in years, it was unquestionably operating to the direct price advantage of producers.

When the government closed the market, it regarded the action as a wartime measure, supported by the fact that the order in council effecting its decision contained an expiry date of July 31, 1945, thus indicating that futures trading would be suspended for a period of two years. Although the government, under wartime circumstances, had come full circle on its philosophical resistance to the principle of a monopoly wheat board, it reconciled its immediate action with its long term policy by setting an expiry date on the monopoly provisions.

The upsurge in wartime wheat demand which placed a strain upon the government's price stabilization policy and led to the closing of the market was the major turning point in the Canadian wheat position during the war. Until 1943, the wartime wheat policy had been characterized by surplus, low prices, income subsidies, and the encouragement to wheat producers to diversify their production into coarse grains and oilseeds. This was the third of the four phases referred to at the beginning of this chapter. The fourth phase — the resurgence of wartime demand — produced a fundamental change in the wartime outlook for wheat. The $1.25 initial payment plus participation in respect of 1943 and 1944 crop deliveries, and participation payments on the 1940, 1941 and 1942 crop accounts relieved the pressure upon the government to subsidize income. From 1943 forward, the search for storage accommodation to house unexportable surpluses gave way to one of finding transportation to move available wheat supplies to markets anxious to take them. This change in the outlook for wheat introduced a new set of policy considerations which remain to be described in Part IV.

In the transition from voluntary to compulsory board several policy-makers and advisers emerged. The obvious policy-makers, the Honourable W. D. Euler and the Honourable James A. MacKinnon, who served successively as ministers of trade and commerce and therefore as chairmen of the wheat committee of the cabinet, were at the same time perhaps the least influential in their contributions. As a minister representing an Ontario constituency, Euler was not only opposed to government intervention in wheat marketing, but he took the eastern side of the debate, along with Ilsley and others, when the east-west confrontation over wheat policy erupted in Mackenzie King's cabinet. Although Euler had made a persistent and effective stand against Gardiner's encroachment on his administrative jurisdiction over grain matters, Euler was on the point of yielding his responsibility for the board of grain commissioners to Gardiner when, in accordance with his wishes, King appointed him to the senate. His successor, the Honourable James A. MacKinnon, made little or no pretense at assuming the role of wheat-policy maker. Unlike Crerar, Dunning and Gardiner, MacKinnon had no roots in the wheat industry. Therefore, he lacked any position of power or representation which his colleagues on the wheat committee possessed, and MacKinnon's interventions in the policy debates were minimal. On the other hand, he made an effective chairman of the wheat committee and he enjoyed announcing the policy decisions which fell within his administrative responsibility.

In the period covered by Part III, one had to look elsewhere than to Euler and MacKinnon for the effective policy-makers. By this time, the Honourable T. A. Crerar had become something of an elder statesman. Nevertheless, his contributions to policy formation were highly effective when the cabinet was split upon the issues and Crerar quietly pointed the way toward acceptable compromise. Crerar was an effective antidote to Gardiner when the latter's political judgment tended to err. The Honourable Charles A. Dunning also helped to curb the more radical of Gardiner's proposals, and he deserves always to be remembered as author of the proposal for an 80 cent initial payment in 1938, to provide urgently needed western farm income support. His successor as minister of finance, the Honourable J. L. Ilsley made a very effective contribution to the formulation of wheat policy, mostly by way of restraint upon Gardiner, not only in the late thirties when he was still minister of national revenue and championed the eastern side in the east-west confrontation, but as wartime minister of finance when he defended the treasury against Gardiner's more sanguine incursions. Ilsley was by no means an obstructionist; he always displayed a keen, personal interest in the problems and he shared in the search for reasonable compromise.

But as wheat policy evolved in the period under review there was scarcely an occasion when the Honourable James G. Gardiner was not the prime innovator; he stood, figuratively, head and shoulders above his colleagues, in his capacity to influence the final result. As his chief, the Right Honourable W. L. Mackenzie King observed, Gardiner was a "loner" among his colleagues, disliked and distrusted by most, but in that environment he displayed a remarkable capacity for getting his way. As a man who unquestionably believed in his mandate to represent the interests of western farmers in cabinet, despite the niceties of conflicting departmental jurisdictions, Gardiner persistently worked to fulfill his self-proclaimed responsibility. Even if Mackenzie King observed in a moment of exasperation that Gardiner's proposals were usually at the expense of the treasury and with an eye to the next election, this was small opprobrium to bear, considering the justification which existed for the restoration of the prairie provinces as a viable segment of the Canadian economy. Although in later years his political power waned and farmers were prone to remember him for some of his equivocal utterances, western agriculture owes a tremendous debt of gratitude to Gardiner for the leadership he furnished in its cause.

Also a word about Mackenzie King, whose delegation of authority stood in sharp contrast to the Right Honourable R. B. Bennett's day-to-day involvement in wheat administration. When King was in office during the 1920's, the government had withdrawn from wheat marketing and few wheat-policy matters commanded the prime minister's attention. The reverse was true of the Bennett administration in the depression years. When King resumed office, he delegated to a cabinet committee the responsibility for recommending wheat policy. Judging by policy announcements in the press and by wheat debates in parliament, one could readily draw from his few interventions that King's contribution to the policy-making process was minimal. The privy nature of cabinet discussions and the relative lack of cabinet secretarial assistance at that time helped to maintain such an illusion. Thus it is only in King's own references to the key policy decisions, which he recorded in his diary, that his own considerable contributions are revealed. The excerpts from the diary quoted in Part III of this review disclose King's real concern and the influence he exerted upon his colleagues as they reached consensus on the more important decisions, including the 80-cent initial payment in 1938 and the successive income support payments during the early years of the war. When cabinet dissension arose, as it did several times on east-west lines, King's role was decisive in the provision of financial support to the west, even if motivated as King acknowledged, in order to avoid more serious consequences.

Among the policy-advisers, the directors of the three pools enjoyed a renaissance in their influence with the cabinet. Whether coming to Ottawa directly, joining in with the Bracken committee, with the newly organized Canadian federation of agriculture, or with the advisory committee to the wheat board (all of which made their contributions in this period), effective advice on behalf of producers came from the pools under the capable leadership of their executives. Mackenzie King was at all times prepared to receive and welcome the representations of these organizations, however carefully he reserved the government's position on acceptance of their advice. Gardiner had a direct and close working association with the pool leaders. He was by no means dominated by them nor did he act as their spokesman; nevertheless Gardiner made a practice of consulting the pools, regardless of whether he had made up his own mind on policies he would recommend. During this period, Mr. J. H. Wesson emerged as one of the outstanding representatives of the pools. His interventions commanded increasing respect among the cabinet members.

As advisers, Mr. J. R. Murray and his successor as chief commissioner of the wheat board, Mr. George H. McIvor, were outstanding. Murray was an adviser, both before and after his tenure as chief commissioner, and it was because of his tenacious belief that Canadian wheat sales could be increased through the existing marketing mechanism, by the maintenance of realistic premiums in relation to competing wheats, through advertising and direct contacts in restoring confidence in Canadian sales policy on the part of overseas buyers that he was so successful in disposing of the government's wheat accumulation. In the latter stages, Murray's task was aided by the record drought of 1937.

George McIvor succeeded Murray as chief commissioner just when surpluses began to accumulate again. McIvor's marketing experience was a great asset; the cabinet wheat committee's confidence in McIvor grew and the ministers accepted him as their primary adviser. Because of wartime exigencies, the Canadian wheat board was asked to take on a wide range of new administrative activities, most of which were unrelated to the board's primary responsibility for marketing wheat. These included such matters as delivery quotas, the processing levy, the administration of grain price ceilings, the administration of the drawback on wheat used for domestic consumption, the implementation of floor prices for oats and barley, the oats and barley equalization funds, the handling of the flaxseed, soybean, sunflower seed and rapeseed crops for government account, and liaison with the railways on the transportation of grain. The board, in fact, attracted these additional responsibilities because of the confidence it enjoyed among ministers and public alike in its administrative competence. For this a large measure of the credit was due to McIvor himself.

Although many other persons could be mentioned among the category of advisers, including officials such as Norman Robertson and Mitchell Sharp, a special word might be said of Clive B. Davidson and Andrew Cairns. While at the bureau of statistics, Davidson had made his mark with Mr John I. McFarland and had organized the educational campaign on acreage reduction which was mounted by the provincial governments in co-operation with the federal government in 1934. With the formation of the wheat board in 1935, Davidson was appointed secretary but he left that position to work for Premier John Bracken, during which time he organized the conference on western farm markets and wrote the briefs for Bracken's committee. After the outbreak of war, Davidson returned to the wheat board as an executive assistant. His forte was in the preparation of briefs for McIvor's use in presenting the board's position to the cabinet wheat committee. When the advisory committee to the wheat board was reestablished, Davidson provided invaluable assistance to that committee in formulation of policy recommendations, especially for the 1941-42 and 1942-43 crop seasons, when wheat production policy underwent a fundamental reexamination. Davidson was responsible for much of the original thinking behind these policy changes, and he followed the various stages through, not only in the drafting of advisory committee and wheat board recommendations, but in the preparation of speeches, which MacKinnon made in the house to announce decisions, and in the preparation of publicity information for distribution to producers. It is a very easy matter to identify the speeches and unsigned documents which Davidson prepared for others to use. The hallmark of identification of Davidson's authorship is the split infinitive which was done deliberately to provide emphasis (as the author learned when he made a modest attempt to edit his drafts).

By way of contrast, Cairns never split an infinitive. His voluminous documentation prepared for an international audience was written in impeccable style. One might wonder why Cairns should be included in the category of policy-advisers as throughout his career he had no direct contact with any Canadian minister except for his one brief exposure to the Right Honourable R. B. Bennett. The members of the cabinet wheat committee, and Gardiner especially, regarded Cairns at a distance and with outright distrust. Cairns was indeed a consummate operator for the cause he believed in, namely an international agency administering the world's wheat marketing in the place of the trade. However impractical that was, it is incredible how Cairns succeeded in nudging governments at every opportunity toward that goal. In Part III it is set out how Cairns refused to abandon his personal hopes for the negotiation of an international agreement, even after war broke out. Instead, he sought British ministry of food sponsorship for an agency to coordinate all wartime wheat purchasing. In this, Cairns's friends in the ministry of food were opposed by the grain merchants who had been recruited to the cereals import branch, and also by the Canadian government which refused to discuss the Cairns proposal. For a time Cairns served on the staff of the ministry of food and also on that of the ministry of economic warfare. He initiated the British move to draw the United States into a discussion of commodity problems generally and more specifically the wheat problem, which led to the convening of the 1941-1942 Washington wheat meeting. He even had a hand in the drafting of the British instructions. Cairns had a following, not only among British but among American and Australian officials, which he used to advantage in getting meetings convened and in involving willy-nilly the participation of the more reluctant governments. Thus, despite their better judgment, the members of the cabinet wheat committee were drawn into negotiations for an international wheat agreement on two separate occasions in 1939 and in 1941. The 1942 memorandum of agreement which resulted was an interim and stop-gap arrangement at best. But it kept alive the prospect for a postwar international wheat agreement, which was the third goal in the western wheat pools' tripartite wheat policy. Notwithstanding the fact that the type of agreement eventually agreed upon was a far different instrument from the type Cairns had envisaged, the ultimate realization of the pools' objective, and its incorporation into federal government policy was due in no small measure to Cairns's initiative. With the 1942 memorandum of agreement in place, and by 1943 a compulsory wheat board created, the pools had taken a notable step forward in the attainment of their basic wheat policy objectives with the unpremeditated help of the federal government.

IV
ASSURANCE OF MARKETS

36

INTRODUCTORY

The "surplus psychology" which Mr. J. H. Wesson had referred to in 1938 had been hanging over the western wheat industry, almost without respite, since the onset of the great depression. Part II of this review related the surplus of the early thirties to the upsurge of government measures, most of them misguided, which were designed to cope with it, and which culminated in the creation of the wheat board. Even so, the creation of the wheat board had been a controversial issue, supported on the one hand by the pools which sought a market system other than that of the open market, and opposed by the grain trade which championed the futures market. The voluntary wheat board created in 1935 represented a compromise between the extremes of a monopoly system and a completely free market. The Liberal opposition and the grain trade representatives persuaded Bennett to amend his legislation by creating a voluntary wheat board in the place of a compulsory grain board.

In the span of the eight years covered by Part III of this review, the futures market continued to operate and producers, in principle, had a choice between delivering to a government board or selling outright on the open market. The choice was governed, nevertheless, by the relation of the board's initial payment to current market prices. If the initial payment proved to be above the market, all producer deliveries went to the board and the government underwrote the board's losses. If the market ruled above the initial payment, deliveries were sold outright and the board was inactive. Thus the Liberal administration had reason to be dissatisfied with the voluntary wheat board system as it worked out in practice, but which it had supported during the legislative process in 1935.

Part III chronicled the efforts the Liberal government made to restore the pre-depression system of co-operatively organized wheat pools operating in competition with the private trade. It had sought through legislation and the guarantee of floor prices to reactivate the producer pools and thereby to obviate the need for a voluntary wheat board. The government's efforts in that direction had been thwarted, nevertheless, by the reluctance of the provincial pool organizations to resume their own pooling operations, by the return of surplus conditions in 1938 and, finally, by the outbreak of war and the European blockade which created a wheat surplus in western Canada far surpassing that of the depression years.

In its reaction to the return of surplus conditions in 1938, and after the outbreak of war, the government had been forced to modify its wheat policy in a fairly fundamental way, first by making an 80-cent initial payment to supplement western farm income at a time when the issue almost split the cabinet on east-west lines and, in the war years, by the introduction of a wheat acreage reduction program implemented by incentives for the transfer of acreage to other crops and by a maximum delivery quota system. In doing so, the government accepted a figure of $325 million as the level at which it must actively support farm income and several subsidy programs were adopted in succession to maintain income at that level. In the process, not only the government became enveloped by the "surplus psychology", but every organization which made representations to the government on behalf of producers, including the provincial pools, the Canadian federation of agriculture, the Bracken committee, the advisory committee to the wheat board and the government's own economic advisory committee became permeated by the same mental attitude. This was why, for instance, Gardiner's 1940 prediction that the surplus could be eliminated within five years was greeted with almost universal incredulity.

The "surplus psychology" requires to be understood in order that, in turn, it may be appreciated why, in the midst of war, the fear was prevalent that once hostilities ceased and the continental countries could resume their peacetime agricultural pursuits, the spectre of surpluses would return to haunt the market. This fear motivated the governments of the four major exporting countries as they signed the 1942 memorandum of agreement. The roots of such fear were embedded in the recollection of inflation during the first world war and the economic and wheat depression which followed the end of hostilities. The"boom and bust" experience of the first great war and its aftermath had prompted the King government to prevent such a recurrence during World War II. One measure of the effect of the King administration's anti-inflationary policy was that whereas wheat had climbed above $3 in the first war before the exchange decided to terminate futures trading, wheat had only risen from 90 cents to $1.20 in 1943, when the inflationary and fiscal implications of that rise inspired the government to order the market closed and to create a monopoly board, thus abandoning its cherished policy of withdrawal from market intervention.

The revival in demand for wheat which prompted that decision marked the major turning point in the wartime wheat position. It helped other people to see, as Gardiner had, that there could be an end to the surplus. In the light of that prospect, the "surplus psychology" waned (without altogether disappearing) as the quest for available storage space was replaced by a search for available transportation to fill the urgent market demand. A parallel shift took place as final payments were made on deliveries to the board from the 1940, 1941 and 1942 crops, and the payments replaced the need for special subsidies which had been devised to maintain farm income. Now that the wheat industry could stand on its own feet, ministers, officials and advisory bodies alike were caught up in the drive to get wheat moving in step with the successful prosecution of the war.

The changed psychological outlook received an appreciable impetus from peripheral bodies concerned with the period of reconstruction after the war.

The Atlantic charter of 1941, even in the generality of its terms, inspired an idealism and charisma in the contemplation and shaping of the postwar world. That idealism was translated into more tangible form by the Hot Springs conference on food and agriculture in May, 1943, which led to the creation of the food and agriculture organization of the United Nations, and also by the conferences which led to the creation of the United Nations itself. Hard on the heels of the Hot Springs conference came the Atlantic City conference of November, 1943, which resulted in the creation of the United Nations relief and rehabilitation administration, more commonly known as UNRRA. That organization, in turn, took over the implementation of the wheat relief commitments of the five governments which had signed the 1942 memorandum of agreement.

Within Canada, planning for the war's end had begun almost from the outbreak of war. In December, 1939, a special committee of the cabinet was formed to study and report upon problems of demobilization and rehabilitation of the armed forces. The cabinet committee forthwith created a general advisory committee of civil servants and others, and subcommittees were formed to examine, in detail, the various phases of the problem. By February, 1941, the assignment was broadened from that of demobilization to include all phases of reconstruction. A committee on reconstruction was formed under the chairmanship of Dr. F. Cyril James, principal of McGill University, and several subcommittees were named including one on agricultural policy under the chairmanship of Mr. D. G. McKenzie, formerly vice-president of United Grain Growers Limited and by then chief commissioner of the board of grain commissioners. The members of that subcommittee included the Honourable J. E. Brownlee, former premier of Alberta; Mr. Paul Farnalls, a director of the United farmers of Alberta and a member of the wheat board advisory committee; Mr. J. S. McLean, president of Canada Packers Limited; Senator Norman Lambert, Dr. W. D. McFarlane of McGill University, and several civil servants (including the author).

The subcommittee's terms of reference encompasssed the domestic and export problems of Canadian agriculture generally, but its contribution in the area of grain policy was not too imaginative (and for that shortcoming the author must accept his share of the responsibility). The subcommittee identified the main problem in the area of trade relations, in which restrictive practices had plagued the grain trade prior to the war. It therefore recommended liberalization of restrictive trade practices as a basic principle of postwar reconstruction. The report recommended that Canada, as an interested and substantial food exporter, should take the lead in pursuit of such a policy, but the subcommittee was ill-equipped to implement that recommendation. More specifically, the committee recommended that by international negotiation Canada should endeavour to have wheat made a free-trade commodity throughout the world. Mr. Paul Farnalls sponsored the idea both in the wheat board advisory committee and in the subcommittee on agricultural policy. Secondly, the subcommittee recommended that the government establish a national wheat marketing council to promote increased exports of wheat and wheat products. It was suggested that the council be financed initially by the government, and thereafter by a levy of not more than one half of one percent on the value of wheat exported.[1] This recommendation was a revival, in somewhat modified form, of the proposal for a Canadian wheat institute advanced by United Grain Growers Limited in 1933.[2] Out of his years of association with that company, the chairman of the subcommittee, Mr. D. G. McKenzie, commended the proposal for inclusion in the report of the subcommittee.

Yet despite the changed environment of a solvent wheat economy in Canada and the attendant interest in anticipating and providing for postwar reconstruction, the concern remained among producers, their representatives and government ranks that wheat surplus conditions would return sooner or later after the end of the war. This concern was expressed through resolutions of the pool central agency and of the Canadian federation of agriculture which sought a system of floor price guarantees at the end of the war. In the bargaining which had taken place between Gardiner and Ilsley over the terms on which the futures market should be closed, Gardiner had suggested a quid pro quo in the form of floor price guarantees for wheat in the transitional period after the war.

Such assurances materialized two years later when, at the end of the war, Mr. Ilsley and one of his key advisers, Mr. Donald Gordon, chairman of the wartime prices and trade board, feared the consequences an international rise in wheat prices would have on the Canadian economy which was still effectively contained by wage, price and profit controls. In September 1945, the government decided to impose, unilaterally, an export price ceiling on wheat of $1.55, in return for which Gardiner secured the concession of a government floor-price guarantee of $1 per bushel over a five-year transitional period. That policy decision, in turn, directly affected the issue whether the open market system should then be restored. It also set in train a chain of developments by which the government attempted, through the international wheat agreement negotiations and the conclusion of a bilateral wheat contract with the United Kingdom, to transfer to the wheat importing countries a share of the responsibility for implementation of the floor price.

The quest for such assurance of markets, which is the theme of this fourth and final part of the review, stemmed directly from the fears of producer and government representatives alike that surplus conditions and low prices would eventually recur. At issue was the marketing system which should survive at the war's end, because each step, such as the guarantee of floor prices and the conclusion of a bilateral wheat contract with Britain, became a justification, in turn, for the retention of a monopoly wheat board. As the private trade saw its hopes vanishing for restoration of the futures market it became critical not only of the government's policies, but it carried its cause to the producers by means of an extensive advertising campaign directed against its old adversaries, the provincial wheat pools. Thus the great debate between the trade and the pools which had been joined with the onset of the depression, but which had been quiescent during the war years, was renewed with fresh vigor at the end of the war. It persisted as the pools pressed for the inclusion of coarse grains in the monopoly board system. It

[1]Advisory Committee on Reconstruction, *I. Agricultural Policy, Final Report of the Subcommittee*, December 16, 1943, p. 4.
[2]See pp. 327-330 and p. 470.

was intensified, but never resolved to the mutual satisfaction of the contending factions, by the implementation of the bilateral contract and the final disposition of the five-year wheat pool. In due course, the bilateral contract was expanded into a multilateral contract for the purchase and sale of wheat exemplified by the international wheat agreement of 1949. The intimate interrelation between the bilateral contract and its conversion into a multilateral agreement produced one of the fascinating passages in the history of Canadian trade relations.

Before embarking, however, on an account of the mainstream of events which followed the end of the war, it is necessary, first, to complete the record of the transition from Part III to Part IV. What transpired by way of annual policy changes from the closing of the market in 1943 to the end of the war reflected the marked change in the demand for wheat and the resulting liquidation of the surplus without, at the same time, erasing the memory of earlier market instability. Thus, Part IV begins with an account of the policy recommendations and decisions from 1943 to the end of the war.

37

GOVERNMENT GRAIN PROGRAMS TO THE END OF THE WAR

To underline the changed tempo of the grain movement which occurred during the 1943-44 crop year, some mention of the total grain movement is in order. In its annual report for that crop year, the wheat board furnished the following comparative figures on the disappearance of commercial stocks:

	Wheat	Oats	Barley	Rye	Flax	Total
			(million bushels)			
1939-40	241	40	23	3	1	308
1940-41	273	34	22	4	3	336
1941-42	280	33	26	7	5	351
1942-43	270	92	63	4	9	438
1943-44	428	136	91	9	15	679

These figures included grain moving commercially into domestic use and export. Wheat and flour exports in 1943-44 totalled 343.8 million bushels of which 160 million moved to the United States. Exports of oats and barley to the United States totalled 65 and 33 million bushels respectively. Barley exports were mainly of malting quality because the feed grades were needed in eastern Canada.

TRANSPORTATION ARRANGEMENTS

From August to December, 1943, the railways loaded 134,000 cars, which was nearly double the rate of loadings a year earlier. By late October when it had become evident that there would not be enough grain at the lakehead to utilize the lake shipping tonnage available before the close of navigation, Mr. Lockwood's emergency grain transportation committee mounted an emergency shipping program which attained the desired results. At that, only nine million bushels of grain were left in lakehead terminals when navigation closed. The emergency program was extended into the winter season to replenish the lakehead stocks, to move feed grains east all-rail from the lakehead as well as directly from western shipping points. Meanwhile, United States boxcars continued to be supplied for the loading of grain at country points for direct consignment to the United States. In addition, the Americans scheduled shipments through Vancouver for their west coast requirements and also through the lakehead for their deficit-feeding areas in the east. A detailed description of the wheat movement to the United States, together with the prices being received, was furnished by MacKinnon to the house on February 14, 1944:

> I wish to inform the house that the United States war food administration, through the commodity credit corporation, is making tentative plans to import 175,000,000 bushels of wheat from Canada during 1944. Of this total, 40,000,000 bushels are intended to be moved by rail direct in United States cars from western country points, 30,000,000 bushels by vessel from Vancouver and other Pacific ports, and 105,000,000 bushels by lake during the 1944 season of navigation.
>
> I wish to emphasize that this is a tentative programme and subject to change in the light of transportation developments and war food administration needs. Purchases by the commodity credit corporation are being made from time to time in amounts broadly corresponding to the quantities for which firm transportation commitments can be made.
>
> With respect to the rail movement, between the dates December 13, 1943 and February 10, 1944, inclusive, the Canadian Wheat Board has sold 10,269 cars (approximately 18,000,000 bushels) of wheat for shipment all rail from country elevators in Manitoba, Saskatchewan and Alberta to destinations in the United States. Of this total, 9,419 cars have been or will be shipped from country elevators in Manitoba and Saskatchewan and 850 cars from country elevators in Alberta.
>
> Since December 13, 1943, United States railways have delivered to Canadian railways a total of 5,561 freight cars owned by the United States railways for the transportation of this wheat. Additional United States cars are being delivered daily at border points to the Canadian lines by United States railways. The volume of future all rail sales to the United States will be largely governed by the number of additional United States cars delivered.
>
> Prices asked for such wheat by the Canadian Wheat Board from December 13, 1943, to February 10, 1944, have ranged between low points for the grades of one, two and three northern of $1.41, $1.38 and $1.36 per bushel, respectively, and high points of $1.47, $1.44 and $1.42 for the same grades, all basis in store Fort William Port Arthur. These sales have been made from day to day and have been within these price ranges, net to the Canadian Wheat Board basis in store Fort William.[1]

To program the grain movement from the opening of navigation to the end of the crop year on July 31, Mr. Lockwood convened a meeting of the emergency grain transportation committee in Winnipeg on April 12, 1944. Throughout the crop year, the wheat board continued to exercise direct control over the allocation of cars to country elevators in order to ensure that the required grain was moved in accordance with the transportation program.

PARTICIPATION PAYMENTS

Although P. C. 7942, of October 18, 1943, had provided authority for participation payments on the 1940, 1941 and 1942 crop accounts, the wheat board encountered some administrative problems in getting the payments under way. A law suit had been entered against the board seeking an accounting of the distribution of board sales among the three crop accounts, which was eventually circumvented by the fixing of the participation payment amounts by order in council. Because the board had kept no record of the issuance of participation certificates to individuals, it

[1] *House of Commons Debates,* February 14, 1944, pp. 433-434.

requested certificate holders to make application for payment to the board. In the main, the applications were returned to the board by the end of March, 1944. At the time, Mr. George W. Robertson, secretary of the Saskatchewan wheat pool, had questioned the propriety of charging the board's expenses for the operation of its acreage, delivery quota and transportation departments which had concerned the delivery of all grains to the wheat crop accounts. McIvor presented the issue to the cabinet wheat committee on March 25, 1944, and, in Ilsley's absence, Sharp acknowledged that these costs should more appropriately be borne by the treasury as they embraced board operations undertaken to implement the government's comprehensive grain policy. With these administrative details settled, MacKinnon was able to announce through a press release on April 15 that the basic participation rates, basis No. 1 Northern, and the anticipated total payments would be as follows:

Crop Account	Cents per Bushel	Deliveries to Board (million bushels)	Total Payments
1940	6⅜	395.3	$25,400,000
1941	14⅞	99.5	14,800,000
1942	11¼	162.5	18,800,000
			$59,000,000

When the board's accounting was completed, the total payment figure rose to $61 million. Payments commenced in April, 1944 on the 1940 crop, in advance of seeding operations, but the rate of payments proceeded slowly. By July 31, 1944, slightly less than half of the 1940 crop payments had been made, and the payments on the 1941 and 1942 crop accounts had not yet commenced. By the end of the calendar year, 1944, the main payments had been made. Considerable balances remained outstanding, however, by July 31, 1945, when the wheat board report disclosed that $7.7 million had not yet been paid out, primarily because of the difficulty in tracing the owners of the certificates, many of whom had moved and disappeared.

In addition to the wheat participation payments, there were also payments due on the oats and barley equalization funds, over and above the advance amounts paid. On the 1942 crop oats and barley accounts a surplus of $18,269 on oats and $452,481 on barley remained payable to producers. These payments were authorized by order in council on June 1, 1943. The 1943-44 oats account resulted in a surplus of $8.8 million and the barley account for that year ran into a deficit of $1.9 million which was borne by the treasury. The oats surplus due to producers was paid out in the 1944-45 crop year. The total wheat participation and oats and barley payments of $71.5 million which represented monies due to producers out of the profits realized by the wheat board from the sale of their products, compared very favorably with the subsidies paid out over a period of the previous five years under prairie farm assistance, the 1941 income supplement and wheat acreage reduction. On April 24, 1944, Gardiner reported in answer to a question the total bonus payments which had been made from their inception up to February 29, 1944: [2]

---

[2] *Ibid.*, April 24, 1944, p. 2275.

	Manitoba	Saskat- chewan	Alberta	Prairie Provinces
		(thousand dollars)		
Prairie Farm Assistance	$ 1,558	$27,130	$ 6,375	$ 35,063
Prairie Farm Income	2,993	10,321	5,681	18,995
Wheat Acreage Reduction	12,046	44,950	24,021	81,017
	$16,597	$82,401	$36,077	$135,075

1944 POLICY RECOMMENDATIONS

The small number of recommendations from the advisory agencies respecting 1944 policy reflected their satisfaction with the policy decisions of September 27, 1943. The degree of their gratification was expressed in the directors' report of Canadian Co-operative Wheat Producers Limited:

Your Board received the announcement of this new policy with great satisfaction, for it represents the culmination of some years of persistent recommendation by the Pools and the Canadian Federation of Agriculture. Ever since the beginning of the war we have urged that the marketing of wheat should be assumed as a national responsibility and regulated in such manner as to make it definitely a part of the nation's war effort. Indeed, before the outbreak of war, with the growing wheat surpluses and the accompanying hedging pressure on the market, the Pools urged upon the Wheat Sub-committee of the Cabinet at a meeting on June 14th, 1938, that a wheat crisis was impending, and that the Wheat Board should be authorized to take delivery of all wheat.

On May 10th, 1940, a delegation from the Canadian Federation of Agriculture was received by the government and presented a memorandum in which, among other things, it was recommended that "the control and marketing of all Canadian wheat should be placed in the hands of the Canadian Wheat Board."

From that date onwards the Pools have persistently and consistently recommended the policy now adopted by the government. We have urged increases in the initial payment and suggested, as this report will show, that the conditions warranted an increase as high as $1.20 but, inasmuch as we could not possibly know as much about the actual situation and the prospects as the federal government, we did not press the $1.20 figure but remained with our repeated request for $1.00, plus, of course, participation certificates. We also asked for a cut-off on previous crop deliveries and for a final payment on the deliveries from those crops. The adoption of this new policy by the government is a complete vindication of the attitude of the organized farmers, towards the wheat problem and its connection with the war effort and, though it comes late and only after strong efforts by the farmers themselves, this recent action by the Dominion Government, taken in conjunction with other concessions made to the agricultural producers, is evidence of the increasing prestige of the organized farmers.[3]

Thus, when the directors of the central agency met with the western agricultural conference on January 21-22, 1944, in the annual meeting of Canadian federation of agriculture on January 27-29, and in the annual presentation of federation recommendations to the prime minister and his cabinet on February 3, 1944, they had nothing to say beyond placing on record their formal approval of the government's wheat policy, and then

[3]Canadian Co-operative Wheat Producers Limited, *Directors' Report 1942-1943*, pp. 63-64.

they turned their attention toward coarse grains. The federation's presentation to the cabinet contained a recommendation that the wheat board be made the sole marketing agency for coarse grains, and that initial payments be based upon the ceiling prices plus the advance equalization payments. For oats and barley, this would have meant initial payments of 61½ cents and 79¾ cents, respectively.[4]

As a carryover of the wheat "surplus psychology", the dominion-provincial agricultural conference of December, 1943, recommended that the area sown to wheat in 1944 remain unchanged from the 1943 level of 17.5 million acres. The recommendation appeared to reflect Gardiner's concern that the wheat surplus should be expeditiously eliminated. The wheat board advisory committee, most of whose members attended the conference, met immediately afterward in Ottawa on December 8-9, 1943, and expressed genuine concern over the advice which had been given to continue restricted wheat production. The wheat board also shared this view that there should be an increase in 1944 wheat acreage to assure continuing wheat supplies during the period of relief and reconstruction. At that time, the wheat board sought to revise the acreages used in its delivery permit system on a station-average basis and to raise the total authorized acreage by 10 per cent over the area sown in 1943. In its report to the cabinet wheat committee, the advisory committee recommended both that the 1944 wheat area be raised by 10 per cent and that for the balance of the current 1943-44 delivery year, the maximum delivery quota be raised from 14 to 18 bushels per authorized acre.

These recommendations were reviewed by the cabinet wheat committee at its meeting on January 10, 1944. The ministers were apprehensive, however, lest any official statement recommending an increase in wheat acreage might induce producers to over-respond. But with the current disposition of wheat promising to exceed by a considerable margin the 280 million bushels represented by the 14 bushel maximum delivery quota, MacKinnon announced on February 3, a few days after the 1944 parliamentary session opened, that the Canadian wheat board regulations were being amended to permit the delivery of 18 bushels per authorized acre.[5]

Shortly after that announcement, Gardiner disclosed during a discussion of his departmental estimates that the government would discontinue wheat acreage reduction payments commencing with the 1944 crop.[6] From Gardiner's statement, producers could infer that the government was not prepared to pay a price for maintenance of wheat acreage at the previous year's reduced level and that, accordingly, some increase in acreage was in order.

When the wheat board advisory committee met again in April, 1944, Mr. Clive Davidson presented a paper in which he encouraged the committee to recommend that the government publicly acknowledge the changed wheat position and give some encouragement to the expansion of production, such as assuring producers that there would be no maximum delivery quota

[4]*Ibid.*, p. 68.
[5]*House of Commons Debates*, February 3, 1944, p. 138.
[6]*Ibid.*, February 18, 1944, p. 638.

imposed on deliveries in the 1944-45 crop year. The committee endorsed Davidson's proposals and approved the following report to the chairman of the cabinet wheat committee:

> The Advisory Committee desires to emphasize once again the important change which has taken place in the grain situation in Canada during the past year. For almost a year the demand for Canadian grain has been rising and stocks of Canadian grain are disappearing at a rate far beyond prospective replacement. There is every prospect that 1944 production and accumulated stocks of Canadian wheat will go into consumption before the end of 1944-45 and there will be a difficult supply position during the first six months of 1945. The fact of the matter is that as far as wheat is concerned we have emerged from the position where available supplies pressed heavily upon limited demand during the early years of the war into a position where the wheat problem of the next year will be largely in terms of receiving and transporting enough wheat to supply the market.
>
> In the opinion of the Advisory Committee the grain supply position in Canada in the face of the current demand is such that a full acreage should be sown to grains throughout Canada in 1944.
>
> In view of these circumstances, the Advisory Committee urgently recommends to the Dominion Government that a complete and authoritative statement be issued forthwith, explaining the present grain situation in Canada, the extent of current demand and the prospective market for Canadian grain during the next twelve months. The Dominion Government and other agencies, including the Advisory Committee, did their full share in publicizing the difficult wheat situation in the two past crop years and the controls which were necessary. The wheat situation during those years and the necessary controls, were accepted generously by the producers of western Canada. Now that the wheat situation has reversed itself, the Advisory Committee is of the opinion that producers are entitled to all the facts of the present position prior to the seeding of 1944 crops. Such a statement should not only contain reference to the essential facts in the wheat situation, but also reference to the supply of, and demand for, other grains. . . .[7]

The report continued by recommending immediate lifting of overall quota restrictions on deliveries in the 1943-44 crop year. In respect of deliveries in 1944-45, the committee recommended that maximum deliveries be related to domestic and export demand which was then estimated at 425 million bushels. While such a figure would permit very large deliveries in 1944-45, the committee did not urge that the question of limitation on deliveries for the oncoming crop year should be determined at that moment, so long as the principle of accepting deliveries to meet the domestic and export demand was openly recognized.

In turn, the government responded to the advisory committee's recommendation by authorizing MacKinnon to make the first official announcement of the changed wheat position. It also acted upon the advisory committee's recommendation to keep its option open on the maximum amount of wheat for which it would accept delivery in 1944-45 as it recognized the principle of accepting deliveries to the full extent of market demand. Mr. MacKinnon said:

> Mr. Speaker, I desire at this time to make a brief statement in connection with some aspects of the 1944-45 grain policy.

[7] *Report of the Advisory Committee to the Honourable James A. MacKinnon, Minister of Trade and Commerce,* April 17, 1944.

The house will recall that last September a major change was made in wheat policy and a basis was established, effective until July 31, 1945, which of course includes the full crop year 1944-45. At that time the fixed initial price of wheat was increased to $1.25 per bushel for No. 1 northern wheat in store, Fort William, Port Arthur or Vancouver. This fixed initial price will be in effect for the coming crop year.

In regard to the wheat policy for 1944-45, the government has yet to determine the quantity of wheat which will be marketable in that crop year. Members will recall that for 1943-44 the limitation was first placed at fourteen bushels per authorized acre and was later increased to eighteen bushels per authorized acre — the understanding being that about 280,000,000 bushels of wheat would be marketable in western Canada during the present crop year.

The government is not prepared at the moment to state the exact quantity of wheat which will be marketable in the coming crop year, owing to the uncertainties of the growing crop and uncertainty in respect to the volume of transportation which will be available for the movement of grains in 1944-45. In establishing the basis of marketings for the coming crop year, which will be announced at a later date, the government will take into account probable domestic and export demand in 1944-45 as well as the volume of grain which the railroads and elevators can handle during the crop year.

I can say at this time that the demand for grain both in Canada and for export is now running at very high levels and that the volume of wheat which will be marketable in 1944-45 will be considerably larger than the limitation in effect during the past two crop years.

I might refer briefly to the present grain position. Accumulated stocks of wheat are moving rapidly into consumption here and abroad and the main problem to-day is meeting demand with the transportation which is available for the movement of grain. It is estimated that the carryover of wheat next July will amount to about 330,000,000 bushels as compared to over 600,000,000 bushels last July. Given adequate transportation the crop year 1944-45 will see our wheat stocks reduced to a nominal figure. Oats and barley are in good demand and there will be no difficulty in disposing of surpluses from the 1944 crop. The expansion in the acreage seeded to these grains in recent years has been more than justified by marketings and the Department of Agriculture is urging that seeding of at least as great an acreage as in 1944.

The government's policy in regard to oats and barley for 1944-45 will be the same as in 1943-44. Minimum prices for these grains will be guaranteed on the same basis as in 1943-44. Equalization funds will again operate and the government will make advance payments free from the equalization funds at the time of delivery. The advance payments are ten cents per bushel for oats and fifteen cents per bushel for barley.

The government has already announced that there will be a guaranteed price for flax of $2.75 per bushel for No. 1 CW flax, basis in store Fort William and Port Arthur or Vancouver. This represents an increase of twenty-five cents per bushel over the guaranteed price in effect in 1943-44.

Respecting sunflower seed and rape seed the government's policy for the 1944-45 crop year is to continue in effect the prices for these seeds established for the 1943-44 season. That is to say, the Canadian wheat board will be authorized to pay five cents per pound for sunflower seed and six cents per pound for rape seed, delivered f.o.b. shipping points to be designated by the board for the top grades.[8]

[8]*House of Commons Debates*, April 27, 1944, p. 2374.

Even with this announcement, Mr. J. H. Wesson, a member of the advisory committee, was not satisfied that producers had been adequately advised. Current private surveys of acreage intentions had shown a successive diminution in producers' intentions to increase wheat acreage to which Wesson reacted by issuing a press statement on May 10, on behalf of the Saskatchewan wheat pool, which took the government to task for not advising producers more candidly about the changed wheat position. Wesson's statement was quoted in hansard as follows:

> The farmers are now in the middle of seeding and we believe they should have the latest information regarding the wheat situation. We also believe they should be frankly advised of the necessity of substantially increased wheat acreage this spring before it is too late. We had hoped that before this eleventh hour a definite statement with final advice would have been made either by the dominion Minister of Agriculture or the Minister of Trade and Commerce. The last statement on production for 1944 was made from Ottawa following the production conference held in Ottawa last December, and the farmer was advised not to increase wheat acreage. The wheat situation has changed from one of large available supplies pressing heavily upon limited demand into a position where the wheat problem next year will be largely in terms of receiving and transporting enough wheat to supply the market.
>
> The wheat glut is gone — our concern now should be a possible shortage in supply in the event of a short crop or crop failure. (We recommend) to farmers as a sound policy for 1944 production:
>
> 1. Make provision for necessary feed grain requirements with some surplus.
> 2. Get back to normal summer-fallow acreage to fit sound farming practice on each farm.
> 3. Sow every available acre to wheat with assurance that every bushel of wheat produced is going to be needed.[9]

In the combination of MacKinnon's and Wesson's statements, producers responded with a 36-percent increase in the 1944 wheat acreage over its wartime low point in 1943. It was not until May 29, 1944, however, that MacKinnon announced that the 18-bushel limitation on wheat deliveries had been removed from deliveries in the 1943-44 crop year. In explanation of the decision, MacKinnon said:

> As members of the house know, during the past year the demand for Canadian wheat, both at home and abroad, has increased substantially. To date in the present crop year, commercial disappearance of Canadian wheat has amounted to about 350,000,000 bushels, as compared with 213,000,000 bushels for the same period last year. We conservatively estimate that commercial disappearance of Canadian wheat for the crop year 1943-44 will amount to 425,000,000 bushels, as compared with 270,000,000 bushels during 1942-43. From August 1, 1943, to May 19, 1944, producers in the prairie provinces marketed 230,000,000 bushels of wheat, or 120,000,000 bushels less than commercial demand for Canadian wheat during the crop year to date.
>
> The Canadian wheat board carefully surveyed remaining farm stocks in the prairie provinces and estimate that producers will market about 265,000,000 bushels of wheat under the eighteen-bushel limitation, and about 305,000,000 bushels if the restriction on deliveries is removed for the balance of the crop year. In other words, with the restriction on deliveries removed for the balance of the crop year, marketings during the present crop year will still

[9]*Ibid.,* June 29, 1944, p. 4378.

remain about 120,000,000 bushels less than commercial disappearance for the crop year.

Available storage space in country elevators has been increasing rapidly in recent months, and at the present time there is over 100,000,000 bushels of space available for the immediate delivery of grain in the three prairie provinces, and grain is being shipped out of country elevators at a rapid rate.

The government's decision removing the restriction on the marketing of wheat for the balance of the crop year is therefore based upon a careful appraisal of domestic and export demand and the storage situation which now exists in western Canada.[10]

Although this announcement marked, in fact, the end of the maximum delivery limitation program which had been introduced in 1941, the government's undertaking in lifting the maximum quota restriction was given for only the remainder of the 1943-44 crop year. Authority to impose a maximum delivery quota at 14 bushels per authorized acre was retained by order in council and by legislation as a standby measure. As will be seen shortly, the government was much more exercised a year later over the level of wheat acreage influenced by the diminished volume of wheat exported to the United States and by its desire that Canada enter the transition from war to peace without a wheat surplus. In the process, resort was made to the government's authority to impose a maximum delivery limitation. Such a warning was made prior to seeding, but was withdrawn in the midst of the harvest.

When MacKinnon reported to the house on August 5, 1944, the initial delivery quotas which had been set by the wheat board for the 1944-45 crop year, he indicated that quotas would be raised when elevator space permitted as had been done in previous years, but he avoided any reference to an upper limit on quotas in the 1944-45 crop year, or to the fact that the authority to impose a maximum limitation still remained.[11]

1945 POLICY RECOMMENDATIONS

Now that the wheat export movement to the United States had declined and Canada was once again dependent upon overseas export markets for the bulk of its wheat exports, the official mood was one of reserve and caution regarding the wheat outlook lest a burdensome surplus be created again.

This attitude was reflected in the dominion-provincial agricultural conference which was held in Ottawa, December 4-6, 1944, and which was much more concerned about the increasing difficulty experienced in filling Canadian meat contracts with Britain than it appeared to be over the need to fill the existing and prospective demand for wheat. The committee, with C. F. Wilson as chairman, which prepared the recommendations on field crop acreages, took account of the continuing high rate of feed grain demand in Canada by recommending increases of 12 percent and 10 percent, respectively, in the areas sown to oats and barley. For wheat, the recommendation was an 8 percent decrease from the 22,444,000 acres sown in the prairies in 1944 to 20,700,000 acres for 1945. Support for such a small wheat acreage reduction came from Wilson's prediction that wheat exports

[10]*Ibid.*, May 29, 1944, p. 3307.
[11]*Ibid.*, August 5, 1944, p. 5969.

in the 1944-45 crop year would amount to 350 million bushels, and that a similar rate of exports could be anticipated in 1945-46. This forecast was based upon the allocations established by the cereals committee of the combined food board and upon our ability to meet that demand on the basis of the Canadian transportation programs which had been set up by the emergency grain transportation committee. However accurate that forecast turned out to be, it was regarded at the time by other officials, especially those directly concerned with livestock feeding, as being much too optimistic. One suggestion advanced during the conference was that the board's initial payment of $1.25 should apply to deliveries in 1945-46 of only 230,000,000 bushels, and that producers having more than their maximum quota to sell should take their chances on an open market.[12] At the end of the conference, Mr. Gardiner declared that now was the time to reduce wheat production and the carryover, and thereby to put Canada in a better position to discuss markets and prices after the war.

In January, 1945, it fell the turn of the western farm conference (the western wing of the Canadian federation of agriculture) and the federation itself, to formulate policy recommendations for the coming crop year. Mr. Gardiner attended the federation meeting and he called for a reduction of from two to three million acres in wheat. He failed to persuade Mr. Wesson, however, who was opposed to any reduction. In the meetings which extended through January 15-20, recommendations were drawn up and presented, in turn, by the federation to the prime minister and members of the cabinet on February 23, 1945. The federation placed its main emphasis upon the need for a permanent food policy including floor price supports. The government had already anticipated that demand by enacting standby legislation embodied in the agricultural prices support act, 1944. The act had established a fund of $200 million for the maintenance of floor prices on all agricultural products, other than wheat, during the transitional period from war to peace, when it was expected that Canada's food contracts with Britain would diminish or expire.

In respect of grains, the federation recommended continuation of the initial payment for wheat at not less than $1.25, with an assurance of deliveries of not less than 280 million bushels, the marketing of oats, barley and flaxseed by the wheat board, and acceptance by the international wheat council that the Canadian delivery quota system would satisfy any international obligation to reduce wheat acreage. These recommendations were set out in detail as follows:

> In the field of grain marketing, we present for your earnest consideration, the following recommendations which were unanimously endorsed by our annual meeting:
> That the Canadian Wheat Board be continued as the sole marketing agency for wheat, and that an initial payment of not less than $1.25 per bushel for wheat for the 1945 and 1946 crops be established;
> That the Wheat Board be instructed to take delivery of all wheat that can be marketed each year, subject to the provision of a minimum delivery of not less than 280 million bushels;
> That the quota system be applied to growers on an equitable basis;
> That, with respect to coarse grains, the Wheat Board be the sole marketing

---

[12] *Winnipeg Free Press,* December 5-6, 1944.

agency for these grains, that the present ceiling on oats and barley be established as the initial payment; that the present equalization payments on these grains be maintained so long as the present policy with respect to furnishing of feed grains to the east is in force;

That the Wheat Board be the sole agency for the marketing of flax and that the Board's paying price for flax be $3.24 per bushel.

In the organization of world trade in wheat, as provided in the international wheat agreement, it is sought to prevent production of wheat in excess of the effective demand. It is our belief that the attempt to regulate the acreage sown to wheat is not the most effective method of regulating production, because of the uncertainty of harvest yields from year to year; rather do we believe that a more effective method is the regulation of the volume actually coming upon the market, by restricting deliveries, and retaining unmarketable wheat upon the farm.

We therefore present the following recommendation for the International Wheat Committee:

That the regulation of supply under the International Wheat Agreement, an exporting Nation be given the right to regulate its marketed volume by applying the quota system of deliveries from the farm, and requiring retention upon the farm of unmarketable wheat, as an alternative to compelling a reduction in the acreage sown; that when a minimum world price is set, it should be on a level which will establish a proper value for this important food commodity.[13]

Next, it fell the turn of the wheat board advisory committee to consider its recommendations. At the committee's meeting held in Saskatoon February 5-6, 1945, the main preoccupation of its members was with the method by which wheat acreage reduction should be encouraged. One alternative considered was the reduction of the initial payment to $1; the other was rigid enforcement of a maximum delivery quota. Producer members held that farmers would not accept delivery restrictions in combination with a reduced initial payment and the committee decided to recommend a firm ceiling on deliveries only. When a motion was put to that effect, including a proviso that if the wheat board found it necessary the maximum limit could be increased, the board took the position that the proviso should be dropped. During the earlier discussion, Mr. McIvor had observed that "an overall restrictive delivery quota had never been tested completely, and pointed out that since the inception of the quota system, the Board has operated under conditions which allowed the removal of delivery quotas each year; therefore, there has been no opportunity to test the producers reaction to the maintenance of an overall delivery quota when space is available in the country elevators."[14] Thus, if the proviso to the motion remained, the advisory committee would be recommending, in effect, that there be no change in the existing quota delivery policy. By removing the proviso, the advisory committee would be recommending to the government a first test of whether maximum delivery quotas could be enforced, in the circumstances in which country elevator space was available. Such a policy, if practicable, would offer a greater deterrent to wheat sowing. The

---

[13]Canadian Federation of Agriculture, *Farmers Meet the Cabinet*, February, 1945, pp. 9-10.

[14]*Minutes of the Meeting of the Advisory Committee to the Canadian Wheat Board*, Saskatoon, February 5-6, 1945.

committee accepted McIvor's point and recommended a 14-bushel limitation without any relaxation as space offered.

One other notable feature of the advisory committee's recommendations was the unanimous agreement among the producer and trade representatives that the board should continue to operate on a monopoly basis in 1945-46. In detail, the advisory committee's recommendations were as follows:

The Advisory Committee recommends that the fixed initial price of wheat for 1945-46 be continued at $1.25 per bushel basis No. 1 Northern in store Fort William-Port Arthur or Vancouver.

The Advisory Committee recommends that the Canadian Wheat Board continue as the sole agency to receive producers wheat in 1945-46.

The Advisory Committee is of the opinion that the grain industry must shortly face the transition from a wartime to a peacetime basis which will involve adjustments in grain policies in Canada as they have been developed during the past six years. It is the view of the Committee that long-range post-war policies should not be influenced unduly by a large carryover of wheat at the conclusion of the war, and after the immediate needs of the liberated areas are provided for. For this reason, the Advisory Committee stresses the importance of a considerable reduction in commercial stocks of wheat between July 31, 1945 and July 31, 1946.

Since the crop year 1941-42, restrictions on the marketing of wheat in each crop year have been based upon the principle of allowing producers to market as much wheat as could be disposed of in the domestic and export markets; a principle that properly assumed that a large stock of wheat should be carried in Canada as a wartime reserve; the Advisory Committee is of the opinion that this principle cannot be applied in 1945-46 and that the overall restriction on marketings for the coming crop year should be such as to provide for a substantial reduction in commercial stocks of wheat in Canada during the coming crop year. On the basis of probable domestic and export demand in 1945-46, the Advisory Committee believes that this purpose can be accomplished by limiting producers' marketings to a maximum of 14 bushels per authorized acre, exclusive of ordinary gristing.

The Advisory Committee, therefore, recommends a firm limitation of wheat marketings to this figure in the western division.

The Advisory Committee recommends that the 1944-45 barley program be continued in 1945-46.

The market for barley, both for malting and feed purposes, has been exceptionally good over the past two years, and this condition promises to continue for the duration of the war, at least. Therefore, the Advisory Committee recommends an increase in barley acreage in areas favourable for its production.

The Advisory Committee recommends that the 1944-45 oats programme be continued in 1945-46. The Advisory Committee points out, however, that the disposal of the 1944 oats crop is proving to be a slow and difficult problem and therefore, the prospect of increased commercial marketings of oats in 1945-46 is disturbing to the Committee, unless new demand appears. The Committee is apprehensive of any increase in the acreage of oats in 1945 that would result in increased commercial marketings.

With regard to the equalization schemes on oats and barley, the Advisory Committee recognizes the serious administrative difficulties but have no practical alternative to offer that would be in line with the Dominion Government's wartime policies on the price ceiling and livestock encouragement.

The Advisory Committee has reviewed the correspondence between the Canadian Wheat Board and Ottawa authorities on (flaxseed), and agree that the 1945-46 price should be fixed and final. It should not involve an initial payment and participation certificates. If the increased supplies are needed, the Advisory Committee is of the opinion that the fixed price of $2.75 per bushel will have to be raised to encourage further seeding in 1945. The Advisory Committee recommends that the fixed price for 1945-46 be $3.25 per bushel.[15]

When the cabinet wheat committee received these recommendations it held two meetings on February 13 and 15, 1945, and it addressed its attention mainly to the recommendation that an unqualified limitation of 14 bushels per authorized acre should be placed on 1944-1945 crop deliveries. Ilsley was concerned about the need for some effective form of discouragement to wheat acreage, and Gardiner indentified the weakness in the advisory committee's recommendation. He recalled the public stance Mr. Wesson had taken a year ago when the latter had criticized the government's policy of holding the line on wheat acreage. At the federation of agriculture meeting in January which Gardiner attended, he had recommended a wheat acreage reduction of 2 million acres, but Wesson remainded opposed to any reduction. Gardiner acknowledged that Wesson had appeared to shift his ground when he supported the advisory committee's recommendation but, even with a 14 bushel limitation, Wesson could still advise producers to increase wheat acreage on the understanding that any excess produced over the maximum quota could be added to reserves held on farms. On the other hand, if Wesson were to renounce his earlier recommendation of a wheat acreage increase and openly support the 14 bushels per authorized acre should be placed on 1944-45 crop that producers would increase acreage whether the maximum delivery limitation was in force or not. Gardiner's analysis convinced Ilsley that the 14 bushel limitation would not work. Both Gardiner and Crerar looked askance at the political practicability of maintaining the limitation on deliveries if elevator space were to become available. Until then the board had consistently removed delivery restrictions as space opened up. An election was in the offing and there was no guarantee that a new government would enforce the limitation. As alternatives to that proposal, the ministers considered a restoration of the wheat acreage reduction subsidy of $2 per acre, and also a reduction in the initial payment to $1. Ilsley saw no sense in paying an incentive $1.25 initial price and counteracting it with a disincentive subsidy. Crerar and Gardiner recognized that producers would not accept a reduced initial payment in combination with a maximum control on deliveries. Crerar even doubted that an initial payment of $1 would act as a deterrent to production. Farm labor was scarce, and less was required in the production of wheat than in the feeding of livestock. As a result, Gardiner withdrew his objection to the 14-bushel limitation, but Ilsley declined to do so because of Gardiner's earlier contention that it would be ineffective. Moreover, Ilsley was playing for time until he received a report from Donald Gordon, chairman of the wartime prices and trade board, who had become alarmed over the current trend in agricultural production policies. Although he did not disclose

[15]*Ibid.*

Gordon's concern at the time, Ilsley declined to accept the delivery limitation proposal. In the impasse, MacKinnon asked that the cabinet wheat committee be called together again after consulting with Ilsley.

Donald Gordon and his officials had been working for some weeks to document in a memorandum their serious concern over the emergence of production trends in western Canada which threatened to produce too much wheat, and too little bacon and butter to fill the contracts with Britain. The shortfall also foreshadowed the reimposition of meat rationing in Canada and a further reduction in the butter ration. Price incentives to stimulate bacon and butter production posed a threat to the continuation of the government's stabilization program, while the current emphasis upon wheat was endangering the postwar outlook for prairie agriculture. In a fourteen-page memorandum, which came to be known as the treasury proposals, Gordon attributed the current maladjustment in production to the wheat policy adopted on September 27, 1943, which raised the initial payment and paid out substantial sums in participation payments. In addition, the oats and barley advance equalization payments had placed a premium on the sale of feed grains for export rather than converting them directly into animal products. Thirdly, the abandonment of the wheat acreage reduction plan had removed the incentive to shift into coarse grains. The result was that, despite the acreage recommendations which had been made a year earlier by the dominion-provincial conference of December, 1943, to increase the areas sown to oats and barley and to hold wheat acreage in 1944 at its record low level of 1943, farmers had sharply increased their wheat areas and had decreased those sown to oats, barley and flaxseed.

In the prairie provinces, where the main wartime expansion in hog production had taken place, the rate of inspected slaughterings had turned sharply downward since September, 1944, and butter production in the west had been falling since July, 1944. Gordon and his officials were convinced that if present policies were not reversed, the shortfall in coarse grain, flaxseed, hog and butter production would be such that financial incentives would have to be paid to increase the production of those products; the effect would be inflationary, necessitating a rise in prices to consumers, and leading to demands for wage increases to an extent which would jeopardize the whole stabilization program.

The continuation of present policies would also lead to increased wheat production. Because of small crops and the extraordinary United States demand, the carryover of Canadian wheat had been reduced from the all-time record of 595 million bushels on July 31, 1943, to 355 million a year later, and a further reduction to 320 million was projected for July 31, 1945. This was still too high a level for the postwar years after relief needs had been met. Thereafter, the outlook for wheat markets was obscure and the recurrence of world surpluses was expected by many observers.

After pointing out the recovery which had already taken place in farm income levels, the memorandum claimed that high agricultural prices would threaten the operation of a floor price system after the war, weaken Canada's competitive position in world markets and stimulate an unwanted rise in agricultural land values.

Because of all these implications, Gordon recommended a definite and urgent change in the direction of grain policy. The fundamental issue was to reduce incentives to wheat growing. A variety of measures was discussed, including a reduction in the initial payment, a statement that market prospects for the 1945 crop were strictly limited, restoration of the wheat acreage reduction payments, an overall limitation on deliveries, and the substitution of an acreage bonus for the advance equalization payments on oats and barley. This latter measure was needed to encourage producers to feed their coarse grains rather than to sell them for cash. In its specific recommendations, the memorandum concluded:

> A completely realistic approach would suggest that as a firm step in the 1945 program the initial price for wheat should be fixed at $1.00. It is recognized, however, that this may not be practicable and the following are put forward as the minimum changes necessary to check and bring about some reversal of the alarming shifts already underway in farm output: —
>
> (1) An initial price of $1.10 per bushel for wheat, basis One Northern, in store Fort William/Vancouver, accompanied by a realistic statement on the prospects for participation.
>
> (2) Limitation on deliveries in the Prairie Provinces to 14 bushels per authorized acre, equivalent to about 280 million bushels of wheat.
>
> (3) Discontinuation of the equalization payments on oats and barley on a bushel basis.
>
> (4) A scheme of acreage payments on land transferred out of wheat into feed crops and flaxseed. As an indication of the scale of payments, these might be $3 to $4 per acre on transfers since 1940, which was the base year for the former plan. The rate might be higher for flaxseed to avoid paying a higher price for needed production.[16]

Although the memorandum had been completed on February 19, it was not circulated until February 27. When the wheat board received its copy it assigned Clive Davidson to prepare a critical commentary on the treasury proposals. Davidson began by pointing out that the 1943 wheat policy had created a controlled price environment for the remainder of the war. In return for that control, producers expected some form of protection in the postwar years. Lowering the initial price in 1945 would be a very disturbing factor in the western economy. Moreover, the reduction of wheat, oats and barley prices, effective as of August 1, 1945, would induce producers to deliver all the grain they could prior to that date which would not only congest the elevator system but decrease livestock feeding during the summer season. Davidson was also concerned whether the export prospects for oats were all that bright. While he was more sympathetic to the firm enforcement of a maximum delivery limitation, he believed that such a limitation was too punitive in combination with the treasury's proposed reduction in the initial payment.[17]

Ilsley did not ask that the cabinet wheat committee be reconvened to consider the treasury proposals. The issue went directly to cabinet where the decision was taken to have the wheat, oats and barley payments unchanged and to place full reliance on the maximum delivery limitation to keep wheat acreage in check. Cabinet authorized MacKinnon to announce the 1945

---

[16]*Memorandum Re 1945 Grain Production,* February 19, 1945, p. 14, Trade and Commerce file 20-141-11.

[17]*Notes on the Treasury Proposals,* Trade and Commerce file 20-141-11.

policy, which he did through a press statement issued on March 2, because parliament had been prorogued since the end of January. Chester Bloom reported the announcement as follows:

The fixed initial price of $1.25 for No. 1 northern wheat, Fort William, will be continued for the crop year, 1945-46, but there will be a limitation of fourteen bushels per acre placed on producers' marketings in that period.

This announcement was made formally Friday night by Hon. J. A. MacKinnon, minister of trade and commerce.

The decision to limit marketings is due to the opinion of the government that the need for a large wartime reserve of wheat is passing. The government wishes wheat acreage reduced and acreages to feed grain substantially increased.

The new policy was adopted after lengthy discussions in the Cabinet, and consultations with members of the Canadian Wheat Board. Great pressure was exerted by some advisers to have the initial price cut from $1.25 a bushel to $1.00. But that plan was defeated. Another scheme proposed was to bonus growers to change wheat to coarse grain acreage. The financial burden would have been too great to carry with other war financing, it was decided. The final conclusion was to limit marketings of wheat producers' crops this year.

Mr. MacKinnon states:

"Wheat policy for 1945-46 involves a continuation of the fixed initial of $1.25 per bushel for No. 1 northern wheat in store Fort William, Port Arthur and Vancouver, and the issuing of participation certificates.

"The change in wheat policy is the inclusion of a firm limitation on producers' marketings in 1945-46 to 14 bushels per authorized acre. In previous crop years the limitation on marketings has been established on the basis of permitting the marketing of as much wheat as could be sold in the commercial domestic market, and in the export market. This policy assumed the carrying of a large wartime reserve of wheat in Canada. In the opinion of the government, the need for a large wartime reserve of wheat is now passing, and market demand in 1945-46 will be supplied out of the accumulated reserves, and 1945-46 marketings by producers. The limitations on marketing to 14 bushels per authorized acre, provides for substantial reduction of commercial stocks of wheat in Canada by July 31, 1946, and represents the application of a new principle, necessary to the transition from a wartime to a peacetime basis."

Mr. MacKinnon stated that the dominion government does not feel that post-war policies should be unduly influenced by large stocks of wheat accumulated during the war.

Mr. MacKinnon stated that he desired to stress the fact that the limitation of marketings to 14 bushels per authorized acre in 1945-46 is final and will not be altered at a later date.

The carryover of wheat at the end of the present crop year plus wheat marketed by producers under the 14-bushel limitation, will provide ample wheat to meet market demand during the coming crop year. The dominion government is announcing its wheat policy now in order to give producers ample time to adjust their 1945 seeding programme to the new policy. It is the hope of the government that wheat acreage will be reduced in 1945, and acreages sown to feed grains substantially increased in accordance with the recommendations of the dominion-provincial agricultural conference.

The 1944-45 programme for oats and barley will be continued in 1945-46. Minimum prices of 45 cents per bushel for oats, and 60 cents per bushel for barley; basis top grades in store Fort William and Port Arthur, will again be effective. Advance equalization payments of 10 cents per bushel on oats, and 15 cents per bushel on barley will continue, and will be made at the time of delivery.[18]

How faithfully the government adhered to its declaration of the 14-bushel limitation of 1945-46 deliveries will be described shortly. Meanwhile, at the February 13 and 15 meetings of the cabinet wheat committee another contentious problem was dealt with which had been created by the exhaustion of the crown wheat account.

REPLENISHMENT OF THE CROWN ACCOUNT

Simultaneously with its consideration of the 1945 grain policy, the cabinet wheat committee had to deal with the issue which had arisen from the exhaustion of the crown account created on September 27, 1943. McIvor notified MacKinnon of the problem by letter on January 6, 1945. Mutual aid and domestic sales had by now utilized all of the stocks in the account, and McIvor recommended that the account be replenished by the purchase from the 1943 and 1944 producers' accounts of 100 million bushels at the export price for commercial sales, or the class 2 price as it came to be called. By the time the cabinet wheat committee first considered the problem on January 27, the crown account already had a deficit quantity of 9 million bushels. Ilsley advised that his department had considered the matter, and that he was prepared to submit a proposal which would involve the continuation of sales from the producers' accounts at $1.25 of wheat for domestic use, the negotiation of a two-year contract with Britain at $1.25 and the balance of export sales being sold for what the market would bear. When Gardiner pointed out that this was at variance with the 1943 policy of giving producers full participation on the 1943 and 1944 crops, Sharp replied that no departure of principle was involved because $1.25 was as much as could be freely negotiated with the British on a long-term contract. It should be noted, in passing, that this was the first time a long-term contract had been proposed with Britain for the immediate postwar period. Gardiner again observed that the effect of such a contract would be to reduce the amount of participation paid. Sharp replied that if this were not done and export sales were made to Britain at the current class 2 price of $1.46, mutual aid expenditures would be increased by $30 million. Gardiner then asked why the cost of mutual aid should be charged to farmers on wheat instead of to the whole of the country. When McIvor observed that export sales to paying countries would amount to 100 million bushels between January and June, 1945, Gardiner asked why the 100 million of mutual aid and domestic sales should not be made at the same prices. Crerar then interjected a cautionary word to the effect that it would not be in the producers' own interest to let wheat prices get too high. Even if Ilsley's proposal meant that the 1945 crop would earn very little participation on the $1.25 price basis, the prospects were that wheat prices would be ruling below $1.25 before the end of the 1945-46 crop year. If, for example, priority were given to sales from the 1944 crop to clean it up and pay participation, sales from the 1945 crop would be postponed, with still less chance of prices coming up to $1.25. If, on the other hand, the initial payment remained at $1.25 for the 1945 crop, wheat acreage would

[18] *Winnipeg Free Press,* March 3, 1945.

rise and lead to a crash later on. On current sales policy, Crerar suggested that the board should sell from producers' accounts at $1.25 plus carrying charges for mutual aid and domestic account, and the balance of exports for what the market would bring. MacKinnon interjected that this would be cheating producers just partly. Gardiner still saw no reason to put the burden on the back of the fellow who was suffering the break and he asked why wheat could not be dealt with entirely outside of the mutual aid arrangements. This brought a rejoinder from Sharp that if wheat were taken out of mutual aid the British treasury would approach the Canadian treasury directly on the price to be paid for the wheat. Gardiner's response was that the Canadian treasury would simply have to tell the British that the prevailing export price was $1.46. Ilsley then reverted to the board's recommendation that the $1.46 apply to domestic sales also. In that event, he cautioned that the domestic price stabilization policy would be wrecked. Since the wheat committee members were far from agreement, the meeting adjourned until January 29.

When the meeting resumed again, McIvor produced a set of three tables which showed the participation results on the 1943-44 crop account if (a) mutual aid and domestic wheat sales were made at class 2 prices; (b) domestic sales at $1.25, and mutual aid and commercial exports at class 2 prices; and (c) domestic and mutual aid sales at $1.25 and other export sales at class 2. The first example resulted in a participation payment of 11.3 cents per bushel; the second 9.5 cents and a treasury savings of $12,800,000 on domestic wheat up to July 31, 1946; and the third in a participation payment of 6.9 cents on the 1943-44 crop and an additional savings to the treasury up to July 31, 1946, of $24,800,000 on mutual aid wheat. Since the meeting two days earlier, the board was now prepared to recommend that it sell domestic wheat from producers' accounts at $1.25 to conform with the domestic stabilization policy, but that mutual aid and other export sales should be made at $1.46, less an allowance of 3 cents on mutual aid sales for possible savings in carrying charges. Once the board had conceded the $1.25 price on domestic sales, the argument continued between Gardiner and Ilsley on the price for mutual aid sales. Gardiner saw no reason why the domestic price policy should be extended to mutual aid. Ilsley's proposal for $1.25 on mutual aid included a long-term contract on that basis. McIvor observed that under those conditions, the initial payment would have to be reduced to $1 if there were to be any effective participation in 1945-46. Crerar then suggested that if the producer were to be given the alternatives of $1.43 on all 1943 and 1944 crop sales plus an initial payment of $1 on the 1945 crop, and mutual aid sales at $1.25 in 1943 and 1944 with an initial payment of $1.25 on the 1945 crop, he would elect the latter. Mr. Gardiner felt he would take the former, but he objected to any change in the policy which had been adopted in 1943. Charging mutual aid sales at $1.25 to the producer rather than letting him have the going price on all export sales would be a departure from that policy. Moreover, he did not consider a $1 initial payment in 1945 would be acceptable. Ilsley was not opposed to an initial payment of $1.25 in 1945, but he felt that the price at which wheat was sold for mutual aid would have to be resolved in cabinet.[19]

[19]*Minutes of the Wheat Committee of the Cabinet*, January 27 and 29, 1945.

When cabinet met on February 2, 1945, Gardiner won the argument and it was agreed that crown purchases of wheat would be made as follows: domestic requirements at $1.25 plus carrying charges, and mutual aid at the board's class 2 price.[20]

When that decision came up in the cabinet wheat committee again on February 13, a new misunderstanding had arisen. The board had prepared a draft submission to council giving effect to the cabinet decision in which it referred to the sale of 100 million bushels to replenish the crown account, Ilsley recalled that the cabinet discussion had related to board sales for mutual aid. He had assumed that the board would sell directly from time to time to the mutual aid board, whereas the board's submission was drafted in terms of a board sale to the crown account which, in turn, would sell to mutual aid.

The practical distinction between the two methods was that an immediate sale of 100 million bushels to the crown would close out the 1943 crop account at once and permit a participation payment of 9.2 cents on that account to be made. If the board were to sell intermittently directly to the mutual aid board, the 1943 account could not be closed for a few months. Gardiner had understood that as a result of the cabinet decision, the 1943 participation payment could be announced at once.

Sharp objected to the sale of 100 million bushels to the crown account. If that were done, the Canadian government in effect would be dictating a price of $1.43 to the British, which the latter would accept resignedly because it was mutual aid and financially of Canadian concern. Wilson contended that on the basis of the board's submission, the Canadian government was free to decide the price at which it would make wheat available under mutual aid to the British. In the absence of a member of the board at the meeting, he explained that the board proposed selling to the crown account 41 million bushels for domestic account at $1.30 including a five-cent allowance for carrying charges, and 59 million for mutual aid at $1.43 which was the board's class 2 price of $1.46 on January 29, less a three-cent allowance to the crown for future carrying charges saved to the board, and that this would permit a participation payment of 9.2 cents on the 1943 crop, which could only be determinate if the 100-million bushel sale was actually made now. Although Ilsley asked that the decision be postponed until he consulted his deputy minister, Dr. W. C. Clark, Gardiner once again had his way and the board's draft submission was approved by P. C. 1116 of February 20, 1945, in which the board was directed:

> (1) To purchase for Crown Account sufficient wheat from the 1943 and 1944 Crop Accounts to cover Mutual Aid sales by Crown for the period January 16th, 1945, to February 28th, 1945, at Class II prices prevailing on the date of each Mutual Aid sale;
>
> (2) To purchase for Crown Account sufficient wheat from the 1943 Crop to cover domestic sales by Crown for the period January 16th, 1945 to February 28th, 1945, at $1.25 per bushel, basis Number One Manitoba Northern in store Fort William/Port Arthur;

---

[20]Mr. A. D. P. Heeney's confirming letter of February 5, 1945 to the Honourable J. A. MacKinnon, Trade and Commerce file, 20-141-11.

(3) To purchase for Crown Account 100 million bushels of wheat from the 1943 and 1944 Crop Accounts at $1.43 per bushel for Number One Manitoba Northern, basis in store Fort William/Port Arthur to cover Mutual Aid sales contracted after February 28th, 1945.[21]

The order in council cleared the way for MacKinnon's announcement on the replenishment of the crown wheat account which he made on March 2 as a part of his disclosure of the 1945 grain policy.[22] The announcement continued:

> Mr. MacKinnon stated that stocks of wheat acquired by the Crown on Sept. 27, 1943, have now been disposed of, and the government has acquired a new stock of wheat for mutual aid purposes. This new supply of Crown wheat has been acquired by the government from the 1943-44 and 1944-45 board accounts on the basis of the board's commercial price on Jan. 29, 1945 less an allowance for carrying charges. The new purchase of Crown wheat will permit the closing out of the 1943-44 board account before the end of the present crop year, and ensures a payment on 1943-44 participation certificates.

> All wheat required for the domestic market between the date of exhaustion of old stocks of Crown wheat, and July 31, 1946, will be provided by the Canadian wheat board from the 1943-44 and 1944-45 board accounts at $1.25 per bushel, basis No. 1 northern wheat in store Fort William, Port Arthur and Vancouver, plus carrying charges. In other words, on sales of wheat from the 1943 and 1944-45 board accounts for domestic use, producers will neither gain nor lose, the board selling wheat for domestic purposes at cost. The basis on board sales of wheat for domestic use takes into account the price control policies of the Dominion Government.

> In providing for participation certificates covering 1945-46 deliveries to the board, the minister pointed out that 1943 and 1944 crops will be sold before sale of 1945 wheat will commence. Actually the board will not start to sell 1945 wheat until 1946, and consequently substantial carrying charges will accrue against 1945-46 deliveries before these deliveries are finally sold.

> The board's fixed price for No. 1 CW flaxseed, basis in store Fort William, Port Arthur, will continue unchanged at $2.75 per bushel for 1945-46 crop year.[23]

MacKinnon's reference at the end of the announcement to the continuation of the fixed price for flaxseed at $2.75 was made after the wheat committee had considered and rejected proposals of the Canadian federation of agriculture that flaxseed be handled by the board on the basis of an initial payment of $3.25.

Although the board had anticipated that the 100-million bushel sale to the crown account would satisfy mutual aid needs until July 31, it reported to the cabinet wheat committee on June 27, 1945, the imminent further exhaustion of the crown account because of heavy mutual aid purchases after VE-Day and the freeing of shipping from the movement of military supplies. Now the board estimated that it would take an additional 25 million bushels to cover mutual aid requirements to July 31, which it offered to sell to the crown account on the same terms as it had sold the 100 million bushels. Only MacKinnon and Ilsley were present for that meeting and they suggested that Gardiner be consulted. The matter came up in the

---

[21] *Report of the Canadian Wheat Board, Crop Year 1944-1945*, p. 14.

[22] See pp. 815-816.

[23] *Winnipeg Free Press*, March 3, 1945.

cabinet wheat committee again on August 8, when it had to consider the continuing mutual aid requirements beyond July 31. After VJ-Day, cabinet decided that all mutual aid procurement should terminate as of September 1, 1945. To provide for wheat supplies under mutual aid to that date, and for the shortfall that had already developed in the crown account, the cabinet wheat committee recommended the purchase from the 1944 producers' account an additional 50 million bushels. Gardiner stood on the principle established in 1943, and continued in the March 1945 purchase, that mutual aid purchases should be made at the prevailing class 2 price. Since the end of March, the class 2 price had risen to $1.55. Because the 50 million bushels were required immediately, no allowance was made for future carrying charges and the committee recommended to cabinet the crown purchase of that quantity for mutual aid pruposes at the board's prevailing class 2 price of $1.55.[24]

1945 ELECTION

By 1945, the nineteenth parliament elected in 1940 neared the end of its statutory life, as the war in the European theatre was reaching its cataclysmic end. The automatic date of dissolution by statute was Monday, April 16. Quite apart from the statutory limitation on the life of the parliament, the government needed a fresh mandate to preside over the transition from war to peace. Accordingly, Mackenzie King announced on April 13 that a general election would be held on June 11. The forthcoming election had unquestionably influenced the cabinet decisions in connection with 1945 grain policy and the crown account. For example, it lent urgency to a decision whether participation on the 1943 crop could be announced forthwith or delayed, and whether cabinet could support the drastic surgery on the 1945 grain program which Donald Gordon recommended, or whether it should proceed on the basis of policies already adopted and announced. It will be seen from the decisions that the government adopted the safer and, as ultimately proved, the more sensible course.

But the time was past when grain policy was a major factor in elections in the prairies. Provincial politics now had their repercussions on the federal scene. The Social Credit party which had elected a government in Alberta in 1935 remained a force, so far as Alberta was concerned, in the federal election. Similarly, the CCF party which had placed the Honourable T. C. Douglas in office as premier of Saskatchewan, dominated the federal campaign in that province.

The 1945 election returned the Liberal party led by Mackenzie King to office with little more than a bare majority. MacKinnon and one other Liberal retained their seats in Alberta. In Saskatchewan only two Liberals were returned, including Gardiner who was declared elected only after a recount. The party standings in the June 11, 1945, election were as follows:

	Manitoba	Saskatchewan	Alberta	Canada
Liberal	10	2	2	125
Ind. Liberal				2
Prog. Cons.	2	1	2	67

[24]*Memorandum to Cabinet*, Trade and Commerce file 20-141-11.

Ind. Prog. Cons.			1
CCF	5	18	28
Ind. CCF			1
Social Credit		13	13
Independent			5
Bloc Pop. Can.			2
Labor-Prog.			1
Total	17	21	17	245

As Gardiner archly observed later that September during the debate on the address from the throne, while welcoming the new members from Saskatchewan he thought he should also congratulate himself for being back in the house at all.[25]

BARLEY POLICY FOR 1945

The drought which reduced the 1945 wheat harvest took an exceptional toll of the barley crop. In southwestern Saskatchewan and southeastern Alberta the barley output was below local feed requirements. The two provincial governments approached the feeds administration and the agricultural supplies board to protect feed supplies in the affected areas. It became apparent to the agricultural supplies board that there was not sufficient barley in Canada to permit exports that year and the supplies board asked the wheat board to suspend the issuance of barley export permits, against which the latter board assessed equalization fees. Because of the threatened loss of revenue to the barley equalization fund, the supplies board and the wheat board presented a series of alternatives to the wheat committee of the cabinet on August 7 and 8.

The discussion of the problem at that time was inconclusive and the matter was postponed until mid-September when the wheat board presented another brief reviewing the alternatives, but recommending that the barley equalization fee be raised from 15 to 20 cents on all deliveries. This increase would give producers the benefit they would have earned on malting premiums paid by United States maltsters had exports been permitted. On domestic sales, the limited requirements of Canadian maltsters would have permitted the payment of the 5-cent premium on only a portion of the crop. This principle was accepted by the wheat committee and approved by cabinet. The wheat board expected that MacKinnon would make the announcement in the house and prepared a statement for his use. But Gardiner claimed that the issue concerned his agricultural supplies board as much as the wheat board, and he made the announcement in the following terms:

> Due to drought conditions extending over the greater part of the crop growing areas of western Canada the yield of barley has been greatly reduced and action has been taken to counteract this condition so that the live stock production programme of Canada will not be jeopardized.
>
> In order to protect Canada's live stock feeding programme and because of the short crop of barley, the agricultural supplies board is of the opinion that all barley marketed in 1945-46 from the 1945 crop should be made available for the domestic market. With this in mind the feeds administrator advised

[25]*House of Commons Debates,* September 24, 1945, p. 402.

the grain trade on August 22 last that no further export permits would be granted during the crop year 1945-46 for barley, whether whole, ground or processed.

To enable farmers to purchase and feed the higher grades of barley, some of which would normally receive a premium, when sold to domestic maltsters or exported, it has been decided as a temporary measure to add five cents to the advance equalization payment, thus raising the amount from fifteen cents to twenty cents per bushel on all barley marked in the prairie provinces, the Peace River block of British Columbia and Creston-Wyndall area, British Columbia, during the crop year 1945-46. This increase will be made retroactive to August 1, 1945, on all barley delivered and sold since July 31, 1945, without receiving the malting premium. If any barley has been marketed and sold since that date without receiving the full five cents per bushel premium, then payment will be made up to the five cents. Regulations in this regard will shortly be released by the Canadian wheat board and these regulations will fix the effective date for payment at country points of the twenty cent advance equalization payments as farmers deliver their barley.

These regulations will also change the present methods of payment of malting premiums by domestic maltsters. Instead of paying the malting premiums to the seller of the barley, the maltsters will be required to pay five cents per bushel on all barley purchased into the equalization fund. The same system of paying the premium into the equalization fund will be used by exporters, if the assurance of domestic supplies will permit the export of some barley later in the crop year. The effect is, therefore, that the increase in the equalization payment replaces for the present crop year the malting premium that would otherwise have been paid to some farmers on barley sold to domestic maltsters or exported.

To further safeguard the feed situation throughout Canada, the present policy of holding reserve stocks of feed grains at Fort William and in eastern Canada, on which the government pays interest and storage charges, has been extended to cover part of the prairie provinces and British Colmbia.[26]

The cabinet decision was confirmed by P. C. 6238 of September 27, 1945.

EXPORT PRICE CEILING AND THE FLOOR GUARANTEE

Since September 27, 1943, the wheat board had calculated its export prices for wheat sold commercially (which excluded mutual aid) by using Chicago quotations and deducting the differential which existed between Winnipeg and Chicago futures prices when the Winnipeg market was closed. As the Chicago market rose from its September 27, 1943, level in the face of the feed shortage in the United States, the board priced its wheat into commercial export at similar rising prices, less the initial differential. These prices were called the board's class 2 prices. The method of their establishment was a valid one as long as the United States was the main commercial outlet for Canadian wheat exports.

By the spring of 1945, however, this ceased to be the case for American wheat imports from Canada had reverted to the small quantity (less than a million bushels) permitted for consumption as flour, and certain quantities used by the Buffalo mills for milling in bond. In fact, the United States had once again become an exporter of wheat in competition with Canadian commercial exports. Export pricing of wheat in the United States was done

[26]*Ibid.,* September 20, 1945. pp. 314-315.

with the help of an export subsidy, because domestic wheat prices in that country would not have been competitive with Canadian export prices. In the dilemma, the wheat board ceased to follow the old formula in establishing the Canadian export price when it reached a level of $1.55 in May, 1945. After that the board left its price at $1.55 as the United States commodity credit corporation matched the competition by a subsidy.

When the board drew its pricing dilemma to the attention of the cabinet wheat committee on June 27, 1945, Mr. McIvor explained that the Americans were awaiting the appointment of a new secretary of agriculture, the Honourable Clinton Anderson, in the Truman administration, to reexamine their export subsidy program. Meanwhile, American officials wanted to follow our class 2 price which until mid-May had been based on Chicago prices. Mr. C. E. Huntting, a commissioner of the wheat board, pointed out that the Chicago market was more affected by the operation of the American domestic wheat loan policy than it was by export considerations.

Because of the uncertainty about how the export price should be determined, the board was content to let it stand at $1.55 for the last few months before the war ended. But after VJ-Day, it raised the matter again, and the issue was taken to council where Mr. Ilsley supported the opinion of the wartime prices and trade board that to allow prices to rise on a product as important as wheat would render it impossible for that board to maintain its control over inflation. At that moment reports had also been received from the London meeting of the international wheat council that agreement could not be reached upon the Canadian proposal of a price range of $1-$1.50 for the next three years. As Gardiner claimed later, both the wartime prices and trade board's representations and the failure to secure international agreement on a range of prices, weighed heavily in the cabinet decision to instruct the board to maintain its export price at $1.55. To justify that action to producers, the government agreed to guarantee a floor price of $1 for the next five years. It is interesting that neither of the two reasons just mentioned for unilateral maintenance of an export price ceiling was cited in the preamble of P. C. 6122 of September 19, 1945, which instructed the board to maintain the ceiling and to implement, if need be, the floor price. The explanation furnished in the preamble of the order ran parallel to that given by Mr. MacKinnon in his announcement of the policy to the house that same day, as he said:

Mr. Speaker, I wish to make a brief statement on wheat prices.

The second world war has concluded with Canadian wheat producers in a particularly strong marketing position. Not only has the general disruption and bad weather reduced production in the war areas, but the Australian and North African crop failures and a small crop in Argentina have left Canada and the United States as the only countries at present having substantial export surpluses of wheat. This has coincided with the release of pent-up demands in the liberated areas.

In these extraordinary circumstances, Canadian wheat might well command for a limited period very much higher prices in the world market. The importing countries, nearly all of them our allies in the war, are buying out of necessity and, to a large extent, on credits. They would be compelled to meet through larger credits or through sacrifice of other food and rehabilitation supplies whatever higher price is demanded for Canadian wheat.

It is in the interest of Canada and of Canadian wheat growers that the importing countries should continue to obtain Canadian wheat at prices not in excess of those prevailing at the end of hostilities. Accordingly the government, by order in council, has instructed the Canadian wheat board to offer wheat for sale for export overseas at prices not higher than the current export price of $1.55 per bushel, basis No. 1 northern, in store Fort William/Port Arthur or Vancouver.

In asking Canadian producers to forgo such benefits as might be realized in the short run through higher export prices, the government recognize the paramount need for relative stability of income to wheat producers. Toward this end, the government undertakes that in the five-year period ending July 31, 1950, producers will receive not less than $1 per bushel, basis No.1 northern, instore Fort William/ Port Arthur of Vancouver on the authorized deliveries for each crop year. For the balance of the 1945-1946 crop year, at least, the Canadian wheat board initial advance will continue at $1.25, where it was set two years ago. By providing a long-term floor price of not less than $1.00 the government will protect producers against the consequences of any sharp reversal in the world wheat position during the next five-year period.

The government, in adopting this policy of a maximum price for overseas shipments for the present and a floor price for five years, is asking the producers, in their own interests, to forgo exceptional short-run advantages in favour of a long-run stability of income. In arriving at its decision on this policy, the government had the following fundamental considerations in mind:

Any further increase in wheat prices now would aggravate the problems of economic and political readjustment of the liberated areas to Canada's detriment in future trade with those areas. There is a moral obligation not to take advantage of our recent allies in their time of compelling need.

Higher wheat prices would encourage the importing countries in a hurried return to wheat production and pre-war policies very directly to the detriment of the wheat exporting countries, particularly Canada. Moreover, production in a number of exporting countries would be unduly encouraged.[27]

It remained for Gardiner, however, to present in an oratorical tour-de-force his defence of the government's wheat policy. This he did during the debate on the address from the throne. On the night of September 27, 1945, he gave extempore a lengthy historical review of wheat policy in the course of which he made several major points, first, that until 1943, the federation of agriculture had consistently recommended a floor price of not less than $1. When the government decided to set the initial payment at $1.25 in 1943, the federation went on record to express its appreciation, but added that it also wanted a continuing floor price guarantee of not less than $1. Secondly, in the late years of the nineteen-twenties Canadian wheat exports averaged 359 million bushels per crop year. In the successive five-year periods since that time wheat exports, however, had never reached that average. This was because many importing countries had undertaken to increase their own production of wheat: a fact which the $1.55 ceiling policy announced the other day had in mind. In all the pool directorates' private discussions with Gardiner, they had called attention to the danger of having an initial payment higher than was necessary to cover operating costs, and had claimed that it was better to depend upon participation payments for

[27]*Ibid.,* September 19, 1945, pp. 289-290.

profits. Thirdly, under the general price ceiling policy adopted in 1941, consumers had been protected ever since by 78-cent wheat, but no ceiling had been placed on the prices received by producers, because the government had not been prepared to do so until wheat prices passed the parity level of $1.42. Now that farmers were getting $1.55 on export wheat, a ceiling could be imposed.

Gardiner then alluded to the special arrangements which had been established between Canada and the recipient countries of mutual aid, and counselled against pressing the price issue while they were buying Canadian wheat, mostly on credit, in the initial stages of postwar readjustment. He also referred to the government's participation in the various attempts to conclude an international wheat agreement, that these negotiations so far had failed to achieve success; that the farm organizations wanted the government to continue the attempt; but that time would be needed for further negotiations which the five-year floor guarantee would provide. Finally, Gardiner declared that the export price ceiling was directly related to the domestic price ceiling policy, and that the $1.55 ceiling would not be continued any longer than domestic ceilings remained on other commodities. The key passages of Gardiner's speech, lengthy in themselves, still impart the flavor of his forensic ability:

Prices of farm products were not raised in the markets in the manner described by someone this afternoon. We were told that we had to take care, in dealing with this particular question, that we did not create a situation whereby we would lose our markets through raising our prices in the markets of the other countries of the world. I think that statement was made by the leader of the opposition to-night.

It was not the other countries of the world that made these prices. The other countries of the world have been getting assistance under mutual aid, which resulted in our being able to pay our farmers higher returns, and that mutual aid came out of the public treasury, a charge on all the people of the country, making it possible for us to pay about the difference between eighty-five shillings and one hundred and thirteen shillings on bacon to farmers through the packing plants for the hogs that were marketed off their farms. A similar condition exists in connection with cheese, in connection with canned milk, in connection with every product that was provided to Britain and other allied countries under the mutual aid arrangement.

Therefore what I want to emphasize in that connection is that in anything we do with regard to ranges of prices on wheat we are not interfering with something which had been established in some other country in recent years during the war. We are dealing with a condition under which this country, under the able leadership of my hon. friend the Minister of Finance (Mr. Ilsley), raised funds with which we paid for Canadian products, and then we sent those products to other countries, taking back from our allies what they could afford to pay under the conditions then existing, and charging the rest of it up to the billion dollars of mutual aid which this government provided in order to help our allies during the war.

It might be said and they have said it — I do not need to say it; our allies have said it — that Canada has done a worth-while job in that regard in carrying that policy through during the last three or four years of the war, and we believe that by carrying that policy through we have created a situation which will make it possible for us to market the commodities we produce in this country in countries which believe that they owe something to us because of the service we gave in their period of greatest trial. That is what the Minister of Trade and Commerce (Mr. MacKinnon) had in mind when he said in this house the other day that we as a government must give consideration to the effects which any price that may be established for our products at the present time, particularly products we are selling in great volume, have upon the economy of the other allied nations alongside of whom we fought. It is in order that we may maintain the proud position which we hold among the allied nations to-day, of having done everything possible to give service in every way in order to assist in the winning of the war. When we have come to the end of it, it is not our intention to do things which might cause us to destroy the good feeling which we established then.

Let me now touch on the position as it relates to the war period and as it relates to the period before the war and to the future. We have been struggling with this wheat question not only ever since the war started but since 1932, when the government of the day sent a delegation from Ottawa, which took with them representatives from the three western provinces, to discuss our wheat problem at that time. It was the problem of a great carryover of wheat which we desired to sell in the European markets. At that time there was set up an organization which has been discussing our wheat problems ever since. As I said here the other day, when this wheat question was being discussed by someone, we have not succeeded in getting any definite arrangements entered into by the five great wheat producing countries of the world in their relationship with the great consuming countries of the world. We have had these people together; we have been discussing their problems and our problems. That has all been helpful, but when it came down to getting definite arrangements as to what the price and the acreage were to be we have always been confronted with some difficulties which have usually resulted in lack of agreement — I would not say in disagreement, but in lack of agreement.

I wish to say to the house to-night that if it is ever possible at any time to lay the records of those discussions, which have been held in camera, before the people of the world, and at the same time before the Canadian people, it will be found that in every case the advances made by this country toward the other countries were in a line which, if they had been agreed to, would have satisfied the demands of farm organizations from one end of Canada to the other. One of those demands has been written down by the farm federation on many occasions. They have said, "What we want is a stabilized price for wheat." They said, "We want a $1 price established." I remember on one occasion that they were saying in one breath they wanted a price established at $1 and in the other criticizing the government at Ottawa because the government would not sign a proposed agreement presented by this committee. I went so far as to say to them: "If you want us to sign the agreement, which is before us at the present time, with the nations of the world, which you have said in one resolution you want, and you want us to accept the price which is in that agreement as the basic price for wheat, then it is lower than $1 a bushel, and the other countries of the world will not agree to its being higher." That was just prior to the war.

Since the war, these discussions have been changed from London to Washington and they have been going on there. What I wish to say to the house is that policies similar to those which have been advocated by the farmers of western Canada with regard to wheat have been submitted to that organization year by year. What the Minister of Trade and Commerce meant the other day when he answered a question from the other side of the house, and when he stated that these countries recently meeting in London had not agreed, was that they had not agreed to a policy which I am sure would have met with the approval of all the farm organizations in Canada.

When that agreement was not reached this government announced its policy in the house the other day. That policy gives us five more years in which to carry on negotiations. That is why the farm organizations, without any coaching on our part, have gone to the press in their own cities of Calgary, Regina and Winnipeg, and said that they are satisfied with the policy that has been announced. Some of them told us clearly that they want us to go ahead and negotiate other steps and arrangements with governments at the present time and hope for any settlement in time to deal with the next crop, let us say, or probably the next crop or two. You cannot depend upon having absolute settlements made among the great number of nations that are involved in this wheat question, while world conditions are what they are.

Therefore what we have said to the people of this country is, that for the present we have asked the wheat board to sell wheat at not higher than $1.55 a bushel. That was the price the market would have paid for our wheat on the last occasion in which we were dealing with the British government just before the policy was announced. Therefore we have said that we are going to sell wheat to the overseas people — we do not say to anyone else — at $1.55 a bushel for the time being. Then we have said that for the next year, down to the end of July, 1946, the initial payment is exactly what it was asked to be by the farm organizations down to that period of time, namely, $1.25 a bushel. Then we have said that in the meantime we are going to carry on with the same policies in relation to wheat and other farm products as we have been carrying on with from 1941 down to the present. And we say — we have not said this in so many words, but I am sure that every member of the government will agree with me when I say it — there is not any intention on the part of the members of this government, or of any one associated with it, to lower the initial payment on wheat below $1.25 a bushel as long as the wheat of this country can be disposed of anywhere at $1.25 a bushel. We are carrying out the policy at the moment just as the circumstances warrant our carrying it out, namely, guaranteeing a floor price of $1.25 a bushel for this year, no matter what happens, and going on with our negotiations with other people as to what the price ought to be, and saying that for the time being, while we are selling wheat overseas to the countries that need our food, we are going to charge them only $1.55 a bushel for it.

I agree with the leader of the opposition that to the extent that we might have got more we are asking the 250,000 farmers who grow wheat to carry that part of the burden for the time being. And we are asked, what are they getting in return for it? We are saying to them that, no matter what happens during the next five years, we are going to see to it that you never have to take less than $1 a bushel for your wheat, basis Fort William. What does that mean? It means that it does not make any difference where the wheat goes on the market, if it goes down to fifty cents a bushel we are going to take the money from all the people of Canada to pay the difference between fifty cents and $1. All we are suggesting to the 250,000 farmers is that, while it is $1.55 or more, and while we have ceiling prices on other commodities in Canada, we are going to ask them to permit us to sell whatever wheat we do sell to our overseas allies at $1.55 a bushel during that time. But at the same time we say to them by inference, if not in words, there will not be any ceiling on your wheat any longer than ceiling prices remain on other commodities in this country. We did not say there was a ceiling of $1.55 for five years. We said there would never be a floor of less than a $1 a bushel for five years; but we have said that as long as wheat is $1.55 or more, and as long as there are ceiling prices on other products in this country, since wheat has gone above parity, to $1.55 instead of $1.42, we are prepared to place a ceiling of $1.55 a bushel on what wheat is sold to our allies.[28]

Thus Gardiner, in his speech, had reflected more fully than either P.C. 6122 of September 19 or MacKinnon's announcement had done, the considerations upon which cabinet had based its decision to impose the export-price ceiling and to compensate it with a floor-price guarantee. In addition to the other reasons given (namely, the opportunity to charge much higher prices to the disadvantage of Canada's wartime allies which were in financial difficulties and in need of time for rehabilitation and, also, the need for relative stability of income at home to avoid the distortion of domestic agricultural production and also abroad to avoid the necessity for recourse to policies of self-sufficiency), Gardiner confirmed that the wheat export-price ceiling was directly related to the continuation of the general domestic price-control policy. The floor-price guarantee was given not only as a quid pro quo for the export-price ceiling and in response to the representations of the farm organizations; but also to provide five more years for the negotiation of other steps or arrangements. Although Gardiner spoke in the context of the international wheat agreement negotiations which had failed, he did not limit the ultimate remedy to that forum. What he was already turning over in his mind was that Canada, on its own, could negotiate with its overseas wheat customers directly.

Meanwhile the $1.55 ceiling and the $1 floor price were noteworthy as the first steps taken by the government in the direction of assuring relatively stable market conditions through the transitional period and in the evolution of Canada's postwar wheat marketing policy.

LIFTING OF THE MAXIMUM DELIVERY LIMITATION

From VE-Day forward, the import demand for Canadian wheat exceeded all expectations. The July 31 carryover, predicted earlier at 320 million bushels, actually amounted to 258 million. The 1945 crop yielded only 306 million bushels. Wheat production on the European continent in 1945 had fallen 600 million bushels below normal output and the cereals committee of the combined food board was hard pressed to allocate available export supplies among the urgent demands of the liberated countries. In this period, the main export responsibility fell upon Canada and the United States. For logistic reasons the lion's share of the responsibility fell upon Canada in the first half of the crop year, and upon the United States in the second half. In the autumn of 1945 the wheat board obtained the approval of the cabinet wheat committee and also of the cereals committee of the combined food board that (because Canada had been Britain's main, if not exclusive supplier of wheat during the war years) it should now give priority in its shipments to meeting British requirements, while the United states concentrated on the needs of other countries, within the allocations set by the combined food board. In meeting all the export demands that year, both Canada and the United States drew down their reserves to a point below the level of prudent year-end supplies. In Canada, by July 31, 1946, the

[28]*Ibid.,* September 27, 1945, pp. 532-534.

carryover of wheat stood at 70 million bushels, of which 27 million was still on farms, and only 43 million in commercial storage.

These simple facts explain the government's decision in October, 1945, to lift the maximum delivery restriction. Had it remained in force, producers would have delivered 15 million bushels less than they did in 1945-46, and the government would have been able to test the efficacy of its control mechanism in circumstances in which there was ample storage space available. But the continuation of the maximum limitation policy would have meant 15 million bushels less wheat available to a hungry Europe, and the government decided that the limitation should be lifted, despite MacKinnon's categoric statement on March 2 that the limitation was final and would not be lifted. That statement had been intended to discourage wheat sowing but producers had, nevertheless, ignored the warning and had maintained their wheat acreage levels in any event. On October 4, MacKinnon offered the following explanation to the house, after he reviewed the earlier history of the maximum delivery limitation:

> When policy was under discussion for the crop year 1945-46 we felt that the transportation situation was such that we would have a carryover of wheat on July 31, 1945, of about 325 million bushels, the equivalent of about a full year's export under the then existing conditions. We thought that a small crop of, say 300 million bushels would give us total wheat supplies of over 600 million bushels in addition to 150 to 200 million bushels of marketed feed grains, or total supplies which would press upon the capacity of our railroads and port facilities having regard to other forms of war-time traffic which they were carrying. We also realized that if the 1945 crop were a large crop we would have to face extremely difficult conditions in respect to the movement of marketed grain. This fact, accompanied by the intensification of the demand for feed grains and live stock products, provided ample grounds for retaining the over-all marketing restriction in 1945-46. We also had another important consideration in mind. We knew we had on hand a very large volume of wheat which could be used to meet overseas requirements in case the war ended; all the wheat which Canada, as one of the wheat exporting countries of the world, could be expected to carry to meet early postwar requirements.
>
> In one respect our calculation of our wheat position early in 1945 was not borne out by subsequent events. V-E day resulted in the raising of exports in the crop year 1944-45 by about 65 million bushels, and the reduction in our July 31 stocks from an anticipated 325 million to 258 million bushels, with, of course some of the post-war European demand already met. The 1945 prairie wheat crop has turned out to be a crop of moderate size—some 300 million bushels. Whereas we expected wheat supplies of perhaps 650 million bushels for the crop year 1945-46, our total supplies will aggregate about 550 million bushels, with an additional 170 million bushels of feed grains to be marketed and transported during the present crop year. The supply of some 150 million bushels less wheat than we expected early in 1945 will, none the less, tax the capacity of our railroads during the first half of the present crop year, and particularly our ability to move grain through available Canadian and United States ports.
>
> During the present crop year we expect to export about 325 million bushels of wheat, leaving between 75 to 100 million bushels of wheat on hand July 31, 1946. Since V-E day over one-half of the wheat going into Europe has been Canadian wheat, and that percentage will be fully maintained during the present crop year.

The average yield per acre in Western Canada this year is not large. Most of the surplus from the 1945 crop will be marketed within the 14-bushel limitation. There are some areas, however, and many producers who will have wheat in excess of the 14-bushel delivery limitation. If the restriction on the limitation on marketings is lifted for the balance of the present crop year, it will probably mean an additional 15 million bushels of wheat available for importing countries during the present crop year. In view of the efforts which this country is making to provide food for Europe, the government feels that if a little more wheat can be provided by lifting marketing restrictions for the present crop year, this action should be taken. It has therefore been decided to remove the 14-bushel limitation for the present crop year.[29]

This still fell short of a promise that the principle of an overall limitation upon deliveries was being abandoned permanently. The 14-bushel maximum delivery limitation had been lifted late in the 1943-44 crop year; it had not been imposed in 1944-45; and now it had been lifted from the 1945 crop before it had a chance to become effective. Although it was not imposed again, the authority to do so was retained by order in council and by subsequent amendment to the wheat board act.

[29] *Ibid.*, October 4, 1945, p. 734.

38

PRICE NEGOTIATIONS UNDER THE 1942 WASHINGTON AGREEMENT

The memorandum of agreement concluded between Britain and the four major exporting countries on April 22, 1942, provided for its administration by establishing an international wheat council on which each of the contracting governments had representation, and the council, in turn, appointed an executive committee to conduct its detailed administration. An organizational meeting of the council was held in Washington August 3-5, 1942. It was intended that Mr. George McIvor should head the Canadian delegation to this meeting, but McIvor was too preoccupied with wheat board affairs in Winnipeg, and Mr. L. B. Pearson who was by now minister-counselor of the Canadian legation in Washington served in his place. Pearson was thoroughly at home with the issues because of his previous exposure to the wheat advisory committee in London. Dean Shaw, Mr. John Deutsch and C. F. Wilson were the other members of the delegation. Wilson had briefed MacKinnon on the agenda which included the election of a chairman, the appointment of a secretary, the approval of a budget and the consideration of the obligations of the member countries under the production control and relief wheat provisions of the agreement. In his memorandum to the minister he carefully prepared the way for the cabinet wheat committee's acceptance, despite their earlier apprehensions, of Mr. Andrew Cairns as secretary of the council. Cairns had served as secretary of the wheat advisory committee since 1933, and he was thoroughly acceptable to the other governments. At the meeting Mr. Paul Appleby, the American undersecretary of agriculture, was elected chairman, Cairns was appointed secretary, a budget was approved, and an executive committee under the chairmanship of Mr. L. A. Wheeler was appointed, with Wilson as the Canadian member of that committee. A discussion took place at the council meeting on the production control measures required to conform with the provisions of the memorandum of agreement; Canada's maximum delivery quota regulations stood it in good stead. Under the relief commitments, the Canadian delegation asked that its current relief contributions to Greece be counted against its obligation, but the chairman objected on the ground that the relief provisions in the agreement were intended to apply to the postwar period only, and the matter was deferred for further consideration.

REOPENING OF THE PRICE NEGOTIATIONS

At that meeting, the United States delegation occasioned some surprise by asking for a reexamination of the price provisions in the memorandum of agreement. Wilson reported to MacKinnon:

> This item was placed on the agenda by the United States delegation. Mr. Wheeler expressed a desire on the part of the United States Government to provide now for some measure of price stability beyond the six-month period provided for in the present Agreement. It was agreed that this question be referred to the Executive Committee to study the matter and to prepare a document for the consideration of the various Governments prior to the January meeting, and that this question be discussed in January. While the following consideration was not mentioned, the Canadian delegation felt that this proposal should be agreed to, in so far as the exploration of alternative price proposals might lead to some satisfactory solution which would not involve the prices paid by the United Kingdom for Canadian wheat during the war with prices to be established under the Agreement.[1]

It will be recalled that the following price provision had been inserted into the 1942 memorandum of agreement as a last minute compromise despite Canadian concern that it would affect future price bargaining on our bulk sales to Britain:

> If no determination of prices has been made on the cessation of hostilities, the five countries will, pending such determination but for a period not exceeding six months, maintain as the export price of wheat the last price negotiated by the United Kingdom for a bulk purchase of wheat from the principal country of supply: . . .[2]

Thus the price issue which had been so recently resolved on the foregoing basis was already reopened by the Americans who wanted a more enduring postwar price guarantee, and by the Canadians who were unhappy about the risks in the existing provision. At the first meeting of the executive committee held on November 28-30, 1942, Mr. Wheeler asked that, as a point of departure for further negotiations, the price on the prevailing contract between Canada and Britain be disclosed. Despite this understandable curiosity on the part of the American, Argentine and Australian representatives, the British representative and Wilson declared that they had no authority to reveal the price. Moreover, Mr. E. Twentyman, the British representative, challenged the whole endeavor to reopen the price question by contending that circumstances had not changed since the memorandum of agreement had been signed. In the result, a noncommittal report was submitted by the executive committee to the council.

In preparation for the January 28, 1943 meeting of the international wheat council, Wilson met with the cabinet wheat committee on January 20 to seek instructions on the American proposal for the renegotiation of prices. In the ministers' view, it was still too early to reopen the price question. Because of the opposing views held by the British and Americans on the issue it was agreed that, if the British maintained their position, the Canadian delegation should suggest that the matter not be pursued at the present time. Before the Washington meeting took place, the Right

---

[1]*Memorandum to Mr. MacKinnon re First Meeting of International Wheat Council, August 3-5, 1942*, Trade and Commerce file 26204:14.

[2]*Memorandum of Agreement, 1942*.

Honourable Malcolm MacDonald, British high commissioner to Canada, confirmed that his government's position was unchanged and Canada replied that if the British delegation would declare their objections to reopening the price negotiations, they would receive support. During the council meeting the British and American positions were restated, and Pearson very skillfully executed a brief in favor of postponement of renegotiations. As a result, the council adopted the following resolution:

> The Council recognizes the critical importance of negotiating at the earliest practical moment, prior to the cessation of hostilities, prices which would rule during the entire interim period. The Council therefore requests the Chairman (a) to call the Council as soon as he is of the opinion that such negotiations can be commenced with reasonable prospects of a definite decision being reached, (b) to maintain contact with members of the Council with a view to keeping the matter under constant review and (c) prior to the calling of the Council to instruct the Executive Committee to prepare comprehensive data, including alternative draft schemes, for submission to the Council at that meeting.[3]

At the time of that meeting, the organization of UNRRA was just under way. The council agreed that the relief obligations under the memorandum of the agreement should be discharged through the council to UNRRA.

CHANGING PRICE ATTITUDES

By the summer of 1943 the feed grain shortage in the United States had materialized, and its impact on the demand for Canadian wheat was reflected in rising wheat prices. In Canada all current deliveries were being disposed of on the open market and, because of its dwindling holdings, the Canadian wheat board was reluctant to commit itself to further bulk sales. In the United States, not only had wheat exports from that country come to a halt, but the department of agriculture proposed a 10 million acre increase in wheat sowings that autumn.

Meanwhile, in pursuance of the council resolution, Appleby took soundings on the prospects of support for the wheat price negotiations. He asked Pearson to discuss the Canadian position with him, and Pearson asked for instructions, in the preparation of which McIvor and Wilson carried on a correspondence which reflected the unsettled conditions of the moment and a consequent wish to be rid of the price clause in the memorandum of agreement. This was reported by Norman Robertson in his teletype message of July 6, 1943, to Pearson:

> Reference your WA-3217 re discussion with Appleby. Wilson has consulted McIvor and Biddulph and they advise as follows for your guidance:
>   1. Immediate uncertainties about trend of wheat prices in North American markets resulting from rapid correction of surplus position make present time a very difficult one for effective progress to be made toward price determination contemplated under price clause of draft convention.
>   2. At the same time Canadian delegation have grave doubts about practicability of present basis, as provided in Memorandum of Agreement, for price determination during first six months after war.
>   3. Present basis, very reluctantly agreed to by Canadian delegation and only because it facilitated conclusion of agreement, was intended in theory to

[3]International Wheat Council, *Minutes,* January 29, 1943.

fix price for first six months at level ruling immediately prior to cessation of hostilities.

4. Method of basing price on last bulk sale very imperfect for accomplishing purpose of paragraph 3. For example, market prices might change substantially between date of last bulk sale and date of armistice.

5. This of utmost importance to Canada because if armistice came within next year or so Canada would be only substantial exporter and the only one of the big four substantially concerned with price. From this standpoint we would welcome removal of present reference to price in Memorandum of Agreement. . . .[4]

Pearson made these points informally to Appleby and suggested that Wilson also speak to him as soon as the position was official. The file discloses that Wilson developed some misgiving over a categoric request to amend the memorandum of agreement, and McIvor suggested that he prepare a paper for submission to the wheat committee of the cabinet. Wilson's memorandum was predicated upon the assumption that the futures market would remain open; a closed market would make the issues considerably simpler. On further assumptions that the United States would resist any attempt to amend the agreement by deleting the price reference and that the Canadian government had an interest in the prices at which they made wheat available for relief, Wilson suggested a floor price of 90 cents, and a ceiling of $1.40, or alternatively a ceiling in terms of some definition of parity. These prices reflected the current level of the board's initial payment, and the government's longer-term price objective for wheat. He spoke to Mitchell Sharp who confided that Dr. Mackintosh and he believed that the American speculators were gaining control of our wheat supplies and that if no corrective action was taken, the Canadian government would have to repurchase the wheat for Britain and relief.

On their next visit to Washington, McIvor and Wilson met with Appleby on July 20, 1943. McIvor told Appleby in confidence that a number of factors were developing in the Canadian situation which might require the futures market to be closed. If that were done, and the price to Britain fixed, Canada could live with the existing price provision. But if the market remained open, his board would soon find itself in a position where it could no longer make bulk sales to Britain. With Britain then forced to come into the market, the price of the last bulk sale referred to in the memorandum of agreement would become meaningless. Appleby confirmed that Mr. Noel Hall, head of the British delegation, had advised Mr. Dean Acheson, assistant secretary of state, that his government hoped there would be no reference to prices on the agenda for the August meeting of the council.

On return to Ottawa, McIvor and Wilson were therefore surprised to receive on August 21 a message through the British high commissioner's office that instructions to the British delegation in Washington had been changed. Although the British government had hitherto opposed reopening the price question they were now prepared, in deference to the wishes of others, to seek a new price arrangement. But instead of attempting to negotiate now on prices to take effect at the end of the war, the British government proposed that the council negotiate on a minimum-maximum

[4] *Trade and Commerce file 26204:14.*

range of prices to take effect as soon as possible and continue until August 1, 1944, when the range should be revised. They had no specific range yet to suggest, and hoped that the executive committee would delay negotiations until October.

In the meantime, Wilson had been devising a workable price clause to replace the last bulk sale clause in the memorandum of agreement and submitted the proposal to Crerar, acting minister of trade and commerce, who was the only member of the cabinet wheat committee in Ottawa at the time. On the same day that the British message was received, Wilson recommended to Crerar that the Canadian delegation be authorized:

> to offer a substitute mechanism for the price of the last bulk sale. One such mechanism would be to have the prices for the first six months after the war based upon a 15 percent range around the average of the actual f.o.b. invoice prices paid by the British Ministry of Food for Canadian wheat within the last month or six weeks prior to the end of hostilities. The range feature would permit markets to function during that period, which would be difficult on a fixed price basis.
>
> Basing the price upon an agreed range around the actual invoice prices paid by the British would meet any one of the following methods of sale which might be in operation at the end of hostilities.
> (1) Bulk sales as at present . . .
> (2) British purchases on an open market;
> (3) Direct sales made because of a closed market.
> Use of the invoice prices ruling just prior to the end of the war would avoid the possibility of any break in prices having to be made because of the Agreement at the end of hostilities. The reason for having this provision in the Wheat Agreement at all is to protect the exporting countries against a collapse in prices after the war, and conversely to protect the importing countries from a sharp rise in prices during that period.[5]

Crerar rejected this proposal in favor of pressing instead simply for the removal from the agreement of the last bulk sale clause. In response to the British cable, however, Crerar suggested that if the British or the Americans advanced any new pricing mechanism, Canada should agree to a tentative exploration only, and refer the matter back to the wheat committee. Accordingly, when the price issue was discussed at the August 26-28, 1943, meeting of the council, Pearson reported that the Canadian delegation had been instructed to request deletion of the last bulk sale clause and invited Wilson to explain the circumstances which had made that arrangement obsolete. When Mr. Hall reported his government's suggestion that a substitute pricing arrangement be discussed in October, Mr. Wheeler tartly inquired what changed circumstances had prompted the suggestion. The only changed condition he knew was that prices had gone up. By the same token, he reported that his government would now find it very difficult to enter into price negotiations. In Wilson's report on the meeting he commented:

> The foregoing complete reversal in the British and American attitude toward reaching a price agreement was the highlight of the meeting. Mr. Hall advised me personally that he had gone to the State Department in July to advise Mr. Acheson that the British Government were not interested in having prices discussed at the August meeting of the Council. When Mr. Appleby learned

---

[5]*Ibid.*

of this, he called in Mr. Twentyman to advise him of his increasing impatience with the British unwillingness to discuss a price agreement. He went so far as to say that unless the British attitude changed, he intended to do some writing which would expose the British reluctance to participate seriously in commodity agreements. These views were communicated to the British Government and Mr. Hall felt they played a considerable part in formulating the changed instructions he had now received. It was perfectly clear that within the past month someone within the United States Government above Mr. Appleby had instructed him not to press for a price agreement any longer. I tried to learn privately where these changed views might have originated, but was unable to obtain any satisfactory explanation. The War Food Administration was ruled out as not having an interest in post-war prices; the Commodity Credit Corporation was suggested as a possibility, with the United States now on an import basis, and the CCC being interested in cheap prices for feed wheat. One speculative suggestion was that Mr. Byrnes' office in the White House was becoming interested in these matters.[6]

In the end, the council adopted the following resolution:

The Council took notice of the strong representations of the Canadian Government that the concluding sentence of paragraph 5 of the memorandum of agreement be deleted.

The Council was of the opinion that that sentence, as interpreted by Minute 5 of the final session of the Washington Wheat Meeting, may no longer be effective for the purpose for which it was designed.

The Council recommends that Governments give earnest consideration to the representation of the Canadian Government with a view to securing either the deletion of the sentence or such substitution or interpretation as may be satisfactory to the Canadian Government at the additional meeting of the Council to be held in October next.[7]

Before the autumn meeting of the council could take place, the Winnipeg wheat futures market had been closed and the Canadian delegation requested deferment of the price question until the council met in January, 1944. In preparation for that meeting the cabinet wheat committee reviewed its position, but could come up with no better alternative than to continue to press for deletion of the price clause from the memorandum of agreement. Pearson, Deutsch and Wilson attended the January 31-February 1 meeting. At Pearson's request Wilson stated the Canadian position and, in doing so, obtained recognition from the other delegations that the bulk-sale price provision in the memorandum of agreement had become obsolete when Canadian bulk sales to Britain had been replaced by mutual aid. Then it was learned that the American delegation had fallen into line behind the British proposal to negotiate a price range to come into effect immediately, subject to revision on an annual or semiannual basis. The other delegations went so far as to assure the Canadians that should the negotiations on a price range not succeed by April 30, 1944, they would approve deletion of the price clause from the memorandum of agreement. Because of this changed position, Wilson telephoned MacKinnon to request his permission to participate in the negotiations to which he agreed. When Wilson reported this to the council the next morning, it adopted the following resolution:

[6] *Ibid.*
[7] *Ibid.*

The Council, having considered the renewed request of the Canadian Delegation that the Memorandum of Agreement be amended by the deletion of the last paragraph 6, (a) recognized that the provisions of this sentence are no longer suitable for the purpose for which they were intended; (b) resolved to proceed at once to a consideration of the possibility of invoking Article V (Price Control) of the Draft Convention, in pursuance of paragraph 6 of the Memorandum of Agreement, and of determining prices under that Article; and (c) agreed to recommend to its constituent governments that in the event of agreement to invoke Article V and to determine prices thereunder not having been reached by April 30, 1944, the Memorandum of Agreement should then be amended by the deletion of the last sentence of paragraph 6.[8]

FAILURE OF THE NEGOTIATIONS

The initial result of this agreement to initiate negotiations on a current price range was the spawning of a variety of proposals which were noted by the sixth meeting of the international wheat council held on April 5-7, 1944. The council's report noted that:

.. 3. (a) The Canadian Delegation suggested a basic minimum price of 125 Canadian cents per bushel for No. 1 Northern in store Fort William-Port Arthur, and a basic maximum price equivalent to the United States wheat ceiling price (the present equivalent being about 172 Canadian cents per bushel for No. 1 Northern in store Fort William-Port Arthur).

(b) The United States Delegation suggested basic minimum and maximum prices of 115 and 135 Canadian cents per bushel for No. 1 Northern in store Fort William-Port Arthur.

(c) The Australian Delegation suggested minimum and maximum prices equivalent in Australian currency to 5/4 and 5/10 per bushel f.o.b. Australia for shipment to the United Kingdom, and higher f.o.b. prices for shipment to nearer destinations such as New Zealand and India.

(d) The United Kingdom representative suggested that the Council should address itself to the consideration of a price range in the neighbourhood of 90 to 130 cents Canadian per bushel for No. 1 Northern in store Fort William-Port Arthur.

(e) The Argentine Delegation was unable to suggest a range of prices pending receipt of instructions from its Government. For the purposes of illustration only, it called the Council's attention to Document W.W.M. (Prices) 2/41, dated 18th November 1941, in which the Argentine Government agreed to a basic minimum price of 8.6 pesos per 100 kilos for resale wheat f.o.b. Buenos Aires and added that if this price, which was based on the level of costs prevailing in July, 1939, were adjusted to take account of the (say) 30 per cent increase in costs over the pre-war period its present equivalent would be about 11.2 pesos per quintal.

4. Following discussion of the foregoing suggestions, the Canadian Delegation proposed the substitution of the commercial export price prevailing in Canada at the cessation of hostilities for the bulk purchase price referred to in the concluding sentence of paragraph 6 of the Memorandum of Agreement.

5. Following discussion, the United States Delegation proposed the substitution of the following clause for the concluding sentence of paragraph 6 of the Memorandum of Agreement:

"Pending such determination the five countries will maintain, from 1st May 1944 and until the termination of the provisions of this Memorandum, export

[8]International Wheat Council, *Minutes,* 5/3, February 1, 1944.

prices of wheat of not less than 100 Canadian cents per bushel, both basis No. 1 Northern in store Fort William-Port Arthur; equivalent f.o.b. prices will be calculated for wheats of the other exporting countries and will be adjusted from time to time to meet substantial changes in freight and exchange rates."

6. The Argentine, Australian, Canadian and United Kingdom Delegations undertook to refer to their Governments the foregoing proposal of the United States Delegation and to request the instructions necessary to enable the Council formally to consider it as its Seventh Meeting, the first session of which will open at 3 p.m. on Monday 17th April 1944.[9]

Pearson sent this report by teletype to Norman Robertson on April 8 and commented in his letter of April 10:

I think you will agree that this is an important document; more especially that the United States proposal in paragraph 5 should be given careful consideration. It is obvious, of course, that there can be no more important single factor in Canada's post-war economic position than a stable and satisfactory price for wheat over a reasonable period of time. The United States delegation felt that their proposal would give that stability. In talking to Mr. Wheeler on Saturday afternoon, he indicated that they certainly could not go below the amount of $1.00 Canadian — though he felt that the United Kingdom might wish to push it down a few cents. His main fear, however, was difficulty from the Argentine. Australia also might be hesitant. The fact that three of the Governments represented on the Council might think that the American proposal involved too high a price, will have I should think, a very definite bearing on our consideration of this matter.[10]

Pearson's letter inspired Robertson's memorandum of April 17, 1944, to the prime minister:

At the meetings of the International Wheat Council held last week, concrete proposals were made for an international agreement on minimum and maximum export prices for wheat to go into effect immediately and to continue for a period of two years after the close of hostilities. The Canadian representatives, acting on instructions from the Wheat Committee of Cabinet proposed that the wartime range of export wheat prices under the Agreement should run from the present Canadian minimum paid by the Wheat Board to farmers ($1.25 per bushel F.O.B. Fort William) to the United States maximum received by United States farmers (which at present is equivalent to 172 Canadian cents F.O.B. Fort William) and that the price in the immediate post-war period should be based on the last wartime commercial export sale. Canadian sales to the United States and to neutrals are now being made at approximately $1.47 and shipments to the United Kingdom of Government owned wheat are charged to Mutual Aid at $1.25. The representatives of all the other countries taking part in the discussions — Australia, Argentina, the United Kingdom and the United States, thought that the Canadian price proposals were too high. The United Kingdom delegation suggested a price range of 90¢ to $1.30. At the conclusion of the meetings, the United States representatives made a compromise proposal for a floor of $1.00 and ceiling of $1.50 both F.O.B. Fort William. All the delegations undertook to refer the United States proposal to their Governments and to request instructions necessary to enable the Wheat Council formally to consider it at its next meeting, which will begin on April 19th.

[9]International Wheat Council (*Conclusion*) 1/44, April 8, 1944.
[10]*Trade and Commerce File 26204:14.*

While not certain, there is a considerable chance that the United States suggestion will, after some discussion, be acceptable to Australia, Argentina and the United Kingdom. However, it can be argued that Canada should adhere to its original proposition, namely a range between the Canadian minimum and the United States maximum. It may be felt that it is not practical (politically) for Canada to agree to a fixed maximum export price which is substantially lower than the probable rising prices which United States farmers will be receiving during a period when the United States is importing heavily from Canada. Under the United States parity price policy, it is quite likely that United States domestic wheat prices will continue to rise for a time.

Depending upon the Canadian attitude it is probable that agreement could be reached on the United States proposal, or some slight modification of it. It is not likely that the Canadian suggestion outlined above will be acceptable to any of the other Governments. If the Canadian position is maintained, the Wheat Agreement, for all practical purposes, will become meaningless and possibly break down altogether. This might have some unfortunate repercussions on the possibility of getting sensible international commodity arrangements in the future. Failure to obtain agreement on a reasonable price might also intensify British caution, and lead her to husband her bargaining power with reference to the purchase of agricultural products generally from Canada during the immediate post-war period.

We must consider also whether, in all the circumstances, export wheat prices higher than $1.50 are really in our interest. During the period of the war and perhaps for a short time after the Canadian Government will have to finance, directly or indirectly, a good part of our wheat exports to the United Kingdom and Russia. The higher the prices the greater the burden on the Canadian Treasury. Also, export prices in excess of $1.50 if maintained for some years are sure to result in an over expansion of wheat production both on the part of ourselves and our competitors, with a renewal in the postwar period of the difficulties of the 'thirties. The Canadian interest lies in a large volume of exports at reasonable prices. This will not be possible for long if the higher cost export competitors in the rest of the world are induced to expand their output considerably. In Canada itself the inevitable extension of production into marginal areas would bring in its train the social and economic problems consequent upon the subsequent readjustment.[11]

Gardiner's reaction to the various proposals was considerably at variance with Robertson's as he wrote to MacKinnon on April 12, 1944:

I have yours of April 10th re wheat prices in the international agreement.

The proposal made by the Canadian delegation that the minimum be the Canadian minimum of $1.25 a bushel and the ceiling be the American ceiling of $1.72 would appear to me to be fair.

The proposal that the minimum be $1.00 and the maximum $1.50 would appear to me to be favorable to the U.S.A. and unfavorable to Canada in view of the fact that the American farmer is protected by a 42 cent duty on 80% of his wheat while the Canadian price to the farmer is regulated by the export price, since he must export 70% of his wheat. It would appear to me that during the existence of any such agreement there should be a free movement of wheat among the agreeing countries. If that were provided then I should see no objection to the proposal of $1.00 minimum and a $1.50 maximum as suggested by the Americans.

[11]*Ibid.*

On the other hand if we were to sign an agreement which ties the Canadian farmer to accept not more than $1.50 for wheat whereas the benefiting country, Britain, provides $1.94 to her farmers and the American government when exchange is at par, with a duty of 42¢, could allow her wheat to run to $1.92, I am afraid we would be open for considerable criticism.

An alternative might be $1.00 minimum with the American domestic price as the ceiling.

I have been wondering what the effect of all this will be on Mutual Aid. Will it be impossible for us to finance wheat to Britain or Russia up to 50% of the value. This would be an indirect way of selling at a price lower than the minimum. If we cannot do that we cannot carry out the arrangement already entered into with others and our own farmers, namely that the wheat taken over on September 28 last would not be sold in competition with new wheat. I do not think this agreement should be allowed to interfere with that arrangement in any way.

I agree that we should not be responsible for blocking the establishment of minimum and maximum prices but hope that does not make it necessary for us to sign an agreement which is inequitable as between our farmers and those of the U.S.A. and Great Britain, who at present are both importers of our wheat. It would seem to me that advancing this agreement on the terms proposed from the end of the war to the 1st of May 1944, is greatly to the advantage of the U.S.A. at the expense of the Canadian farmers.[12]

It should be noted, in passing, that the minimum of $1.25 in the Canadian proposal for a price range was based upon the board's recently raised initial payment and the price at which crown wheat was made available under mutual aid. The $1.75 maximum was related to the United States ceiling price of $1.72, basis Chicago, which was the upper limit of what might be realized on the commercial sales of Canadian wheat to the United States. On the other hand, should the American ceiling be raised, Canada reserved the right to sell in that market at any higher prevailing prices.

Recognizing, however, that the American proposal for a range of $1 - $1.50 was the one on which agreement could most probably be reached, the cabinet wheat committee authorized the Canadian delegation to support it, subject to the proviso that the maximum price be revised if the American ceiling were to be raised above $1.72.

On his return to Ottawa, Wilson reported to the cabinet wheat committee on April 25, 1944, that the various governments had agreed to the American proposals, subject (a) to a Canadian-American resolution of the problem related to any change in the American wheat ceiling (b) to a British proviso that the agreement remain in effect to August 1, 1946, or to the end of the European war, whichever was later, and (c) to the settlement of a dispute between the British and the Australians on the Australian price equivalents. The British had also proposed a continuing agreement beyond August 1, 1946, for another two years or until the end of the war with Japan, whichever was later, with a floor of 90 cents and a ceiling of $1.30. The Americans had intimated that they would oppose the British proposal for a lower range during this later period. Wilson also reported upon a private conversation with the British delegation in which they had suggested as an alternative a five-year agreement with a floor of 90 cents, with no ceiling, and with an undertaking on their part not to buy wheat from any exporting

[12] *Ibid.*

country inside or outside the agreement at less than 90 cents. The ministers were rather taken by this unilateral obligation offered by the British, and Wilson was instructed to explore it further should agreement be not reached on the American proposal. Meanwhile, he could continue to support the latter, provided that Canada would not be bound by the $1.50 maximum, should the American domestic ceiling rise above $1.75.

At the eighth meeting of the council held on April 28, 1944, the Canadian problem over changes in the American wheat ceiling was referred to the Canadian and American delegations for direct consultation. A disagreement arose over the duration of the proposed agreement on a price range, the British wanting a shorter period and the Canadian delegation a longer. At that stage, Wilson proposed that the agreement remain in effect for three years after the end of hostilities, and the British wanted only two. A British-Australian dispute had also arisen over the Australian price equivalents to be incorporated in the price agreement. It was now April 28, and the council had earlier resolved that if no agreement on a price range had been reached by April 30, the bulk sale price clause would be deleted from the memorandum of agreement. Rather than force the issue, however, the council decided to keep its eighth meeting in session until agreement was reached.

On April 29, 1944, the Canadian and American delegations met to discuss the ceiling price proviso. At first it was proposed that the matter be dealt with by an exchange of notes, rather than by incorporation into an agreement. Notes were drafted, and an exchange of notes was also projected between the British and Canadians to insure British concurrence. Shortly afterward, however, the Americans came up with a much simpler solution by proposing a clause in the agreement to the effect that the obligation to observe the price range would not apply to transactions between member exporting countries. The text of the American clause was as follows: "Inasmuch as trade in wheat between exporting countries arises largely from dislocations resulting from the war these minimum and maximum prices shall not apply in respect to such trade."

The British, in turn, had reservations over this clause based on the fear that the attractiveness of the United States market might prevent Canada from supplying all the wheat the British required within the price range. Consequently, they requested an exchange of notes in which the Canadian government would give such assurance.

The British-Canadian dispute over the duration of the price agreement was also pursued bilaterally. At the April 28, 1944, meeting of the council Mr. E. Twentyman had proposed: "That a range of $1.00 to $1.50 should be maintained from the date agreement is reached until August 1, 1946 or until the first August 1 occurring not less than two years after the cessation of hostilities in Europe, whichever be the later date."

Wilson had countered with the proposal: "That the range of $1.00 to $1.50 be maintained from the date agreement is reached until August 1, 1947, or the expiry of three years after the cessation of hostilities in Europe, whichever be the later date."

The effect of the British proposal would have been to terminate the agreement two years after the end of European hostilities at the shortest, and three years at the longest, while the Canadian proposal would have made the three-year duration definite. The issue was transmitted by the secretary of state for external affairs to Massey, high commissioner in London on May 29, 1944, to pursue with the British secretary of state for dominion affairs. On July 18, Massey reported a British compromise proposal that the price range should last until August 1, 1947, or until the first August 1, two years after the cessation of European hostilities, whichever was the later date. This, in turn, assured an agreement of three years' duration and was accepted by the Canadian government.

The remaining outstanding issue was that of Australian price equivalents. The basic prices in the proposed agreement were stated in terms of No. 1 Northern wheat, in store Fort William. Price equivalents for United States, Argentine and Australian wheats were to be worked out, after allowing for quality differentials, by adding to the Fort William price the costs, including freight, from Fort William to Liverpool or London, and then deducting the costs of moving wheat from American, Argentine and Australian ports to Britain. This method of establishing equivalent prices was satisfactory to the United States and Argentine delegations, but not to the Australians. Because of the high freight charges from Australia to Britain, the Australian equivalents produced a low figure, in their terms, at which that country must sell in order to compete in British and European markets. But such equivalent prices were lower than the Australians could obtain competitively in their nearby markets. For that reason, the Australians held out for a two-price system for Australian wheat to which all the other delegations were opposed. The Australians had a valid argument in equity, and the issue was referred by council to the Australian and British governments to discuss bilaterally.

Those discussions took an interminable time, as the eighth session of the council remained, technically, in existence. When that session held its fifth meeting on January 30, 1945, the council was informed that no progress on the price-equivalents issue had been made. The executive committee also continued to meet in April and July of that year, but the Australian two-price issue remained unresolved. The American delegate advocated that export quotas be introduced along with the price range, but this found little support. At a meeting of the executive committee held on July 19, 1945, the committee recommended that the ninth meeting of the council be called, to which the committee would report its inability to reach agreement upon equivalents and recommend the deletion of the bulk sale clause from the memorandum of agreement.

Because several of the council delegates planned to be in London in August, 1945, the seventh meeting of the eighth session of the council was held there on August 31-September 1. Biddulph was briefed to represent Canada because Wilson was ill. Mr. Leslie A. Wheeler was elected chairman of the council in replacement of Mr. Appleby. George McIvor had been approached to become chairman, but the cabinet wheat committee felt it would be a mistake for him to do so with such little prospect of anything tangible ensuing from the stalemate in reaching a price agreement. At the meeting, Mr. Herbert Broadley of the ministry of food and Mr. R. Tadman of the Australian wheat board had been unable to resolve the price-equivalents dispute. The council thereupon recommended to governments the deletion of the price clause in the memorandum of agreement. On behalf of Canada, Biddulph withdrew support of the $1.00 - $1.50 price range which had awaited resolution of the price-equivalents issue. Mr. Carl Farrington of the commodity credit corporation who represented the United States remarked on the inappropriateness of bringing the export quota proposals of the draft convention into operation in view of the unprecedented demand for wheat and the efforts of his government to meet relief needs. The eighth meeting of the council was then adjourned.

Because of the desultory reports sent to Ottawa during the course of that meeting, Gardiner became convinced that the international approach afforded no hope of the postwar assurance of markets and of price stability that western wheat producers so urgently needed. Thereafter he directed his attention to obtaining the same result by other means.

The ninth meeting of the council held in Washington on September 1, 1945, resolved to invite the following countries to join the council in the preparation of a new wheat agreement: Belgium, Brazil, China, Denmark, France, India, Netherlands, USSR and Yugoslavia. The action seemed dubious to those in Canada who believed that no more hope of agreement could come from a larger body if the principal participants, Britain and the four major exporting countries, continued to find it impossible to find a compromise. In response to Mr. Broadley's urging that prices be held at the lowest possible levels pending agreement on a price range, the council adopted the following resolution:

> Having regard to the grave danger of a recurrence of a state of disequilibrium in the world wheat situation resulting from the uneconomic high-cost production of wheat which will be stimulated by the present high level of wheat prices, the Council recommends to its constituent governments (a) that they take every possible step to maintain during the period ending 31st July 1946 export prices of wheat at the lowest possible levels, and (b) that accordingly they instruct their representatives to inform the Executive Committee at its next meeting (which meeting shall be held in Washington not later than 5th October 1945) of the ceilings on export prices of wheat which they will maintain during that period.[13]

At the executive committee meeting held on October 5, 1945, Wilson pursued the cabinet wheat committee's view that it would be futile to enlarge the council's membership while the price negotiations remained unresolved. Instead, he recommended that the price negotiations be pursued by the existing members. The United States delegation was in an embarrassing position because it had been unable to secure any formal instructions. The Honourable Clinton Anderson had replaced the Honourable Claude Wickard as secretary of agriculture. Anderson was by no means as keen on an international wheat agreement as his predecessors, Wallace and Wickard, had been. Mr. James Byrnes, a former presidential assistant was now secretary of state. His undersecretaries, Edwin Stettinius and Will Clayton, were known to be opposed to commodity agreements which might stand in the way of the resumption of complete trade liberalization after the war. Paul Appleby had resigned as undersecretary of agriculture, and with the United States hierarchy now broadly out of sympathy with the market

[13]International Wheat Council, *Minutes*, 9/2, September 1, 1945.

sharing objectives of its predecessors and opposed to any price or quota limitations which might impede trade in the immediate postwar period of short supplies, Wheeler and Farrington could get no instructions. Within the international wheat council, the position was such that the United States could be blamed for the breakdown of international negotiations, as Wheeler requested time in which to seek instructions.

As for the council's resolution that the executive committee receive reports on measures taken by member governments on the maintenance of ceiling prices on wheat, Wilson was quoted as follows:

> Mr. C. F. Wilson stated that, as a result of the failure of the Council to come to agreement on price equivalents, the Canadian Government had been faced with having to take a decision as to its future export price policy. His Government recognized that the United States was the only other present source of supply able to help meet the paramount needs for food of liberated Europe. It also recognized that the present export price of United States wheat — equal to the domestic ceiling price which was supported by a parity relation to non-farm products — was equivalent to a Canadian export price of approximately $2.00 per bushel at Fort William. It was nevertheless felt that it would be a mistaken policy on the part of the exporting countries, in view of their long term interests, to continue to allow prices to rise and unduly stimulate the domestic production of wheat in both importing and exporting countries. The Canadian Government had, therefore, by order-in-council set the export ceiling price on Canadian wheat at the same level as that ruling at the cessation of hostilities, namely $1.55 per bushel for No. 1 Northern in store Fort William-Port Arthur or Vancouver. While no time limit had been set upon the continuation of this ceiling price his Government had, in asking its producers to forego the benefits of their present strong marketing position guaranteed to them a minimum price of $1.00 per bushel for No. 1 Northern in store Fort William-Port Arthur or Vancouver on the authorized deliveries for each crop year for the five year period ending 31st July 1950.[14]

The chairman, Leslie A. Wheeler, reported on the ceiling price in effect in the United States, but the Argentine and Australian members had nothing positive to report. As a result, the committee adopted the following innocuous resolution:

> The Executive Committee, in accordance with the resolution adopted by the Council at the second meeting of its Ninth Session held in London on 1st September 1945, received reports from the representatives of Argentina, Australia, Canada and the United States with regard to the establishment of ceiling prices and considered anew the possibility of continuing negotiations on Argentine, Australian, and United States f.o.b. equivalents of the agreed minimum and maximum basic prices.
>
> Having a common anxiety to ensure the successful continuation of the International Wheat Agreement the members of the Executive Committee recommend that governments give further consideration to the problem with a view to instructing their respective representatives to continue discussions on price equivalents at the next meeting of the committee to be held at the call of the Chair.[15]

In their efforts to escape the predicament that American disinterest was at the root of the breakdown in price negotiations Wheeler and Farrington

---

[14]International Wheat Council, (*Executive Committee: Resume*) *16/45*, October 5, 1945. See also pp. 46-48.

[15]*Ibid.*

convened an informal meeting of the executive committee on November 30, 1945, on very short notice and Mr. A. E. Ritchie of the Canadian embassy attended as an observer. At the meeting Farrington disclosed that he was authorized to propose for the consideration of the council at its next meeting:

> (a) that the five countries signatory to the Memorandum of Agreement should maintain from 1st August 1945 until 31st July 1950 basic minimum and maximum export prices of wheat of 100 and 150 United States cents per bushel for No.1 Manitoba Northern in store Fort William-Port Arthur and for No. 1 Heavy Dark Northern Spring, containing not less than 14 per cent protein, in store Duluth, Minnesota; (b) that f.o.b. prices comparable to the foregoing be agreed for Argentine and Australian wheats; and (c) that should the Executive Committee of the International Wheat Council determine, at any time during any one of the four crop-years August/July 1946/47-1949/50, that the aggregate estimated supplies available for export from Argentina, Australia, Canada, and the United States in any one of the aforementioned crop-years, or part thereof, would exceed the effective world demand at the maximum price specified above for wheat imported from those four countries as a whole the provisions of Article IV (Export Control) of the Draft Convention would automatically come into effect and be applied by the International Wheat Council.[16]

The proposal as it stood seemed far from acceptance; it assumed that price equivalents could be agreed, and that the British would accept a price commitment terminating four and a half years hence.

When Wilson reported the position to the cabinet wheat committee, Gardiner asked quite pointedly about the chances for a successful outcome of the negotiations; Wilson replied that they were almost nil. With that point reconfirmed, Gardiner pressed ahead with a scheme of his own for the assurance of postwar price and market stability.

---

[16]*International Wheat Council (Executive Committee: Resume)* 17/45, November 29, 1945.

39

CANADA-UNITED KINGDOM WHEAT CONTRACT AND THE FIVE-YEAR POOL

In his September 27, 1945, speech justifying the $1.55 export price ceiling, Gardiner referred to the government's participation in the prolonged negotiations for a postwar international wheat agreement and he gave as one reason for Canada's unilateral price action the fact that the international attempt had failed until now, and that the government's floor price guarantee would afford more time to revive it. Privately, Gardiner had little faith that the multilateral approach would succeed and he was not prepared to wait indefinitely on the outcome, because he believed there were other ways of stabilizing the Canadian postwar wheat position.

Part III of this review has recorded Gardiner's role as the de facto wheat-policy maker, in addition to the discharge of his departmental responsibilities in which he had been outstandingly successful in his contractual negotiations with the British ministry of food for the supply of other food products. The existence of these contracts had helped the government to underwrite floor prices and to expand the production of other foodstuffs throughout the war. Although the British were hard bargainers, they had their counterpart, if not a match, in Gardiner, and the resulting contracts had provided a firm basis of market assurance. In their negotiation, Gardiner had acquired full confidence in the exchange of oral commitments modified only by necessity of force majeure, and he carried his faith inspired by his experience with the other food contracts into the conception of a major contract for wheat. The existing contracts for bacon, cheese, eggs and frozen meats were shortly coming up for renewal, and Gardiner saw no reason why a similar contract could not be negotiated for wheat.

The first inkling of Gardiner's thinking in that direction was revealed in a meeting of the cabinet wheat committee held on December 4, 1945. The principal topic under consideration was the wheat board's monopoly status now that the war was ended, and the board had properly raised the question in a memorandum to the minister. It had ascertained that the British intended to continue their monopoly purchasing arrangements through the transitional years. This appeared to prejudice our reversion to an open market system, just as it had done after World War I when the first wheat board was created. The board's immediate responsibility was to conform with the government's directive on the export price, and later on it might have to implement the five-year floor price. Either responsibility appeared to justify the retention of a monopoly board. But the government had promised to continue the ceiling only "for the time being" as a result of which the board was inhibited in making forward sales, and the ministers were not prepared to predict how long the "time being" might endure. If, for example, the ceiling were to be removed within a few weeks, the board could only go by the rough criterion provided by the American markets in setting its own prices. The question of legislative authority for the board's monopoly powers also arose. The ministers' initial reaction was that the board should have draft amendments to its act ready, as a standby measure, for the next session of parliament. As events transpired however, the board's monopoly powers were continued under authority of the national emergency transitional powers act until 1947.

The board also asked for a review of its instructions on the priorities to be given in its wheat sales. First priority had already been accorded to the British and second priority to the European allied countries, but the board's stocks were now at a point where there were no longer supplies to cover residual sales to the USSR, nor to our traditional customers among the neutral countries of Europe and South America. Despite demands of these other markets, the ministers agreed that the existing priorities should remain.

Although the international price negotiations were not on the agenda for that meeting, Gardiner queried Wilson, nevertheless, on the latest developments in that area. He wanted to know what the executive committee had accomplished that autumn toward reviving the negotiations and Wilson could only confirm that the results had been very poor. Gardiner attached great importance to that fact, although the significance of his reaction was not apparent at the time. To Gardiner it was the only prerequisite he needed for taking his own initiative to assure market security. When, during the course of the discussion, Mitchell Sharp referred to Mr. Graham Towers' suggestion made elsewhere that afternoon that first priority accorded to wheat shipments to Britain should be used as a bargaining weapon in the pending loan negotiations with that country, Gardiner countered with an alternative proposal of his own. He mentioned that he would be heading a delegation to London shortly on the renegotiation of the other food contracts, and that it would be preferable to use both the priority and export ceiling as levers in the negotiation of a five-year wheat agreement with Britain. Such an agreement could underwrite or replace the floor-price commitment which the Canadian government had given in compensation for the ceiling. The transfer of that responsibility to the British could be expected to appeal to his cabinet colleagues.

COMMENCEMENT OF THE NEGOTIATIONS

Following the December 4, 1945, discussion in the cabinet wheat committee, Gardiner arrived in London on December 22 on what appeared to be an informal errand. He had not left Canada with any cabinet authority to negotiate on wheat. What he sought was some encouragement from the British before making a recommendation to cabinet. He was met upon arrival in London by Mr. R. V. Biddulph, the wheat board's representative, who arranged a luncheon for Gardiner with Messrs. James Rank and Alfred Hooker on December 26. With the two British grain men in charge of the imported cereals division, Gardiner explored, over the course of two hours, the possibility of a long-term wheat contract with Britain. Gardiner dwelt upon the wartime effort Canadian farmers had made to keep Britain supplied with wheat on reasonable terms and used that as an argument that Britain should offer some tangible assurance of a market for wheat over the transitional period. This could take the form of a long-term contract or, at least, Britain could underwrite the five-year floor guarantee of $1 to which the Canadian government was committed. Rank acknowledged the help Canadian farmers had provided during the war in return for which Britain should consider some form of long-term commitment. On the other hand, Hooker hoped that the open market could be restored as quickly as possible. One suggestion was that for the short term Britain should buy all Caanadian wheat supplies and distribute any residual quantities to other markets in Europe. While Rank subsequently backed away from the long-term contract proposal, he was prepared to recommend that Britain guarantee a floor price. In any event, the two men were now in a position to inform the ministry of food of the exploratory discussions. Sir Ben Smith was away from London at the time, and any further discussion had to await his return.

Gardiner was aware that he was initiating contract discussions in an area which was the prerogative of MacKinnon, as the minister directly responsible for wheat marketing policy, and he kept him informed. At that time MacKinnon's trade officials were lining up trade missions for him both in Europe and in Latin America. After their meeting with Rank and Hooker, Gardiner and Biddulph went to Paris, Brussels and the Hague for the purpose of exploring informally, also, the prospect of long-term wheat contracts with those countries. Gardiner's return to London in mid-January, 1946, coincided with MacKinnon's arrival in London. Thereupon Gardiner and MacKinnon, Dr. Barton, deputy minister of agriculture, and Biddulph met with the British minister of food, Sir Ben Smith, and his officials, including Rank, Hooker and Pillman of the imported cereals division. Over the course of several meetings, a long-term wheat contract was discussed. Gardiner wanted a five-year agreement, but was prepared to settle for four years. He wanted the British to agree to $1.55 as a fixed price for at least two years, with an arrangement for subsequent agreement on prices for the latter years. Gardiner was concerned about a long-term guarantee. The longer it extended the more certain he was that he could commit western farmers to acceptance of a price below the market in the immediate future. On the other hand, the British believed their interests lay in a short-term contract, with nothing more than a floor-price guarantee in subsequent years. MacKinnon had to leave London while the discussions continued and, according to the British account of the talks after MacKinnon left, Gardiner suggested a four-year contract at a fixed price of $1.25 for its duration.[1] Gardiner failed to report that he had made such a proposal and, if he did, it was on an exploratory basis as something, if acceptable to the

[1] R. J. Hammond, *Food*, pp. 779-780.

British, he might be prepared to recommend to his own cabinet. If he made it, the offer displayed his concern over a decline in open market prices in the later years of the agreement.

In the closing stages of the London talks, Sir Ben Smith proposed a two-year contract for 120 million bushels at $1.55. Gardiner rejected the offer as something he could not recommend to his government. Gardiner's negotiating weapons were the removal of the export-price ceiling and the priority on wheat sales to Britain, and Sir Ben finally proposed that the negotiations continue in Ottawa on a basis of somewhat larger quantities at a fixed price of $1.55 for two years, and a floor price guarantee of $1.00. for another two years. Although MacKinnon had left just before this position was reached, he gave a press interview on his departure from London, which was reported as follows:

Canada will supply to the United Kingdom 200 million bushels of wheat a year during the next two years at a price which has been fixed at $1.55 a bushel, Hon. James MacKinnon, minister of trade and commerce, disclosed here Thursday night.

Head of the Canadian trade delegation to Britain, Mr. MacKinnon, left by air, Friday, for Canada to get final government approval of a grain deal which will mean that all wheat produced by Canadian farmers during the next few years is sure of finding a market outlet, both here and in Europe.

Mr. MacKinnon said that the two year agreement was only an interim measure, and that he felt formal long-term contracts would be signed with Britain soon extending interim agreement for "several years".

"Britain is to be our biggest permanent peace-time customer," he declared.

To be decided on his return, he stated, was whether annual carryover would be marketed or whether it would be retained in event of poor crops. He said that every bushel of wheat including carry-over now in storage in Canada could be sold immediately to Britain or to the nations of Europe.

Price of $1.55 is not fixed in any written contract, but has been only verbally agreed upon and could vary from time to time according to Mr. MacKinnon, although it was not likely to do so.

France is clamoring for all Canadian wheat that the dominion can export, said the minister. The only way that French allotment could be increased, however, would be by cutting the amounts imported by other nations, and this matter is under consideration.[2]

Hammond recorded that MacKinnon's premature disclosure of the contract exploratory talks had "proved a little embarrassing to both governments". Also, MacKinnon's reference to a quantity of 200 million bushels was far higher than the British were prepared to contemplate, although it reflected Gardiner's objective, as Gardiner reported to cabinet directly upon his return to Ottawa on February 7, 1946:

On Friday, February 1, 1946, Mr. Biddulph, representative of the Wheat Board in London; Dr. Barton, Deputy Minister of Agriculture; Mr. Robertson, representative of the Department of Agriculture, and I met Sir Ben Smith, Minister of Food, Mr. James Rank and Mr. Hooker of the Cereals Committee of the Food Ministry, and others, to discuss wheat. Mr. MacKinnon had discussions before he left for Canada and asked me to continue them to a conclusion.

[2] *Winnipeg Free Press*, January 29, 1946.

It was finally agreed that I would report to the Government in Ottawa that the Food Ministry was prepared to discuss the possibility of reaching an agreement on the following basis:

1. The United Kingdom would take stated supplies of wheat from Canada to December 31, 1947, at $1.55 a bushel No. 1 Northern basis Ft. William.

2. That in the fall of 1946 a meeting would be held to determine what the price would be beyond 1947.

3. That the United Kingdom undertake that at no time during the crop years covering the crops of 1946-47-1948 or 1949 would Canada be asked to accept less than $1.00 a bushel No. 1 Northern basis Ft. William.

4. The question of quantity each year covering the entire period is to be taken up as discussions proceed.

I may state that the quantities discussed were from 180,000,000 to 200,000,000 per year, I do not think an agreement would be very helpful unless at least 180,000,000 bushels were taken.

I may say that the Minister of Agriculture in France was prepared to discuss the possibility of a similar contract.

If we could make a contract for twenty to thirty million in France and about the same amount over the countries north of France our supplies would be well taken care of. . . .[3]

After discussing Gardiner's report, cabinet decided to refer the proposal to the food requirements committee for study. In that committee the trade and commerce member took the position that the matter was one which should be considered by the cabinet wheat committee, as the annotated agenda for the next meeting of that committee recorded:

Mr. Gardiner's report was submitted to the Cabinet about two weeks ago and referred for consideration and report by the Food Requirements Committee. When the committee met, the officials of Trade and Commerce took the view that the committee should not take any action on Mr. Gardiner's report, but rather that the report could more appropriately be considered by the Wheat Committee of Cabinet. The present position, therefore, is that Cabinet is still awaiting advice on Mr. Gardiner's report—the nature of which cannot be determined until the report has been discussed by the Wheat Committee. The Chief Commissioner of the Canadian Wheat Board has stated that the Board will be prepared at the next meeting of the Wheat Committee to give its views with regard to the main points set out in Mr. Gardiner's report. From the standpoint of long-term marketing policy, the Wheat Board has intimated informally that the Board will seriously question the advisability of a four-year contract with the U.K., except for an amount substantially less than 180 million bushels per year—also that the proposed contract with France should be considered only on a basis that would leave the Board free to supply the other European countries that have been more regular customers for Canadian wheat, e.g., Belgium, the Netherlands, Norway, and possibly Switzerland and one or two others.[4]

At that stage, the cabinet wheat committee could do little more than await Sir Ben Smith's projected visit to Ottawa. When he arrived in March to plead for increased wheat production in 1946 and to continue contract negotiations, the two governments appeared to be close to agreement on terms which included $1.55 for the first two years and a minimum of $1.00

[3] *Trade and Commerce File 20-141-11.*
[4] *Ibid.*

on the last two. On quantities, the British countered Gardiner's suggestion of 200 million bushels with 160 million, and it appeared that a compromise could be reached on 180 million. Smith took the proposal back to London and George McIvor followed him over in April.

As a result of the negotiations which had proceeded so far, MacKinnon wrote to McIvor on April 3 informing the wheat board of the developments and requesting the board to study the matter and its implications if a contract were to be concluded. At the same time an interdepartmental committee was named to give similar consideration to the contract. This committee included Dr. G. S. H. Barton, deputy minister of agriculture, Dean A. M. Shaw, chairman of the agricultural supplies board, Mitchell Sharp, special assistant in the department of finance, M. W. Mackenzie, deputy minister of trade and commerce and C. F. Wilson.

During McIvor's visit to London in April, he was informed that the British were prepared to agree upon the prices and quantities discussed in Ottawa in March, with the addition of two provisos. These were the resale and fall clauses worded as follows:

(a) That the United Kingdom will have full discretion in regard to price and destination in the disposal of this quantity of Canadian wheat and shall not be required to utilize it only in the United Kingdom.

(b) If Canada were to sell wheat to other buyers at prices lower than the United Kingdom is currently paying under the terms of the contract, the United Kingdom would be entitled to receive a similarly favourable treatment.[5]

What the British had in mind in the resale clause was their supply responsibility in the occupied zone of Germany, but the unqualified clause as drafted would have permitted Britain, if it were to her advantage, to resell Canadian wheat competitively in Canada's commercial markets. The fall clause provided that the contract price would be reduced if Canada were to sell wheat more cheaply to any other customer. As the Canadian government was offering, on behalf of producers, to accept lower than prevailing market prices at the outset of the contract, that clause would have denied producers any hope of recouping their losses later on when the contract prices were above those in other markets. For this reason, the fall clause was unacceptable to the Canadian side. As McIvor and his board members advised: "The latest proposal received from the United Kingdom is not one which can be given serious consideration. In effect, it is not a contract either in respect to quantity or in respect to price."[6]

WHEAT BOARD RESERVATIONS

Meanwhile, the board had been at work on its reply to MacKinnon's query of April 3 on the merits of a contract. On April 28, McIvor forwarded a confidential memorandum to MacKinnon and circulated copies to the members of the cabinet wheat committee and to the members of the interdepartmental committee which had been named. While the members of the board had more serious reservations about the wisdom of the contract than their memorandum displayed, their comments were circumspect

[5]*Ibid.*
[6]Canadian Wheat Board, *Observations on Proposed United Kingdom Wheat Contract*, April 26, 1946, Trade and Commerce File 20-141-11.

because they were reluctant to intrude their views upon what was primarily a political decision. Nevertheless, the memorandum did query the risk of tying up too large a portion of Canada's available wheat supplies in a contract with one customer, which would deny to Canada's other traditional customers similar access to Canadian contractual supplies and prices. The board also pointed out that a long-term contract would necessitate continuation of a monopoly board. If the contract were signed, the government would have to postpone reversion to its prewar policy of restoring wheat marketing to the open market or at least to a voluntary board. Thirdly, it counselled the government that the provisions of a bilateral contract should not preclude negotiation of an international wheat agreement for which the western farm organizations had declared their support. Lastly, the board demonstrated the extent to which the proposed contract quantities would distort the traditional pattern of our export distribution. The issues the board raised were of such importance that the relevant passages of its memorandum are quoted:

(1) The signing of a long-term contract between Canada and the United Kingdom for the sale and purchase of fixed quantities of wheat at specified prices over a period of years constitutes a new departure in the marketing of Canadian wheat. It is not easy to adequately appraise all the complex factors involved in this type of approach to our largest overseas market.

(2) Such a contract can only be appraised *in part* by those responsible for the marketing of wheat. Problems of security, trade and finance are involved, and the views of those more familiar with these wider fields should be a part of an adequate appraisal.

(3) *Affirmative or negative appraisal of the wisdom of the proposed contract must largely depend upon our estimate of international conditions which will prevail during the next five years.* If we are in for an unsettled world economy where nationalism and political blocs limit the movement of goods and determine the direction of trade, then a contract with the United Kingdom has a great deal of merit. On the other hand, if we are about to work into an era of expanding international trade, our interests lie in the direction of the broadest possible approach to all available wheat markets. Superficial knowledge indicates that the former rather than latter alternative will prevail for the next five years.

(4) The contract for the sale of wheat to the United Kingdom under certain circumstances should be capable of forming the pattern of a broader international wheat agreement. This is an important consideration because the organized grain producers in the Prairie Provinces appear to have placed their faith in such an international agreement as a stabilizing factor in their industry. In negotiating the proposed contract with the United Kingdom, care could be taken that the terms of the contract do not bar the way for either Canada or the United Kingdom to take an effective part in an international wheat agreement if such an agreement is the sincere desire of the great majority of importing and exporting countries.

(5) In the opinion of the Board, the carrying out of a contract for the sale of fixed quantities of wheat at specified prices over a period of years involves the continuance of a monopoly Wheat Board for the duration of the proposed contract. There does not appear to be any way in which an open market could operate with a large proportion of Canadian wheat exports under contract in respect to both volume and price. . . .

There followed a lengthy discussion of the constitutionality of a monopoly wheat board act and the memorandum continued:

(8) If this contract is proceeded with and a Monopoly Board virtually decided upon for some time to come, we have taken an important step in the direction of the nationalization of the grain trade in Canada. The Board believes that there should be no mistake about the direction in which we are moving when the proposed contract with the United Kingdom is signed and perhaps, contracts with other countries are similarly negotiated. During the War, the Board has, in accordance with its statute and under the direction of the Government, maintained the various branches of the trade in operation, it being presumed that these services would then be available should the eventual decision be in favour of the so-called competitive method of marketing. If a long-term contract is signed, it seems that our marketing course is set in favour of monopoly assumption and operations of the various wheat marketing services, whether this is done at once or over a period of time.

(9) The proposed contract should be examined from the standpoint of our ability to fulfill such a contract. The proposed contract calls for the delivery of a specified quantity of wheat to the United Kingdom each year, in spite of the fact that annual yields are extremely variable in the Prairie Provinces. The quantity involved in the contract should be such that fulfillment is possible even in years of moderate wheat production in Canada. If the British contract were supplemented by contracts with other importing countries — a natural development if this type of marketing is decided upon — it would be necessary for Canada to carry a considerable reserve of wheat against the contingency of short crops.

(10) In negotiating the proposed contract, the Canadian Government should give very careful consideration to the extent to which it desires to direct the flow of Canadian wheat and flour to the United Kingdom and away from other countries. For instance, supposing it were possible to contract with the United Kingdom for the purchase of 200 million bushels of Canadian wheat per year: What effect would such a contract have upon the basis of Canadian trade with Belgium, the Netherlands, France, Norway and South American countries: Under these circumstances would the national interest be served by such a contract? In the opinion of the Board, the terms of any contract entered into with the United Kingdom should not preclude the possibility of our supplying wheat to our old established markets in other countries in terms of their normal purchases from Canada. This could be accomplished through a supply of uncommitted wheat or through the negotiation of individual contracts along the lines of the contract finally agreed upon with the United Kingdom. Most likely those interested in the field of Canadian trade would support the view that Canadian wheat should still play an important part in our trade with a considerable number of importing countries.

(11) Thought should be given to the probable reaction of Argentina and Australia to Canada's effort to build up a secure position in the post-war years. It can be expected, in the lack of an international accord in respect to wheat, that these countries will take steps to protect their respective positions. If their response is in the form of a lowering of export prices they could go a long way in undermining Canada's programme based on long-term contracts.

. . .

(15) The proposed contract has specific advantages which should be mentioned. If we are to have an unsettled world it will provide a measure of price and market stability for the wheat farmer. The Dominion Government

will have a good deal of protection in respect to the guarantee it has already given to wheat producers for a minimum price of at least $1.00 per bushel until July 31, 1950. The proposed contract would also end the unilateral approach involved in the $1.55 ceiling and would represent an effort to establish a quid pro quo on the part of our principal customer.

(16) If the Dominion Government decides to proceed with the negotiation of the British contract, the Board is of the opinion that similar contracts should be offered to those countries who have demonstrated a persistent interest in Canadian wheat. The Board further believes that the price basis finally decided upon in the British contract should be generalized. The Board would not want to see a two-price system established in respect to Canadian export wheat. The dangers of a two-price system are apparent, particularly in its denial of the principle of "free access".

(17) Any long-term contract for the sale of Canadian wheat should have the confidence of the organized wheat producers in Western Canada. In order to prevent misunderstanding and in order that the proposed Canadian-United Kingdom agreement may be appraised on the basis of relevant facts, the actual signing of the agreement should be preceded by some degree of public discussion. For instance, the general terms of the agreement should be discussed in advance with the producers' organizations in the Prairie Provinces. They should be acquainted with the main terms of the agreement, with the relationship which exists between the agreement and international co-operation in respect to wheat and the main factors which have caused the Dominion Government to look to the United Kingdom market for the next three to five years in terms of a fairly inflexible contract.

(18) The contract now under discussion is not a contract as generally understood in the grain trade. It is, in the Board's opinion, in the nature of a treaty between the Government of Canada and the Government of the United Kingdom. No doubt the document which is signed by His Majesty's Government in Canada and His Majesty's Government in the United Kingdom will define the general terms of the arrangement and will provide *suitable machinery* for working out the initial detail and continuing problems in respect to the agreement. . . .

At the end of its memorandum, the board analyzed Canada's prewar and wartime wheat export distribution and recommended target figures for the postwar period, as follows:

	United Kingdom Imports	Continental Europe	Orient	Other Countries	Total
		(million bushels)			
Average 1925-26 to 1938-39 (1937-38 omitted)	90.0	122.0	14.0	24.0	250.0
Average 1939-40 to 1944-45	148.0	39.0	1.0	70.0	258.0
Wheat Board's suggested postwar distribution	145.0	65.0	5.0	35.0	250.0

The memorandum concluded with a recommendation that not more than 145 million bushels be committed to Britain annually, and that Canada's exports to the European countries be covered by similar contracts to avoid a two-price export system.[7]

At the same time, McIvor wrote to McKinnon on another pressing issue, namely the continued application of the $1.55 export price ceiling. Prices on commercial export markets had already begun to climb substantially and were crowding the $2.00 level. The government had never defined how long it would maintain the ceiling and, in the expectation that it would soon be lifted, producers had almost stopped delivering from farms at a time when the wheat was urgently needed. In the absence of other considerations, the time had come when the ceiling should be removed.

CABINET WHEAT COMMITTEE CONSIDERATION

With these issues before the ministers, Wilson arranged a meeting of the cabinet wheat committee on May 2, 1946. With Ilsley unavailable, and Crerar already in the senate, MacKinnon and Gardiner were the only members present. The three commissioners of the wheat board, Messrs. George McIvor, Charles E. Huntting and William C. McNamara attended, as did Dr. T. W. Grindley, secretary of the board, Mr. M. W. Mackenzie, who had been appointed deputy minister of trade and commerce on March 31, 1945, and Mr. J. B. Lawrie, recently recruited as assistant director of the wheat and grain division. Lawrie had been associated with the Alberta wheat pool for a number of years.

The ministers directed their attention, first, to the board's letter on the export ceiling, and they recognized the impracticability of prolonging it on a unilateral basis. Gardiner's solution was to have the contract supersede the ceiling. Until the contract could be concluded, however, Gardiner recommended that producers be paid $1.55 on wheat sold in the domestic market, instead of the $1.25 they were now receiving, which he believed would satisfy their price expectations. Any change in the domestic price, however, would have to be approved by Mr. Ilsley, and that issue involved, in turn, the gradual phasing out of domestic price controls.

Then the principle of the contract was discussed. Mr. Mackenzie had been chairing an interdepartmental committee on the broader aspects of Canada's postwar trade policy and was seeking to keep the Canadian position flexible enough to shore up with the proposals contained in a recently issued United States state department white paper on trade policy, but his warnings against a bilateral contract fell on deaf ears.[8] Gardiner believed that Canada could safely tie up a minimum of 160 million bushels in a contract with Britain and that smaller contracts could be negotiated with other countries. However, for bargaining purposes, he proposed that Canada should continue to press for 180 million bushels per year to Britain. Mr. Huntting took issue with the British proposal to limit the $1.55 price to two years; in order to compensate producers who would be accepting below-market prices in the earlier period of the contract, he thought that the firm price of $1.55 should apply also in the third year. There was also a discussion about what quantities of flour should be stipulated in the contract.

During the discussion, the ministers considered at length the board's

[7] *Ibid.*

[8] See Department of External Affairs Conference Series 1945, No. 3, *Proposals for Expansion of World Trade and Employment* communicated by the United States government.

warning that the signing of a long-term contract would necessitate the continuation of a monopoly board. The mechanics of implementing the contract were discussed, and it was obvious that the board would have to maintain control over all wheat supplies. Too thin a trading volume would remain to permit the reopening of the futures market for sales outside the contract. The point which the board had raised in December, 1945, remained valid that the implementation of the export ceiling required a monopoly board. The board had raised the issue again in March when a discussion took place on the form of enabling legislation. At that time the cabinet wheat committee shied away from the prospect of a lengthy debate in the house, which an amendment to the Canadian wheat board act might provoke. Moreover, the monopoly powers would not be necessary if the ceiling export price were to be abandoned and the market reopened. By now, the ministers were acutely aware that the decision to conclude a contract with Britain entailed a consequent decision to retain a monopoly board. They accepted that as necessary to assure markets through the postwar transitional period. They disposed of the consequential question of legislative authority by deciding that the monopoly powers could be conferred, temporarily at least, by the national emergency transitional powers act. Undoubtedly, the decision was eased by the stature the board had acquired through its competent administration of complex problems in the war years, and by the current strength of the farm organizations' support for a monopoly board handling all grains. Nevertheless, the contract had precipitated the issue, and the government's prewar policy of eventual withdrawal from marketing operations and of restoring them to the pools and to the private trade was thereby summarily reversed. On a subsequent occasion, Gardiner declared that he was not opposed to a board accepting all deliveries as he had been to the voluntary board created in 1935 which received deliveries only when the initial payment was above the market level, and the government incurred all the losses.

Toward the end of the meeting, Gardiner and MacKinnon readily accepted the board's recommendation that the terms of the proposed contract be made subject to any terms that might be negotiated under an international wheat agreement. Because of the continued resolutions by the farm organizations in support of the negotiation of an international agreement, and also because there seemed so little prospect of a successful outcome, the ministers thereupon gave Wilson authority to see what could be done to revive the multilateral negotiations.

Despite all reservations McIvor and Mackenzie expressed in terms of trade policy, Gardiner was determined that the contract negotiations should proceed. Accordingly the ministers decided that McIvor should resume them through Sir Andrew Jones, the newly-arrived head of the British food mission in Ottawa, who:

> should be advised at once that Canada was prepared to proceed to negotiate a five-year contract on the basis of $1.55 per bushel No. 1 Northern for the crop years 1946-47, 1947-48, 1948-49; not less than $1.00 per bushel for 1949-50 and 1950-51 with the actual price to be determined a year in advance. The quantity involved would be 180 million bushels per year, a stated percentage to be in flour, the actual amount to be subject to negotiation.[9]

[9]*Minutes of the Wheat Committee of Cabinet,* May 2, 1946.

RESUMPTION OF THE CONTRACT NEGOTIATIONS

On May 3, 1946, McIvor communicated by letter to Sir Andrew Jones the terms of the Canadian proposal which had been decided upon by the cabinet wheat committee. On May 16, Sir Andrew replied with a counterproposal from his government for a four-year agreement with a fixed price for the first two years, a fixed price of $1.25 in the third year, and a minimum price of $1.00 in the fourth. At the same time the British government suggested that experts from the two sides get together to resolve the differences between the two proposals. On May 20, McIvor advised Sir Andrew Jones that the Canadian government would welcome such a meeting and suggested that it take place in Ottawa.

There was some delay, however, in getting the two sides together because the British had somehow gained the impression that the Canadian government desired the delegations to be headed by ministers. The Right Honourable John Strachey had just replaced Sir Ben Smith as minister of food and he needed time for briefing on his new responsibilities.

In the interval, Norman Robertson visited London and met Rank and Hooker on June 5, from whom he learned that the British government was predisposed to proceed with the negotiations out of appreciation for Canada's wartime effort in meeting Britain's food problems, and also because it believed a long-term contract was necessary to stimulate Canadian wheat acreage in response to the world food shortage. By now Rank was definitely opposed to a long-term contract and he declined to join the British negotiating team. He believed that, in the circumstances, the Canadian government should simply set its own price, but the British treasury officials were disturbed by the immediate price trend and saw in a contract the possibility of securing British wheat requirements at prices below the world level. Robertson mentioned that the British appeared to think that the Canadians wanted the delegations to be headed by ministers which had caused him some surprise.

In due course Strachey arranged to head a negotiating team to Canada. The team preceded him by a few days. On the eve of his departure from London, Strachey made a radio speech which Canada House reported to Ottawa on June 16, 1946:

> Tomorrow I'm flying to Canada. There I hope to sign an agreement with the Canadian Government under which we shall buy our main supply of wheat in the coming period. The Canadian farmers have stuck by us through this war. They've supplied us with almost all our wheat and they haven't tried to wring the last shilling out of us. Now they want the security of a firm, stable agreement, under which we will go on buying wheat from them at a fair price. Don't you think that we owe that to them? I do. And I also think that such an agreement, on reasonable terms, will be just as much in our interests as in theirs, for by giving security to the farmers it will help to prevent our ever getting into a mess over our wheat supply again.

The negotiating team which Strachey headed included Mr. Herbert Broadley, deputy secretary of the British food ministry, Mr. E. G. Harwood, undersecretary, Mr. R. E. Furness, British food mission in Washington, and Sir Andrew Jones, head of the British food mission in Ottawa. The Canadian negotiating team was headed by Gardiner and MacKinnon and it included the three members of the wheat board, McIvor, Huntting and

McNamara, and the Ottawa officials who had earlier studied the contract proposal including Messrs. Barton, Mackenzie, Sharp, Shaw and Wilson. With the exception of Broadley who travelled with Strachey, the two negotiating teams commenced their meetings in Ottawa on June 14. They met through the week end and had made considerable progress by the time Strachey arrived on June 18.

In the negotiations held at the official level, the Canadian team held out for an agreement of five years with the $1.55 price fixed for the first three years; and for uniform quantities throughout the contract at levels sufficiently low to permit the reestablishment of our wheat trade with our other normal customers. By June 18, the team had yielded to the British insistence upon a four-year contract, and had accepted the resale clause and the British, in turn, had agreed to drop the contentious fall price clause.

The officials, however, had failed to reckon upon Gardiner's personal propensity for negotiation because, on June 18, the day Strachey spent in Ottawa, Gardiner explored matters with him and one or two of his officials. In their talks, Gardiner and Strachey agreed upon a four-year contract for 160 million bushels in each of the first two years, and 140 million thereafter. The $1.55 price was fixed for the first two, and floor prices of $1.25 and $1.00 were agreed for the third and fourth years. Their agreement was ad referendum, of course, to both governments.

ORIGIN OF THE "HAVE REGARD TO" CLAUSE

Because the $1.25 floor price for 1948-49 and the $1.00 floor price for 1949-50 were minimum guarantees, and no ceiling levels were specified, it was important that provision be made for subsequent negotiation and agreement upon the actual prices to apply in those years. The original Canadian proposal of May 3, 1946, had suggested that these prices be negotiated a year in advance. In Gardiner's and Strachey's talks it was agreed that the deadline for such negotiations should be seven months in advance, that is, by December 31, 1947, for the price applicable to 1948-49, and December 31, 1948, for 1949-50. Gardiner believed strongly that the actual prices to be agreed upon for the last two years should take care of any losses below world prices Canada might realize in the first two years and that, if such losses occurred they should be added on to the world price in the last two years. He discussed this principle with Strachey, Broadley and Harwood, and he recorded their reaction in his statement to the house some two months later:

> We on behalf of the government — that is, the Minister of Trade and Commerce and myself — suggested that in view of the fact that Great Britain was going to get wheat at some margin below the world price in 1946-47, they should be prepared, no matter whether wheat is below or above $1.25 or even above $1.55, to take into consideration any advantage that they get by obtaining wheat at a low level during these first two years. Without any reservations whatsoever those with whom we were discussing it came right back and said, "That is absolutely fair. We would have no reason for refusing to do it, and we ought to do it." . . .
>
> Mr. Castleden: You admit they will take it into consideration, but no actual basis is set out.
>
> Mr. Gardiner: No; the actual basis will have to be established in the light of the facts as they are at the time. Still I am satisfied that the British would say

this: "If we got the wheat at 20 or 30 cents a bushel less than the world price during that period, certainly we are prepared to negotiate a satisfactory basis." I do not think they would say they would consider the difference to the extent of 100 per cent and go on that basis; it would depend on the number of bushels they were buying. . . .[10]

Gardiner firmly believed that in his June 18 talks he had reached a gentlemen's agreement with Strachey on the principle that the prices in the last two years would compensate, in large measure at least, for any losses incurred in the first two years. As a result of his experience in negotiating the other food contracts, he was prepared to place full faith in the verbal understanding. He left it to the British side to draft a form of words to give effect to the agreement, and on the following morning Sir Andrew Jones handed Wilson the British draft for our consideration. In all probability it had been prepared by a treasury official as a cockshy or try on. The draft was precisely as written into the contract and it read as follows:

> The actual prices to be paid for wheat to be bought and sold within the crop year 1948-49 shall be negotiated and settled between the United Kingdom Government and the Canadian Government not later than the 31st December, 1947, and prices for wheat to be bought and sold within the crop year 1949-50 shall be negotiated and settled not later than the 31st December, 1948. In determining the prices for these two crop years, 1948-49 and 1949-50, the United Kingdom Government will have regard to any difference between the prices paid under this Agreement in the 1946-47 and 1947-48 crop years and the world prices for wheat in the 1946-47 and 1947-48 crop years.[11]

Wilson fully expected the Canadian negotiating team to take a long, hard look at this draft, and that it would be subject to further negotiation and revision. The last sentence of the draft appeared to express the principle of compensation in the last two years for losses incurred in the first two, but there was no way of prejudging months in advance what world prices were going to be, and therefore no predetermined base to which the compensation could be added. The draft should have had a thorough vetting, but the time factor frustrated such precaution. Gardiner had the agreement in grasp and he wanted it to be approved immediately by cabinet. Thus the draft had barely arrived on June, 19, when Gardiner intervened to demand its acceptance. He had looked over the draft; he was convinced that it embodied the gentlemen's agreement in a way which no refined legal drafting could improve upon; and he telephoned MacKinnon to instruct Wilson to accept it without change. Wilson can still recall the look of incredulity which swept over Sir Andrew Jones's face as he was told of the acceptance of what was to become the celebrated "have regard to" clause.

CABINET DELIBERATIONS, JUNE 18-20, 1946

With Gardiner pressing for immediate cabinet acceptance of the agreement he had just put together with Strachey, it fell the lot of the department of external affairs to forewarn the prime minister of the trade implications in Gardiner's proposal. Pearson was concerned about consultation with the United States on a matter which cut across American trade policy, and Robertson was as concerned as the wheat board had been about the

---

[10]*House of Commons Debates*, August 15, 1946, p. 4834.
[11]*Ibid.*, August 15, 1946, p. 4848.

implications for Canadian trade policy. The trade issue was touched off by Pearson's telegram from Washington on June 14, 1946:

> I heard today from United Kingdom sources here that the new Minister of Food, John Strachey, would arrive shortly in Ottawa and come on later to Washington for the first meeting of the International Emergency Food Council on June 20th. I also heard from the same sources that while in Ottawa he hoped to sign the long-term contract with Canada, the difficulties in the way of which seem to have been removed. I do not know anything about this contract, its terms, conditions, etc., but I think I should point out that an agreement of this kind will probably be very unpopular in United States official circles, who are notoriously sensitive to such arrangements (at least when concluded by others) as prejudicial to the success of the forthcoming international trade discussions. I feel that we should be prepared for United States criticism on this score, which is my reason for bringing the matter to your attention. I would, of course, be in much better position to report on the United States reaction if I knew more about the proposed United Kingdom-Canadian arrangement.[12]

Norman Robertson followed up Pearson's message by forewarning King of the trade implications and of the paucity of alternatives open to the government in a memorandum he addressed to King on June 17:

> I think the Government is drifting into a very difficult position in the discussions for the negotiation of a bulk wheat contract with the United Kingdom, which are now taking place in Ottawa. The initiative in these negotiations has been taken by our Government, which originally desired to conclude an agreement with the United Kingdom under which the latter would take 180,000,000 bushels of wheat each year for the next five years, at fixed prices negotiated in advance. I enclose a note showing the present status of the negotiations.
>
> I feel very strongly that the conclusion of such a contract is not in the long-run interests either of Canada or the United Kingdom, and would be in direct conflict with the general policy of freer international trade to which the Government is committed. The officials who have been entrusted with the negotiations on our side share most of my misgivings, but feel they are under direct instructions from the Cabinet to press forward the negotiations. I cannot think that the Cabinet, in authorizing the negotiations, had the full implications of this decision put before it. It has been said that a long-term bulk purchase contract with the United Kingdom is the only alternative to a drastic increase in the price of wheat, which in itself would have a very serious effect on the maintenance of our present prices and wages policy. The situation is admittedly an extremely difficult one, but I think every effort should be made to find some third course which would not have the really disastrous consequences I foresee from either of these alternatives.
>
> I shall try to do a proper note on the subject for tomorrow. In the meantime, I thought I had better put in this immediate word, as Strachey of the United Kingdom Ministry of Food is arriving in Ottawa tomorrow and, according to his broadcast from London last night, expects to return here next week, after the Combined Food Board meeting in Washington, to sign a concluded contract.[13]

Robertson's memorandum led to a long conversation with King, as a result of which the prime minister invited McIvor and Robertson to attend the cabinet meeting on June 19. Consideration of the contract had already

[12]*King Papers.*
[13]*Ibid.*

begun in cabinet the day before. King left his own record, however, of the deliberations in council on June 19:

> We had up for consideration the contract with the U.K. which Gardiner has been negotiating and which Strachey is here to sign which contemplates purchase for 4 years of a large percentage of Canada's total wheat. The contract itself while it has advantages with regard to stabilization for the farmers has nevertheless elements which are in the nature of a great gamble, as, for example, the certainty that the British Govt. will pay a higher rate than may be the current rate in a couple of years hence, to make up for their getting wheat at the present time at less than the current rate. Also whether we would not be blamed for entering into a bi-lateral agreement that destroys the multilateral plan which lies at the basis of the U.S. policy for freer trade among nations and an ultimate world price for wheat. Still further whether it may not cost us some of the markets we should be able to have with other nations.
>
> Robertson had spoken to me about this over the 'phone at some length. I brought the matter up yesterday but brought it up anew today in considerable detail. I had Robertson come in to the Cabinet along with McIvor of the Wheat Board. Robertson outlined the dangerous position in which we might get Canada vis-a-vis the U.S. in negotiations. Looked very tired and it was embarrassing for him with Gardiner more or less abrupt in his way of meeting statements.
>
> The trouble is no one knows what he is saying is altogether in accord with the facts or whether—or what is perhaps more to the point he may be on true ground as regards purely departmental arrangements and negotiations with some Board but quite wrong when he assumes that the U.S. Govt. etc. in relation to making a world peace have been kept informed as they should. The real truth is that enough people have not been safe-guarding the situation in any of the country and that transactions in any large order are left to the last moment and then put through as a result of pressure in one dirction or another without the knowledge of more than a very few persons.
>
> While I was very tired, I managed to keep my mind and the mind of Council concentrated on this problem for a couple of hours and ultimately get agreement in a position from which there is no satisfactory solution. It was the choice of a lesser of two evils. We had a certainty in the matter of agreement against an uncertainty as to what American negotiations might come to. What I stressed, however, was we must let the Americans know our position before we sign any contract so that they could not say they would have objected had they known and wished we would have told them in advance, etc. It was agreed Pearson should tell them the situation.
>
> Strachey was to go to New York and contract was not to be signed until after his return, nothing to be said of it meanwhile. If agreement was reached while he was there, with approval by the Americans, well and good. Gardiner had insisted that Clayton of the Secretary of State's Dept. had been present at negotiations with the Food Board of which he, Gardiner, had explained the situation. Ilsley is very fearful of all these things but seems unable to suggest alternatives. The Cabinet, however, were unanimous as to what seemed possible to do in the light of the circumstance as they existed. I felt I had helped to save a very serious situation by keeping the discussion on the level it was this morning and getting the (external affairs) position properly registered.[14]

Despite Gardiner's assurance that he had explained the situation to William Clayton, assistant secretary of state for economic affairs, Robertson

[14]*King Diary.*

telephoned Pearson as soon as he left the council chamber to ascertain whether the Americans had been adequately informed. Pearson wired back that same evening:

> After our telephone conversation this afternoon I informed the State Department that the Canadian Government was considering with the United Kingdom Government a wheat contract along lines which you indicated to me and that there was every likelihood of an early conclusion of this negotiation. The Acting Secretary of State, Mr. Acheson, the Assistant Secretary, Mr. Clayton, and Mr. Hickerson all expressed alarm and disappointment at this information. They had had no knowledge of the matter as apparently Mr. Wilcox had not yet delivered to them Sir John Magowan's note on the subject and which I referred to in WA-2501 of June 18th. In any event, this note was more general in terms than the information I gave them. Clayton urged in strong terms that we hold up our signature until they have had an opportunity to talk the matter over with us. He felt that an announcement of an agreement of this kind at this time would seriously prejudice the British loan which now is about to reach the House of Representatives for final determination. I pointed out that this is a matter of more concern to the United Kingdom than to us and that no doubt they would take this aspect of the question up with Mr. Strachey. Mr. Clayton referred to the recent closing of the Liverpool Cotton Exchange which had antagonised the cotton bloc in Congress. If the wheat bloc were also to be antagonised, the effect on the loan would be deplorable.
>
> Insofar as international trade proposals are concerned, the State Department officials thought our proposed Agreement with the United Kingdom would cut right across the middle of the whole multilateral idea. I pointed out that they had largely themselves to blame for this because of the uncertainties and delays of their own policy. There was general appreciation of this, but it was nevertheless felt that a wheat contract of this kind would knock the props from under anything we all might hope eventually to accomplish. They were also worried about the effect of an arrangement of this kind on their own plans for food relief and feared that, notwithstanding escape clauses, it would be felt here that the United Kingdom were going ahead to safeguard their own position at any cost and that Canada was lending itself to this policy. They felt that an arrangement of this kind would make difficult and possibly impossible, United States plans for directing wheat in the future to high deficiency areas. I think their fears in this regard are exaggerated, but they are certainly not to be dismissed as completely groundless. I pointed out that price and other policies in this country were largely responsible for efforts being made by other countries to protect their own economic positions in the present difficult circumstances and that, if the United States had given a stronger and speedier lead in international economic policies, such contracts as the one under discussion might not have been necessary. The Americans, while recognizing the force of this, still remain highly disturbed at our proposed contract and feel that they should at least be given a chance to see if something could not be worked out which would make it necessary for us or the United Kingdom to proceed along these lines.
>
> I am passing on this information to the United Kingdom authorities here.[15]

King took Pearson's message into cabinet with him next morning, and he recorded the June 20 continuation of the cabinet discussion:

> The morning . . . was mostly taken up with the wheat agreement. When I read a long despatch from Pearson which brought up the feelings of Americans,

[15]*King Papers.*

now that they knew what was being arranged; a letter from Parker, of the Winnipeg Grain Pool, and a statement sent in by Lambert and Senator Paterson which dealt with the dangers of the contract itself as Gardiner was seeking to have it arranged—after a very full discussion, it was agreed that Strachey who was now in Washington should go to see the State Dept. and explain the whole situation and get something worked out with them which would be satisfactory to Britain and the U.S. Word was to be sent to Pearson to let the Americans know the whole situation. Tell them we are prepared to hold up the signing of the agreement to see if they could work out something that would be satisfactory to both; if they could not, then we might have to sign when Strachey returned. Gardiner seemed anxious to have permission to 'phone Strachey which was given. I told him to speak at once to Robertson and have him 'phone Pearson.

Later Gardiner 'phoned me that Pearson and Strachey were seeing the State Dept. Robertson 'phoned me to say that Pearson had said Gardiner had told Strachey we were all agreed on the terms. The whole thing is unfortunate. I gave word to Robertson to 'phone Pearson exactly on the line he had read over to me, and that Heeney had recorded in Council, and have Pearson let the State Dept. know and Strachey know, that I thought they ought to let the British Embassy know what the position was; how far we were prepared to hold back, and how far we were prepared to go. Gardiner meanwhile has left for the West.[16]

Mr. A. D. P. Heeney, secretary of the cabinet, advised Norman Robertson of the cabinet's decision in his memorandum of June 20:

The conclusion reached by the Cabinet this morning, when the Prime Minister read a message which had been received from Pearson . . . was as follows:

It was agreed that, in the circumstances, action upon the proposed U.K. contract be suspended temporarily, pending discussion in Washington between the U.K. Minister of Food and U.S. authorities of the considerations raised in Mr. Pearson's message; the government would be prepared to give consideration to any alternative proposals which might be worked out in such U.S.-U.K. discussions; if, on the other hand, no other course satisfactory to Canada were to be suggested, it was recognized that, before Mr. Strachey returned to Britain, Canada might have to conclude a contract with the United Kingdom along the lines proposed.

It was also agreed that Mr. Pearson should be instructed to get in touch with Mr. Strachey at once and inform him of the government's attitude and that the whole question would be considered again at a meeting early next week.

As you know, I sent a teletype to this effect to Pearson this afternoon.[17]

Heeney also telephoned immediately to Pearson and confirmed the message by telegram in which he quoted the cabinet conclusion and added: "As I said to you on the telephone, the Cabinet wished to have you get in touch with Mr. Strachey at once and inform him of the government's attitude so that he in turn might take up immediately with the U.S. authorities the important considerations which Mr. Acheson, Mr. Clayton and Mr. Hickerson raised in their conversations with you yesterday."[18]

The cabinet decision had clearly been to hold the conclusion of the contract in abeyance pending formal consultations with the United States

[16]*King Diary.*
[17]*Privy Council Office files.*
[18]*Ibid.*

and to provide the American authorities an opportunity to come up with a constructive alternative to the contract which would, nevertheless, provide the desired market assurance for Canada. To King's regret, the decision to suspend the contract negotiations temporarily had been compromised by Gardiner's telephone call to Strachey intimating that the contract terms had been agreed. As Gardiner had left for the west immediately after phoning Strachey, King followed up by wiring Gardiner that he was not to make any announcement concerning the agreement.

On the following day, June 21, Robertson sent the prime minister a note mentioning a visit he had received from the Honourable T. A. Crerar which underscored the representations against the contract already made by Mr. W. J. Parker and the Honourable Norman Lambert. Robertson wrote:

> Senator Crerar came in this morning to say that he was very worried about what he had read in the press on the proposed Canada-United Kingdom wheat agreement. His general line was very much that of Parker's letter and of the memorandum which Senator Lambert left with you. He thought that when the Americans learned of such a contract they would be very much upset and would regard it as conflicting with the general commercial policy proposals which they had sponsored. I told him this was an aspect of the whole very difficult position which was much on your mind, but did not indicate that we were already in communication with the United States on the subject.[19]

When Strachey passed through Ottawa again on June 25 before returning to London, he saw King who made a brief reference in his diary:

> I . . . had a talk with Strachey, the Minister of Food, who has come back from Washington. He admitted it was fortunate he had been there and that no statement had been made of our agreement prior to the settlement of the loan question. He admitted it might have prejudiced the loan. He was entirely agreeable to have the agreement wait but felt it would be doubtful if we could do anything better in the end. Said the Americans had nothing constructive to offer.[20]

King reported his conversation with Strachey to cabinet on June 27, and it was agreed that approval of the contract should continue to be deferred pending congressional action on the loan to Britain.

Strachey's return to London was greeted by disappointment in the press over his failure to bring home the contract he had promised on his departure, and over his announcement of the commencement of bread rationing in Britain.

CANADIAN PROTESTS AGAINST THE CONTRACT

Before continuing with the account of the Washington consultations, one should take note of the protests against the contract negotiations which originated in Canada. As King mentioned, Senators Lambert and Paterson had submitted a memorandum and W. J. Parker had written a letter. While these two documents are not among the King papers, their substance may be inferred from speeches subsequently made in the senate and from Parker's public utterances. A year later when the wheat board act was being amended to provide for the continuation of a monopoly board which the

[19] *King Diary.*
[20] *Ibid.*

contract necessitated, Senators Paterson and Crerar attacked the contract as "the greatest short sale in the history of the world".[21] Mr. W. J. Parker had publicly criticised the contract proposal on June 27, 1946, a few days after he had written to the prime minister.

These criticisms had come from interested parties who were not privy to the negotiations. The most telling protest of all, however, came from George McIvor who had headed the Canadian negotiating team. Just after he returned to Winnipeg from the meetings in Ottawa, McIvor wrote to MacKinnon on June 22:

> I feel that in consequence of the turn of developments during the past week in regard to the proposed United Kingdom contract, you should have the Board's resume and their views on this subject.
>
> On April 3rd, 1946, you wrote to Mr. Huntting asking for the views of the Board in regard to the proposed wheat contract with the United Kingdom. After consideration and study on the part of the Board, we prepared a document containing observations which the Board felt the Government should take into consideration in arriving at a decision in regard to the contract. In the document, copies of which were forwarded on April 28th, 1946, to the Wheat Committee of the Cabinet, and the inter-departmental committee established to consider the contract, we tried to weigh the pros and cons of the proposed contract. We felt that such a contract would provide a measure of price and market stability for the wheat farmers during the uncertain years which would be covered by such a contract. At the same time, we made it clear that there were important difficulties involved in a long-term wheat contract with the United Kingdom. We pointed out that the implementing of such a contract required the continuation of a monopoly Wheat Board in Canada and that very grave doubts existed as to the legal and constitutional basis of such a Board in peacetime.
>
> We pointed out that the proposed contract was not in line with the general desire to promote broad international trade as between Canada and other countries and that there would be international repercussions. We indicated that wheat producers in the Prairie Provinces were interested not only in the price they received for their wheat but in the goods and services which their wheat income would make available to them. We also indicated that such a contract would lead the Dominion Government in the direction of further nationalization of grain handling and services.
>
> In spite of the many disadvantages of the proposed contract, the Board, if called upon to do so, was prepared to approach the matter in a realistic manner and felt that it was not impossible to arrive at a contract which would be advantageous to wheat producers for the next four or five years. The Board felt that if such a contract could be obtained the immediate and basic difficulties would have to be worked out in the general interest of the wheat producers of the Prairie Provinces.
>
> On May 2nd, 1946, the Board was advised by the Wheat Committee of the Cabinet that it was the intention of the Government to open negotiations with the United Kingdom, looking towards a long-term wheat contract. I was instructed to convey a proposal to the United Kingdom Government on behalf of Canada in a letter to Sir Andrew Jones. This letter was forwarded on May 3rd, 1946, after consultation with Mr. Mackenzie, Dr. Barton and Mr. Shaw. The United Kingdom replied on May 16th, 1946 with a counter-proposal and suggested that experts of the two countries meet together for further discussion. On May 20th, 1946, I advised Sir Andrew Jones that it was the

[21] *Senate Debates*, April 23, 1947, pp. 257-263.

desire of the Canadian Government that the United Kingdom send representatives to Canada to open negotiations on the basis of the Canadian proposal of May 3rd, 1946 and the British counter-proposal of May 16th, 1946.

On Friday, June 14th, Canadian representatives met with the United Kingdom representatives in Ottawa and commenced the task of negotiating a contract. The Canadian representatives consisted of members of the Board and officials of the Department of Trade and Commerce, the Department of Agriculture and the Department of Finance.

In the negotiations with the British representatives, we, and I believe Departmental representatives were firm in respect to three important elements in the proposed contract. We proposed that the contract should include the following basic considerations:

(1) That the quantities of wheat involved in the contract should be the same in each year covered by the contract;

(2) That the quantities involved in each year should be moderate and not such as to prevent our continuing (a) to sell Canadian wheat in other traditional markets, and (b) to maintain our flour exports;

(3) That the $1.55 price should be effective for the first, second and *third* years of the contract.

In regard to (1) the Board felt that it would not be wise to commit larger quantities of wheat to the United Kingdom in 1946-47 and 1947-48 than in succeeding contract years. We felt that it would not be wise for Canada to withdraw from other traditional markets for the next two crop years and then have to establish a position once again in these outside markets. We thought that this point was important, especially in view of the general outlook for 1946 wheat production and our present extremely low stock position.

In regard to (2) we felt that the annual quantity of wheat involved in the United Kingdom contract should be in terms of a quantity which would permit us to continue to supply other traditional markets and to maintain our position in these markets for the duration of the United Kingdom contract. We also felt that if the United Kingdom contract were signed, Canada should be in a position to negotiate similar contracts with other countries.

In regard to (3) the Board was of the opinion that advantages under the contract would probably pass from the United Kingdom to Canada in the third year. We know that wheat producers have received much less than the world price for wheat during the present crop year. We believe that the $1.55 price will be less than the world price in 1946-47 and probably for part or even all of 1947-48. We felt that adequate stability and some recompense for income given up by producers in 1945-46 and in the first two years of the proposed contract demanded the continuation of the $1.55 price in the third year of the contract.

These three points were being pressed by the Canadian representatives in the negotiations with the British delegation, and to protect these elements in the contract we offered to reduce the period of the contract from five to four years.

On Wednesday, June 19th, however, the proposed contract became a matter of Cabinet discussion. I was asked to attend Cabinet discussions on Wednesday morning and in the course of these discussions advanced these points which were being stressed by the Canadian negotiators. On Wednesday afternoon the Hon. J. G. Gardiner, Minister of Agriculture, asked for a meeting with Mr. Shaw and myself and advised us that the Canadian representatives were instructed to negotiate with the British representatives on the basis of a four-year contract as follows: For the first two years of the contract the quantity was to be 160 million bushels and the contract price was to be $1.55 per bushel. For the third and fourth years of the contract the quantity was to be 140 million bushels in each year. The contract price for the third year was to be not less than $1.25 per bushel with the actual price to be negotiated not later than December 31st, 1947, and the price for the fourth and final year of the contract was to be not less than $1.00 per bushel with the actual price to be negotiated not later than December 31st, 1948.

These were the terms that we were asked to place before the British representatives. The Canadian representatives had no alternative but to abandon negotiations on the basis of the discussions of the preceding four days.

As far as the Board is concerned, we feel that these instructions do not constitute an adequate basis for a contract with the United Kingdom. As a Board, we do not agree that the quantities should be variable; we think the quantity of wheat included for the crop years 1946-47 and 1947-48 is too high, especially in view of our lack of reserves at the present time, and we feel that the price basis for the third year of the contract is not satisfactory from the producers' standpoint in view of the sacrifices in income which producers will have made by the time the third year of the contract is reached.

My colleagues and I, having been asked to take part in the negotiation of the proposed contract, feel that it is our duty to place our views before you at this time.[22]

CONSULTATIONS WITH THE FARM ORGANIZATIONS

In the account given thus far of the contract negotiations, the record is abundantly clear that the initiative had been entirely Gardiner's. Gardiner had obtained MacKinnon's acquiescence from the beginning and he had held exploratory talks with the British before seeking authority from cabinet to proceed with the negotiations. In fact, the cabinet did not appear to have become fully apprised of the implications of Gardiner's proposals until the debate which took place on June 18-20. On a matter of such major importance, the question arises about the extent to which farm organizations were consulted.

The wheat board's confidential memorandum which it submitted on May 2 contained a curious recommendation that the ministers take the organized producers of western Canada into their confidence on the contract negotiations. Gardiner was accustomed to do so on matters of policy as he frequently met formally with the organizations and informally with their leaders. But, on this occasion, the board must have gained the impression from the farm leaders that they were not being consulted; otherwise there would have been no point to the board's recommendation. The consultations which did take place, however, early and late in the proceedings, confirmed that Gardiner had taken the initiative in recommending the contract. The farm organizations accepted it for its stabilizing value in lieu of the immediate attainment of an international wheat agreement, and as a bridge to the latter.

The first consultation took place on March 28, 1946, when the Canadian federation of agriculture made its annual presentation to the prime minister and his cabinet. Headed by Mr. H. H. Hannam, president, and Mr. W. J. Parker, vice-president, the delegation of 14 included Messrs. R. S. Law and

[22] *King Papers.*

Lew Hutchinson. Fourteen out of twenty cabinet ministers also attended. The federation brief listed the following items in its recommendations on grains:

1. That the Canadian wheat board be established as the sole institution for the marketing of all Canadian cereal crops. (One member body desires to record non-concurrence on this item.)[23]

2. That in view of the announcement by the Government of a floor price of not less than $1 bushel for wheat for the next five years, the Wheat Board Act should be amended to make the initial payment which may be made by the Wheat Board $1.00 bushel instead of the 90¢ now specified by the Act.

3. That the Government of Canada give aggressive leadership in working out an international wheat agreement, and in the negotiations on this subject, should endeavor to:

(a) secure from wheat importing countries assurances against restraints in the future of international wheat trade;

(b) obtain assurance of practicable measures designed to maintain a reasonable minimum level of wheat prices in international trade, in return for which this country might reasonably agree to measures designed to prevent prices becoming unduly high during periods of scarcity;

(c) To bring about a system of international wheat marketing based on such principles, which would be regarded by producers as superior to the system which has prevailed in the past and which has resulted in very wide price fluctuations.

4. That the principle of the quota system of deliveries from the farm to the elevator be retained.

5. That the Government investigate the wheat price situation in respect to the discrepancy between the domestic and the export price of wheat, and make an adjustment so that the wheat producer is not called upon to bear more than his share of the responsibility of keeping down the price of bread to the consumer. . . .[24]

Mr. R. G. Robertson of the privy council office prepared a minute of the meeting:

. . . Following the reading of the brief by Mr. Hannam, Mr. W. J. Parker spoke concerning the Federation's views with regard to the price policy of the government. He said that they accepted the export price of $1.55 on the understanding that it was a temporary measure and represented what the government thought was the best price at the moment to prevent future dislocation. They felt that any increase in the price at present would upset the general programme of agricultural production unless parallel increases in prices of agricultural products were made all along the line. At the same time, while approving the export price, the organization was doing so on the understanding that the government would do all it could to secure a postwar agreement between the wheat exporting countries as to marketing policies. If this were not done, the Federation felt that there was no probability of future stability and they would have to reconsider their support for the export ceiling price.

While the Federation approved the export price and while they felt that wheat was the essential commodity to be stabilized inasmuch as changes in its price had far-reaching effects on other agricultural products, nevertheless the Federation had in mind at the same time that costs for the producer were steadily increasing. Moreover, industrial workers were making demands for,

[23]United Grain Growers Limited
[24]Canadian Federation of Agriculture, *Farmers Meet the Cabinet,* March 28, 1946.

and getting, better pay standards. If price and wage levels changed significantly, this would affect the agricultural position and might require an increase in the $1.55 level.

In general, Mr. Parker said that the Federation feared instability more than they feared any loss from a presently low price level. They thought that too high a price in wheat would vitiate any later argument for placing a floor under prices, and they also feared that it would constitute an incentive to marketing countries to increase their domestic acreage. . . .

With regard to international agreement on wheat marketing, Mr. MacKinnon said that the government had been trying for some time to secure agreements with other wheat exporting countries. There was certainly no opposition in the Cabinet to the achievement of a binding agreement.

In connection with this, Mr. Gardiner asked whether the Federation had been referring to a single overall agreement that would embrace all exporting countries or whether they rather had in mind the conclusion by Canada of agreements with importing countries to ensure in advance that the total Canadian production would be taken up in any given year. In reply to this, Mr. Parker said that what they had in mind was a general agreement between exporting countries. They felt that this should be the long-term objective and that only this would secure future stability.[25]

Later, prodded by the *Winnipeg Free Press,* Parker declared that at this meeting the "principle of a bilateral agreement was discussed at some length" to which the federation had expressed its opposition and "just as definitely supported a multilateral arrangement embracing all countries, exporting and importing alike".[26] Parker also wrote to the prime minister in the same vein about mid-June and his letter was read to cabinet, but the letter is missing from the King papers.

After the March 28 meeting there was a considerable hiatus in the consultations. This was implied in the wheat board's memorandum and may have been attributable to the initial rebuff Gardiner's idea had received from the federation, to the fluid state of the negotiations and to a rather prolonged absence of the pool leaders as they left Canada in May to attend the organizational meeting of the international federation of agricultural producers in London, and returned in late June. Their London meeting was addressed by the Right Honourable Ernest Bevin, British foreign secretary, who commended $1 per bushel at Fort William as a means of providing postwar price stability for producers. Bevin's statement provoked Wesson's retort that he hoped the foreign secretary was speaking facetiously. Had Mr. Bevin mentioned $1 as a floor, Wesson declared that he would not have taken it so hard. At that meeting, the Canadian delegation continued to advocate the signature of an international wheat agreement.[27]

Shortly after the delegation's return to Canada, a meeting may have taken place between Gardiner, MacKinnon and the heads of the three pools, a few days after the June 14-19 negotiations. The only reference to it appeared half a year later when Mr. R. C. Brown, vice-president of United Grain Growers Limited, charged that Wesson was attending such a meeting when he should have been present for the June 27, 1946, meeting of the

[25] *King Papers.*
[26] See pp. 871-873.
[27] *Winnipeg Free Press,* May 23, 1946.

advisory committee of the Canadian wheat board. The discussion which took place at the committee's meeting of January 9-10, 1947, pointed up the fact that the government had not formally consulted the advisory committee during the contract negotiations. After an expression of indignation over the slight by the trade members of the committee, Mr. Wesson wryly observed that if the committee had been consulted, it could not have agreed upon a recommendation.[28] The none too well documented meeting with the three pools at the end of June was the only other consultation with farm leaders during the course of the negotiations. The Canadian federation of agriculture, including the pools, United grain growers, and Ontario wheat producers were invited to a meeting with Gardiner and MacKinnon in the latter's office on July 24, 1946, the day the contract was signed. With the contract by then a fait accompli, the discussion at that meeting was directed toward the creation of the five-year pool. Reference to that meeting is made below.[29]

PUBLIC DEBATE

While the contract was still under negotiation, a public debate was touched off by Strachey's radio address, and the arrival of the British negotiating team in Ottawa. *The Winnipeg Free Press* led the attack. In its editorial of June 20, 1946, the *Free Press* referred to the United States state department white paper on "Proposals for expansion of world trade and employment" which culminated later in the negotiation and signing of the Havana trade charter, and the editorial commented:

> ... Right here, it is to be recalled that this policy is no longer a matter of improvisation or of pragmatic approach. The principles which are to govern the trade policy of this country, of the United States, the United Kingdom, Australia, New Zealand, France and many other countries have been laid down in the trade white paper issued last November. This paper took the form of proposals by the United States government, proposals of which have been agreed to by all countries mentioned.
>
> These proposals deal with commodity agreements in detail. Rules are laid down as to their character and operation. Deviations from these rules could only be construed as a repudiation of the proposals and a refusal to proceed with the task of freeing the world's trade. ...

The editorial then cited the rules for commodity agreements set out in the white paper, the first of which stressed their multilateral applications: "The agreements should be open to accession by any member on terms not less favourable than those accorded to member parties thereto. ..."[30]

After his brief visit to Washington, Gardiner flew to Saskatchewan to address a farmers' meeting and to defend the bilateral contract proposal against the publicity which the pools had given to their demand for an international wheat agreement. From Kenosee, Saskatchewan, on June 22, Gardiner was reported as follows:

> The government, prior to the last election, announced that it intended to maintain returns to farmers during the transitional period at a level which would produce net returns to farmers comparable with those of the last three years of the war. So said Hon. James G. Gardiner, minister of agriculture, in

[28]*Minutes of the Advisory Committee to the Canadian Wheat Board,* January 9-10, 1947.
[29]See pp. 886-887.
[30]*Winnipeg Free Press,* June 20, 1946.

an address to the Canadian Federation of Agriculture at the annual farm holiday celebrated here Friday afternoon. . . .

Speaking on the contract for marketing of wheat, he said: the idea dated back as far as (1932). Under it acreage and price would be controlled among the chief exporting and importing countries.

"So far as I know, " he said, "it hasn't accomplished anything. They were prevented from doing anything because one, or more, countries refused to sign any agreement. Finally in 1942 the countries did sign. But the terms of the agreement were such that when trading was suspended on the Winnipeg grain exchange to all intents and purposes, there was no agreement as to price."

By this time, he continued, wheat had reached a price of $1.55 a bushel. Canada had then to decide whether she was going to allow uncontrolled wheat prices, or whether to have stabilized prices. Under the control system farmers could be protected against possible declining prices.

He discussed the placing of a floor of $1 a bushel under wheat for five years without assurance of anyone but Canada that they would maintain wheat above $1. This, he said, would necessitate placing the present ceiling of $1.55 a bushel on wheat sold to Britain and other overseas allies. Britain he said was prepared to sign an agreement covering a four-year period which is satisfactory to the Canadian government.[31]

The *Free Press* returned to the attack in its editorial of June 26 headed "The Time To Speak" which put the farm leaders on the spot:

A surprising and puzzling feature of the wheat negotiations presently proceeding between the Canadian and the United Kingdom governments is that there have been no public expressions of views from the organized farm groups in this country.

Broadly speaking there is no difference of opinion among primary producers as to the need of scaling down and, if possible, removing barriers to trade. All are ardently in favor of multilateral as opposed to bilateral trade practices and all have said so repeatedly. This unanimity, however, stops short when future marketing policy with regard to certain farm products, of which wheat is the chief example, is under discussion. On the one hand there is the group which believes in the market system, and on the other there is the group — which embraces organized farm bodies, such as the Canadian Federation of Agriculture and the Wheat Pools — which believes in international commodity agreements. The Free Press holds wholeheartedly to the market system and desires not to be misunderstood in that regard in the discussion which follows.

The editorial referred at length to speeches Mr. H. H. Hannam and Dr. G. S. H. Barton had delivered to the founding conference of FAO at Quebec City in October, 1945, in which both had endorsed the the principle of multilateral trade arrangements. Then the editorial concluded: ". . . The report of the press conference given at Washington on Friday by Rt. Hon. John Strachey, minister of food in the United Kingdom, indicates that the negotiations at Ottawa will continue for some time. This being so, an expression of opinion from organized farm bodies of the west with respect to bilateral wheat agreements would be timely."[32] The editorial evoked an immediate reply from Mr. W. J. Parker, who, speaking at a Manitoba federation of agriculture dinner in Winnipeg was reported as follows:

[31]*Ibid.*, June 22, 1946.
[32]*Ibid.*, June 26, 1946.

His organization wants a wheat agreement embracing many exporting and importing countries, rather than the kind of bilateral pact now being negotiated between Canada and Great Britain, W. J. Parker, president of Manitoba Pool Elevators, declared Tuesday evening.

Recently returned from an international farm conference in London, he was addressing delegates of the Manitoba Federation of Agriculture and Co-operation at a dinner in connection with their three-day annual convention being held at the Marlborough Hotel. The function, sponsored by the Scottish Co-operative Wholesale Society, was presided over by James T. Prosser.

Mr. Parker's argument was that for Canada and (Britain) to make a separate wheat agreement would antagonize the United States and other interested countries.

Referring to an editorial in (the) Free Press which wanted to know how organized farmers felt about the proposed two-way agreement, the Manitoba Pool president stated that the dominion government had never asked for the opinion of the prairie pools.

"However," he added, "the government must be aware of our position, because this principle of a bilateral agreement was discussed at some length last March when the Canadian Federation of Agriculture met the cabinet. At that time we very definitely expressed our opposition to this principle, and just as definitely supported a multilateral arrangement embracing all countries, exporting and importing alike.

"This is still the attitude of the Manitoba Pool, and it is still the attitude of the Canadian Federation of Agriculture.

"If however the government feels that it must negotiate some kind of a contract with the United Kingdom now," Mr. Parker continued, "because it feels it can't get the broader plan, then we have these reservations regarding such a bilateral agreement:

"1. It should be for a period of not less than three years.

"2. The government must realize that any price determined today may be completely out of line later, and therefore it must be prepared to maintain domestic price controls. Or if these controls are abandoned and inflation takes place, it must be prepared to establish subsidies and so restore the price relationships now existing.

"3. Washington should be kept closely advised of the present negotiations.

"4. Assuming an agreement, a joint statement should be issued by the United Kingdom and Canadian governments to the effect that they have taken this step because it was found impossilbe to get a wider wheat agreement at the present moment; but that the door is wide open for any country interested in wheat, exporting or importing, to come into the arrangement; and that the original parties would be willing to negotiate the terms of the contract so as to accommodate other interests, even during its lifetime."

As to the matter of price, Mr. Parker decried the violent controversy he found on his return from overseas. "People who are worrying about the price of wheat should go to Europe and see what they have to live on over there," he said. "It might be well to try to recapture some of the idealism of the war years.

"I feel sure our farmers don't want to grasp at the shadow of an immediate economic or political advantage and lose the substance of long-term stability and peace."[33]

[33]*Ibid.*, June 27, 1946.

In its editorial of June 28, the *Free Press* congratulated Mr. Parker for "standing firmly on principle" as it quoted a statement by Mr. J. H. Wesson which had appeared in the June 19 issue of the *Regina Leader Post*:

> We have urged both the Canadian and British governments that the situation can best be met by an international wheat agreement between surplus producing and consuming countries which would establish minimum prices for the protection of the producer and maximum prices for the protection of the consumer. We fully realize the difficulties in the way of such an agreement. At the same time we believe that world peace and security can only be achieved by international action and agreement. So far as the newspaper story from Ottawa is concerned, we believe that until international agreement can be achieved, it is in the interests of western wheat growers that a marketing agreement should be reached with Great Britain covering a substantial part of our exportable surplus, at a fair price to both parties. This will ensure a degree of stability vital to present day conditions.

Then the *Free Press* editorial continued:

> With Mr. Wesson the case is different. Either Mr. Wesson is confusing, or is confused by, the issue. He says, in effect, that the Saskatchewan pool has always favored a world wheat agreement on a multilateral basis but as this is obviously difficult to bring about, it would be a good thing meantime to have a bilateral deal. In plain language, Mr. Wesson's argument is that as it is hard to get importing and exporting nations to agree on a division of the world market and the price, the next best thing is to make a private deal with the largest importer, to the disadvantage of everybody else. How he calculates that you can induce friendly feelings and co-operation by blackening the other fellows' eyes, is not clear. He is like the man that believes with all his heart in free trade but, because it is not easily achieved, proposes to go in for higher tariffs.[34]

Despite Parker's open opposition to the bilateral contract as a substitute for a multilateral agreement he closed ranks with the other pool leaders in support of the bilateral contract as an interim measure in the cause of market stability pending conclusion of a multilateral agreement.

CONSULTATIONS WITH THE UNITED STATES

Although the account of the contract negotiations was interrupted to take note of the minimal consultations with the farm leaders and the public controversy which the negotiations had provoked, it will be recalled that after Pearson's and Robertson's warnings, cabinet had decided to delay approval of the contract until consultations with the United States authorities could take place and disclose whether the latter could suggest a practical alternative.

While the cabinet was justifiably concerned about the possible repercussions on our own trade relations with the United States, the British government had much more at stake in the consultations, because the Truman administration had just submitted to congress for approval a $3,750,000,000 loan to Britain. Earlier that year, Ilsley had put a bill through parliament approving a Canadian loan to Britain of $1,250,000,000. The need for such loans underlined the critical state of Britain's balance of payments position.

[34]*Ibid.*, June 28, 1946.

Because of the loan consideration, the formal consultations took place between the British ambassador and the United States secretary of state. After the initial consultations, the state department left an aide-memoire with the British ambassador on July 1 expressing hope that the contract (unless substantially modified) would not be signed. The note took exception to the preferential treatment accorded to Britain and Canada in a long-term arrangement which appeared to be based on other than commercial considerations. In that respect, the contract was contrary to the accepted proposals for the expansion of world trade and employment. It also appeared to jeopardize the negotiation of a multilateral agreement.[35] In the aide-memoire, no reference was made to the pending loan, but its implications were obvious and the British government withheld its reply until after the loan had been approved.

While the formal consultations were in progress, informal consultations between Pearson, Robertson and the American officials were pursued in detail to determine whether the Americans could propose an alternative to the contract satisfactory to Canada for which King had insisted that an opportunity be provided. In his conversations with Messrs. William Clayton and John Hickerson of the state department, Pearson got to the heart of King's question regarding an alternative. In the process, he also disclosed how widely the state department and the department of agriculture had been apart in their attitudes toward an international wheat agreement which, were it negotiable, could have been the alternative King was seeking, but in which Clayton had no faith. Mr. Pearson prepared a memorandum on the June 27 discussions:

> Mr. Clayton and Mr. Hickerson lunched at the Embassy today with Mr. McIvor and Mr. Stone and myself.
>
> In the course of the luncheon Mr. McIvor gave Mr. Clayton a brief review of Canadian Wheat Policy during the past 15 years and the role therein of the Canadian Wheat Board. We then discussed the proposed Canada-U.K. wheat contract.
>
> Mr. Clayton put forward his views on this contract in no uncertain terms and with strong feeling. Our discussion of the contract was long and I can only indicate below, briefly, the views which Mr. Clayton put forward at greater length.
>
> I have already reported the views of the State Department in respect of the possible adverse effect of an announcement of the signing of the contract on the British loan. Mr. Clayton went further today. He said that he would regard the conclusion of this contract as a violation of the spirit, at least, of the U.K. loan agreement. He added that there were some people in the State Department who would regard it as a violation of the letter of the loan agreement and while he was not yet prepared to go so far himself, further study of the matter was being made. In any case, he said he felt that the loan agreement, in spirit, was designed to make unnecessary exactly this sort of unilateral arrangement. He felt this so deeply that if the contract were to be signed he could not, in all conscience, in his discussion with members of Congress use any more the argument that the passage of the loan would dissolve the Sterling Bloc, open British markets to all comers, and make hard currency available to the United Kingdom. This was, moreover, one of the strongest and most effective arguments that they had put forward. While he

35 *King Papers.*

did not wish to overemphasize the adverse effect of this contract on the loan (as he said before, he would regard it as just another serious obstacle to the passage of the loan about which he is not over-optimistic at the moment), he repeated his views as to the contract's violation of the spirit of the loan agreement, views which would naturally hold even if the contract were signed **after** the passage of the loan by Congress.

Mr. Clayton's next and perhaps most emotional argument against the contract was that it would be contrary to the whole multilateral trade idea envisaged and supported by all of us, including particularly the United Kingdom, in the proposals for an international trade organization. I observed that plans in this connection were not going ahead very fast and that, in the meantime, the United Kingdom had a natural desire to assure its supplies of reasonably priced wheat and we had a natural desire to assure our sales of wheat at such a price in the three or four difficult years ahead.

Mr. Clayton then went into the possible international trade programme. He foresaw the nuclear countries completing their preliminary work in about three months from their first meeting, that is to say, April or May of 1947, and he thought that this preliminary work would, in effect, put the stamp of approval on the general idea of lower tariffs, multilateral trade and open world markets; an idea to which any Canadian-U.K. unilateral wheat contract would be definitely contrary. He foresaw the meeting of the full international trade organization as coming about late summer or early fall of 1947, and he allowed some months for the ratification of the various agreements arising out of this conference. In view of past experience, I am inclined to accept any United States estimate of timing in these matters with a grain of salt and I implied as much to Mr. Clayton. He stood his ground however.

I asked Mr. Clayton what his feelings would be if the wheat contract, in its terms, took into account (as in fact I believe it did, although I was not sure of the text) the possibility of the organization of wider international trading arrangements during its life. He was not impressed with the idea and did not see how any contract of this kind could be "fitted in" nor how it could carry any cancellation clause which would become operative on a date which would be as difficult to determine as this date would be.

Mr. Clayton also holds strong views as a trader and as an economist on the proposed wheat contract. As a trader he could see nothing in it but a large scale and long-term guess on the markets by two governments. As an economist, he regarded it as a weak instrument for stabilizing prices and he thought that what it hopes to achieve in this respect could be much more adequately and easily achieved by other methods. He was a little indefinite as to what these other methods might be in Canada and almost equally indefinite as to what they could be in his own country in respect of which he could only say that the United States is trying to maintain control. He referred, several times, to the effect on the contract of a wide-range inflation and the world price of wheat going up to, say, four or five dollars. We pointed out to him that the United States price of wheat was already fifty cents above the Canadian price and that the Argentinian wheat was being bought at $3.15 now and that our farmers seem to be prepared to accept a lower present return which is accompanied by a guarantee of a future minimum. He argued that this present attitude of the farmers would not stand up against really high world prices and that, while the Western farmer might not worry much about a wide discrepancy between his price and an Argentine price, he doubted that he would stand for a very much higher differential than already exists between the Canadian and the United States prices.

Mr. Clayton had no alternatives to offer. He made it quite clear, for instance, that he considered any world wheat agreement as impracticable and unenforceable. He said that the State Department has always held this view but that they were pushed into the advocacy of a world wheat agreement some time ago by Agriculture. When we told him that Agriculture now had apparently abandoned this advocacy, he seemed relieved.

Mr. Clayton emphasized two or three times that he was not considering the proposed Canadian-U.K. contract from any selfish point of view but that he was looking at it in the light particularly of the general world picture and its effect on the possibility of our achieving in international trade those objectives of an expanding and free economy towards which we are all working so hard.[36]

Pearson's arguments had evidently weighed with Clayton because he telephoned Robertson on July 3 to record his better appreciation of the Canadian dilemma arising out of American wheat price policies. Robertson reported the conversation in a memorandum to the prime minister:

Mr. Will Clayton telephoned me today from Washington about the wheat position. He had learned from Atherton that we had been disappointed in the negative and quite unhelpful attitude he had taken in his earlier talks with Strachey and Pearson. He had told Atherton that he would like to think over the position again, and would call me direct if he found he had anything to add to the views he had expressed in his earlier conversation with our Ambassador.

Clayton said he had been reviewing the American position with the Secretary of Agriculture, who had just returned to Washington after an absence of ten days. They were both concerned about their whole price policy, and realized why we were worried about the effect of an increase in the price of wheat on the general price structure. With the ending of O.P.A., the United States Administration had, at present, no power to control either domestic or export prices. If Congress restored O.P.A. authority, they would be in a position to consider a wheat agreement. Alternatively, he did not exclude the possibility of going to Congress for authority to make special arrangements about wheat. He asked if we were equally concerned about the course of their domestic price for wheat and their export price. I said that we had been used, over the years, to tariff-made disparities between domestic wheat prices in Canada and the United States and, moreover, recognized that, under present conditions, it was the generally higher level of prices in the United States which blurred the comparison between domestic wheat prices in the two countries. It was the uncontrolled American export price which was prying the lid off our export wheat price ceiling.

I said it was very difficult for us to justify and maintain our present export price of $1.55 alongside an American price to the same customers of $2.15. At the same time, we had to recognize that our present export price and the related return to farmers represented a relatively adequate incentive price. Any major change in this price would force radical readjustments right across the board, which would materially affect our general price control policy. The only way we could see of justifying to our producers the maintenance of present wheat prices lay in giving them some guarantee of a stable income over the next three or four years. This was the object of the draft bulk purchase agreement with the United Kingdom. I told Clayton that the maintenance of our export wheat price during the current year had represented, in effect, an export subsidy of $140,000,000, which was a very

[36] *Ibid.*

sizeable supplement to the assistance we had given Allied countries in the form of loans, export credits and UNRRA contributions. UNRRA contributions would probably be coming to an end, but this did not mean that the recipient countries could automatically put themselves on a pay as you go basis. He agreed, and said that Italy and Austria, in particular, would need substantial relief and assistance in 1947. I suggested the United States consider an agreed policy of subsidizing a staple export like wheat as a means of helping to bridge the gap between the real needs of the European countries and their immediate capacity to pay.

Clayton agreed that letting wheat prices ride without control would have the effect of stimulating uneconomic wheat production in all sorts of countries, which it was certainly not in our interest to encourage past the point of actually averting famine. He seemed to think the risk of world over-production in three or four years' time was a serious one, and agreed that it might be not only in the long-run interest of the exporting countries but a real aid to the general commercial policy programme if a staple of international commerce like wheat could move in quantity and at reasonable prices during this period of acute shortage.

In conclusion, he said he would go into the whole position again with Clinton Anderson and get in touch with us again as soon as Congress had decided what powers over prices were going to be entrusted to the Administration. Altogether, his opinion seemed to have moved a very considerable distance from the position he had taken in conversations in Washington last week.[37]

Although the Americans had submitted no practical alternative to the contract, beyond recommending that Canada and Britain await the outcome of the trade policy conference, cabinet continued to delay action on the contract pending the British reply to the American aide-memoire. While waiting, King made an attempt to meet the American objections that the contract might prejudice the pending multilateral trade negotiations. The June 20 draft contract had commenced with the first operative clause stating the purchase and sale undertakings. King recommended that the operative clauses be preceded by a preamble in which the governments recognized that their mutual interests could best be served by "international co-operation in the expansion of world trade and employment" and that the contract was a means to that end.[38] King also modified clause 7 which made the terms of the contract subordinate to any international agreements or arrangements subsequently entered into, by prefacing the clause with the words "Having in mind the general purposes which this agreement is designed to serve," ... [39] These amendments were accepted by the British.

After the loan was approved, the British ambassador left an aide-memoire with the secretary of state on July 19 which denied that other than commercial considerations were involved in the contract. It declared that the quantities over the four-year period were well within Britain's actual requirements and, with reference to the inference of discrimination, the British government indicated that it was prepared to enter into similar contracts with other suppliers at negotiated terms.[40]

[37] *Ibid.*
[38] See p. 878.
[39] See p. 879.
[40] *King Papers.*

The message was of scant comfort to the Americans, but the Canadian cabinet insisted upon withholding approval of the contract until the British reply had been made. Even at that late date, the flour quantities to be included in the contract had not yet been agreed. When word came through that the British government had accepted the flour quantities, the cabinet approved the terms of the contract on July 24, 1946, and it was signed in Ottawa that same day by the Honourable James A. MacKinnon, on behalf of Canada, and by Sir Alexander Clutterbuck, the British high commissioner, on behalf of Britain.

ANNOUNCEMENT OF THE CONTRACT

The agreement was announced simultaneously on July 25 by MacKinnon and Strachey in their respective houses of commons, and the text of the agreement follows:

The government of Canada and the government of the United Kingdom, recognizing that their mutual interest in the maintenance of reasonable prices and adequate supplies of wheat for consumers and of steady and remunerative prices for producers can best be met by international cooperation in the expansion of world trade and employment, have entered into the following arrangements designed to ensure a measure of security in the supply and of stability in the price of wheat supplied by Canada to the United Kingdom:

1. (a) The United Kingdom government undertakes to purchase and the Canadian government undertakes to sell the following quantities of Canadian wheat, which quantities include wheat to be processed into flour for sale to the United Kingdom government:

   (i) within the crop year 1946-47, 160,000,000 bushels;
   (ii) within the crop year 1947-48, 160,000,000 bushels;
   (iii) within the crop year 1948-49, 140,000,000 bushels;
   (iv) within the crop year 1949-50, 140,000,000 bushels;

A bushel shall be the weight of 60 pounds avoirdupois.

   (b) In the event of the United Kingdom requiring from Canada any additional quantities of wheat that the Canadian government is prepared to make available, such additional quantities which the Canadian government offers and the United Kingdom government accepts shall in all respects be subject to the provisions of this agreement.

   (c) Of the total quantities of wheat specified above for each crop year, the United Kingdom government agrees to take the following quantity in long tons in the form of flour:

1946-47 — 500,000 tons as a minimum, with an additional quantity not exceeding 140,000 tons to be determined by negotiations in the light of the out-turn of the crop.

1947-48 — 400,000 tons as a minimum, with an additional quantity not exceeding 140,000 tons to be determined by negotiations in the light of the out-turn of the crop.

1948-49 — 300,000 tons as a minimum, the actual tonnage to be negotiated by the 1st July, 1947.

1949-50 — 300,000 tons as a minimum, the actual tonnage to be negotiated by the 1st July, 1948.

   (d) The rate and place of deliveries of wheat and flour shall be determined from time to time by mutual agreement.

2. (a) The price per bushel to be paid by the United Kingdom government to the Canadian government on the basis number one Manitoba northern, in

store Fort William/Port Arthur, Vancouver or Churchill, shall be as follows:

    (i) In respect of wheat bought and sold in the crop year 1946-47, $1.55.

    (ii) In respect of wheat bought and sold in the crop year 1947-48, $1.55.

    (iii) In respect of wheat bought and sold in the crop year 1948-49, not less than $1.25

    (iv) In respect of wheat bought and sold in the crop year 1949-50, not less than $1.

(b) The actual prices to be paid for wheat to be bought and sold within the crop year 1948-49 shall be negotiated and settled between the United Kingdom government and the Canadian government not later than the 31st December, 1947, and prices for wheat to be bought and sold within the crop year 1949-50 shall be negotiated and settled not later than the 31st December, 1948. In determining the prices for these two crop years, 1948-49 and 1949-50, the United Kingdom government will have regard to any difference between the prices paid under this agreement in the 1946-47 and 1947-48 crop years and the world prices for wheat in the 1946-47 and 1947-48 crop years.

(c) The prices to be paid for grades other than number one Manitoba northern to be delivered under this agreement shall be determined yearly in consultation between the United Kingdom government and the Canadian government.

(d) In addition to the prices detailed in Section (a) of this article, the United Kingdom government undertakes to pay such carrying and forwarding charges as may be mutually arranged.

(e) Payment shall be made in full in Canadian funds at par Winnipeg by the United Kingdom payments office against presentation of completed statements of claim or otherwise as may be mutually agreed.

3. It is agreed that the United Kingdom government may sell or dispose of the wheat and flour purchased under this agreement in whatsoever manner the United Kingdom government may deem expedient both in regard to destination and price.

(b) The United Kingdom government will use its best endeavours to arrange for the provision of the required ocean tonnage within the stipulated dates and in accordance with the rates and places of delivery determined under section (d) of article 1 of this agreement.

5. It is agreed that the detailed terms and conditions relating to such matters as carrying and forwarding charges, grades, routing of shipments and all other matters incidental to the fulfilment of this agreement shall be discussed and settled from time to time and incorporated in documents to form annexures to this agreement.

6. It is mutually understood that matters arising from, or incidental to, the operation of this agreement may at the insistence of either party become subjects of discussion between the parties to this agreement.

7. Having in mind the general purposes which this agreement is designed to serve, the two governments have agreed that its terms and conditions shall be subject to any modification or amendment which may be necessary to bring it into conformity with any international agreement or arrangements hereafter entered into to which both governments are parties.[41]

The British press hailed the announcement. In the American press, the contract was greeted with dislike and suspicion at the official level, and one senator viewed the deal as a British purchase of Canadian wheat with United States dollars from the loan which had just been approved. In

---

[41]*House of Commons Debates,* August 15, 1946, pp. 4848-4849.

Canada, there was no immediate official reaction from the Winnipeg grain exchange, although unidentified members claimed that "the Canadian grain farmer, millers and export trade generally have been sold down the river".[42] The *Free Press* produced another series of editorials criticising the agreement in terms of its price gamble, its distortion of Canadian wheat export trade patterns and its departure from the principles of multilateral trade.

The press had failed to report, however, on representations which the exchange had made directly to the government. As in September, 1943, when the market was closed, the Winnipeg grain exchange had sent a delegation to Ottawa in July, 1946, when it also failed to get a hearing before the final decisions were made. On this present occasion, Mr. George S. Mathieson, president of the exchange, wrote to the prime minister on July 22, regretting the delegation's failure to obtain an interview and enclosing a six-page memorandum, which Mathieson circulated to all members of the cabinet. The memorandum opposed the government's monopoly control of wheat marketing, supported a floor price for producers and retention of a voluntary wheat board to administer it and even a monopoly board in immediate circumstances but that, under normal conditions, producers should have a choice of selling to the board or on an open market. In the meantime, the board should be pricing wheat on the basis of the world market. The memorandum espoused an expansionary multilateral trade policy and criticized the contract as a violation of that principle, which would draw the government inevitably into increasing control and regulation of the whole grain industry.[43]

The pool leaders in turn left it to Mr. H. H. Hannam, president of the Canadian federation of agriculture to speak on their behalf. Hannam issued the following press release on July 26:

> The new contract with the United Kingdom for sale of wheat, just concluded by the Canadian government, providing some stability of market and price over a period of years, is, generally speaking in line with the thinking of organized farmers across the Dominion. "This contract typifies what organized agriculture through the Federation, has been urging upon the government for a long time," said H. H. Hannam, President of the Canadian Federation of Agriculture, in a statement issued to-day on behalf of the Federation, which includes within its membership over 200,000 organized wheat farmers in the west.
>
> With many years of sad experience under the old unstable, speculative marketing system, producers believe it is wiser to forego the temptation of grabbing all they could get at the moment for the sake of securing instead the guarantee of remunerative prices for a number of years in advance. Because of their level-headed reasoning on this matter, they were not misled by the private grain trade and leaders of the grain exchange at Winnipeg, who have been spending an obviously enormous amount of money recently in a campaign to prevent the adoption of this particular type of wheat marketing program. Wheat farmers know only too well that the men behind such a campaign were those who through the years have prospered in the business of buying and selling the farmers' wheat under the old speculative system of marketing, and the success of whose campaign would have resulted in the

[42] *Winnipeg Free Press,* July 26, 1946.
[43] *Ibid.*

resumption of this system, with prospect of easy profits for themselves. It is gratifying also to note that the government apparently was not misled by this campaign.[44]

The federation's broadside against the exchange exemplified the revival of the feud between the pools and the trade which had quieted down during the war, but had broken out anew as the postwar wheat marketing policy of the government took shape. The feud became intensified as the Winnipeg grain exchange carried its case to the farmers by means of an extensive advertising campaign and the pools replied in kind.

CREATION OF THE FIVE-YEAR POOL

Just as the concept of the bilateral agreement with Britain had originated with Gardiner, so did also the concept of a five-year pool. The object of the contract had been to create relative stability of markets in the transitional period. Now that Gardiner had secured an assurance of the British market in a quantity larger than anyone but he desired, the time had come to relate the contract to what producers could expect by way of an initial payment on their deliveries. There was no legal basis for the creation of more than a one-year pool under the authority of the Canadian wheat board act, but that served as no deterrent to Gardiner's conception of a five-year pool with an initial payment guaranteed for four years ahead instead of for one year as specified by the act. The longer-term guarantee of the initial payment was the essence of the continuing assurance of markets at stable prices which the contract afforded.

The concept of the five-year pool had originated with Gardiner in the government's guarantee of the $1 floor for five years which had been given on September 19, 1945. He subsequently claimed that the five-year plan had originated with that guarantee; it had been basic in his discussions with the British in terms of a five-year contract for which he had pressed until the end, in his discussions in cabinet, with the wheat board and the farm organizations and that "no one ever suggested that it ought to be anything else but a five-year programme".[45]

However, when the five-year pool fell under the fire of the provincial wheat pools, Gardiner shifted his explanation to account for the fact that he had originally discussed with the farm organizations on July 24, 1946, as the contract was being signed, an immediate payout of the surplus in the 1945-46 crop account according to statute, and the creation of a four-year pool commencing August 1, 1946 and ending on July 31, 1950. This was how Gardiner described MacKinnon's and his consultations with the farm organizations both on the initial payment and on the duration of the pool:

> Now I come down to the last week before the British agreement was signed, when we knew all the facts with regard to it. The Minister of Trade and Commerce and I met — I have stated this in the pool board meetings in western Canada and I have their consent to state it anywhere — we met the representatives of all the farmers' grain handling organizations in western Canada — the Saskatchewan wheat pool, the Manitoba wheat pool, the Alberta wheat pool, the United Grain Growers. These organizations were all present, together with the president and secretary of the Canadian Federation

[44]*King Papers.*
[45]*House of Commons Debates,* February 28, 1947, pp. 897-898.

of Agriculture, and a representative of the wheat growers of Ontario. The meeting was held for the purpose of discussing what the initial payment ought to be following this agreement. We were in a position at that time to inform them what that British agreement was, because it had all been agreed to. The agreement was signed I think two days later.

Mr. Coldwell: What was the date of that meeting?

Mr. Gardiner: It was some time last summer — I think in July. The first question I asked the representatives of the farm organizations when we settled down was this. I said: Am I right in believing that the highest initial payment that has been asked for officially by the farm organizations is $1.25 a bushel? Without any exception they said yes. The next question I asked was: Am I right in believing that the farmers would like to have a price which might be termed parity? The answer to that was yes. Beyond that I do not know that I had their consent to this, but in all the previous meetings it had been agreed that parity based upon the price which had been received for wheat from 1926 to 1929 was $1.41 a bushel. Therefore I said: Am I right in believing that you now would like to have an initial payment of about $1.40 a bushel in order that it may be somewhere near the parity prices as it has been calculated? And they said yes. As a matter of fact, Mr. Chairman, they then submitted arguments as to why the advance payment ought to be $1.40.

I tell this story in order to show that the first time anyone ever suggested that participation be paid on the 1945 crop was during that discussion. It was not suggested by the farm organizations; it was suggested by myself, and every one of the farm organizations will agree that that is so. Why was it suggested? When the proposal was made that we should start off with $1.40, the argument was used which I have twice used in the committee, namely, is it not much better for the farmer to be in a position to say that whatever price he is getting, he is getting it for his own wheat, paid for by the people of Canada, paid for by the British or anyone else who wants to buy it? It is better that way if we can arrange it, and everyone, I think, was agreeable to that.

The next thing was to calculate how much could be paid without any fear of loss. It was suggested that $1.35 was the highest price that could be paid without any fear of loss, on the calculating that had been done by those who look after matters of the kind for the government. Others checked it and it was agreed that that was as high as one could go if all the crop years were taken into consideration.

Then the suggestion was made that since we could not pay more than $1.35 over the whole five years without involving someone other than the farmers themselves, probably we could develop a plan based on four years and pay the participation on the first year at the end of the year 1945. We asked the definite question whether it would be more satisfactory to the farmers if we paid the participation on the 1945 crop and then paid $1.35 through for the four years. The representatives of the farm organization said that would be more satisfactory to them. It was not their proposal; it was our suggestion to them.

A few days following that they held a meeting in Winnipeg and submitted the question to that meeting. It was discussed behind closed doors by the representatives of the farm organizations. We continued to make our calculations and finally had to come back and say that after calculating the matter as we had done previously it would be impossible to maintain the floor at $1.35; we would have to come down to a lower floor in order to maintain the position that we had taken previously, if we had paid the 1945 participation and put it on a four-year basis. Therefore the question would have to be discussed again from the point of view of the five-year period.

Representatives of the farm organizations flew from Ottawa to Winnipeg to complete the discussion in Winnipeg and finally received the agreement of the organizations under some protests that it would be satisfactory to proceed on that basis. Hon. members know what results from discussions of that kind. When discussions of that kind are started—and we assumed the responsibility for starting them, not the farm organizations—it is not easy to stop them, particularly when you start them in that way. These matters have been discussed in farm organizations ever since. Farm organizations have been passing resolutions about it here and there. But the heads of the organizations know what the discussions were which took place and the reason for them. They know what was involved in them, and when they come to talk to us they are not talking of this year-by-year proposal of the leader of the opposition. In the statement they made to us today they asked for payment of the 1945 participation, thereby going back to the suggestion which was made to them by us last summer. They suggest that that ought to be paid. . . .[46]

Gardiner's explanation was that he had offered the farm organizations on July 24, 1946, an immediate payment of the surplus which had accrued from the disposition of the 1945 crop and then, commencing August 1, 1946, a four-year pool with an initial payment of $1.35. After the provincial pool leaders had returned to the west, the government, at the insistance of the department of finance, had concluded too great a risk was involved in the guarantee of $1.35. On the export side, the contract price was firm at $1.55 for two years, but only at $1.25 and $1.00, respectively, for the last two years. The contract terms could, therefore, barely justify the $1.35 figure. But it must also be remembered that the board's price for domestic sales was still restricted to $1.25, and there was no assurance whatever of what the residual quantities of wheat could be sold for in other export markets. The matter was further complicated at the time by an adjustment in the proceeds accruing to the 1944-45 and 1945-46 pool accounts. Rather than drop the initial payment below $1.35 on a four-year pool, Gardiner fell back on the argument that everyone until then had been discussing a five-year plan. By taking the 1945-46 pool account retroactively into five-year period commencing August 1, 1945, to coincide with the date of commencement of the five-year floor guarantee, there was a sufficient surplus remaining in the 1945-46 board account which, instead of being paid out, could be put into a five-year pool and justify the retention of the $1.35 initial payment. Thus cabinet approved Gardiner's recommendation on a five-year pool on July 30, 1946, and MacKinnon made the following announcement in the house:

Mr. Speaker, as the house has been advised, the government's attention has been directed for some time to the question of wheat policy for western Canada. The United Kingdom-Canada wheat contract, signed on July 24 and announced to the house on July 25, is an important element in the new policy for western producers that I now wish to describe. The contract establishes a market for a considerable proportion of the next four western wheat crops, with underlying price guarantees. This factor, along with the continued shortage of foodstuffs and the high prices of competing wheats, makes it possible to deal more generously with the wheat producer than I indicated in this house on March 20, 1946. At that time, I announced the continuation of the initial price at $1.25 per bushel basis No. 1 Northern in store, Fort William-Port Arthur or Vancouver, for the 1946-47 crop year.

[46]*Ibid.*, pp. 898-899.

The new policy is based upon an initial price of $1.35 per bushel basis No. 1 Northern in store Fort William-Port Arthur or Vancouver, applicable to all the wheat delivered to the Canadian wheat board in the five-year period from and including August 1, 1945, and July 31, 1950. The 1945-46 deliveries, based on an initial price of $1.25 will be brought up to a $1.35 basis by payment of a flat ten cents per bushel on all grades.

As the house has been informed, the payment of about 12 cents per bushel as participation on the 1943 crop is now under way. This participation payment will be followed by one on the 1944 crop the sale of which has progressed to a point where I am safe in saying that the participation payment will be upwards of 16 cents per bushel. After the ten cent payment on the 1945 crop has been made—to bring the initial payment up to $1.35—the plan is to place the remaining surplus from that crop in a five-year pool with the succeeding four crops of 1946, 1947, 1948 and 1949. Participation certificates will be issued in the usual way, but the payment on these certificates will not be made until after the conclusion of the five-year pool at July 31, 1950. In other words, the deliveries of all five years will be bulked in one pool, with the same initial price of $1.35 ruling throughout the period and the suplus resulting from the marketing of these crops will constitute the participation payments.

In connection with deliveries, there was, of course, no restriction on 1945-46 deliveries and it was the intention of the government to instruct the Canadian wheat board to accept all the wheat that producers wish to deliver in 1946-47. The best information we can get indicates a continued overall world shortage of wheat and wheat flour in the coming crop year. Deliveries in the last three years of the pool will depend upon conditions of production and of markets. It will be provided in the new orders that the deliverable quantities will be determined by the governor in council before each crop year, but in any event, the deliverable quantity shall not be less than 14 bushels per authorized acre. The latter provision should safeguard wheat producers against an extreme reduction in deliverable amounts, should available markets be smaller than we expect.

I should also mention the provisions for domestic and export prices. In the interests of general price control that benefits the wheat producers along with other Canadians, the domestic price of wheat will be continued at $1.25, with the government assuming the carrying costs on the amounts of wheat used domestically. The government will continue to pay a drawback to millers covering the difference between 77⅜ cents and 125 cents per bushel on wheat used in Canada for human consumption. This is, of course, not a direct charge against the producer. With regard to export prices, the supplies for the United Kingdom will obviously be sold within the terms of the contract. In sales to non-contract countries, a serious effort will be made to sell at prices roughly corresponding to those of the other principal supplier—now, the United States. To this end, order in council P. C. 6122 of September 19, 1945, has been revoked. It will be remembered that through this order the government directed the Canadian wheat board for the time being not to exceed a sales price of $1.55 per bushel for No. 1 Northern in store Fort William-Port Arthur or Vancouver in its export sales.

It will be apparent from what I have just said and from the terms of the United Kingdom-Canada wheat contract that the government considers it wise and advisable to continue the Canadian wheat board as the sole purchaser of western Canadian wheat from the producers. The government believes that the great majority of western producers are satisfied, for the present at least, with this method of marketing. The present powers of the

Canadian wheat board will be extended under the National Emergency Transitional Powers Act for the duration of this statute. When it expires, the government will direct its attention to the form and authority under which the board's powers may be further continued.

Other powers of the board, such as delivery quotas, will continue to be employed as in the past. For 1946-47, however, the quotas will not be finally restrictive but employed for the purpose of fairly dividing elevator space and railway cars among all the producers.

The representations that have been made to the government by spokesmen for the organized producers of western Canada stress their great desire for stability, so far as it can be attained by government action, during the post-war years. I think it can be fairly said that the policy I have outlined helps the producers materially toward that objective. There is no question that the wheat producers have made possible the success of domestic price control by immediate sacrifices in their 1945-46 and current export prices. These sacrifices have also assisted in overseas rehabilitation. The government is convinced that the outlined policy will give fair and comparatively stable returns to the producers, so far as it is within the power of the government.[47]

Thus the five-year pool was created, commencing retroactively on August 1, 1945, and extending to July 31, 1950. In the announcement, MacKinnon had indicated that final payments would be made on the 1943 and 1944 crops but that, instead of a final payment on the 1945 crop, an interim payment of 10 cents only would be paid to raise the level of the initial payment for that crop to $1.35. Any residual surplus on the 1945-46 crop account would be put into the five-year pool. MacKinnon also declared that the monopoly powers of the wheat board would be retained under authority of the national emergency transitional powers act. Although MacKinnon made no reference to it, the five-year pool was created by order in council under authority of the same act, thereby setting aside the one-year pooling provision of the wheat board act.

In his announcement that export sales to non-contract countries would be made at class 2 prices, MacKinnon tacitly inferred that contracts similar to the British would not be entered into (as Gardiner had initially envisaged) with the continental European countries. Later that year, Gardiner attended the FAO conference in Copenhagen and defended Canada's preferential treatment to Britain. Although Gardiner claimed that French, Belgians, Dutch and Norwegians did not press for contracts on British terms, representatives of these countries in Ottawa all indicated interest in contracts at the same prices. They were told that the board's limited supply position made further quantity guarantees unrealistic. At the same time C. F. Wilson urged representatives to elicit their governments' support for the international wheat agreement negotiations, through which several exporting countries could offer a collective guarantee on quantities and which offered a greater assurance of supplies than one exporting country could provide on its own.

FURTHER PUBLIC REACTION

Mr. George Mathieson, president of the Winnipeg grain exchange issued an official statement on July 30, 1946, the day of the announcement of the

[47]*Ibid.,* July 30, 1946, pp. 4035-4037.

five-year pool. His statement was directed to the contract, and Mathieson commended it for the benefits it conferred upon producers, while taking the government to task for selling to the British at a price so far below the world market level, and for allowing Chicago and Minneapolis markets to take the lead in price making as he said:

> It is gratifying that farmers are assured of a higher price for the past year and for the next four years. But the price of $1.35 is still about 60¢ below present world values. What the participation certificates will bring to farmers at the end of the pooling period and over and above this initial payment of $1.35 cannot at this stage be gauged. The chances of an initial payment would have been greater had sales to the British government been made at near world values. The intended use of United States values as a yardstick is, however, an admission of the importance of an open market in arriving at sales prices.[48]

The press featured the fact that Canadian wheat would be sold to all export markets other than Britain at United States export prices to which the board's class 2 price would be related. As at the end of July, 1946, the board's class 2 price was quoted at $2.05.

In the wake of the July 30 announcement, the pool leaders continued to withhold official comment but they welcomed, without attribution, the stability afforded through the five-year initial payment of $1.35. At the same time they deplored the retroactive inclusion of the 1945 crop in the pool. The annual report of the directors of the three pools disclosed that when they met in Winnipeg on July 25-26, 1946:

> The meeting . . . discussed the Canada-United Kingdom Wheat Agreement. It was agreed that action be taken to have the 1945-46 crop excluded from the pool set up by the government in connection with the agreement and dealt with according to the terms of the Wheat Board Act. Some dissent was registered to a four-year pool, and strong opposition was expressed to the $1.25 domestic price.[49]

Elsewhere the report indicated:

> The inclusion of the 1945-46 crop in the five-year pool created some dissatisfaction among farmers and to the layman at least would seem to be of doubtful legality in the light of the provision of the Wheat Board Act that participation certificates issued in connection with any crop entitles the producer to share in the equitable distribution of the surplus accruing from the sale of that particular crop.[50]

When the opposition parties sought an opportunity to debate the five-year pool based on the contract with Britain, MacKinnon promised that one could take place during his departmental estimates. Thus, when the item covering the wheat and grain division was called on August 14, 1946, the debate began and extended over two days. During its course, no opposition member condemned the contract with Britain outright. The Honourable John Bracken, leader of the opposition, prefaced his remarks by saying:

> I rise at this time to criticize the government's wheat policy. But before doing so, let me say this, with respect to the United Kingdom wheat agreement. Any agreement such as this which tends to level out the inequalities, and the wide fluctuation of prices in the past, is a step in the right direction. Even this

[48] *Winnipeg Free Press,* July 31, 1946.
[49] Canadian Co-operative Wheat Producers Limited, *Directors' Report 1945-1946,* p. 85.
[50] *Ibid.,* pp. 82-83.

agreement is better than no agreement at all; because, as the Minister of Agriculture pointed out, those of us who went through the price depression following the last war know the danger of proceeding without some kind of plan to try to avoid wide fluctuations in price.[51]

Then he proceeded to question the firmness of the government's commitments to producers under the five-year plan and to attack the implications of the contract for trade policy. Messrs. M. J. Coldwell and Robert Fair, speaking for the CCF and Social Credit parties endorsed the contract but decried the fact that producers were not being dealt with more generously. MacKinnon left it to Gardiner to defend the contract and the five-year pool. Gardiner did so with characteristic vigor.[52] In the conclusion of the contract and the creation of the five-year pool, Gardiner had reached the zenith of his career; hereafter he could only recede as the wisdom of the contract was increasingly challenged. One byproduct of the contract, little realized at the time, however, was the considerable impetus it gave to the renewed effort to conclude a multilateral wheat agreement whereby the same terms of access could be extended to all importing countries.

[51]*House of Commons Debates,* August 14, 1946, p. 4811.
[52]*Ibid.,* August 14, 1946, pp. 4802-4810.

40

REVIVAL OF THE
MULTILATERAL NEGOTIATIONS

The preceding chapter illustrated how tenaciously the pools, with the support of the Canadian federation of agriculture, continued to advocate the negotiation of an international wheat agreement. The pools had done so after they were forced to abandon their own co-operative marketing activities with the onset of the depression. They envisaged a government monopoly grain board reinforced by an international agreement as the most effective means of assuring market stability and security which, in their opinion, the open market system had failed to provide.

On the other hand, Gardiner had been substantiated in his belief that an international agreement on wheat prices could not be negotiated. Furthermore, he shared the general belief that the postwar demand for wheat was ephemeral, and that producers would find themselves in need of price protection again two or three years hence. Gardiner sponsored the bilateral route to market assurance because it offered some practical prospect of success.

Nevertheless, so long as he had his contract in hand, or the authority to negotiate it, Gardiner was by no means averse to placating the pools by endorsing the multilateral negotiations. At the federation's March 28, 1946, meeting with the government, MacKinnon had reassured Parker that the government was actively promoting the multilateral approach, while Gardiner sounded out the pools on the bilateral alternative. Thus there was no inconsistency in Gardiner's and MacKinnon's decision on May 2 to press forward on the bilateral front on the one hand, and issuing instructions to Wilson on the other, to do whatever could be done to revive multilateral negotiations.

INFORMAL DISCUSSIONS

At that moment the international wheat council was in a quiescent state; at its most recent meeting on February 27, 1946, the price provisions of the 1942 memorandum of the agreement had been finally deleted, the life of the council extended, and a decision taken to invite the governments of Belgium, Brazil, China, Denmark, France, India, Italy, the Netherlands, USSR and Yugoslavia to become members of the council. Despite the critical wheat shortage and its turbulent effect upon wheat prices, the council, had seen fit to postpone further price discussions until an enlarged body could deal with the issue sometime in August. One of the significant factors in that decision was that, in the changed circumstances, the United States department of agriculture had abandoned its drive to conclude an agreement. The 1942 draft convention had assigned a very small proportion of commercial exports to the United States. Now it was shouldering its full share of the burden of postwar relief wheat shipments; prices were strong, and the United States would have to subsidize its export prices heavily in order to participate in a wheat agreement. Although it was natural that the exporting countries should relax their efforts in the pursuit of an international agreement during the period of wheat shortage, it also followed that when surpluses reappeared, they would find the importing countries less interested in extricating suppliers from their difficulties.

It was on this theme—if the exporting countries were to make a deal with the importing countries, they should do it when prices were high and supplies short—that Wilson tried to revive the discussions. Under such circumstances the exporting countries could offer price concessions in return for importers' support of prices later on.

When the executive committee of the council met in Washington on May 2, 1946, it was advised that only four of the invited governments had accepted membership in the enlarged council, and the next meeting of the council was put off until August. As there was no hope of a formal meeting before then, Wilson secured MacKinnon's approval and McIvor's encouragement to approach the key delegates individually and to urge that more precipitate action be taken. Such an opportunity presented itself when a special meeting on urgent food problems was convened in Washington by the fledgling food and agriculture organization of the United Nations, at which governments were to be represented by ministers and their senior officials. Gardiner headed a rather large Canadian delegation to which Wilson was named. The meeting opened on May 20, 1946, and as opportunities presented themselves outside the conference, Wilson pressed his argument on the timing of the wheat negotiations with Herbert Broadley and Maurice Hutton of the British delegation, L. A. Wheeler of the United States and J. U. Garside of Australia. As a result, the others agreed to hold an informal meeting of the executive committee of the wheat council on May 31. On the following day Wilson reported to MacKinnon:

> I opened the discussion by stating that although price negotiations had proved fruitless over the past two or three years in trying to set up a price range to meet a future situation, we had this past year reached a point where the level of export prices in each of the exporting countries had become an immediate and very practical consideration. The exporting countries in the past had looked to the importing countries for support in guaranteeing an international floor level of prices, but by the same token the importing countries had a right to expect that the exporting countries under the present sellers' market would exercise some control over the prevailing high prices of export wheat. In the export level of prices in the 1946-47 crop year, the cumulative effects of encouraging expanded wheat production to meet the immediate food crisis would sooner or later give rise to another wheat surplus. Prices could then be expected to collapse from the prevailing high levels, and unless the exporting countries were prepared now to sell to the importing countries at an agreed

price level, they could not expect the cooperation of the importing countries later on to refrain from taking advantage of low wheat prices.

Mr. Broadley supported this position fully, saying that there was a tendency now on the part of certain British officials to wait out the period of prevailing high prices in the expectation that having entered into no commitment on price levels they could take full advantage of low prices later.

Mr. Wheeler, for the United States, expressed sympathy with the need for international stabilization of prices, but pointed out that while the present time might be most opportune for the other countries, for the United States the present was the most difficult period for them to enter into an agreement.

Under normal conditions the United States could expect an export quota of 16 per cent of the total world net exports. During the present crop year they have had to export more wheat than any other country and might have to do so again in the 1946-47 crop year. With an abnormal high level of exports from the United States going to claimants such as UNRRA and India, which do not represent normal commercial markets, and with the pressure exerted upon the United States to maximize these exports under present conditions, it would be difficult to get Congress to approve the amount of the subsidy necessary to bring United States export prices into line with the $1.00-$1.50 range in United States funds envisaged under an International Wheat Agreement. Notwithstanding, he was prepared to seek further instructions from his Government to see if any new proposal could be supported by the United States. . . .

Mr. Viacava, the Argentine representative, stated that his Government had always been prepared to support an international range of prices. However, with the conclusion of hostilities his Government had insisted that the importing countries, rather than the United Kingdom alone, be fully represented in the negotiations. He would be prepared to proceed, so long as the additional importing countries which had been asked to join the Wheat Council were brought into the negotiations.

Mr. Bulcock, for Australia, did not think that any objections would be raised by his Government to another attempt at reaching international agreement on prices. He thought, however, some solution would need to be found for a preferred price in Australia's nearby markets.

It was finally agreed that Mr. Wheeler should write to the five governments, there represented, requesting that each delegate a representative to take part in a preparatory committee which would meet in Washington during the third week in June. Each of the delegates would be expected to put forward the proposals covering the duration of the price agreement, the range of prices and possibly the future operation of export quotas which their Government would be prepared to support. These proposals would need some reconciliation in the preparatory committee, which would then report to the Executive Committee the last week in June. A full meeting of the International Wheat Council involving some fifteen governments in all would be called about the middle of July. At that meeting it is hoped definite price proposals could be presented. A further meeting of the full council would also be called for the middle of August after the newly joined importing country governments would have an opportunity to consider the price proposals.[1]

---

[1]*Trade and Commerce File 26204:14.*

CONSULTATIONS WITH ROBERTSON, MACKENZIE AND SHARP

Before the executive committee met again, Wilson had a conference with Robertson, Mackenzie and Sharp. This took place immediately after the critical cabinet meeting on June 19, when Robertson had queried the wisdom of the contract on trade policy grounds, to Gardiner's evident chagrin. The cabinet had decided to provide the Americans with an opportunity to propose an acceptable alternative, and when Wilson informed Robertson of the initiative taken to revive the multilateral negotiations, he endorsed the project wholeheartedly as one way of providing the alternative for which the cabinet was groping. Robertson perceived more clearly than the others that the multilateral approach still offered the best hope of extricating Canada from the discriminatory trade posture implied in the bilateral contract. The possibilities were discussed of streamlining the provisions of the 1942 draft convention, many of which seemed unnecessarily complex and of doubtful negotiability. It was recognized that in the multilateral negotiations a price agreement had become the paramount issue and that other matters such as export quotas, reserve stocks and the regulation of production were expendable, at least, until prices reverted to lower levels. With the support of the cabinet wheat committee, McIvor and these senior officials, Wilson continued his endeavors in Washington..

EXECUTIVE COMMITTEE MEETINGS

When the executive committee met on June 28, no progress could be made beyond ascertaining what the discrepencies were in the export prices of the four major exporting countries. The meeting was adjourned until July 8 when the United States representative explained how difficult it would be for his government to subsidize export prices to the necessary extent. Nevertheless, he declared that the department of agriculture was still sympathetic to the international approach, and Wilson pressed on with the presentation of a simplified draft agreement. He also learned something of the state department position and reported from Washington to Robertson on July 10, 1946:

> At a meeting of the Executive Committee of the International Wheat Council Monday afternoon, C. C. Farrington reported that the Department of Agriculture continues to favour the wheat agreement approach to the international wheat problem, and would like to participate in an agreement operative during the 1946-47 crop year. However, the Department had reexamined its position regarding available funds for export subsidies which they still regarded as inadequate even on the assumption of limitation of the subsidy to commercial sales. Section 32 of the Agricultural Adjustment Act requires that one-third of all Customs revenues be made available to the Department of Agriculture for agricultural subsidies, but there has since been a proviso that fifty percent of the funds be devoted to domestic subsidies. The Departmental receipts from customs revenues run to 100 to 130 million dollars annually, so that fifty percent of this amount for export subsidies would amount to approximately 60 million dollars. There was the further difficulty of lack of any domestic ceiling for the present on wheat prices.

In view of Mr. Farrington's statement that from an administrative viewpoint they would like to take part in a wheat agreement, I urged that the negotiation of an agreement take place immediately, suggesting that the Executive Committee prepare and submit a draft agreement to the enlarged Wheat Council within a week's time in order that the draft might be studied by Governments and reported back to the Wheat Council at an August meeting. The agreement might then be published and invitations issued to all interested Governments to accede. ...

It was agreed ... that a meeting of the enlarged Council, including representatives of Denmark, the Netherlands, Belgium, France, Italy, Brazil, China and India, who had accepted membership on the Council, be called for next Monday, July 15th. At this meeting, it is suggested that a Preparatory Committee be appointed to review the Draft Convention and to make recommendations regarding the terms of an agreement to be submitted to an international Conference. The Council would then request the United States to call the Conference. ...

Before the meeting adjourned, it was decided to hold a further meeting of the Executive Committee tomorrow morning, at which time I would present a document which I have drafted today making specific proposals regarding the content of an agreement. This has been done along the lines discussed with Mackenzie, Sharp and yourself, and will be presented at tomorrow morning's meeting. The purpose of the meeting is to see if any general accord can be reached among the four exporting countries particularly before the matter goes to the larger Preparatory Committee following next Monday's meeting of the Council, and I hope some progress can be made at reaching an agreement. ...

Prior to Monday's meeting of the Executive Committee, Stone invited Hickerson and Wheeler and myself to lunch. In the conversation, it developed that Wheeler was personally still as interested as ever in getting an international wheat agreement in operation. He pointed out the need of the Administration's going to Congress for additional subsidy funds before the Unites States could adhere to an agreement. Apart from the fact that it appears to be physically impossible because of the jam in legislation to put anything new before Congress during the present session, Wheeler thought it would be a mistake to raise the issue with Congress now, but rather to wait until the January session. In this Hickerson concurred. Wheeler then questioned Hickerson about the State Department's attitude toward commodity agreements. He contended that, while the Department of Agriculture's position had remained unchanged, there had been some reason to believe that the State Department's attitude might not be the same. He asked if the State Department believed that open future markets were to be given a first priority as a solution to commodity problems. Hickerson denied this and stated his personal view that the proposition of a wheat agreement should be advanced now even if the United States could not give effect to it until January.

Hickerson then asked me if, with the publication of a draft agreement, Canada could confine itself to a one-year contract with the United Kingdom to tide over the gap. I replied that without the certainty of an international wheat agreement a one-year contract would be most impractical. It would have to be at a much higher price since there would be no quid pro quo to the producers in subsequent years. I added that, if prompt arrival at an international wheat agreement could not be accomplished, I saw little alternative to a four-year contract with the United Kingdom.[2]

[2]*Ibid.*

All this had transpired in the midst of the consultations conducted at a higher level with the United States government on the Canada-United Kingdom contract.[3]

PROPOSAL FOR A SIMPLIFIED AGREEMENT

A simplified agreement along the lines discussed with Messrs. Robertson, Mackenzie and Sharp was submitted to the July 10 meeting of the executive committee. The purpose of the draft was explained in the following terms:

The preamble of the draft convention contemplated a postwar surplus situation; consequently the provision therein for production control, export quotas, minimum and maximum reserve stocks. Consideration at that time was also given to the operation of an agreement under conditions of scarcity, hence the provision for maximum, as well as minimum, export prices, and the provision for minimum, as well as maximum stocks. Notwithstanding, the current situation was not fully anticipated, a situation in which all limitations would have to be suspended on production control, export quotas and minimum reserve stocks, thereby leaving the maximum export price provision the only one which might now have been operative. To the extent that an international wheat agreement is desirable now, a major reorientation of approach would be required, particularly in respect of the timing of its several provisions.

In contrast with the 1941-42 negotiations, there is the advantage of dealing now with known elements of the current situation. It is evident that the most urgent problem is that of immediate recognition by the exporting countries of an obligation not to charge "all the traffic will bear" in an acute sellers market if there is to be any hope for recognition by the importers of their obligation to support a minimum export price level as soon as the market situation is reversed. Secondly, there is the problem of the current disparity between national export price levels. The immediate choice is between following an unstable export market situation up and down and the securing of a long-run measure of international price stability or, alternatively, a series of bilateral contracts between exporting and importing countries seeking piecemeal a similar end.

If wheat export prices were unlikely to rise further during 1946-47, thereby avoiding additional incentives to surplus production, and if there were no economic and political pitfalls in the path of "an expanding world economy" much could be said for the first alternative. In the absence of such assurances, the argument shifts in favour of a multilateral approach to a measure of stability in prices, production and export markets. Many considerations may be adduced in favour of multilateral against bilateral action if the multilateral approach can be accomplished.[4]

The terms of the draft included a four-year agreement to come into effect upon acceptance by at least three major exporting countries and ten importing countries. The significance of specifying three exporting countries at that time was that the constitutional procedures of Argentina, Australia and Canada permitted sufficiently prompt ratification to bring the agreement into operation in the 1946-47 crop year. Senate ratification in the United States would take longer, but there was no reason the other exporting countries should delay the implementation of the price range pending the adherence of the United States. The draft article on prices was explicit, except for the actual range of prices agreed. Basic export prices would be set for each exporting country, with provision for adjustment as necessary to keep the f.o.b. equivalents in line. An operating committee of grain experts would supervise these adjustments. Member exporting countries would undertake to sell within the price range to member importing countries for the duration of the agreement. Member importing countries would undertake not to increase their average purchases from non-member exporting countries when prices reached the minimum of the range.

Additional provisions relating to production in exporting and importing countries, export quotas, reserve stocks, etc., would be brought into operation only on such terms and at such times as approved by a two-thirds vote of the council. The two-thirds vote proviso had an implicit appeal inasmuch as it conferred upon Canada virtually power of a veto.

The reaction of the other members of the executive committee was that the streamlining of the 1942 draft convention had been too stark. Wheeler believed that production control in the importing countries was still important; otherwise policies of self-sufficiency would become entrenched. On this issue, Wilson considered compromise was in order to retain American support for the price agreement. Cairns took a hand in redrafting the skeleton draft. In the result, it was not quite so simple a document. It was submitted to the first meeting of the enlarged council which was held on July 15.

APPOINTMENT OF PREPARATORY COMMITTEE

The new members of the council displayed considerable interest in Wilson's proposals and approved the appointment of a preparatory committee whose function was to ascertain if a sufficient basis of agreement could be reached to warrant the calling of a full negotiating conference. As Wilson reported on the July 15 council meeting:

> Each of the eight new governments was represented including Belgium, Brazil, China, Denmark, France, India, Italy and the Netherlands. The Chairman welcomed the new delegates and, for their information, reviewed the activities of the Council from its inception in 1942 to date.
>
> The main business was the appointment of a Preparatory Committee to revise the Draft Convention, or in other words to draw up a new draft agreement that would be workable for the present, and to report to the next meeting of the Council which was set for August 19th.
>
> In the discussion leading to the appointment of the Preparatory Committee, I emphasized the need of bringing a price agreement into operation as quickly as possible, and this appeared to elicit the immediate interest of the new importing Government representatives. They agreed to the appointment of the Committee and all appeared interested in being represented thereon. My Document No. 2 outlining the scope of a new agreement was circulated and the first meeting of the Preparatory Committee is called for Wednesday afternoon, July 17th, at which time there will be opportunity to discuss and to explain the proposals in order that all representatives may make adequate reports to their Governments thereon. It then appears most probable that the Preparatory Committee will adjourn for a fortnight while Governments are being consulted, and re-convene early in August to reconcile the various

instructions, if possible, in order to make a report on a new draft agreement for submission to the August 19th meeting of the Council.[5]

When the preparatory committee met on July 17, Wilson was elected chairman. It was agreed to submit the redraft of his original proposals to governments for instructions in the hope of getting responses by August 15 before the committee would meet again to prepare a report to the council.

AUGUST 1946 COUNCIL MEETING

The August 19 meeting of the council had been called for the purpose of hearing reports from the members on the initial reactions of their governments to the proposal that negotiations proceed on the basis of the new draft. At that meeting, only the French delegate had been instructed to oppose negotiations within the international wheat council because the issue of commodity agreements in general had been referred for consideration to the FAO preparatory commission on world food proposals. Because the French delegate was in a minority, the council agreed that price negotiations should commence in the preparatory committee by August 27. The French position was worrisome, however, because governments of some of the other importing countries were subsequently attracted to it. Through the autumn of 1946, therefore, the wheat agreement had to be discussed in two forums, that of the international wheat council and of the FAO preparatory commission.

COMMENCEMENT OF PRICE NEGOTIATIONS

The meeting of the wheat council's preparatory committee which had been authorized to commence the price discussions was held August 27-29. On the opening day the British delegate suggested a range of $1 minimum, $1.55 maximum, which was compatible with the terms of the Canada-United Kingdom wheat agreement. The American delegate countered with a price range of $1.25-1.75. Wheeler told Wilson after the meeting that the $1.25 floor was more critical to the Americans than the $1.75 ceiling, and on the second day a Canadian compromise proposal was made of $1.25 - 1.55. As Wheeler pointed out, the $1.25 floor was consistent with the terms of the bilateral contract for at least three of its four years. As there was no immediate acceptance of the suggested compromise, the preparatory committee agreed to refer the three price proposals to governments for instructions by September 16, with a view to permitting the council to convene a full international wheat conference that autumn. After some delay, the preparatory committee met again on September 24 in what proved to be an abortive meeting because the British delegate was still without instructions and the Argentine delegate was in Buenos Aires.

In the interim Wilson arranged with Pearson, who had just succeeded Robertson as undersecretary of state for external affairs, to make direct representations to the British on acceptance of the $1.25 - 1.55 range and the British reply had been expected by September 24. Wilson reported on the meeting to MacKinnon:

> Just prior to the meeting, I learned from the British delegation that the price instructions they expected from their Government did not arrive in time for

the meeting. In view of the discussions Mr. Robertson and Mr. Mackenzie had with Sir Alexander Clutterbuck ten days earlier, it was hoped that the British would have been able to take a definite position at last Tuesday's meeting.

The other importing countries, particularly those of Northwest Europe, in my opinion, are partly waiting for the United Kingdom to take a lead in these discussions and also partly waiting to see if Canada enters into any additional contracts. These considerations, which were not brought out in the discussion at Tuesday's meeting, were fairly evident, however, and I thought it best to agree to another postponement until the second week in October, to give the British ample time to state their views and when our policy on further contracts might be decided.[6]

That message provided corroborative evidence that the European countries hoped to conclude bilateral contracts with Canada too. On October 17, when the preparatory committee met again, the British delegate reported that his government desired to hear the views of other importing countries and of the Argentine government before discussing the price proposals further. Viacava had still not returned from Buenos Aires. The French delegate had enlisted support for delaying the proceedings pending the FAO deliberations. Thus, while the British, Argentine and some of the European delegations engaged in procedural delays by contending that others should make the first move, it appeared that the price negotiations were foundering again.

POOL REPRESENTATION ON THE CANADIAN DELEGATION

In the midst of the desultory progress in Washington, the central executive of the pools, unaware of the impending stalemate, passed a resolution recommending that the pools be represented on the Canadian delegation. It was not the first time that such a suggestion was made. There had been complaints in the past that the negotiations were too secretive, and that their substance had not been communicated to their friendliest supporters. For the past year the wheat board's advisory committee had been reviewing the history of the negotiations which had taken place since the conclusion of the 1942 memorandum of agreement. For the benefit of the advisory committee, Dr. T. W. Grindley had prepared a detailed review and a critical analysis of the type of agreement projected in the 1942 draft convention. Grindley had questioned the wisdom and negotiability of its many complex provisions.[7] As a result, the advisory committee reported to the government on May 21, 1946, the divided views of its pool and trade members on the merits of international commodity agreements in general. Nevertheless, on the assumption that negotiations toward an international wheat agreement would continue, the advisory committee recommended several guidelines including the need for practical grain men, as well as diplomats and economists, to participate in the negotiation of any such agreement.[8]

The simplification of the draft agreement was one response to the advisory committee's recommendations. The other was an attempt, on

---

[6] *Trade and Commerce File 26204:14.*
[7] T. W. Grindley, *International Wheat Agreements,* prepared for the Advisory Committee to the Canadian Wheat Board, 1945.
[8] *Trade and Commerce File 26204:14.*

Wilson's part, to have respected grain men such as Gordon Smith added to the Canadian delegation for the July 15 meeting of the council. At the last minute, however, the invitations were withheld and the matter did not come up again until a resolution from the pools was received. MacKinnon was in the west when this happened and he wired Oliver Master, his acting deputy minister, on October 24: "I think that steps should be taken to have the western pools represented at next international wheat meeting. It looks to me that nothing is going to result and I think in view of this that it is especially important that the pools be represented."[9]

MacKinnon's assessment of the prospects was warranted and there was no reason the pools should not see the fruitless effort the government's representative had been making. Accordingly, Ben Plumer, J. H. Wesson and W. J. Parker were invited to attend the November 8 meeting of the preparatory committee. For that particular meeting, however, Wesson could not attend and he requested that George W. Robertson should go in his place.

At that meeting, despite the forewarnings from the Argentine embassy that Viacava's instructions would be completely negative, Viacava reported that his government would be interested in the reaction of the importing countries to the proposed price range. In addition to this slight encouragement, a major breakthrough in the price negotiations occurred when the British delegate accepted the $1.25 - 1.55 price range for three years, with a floor of $1 in the fourth year. Although not proposing a ceiling figure for the fourth year, the British delegate acknowledged that $1.75 would be reasonable. In response to this information, the committee agreed to meet again on November 12 to prepare a report and to resolicit the views of governments. The pools were represented for the first time at the November 8 meeting and they were well satisfied with the progress. Messrs. George W. Robertson and W. J. Parker met with Maurice Hutton, head of the British food mission, and they discussed the feasibility of a multilateral agreement without Argentine participation. Hutton believed it was practicable as long as Britain could purchase the same quantities from Argentina, whether in periods of scarcity or surplus. The concept of a viable agreement without Argentine participation added a surprising new dimension to the negotiations, because of everyone's recollection that the 1933 agreement had foundered upon the failure of Argentine compliance. Now it appeared that a different type of agreement could be devised which could function, with or without Argentina as a member.

Upon Wilson's return to Ottawa, MacKinnon agreed that Canadian missions abroad should be requested to approach the governments of the importing countries directly. This was arranged by Mr. Pearson, the undersecretary of state for external affairs.

In preparation for the November 8, 1946, meeting, the preparatory committee had been asked to present a complete draft agreement, and also an alternative draft if Argentina declined to participate. However much the other delegates desired the inclusion of Argentina in an international agreement, the committee, nevertheless, determined that the negotiations should not be frustrated by that issue, and that they should proceed in any

[9] *Ibid.*

event. The council set a tentative date of March 1, 1947, for the convening of an international conference. In deference to the wishes of the importing countries it was decided that the conference should be held in Europe.

FAO PREPARATORY COMMISSION

During the whole of that autumn, the members of delegations on the preparatory committee were also preoccupied with the progress of the discussions on commodity agreements in another place, namely, the FAO preparatory commission, which was also scheduled to meet in Washington. That commission had been convened for the purpose of considering the world food board proposals advanced by the FAO director general, Sir John Boyd Orr. The principle of commodity agreements had been included on the agenda and it was also under special study by the ITO preparatory commission which had been convened to implement the United States state department proposals.

The FAO preparatory commission met from October 28, 1946, until mid-January, 1947. The Right Honourable Harold Wilson, by now a junior member of the Attlee government, and Dr. C. F. Wilson were the British and Canadian representatives, respectively, on the FAO commission's committee on price stabilization and commodity policy. In that committee Harold Wilson presented the British position which weighed heavily in favor of buffer stocks and long-term contracts. The preparatory commission also invited Andrew Cairns to assist in the drafting of its commodity report. The result was a draft of another comprehensive type of commodity agreement with the British proposal for buffer stocks superimposed.

In the end, the report of the FAO preparatory commission turned out to be helpful, inasmuch as it recognized the jurisdiction of the international wheat council in the convening of an international wheat conference. Until then the FAO deliberations had provided a convenient excuse for those governments which wanted to delay progress toward an agreement under the aegis of the international wheat council. By January 1947, however, that pretext was removed by the FAO report, and the international wheat council pressed ahead with the preparation of its own draft agreement for use as an annotated agenda for a negotiationg conference.

As the report of the FAO preparatory commission was taking shape, the international wheat council met again on December 11, 1946. In advance of that meeting, and on the basis of replies received from the importing countries, the preparatory committee decided to recommend to council that a sufficient area of agreement had been reached to warrant the convening of an international wheat conference. In doing so, the preparatory committee took note of the British representative's interest in pursuing a "partial" agreement if Argentine support failed. On December 11, the wheat council accepted the committee's report and set the date for the council's next meeting on January 15, 1947.

PREPARATIONS FOR A NEGOTIATING CONFERENCE

The December 15, 1946, meeting of the council had requested Cairns to produce a new draft of an international agreement for its consideration in January. In doing so, Cairns took aboard all the ideas which had been projected during the deliberations of the FAO preparatory commission, and he reproduced the old comprehensive type of agreement with a buffer stock scheme added. Wilson's overriding concern was that any elaborate draft of an agreement would be difficult to negotiate. An attempt to regulate production within the importing countries was just one case in point, but Cairns had drafted such a clause in deference to the American position.

As mentioned earlier, Wilson had been receiving representations from Ottawa representatives of the European importing countries for contracts on similar terms to that of the United Kingdom ever since that contract had been signed. Also, as mentioned, he played upon their concern over equal access to the British preferential terms by urging their support for the multilateral negotiations. Moreover, a collective contract could dispose of the issue whether effective co-operation could be expected from the Argentine government, which had been preserving its bargaining power by keeping its participation in doubt. To bypass the uncertainty of Argentine participation, a collective contract appeared feasible which could be signed only by those countries which desired to share in the arrangement. Therefore, when Wilson saw Cairns's draft of a comprehensive agreement which included all the old clauses concerning production control, export quotas and the like which required the participation of all exporting countries, including Argentina, for effective operation, he prepared an alternative draft modeled on that of a collective contract for the purchase and sale of wheat within an agreed range of prices. Such form of an agreement could be signed by as few or as many of the exporting and importing countries as wished to do so, and still operate effectively.

When the council met January 15, 1947, it appointed Wilson chairman of a drafting committee to revise Cairns's draft along the lines he had recommended. Within the next several days the drafting committee adopted the new draft and referred it to governments as a basis upon which the negotiating conference could proceed. Although a new agreement format had emerged, its price range remained to be resolved. Three price proposals were listed in the draft. Wilson's compromise proposal of a $1.25 - 1.55 range for four years, proposed the previous July, still stood and was supported by the majority of governments. The British proposal of $1.25 - 1.55 for three years, and $1 - 1.55 for the fourth year, and the American proposal of $1.25 - 1.80 in the first three years and $1.00 - 1.55 in the fourth year, were included as alternatives. At its concluding meeting on January 28, 1947, the council voted that the negotiating conference be convened in London in March. The British government graciously undertook to be host for the conference.

Upon Wilson's return to Ottawa at the end of January, the cabinet decided to refer the draft agreement to a subcommittee of experts under the aegis of the cabinet committee on external trade policy. The subcommittee consisted of A. M. Shaw, James E. Coyne, John Deutsch, Sydney Pierce, Mitchell Sharp and C. F. Wilson. The majority of the subcommittee favored a price arrangement with export quotas only. Coyne foresaw that a system of export and import guaranteed quantities would minimize export competition and would thereby impair the determination of actual prices within the agreed range. On the other hand, Wilson foresaw the price range as merely marking the outside limits within which competitive factors could continue to operate. Within that framework he believed that even the futures market could be restored. Coyne believed, however, that under a collective contract system, a fixed price would be more practicable than a price range, such as had been agreed upon in the bilateral contract. In that case, however, there could be no scope for a futures market.

Because of the interest the advisory committee to the wheat board had taken in the international wheat agreement negotiations Wilson was invited to report to it on the latest developments at a meeting which was held in Toronto on February 19, 1947. He explained the conversion of the agreement into a multilateral contract proposal and, because of Coyne's concern, raised the issue of a fixed price versus a range of prices. The Canadian wheat board act was about to be amended and the constitutionality of a monopoly board remained in question. As a range of prices was compatible with either a board or an open market system, he secured the committee's support for a range.

By February 24, 1947, the subcommittee of experts on the draft wheat agreement reported to their deputy ministers L. B. Pearson, M. W. Mackenzie, David Sim, Dr. G. S. H. Barton, and Graham Towers. Following that meeting, Wilson drafted a report to the cabinet committee on external trade policy, on the type of agreement to be sought:

Alternative A
An agreement providing for a price range of $1.25 to $1.55, preferably for four years, plus export quotas.

Alternative B
An agreement providing for a price range of $1.25 to $1.55, export quotas, import quantities agreed for each signatory importing country, minimum and maximum reserve stocks in signatory exporting and importing countries, marketing control, or alternatively production control in signatory exporting countries, and sales at special prices.

Note on Alternative A
This type of agreement is more practical from an operational viewpoint. The Canadian delegate commenced negotiations last July with a recommendation for agreement on a price range only, but the delegates of other governments at the Wheat Council meetings and at the F.A.O. Preparatory Committee in Washington have already insisted upon recommending a more comprehensive agreement including import quantities to be agreed, minimum and maximum reserve stocks in both exporting and importing countries, plus either marketing or production control in the exporting countries, and permission to make sales below the floor price for nutritional programs in importing countries. These additional provisions are set out in the draft wheat agreement already referred to all governments for consideration.

To reject these additional provisions at the Conference would be to delay — if not to break up the Conference. This would imperil the bargaining position the exporting countries now have in their endeavour to bring the price range into effect on August 1, next. The United States winter wheat crop is in peak condition at the moment, and fall moisture supplies, which were the best in years in both the Canadian and United States spring wheat areas, have placed the seed bed in excellent condition. If an international wheat agreement is desired at all, the negotiations at the March Conference should be facilitated, bearing in mind particularly the need for United States Congressional action prior to August 1.

Under this alternative, a serious problem arises if Argentina stays outside the agreement. Provision would need to be made to limit purchases by signatory importing countries from non-signatory exporting countries. Such commitments have already proved difficult to obtain.

Note on Alternative B

Export quotas dividing up among signatory importers the sum of agreed import quantities make this type of agreement essentially a collective long-term contract, within a price range, instead of at fixed prices.

This type of agreement is embodied in the Draft Wheat Agreement prepared by the International Wheat Council in January and in the F.A.O. Preparatory Commission Report. Acceptance would facilitate the conclusion of the Conference.

It would assist in resolving the Argentine position. If Argentina is prepared to adhere, the agreed import quantities for each signatory importing country would be correspondingly larger than would be the case if it were necessary to allow for reasonable imports by the signatory importing countries outside the agreement from Argentina.

Questions should be raised regarding provision for maximum reserve stocks, marketing or production control in the exporting countries and sales at special prices. If the signatory importing countries accept agreed import quantities, signatory exporting countries are not concerned about domestic production and price policies within the signatory importing countries. . . .[10]

On February 25, Mackenzie and Wilson presented the report to the ministers who approved the second alternative and a list of delegates to the London conference. Cabinet appointed Mr. Norman Robertson, Canadian high commissioner in London to head the delegation with Wilson as his alternate. Advisers were Messrs. R. V. Biddulph, European commissioner of the wheat board, J. J. Deutsch, department of finance, and A. M. Shaw, department of agriculture. Messrs. R. C. Brown, vice-president of United grain growers, Paul Farnalls, a member of the wheat board advisory committee, C. E. Huntting, formerly assistant chief commissioner of the Canadian wheat board, Ben S. Plumer, chairman of the Alberta wheat pool and J. H. Wesson, president of the Saskatchewan wheat pool were named as technical advisers.

[10]*Ibid.*

41

LONDON WHEAT CONFERENCE, 1947

As arranged, the British government invited all members of the United Nations or of FAO to attend the negotiating conference which opened at Lancaster House on March 18 and continued, except for an Easter recess, until April 23, 1947. The governments of Argentina, Australia, Belgium, Brazil, Canada, China, Colombia, Czechoslovakia, Denmark, Dominican Republic, Egypt, Ethiopia, France, Greece, Guatemala, Hungary, India, Ireland, Italy, Lebanon, Luxembourg, Mexico, Netherlands, New Zealand, Norway, Peru, Poland, Portugal, Syria, United Kingdom, United States, and Uruguay responded by appointing delegates, and the governments of Austria, Bulgaria, Cuba, Iran, Romania, Sweden, Switzerland, Turkey and Yugoslavia sent observers. Sir Herbert Broadley (who had been knighted for his wartime contribution in the ministry of food) headed the British delegation as did Mr. L. A. Wheeler, the United States delegation. The Right Honourable John Strachey, who had just returned from Canada, presided over the opening meeting of the conference, and Sir Gerard Clauson, a colonial office expert on commodity problems, was elected chairman.

In preparation for the opening of the conference, the Canadian delegation conferred with Norman Robertson and also prepared its own formulation of a draft agreement which could be presented to the conference in the hope of streamlining the council's draft. In the Canadian draft, emphasis was strictly upon the price range and a balanced list of export and import guaranteed quantities. If agreement could be reached on those provisions, all other commitments could be dispensed with. In preparing this draft one important point of difference with the international wheat council's January draft was discovered. The latter had made the maximum and minimum prices applicable to all wheat transactions of the signatory countries. The Canadian draft limited the applicability of the price range to wheat sold within the quantities specified in the agreement. Otherwise transactions could take place at the class 2 or spot market prices. This modification was later accepted by the conference.

When the conference got down to business on March 19, the chairman called for opening statements from delegations, giving first priority to countries which had been party to the 1942 memorandum of agreement. This provided an opportunity for delegations to disclose their instructions, particularly those relating to the price range.

OPENING STATEMENTS
The key statements were those of Mr. Wheeler, Sir Herbert Broadley and Norman Robertson. Mr. Edwin McCarthy, who headed the Australian delegation took a flexible position, and Sr. Anselmo Viacava, the Argentine delegate had not yet received his instructions. Wheeler spoke first and reviewed the historical support the United States had given to the negotiation of a wheat agreement. He disclosed how firmly his delegation still supported a comprehensive form of agreement, with a price range of $1.25 - 1.80 as he had indicated to the council in January. Wheeler said:

... Before setting out in some detail our position with respect to the specific draft proposals which the International Wheat Council had recommended for our consideration, I should like to refer briefly to the historical attitude of the United States Government toward the question of an international agreement on wheat.

Since 1933, when an International Wheat Agreement was negotiated in this city, we have consistently supported the principle of multilateral negotiation and agreement with respect to wheat. It has been our view that wheat presented a problem which, in the long run, could only be solved by international action.

This problem consists fundamentally in an inherent tendency toward a disequilibrium between world export supplies and effective world import demand. We do not believe that this disequilibrium, which results in enormous price fluctuations in the world market, will be corrected by free competition. Nor do we believe that unco-ordinated national actions or any series of limited bilateral agreements will lead toward stability in world wheat prices at levels reasonable to both producers and consumers. Such stability, we believe, will be achieved only by effective co-ordination of national actions, i.e., by international agreement.

There is one further general aspect of this matter to which I should like to draw attention. That relates to the importance of wheat in the world general economic situation. We feel strongly that, as one of the principal staples of world consumption and trade, what may be accomplished with respect to international cooperation on wheat will have a great influence—proportionately much greater than its relative importance in the world economic sphere—in furthering effective international co-operation in other fields.

I come now to a statement of the position of the United States Delegation on the Memorandum on The Proposed International Wheat Agreement which was prepared by the Wheat Council as an annotated agenda for this Conference.

In the first place, and as a general comment, we believe that the Memorandum contains all the provisions essential to an effective international agreement. Not only that, we believe that the articles included therein, although naturally of varying degrees of importance, are all necessary to a well-rounded agreement.

I shall not at this time attempt to comment on each and every article. There are some that are more important than others and it is in respect of these articles that I wish to devote the time at my disposal. The articles which we consider to be of the greatest importance are those concerning prices (and the related question of the duration of the Agreement), export programs, stocks, special prices, and the obligations of importing countries with respect to imports and production. . . .

We consider an article on price a *sine qua non* of an international wheat agreement. We do not believe that the question of basic price objectives can or should be left to the determination of an international administrative body. This is not to say that we believe price objectives should be rigid and unalterable. On the contrary, we favour a reasonable degree of flexibility.

We therefore welcome the general idea expressed in the Memorandum that there should be established an agreed price range for wheat traded internationally to which signatory governments would commit themselves to adhere. We believe that price arrangements should be agreed covering a period of five years.

As regards specific price ranges, we support the proposal made by the United States representative during the fifteenth session of the International Wheat Council for a range of prices at the outset between $1.25 and $1.80 on the basis of No. 1 Manitoba Northern wheat in store at Fort William, Canada. We believe that the proposal of $1.80 as a price ceiling is, under present circumstances, reasonable and realistic.

I must remind my colleagues from other countries that, when this problem was being discussed in Washington during the month of January, the export price of wheat in the United States, and also in Canada except for quantities sold to the United Kingdom under special agreement, was in the neighbourhood of $2.15 a bushel. Since that time this export price, which for the United States is also the domestic price, has risen to the point where it is now in the neighbourhood of $2.75 a bushel. We believe that it is both unrealistic and unreasonable in the face of this situation to expect to start an international agreement on the basis of a ceiling price as low as $1.55. However, we would be willing to consider something less than $1.80 as the ceiling for the later years of the agreement. . . .[1]

Sir Herbert's statement was more expansive as he disclosed a rather unaccommodating negotiating position, from which the following excerpts are quoted:

. . . Our prospective balance of payments difficulties are by now known to the whole world. It is vital to this country that we should expand our exports and obtain our essential imports as reasonably as possible, if we are to establish a state of solvency and be able to play our part in developing world prosperity. We cannot contribute to the successful operation of a Wheat Agreement unless we frankly recognise this. It would be folly for us to accept obligations which place an added strain upon our economy and make it all the more difficult to achieve the solvency which we desire and the world expects us to establish. Subject to the recognition of these facts we will render any assistance in our power to achieving a Wheat Agreement. To ensure adequate supplies, to eliminate disastrous price fluctuations, to expand consumption, to encourage the more efficient producer—these are great objectives which will confer continuing benefits on producer and consumer alike.

Nevertheless, because of the difficulties to which I have referred and the uncertainties of the immediate future we feel that there might have been much to be said for postponing the conclusion of a Wheat Agreement until the sky was a little clearer and we could see the way in which the world is tending. . . .

We do feel, however, that in so uncertain a state of affairs it would be unreasonable at this moment to ask the different countries to bind themselves for unduly long periods of time, should we agree, as I hope we will, that a satisfactory Wheat Agreement can be concluded at the present Conference. In the view of the United Kingdom a period of three years, in these uncertain days, is a sufficiently long time to enter into commitments regarding wheat. If

[1] *International Wheat Conference, London, March 19, 1947, Verbatim Report.*

we can reach an agreement to cover this period it will give us time to look around and study the longer term problems. Then, at the end of those three years, we can plan afresh having not only the experience of those three transitional years with us, but the opportunity of seeing the future, possibly rather more clearly and definitely than we can see it today. . . .

As I have just said, any Wheat Agreement must be based upon a price range which is satisfactory to exporting and importing countries alike. The United Kingdom and Canada have entered into a four year contract, the terms of which are known to all. . . .

We would suggest that the Agreement should prescribe the following basic price range for Canadian No. 1 Manitoba wheat, not only for purchases by the United Kingdom, but for purchases by any other importing country which is a party to the Agreement:—

> 1947/48 - minimum $1.25 - maximum $1.55
> 1948/49 - minimum $1.25 - maximum $1.55
> 1949/50 - minimum $1.00 - maximum $1.25. . . .[2]

Norman Robertson then gave the Canadian position:

Canadian wheat producers, as represented through their organisations, and the Canadian Government have long been in favour of an international wheat agreement. Canada was one of the signatories of the 1942 Agreement which envisaged the calling of this Conference. That Agreement provided for certain price measures in the immediate post-war period pending the calling of a Conference. The price measures failed, however partly because of their faulty mechanism and partly through the absence of unanimity among members of the original Wheat Council to adopt an appropriate substitute, as evidenced in the record of the meetings of the International Wheat Council held in London at the end of August, 1945.

This morning I wish to refer to the main developments both in Canadian Government policy and in the deliberations of the International Wheat Council which have led to this Conference. I shall then briefly say something about the principal matters of policy which the Canadian Delegation desires to submit in connection with the draft Agreement.

Despite the unsatisfactory results of the International Wheat Council meeting held in August, 1945, the Canadian Government a few weeks later announced that it was instructing the Canadian Wheat Board not to offer wheat for export for the time being at prices above $1.55 for No. 1 Northern Wheat, basis in store Fort William, Port Arthur or Vancouver. This export price of $1.55 was held throughout the 1945/46 crop year, despite a substantial rise in the export prices of Canada's principal competitiors. A declared intention of this single-handed and rather one-sided effort at export price control was to take into consideration the position of our historic customers which were in most cases immediately confronted with major economic and financial readjustments following the conclusion of hostilities.

During the 1945/46 crop year the Canadian representative on the International Wheat Council supported an agreement on the international range of prices, but the Council was unable to agree on the immediate practicability of this step. Although the membership of the International Wheat Council was expanded in May, 1946, it was not until July of last year that the enlarged Council met and set up a preparatory Committee to undertake the negotiations of a suitable price range.

[2]*Ibid.*

In the considerable uncertainty which surrounded the possibility of reaching an agreement, the Canadian Government was concerned about its unilateral control of export prices. As a half-way measure it concluded with the Government of the U.K., the largest buyer of Canadian wheat, a contract extending for four crop years, the prices in the first two years of which were to continue at the $1.55 level. Commencing on 1st August, 1946, this price was made only on contractual sales, with spot prices applying to noncontractual sales. Since that time, however, the Canadian Government through its representative on the Preparatory Committee of the International Wheat Council has urged that the co-ordination of export wheat prices be attained.

Fortunately, by December, 1946, the Preparatory Committee was able to report to the International Wheat Council that substantial agreement had been reached on a range of prices and, as a result of this report, the International Wheat Council at its January, 1947 meeting prepared a draft wheat Agreement which is before us for consideration, and recommended that this Conference be convened.

Turning now to the principle embodied in the Draft, the Canadian delegation regards as essential features the provisions for a range of prices, export programmes and agreed import quantities. We feel that a measure of price stability applying to the great bulk of international transactions in wheat is much to be preferred to a $3 price for spot wheat now, together with the possibility of 50 cents for spot wheat some time later. Relative stability of prices could be expected to contribute much to the general economic stability and post-war reconstruction in both wheat exporting and importing countries.

Secondly, the Canadian delegation regards as essential the acceptance of agreed import quantities by the importing countries. This is important to the importing countries in assuring their desired supplies at the agreement prices. It should assist the importing countries in arriving at a more satisfactory determination of their post-war domestic agricultural production policies. In the same sense, it should assist the exporting countries to direct their agricultural policies in the light of a certain assured market for export wheat.

Thirdly, for the purpose of avoiding misunderstanding among the exporting countries in respect of their relative share of the assured import market, we consider it essential that the basis for export programmes be determined in this Conference to be applicable, if need be, during the life of the Agreement.

The Canadian Government are anxious that an Agreement be concluded in the simplest terms possible, having in mind its successful operation which would be facilitated by avoidance of complex administrative details that might lead to embarrassment to individual signatories or to misunderstanding among the countries concerned. Although we feel that the objectives embodied in the Draft Articles on stocks, production and sales at special prices have much to commend them, it is our opinion that these objectives would best be served by permitting complete freedom of action by individual Governments in these matters.

It is obviously the desire of both exporting and importing countries to build up adequate working and reserve stocks as soon as this can be done after meeting current consumption requirements. Prudence will dictate to individual Governments such disposal or adjustments as might eventually appear desirable, should surpluses ultimately appear too large. Without specifically providing for sales at special prices, we nevertheless feel that any signatory

Governments interested in concluding these transactions should be entirely free to do so over and above the commericial transactions provided for in the Agreement.

Rather than go into more detail at this stage on our views about the Draft Wheat Agreement, I think it would be more useful to the Conference if the Canadian delegation were to submit a paper embodying the revisions in the draft which it considers desirable, and I would like to hand this draft to the Secretary for distribution to the Delegations.

The Government of Canada desires to co-operate fully in seeking an international agreement which will provide long-term price stability and the possibility of a steadily expanding world trade in wheat in the interests of both exporting and importing countries.[3]

There followed the statements of several other delegations, but the prices issue had been joined on the first day of the conference. Between the extremes of the British and American positions on prices, a compromise was never quite reached. To continue the work of the conference, two committees were formed; the first to conduct the negotiations and to draft the substantive clauses, and the second to deal with the administrative clauses of the agreement. As soon as the committees were formed, Norman Robertson left the day-to-day negotiations with Wilson. The delegation, as a whole, conferred regularly with Robertson. The presence of producer representatives on the delegation, (Wesson, Plumer, Brown and Farnalls) helped immeasurably in making decisions. What the producer representatives could accept was likely also to be acceptable to the Canadian government. Huntting's and Biddulph's advice was also helpful on the trade side.

GUARANTEED QUANTITIES; RIGHTS AND OBLIGATIONS

By dint of constant pressure in the two committees, the Canadian delegation kept working for a draft agreement along the lines of multilateral contract as others, notably the Americans, championed the old notion of a comprehensive agreement. A major modification in the form of a multilateral contract was introduced, however, after the British examined the prospects for competition within the price range when importers guaranteed in advance the quantities they would purchase. It was the same point James Coyne had raised in Ottawa, and the British contended that exporters would hold prices at the ceiling so long as they were assured of sales. They had obviously given a great deal of study to the problem and, as they told Wilson, Professor James Meade, (then with the economic section of the British cabinet office), who was an adviser to the British delegation, had originated the suggestion that the article on quantities should be drafted in terms of a balance between exporters' and importers' rights and obligations. More explicitly, the exporting countries should have the right to sell their guaranteed quantities, only if offered at floor prices; conversely they should have an obligation, only at ceiling prices, to sell their guaranteed quantities upon the demand of importers. The importing countries, in turn, had an obligation to purchase their guaranteed quantities at floor prices, and a right to purchase them at ceiling. Rights and obligations would not apply to transactions within the price range where

[3]*Ibid.*

competition would determine actual prices. Wheat sold and purchased within the price range would be recorded, however, in discharge of the guaranteed quantity commitments. Although Meade's proposal denied exporters the right to sell their guaranteed quantities except at the floor, the precision of his proposal appealed to the great majority of the delegations and it would have been unwise to oppose it unless, as an alternative, the Canadians were to seek support for a fixed price instead of a price range. At one stage in the negotiations they did, in fact, propose a fixed price but found no support. Thus the Meade formula was incorporated into the conference's draft agreement; it was never questioned thereafter and it survived in the basic structure of the international wheat agreement signed in 1949. The import and export rights and obligations were spelled out for the first time in a March 29, 1947, working draft as follows:

1. The quantity of wheat set down in Annex I against the name of each importing country shall be called that country's "guaranteed import quantity" and shall represent the quantity of wheat which that country: —
(a) in accordance with paragraph 2 of Article IV may be required to purchase at the minimum price specified in Article VI for shipment during each wheat year from the exporting countries, or
(b) in accordance with paragraph 1 of Article IV may require the exporting countries to sell to it at the maximum price specified in Article VI for shipment during each wheat year.
2. The quantity of wheat set down in Annex II against the name of each exporting country shall be called that country's "guaranteed export quantity" and shall represent the quantity of wheat which that exporting country: —
(a) in accordance with paragraph 1 of Article IV may be required to sell at the maximum price specified in Article VI for shipment during each wheat year to the importing countries, or
(b) in accordance with paragraph 2 of Article IV may require the importing countries to purchase from it at the minimum price specified in Article VI for shipment during each wheat year.
3. The Council shall at its first meeting compare Annexes I and II and make such adjustments by mutual agreement as will make the totals of the two Annexes equal to one another.
4. The Council may at any meeting approve an increase in any figure or figures in either Annex if an equal increase is simultaneously made in a figure or figures in the other Annex.[4]

ARGENTINE DECLARATION

On March 26, 1947, Sr. Viacava, who had until then been without instructions, reported the extremely negative position of his government as follows:

The Argentine Government, as a signatory of the Agreement concluded at the meeting of the Wheat Conference held in Washington in 1942, has taken part in the deliberations held in that City in 1945 and 1946, with the object of arriving at a general agreement which, on the basis of the Draft Convention approved in 1942 by five countries, could also be extended to all the other countries which have a substantial interest in the wheat trade. I should add, with regard to my country's participation in the past in international meetings from the very first, which took place in London in 1933, when the first Wheat Agreement was drawn up. This Agreement, in which Argentina participated,

[4]*Draft Wheat Agreement, March 29, 1947, Article II.*

was the first experience in this class of international agreement. Argentina was subsequently represented at the Conference held in London in 1939 and formed part of the Preparatory Committee which, after nine months' discussions, had agreed on the fundamental points when war broke out and the deliberations were suspended.

From the last meetings held in Washington to which I have referred emerged the Draft International Wheat Agreement, which forms part of the agenda of this Conference. This Draft Agreement covers in very full and detailed form, among others, the same four fundamental points contained in the 1942 Draft Agreement, namely, price control, stocks, exports and production.

From the discussion which has taken place during the past days of this Conference we have been able to gather the importance attached to the Article in the Draft Agreement under consideration dealing with the price of wheat and quantities to be purchased at that price. Undoubtedly the price factor is the fundamental one in the wheat trade, as in the trade of any other product. At present the world is passing through a period in which the prices of wheat as well as of many other products are undergoing great fluctuations. When a few months ago we were speaking in Washington of a price level of one dollar fifty-five per bushel and wheat was selling at two dollars fifteen, none of us present at those meetings would have imagined that a few months later prices would rise up to three dollars. This instability in price occurs also in a large number of manufactured goods, machinery and industrial equipment, and even in the case of second-hand machinery and equipment which can only give service for a short time. For the Argentine Government, whose supplies of materials and industrial plant for her population depend on imports, this instability of prices, as I mentioned some days ago, is a matter of deep concern.

To this instability of prices is added the circumstance that the Argentine Government is in the middle of the reconstruction of the country's general economy, the plan for which has already been made public, and includes 28 laws. The final provisions of these laws will show the extent of the commitments that they will be able to undertake in the future.

For these reasons the Argentine Delegation makes it very clear to this Conference that, with regard to the question of prices, which is the fundamental one of this Conference, it will abstain from accepting any of the price levels which have been proposed.

In our opinion the Article dealing with prices would have to be held over for consideration until such time as the present abnormal disparity between supply and demand has disappeared, or has diminished sufficiently to make it possible to see more clearly what the definite price level for wheat and industrial products is going to be.

In the Draft Agreement of 1942 it was stipulated that the prices to be fixed for wheat should be such as in the opinion of the Council would bear a reasonable relationship to the prices of other commodities. For Argentina, in whose economy wheat represents an item of great importance, it would be hazardous to fix its price independently of that of other commodities. Neither in the Draft Agreement of 1942 nor in any previous draft agreement was it considered wise for some reasons to include in the text the figures corresponding to the price which wheat should command in the international market during the life of the agreement. It was decided, on the contrary, to establish in the agreement the fundamental factors on the basis of which the prices should be determined from time to time, taking into account also the result which would be obtained from the application alone of the remaining articles of the agreement. The delegates here today who took part in the discussions of 1939 in London will recollect that it was considered that the regulation of production and exports and the maintenance of adequate stocks would automatically, through the interplay of these natural factors, lead to the achievement of a desirable price level in the international market.

The Argentine Delegation fully appreciates the desire of the other delegations to know whether the Argentine Government will finally participate in the agreement resulting from this Conference. For the reasons I have already pointed out, this Delegation can only state that the Argentine Government does not consider it prudent at this moment to undertake any obligations deriving from such an agreement. It attaches, however, great importance to this Conference and its interest is evidenced by the fact that, in spite of the situation already referred to, a Delegation has been sent over to attend it.

Experience in international meetings of this kind is that sometimes governments may not at the moment at which they take place be in a position to undertake the obligations which may arise as it may also happen that sometimes governments are prepared to undertake such obligations and subsequently there may be reasons to prevent them from putting them into practice. Our Delegation is inclined to think that the Argentine Government at present finds itself in the first of these cases and therefore considers that it should continue to collaborate in the Conference in order to keep that Government informed with regard to its work and the alterntives that the resulting agreement may present.[5]

Clauson, Broadley, McCarthy and Wheeler all expressed their understanding of the Argentine position and their profound regrets, but the question had now to be squarely faced whether an agreement could be reached in the absence of Argentine participation. Wheeler's statement appeared to be ominous, as the minutes showed:

. . . In its opening statement at the second plenary session of the Conference the United States Delegation voiced its hope that the Conference would achieve two broad objectives, namely to secure an international agreement which would make a contribution to a more stable world market price for wheat, and through that contribution to make a further one to a more stable world economic position as a whole. He felt that it was not possible to secure a more stable world price for wheat in an agreement in which only three of the four principal wheat exporting countries participated. Such an agreement would produce at least two world market prices for wheat. Thus instead of contributing stability to the world market such a partial agreement might well contribute instability. The second objective was now beyond their reach. He had understood Senor Viacava to state that the Argentine Government considered it inappropriate and undesirable to try to bring down and stabilise the price of wheat, because prices of manufactured foods were so high. Although the prices of such goods were higher than formerly, the prices of the world's major agricultural staples, including wheat, were relatively higher. In the light of this fact the United States Delegation felt that it was highly appropriate to start with the agricultural staples, and particularly with wheat, upon which commodity there had already been a good deal of preparatory work and at least some prospect of reaching an international agreement. He could not, therefore, accept the position that a start should not be made with wheat because the prices of other goods were high. If such a position were accepted the Conference would get nowhere at all and might as well discuss

[5] *Resumé of Proceedings of Third Meeting of Committee I,* Wednesday, March 26, 1947.

which came first, the hen or the egg. It would be clear to all from his remarks that the United States Delegation was extremely disappointed with the statement made by the Argentine Delegation on the position of its Government. The United States Delegation found it very difficult to foresee how the Conference could achieve the two principal objectives he had enunciated. Nevertheless, the Delegation of the United States was prepared to examine any proposals made at the Conference, particularly the proposals made by the representatives of the Governments of the importing countries, in the light of the situation which now confronted the Conference.[6]

Wheeler's query prompted the Netherlands and Italian delegates to declare that in view of the price concessions offered by the other three exporting countries within an agreement, their governments would have to divert their wheat purchases to them. Then Wilson stated the Canadian position in the following terms:

Mr. Wilson (Canada) concurred in the statements by other Delegations on the mutual disappointment felt as a result of the decision of the Argentine Government not to participate for the time being in the proposed international wheat agreement. He felt however that the Conference must face this decision as a fact. He concurred in all Mr. Wheeler's remarks, with one possible exception. Mr. Wheeler had stated that a partial agreement would contribute to the instability rather than the stability of prices. If, as he had every reason to hope, the quantities which signatory importing countries bound themselves to take during the life of the agreement from signatory exporting countries were substantial, he could not accept Mr. Wheeler's statement regarding the contribution of the agreement to price instability. In order to remove any possible doubt in the minds of the representatives of importing countries, he desired to state that for a long time there had been uncertainty with regard to the position of the Argentine. Although Canada had hoped until the last minute that Argentina would be an active participant in the Agreement, the Canadian Delegation had nevertheless come to the Conference prepared for the contingency which now faced it. He was fully satisfied that an Agreement could be reached between the importing countries and the three principal exporting countries other than Argentina, and such of the smaller exporting countries who desired to join the Agreement. He was convinced that such an Agreement could be framed in very precise terms and contain obligations which would embrace very clear-cut understandings. In view of the decision of the Argentine Government not to participate he felt it all the more desirable to provide for what the French representatives had referred to in the Working Party as a "parallel" market. There could be no illegality about such a market, as one market would be provided within the legal framework of the Agreement and one market would remain free outside the terms of that Agreement. The representatives of the exporting countries which would be signatory to the Agreement would now be even more interested in the size of the quantities which the importing countries would be prepared to undertake to obtain from the signatory exporting countries. This was particularly true with reference to the later years of the Agreement when there could be no doubt of the ability of Australia, Canada and the United States to meet in full all the requirements the importing countries were now prepared to undertake to buy. He was most gratified to hear the declarations of the representatives of the Netherlands and Italian Governments that if the Government of Argentina did not join the Agreement then the importers must turn to the other three exporting countries to obtain their imports.[7]

[6] *Ibid.*
[7] *Ibid.*

The indication that other countries were prepared to press ahead to conclude a "partial" agreement embracing the wheat trade of the residual "big three" exporters had a salutary effect upon the morale of the conference which had been depressed by the Argentine statement. The negotiations proceeded now in terms of participation of the other three exporting countries only. This was practicable on the basis of a collective contract, and it put an end to the support which had existed until then for a comprehensive form of agreement embracing export quotas, production controls, minimum and maximum reserve stocks and concessional sales which depended upon the participation of all the major wheat exporting countries.

The guaranteed quantities also presented a negotiating problem. Australia, Canada and the United States were prepared to put in guaranteed quantities based on their average export capabilities, and in constant quantities for each crop year of a four or five year agreement. The majority of the importing countries which were regular importers were also prepared to put in their average import requirements from the three exporting countries as constant quantities over the life of the agreement. Uniform quantities through the agreement presented no problems, because they assured that importers would buy as much wheat, if offered to them at the floor in the later years of the agreement, as they purchased at the ceiling when non-agreement prices were at much higher levels. But countries such as France, India and Uruguay had immediate import needs which were much higher than their anticipated requirements one or two years hence. The exporters, notably the Canadian delegation, took exception to their proposals for declining import quantities, on grounds of equity. The issue was debated for the remainder of the conference but, in the end, the draft agreement authorized the council to balance the totals of the guaranteed quantities of the importing countries with those of the exporting countries, which eliminated the possibility of securing importers' guaranteed quantities on a descending scale. During the conference, each country filed the figures it sought in each of the crop years. In total, the importers' figures exceeded the exporters' ability to supply, which underscored the world shortage of wheat at the time. Had the agreement come into operation, adjustments in the figures for each country would have had to be made in any event.

PRICE NEGOTIATIONS

The price negotiations were referred to a commission chaired by Sir Gerald Clauson. There it was recognized that the price issue was interrelated with that of the duration of the agreement. The Americans had advocated a five-year agreement, whereas the British were prepared to support only three years. Because of the difficulties of negotiating within the full commission, a small working party was appointed in turn, which included the delegates of Australia, Britain, Canada and the United States.

The first casualty in that small forum was the Canadian proposal for a $1.25 - 1.55 price range. Wheeler contended that the ceiling was not sufficiently high, and Broadley contended just as vigorously that the floor was not sufficiently low. As a compromise Wilson, for Canada, suggested that the prices specified in the Canada-United Kingdom contract be projected a year forward and adopted without further change in the international agreement. This alternative was equally unacceptable to Wheeler, who objected to the $1.55 fixed price.

In order to move away from his original negotiating position, Broadley proposed, in the absence of formal instructions, two further alternatives. The first included a fixed price of $1.60 in the first year, and a $1 - 1.50 range for the next three years. The second was a descending price range through the four years, $1.40 -1.70; $1.25 - 1.55; $1.10 - 1.40; and $1 - 1.40.

Wheeler, in turn, proposed a five-year agreement with an outside range of $1.05 - 1.75, including a formula designed to prevent major fluctuations within the extremes of the range. His formula proposed that the price range would commence with $1.35 - 1.75 in the first year, and vary by only 20 cents in either direction in subsequent years from the average prices actually paid in each previous crop year.

The essential difference between the British and American proposals was that the former sought to predetermine a downward trend in prices whereas the latter tried to effect some orderly transition from one year to the next depending upon the level at which wheat had been previously trading. This point in the discussions had been reached by March 25 when the delegates were requested to report back to governments for fresh instructions. So far as the Canadian delegation was concerned it mattered very little what instructions were given at the moment because the price issue depended now upon a reconciliation of views between the Americans and the British.

It had been everyone's intention to conclude the conference before Easter, but the price question remained unresolved by April 3 when the meetings were recessed until April 14, 1947. The prospects for an agreement still seemed bright, however, until serious reflection was triggered by the implications of the British preparedness to consider a fixed price, or a ceiling price, at American insistence, above the level of the prevailing bilateral contract price of $1.55. When the British first suggested a ceiling price of $1.70 for the 1947-48 crop year, it was assumed that it would replace the contract price under clause 7 of the contract which subordinated its terms to the extent necessary to comply with any subsequent international agreement. Norman Robertson had also looked upon the guaranteed quantities in the agreement as replacing Canada's quantity commitment of 160 million bushels under the contract. He had always been opposed, as had wheat board, to the high quantity commitment in the contract, and saw the international agreement as a release from that obligation in order to deal more equitably with our customers in Belgium, Netherlands and Norway. But it occurred to Robertson that a clear understanding should be established with the British delegation to the effect that the new agreement terms would abrogate those of the bilateral contract. On April 14, as the conference resumed Wilson raised the point with Broadley. It was discovered that each was interpreting clause 7 differently. Broadley's position was that so long as the contract terms did not conflict with those of the new agreement, the former should continue to be honored. On the following morning, April 15, Broadley handed Wilson a letter requesting Canadian concurrence in his understanding.

Wilson took the letter and the delegation to Canada House to confer with Robertson who, in the same urgency, sent the following telegram to Pearson, the undersecretary of state for external affairs:

1. The Chairman of the United Kingdom delegation has now raised in a letter to Wilson the relationship of the Canada-United Kingdom Wheat Agreement to the proposed International Agreement. He enquires whether Canadian Government share their views:

(1) That if the price range for the first year of the Agreement is such that the price of $1.55 per bushel specified in the contract is between the new minimum and maximum, the price provisions of the Agreement will not affect the $1.55 price;

(2) That the undertaking in respect to quantities to be delivered in 1947, 1948 and subsequent years from Canada to the United Kingdom will continue to be maintained within the framework of the International Agreement.

2. In asking for our confirmation of their understanding that these provisions of the Canada-United Kingdom Wheat Agreement will stand, the letter continues:

"You will of course appreciate that this is a matter of great importance to us, as we wish to continue importing from Canada on the scale described in the contract. On the basis of any other interpretation which might mean that you were not able to supply us with the quantities specified in the contract, we should not be able to proceed with the Agreement."[8]

During the morning the possibility of renegotiating the contract was considered. If, for example, the British would pay in 1947-48 the $1.70 they had proposed, or the American figure of $1.80, the producer representatives on the delegation were prepared to trade that against the obligation the British were incurring in 1946-47 under the "have regard to" clause. After the meeting Robertson addressed a long telegram to Pearson on the afternoon of April 15:

1. After reviewing position with our wheat delegation this morning, I am inclined to think that the elements of the solution of our present difficulty may lie in proposing to the United Kingdom certain substantial amendments to the Canada-United Kingdom wheat contract which would be directly related to the coming into force of the International Wheat Agreement, and could be justified by both Governments as the logical fulfilment in changed circumstances of the steps they took together last year.

2. The argument for this course rests on four assumptions:

(a) That the provisions of the wheat contract do not, in fact, conflict with the proposed International Wheat Agreement as presently drawn up;

(b) That it would be very difficult for the Government of Canada to become a party to a new International Wheat Agreement which fixed a ceiling of, say, $1.70 per bushel for the next crop year while we continued to be bound by our undertaking to provide the United Kingdom with 160,000,000 bushels during that period at a fixed price of $1.55, since, under this new arrangement, Canadian farmers would receive a lower average return for wheat sold abroad than they do at present;

(c) That it would not be right or feasible for our delegation to take the initiative in revising the terms of the International Wheat Agreement so that it would, in fact, compel the amendment of the bilateral Canada-United Kingdom contract.

[8] *Privy Council Office files.*

(d) That, in these circumstances, our best course would be to try to persuade the United Kingdom to agree to certain substantive changes in the wheat contract which would bring it more nearly into conformity with the general purposes and spirit of the new International Agreement.

3. On the assumption, which appears to be generally accepted, that the maximum price in the range set for the first wheat year under the new Agreement will, in fact, be the operative price at which all freely sold wheat will change hands, I would ask the United Kingdom to pay this price for the whole quantity promised by Canada. The Americans and Australians have been holding out, with our general support, for an initial maximum price of $1.80 per bushel. If we hope to persuade the United Kingdom to pay a single price for all their wheat imports under the Agreement, then I think we should support their effort to get the ceiling, lowered, say to $1.70. In consideration of the United Kingdom voluntarily agreeing to pay $1.70 instead of $1.55 per bushel from Canada next year, I think we should absolve them from their contingent obligation to "have regard to" the differential between contract and market prices in the first year of the Agreement in negotiating the prices to be agreed for the third and fourth years of the contract. The position then would be that in 1948-49 and 1949-50 the price range determined by the Wheat Agreement formula would set the limits within which Canadian-United Kingdom prices would be negotiated. I see no objection to continuing the $1.25 floor price for the third year of the contract and the second year of the Agreement as a special stop-loss provision linked with our continuing to furnish the quantities promised under the original contract.

4. The foregoing outlines a possible compromise solution, which I fear would have no chance of success unless the United States agreed to a somewhat lower price ceiling than the $1.80 they have been insisting on, and an Agreement with a formal duration of something less than five years. I do not think that the United Kingdom would agree to it unless it could be successfully put to them that some such deal was necessary in order to reinsure their effective receipt of the quantities promised them under the contract. From our point of view, it means giving up the hope of redistributing our exports, to which I had always attached some importance, in return for a price formula which would strike the Canadian farmer as fair and reasonable. I myself, would think it a great advantage to both Canada and the United Kingdom to liquidate as promptly as possible the open-ended undertaking in the present wheat contract which implies an obligation on the part of the United Kingdom to pay more than the world price of wheat at the time when its exchange position is likely to be even more straitened than it is now.

5. This general line of approach carries the judgment of all the members of our wheat delegation. If it is approved by the Government, then I think we should take immediate steps to sound out the other countries as to its acceptability.[9]

The proposal that the "have regard to" clause should be settled immediately in the terms Robertson suggested was unacceptable to Gardiner and MacKinnon. Meetings of the cabinet wheat committee were held on April 16 and 17. A draft reply was prepared and cleared with the secretary of state for external affairs, Mr. St. Laurent, before Pearson sent it to Robertson on April 19:

1. Cabinet Wheat Committee discussed this matter on April 16th and, provided that there is a prospect that an International Wheat Agreement will

[9]*Ibid.*

be adopted, wishes you to base your talks with the United Kingdom authorities on the following considerations.

2. Anxious as we are that an International Wheat Agreement be adopted, we could not become a signatory if it would in fact mean the establishment of a world price higher than one dollar and fifty five cents a bushel while Canada was expected to continue sales to the United Kingdom at the original contract prices. We can probably give assurance of continuing our programme of shipments to the United Kingdom in the quantities specified in the contract, but would expect the contract price to be brought in line with any maximum adopted by the International Wheat Agreement which was, in fact, the operative price on the effective date of the agreement.

3. In the interests of reaching agreement, we should therefore be prepared to give our support to a maximum international price of one dollar and seventy cents on the understanding outlined in Paragraph 2 above.

4. As regards the arrangements, contemplated in Article 2 (B) of the Wheat Contract, for the negotiation of prices on 1948-49 and 1949-50 shipments, the Cabinet Wheat Committee feel most strongly that we cannot agree to any modification of the United Kingdom Government's undertaking with respect to the contract prices to be established for the later years. Mr. Gardiner and Mr. MacKinnon who have represented us in all these discussions are very firm in their view that in establishing these later years prices due regard must be given to any differences between contract and world prices in the first two years of the contract. It is their view and ours, that if the International Agreement is successfully concluded the savings to the United Kingdom on immediate imports will counterbalance the adjustment required both now and for later years.

5. In the light of the present world food situation and of present prices on the free wheat markets, we consider our position as outlined above a reasonable one. If the United Kingdom Government does not find it acceptable, and for that reason feels it could not agree to the international arrangements proposed, we wish to make it clear that we would not consider Canada responsible for the resulting failure to conclude the International Wheat Agreement.[10]

Upon receipt of that telegram Robertson explained the Canadian government's reaction to Broadley. He acknowledged its reasonableness and undertook to report to his ministers who had mixed feelings over the merits of an international agreement. Thus it came as no surprise that the British government insisted upon the retention of the bilateral contract terms. Although both the British and Canadian delegations guarded the issue which had arisen between them with the utmost secrecy from the other delegations, the conference moved swiftly toward an unsuccessful conclusion. By April 22, 1947, the conference agreed to prepare a final document which remained unaccepted by governments, but which embodied the collective contract form of an agreement and the final American price proposals. Wilson telephoned MacKinnon to report the situation which had developed and confirmed the message by telegram:

1. Ten importing countries today supported American proposal as follows:

First year	$1.40 - $1.80;
Second year	$1.30 - $1.70;
Third year	$1.20 - $1.80;
Fourth year	$1.10 - $1.80;
Fifth year	$1.00 - $1.80.

[10]*Trade and Commerce File 26204:14.*

With provision to negotiate narrower ranges if agreement can be reached before commencement of third, fourth and fifth years.

2. Five importing countries, the United Kingdom, India, France, China and Norway, said that under present instructions they could not accept the American proposal for $1.20 and $1.10 floors in the third and fourth years, and they are asking $1.00 floors in those years.

3. Nevertheless, these five importing countries were prepared to release the final Conference document this Thursday which would disclose the price range proposed as above by the Americans.

4. Upon receipt of last week's Cabinet Wheat Committee instructions, we did our best to persuade the British separately to make contract conform to the proposed agreement price provisions but British delegates' consultation with British Cabinet revealed they are not immediately prepared to make any change. However, they did propose release of the Conference document unaccepted by the Governments concerned. Between now and June 1st, which is the final date for signature of the Agreement, they propose that these differences in views between British and ourselves be resolved if possible by direct negotiation. Otherwise they, like ourselves, are not prepared to sign the Agreement.[11]

Despite the disagreement between the British and Canadians, the British had not accepted the American price proposals either. In the last few days of the conference the British and Americans attempted to reconcile their price differences. The Americans had tried to compromise by offering a ceiling of $1.70 in the second year of the agreement, and the British then declared that the floors of $1.20 and $1.10 in the third and fourth years were unacceptable. They had secured the support of four other importing countries for their position. As the conference ended, Broadley stated that disagreement over the level of the floor prices had prevented his government from accepting the agreement.

In the final plenary session of the conference held on April 23, 1947, the Right Honourable John Strachey presided. Sir Gerard Clauson reported to him in the following terms:

Since that date very much has happened, and the Agreement which is presented to you now is a very different one from the draft agreement prepared by the International Wheat Council at its meeting last January which was the agenda of this Conference. The chief reason for the very great change in the document is the fact that at an early stage in our proceedings the Argentine Delegation stated that their Government were not at present in a position to bind themselves to adhere to an Agreement. From the moment that statement was made it was clear that the Agreement had to be drafted in a form which would work whether the Argentine were party to it or not. Instead of being an Agreement for regulating all the transactions in wheat between the parties it has become in effect a long-term contract for the purchase and sale of stated quantities of wheat. Countries will join either as importing or as exporting countries, stating when they sign whether they are joining it as importing countries or as exporting countries and what quantities of wheat they contract to buy or sell as the case may be over the period of the Agreement. . . .

The document as presented is substantially an agreed document. It contains 22 Articles, and all except one paragraph of one Article seems to be agreed. But it would not be frank of me to say that agreement had been reached on that particular paragraph, because it has not. Certain Delegations have

[11] *Privy Council Office files.*

expressed doubts on other points, but the major point of difference is paragraph 3 of Article VI, which provides minimum prices in the third, fourth and fifth years. That paragraph is agreeable in its present form to the exporting countries, and to certain importing countries. It is not agreeable to certain other importing countries. The position is the paradoxical one that more importing countries are prepared to agree to it than are not prepared to agree to it, but they represent a smaller tonnage of wheat than the importing countries that are not prepared, as at present advised, to agree.

Certain Delegations are anxious to sign the Agreement before they return to their countries, and the Conference will no doubt consider whether they wish to invite the United Kingdom Government, as the host Government, to instruct the Treaty Department of the Foreign Office to have the document made available for signature as soon as that can be done. . . .

I think, Mr. President, the first business is for you to put the draft Agreement . . . to the present meeting of the Conference, and ask them to declare whether, without prejudice to their Governments' positions, they are prepared to invite the United Kingdom Government to have the document prepared for signature . . . or whether they have any remarks to make.[12]

Mr. Wheeler followed by stating that his delegation was prepared to recommend signature of the draft agreement to the government of the United States, and he moved that the British government be invited by the Conference to open the agreement for signature. But there was no seconder. Sir Herbert Broadley presented the British position in the following terms:

Mr. President, I am sorry to have to announce that the United Kingdom Delegation is unable to associate itself with this Wheat Agreement. With its general plan we are in complete agreement, and the United Kingdom Delegation took a substantial part in shaping it. In fact in many ways we regard it as a model for future commodity arrangements. It preserves the opportunity for freedom of trade so that the price finds its own level, and at the same time it provides maximum and minimum wheat points, rather like gold points, so that the consumer is protected against too high prices, and the producer against too sudden and too deep a fall.

It is the prices themselves, Mr. President, with which the United Kingdom Delegation are unable to agree. We regard certain of these prices as excessive. We do not admit that the present and future wheat prices quoted on particular markets are any indication of what should be a reasonable price for wheat either now or in the coming years. At the same time we agree that some of the low prices that ruled before the war were equally unjustifiable. What the United Kingdom seeks is a price which is fair to the producer and the consumer alike. The world must face much lower prices for wheat than those which rule at present, and we want to see these lower prices achieved in a manner which protects the producer against hardship and enables such arrangements as are necessary for every form of agriculture to be made without serious dislocation and disaster.

But having said that, and being prepared to recognise the system which contains these safeguards, the United Kingdom Delegation must place on record its feeling that the price scheme proposed in the Agreement in article VI does not enable the price to come down to a reasonable figure sufficiently quickly. The United Kingdom cannot afford to pay excessive prices for its imports, and the reduction of the cost of our imports is a corollary to the expansion of the volume of our exports.

[12] *Verbatim Record of Open Plenary Session,* April 23, 1947.

In making this statement on behalf of the United Kingdom Delegation I do so without in any way opposing the particular resolution before the meeting. We should certainly have no objection to a final text being prepared on the lines proposed by the United States Delegation.[13]

Norman Robertson then recommended that the conference be adjourned until the British and American price differences could be resolved. He made no reference to those existing between Britain and Canada beyond a tacit suggestion to the British that the way out of the difficulties might be found in agreeing upon a fixed price for the first year of the agreement, as he said:

Mr. Chairman, the draft scheme for an International Wheat Agreement which is being released this morning will require very careful study and consideration by all Governments. In this they will wish to have the benefit of the advice and experience of their technical advisers who have taken part in these protracted discussions. In the meantime it would be wise for us all to remember that we have not quite reached an agreement in substance to the extent that the form of the draft might suggest. The fact that there has not yet been a meeting between the United Kingdom and the United States points of view about the price range in subsequent years may be of decisive importance, because it is not possible for us to think of an Agreement to which they are not both parties. in these circumstances while we must keep the target date of August 1st clearly in mind, I do not think that we should feel ourselves limited by the intermediate timetable suggested for signature and acceptance. Some of us feel that another effort might usefully be made to work out some kind of supplementary "second preference" scheme which would help meet the acute short-run supply position of a number of importing countries by bringing such surpluses as Providence and good weather may bring us, within the scope of the Agreement. Other countries may also think as we do that a fixed price for the first year of operation of the Agreement would be more realistic and appropriate than the suggested range.

This is a very big project to which our Governments have put their hands, and it is important, not only for the solution of the wheat problem, but for the furtherance of the great effort for the freeing and expansion of world trade, to which our Governments are committed, that we achieve an Agreement that has the best possible chance of continuing successful operation. We cannot let an understandable impatience and a real sense of urgency deter us from doing a really thorough job. For these reasons it may well be necessary for us to meet again — briefly, I hope — to attempt to reconcile the outstanding points of difference before an Agreement can be brought into operation.

In these circumstances I am inclined to think it would be unwise to proceed at once with the preparation of a formal text for signature.[14]

Despite the great care taken to prevent the British and Canadian disagreement from becoming known to the Americans, Wheeler inferred, at least, from Robertson's statement that the Canadian government had its own difficulties in accepting the agreement, as he observed:

I have been very much interested in the statements that have been made by the different Delegations. I have been particularly interested in the proposal made by the Canadian Delegation. I am not quite clear what the significance of that suggestion is, but it occurs to me that if the significance of it is that the Canadian Government is not prepared to sign this Agreement, and the United Kingdom Government is not prepared to sign this Agreement, I

[13]*Ibid.*
[14]*Ibid.*

suggest it would be rather futile for the Government of the United Kingdom to go forward with the formality of preparing a text for signature.

I agree with Sir Herbert Broadley that this Conference has made a great deal of progress. It happens that, like some of you, I have been attending Wheat Conferences personally since 1933 in London, and I can say without any reserve that this Conference has done more work and got nearer to agreement on the question of an International Wheat Agreement than any Conference that I have had the opportunity to attend. For that reason I think it would be very undesirable not to try and build on the gains we have made here. But I have to bring forward again, Mr. Chairman, as I have done in other meetings, the particular position of the United States.

The position of the United States is that the Congress of the United States will have to approve this Agreement before it comes into effect. I think that all Delegates are familiar with that fact. That being the case, due to the particular schedule of Congress, we could not be at all certain of getting such an Agreement before Congress and actually settled in any short period of time. I am very much afraid that if we take the procedure suggested by the Delegate of Canada there would not be time for the United States to accept this Agreement in time for it to come into effect on August 1st of this year.

I myself am inclined to make this suggestion as an alternative to the suggestion made by the Delegate of Canada. I think we have forgotten from time to time in our deliberations here that there already exists an International Wheat Council which has been formed for the purpose of exchanging views and ideas in regard to wheat. That Council was developed at a meeting in 1941, and has since that time expanded to include many other countries which are represented at this Conference. There would be nothing in the way of all countries joining that Council for the purpose of further consideration of this problem.[15]

As a result of Wheeler's suggestion, the draft agreement was referred to the international wheat council and the 1947 London wheat conference terminated in failure. All that had been achieved was an agreement upon the form of a multilateral contract which had been inspired by the bilateral contract, and which it was intended to replace.

[15]*Ibid.*

42

BILATERAL AND MULTILATERAL CONTRACT DEVELOPMENTS

There were a number of related matters in 1947 most of which can be covered under the fairly broad category of bilateral and multilateral contract developments. In the first place, the government responded to the representations from the Canadian federation of agriculture, with Gardiner's support, to raise the wheat board's price for domestic sales to $1.55. For a time, the government continued to subsidize wheat purchases for human consumption at the 1942 ceiling rate of 77⅜ cents, but it now transferred the whole of that subsidy to the treasury, rather than recovering it partially at the expense of the wheat growers who, until then, were paid only $1.25 on domestic sales. The subsidy on wheat sold for feed remained unchanged at 25 cents, however, and feed users now had to pay an additional 30 cents. As Mr. MacKinnon announced the new policy in the house on February 17, 1947, he explained that due to the world food shortage, the use of wheat for feed was being discouraged. His statement ran in part:

... The field of price control in Canada is being progressively narrowed and the government is of the opinion that the Canadian wheat board should no longer be required to sell wheat for domestic consumption at $1.25 per bushel. Accordingly the government has decided that wheat shall be sold for domestic consumption on the same basis as provided in the United Kingdom contract. The government has therefore directed the Canadian wheat board to advance the domestic price of wheat to $1.55 per bushel plus carrying charges. This direction is effective at once.

I wish to state explicitly that prevailing ceiling prices on flour, bread, mill feeds and other wheat products are not affected by this change in the board's selling price of wheat for domestic consumption. The government, through the treasury, will continue as in the past to make wheat available to millers and other processors at prices appropriate to these ceilings. The government regards this continuation of price ceilings on flour, bread and other wheat products as a necessary part of its programme of orderly decontrol.

The feed wheat subsidy of 25 cents per bushel is being continued, but the increase in price to $1.55 per bushel plus carrying charges will mean an increase of slightly over 30 cents per bushel in wheat used for feed in Canada. Because of the continuous demand for wheat for human food, the government feels that as far as possible grains other than wheat should be used for feed purposes in this country.[1]

[1]*House of Commons Debates,* February 17, 1947, p. 462.

STRACHEY'S VISIT TO CANADA

In late February, 1947, Strachey visited Canada and continued on to Washington in connection with food contracts. Strachey arrived in Ottawa on February 20 and, apart from his talks with Gardiner, he conferred with MacKinnon on February 21 about the rate of wheat shipments under the contract. Severe weather conditions had slowed down the grain movement in Canada, but Strachey was assured that shipments had a top priority and that the quantity commitment in the current crop year would be met.

Because of the controversy which had developed within Canada over the precise meaning of the "have regard to" clause Strachey accepted an invitation to address the Canadian club in Winnipeg on February 25 at which he said:

In London I often have to meet strong criticism of the Canadian wheat agreement. Our British Conservatives tell me that I have made a very poor bargain. They tell me that the result of the agreement will be that the British people will in the end have to pay millions of pounds more for their wheat than if no agreement had been made.

So that I rather wish that I could have had them with me in Ottawa last Friday to listen to the Canadian opposition speakers alleging that I had made far too good a bargain, that under the agreement the Canadian farmers would sell their wheat to us for much less than if there had been no agreement . . . It is monstrous to suggest that any British government would ever break the terms of a solemn agreement such as this. And in this I am quite sure that I speak for the Conservative opposition in the British House of Commons as well as for my own government. The British Conservatives might not have made the wheat agreement, but once made, they, and all other parties in Britain, are bound by it. In fact the Conservative critics of the agreement whom I face in the House of Commons have complained precisely that we of the labour government have irrevocably bound Britain to this agreement, which in their view will mean paying a far higher price to the Canadian farmers.

How then will the actual prices be fixed in the third and fourth years of the agreement? They will be determined by negotiations between two parties and the agreement laid it down in these precise words that I quote.

"In determining the prices for the two crop years 1948-49, 1949-50, the United Kingdom government will have regard to any difference between prices paid under this agreement in the 1946-47 and 1947-48 crop years, and the world prices for wheat in the 1946-47, 1947-48 crop years."

Now these words mean neither more nor less than they say. They mean that the fact that we have bought our wheat from you this year below world prices—and that we may do so again next year—will be one of the factors in negotiating the actual prices to be paid in the third and fourth years. I and my government, and I am quite sure that this applies also to the Canadian government, would resist any attempt to add to or subtract from this clear and definite statement as written into paragraph two subsection (b) of the wheat agreement . . . And, therefore, I personally hope that an international wheat agreement modelled on our Anglo-Canadian wheat agreement does come out of the forthcoming conference in London. But be that as it may, we in Britain and in Canada have already done our part to put our economic relations on a stable basis.[2]

[2]*Ibid.*, March 8, 1951, pp. 1062-1063.

Strachey's observations on the "have regard to" clause strengthened producers' expectations that the prices in the last two years of the contract would compensate in good measure for the concessions they were making at the current contract price. They also assured Gardiner that his gentlemen's agreement was intact.

CANADIAN FEDERATION OF AGRICULTURE RECOMMENDATIONS

The federation of agriculture made its annual presentation to the cabinet on February 28, 1947. Although the prime minister was ill, 12 members of the cabinet were present and the federation was represented by 30 of its directors. In respect of the marketing of wheat and other grains, the federation submitted:

> We commend the government for having made necessary adjustments to give wheat growers the benefit of the $1.55 price for domestically-consumed wheat, but we protest the action of the government in not retiring participation certificates on wheat delivered to the Canadian Wheat Board during the crop year 1945-46. We cannot but regard the withholding of these payments as contrary to the understanding which wheat growers had with the government during the whole of that crop year. We strongly urge that any surplus on hand resulting from the operations of the crop year 1945-46 be paid to producers now and not pooled with the operations of subsequent years. . . .
>
> We desire to express our confidence in the operations of the Canadian Wheat Board and the management under its present chairman. We commend the principle of the bill now before Parliament which ensures permanence of the Wheat Board and continuance of operations. We recommend (with one member body not concurring) that the board be made the sole marketing agency for all commercial grains grown in the provinces of Manitoba, Saskatchewan and Alberta.
>
> The Federation of Agriculture recommends that the Canadian Government should endeavor to:
>
> (a) Secure from wheat importing countries assurances against restraint in the future of international wheat trade.
>
> (b) Obtain assurance of practicable measures designed to maintain a reasonable minimum level of wheat prices in international trade in return for which our country reasonably might agree to measures designed to prevent prices becoming unduly high during periods of scarcity.
>
> We recommend the efforts of the government to bring about a satisfactory international wheat agreement to be signed by both importing and exporting countries.[3]

WHEAT BOARD LEGISLATION

The legislation referred to in the federation's brief had already been introduced in the house by resolution of February 10, 1947. The amending bill had been drafted to provide the Canadian wheat board with the monopoly powers required to administer the Canada-United Kingdom wheat contract. Until now, these powers had been provided by order in council under authority of the national emergency transitional powers act, but it was not expected that the latter act would remain in force much

[3]Canadian Federation of Agriculture, *Farmers Meet the Cabinet*, February, 1947, pp. 6-7.

longer. In the debate which commenced on February 18, Mr. MacKinnon explained the intention of the bill as follows:

> Mr. Speaker, the purposes and essential features of the bill to amend the Canadian Wheat Board Act may be briefly described as follows:
>
> It is the desire of the government to have certain powers of the Canadian wheat board which are at present authorized by order in council continued by parliament in the form of an amendment to the Canadian Wheat Board Act.
>
> During the war years and since, the Canadian wheat board has derived its powers and authority from the Canadian Wheat Board Act, 1935, as amended, and from orders in council passed under the War Measures Act and the National Emergency Transitional Powers Act. In this period the Canadian wheat board, at the request of the dominion government undertook a series of exceptional operations relating to wheat and other grains. It is not the intention of the government to extend the powers authorizing such operations in respect to grains other than wheat beyond July 31, 1947.
>
> The bill proposes to provide the government and the Canadian wheat board with more powers than are provided by the present act, but with less power than was provided by order in council.
>
> The general purposes of the proposed amendment to the Canadian Wheat Board Act, 1935, are as follows:
>
> 1. To authorize the regulation by the Canadian wheat board of the interprovincial and export trade in wheat for the purpose of meeting the requirements of the wheat contract with the United Kingdom;
> 2. To make a corresponding adjustment in the pool period in relation to the wheat contract with the United Kingdom;
> 3. To make necessary changes in the provisions fixing the price to be paid to producers of wheat by the Canadian wheat board;
> 4. To permit the board with the special approval of the governor in council to deal in grains other than wheat.
>
> With respect to wheat, the proposed amendments authorize the regulation of the interprovincial and export trade in wheat by the board and the conduct of all of such trading through the board until July 31, 1950. In regard to other grains, the amendment enables the board, with the approval of the governor in council, to buy, sell and deal in other grains.
>
> In addition to making provision for implementing the wheat contract with the United Kingdom, the proposed amendments provide for a five-year pool period from August 1, 1945, until July 31, 1950, during which time producers of wheat are guaranteed a fixed initial price of $1.35 a bushel.[4]

The drafting of the bill had been undertaken by Mr. Henry Monk, the Canadian wheat board's solicitor, who worked with the law officers in the department of justice. Monk's draft was considered, in turn, by a cabinet committee including Messrs. St. Laurent, Ilsley, Abbott, Gardiner and MacKinnon on February 11, 1947. The officials included McIvor, Monk, Sharp, David Mundell of justice department and Wilson. The key issue was the constitutionality of the monopoly powers being assigned to the board, and the lawyers relied upon the federal government's authority to regulate deliveries to elevators and to railways within the terms of the British North America act. A new part II of the act was inserted on the control of elevators and railways. The bill also confirmed the creation of the five-year pool and an initial payment of $1.35 throughout the five-year period. Because of the

[4]*House of Commons Debates,* February 18, 1947, p. 575.

increasing pressure from producer organizations to place grains other than wheat under the control of the board, authority was provided through the introduction of a permissive clause: "Except as directed by the Governor in Council, the Board shall not buy grain other than wheat". A year later, the act was amended to make more explicit provision for board handling of oats and barley. All of the monopoly powers assigned to the board, as well as the five-year pool were to terminate as of August 1, 1950.

The introduction of the bill provided opportunity for an extensive debate on the government's current grain policies. Third reading came on March 13, and royal assent to the bill was given on May 14, 1947.[5]

NEGOTIATION OF THE 1948-49 CONTRACT PRICE

According to the terms of the Canada-United Kingdom wheat contract, the price to be paid for 140 million bushels in the 1948-49 crop year, under any circumstances, not less than $1.25, was to be negotiated by December 31, 1947. Under the "have regard to" clause the British government had undertaken to "have regard to any difference between the prices paid under this agreement in the 1946-47 and 1947-48 crop years and the world prices for wheat in the 1946-47 and 1947-48 crop years."

Long before the time approached for the first price negotiation, the Canadian wheat board had been concerned over the dilemma in which the Canadian government would find itself in carrying out its intention to seek compensation in the last two years of the contract for any concessions below world levels which resulted from the price fixed for the first two years. As the board correctly pointed out, the December 31, 1947, deadline for the first negotiation fell seven months in advance of the start of the 1948-49 crop year and nineteen months in advance of its completion. It was impossible to predict that far ahead what the average level of world prices would be in 1948-49, so that there was no firm base to which the known concession in the first year of the contract could be added. In a letter of June 20, 1947, to MacKinnon, George McIvor estimated that the difference between the board's class 2 prices and the $1.55 fixed price on 160 million bushels of sales would amount to $140 million or nearly 90 cents per bushel. On the one hand, the world price in 1948-49 would have to fall to a very low level if full compensation were to be recovered; on the other hand, compensation added to the existing world level would put the price well beyond the scope of the proposed international wheat agreement. McIvor mentioned that the board had considered the advisability of extending the $1.55 price for the life of the contract, but believed that $1.80 in the last two years would come closer to adjusting prices on the basis of the intention of the "have regard to" clause, as he contended that a serious effort should be made immediately to reach agreement on prices for the last two years of the contract and to eliminate, thereby, the ambiguity of the "have regard to" clause in the interest of price stability.[6]

No reference was made to the desirability of settling the "have regard to" clause in order to expedite the signature of an international wheat agreement. The June 1 deadline had already passed, beyond which it would

[5]*Statutes of Canada,* 11 George VI, Chap. 15.
[6]*McIvor's letter of June 10, 1947,* Trade and Commerce file 20-141-U2.

have been impossible for the ratification procedures to be taken in time to permit an international agreement to operate as from August 1, 1947. However, McIvor's letter had some influence in advancing the date of the negotiations on the contract price for the 1948-1949 crop year. On August 20, 1947, Gardiner submitted a negotiating position to cabinet, and it was approved subject to referral to the interdepartmental committee on external trade policy which met later that afternoon and concurred in Gardiner's suggestions.

To assist him in the negotiations, Gardiner requested that Wilson accompany him. They visited Geneva briefly beforehand to attend an FAO meeting. Mr. Leslie Wheeler also attended, as did several leaders of the America farm organizations. Wheeler invited Gardiner and Wilson to meet his delegation and the invitation was accepted, only to find out that he wanted to discuss the international wheat agreement negotiations. Wheeler vigorously charged Canada with responsibility for the breakdown of the London negotiations. Specifically, he claimed that it was the discrepancy between the contract price and the proposed ceiling price which had caused the Canadian government to refuse to sign the agreement. Wilson contended just as vigorously that the Canadian delegation had gone to London with instructions to sign an agreement with a ceiling of $1.55 or on straight Canada-United Kingdom contract terms. The outright refusal of the American delegation to consider a ceiling at that level was more responsible for the breakdown of the negotiations than the Canadian position had been. But, quite apart from the attempts to pin responsibility on one country or another for the breakdown, Gardiner inferred from the confrontation that the American government, with producer support, was still very interested in the negotiation of a multilateral agreement. He carried that impression away with him as he proceeded to London for the contract negotiations with the British.

In London Gardiner and Wilson were joined by Biddulph and by Mr. J. G. Robertson, the agricultural commissioner at Canada House. They met with Strachey and his officials, Sir Percivale Liesching, permanent secretary of the ministry of food, and Harwood, during the first week of September, 1947. Harwood had taken part in the Ottawa negotiations in June 1946. Sir Herbert Broadley was ill at the time.

The London talks were opened between the two ministers and their attending officials. Although Wilson had taken along price statistics which demonstrated the discrepancy between the contract price and the board's class 2 price in 1946-47, Strachey contended that there could be no arithmetical settlement particularly because the world level of prices which might rule in 1948-49 could not yet be ascertained. Gardiner acknowledged this difficulty, and suggested that if the price now negotiated failed to compensate for the first year's losses in 1948-49, any remaining obligation should be carried forward to 1949-50. The final talks were conducted by Gardiner and Strachey alone, and Gardiner informed the others afterward that this had been their understanding. As Wilson reminded the Right Honourable C. D. Howe some two and a half years later:

The December 31 dates ... which were seven months in advance of the beginning of the crop years concerned, ruled out any practical possibility of foretelling that any price agreed upon would yield Canada compensation for the losses in the first two years, rather than incurring for us an additional deficit.

Mr. Gardiner was aware of the difficulty arising from this ... point when he met Mr. Strachey in London, in September, 1947, to negotiate the price for the 1948-49 crop year. The understanding he reported to his officials immediately after his final meeting with Mr. Strachey was that the tentative price of $2.10 (subsequently agreed by both governments at $2.00) did not settle the United Kingdom "have regard to" obligation for the 1946-47 crop year, but that the course of market prices during the 1948-49 crop year would be taken into account, and if the obligation arising from the 1946-47 crop year were not in fact discharged by the price for 1948-49, any remaining obligation would be taken into account in the negotiations a year later on the price for the fourth year, 1949-50.[7]

Wilson added that the understanding between Gardiner and Strachey had been verbal, and that the British were arguing away from it a year later.

After Gardiner's return to Ottawa the two governments settled by telegram the figure of $2 for 1948-49, and also the terms of an agreed press release. Gardiner had wanted the announcement to state more specifically that the British recognized their obligation to pay substantially more than the floor price of $1.25 named in the contract but that suggestion was dropped. When cabinet met on September 30, 1947, it formally approved the $2 price for 1948-49; a draft statement which, when cleared with the British, would be made by the prime minister rather than by Mr. Gardiner; and it also agreed that when the Canadian wheat board act came up for amendment in the spring again it would recommend to parliament that the initial payment be increased from $1.35 to $1.55 for the entire period of the five-year pool. The cabinet gave some thought to including in the announcement its intention to increase the initial payment, but decided that it would be premature. Accordingly, the prime minister issued a press release on October 1, 1947, in the following terms:

> The Prime Minister, Mr. Mackenzie King, made the following announcement: "A wheat price of $2.00 per bushel for the third year of the Canada-United Kingdom wheat contract has been agreed upon by the governments of Canada and the United Kingdom.
>
> The price, basis in store Fort William, Port Arthur, Vancouver or Churchill for number one Northern wheat, applies to 140 million bushels of wheat to be sold to the United Kingdom in the 1948-49 crop year under the terms of the contract which requires that the price for the third year be negotiated and settled not later than December 31, 1947.
>
> In the negotiations which took place during the past month both parties recognized the obligation contained in clause 2 (b) of the Agreement, which requires that in settling the price to be paid in the last two years of the Agreement period regard should be had to the difference in the first two years between the world prices and the agreement price. Having in mind the magnitude of the agreement and the long term security which it provides, a precise arithmetical calculation of the difference in price was not suggested. The government is satisfied that the considerations which have prompted the

---

[7]C. F. Wilson's memorandum of May 5, 1950, to the Right Honourable C. D. Howe re *Settlement of Obligations under the Canadian-United Kingdom Agreement.*

United Kingdom Government to offer and the Canadian Government to accept a price of $2.00 a bushel for 1948-49, will apply, fully and in the same spirit, in the negotiations for the settlement of the prices to be paid in 1949. The negotiations for this purpose are to take place before the end of 1948."[8]

DIFFICULTIES OVER THE OTHER FOOD CONTRACTS

In the midst of its balance of payments difficulties in the autumn of 1947, the British government made a strenuous effort to reduce the volume of its hard currency imports including foodstuffs. This entailed a further reduction in British meat rations and, in the process, the British government sought to cancel some of its existing food contracts in Canada. A mission headed by Sir Percivale Liesching arrived in November, 1947, to negotiate the cancellations. For specific commodities, such as bacon and eggs, which were now available from Denmark against payment in sterling, Liesching sought to cancel their dollar contract commitments. To protect the Canadian supply position which had been geared up to meet the British requirements, cabinet took the strong position that the British could not select among the food contracts for cancellation. If any were to be cancelled, all would be, including wheat which would be placed on the open market, and food supplies from Canada could all be negotiated afresh, with the bargaining based upon open market prices. As the talks proceeded, the cabinet rejected a British proposal to purchase only $65 million of foodstuffs other than wheat and cheese in Canada during 1948, for which the British asked to draw $229 million under the Canadian credit. As for use of the credit, the cabinet would approve only $10 million per month, for a period of three months, after which the position would be reviewed. The monthly drawing figure was later raised to $15 million. With both countries in balance of payments difficulties, neither government wanted to see the negotiations break down. In the end, an agreed announcement was made in the house on December 18, 1947. Tacit public acknowledgment that the cancellation of the bilateral wheat contract had figured in the negotiations came in King's declaration that the wheat agreement with the United Kingdom would be continued, as he said:

Mr. Speaker, I wish to give the house a statement on trade and financial arrangements between the governments of the United Kingdom and Canada, for which hon. members have been waiting.

As the house is aware, it was recently agreed with the United Kingdom government that a mission should come to Ottawa to discuss the trade and financial arrangements between the two countries, with special reference to the United Kingdom's purchasing program of Canadian supplies in 1948.

The mission headed by Sir Percivale Liesching, Permanent Secretary of the Ministry of Food, arrived in Ottawa on the 25th November. There has since been held with them a series of most valuable and comprehensive discussions covering the whole field of our trade with the United Kingdom, and I am happy to announce that as a result of the exchanges which have taken place agreement has now been reached with the United Kingdom government on all matters under review.

Both countries at the present time face a common difficulty, namely, a shortage of United States dollars. From the Canadian standpoint, this and

[8]*House of Commons Debates,* March 8, 1951, p. 1064.

other factors limit the extent to which the balance of the credit, provided for under the Financial Agreement Act of 1946, can be drawn on in order to make supplies available to the United Kingdom. . . .

The agreed arrangement provides for the continuance of the wheat agreement with the United Kingdom and for the continuance and renewal of the contracts for livestock products at prices adjusted accordingly. Thus the balance of Canadian agricultural production will be preserved, and there will be no interruption in these supplies to the British market.

The arrangement also provides for continued supplies to the United Kingdom of certain raw materials needed for reconstruction purposes, in particular timber and non-ferrous metals, though the quantities have been adjusted in relation both to United Kingdom needs and the demands for these products from other countries.

In estimating the probable trading deficit on this basis, account has been taken of the increased exports from the United Kingdom and the sterling area which, following these discussions, are expected to be made available for the Canadian market during the coming year. The arrangement provides that in the three months period up to the 31st March next, the expected deficit of 145 million dollars should be financed by drawings on the Canadian credit up to 45 million dollars and by the payment by the United Kingdom of 100 million dollars. Our government will review the position at the end of the three months period.

A statement substantially similar to this is being made today in London by the United Kingdom Prime Minister.[9]

MEETINGS OF THE INTERNATIONAL WHEAT COUNCIL

The London draft agreement had been referred back to the international wheat council which was requested to enlarge its membership again to include all the countries which had participated in the London negotiations. A first meeting of the enlarged council was convened in June, 1947, but the Canadians were forewarned that there were no prospects of reviving the negotiations then by the acting high commissioner in London who cabled on June 17:

Liesching now confirms what I conveyed to you in my earlier telegram — that the Minister is not sending any special delegation from London to the Wheat Council. By way of general comment he informs me that they have not been able to see much prospect at present of it being possible to overcome difficulties which prevented acceptance of the draft Agreement when the discussions in London ended.

Broadley has been ordered on three months leave on medical advice and will not now be back on duty until September.[10]

When the council met again on December 8, 1947, the 1948-49 price of $2 in the bilateral contract had been announced for some time, and class 2 prices prevailed at still higher levels. The bilateral contract price agreement at $2 contributed as much as anything to the renewed hopes for the negotiation of an international wheat agreement because it surmounted the issue which had risen between the British and Canadian governments at the end of the London wheat conference earlier that year. The conditions were now right for another attempt to reach agreement. The delegates of the importing countries and those of the exporting countries, except Argentina,

[9]*House of Commons Debates,* December 18, 1947, pp. 423-424.
[10]*Trade and Commerce File 26204:14.*

all favored a resumption of the negotiations. The December 8 council meeting agreed that the London draft agreement could serve as the basic framework of an agreement and that the council itself could convene a special session in Washington commencing January 28, 1948, to which all member governments of the United Nations or of FAO could be invited. A special committee of representatives of Australia, Brazil, Britain, Canada, France, India, the Netherlands and the United States was appointed to do any necessary preparatory work in anticipation of the January 28 meeting. The committee, under the chairmanship of the Indian delegate, Mr. J. Vesugar, held four meetings which pointed up the importers' preference for a four-year agreement and the exporters' preference for five-years' duration. The price range which had been set in the London draft agreement within outside limits of $1.00 - 1.80 was now set at $1.20 - 2.00, to which the American delegation added its proviso that the price range in any crop year be limited to a maximum variation of 40 cents. Stress was placed on the need to equate the guaranteed export and import quantities, and a price equivalents committee was proposed for the purpose of equating American and Australian qualities and locations of wheat with the basic miminum and maximum prices expressed in terms of No. 1 Northern wheat in store Fort William.

The changed attitude of the British government toward an agreement was summed up in Pearson's letter of January 15, 1948, to Mackenzie:

> I have had a letter from Norman Robertson in London in which he tells me that Sir Herbert Broadley, the Deputy Under-Secretary of the Ministry of Food and leader of the United Kingdom Delegation at last year's Wheat Conference, is planning to arrive in Washington three or four days before the official opening of the Wheat talks on January 28th. He hopes that Charlie Wilson might be able to come down, say by the 23rd or 24th, so that any question arising out of the relationship between Canada-United Kingdom Wheat Contract and a possible international agreement could be canvassed informally before the official talks begin. I believe that there is also a possibility that the Australian representative will be present for these preliminary talks.
>
> Following is account of talks which our High Commissioner had with Sir Herbert Broadley some weeks ago on the same subject. "When I was last talking to Broadley on wheat questions some weeks before Christmas, he said that the United Kingdom Treasury, which had never been very keen on the idea of a wheat agreement, now looked back with some regret at the possibility of an agreement with a $1.00 to $1.80 price range, which seemed near enough in April last year. I asked him today if the United Kingdom delegation to the forthcoming Wheat Conference would start with a more realistic set of price ranges in mind that in no circumstances would they sponsor or support any proposal for an international agreed price range which would appear to have the effect of chiselling at the $2.00 price negotiated for the next crop year deliveries under the Canada-United Kingdom contract. He has the point clearly in mind, and will not, I am sure, suggest a price range which would shade $2.00 a bushel for 1948-49. Once we are satisfied that the United Kingdom will not try to undercut the contract price, then I think both our Governments have an overwhelming interest, both political and economic, in trying to secure a new International Wheat Agreement."
>
> I should be glad to know whether it would be possible for Wilson to fall in

with this suggestion, as I think Norman Robertson would like to be informed.[11]

The stage was now set for a resumption of the international wheat agreement negotiations under the aegis of the international wheat council in Washington on January 28, 1948. These negotiations are described in the next chapter.

CHANGES IN PERSONNEL

It is difficult, while concentrating on an account of the policy developments, to keep abreast of all the changes in personnel at the time they occurred in the cabinet wheat committee, the wheat board, and the senior officials in Ottawa and abroad, all of whom made an input to policy decisions at one time or another. Hence the need for some sort of a chronological record of the changes.

Crerar's appointment to the senate on April 18, 1945, touched off the first of the postwar changes in the membership of the cabinet wheat committee. After a considerable hiatus, the Honourable J. A. Glen, who had been sworn in as minister of mines and resources after the 1945 election, took Crerar's place on the committee. Because the original order in council appointing the cabinet wheat committee in 1935 had referred to the members in their departmental capacities rather than by name, Glen qualified for membership as minister of mines and resources. He was also the Manitoba representative in the cabinet as Crerar had been.

The next change in the cabinet wheat committee took place when King transferred Ilsley, who had become physically exhausted from his wartime finance responsibilities, to the justice portfolio on December 19, 1946, and the Honourable D. C. Abbott was sworn in as minister of finance. This automatically qualified Abbott for membership on the cabinet wheat committee.

By the autumn of 1947, the Right Honourable C. D. Howe, formerly minister of munitions and supply and now minister of reconstruction and supply, had been dismantling the large wartime staff he had borrowed from industry and he was minister of a shadow department when the United States government introduced the Marshall aid plan. The aid to war-torn countries including Britain was so massive that the recipient countries were allowed to make offshore purchases with American funds, and the expectation was that extensive purchases would be made in Canada. King wanted Howe to oversee this trade opportunity, but Howe needed a department for the purpose. Accordingly, on January 18, 1948, Howe was sworn in as minister of trade and commerce and, in doing so became chairman of the cabinet wheat committee. McKinnon served briefly as minister of fisheries until, upon Glen's resignation, he was sworn in as minister of mines and resources on June 11, 1948, and was reinstated as a member of the cabinet wheat committee.

After he had taken appropriate soundings among the British authorities, Mackenzie King had five of his ministers sworn in as members of the imperial privy council. Ilsley and St. Laurent were the first; their appointments were announced on January 1, 1946. Howe followed with an appointment on June 13, 1946, and Ian Mackenzie and Gardiner on

[11]*Ibid.*

January 1, 1947. With their appointments they assumed the imperial privy council designation of "Right Honourable".

Because of frequent and sometimes long absences from Ottawa, C. F. Wilson could no longer serve regularly as secretary of the cabinet wheat committee. After the war he was the only cabinet committee secretary who was unattached to the privy council office; this was a matter of concern to Mr. Arnold Heeney, secretary of the cabinet. Heeney had brought order out of chaos by recording and distributing all cabinet decisions. Wilson regularly forwarded copies of the cabinet wheat committee minutes to him but, during one of his absences, Heeney asked MacKinnon to appoint, as assistant secretary to the committee, one of his privy council staff. This served to fill the void until Wilson went to Washington for the January - March, 1948, special session of the council. During his absence, Heeney arranged with the newly-appointed minister of trade and commerce, Mr. Howe, to appoint Mr. J. R. Baldwin as secretary, and to designate Wilson as an adviser to the committee. The change was effected by an exchange of letters on February 20, 1948. Later that year, Heeney also arranged a merger of the wheat committee with two other cabinet economic committees and, for a time, the wheat committee lost its identity. At that point the cabinet wheat committee included Howe, Gardiner, Abbott and MacKinnon. Of the four, only Gardiner had been an original member.

Just as Gardiner had provided continuity in the wheat committee, so had Mr. George McIvor in the wheat board. He had been a member of the board since December, 1935, and his service with Canadian Co-operative Wheat Producers, Limited had extended back beyond that. On Mr. J. R. Murray's resignation in 1937, McIvor became chief commissioner of the board. During the war years, Mr. C. Gordon Smith served as assistant chief commissioner and Mr. W. C. Folliott as commissioner, until the latter's death on March 13, 1943. Mr. D. A. Kane filled the vacancy on June 1, 1943. When Mr. C. Gordon Smith resigned in December, 1944, Mr. Kane became assistant chief commissioner, and Mr. C. E. Huntting was appointed commissioner. In September, 1945, Mr. Kane's health prompted a transfer and Mr. Huntting became assistant chief commissioner as Mr. W. C. McNamara was appointed commissioner. In February, 1947, when Mr. C. E. Huntting resigned, Mr. McNamara replaced him as assistant chief commissioner and Mr. F. L. M. Arnold was appointed commissioner. When Mr. Arnold resigned in May, 1948, Dr. T. W. Grindley replaced him as commissioner. In July, 1950, Dr. Grindley resigned and Mr. W. Riddell was appointed commissioner. Until Mr. McIvor's resignation on April 30, 1958, the McIvor, McNamara, Riddell board remained intact, with the appointment of a fourth commissioner to the board, Mr. W. E. Robertson, in November, 1953.

Meanwhile, Wilson's wheat and grain division in the department of trade and commerce, which had been a one-man operation until the end of the war, secured excellent recruits from the armed forces as Messrs. J. B. Lawrie and R. M. Esdale joined him. The division, without premeditation, provided a training school for Canadian wheat board commissioners. Mr. Lawrie left the division in November, 1948, to join the board staff, and subsequently become a commissioner. To replace Mr. Lawrie, Mr. G. N.

Vogel was recruited; he succeeded Mr. McNamara as chief commissioner of the board in 1971, and Mr. R. M. Esdale was appointed a commissioner. On his retirement from the board, Mr. McNamara was appointed to the senate.

As already noted, Mr. M. W. Mackenzie was appointed deputy minister of trade and commerce in 1945. In 1950, Mackenzie recruited Mitchell W. Sharp, who had served until then as a special assistant in the department of finance, as assistant deputy minister of trade and commerce, while Wilson headed a Canadian grain mission to Britain and Europe, accompanied by Mr. Roy W. Milner, chief commissioner of the board of grain commissioners, and Mr. J. B. Lawrie, who was then an executive assistant of the Canadian wheat board.

In the department of external affairs, Messrs. Norman Robertson and Lester B. Pearson shared the longest continuity in respect of wheat policy matters. Robertson became undersecretary of state for external affairs following the death of Dr. O. D. Skelton in 1941 when (as Pearson has described in his Memoirs) he was brought back from London as Robertson's second in command. Then Pearson was posted to Washington in 1942 where he served under Mr. Leighton McCarthy, and succeeded him in January 1945 as Canadian ambassador to the United States. In the autumn of 1946, Norman Robertson succeeded Vincent Massey as Canadian high commissioner in London, and Pearson returned to Ottawa as undersecretary of state for external affairs. Hume Wrong, in turn, was appointed Canadian ambassador to the United States. As these transfers took place, Prime Minister Mackenzie King transferred his external affairs portfolio to Mr. St. Laurent, who had been minister of justice until then. Some two years later, on November 15, 1948, Mackenzie King resigned from office, and Mr. St. Laurent was sworn in as prime minister. Just prior to that event, Mr. Lester B. Pearson was sworn in as secretary of state for external affairs. Upon Pearson's appointment to the cabinet, Norman Robertson returned to Ottawa to resume his former post as undersecretary and Mr. L. D. Wilgress succeeded him in London as Canadian high commissioner.

1949 ELECTION

After he became prime minister, the Right Honourable Louis St. Laurent toured western Canada in the spring of 1949, dissolved parliament and called a federal election for June 27, 1949. In the election, he won a resounding victory; of interest here was the western vote. The new prime minister's popularity was a primary factor in the result but, in the prairie provinces, there was also general satisfaction with the government's grain policies as the results showed:

	Manitoba	Saskatchewan	Alberta	Canada
Liberal	12	14	5	190
Independent Liberal	—	—	—	3
Independent	—	—	—	5
Progressive Conservative	1	1	2	41
CCF	3	5	—	13
Social Credit	—	—	10	10
	16	20	17	262

Thus, the Liberal party regained seats lost in the 1945 election in all three provinces, with a major swing back from the CCF party in Saskatchewan. The 1945 election in that province had returned two Liberals, one Progressive Conservative and 18 members of the CCF party. In the 1949 election in Alberta, the Liberals gained three seats from the Social Credit party.

43

SPECIAL SESSION OF THE WHEAT COUNCIL, WASHINGTON, 1948

Upon receipt of Leslie Wheeler's invitation to send a delegation to the special session of the international wheat council commencing on January 28, the Canadian government named Wilson as chief delegate. W. C. McNamara, assistant chief commissioner of the Canadian wheat board, was named as alternate delegate. C. C. Boxer, Washington representative of the wheat board, G. R. Paterson, commercial counsellor Canadian embassy, and A. M. Shaw, chairman of the agricultural supplies board, were named as advisers and R. C. Brown, United grain growers, Paul Farnalls, farmer, B. S. Plumer, Alberta wheat pool and J. H. Wesson, Saskatchewan wheat pool, as technical advisers. George W. Robertson, secretary of the Saskatchewan wheat pool accompanied Wesson as an observer. W. C. McNamara was a fortunate choice as alternate. Having served for years in the Saskatchewan wheat pool, he was an advocate of orderly marketing and of the price stability the pools sought in an international wheat agreement. His infectious enthusiasm and sense of humor appealed to the other delegations and made many friends for Canada and the board. With Brown, Farnalls, Plumer and Wesson on hand for daily conferences, one could be confident that what they agreed to would have their subsequent support when it became a government commitment. Although the meeting was convened as a special session of the council, it was a negotiating conference, in every respect, just as the London wheat conference had been a year earlier.

BILATERAL CONTRACT ISSUE AND THE CONFERENCE

As Broadley had requested, Wilson went to Washington early to discuss the implications of the terms of the agreement for the Canada-United Kingdom contract. Broadley's concern over this issue, which had caused a breakdown in the London negotiations in 1947, was shared by members of the cabinet wheat committee who felt strongly that the terms agreed upon in a multilateral contract should in no way abrogate Canadian rights under the provisions of the bilateral contract. The meeting confirmed the continuing difference of views. After arrival of the rest of the delegation and consultation with them, Wilson wired on January 28 to Mr. Howe and the other members of the cabinet wheat committee as follows:

> Broadley, Head of British delegation, has disclosed that he will make an opening statement to the Conference beginning today that the United Kingdom will accept (1) a four-year agreement based on a price range of $1.20 to $2.00, or alternatively (2) a five-year agreement based on the same range, except that in the fifth year the floor would be set at $1.00.
>
> No doubt other countries will interpret such a statement as greatly enhancing the prospects of reaching agreement, as both the United States and Australian representatives have said earlier they would support a $1.20 to $2.00 price range for five years. The Conference will be expecting the Canadian delegation to support this price range, but at the moment we see in it the danger of another misunderstanding between the British and ourselves on the status of the Canada-United Kingdom contract under an international agreement.
>
> Broadley has asked privately if Canada would continue to carry out such terms of the contract as would not be inconsistent with the terms of an international agreement, but specifically he is interested in our quantity to the United Kingdom remaining at 140 million bushels in each of the next two years. My tentative reply was that we would be more concerned over retaining other provisions of the contract under an international agreement, including carrying charges in addition to the price, Vancouver at price parity with Fort William/Port Arthur, the flour commitments, and most importantly Clause 2 (b) known as the "have regard" clause.
>
> Broadley's view is that the international agreement would place a ceiling of $2.00 on the price in the fourth year of the contract and would free the United Kingdom from paying carrying charges in addition to the $2.00 price. The latter is undoubtedly a material consideration in the United Kingdom Government's support of the proposed price range.
>
> These issues were discussed at length in our own delegation who hold the view that all the contract provisions should stand, including the "have regard" clause. The delegation mostly favours a five-year agreement with the $1.20 to $2.00 price range throughout. Specifically this means that in negotiations which are scheduled to take place next autumn between Canada and the United Kingdom, Canada would have to accept a maximum of $2.00 for the wheat price in the fourth year of the contract but should be free to negotiate a financial or other settlement in discharge of the United Kingdom's obligations under that clause.
>
> In order to avoid having the international negotiations here proceed on the basis of any misunderstanding between the British and ourselves, or delaying the negotiations until these matters are settled, we would appreciate being advised if it is your desire that the British should be told now that their obligations under the contract will not be reduced by the proposed terms of an international agreement. If the Wheat Committee desires a fuller discussion of these matters I could arrange to be in Ottawa Saturday morning.[1]

As anticipated, when the conference opened, Broadley made his opening statement and set the conference tone in an air of expectancy, while maintaining the British position on a declining range of prices over the period of the agreement. Excerpts from his speech are as follows:

> ... I would like to say personally how sorry I was we did not succeed in reaching full agreement in London last spring. Nevertheless, we did come

[1] *Trade and Commerce File 26204:14.*

very near to it and, as a result of the efforts made by all the delegations attending the London Conference, reduced our points of difference to a very limited range.

If the other delegations are generally agreed that the London draft provides the basis of a satisfactory agreement then the main issues which we shall have to debate will be:

1) Prices

2) Duration

3) The adjustment of the total guaranteed export quantities and the total guaranteed import requirements.

4) Special emergency measures in periods of short supply.

Price and duration are related. I may say at once that the United Kingdom delegation is prepared to accept an initial maximum price of $2.00. Last spring we considered $1.80 a reasonable initial maximum. Market changes and current conditions probably make some increase justifiable in the first year of an agreement. But it cannot be argued that these circumstances can affect our estimates of a fair price for three, four, five years ahead. What we considered last spring a fair price for 1950-51 or 1951-52 must surely still be a fair price for those years. We have no new information as to the supply/demand position so far ahead that would justify any increase or decrease of those prices. Nevertheless, we generally accept in principle a minimum price of $1.20 for a four year agreement. Last spring we were all satisfied with a minimum price of $1.10 for 1950-51 and $1.00 for 1951-52. Under a four year agreement starting on 1st August, 1948 we are prepared to concede a minimum of $1.20 for both these years. I hope this will be taken as proof of the willingness of the United Kingdom to help to the best of their ability to frame an agreement satisfactory to all interests. But if the Council desires a five year agreement, the United Kingdom would be prepared to accept an agreement for that period only on the condition that the minimum price in the fifth year (that is for 1952-53) was $1.00.

In other words, we will accept a *four* year agreement with a range of $2.00 maximum and a $1.20 minimum. or a *five* year agreement with a range of $2.00 maximum and a $1.00 minimum, the latter figure to operate for the fifth year.

For the intervening years we would like to see an arrangement on the lines discussed in London whereby the price range descends by regular steps over the four or five years over which the agreement operates. At that time we all agreed to $1.80 to $1.40 for the first year, and $1.70 to $1.30 for the second year. We wish the same principle adopted for the new agreement in relation to our revision of the overall price range. Such an agreement would, we feel, fulfill the obligation which the original Wheat Agreement expressed of determining a price fair to importers and exporters alike. I think it will be generally agreed that over the next four years, as the world recovers from its wartime devastation, wheat supplies throughout the world will increase and if there was no Wheat Agreement in operation the price would fall. Indeed, it might slump disastrously as only a small marginal quantity over and above world requirements could lead to a very substantial fall in prices. We therefore support the idea of graduating the price range downwards over the next four years so as to ensure that the probable fall in prices will operate gradually and without due hardship to producers and will be on a predetermined basis so that producers can adjust their production programme well in advance.

We have studied the pros and cons advanced in the report of the Special Committee for a method of determining the price range for succeeding years of the agreement on the basis of the average realized price of the previous year. This method was discussed at considerable length in London and in the end it was not incorporated in the draft agreement. So far as the United Kingdom is concerned we stand by the line we adopted at the London Conference that we cannot accept such an arrangement. It would have the effect of artificially maintaining high prices when the supply/demand position justified a reduction and would put a strain on the maintenance of the Wheat Agreement which it might not be able to bear . . .

Although we reject the proposal to relate the price range to the average price of the previous year we should be prepared to examine any alternative proposals for determining in advance a series of annual price ranges which will ensure that both producers and consumers know in advance the limits of return they can count on and the extent of their commitments respectively. If no plan finds general acceptance, then it may be necessary for us to adopt the expedient we devised in London of maintaining the maximum and minimum price over the whole period; but that in that case we would press, as the London draft provides, for the minimum prices to be fixed over the period of agreement at figures descending by regular steps from $1.50 to $1.60 in the first year to $1.20 in the fourth year or $1.00 in the fifth year . . .[2]

As Broadley continued his statement, he endorsed equal guaranteed quantities for each country throughout the life of the agreement and several emergency provisions which had been proposed in the report of the special committee, but he made no reference to the Canada-United Kingdom wheat contract as he concluded with an eloquent expression of hope that governments would avail themselves of this second chance to conclude an agreement, and that all exporting and importing countries would participate.

In Wilson's opening remarks, he said:

Mr. Chairman — In response to your invitation the Canadian Government has once again appointed a representative delegation to participate in the negotiation of an International Wheat Agreement. We are here to assist in the reaching of an agreement. As the negotiations develop we will indicate our views in detail on the terms which may be suggested, subject of course to their final acceptance by the Government we represent.

At this stage I should like to refer very briefly to the points arising from the report of the Special Committee. We appreciate the fact that the representatives of Australia and the United States have already insisted on a five-year agreement. Although a majority of representatives of importing countries have indicated their preference for a four-year agreement, they have also indicated certain conditions under which they would accept a five-year agreement. One of these conditions has been a reduction in the floor price for the fifth year. In the view of our delegation the basic minimum and maximum prices should remain constant throughout the five-year period. We favour, in principle, the proposed $1.20 to $2.00 price range. This is without prejudice to compensation for carrying costs which we shall discuss in the price Equivalents Committee. With reference to the price range, however, I feel bound to point out that it had implications regarding the final settlement of the Canadian wheat contract with the United Kingdom which are only of indirect concern to the conference, but on which a separate understanding must be reached between the Governments of Canada and the United Kingdom. We are taking steps to have these matters clarified before the conclusion of the Conference.

[2]*Ibid.*

We are concerned about the width of the proposed price range. We find no equity in the suggestion that the exporting countries, after accepting less than the market price by means of a ceiling should expect to get little if anything more than the market at the floor. We favour the United States proposal for a formula determination annually within a 40¢ range. We are definitely opposed to the predetermined scaling down of both the ceiling and the floor.

We are in sympathy, however, with the British proposals regarding the equation of guaranteed export and import quantities. This Conference is faced with the reality that the agreement will not embrace all the wheat entering into international trade. The only feasible solution to this situation which has been suggested so far is the London draft agreement involving the principle of a multilateral bulk contract. This implies equality of commitment in both the earlier and later stages of the contract.

In conclusion, this contract will only succeed if it is entered into in the spirit that it be kept, not broken. This concerns the issue over emergency provisions on which I have stated my views in the report of the Special Committee. It also concerns the escape clause presently provided on the balance of payments grounds. The Agreement will accomplish its purpose only if its primary obligations on both sides are carried out. If it fails in operation it can hardly expect a second chance.[3]

It will be noted that Wilson referred openly to the need for an understanding between Britain and Canada on the bilateral contract implications, about which he had just wired to Howe. The immediate reaction to his telegram of January 28 was to call Wilson to Ottawa for a meeting of the cabinet wheat committee to be held on Tuesday, February 2. However, in the end, Mr. M. W. Mackenzie, the deputy minister, attended the meeting at which the ministers decided that Howe should communicate directly to Strachey. Mr. L. B. Pearson sent Howe's message through Norman Robertson to Strachey on February 2:

From the negotiations for an international wheat agreement now in progress in Washington it has become apparent that some questions will arise between our two governments on the status of the terms of the Canada-United Kingdom wheat contract in the event that we become parties to an international agreement. It would appear to us to be very important that these questions be dealt with by our two governments at the present time, rather than have the negotiations proceed to a point where non-settlement of these questions would be embarrassing to both governments.

Your delegate has already asked our delegate if we would agree to the continuation of such terms of our contract as are not excluded by the terms of an international agreement, and in particular whether we would supply the United Kingdom with 140 million bushels of wheat in each of the next two years.

In reply, we feel that all the contract terms should be carried out between us under an international agreement. This includes settlement of the 1949-50 price prior to the 31st December, 1948, in which regard will be had for any difference between the $1.55 price and world prices in the 1947-48 crop year. With only half of the 1947-48 crop year elapsed we consider it premature to discuss at this stage what the actual settlement for 1949-50 might be, but we do not feel that the negotiations to take place next autumn should in any way be restricted by the terms of proposed International Wheat Agreement, which

[3] *Ibid.*

might otherwise imply that not more than $2.00 could be paid in the fourth year of the contract.

If such an understanding is satisfactory to you, our respective delegations could be instructed to proceed with the Washington negotiations accordingly.[4]

This message was repeated to Wilson in Washington, and Mackenzie sent a further wire:

At evening continuation of (cabinet wheat committee) meeting further suggestion was made and agreed that as an addendum Broadley should be told that any complications that might arise from an International Agreement need not interfere with completion of such an Agreement since we would be prepared to discuss now with the British a settlement of the "have regard to" clause.[5]

Accordingly, Wilson met with Broadley again on February 4. Because the issue was of such consequence to the two governments, both were particularly careful that no misunderstanding of interpretation should arise in verbal discussions. Therefore, the practice was adopted of exchanging written memoranda on the points being made (in diplomatic usage called aide-memoires). Henceforth, for the next month, as Broadley and Wilson pursued the issue of the status of the bilateral contract in relation to the multilateral agreement, they engaged in a conflict armed with aide-memoires. These memoranda, however, form an integral part of the record of the negotiations which took place over the reconciliation of the terms of the multilateral and bilateral contracts which had to be made before either the British or Canadian governments were prepared to sign the international agreement. They are quoted at length, for that reason. Thus, at the meeting on February 4, Wilson left with Broadley the following aide-memoire:

In our discussions on the 26th of January you asked if we would agree to the continuation of such terms of the Canada-United Kingdom wheat contract as would conform with the terms of an international wheat agreement, and in particular whether Canada would supply the United Kingdom with 140 million bushels of wheat in each of the next two crop years.

I have since had the opportunity of consulting my Government, and I am authorized to convey to you their view that all the terms of the contract should be carried out between us under an international agreement.

In addition to the quantity and other terms, this includes settlement under the terms of Clause 2 (b) of the contract, commonly known as the "have regard to" clause. In our view, such settlement should not be reduced in substance by the terms of the proposed international agreement, since it relates to the first two years of the contract which will have elapsed before the international agreement comes into operation.

If there is any question in the minds of the United Kingdom authorities with regard to the continuance of the terms of the contract, then it is suggested by my Government that these complications need not interfere with the reaching of an international agreement. Accordingly, they would be prepared to discuss now a settlement of the "have regard" clause in the contract.[6]

Broadley after a meeting on February 7 left his aide-memoire in reply:

I have consulted my Government on the points raised in your Aide Memoire

[4]*Ibid.*
[5]*Ibid.*
[6]*Ibid.*

of 4th February regarding the effect on the terms of the Canada-United Kingdom wheat contract of any International Wheat Agreement which may be concluded.

My government authorise me to state that they have noted the contents of your Aide Memoire and desire me to state in reply that for their part:

(a) They would not be prepared to be committed to a price for Canadian supplies of wheat for 1949-50 under the Canadian contract which would be in excess of the maximum price for that year under an International Wheat Agreement.

(b) They would prefer that negotiations for the 1949-50 price should take place towards the end of 1948 as provided in the Wheat contract itself.

(c) If prices and other conditions which the U. K. Government are able to accept are put forward in the International Wheat Agreement discussions they would subscribe to such an Agreement and that this would involve bringing the U. K.'s obligations under the Wheat contract within the overall obligations of the International Wheat Agreement as required by Article 7 of the contract and Article 19 of the Draft Agreement of April 1947.[7]

Wilson then left the conference for Ottawa to confer with Howe. For Howe's consideration, he prepared a memorandum setting out his views on how a reconciliation of the British and Canadian positions might be effected. This involved an extension of the contract until eventually some compensation would be received for price concessions we had made in its first two years. The memorandum read:

From Broadley's aide-memoire attached, it is clear that the United Kingdom government are not prepared to pay more than $2.00 for Canadian wheat in 1949/50. They would prefer to negotiate the actual price for 1949/50 late in 1948.

Broadley personally admits that the United Kingdom has much to gain if they are able to modify the terms of both their Canadian and Australian wheat contracts through an international agreement.

Since the floor price under the international agreement may be fixed as high as $1.60 in 1949/50, very little scope would be left for compensation under the "have regard" clause of the contract.

This raises the question of whether we should stand on allowing room for compensation above $2.00 in 1949/50, at the risk of letting the international agreement go, or whether we should further seek an understanding on the "have regard" clause.

A possible compromise would be to extend the contract terms for the life of the international agreement. Although we could not go above $2.00, we could negotiate annually for a fixed price of $2.00 until sooner or later we would be receiving more than the market price from the United Kingdom in compensation towards our price sacrifice in the 1946/47 and 1947/48 crop years.

Had the United Kingdom agreed with us on settling the 1949/50 price now, it could develop through such pre-fixation of the prices that we had accepted prices below the market in three, and possibly all four years of the contract.

By extending the contract period for three more years to cover the five years of an international agreement, we could protect our right to compensation for our price sacrifice in the first two years of the contract, and at the same time assist in reaching an international agreement.[8]

[7]*Ibid.*
[8]*Ibid.*

Howe called the cabinet wheat committee together on February 11, 1948. Because of the issue before the committee, he invited the recently retired chairman, James A. MacKinnon, and the minister of external affairs, the Honourable Louis St. Laurent, to attend as well as the other members of the committee, Messrs. Gardiner, Abbott and Glen. George McIvor had come down on other business from Winnipeg and he prepared a note on the meeting for the benefit of the other members of his board:

> This meeting was called at 4:30 Wednesday afternoon for the main purpose of discussing the difficulties which had arisen in respect to the "have regard" clause in the Canada-United Kingdom Wheat Agreement and its effect on the proposed signing of an International Wheat Agreement. Dr. Wilson was on hand from Washington and he read to the Wheat Committee of the Cabinet a short memo which contained the reply of the United Kingdom Government to the Canadian request that discussions should be opened up with a view to settlement of the "have regard" clause in relation to the Canada-United Kingdom Agreement. The British Government *seemed* to take the view that once the International Wheat Agreement was signed the terms of this Agreement would apply to the Canada-United Kingdom Agreement. It was not entirely clear in the minds of at least some of the Ministers that this meant a sign-off insofar as the cumulative concessions which had been made by Canada were concerned. For that reason, Dr. Wilson was asked to return to Washington, and a prepared brief memorandum given to him in the form of an aide memoire, which he was to hand to Sir Herbert Broadley, asking the United Kingdom Government to authorise Sir Herbert or some other party to come to Ottawa with the view of undertaking discussions on this important question in order that a settlement should be arrived at before the Agreement was initialled by the signatory nations; provided, of course, that an Agreement will be achieved.[9]

In addition to the aide-memoire Wilson was to hand to Broadley, Howe suggested that the committee agree on Wilson's own instructions for the conduct of the negotiations within the conference. Because of the possible conflict in the terms of the bilateral contract and the proposed wheat agreement, St. Laurent dictated instructions in the following terms:

> The Wheat Committee's decision is that the Canadian delegation cannot initial an international agreement which, under Clause seven of the bilateral agreement, would necessitate any modification or amendment thereof without prior agreement with the Government of the U. K. as to the terms and conditions of the consideration for which the Canadian Government would accept the necessary modification or amendment.[10]

Strachey's reply to Howe's message of February 2 was reflected in an aide-memoire Broadley left with Wilson on February 19:

> On the 7th February I handed you an aide memoire in reply to your aide memoire of the 4th February regarding the effects on the terms of the Canadian-United Kingdom wheat contract of any international wheat agreement which may be concluded. Since that exchange of documents further discussions between us have taken place. I have now received instructions from the United Kingdom Government to inform you as follows:
>
> The United Kingdom Government are prepared to enter an international wheat agreement with the following price ranges:

[9]*Ibid.*
[10]*Ibid.*

1948/49	$2.00 — $1.60
1949/50	$2.00 — $1.50
1950/51	$1.80 — $1.30
1951/52	$1.70 — $1.20
1952/53	$1.60 — $1.10

The United Kingdom Government recognize their obligations under Clause 2B of the Canadian/United Kingdom wheat contract and they stand by the declaration made by the Minister of Food in his speech in Winnipeg on 25th February, 1947. The United Kingdom Government are satisfied that these obligations can be met within the price ranges set out above.

Agreement has already been reached that the price for the third year of the contract shall be $2.00 per bushel. This is the maximum price for the year 1948-49 under the proposed international wheat agreement, and the actual world price for that year may well be below the maximum prescribed in the agreement.

For the fourth year of the contract (1949/50) the United Kingdom Government are prepared to agree now to pay $2.00 per bushel, which is the proposed maximum for that year under the proposed international wheat agreement. This price, together with the guaranteed payment of $2.00 per bushel in 1948/49 would, so the United Kingdom Government feel, permit of fulfillment of their obligations under Clause 2B of the contract.

The only alternative is to leave the actual price for 1949/50 to be negotiated before the 31st December, 1948, as provided in the contract in the light of the conditions then existing; but if an international wheat agreement should be reached the price would have to be within the range prescribed in the agreement.[11]

Wilson wired the text of the aide-memoire to Howe and in a separate teletype of February 20 he reported on the reaction of the three exporter delegations:

Reference my teletype WA-546 of today's date, the United Kingdom Government's new proposal on price ranges, was submitted by Broadley yesterday afternoon to the Prices Committee of the Conference.

The immediate reaction of the United States, Australian representatives and myself was that under no circumstances would the exporting countries accept a lowering of the ceilings as set out in the British proposal. The position I took was that if the British expected a downward trend in wheat prices, their position was safeguarded by the declining floors. If, however, their prediction on the price trend is wrong, it is unfair to the exporters to predetermine the position now by a declining ceiling that could be against the price trend.

Last evening Broadley handed me his aide-memoire containing the United Kingdom Government's offer to agree now to pay $2.00 per bushel in the fourth year of the contract. I have not disclosed this offer to our delegation, except to McNamara of the Wheat Board, this being a matter between Governments.

At nine this morning the delegations of the three exporting countries met together, the Americans being represented by N. E. Dodd, Under-Secretary of Agriculture, and the Australians by E. McCarthy, Assistant Secretary of Commerce and Agriculture. It was agreed that the three exporting countries should prepare a unanimous and final offer on prices to the importing countries. After discussion, in which both Dodd and McCarthy stated they would accept declining floors down to the British $1.10 in the fifth year in

[11]*Ibid.*

order to reach agreement, and Dodd went further by suggesting $1.50 and $1.40 for the first two years in the place of the British $1.60 and $1.50 for those years, which the Americans considered to be an inconsequential concession but one which might be helpful in reaching agreement, and after I had polled all the members of the Canadian delegation who concurred, the three exporters agreed on the following as a final offer to the importing countries to be accepted by them if there is to be an agreement:

1948/49	$2.00 — $1.50
1949/50	$2.00 — $1.40
1950/51	$2.00 — $1.30
1951/52	$2.00 — $1.20
1952/53	$2.00 — $1.10

At the meeting of the full Conference at 10:30 this morning, the Chairman announced the new British proposal on prices, together with the exporters' agreed reply, on the basis that this was a final offer by the exporters. The exporters then left the meeting to allow the importers to consider the exporters' offer.

Since the agreement will be held open for signature until April 1st, and subject to formal acceptance by July 1st, the text of the agreement could be completed by Monday next, if the majority of importers accept the exporters' price provisions, and the Conference concluded. Needless to say, I will not sign unless I am instructed to do so.[12]

Also, on that same day, the Canadian delegation received some unexpected help from the New Zealand delegate, Mr. R. W. Marshall, who proposed that the provisions of the Canada-United Kingdom contract should be exempted from those of the international agreement, and he presented a conference resolution in the following terms:

So long as this Agreement remains in force, it shall prevail over any provisions inconsistent therewith which may be contained in any other Agreement previously concluded between any of the signatory Governments, provided that should any two signatory Governments be parties to an Agreement, entered into prior to 1st March, 1947, for the purchase and sale of wheat, the Governments concerned shall supply full particulars of transactions under such Agreement so that quantities, irrespective of prices involved, shall be recorded in the register of transactions maintained by the Council in accordance with Article III and so count towards the fulfillment of obligations of importing countries and obligations of exporting countries.[13]

This paragraph was inserted as Article XIX of the agreement under the heading of relation to other agreements. Without referring specifically to the Canada-United Kingdom wheat contract, it found a means of recording all the transactions under that contract in discharge of the British and Canadian quantity obligations under the multilateral agreement without regard to price terms which might be agreed upon under the bilateral contract, and this met the Canadian position. The text of this was wired to Ottawa.

Upon receipt of a copy of Broadley's aide-memoire of February 19, Howe continued to insist that the best arrangement would be for Broadley to visit Ottawa to discuss the settlement of the "have regard to" clause. But when Broadley received instructions from London that he must stand firm on the declining ceiling proposals which the exporters had rejected, the negotia-

[12]*Ibid.*
[13]*Ibid.*

tions appeared to be heading for still another breakdown and Wilson telephoned on February 25 to Max Mackenzie who made a note of the conversation:

Dr. Wilson called this morning to advise that Broadley had advance information from London to the effect that the British would stand by their original proposal, that is, a declining ceiling, and would not agree to the offer of the exporting countries. Full instructions should reach Broadley this afternoon.

In discussion with Wilson, Broadley suggested that there would, under these circumstances, be no reason for his coming to Ottawa. I told Wilson that I was sure Mr. Howe would want Broadley to come, in any event, and that I also felt that the British proposal would not be acceptable to the Canadian Government, but that this would have to be referred to Ministers.

I called Mr. Howe to advise him of the foregoing, who confirmed that he was most anxious to have Broadley come to Ottawa, in any event, and that we should maintain our stand for a flat ceiling, but that, if the Americans were prepared to weaken on this stand, we might well be prepared to go along with them. We should not, however, take any initiative to alter the position already taken.

Wilson called me back a few minutes later to say that Broadley would announce to the full meeting that his instructions from London did not permit him to sign the agreement, at which point another delegate had been primed to propose that the exporters' offer be written into the agreement, and that the meeting would break up on the understanding that the agreement was open for signature until April 1.

It is expected that the final meeting of the International Wheat Council will be held some time to-morrow, and that, on that basis, Broadley could not be here before Friday. Wilson will, of course, keep us posted on any further developments.[14]

Howe's reaction to these latest developments was to make another direct approach to the British government. He arranged this through Mr. St. Laurent, and Pearson sent off the following cable on February 28 to Robertson:

The negotiations for an international wheat agreement have progressed in Washington to the point that the only remaining disagreement is on prices. On February 19th the British Government, through Broadley, proposed the following price ranges:

1948/49	$2.00 -	$1.60
1949/50	2.00 -	1.50
1950/51	1.80 -	1.30
1951/52	1.70 -	1.20
1952/53	1.60 -	1.10

On February 20 the Canadian, United States and Australian delegates countered with an unanimous and final offer on behalf of the exporting countries:

1948/49	$2.00 -	$1.50
1949/50	2.00 -	1.40
1950/51	2.00 -	1.30
1951/52	2.00 -	1.20
1952/53	2.00 -	1.10

The British in making their offer were evidently influenced in their attitude toward desiring an international agreement by the recent developments in the

[14]*Ibid.*

Chicago market. Accordingly, their new proposal involved a decline in prices if the over-all wheat developments hold them to the floor. On the other hand, if inflationary factors continue to operate, the proposal would require the exporters to reduce prices in the later years contrary to the general price trend.

The three exporters, while accepting the British proposals for declining floors and even reducing the floors in the first two years beyond the levels proposed by the United Kingdom, were unanimous in their insistence on a level ceiling at $2.00 throughout the agreement. Therefore the price issue revolves around the price ceilings in the last three years of the agreement.

By February 24th Strachey, in consultation with Cripps, was prepared to turn down the agreement unless the British proposals were accepted. Their final refusal was postponed, however, until a meeting of the Economic Policy Committee of the British Cabinet which was to have been held on February 27. Meanwhile, however, Broadley has asked that the British Cabinet meeting be postponed until consideration could be given to the political as well as the economic implications of their refusal to enter an agreement, except on a "Heads I win, tails you lose" basis, with the exporters.

At the February 26th meeting of the Washington Conference the representatives of the three exporters reaffirmed their position on the exporter's offer. The delegates of the importing countries, apart from the United Kingdom, all indicated that they were prepared to accept the exporters' offer, although some of them emphasized that it would be impracticable to have an agreement without the United Kingdom participating. Some of the importers expressed their concern that the United Kingdom's attitude was preventing their receiving the benefit of prices lower than those currently prevailing which would be available under an international agreement. The Americans, apart from desiring the agreement on other grounds, are interested in the effect of the agreement on the use of E. R. P. funds for wheat. Our producer organizations take a very strong interest in the securing of an international agreement, and the refusal of the United Kingdom to participate could materially reduce their support for the contract existing between the United Kingdom and ourselves.

On February 19th the United Kingdom made a firm offer to pay $2.00 per bushel in the fourth year of the contract (1949/50) in fullfilment of their obligations under Clause 2(b) of the contract, and we have been waiting since for Broadley to come to Ottawa to discuss this settlement.

Since Cripps apparently is already party to the idea that the British turn down the international agreement, except on terms unfair to the exporters, it would be most useful if you could have a talk with him prior to their Cabinet meeting for the purpose of emphasizing the political considerations involved and the repercussions of the United Kingdom alone refusing to make this agreement possible.[15]

Robertson's reply came on March 1 and it reported the Right Honourable Ernest Bevin's intervention in favor of coming to an agreement:

I understand that United Kingdom cabinet agreed over the weekend to the exporters prices range, at the strong insistance of Bevin, who took a very serious view of the political consequences of failure to achieve an International Agreement at this time.

The basis of the United Kingdom reluctance, which the Ministry of Food and the Treasury share, to enter into a four year Agreement with a constant ceiling, has been their fear that the Negotiating Committee contemplated in

[15]Ibid.

the Agreement would not in practice be free to negotiate annual prices which would reflect world supply-demand relationships, but would tend, under collective pressure from exporters, to fix a price at or near the ceiling, which would thus become the operative factor in price-making under the Agreement.

Before definitely accepting the exporters' offer, I believe they are asking Inverchapel to see if he can get an assurance from the United States that the exporters will not in fact gang up in restraint of trade to use the quasi-monopoly position which they will have under the Agreement to fix annual prices within the agreed price ranges at levels higher than those which the free operation of market forces within the framework of the Agreement might be expected to establish.[16]

Bevin's influence in persuading the other British ministers to modify their position was crucial to the success of the 1948 negotiations. Until then it had appeared that another breakdown would occur. It was an occasion of great relief, therefore, on March 4, when Broadley happily announced to the steering committee that his instructions had been changed and that he was now authorized to sign the agreement.

SIGNATURE OF THE 1948 AGREEMENT

Plans were immediately made for the closing ceremony of the conference on March 6, at which the agreement would be opened for signature and remain open until April 1. Because the British and American delegations were prepared to sign on March 6, Wilson telephoned Howe on March 4 and requested full powers to sign on behalf of Canada on the same day. After consulting his colleagues, Howe telephoned on March 5, and confirmed his message by telegram:

In accordance with our telephone conversation you are instructed to initial the International Wheat Agreement on behalf of Canada but before doing so to deliver to Sir Herbert Broadley representing the United Kingdom an aide-memoire in the following terms; Canada will sign the International Wheat Agreement but only upon the condition that the United Kingdom agrees notwithstanding the terms of section seven of the Canada/United Kingdom wheat contract that such action shall be without prejudice to Canadian claims arising under section two (b) of the said wheat contract.[17]

Section 7 of the bilateral contract was the one which rendered it subject to the terms of any subsequent international agreements or arrangements to which both governments are parties. The ministers wanted no misunderstanding to arise with the British, on the point that the "have regard to" clause in the bilateral contract remained in force, despite the signing of the international agreement. Wilson duly delivered the aide-memoire to Broadley and the Canadian ambassador, Hume Wrong, notified the state department that a full power was en route authorizing Wilson to sign the agreement. At its final meeting before the signing took place, the conference established a preparatory committee under the chairmanship of Sir Herbert Broadley to make the necessary arrangements for the new international wheat council to administer the agreement commencing August 1, 1948. Broadley called two such meetings in London in April. On April 2, Mr. C. C. Boxer wired from Washington that all 33 importing countries as well as

[16]*Ibid.*
[17]*Ibid.*

the three exporting countries which had actively participated in the negotiations had signed the agreement.

BROADLEY'S VISIT TO OTTAWA AND THE "HAVE REGARD TO" CLAUSE

In response to Mr. Howe's persistent invitation, Sir Herbert Broadley came to Ottawa after the conclusion of the conference. When he met with the cabinet wheat committee, however, all he could do was to confirm his government's offer of a $2 price in 1949-50 in settlement of the "have regard to" clause which the Canadian ministers understandably regarded as insufficient. They had already said so, in effect, through the last aide-memoire handed Sir Herbert in Washington. Thus, any further proposals the ministers could put to Broadley had to be referred by him to his government.

The cabinet wheat committee met twice on March 8 and 9 to consider its course in the light of Broadley's position, and Mr. J. R. Baldwin, newly-appointed secretary of the committee, made minutes of its decisions. The committee had considered three alternatives, namely, that Gardiner should proceed to London forthwith to complete the negotiations on the 1949-50 price and settlement of the "have regard to" clause; an arrangement suggested by Mr. St. Laurent (who had been invited to attend the wheat committee meetings) by which a cash settlement of the "have regard to" clause would be made from the outstanding balance of the Canadian credit to Britain; or thirdly, acceptance of the $2 offer for 1949-50 with a proviso that, if need be, any residual obligation under the "have regard to" clause be taken into account in setting the price to be paid by Britain for Canadian wheat within the provisions of the international wheat agreement in the crop year 1950-51.

With these three alternatives in hand, Gardiner had a negotiating position he could take to London. Howe reported, in turn, to cabinet on March 9, 1948, that Canada had signed the international wheat agreement provisionally, pending a satisfactory settlement of the "have regard to" clause. He also recommended that Gardiner go to London for that purpose before the end of March.

Howe followed up by cabling Norman Robertson on March 18:

> In discussions which Broadley had with the Cabinet Wheat Committee on March 8 and 9 Broadley was informed that in addition to the $2.00 fixed price in the fourth year of the contract offered by the United Kingdom Government we desire agreement in the following terms:
>
> "If the two countries should not be agreed that the price arrangements for 1948 and for 1949 have provided adequate settlement under the "have regard to" clause, that clause will also be taken into consideration in setting the price for that proportion of the United Kingdom quota under the International Wheat Agreement, which is taken from Canada in 1950/51."
>
> Such agreement would extend for one additional crop year the period in which we might receive compensation under the "have regard to" clause bearing in mind the fixed prices of $2.00 for the third and fourth years of the contract and the lower limit of world prices of $1.50 and $1.40 respectively set for those years by the International Wheat Agreement which could result in less than a fair ultimate settlement under the "have regard to" clause if no

provision were made beyond fixing a price at $2.00 for the fourth year of the contract.

Broadley agreed to cable our proposal and also to discuss it with his Government upon his return to London. He sailed from New York on March 12, and should be arriving in London late this week.

We are interested in getting the British Government's reply and would appreciate your following this up through Broadley.[18]

The British government did not respond to the representations made through Broadley and Robertson, and Howe cabled again on April 5 to find out where matters stood. As he advised Robertson then, the Canadian government would withhold its ratification of the international wheat agreement until agreement was reached on the basis for settling the bilateral contract. Howe followed by making formal representations through the British high commissioner, Sir Alexander Clutterbuck, but still there was no reply.

By the beginning of June, Wilson had become quite apprehensive about the delay in Canadian ratification of the international agreement, and reported on the position to Mackenzie:

Washington officials concerned are guessing that the agreement has a 50-50 chance of ratification by the United States Senate. The Senate Sub-Committee on Foreign Relations which held open hearings May 14-18 has still made no report to the Senate. The officials were confident of its passage until the grain trade got under way with their opposition and an active lobby is being carried on against it. Meanwhile the heads of three United States farm organizations have wired Senator Vandenberg supporting it. The Senate must act before its adjournment on June 19 for it will not reconvene again until late July and formal acceptance of the agreement is required by July 1.

Biddulph reports from London that the United Kingdom government are not submitting the agreement to parliament for ratification, but intend to give formal acceptance on their authority as a government.

Although it would expedite passage here if the agreement had already been ratified by the United States, or would save waste motion here if they failed to ratify, I think it is out of the question to wait until June 19 before commencing with the resolution in the House. There would be only one effective week for getting the resolution through and not only is there the difficulty of getting precedence over the other business, but the Senate will require certain notice and will undoubtedly refer the resolution to a Committee. For these reasons, I would suggest getting started in the House by June 14, or earlier if possible, and in the meantime we will be getting reports on the progress in the United States Senate.

The major question here is the United Kingdom contract in relation to the agreement. There has been no reply yet to the second approach to the United Kingdom government and it should be decided whether:

1. to close off with $2.00 in the fourth year;
2. to send a stronger note that our government would like prompt concurrence in our earmarking of $100,000,000 of the credit balance; or
3. our government should take the position that the International Wheat Agreement does not affect the final settlement to be made under the "have regard to" clause, which can be decided under the terms of the contract by December 31, 1948.

[18]*Trade and Commerce file 20-141-11.*

This decision should be sought at once, since the second alternative requires further consultation with the British before the International Wheat Agreement is brought into the House.[19]

As a result Howe cabled to Robertson again who reported back on June 9, 1948:

> United Kingdom ministers have been unable, so far, to agree on reply to be sent to your letter to Clutterbuck, with Treasury arguing that they cannot accept a contingent dollar liability of unspecified magnitude for a fifth year under the wheat contract. Present indication is that United Kingdom will propose an agreed announcement now that the price for the 1949-50 crop year will be arranged between the two Governments before the end of this year in accordance with the contract. They will probably say, though they will not wish to have this made public, that in the course of negotiating the 1949-50 prices they would for their part not exclude the possibility of the two Governments then agreeing on a fifth year extension of the contract if at that time implementation of the "have regard to" clause appears to require a fifth year for its fulfilment.[20]

Clutterbuck eventually wrote to Howe on July 14, 1948, acknowledging Howe's suggestion that the "have regard to" clause could be settled by payment from the balance of the Canadian credit but that his ministers had not viewed this as solving all the difficulties. Because of the failure of the United States to ratify the international wheat agreement, the matter no longer seemed urgent, and Clutterbuck proposed that the outstanding issues be settled in accordance with the provisions of the contract.

CANADIAN RATIFICATION

As a result of the delay over the attempt to settle the "have regard to" consideration, Howe postponed the moving of a resolution in the house to approve the agreement until June 21, 1948. It was not necessary for the government to submit the agreement to parliament for approval but, as a matter of policy, the government preferred to have parliamentary endorsation. By the time the action was taken it was already known that the United States senate would not act upon a similar resolution before the deadline of July 1 for ratification prescribed within the agreement. Nevertheless, the Canadian government proceeded with its resolution in order to avoid sharing the blame for failure to bring the agreement into operation. Wilson drafted a speech for Mr. Howe which he made on June 21, without referring to the United States dilemma:

> Mr. Speaker, in moving this resolution I am asking the house to approve Canada's participation in the international wheat agreement which was opened for signature at Washington on March 6, 1948, and signed on behalf of thirty-six countries, including Canada. No additional legislation is required to implement this agreement so long as the present authority remains under the Canadian Wheat Board Act or under the Export and Import Permits Act.
>
> Formal acceptance of this agreement is required by July 1 of each of the countries whose legislative bodies have been in session since the agreement was signed. For example, I understand that the agreement is now before the United States senate for ratification as a treaty, in order that the United States

[19] *Ibid.*
[20] *Privy Council Office file.*

government may give its formal acceptance by July 1, and in order that the agreement may become operative commencing with the new crop year on the first of August.

I think that members will be interested in hearing something of the background leading up to this agreement. I need not dwell on the prewar period, or on the international agreements and proposals of those days, beyond pointing out that the terms of those earlier agreements were quite different from the terms of the agreement we have before us for approval today. The old idea was to influence prices indirectly by regulating or restricting supplies. The present agreement is a multilateral contract covering the sale of wheat. It is a price and quantity agreement drawn up between three exporting countries and thirty three importing countries, and does not in any way affect additional wheat transactions, either between member countries or with non-member countries once the transactions provided in the agreement are met.

Since the end of the war, this government has consistently supported the objective of obtaining a measure of stability in international wheat prices. With the hearty support of our wheat producer's organizations we instructed our officials to further these views with other governments, both through the international wheat council and through the food and agriculture organization.

By the spring of 1946 it was apparent that an international agreement on wheat prices could not be reached in time to affect the 1946-47 crop year, and in lieu thereof Canada concluded a bilateral contract with its principal wheat customer, the United Kingdom. In the meantime, negotiations toward an international wheat agreement were continued, one conference being held in London in the spring of 1947, at which agreement was almost reached, and the second conference being held in Washington early this year, at which the present agreement was concluded.

The agreement involves the annual sale of 500 million bushels of wheat over a period of the next five crop years, of which Canada's share is 230 million bushels. This figure represents our normal export surplus from crops grown on our existing acreage. The agreement provides for a range of prices all based on No. 1 northern wheat, in store Fort William-Port Arthur, with a uniform ceiling of $2 over the five-year period and floors commencing with $1.50 in the first year and declinging by ten cents per year until the floor of $1.10 is reached in the fifth crop year. Each of the importing countries is assigned a share of the total 500 million bushels, and they have the right to buy and the exporting countries have an obligation to sell these quantities at the ceiling prices. Conversely, the exporting countries have a right to sell and the importing countries an obligation to buy these same quantities at the floor prices. In brief, this means that the importing countries have an assurance of supplies at not more than ceiling prices, and the exporting countries have the assurance of a market at not less than floor prices to the extent of the agreement quantities.

As I mentioned before, the agreement in no way affects wheat purchases by the member-importing countries in excess of their commitments under the agreement from any source whatever, nor does it affect the sales of the member-exporting countries if they have wheat for sale in excess of their commitments. The 500 million bushels in the agreement by no means exhausts the current volume of the world wheat trade, which is running upwards of 850 million bushels per year.

It has been frequently mentioned that Argentina and Russia are not parties to this agreement. They were given every opportunity to join, but they declined. Because the agreement is in the form of a sales contract, its operation and the interests of its member countries are not affected by the absence of these two countries. Under surplus conditions, it can be assumed that Argentina and Russia will offer their wheat below the floor prices set out in the agreement. Canada, Australia and the United States, however, have the protection of floor prices on their normal export surpluses, and are free to meet Argentine and Russian competition on any additional quantities they may desire to sell. On the other hand, should the importing countries produce more of their own wheat, their imports will be maintained from Canada, Australia and the United States, while diminishing from other sources.

The international agreement does not limit our rights under the Canada-United Kingdom wheat agreement. The fixed price of $2 per bushel for the third year of that agreement will continue in force for the 1948-49 crop year on our sales under the contract to the United Kingdom. The price for the fourth year of the contract is to be negotiated under the terms of the contract before December 31 of this year.

The agreement is noncommittal on the issue of state versus private trading between the member countries. Under the same agreement the Canadian and Australian wheat boards will continue for the present to make wheat sales for their respective countries, while wheat sales from the United States will be made by the private trade. Flour exports from each of the three exporting countries are to continue under private trade. Because of the breadth of the price ranges there is ample room for the operation of markets within the limits of the price ranges. What the agreement accomplishes is to rule out the extreme situations beyond either end of the price range which have hitherto brought undesirable consequences in their wake and which have been the main source of resentment against the open market system as it has operated in the past.

Because of the variation in our crop yields and consequent uncertainty of supplies, it has been impossible for us to deal as a single exporter with a number of our other wheat customers on the same basis as we have been dealing with the United Kingdom for the past two years. By combining the resources of the three wheat exporting countries under an international agreement, it will be possible for us to deal with all our wheat customers alike in return for like obligations on their part, and on the same terms in which they are being dealt with by the United States and Australia, if the international wheat agreement is formally accepted by the countries concerned.

It seems to me, Mr. Speaker, that this wheat agreement is very much in the interests of Canada, and I recommend its acceptance.[21]

Although the Conservative opposition tended to line up behind the Honourable John Bracken in criticism of the motion, the CCF and Social Credit members endorsed the agreement, and Howe wound up the debate in eloquent extempore fashion:

As hon. members are probably aware, the question before us is whether we shall or shall not ratify an agreement that has already been made. The agreement was made by delegates of the government, among whom were included the leaders of the three largest wheat marketing organizations in Canada, as well as other men whose reputation as market experts is well established. The unanimous recommendation of Canada's delegates was that the agreement be ratified, as being in the best interests of the Canadian producer. It is significant that the favourable report was not confined to farm

[21]*House of Commons Debates,* June 21, 1948, pp. 5561-5562.

organizations in Canada. The leading farm organizations in the United States also recommended to their government that the agreement be ratified. The leading farm organizations of the United Kingdom made the same recommendation to their government. The farm organizations of other countries supported this agreement as being a satisfactory outcome of the efforts of the thirty-six countries which during the past several years have met together in attempts to bring about stability in international wheat trading.

What is the purpose of the agreement? The purpose is to take out a mutual insurance policy. The three producing countries obtain a firm guarantee, first, that they will be able to dispose of the quantities allocated to them under the agreement — in the case of Canada 230 million bushels — and second that they will be able to dispose of that quantity of wheat at a price. It is interesting to hear people laugh off the idea that there may be surpluses in this country, and that there may be difficulty in disposing of surplus wheat. Memories are very short. I was around in the thirties and I know that the most difficult problem of the country in those days was the disposal of our wheat. I know that if any minimum price had been available there would not have been much question as to what the minimum was; if we could have moved the quantity and got any price that seemed reasonable even in those days, that privilege would have been a very welcome insurance policy indeed.

As I say, the insurance policy for the producing countries is that they will be able to sell a definite quantity of wheat at a definite price. The insurance to the consuming countries is that they will be able to buy a definite quantity of wheat at a maximum price of $2 a bushel. As I say, the experts of all these countries believed that that is a desirable arrangement. I believe it is a desirable insurance policy. I believe that it will do a great deal to stabilize world markets and world price. I believe that Canada should ratify the agreement.

The question has been raised as to how many countries have ratified the agreement. I cannot say the number; I do not know how many. The date of ratification is the first day of July, and we have not as yet reached that date. We have had informal but definite advice to the effect that the United Kingdom intends to ratify the agreement. Several countries on the continent already have ratified the agreement. Australia has done so. The United States senate has adjourned temporarily without ratifying the agreement, and it is obvious that that country will not ratify it before July 1, but indications are that there is a fair chance that it will be ratified later this year.

As far as the position of the Canadian farmer is concerned, based on whether the agreement is or is not ratified within the next month, may I say that it does not make the slighest difference. Canada's export of wheat is contracted for, for the 1948 and 1949 crops.

The hon. member for Portage la Prairie (Mr. Miller) says it is obvious that the promises of the Minister of Agriculture (Mr. Gardiner), and the promises of the Minister of Agriculture of the United Kingdom, would not be carried out if the agreement was signed. I may tell him that he is mistaken about that. Conversations have taken place with the United Kingdom government, and it is clearly understood between the two parties to the United Kingdom wheat agreement that the settlement of the current wheat agreement will be made whether the multilateral agreement is signed or not.

It is all very well for hon. members to make speeches about the price of wheat, and to compare the prices obtained under the Canada-United Kingdom agreement with the domestic price in the Chicago market; for the latter is the price they are talking about. They can call it the price of No. 2 wheat if they like. The price of No. 2 wheat has been the price in the Chicago domestic market. Our No. 2 wheat price is the quotation from day to day on the Chicago grain exchange. The quantity of No. 2 wheat that Canada had to sell was small, and as a price had to be fixed, the day to day Chicago price was adopted as reasonable in the circumstances. We know that dentists, doctors, oil men and persons engaged in various professions were dabbling in the Chicago market at that time, and that the United States government was itself alarmed at speculation in that market. Nevertheless hon. members opposite like to talk about $3.20 wheat and compare that with the price obtained for Canadian wheat. We never hear the fact mentioned that the price already paid the western farmer for the 1945 Canadian crop is higher than that obtained for the 1945 crop by any other country in the world, and the final payment on that crop has not yet been determined.

No one knows what will be the final price for the pool wheat of the crops of 1945, 1946, 1947, 1948 and 1949, and I suggest it might be well to wait for the determination of that price before comparisons are made. I say that any man who attempts to base a comparison on the peak Chicago price for domestic United States wheat is attempting to deceive his listeners, and I say that without qualification.

It has been suggested that this resolution should go to the banking and commerce committee. If there were any possibility of varying the terms of the agreement, that might be worth while; but when it is a simple decision, whether Canada will or will not be a party to the agreement, it seems to me that question is sufficiently clear to make unnecessary any reference to a committee.

Questions have been asked about the details of the agreement. The agreement requires no great comment. The price fixed is the price between countries. It does not interfere with the policy of any country regarding its domestic wheat. We know that the United States intends to fix wheat prices for the current year somewhat above the maximum price provided for in the agreement for wheat sold to any export markets. Any country can do the same. I think that covers the situation.[22]

The motion was approved on division, and the United States state department was formally notified of Canada's acceptance of the agreement.

AMERICAN RATIFICATION

The United States state department decided that the agreement should be submitted to the senate for ratification as a treaty, rather than as an executive agreement. International treaties required senate approval by a two-thirds majority whereas executive agreements could be approved by a simple majority. By letter of April 30, 1948, from the White House, President Harry S. Truman transmitted the agreement to the senate with accompanying letters of explanation from the secretary of state and from the acting secretary of agriculture with a request for the senate's earliest possible consideration of its formal acceptance.

The senate referred the agreement to its committee on foreign relations which appointed a sub committee consisting of Senators Lodge (chairman), George and Capper to consider the agreement. Senator Capper was also chairman of the senate agricultural committee. Lodge and Capper were Republicans and George a Democrat, which reflected the Republican control of the senate. The sub-committee opened public hearings on May 14, 1948. Presentations were made by Willard A. Thorp, assistant secretary

[22]*Ibid.,* pp. 5580-5581.

of state for economic affairs, and by N. E. Dodd, acting secretary of agriculture. Dodd was cross-examined at length and made a good case for the agreement. The farm organizations were represented by Mr. H. A. Fraser, American farm bureau federation, Mr. J. T. Sanders, National grange, and by Mr. Arthur H. Booth, United Farmers of America Incorporated. The first two supported the agreement, but Booth opposed it. The hearings continued until May 17, during which time, Mr. John Locke, president of the miller's federation, Mr. W. C. Schilthuis, appearing on behalf of the North American export grain association and of the National grain trade council, and Mr. Walter C. Berger, president of the American feed manufacturers' association, all presented briefs in opposition to the agreement, on the general ground that the agreement was an instrument of state trading which conflicted with the government's trade liberalization policy as well as upon their concern over the adminstrative details of the agreement. The National grain trade council distributed a brochure criticising the agreement, of which Mr. Charles E. Huntting, who had returned to private business in Minneapolis, had been co-author.

In response to questioning by the the sub-committee, witnesses provided estimates ranging from $50 to $300 million on the cost of the federal subsidy required to subsidize export prices from their domestic level in order to conform with the ceiling price in the agreement. By June 1, administration officials were genuinely concerned whether the foreign relations committee would report the agreement back to the senate before its adjournment date of June 19. The real blow fell on June 9 when Senator Lodge informed the department of agriculture that his sub-committee had voted not to take action on the agreement at that session of congress. Secretary Charles F. Brannon declared that this spelled the end of the multilateral agreement and that the United States could expect a prolification of long-term bulk contracts on the lines of the Canada-United Kingdom bulk contract. All these details were reported to Winnipeg and Ottawa by Mr. C. C. Boxer, the Washington representative of the Canadian wheat board who attended the senate sub-committee hearings.

JULY 1948 MEETING OF THE
INTERNATIONAL WHEAT COUNCIL

The consequences of the senate sub-committee's decision were summed up in a brief message from Hume Wrong, the Canadian ambassador in Washington, on June 21:

> Congress adjourned early yesterday morning without any action by the Senate to approve ratification of the International Wheat Agreement. The Agreement, therefore, cannot come into effect and must be regarded as dormant if not dead.
>
> Mr. Andrew Cairns has telephoned today to say that it has been agreed that the meeting of the new International Wheat Council which had been set for June 29th is being cancelled, and that there is being substituted for it a meeting of the old Wheat Council to be held on July 6th. He will confirm this by letter. He added that the meeting of the old Wheat Council would be in the nature of a funeral gathering and it was not expected that representatives of other countries would come specially to Washington to attend it.[23]

[23]*Trade and Commerce file 26204:14.*

Some notable changes, however, did take place in the personnel who attended the July council meeting. Its Chairman, Mr. Leslie A. Wheeler, had opted for early retirement and his continuous association with all the wheat agreement negotiations since 1933 came to an end. Andrew Cairns, the secretary, was the only remaining person whose participation stretched back to 1933. Among the delegates, Wilson's participation since 1939 made him an informal dean of the corps. Mr. Norris E. Dodd, undersecretary of agriculture, had just resigned to accept an appointment as director general of FAO in succession to Lord Boyd Orr, and Sir Herbert Broadley had been recruited to join him as deputy director general of that organization. For purposes of the July council meeting, however, Broadley came to Washington and chaired that meeting. He brought with him his next senior officer in the ministry of food, Mr. Frank Sheed Anderson, who now headed the British delegation. Anderson had been a member of the British delegation at the 1947 London wheat conference, but he had not taken part in the special session of the council which had met in Washington earlier in 1948. From thenceforward, Anderson served as the British delegate and he was elected as chairman of the council after the agreement became operative in 1949. Secretary Brannan represented the United States at the July 1948 council meeting.

As matters turned out, a meeting of the new council established by the 1948 agreement had to be called in order that governments which had already ratified that agreement might have a legal means of withdrawal in the light of the American failure to ratify. When Broadley opened the meeting on July 6, Secretary Brannan regretfully reported the United States position that unless congress were reconvened, its next regular session would not commence before January 1949. Under instructions from his government, Anderson gave formal notice of Britain's unconditional withdrawal. The Australian delegate also notified his government's withdrawal. Before the meeting opened, Anderson had strongly urged Wilson to support him by withdrawing on behalf of Canada. But Wilson had sought no such instructions, in the hope that some means could be found for extending the time for the United States to come into the agreement. He explained the Canadian position to the council:

> The International Wheat Agreement, which was signed by the Representative of Canada on March 6, 1948, was submitted by my Government to the House of Commons and to the Senate in Canada for approval. Notice of the motion was placed on the Order Paper in May and it so happened that in order of Government business the Wheat Agreement came up for discussion in the House on June 21 and in the Senate on June 24. I mention those dates particularly because, at least when the approval of the Agreement came under discussion in both the House and the Senate, it was already known that the United States Senate had adjourned without ratifying the Agreement. Nevertheless, it was the express desire of my Government to have this Agreement approved, as it was approved by both Houses of Parliament, in order that if it were impossible for the United States Government to ratify by the deadline of July 1 it might be possible by some device or other to bring this Agreement into operation later during the present crop-year.[24]

As the chairman polled the delegates, several others gave notice of

[24]*Verbatim Minutes, International Wheat Council,* July 6, 1948 p. 5.

immediate withdrawal and, in the result, only the delegations of Austria, China, Dominican Republic, Egypt, India and Switzerland remained in the same position as Canada. Without formally withdrawing, these delegations resolved to recommend to their governments that in the light of the circumstances, the agreement should be inoperative among them. Although there was little hope of having the agreement come into operation in 1948-49, wider support for that resolution instead of formal withdrawal would have kept the possibility alive.

The next important question was to provide some machinery for reviving the negotiations should the United States position change. Wilson was rather outspoken against the suggestion that the issue be referred to the old wheat council which had been created by the 1942 memorandum of agreement. The record of negotiations under that aegis had been a sorry one and it appeared there would be a greater chance of success if some government, such as that of the United States, would take the initiative in reconvening a negotiating conference when the prospects for success were more promising. The American delegation were quite prepared to accept such responsibility on behalf of their government, and the council passed a resolution:

> This meeting of representatives of the countries which signed the International Wheat Agreement, concluded in Washington on 6th March 1948, appoints a Preparatory Committee, consisting of the countries represented on the Preparatory Committee, appointed by the final plenary meeting of the Special Session of the International Wheat Council, held in Washington on 6th March 1948, to keep under review the prospects of concluding a new international wheat agreement, and invites the United States Government to convene a meeting of the Preparatory Committee now appointed, after consultation with the Chairman of that Committee.[25]

Immediately after the adoption of that resolution on July 7, the new wheat council created by the 1948 agreement adjourned, and a meeting of the old council created by the 1942 memorandum of agreement was convened. The difference in substance was that the governments of Argentina and Uruguay were members of the latter, but neither had signed the 1948 agreement. This meeting was informed of the resolution which had just been passed by the new council, which indicated the agreed arrangements for reviving the wheat agreement negotiations again, and the question arose what disposition should be made of the old council. With some feeling, but rather inadvisedly Wilson moved its dissolution. The majority of delegates believed that it should be continued for another year, pending the possibility of another negotiating conference. The old council was therefore kept formally alive by electing Mr. J. C. Van Essche, the Belgian delegate as chairman and Wilson as vice-chairman.

Thereupon, the meeting of the old council adjourned and a meeting of the preparatory committee appointed earlier that afternoon by the new council was convened. Australia, Benelux, Brazil, Canada, Egypt, France, India, and United Kingdom and the United States had been named to that committee. Wilson was elected chairman and Van Essche the vice-chairman. Wilson's responsibility in that capacity was to await consultation from the United States government regarding the convening of the committee

[25]*Ibid.*, July 7, 1948, p. 3.

whenever that government considered the time propitious to negotiate a new international wheat agreement.

SPECIAL SESSION OF CONGRESS

The question of ratifying the wheat agreement had become a partisan consideration in the United States presidential election campaign as soon as the sub-committee of the senate committee on foreign relations had voted against reporting the agreement to the senate. The issue had arisen between a Democratic administration and a Republican controlled senate. When the Republican party convention was held in Philadelphia, it was reported that, despite the representations of the major farm organizations, the platform committee, under the chairmanship of Senator Henry Cabot Lodge of Massachusetts, had refused to support the principle of international cooperation in the marketing of crops. Lodge was credited with having led the objections.[26]

For the purpose of reintroducing several domestic legislative measures, to which he added the ratification of the wheat agreement, President Truman summoned a special session of congress which opened on July 27. The wheat agreement was then referred to the main foreign relations committee under the chairmanship of Senator Arthur Vandenberg. Both closed and open hearings were held as the administration and the farm organizations pressed for action. On August 6, Vandenberg reported the unanimous decision of the committee:

> The Senate Committee on Foreign Relations reports the international wheat agreement to the Senate Executive Calendar because of the Committee's earnest belief that the principle of surplus marketing by international agreement is sound and because it wishes to encourage this objective. It will not ask for Senate consideration until early in the next Congress because of contingent factors which make it impossible, as it is also unnecessary, to apply the agreement to this year's wheat crop, and because these factors can more wisely and safely be resolved at that time.
>
> One of these factors involves resignature to the agreement by other countries which have withdrawn since July 1 and which are necessary in order to make the agreement effective. Another involves the necessity for implementing the treaty with general legislation to authorize the Commodity Credit Corporation to finance these export deficits when they occur. There are other factors which the Committee believes can be helpfully explored in the interim to create a better domestic understanding of the issue and the widest possible degree of agreement upon the treaty.
>
> The committee regrets that it was physically impossible to complete work on the treaty at the recent regular session in the relatively few weeks available for this purpose. In view of its novelty and its complications and its controversies, there was no chance to reach a responsible finality. These complications increased in the brief recess preceding the present special session. But so also did the conviction that a useful principle is involved. So also did the committee's desire to revive the treaty and keep it open for ratification or renegotiation.[27]

Immediately afterward, Senator Vandenberg held a press conference which was reported as follows:

[26] *Winnipeg Free Press,* June 23, 1948.
[27] *The Congressional Record,* August 6, 1948.

The Senate Foreign Relations Committee by a 13-to-0 vote today approved the International Wheat Agreement as the first step toward revival of the agreement. . . .

Chairman Vandenberg said that this action would serve "to keep the concept vigorously and effectively alive." He said also that it would give other countries which have withdrawn a chance to sign again and Congress a chance to pass enabling legislation to cover new principles involved in the treaty. He added that it would even permit renegotiation if necessary. . . .

Mr. Vandenberg emphasized that the time limit on the present session of Congress was no factor in the committee's hold-over action. President Truman had made ratification of the agreement his only foreign policy recommendation for the extra session.

The Michigan Senator urged that in the interim a better domestic understanding on the treaty be promoted and that all interested factions seek the widest possible agreement on the many complicated and controversial phases.

He termed today's action "the friendliest possible that can be taken from the standpoint of the friends of the proposal itself." He also said that "it is the pretty general belief of the committee that when all available factors are adequately explored it is going to be possible to work out a complete agreement."

Underlining the necessity for careful consideration of the agreement is the fact that it may well prove to be a precedent for other commodities in international trade, Mr. Vandenberg said.

He cited as the chief obstacle to immediate ratification the withdrawal of five nations — the United Kingdom, Australia, New Zealand, Ireland and Denmark.

He said that, while those nations' withdrawals probably resulted from the failure of the United States to ratify by the time limit of July 1, this year, it was "obviously wholly impractical to contemplate operating with any such limited cooperation" as would be afforded by the nations remaining under the compact — Austria, Canada, the Dominican Republic, Egypt, India and Sweden.

"It is contemplated by the proponents of the treaty that if the Government of the United States indicates any degree of interest in the treaty in its basic concepts the signatures withdrawn probably will be restored," the Senator added.

Asked what would happen if they did not sign again, he replied: "They no longer can relate their refusal to lack of interest on the part of the Government of the United States."[28]

The refusal of the foreign relations committee to ratify the agreement forthwith, however, gave President Truman another issue as he fought his uphill battle for reelection. Meanwhile, the fate of international wheat agreement turned on the outcome of that election.

[28]*New York Times,* August 6, 1948.

44

BOARD HANDLING OF
OATS AND BARLEY

Although the bilateral wheat contract and its attempted conversion into a multilateral contract had dominated the direction of postwar wheat policy, the government's policy on coarse grains remained to be determined. It will be recalled that during the war, the wartime prices and trade board had established price ceilings on oats and barley and that the government had also set floor prices which were implemented, if need be, through the wheat board. Because of the feed demand in the United States, higher prices were obtainable there than at the ceiling in Canada. To control supplies, the wheat board issued export licences, and collected the difference between the Canadian and United States prices as an export tax on the issuance of licences. The proceeds of the tax accrued to producers through equalization funds for each grain in each crop year, and from which advance equalization payments of 10 cents per bushel on oats and 15 cents on barley were made at the time of delivery, and any remaining surpluses in the funds paid out after the end of the crop year.

Now that price controls were being removed and prices entering into farm production costs were rising, it was no longer possible to retain the price ceilings on oats and barley and, in the absence of any other policy, oats and barley could have reverted to the open market system. Canadian producers could thereby have been assured of export values on both their export and domestic sales. The open market offered producers no assurance, however, that such prices would remain high. On the other hand, domestic users of feed grains, notably the farmers in eastern Canada, were faced with much higher feed costs.

The Canadian federation of agriculture which embraced in its membership the farm organizations of both eastern and western Canada had annually placed its members, with the exception of United Grain Growers Limited, on record as favoring a monopoly grain board in which all grains would be handled on the same basis as wheat. With the disappearance of the wartime price controls, the issue became more relevant because a choice must now be made to opt for a board system or for the open market system on coarse grains. Unlike wheat, however, most feed grains were consumed on farms where produced, or sold to neighboring farms. A smaller percentage moved into interprovincial trade, mostly between western and eastern Canada, and a still smaller percentage was exported. But with the preponderance of users as well as the producers in Canada, the criterion for prices became very involved. The open market could have made daily prices with which both producers and consumers would have to abide. If the producers and consumers, however, sought greater security by assigning the price-making function to a government board, the board would be caught inescapably between the conflicting interests of producers and buyers.

The government had only partly faced the issue when it amended the Canadian wheat board act in 1947. As Mr. Ilsley, minister of justice, had explained in that debate, the form of authority requested by the government to extend the provisions of the act to oats and barley did not require it to provide for the monopoly handling of those grains. If exercised, the authority could be used to provide for board handling on a voluntary basis, in which case the operations would be unquestionably intra vires. On a complusory basis, however, the board's constitutional authority was seriously in question. The British North America act established federal jurisdiction over interprovincial trade, but transactions within a province fell under provincial jurisdiction. Trade in coarse grains was predominantly intraprovincial, and federal complusory marketing would be ineffectual if confined within constitutional bounds, or unconstitutional if effective.[1] When pressed by the opposition to declare where they stood on the complusory marketing of coarse grains, neither Ilsley nor Gardiner was prepared to support the policy at that time.[2]

Within a year, however, as eastern feeders became increasingly concerned over the rising costs of feed grain, the government realized that it was facing a political issue of national dimensions. If it failed to respond it could be blamed for thwarting the marketing preference of most of the farm community, and a federal election was not that far in the offing. A joint solution to the political and constitutional problems was found by making proclamation of the federal legislation conditional upon the enactment of complementary legislation by the governments of the three prairie provinces. With provincial legislation also in force, compulsory marketing of western oats and barley, whether interprovincially or intraprovincially, would be constitutional. Legislative action by the provinces would assure beyond doubt the political acceptance of the policy. Should any of the provincial governments fail to respond, it would have to justify its position to producers.

Provincial support could be expected from the Alberta and Saskatchewan governments where the influence of the farm organizations was strong, but the situation in Manitoba was complicated by the influence of the private grain trade and of the *Winnipeg Free Press.* In recent years the Winnipeg grain exchange and other organizations, notably the Searle Grain Company, Limited, had conducted an extensive publicity campaign to persuade producers that the monopoly system of marketing, the bilateral contract and the international wheat agreement were not in their best interests.

In parliament, moreover, many Liberal members felt that monopoly marketing violated the basic Liberal philosophy of free enterprise and they

[1]*House of Commons Debates,* February 27, 1947, p. 867.
[2]*Ibid.,* p. 868.

equated it with state socialism. The Progressive-Conservative party as a whole championed the open market system. Therefore government sponsorship of board marketing could be expected to provoke a protracted debate.

There was disagreement over the issue even within the cabinet as the prime minister attested in his diary on February 12, 1948:

> There was a most difficult discussion on the question including oats and coarse grains under the powers to be given to the Wheat Board in certain emergencies. The three western ministers Gardiner, MacKinnon and Glen were all strongly of the opinion that if this were not done, the party would lose the West entirely. The C.C.F. would sweep everything. Garson, of Manitoba, was strongly for the inclusion of this extension of power. Gardiner doubted if all provinces — Ontario — would agree to the legislation. It would not become law without their concurrence.... Howe who is, as Minister of Trade and Commerce, fathering the legislation, is strongly opposed to it as is also the Minister of Finance. They both feel it may further socialistic aims and lead to state marketing of goods, etc.
>
> I had to give the decision; in doing so, I stated that I thought the Cabinet could not, on a matter affecting Agriculture, go contrary to the strong views of representatives of three Western Provinces. Howe immediately said: carried, and that ended the discussion of one of the most difficult matters we have had to deal with.

Cabinet also had approved a package of amendments to the wheat board act including a pension scheme for the board and its staff, authority to control the interprovincial sale of wheat products as well as wheat, and authority to increase the initial advance applicable to the five-year pool. It was anticipated that the urgency for an increase in the initial payment for wheat would help to carry the contentious clause concerning oats and barley. The Right Honourable C. D. Howe, who had just recently assumed the trade and commerce portfolio, proceeded to honor his commitment to pilot the controversial legislation, as he introduced the amending resolution in the house on February 16, 1948.

FEDERATION OF AGRICULTURE REPRESENTATIONS

Government policy respecting oats and barley was decided after the Canadian federation of agriculture had held its annual meeting at Brockville in January, 1948, but before the federation made its annual presentation to the cabinet on February 26. The location for the annual meeting reflected the concern of eastern feeders over feed grain prices and supplies. At that meeting, members of the federation discussed the coarse grain situation at length. Except for United grain growers, the western and eastern members resolved once again to recommend that the wheat board be given monopoly powers over the marketing of western oats and barley. The western and eastern members believed that they could agree from time to time on prices at which the board should sell the grain, and could so advise the government.

In the federation's annual presentation to cabinet, Mr. H. H. Hannam led a delegation of 17 representatives and 10 members of the cabinet attended. Mr. St. Laurent took the place of Mackenzie King who was ill. In its formal brief the federation referred to the international wheat negotiations in the following terms:

In respect to international marketing we have consistently advocated the use of international commodity agreements for staple products entering extensively into international trade; and we have wholeheartedly backed the efforts of the government in working for an international wheat agreement.

In representations to the government the Canadian Federation of Agriculture has always advocated moderate prices, and have never asked for "all that the traffic would bear." Canadian farmers have consistently supported stabilized prices fair alike to producers and consumers of our farm products.[3]

On the subject of coarse grains, the brief continued:

As we have indicated, our dairymen, poultrymen, and live stock feeders are keenly concerned over the rise and fluctuations in the cost of feeds since decontrol, and are urging measures to stabilize these costs.

Our main recommendation in this respect is contained in a resolution passed by our annual convention, which urges once more that the Canadian Wheat Board become the sole marketing agency for all other grains in addition to wheat. (One member body has recorded its dissent.)

This resolution asks that the necessary amendments to the Wheat Board Act do not disregard the principle that the Wheat Board be an agency operating primarily for the benefit of, and in the interests of grain producers; it asks that the purpose of the legislation be to enable the Board to stabilize grain prices and prevent short-term fluctuations; and that it be provided always that the Board's domestic operating and selling policy shall carry out the spirit and intent of a general agricultural policy that shall effect a proper relationship between grain and livestock prices, as determined by the Federal Department of Agriculture after consultation with the Canadian Federation of Agriculture.

Our convention also asked that steps be taken to stabilize the costs of millfeeds and protein concentrates, and that a federal board should be set up to control protein feeds manufactured in Canada, with power to set the price of the product in Canada, in keeping with farm product prices, and to control the export of any surplus protein feeds.[4]

The federation offered an intriguing formula for the reconciliation of the conflicting price interests of the producers and users, but it failed to provide a precise definition of pricing policy, and could not be adopted as a practical selling policy by the board.

DEBATE ON RESOLUTION

Although Howe had moved his amending resolution on February 16, debate did not commence until February 27, a day after the federation had presented its annual policy recommendation to cabinet. The debate extended over two sittings on February 27 and March 11 before first reading of the proposed bill was given. In opening the debate, Mr. Howe explained the reasons for each amendment, as he said:

The fourth amendment proposes to empower the governor in council by regulation to extend to oats and barley the regulations now applicable to wheat. Strong representations favouring the marketing of oats and barley through the wheat board have been received from farm organizations in both western and eastern Canada, among them the Canadian council of agriculture. The government desires to meet the wishes of farm organizations in this regard, provided a workable plan can be agreed upon. However, the

---

[3]Canadian Federation of Agriculture, *Farmers Meet the Cabinet*, February, 1948, p. 3.
[4]*Ibid.*, pp. 6-7.

government is well aware that the compulsory marketing of oats and barley through the board represents serious difficulties. The success of such an enterprise must be dependent on a large measure of agreement on policy matters as between organized farmers of both the producer and the consumer class, as well as on the co-operation of provincial governments. Therefore this government will wish to have concrete evidence of such agreement and such co-operation before it can assume the responsibility for putting this amendment into effect.

The difficulties of which I speak stem from the basically different uses made of wheat on the one hand and of oats and barley on the other. Wheat is pre-eminently a grain for human consumption, "the staff of life," the most efficient and economical foodstuff known to the human race. About three bushels out of every four of the Canadian crop are consumed as food by people at home and abroad and, of the balance, about half is required for seeding the next crop. The great bulk of the crop — on the average over eighty per cent — must be moved across interprovincial and international boundaries. Consequently the federal government can, under its legal responsibilities, regulate and have effective control of the wheat trade as a whole.

Oats and barley, on the other hand, are pre-eminently animal feed crops. Human use, including porridge, beer and whisky, amounts to less than two per cent of the oats crop and five per cent of the barley crop of Canada. In fact, only about thirty per cent of the oats and forty per cent of the barley ever leave the farms on which they are grown, except in the form of livestock. A large proportion of these grains that leave the farm are sold as feed or seed to other farmers. In recent years only about twenty per cent of the prairie oat and barley crops have moved, under the government's freight assistance policy, to eastern Canada or to British Columbia. Incidentally this is a far greater proportion of the crop than had ever moved out of the prairie provinces prior to the initiation of the government's freight assistance policy.

Normally a relatively insignificant portion of these crops moves into export. In short, the movement of oats and barley is from farmer to farmer. This presents peculiar problems in establishing and maintaining prices which would be accepted as fair in both the east and west, under a federal government monopoly of interprovincial trade. To put it another way; while the wheat board is handling wheat it is primarily concerned — to quote the Canadian Wheat Board Act — with "promoting the sale of grain, produced in Canada, in world markets." The wheat board, in handling oats and barley, would be concerned primarily with sales of western grain to eastern farmers, at prices that both seller and buyer will consider fair and reasonable. I am informed that at a recent meeting of the Canadian federation of agriculture this possible conflict of interest between farmer buyers and farmer sellers was recognized. . . .

The point I am making is that while wheat, oats and barley are all classed as grains, their marketing, from the point of view of their place in the whole mechanism of production and trade, as well as their use and customary manner of handling, are quite different and distinct. This raises not only practical marketing problems but also constitutional questions. As my colleague the Minister of Justice (Mr. Ilsley) observed last year, speaking of the dominion government entering this field alone — if I may be allowed to paraphrase him — a scheme that would work for oats and barley would not be constitutional, and a constitutional scheme would not work.

It is with this dilemma in mind that we are introducing the present legislation. There is no question of the dominion's constitutional authority to regulate interprovincial trade or export trade in oats and barley, but there is very considerable doubt as to whether that limited power would in itself provide effective control of commodities which are so largely marketed locally. This amendment to the wheat board act will open the door as far as the federal government is concerned. The next step will be to determine whether the three provincial governments most directly concerned — that is, in the prairie provinces — wish to join with us in placing compulsory regulation of the trade in oats and barley in the hands of the wheat board.

Presumably this could be done most conveniently by use of the device known as "conjoint" or "complementary" legislation. The device of "enabling" legislation, once employed in a number of fields of agricultural production marketing, has been held ultra vires by the privy council as a method of delegating provincial powers to the dominion. Co-operative arrangements have, however, been worked out and given the force of law in several fields of agricultural marketing, by "conjoint" or "complementary" legislation. In such cases the province or provinces concerned that wish to take advantage of the dominion legislation pass directly whatever complementary legislation is necessary and within their power, and appoint the dominion administrative agents as provincial agents as well. This may perhaps indicate a path for provincial co-operation which must be a preliminary to bringing this legislation into force.

The government is prepared to take whatever steps lie within its power to assist in establishing marketing arrangements that will help to maintain economic and stable prices for Canadian agricultural products. The government must, however, be satisfied that any given scheme for this purpose is a practical one, a constitutional one, a workable one and one that will command the support of the interested groups concerned. Until it is satisfied that these conditions have been met, the government will not be prepared to undertake the marketing of oats and barley through the wheat board. It will be noted in the resolution that marketing arrangements shall come into force only at the beginning of a crop year. I believe the attitude of the government in this regard will be understood by all hon. members who are familiar with grain marketing and related agricultural problems.[5]

During the debate, Mr. J. A. Ross (Souris) moved an amendment to divide the bill into several bills which would have permitted separate consideration of the oats and barley clause but which, for technical reasons was ruled out of order.[6]

HOWE CORRESPONDENCE WITH DOUGLAS AND GARSON

The Honourable Stuart Garson, premier of Manitoba, had initially supported legislation by the federal house but he found himself in a considerable quandary over Mr. Howe's declaration that the oats and barley amendment would also require complementary provincial legislation. He was also caught in the middle of the controversy between the pools and the trade. Accordingly, Garson initiated a public correspondence with Howe which provided fuel for the debate on the amendment until it received royal assent.

Unlike Garson, the Honourable T. C. Douglas, premier of Saskatchewan, had no such difficulty as he wrote to Howe asking for a draft of the federal

[5] *House of Commons Debates*, February 27, 1948, pp. 1677-1678.
[6] *Ibid.*, February 27, 1948, p. 1681, and March 11, 1948, pp. 2112-2113.

bill and for the form of complementary provincial legislation Howe would like to have passed. Howe sent Douglas a very straightforward reply on March 4, 1948:

> I have referred to the Department of Justice your recent request for a draft of approved legislation for the control of the marketing of oats and barley within Saskatchewan to be complementary to the proposed amendments to the Canadian Wheat Board Act. I am informed that the control of the marketing of oats and barley within a Province can be established under Provincial legislation by several different methods, and that the necessary Provincial statute can take one of several forms, depending on the scheme of control to be employed. As you know, it is contemplated that complementary legislation for this purpose should be passed not only in Saskatchewan but in other Provinces, and it is felt that the controls to be established by the Provinces should be uniform in form and effect in each Province, and that such Provinces should mutually agree to the duration and form of the Provincial legislation.
>
> I feel that it is the responsibility of the Provinces, rather than the Dominion, to select the form and to determine the duration of the legislation and the form of the controls to be established in relation to the marketing of oats and barley within each Province. Until the Provinces have agreed to a uniform scheme of control and have determined the duration of that scheme, it does not seem advisable for consideration to be given to the drafting of a statute for any one Province. When such agreement has been reached, I feel that a uniform statute can be prepared by the legal advisers to the Provinces.
>
> I have discussed the subject of complementary legislation with Mr. R. H. Milliken, K.C. of Regina, solicitor for the Saskatchewan Wheat Pool, who seems to be thoroughly familiar with the problems involved.[7]

On March 16, 1948, Garson in turn addressed a lengthy letter to Howe which was couched in political overtones. In it he upbraided Howe for not consulting him on the issue, and he asked for a copy of the legal opinion on which the need for complementary legislation had been established. Then he pointed out that ever since P.C. 7942 of October 12, 1943, had created a monopoly board, the latter had been an agency of the crown, subject to government direction in pricing rather than the agent of producers and selling to their best advantage. Garson continued:

> ... What we would like to know is whether in the legislation which you will ask us to complement, these same principles or policies will be followed with regard to oats and barley? Is the Wheat Board to be the agent of the producer of oats and barley charged with the responsibility of securing the best price possible in all available outlets? Or is the Board to be the agency of the Government, buying oats and barley at a price set by the Government for reasons not necessarily related to, and even incompatible with, the securing of the best price? Is the price to be set for example, at a certain level to keep down the cost of living in Canada or to provide livestock raisers with feed at a reasonable figure? In this latter case if the Wheat Board fixed a price for oats and barley below what they can be sold for, will the resulting loss be left with the producer of oats and barley? Or will this loss be paid by the whole Canadian people? To put this in another way, will it be the policy of the Wheat Board in handling oats and barley to hold down the price to the buyer of them by open or hidden subsidies? If so, who will pay the subsidies, the

---

[7] *Privy Council Office files.* For the complete Howe-Douglas correspondence, see *House of Commons Debates,* March 12, 1948, pp. 2172-2173.

producer of oats and barley or the Federal Government representing and taking the whole body of the Canadian people?

At the present time our export trade in oats and barley is shut off by a general export ban. Some of our traditional markets for oats and barley, particularly malting barley, have been passed by for sometime in the interests of maintaining a supply of feed grains in Canada in order to meet the requirements of the British contracts and our domestic needs in the production of animal products. Our trade to Great Britain is regulated by government agreements which fix our prices for our wheat, beef, pork, poultry and dairy products. As long as these conditions continue, it would be relatively easy for the Wheat Board to set the price for oats and barley; for the Wheat Board could not get any greater price than these government policies will make possible, even if it were acting as the agent of the producer of oats and barley. But the price so determined would not necessarily be fair to the producer and could be most unfair.

Let us suppose, however, that the time comes when it is impossible or unwise to renew these British contracts and to maintain this export ban. In such a case we should have to seek a re-establishment of our former export markets for oats and barley and their products. If at that time the Wheat Board were the agent of the producer of oats and barley, it would be under obligation to get for him the best price available for his oats and barley in the export and Canadian markets. If, on the contrary, the Wheat Board were the agent of the Government, the Wheat Board would fix the price in accordance with the Government's instructions; but, with export markets available, surely it would do so in some kind of relation to market prices in the export and Canadian markets? In such event, under your proposed policy and legislation, who will defray the difference, if any, between the market price and the Wheat Board price, the nation or the producer of oats and barley? . . .[8]

The letter continued in like vein as Garson posed seven questions of detail and ended by asking why complementary legislation was not being required from Ontario and Quebec. Without it eastern farmers could sell their own feed grains at high prices and replace them by price-controlled western grain.

Howe replied to Garson on March 20:

I wish to acknowledge your letter of March 16 with reference to complementary legislation to Bill 135, which is presently before Parliament.

I believe that the facts in support of this legislation are as well known to you as they are to me. The Canadian Federation of Agriculture, purporting to represent the views of the considerable majority of farmers in Western and Eastern Canada, has recommended the placing of the marketing of coarse grains under the Canadian Wheat Board. In our discussions with the Canadian Federation of Agriculture, they have indicated the need of complementary legislation by the legislatures of the three Prairie Provinces, and have urged the early passage of legislation on our part in order that the provincial legislatures may act while they are presently in session.

I have no doubt that the representations that have been made to the federal government have also been made to the government of Manitoba. As a matter of policy, so far as the federal government is concerned, we have made our decision as indicated by the introduction of Bill 135 and by my statement from which you have quoted. Your policy in the light of these representations is a matter for the government of Manitoba to decide, and any ensuing complementary legislation is a matter for your decision.

[8]Province of Manitoba, *Manitoba's Position on Oats and Barley Marketing,* 1948.

In general reply to your questions regarding administration, I might say that we would look to the Canadian Federation of Agriculture to recommend prices for oats and barley satisfactory both to producers and feeders. In respect of your detailed questions of administration, however, these are matters of government decision to be announced in due course.[9]

Howe's reply was intentionally of cold comfort to Garson and the latter wrote back on March 23:

Thank you for your letter of March 20th, 1948.

You say that the facts in support of your bill 135 are as well-known to me as they are to you. Unfortunately this is not so. These facts are not well-known to us. Contrary to your impression, no representations whatever in this matter have been made to the Government of Manitoba by the Canadian Federation of Agriculture. That is our difficulty. We do not have facts.

Since you and I are exceedingly busy I would not have troubled you with my long letter of March 16th, if there were any other authoritative source from which I could get the information which we must have if we are to deal with this important matter in an intelligent manner. I do not know of any other person who could speak upon this matter with as great authority as yourself, both as the responsible Minister and as the sponsor of federal bill 135.

You are quite right in stating that our policy is a matter for the Government of Manitoba to decide, and that any ensuing complementary legislation is also a matter for our decision. But before we complement your bill 135 with provincial legislation which will substantially affect many thousands of farm homes in Manitoba, we must know the facts in order that we may judge whether the legislation which you propose that we should conjointly provide, is adequate and workable. No one has consulted us concerning this legislation on which our co-operation is sought. We do not stand on any ceremony in this regard, but surely we are entitled to ask for a statement of facts and policy. Otherwise it would appear that we are to blindly endorse as an accomplished fact a policy in which we have had no say, based upon facts undisclosed to us.

Your letter of March 20th is not completely helpful. For example, if, as you state, you are passing this legislation because the Canadian Federation of Agriculture asked you to do so, one would think that your legislation would be based upon the principles stressed in the Brockville resolution of the Canadian Federation of Agriculture. One of these principles is contained in the second sentence of that resolution, which reads:

"That such legislation be based upon the principle that the Wheat Board shall be an agency operating primarily for the benefit and in the interests of grain producers."

There is no indication in your speech or in your letter or in the bill itself that it is your policy that the Wheat Board in handling oats and barley shall be an agency operating primarily for the benefit and in the interests of the grain producers. On the contrary, as nearly as we can gather from bill 135, a copy of which I saw for the first time only yesterday, it is provided in Section 29A(1) —

"The Governor-in-Council may by regulation extend the application of Part III or of Part IV or of both Parts III and IV to oats or to barley or to both oats and barley."

This seems to indicate that the Wheat Board as it is now constituted would take control of oats and barley. As I pointed out in my letter of March 16th, the Wheat Board as now constituted is not an agency operating primarily for the benefit and in the interests of the grain producers.

Your letter states that you plan to look to the Canadian Federation of Agriculture to recommend prices for oats and barley satisfactory to both the producers and feeders. But we note that there is no provision to this effect in your bill 135. If you are prepared to amend the bill to provide that prices for oats and barley should be set upon the recommendation of the Canadian Federation of Agriculture, and if that body which is representative of both growers and feeders were prepared to accept this responsibility, these facts would be a most important factor which we would want to take into consideration. Are you willing to include such a provision in your bill? Have you inquired whether the Canadian Federation of Agriculture is willing to accept this responsibility? This is exactly the kind of information which we require in properly discharging our own responsibility. If the price so recommended happened to be a price less than would otherwise be available, do you plan to leave the loss of the difference upon the producers of oats and barley or to make it good from the Federal Treasury? This is not a detailed question of administration. This is a fundamental matter of principle without information upon which no provincial legislature can intelligently or honestly deal with this matter.

Again when we ask for a copy of the legal opinion upon which you base your view that complementary provincial legislation is essential, we are making a serious, and we think, a reasonable request, which was suggested to us by the legal counsel whom we have asked to advise us in this matter. What is the purpose of this arrangement which we are considering? Is it not the setting up of a government board which amongst other things will fix the prices of oats and barley and allocate them as between export and domestic use? On both pricing and allocation there is a distinct conflict of interest between those who grow oats and barley and those who purchase them for feeding and other purposes. The making of decisions under political auspices upon these potentially controversial points is bound to be attended with some difficulty. Once Manitoba is tied into this business by means of complementary legislation, Manitoba citizens—and rightly so—will look to us to see that without being unfair to any other Canadians, the interests of Manitoba farmers are protected. If you have a legal opinion with which our law officers can concur that complementary provincial legislation is really essential and if at some later stage this scheme does not work out as satisfactorily as planned, we can by repealing our provincial legislation withdraw our citizens from its operation. For this and other reasons we are very much interested in such an opinion. That is why we ask you for a copy of it.

It is for similar reasons that we think it not unreasonable to ask you to let us have a copy of the legal opinion, if any, which you have, indicating that although complementary provincial legislation is required in Alberta, Saskatchewan and Manitoba, it is not required in Ontario and Quebec, where oats and barley in large quantities are also grown, purchased and consumed.

We have no objection to going elsewhere for this information if there were another more authoritative source, but as there is not, I must respectfully press for a reply to my questions.[10]

In response, Howe shifted his defence of the complementary legislation requirement from legal to political grounds. The federal government had done its part by passing the federal legislation. It need not be proclaimed in

---

[10]*Ibid.*

the absence of complementary legislation, but the Manitoba government could answer to the Manitoba federation of agriculture if it withheld action. Howe wrote on March 25:

> Thank you for your letter of March 23rd, which I have read with care.
>
> Bill 135 has now been enacted into law, to be proclaimed after the conditions set out in my speech on the Resolution have been complied with. It seems to me that this Government has discharged its immediate responsibility in the matter, and should not be called upon to advise other governments in the matter of complementary legislation.
>
> You ask for a copy of the legal opinion upon which we base our view that complementary provincial legislation is essential. This would seem to be a policy matter rather than a legal matter. Representations made to us indicated that those sponsoring government marketing were themselves convinced that complementary legislation is necessary to produce a workable plan, and my own study of the matter confirms this opinion. The position of the Federal legislation is not in doubt. Further, there is no doubt that Federal legislation cannot control marketing of oats and barley within a Province.
>
> Complementary legislation in Alberta, Saskatchewan and Manitoba is required to make Wheat Board prices effective. Provincial legislation in Ontario is desirable, but perhaps not necessary, as the competitor situation as between Western coarse grains and Eastern coarse grains will tend to hold prices in line.
>
> The next step of this Government will be to review the position in early July with the Canadian Federation of Agriculture, in order to determine whether the then existing situation warrants proclamation of Bill 135.
>
> It seems to me that the above is all the information that I can usefully give you at this time.[11]

Garson published the exchange of correspondence with Howe, and defended his position in a radio address.

DEBATE ON SECOND READING

Debate on second reading of bill 135 to amend the Canadian wheat board act commenced on March 12, 1948. In order to foreshorten the anticipated length of the debate, Howe offered at the outset to divide the bill into two separate bills at the appropriate time when it reached the committee of the whole. This would have facilitated due consideration of the oats and barley clause. Nevertheless, a lively debate ensued until March 19 when the bill received second reading. Thereupon Howe moved the split but only a handful of Liberals supported him, as did the Progressive-Conservative and Social Credit opposition. The CCF party and a majority of the Liberals voted to defeat the motion.[12] Inside and outside the house, Howe was accused of engineering the defeat.[13] Yet in keeping his whole package intact, Howe ensured the acceptance of the oats and barley clause. The bill embracing all amendments to the wheat board act was then examined in committee of the whole, following which it received third reading on March 19.

DEBATE IN THE SENATE

With Easter adjournment only two days away, the bill was read for the first time in the senate on March 22. Special consent was required to proceed

[11]*Ibid.*
[12]*House of Commons Debates,* March 19, 1948, pp. 2411-2412.
[13]*Winnipeg Free Press,* March 23, 1948.

with second reading on March 23. In the debate, the Honourable T. A. Crerar and the Honourable Norman Lambert, both Liberals, joined the leader of the opposition, the Honourable John T. Haig, in their objections to the oats and barley clause. Lambert and Crerar made eloquent speeches in defence of the Liberal philosophy of free enterprise.

Crerar's record on his position was impressive. In the house of commons in 1920 he had declared himself as being entirely opposed to any permanent policy involving control of the marketing of grain.[14] In 1923 he had advised the United farmers of Manitoba that nothing could be done by government boards which could not be done better by co-operation.[15] The co-operative company whose policy he had guided from 1907 to 1929 had consistently defended the open market system against the consensus for board marketing which emerged among other co-operative organizations. As a minister of the crown he had acquiesced in the creation of a monopoly board in the particular circumstances of 1943, but he reasonably expected that the need for it would be temporary. In 1946 when the proposed bilateral contract implied an extension of monopoly control over the marketing of wheat, Crerar interceded through Norman Robertson as his colleagues, Norman Lambert and Norman Paterson, protested in writing to Mackenzie King.[16] Now that monopoly marketing was being extended to oats and barely, the three tried their utmost to defeat the measure in the senate.

After debate on March 23, the bill was referred to the senate committee on banking and commerce where it was discussed that evening and on the following morning. Both Howe and George McIvor, chief commissioner of the wheat board, were called as witnesses. Howe answered questions on government policy and McIvor those that related to the current board operations and the way in which the board might undertake the marketing of oats and barley. During the hearings, Crerar and Lambert recruited enough support to have the bill reported back with a recommendation that the oats and barley clause be deleted, which the committee approved by a 15-8 vote.[17]

That afternoon, when the committee's decision was reported to the senate, it fell to the government house leader, the Honourable Wishart Robertson, to rally support for rejection of the report. At the end of the debate he succeeded by a 25-17 margin but, in doing so, he watched nine of his fellow Liberals cast their votes with the meager opposition. The Liberals who voted aginst the oats and barley clause were W. A. Buchanan (Lethbridge), Thomas A. Crerar (Churchill), W. D. Euler (Waterloo), J. P. Howden (St. Boniface), A. K. Hugessen (Inkerman), G. Lacosse (Essex), Norman P. Lambert (Ottawa), Norman McL. Paterson (Thunder Bay), and Cairine R. Wilson (Rockcliffe).[18] For the most part the 25 Liberal senators who supported the clause were identified with the deficit-feeding areas. Now that the issue was settled, the bill received third reading and the

14See p. 169.
15See pp. 201-202.
16See pp. 863-864.
17*Senate Debates*, March 24, 1948, p. 309.
18*Ibid.*, p. 316.

Canadian wheat board amendment act, 1948, received royal assent on the evening of March 24, immediately prior to the Easter recess.

As a postscript to the policy confrontaion which had arisen in the senate, Mackenzie King recorded the following in his diary:

> At the H of C, had a talk with Wishart Robertson who told me that in the Banking Commerce Committee, Howe had lobbied against the clause re handling of coarse grains by the Wheat Board. Had the clause deleted from the Bill. Robertson had been terribly put out. Said he had spoken very strongly to Howe who had admitted that he had 'phoned to Lambert or Crerar to take this course which was a frightful thing for him to have done but he had since told Howe that he would have to tell them they must support the Bill in the Senate. He asked my advice as to whether he should let the Bill come over to our House — have the clause reinserted or fight for reinsertion of the clause at the start. I told him to adopt the latter course. Let it be known that he had talked with me and that the govt. wanted this measure through.
>
> Robertson made a successful fight. In the House, when the Bill had carried, Howe came and told me that he had spoken to several to make sure that it would be carried. I do not like that sort of thing.[19]

The Honourable Wishart Robertson, minister without portfolio and government leader in the senate, had been understandably upset by the opposition to a government bill which Liberal senators like Crerar, Lambert, Paterson and Euler had engendered. If, in his confrontation with Howe, Robertson had implicated him in the insurrection, Howe may easily have responded in characteristic fashion to his cabinet colleague by going on the offensive. Undoubtedly a contretemps had flared up between the two, but it is hard to lend credence to the charge that Howe was quietly manoeuvring defeat of the bill, however much the latter offended his personal convictions. Howe's record in piloting the bill through the house and in his testimony before the senate committee on banking and commerce was one of unqualified sponsorship of the controversial measure which he had agreed in cabinet to give when Mackenzie King had concluded that the measure must go through.

Moreover, Senators Crerar, Lambert, Paterson, Euler and the others were in no need of prompting from Howe to defend their lifelong principles. They would have done so in whatever event. Their Liberal philosophy which championed free enterprise against the encroachment of what they considered to be socialism actually had its principal protagonist in Mackenzie King, except when the overriding threat of political consequences persuaded him to bend with the wind.

PROVINCIAL LEGISLATION

After receiving Howe's letter of March 4, 1948, Premier T. C. Douglas proceeded forthwith to enact provincial legislation. In Saskatchewan, the coarse grain marketing control act received royal assent on March 25. The substantive provisions of the act were very simple. Section 4(1) provided that:

> No producer shall sell ... grain ... for delivery within the province to any person other than the Canadian Wheat Board.

[19]*King Diary,* March 24, 1948.

Section 4(2) made an exception for farm-to-farm transactions for feeding purposes:

> Notwithstanding the provisions of subsection (1) a producer may sell . . . for delivery to a producer or to an owner of live stock or poultry within the province.[20]

No legislative action was taken in 1948 in the provinces of Alberta and Manitoba, however, and the western conference of the Canadian federation of agriculture which met in Saskatoon on January 20-22, 1949, reverted to the matter by passing the following resolution:

> Be it resolved that a joint effort be made to enable the Canadian wheat board to be the sole marketing agency of coarse grains, and that any legislation giving the Canadian wheat board the same exclusive powers over the marketing of other grains as it now exercises over wheat, shall be based on the principle that the Canadian wheat board shall be an agency operating for the benefit and in the interest of grain producers, with a duty to sell grain for the best available price whether in export or domestic markets, and shall not be used as an instrument of government control domestic policy; but full recognition of the importance of the livestock industry shall be given by the government of Canada, and that the government shall take adequate measures to establish necessary reserves of feed grains whenever such action is deemed necessary.[21]

The resolution was approved by the Canadian federation of agriculture at its annual meeting, January 24-28, 1949. Then, on February 21, Howe received a delegation from the western members of the federation and also the three western premiers to discuss the coarse grains marketing policy. The pool leaders wanted to know if the federal government, in proclaiming the coarse grains amendment to the Canadian wheat board act, would meet its "letter and the spirit". Also, they wished to know whether the federal government still considered it necessary for the provinces to enact complementary legislation. Howe, in turn, stood his ground on the need for provincial legislation, and he baulked at the apparent ambiguity in the federation's resolution which would have required the wheat board to sell coarse grains to best advantage on behalf of producers, on the one hand, while on the other the federal government would be expected to protect the livestock industry. Either the pools could accept wheat board responsibility for selling to best advantage without further obligation on the federal government or they could set up co-operative marketing pools on their own. As Howe explained the government's position to the house on March 14, 1949:

> The resolution forwarded by the Canadian Federation of Agriculture, which has been carefully reviewed, is not acceptable to the Government. In the first place, if this resolution is intended to suggest that the Canadian wheat board as now constituted does not function in the best interests of the Canadian producers, this is a suggestion which I strenuously deny. Further, this resolution by its terms is contradictory, in that it would, on the one hand, require the board to sell "for the best available price whether in export or domestic markets" and at the same time to the "full recognition of the importance of the livestock industry".

---

[20]*Statutes of Saskatchewan,* 12 George VI, Chap. 66, assented to March 25, 1948.
[21]*House of Commons Debates,* March 14, 1949, p. 1421.

In discussing the marketing of crops that are largely consumed within Canada, it is obvious that the government of Canada cannot give any undertaking that it will become responsible for marketing coarse grains solely in the interests of the producer, and without regard to the interests of the consumer of those products. If the coarse grain producers of western Canada are not satisfied that the wheat board, as now constituted, is a satisfactory marketing agency for their coarse grains, then an obvious alternative is for the producers of coarse grains in western Canada to establish their own marketing agency. My colleague, the Minister of Agriculture, has on the order paper legislation designed to complement the marketing legislation of provincial governments. Under such legislation, the producers can themselves establish a board to sell "for the best available price, whether in export or domestic markets". This assumes that to obtain "the best available price, whether in export or domestic markets," is in fact always in the best interest of the producers, which in my opinion is questionable, to say the least.

If, on the other hand, the westen producers wish to market their oats and barley through the Canadian wheat board, and provided that their provincial governments will enact the necessary legislation, this government's position has not changed since I introduced Bill 135 in response to specific requests then made by the farm organizations.[22]

The upshot was that the Alberta and Manitoba governments passed complementary legislation in identical form to that already passed in Saskatchewan. Royal assent was given to the Alberta act on March 29, 1949, and to the Manitoba act on April 22, 1949. In the meantime, the Honourable Stuart Garson had resigned as premier of Manitoba to accept the justice portfolio in Ottawa when Mr. St. Laurent became prime minister. The Honourable Douglas Campbell succeeded Garson as premier, and he put through the Manitoba legislation.

APPLICATION OF THE WHEAT BOARD ACT TO OATS AND BARLEY

With the enactment of the Manitoba legislation the way was clear for the federal government to place the marketing of oats and barley exclusively in the hands of the board. On July 20, 1949, P.C. 3713 extended parts III and IV of the Canadian wheat board act to oats and barley for the 1949-50 crop year commencing August 1. The governments of Manitoba, Saskatchewan and Alberta followed suit by proclaiming their legislation. On July 20, Mr. Howe issued the following press release:

> Effective August 1st, 1949, oats and barley produced in the three Prairie Provinces will be marketed through an oats pool and a barley pool operated by the Canadian Wheat Board, it was announced today by the Right Honourable C. D. Howe, Minister of Trade and Commerce.
>
> Initial payments will be made on the basis of the 1949-50 support prices announced by the Dominion Government on March 15th, 1949, less all charges before delivery in store Fort William or Port Arthur. The 1949-50 support prices announced last March were 61½ cents for oats and 90 cents for barley basis No. 1 Feed grades in store Fort William or Port Arthur.
>
> In explaining the adjustments to be made in determining the new initial payments Mr. Howe pointed out that deductions would include an allowance of 1½ cents per bushel on oats and 3 cents per bushel on barley, this to constitute a reserve against country carrying charges and pool operating

[22]*Ibid.*

expenses to the Lakehead. Mr. Howe said that total deductions under the pool system including the reserve of 1½ cents for oats and 3 cents for barley would be about equivalent to deductions which have been made at country elevators under the price support policy.

The Dominion Government guarantees a minimum return to the oats and barley pools of 61½ cents for oats and 90 cents for barley on the basis of No. 1 Feed grades in store Fort William or Port Arthur for the total handling of the pools.

The Canadian Wheat Board will establish related initial payments for other grades of western oats and barley and these will be announced before the end of July. These will include initial payments for the basic grades of oats and barley set forth in Section IV (a) of The Canadian Wheat Board Act. These basic grades are for oats, Grade No. 2 Canada Western, for which the initial payment will be 65 cents per bushel basis in store Fort William or Port Arthur, after deduction of the allowance; and for barley, Grade No. 3 Canada Western Six Row, for which the initial payment will be 93 cents per bushel on the same basis.

Producers will receive the established intial payments at the time of delivery and sale of their oats and barley to the Board. At the same time they will receive a producer's certificate covering the quantities and grades so delivered and sold, which entitles producers to share in any surpluses accumulated by the Board in the sale of oats and barley delivered to the Board between August 1st, 1949 and July 31st, 1950.

Mr. Howe stated that both the Government and the Board had given consideration to the manner in which selection premiums would be paid to producers for special qualities of western oats and barley. It has been decided that the Board will purchase oats and barley on the basis of initial payments applicable to the established grades and that special quality premiums will be reflected to producers by handling companies in the same manner as in the past. The producer should therefore make his own arrangements with the handling companies for malting and other premiums, The Canadian Wheat Board being responsible only for the basic grade price.

Mr. Howe said that The Canadian Wheat Board would shortly be announcing further plans in respect to the handling of oats and barley in 1949-50, but in general it is the intention of the Board to use existing facilities for the distribution of these grains.

On August 1st, 1949, Parts III and IV of The Canadian Wheat Board Act will be brought into force by The Canadian Wheat Board Regulations approved by the Governor-in-Council. The authorities in the three Prairie Provinces will be consulted with a view to having their Acts proclaimed.[23]

BOARD SALES POLICY

The original proposal that the Canadian federation of agriculture recommend the prices at which the board shall sell oats and barley held promise of reconciling the conflicting interests of producers and users but, if it did nothing more it would have created a strain within the federation, and the board fell back upon recommending that it follow the intention of the wheat board act in selling to producers' best advantage. In order to do so, the board still needed a price indicator, which could most readily be provided by the futures market. Once the market had absorbed the outstanding stocks of oats and barley, however, the board would become the dominant seller of futures and could make or break futures prices by its operations.

[23] *Report of the Canadian Wheat Board,* Crop Year 1949-1950 pp. 10-11.

Accordingly, in regulating the flow of sales to the market, the board could only be guided by the trend in United States market and by the cost of imported feed grain, mainly corn. On August 4, 1949, the board issued a statement on its sales policy:

> At this time the Board has the following comments to make in regard to the sale of oats and barley:
>
> (1) The Board intends to sell oats and barley freely and to the best advantage, using the methods which suit these purposes;
>
> (2) The Board will sell oats and barley to dealers and others for distribution to users of these grains;
>
> (3) The Board recognizes that there are stocks of old crop oats and barley in Canada which are not the property of the Board and which are in the process of being marketed by the present holders.
>
> With these considerations in mind, the Board will use the sales procedures which it considers desirable and advantageous. The Board will use the futures market in the selling of oats and barley. At the same time, the Board is prepared to make outright sales of oats and barley in store Fort William/Port Arthur where buyers wish to purchase on this basis. To give effect to this policy, the Board will quote prices for principal grades of oats and barley basis in store Fort William/Port Arthur. The Board will also establish prices of oats and barley for sale at country points in Western Canada and for shipment to British Columbia. These Board sale prices will be on a Fort William/Port Arthur basis.
>
> It will be appreciated that the Board is concerned only with oats and barley delivered by producers on and after August 1st, 1949. It will therefore be several weeks before the Board has stocks of oats and barley available at the Lakehead. However, the Board is prepared to sell limited quantities of cash oats and barley for delivery at the Lakehead in forward positions and the Board will also sell futures.[24]

Thus, the placing of oats and barley within the ambit of a monopoly grain board completed the structure of the Canadian wheat board's responsibilities, which continued without change for the next quarter of a century.

MANITOBA PLEBISCITE ON COARSE GRAIN MARKETING

After the Canadian wheat board had been marketing oats and barley for year and a half, Premier D. L. Campbell announced, on February 9, 1951, in the Manitoba legislature that his government would introduce legislation to provide a producer plebiscite on coarse grain marketing, with the vote to be taken as soon as possible after the results of the 1950-51 crop year sales by the board became known. In October, 1951, Premier Campbell announced that the plebiscite would be held on November 24, and the question to be put to a "yes" or "no" vote by qualified producers was worded as follows:

Do you wish to market your oats and barley as at present?

In due course, the results of the referendum were announced. Out of 51,803 eligible voters, 34,898 voted; 31,052 voted "yes", and 3,846 voted "no".

Although the holding of a plebiscite came as a surprise to the Manitoba farm organizations, they were not apprehensive about the way producers might vote, as the Manitoba federation of agriculture and co-operation

[24]*Ibid.*

organized a campaign in support of a "yes" vote. The only trade criticism of the plebiscite when the results were in, ran to the effect that the wording of the question put to producers did not afford them the option of voting for voluntary pools operated by the Board alongside an open market.[25]

[25]*Manitoba Co-operator,* February 15, October 18 and November 29, 1951.

45

1949-50 BILATERAL CONTRACT PRICE NEGOTIATION

As will be recalled from Chapter 43, the negotiation of the 1949-50 price, which needed also to take into account the "have regard to" clause, had commenced with Broadley's arrival in Washington for the special session of the international wheat council in January, 1948. Both governments were concerned that the fulfilment of the bilateral contract should not impede the international negotiations and, as a gesture toward that end, the British government had offered on February 19 a price $2 for the 1949-50 crop year and as a settlement of their obligations under the "have regard to" clause. The $2 price created no conflict with the proposed price range in the international agreement, but the Canadian government hastened to reply that it would necessarily not assure the fulfilment of Britain's obligation under clause 2 (b). The direct negotiations continued to drag on until it was finally decided in July, 1948, to let the determination of the 1949-50 price and the settlement take their course as originally provided in the contract which meant that they should be determined not later than December 31, 1948. Because the views of the two governments remained wide apart on the substance of the settlement to be made, nothing further transpired until Sir Stafford Cripps raised the matter that autumn.

Early in November, 1948, Sir Stafford Cripps wrote to the Honourable D. C. Abbott that he would like to settle the procedures for discussing British food purchases from Canada in 1949 involving the renegotiation of several other contracts and the price to be paid for wheat in 1949-50. Abbott replied on November 10 that the negotiations on bacon, eggs and cheese could commence immediately, but that the Canadian government was not yet in a position to discuss the wheat price. Gardiner would do that later and was prepared to go to London early in December. This varied the procedure adopted a year earlier when all the contracts had been regarded as one package, and it did not please Cripps who agreed to negotiate forthwith on bacon, cheese and eggs but on condition that no approval of the contracts would be forthcoming until the wheat price was agreed. He also pointed out that all such agreements required ECA approval. Gardiner announced that agreement had been reached on the other contracts, however, as he addressed the dominion-provincial agricultural conference in Ottawa on December 8, 1948. On the same day, cabinet authorized Gardiner to proceed with the wheat negotiation on a basis of $2 for 1949-50 and an affirmation by the British government that the extent of its obligation under clause 2(b) would be the subject of further negotiation.

LONDON NEGOTIATIONS

Gardiner left immediately afterward for London and he invited his parliamentary assistant, Mr. Robert McCubbin, M. W. Mackenzie and C. F. Wilson to accompany him. The talks got under way on December 11, 1948, when Strachey presented a first offer of $1.75 for 1949-50, plus a floor of $1.40 on 100 million bushels in 1950-51 to be exercised at Canada's option if declared before April 30, 1950. This was the first attempt made from the British side to extend the settlement of clause 2(b) into 1950-51. Gardiner declined the offer on the grounds that (a) Canada could not agree to a 1949-50 price less than $2 while class 2 prices were still considerably above that level, (b) grain exchange critics had calculated Canadian losses already incurred under the contract at $320 million, which was more than the government was claiming. He believed agreement could be reached on a lower figure, and (c) Canada could not accept an option for 1950-51 which had to be exercised several months in advance of the crop year during which actual prices might entail further losses for Canadian producers. At that stage it was agreed that the officials should meet on Monday, December 13 to seek some common ground. When the meeting was held, however, the British officials had no authority to go beyond their opening position.

The meetings resumed on Wednesday, December 15, with Strachey, Gardiner and their officials present, but on this occasion the British team was augmented by treasury officials and Strachey declared that he was speaking for Cripps as well as himself. Strachey contended that the British could not accept an arithmetical approximation of the Canadian losses already incurred on the contract, and suggested if any sum were considered it would be added to the $1 floor for 1949-50 in the contract rather than to some arbitrary notion of what the world price might then be. Nevertheless, Gardiner proceeded to make such a calculation of the loss which, even if added to the floor, would justify a price of $2.50 in 1949-50.

At that meeting Mackenzie and Wilson were named to meet with two officials representing the ministry of food and the treasury to explore a solution to the "have regard to" obligation, by projecting purchase guarantees into the future. The results of that exploration were set out in the following draft:

> The Government of Canada and the Government of the United Kingdom having negotiated, as provided for in Paragraph 2(b) of the Anglo-Canadian Wheat Agreement dated July 24, 1946, the price to be paid for 140 million bushels of wheat, and wheat processed into flour, within the crop year 1949/50, and having taken into account the interest of both Governments in the satisfactory outcome of the forthcoming discussions for an International Wheat Agreement and the desirability that the settlement of the price to be paid in the crop year 1949/50 should not prejudice the free determination by importing and exporting countries of agreed international price ranges,
>
> are agreed that, irrespective of the outcome of those international discussions: —

(a) The United Kingdom Government shall purchase and the Canadian Government shall sell, within the crop year 1949/50, 140 million bushels of wheat including wheat processed into flour, as defined in the Anglo-Canadian Agreement and the Annexure thereto.

(b) The United Kingdom Government shall pay to the Canadian Government on the basis of Number One Manitoba Northern, in store Fort William/Port Arthur, Vancouver, or Churchill, a price $2.00 per bushel, for the quantity of wheat and flour referred to in (a) above.

(c) Should the average price at which Canadian wheat is sold for export, otherwise than under the Agreement of July 24, 1946, in 1949/50 fall below $1.50 per bushel, on the basis of Number One Manitoba Northern, in store Fort William/Port Arthur, Vancouver, or Churchill, the United Kingdom Government shall have made full and final discharge of all obligations arising under the terms of Paragraph 2(b) of the Agreement of July 24, 1946.

(d) Should the average price referred to in (c) above fall below $1.75 but not below $1.50, the United Kingdom Government shall undertake to purchase within the 1950/51 crop year at the option of the Canadian Government, which option shall be declared before August 15, 1950, (100) million bushels of wheat including such quantities of flour as may be agreed by August 15, 1950 at a price of ($1.40) per bushel, and the United Kingdom shall have made full and final discharge of all obligations arising under the terms of Paragraph 2(b) of the Agreement of July 24, 1946.

(e) Should the average price referred to in (c) above equal $1.75 or higher the United Kingdom Government in addition to the undertaking in (d) above shall undertake to purchase within the 1951/52 crop year, at the option of the Canadian Government, which option shall be declared before August 15, 1951, (100) million bushels of wheat including such quantity of flour as may be agreed by August 15, 1951, at a price of ($1.40) per bushel, and the United Kingdom Government shall have made full and final settlement of all obligations arising under the terms of Paragraph 2(b) of the Agreement of July 24, 1946.[1]

When Gardiner saw the first draft of that proposal, he foresaw little chance of its acceptance by his government. An improvement in the prices and quantities might help.

When Gardiner saw Strachey alone on December 17, Gardiner requested a further meeting with both Strachey and Cripps. This was arranged on December 18, and Cripps heard Gardiner's detailed proposal for an arthimetic calculation of not more than $100,000,000 in settlement of the "have regard to" clause. Cripps thereupon claimed that there had been no agreement that the British should take care of losses, and the ambiguity in the wording of clause 2(b) was now painfully apparent. Gardiner claimed that Cripps's interpretation was completely at variance with the verbal understanding he had reached with Strachey in June, 1946, and with Strachey's Winnipeg speech on February 25, 1947. Even when Cripps had been in Ottawa in September, 1948, no such interpretation as Cripps was now making, had been made. Had that been the understanding, Gardiner contended, the Canadian government would have been justified in cancelling the contract and reverting to the open market as had been proposed in November, 1947. Cripps replied by handing Gardiner the draft which had been worked out by the officials. As Gardiner observed, either of the options for 1950-51 and 1951-52 would have to be exercised in

[1]*Supporting Documents, Canada-United Kingdom Wheat Discussions, May, 1950.*

advance and without precise knowledge of the trend of prices and whether acceptance would incur further losses. In the circumstances, Gardiner said that he would have to report the British offer to the Canadian cabinet for consideration, and he made an appeal to Cripps to consult his colleagues and officials who had participated in the previous negotiations, because he was certain that Cripps would find his present interpretation of the meaning of clause 2(b) was at variance with the earlier understanding. As no agreement had been reached by the end of the London talks, Cripps offered to send a delegation to Ottawa to continue the negotiations.

When the cabinet considered the draft proposal on December 23, 1948, the ministers expressed concern over paragraph (c). If, in fact, average wheat prices fell to $1.50 in 1949-50, the additional 50 cents paid by the British on 140 million bushels would be calculated by producers to have produced $70,000,000 only in settlement of the "have regard to" clause. Therefore they wanted the option terms in paragraph (d) and (e) above to appear as favorable as possible. Hence they suggested that the price the British should pay, if the options were exercised, be raised to $1.55 from $1.40.

They also proposed that the quantity guarantees be raised from 100 to 140 million bushels. On December 24, the minister of external affairs wired Robertson to make as strong representations as he could in support of these changes. While these issues were still outstanding, the two governments agreed, on December 29, that the deadline for settlement should be extended from December 31, 1948 to January 15, 1949.

On January 6, 1949, Sir Alex Clutterbuck, British high commissioner called on Pearson to convey his government's rejection of the Canadian proposals in the following note:

United Kingdom Ministers have carefully considered the proposals put forward by the Canadian High Commissioner in London to the Chancellor of the Exchequer on the 24th December.

2. As regards **quantity**, United Kingdom Ministers feel that the request that this should be increased to 140 million bushels in the two options raises extreme difficulty, for the following reasons: —

(1) Total United Kingdom requirements of wheat and flour may be taken to be of the order of 220 million bushels of wheat. Of this quantity it is hoped to obtain 60 million bushels from Australia, and 20 million from the other non-dollar sources of supply. If we were committed to obtain the whole of the remaining balance of 140 million bushels from Canada, not only would our supply programme be deprived of any margin of flexibility but we should be placed in a very difficult position in relation to any International Wheat Agreement. Indeed, the effect would be that we should be virtually contracting out of the Agreement for a period of three years. This would be likely to meet strong objection from the United States, and the prospects of securing a satisfactory International Agreement might be fatally prejudiced.

(2) It is vitally important to us (and also, it is suggested, to Canada) that our wheat supplies from Canada should continue to be secured by off-shore purchases under E. R. P. An International Agreement would guarantee the Americans a market for an agreed quantity of wheat but it would not guarantee a price above the floor price. If the United Kingdom import programme were to be wholly committed in advance as in (1) above, and given also a continuance of heavy crops in the United States, it might well be that the Americans would be compelled to accept very low prices for any

wheat that was not covered by E. C. A. finance. In such circumtances the strain on the off-shore purchase system would clearly be insupportable.

(3) The conclusion is unavoidable that if we are to be assured of a continuance of E. C. A. finance for off-shore purchases of wheat from Canada, the quantities **to which we are committed in advance** must, in order to be proof against criticism from the United States standpoint, bear reasonably close relation to the pre-war volume of supply. During the years 1921-38 inclusive the average United Kingdom retained imports of wheat and flour from Canada were substantially less than 100 million bushels in terms of wheat equivalent.

Hence the insertion of the figure of 100 million bushels in the United Kingdom proposals, as the maximum figure likely to be acceptable from the standpoint of E. C. A. finance. The adoption of this figure would not of course mean that the United Kingdom would not in practice take more than 100 million bushels in any circumstances; it would, however, mean that the United Kingdom would not be committed in advance to take more than 100 million bushels, and that the question of filling the balance of its import requirements would be left to be determined in the light of supply and financial conditions at the time.

3. As regards **price**, on this head too the proposals of the Canadian Government raise serious difficulty. The price of $1.40 suggested by the United Kingdom Government in the two options is above the floor proposed in the draft International Wheat Agreement. To increase this price to $1.55 would raise it still further above the floor and would indeed introduce a new conception into the options.

The options were devised, in an effort to meet the Canadian Government, with the object of putting Canadian farmers in a specially favourable position compared with other producers by giving them a guaranteed floor price in the years in question higher than the floor proposed in the draft International Agreement. At the same time Canadian hands are not tied in any way. There is nothing to prevent Canada from seeking to sell at higher than floor price, and indeed there is no commitment on Canada's part to sell to the United Kingdom at all. Thus the options are heavily weighted in Canada's favour, the United Kingdom obligating herself to buy at a specially favourable floor price if Canada requires her to do so, but being left in a position of complete uncertainty as to her forward supply position.

To advance the proposed floor price to $1.55 would weight the options still more heavily in Canada's favour while leaving the United Kingdom in the same position of uncertainty. Moreover, a **floor** price of $1.55 would be wholly out of line not only with the contemplated floor prices in the International Wheat Agreement, but also with any realistic estimate of world supply prospect in eighteen months' time.

4. In these circumstances United Kingdom Ministers feel that, if difficulties are seen in the proposals communicated to Mr. Gardiner in London, a solution might best be found in an alternative line of approach.

For the reasons stated they fear that there would be serious risk of difficulty with the United States over the provision of E. C. A. finance if the quantities envisaged were to be in excess of 100 million bushels. In order, however, to meet the Canadian Government they would be prepared, if what follows is acceptable, to agree to a figure of 120 million bushels for 1950-51 while leaving the figure of 100 million bushels for 1951-52, and they would do their utmost to justify these figures to the E. C. A.

If an increase in price to $1.55 is desired, it is clear to United Kingdom Ministers that this could only be justified and defended to E. C. A. and to other signatories of the proposed International Wheat Agreement if the proposal was not an entirely one-sided one, related only to a floor price, but carried with it an obligation on the part of Canada to sell as well as an obligation on the part of the United Kingdom to buy. Even so, while they would be prepared on this basis and in order to achieve a settlement, to envisage a price of $1.55 for 1950-51, they do not feel that they could reasonably go further than $1.45 for 1951-52 when the supply position may be expected to be very substantially easier.

5. Accordingly they would urge on the Canadian Government the merits settlement on the following lines, the proposition to be considered as a whole: —

(1) Payment of $2.00 for 140 million bushels in 1949-50, the last year of the existing Agreement.

(2) A firm commitment on the part of the United Kingdom to buy, and on the part of Canada to sell, 120 million bushels in 1950-51 at a price of $1.55

(3) A firm commitment on the part of the United Kingdom to buy, and on the part of Canada to sell, 100 million bushels in 1951-52 at a price of $1.45.

(4) Recognition that on the above basis the obligations of the "have regard" clause in the existing Agreement will be fully satisfied.[2]

UNITED STATES INTERVENTION

That the United States government had a stake in the settlement terms was evidenced by the concern expressed in the British reply about American approval. By that time the great part of British wheat purchases from Canada was being financed by Marshall aid or economic co-operation administration funds allocated to the recipient allied governments for offshore purchases. The continued availability of these funds had already been jeopardized by the availability of wheat in the United States resulting from the large 1948 harvest. The American congress understandably could not be depended upon to continue to approve the use of ECA funds for offshore purchases if American wheat were to become in surplus supply. Such contingencies heightened Canadian interest in securing forward quantity commitments on British purchases. When the Americans were informed in January, 1948, of a possible settlement of the British obligation by means of quantity guarantees extending beyond 1949-50 the state department made representations to both the British and Canadian governments and, so far as the latter were concerned, the quantity guarantees were reluctantly dropped.

JANUARY 1949 DECISION TO POSTPONE THE SETTLEMENT

Because of the American representations, there was little left for the Canadian government to do beyond proposing that the price for 1949-50 be accepted, on condition that the whole question of the "have regard to" settlement be postponed for later consideration. Following a cabinet meeting on January 7, 1949, Prime Minister Louis St. Laurent called in Sir Alex Clutterbuck and made a proposal to that effect. By letter of January 12, 1949, Clutterbuck conveyed to St. Laurent the British government's reply:

[2] *Ibid.*

I reported at once to my Government the proposal which you put to me at our meeting on Friday, and I am happy to say that I have now been authorized to inform you that they are ready to agree in all the circumstances, and especially in view of the representations made by the United States authorities both in Washington and London, to leave the matter as you suggested.

It seems to United Kingdom Ministers that the following points arise: —

(1) Bearing in mind the terms of Article 7 of the Canadian/United Kingdom Wheat Agreement, Ministers regard it as very desirable, and they feel sure that the Canadian Government will agree, that we should take such steps as are possible to avoid having representations made by any of the Governments who will be represented at the forthcoming International Wheat Conference to the effect that, whatever may be the ceiling fixed for the purposes of the International Wheat Agreement (should one be negotiated) the Canadian price must be brought within that ceiling for the crop year 1949-50.

(2) In this connection my Government have in mind particularly the attitude of the other importing countries some of whom have already expressed interest in the price likely to be fixed for the fourth year of the Canadian/United Kingdom Agreement. Under the draft International Wheat Agreement of 1948 the other importing countries would have taken 320 million bushels out of the total of 500 million bushels and Canadian wheat to the amount of up to 90 million bushels would have gone to them. It is evident therefore that, if there is to be an International Wheat Agreement, the other importing countries will wish to feel that their freedom to negotiate ceiling and floor prices has not been prejudiced by the fixing of a $2.00 price for the last year of the Canadian/United Kingdom Agreement, and it seems to United Kingdom Ministers that the only way in which this can be assured is for the two Governments now to say plainly that, if prices under an International Wheat Agreement differ in 1949/50 from $2.00 this will subsequently be taken into account in making a final settlement of any balance of the United Kingdom obligation under the "have regard" clause.

(3) At one stage during the discussions with Mr. Gardiner in London the Canadian representatives handed to the United Kingdom representatives for consideration some pro forma clauses for an agreement of the kind we are now contemplating. These clauses are contained in the minutes held at Montagu House on the 14th December. It is not suggested that there should be any formal document of the kind then contemplated, but Ministers regard it as important that the two Governments should agree upon a joint announcement which will make it plain that United Kingdom agreement to pay $2.00 in 1949-50 will in certain circumstances be taken as having at least partly settled our "have regard" obligation. I enclose for your consideration a suggested text for such an announcement, which incorporates some part of the wording proposed by the Canadian representatives on the 14th December.

Accordingly, with the foregoing considerations in mind, I am asked to inform you that the United Kingdom Government agree to a price of $2.00 a bushel for 1949-50 and to your proposal that the question of liquidating the "have regard" clause should be left over for further discussion during 1949-50, on the understanding that both Governments make as plain as possible what they are doing by issuing simultaneously an announcement on the lines suggested above.

In this connection I have been instructed to add for the record that the United Kingdom Government do not regard the type of arithmetical calculation which was presented to them in the London discussions as forming a satisfactory basis for settling the "have regard" obligation. Accordingly, in the later negotiations, when the matter comes up again, they will hope to be able to reach agreement to link final liquidation of our obligation under the "have regard" clause, if any still remains, with the further purchases of wheat which we shall no doubt desire to make from Canada in subsequent years. In order to prevent any possible misunderstanding on this point I am asked to make it clear that in the view of Ministers it would not be satisfactory from the United Kingdom standpoint to have to make a further cash payment in respect of any of the wheat coming within the four years of the 1946 Agreement.

The next step is to agree upon the wording of a simultaneous announcement, and I should be most grateful if you would let me know whether the draft announcement enclosed is acceptable to you. It will of course be necessary to clear the agreed draft with E. C. A. before the announcement is issued by the two Governments, and I am in consultation with our representatives in Washington with a view to their standing ready to take this up immediately agreement on the wording has been reached between us.[3]

The draft announcement attached to Clutterbuck's letter read as follows:

Representatives of the United Kingdom and Canadian Government have had discussions on the price to be paid by the United Kingdom for Canadian wheat in 1949/50, the fourth and final year under the United Kingdom-Canadian Wheat Agreement of 1946. After taking account all relevant considerations, including the United Kingdom obligations under Clause 2(b) of the Agreement, the two Governments have agreed upon a price of $2.00 per bushel.

The two Governments have also agreed that their representatives shall meet not later than 31st July, 1950, to settle any obligations of the United Kingdom which may then still be outstanding under Clause 2(b) of the Agreement. The extent to which any such obligations will remain will depend largely upon the actual prices ruling for wheat during 1949/50. Further, in the event of an International Wheat Agreement operating in 1949/50, the two Governments are agreed that any excess of the price of $2.00 over the average price for wheat falling under the International Wheat Agreement shall be taken into account in the final settlement.[4]

On January 13, 1949, the prime minister replied to Clutterbuck as follows:

I have considered with my colleagues your letter of the 12th instant and the annexed draft of announcement regarding the wheat price for the crop year 1949-50.

With regard to the points numbered (1) and (2) in your letter, the Canadian government is in agreement. As for the point numbered (3) our government is pleased that the United Kingdom government agrees to a price of $2.00 per bushel on the understanding that the question of additional consideration under the "have regard to" clause should be deferred for settlement during 1949-50. We have noted that the present view in the United Kingdom is that they would prefer to link settlement of any obligation under the "have regard to" clause with further purchases of wheat in subsequent years rather than have to make a further cash payment in respect of any of the wheat delivered under the 1946 agreement.

[3] *Ibid.*
[4] *Ibid.*

As for the draft announcement, we suggest that the second sentence of the first paragraph be amended to read:

"After taking into account all relevant considerations, but without attempting to reach a final settlement of the United Kingdom obligations under Clause 2(b) of the agreement, the two governments have agreed upon a price of $2.00 per bushel."

We suggest further that the final sentence should be amended to read as follows:

"Further, whether or not an International Wheat Agreement is in operation during 1949-50, the two governments are agreed that any difference between the price of $2.00 per bushel and the average price at which Canadian wheat is sold for export outside the contract shall be taken into account in the final settlement."

Subject to these amendments, which have been included in the draft annexed hereto, we are prepared to issue the joint statement, and to regard it as expressing the terms of our agreement.[5]

St. Laurent's revised draft of the announcement attached to his letter ran as follows:

Representatives of the United Kingdom and Canadian Governments have had discussions on the price to be paid by the United Kingdom for Canadian wheat in 1949-50, the fourth and final year under the United Kingdom-Canadian Wheat Agreement of 1946. After taking into account all relevant considerations including but without attempting to reach a final settlement of the United Kingdom obligations under Clause 2(b) of the agreement, the two governments have agreed upon a price of $2.00 per bushel.

The two Governments have also agreed that their representatives shall meet not later than 31st July, 1950, to settle any obligations of the United Kingdom which may then still be outstanding under Clause 2(b) of the Agreement. The extent to which any such obligations will remain will depend largely upon the actual prices ruling for wheat during 1949-50. Further, whether or not an International Wheat Agreement is in operation during 1949-50, the two governments are agreed that any difference between the price of $2.00 per bushel and the average price at which Canadian wheat is sold for export outside the contract shall be taken into account in the final settlement.[6]

The draft was referred to the United States authorities who took exception to the clarification of the terms of any settlement in relation to the resumption of negotiations on the international wheat agreement, and they asked that the last sentence in the second paragraph be dropped. With that deletion the British and Canadian governments made the announcement simultaneously on January 20, 1949.

As an afterthought to that announcement, Sir Stafford Cripps, chancellor of the exchequer, issued a statement on British food procurement in Canada to The Canadian Press on February 23, 1949, in which he said:

Perhaps a special word should be said about United Kingdom food purchases in Canada. Since the end of the war we have been buying foodstuffs from Canada under bulk contracts negotiated by the Ministry of Food. If the terms of these contracts are examined, it will be seen that although the volume of purchases of bacon, eggs and cheese had to be somewhat reduced in the face of the acute world dollar shortage which hit the United Kingdom especially

[5] *Ibid.*
[6] *Ibid.*

hard in 1947, we are nevertheless continuing to buy a substantial part of our total requirements from Canada. In 1948, for instance, Canada was our largest single source of supply for wheat and wheat flour (three-quarters of total United Kingdom imports), bacon (three-quarters of total imports), shell eggs (just under one-third of total imports) and dried eggs (three-quarters of total imports).

As regards wheat, we shall continue to depend on Canada for the greater part of our supplies. The four year contract negotiated in 1946 will expire in 1950, and we have recently agreed upon a price of $2 a bushel for the 1949-50 season. We think there is every possibility of the world price falling below the $2 level before the end of the contract, either because of the general improvement in the supply position or as a condition of any international wheat agreement which may be concluded in the near future. If this should be the case, the Canadian farmer will enjoy a favoured position by virtue of the fixed price on which we have now agreed. This might prove to be fair compensation for the earlier years when he was selling us wheat at below the world price. It depends of course upon how far prices actually fall. But in any case we have agreed to discuss this matter further with the Canadian government some time towards the middle of 1950.[7]

[7] *Privy Council Office files.*

46

WASHINGTON WHEAT CONFERENCE, 1949

In July 1948 the preparatory committee appointed by the new wheat council had been left as a caretaker group to revive the negotiations whenever the circumstances were propitious, and Wilson was chairman of the committee. After the Vandenberg report had paid lip service to the agreement and then tabled it until after the November presidential election, Cairns made a valiant effort to salvage the remains by proposing, on his own initiative, a protocol by which the governments not categorically withdrawing from the agreement would roll back prices to August 1, 1948 on wheat transactions made above the $2 ceiling, in the hope that before the crop year expired the agreement might become viable. Governments responded to Cairns's proposal with reminders that any new initiative must come from the government of the United States in consultation with the preparatory committee.

1948 PRESIDENTIAL ELECTION

Contrary to most predictions, President Truman won an upset victory in the November election. Because Truman had made the international wheat agreement a campaign issue, hopes were revived that a new initiative would be taken by the United States government.

Arrangements had been made that year to hold the annual FAO conference in Washington in November. During the FAO meeting in progress, President Truman and his entourage made a surprise entrance; Truman mounted the podium and after the proper amenities ventured his opinion that if the international wheat agreement could be renegotiated, he had reason to believe that the senate would ratify it. After his speech, Truman received the delegates; Wilson was introduced to him as the chairman of the preparatory committee and was invited to get the negotiations under way again. This was done by one short meeting of the committee and a confirming communication to its members. Government responses were unanimous, and the United States government formally invited all members of the United Nations or of FAO to attend a conference in Washington commencing January 26, 1949, which that government would host.

1949 NEGOTIATIONS

The Canadian government responded by reappointing the delegation with its advisers from the farm organizations which had attended the 1949 special meeting of the international wheat council. Once again, Wilson had the able assistance of W. C. McNamara as alternate delegate and of R. C. Brown, Paul Farnalls, Ben S. Plumer and J. H. Wesson as technical advisers. Now that Sir Herbert Broadley had transferred to FAO, the British delegation was headed by Mr. Frank Sheed Anderson. Secretary of Agriculture Charles F. Brannan headed the American delegation and served as chairman of the conference. Mr. J. C. Van Essche was elected vice-chairman and presided over the working sessions. Both Argentina and the USSR sent delegates, the former in a passive and the latter in an active capacity, as Wilson reported to Ottawa through Hume Wrong, the Canadian ambassador, on January 27:

A - January 26th - Opening Session
1. The welcoming address was delivered by United States Secretary of Agriculture Brannan. Representatives of forty-nine nations, F.A.O., the Monetary Fund, and the Interim Co-ordinating Committee of I.C.A. were in attendance.
2. Elections to the executive posts of the Conference were unanimous. Secretary Brannan was appointed Chairman, Mr. Van Essche of Belgium, first Vice-Chairman (proposed by Canada), and Mr. O'Connell of Ireland, second Vice-Chairman.
3. The Conference approved the nomination of the following as members of the Steering Committee: Australia, Brazil, Canada, Egypt, France, India, the Netherlands, United Kingdom, United States, together with the permanent Chairman and the two Vice-Chairman as ex officio members.
4. The 1948 Agreement was accepted unanimously as the annotated agenda for the Conference.

B - January 27th - Morning and Afternoon Sessions
1. Opening statements were made by the delegates of thirteen countries, commencing with the United Kingdom and immediately followed by Canada. (I gave you the text of Wilson's remarks in my message WA-216 of today's date).
2. The United Kingdom delegate stated that his country would be willing to take 180 million bushels if the same quantity as last year (500 million) was offered. He said that the United Kingdom would welcome a four-year agreement, although it may accept a five-year agreement depending on the prices agreed upon. He finally stated that his country expects substantial price reductions, particularly in the ceiling prices, owing to the improved wheat supply situation and their dollar difficulties.
3. India, Italy, Ireland, Lebanon and the Netherlands also asked for price adjustments on the same grounds, and favoured a four-year agreement, though they will not oppose a five-year one.
4. Under-Secretary of Agriculture Loveland, speaking for the United States delegation, supported a five-year agreement and stood for a maximum price of not less than two dollars. He stressed that, according to the President's recent budget message, it would cost the United States Treasury $56 million during 1949-50 to finance United States participation in a wheat agreement with a two dollar ceiling.
5. In the absence of their Chairman, the Australian delegation deferred the statement on their position.

6. At the afternoon session the Argentine delegate indicated, among other things, that he is not prepared to submit quantitative figures. The Conference thereupon decided to proceed, for the time being, on the assumption that Argentina will not participate.

7. The Soviet delegate, on the other hand, said that he would be submitting quantitative figures shortly. In private conversation with the United States delegation, we agreed that the question of Soviet membership on the Steering Committee should not be discussed until the U.S.S.R. have made known their export quantities.

8. Of interest was the announcement made by the French delegate that his country was now an exporter and that he would submit quantitative figures to the Conference. He indicated, however, that these figures would not be large.

9. The questions of submitting and balancing the guaranteed sales and purchases were referred to a working party, composed of the five exporters and India, United Kingdom, Holland, Italy, Egypt, Brazil and Belgium, which will meet Monday morning, January 31st. The question of prices and duration were referred to the Steering Committee which will begin their discussion tomorrow morning.[1]

The British, Canadian and American statements furnished the key opening positions. On the substantive points Anderson said:

In the United Kingdom view, the first issue which should be tackled is that of guaranteed quantities. Until importing countries have some indication of the supplies likely to be available under an agreement, it will be difficult for them to indicate their requirements. And, similarly, until exporting countries know what importers' requirements are likely to be, it will be difficult for them to evaluate the worth of an agreement. Perhaps it will help if I say that, providing the total quantity to be guaranteed under an Agreement is to be 500 million bushels as last year, then the United Kingdom is prepared, subject to agreement on other issues, to guarantee a purchase of 180 million bushels as last year. But on this issue it is important for us to know as early as possible the views of representatives from exporting countries. With more adherents to an Agreement, we would wish to consider raising our guaranteed purchases.

So far as concerns the duration of the Agreement, the United Kingdom accepted last year an agreement for five years extending until the crop year 1952/53. If an Agreement coming to an end then could be concluded at this Conference, i.e. one for 4 years, it would be welcomed by the United Kingdom. But we do not rule out an extension to five years. Any such extension would be related directly to other terms, however, particularly price terms, and in our view cannot very well be considered in isolation.

As regards prices, I cannot at the moment be very specific and must content myself with one or two observations. First and foremost, I must say that in view of the change in wheat prospects to which I referred earlier, the United Kingdom expects a substantial reduction in the price figures contained in Article VI of the 1948 Agreement, particularly so far as concerns the maxima. If changed wheat prospects justify the request for such substantial reduction, the position of the economies of the United Kingdom and Western European countries emphasizes the need for it. Without it, a balance of trade between Europe and the Western Hemisphere is not possible. Secondly, I must refer to the price scale under an Agreement. Last year we agreed to a maximum price for the first year of the Agreement which was maintained throughout its course. Reflection since then has only served to convince us that the views

[1]*Trade and Commerce File 26204:14.*

advanced on behalf of the United Kingdom last year in support of a graduated maximum price are logically unassailable. The scale can be so graduated as to operate without undue hardship to producers and, by avoiding a widening range of prices year by year, will serve to provide that element of stability which it is the object of a Wheat Agreement to secure.

On these three issues of quantities, duration, and price, it seems to us that attention must be concentrated. If agreement on them can be obtained, then the United Kingdom believes that machinery is at hand which will work under the conditions of today. Such machinery will serve to provide, for consumers, security and, for producers, the avoidance of undue fluctuations in prices and incomes. If at this Conference we can set up such machinery, we shall have deserved well of our day and generation.[2]

Wilson's statement immediately followed Anderson's:

Mr. Chairman I appreciate this opportunity of conveying the sincere thanks of my Government to the Government of the United States for convening this Conference. It is just a year ago that most of the delegations that are present here today convened for a similar purpose under the auspices of the International Wheat Council. I am very happy that one of the negotiating Governments had taken the initiative in convening this Conference. It is one manifestation of the fact that Governments themselves are taking a direct interest in balancing the interests and improving the welfare of their producers and consumers by means of an International Wheat Agreement. . . .

Mr. Chairman, I should like to enlarge a little upon the fact that not only were the objectives of an international wheat agreement defined in principle in the 1948 Agreement, but they were also given specific definition in the guaranteed purchases and sales of 500 million bushels between the then signatory Governments within a specific price range of $2.00 at the ceiling and $1.50 to $1.10 at the floor scaled down over a five year period. I would like to recall that in our negotiations of last year it was recognized that a basic price of $2.00 represented equity between producers and consumers under conditions of scarcity and that the declining floors of $1.50 to $1.10 represented equity between producers and consumers under conditions of surplus and lower production cost.

In the interval which has transpired between last year's negotiations and those we are now entering, the world's wheat position has altered from one seriously weighted on the side of scarcity to one in which supplies and effective demand are approximately in balance. The present situation instead of increasing our difficulties should, in my judgment, enhance the prospects of our reaching an agreement. Undoubtedly, some delegations may read into the present circumstances an opportunity to seek different terms than those which were agreed upon a year ago. Because of that possibility, I should like to mention that the only prices relevent to conditions of surplus are the floor prices; and I should like to emphasize that the floor prices agreed upon last year fully discounted the possibility of changed supply conditions. They have already been recognized as equitable to producers and consumers under conditions going far beyond the present position of balanced supply and effective demand into actual surplus conditions.

For these reasons, Mr. Chairman, in our forthcoming deliberations the Canadian delegation will support the price ranges as agreed upon last year as being appropriate to give effect to the objectives of an international agreement whether wheat is in scarcity or in surplus. . . .[3]

[2] *Verbatim Minutes,* Second Plenary Session, January 27, 1949.
[3] *Ibid.*

Later, Undersecretary of agriculture Albert J. Loveland stated the American position:

It might be helpful if at this time I briefly outlined the position of the United States on three specific questions which are before us; namely quantity, price, and duration of the Agreement.

The United States hopes that the new Agreement will cover a substantial portion of the international trade in wheat. The volume of wheat import demand has increased far above pre-war levels and there is some indication that it will remain considerably higher than it was before the war. Recognition of the increasing need of importing countries for wheat, production in the post-war periods has been greatly expanded in the United States. The result is that the United States alone is now exporting as much wheat as all other nations of the world did in some prewar years. The United States Delegation feel that in determining our share in the world some consideration should be given to the contribution made by the wheat growers in this country to feeding a hungry world.

Furthermore, I might note that the United States still feels a great responsibility for maintaining supplies sufficiently large to be a protection not only for our own people but also for wheat-importing countries against a crop failure.

As to price, we are all aware that within the last year the general price level in this and most other countries has gone up. The cost of producing wheat has gone up. We have some figures that indicate this increasing cost of wheat production but I won't burden you with them at this time. These factors, coupled with the prospects for a continued high level of economic activity throughout the world, point to a continuation of very high wheat prices for some years. However, in spite of the increased cost of wheat production and the prospects for continued high prices, the United States would be willing to agree to a maximum price of $2.00 a bushel as provided in the 1948 Agreement, provided relatively favorable provision can be obtained on other points. We estimate that to sell wheat at this price next year would cost this Government a great amount of money. I call your attention to the fact that the President's budget for the next fiscal year presented to Congress provides as a rough estimate for $58 million to cover the anticipated loss to our Treasury under a Wheat Agreement providing for a $2.00 maximum.

With respect to duration, the United States has always believed and still believes that the agreement should cover a period of five years. A shorter period would not give the assurances of stability and insure an opportunity to plan ahead which is the final objective of an agreement.[4]

As the conference got under way, the Canadian delegation received encouragement from the Canadian federation of agriculture. Mr. H. H. Hannam, president, telegraphed from its annual meeting in Regina on January 27:

Following resolution has been forwarded your minister at Ottawa quote that the Canadian federation of agriculture in annual meeting assembled desire to record their extreme satisfaction that efforts to convene a further international wheat conference in which the Dominion Government has shared have been successful and such conference has now been convened stop We express confidence that representatives of the Government will exercise every effort to reach an agreement which will recognize the important place which the Dominion holds in the production and export of wheat and we trust an agreement will be reached which will give greater stability to wheat prices and

[4]*Ibid.*

greater security to those engaged in the production of the essential food commodity unquote.[5]

By January 31, the working party on quantities and the steering committee on prices and duration held their first meetings. As Wilson reported through the ambassador on February 1:

1. At yesterday morning's session the Working Party on Quantities received provisional estimates from twenty importing countries. Several of the countries submitting figures shaded the quantities they were prepared to take a year ago. Since the figures were incomplete the meeting was adjourned pending receipt of the other importers' estimates. Australia, the United States and Canada have submitted eighty-five million, one hundred and eighty-five million and two hundred and thirty million bushels respectively, as they did last year. France has offered to export three point seven million bushels, but so far, the Soviet delegate has given out no figures, although he had already indicated that he would do so.

2. The Steering Committee on Prices and Duration met in the afternoon. The United Kingdom Representative, speaking on behalf of the other importers as well as of his own Government, proposed a declining ceiling price as well as declining floor price over a four-year period as follows:

1949-50	$1.65	$1.40
1950-51	1.60	1.30
1951-52	1.50	1.20
1952-53	1.40	1.10

He said that in exchange for the importers' acceptance of the floor prices specified for the crop years referred to above, and which are the same as in the 1948 Agreement, the importers expected from the exporters a reduced and declining ceiling price which would reflect the following factors:

(a) The increasingly plentiful supply of wheat brought about by increased acreage and yields in exporting countries, and by increased indigenous production in importing countries.

(b) The need for exporters to avoid wide fluctuations in prices against small shifts in supplies and demand.

(c) The necessity for Western European countries achieving rapid viability. For that purpose they must apply their very limited dollar purchasing power where it will help most.

3. Commenting on the announcement by the United States delegate that a two dollar ceiling agreement would cost the United States Government $58 million, the United Kingdom delegate feared that this would mean that the United States would try to hold the price of wheat at the two dollar maximum.

4. He thought that his proposed floor price scale would cover wheat production costs in Australia and Canada, and eventually in the United States, where he believed that technical improvements coupled with higher yields and acreage would gradually decrease production costs.

5. The delegates of India and the Netherlands supported the United Kingdom views. So did also the Irish delegate who stressed that high ceiling prices and the dollar shortage would force some importing countries to engage in uneconomical production of wheat.

6. Wilson took the position that there was no justification for declining ceilings and he reiterated his view that while floor prices are tied in with conditions of surplus, ceiling prices are related to conditions of scarcity. He added that ceilings at $1.65 were too low for Canada to consider.

[5]*Trade and Commerce File 26204:14.*

7. The Australian and United States delegates spoke of the rise of the cost of wheat production in their countries and emphasized that production can only be kept up if the ceiling price pays for the cost of production.

8. Discussion of prices in the Steering Committee will not be resumed until the Working Party on quantities has received the requirements of the importing countries.

9. Today the Canadian, United States and Australian delegates are meeting informally to discuss the situation in the light of the importers' price proposals. . . .[6]

At a meeting of the steering committee held on February 3, the members defended at length their respective price positions but no attempt at reconciling the exporters' and importers' differences was made. In the working party on quantities, the guaranteed quantities filed by the importing countries reflected the declining requirements of France and Brazil. France was now negotiating to become a member exporting country. On February 7, Secretary Brannan met with the steering committee and maintained the American position by reaffirming that the United States could not accept price provisions less favorable than those of the 1948 agreement. But, to avoid further debate and to get on with the negotiations, the steering committee appointed four representatives to explore the possibilities of a compromise. Although a complete record of the negotiations is available in the verbatim minutes, they were summarized day by day in telegrams sent off to Ottawa through Hume Wrong. On February 11, the report went as follows:

1. Prices. The price discussions were referred by the Steering Committee last Monday to the delegates of the United Kingdom, India, United States and Canada. These four representatives held talks on Tuesday and Wednesday on an exploratory basis beyond the limits of their instructions in order to find some compromise proposal which could be referred back to all Governments. At the conclusion of these talks on Wednesday all four were agreed upon floors of $1.50, $1.40, $1.30 and $1.20 if the duration is to be four years and the two importers offered $1.10 for a fifth year floor. As for the ceilings, the United Kingdom and India offered first a level ceiling at $1.70 and finally at $1.75 as being their last word on the extent to which they would be prepared to ask for new instructions. The United States and Canadian delegates on the other hand offered to seek new instructions for $1.90 ceiling. Thus there is a gap between $1.75 on the one side and $1.90 on the other side that still remains to be resolved.

2. Apart from these direct talks with the United Kingdom and Indian representatives, the Australian, United States and Canadian representatives have held separate talks. Both McCarthy (Australia) and Wilson have made plain to the Americans their opinion that the highest ceiling upon which agreement could be reached is $1.80. They also urged that the Americans come down now to $1.85 and if there were a ten cent gap between exporters' and importers' positions referred back to the United Kingdom Government in particular there might be more hope of a compromise on $1.80 than if we offered $1.80 straightaway. All the members of the Canadian delegation are prepared to support an agreement with outside limits of $1.80 on the ceiling and $1.20 on the floor.

In separate talks which Wilson and McNamara have had with the Russian delegation the latter were prepared to support $1.80 and the individual

[6] *Ibid.*

delegations of several of the lesser importing countries also appear to be prepared to settle on that basis.

3. So far the real delay in making progress had been the American reluctance to go below $1.90. All conversations on prices were stalemated yesterday during which time the American officials were consulting their Advisory Committee including farm organizations and the latest word last night was that Secretary Brannan intended to take the price issue into this morning's meeting of the Cabinet for consultations with the President and the Secretary of State.

4. Regarding quantities, the Working Committee on Quantities reported on Wednesday that importers collectively were prepared to take 501.6 million bushels on a five year basis assuming that Russia would be included with, and Argentina excluded from, the exporters. These figures indicate an increase of 38 million bushels as a result of the inclusion of Russia. Yesterday (February 10th) at the request of the Russian delegation, the exporters met to discuss the division of the import figures amongst the exporters. The Russians have of course asked for twenty percent of the total import requirements representing much too large a concession on the part of the other exporters and with Wilson in the Chair the debate took place principally between the Australians, Americans and the Russians. The one concrete result of the meeting was an admission on the part of all the exporters including Russia that they were prepared to compromise on their original figures in order to settle this problem, and a further meeting on this subject should be held sometime today.

5. The Americans have just advised us at noon today that they will not be in a position to say anything further on prices before Monday.[7]

When Mr. Howe saw the $1.75 figure which Anderson was prepared to recommend to the British government he brought Wilson back to Ottawa for fresh instructions. Despite the daily reports, Howe had become concerned about the slow pace of the negotiations, and he wanted to be sure that nothing in the Canadian position was standing in the way of reaching an agreement. Because of the developing surplus situation he did not want to see the agreement slip through his grasp. Howe told Wilson, in confidence, that if Anderson could get approval for a $1.75 ceiling, he would be prepared to recommend the same figure to cabinet. Wilson explained that the real problem in the negotiations was to get the British and the Americans together on price. A separate Canadian offer would be of little avail if the Americans were not prepared to go along and Wilson counselled patience with the rather cumbersome procedures they had to go through whenever they sought to get instructions changed. Nevertheless, Howe wanted it understood that Wilson had authority to offer $1.75 whenever it might help to bring about an agreement.

Meanwhile Mr. Gardiner had been reading the reports and he wrote to Howe on February 12:

> I have been reading the teletype reports on the wheat discussions, and note that the importers are asking $1.75 as the ceiling and the exporters $1.90. I note also that the discussions ranged about receding floors beginning at $1.50 and ending at $1.20 on a four-year agreement, or $1.10 on a five-year agreement.
>
> I think there is much to be said for a narrower margin between ceilings and floors with a flat floor instead of a receding floor. It seems to me there would

[7]*Ibid.*

be a much higher degree of stability established with a flat floor and a flat ceiling. The discussions of last year started at $1.65 ceiling and $1.25 floor, with both maintained throughout the five years. It seems to me that that was a much sounder basis of prices, namely, to have a flat ceiling and a flat floor without so great a margin between them than what is being discussed now.

I would hope that Canadians will not find it necessary to reduce the quantity below two hundred and thirty million bushels.[8]

Howe replied to Gardiner on February 15:

Thanks for yours of February 12th. I agree completely on the desirability of our delegation attempting to bring the floor and ceiling more closely together, even though this involves a lowering of the ceiling. Mr. Wilson understands my view on this and, subject to the guidance of his Advisory Committee, I am confident that he will do what he can in that direction.

Wilson must, of course, take account of the fact that the U. S. delegation are fighting for the highest possible ceiling and are not much interested in the floor. Other than putting forward the Canadian viewpoint, I doubt if Wilson should openly take an independent line at this time, for fear that it might further complicate an already complicated situation.

I share your hope that Canada will not find it necessary to reduce the quantity below 230,000,000 bushels. I know that Wilson will fight to hold his position.[9]

On February 16 Wilson reported afresh on developments:

1. The small Exploratory Committee on prices (United Kingdom, India, United States and Canada) met for the first time yesterday afternoon since its meeting on Wednesday, February 9th. In the interval the discussions had been postponed in order to permit the Americans to clarify their own position. This was evidently a complicated undertaking, involving discussions within the American delegation, between the American delegation and its Advisory Committee comprised of representatives of the farm organizations and the trade, discussions at the Friday morning Cabinet meeting and also discussions between Secretary Brannan and a small group of congressional advisers. The American delegates were obviously embarrassed over the time consumed in arriving at their own position.

2. Apparently there resulted from the discussion in last Friday's Cabinet not only the weekend top level approach to ourselves but also an approach on Monday by Secretary Acheson to Sir Oliver Franks, the British Ambassador. Anderson who accompanied the British Ambassador to the meeting told Wilson that Secretary Acheson suggested the conference was bogging down as a result of too rigid instructions on either side and that with the President taking personal interest in the successful outcome of the conference it would be desirable for both sides to seek more flexible instructions. No specific mention was made during their meeting of actual prices upon which a compromise might be reached. It may be significant however that the Americans have taken the first step toward negotiating the differences through diplomatic rather than conference channels.

3. In yesterday afternoon's meeting of the Exploratory Committee Anderson stated that his position was unchanged from a week ago, namely $1.75 for the maximum in each year of the agreement and floors of $1.50 declining by ten cents each crop year to $1.10 in the fifth year. Smith and Rossiter for the Americans stated that they were prepared to recommend to their own people $1.85 maximum for four years with floors of $1.50, $1.40,

[8] *Ibid.*
[9] *Ibid.*

$1.35 and $1.25, or alternatively a five year agreement with a uniform maximum of $1.85 and floors of $1.50, $1.40, $1.30, $1.20 and $1.20. Anderson replied that he would report the American proposals and would recommend the $1.75 maximum and the floors he previously mentioned and would hope that these matters would be before the British Cabinet on Thursday.

4. After suggesting that the British and American positions were probably the firmest on either side Wilson asked if both the British and American delegations would go further and seek sufficiently flexible instructions to permit a settlement. Anderson replied that his Government would appreciate the gap which remained and that any more flexible instructions would be for his Government to decide. It was evident from this meeting that no further progress could be made in the price discussions until Anderson receives fresh instructions in the light of all these developments.

5. In separate conversations between the Americans and ourselves, Rossiter told Wilson that Secretary Brannan had intended to invite the Exploratory Group in for further discussions. In view of Anderson's present position, however, Rossiter doubted that Secretary Brannan would carry out his intention. Wilson suggested to Rossiter that the Americans having commenced discussions with the United Kingdom on the diplomatic level might yet have occasion to advance the discussions further on that level.

6. With the present gap remaining between $1.85 and $1.75 a settlement at $1.80 is plain for all to see. This could be misleading, however, since the Americans will probably face as strong Congressional objection to $1.80 as the United Kingdom Government will be reluctant to come up to that level. Anderson is meeting with the other importers represented on the Steering Committee today in order that those who need to may get fresh instructions. Gupta, the Indian delegate, has privately admitted his readiness to settle for $1.80 with floors declining to $1.20.

7. Meanwhile the full conference is meeting daily to discuss drafting changes in the text of the Agreement. On Monday, February 14th, the exporters met separately to discuss a division of the overall quantities amongst the exporters. The Russians have not moved from their initial position of asking 20 percent of the total quantity, a proportion which at the least is twice too high. Before pursuing this touchy debate, however, it was agreed that Argentina be invited to declare its position not later than Thursday of this week, which was done at Monday afternoon's meeting of the full conference, the Argentine delegate appeared to welcome this pressure in getting instructions from his Government and late this week the debate among the exporters on quantities should continue after the Argentine declaration as to whether they are in or out. Naturally the importers' figures would be increased if Argentina were to come into the agreement, and in any event we have probably not heard the last word from the importers on their figures.[10]

The American price position was clarified on February 18, but Anderson had not yet had fresh instructions from his government, Wilson reported again:

1. Anderson (United Kingdom) informed Wilson this morning that the price issue would not come before the British Cabinet until Monday.

2. Smith and Rossiter (United States) let Wilson and McCarthy (Australia) know that as a result of further discussions with Secretary Brannan and his

[10]*Ibid.*

Congressional Committee the Americans could consider two further price bases both involving five year agreements as follows:

	$1.80	$1.80	$1.80	$1.80	$1.80
or	$1.50	$1.40	$1.30	$1.25	$1.25
	$1.90	$1.90	$1.80	$1.80	$1.80
	$1.50	$1.40	$1.30	$1.20	$1.20

After discussion with McCarthy and Wilson the Americans agreed not to submit these two new alternatives to Anderson until he has fresh instructions from the British Cabinet on the basis of the present $1.85 — $1.75 gap. Otherwise it would be construed that the exporters' position could be further weakened.

3. At this morning's conference session the Argentine delegate announced that Argentina would not participate in the agreement.[11]

The long-awaited British reply came on February 28. As that government remained firm on a ceiling of $1.75, the exporters consulted on their position as Wilson reported to Ottawa:

1. Reference paragraph one of my WA-437 of February 18th the British Cabinet dealt with their reply on the price issue on Monday, February 21st. Since the American representations had been made through the Secretary of State to the British Ambassador the reply came through this channel and could not be transmitted to Secretary Acheson until Friday, February 25th, when the latter had recovered from an indisposition. Secretary Brannan, in turn, was out of town and returned to Washington today.

2. This afternoon Secretary Brannan called in Wilson and McCarthy (Australia) to inform them of the British reply which was to the effect that the United Kingdom were not prepared to go beyond a four year agreement with ceilings of $1.75 in each of the four years and with floors of $1.40, $1.30, $1.20 and $1.10.

3. In view of this position Secretary Brennan proposed that the exporters agree upon a uniform reply. McCarthy and Wilson agreed that this would be a desirable approach, but McCarthy indicated that his present instructions would not permit him to accept less than $1.90 for the ceiling although he thought on due consideration his Government would alter its position when they appreciated that the other exporting countries would settle for a lower ceiling with the possibility of reaching an agreement in which Australia would not be included. Wilson stated that his present instructions would permit him to accept a ceiling of $1.80 with a floor not going below $1.20 in the final year. He suggested that this be our present negotiating basis although he thought both Secretary Brannan and McCarthy should appreciate that in the last stage of the negotiations, rather than breaking off without an agreement, he would be prepared to recommend to the Canadian Government with some hope of acceptance a ceiling of $1.75 with the floors not going below $1.25. Secretary Brannan then stated that he had discussed the American position with his own officials and that he would be prepared to recommend a four-year agreement with the ceiling at $1.80 and floors of $1.50, $1.40, $1.30 and $1.20. When Wilson and McCarthy agreed that this should be the present basis for an exporters' united front Secretary Brannan undertook to clear this proposal later in the afternoon with his Congressional advisors, with Secretary Acheson and with the President. His hope was that the Secretary of State could give this position to the British Ambassador tomorrow and that by Wednesday at latest the exporters could declare their position to the Conference.

[11]*Ibid.*

4. It was also suggested that the exporting countries make their offer on the basis of the importing countries putting in sufficient quantities to make an agreement feasible. In this regard Lee Smith for the Americans suggested that Canada, the United States and Australia take a five percent reduction from last year's figures which would mean 230 million bushels for Canada less five per cent. The total quantity for the importing countries however would have to be 475 million bushels from Canada, the United States and Australia instead of 500 million bushels as was provided last year, but added to the 475 million bushels would have to be the quantities the importing countries desire to take from the U.S.S.R.

5. Before going to this afternoon's meeting Wilson consulted the other members of his delegation with the exception of Mr. Farnalls. It happened that the position which developed in the talk with Brannan was anticipated in the delegation meeting. Messrs. MacNamara, Wesson, Plumer and Brown were agreed that they would accept a four year agreement with a ceiling of $1.80 and floors not going below $1.20, or if need be, rather than have no agreement they would accept a four year agreement with a ceiling of $1.75 and with floors not going below $1.25.[12]

By March 2 the American position had been confirmed on a four-year agreement with a price ceiling of $1.80 and floors descending yearly from $1.50 to $1.20, on condition that the guaranteed import quantities were at least 550 million bushels. This position was conveyed to the steering committee on March 3, and reported to Ottawa:

1. Reference paragraph 3 of my WA-526 of February 28th. The Americans advised Wilson yesterday morning that their position had been fully cleared with the authorities concerned on a firm offer of a four-year agreement with a price ceiling of $1.80 in each of the four years and floors of $1.50, $1.40, $1.30 and $1.20. Wilson thereupon called a meeting of the exporters, at which Smith and Rossiter for the United States added to their proposed price range a condition that the importers collectively take at least 550 million bushels per year under the agreement. Rossiter and Smith also indicated that the prices above mentioned were as far as the United States was prepared to go in order to reach an agreement.

2. McNamara stated that for purposes of continuing the negotiations the Canadian delegation would support the American proposals. The French delegate also declared his support.

3. McCarthy (Australia), Borisov (U.S.S.R.)and Yriart (Uruguay) stated that their present instructions did not permit them to go below a ceiling of $2.00. In order to make progress, however, they agreed that Wilson on behalf of the exporters, should make a statement to the Steering Committee today, to the effect that, while all the exporters were not presently prepared to go that far, a considerable element among the exporters, as a contribution towards reaching an agreement, were agreed that they should accept a four-year agreement with ceilings of not less than $1.80 and floors of not less than $1.50, $1.40, $1.30 and $1.20. Together with this price range, however, was attached the condition that the importing countries raise their total quantities to a level of at least 550 million bushels.

4. This position was reported to the Steering Committee this afternoon. Inasmuch as the delegates for the importing countries probably heard for the first time that the exporters would attach a minimum quantity requirement to their price proposals, the delegates of the importing countries on the Steering Committee asked for further time to consider this aspect of the exporters'

[12]*Ibid.*

proposals, and also urged that the exporters define the proportions by which the exporters' total would be divided amongst the exporters, because until the importing countries had this information they would be handicapped, through uncertainties regarding the sources of their wheat, in stating how much they would be prepared to take from the exporters collectively.

5. Following this afternoon's meeting of the Steering Committee, the Committee of the Whole agreed to break into separate groups of importers and exporters, and presumably the delegates of all the importing countries learned of the exporters' proposals at their importers' meeting. The exporters, in turn, agreed to reopen the discussion of the division of the quantities amongst the exporters at a meeting among themselves tomorrow morning.

6. Instead of the Steering Committee reporting directly to the Committee of the Whole, this was postponed for another day. Since there could be no agreed press release from the Committee of the Whole, the Americans decided, in turn, that they themselves would not make a press statement today, although both President Truman and Secretary Brannan had agreed that the United States' position should be made public and the press had been invited to be on hand at the end of this afternoon's meeting.

7. Wilson will watch the developments regarding any publicity tomorrow and, as cleared by telephone this afternoon, if the occasion arises, say that, according to his understanding, the position of the Canadian Government is in accord with that taken by the Government of the United States.

8. Borisov has told Wilson privately that the U.S.S.R. could probably agree on a $1.80 ceiling. The Australian position remains as stated in paragraph 3 of WA-526.[13]

Over the next few days there were several meetings, but no progress was made toward a solution of the exporters' guaranteed quantities as the Americans held firm to their original objective and the U.S.S.R. delegate's instructions prevented him from considering any realistic figure for his country. Wilson's report of March 5 recorded the extent of the disagreement over quantities and the attempts that were made to reconcile the differences:

1. Reference my WA-576 of March 3rd Wilson called a meeting of the exporters on Friday morning to consider the request of the importers, as reported in paragraph 4 of WA-576, that the exporters give an indication of the way the total export figure would be divided amongst the exporters. This was an almost futile meeting with the Americans on the one hand not prepared to put forward the five percent reduction proposal which they had advanced to Wilson last Monday as reported in paragraph 4 of my WA-526 of February 28th. Instead they said that if the total quantity were to be 550 million bushels the United States would ask for 200 million bushels which was 15 millions more than they had in last year's agreement. On that basis, the Canadians and Australians in turn said they would have to stand on last year's figures of 230 and 85 million bushels, while the Russians maintained their demand of 20 per cent of the total or 110 million bushels. Allowing 5 million bushels for France and Uruguay combined this gave a total of 630 million bushels against the 550 million bushels target. No delegate would offer any specific compromise although before the meeting ended each delegate admitted there would have to be some compromise, including Borisov (U.S.S.R.) who pointed out that his instructions would have to be changed if he were to accept anything less than 20 per cent.

[13]*Ibid.*

2. Yesterday afternoon the Steering Committee met, at which Anderson (United Kingdom) on behalf of the importers reported on a meeting he had with all the importers the previous afternoon. He said that the importers had undertaken to cable the exporters' offer to their Governments on Thursday and that the delegates of the importing countries had then discussed among themselves the exporters' firm condition that the quantities must be at least 550 million bushels. The opinion of the importing country delegates was that the most that the importers' figures could be extended beyond the 493 million bushels they had previously indicated was another ten to twelve million bushels making an outside possible figure of 505 million bushels. After supporting his argument that this was the most the importers could enter an agreement upon, he then insisted on knowing whether the exporters' figure of 550 million bushels was a firm and final figure. If so, there could be no need for exploring further a settlement of the other issues because the negotiations would break down over failure to agree upon quantities. Without consultation with the other exporters, particularly the United States, Wilson could only maintain that the 550 million bushels figure was a firm condition.

3. The meeting of the Steering Committee was followed by a meeting of the Committee of the Whole and the same position which had developed in the Steering Committee was reported to the Committee of the Whole. At the request of the Indian delegate to refer the whole question on quantities again to the Quantities Committee which had been set up earlier in the Conference where the importers and exporters might together discuss the quantities, Rossiter (U.S.) agreed thereby leaving the implication at least that the firm figure of 550 million bushels was no longer firm.

4. It was also agreed that Van Essche, Acting Chairman of the Conference, would hold a press conference at the end of yesterday afternoon's meeting at which Wilson on behalf of the exporters would disclose the exporters' offer and Anderson would report on behalf of the importers their reaction to the quantity condition.

5. Another meeting of the exporters was called this morning at which it was agreed that the exporters would have to address themselves to the figures the importers were prepared to put in. Again there was no tendency to move toward any acceptable compromise. Thereupon McNamara put forward the proposal which had originated with the Americans that Australia, Canada and the United States cut back five per cent on last year's figures to a total of 475 million bushels giving the Russians 25 million bushels firm, France and Uruguay 5 million bushels, making up the present import total of 505 million bushels and offering the Russians any increases that the importers might make. This was immediately unacceptable either to the Russians or to the Americans. Wilson (in the Chair) then compared the figures which the importers had put in this year totalling 405 million bushels as against the 500 million bushels last year. Importers who had dropped out or decreased their figures this year accounted for a total reduction of 66 million bushels whereas the new importers and those who had increased their figures had put in an offsetting amount of 59 million bushels. Pursuing one of the Russian arguments that the original exporters had lost markets in the agreement of 66 million bushels from last year Wilson examined each of the countries which had put in new or additional figures this year and it was generally admitted that the Russian participation could account for approximately only 24 million bushels of the 59 million bushels increase. Borisov thereupon declared that such a figure for Russia was quite unrealistic and that without fresh instructions he was not prepared to go below 100 million bushels. Wilson expressed his regret to the exporters that they could not furnish the importers

at the meeting scheduled for Monday morning with the information the importers had properly asked on how the exporters' shares would be divided. He pointed out that the conference had gone beyond the stage where it could await the instructions of one Government in turn and then another and that some precipitate action on the part of the exporters would be required.

6. After this morning's meeting of the exporters Wilson and McNamara met separately with the United States and Australian delegations. Wilson suggested to the Americans that they quickly weigh the alternative of making a proportionate concession together with Canada and Australia of an additional quantity to the Russians as a token gift of our markets to have them inside the agreement or of telling the Russians forthwith they must either accept the 25 million bushels or withdraw from the negotiations. In view of the rapidly developing competition from Russia as an exporter Wilson argued that there would be a definite advantage in having such a competitor in the agreement rather than shutting him out and inviting the competition. The Americans, including Under Secretary Loveland, appeared to favour the other alternative, arguing that in order to obtain the necessary congressional approval on their side they felt this would be impossible if it could be demonstrated that through the agreement the United States had contracted away a part of its markets to Russia. A further meeting with the Australians and Americans with possibly Secretary Brannan and someone from the Soviet Division of State Department present was arranged for tomorrow Sunday afternoon in the hope of agreeing on a course of action for Monday.[14]

Over the weekend, Wilson and McNamara met with Australian and United States delegates and a Soviet specialist in the state department and agreed upon a plan to resolve the quantity issue, as reported on March 7:

1. Reference paragraph 6 of my WA-605 of March 5th, Wilson and McNamara met on Sunday afternoon with the Australian and United States delegations, the latter including Under-Secretary Loveland and Secretary Brannan. After pointing out the urgency of resolving the exporter's riddle on the division of the quantities so that the importers would be unable to insist that this issue take priority over a reply on their part to the exporters' price offer Wilson then put forward a proposal which had been agreed within the Canadian delegation with Messrs. Barton, Deutsch and Beaupre also present.

2. The proposal was that instead of continuing a bargaining approach with the Russians which could be time consuming to the defeat of the negotiations, the three exporters, United States, Canada and Australia should first declare a firm position to the Russians of their preparedness to allocate the importers' figure of 505 million bushels as follows: 5 million bushels for France and Uruguay; 50 million bushels for Russia; 450 million bushels for the original three exporters. The 50 million bushels for the U.S.S.R. would undoubtedly involve some element of a gift of our markets to the U.S.S.R. but it was generally admitted that the 24 million bushels figure which we had argued with the Russians on Saturday as being the extent of the importers' interest in Russian wheat, was actually an understatement of what the importers would take from the U.S.S.R. if larger quantities of Russian wheat are actually available to them, and it was felt that 40 million bushels is a more realistic approximation of the importers' interest in Russian wheat. However on the basis of the 50 million bushels offer the three exporters might agree that the Russians should be told that their participation in the agreement was conditional upon their acceptance of the 50 million bushels figure. Otherwise

[14]*Ibid.*

the three exporters would promptly tell the importers that it was impossible to come to an agreement with the U.S.S.R. on quantities and that Australia, Canada and the United States would be prepared to proceed immediately with the conclusion of an agreement with the importers without Russian participation.

3. After a long discussion in which Secretary Brannan, with the assistance of his own Departmental advisers and two State Department advisers including one from the Soviet Division, weighed the alternatives of making or breaking with the Russians on 40 million bushels instead of 50 million bushels, he decided to go along with a firm offer of 50 million bushels. The State Department officials held the view that the Russians would not come into the agreement for 50 million bushels. Secretary Brannan felt that if he had to defend why no agreement was reached with the Russians he could do it better on the 50 million bushels rather than the 40 million bushels figure. One the other hand if the Russians accepted he would have a harder time justifying the 50 million bushels offer in seeking Congressional ratification of the agreement. Nevertheless he accepted the higher figure and arrangements were made to meet Monday morning first with the exporters including Russia, where the "take it or leave it" offer would be made known to the Russians, following which we would go into the meeting on quantities with the importers and make this offer known in order that the importers could be told how the quantities would be divided if Russia participates in the agreement.

4. As for the division of the 450 million bushels among Canada, United States and Australia, McCarthy (Australia) said that 80 million bushels was the minimum figure on which he had instructions to accept. Secretary Brannan said that there would be no hope of carrying Congress on a figure lower than 170 million bushels. Wilson said that the remaining 200 million bushels was the smallest figure that the Canadians could consider. However there was still some hope of a small increase in the importers' figures and Secretary Brannan suggested it was time that the French were told they had no place in the agreement. Should any additional quantities materialize it was agreed that Canada would get the benefit until we had an exact proration on the basis of the quantities agreed last year.[15]

The position agreed upon by the three major exporters was communicated to the importers. In the prospect that the totals of the importers' and exporters' guaranteed quantities could be reconciled, hopes for an agreement were revived at a stage when the negotiations had virtually ended in failure. Wilson reported the changed position on March 8:

1. At the various meetings held yesterday the proposals of the United States, Canada and Australia referred to in my WA-606 of March 7th were made known to the Conference. A meeting was first held with all the exporters present at which Wilson made known to the Russians the proposal of the three exporters that 50 million bushels out of 500 million bushels was as far as the three exporters could go in making an agreement with Russian participation. The Russian delegate replied that until he had new instructions his position remained that his Government desired 20 per cent of the total or 100 million bushels. While making no comment on our offer he did not assert that it was beyond their consideration as he had done during earlier meetings when the Americans and others were talking about a figure of 24 million for Russia. He had no objection to the three exporters making their proposals known to the importers.

[15]*Ibid.*

2. Later in the morning the exporters met with the importers in the Quantities Committee of the Conference and Wilson on behalf of three exporters stated that although they were shocked at the indication given last week by the importers to the effect that the importers could not raise their figure above 505 million bushels, they were nevertheless prepared to face the facts and that the exporters who had made the offer last week on the basis of a four year agreement with the range as previously stated would now amend their conditional quantity to a minimum of 505 million bushels in the place of 550 million bushels. Then he mentioned the proposal that had been put to the U.S.S.R. adding that the 450 million bushels would be prorated to Canada, United States and Australia approximately on the basis of last year's agreement or in other words that they would each take approximately a ten per cent cut. The importers appreciated the inference from Wilson's remarks that if the 50 million bushels proved unacceptable to the U.S.S.R. the Conference would have to proceed with an agreement without Russian participation.

The effect of this information on the importers was that it revived a rapidly deteriorating Conference. Later in the afternoon the importers replied that they were prepared to proceed on the assumption of allocations amongst the exporters as had been indicated to them, that they would naturally accept the four year agreement and that in respect of prices they hoped to be able to reply to the exporters' offer in the next two or three days. Other arrangements were made to revive the activities of all the Committees working toward the preparation of a clean new draft. Some of the importers were sufficiently optimistic that an agreement could be signed about the end of next week.[16]

A similar break on the price issue came a week later when Anderson informed the working party on prices that he had received instructions to accept the $1.80 price ceiling. Wilson reported on March 15:

1. The first progress was made today since my previous report in WA-621 of March 8th. Anderson (United Kingdom) and Abhyankar (India) met this morning with Smith (United States) and Wilson, and Anderson stated on behalf of the importers that they were prepared ultimately to accept the price offer advanced by the "considerable element" of the exporters namely a maximum of $1.80 for four years with successive floors of $1.50, $1.40, $1.30 and $1.20. Anderson added that his instructions from his own Government were to make a last try for $1.75 and if this failed to accept $1.80. He expects to go through the motions of a last try at a meeting of the Steering Committee to be held tomorrow but said that he already appreciated from individual talks with the exporters that $1.75 would be unacceptable. The importers' acceptance of this price offer is based on participation by all four exporters but when Wilson questioned this condition Anderson made plain that it was the quantities they were concerned about rather than the prices in the event say that Russia were to drop out. In Anderson's opinion the importers would put in collectively for scarcely any more than the 450 million bushels already proposed for Canada, the United States and Australia if these three exporters were to go into the agreement without Russia.

2. McCarthy (Australia) informed Wilson this morning of a cable he had received overnight advising that the Australian Cabinet had discussed the agreement yesterday and had decided not to change McCarthy's instructions (i.e. $2.00) until a Sub-Committee of their Cabinet held a meeting with the Australian Wheat Growers Federation scheduled for tomorrow. It could be inferred from this telegram that the Australian Government wished to obtain

this producers' organization's consent to the terms now under negotiation before committing themselves as a Government. McCarthy is expecting a further cable Thursday morning.

3. Late this afternoon the exporting country delegations met at which Borisov (U.S.S.R.) stated that he had not received any new instructions. Rossiter (United States) suggested that we wait until Wednesday noon for word from the U.S.S.R. delegation but failing acceptance of the three exporters' proposal for 50 million bushels out of 500 million bushels for the U.S.S.R. and that the exporters were prepared to make an agreement with the importers without Russian participation. Borisov remarked that this was an ultimatum. Wilson (in the Chair) suggested that as soon as the importers make known in the Steering Committee their preparedness to accept the $1.80 maximum and $1.50, $1.40, $1.30, $1.20 minima, the three exporters would proceed as Rossiter has suggested but that Borisov might inform him at any time before the meeting of the Steering Committee if he had new instructions. This suggestion was accepted by Borisov and the issue should come to a head tomorrow.[17]

Anderson informed the steering committee on the following day that all the importers were prepared to accept the $1.80 ceiling. Agreement was now in sight without resort to the lower limit of the instructions Howe had given Wilson on the ceiling. On March 16, Wilson reported the day's developments:

1. Before the Conference opened this morning Borisov (U.S.S.R.) requested a meeting of the exporters at which he informed the others of instructions received from his Government to the effect that while they were interested in participating in an agreement they were not prepared to come in with a figure less than 75 million bushels on the basis of 500 million bushels for the four exporters. The delegates of the other three exporting countries re-affirmed their position that their 50 million bushels proposal on the basis of 500 million bushels had been a generous one and which the figures as submitted by the importing countries did not fully support. The Australian, Canadian and United States delegates agreed that there was no alternative but report to the importing countries that the four major exporters could not reach agreement on the division of the 500 million bushels and Borisov made no objection to the other three informing the importers of their preparedness to propose an agreement in which Canada, Australia and the United States would be the major exporters.

2. This position was reported by Wilson at a meeting of the Steering Committee this afternoon. Borisov reiterated that his original instructions were for twenty per cent of the total. He had later recommended to his Government and obtained consent for acceptance of at least 75 million bushels out of the 500 million bushels but his Government would not consider participation at a figure lower than 75 million bushels. The three exporters then proposed that the importers re-examine the figures on the basis of non-participation by the U.S.S.R. and the importers agreed to do so. They held a meeting late this afternoon for this purpose.

3. At the same meeting of the Steering Committee Anderson (United Kingdom) reported on behalf of all the importers that subject to participation by the four exporters and agreement being reached on the other provisions the importers were prepared to accept an agreement of four years' duration with the maximum price $1.80 in each of the four years and floors of $1.50, $1.40, $1.30 and $1.20. He said that in the judgment of the importing

[17]*Ibid.*

countries, considering that the floors now agreed upon were 10 cents higher in each of the four years than were provided for the same years in last year's agreement, and considering also the changing supply situation, the importers felt that a ceiling of $1.75 would have been equitable. Nevertheless, they realized the difficulty that a maximum of $1.75 would present in getting agreement and ratification on the part of the exporting countries; therefore they were prepared to concede the $1.80 ceiling. It was clarified in the discussion which followed that the importers reservation on participation of all four major exporters concerned quantities rather than prices and that they naturally reserved the right to lower their quantities if only the three exporting countries were to participate.

4. At the conclusion of the meeting of the Steering Committee Anderson stated that he was prepared to make the importers' agreement on prices public and Borisov requested that the exporters' position on the disagreement on quantities also be made public forthwith. Therefore the Committee asked the Chairman, Van Essche, Anderson representing the importers and Wilson representing the exporters to meet the press which they did at 5:30 giving the substance of the above developments.[18]

In the remaining stages of the conference, McCarthy reported his government's acceptance of the $1.80 ceiling. To deal with the Soviet withdrawal, Anderson proposed that the importing countries meet with Borisov to discuss the quantities that they would be prepared to purchase from the USSR. But the importers' figures failed to come anywhere near the 75 million bushels the USSR had requested so Anderson reported that no agreement with the USSR could be reached, and regrets were expressed in the committee of the whole that the USSR could not be party to the agreement. On behalf of the five remaining exporting countries including France and Uruguay, Wilson informed the committee that the exporters' group could all accept a four-year agreement at the prices proposed. The only problem outstanding was to make a final reconciliation of the exporters' and importers' quantities. Even as late as March 20, it turned out that some of the importers had reduced their quantity figures by more than their normal purchases from the USSR. Several of the Latin American countries had reduced their figures, and as none of them bought from the USSR, it appeared that Argentina had been active in signing bilateral agreements. As a result the United States state department cabled its ambassadors in the countries concerned, and Secretary Brannan interviewed the delegates.

On March 23, the closing day of the conference, Wilson reported:

1. Reference my WA-792 of March 20th, the final revisions in the importers' quantities were not completed until late Tuesday night. Nevertheless the weekend drive to get these quantities revised proved successful and the total import quantities going into the agreement are 456,283,389 bushels.

2. Until yesterday (Tuesday) afternoon the exporters had no precise idea of the total quantity they would have to divide among themselves. During the afternoon, however, Wilson and McNamara met with Rossiter, Smith and Zaglitz (all United States) and McCarthy (Australia). The Americans made a considerable issue to the effect that Canada should accept 200 million bushels even, thereby making it possible for the Americans to get up to 170 million bushels. Wilson and McNamara had indicated to the Americans two weeks

[18]*Ibid.*

ago, when the 50 million bushels offer was made to the U.S.S.R., that the 200 million bushels figure was the bare minimum below which Canada could not go but pointed out at the time that if the Russians were not involved they would accept a reduction on the basis of a straight proration from last year's figures. Yesterday afternoon McNamara, in a superb bit of eleventh-hour negotiating, secured an extra 3 million bushels above our 200 million bushels minimum while the Americans went below their 170 million bushels figure by 2 millions to settle their figure at 168 millions.

3. Even on the above figures Canada has taken a 12 per cent reduction from last year's figure of 230 million bushels and the United States has taken nearly a 10 per cent reduction from last year's figure of 185 million bushels. The Australian figure was agreed at 80 million bushels which is only 6 per cent below last year's figure of 85 million bushels. As for Australia the negotiators were confronted with Hobson's choice: if the Australian figure were reduced the figure for India on the importers' side would have been correspondingly reduced.

4. As for France and Uruguay, they have taken figures mainly for reasons of national prestige and to recognize that they are producers who should be participants in the Agreement. . . .

5. The Agreement to be opened for signature this afternoon includes 37 importing countries and 5 exporting countries. About 29 of the countries, including all the important ones as to quantity, will sign this afternoon and the Agreement remains open for signature for the rest until April 15th. Wilson will sign for Canada this afternoon, and is returning to Ottawa on Thursday. . . .[19]

THE INTERNATIONAL WHEAT AGREEMENT, 1949

The text of the 1949 international wheat agreement with all its administrative clauses ran into a lengthy document. Its essential provisions, however, were the guaranteed quantities, the price range and the article on rights and obligations which required the exporting countries to offer up to the limit of their guaranteed quantities at the ceiling, if required by the importing countries and, in turn, required the importing countries to purchase up to the limit of their guaranteed quantities if offered by the exporting countries at the floor prices. These provisions were the essence of the multilateral contract entered into by the signatory countries. Although varying slightly in form, because of the price range and the defined rights and obligations, it was no more than a collective version of the bilateral contract signed in 1946 by Canada and the United Kingdom which had inspired and given form to the multilateral contract. The following key provisions from the 1949 agreement are quoted:

Part 2 - Rights and Obligations

Article III

Guaranteed Purchases and Guaranteed Sales

1. The quantities of wheat set out in Annex A to this Article for each importing country represent, subject to any increase or reduction made in accordance with the provisions of Part 3 of this Agreement, the guaranteed purchases of that country for each of the four crop-years covered by this Agreement.

[19]*Ibid.*

Annex A to Article III

Guaranteed Purchases

Crop-Year August 1 to July 31	1949/50	1950/51	1951/52	1952/53	Equivalent in bushels for each crop year
	.... thousands of metric tons[1]				
Austria	300	300	300	300	11,023,113
Belgium	550	550	550	550	20,209,040
Bolivia	75	75	75	75	2,755,778
Brazil	360	360	360	360	13,227,736
Ceylon	80	80	80	80	2,939,497
China	200	200	200	200	7,348,742
Colombia	20	20	20	20	734,874
Cuba	202	202	202	202	7,422,229
Denmark	44	44	44	44	1,616,723
Dominican Republic	20	20	20	20	734,874
Ecuador	30	30	30	30	1,102,311
Egypt	190	190	190	190	6,981,305
El Salvador	11	11	11	11	404,181
Greece	428	428	428	428	15,726,308
Guatemala	10	10	10	10	367,437
India	1,042	1,042	1,042	1,042	38,286,946
Ireland	275	275	275	275	10,104,520
Israel	100	100	100	100	3,674,371
Italy	1,100	1,100	1,100	1,100	40,418,081
Lebanon	65	65	65	65	2,388,341
Liberia	1	1	1	1	36,744
Mexico	170	170	170	170	6,246,431
Netherlands[2]	700	700	700	700	25,720,597
New Zealand	125	125	125	125	4,592,964
Nicaragua	8	8	8	8	293,950
Norway	210	210	210	210	7,716,179
Panama	17	17	17	17	624,643
Paraguay	60	60	60	60	2,204,623
Peru	200	200	200	200	7,348,742
Philippines	196	196	196	196	7,201,767
Portugal	120	120	120	120	4,409,245
Saudi Arabia	50	50	50	50	1,837,185
Sweden	75	75	75	75	2,755,778
Switzerland	175	175	175	175	6,430,149
Union of South Africa	300	300	300	300	11,023,113
United Kingdom	4,819	4,819	4,819	4,819	177,067,938
Venezuela	90	90	90	90	3,306,934
Total (37 countries)	12,418	12,418	12,418	12,418	456,283,389

[1] Unless the Council decides otherwise, 72 metric tons of wheat-flour shall be deemed equivalent to 100 metric tons of wheat for the purpose of relating quantities of wheat-flour to the quantities specified in this Annex.
[2] Quantity listed for the Netherlands includes for each crop-year 75,000 metric tons or 2,755,778 bushels for Indonesia.

2. The quantities of wheat set out in Annex B to this Article for each exporting country represent, subject to any increase or reduction made in accordance with the provisions of Part 3 of this Agreement, the guaranteed sales of that country for each of the four crop-years covered by this Agreement.

3. The guaranteed purchases of an importing country represents the maximum quantity of wheat which, subject to deduction of the amount of the

Annex B to Article III

Guaranteed Sales

Crop-year August 1 to July 31	1949/50	1950/51	1951/52	1952/53	Equivalent in bushels for each crop-year
	.... thousands of metric tons[1]				
Australia	2,177	2,177	2,177	2,177	80,000,000
Canada	5,527	5,527	5,527	5,527	203,069,635
France	90	90	90	90	3,306,934
United States of America[2]	4,574	4,574	4,574	4,574	168,069,635
Uruguay	50	50	50	50	1,837,185
Total	12,418	12,418	12,418	12,418	456,283,389

[1] Unless the Council decides otherwise, 72 metric tons of wheat flour shall be deemed equivalent to 100 metric tons of wheat for the purpose of relating quantities of wheat-flour to the quantities specified in this Annex.
[2] In the event of the provisions of Article X being invoked by reason of a short crop it will be recognized that these guaranteed sales do not include the minimum requirements of wheat of any occupied Area for which the United States of America has, or may assume, supply responsibility, and that the necessity of meeting these requirements will be one of the factors considered in determining the ability of the United States of America to deliver its guaranteed sales under this Agreement. ...

transactions entered in the Council's records in accordance with Article IV against those guaranteed purchases,

(a) that importing country may be required by the Council, as provided in Article V, to purchase from the exporting countries at prices consistent with the minimum prices specified in or determined under Article VI, or

(b) the exporting countries may be required by the Council, as provided in Article V, to sell to that importing country at prices consistent with the maximum prices specified in or determined under Article VI.

4. The guaranteed sales of an exporting country represent the maximum quantity of wheat which, subject to deduction of the amount of the transactions entered in the Council's records in accordance with Article IV against those guaranteed sales,

(a) that exporting country may be required by the Council, as provided in Article V, to sell to the importing countries at prices consistent with the maximum prices specified in or determined under Article VI, or

(b) the importing countries may be required by the Council, as provided in Article V, to purchase from that exporting country at prices consistent with the minimum prices specified in or determined under Article VI.

5. If an importing country finds difficulty in exercising its right to purchase its unfulfilled guaranteed quantities at prices consistent with the maximum prices specified in or determined under Article VI or an exporting country finds difficulty in exercising its right to sell its unfulfilled guaranteed quantities at prices consistent with the minimum prices so specified or determined, it may have resort to the procedure in Article V.

6. Exporting countries are under no obligation to sell any wheat under this Agreement unless required to do so as provided in Article V at prices consistent with the maximum prices specified in or determined under Article VI. Importing countries are under no obligation to purchase any wheat under this Agreement unless required to do so as provided in Article V at prices consistent with the minimum prices specified in or determined under Article VI.

7. The quantity, if any, of wheat-flour to be supplied by the exporting country and accepted by the importing country against their respective

guaranteed quantities shall, subject to the provisions of Article V, be determined by agreement between the buyer and seller in each transaction.

8. Exporting and importing countries shall be free to fulfill their guaranteed quantities through private trade channels or otherwise. Nothing in this Agreement shall be construed to exempt any private trader from any laws or regulations to which he is otherwise subject.

Article IV
Prices

1. The basic minimum and maximum prices for the duration of this Agreement shall be:

Crop-Year	Minimum	Maximum
1949/50	$1.50	$1.80
1950/51	$1.40	$1.80
1951/52	$1.30	$1.80
1952/53	$1.20	$1.80

Canadian currency per bushel at the parity for the Canadian dollar, determined for the purposes of the International Monetary Fund as at March 1, 1949 for No. 1 Manitoba Northern wheat in bulk in store Fort William/Port Arthur. The basic minimum and maximum prices, and the equivalents thereof hereafter referred to, shall exclude such carrying charges and marketing costs as may be agreed between the buyer and the seller.[20]

The balance of Article VI was concerned with the determination of equivalent maximum and minimum prices for other grades of Canadian wheat and for United States, Australian, French and Uruguayan wheats.

RATIFICATION OF THE 1949 AGREEMENT

Ratification of the 1949 agreement in the Canadian parliament, was fairly routine. In the absence of Mr. Howe, Prime Minister St. Laurent moved a resolution in the house on April 29, 1949 to approve the agreement, and he said:

Mr. Speaker, in moving this resolution that the house approve of Canada's participation in the international wheat agreement which was opened for signature at Washington on March 23, 1949, I do so on behalf of the Minister of Trade and Commerce (Mr. Howe), who, as hon. members know, is absent from the country on official business in the United Kingdom.

Hon. members will recall that last June parliament approved a similar resolution relating to the agreement signed in 1948. The 1948 agreement did not come into operation, primarily because the United States did not approve the agreement before July 1, the deadline last year. I should like to review the developments leading up to the renegotiation of the agreement this year. I might point out that it does contain, similar to the agreement of 1948, a clause whereby the signatories are required to ratify their signatures by the 1st of July, 1949. It does not come into force unless seventy per cent of the purchasing countries and eighty per cent of the supplying countries have ratified by that date. As Canada is a supplying country to the extent of 203 million bushels out of the total of 454 million bushels, if Canada does not ratify it prior to the 1st of July, 1949, the agreement cannot come into effect.

[20]*International Wheat Agreement, 1949,* Canada Treaty Series No. 10, 1949.

It will be recalled that the ratification of last year's wheat agreement was one of the issues, upon which President Truman reconvened congress. When the senate again failed to approve the agreement it became one of the issues raised in the United States election. Following the election President Truman addressed the conference of the food and agricultural organization of the United Nations in late November and stated that if the international wheat agreement could be renegotiated he would submit the agreement to congress and that he had reason to believe it would be approved this time.

Shortly afterwards the government of the United States invited all the interested governments to attend a conference which met in Washington from January 26 to March 23 of this year. Because last year's agreement was not ratified in time, all of its terms were subject to renegotiation. In the light of the changes which had taken place in the world wheat situation during the past year, the importing countries were not under the pressure of shortage of supplies, and both exporting and importing countries undertook the negotiations under more balanced conditions. The result, after eight weeks of negotiations was that a new agreement was reached and the text was tabled in the house, and printed in Votes and Proceedings on March 28 last. The agreement has already been referred to the United States senate for consideration as a treaty.

Hon. members know that means that it will have to get the approval of a two-thirds vote in the senate in order to be validly ratified as a treaty. Since the same principles are embodied in this year's agreement as in the one which received the approval of the house last year, I shall outline briefly the changes which have taken place in the actual terms of the new agreement.

Altogether thirty-seven importing countries actively participated in the negotiations and by April 15, the closing date for signatures, all but one, Paraguay, signed the agreement. Last year thirty-three importing countries signed. This year two minor exporting countries, France and Uruguay, have joined the main exporting countries, Canada, the United States and Australia. This year's agreement is a four-year agreement covering the last four years of the period covered by last year's five-year agreement.

For the quantities stated in the agreement, the exporting countries guarantee maximum prices of $1.80 per bushel, basis No. 1 Northern wheat in store Fort William-Port Arthur, and the importing countries guaranteed floor prices of $1.50, $1.40, $1.30 and $1.20 in the first, second, third and fourth years respectively. Each exporting country undertook to sell the quantities agreed upon by each of them at a maximum price of $1.80 and the importing countries undertook to bid for that at the minimum price of $1.50 the first year, $1.40 the second year, and $1.30 and $1.20 respectively in the following years. It is evident there will have to be agreement to bring about a sale.

Mr. Bracken: Will the Prime Minister permit one question? I did not hear the number of importing countries that he said had signed this agreement. Will the Prime Minister repeat the number?

Mr. St. Laurent: Thirty-six, thirty-six instead of thirty-three last year. There are five exporting countries this year instead of three exporting countries as in last year's agreement because France has taken the rank of an exporting country for the small quantity indicated in the agreement. Uruguay has also signed as an exporting country for a very small quantity. Although the ceiling prices are twenty cents a bushel lower than in the 1948 agreement, the floor prices are ten cents per bushel higher than were the floor prices for the same years of the old agreement.

Last year's total quantity was 500 million bushels, but this year's quantity is reduced to 456 million bushels. The reduction is due primarily to the altered position of France, which last year required heavy imports but now, under ECA, is endeavouring to improve its balance of payments situation by becoming a net exporter of grain. Of this year's total quantity, Canada's share is 203 million bushels. Because of Paraguay's failure to sign, involving 60,000 tons and the reservation by the government of Peru that their quantity should be reduced by 50,000 tons, an amount of about 4 million bushels will require to be adjusted when the international wheat council meets in July. Although our stated quantity is 203 million bushels of the 456 million bushels, there will probably be a proportionate reduction of about 4 million bushels. this will be made either by having the other importing countries take up this quantity or by the exporting countries sharing a proportionate reduction or by a combination of both, in order that the total import will balance with the total export quantity.

Both Argentina and the U.S.S.R. attended the conference and were given every opportunity to participate. From the outset of the negotiations, however, it was apparent that Argentina had no intention of coming into the agreement. The U.S.S.R., however, took an active part in the negotiations and withdrew only towards the end of the conference when it was apparent that neither the importing countries nor the exporting countries could agree to the share of the total quantities which the U.S.S.R. delegation demanded. Our representative felt that, of the total quantity to be purchased, the U.S.S.R. wanted too large a share. The non-participation by Argentina and the U.S.S.R. is not a complicating factor in the operation of the agreement because the agreement is in the form of a multilateral contract, the terms of which stand among the participating countries regardless of any additional trade in wheat which they may conduct among themselves or may wish to carry on with countries which are not parties to the agreement. These importing countries have undertaken to purchase at the floor prices the quantity mentioned and the exporting countries have undertaken to sell at the ceiling prices the quantities mentioned, but this does not prevent the exporting countries from selling to others or from selling larger quantities. It does not prevent the importing countries from purchasing from others or purchasing larger quantities from the exporting countries.

This is an outline of the developments which led up to the conclusion of this new agreement and the way in which its terms compare with the agreement which was approved by the house last June. Having in mind the changed wheat situation and all the uncertainties which may face the marketing of Canadian wheat without such international co-operation as this agreement provides, I move the adoption of this resolution as one of particular interest to our wheat producers and in the general interest of Canada over the next four years. I think its ratification will also improve our situation and make easier for both parties the carrying out of our wheat agreement with the United Kingdom; because the international agreement does recognize our right to be exporters to these importing countries of a quantity of approximately 200 million bushels. Even if wheat were declared a surplus in the United States, the United States would nevertheless be a party to an agreement which recognizes our right to have these importing countries take approximately 200 million bushels of our wheat. On the whole, I think that this international agreement is an interesting step in these international arrangements that are now being made to try to stabilize the economies of the participating countries, and that it may be a valuable complementary agreement to the North Atlantic pact for the maintenance of stable and peaceful conditions among the nations which trust each other and believe that, when they have made international agreements, those agreements should be carried out.[21]

After the leaders of the other parties spoke, the resolution was approved that same afternoon. Almost simultaneously, a similar resolution was approved in the Canadian senate on April 29, 1949.

On April 19, President Truman submitted the agreement to the senate for ratification and it was referred to the committee on foreign relations. On this occasion, the senate and its committees were under Democratic control. On May 5, Senator Connolly of Texas appointed a subcommittee under the chairmanship of Senator Thomas of Utah to study and report on the agreement. On June 6, Senator Thomas reported the agreement favorably and senate approval came on June 13, 1949.

INTERNATIONAL WHEAT COUNCIL

The 1949 agreement was administered by the international wheat council which had been created under the provisions of the agreement. The agreement provided that the seat of the council should be in London. After a preparatory committee had drawn up a set of rules and regulations for the council, the agreement became operative in London as from August 1, 1949. Although the negotiation of the agreement had been undertaken as a direct government responsibility, its administration from the Canadian side became the responsibility of the Canadian wheat board, whose monopoly powers had been continued for the purpose of administering the Canada-United Kingdom wheat agreement. For a year the bilateral contract overlapped the international wheat agreement. According to a proviso in the terms of the latter agreement, the price applicable to our sales of 140 million bushels of wheat under the bilateral contract continued at $2 in Canadian funds. On September 19, 1949, the Canadian dollar was devalued by 10 per cent. Because prices in the international wheat agreement had been defined in terms of parity of the Canadian dollar determined for purposes of the international monetary fund as of March 1, 1949, this had placed a gold value on the agreement's prices. Accordingly, the agreement ceiling now became $1.98 in terms of the devalued Canadian dollar. Also, because no such gold definition of the Canadian dollar had been placed in the bilateral contract with Britain, Canada continued to sell to that country through 1949-50 for $2 in devalued Canadian funds.

IMPACT OF THE AGREEMENT ON CANADA

The international wheat agreement became operative during the last year of the bilateral contract, and it ruled out any serious consideration of renewing the latter.

As the years of the contract progressed, it had become possible for the government to raise the amount of the initial payment applicable to the five-year pools. On March 25, 1948, the Right Honourable C. D. Howe announced that the payment would be raised from $1.35 to $1.55 forthwith for the whole pool period and, a year later, he announced a further increase to $1.75. Those increases had been facilitated by the contract prices of $2 which had been negotiated for the 1948-49 and 1949-50 crop years.

[21]*House of Commons Debates*, April 29, 1949, pp. 2779-2781.

Now, with the expiry of the contract imminent and its replacement by the international agreement already in effect, the government had to look to the range of prices provided by the latter in determining the initial payment for the 1950 crop. The price range for the 1950-51 crop year in the agreement had been set at $1.40 - 2.00 and there was assurance that the Canadian guaranteed quantity could be sold, only if offered at $1.40. Accordingly, Mr. Howe announced on April 5, 1950, an initial payment of $1.40 for the 1950-51 crop year. The agreement floor was equivalent to $1.40 in United States funds, and the initial payment in the recently devalued Canadian funds afforded the government some additional protection in the floor price guarantee.

Canadian participation in the international wheat agreement had warranted an extension of the wheat board's monopoly powers which had been granted earlier by parliament for the life of the bilateral contract. Now an amendment to the Canadian wheat board act was introduced to extend the monopoly powers for the duration of the international wheat agreement to July 31, 1953, and to revert to the system of annual pools in the place of the five-year pool. As Howe opened the debate on the resolution on April 20, 1950, he reviewed the progress under the contract and the prospects for the international agreement as he said:

> We are now drawing toward the close of the five-year producers' pool and the close of the four-year contract with the United Kingdom, and at this time we find that the Canadian wheat position is essentially sound. The test of soundness is what we have to sell in relation to the demand for it. In this regard we have not had large wheat stocks in Canada since the end of the war. By the date that our contract with the United Kingdom came into operation, our wartime surplus of wheat had been disposed of, and now at the end of four years we are still working with wheat stocks about as small as we had on hand when the four-year contract was negotiated. There appears to be an active demand for the small quantities that remain to be sold from the 1949 crop. Apart from any other factors in the world wheat situation today, Canada will be entering into a new crop year next August without any burdensome legacy of unsold stocks from our previous operations, which is a sound position for us to be in. . . .
>
> Certainly the favourable position in which we find ourselves today has not always, nor has it usually, been the rule. Out of the experience of the early thirties we have had to devise means of handling surplus situations, and it was because of this experience that the Canadian wheat board was established. Up until 1943, the wheat board operated a voluntary pool, which was supplementart to the open market. Under wartime conditions, futures trading in wheat was discontinued, and since 1943, the Canadian wheat board has continued as the sole agency through which producers might market their wheat. This policy received full and careful review by this house during the 1947 session, when amendments were made to the Canadian Wheat Board Act which provided for the board being the sole marketing agency for wheat during the lifetime of the Canada-United Kingdom wheat agreement.
>
> The agreement between Canada and the United Kingdom was entered into at a time when the prospects for sound marketing conditions were clouded by many uncertainties as to the way in which our principal customers, who have suffered the ravages of war, would be able to adjust themselves in the immediate post-war period. Although we had seen the effects of the pent-up demand from some of these countries after their liberation, there were no

indications that this was more than a transitory situation. Our desire to obtain stability inspired a search for a more dependable basis in dealing with our customers than that of the seller taking all while wheat was scarce, only to be at the mercy of the buyer when surpluses returned. In our past experience, periods of scarcity were of much shorter duration than the periods of surplus.

The first step in the direction of dependable trading was taken when we entered into the four-year contract with the United Kingdom. This contract assured us a market, and assured the United Kingdom of supplies at negotiated prices, for a long period, and in this way served as an insurance policy to both contracting parties against instability, which could hardly have been insured against in any other way. Now that we are drawing toward the end of the contract period and can begin to evaluate the results, it is apparent that the United Kingdom has obtained the bulk of her wheat requirements for three the four years at prices lower than she would otherwise have had to pay. On the other hand, we should not overlook the fact that if nothing more were to be paid from the five-year pool — and there will be another payment — our producers have had the best returns from wheat that they have had in any five-year peacetime period of their history. . . .

An important element in our post-war policy on wheat, which was obscured by several factors at the time, was our desire to deal with all our normal customers for wheat on the same basis as we were prepared to deal with the United Kingdom. Had there been any means of making effective firm guarantees of supplies, we would have been glad to extend the provisions of our contract with the United Kingdom to other importing countries during that period. As it was in 1946, this government actively sought to get ahead with the negotiation of a post-war international wheat agreement, but could find no concerted view among the other countries at the time that an international agreement should be made. Thus when we entered into the contract with the United Kingdom we did so in the knowledge that no arrangements of an international character could be secured at the time. Notwithstanding, reference to the final clause of the Canada-United Kingdom agreement will remind us that both countries envisaged that an international agreement might be reached, and that if this were accomplished, the terms of the contract would be brought into conformity with the terms of an international agreement.

I need not dwell upon the successive negotiations which took place to bring the international agreement into operation, beyond mentioning that over the three conferences which took place from 1947 to 1949, there developed among the other countries of the world a growing appreciation of the benefits which would accrue to exporters and importers alike if a stabilizing influence could be introduced into the world wheat trade. As a result, negotiation became possible of an agreement which was duly ratified and came into operation last August 1 for a four-year period ending July 31, 1953. This multilateral agreement is not dissimilar in nature to that of our agreement with the United Kingdom, except that a range of prices was adopted rather than a fixed price, and that by pooling together the export potentials of Canada, the United States and Australia, we were able to offer a four-year contract on equal terms to some thirty-six importing countries.

I hardly need to elaborate on what this agreement means to Canada. The agreement received the unanimous approval of this house a year ago. It is recognized as an experiment, which we all hope will succeed. It holds no panacea for all our wheat problems, nor does it settle the problem of exchange. There is no guarantee of its implementation beyond the commitments governments have given to carry out its terms. We are dependent upon their good faith. The agreement does, however, set a standard for reasonable prices to both buyers and sellers, and assures supplies to the buyers and markets to the sellers. As such it is well worth the best implementation we can give to it. . . .

There is little doubt that we are passing from a seller's market to a buyer's market, in which there is not likely to be a shortage of supply. The situation will be helped by the international wheat agreement, which is intended to provide both a ceiling and a floor for wheat prices. The agreement has not been tested under conditions of oversupply, but I for one believe that the agreement will have a stabilizing effect on wheat prices.

One can be either an optimist or a pessimist about the ability of Canada to dispose of her wheat at reasonable prices in the trading world today. I prefer to be an optimist. In fact, if I were not an optimist at this stage, I would be a poor selection for the minister in charge of our wheat-selling organization. I believe that we can sell our surplus wheat at prices that will return a profit to our farmers in the future as we have in the past. The reputation of Canadian wheat is unquestioned in world markets. Under the trading conditions of today, price and quality are not always the determining factor to the extent that they were in pre-war days, but price and quality still count for much. Canada has established a reputation in world wheat markets for fair dealing, which will stand us in good stead. The deficit countries of the world will continue to require wheat, and I believe that Canadian wheat will continue to find a market in those countries. The Canadian wheat board has demonstrated its ability to handle Canada's wheat marketing problems efficiently, and I have every confidence that this ability will be further demonstrated in the years to come.[22]

In the immediate wheat situation, Howe had need for optimism. Britain's purchases of wheat within the past year had been facilitated by an American ECA authorization of $175 million for offshore purchases of wheat in Canada. Now the Americans had to terminate such assistance in the face of an emerging wheat surplus position in their own country. It was uncertain therefore how competitive the Americans might yet become. Because of the British and Canadian balance of payments difficulties reflected in their exchange devaluations, the British had asked for, and been granted, a postponement of the purchase of 12½ million bushels out of the 140 millions they had undertaken to purchase in the last year of the contract, in order to make it possible for them to make other essential purchases in Canada. It was in that atmosphere that Howe sought to assure a continuing priority for Canadian wheat in the British market.

[22]*Ibid.*, April 20, 1950, pp. 1730-1734.

47

FINAL SETTLEMENT OF THE "HAVE REGARD TO" CLAUSE

It will be recalled, from Chapter 45, that the Canadian and British governments had agreed to meet not later than July 31, 1950, to settle any obligations which might then remain outstanding under clause 2(b) of the bilateral agreement.

From the time that the contract was first announced, Gardiner had ruled out any precise arithmetical calculation of the difference between the contract price of $1.55 and world prices in the first two years, and Mackenzie King, in his October 1, 1947, announcement of the $2 price for 1948-49 had confirmed that "a precise arithmetical calculation of the difference in price was not suggested". Nevertheless, on the strength of Gardiner's interpretation of what the "have regard to" clause meant, expectations had been built up that if the British realized a "break" on prices during the first two years of the agreement, they would make up for it in the prices to be negotiated and to be paid in the last two years. This interpretation was confirmed in the minds of western Canadian farmers and their organizations by the dramatic speech which Strachey made in Winnipeg on February 25, 1947. That was the popular and reasonable interpretation put on the intent of the "have regard to" clause, but that construction was, unfortunately, not borne out by the actual wording of clause 2(b) which required that such considerations be embraced in the price negotiations for the 1948-49 crop year to be completed before December 31, 1947, and for 1949-50 before December 31, 1948. Thus the "have regard to" clause carried a double entendre, interpreted one way by the western farmers and the two original negotiating ministers, and another way by other ministers when the settlement was made.

PREPARATIONS FOR MR. HOWE'S MISSION

When the time came for the negotiations of the final settlement of clause 2(b), it was Howe, rather than Gardiner, who undertook the assignment. The cabinet was concerned over the continuing balance of payments difficulties of both countries. The British pound and the Canadian dollar had recently been devalued. Unemployment had emerged as a problem in Canada that winter, and some of the food contracts had been cancelled by the British. The most important immediate factor had been the American withdrawal of ECA funds for British offshore purchases of wheat in Canada, and it was unknown whether the Americans would go further by subsidizing the sale of their own surplus wheat in Britain. It was in that economic environment, that Howe undertook the mission. In preparation therefor, Howe asked Wilson to brief him upon the "have regard to" negotiations which had taken place to date, and upon the terms of a possible settlement. Wilson put together a departmental "black book" with all the relevant documents together with his memorandum of May 5, 1950, regarding the settlement of obligations under the Canada-United Kingdom agreement. The memorandum contained a summary of the September 1947 and the December 1948 negotiations which Gardiner conducted, and then proceeded with an analysis of the merits of settling the "have regard to" obligation by a further payment into the five-year pool and, alternatively, of settling the obligation by means of a further quantity guarantee. In doing so, he assessed the merits of the financial claims advanced on behalf of producers by the critics of the agreement, and of those made at various times by Gardiner as he wrote:

Dealing first with the issue of a cash settlement, we should bear in mind that the settlement involves the price discrepancies in the first two crop years only, and the following is the comparison most frequently used by the critics of the agreement:

Crop Year	Contract Quantity (incl. allow- ance for offals) bushels	Weighted Average Class II Price	Contract Price (incl. 3½¢ carrying charge)	Differ- ence	Total "Loss"
1946/47	169,000,000	$2.43	$1.58½	.84½	$142,805,000
1947/48	170,600,000	2.88	1.58½	1.29½	220,927,000
					$363,732,000

It can also be shown that in the 1948/49 crop year there was a further "loss" of $26,520,000, although the United Kingdom has no obligation under the contract to compensate for this. Further, in the 1949/50 crop year, assuming that the International Wheat Agreement price remains at the ceiling until July 31, the United Kingdom could claim that there has been compensation to Canada of $11,530,000, this sum representing the additional cost on contract terms to the United Kingdom over what they would have had to pay in 1949/50 under International Wheat Agreement terms.

Supporters of the contract, of course, have not admitted that validity of the "loss" shown above when calculated on the differences between contract and Class II prices. They have claimed that it is impossible to tell what prices would have been received if the whole of the Canadian supplies had been offered on Class II markets.

A different approach from the above on the calculation of the "loss" has been made by Mr. Gardiner. He would have been satisfied to establish evidence that, after allowing for the "normal" disparity of Canadian farm prices for wheat below those in the United States the Canadian producers' returns from wheat during the five-year pool period were as good as those of the American producer. Whereas two years ago, when Mr. Gardiner first developed this approach, there appeared to be some hope of establishing such a position, Mr. Gardiner's calculations brought up-to-date show that it would be impossible to do so now. Allowing for the war-time Canadian dollar discount, Canadian farm prices for wheat averaged 20 cents below American farm prices during the ten crop years 1935/36 to 1944/45. Dominion Bureau of Statistics surveys have shown that Canadian wheat prices for the average grade at the farm have averaged 20 cents below Lakehead or Vancouver prices for No. 1 Northern. Thus the $1.75 for No. 1 Northern already paid, teminal basis, during the pool period, plus 5 cents still due from the pool would bring the farm price to $1.60 in each of the five years. From the 1945/46 and 1949/50 Canadian farm prices should be deducted 15 cents because of the discount on Canadian funds in those years. This adjustment should be made, because the exchange discount increased the disparity between Canadian and American farm prices during the war years. With these adjustments the comparison can be made as follows:

Crop Year	U.S. Average Farm Prices	Cdn. Average Farm Prices (incl. further 5¢ pay- ment)	Ten Year Average 1935/36- 1944/45 differ- ence between U.S. & Cdn. farm prices (inc. exchange adjust- ments)	Net differ- ences between Cdn. & U.S. Farm Prices	Cdn. Farm Deliv- eries (000 bu.)	Net "Loss"
1945/46	$1.49	$1.45(¹)	.20	(.16)	235,438	$(37,670,000
1946/47	1.90	1.60	.20	.10	335,154	33,515,000
1947/48	2.29	1.60	.20	.49	243,941	119,531,000
1948/49	1.99	1.60	.20	.19	293,015	55,673,000
1949/50	1.87	1.45(¹)	.20	.22	309,000	67,980,000
						$239,029,000

(¹) exchange discount deducted

It is evident that no source will yield $239,000,000 to make good the argument based on this comparison. In December, 1948, Mr. Gardiner calculated that $150,000,000 would be required to bridge the gap, and handed Sir Stafford Cripps such a calculation. At that time, Mr. Gardiner appeared to be prepared to settle for $75,000,000.

If Mr. Gardiner's method of calculation is confined, however, to the contract quantities rather than to the total farm deliveries, and also to the 1946/47 and 1947/48 crop years which actually concern the United Kingdom's obligation, we have the following results:

Crop Year	Contract Quantity (incl. allow- ance for offals) (bushels)	Net Difference between Cdn. & U.S. farm prices (see above)	Total "Loss"
1946/47	169,000,000	.10	$ 16,900,000
1947/48	170,600,000	.49	83,594,000
			$100,494,000
Less U.K. "compensation" to Canada in 1949/50			11,530,000
		Net "Loss"	$ 88,964,000

This figure of $89,000,000 comes much closer to the realm of practical consideration. If the United Kingdom government were to find means of paying it, such a settlement has much to commend it, for the following reasons:

(a) Since very few producers concerned are likely to be entirely satisfied, whatever the settlement, the sooner a final settlement is made the better.

(b) Western producers are looking for a further cash payment to the producers' pool. The representatives of the three pool organizations who met with ministers on March 24 were quite definite that they expected a "further substantial adjusting payment" in settlement of the "have regard to" obligation. Their attitude was that they were not particular what source the payment comes from so long as it is made. It could be taken for granted that the non-pool supporters hold this view even more strongly. If such a payment were made by the United Kingdom, it would have the advantage of being a definitive settlement of issue—that is, the Canadian government would have negotiated the issue with the United Kingdom and $89,000,000 or other sum would be what actually resulted from the negotiation. In other words, producers would accept the settlement because the United Kingdom in its present circumstances had paid for it. Perhaps the most likely source of such funds would be the unexpected balance of the Canada-United Kingdom Credit, the United Kingdom accepting the obligation under the Credit.

On the other hand, if the Canadian government were to attempt a settlement with the producers in lieu of the United Kingdom government, the settlement would probably not be definitive.

With the Canadian government putting up the funds in default by the United Kingdom, no specific sum short of the $363,732,000 shown on page 3 would satisfy all the Canadian critics, and whatever sum provided would generate its own controversy. In my opinion, however, it would be unrealistic not to seek a cash settlement from the United Kingdom, despite the arguments that will be advanced from their side that any cash settlement will have the effect of curtailing purchases on current account, whether of wheat or other commodities from Canada.[1]

In the foregoing, Wilson left no doubt about his own views that a further payment should be made, and that it should be made by the British using, if necessary and as Mr. St. Laurent had earlier suggested, the undrawn balance remaining in the Canada-United Kingdom credit. Then he proceeded with an analysis of a further quantity guarantee:

Turning now to consideration of a forward quantity guarantee, such a scheme was developed during the December 1948 discussions. This scheme varied in its terms according to the actual level of prices ruling in 1949/50 as follows:-

(a) if the average price in 1949/50 received by Canada from other countries were to fall below $1.50 per bushel, the United Kingdom would have made full and final discharge of its "have regard to" obligations.

(b) If the above average price were to fall between $1.50 and $1.75 the United Kingdom would give Canada an option on the sale of 100-140 million bushels of wheat at a price of $1.40-$1.55 for the 1950/51 crop year, such option to be exercised before the beginning of the crop year.

(c) If the above average price were to be higher than $1.75 in 1949/50 the option would be repeated for the 1951/52 crop year.

[1] *C. F. Wilson, Memorandum of May 5, 1950, to the Right Honourable C. D. Howe re Settlement of Obligations under the Canada-United Kingdom Wheat Agreement,* Trade and Commerce file 20-141-U2.

The quantities and prices in the options were never agreed, the ranges shown indicating the differences between Canadian and the United Kingdom views. Consideration of these options was abandoned because of representations from the United States government.

Although there are several advantages of a forward quantity guarantee which will be mentioned below, in my opinion options of the type outlined above are of very doubtful value from the Canadian standpoint. Their first weakness is that the options are conditional upon the future trend of prices. Their main weakness, however, is that the United Kingdom authorities have insisted that the options be exercised in advance of the crop year to which they apply. This is the same weakness that lay in the "have regard to" clause which required the United Kingdom obligation to be settled by prices determined well in advance of each of the last two crop years. Exercising options in advance of the crop year would involve the Canadian authorities in a major speculation — if we were to take up the option, subsequent price developments might easily show that we had sold to the United Kingdom too cheaply, and if we let the option lapse a reverse in prices could make us look foolish for not having taken it up.

Canada's interest lies essentially in a quantity guarantee without any price commitment; the United Kingdom's interest is in tying a cheap price to any quantity guarantee. From Canada's standpoint we should seek a firm quantity, with the price free to follow the level of our other sales under the International Wheat Agreement. On price we could undertake that the price of current shipments to the United Kingdom would be no higher than the price at which we are currently selling to other countries under the International Wheat Agreement. This basis would abandon any thought of eventually obtaining a higher price from the United Kingdom than on other sales in "have regard to" compensation, but there appears to be no satisfactory way of reaching for a higher price without assuming the risk that any forward price might again turn out to be under the market.

A firm quantity guarantee, on the other hand, has definite advantages. With two more years of ECA, such a guarantee would serve as protection against any substantial movement of United States wheat into the United Kingdom market. it might be argued that we already have protection on quantity under the International Wheat Agreement, but this protection is at floor prices. A quantity guarantee from the United Kingdom should apply at higher than floor prices if prices on our sales to other countries are ruling above the floor. A quantity guarantee on wheat also provides the opportunity to negotiate a quantity on flour.

One of the main considerations in a quantity guarantee would be its size. During and since the war Canada has exported much larger quantities of wheat and flour to the United Kingdom than in the pre-war years. On the average from 1924/25 to 1938/39 Canada exported 87,300,000 bushels of wheat and flour per year to the United Kingdom, including 227,000 long tons of flour. During the war years these quantities picked up sharply, and reached their height during the first years of the war when, for example in 1940/41, the United Kingdom took 191,300,000 bushels from Canada. The quantities remained heavy during the first years of the Canada-United Kingdom contract when the postwar wheat shortage was at its height.

From these figures it appears that we should strike at least a "half-way house" between the pre-war years and the war and post-war period, and settle for firm quantity guarantees in the next two years of at least 120 million bushels of wheat, including 300,000 or 350,000 long tons of flour. If such quantities could be guaranteed by agreement with the United Kingdom,

Canadian Wheat and Flour Exports to the United Kingdom

Crop Year	Wheat and Flour (bushels)	Flour Only (long tons)
Fifteen-year average 1924/25 - 1938/39	87,300,000	227,000
Seven-year average 1939/40 - 1945/46	148,200,000	524,000
1946/47	169,000,000	640,000
1947/48	170,600,000	750,000
1948/49	146,300,000	450,000
1949/50	145,600,000	400,000

without a price commitment other than that we are selling to others for under the International Wheat Agreement, such a guarantee would have the advantages already referred to above, and would have only minor technical disadvantages.[2]

In that analysis, Wilson had stressed that Canada's interest lay in a quantity guarantee without any price commitment. What was needed was a continuing priority of treatment in the British market as protection against the possibility of the inroad of American subsidized wheat. But he left no doubt about his belief that producers would prefer a cash settlement as he concluded the memorandum:

> The decision as to whether the advantages of a quantity guarantee compensate sufficiently to forego a financial settlement with the United Kingdom and any financial contribution to the producers' pool must be a ministerial one. In my own judgment a financial settlement would be more acceptable to western producers than a quantity guarantee.[3]

After contemplating the alternatives, Howe had no difficulty in making up his own mind that the issue of paramount importance to producers was a forward quantity guarantee uncluttered by any price commitment. To maintain a continuing volume of sales in our largest market was the primary consideration. In Howe's mind, this transcended in value the cash settlement Gardiner cherished in order to honor the undertakings he had promised in settlement of the expiring contract. The issue was not squarely joined in cabinet, however, before Howe's departure for London. Instead, when the matter was raised, Gardiner urged that the time was premature to negotiate the final settlement of the contract. Accordingly, he asked that Howe be instructed to request an extension of the agreed deadline of July 31, 1950, for those negotiations; Howe readily agreed. This was the understanding reached in cabinet as Howe was authorized to seek his own objective of securing a forward quantity guarantee.

LONDON NEGOTIATIONS, MAY 22, 1950

On his trip to London, Mr. Howe was accompanied by the Honourable L. B. Pearson, the recently appointed minister of external affairs, Norman Robertson, who was now Pearson's undersecretary, Max Mackenzie and George McIvor. The party was joined in London by the newly-appointed Canadian high commissioner, L. Dana Wilgress. On May 22, 1950, the Canadian party met with Sir Stafford Cripps, chancellor of the exchequer,

[2]*Ibid.*
[3]*Ibid.*

P. Gordon-Walker, secretary of state for commonwealth relations, Hugh Gaitskell, minister of state for economic affairs, M. Webb, minister of food and their senior officials. Webb had succeeded Strachey as minister of food on February 28, 1950.

Despite the best of intentions in accordance with the understanding he had reached with Gardiner in cabinet about avoiding discussion of the final settlement during his visit, Howe was confronted by Sir Stafford Cripps who was just as determined that the issue should be dealt with then. Cripps was aware of his previous encounters with Gardiner who had insisted that the "have regard to" negotiations be dealt with separately from considerations such as the other food contracts. Therefore, Howe listened to the British representations and discussed them at length, but on the understanding that he had no authority to negotiate the settlement and could only report the British views back to his government. After their meeting, the British prepared a minute on the discussions which was accepted by the Canadian delegation. The minute, however, simply listed the conclusions reached so that there was no record of the extent, if any, to which a financial settlement was discussed before the parties agreed to a forward quantity guarantee. This was Howe's main objective, of course, but the minutes made clear that the British did not wish it to be construed as a quid pro quo for their clause 2(b) obligation, but rather as something they wished to do in any event. By implication, the minute suggested that the British obligation had already been discharged in the prices which had been negotiated for the third and fourth contract years. The text of the agreed minute read:

United Kingdom-Canadian Wheat Talks
May 1950

Agreed record of a Meeting in the Foreign Secretary's Room in the House of Commons at 2:30 p.m. on Monday 22nd May 1950.

Present:

United Kingdom: Chancellor of the Exchequer; (in the Chair): Secretary of State for Commonwealth Relations; Minister of State for Economic Affairs; Minister of Food; Sir Percivale Liesching; Sir Henry Wilson Smith; Sir Frank Lee; Mr. A. E. Feavearyear.

Canada: Mr. C. D. Howe; Mr. L. B. Pearson; Mr. L. D. Wilgress; Mr. Norman A. Robertson; Mr. M. W. Mackenzie; Mr. G. H. McIvor.

Secretary: Mr. F. Hollins.

1. The meeting considered the following three questions in the light of the discussions that had taken place since Friday, 19th may:

(a) The quantity of wheat to be bought by the United Kingdom from Canada in the crop year 1950/51.

(b) The proportion of the quantity at (a) which the United Kingdom would take in the form of flour.

(c) The final settlement of any question still outstanding under Clause 2 (b) (the "have regard to" clause) of the United Kingdom/Canada Contract of 1946.

2. The conclusions reached on these three subjects were as follows:

(a) The United Kingdom and Canadian governments would both make agreed announcements on the results of the conversations in the terms of the statement at Annex A. The United Kingdom government would have no objection to Mr. Howe stating publicly on his return to Canada, if he considered it desirable, that he thought it reasonable to assume that in 1950/51 Canada would be able to sell to the United Kingdom at competitive international wheat agreement prices somewhere between 100-120 million bushels of wheat. This quantity would include the carry-over of 12.5 million bushels bought under the terms of the four-year contract. The Chancellor of the Exchequer would also be prepared to make a public statement to the effect that the United Kingdom government hoped that they would be able to meet their requirements for dollar wheat from their traditional market in Canada within the international wheat agreement, and that this would be possible provided that such wheat could be purchased on terms as to price, quality and position not less favourable than those obtained by any other buyer in the dollar market whether in the United States of America or Canada.

(b) As part of its purchases of Canadian wheat in the crop year 1950/51 the United Kingdom would agree to take 300,000 tons of flour, provided that it could be purchased on terms not less favourable as to price and quality than those obtained by any other buyer of flour in the dollar market, whether in the United States of America or Canada. The United Kingdom representatives made it clear that the purchase of 300,000 tons in 1950/51 would be without prejudice to a possible lower scale of purchase in 1951/52.

(c) The United Kingdom was anxious not to be represented as having given assurances regarding wheat purchases in 1950/51 in return for the waiver of a claim by Canada under the "have regard to" clause. The United Kingdom expected to make large purchases of wheat from Canada in any event. Nevertheless, in the context of these discussions, the United Kingdom representatives felt that it would be reasonable that all obligations under the "have regard to" clause might be considered to have been taken care of. Mr. Howe said that this was a matter which could only be settled by the Canadian cabinet on his return.[4]

AGREEMENT OF MAY 30, 1950

Howe returned to Ottawa to report to cabinet the results of his discussions. In cabinet the issue of the settlement was debated at length, with Gardiner adhering to his original understanding of the "have regard to" clause, and Howe to the interpretation which Sir Stafford Cripps had placed upon it. In the debate, Howe likened the contract to an insurance policy as he had done in his earlier statements with reference to the contract and to the international wheat agreement. Although too high a premium might have been paid for assurance against unstable markets and prices during the transitional period, one did not ask for a return of the premium after the calamity had been avoided. Gardiner maintained that if a further payment were not forthcoming from the British, the Canadian government would have to make good the default. Norman Robertson, who had accompanied Howe to the London meeting and had attended two days of cabinet discussion, prepared a memorandum for Prime Minister St. Laurent on June 26, 1950, in which he weighed the alternatives. Because the British had refused further payment, and Gardiner had proposed a payment in lieu thereof from the Canadian treasury, Robertson wondered if the producers' reasonable expectations could be met in another way by a Canadian government undertaking to guarantee a price of $2 on the marketings from the 1950-51 crop. Such a guarantee would tend to hold world prices at the international wheat agreement ceiling and avoid the need for a supplemen-

[4]*House of Commons Debates,* March 15, 1951, pp. 1306-1307.

tary estimate to cover a payment into the five-year pool during the current session of parliament.

Robertson's proposed solution found little support in cabinet which continued to debate the "have regard to" settlement, with Howe adhering to the Cripps position and Gardiner contending that a further payment was due. On May 30, 1950, cabinet decided to accept the agreed record of the May 22 meeting in London and to approve a statement to be made by Howe to the house on the extended quantity guarantee. The draft statement had also been drawn up in London. At the same time, cabinet decided to defer for further consideration the issue of the final settlement. Accordingly, immediately after the cabinet meeting on May 30, Mr. A. D. P. Heeney, secretary of the cabinet, forwarded with a covering letter to Sir Alexander Clutterbuck, the British high commissioner, a message for Sir Stafford Cripps from Howe:

Following for the Chancellor of the Exchequer from the Minister of Trade and Commerce, begins:

I have reported to my colleagues in the Cabinet on our recent wheat talks in London, and wish to let you know that they are in accord with the conclusions recorded in paragraph 2 (a), (b) and (c) of the agreed record of the meeting which we held in the Foreign Secretary's room in the House of Commons on Monday, May 22nd.

In the circumstances, I should very much like to make public the agreed statement today, May 30th, if possible at 3:00 p.m. Ottawa time.[5]

With his message delivered to Cripps, Howe announced the results of the London discussions to the house in the following terms:

In connection with my recent trip to the United Kingdom, I should like to read into the record an agreed statement by the United Kingdom and Canadian government recording the result of our wheat discussions.

"The Canadian Minister of Trade and Commerce held discussions in London with United Kingdom ministers on the subject of the United Kingdom's wheat requirements in the crop year 1950-51 within the framework of the international wheat agreement."

"Both governments have now reviewed the results of those talks. They are agreed that the international wheat agreement removes the need for a contract to replace the existing Ango-Canadian wheat agreement which expires at the end of July."

"The United Kingdom government has made it clear that out of its total wheat import requirements in 1950-51, it expects to buy a large proportion in Canada which, quite apart from the special contractual arrangements for the past four years, is, and it is hoped will remain, the traditional source of supply for the United Kingdom. The Canadian government, for its part, is satisfied that Canadian wheat growers will continue to find in the United Kingdom a market for a very substantial part of their exportable wheat."

I should also mention that the United Kingdom has agreed to take 300,000 tons of Canadian flour at competitive North American prices as part of its purchases of Canadian wheat in the crop year 1950-51.

In the light of all our discussions, I think it reasonable to assume that in 1950-51 the United Kingdom will purchase from Canada between 100 and 120 million bushels of wheat. It is understood that such wheat will be offered upon international wheat agreement terms as to price, quality and position

---

[5]*Ibid.*

not less favourable than those obtained by any other buyer in the dollar market, whether in the United States or in Canada.[6]

Opposition members were well aware of the July 31, 1950, deadline for the final settlement which had been announced in January 1949, and Mr. J. A. Ross asked Howe immediately if the settlement had been discussed. Because that issue had not yet been decided by cabinet, Howe fielded the question as he replied to Ross by saying: "I understand the wheat board act will be discussed later in the session and I do not care to amplify this statement at the moment."[7]

The debate on the wheat board act came up in the house shortly thereafter, and Ross continued to press for an answer to his question whether the settlement had been discussed in London. On that occasion, on June 5, 1950, Howe proceeded to answer Ross by stating the Cripps version of the "have regard to" clause. He read the text of clause 2(b) into Hansard and said:

> That is the "have regard to" clause in the agreement. I suggest that regard was paid in fixing these prices. The price for the first two years of the agreement was $1.55. After negotiation the price for the third year was fixed at $2, and after negotiation the price for the fourth year was fixed at $2. What does my hon. friend read out of the agreement beyond the fact that the price for the last two years would be settled having regard to world prices in the first two years?[8]

When Ross replied by referring to the January 1949 announcement that the final settlement would be extended to July 31, 1950, Howe responded with the following extempore explanation:

> The matter of the "have regard to" clause was discussed in great detail during our sessions with Sir Stafford Cripps and other ministers of the United Kingdom government. The whole situation was reviewed. The United Kingdom is just as positive as I have been in my statements in the house as to what the world price of wheat really was in those periods. My hon. friend said the world price was the price in a local market to which Canadian grain is not permitted access. I wonder what the world price would have been if we had been able to ship our Canadian grain to the Chicago market, which he says is the great criterion for world prices. We went over the agreement while in London. We asked the United Kingdom government what further settlement it is to make on account of the "have regard to" clause. The United Kingdom government took a very strong position that they had fulfilled all obligations under that clause, and so far as the United Kingdom was concerned. We agreed on behalf of Canada that considering all the circumstances that was the case.[9]

The presumption was strong that the explanation Howe gave was done without cabinet approval, in which case there would have been a formal statement. Evidence that Howe prejudged the issue lay in the fact that the cabinet continued to debate the settlement on June 22-23 and was still unable to resolve it. Nevertheless, Howe's message of May 30 to Cripps and his remarks in the house on June 5 convinced the British authorities that the Canadian government had accepted the British position.

[6]*Ibid.,* May 30, 1950, p. 2985.
[7]*Ibid.*
[8]*Ibid.,* June 5, 1950, p. 3221.
[9]*Ibid.*

REOPENING OF THE ISSUE

There was a delayed shock reaction through the west to Howe's statement of June 5. A good crop was looming up but, in the result, the 1950 crop was heavily frosted. The amount of the final payment from the five-year pool still remained to be announced, and the expectation was that a larger final payment could be made than the remaining funds warranted. As the representatives from the west began to mount a campaign for a further payment either by the British or by the Canadian government, Gardiner reopened the question in cabinet. In a 14-page memorandum he submitted to cabinet on October 11, 1950, he reviewed the whole history of the government's intervention in the wheat industry, including the origin of the bilateral contract and the negotiations he had undertaken thereunder in 1947 and in 1948, in London. Gardiner placed squarely upon Sir Stafford Cripps the responsibility for the literal interpretation of clause 2(B) under which Cripps contended that regard had been had in negotiation of the 1948-49 and 1949-50 prices, and that no further obligation had been incurred. This was directly at variance with the verbal understanding Gardiner had reached with Strachey, both during the contract negotiation in June, 1946, and during the 1948-49 price negotiation in September, 1947. At the end of his memorandum, Gardiner contended that he had shown beyond doubt that Britain had agreed to pay more for the 600 million bushels she had received during the life of the contract than had yet been paid. He recommended that discussions be reopened with the British government to pay $100 million additional or, at any rate, not less than $65 million. The funds could be taken, if need be, from the undrawn balance of the Canadian loan. Failing that, Gardiner contended, the Canadian government should consider what amount it was prepared to pay into the five-year pool. Gardiner's long submission to cabinet was prepared, characteristically, by himself. In it he reproduced all the relevant history of the contract developments as he recalled them. Because it sheds such light upon his own interpretation of the events and also upon Gardiner's personality, the memorandum entitled "A History of the Wheat Position" is reproduced in Appendix 6.

When the wheat board disclosed that, in the absence of any further contribution, the final payment on the five-year pool would not amount to more than four cents a bushel, the three wheat pools sent a delegation to Ottawa to plead the case for a supplementary payment. Messrs. Parker, Wesson and Plumer met with several cabinet ministers on November 28, 1950, and presented a brief in support of a further payment.

MR. ST. LAURENT'S INTERVENTION

Because of these representations, Prime Minister St. Laurent undertook to reopen the question with Prime Minister Attlee during the latter's visit to Ottawa on December 9-12, 1950. Attlee had gone to Washington to consult with President Truman at a critical stage in the Korean conflict and he returned to London via Ottawa. Mr. St. Laurent reported the substance of his discussion on wheat with the British prime minister to the house after the leader of the opposition, Mr. Drew, claimed that the Canadian government had proposed to the British government use of the $65 million balance in the credit as a final payment on the contract. Mr. St. Laurent replied:

> There was no proposal by the government that they draw this amount and pay it over. There was the statement that they could do so if they saw fit to do it. But there was no request at all made by the government to the British government to make any further payment. It was always recognized that there was no further legal obligation upon them. But I felt that it was only fair that I should point out to the prime minister of the United Kingdom when he was here that there was a prevailing feeling that they had not carried out the "have regard to" clause in the manner in which it had been expected they would carry it out; and those expectations were a result of statements that had been made in this country by one of his colleagues after listening in this house to discussions taking place here and having gone out to Winnipeg to make the position clear. I felt that they should know that those expectations existed; that they should know that there would be serious disappointment if they did nothing further about the "have regard to" clause. I told the prime minister of the United Kingdom that we had accepted as their position in May or June their statement that they had done all they intended to do under the "have regard to" clause, and I said: "I am not asking you to do more, but I am asking you if you do not think, in view of what I am saying to you now, that I should bring those facts to the attention of the chancellor." He agreed that I might bring them to the attention of the chancellor. When I went over in January, I did so.[10]

As arranged with Prime Minister Attlee, Prime Minister St. Laurent raised the matter again with the Right Honourable Hugh Gaitskell, chancellor of the exchequer, who had succeeded Sir Stafford Cripps in that post, on October 19, 1950. Gaitskell had attended the meeting with Howe and Pearson on May 22 of that year. In the course of the commonwealth prime ministers' conference in London, St. Laurent met with Gaitskell on January 6, 1951, and left with him a very diplomatically worded aide-memoire. In it, St. Laurent reviewed the background of the "have regard to" negotiation including the postponement of the settlement which had been agreed in January, 1949, and also the agreed minute of May 22, 1950, which he claimed had not gone farther than to state that the question of the "have regard to" clause would have to be referred to the Canadian cabinet. Nevertheless, the Canadian government was not now claiming that there was any further obligation upon the British in the strictly legal sense, and was not making representations upon that basis. The Canadian government believed, however, that the British authorities should be made aware that British ministerial statements in Canada had led Canadian wheat growers to believe that an obligation remained. The Canadian government was, therefore, prepared to discuss an arrangement whereby a payment could be made from the undrawn balance of the Canadian credit in order to avoid a strain upon the British dollar position.

St. Laurent gave copies of his aide-memoire to the secretary of commonwealth affairs, Mr. Patrick Gordon-Walker, and also to the Right Honourable Herbert Morrison. After his return to Ottawa, Sir Alexander Clutterbuck conveyed to St. Laurent on January 30, 1951. Mr. Gaitskell's reply to the effect that, after considering Mr. St. Laurent's representations, the British government had decided not to reopen the matter.

[10]*Ibid.*, March 13, 1951, pp. 1227-1228.

When Mr. St. Laurent reported the position to his cabinet colleagues, Mr. Gardiner still believed that another attempt should be made to reopen the question. He asked for, and received, cabinet approval to go to London and to take Mr. J. H. Wesson with him to present his version of the "have regard to" understandings and to present the producers' case. Wesson had participated in the Canadian federation of agriculture's annual presentation to the cabinet on February 15, 1951. In its brief, the federation said:

1. We wish to express our appreciation of the efforts of the government to obtain from Great Britain adequate recognition of the "have regard" clause in the Canadian-United Kingdom wheat agreement.

2. We wish to point out that the government of Canada has a vital responsibility to see that wheat producers are treated fairly in the final settlement of the five-year pool, because the returns to wheat producers for those years were prescribed by government policy sale of wheat in the domestic market and by the terms of the contract which the government made with the government of the United Kingdom in 1946.

Our producers feel that balance of the actual proceeds of the sales of wheat during the five-year pool is not sufficient to provide a satisfactory settlement. Our convention was unanimous in asking that a very substantial contribution per bushel should be made by the government of Canada to the final settlement of the five-year pool.[11]

MR. GARDINER'S APPEAL

When Mr. Gardiner met with Mr. Gaitskell and his officials on February 20, 1951, he was accompanied by Mr. J. H. Wesson, the Honourable T. C. Davis, Mr. L. Dana Wilgress, Canadian high commissioner, and Mr. J. H. Warren on Mr. Wilgress's staff. Following Mr. St. Laurent's lead, Mr. Gardiner did not present a case on legal grounds, but on the moral issue raised by western farmers that they were entitled to further consideration on the basis of Mr. Strachey's statements. Gardiner's argument was effectively supported by Wesson who described the farmers' expectation of a further payment in the circumstances which had developed, and also by Davis who had attended the Canadian Club dinner in Winnipeg on February 25, 1947, which Strachey had addressed.

In reply, Gaitskell recalled the meeting with Howe on May 22, 1950, when Cripps had insisted that the British were under no obligation to make a payment and that they did not intend to do so. Gaitskell was still of that opinion. He had been surprised by Mr. St. Laurent's claim in his aide-memoire that the Canadian government in accepting the agreed minute, had not gone beyond acknowledging Howe's declaration that he must refer the issue of settlement back to his government, but Gardiner confirmed that this was all the Canadian government had intended. In doing so, he acknowledged that the British had declared they felt under no further obligation by the terms of the agreement, and that the Canadian government was not in a position to compel payment.

Then Gardiner proceeded with his settlement proposal and he suggested that if the British recognized a moral obligation they could

[11]*Ibid.*, March 9, 1951, p. 1082.

use the unexpended balance of the loan amounting to $65 million as a final payment. Gaitskell's response was that he was about to announce that the British government would make no further drawing on the loan. In the light of the announcement he would make in the British house that afternoon, it was not for him to suggest what the Canadian government might do with its own funds.

Gardiner's response was to propose a joint declaration whereby the British would disclaim any liability but would understand the Canadian government's action in making the payment as a means of removing any misunderstanding. Gaitskell thought that some such phraseology might be worked out.

At the conclusion of his meeting with Gaitskell, Gardiner asked if he could have an appointment with Mr. Attlee. He also addressed a letter on the "have regard to" issue to Mr. Attlee. The appointment was kept on February 22 when Gardiner, in half an hour, presented his case to the British prime minister. Attlee gave his response to Gardiner by letter that same day to the effect that his representations had been carefully considered, but the decision already communicated to him orally represented the views of the British government.

ANNOUNCEMENT OF THE FINAL SETTLEMENT

No one in the Canadian cabinet was surprised by Gardiner's negative report on his mission. Yet the position of the producers' representatives remained unchanged that an obligation existed, whether met by the British or the Canadian government, and the cabinet had by now become persuaded to this view. Gardiner's representations to the British authorities that the latter should use the $65 million balance in the loan to make final settlement had been directly witnessed by Mr. J. H. Wesson, and it was his reasonable expectation that, if the British government refused payment, the Canadian government should pay a similar amount into the five-year pool. The cabinet decision to that effect was taken on March 2, 1951, and Mr. St. Laurent announced it to the house:

Mr. Speaker, I have a brief statement to make concerning the final settlement of the five-year wheat pool. . . .

As the house is aware, there have been discussions with the United Kingdom government on several occasions concerning article 2(b) of the wheat agreement entered into in 1946—the so-called "have regard to" clause. The United Kingdom government has made it clear that no further payment will be made by them under the agreement. Hon. members may also have seen an announcement by the Chancellor of the Exchequer on February 20 that the United Kingdom will not draw further on the remainder of the credit of $1,250 million which was made available in May, 1946, and which expires on December 31, 1951.

The government has decided to recommend to parliament that an amount equal to the balance of the United Kingdom credit, namely, $65 million, be added to the sums now awaiting distribution in settlement of the five-year pool. The amount will be included in the final supplementary estimates for the fiscal year 1950-51 which are shortly to be placed before the house for approval.

The contribution we will be asking parliament to make is equivalent of about 23 cents per bushel on the deliveries made during the last two years of the agreement to which article 2(b) had reference. The addition of $65 million to the pool would make a total of approximately $120 million for distribution. On the basis of deliveries of 1,428 million bushels during the period of the five-year pool, this would provide a final payment of about 8.3 cents per bushel. Final payments will be made as soon as possible after parliament has dealt with the supplementary estimates.[12]

THE DEBATE ON THE FINAL PAYMENT

An opportunity for debate upon the merits of the final settlement announced by the prime minister came a few days later on March 8, 1951, when Howe moved second reading of a bill to amend the Canadian wheat board act. The amendment was designed to speed up the closing of the annual pool accounts and to permit the issuance of participation payments more promptly. Mr. J. A. Ross moved an amendment to the effect that second reading be deferred until the house had an opportunity to review the government's decision on the final settlement. Thus a prolonged debate commenced in which Gardiner led off by reviewing the history of the government's wartime wheat policy culminating in the export price ceiling, the floor price guarantee, the bilateral contract and the five-year pool. He recalled the early public debate which had taken place whether the British government would honor the contract and he quoted Strachey's Winnipeg statement. As he spoke Gardiner offered his own version of all the negotiations which had taken place on the "have regard to" obligation:

Clause 2 (b) in the greement, better known as the "have regard to" clause, provided for two discussions of price, ane before December 31, 1947, and another before December 31, 1948. I was in London in September of 1947 on my way back from Geneva, and had the first of those discussions with Mr. Strachey, minister of food. The meeting was held at that time partly because of discussion I had with the international wheat committee while in Geneva. They were anxious to know at once what the terms of the contract were going to be for that year, because they were discussing what was to be the price under the international contract. The critics who had maintained that when the time came the British would not agree to advance the price above $1.55 a bushel proved to be wrong. No one in London questioned our right to discuss a payment far above $1.55. The price was then around $3.00 a bushel, as the hon. member for Souris has said. We suggested that with the Marshall plan in existence and the Canadian 1946 loan operating to give purchasing power there was little chance of wheat dropping below $2 a bushel over the next two years, which would carry us to July 31, 1949. We stated that instead of asking Britain to pay on the basis of what the price of wheat had been, we were prepared to accept a temporary payment of $2 a bushel, with the final calculation of what we were entitled to left over to the end of the 1948-49 crop year. This was a definite change in the agreement consented to by both parties, so that when today persons quote the original terms of the agreement and say the $2 was a final payment of the price for the third year of the contract, they entirely lose sight of the fact that we had an agreement at the time which changed the terms of the original agreement with regard to that matter.[13]

[12]*Ibid.*, March 2, 1951, p. 833.
[13]*Ibid.*, March 8, 1951, pp. 1063-1064.

Gardiner quoted Prime Minister Mackenzie King's press release of October 1, 1947, and he continued:

> The discussions on the payment to be made on the 1949 crop were carried on in December, 1948, by myself with Right Hon. John Strachey and Sir Stafford Cripps. For the first time the meaning of the "have regard to" clause was questioned by a minister of the government of Great Britain; it was questioned on that occasion by Sir Stafford Cripps. The final news release, however, did not question it. The questioning was done in the discussions we had. We threshed out the matter, and after it was threshed out a press statement was issued.[14]

Gardiner then quoted Prime Minister St. Laurent's press release of January 20, 1949, and also the press statement which Sir Stafford Cripps issued on February 23, 1949, and he continued:

> Now, I do point out that is the first time that anyone to my knowledge who had been dealing with this question used the word "compensation". It is not our term. It is a term used by the chancellor of the exchequer in Great Britain. He said we were entitled to compensation, and the extent to which we would obtain compensation would depend upon the extent to which wheat in 1949-50 dropped below $2 a bushel. We all know now that in so far as most markets were concerned it did not drop below, but I will go into that in a few moments and make allowance for what was said.
>
> My colleague, the Minister of Trade and Commerce (Mr. Howe), went to London in May, 1950, and took with him the members of the wheat board to discuss deliveries of wheat to the United Kingdom under the international wheat agreement. Before he left it was suggested that he arrange to have the date for final discussion of the "have regard to" clause postponed until all the facts were known. Some of us thought it might be a good thing to have all the facts before us when we discussed this matter finally. It was then acknowledged by everyone that there had been no drop in prices, which was going to create a situation, and we tried to have it arranged that the discussion would take place after July 31, 1950. He reported on return that Sir Stafford insisted on discussing and declaring closed the four year wheat agreement. The Minister of Trade and Commerce indicated he was not prepared to discuss the matter at that time, but agreed to report their attitude back to Ottawa but refused to agree with their view.
>
> In other words, he said the matter had to be discussed back in Ottawa, and no matter what position they took he was not there to agree on that question. He did so report, and the government here unanimously agreed that if the British refused to acknowledge any obligation under the agreement, any further obligation under agreement, it was not drawn in such terms as permitted of our enforcing the agreement. I think I am right in saying that even if it had been in legal terms we would not have considered taking the matter to the international court. We have not been in the habit of dealing with matters of this kind, as between ourselves and Great Britain, in any such manner. Even had the terms of the agreement been drawn in different terms from what they were drawn—and I am not admitting that there were any weaknesses in the terms of the agreement—it was fully understood and everyone agreed as to what the meaning was down to a certain time, then there was some disagreement. . . .
>
> We just could not reach agreement that there would be a final discussion of the matter at a later date. That was the question under discussion, could we reach an agreement that there would be a discussion at a later date. We just

[14]*Ibid.*

could not reach an agreement that there would be discussion at a later date. ...

The government of Canada continued to make representations to the United Kingdom to the effect that further consideration be given to the opinion widely held in Canada that the terms of the agreement had not been met.

When it was suggested that there was a shortage of dollars, it was pointed out that there was $65 million left in the loan which might be utilized and save dollars for the present. It was suggested both in this house and outside that the government had announced agreement with the British in their contention that they had met their obligations. That was not the case, and in the hope that a removal of that opinion might change the decision the re-opening of the discussions were pressed. ...

The Prime Minister re-opened the discussions while in Britain in January. After his return we were notified that the United Kingdom government preferred to consider the matter closed.

It was thought wise that because I had carried the negotiations five years ago and when the payment for the last two years was arranged I should make an effort to have the question re-opened. ...

I got to Britain on Sunday. I was in touch with the government immediately. I was in touch with them again on Monday, and I was in touch with them again on Tuesday, and the announcement was not made until Tuesday afternoon.

While I was in Britain I was informed that notwithstanding the views of the Canadian government the United Kingdom government had determined that they would not make further payment, they would not make use of the $65 million remaining in the 1946 loan for the purpose and that it was their intention to declare that they did not intend to utilize the remaining part of the loan for any purpose. They so declared on Tuesday, February 20, while I was in London and after the matter had been discussed. ...

All that was necessary to put us all behind such a settlement was the consent of the British government. I am sorry I was unable to obtain that consent.[15]

Throughout his explanation Gardiner continued to leave the impression that the British had a moral obligation to make a further settlement. The notion was consistent with his original understanding of the gentlemen's agreement which he thought had been embodied in the "have regard to" clause.

The members of the opposition were quick to discern the difference between Gardiner's presentation of the issue, and Mr. Howe's statements of May 30 and June 5, 1950. When pressed on the difference, Howe explained:

Mr. Speaker, on a question of privilege, I am entitled to keep the record straight so far as I am concerned. I may say that the discussions about the disposal of the 1950 crop took place before there was any mention of the five year pool. That matter was discussed and settled and then discussions were opened on the five year pool, against our wishes really. I made it clear at the outset I had no authority to discuss or settle. I told those present that we looked to the minister who negotiated the agreement in the first place to negotiate the settlement, and that all I could do was carry back a report of the discussions. Nevertheless when the discussions continued I got a very positive statement from the chancellor of the exchequer, and there were other

[15]*Ibid.,* pp. 1065-1068.

ministers present. I had to take their views back to my colleagues as the position of the United Kingdom government. I reported that position to them. The decision, if there was any decision, was made after I returned.[16]

In the continuation of the debate on March 12, Howe delivered a major speech which had been drafted in part by Mr. Mitchell W. Sharp, his newly-appointed assistant deputy minister. Howe defended the agreement in the following terms:

I think I said before, and I say again, that the time when you must decide whether an agreement is good or bad is when you sign on the dotted line, and we signed on that dotted line in 1946. That is when the decision had to be made and that is when it was made. . . .

When an opportunity arose to sell 600,000,000 bushels of wheat at assured prices to our best customer—more than had ever before been sold by Canada to that customer in any comparable period—we accepted. That decision was supported by the great majority of the western grain growers and I am confident that they still support it. Everyone recognized that there were risks in such an agreement. There were risks on both sides. But it must never be forgotten that there were even greater risks in not entering into the agreement. The advantage of the agreement was that it minimized the risk. The wheat agreement was similar to an insurance policy. Because a man who buys an accident policy never claims under it that does not mean the policy should not have been taken out, or that the premiums should not have been paid. It is well to keep that in mind. If wheat prices in the last two years had fallen very substantially the shoe would have been on the other foot, and I do not think it would have been proper for the United Kingdom to ask us to accept less than the floor prices provided in the agreement in order to reduce average returns to the open market level.

As I shall point out later, the have regard to clause is important but it did not mean, and we have never argued that it meant, that the United Kingdom should make up in the final two years any mathematical calculation of losses in the first two years. Five years ago the western wheat grower supported a policy of stability at reasonable prices. Today, unless I am seriously mistaken, he still supports that policy. There are some, however, who do not believe in the policy of stability at reasonable prices. Some of those people are today criticizing the five year pool and the British agreement. I suggest to those who now think they see an opportunity of gaining some political advantage by attacking the government on the results of the five year pool and the British agreement that they should consider carefully whether they are not playing into the hands of those who prefer to return to the old boom and bust type of wheat marketing.

The test of any policy is its results; and I believe the results of a policy which returned an average of $1.83 a bushel on the basis of No. 1 Northern in store Fort William for nearly 1.5 billion bushels of wheat sold over a five year period require no apology; and I am making none. The wheat economy prospered during that period as it deserves to prosper and as I hope and believe it will continue to prosper. If a policy can produce that kind of result it meets the only test that matters. The essential fact is that producers are being paid on the basis of $1.833 on their deliveries for five successive crops. . . .[17]

Howe proceeded to analyze the results, crop year by crop year from 1945, and he continued:

[16]*Ibid.,* p. 1072.
[17]*Ibid.,* March 12, 1951, p. 1169.

From 1947 to 1949 the United States permitted Marshall aid funds to be used for the purchase of Canadian wheat, and though large stocks of wheat were accumulating in the United States that government respected the United Kingdom-Canada agreement and did not demand that the Marshall aid funds be used to purchase United States wheat instead of Canadian wheat. However, before the 1949 crop came on the market United States wheat was declared in surplus supply, which automatically stopped the use of Marshall aid funds to buy Canadian wheat. Just think of the importance of that agreement during those years. Because of the agreement, the United States paid money to Canada for supplying wheat to Britain, instead of giving away her own surplus wheat to England, at a time when the surplus in the United States was becoming burdensome. Those who are making up the equation to show losses might very well put in that intangible for a very considerable price indeed.

Passing on now to the 1948-49 crop year, which was the third year of the contract, producers will receive $1.83 for deliveries of 293 million bushels. Throughout this crop year the payment difficulties of the United Kingdom continued acute. To put it bluntly what we faced here in Canada was the very real possibility that the United States would drive Canadian wheat out of our traditional markets. This actually occurred in the European markets with the exception of the United Kingdom, and the fact that the Canada-United Kingdom wheat agreement was of the greatest value at this time in retaining our position in the United Kingdom market. As a matter of fact we have a very serious problem ahead of us in regaining markets in continental Europe which are now being supplied by the United States under Marshall aid. It was for that reason the government sent a mission to Europe last year for the express purpose of finding out how to regain a foothold in some of those markets. What the Canada-United Kingdom wheat agreement actually accomplished was to enable us to hold our position in the United Kingdom market. The United States government respected the agreement, and in fact went so far as to provide a very substantial amount of United States dollars, $175 million to be exact, which enabled the United Kingdom to finance her wheat purchases from the 1949 wheat crop under the agreement. This amount was provided as the result of negotiations which took place in Washington early in September, 1949. . . .[18]

Howe quoted a letter of September 13, 1949, from Mr. Paul G. Hoffman, ECA administrator, to the Honourable Charles F. Brannan, secretary of agriculture, in corroboration of his statement that the bilateral contract had helped to maintain the Canadian position in the British wheat market. The mission to Europe to which Howe referred was the one which Lawrie, Milner and Wilson undertook in the autumn of 1950.

Howe then turned to the question of whether the British government had lived up to the terms of the agreement, and he continued:

It will be noted that the price for the 1948 crop was to be determined before December 31, 1947, and the price for the 1949 crop before December 31, 1948. In other words, the prices were to be determined seven months ahead of the beginning of the relevant crop year. Our two governments met in the autumn of 1947 and determined upon a price of $2 per bushel for the 1948-49 crop year. Again in December, 1948, we met and determined upon a price of $2 per bushel for the 1949-50 crop year. If we knew then what we know now about world wheat supply and demand in the months that lay ahead, we might have been able to negotiate a higher price. In the circumstances then prevailing, $2

[18]*Ibid.*, p. 1170.

plus five to six cents carrying charges looked like a good price for 140 million bushels of wheat, and I think it was a good price at which to sell such substantial quantities of wheat, particularly as the United Kingdom at that time anticipated that the international wheat agreement price would be $1.70 per bushel and that wheat could be purchased from countries other than Canada for the international wheat agreement price.

In January, 1949, it was agreed that final settlement under the have regard to clause would not be made at that time, but would be made before July 31, 1950. I went to London in May, 1950, for discussions having to do with marketing the 1950 crop. While there I discussed the wheat agreement, at the request of the United Kingdom. I reported thereon to the cabinet and to this house following my return. I had no authority, or indeed no reason to conclude any agreement with the British government. All I could do, and all I did do, was to report the position taken by the British government.

In brief the British government stated positively that they had discharged their obligations under the agreement. They pointed out what I have pointed out in this statement, namely that there were risks on both sides in entering into an agreement for four years ahead covering such large quantities of grain.

That was an understandable attitude and, while I might have wished that the British government could have seen the advantage to them of making further payments to Canadian wheat growers, I could not conscientiously say that they were in default under the agreement. I so reported to the cabinet, to this house and to the western wheat producers.

My own words in Hansard on June 5 of last year, though uttered on the spur of the moment and in the heat of debate, put the position as I have just stated it and I have no desire to alter them in any way.

On November 13, 1950, I gave a speech in Regina to the Saskatchewan wheat pool during which I dealt with the same point and perhaps with greater decision. I quote from my remarks at that time:

"Now I personally went to London in May of this year for these final discussions. I found the attitude of the British government to be an understandable one. British authorities felt that they had taken sufficient forward risks during the life of the contract in guaranteeing us a market and they considered they had discharged their obligations under the "have regard" clause.

"Quite apart from this issue, however, but out of respect for the way in which Canada and the United Kingdom had worked together in each other's interest in these post-war years, the United Kingdom undertook to purchase from Canada in the 1950-51 crop year ... its full requirement for North American wheat, provided price and quality to be not less favorable than that obtainable from other North American sources. Probable United Kingdom requirement was estimated to be from 100 to 120 million bushels of wheat and flour on international wheat agreement terms. This undertaking was given with the knowledge that there would be little if any E.C.A. aid on purchases in Canada, and I have no doubt that the eminently fair way with which Canada has dealt with the United Kingdom under the contract these past four years had much to do with their giving us a forward assurance of a market for the present crop year, even though E.C.A. finance is available for any wheat or flour purchases in the United States."

As I have said, the British government has discharged its legal obligations under the agreement and is not in default. Subsequently, however, the Canadian government considered it advisable to inform the United Kingdom government of the views of certain producers' groups to the effect that sufficient account had not been taken in the final settlement of the so-called "have regard to" clause.

Accordingly, the Prime Minister (Mr. St. Laurent) mentioned the matter to Mr. Attlee when he was on a visit to Canada at the end of last year and again the Prime Minister had discussions in London in January. It was never suggested to the British government at any time that they were in legal default under the agreement. It was pointed out, however, that the existence of dissatisfaction among wheat producers in Canada about the results of the agreement could have unfortunate consequence for future trade relationships between our two countries and that the British government might wish to reconsider their earlier decision. My colleague, the Minister of Agriculture (Mr. Gardiner), made similar representations a few weeks ago. As the house knows, however, the British government did not see fit to make any further payments.

That was a perfectly legal and proper decision for them to make under the agreement. The Canadian government, while recognizing that the legal obligations of the British government under the agreement had been fulfilled, took a different view of the over-all results and decided to pay into the five-year pool the $65 million that remained under the United Kingdom loan act.

Personally, I think it was a mistake that there should have been included in the agreement such a loosely-worded "have regard to" clause. It has been a source of much misunderstanding in both the United Kingdom and Canada. I think the British government itself is partly to blame for the misunderstanding, for the speech by Mr. Strachey in Winnipeg undoubtedly led many producers to believe that the United Kingdom would act on a more generous interpretation. Nevertheless, the agreement without that clause was by no means one-sided. It produced substantial benefits for Canadian producers as well as British consumers. It resulted in the highest average price for wheat over a five-year period. But the "have regard to" clause was included, at the suggestion, as I recall it, of the United Kingdom government. Such a clause is not capable of precise meaning. The United Kingdom government took one view of it, which from their point of view was understandable. Our producers took another attitude which was equally understandable. Nevertheless, a clause in an agreement that is not subject to legal interpretation must inevitably be interpreted by the party that must do the paying. The other party may not agree, but he has no option but to accept.

That hon. members of the House of Commons, is my view of the United Kingdom-Canada wheat agreement. I believe it was a good agreement. I believe it has been greatly to the advantage of the Canadian producers that that agreement was made. I cannot believe that we would have been able to deal with all the hazards involved in the marketing of those five crops without the British wheat agreement. I presume that we shall continue to have arguments as to the losses under the agreement. I do not know just from what point of view losses can be reckoned. . . .

This year we would have had practically the entire British market had we been able to fill it. Unfortunately the frost damage in western Canada has made it impossible for us to fill even our quota under the international wheat agreement, as far as Britain is concerned; but they are taking anything we can offer them in the way of milling wheat.

It is well to keep in mind that our second market in the prewar days was the Netherlands; and I may tell hon. gentlemen that we have hardly sold a bushel of wheat to the Netherlands since the war ended. Our next biggest market was Belgium. Belgium has supported our wheat, has bought sizeable quantities in the postwar years, for the reason that their supply of United States dollars was somewhat better than other countries. Italy was a great market. We are just now getting back into the Italian market in something like a substantial way, but there are other markets, which we have lost entirely for the reason that they were quite happy to buy wheat from the United States with E.C.A. funds.

If anyone can view the position of Canada as a result of the five year agreement and say that it was a bad agreement, and quibble about whether we lost money under it or made money under it, that is their privilege; but I say that I am very happy the agreement was made. I am happy the way it has worked out, and I deplore the suggestion that the British government has not played fair with the Canadian people.[19]

In the speech, Howe had emphatically denied that the British government had not lived up to the terms of the agreement, and that appeared to conflict with the reference Gardiner had left from his pursuit of a settlement to the end. Moreover, in the whole of Howe's speech he made no attempt to establish a case for the payment of $65 million from the Canadian treasury into the five-year pool, whereas Gardiner's speech had been directed toward that end. As a result, the Honourable George Drew, leader of the opposition, in the continuation of the debate on March 13, alleged a breach of cabinet solidarity as he said:

Mr. Speaker, one of the basic and fundamental principles upon which our parliamentary system depends is that the members of the house can rely upon statements on behalf of the government in dealing with questions before this house. That is so deeply imbedded in the traditions of our system that a member of the government speaks on behalf of the government collectively, or he must be disavowed by the government itself.

The Minister of Agriculture has made one statement in this house, and through this house to the people of Canada, and the Minister of Trade and Commerce had made another, and those two statements are entirely different in their basic proposition. Those two statements are statements which can only be reconciled by the Prime Minister himself explaining to us exactly what the situation is, and exactly how the government has arrived at the figures which it has put before the house.[20]

With that confrontation, St. Laurent picked up the challenge. As he rose to put to rest the issue of cabinet solidarity and to justify the payment from the Canadian treasury, he said:

I intend to reply very briefly, first about this alleged divergence of opinion which is now referred to as a conflicting position in the government, and then about the principle under which the payment is being recommended. Obviously in any government under parliamentary system all ministers—and I am not speaking of this government in particular—do not necessarily always have the same thoughts, nor do they necessarily always use the same expressions in communicating their thoughts. There are many matters of interest to human beings about which they do not always have the same views. If it were otherwise it would be very much simpler to have a one-man government. Our system is cabinet government, and cabinet government involves cabinet responsibility and cabinet solidarity. As I understand it cabinet solidarity requires agreement on policies and on conclusions. With respect to this "have regard to" clause, all the members of the government are

[19]*Ibid.*, March 12, 1951, pp. 1171-1173.
[20]*Ibid.*, March 13, 1951, p. 1229.

agreed on the four essential points, and they are the only points which affect policy and conclusions.

The first point is that the United Kingdom had discharged all its legal obligations under the wheat agreement. Everyone recognized that was a binding contract for two years at $1.55 per bushel, and it was a contract which bound the United Kingdom government to take the number of bushels stipulated in the third and following year at a price to be agreed upon, which would not be less than $1.25 for the third year and $1 for the fourth year. That was all there was in the agreement as a binding agreement on the parties. There was a statement that in fixing the prices, which would not be less than $1.25 in the third year, the United Kingdom government would have regard to the price that was paid as the agreed price for the first two years; and that in fixing the price for the fourth year they would have regard to the price that was paid during the first year; the price for the fourth year being not less than $1. There was no obligation on them other than the undertaking to take the stipulated quantity in the third year at a price which they did not have to agree would be more than $1.25, and to take the agreed quantity in the fourth year at a price which they did not have to agree would be more than $1. No one contended there was any other legal obligation.

The second point on which there was agreement was that, at the end of May, 1950, the Canadian government accepted as the decision of the United Kingdom government that they had discharged all their legal obligations under that contract. The third point was that the Canadian wheat growers believed there was a continuing obligation under the "have regard to" clause which had not been discharged in full and that, in the words of the Minister of Trade and Commerce (Mr. Howe) in the speech referred to by the leader of the opposition (Mr. Drew), "the British government itself was partly to blame" for this expectation of the wheat producers because of the speech that had been made in Winnipeg by the Right Hon. Mr. Strachey, after he had listened from the galleries of this House of Commons to a speech delivered by the then leader of the opposition, Mr. Bracken.

Now, we all felt the Canadian wheat growers had understandable grounds for this expectation that there would be more done under the "have regard to" clause than had been done, and our government hoped—again I use the words of the Minister of Trade and Commerce in the speech referred to by the leader of the opposition—"that the British government could have seen the advantage to them of making some further payments to the Canadian wheat growers." On that third point we were all agreed.

The fourth point upon which we were agreed was that the Canadian government should make a contribution to the five-year pool because producers had been led. both by the United Kingdom ministers and by Canadian ministers, to expect that something more substantial would be done under the "have regard to" clause than had been done, and because the government of the United Kingdom had not seen fit to do anything more under that clause. I repeat that all members of the government are agreed on these four points, and these are the only points about which there is any matter of policy or any matter of conclusion. . . .

There is no doubt that when the government of the United Kingdom took the position that all obligations, in the sense of obligations, had been fulfilled, and that nothing more was to be done by them as a consequence of the "have regard to" clause, those expectations were not met. I think that is indisputable. We were all agreed we were not alone responsible for those expectations in the minds of the wheat producers of the western provinces. Because of the principle of solidarity invoked by the leader of the opposition, and because of the declarations that had been made by the Minister of Agriculture, by the then minister of trade and commerce and by the right hon. gentlemen from the United Kingdom, we all felt that those having such expectations should not remain in the disappointed state in which they were left by the position taken by the government of the United Kingdom that it would make no further payment as a consequence of the "have regard to" clause.

Hon. members recall that when the price for the third year was being discussed it was expressly agreed that a price of $2 would be paid for that crop, and that the matter of giving consideration to the "have regard to" clause would be postponed. When the price for the fourth year crop was fixed at $2 it was agreed that consideration of what should be done under the "have regard to" clause would be still further postponed. It was not until the matter was raised by the representatives of the British government when the present Minister of Trade and Commerce was in London in May of 1950 that the matter came to a head. The position they then took was that they had fulfilled all obligations under the contract. We felt that they had fulfilled all legal obligations, but that they had not met the expectations that had been raised by the declarations made in 1946 in respect of the effect this "have regard to" clause would have on the amounts put into the pool. We came to the conclusion that the government of the United Kingdom having decided that it would do no more, we would recommend to parliament that the sum of $65 million would be put into the pool to be added to what was left there for distribution as a final payment. . . .

When this decision was made and accepted by the government of Canada as being the position taken, and the position they were entitled to take, in the United Kingdom, there was still $65 million that had not been drawn from the credit provided by the agreed loan of $1,250 million. Had the government of the United Kingdom seen fit to draw that amount of $65 million and use it as a settlement of anything legitimately or properly expected under the "have regard to" clause, the government of Canada would not have felt required to do anything more, and would have been quite content to say that everything that could reasonably be expected as a consequence of the "have regard to" clause had been discharged by that payment. . . .

Without attempting to make any mathematical calculation, but taking a rough approximation of what could be regarded as just and fair, the Canadian government decided to recommend to parliament that a sum equal to the $65 million be put into the pool because that placed no heavier burden on the production of this year than would have been placed upon it by the drawing and use for other purposes of the available $65 million of the credit. There was no other calculation made or attempted.

On all these points there was agreement. It seems to me that it is not going to make much difference to the producer in western Canada what I, or the Minister of Agriculture or the Minister of Trade and Commerce (Mr. Howe) may think it would have been desirable for the United Kingdom to have done because of the expectations that had been raised in 1946 and that had continued as a result of the postponing of consideration of what should be done about the "have regard to" clause right up to the time the contract had been completely fulfilled. It is not going to matter much to them whether I think we should have done it or whether I think that the government of the United Kingdom should have done it. It is not going to matter much to them whether, it being done by us, it is limited to that amount or whether, in their opinion, it should be more, or whether in the opinion of someone who does not derive any benefit it should be less. On the facts we in the government are agreed. On the policy we are agreed. On the recommendation we make to parliament we are agreed. On the question of one's personal opinion of how each party has behaved not under a contractual, enforceable obligation but under a set of expectations raised by the declarations made by cabinet ministers, we are not going to have much effect upon the thinking of those who are interested as producers or those who are interested as taxpayers.

I do not think there is going to be much cheering anywhere over this decision. But I think it is the kind of decision that no one can say is an unfair and unreasonable one to make under all the circumstances which have now been quite fully discussed.[21]

At the end of St. Laurent's speech, Mr. Coldwell, leader of the CCF party pursued the interpretation about Mr. Howe's involvement after he had returned from London, and between his formal announcement on May 30, 1950, and his June 5 extempore explanation. Mr. St. Laurent volunteered the following explanation:

There was one communication which I think we will lay on the table. I am told that an answer has been received from London, and I think I shall be able tomorrow to file a minute of the discussions in London and the communication that was sent from Canada on that minute before June 5, 1950.

But following June 5, 1950, as hon. members will recall, last summer there were many things which I at least had to regard as matters of urgency and priority. The first that occurred was the unexpected death of the former prime minister; the next was the unexpected death of the former minister of labour. There were other special circumstances arising in connection with the Korean crisis and the decisions we had to make in respect thereof. That was followed almost immediately by, first of all, the threat and then the realization of a general tie-up in transportation which necessitated the calling of a special session of parliament somewhat earlier than we had intended to call it for the purpose of dealing with the Korean situation. Just as soon as those matters which, I must confess, occupied my mind to the exclusion of domestic problems other than the railway strike at that period, had been dealt with, I came to realize to what extent there was this persisting feeling of disappointment at the attitude taken by the United Kingdom government in respect to the "have regard to" clause. I knew that we had accepted that as the decision of the United Kingdom government, and it was understandable that they would consider that it should not be mentioned to them again. I felt that it would be unfair to the government of the United Kingdom not to bring to their notice what I knew about the feeling as it existed in Canada, and about the way in which that feeling and this expectation had developed, and why it had developed.

When Mr. Attlee was here I ventured to mention it to him, telling him that I was not making any request on behalf of our government that the United Kingdom do anything more, but that I felt it would not be fair for them not to know what the situation was. I suggested that if he had no objection I would raise it again with the chancellor of the exchequer when I went over for the prime ministers' conference in January; and I did so. But at no time did I suggest that there was any legal obligation, and at no time did I suggest that we had not accepted their position, the one they took in May of 1950. But I did suggest to them that they should consider whether or not in their own interest it would be wise to do something more about the "have regard to" clause, and I put the facts, as they had been placed before the members of this house, before them. Shortly after my return I was informed that they had considered my representations and had come to the conclusion that they were not going to re-open the matter.

Thereupon there was a suggestion that the right hon. Minister of Agriculture himself go over and see if he would not be able to persuade them that it would be in their interest to do something more. While it was suggested to my colleague the Minister of Trade and Commerce, and to me, that that might be some reflection on us because we had both discussed the matter, we both said that we were not sensitive on that point, and that if the Minister of Agriculture could bring about any other decision we would rejoice with him in that other decision.

Now, when he returned and told us that it was useless we said, there is nothing more we can do that will have any possibility whatsoever of getting anything further done by the government of the United Kingdom, and we have to decide whether or not in these circumstances there is responsibility upon us to do anything; and we decided—and we come before parliament agreed upon that policy and conclusion—to recommend to parliament this contribution of $65 million to be added to the price of the 1,400 million odd bushels of wheat put into the pool in the five years to which it applies. . . .

There was no consultation with the advisory board or the wheat pool between the return of the minister and the acceptance of the proposals. The proposals were proposals for the purchase of a certian portion of the 1950 crop. We did not treat as a proposal their declaration that they had fulfilled all their obligations under the contract. We treated that as their decision, and we accepted it as their decision. . . .

There was no consultation at that time. We accepted that as being the decision arrived at, and being the decision which implied that they had fulfilled all the legal obligations that the contract provided.[22]

It remained for an item of $65 million in the supplementary estimates to be approved. The item was placed in the department of agriculture estimates, and it came up in the house a few days later on March 15. As Gardiner opened the discussion of the item he endeavored to justify the amount in terms of a financial obligation still due, had it been paid by Britain. It took an afternoon and an evening to get the item passed, but much of the time was spent in a political debate which had little to do with the merit of the item.

There the matter ended in parliament, but the issue still remained to be pursued by the farm organizations.

By now a rival farm organization was being formed in the western provinces, under the name of the farmers' union. Manitoba, Saskatchewan and Alberta farmers' unions had been organized and they, in turn, became the nucleus of the National farmers union. Mr. Joe Phelps was president of the Saskatchewan organization, and he led a delegation of the three provincial unions to Ottawa on April 10, 1951, to meet a committee of cabinet ministers and to present a brief demanding an additional payment. Mr. H. H. Hannam, president of the Canadian federation of agriculture, made similar representations. On April 16, the Legislative Assembly of Saskatchewan endorsed the resolution the Saskatchewan farmers' union had presented to cabinet. A further brief from the farm organizations was received on May 2, 1951, but the cabinet turned a deaf ear to all these

[22]*Ibid.,* pp. 1284-1285.

representations. On April 10, after it had received the delegation from the western farmers' unions, the cabinet agreed that no further payment would be made in addition to the $65 million. In their rebuff of all further claims, the cabinet could sympathize with producers to the extent that it, too, had been rebuffed by another government. In all the circumstances, however, its conscience was clear that, on its own initiative, it had already responded in rough justice at least to the producers' reasonable expectations.

48

POLICIES, INSTITUTIONS AND PERSONALITIES

The time has come for a concluding word on the evolution of grain policy, the institutions it created and the people who were responsible for them. The main components of the review have traced developments up to 1930, through the policy-forming years of the thirties and the early years of the war which resulted in the creation of a monopoly wheat board and in a postwar quest for the assurance of markets. The need remains now only to glance back over the whole period covered by the review, to recall some of the highlights and to offer a few concluding observations. The account, which began with the opening up of the west, has traced the interaction between producers and government until, during the interwar years, the wheat industry had become not only Canada's dominant export industry but also Canada's dominant internal economic concern. In the process, it has traversed one of the fascinating periods in Canadian economic history.

During the frontier period in the west, there was opportunity for commencement of a new life whether in homesteading and farming or in private business associated with the movement and handling of grain. The first real demand for government intervention arose from the plight of the grain warehousemen when they found themselves cut off from access to the railways which sought to encourage technological advance and greater handling efficiency through the construction of country elevators. The result was a temporary monopoly in grain handling by the newly-formed line elevator companies about which the Reverend James Douglas, the member for East Assiniboia, complained to parliament. His intercession led to the enactment of a grain handling regulatory act, to the creation of the car order book and to the requirement placed upon the railways to erect loading platforms on demand and thereby to afford a measure of freedom of choice to producers in the manner by which their grain could be marketed. The next series of producer grievances arose when a shortage of boxcars developed at harvest time in moving grain from country points to the lakehead. During the "wheat blockade" of 1901, the elevator companies were forced to widen the spread between prices at country points and at the terminals because of their inability to move grain out of the country elevators before the close of navigation. Investigations were demanded and made, but the solution lay in more adequate provision of rail equipment.

Meanwhile, the Winnipeg grain exchange which included in its membership the line elevator companies, took a great step forward in the creation of a futures market for grain in 1904. The futures market helped to minimize the price risks incurred in the handling of grain and thereby to reduce the grain handlers' margins. Not only was the futures market mechanism of immediate benefit to producers but it helped to strengthen the marketing system the line elevator companies provided. That marketing system has survived until today as one of the marketing alternatives, and much of the intervening history of grain policy has had to do with the rivalries between that system, the voluntary co-operative marketing system which later evolved, and the third alternative of a monopoly board. Except in the case of the latter, these were not necessarily mutually exclusive systems. For example, the futures market functioned alongside the co-operative marketing pools and the voluntary wheat board.

Out of continuing dissatisfaction with the availability of marketing alternatives, such as were provided by the line companies and the loading platforms, producers took two further initiatives by forming co-operative elevator companies and by demanding the public ownership of elevators. Partridge's initiative in the organization of the Grain Growers Grain Company Limited, and the subsequent formation of the Saskatchewan and Alberta farmers' co-operative elevator companies will be recalled. In the process, these companies launched such leaders as Crerar, Dunning and Motherwell on their business and political careers. The demand for public ownership of elevators provided rather desultory results. One provincial experiment ended in failure as the federal government responded guardedly with the construction of interior terminals and some public terminals at the lakehead, in the east, on the west coast and eventually at Churchill.

Until the first world war, the basic marketing system was dominated by the line elevator companies and the emerging co-operative companies, both of which used the hedging facilities provided by the Winnipeg grain exchange. It was only when the element of competition disappeared from the overseas buyers' side, under the circumstances of war, that the futures market failed to function satisfactorily. A corner created by the monopoly purchasing agency forced a cessation in wheat futures trading and its replacement by government boards. During the two remaining years of the great war, the board of grain supervisors operated on a fixed-price basis which was appropriate only to the circumstances of the time. That board was surpassed in interest by it successor, the first Canadian wheat board. It was the format of the latter, for which Mr. C. B. Watts deserves much of the credit, that held producers' continuing attention. Pooling wheat deliveries against an initial payment, selling to best advantage and returning any surplus earned to producers through participation payments caught the producers' imagination as a viable alternative to the open market system. As soon as competitive conditions were restored to overseas buying, however, the government of the day terminated the wheat board and restored wheat marketing to the trade. In the philosophy of those days no government, of whichever party, would have wished to do otherwise.

It was unfortunate that in the deflationary debacle which followed the uncontrolled wartime inflation, the futures market had to reflect as efficiently as it did the deteriorating wheat market conditions. The futures market has been rightly credited for its ability to reduce the amplitude of daily price fluctuations which would have been experienced if trading had to be conducted on a basis of cash markets only, but no one has ever claimed on its behalf the capacity to provide continuing price stability. On the other hand, it was the belief of producers that co-operative marketing organizations or government boards could somehow provide such stability that resulted in sporadic and, at times, intensive demand for the replacement of the open market by some alternative system.

The first of such periods of intensive demand came with the 1921-1923 agitation for reinstatement of the Canadian wheat board. The producers' organizations and the members of parliament they could influence pressed the federal and provincial governments for reinstatement until, eventually, Mackenzie King succeeded in transferring the issue to the provinces where it foundered. This disappointment served only to divert the producers' drive into the organization of co-operative marketing pools.

The period from 1923 to 1930 was characterized by the formation and growth of the three provincial wheat pools which operated upon the same format as that of the government wheat board, with the exception of its monopoly feature. Under contract, the pools offered an initial payment, sales to best advantage, whether direct or through the futures market, and the pooling of returns through participation payments. These voluntary pools succeeded within a short time in signing up enough producers under delivery contracts to make them responsible for the marketing of half the wheat crop of western Canada. Two of the provincial organizations also operated coarse grains pools. With the other half of the business handled by the line elevator companies, the combination of pool and line elevator responsibility for the marketing of grain represented, from the government standpoint, a normal and almost ideal state of the industry. The government itself was no longer directly involved in marketing; it operated several terminal elevators and a regulatory service for the industry through the board of grain commissioners. As for the pools and the private trade, the situation was one of intense competition.

This state of affairs might have persisted had it not been for the great depression and the severity of its impact upon wheat prices and markets. The inability of the pools to sustain an initial payment on a falling market resulted in the termination of their marketing function and in the transfer of their interest primarily to the operation of their elevator facilities. At the same time, producers renewed their pressure for a government grain board and they gained their objective, partially at least, in the Canadian wheat board act of 1935. In doing so the pools lost interest in the restoration of co-operative grain marketing. Even when the government urged them to do so by undertaking to guarantee their initial payments, the pools declared their preference for a government board.

Although United grain growers and the line elevator companies remained solvent through the depression thanks, in part at least, to their use of the hedging facilities of the futures market, that mechanism failed to emerge unscathed from the depression. When the market failed to display any self-generating recuperative power under depression conditions, the government provided much-needed support through the purchase and accumulation of futures. In time the accumulation itself became a market depressant. Just as the futures market had failed to function smoothly when competitive conditions were disrupted during the first world war, it encountered difficulties of another sort under the abnormal conditions of the depression. After a long period of support, Bennett gave up in despair as he joined forces with Brouillette and Bredt to create a monopoly grain board. In the process of doing so, Bennett paid heed to the grain trade executives who appeared before his special committee to plead against the confiscatory implications of the monopoly bill, and to the opposition members of his committee who supported them. The result was the creation of a voluntary wheat board which was hailed at the time as a victory for the grain exchange.

The Liberal administration which inherited the wheat board in 1935 espoused it as a temporary measure only, and soon had occasion to find fault with the "heads you win, tails I lose" basis of its operation, depending upon whether the market ruled above or below the level of the initial payment. As soon as conditions permitted, the government sought to get out of the wheat marketing business and, as a means of doing so, it eyed nostalgically the state of the industry as it had existed prior to the depression. In 1938, Gardiner requested and readily obtained instructions to negotiate with the wheat pools the restoration of co-operative grain marketing backed by a government guarantee. The attempt had barely failed when war broke out, and the government refused a British request to close the futures market in the hope that the latter would reflect better returns to producers. Although the Nazi occupation of western and northern Europe dispelled that prospect, the government continued to gear its marketing policy to the open market system until, in 1943, it became caught up in a threat to the maintenance of its general price control policy. The wheat futures market was closed at Ilsley's insistence to put a ceiling on the cost of wheat to the Canadian treasury and to preserve the price ceiling policy in other areas; it was not done in response to the persistent recommendations of the Canadian federation of agriculture, however much it welcomed the move.

One would have expected, nevertheless, that at the end of the war, the government would revert to its prewar wheat policy by terminating the monopoly board. But the memory of price debacles in the early twenties and in the depression years had instilled in producers and government alike the dread of a price recession after the war. When the end did come scarcity, rather than surplus conditions, prevailed but without abating the fear. Public concern for the future was reflected in the return of the government in the 1945 election with a bare majority, when Gardiner made it back to Ottawa on a recount. In his near defeat, Gardiner recognized the need of doing something spectacular on behalf of producers in order to regain his popularity. While this may have accounted for Gardiner's personal motivation, it was his ability to assess and to capitalize upon the basic fear that led him to promote the bilateral contract. Even if it involved a fundamental reversal of his prewar wheat policy, Gardiner was determined to pursue the contract. What the Canadian federation of agriculture was demanding was a monopoly wheat board supported by an international wheat agreement as a means of assuring market stability. To provide forward market assurance, Gardiner was all too aware that the futures market, however consummate a guide to current values, would reflect just as quickly any change. Therefore it could not be used as vehicle for stabilizing returns to producers. Nor could he rely on the vehicle recommended by the farm organizations, namely an international wheat agreement. Gardiner promptly seized upon the persistent failure of the international wheat council to come to terms on a price agreement. By way of contrast, he had been highly successful in his wartime negotiations with the British ministry of food on other food contracts. In the vacuum which had been created by the international negotiations, Gardiner envisaged the largest of all contracts in a wheat agreement with the United Kingdom.

In putting the contract through, Gardiner encountered no effective opposition from his most serious critics in Canadian and American official circles for the reason that they had no viable alternative forms of market assurance to offer. Anyone could carp at the excesses of the contract in terms of price, quantity and trade discrimination, but no one could challenge the contract in its entirety because he could suggest no more effective means of providing market security. Over an extended period of time, the international agreement had already proved to be nonnegotiable and any hope of creating an international trade organization to do the job was still a year in the offing.

The interplay between the bilateral contract and the international wheat negotiations and the contributions each made to bringing the other into being, was one of the fascinating episodes of that period. The failure of the international negotiations had spawned the bilateral contract. Once it was realized that for reasons of supply limitations, Canada would be unable to enter into similar bilateral contracts with other countries, the importing countries seeking such contracts now had a new incentive to support an international wheat agreement. The American wheat position was such, however, that the American government could not contemplate the subsidizing of its wheat exports down to the level of the bilateral contract price. Therefore the first attempt to negotiate a multilateral contract patterned on the bilateral contract foundered in London in 1947. But as soon as the British and Canadian governments agreed upon a $2 price for the third year of the contract in the autumn of that year, an international agreement once again appeared to be attainable, and it was reached in Washington in the early months of 1948. That result was possible only because all the contracting parties agreed that the negotiations under the "have regard to" clause of the bilateral contract would not be restricted by the price limits agreed upon in the international agreement. The 1948 agreement did not become operative, however, because of the American failure to ratify. A year later when the terms of trade had already begun to turn against the exporters, the agreement was negotiated afresh and came into operation in 1949. The existence of the international agreement removed the need for renewal or extension of the bilateral contract.

A last great debate arose over the final settlement of the "have regard to" clause. The debate had been waged ever since the contract had been signed between Gardiner and the pools on the one side and members of the Winnipeg grain exchange and the *Winnipeg Free Press* on the other, but it came to a head when the final settlement was announced. The two contending factions carried the issue to the producers and strong feelings arose (which even now have not wholly subsided) whether the producers had been badly bilked by the deal. In the opinion of the author, the argument was incapable of resolution. One could readily point to the fact that the board's class 2 prices as a measure of world prices never fell below the contract prices over the four-year span of the agreement. In terms of these two price comparisons, the losses could be made to appear to have run into hundreds of millions of dollars. Gardiner advocated a much more modest basis of calculation but he believed, nevertheless, that losses had been incurred and he expected them to be redressed under the "have regard to" clause. On the extent of the losses there can be no conclusive evidence. The class 2 prices on which arithmetical comparisons were based applied to fringe sales which reflected the high prices importers were prepared to pay for relatively small quantities of wheat. Had the whole volume of Canadian wheat exports been disposed of through an open market, the presumption is strong that prices would not have ruled as high as those which were obtained on the fringe. Britain, its principal customer, was in acute balance of payments difficulties. Indeed, her imports were made possible by the Canadian and American loans and by Marshall aid. Any increased cost of wheat imports would have had to be countered by more severe bread rationing or by inroads on other essential imports. Had her wheat purchases been made through an open market, there is no way of reconstructing what the actual price results would have been.

In the result, Howe agreed with Gardiner to the extent that there had been some losses, although he favored the Cripps version rather than the Gardiner interpretation of the meaning of the "have regard to" clause. Howe and Gardiner presented a striking contrast in personalities, the one the epitome of the business mentality, and the other that of the dedicated politician. Howe was disposed simply to write off the losses in terms of the insurance analogy that too high a premium had been paid for the coverage. But he never questioned the need for coverage and he defended the contract as a good one, even without the ambiguous "have regard to" clause. As it was, the contract had resulted in five years of unprecedented returns. Also, Howe asserted that the time to form a judgment whether it was good or bad was when the agreement was signed, nor after it was all over. It was a businesslike assessment. Howe also expressed his opinion that it had been a mistake to have such a loosely-worded clause in the agreement (In Canada the words "have regard to" have survived only in derisive terms as a meaningless phrase, and have been eschewed in official usage ever since).

The bilateral contract and its multilateral successor had another significant result, however, in propelling the monopoly wheat board along the way to its eventual acceptance as a permanent institution in 1967. From 1943, when the monopoly powers were first conferred upon the board, those powers were extended by periodic amendment to the act until, in 1967, a terminal date on the board's powers was removed.

This recapitulation of the evolution of grain marketing policy has deliberately avoided any attempt to assess the relative merits of the alternative marketing systems which emerged. That issue remains from time to time the subject of lively debate upon which strong views are held. Rather, the purpose of the review has been to recall and to clarify the circumstances in which each system came to be adopted and integrated into today's grain marketing structure.

But the story is only half told if it fails to take into account the colorful personalities who contributed to the result. The industry has been blessed in the capacity of the men who helped to shape it. In earlier parts of the review tribute has already been paid to the more notable policy-makers and advisers, Sir George Foster, Dr. Robert Magill, Mr. James Stewart, the Right Honourable R. B. Bennett and Mr. John I. McFarland. These are singled out for special mention because of their input from the government side. The founders of the elevator companies and grain firms were all mentioned in the early part of the review as were the leaders within the co-operative movement. The calibre of the leaders among the private trade was reflected by those who were elected to the presidency of the Winnipeg grain exchange, and who made representations to government. Without in any way attempting an adequate list of such persons, the names of John Charlie Gage, W. R. Bawlf, F. J. Anderson, James A. Richardson, Sidney T. Smith, Roy W. Milner, Robert McKee, Henry Gauer, Alex Christie, W. J. Dowler, George Mathieson, and K. A. Powell have been associated with the various policy recommendations. To these names should be added those of C. Gordon Smith and Charles E. Huntting who as grain men also served for a time on the Canadian wheat board, and who made their impact as policy-advisers. The co-operative movement similarly produced men of great stature, such as Thomas Crerar, Charles Dunning, Dr. Motherwell, Henry Wise Wood, Alexander J. McPhail, L. C. Brouillette, Paul Bredt, George Bennett, Lew Hutchinson, Ben Plumer, Dr. W. J. Parker, J. H. Wesson and George W. Robertson.

More extended reference, however, still remains to be made about the policy-makers and advisers who shaped the events through the latter part of the review. In 1935, it was only natural that the incoming Liberal administration should adopt a policy stance at variance with that of the Right Honourable R. B. Bennett and John I. McFarland who, until then, had dominated the scene. As a reflection of his difference in temperament from Bennett, King presided over wheat policy in the anonymity of cabinet. His incisive interventions on occasion to adjudicate contentious issues would have been forgotten, except for the record he kept in his diary. For the day-to-day decisions on wheat policy, King decided to appoint a cabinet wheat committee, and he may have been influenced in doing so by his desire to have the Honourable James Garfield Gardiner represent Saskatchewan in his cabinet. Gardiner had a compulsive desire to be responsible for wheat policy which he could share, if not dominate, as a member of the cabinet wheat committee. King was predisposed to trust Gardiner's judgment in the interpretation of producer attitudes and needs.

Nevertheless, King deserves credit himself as a policy-maker to the extent that he intervened on several occasions in crucial policy decisions. His well-known and overriding consideration for the unity of Canada extended into wheat policy. He was keenly aware of the post-depression plight of the western producers. Perhaps the best example of King's several interventions occurred in connection with the setting of the initial payment at 80 cents in 1938. The country was split on the issue of any special subvention for the western farmer as the Hepburn and Macauley outbursts in Ontario attested. Even the eastern and western members of King's own cabinet were split, but King had the sense to back Dunning's recommendation for an 80-cent payment to forestall worse events. Nowadays when much larger subventions are made in whatever part of the country the need is warranted, it is interesting to look back upon the east-west confrontation of those days and to see how much the sorely-needed income supplement in western Canada was begrudged. King vigorously defended the government's 1939 grain legislation when he met with the Bracken committee on western farm markets and he appeared to relish the annual presentations of the Canadian federation of agriculture. He was prepared to face the farmers' delegation in 1942 and to support ameliorative action in the setting of the 1942 initial payment. King also supported Gardiner in the latter's opposition to a wartime ceiling upon the price of wheat.

But to revert to Gardiner's contribution to wheat policy, his influence was felt in the abrupt change of direction which followed the election of 1935. The Liberal party had rightly claimed joint authorship of the voluntary wheat board but, even in its election platform, Gardiner had insisted that the board should operate only during the period of the emergency. The next step was the replacement of the McFarland board by the Murray board. The sales effort mounted by the new board was successful to the point of encouraging the government to believe that it could soon get out of the wheat marketing responsibility. Murray's effectiveness as a policy-adviser transcended by far his brief interlude as chief commissioner of the board. He convinced his ministers that the surplus could be moved and he backed up his advice with action. In the brief time that the surplus was out of the way, Gardiner set about in earnest to reshape the government's wheat policy. As the Turgeon report recommended, Gardiner undertook the bizarre task of persuading the pools to resume their co-operative marketing function. But the pools which had fathered the co-operative marketing system had lost confidence in their progeny and persuaded the government instead to continue in the marketing role. In 1938-39, the government came as close as it had ever done to opting out from its commitment; from thenceforward events reshaped the government's marketing policy as evidenced in the creation of the monopoly board in 1943 and its retention in the interest of assuring markets through the postwar transitional years. Although Gardiner was not the sponsor of the policy decision in 1943, he was responsible for the retention of the monopoly board after the war, by which time he had already become undeniably the predominant wheat-policy maker.

Apart from Gardiner's propensity to negotiate contracts, his skill lay in his ability to wrest subventions from the treasury to bolster farm income. He led the attack to increase the initial payment in 1938. Then when he analyzed the results in a disproportionate payment to Alberta producers at the expense of those in Saskatchewan, Gardiner attempted to trade a reduction in the initial payment against other desirable legislation to distribute treasury subventions more equitably among producers. With the outset of war he turned to the negotiation of food contracts with the United Kingdom which had the effect of providing floor prices and market assurance for the food staples other than wheat.

One of Gardiner's great efforts on behalf of producers was when he stood off the application of the general wartime price-ceiling policy to wheat. Had Gardiner not protested vigorously, a wartime ceiling of 82¾ cents would in all probability have been imposed on wheat. In that event, the inequities attendant upon an unduly depressed industry would have been prolonged to the war's end. Another of Gardiner's great efforts was in getting the initial payment raised from 70 to 90 cents, despite the surplus conditions, in 1942. Earlier he had fought persistently to have the government honor its commitment to maintain prairie farm income at a level of $325,000,000.

Nevertheless, Gardiner's major policy contribution lay in his endeavor to assure a stable market for western producers through the uncertain postwar transitional period. The issue was of prime concern to producers, and the means of resolving it were the bilateral contract and the five-year pool, both of Gardiner's devising.

If Gardiner deserves, as he surely did, to be ranked foremost among the policy-makers, the Right Honourable C. D. Howe also deserves honorable mention. Howe brought to the chairmanship of the cabinet wheat committee a wealth of background and a businesslike approach to the grain industry. He fully shared Gardiner's concern over the need for market assurance during the postwar transitional period, and he vigorously defended the signing of the bilateral contract, however much he may have disagreed with Gardiner over the means of its final settlement. Howe also gave unwavering support to the negotiation of the international wheat agreement for the same reason that, like the bilateral contract, it provided an insurance policy underwriting an assurance of markets. Even as the bulk contract expired, Howe pursued the bilateral negotiations with the British government to assure that British purchases of Canadian wheat would not diminish. In response to farm organization demands, Howe also devised the strategy by which the Canadian wheat board was made the sole marketing agency for oats and barley.

Among the policy-advisers, Mr. George McIvor deserves recognition as the most outstanding. McIvor followed two great and colorful men in John I. McFarland and J. R. Murray, and had been a principal assistant to both. Little known to the members of the cabinet wheat committee, McIvor was commended by Murray as his successor, and McIvor quickly justified the confidence placed in him. Over the 20-year period which followed until his retirement, McIvor consistently tendered well-considered advice. In his presentations to the cabinet wheat committee, McIvor probed thoroughly into the implications of each policy issue and he generated confidence in his recommendations. McIvor gathered about him a remarkable support staff who were just as thorough in their spheres. As a consequence of the recognized competence of the board, other agencies turned to the wheat board, during the war years, to discharge a number of responsibilities having little to do with the sale of wheat. It was due in no small measure to McIvor's direction that the board transcended the political image of its early days. Even if it were counted by some to be a doubtful accomplishment, McIvor should be credited with the fact that the public confidence engendered by the board contributed to its retention as a permanent institution after the war.

The emergency grain transportation committee, thanks to Mr. T. C. Lockwood's chairmanship, to the active co-operation of the railway representatives and to McIvor's participation, contributed in no small measure to the successful movement of grain through the wartime transportation crisis. McIvor's chairmanship of the cereals committee of the combined food board and its successor, the international emergency food council, earned the confidence of the claimants for wheat supplies that their interests were at least equitably safeguarded. In that capacity, McIvor won for Canadian producers a host of international friends by his level-headed and impartial handling of wheat export programs during a period of critical world shortage.

Prominent mention among the policy advisers is due to Norman Robertson, Mike Pearson and Mitchell Sharp. Sharp was concerned with wheat policy matters from the time he was called in as a wartime assistant to Ilsley, although his principal contributions both as policy-adviser and policy-maker were yet to come in the period subsequent to this review. Pearson first became involved in the wheat problem when he served as secretary of the Stamp Commission. In both his London and Washington posts he was involved in the affairs of the wheat advisory committee and the international wheat council. His reports from Washington on the American attitude to the bilateral contract gave cabinet reason to pause. Eventually, as minister of external affairs, Pearson accompanied Howe to London on what proved to be the final settlement of that contract.

Norman Robertson (a British Columbia Rhodes scholar without roots in the grain industry) became even more directly exposed as a wheat policy adviser. As a young external affairs officer, Robertson had made a study of the numerous conferences on wheat which preceded the London conference of 1933, and he accompanied Bennett to London as his principal adviser during the negotiation of the 1933 agreement. He followed the activities of the wheat advisory committee with interest and produced a report of more than a hundred pages, which remains as an invaluable record of the events of those days. Robertson prepared the innocuous instructions sent to the Canadian representatives on the wheat advisory committee in the days when the cabinet wheat committee would take no stand. He was still doing so, when McIvor, Shaw and Wilson arrived in London in 1939, cutting across the instructions he had already sent to Massey.

As King's principal adviser during and immediately after the war, Robertson interceded when he saw the conflict between Gardiner's proposed contract and the postwar trade policies the Americans had sponsored and the Canadian government had already espoused. As head of the Canadian delegation to the London wheat conference in 1947 he did his utmost to mesh the bilateral contract terms with those of the proposed international agreement. It was not his fault that he failed. When Robertson returned to Ottawa after St. Laurent became prime minister, he resumed among his other duties his role of wheat-adviser to his new chief.

Looking farther afield, one should also make brief mention of the British and American contributions to the shaping of Canadian wheat policy. From the first world war until well after the end of the second, British buyers whether government or private afforded the largest single market for Canadian wheat. Through two world wars, Canadian propinquity to the

British Isles placed Canada in the position of Britain's dominant supplier. In the circumstances the propensity was strong, under wartime conditions, to enter into bulk contracts. Foster had made such an attempt which fell through to the disadvantage of the buyer judged by subsequent events. Crerar's proposal, rejected by his colleagues, would have benefited producers. Even though both buyer and seller might be bearish on the outlook, the buyer tended to be the more so. Eventually when a large bulk contract was made, it proved to be of disadvantage to the seller, the extent of which defies any accurate assessment.

Some lessons have been learned, however, by both sides. On the one hand, Canadian marketing policies were unable to survive on the hypothesis that the seller could make the market and thereby create his own price stability. On the other, the buyer has come to recognize that his economy cannot thrive upon agricultural distress among the supplying countries. It is interesting that it was Prime Minister Harold Wilson who, in his student days, established a direct relation between agricultural depression abroad and unemployment in Britain. By the same token, industrial Canada cannot thrive upon rural distress nor upon the ever-shrinking rural population. Such economic wisdom dominated the policies of British governments sufficiently since to ensure the co-operation of the latter in the negotiation of an international wheat agreement. The stabilization of wheat supplies and markets contributed in turn to stability in the prices of related commodities. It was one thing to set an arbitrary price between buyer and seller in a bilateral contract, but quite another to set a range on the bulk of world wheat prices in a multilateral contract.

Even more importantly, mention should be made of the Right Honourable Ernest Bevin. It was he who gave practical expression to Wilson's philosophy in 1948 when he intervened to reverse a British cabinet decision which would have terminated the international wheat agreement negotiations. In that respect, he helped to make the 1949 international wheat agreement possible.

The Americans, on the other hand, have been traditional competitors. Varying degrees of co-operation were developed in the two world wars and on two occasions Canadian supplies were drawn upon to meet American deficits. Otherwise competition prevailed until it led eventually to the exclusion of each country's wheat from the other's internal markets. In these policies the Americans led the way, necessitated by domestic price-support policies which would have attracted an abnormal inflow of foreign grain. Traditionally, the Americans have been more generous in redressing the economic problems of their producers. Canadian policies took different shape and at much less cost, justified on the ground that the Canadian treasury could not support an export industry to the extent that the American treasury could support its predominantly domestic industry. It would be a mistake to fail to recognize, however, the extent to which the more dramatic American measures have influenced Canadian policy.

In the field of international co-operation, it was the Americans who led the way. With the incoming Roosevelt administration in 1933, Secretary of Agriculture Henry A. Wallace sponsored an international wheat agreement and sought the support of other governments. It was only in the absence of adroit American representation at the London conference in 1933 that

Bennett moved into the breach, took over the chair and forced the 1933 agreement through. When Bennett discovered in practice that the formula of export quotas was not sufficient by itself to raise the level of world wheat prices, he lost interest in the agreement. For several years thereafter Canadian support for the revival of the agreement waned. In that interval it was American persistence that brought the key countries to the negotiating table in 1939 and again in 1941. By then, for reasons of wartime diplomacy, the Canadian government attitude toward an international wheat agreement had begun to change.

By the war's end, the wheat position had altered so dramatically that the American administration, including the department of agriculture as well as the department of state, would have been content to let the international negotiations lapse. It was purely coincidental that Gardiner's pursuit of the bilateral contract inspired interest in other official quarters in an international agreement as a more palatable trade alternative. The result was that Canada took over from the Americans the initiative and organizational drive which led eventually to an operative agreement in 1949. Success had been almost attained a year earlier when the agreement foundered on the American senate's failure to ratify. President Harry S. Truman made the international wheat agreement an election issue. In doing so, his presidential intervention was unique.

Whether in Canada, Britain or the United States it seems almost incredible in retrospect that so many of the distinguished corps of civil servants of that era were involved in one way or another with the formulation of wheat policy; likewise the number of ministers, prime ministers and presidents, either in office or on the way up. Throughout the review, the actual producers of wheat have remained anonymous. Although his figure was on the high side, Gardiner counted them at 250,000. The mental image officials had of them, however accurate or otherwise, was that they were individualists and inveterate optimists, capable of enduring untold hardships and of reaping occasional rewards. Collectively, they presented their grievances with credibility and dignity; their political force was reflected in the deference policy-makers and advisers displayed toward their interests. In terms of quality of human input from either side, the record is astonishing and the conclusion inescapable that, with little debatable exception, producers' interests were well served.

APPENDIX 1

OPERATIONS OF THE BOARD OF GRAIN SUPERVISORS FOR CANADA JUNE 11th, 1917 TO JANUARY 31st, 1920

I. WHY THE BOARD WAS CREATED

The Government created the Board because the accumulating effect of the war upon international trading in general, and trading in wheat in particular, made some such step necessary. The financing of the war by the various countries involved had led to a vast extension of credit and currency in those countries, and this tended toward a general increase in price levels. This was accentuated as regards wheat by several powerful contributory causes. The wheat surpluses of Russia, Australia, India and the Argentine were either inaccessible altogether, or difficult to secure by reason of the increasing shortage of tonnage. Not only the allied peoples in Great Britain, France, Belgium and Italy, but also the neutral countries in Northern Europe, were dependent upon North America for their necessary wheat supplies. And the methods by which the Governments of these countries bought their wheat in North America in 1915 and 1916 added to the difficulty. Their agents bought wheat, for example, at Winnipeg in competition with each other, and with Canadian and American millers, and in some cases the same Government had different buyers for Canadian wheat and flour. The primary object of these buyers for the European Governments was to secure quantities of milling wheat; the price was a secondary consideration. And as the Grain Exchanges in North America were still open and unrestricted, these government buyers soon became the dominating operators.

The effect of all this was not only an increase in the price of wheat, with occasional violent fluctuations, but was in a word the disintegration of the grain exchanges both in Canada and in the United States.

This disintegration appeared dramatically in Winnipeg in the spring of 1917. During the previous winter months the agents of the Allied Governments had

Source: *Trade and Commerce File T-14-144*, Public Archives of Canada. Dr. Robert Magill gave the above title to his final report on the operations of the Board of Grain Supervisors. The report was written in the form of a departmental memorandum for future official reference and was unpublished.

bought wheat freely to be delivered in May and July. They bought this wheat mainly, if not altogether, from the operators of country elevators, who as they bought wheat from the farmers from day to day sold it for May and July delivery. Neither the buyers for the Allied Governments nor the elevator operators who sold the wheat were gambling in futures. The buyers were providing to the best of their judgment for the future needs of the countries they represented, and the sellers were securing their loans from the banks by hedging their purchases in the only way known to commercial men of providing against risk. These future contracts called for grades 1, 2 and 3 Northern. It turned out that much of the wheat thus sold or hedged did not measure up to these contract grades. As a rule, and under normal conditions, this presents no great difficulty, because the buyers are willing to accept lower grades on the contracts at fair discounts. This, indeed, is a well-established commercial practice. In the Spring of 1917, however, the British representatives intimated that they were unwilling or unable to accept lower grades at discounts, and that they would require the contract grades. This forced the sellers to try to buy the higher grades on the open market, with the result that the prices of these grades went skyrocketing. As prices soared the sellers were called for increasing sums of money, and the limit of their credits was soon reached. In effect the market was cornered and a disaster upon a large scale was impending.

To avert this the Winnipeg Grain Exchange investigated the conditions, found them as above, closed the market for futures, and by the aid of the Dominion Government secured the consent of the British authorities to a settlement along commercial lines. As a result, the British accepted the lower grades of wheat on the contracts at fair discounts, the discounts were speedily fixed and the situation cleared up.

While, however, the situation within the Grain Exchange was cleared up for the time, there remained the possibility that a similar crisis might develop at any time so long as the British and European Governments continued their methods of buying in an open market at Winnipeg, and this possibility alarmed the grain trade. In the meantime, the increasing cost of living was alarming consumers in North America generally, and the United States had established its food control system. The dependence of Great Britain and her Allies and of European neutral countries upon North America for wheat meant that there was no limit to the price to which wheat might go, except ability to pay. Under these circumstances, a delegation from the Winnipeg Grain Exchange waited on the Dominion Government, and asked for government control of the grain markets during the war.

At that time Mr. Balfour was in the United States on his mission, and the Vice-Chairman of the British Cereal Commission, Mr. Anderson, was one of his party. Mr. Anderson came to Ottawa, bringing with him Messrs. Robson and Stewart of the Wheat Export Company, the agency of the British Royal Commission, and a series of conferences took place between the Canadian Government, the British representatives and the delegates from the Winnipeg Grain Exchange. These conferences resulted in the creation of the Board of Grain Supervisors.

II.   PERIOD OF OPERATION

The Board was created by Order-in-Council under the War Measures Act on the 11th June, 1917, and it was dissolved on the 31st January, 1920. It was in operation for a period of thirty-two months, and the period of its operation was that in which the war reached its critical stages and finally its end.

During this period the Board marketed the balance of the wheat crop of 1916, and the whole of the wheat crops of 1917 and 1918, making a total of about 350,000,000 bushels of wheat.

III.   COARSE GRAINS

The Board did not market oats, barley, flax and rye. Its reason was not that these grains are not human food, or that they are unimportant, or that the Board wished to leave something to private enterprise. The reason was that it could not find buyers who would agree to accept the surpluses of these grains at fixed prices satisfactory to the Board. It would have been as easy to fix the prices for these grains as it was to fix the price of wheat. But to fix the prices without the certainty that the whole of the grains would be sold at the prices fixed would have incurred a risk of serious financial loss which the Board would not face.

The coarse grains, therefore, were not marketed by the Board, but by private enterprise, and difficult as were the conditions of trading during the years 1917 and 1918, the grain trade were able to market the coarse grains successfully.

IV.   THE BALANCE OF THE CROP OF 1916

Great Britain and her Allies needed the whole of the balance of the crop of 1916, and the United States did not need any of it. The Board took measures, therefore, to sell the whole of the remaining exportable surplus to the Wheat Export Company for shipment overseas. In doing so the Board protected such contracts as had been previously made with buyers in the United States, and it did not interfere with the courtesy custom extended to wagon-loads hauled across the boundary line to nearby American elevators. Upon the balance of wheat remaining the Board fixed a maximum price of $2.40 per bushel for One Northern Wheat in store Fort William, and at that price, with commercial spreads for lower grades, sold the balance of the remaining surplus of wheat to the Wheat Export Company.

V.   MARKETING METHOD OF THE BOARD

The main work of the Board was to market the crops of 1917 and 1918, and its chief problem immediately after its creation was to formulate a satisfactory method for marketing the crop of 1917. Speaking generally, there were two alternatives open to it, and these alternatives may be briefly described thus: The Board might either supplant the grain trade altogether, or it might utilize the grain trade as its agents.

The Board decided upon the second alternative, and this method was pursued during two years, and indeed is still being operated.

As wheat is grown in every province of the Dominion, as many farmers sell their wheat to the elevator, warehouse or mill in their neighborhood, and as the quantity of wheat grown yearly in Canada is so large, the organizations created by commercial evolution for the marketing of wheat are numerous, are widely scattered and are highly developed.

Theoretically, a Board with the requisite statutory powers might undertake to throw all these organizations aside and to interpose itself and its employees between producer and consumer instead. It might take over all the physical machinery, especially the grain elevators, and by operating the elevators itself, and by buying the wheat direct from the farmers at some 4,000 elevators and over a thousand mills on the one hand, and selling it to millers and exporters on the other, it might nationalize the grain trade, and do away with private enterprise altogether so far as the merchandising of grain is concerned. Were this method adopted, while transportation costs by rail and vessel, and insurance and interest costs, would still remain as under private trading, elevator costs, commissions for buying and selling, and merchandising profits, would be taken over from private enterprise, and be converted into revenues of a nationalized system.

Obviously, however, such a comprehensive scheme could not be attempted by a Board created for emergency purposes, and such a comprehensive scheme has not yet been formally attempted, nor, indeed, formally advocated.

The general plan adopted by the Board of Grain Supervisors for 1917, continued in operation during 1918, was quite different. It was that of employing the grain trade organizations as they were to do the work, and of prescribing and enforcing the terms and conditions under which the work should be done. To speak of this as nationalizing the grain trade is a misnomer.

VI.   STABILIZED WHEAT PRICE

Translated into plain language, a stabilized price means a price which does not vary through the crop year. Could the price be so stabilized the difficulties incident to fluctuations would be avoided, and this would be a relief to producers, dealers, bankers and millers.

VII.   GUARANTEEING THE PRICE

Naming a price is one thing — it is quite another to find a purchaser who will contract to take the article at the price fixed throughout the whole of the twelve months. For the crop of 1917 there was no difficulty in this respect. The Allies needed the whole exportable surplus wheat of Canada. They were willing to buy the whole surplus at the price fixed, and they gave a guarantee to that effect. In this respect, wheat was in a different position from coarse grains.

It was different with the crop of 1918. No guarantee was obtained from the representatives of the British Royal Commission with regard to the surplus of the crop of 1918, and when the Armistice was signed there was considerable difficulty in selling the balance of wheat still remaining in Canada. Having, however, fixed a price for the wheat of 1918, and having arranged for the purchase of wheat from the farmer by the trade on that basis, a guarantee was necessary and it was given by the Dominion Government. Fortunately, the Allied countries needed the wheat, and in the end the balance of the crop of 1918 was sold at the fixed price.

The experience of these two years illustrates the fundamental difficulty in fixing the price of wheat. To fix the price without the certainty that the wheat can be sold on the basis of the price fixed is to run the risk that at the end of the year the wheat would either not be sold or could not be sold except at a loss. This risk would be great in years when wheat exporting countries had good average crops — it would be less when there was a world shortage in wheat.

VIII.   FIXED TERMINAL PRICES

The next difficulty in stabilizing the price of wheat in Canada arises from the fact that the wheat growing areas are so widely scattered. Wheat is grown in the Maritime Provinces and in the valleys of British Columbia, as well as in Ontario and the Prairie Provinces. The scale of prices must be based on a parity commercially sound. This was done eventually by taking Montreal as the terminal point for wheat grown in the eastern provinces, Vancouver for wheat grown in British Columbia, and of course Fort William for wheat grown in the Prairie Provinces.

IX.   VARIETIES AND GRADES

The next difficulty arises from the number of varieties of wheat grown and the number of grades in each variety. Theoretically, it is its milling and baking value that should determine the price of any lot of wheat. The Board took One Manitoba Northern Wheat in store Fort William as the basis. Having fixed the price of that grade for the 1917 crop at $2.21½ per bushel, it used this as the basis or standard throughout, and after long conferences with producers and millers, it completed its long list of prices for the different varieties and the different grades; in store Montreal for wheat grown in the eastern provinces; in store Dominion Government Elevator, Vancouver, for wheat grown in the Prairie Provinces.

In all this work there was a plethora of detail that cannot be embodied in a report, and there were opportunities for differences of opinion that might well have given rise to considerable trouble. It is pleasant to be able to report that in this part of the work, once the basis price was agreed upon, the Board enjoyed the co-operation and good-will of producers, merchants and millers alike, and that while doubtless the sale of prices fixed contained features open to criticism, still on the whole there was no strong objection to it from any quarter.

X. STREET PRICES

The fixing of prices at the terminal points is, however, only the beginning, though an essential one. Wheat is sold by farmers to the local elevator or warehouse operator both east and west. This is known as "street" wheat. And in by-gone days the prices paid for street wheat were a perennial source of complaint. After careful consideration the Board decided that the price of wheat should be stabilized at country points also.

XI. CARRYING CHARGES ON WHEAT

From harvest to the close of navigation at Fort William there is only a limited period of time. It is physically impossible, and it is economically undesirable, to ship out the whole of the western wheat surplus in that period. Considerable quantities are delivered by farmers to country elevators during harvest which cannot be transported to Fort William before December, and considerable quantities are hauled from the farms to country elevators during the Winter months. Western wheat must still be hauled east. The Panama route is not yet effective, Canada has no outlet such as the United States enjoys in the Gulf of Mexico, and the milling industry of the Dominion cannot yet absorb as large a proportion of the total Canadian wheat as the milling industry in the United States can of United States wheat.

Under these conditions a large quantity of wheat in Western Canada must be carried over every year during the Winter months—some of it on the farms, some of it in country elevators, and some of it in the terminal elevators at the head of the lakes.

Every one understands that if wheat is worth $2.21½ a bushel at Fort William, it is worth more at Montreal by the cost of transporting it there. It should be equally obvious that if wheat is worth $2.21½ per bushel at Fort William in the month of December, it is worth more the following May by the cost of keeping it there. That cost includes storage, insurance and interest. And with wheat at $2.21½ per bushel, these carrying charges, as they are called, amounted to practically 2¢ a bushel per month.

In normal times all accruing charges, whether handling charges at the elevator, or freight charges by lake and rail, or carrying charges in an elevator, became part of the price of wheat, just as do the costs of production, and all commercial experience shows that this is the simplest and most economical way of handling them.

It is somewhat curious that while the notion of stabilized prices was supposed to be consistent with these variations that were due to freight rates, it was decided that it was inconsistent with those variations that were due to carrying charges. In the United States considerable importance was attached to this, possibly because the carrying charges do not bulk quite so largely there as in Western Canada. In Canada, at all events, the cost of carrying wheat from Fort William when the price was fixed at $2.21½ per bushel was, as stated above, 2¢ a bushel per month. Who was to pay this 2¢ a bushel per month, and how, if it could not be incorporated in the price of wheat?

XII. STREET PRICE MARGIN

With regard to street prices, the principle adopted by the Board was that if the price at the terminal point was fixed, the country price should also be fixed. And this was done simply by deducting the freight rate from the Fort William price, and in addition whatever amount the elevator was fairly entitled to for its services. The board set this latter amount at a maximum of 5¢ a bushel, with the result that the street price at any particular point in the west was the Fort William price minus freight and minus a maximum of 5¢.

In reaching this maximum the Board considered that the Canada Grain Act allows country elevators a maximum of 1¾¢ per bushel for handling wheat through the elevator, that the Winnipeg Grain Exchange fixes 1¢ a bushel for selling it, and that the difference between the sum of these two and 5¢ would be sufficient to protect the country elevator operator against loss in grades and weight and give him his profit.

As stated above, in bygone days street prices gave rise to much trouble. The maximum margin set by the Board for straight grade wheat was 5¢ and at no time during the crop years of 1917 and 1918 did the Board receive a single protest from producers in regard to that margin. For some of the lower grades, or the "no grade" grain, it was admitted on all sides that the margin was too low, and this was provided for as time went on.

When the street price problem had been thus far solved, the question of carrying charges became still more urgent. A five cent margin would not enable a country elevator to carry its purchased wheat long when the carrying charge cost at Fort William was 2¢ a bushel per month. In other words, the street price margin could only be fixed at a maximum of 5¢ provided the carrying charges—storage, interest and insurance—were paid to the elevators by the Board. There were two alternatives—the Board must either pay the carrying charges, or the elevator must be permitted to collect them from the producer. An in the case of street wheat that would mean a margin very much larger than 5¢ a bushel.

It may be said that the Board could have added 2¢ a bushel per month to the terminal price, and have met the carrying charges in that way. And in fact this was the method which the Board at first contemplated. This plan would have followed commercial practice, as in normal times the price of May wheat at Fort William is higher than the price of previous December wheat by the cost of carrying. While the Board contemplated this method favorably, however, there was a very serious objection from the United States. If the Fort William price in November was $2.21½, and if 2¢ a bushel per month were added to it, the Fort William price in May would be some ten cents per bushel higher than the price in Duluth, grade for grade, because the United States authorities had determined to maintain the same nominal price for wheat at the same point the year through. The United States authorities recognized that carrying charges in Western Canada were an important thing. The Board, on the other hand, recognized the desirability of keeping the prices on the two sides of the boundary in line, and a way out was found by separating the carrying charges from the price of wheat, and handling them through the Board's offices by means of a special fund.

This was not a method which the Board ever regarded with pleasure. It was an untried method for which there was little or no guidance in previous commercial experience. It meant imposing an assessment on the wheat sold to millers and exporters. It meant the creation of Collecting and Disbursing Departments. It meant elaborate and accurate records of the purchases of wheat at every country elevator, of all quantities sold to exporters, and of all quantities ground into flour at the mills. It meant a system of checks and a machinery to enforce payment. It meant a heartbreaking audit of the books of all the elevators, grain companies and millers of the Dominion. It meant the possibility of misunderstandings about the nature of the tax; of litigation about payments; and worst of all it meant the possibility of the abuse of public money. It is a method which should not be tolerated, or should be tolerated only so long as it is forced by imperative conditions. It has no other defence. It was adopted by the Board because there was no other way out. To maintain an identical price for twelve months at the terminal point meant that the carrying charges must be either assessed on the buyer in the form of a special payment to the Board, or taken out of the producer by giving him a lower price for his wheat. After considerable hesitation, therefore, the plan was adopted. The consumer paid and the producer benefited. It should be emphasized that the one party who profited by this method was the grower of the wheat. And this in spite of the fact that some have misunderstood the whole matter so thoroughly as to state that the producer paid these carrying charges. The exact opposite is the fact — the consumer paid them and the producer received them less the administrative costs of the Board.

XIII.   THE RATE OF ASSESSMENT

Having decided to adopt the plan the next difficulty was as to what rate of assessment should be. On this question the Board had little to guide it. It did not know at what rate the wheat would be hauled from the farm to the country elevator, from the country elevator to the terminal point, or from Canada across the seas. Yet this was the most material factor in the problem. The Board could guess at the total yield — everybody does that. It could tell how much the carrying charges would amount to per bushel per month, and from commercial experience it could ascertain that in pre-war days, and when wheat was selling far below a dollar a bushel, the average excess of May over previous December for a period of some twelve years was a fraction above 5¢ a bushel. Making the most of all such considerations the Board began by fixing the assessment at 2¢ a bushel to be paid by Canadian millers and 4¢ a bushel to be paid by exporters upon all wheat sold to them.

In comparison with the above named average excess of May over December, this rate was low, but the reason was that by assessing all wheat shipped a lower rate would suffice.

The representative of the British Royal Commission naturally objected to being assessed a higher rate than Canadian millers, and he was somewhat sceptical about the value of the consolation offered him by the Board, namely, that in the event of a surplus accruing at the end of the year, the inequality would be met. As it happened, at the end of the year there was a considerable surplus, and the Board gladly implemented its promise by refunding to the British authorities the sum of two and a half million dollars. The balance of the surplus was used by the Board in reducing the rate on the crop of 1918. During that year the rate was equal, and both parties shared in the reduction.

XIV.   EASTERN MILLS

Having fixed the assessment for carrying charges and created its machinery for collecting and paying them, the Board began to breathe. It soon appeared, however, that the total cost of wheat to Canadian mills must be somehow equalized under a system of stabilized wheat prices.

The most intolerable feature of the regulation of commerce, especially of international commerce, is that no mortal mind can foresee the series of effects that one apparently simple regulation may start.

International trading in grain is such a complicated matter on the one hand, and on the other hand the machinery for handling it evolved during centuries of commercial experience is so delicately balanced, that one never knows what the result of any artificial interference with it will be. The terminal prices had been nicely fixed by the Board. The producer's prices had been fixed. The Western millers who could secure their wheat supplies from the ample streams flowing past their doors were also nicely fixed. But the Eastern miller found himself in a different position because he paid $2.21½ for his wheat at Fort William; in addition he paid 2¢ a bushel to relieve the farmer of carrying charges, while at the same time he had to provide for the carrying of his own wheat. The miller, however, is audible even while he is in Toronto or Montreal and his listener is in Winnipeg, and upon investigation the Board undertook to carry all wheat for all millers. To do this it increased the assessment to be paid by Canadian millers by a cent and a half a bushel.

When it reached this stage the Board found itself paying the carrying charges on all wheat in all public elevators, all mills, and all Winter storage boats except the wheat sold for export.

XV. GRISTING MILLS

There are little mills throughout the country that do only a gristing business. They are very useful institutions in their communities. They take a farmer's wheat, grind it and return him the flour made therefrom. The Board decided that such mills as did only a gristing business in this sense should be exempt from the assessment, but it could not grant exemption to any mill that did a commercial business, even though it did at the same time a gristing business.

XVI. CARRYING CHARGES IN ONTARIO

One feature of this plan of handling carrying charges that was a source of anxiety to the Board was that it might tend to delay the movement of wheat. Delay in movement in 1917, when the allied communities in Europe were suffering from shortage of flour, would have been criminal. The Board refused to pay carrying charges to any elevator or warehouse throughout 1917 that could sell the wheat either for milling in Canada or for export. The Board never regarded the carrying charge fund as an endowment to anybody — the Board regarded it as essential toward giving the farmer his proper share of the stabilized price. And it was the determination of the Board that if there was evidence to warrrant the belief that any elevator or warehouse was holding back wheat in order to make carrying charges out of it, that elevator or warehouse would be dealt with most drastically.

In 1917 there was no reason so far as the Board could ascertain why any warehouse in Ontario should hold wheat. The conditions there are more akin to those in the United States. The Ontario warehouseman could ship his wheat any day during 1917 to a mill or to the Wheat Export Company. The Board therefore allowed no carrying charge there.

In 1918 a different situation developed. For some reason or other the Canadian Food Board desired warehouses in Ontario not to ship their wheat out for a time, and no orders were given by the Wheat Export Company for Ontario wheat or flour made therefrom for a time. The Board of Grain Supervisors did not see its way to pay bills which it did not incur, and for which it was in no way responsible, but as an injustice was done to the Ontario warehouses the Board recommended payment of carrying charges under those conditions.

XVII. THE CONSUMERS PAID

Some have said that carrying charges were paid by the producer, and others have stated that they were paid by the miller and exporter. It has been shown above that they were not paid by the producer, but to the producer. So far as the millers were concerned, the carrying charge assessment was simply added by them to the total price of wheat and provided for in the price of flour. The consumer paid the carrying charges, and the consumers of Great Britain, France and Italy paid their share of them. If consumers considered such an assessment to be unfair, the only reply that can be offered is that they would certainly have paid much more for the wheat had the price of wheat not been fixed, and that they would most probably have paid more had a monthly addition been made to the fixed price at the terminal point to meet the carrying charges.

XVIII. DISTRIBUTION OF THE WHEAT

The first claim on Canadian wheat is that of the Canadian consumer for bread and seed. The Board therefore estimated the quantity needed for those purposes, and retained it. In doing this the Board was confronted with a serious shortage in wheat in Alberta and Saskatchewan both in 1917 and in 1918. The Board limited and regulated the shipments from the districts in which there was a shortage, and made special provision for the holding back of sufficient quantities to meet the needs of those districts, and of British Columbia.

The second claim is that of the Canadian milling industry for such an additional quantity as the millers can export in the form of flour to the Allies, to Newfoundland, and to the West Indies. This quantity in the years dealt with depended mainly upon the orders for flour received by the millers from the British Royal Commission. The Board retained sufficient wheat for this purpose also.

The total quantity retained in Canada for milling was distributed amongst the millers on principles agreed upon between the Board and the millers, and the terms and conditions were also arranged.

Taking the two years together, the Board supplied the Canadian mills to the full capacity required by their orders for flour, and there was practically no complaint as regards wheat supply from the millers. And on the other hand, when, in the Winter of 1917, there was an urgent call from overseas for wheat, the millers cordially assisted the Board to meet that demand by shipping from their stocks at the Board's request.

The balance of the wheat after provision had been made for Canadian consumers and millers was sold to the Wheat Export Company. There was no difficulty in selling the balance of the 1917 crop. The need of the Allies was urgent and the war was not ended. It was not so easy to sell the balance of the crop of 1918, or that part of it which was still in Canada when the armistice was signed. Indeed, for a considerable period it looked as though that quantity could not be sold at all, or could only be sold at a loss. The British Royal Commission had ceased buying, and the Board through the grain trade had bought the wheat as it reached Fort William, and carried it there. The Board could have sold some of it at an earlier date to United States millers, but had declined to do so because they were told that the Allies needed it. After the armistice was signed, the Board learned that they could not sell the wheat to neutral countries in Europe because of certain treaties made by the Imperial Government, and that the Imperial authorities did not need any more Canadian Wheat. In the end, however, the British Royal Commission bought the wheat.

XIX. MOVING THE WHEAT

Taking the two years together, there is little doubt that the system of price fixing adopted tended to slow down the movement of wheat from the farm to the local elevator, and in all districts where the yield was only fair or short, from the local elevator to the terminal point. There was no sign of any deliberate attempt to hold back wheat either by the farmers or by the elevator operators. But the incentives to prompt shipment were no longer in operation as in the days of open markets, of varying prices, individual initiative and keen competition for cars. And the absence of such incentives was reinforced by the failure of the crop over considerable areas, and by the conditions of car supply.

So far as the crop of 1917 is concerned, it is only necessary to say that because of the needs of the Allies in Europe every effort was made to move the wheat. During the Winter months the Board commandeered wheat throughout the prairie provinces, arranged for the handling of it through the Government interior elevators, and by the co-operation of the country elevator operators and the train men shipped a considerable quantity all-rail. It is, of course, easy for the Board to order men to ship wheat and claim credit for so doing. But in this case the credit must be given to those country elevator operators and those train crews who, in January and February, when the thermometer showed from 30 to 45 degrees below zero, loaded, shunted and dispatched the cars. During that year elevator men, railway men, grain men, and millers, all worked to move the wheat.

In regard to the moving of the crop of 1918, a special report was written by the Board dated March 19th, 1919. It is unnecessary, therefore to write about it here. Speaking generally, the conditions had changed in one essential respect. viz., that the American crop of 1918 was larger than the preceding crop, that the danger point in supplies had been passed by the allies, and that there was not the same eagerness in regard to the 1918 crop that had been shown for the previous crop. During the Winter months the agent for the allies ceased buying, and when the armistice was signed as stated above there was difficulty in disposing of the wheat.

XX.   INTEREST AND COST OF ADMINISTRATION

The fund created by the Board for the payment of carrying charges was disbursed regularly, but there were balances left from day to day in the banks to the credit of the Board. On these balances the Board secured interest from the banks, and for a time it increased the interest earning by buying government bonds, which were just as liquid as bank credits. In this way the Board earned $149,193.37 during the period of its operation in the form of interest on its unused balances. The total expense of the Board for all purposes were $146,621.65, so that the interest earned did a little more than pay the administrative expenses.

XXI.   CARRYING CHARGE FUND

The total receipts from the fund created for the purpose of paying carrying charges amounted to $10,425,248.37. This amount includes the interest above referred to, namely, $149,193.37.

Out of this the Board paid for carrying the wheat $7,341,843.26. It refunded on the crop of 1918 to the Imperial Government $2,500,000.00. It handed to the Government of Canada as a surplus for which it had no use $350,000.00. And in addition to this, when it was dissolved on January 31st, 1920, it had as cash on hand and in the banks $75,843.46, and also a travelling expense advance to auditors of $900.00

This cash on hand, amounting to over $75,000.00, will not all be needed. A considerable portion of it will be added to the above surplus of $350,000.00.

XXII.   COST OF THE BOARD

As stated above, the total cost of the Board during those thirty-two months amounted to $146,621.65. The items of this amount are as follows:

Salaries of members of the Board	Nil
Travelling expenses of members of the Board	11,064.48
Salaries of employees of the Board	96,819.13
Travelling expenses of Auditors of the Board	9,265.87
Rentals	7,694.97
Printing	6,213.83
Telegrams	4,758.98

Telephones	354.10
Postage and express	2,139.90
Stationery	2,510.00
Sundry expenses	1,993.51
Legal expenses	2,131.91
Advertising	494.38
Office equipment	1,180.59
	$146,621.65

As the total quantity of wheat marketed was 350,000,000 bushels, the curious and the critical can figure the per bushel cost of the Board's administration. It is more important to note the reasons for such a low cost.

The first is that members of the Board received no salaries, and no allowances for attending sessions, and no expenses other than for such travelling expenses as they incurred when away from home on the work of the board.

The second is that by utilizing the grain trade as above stated the Board avoided the necessity of creating large and expensive establishments.

The third is that in regard to the extensive office work involved the Board was able to utilize the Winnipeg Grain Exchange Clearing House and the Lake Shippers' Clearance Association on most favorable terms. Here, too, should be mentioned the fact that the Winnipeg Grain Exchange gave the Board the free use of its Board Room for public sessions, of its Council Room for the Board's Executive, and an office for the Chairman, all of which reduced the Board's expenses for rent, equipment and telephone service.

It only remains to add that more than one-half of the total cost of administration, as given above, was due to the method of meeting the carrying charges on wheat. Had the Board been able to provide for these charges by additions to the price of wheat sufficient to meet them, the cost of the Board would not have been much more than $50,000.00 for the whole period of its existence. On the other hand, the Board would not have received any revenue from interest.

XXIII. ECONOMIES OF NATIONAL SELLING

It must not be supposed that the Board's cost as above was the total cost of taking that large quantity of wheat from producers and putting it into the hands of millers in Canada and the United Kingdom. The most elementary knowledge of commerce would indicate that apart altogether from the administrative costs of the Board, few, if any, of the costs of taking the wheat from the producers and delivering it to millers were affected by national selling. The banks received their rates of interest on the capital required to finance the wheat, the railway companies and the lake and ocean carriers received their freight rates, and the marine and fire insurance companies received their premiums, under national selling just as under private trading. Further, the country elevators throughout the West, the terminal elevators at the head of the lakes, and the transfer elevators in Eastern Canada, received their handling charges in accordance with the tariffs approved by the Board of Grain Commissioners, under national selling just as under private trading. Further, at every little warehouse in Ontario, at every country elevator throughout Canada, Prairie Provinces, and at every mill throughout Canada, wheat was sold, and at all of these markets — numbering four or five thousand — grain merchants or millers bought wheat direct from farmers in accordance with the plans and orders of the Board, and were allowed a profit for so doing. Commission merchants and track buyers earned their fees on the wheat they handled, and in 1918 even shippers and exporters earned a commission for forwarding wheat to Canadian mills or to the Wheat Export Company at the seaboard.

It is not correct, therefore, to say that national selling interfered with most of the costs of purchasing wheat from the producer and delivering it to the miller. It interfered with very few of these costs, and it is a question whether it lessened any of them. The Wheat Export Company in shipping wheat from Fort William and across the sea incurred expenses in so doing, and when the exported wheat reached Great Britain it was distributed to millers by British grain merchants, who were paid by the Royal Wheat Commission 2 cents a bushel for their services.

National selling did, and does, interfere with grain marketing by private enterprise. But the nature and limits of this interference and the economies resulting from it, have been much misunderstood. So long as there was not only a fixed price, but a guarantee by either the British or Canadian authorities of the price fixed, there was no financial risk in buying on the basis of the fixed price. Bankers, grain dealers and millers could rely upon the guarantee of the British or Canadian government, and that being the case there was no need to insure the purchases of wheat made from day to day in the country by selling them for future delivery at Winnipeg. In other words, there was no need of future trading, and the market for futures was accordingly closed. And as in the minds of many the market for futures appears to be the most prominent thing in the grain exchanges, there followed the misapprehension that the grain trade were put out of business and that all their alleged profit would, under national selling, be saved and divided among producers and consumers. The facts of the case are quite different. The only sections of the grain trade that were seriously affected were those that were engaged in exporting Canadian wheat across the seas, those that sold wheat from Winnipeg and Fort William to eastern mills, and those that received orders to buy or sell wheat for future delivery. These were indeed seriously affected. It should be recognized, however, that a fixed and guaranteed price rendered future trading unnecessary and impossible, and on that score there was no complaint from the grain trade during the war period. There was a serious complaint — and in the opinion of the Board a just complaint — because the British Royal Commission through the Wheat Export Company supplanted shippers and exporters first in the purely domestic trade of Canada, namely, supplying Canadian wheat to Canadian mills, and second, shipping the exported wheat from Fort William to the seaboard. The Canadian grain trade believed, and rightly believed, that they should not have been supplanted in these respects, and this view was put before the Canadian Government, with the result that for the crop of 1918 the Wheat Export Company accepted delivery of the wheat for export at the seaboard, the Canadian grain trade delivered it at the seaboard, and the Wheat Export Company withdrew from the purely domestic trade of Canada altogether.

There was, indeed, one great economy effected by national selling. Throughout the year 1917 Great Britain and her Allies in Europe, along with neutral countries in Europe, were so dependent upon North American wheat on the one hand, and on the other the supplies of North American wheat were so short, that had the price of wheat in North America not been fixed by the Canadian and American governments it would have risen to a degree that would have placed an intolerable burden upon consumers in Canada, Great Britain and the Allied countries. This was the main economy effected by national selling, and it was purely in the interest of consumers. There was no economy in the interest of producers, although the price fixed in the United States and Canada was surely a price that was sufficient to pay any producer who had a fair yield of wheat.

It is worth while to summarize this section — national selling of wheat did not affect these charges:

1. Interest on the capital needed to finance the wheat.
2. Freight rates — by land, and lake and sea.
3. Insurance premiums — fire, marine and shortage.

4. Elevator charges — country, terminal and eastern.
5. Returns for buying in the country and shipping to the terminal points.
6. Commissions for special work, viz., consignments.
7. Commissions for selling and forwarding wheat to millers and to the Wheat Export Company at the seaboard.

National selling did affect:

1. Canadian exporting houses and houses engaged in forwarding wheat from Fort William.
   These houses were displaced by the British Royal Commission; then for the crop of 1918 they were restored by the Canadian Government, and as a result they forwarded the wheat from Fort William to the seaboard for stated fees.
2. The Market for futures — a guaranteed price removed the need for hedging wheat.
3. Price limit. Above all, national selling held the price steady under conditions that had there been no price control the price would have been forced to an intolerable figure.

XXIV. INTERNATIONAL CO-OPERATION IN WHEAT

The Board were desirous of working in close harmony with the representatives of Great Britain and the authorities in the United States. And on the whole, considering the nature of the work and the conditions under which it was done, there was very little friction. It would however, be a grave mistake to ignore the fact that there were difficulties in attaining harmony, and that these difficulties were by no means unimportant, and might have led to serious trouble.

Taking the two crops as a whole, the United States did not purchase a large quantity of Canadian wheat or flour, while the British Royal Commission did. The relation of the United States authorities to the Canadian method of handling the wheat was therefore different from that of the British authorities. The former were rather spectators, though deeply interested spectators — the latter were the buyers, and the interests of buyer and seller cannot be made identical. The United States authorities obviously could not approve of a higher price being paid for Canadian than for American wheat of the same grade and in the same relative position, especially as they assisted in the financing of the British purchases of Canadian wheat. This was fully recognized in Canada, and the price basis adopted was the same in the two countries.

In regard to the carrying charges of wheat, as explained above, the Board favored an increase in the terminal prices to take care of those charges. The Board, however, recognized that if that method were adopted in Canada, the nominal prices in the two countries would soon be very much out of line. The United States authorities recognized on the other hand that the matter was a vital one in Western Canada, and they did not object to the Board paying those charges by the method adopted.

There were some matters pertaining to lake transportation, especially marine and shortage insurance, on which there was a difference of opinion, but in order to secure American tonnage for wheat the Board waived their views.

The British buyers were naturally eager to make the best bargain possible. The Board felt that the price being fixed at a point much below what it would otherwise have been, the buyer's interest was provided for. As time went on it became clear that so long as the British buyers took delivery of the wheat at Fort William and negotiated with the transportation companies for cars and vessels, they could control the domestic business in wheat at the expense of Canadian shippers. It is not a secret that after the year's experience the Board sought additional powers from the

Government, with the result that the British buyers took delivery at the seaboard and that Canadian firms were to a limited extent enabled to (do) business.

It is a very superficial mind that can entertain the belief that international trading is an easy matter, or that it can be carried on without serious difficulties. In ordinary times when trading is done along commercial lines these difficulties are worked out in keen and open competition. When commercial methods are displaced, and when the trading is done by Government representatives, the difficulties still appear, but they no longer work out by competition; they become subjects of diplomatic negotiations. They are taken from the commercial into the political arena, and sooner or later they will result in bad feeling between the governments concerned, if not in the complete surrender of commercial independence on the part of the selling country, especially if it happens to be a weaker power selling to powers very much stronger and wealthier.

APPENDIX 2

THE CANADIAN WHEAT BOARD CHAIRMAN'S REPORT

For two years prior to the appointment of The Canadian Wheat Board, grain markets in Canada had been under the control of the Federal Government. In the two concluding years of the war, and including the two crop seasons 1917-18 and 1918-19, the handling of Canadian wheat within the bounds of the Dominion, was done through a governmental agency, known as the Board of Grain Supervisors. In addition to that Canadian board, the British Government also had representation in Canada in the form of the Wheat Export Company, which performed the function of sole exporter of wheat from the Dominion to the United Kingdom, France and Italy. The Wheat Export Company was simply one of many grain purchasing agencies which the British Government established in every accessible grain exporting country throughout the world during the war, and its head was the Royal Commission on Wheat Supplies in London, England. Through the Board of Grain Supervisors assembling and distributing wheat within Canadian territory, and through the Wheat Export Company taking charge of exportable surpluses and transporting them overseas, the crops of this country were marketed during the two seasons of 1917 and 1918. And during these two years the price of wheat in Canada, as in the United States, was fixed on the guarantee of the Federal Government.

The Armistice was signed in November, 1918, and the Allied Peace Conference met in Paris early in 1919. As soon as the armies stopped fighting in Europe, a certain relaxation of the machinery of Government Control as it affected the purchase and distribution of food supplies, took place, and the remainder of the crop season of 1918-1919 was spent by many people on either side of the Atlantic Ocean in wondering whether or not the grain markets would be subject to continued control during the following season of 1919-20. A few months after the Armistice the co-operative and concentrated arrangement which had existed among the Allies and certain neutral nations for the purpose of buying wheat and other supplies automatically disappeared. The exigencies of the war forced the Allies and principal neutral countries of Europe into one efficient food collecting and distributing organization, the executive body of which was the Royal Commission on Wheat

Source: The report was submitted to the Rt. Hon. Sir George E. Foster, G.C.M.G., Minister of Trade and Commerce, Ottawa, by James Stewart, Chairman, January 28, 1921, and printed in Winnipeg.

Supplies. But with the commencement of peace negotiations at Paris, each of the Allied, as well as each of the neutral, nations became inoculated with the germ of independent action, and the Royal Commission on Wheat Supplies ceased to be anything more than a purveyor of grain supplies for Great Britain. In August, 1919, however, the Supreme Economic Council, which had been organized out of the Peace Conference in Paris, brought into existence the Consultative Food Committee and made the old Royal Commission on Wheat Supplies the centre of this new body, which, amongst other duties, continued to buy wheat for the former Allies. At the outset of the Canadian crop season of 1919-20, therefore, the situation in Europe, so far as controlled grain markets were concerned, was as follows:

The Royal Commission on Wheat Supplies had become again the purchaser of wheat for Great Britain, France and Italy, each nation, now, however, being responsible for providing its own finance and shipping tonnage;

Continued Governmental control of the purchase and distribution of wheat in Belgium, Holland, Denmark, Sweden and Norway, each of these countries, while under Government control, competing with the other in the purchase of wheat.

In 1918 when the Government of the United States established its Grain Corporation, under the direction of Mr. Julius Barnes, it also fixed and guaranteed the price at which the farmers of that country marketed their wheat for that season. In the following season, Government control in the United States assumed the form of a fixed and guaranteed minimum price. Under this arrangement, the United States Grain Corporation was in readiness to receive the farmers' wheat at $2.25 per bushel, if the grain trade of the United States refused to take it at an equal or higher price. Canada alone was faced with the problem of determining what form of control her Government would adopt in connection with the marketing of her wheat during the season of 1919-20.

APPOINTMENT OF CANADIAN WHEAT BOARD

The Dominion Government called a conference at Ottawa early in June, 1919, to consider the problem of the marketing of the wheat crop of 1919. A second conference was called towards the end of July. As a result of this latter conference the Government decided to create the Canadian Wheat Board, which was duly brought into existence by an Order-in-Council passed on July 31st, 1919. The plan upon which the Canadian Wheat Board was based resembled very closely that which was in existence in Australia. A central feature of it was the "pooling" of returns from the sale of the nation's wheat. The instructions given to the Canadian Wheat Board were very simply stated. The Board was instructed to sell the Canadian wheat crop of 1919 at a price which would bring the greatest possible benefit to the Dominion as a whole. The Board was given power to control the sale of wheat in the home market as well as for export, and, in addition, it controlled the export trade in flour. For the first six months of the crop season of 1919, the Board also controlled the price at which millers could sell flour in Canada. An initial minimum price for wheat, which assumed the form of an advance to the farmer, was another feature of the Wheat Board's plan of operations. Participation Certificates were issued to the producers of wheat, and the holder of these Certificates was to receive at the end of the season his share of whatever amount the Board's pool would yield, or, in other words, the amount which the Wheat Board had been able to secure for the crop over and above $2.15 per bushel, basis No. 1 Northern, Fort William. The three features of the plan of control adopted by the Canadian Wheat Board, therefore, were: An initial advance payment to the producer of wheat, issuing Participation Certificates, and pooling of returns.

The personnel of the Board was selected with a view to creating a body which would be truly representative of those interests in the country most immediately affected by the movement of the wheat crop.

In addition to the Chairman, who previously had been President of the Wheat Export Company, the following were appointed to the Board: H. W. Wood, Carstairs; Frederick William Riddell, Regina; and Lieut.-Col. John Z. Fraser, Burford, Ontario, representing the organized farmers of Canada; W. A. Black, Montreal; C. B. Watts, Toronto, and William A. Matheson, Winnipeg, representing the flour milling interests of Canada; Norman Macleod Paterson, Fort William; Frank O. Fowler, Winnipeg; William Howard McWilliams, Winnipeg, and Joseph Quintal, Montreal, representing the grain trading interests, and William L. Best, Ottawa, representing organized labor. The selection of the personnel of the Board was completed on August 7th. As Secretary, the Board was fortunate in securing the services of Mr. H. Tooley, who had had previous valuable experience as Secretary of the Board of Grain Supervisors.

The Chairman was entrusted with the responsibility of selling the crop, and his relations with his fellow members were necessarily modified somewhat by the secrecy which had to be maintained in connection with the various transactions of the year's business. The Vice-Chairman, during the frequent absence of the Chairman in Eastern Canada and the United States, assumed control of affairs at the Head Office, and in March, 1920, in company with Mr. W. A. Black, represented the Board in London, England, in connection with the settlement of a contract which had been made with the Greek Government.

While the Order-in-Council creating the Canadian Wheat Board laid no obligation upon it to utilize the existing machinery of the grain trade, the Board, having regard to the fact that its term of life was limited to one crop period, considered it advisable to maintain the grain trading facilities intact as far as possible. In doing this, the Board thought that the trade would be better able to resume the handling of the wheat at the expiration of the controlled period.

PLAN OF ORGANIZATION

As set forth in the Order-in-Council, the Canadian Wheat Board was created because the Federal Government realized that the usual channels of trade were unlikely successfully to perform their proper function. The Winnipeg Grain Exchange, which had been open for one week, was closed, and as the new crop was beginning to move, the Board was obliged promptly to organize some machinery which would enable producers to dispose of their wheat at primary markets. Realizing the importance of facilitating a free movement of wheat to market by preventing any unreadiness on the part of country or terminal elevators to receive and handle grain in the usual manner, the Board practically from the first day, and indeed before its members became acquainted with each other, set to work to evolve plans whereby this end could be attained with the least possible delay. Within one week from the first meeting of the Board, a system was devised; and within a fortnight, rules and regulations governing that system were in effect. Practically every branch of the trade thereby was enabled to proceed with business. That virtually no change was necessary throughout the season in the system thus devised would indicate that, as originally conceived, it was sound.

Within four days from the date of the selection of its personnel, the first meeting of the Board was held in Winnipeg—on August 11th, 1919.

A public meeting was held in Winnipeg on August 13, 1919, at which representatives from the Canadian Council of Agriculture, Winnipeg, Calgary and Fort William Grain Exchanges, Canadian Millers' Committee, Brandon Board of Trade, as well as bakers and representatives from other industries presented their views.

A public sitting was also held in Toronto on September 8th, 1919, at which delegates from the United Farmers of Ontario, Ontario Milk Producers' Association, Ontario Grain Dealers, Dominion Millers' Association, and other various interests addressed the Board.

In order to ascertain the views of the various interests in the Western Provinces, a Committee consisting of Mr. W. H. McWilliams, Chairman, and Messrs. F. O. Fowler, H. W. Wood and W. A. Matheson, held a public meeting at Calgary on September 17th, 1919, at which members of the following organizations contributed to the discussion: Grain Dealers, Millers, organized and unorganized Farmers, Railways, Government Seed Commission, and the Municipal Department of the Government of Alberta.

A further session was held in Regina on September 19th, 1919, at which representatives from the Provincial Department of Agriculture of Saskatchewan, the Saskatchewan Grain Growers' Association, Government Seed Commission, Saskatchewan Co-operative Elevator Company and various individual farmers presented their views.

Notwithstanding the fact that representatives from British Columbia were heard at Calgary and elsewhere, the Board considered it advisable, in view of the different conditions prevailing in British Columbia, to hold a public meeting at Vancouver, on October 6th. On that occasion delegates from the Farmers' Institute of British Columbia, the Provincial Department of Agriculture, Grain Dealers, Flour Millers and Flour and Feed Dealers of British Columbia, presented their views.

In addition to the special public hearings held during the first months of the season, general meetings of the Board were held at regular bi-monthly intervals throughout the year. The majority of these sittings were held in Winnipeg, the other meeting places being Toronto, Montreal and Fort William.

A THORNY PATH

At the outset of its brief career, the Wheat Board was confronted by numerous obstacles and difficulties. Some of these disappeared naturally within a few weeks, while others remained immovable.

In the first place, the Board, in adopting the plan of operations outlined in the Government's instructions, had to blaze a new trail. There was no precedent to follow. While a wheat "pool" was being tried in Australia, its success had not been established, and it seemed to be regarded with more or less disfavor by some important sections of that country. In North America nothing of the kind had ever been attempted. Some of the ablest men in the North American grain trade considered the plan as too "communistic," and doomed to failure. This impression was not confined to grain men alone, but was quite prevalent among our bankers and in other business circles. Large sections of the rural communities in the various Provinces, too, protested, by resolution or delegation, against the creation of the Board, and, as an alternative, seemed bent upon having the Government either purchase the crop outright, at a fixed price, or establish an organization similar to the United States Grain Corporation.

In the rural districts along the International Boundary, particularly in Southern Manitoba and South-Eastern Saskatchewan, the cry during the autumn months of 1919 was for an open market, as prices prevailing just across the border were higher than the initial price paid to Canadian farmers. Naturally, they preferred to dispose of their wheat at whatever price was obtainable over $2.15, than to place any faith in the ultimate value of the Participation Certificate.

RELATIONS WITH THE UNITED STATES

In the United States, the director of the United States Grain Corporation, Mr. Barnes, in order that the Government's guarantee of $2.25 per bushel for wheat to the American farmer should be protected, and domestic wheat prices in that country be prevented from breaking, had the power to place an embargo against importation of any wheat into the United States. Up to December 15th, 1919, by which date over three-fourths of the Canadian crop had been marketed by the Canadian farmer, this embargo was in effect, insofar as shipments of wheat or flour, other than in waggon-load lots across the boundary, were concerned. Under these conditions, Canadian farmers living close to the International boundary were placed in a much more favorable position early in the season than farmers living distant therefrom ten miles or more. The Canadian Wheat Board, in co-operation with the United States Wheat Director, granted permits to Canadian farmers who lived nearer to an American elevator than a Canadian elevator, to haul their grain across the border line, if they so desired. Subsequent to December 15th, however, when the general embargo against Canadian wheat was lifted, the Board ceased granting these permits to individual farmers. This was done because the Board was then in a position to take advantage of any higher prices which might be obtainable on the United States markets, and therefore desired to place all Canadian farmers on an equal basis, but practically all of the Canadian wheat tributary to the United States boundary had already been hauled across the border or marketed in Canada prior to December 15th.

Notwithstanding the lifting of the embargo in the United States on December 15th, comparatively little grain passed across the line until the following May. The railways were a large factor in bringing about that condition. A dearth of foreign cars prevailed throughout Western Canada during all the long winter of 1919-20, and it was next to impossible to persuade our railways to permit any of their equipment to cross the line, the number of their grain cars distributed throughout the neighboring Republic being far in excess of the number of American cars of similar character on the Canadian roads. In spite of every effort to increase the movement of wheat across the border between December 15th, 1919, and May, 1920, only some 500,000 bushels could be shipped, and that was mainly for seed purposes, for which American equipment was obtained.

It must be remembered that the method of handling the wheat crop in the United States was entirely different from that adopted by this country. The United States gave the producer a minimum guaranteed price, which, while it protected the producer against a decline, also precluded the Wheat Director from paying any higher price. This fixed minimum price also enabled millers and grain dealers to withhold their demands from the market whenever they felt so disposed, as the Government's guarantee was always available. Therefore, although the Grain Corporation handled less than 150,000,000 bushels during the year, statistics indicate that much more than that amount was sold by the farmers direct to the trade at from one to a few cents above the minimum price. This applied particularly to Winter wheat, both hard and soft. The American Spring wheat on the whole, however, being a poorer quality than usual, fairly high premiums were obtainable for the better grades. This condition was noticeable from the commencement of the American crop year, and became more pronounced as the season developed. The volume of this high grade Spring wheat required by the United States markets, was not large, and the wide "spread" prevailing between cars of good Spring wheat and cars of slightly lower quality were very marked. The Canadian Wheat Board, in order to keep itself fully and correctly informed as to the values prevailing in Minneapolis and other markets, always kept a car or two en route to Minneapolis, which were disposed of on arrival. In this way, while realizing that a free flow would depress prices, the Board nevertheless kept posted on the best prices obtainable for odd cars, thereby enabling it to appreciate when good bids were received from countries other than the United States. For instance, on May 17th, 1920, the Board was able to sell abroad a few million bushels, basis One Northern, at the equivalent of $3.50 in store Fort William, while the best price obtainable on the Minneapolis market on the same day was about $3.28 for odd cars. Indeed, according to advices received from the Board's New York correspondent, the highest price received for American wheat on the 1919-20 crop was about $3.40 f.o.b. steamer New York, as against $3.60 for Canadian wheat secured by the Canadian Wheat Board f.o.b. steamer Montreal, both U.S. funds. And this was done despite the fact that the Montreal ocean freight rate to Europe was invariably higher than that prevailing from New York.

MAINTAINING BALANCE BETWEEN EAST AND WEST

One of the outstanding difficulties which confronted the Board was a tendency towards a conflict of varying interests within the Dominion itself. The Act creating the Canadian Wheat Board prescribed that the price of wheat to mills was to be governed as nearly as possible by the price obtainable at the same time in the world's markets for wheat of equal value, regard being had to cost of transport, handling and storage. The Act also gave power to the Board to fix the price at which flour could be sold for domestic purposes, as well as the prices of other wheat products. From the commencement of its operations, therefore, the Board endeavored to maintain an equilibrium of prices between wheat, flour and mill offal. This inevitably resulted in a conflict of interests between the livestock and dairymen of Eastern Canada and the grain producers of Western Canada. Mill offal, such as bran and shorts, had to be regulated as well as flour, and the maximum prices of $45.00 and $52.00 per ton for bran and shorts respectively, basis f.o.b. cars Montreal, were fixed by the Board on November 15th, 1919.

SEED GRAIN

Another factor which had to be taken into consideration at the very outset of the Board's operations was the pressing need for seed grain in certain localities which had been seriously affected by drought. The Board met this need by co-operation with Mr. A. E. Wilson, Seed Commissioner, in establishing reserves of the best seed grain at Saskatoon, Moose Jaw and Calgary. That was done by diverting grain to those points from the more fortunate districts, instead of shipping direct to the Upper Lake Front Ports. About one million bushels was turned over to the Seed Commissioner in this way. In addition, the Board, in the following Spring, made supplies of seed grain available to farmers at $2.45 per bushel, basis One Northern in store Fort William, notwithstanding the fact that the fixed price for domestic consumption at that time was $2.80 per bushel, basis One Northern in store Fort William. From the areas which had suffered from drought wheat shipments to Lake Terminals by elevator operators were strictly regulated, with the object of providing convenient supplies until seeding was completed.

PROSPECTS FOR SELLING THE CROP

Owing to the prospects in the summer of 1919 of very large crops in the United States, the views of European Governments as to values were very "bearish," and as indicative of their minds, we quote from cables received from Mr. Lloyd Harris, Chairman of the Canadian Mission in London, on August 6th and 7th, 1918:

August 6th. "Situation here is that Government is uncertain as to United States action reference their wheat arrangements (stop) ... reduced price of wheat in United States on account of internal situation will result in lower price than United States fixed price for export (stop) ... It is very important from Canadian standpoint that we meet them in every way possible as if shipping is withdrawn from Canada for movement of our crop there would be great difficulty in hauling same (stop) ... We would like to suggest to ... that they pay last year's fixed price for wheat and in the event of there being a reduction later in export price we will refund them difference ...."

August 7th. "In order to keep purchasers interested . . . definite contract if possible for their supply at last year's fixed price with an understanding to refund any difference between such price and price which may eventually be definitely fixed by American Government for export (stop) . . . are in market for further quantities but have considerably lower quotations for Australian wheat (stop) . . . here and they would contract I think on basis of paying last year's Canadian fixed price if we agree to refund any difference should American export price be lowered later . . . ."

On account of the limited time for investigation at the Board's disposal, the foregoing was the only reliable information about European values and ideas which the Board could then obtain. The Board, however, decided to fix the initial payment to the Canadian farmer at $2.15, basis One Northern in store Fort William, and the first export sale was made on September 1st, 1919, at $2.44 f.o.b. steamer Montreal, basis One Northern. The tone of the cables from Mr. Harris continued to be of the same depressing nature, and the demand for our wheat at reasonable levels was very indifferent during September and October. The reason for this condition was largely that Australia and the United States were underquoting Canada, and it will be remembered that, particularly in the United States, there was a very large surplus to dispose of. True, this wheat was not of such high milling quality as ours, but, nevertheless, the European countries were not necessarily demanding high quality in bread flour. At this point, too, the embargo against imports into the United States existed, thus preventing the Board from taking advantage of prices prevailing for the higher quality wheat in the Northwestern markets of that country. In any event, even if the United States markets had been open, it is reasonable to assume that the premiums then quoted across the line would have vanished as soon as any quantity of wheat had been shipped there. Fortunately, however, the first sale made by the Board represented the lowest price at which any of our wheat was sold during the year.

THE COURSE OF WORLD DEMANDS

Approximately fifty per cent of the exportable surplus of the Canadian wheat crop was disposed of before December 31st, 1919. Prices on the Minneapolis market advanced rapidly after the close of navigation in 1919, but, as stated previously, Canadian railroads would not load any of their equipment for United States points owing to the difficulty of having their cars returned. Consequently, all that could be sent to the United States during January, February and March, consisted largely of wheat shipped from Western points in foreign cars, and aggregated about one half million bushels.

Reports of the United States Bureau of Statistics indicate that prices prevailing during the later part of January and early February in the United States, suffered a considerable decline, resulting in some wheat being turned in to the Wheat Director at the minimum fixed price. Owing to this depression, and the very poor demand for flour in Europe, the Board found itself at the beginning of 1920 with approximately one million barrels of flour on its hands, unsold. The Board was not satisfied that justification for such a decline existed, and consequently withheld Canadian stocks of flour and wheat from the markets. Prices began to improve during the earlier part of March, and the balance of our wheat and flour was then disposed of at more advantageous prices.

The Spring of 1920 opened rather late in Canada. Seeding was delayed, and the wheat acreage was curtailed. Under normal circumstances, it takes about ninety days from the time wheat is sown until it is ready to harvest. In that season, however, the bulk of the wheat ripened in from eighty to eighty-five days, and the harvest season being ideal, new wheat was on the market in large volume during the early part of August. Consequently, the normal grain reserves retained by the millers all through the Dominion were not required. Therefore, during the latter part of August, 1920, millers returned to the Board over five million bushels of wheat, leaving the Board at the end of the season with an unsold surplus of about five million bushels. The prices, by that time, had receded considerably from the high levels prevailing earlier in the summer. Had this country experienced wet or backward weather during harvest, all of that five million bushels of surplus wheat would have been required for domestic consumption. The Board fully realized that it was better to have a good margin of safety in the matter of providing for domestic requirements than to have the crop oversold.

NEWFOUNDLAND AND BRITISH WEST INDIES

Canada being the natural market for the importers of flour in Newfoundland, and the Board being only of a temporary character, and endeavoring to retain for Canadian millers their export connections, consistent with carrying out their duties, as specified by the Act, arrangements were made with the Food Controller of Newfoundland on January 6th, 1920, whereby, in effect Newfoundland agreed to adopt the same regulations regarding flour prices as prevailed in Canada. In consideration of Newfoundland receiving flour at Canadian domestic prices, it was agreed that all flour purchases by that country should be made in Canada until the end of the period of control in the Dominion.

The British West Indies, having reciprocal trade agreements with the Dominion, the Board, early in 1920, made arrangements whereby, on proof being given that consignments of flour to those Islands were destined for consumption there, shipments could be made on the same basis as the domestic market.

The Board, further, in its desire to enable Canadian millers to take advantage of markets in the Orient and Western Hemisphere, excepting the United States, issued a circular to the Canadian Millers' Committee, and the Dominion Miller's Association, for distribution among their members, as follows:

Winnipeg, Man., March 1st, 1920.

"Millers can effect sales of flour to Newfoundland on same basis, and under same conditions as prevail for sales within the Dominion, excepting that before shipment is made an import permit is necessary from the Food Control Board of Newfoundland, as well as export permit from this Board. Regular patent flours can be manufactured and exported to Newfoundland. No permits will be granted for shipment beyond sixty days.

"The British West Indian market is also open to the Canadian milling trade, on the same basis as the domestic market, excepting that an export permit must be obtained, and in the event of any change in the price of wheat only export permit, or application therefor prior to date of wheat price revision, will be considered in adjustments. No permits will be granted for shipment beyond thirty days.

"To other markets in the Western Hemisphere, excepting the United States, millers can from time to time ascertain prices from the Board at which they may sell flour. Such quotations will fluctuate, and reflect as nearly as possible the relative value of wheat in the world's markets at time same is given. This applies also to the Orient and Africa, excepting Egypt, but not to Europe."

DECONTROL OF FLOUR

At a meeting of the Board held in Montreal on Friday, March 19th, 1920, the following motion was carried unanimously:

"That the Chairman be requested to advise the Government of the Board's recommendation that its control of the prices of flour, bran and shorts for domestic consumption be discontinued; and further, if for any reason such decontrol cannot immediately be put into operation, the Chairman be authorized to take such action as he considers advisable in connection with the prices of flour, bran and shorts."

This resolution was passed by the Board after long and careful consideration of a request from the Canadian Millers' Committee for an increase in the maximum price of flour, and also of statements prepared by the Board's Chief Auditor and Milling Expert.

Notwithstanding strong representations to the contrary made to the Government by the Canadian Millers' Committee, the Board, on April 8th, made the following public announcement:

"Considering the time opportune, the Canadian Wheat Board, as a preliminary step towards general decontrol, propose as from this date to withdraw the maximum price on flour sold for domestic purposes, whilst retaining control of the price of wheat.

"The Board will temporarily continue to control the maximum wholesale price of mill offal.

"Expert cost accountants have audited the books of several representative milling companies, and the Board being thus in possession of certified milling costs, and having the price of wheat under control, can and will see that no abuse occurs. There is every reason to believe, however, that competition among millers will amply protect the consumers."

PAYMENT OF DIVIDENDS ON PARTICIPATION CERTIFICATES

As considerable trading in Participation Certificates had evidently been taking place during the entire season, and the Board, realizing that farmers were unnecessarily parting with their Participation Certificates at less than they were likely to be worth, made an announcement on May 5th, 1920, to the effect that wheat represented by the Board's Participation Certificates would be worth not less than forty cents per bushel. It was realized that whatever figure was given out might be regarded as the outside figure, and consequently it was made as liberal as possible. That the Board's judgment in this matter was correct is evidenced by the fact that even after the announcement on May 5th, advices were received of Participation Certificates changing hands on the basis of thirty-eight cents per bushel on the wheat represented thereby. Co-operation of the press and the grain trade was sought to endeavor to dissuade the farmers from parting with their Participation Certificates to speculators. The grain trade circularized their Agents accordingly, and, as a whole, remarkably few instances were found of men, associated directly or indirectly with the business, who acted other than to discourage the farmers from selling their Participation Certificates.

Early in the summer, on its becoming evident that a considerable amount of surplus money would be at the Board's credit in the Banks, and on which it could only secure 3% interest, it was decided that an interim dividend should be made against the Participation Certificates. This necessitated an outlay, in the matter of revenue stamps on cheques, together with extra labor and stationery involved, of approximately $100,000.00, but, as it was found that producers were obliged to pay interest to Banks at from 7% to 8%, wherever they could secure advances, it was estimated that it was very much to the Producers' advantage to receive an interim payment, rather than be borrowing funds from Banks or Loan Companies. The Producers took full advantage of this payment, which was announced as commencing on July 15th. Before the end of October, some thirty-eight million dollars were paid on this interim dividend against the Participation Certificates.

The final announcement as to the value of the Participation Certificates was made on October 30th, 1920. The price realized for the whole crop, basis One Northern in store Fort William, was $2.63.

The average freight rate from shipping points in Manitoba, Saskatchewan and Alberta during the season had been under thirteen cents, so that the average price realized by the farmer at the shipping point has been $2.50. Calculations made from the reports of the United States Bureau of Statistics indicate the average price paid to farmers at shipping points in the United States was approximately 25¢ per bushel less than that realized by the farmers in Canada.

While this was so, the price of bread in this country, according to records of the Board of Commerce, was 1½¢ per lb. less than that paid by the consumer in the United States.

"SPREADS"

One of the salient features of the operations of the Canadian Wheat Board was the small differences between the prices paid to the producer for the various grades of wheat at country points. These "spreads" were never before so narrow in the history of the trade. From the very commencement of the season to the close, notwithstanding the several advances in price made by the Board, the "spreads" between the prices paid for the different grades of wheat remained constant.

On the other hand, when sales of this same wheat were made, the Board was able to preserve corresponding "spreads" between the different grades in the prices that were realized. For example, on an actual sale of wheat that was negotiated on the basis of $4.02 per bushel for One Northern at seaboard in Canadian funds, the Board was able to get $3.99 for Two Northern, $3.95 for Three Northern, $3.89 for Number Four, $3.78 for Number Five, $3.68 for Number Six, $3.91 for Rejected One Northern, and $3.96 for Tough One Northern.

BRANCH OFFICES OF THE BOARD

As soon as preliminary steps were agreed upon, and the machinery of the Board was set in operation in the three Prairie Provinces and British Columbia, the Chairman proceeded to Eastern Canada to survey the situation there and establish necessary offices. On September 11th, 1919, a general meeting of the Board was held in Toronto, and plans were laid for the handling of the crops of Ontario and Quebec. Offices were immediately established at Montreal and Toronto; the function of the Montreal office being very largely to look after the forwarding and transportation of the grain from Georgian Bay Ports to the seaboard, as well as to pay shippers for wheat which might be forwarded under instructions from the Board, from Terminal Elevators at Fort William to the Atlantic seaboard. For these services Mr. A. E. Clare, of Montreal, who had had considerable previous experience in such matters, was secured.

The function of the Toronto Office was very similar to that of the Winnipeg Office. The Ontario Grain Dealers reported there, instead of to Winnipeg, and Licensees received their Participation Certificates from that point in the same manner as the Licensees of the West received their Participation Certificates from Winnipeg. The services of Mr. Lincoln Goldie, a gentleman well known in the Ontario wheat and flour trade, were secured for Toronto. In addition, in order that many difficulties incidental and peculiar to the Ontario trade be dealt with and solved promptly, a Committee, consisting of Colonel J. Z. Frazer as Convenor, with Messrs. W. A. Black, C. B. Watts and J. Quintal, was appointed to advise and make recommendations to the Board. Mr. Goldie's duties extended over Ontario, Quebec and the Eastern Provinces, and required much tact in dealing with grain dealers, millers and farmers.

An office was established at Fort William, under Mr. C. S. Langille, to attend to the loading and grading of shipments, particularly shipments of rejected and low grade wheat.

Later in the season, in order to keep itself fully posted, the Board opened an office in New York, under the general supervision of Mr. J. J. O'Donohoe. It was considered necessary to have this connection in New York, so as to keep informed as far as possible about ocean freight rates and values of wheat which might be entering into competition with our wheat on the European and other markets.

The services of Mr. John Fleming, of Winnipeg, were secured to represent the Board in British Columbia, and an Office was established in Vancouver from October, 1919, to March, 1920.

The Representative of the Canadian Trade Mission in London, Mr. Lloyd Harris, was used by the Board from the commencement of its operation until the latter part of October, when he returned to Canada. The Board, deeming it advisable that it should be kept informed as far as possible as to the situation in Europe, was then fortunate in securing the services of Mr. W. Sanford Evans. Mr. Evans sailed for London on November 25th, 1919, and although his chief function was to advise the Board regarding the flour business and wherever possible to negotiate contracts for flour, the information obtained by him in regard to food conditions in the various European countries was invaluable as a guidance to the Board.

One of the most important duties incidental to the marketing of the wheat crop, and making returns therefor to the producers, was the registration of Participation Certificates, and keeping account of the wheat marketed through the Board's Licensees. Such a position required experience and sound organizing ability. Mr. F. W. Young, of Winnipeg, agreed to combine these duties with that of his position as General Manager of the Lake Shippers' Clearance Association. The general satisfaction and smoothness with which this work proceeded gave excellent testimony to the worth of this branch.

A most important branch of the work was the accounting and auditing of the business, transacted by the Board, directly and indirectly through its Licensees. Mr. B. F. Griggs, C.A., was placed in charge of this branch as soon as possible after the commencement of the Board's operations. A staff of efficient and loyal auditors was gradually developed under his supervision, and, notwithstanding that the aggregate business involved a double turnover of between eight and nine hundred million dollars, involving the auditing of the accounts of about 1,100 Licensees, I am able at this date to report the completion of the auditing of practially all Licensees' Accounts. Indeed, the independent Government auditor has signed the Financial Statement as at December 31st, 1920, certifying its accuracy.

Mr. George H. Kelly, Milling Expert, was in charge of the Flour Department. His extensive knowledge, throughout the Dominion, of mills and milling was of invaluable assistance to the Board, and his well-known impartiality inspired and maintained the confidence of the entire milling trade. Approximately seven million bags of flour were handled through this Department, and although our stocks on order, in transit or in store, exceeded one million barrels at times, not one single bag was lost through deterioration or through not being accounted for.

The success of any organization is always interwoven with the loyalty and ability of its employees, and the case of the Canadian Wheat Board was no exception to this rule.

WHOLEHEARTED CO-OPERATION

In conclusion, as Chairman of the Board, I desire to record an expression of personal appreciation of the wholehearted co-operation and unselfish devotion manifested by my colleagues in the work of the Canadian Wheat Board during the entire period of its existence. Composed of the representatives of varying interests, the Board, in its work during the past eighteen months, in a very practical way has afforded the country an example of the possibilities of co-operation. On many occasions during the period of the Board's existence, it was necessary to seek the advice and judgment of the members, bearing upon transactions of vital national importance. Always, consideration of the national welfare was uppermost. Without this spirit and valuable practical contributions of support to the Chairman, any achievement by the Canadian Wheat Board would have been impossible.

The various departments of the grain trade of the Dominion, as well as the flour milling interests of Canada, have also co-operated with the Board wholeheartedly in lending their operating facilities to the needs of the country during the season's operations. For their strict adherence to the many regulations of the Board, involving, as was inevitable, many inconveniences in the conduct of the "trade," this report would be incomplete without expressing sincere appreciation.

Attached hereto is the Balance Sheet, covering the period from the inception of the Board to the 31st December, 1920. From the very nature of the business, this Report is necessarily not final. This Balance Sheet shows ten and one-half million dollars on deposit in various Banks and elsewhere, against which there was outstanding, as at the same date, liability on Participation Certificates aggregating slightly over ten million dollars. Up to this date, about $9,000,000.00 has been paid, leaving a balance of $1,000,000.00. Of this balance, claims are already filed with the Board for between five and six hundred thousand dollars, covering lost, stolen, or destroyed Participation Certificates, leaving approximately, perhaps, Participation Certificates aggregating over four hundred thousand dollars unaccounted for.

Including the disbursing of the interim and final payments, which by themselves will have cost $200,000.00, the costs of administering the Board, including general expenses, auditing, registration of Participation Certificates, payment of Participation Certificates, collection of assessments, statistical, and all other branches, will have been less than one-half cent per bushel on the volume handled.

THE CANADIAN WHEAT BOARD

BALANCE SHEET
As at December 31st, 1920

ASSETS

Cash on Hand		$ 3,438.38
Balances at Bankers:		
Current Accounts	$ 788,853.17	
Deposits at interest	8,224,309.82	
		9,013,162.99
Province of Manitoba 6% Treasury Bills		1,555,000.00
		$10,571,601.37
Sundry Debtors		263,238.51
Advances to Officials		1,001.17
Furniture and Fixtures		30,346.18
Grain Exchange Seat—Fort William		200.00
		$10,866,387.23

LIABILITIES

Private Elevator Deposits	$ 10,000.00
Sundry Creditors	11,529.81
Items in Suspense	246,692.20
Participation Certificate Distribution Payable	10,158,470.14
Balance at credit, Profit and Loss Account	439,695.08
	$10,866,387.23

APPENDIX 3

NOTE OF AGREEMENT BETWEEN THE OVERSEAS WHEAT EXPORTING COUNTRIES, JUNE 30, 1933

The world wheat situation has altered to so considerable extent since the discussions between the four oversea exporting countries commenced that it is necessary to restate the position.

The basis of any plan agreed to between the oversea exporting countries is to bring about an adjustment of production so as to allow of the liquidation of existing surplus stocks within a period of two years.

The following data represents the best available indication of the present position:

(a) World import demand in 1933-34 is assumed to be 750 million bushels, but this figure may vary by 50 million bushels up or down;

(b) Exports from new crops in 1933-34 are estimated at: —

Canada

Crop from 395 to 400, say	400
Domestic requirements	117
Exportable surplus	283

Argentine — no crop estimate possible, but on estimate of 3-year-average and of yield

Crop	240,000,000
Domestic requirement	90,000,000
Exportable surplus	150,000,000

Australia — based as in the case of Argentina

Crop	192,000,000
Domestic requirement	50,000,000
Exportable surplus	142,000,000

Source: *United States Treaty Information Bulletin No. 48, September, 1943*, pp. 24-27. Also in N. A. Robertson's memorandum on *The London Wheat Agreement, Annex I*, Bennett Papers.

It is estimated that the other exporters will need 75,000,000 bushels. The position in regard to new export wheat may, therefore, be expected to be as follows:

Canada	283 million bushels
Argentina	150 million bushels
Australia	142 million bushels
Other exporters	75 million bushels
	650 million bushels

The residual exports after allowing for the marketing of new wheat is therefore estimated at 100 million bushels which may, however, vary upwards or downwards by 50 million bushels according to the variation of the requirements of the importing countries.

The U.S.A. Position:

The U.S.A. 1933-34 crop is estimated at from 520 million bushels to 575, say 540, and the U.S.A. domestic requirements at 610, leaving a deficiency of 70 million bushels. The above estimates allow of the following method of dealing with the 1933-34 situation:

(a) Export quotas are allotted to deal with new wheat 575 million bushels

(b) The U.S.A. surplus stocks are 240 million and Canada at 140 million. The U.S.A. 1933-34 deficiency of 70 will reduce the surplus to 170. To bring about equality between the U.S.A. and Canada in regard to surplus, an initial figure of 30 million bushels should be allotted to the U.S.A.

(c) This leaves a figure of 70 million bushels as a final residual subject to considerable fluctuations up or down. This should be divided equally between U.S.A. and Canada for the absorption of surplus stocks. The method of dealing with reductions in the world import demand will be discussed in the next paragraph. It is felt that any increase in the possibilities of reduction of surplus due to failure of 1933 crops to reach the estimate of 541 million bushels for U.S.A. and 400 million bushels for Canada should be utilized by each country and that no attempt should be made to allot such figures between the two countries. Any increase of the marginal surplus due to increased world import demand should be shared equally between U.S.A. and Canada.

(d) If world import demand were below 750 million bushels, it is suggested that each of the four countries should share the necessary diminution of exports on a basis proportionate to their exports. Thus, if the world imports were 25 million bushels less than in 1933-34, the diminution

Canada	47%=a diminution of 11,700,000
Argentina	22%=a diminution of 5,500,000
Australia	21%=a diminution of 5,200,000
U.S.A.	10%=a diminition of 2,500,000

In the event of Australia or the Argentine not being able to fulifll their respective export surpluses in 1933-34 the difference between actual exports and export quota shall be available, upon the advice of the Advisory Committee, firstly, to enable the whole of the new wheat of the 1933-34 crop to be marketed by an increase in the allocation to any country with a larger exportable surplus than provided for in the quota and, secondly, in so far as such difference is not needed to cater for new wheat, to be equally divided between U.S.A. and Canada for the disposal of surplus stocks. If either Australia or the Argentine thus surrenders a part of its export quota, the quantity so surrendered shall be added to the export quota of that country for 1934-35.

During the second year of the scheme the surplus stock position will, on the basis of the foregoing estimates, be a total of 210 bushels equally divided between U.S.A. and Canada.

Since an essential part of any scheme must be effective cooperation of the European importing countries, it is felt that even if higher prices cause some diminution of demand in the Far East, yet total world import demand should be taken as 800 million bushels instead of 750 million bushels.

Each of the four countries agree to bring into effect a reduction of production of wheat to the extent of 15%.

The position of each country in 1934-35 is estimated to be as follows:

Australia 15,000,000 acres at 12.8 bushels=192,000,000 bushels less 15%=163.4 bushels less domestic consumption 50,000,000 bushels leaves an export quota of 113,000,000 bushels.

Argentina 20,000,000 acres at 12 bushels per acre=240,000,000 less 15%=214 million bushels, domestic consumption 90 million bushels=export quota 114,000,000.

Canada 26,300,000 acres at 17.24 bushels per acre=453,000,000 less 15%=380,000,000 bushels. Domestic consumption 117 million and export quota of 263.

Other Exporting Countries. 75,000,000 bushels. The total of the above allocations amounts to:

Australia	113 million bushels
Argentina	114 million bushels
Canada	263 million bushels
Other exporters	75 million bushels
	565 million bushels

U.S.A. is estimated in 1934-35 to have the following position: 62,400,000 acres at 13.1=816 million bushels; less 15%=694. Domestic requirements 610 million bushels, and export quota of 84 million bushels.[1]

The addition of the U.S.A. export figure gives a total export from new 1934-35 crop of 649 million bushels.

With a world import demand of 800 million bushels this leaves a total of 151 million bushels to be divided between U.S.A. and Canada on an equal basis for the reduction of surplus stocks.

The deduction of 151 million bushels from the 204 million bushels surplus total at the end of 1933-34 leaves at the end of 1934-35 a total of 53 million bushels or 26.5 million bushels in each country.

This is the Agreement of 30th June, 1933.

> R.B.B
> F.E.M.
> T.A.LeB.
> F.L.McD.[2]

---

[1]The figure accepted by the U.S. was 90 million bushels. (Footnote on advance copy)
[2]The initials are those of R. B. Bennett (Canada), F. E. Murphy (United States), T. A. LeBreton (Argentine), and F. L. McDougall (Australia).

APPENDIX 4

ANNEX OF AUGUST 21, 1933, TO JUNE 30, NOTE OF AGREEMENT

While the foregoing statement represents the basis of agreement between the four great exporting countries, the changes which have taken place in the world wheat situation since June 30th, 1933, render necessary a series of adjustments:—
The main changes in the situation are as follows:—
1. Owing to highly favorable weather conditions in Europe and to reports of good crops of wheat in the extra European importing countries the world demand is now assumed to be 560,000,000 bushels in place of 750,000,000.
2. The relative failure of crops in North America have resulted in the following changes:
The Canadian crop is now estimated at 300 million bushels which after allowing for domestic requirements leaves an exportable surplus of 183,000,000 bushels. The figure of 75,000,000 bushels allowed to meet the requirements of other exporters has to be amended upwards to 100,000,000 bushels.
The 1933 crop in the U.S.A. is now estimated at 500,000,000 bushels. The estimated surplus stocks in the U.S.A. are now taken as being 261,000,000 instead of 240,000,000 while those in Canada are taken as being 179,000,000 in place of 140,000,000.
In order to meet the altered situation the four overseas exporting countries are prepared tentatively to adjust their respective allocations in the following ways.
The U.S.A. will accept an export quota of 45,000,000[1] bushels being roughly 8½% of the estimated world import demand.
Canada will receive an export allocation of 200,000,000 bushels.
The position in regard to Argentina and Australia is as follows:—
These countries have been allotted export quotas for the crop years 1933-34 and 1934-35 of 258,000,000 bushels in the case of Argentina and 255,000,000 bushels in the case of Australia.

Source: *United States Treaty Information Bulletin No. 48*, September 1933, pp. 27-28. Also *The London Wheat Agreement*, Bennett Papers.

[1]Originally typed as 47,000,000 but altered to 45,000,000 by Bennett on signing. See final paragraph. (Footnote on advance copy)

Since it is impossible to estimate the actual crops in the Southern Hemisphere for at least two months, and since present reports of crop growth are not wolly favourable in either country, Argentina and Australia are prepared to undertake not to export more than for Argentina 110,000,000 bushels and Australia 105,000,000 bushels of the above export quotas prior to July 31st, 1934.

The Argentine Delegation declared that they subscribed to this agreement on the understanding that the distribution of the surplus export of the harvest of 1933-34 was that already fixed under letter (b) of the Draft approved by the exporting countries during the Economic and Monetary Conference; but up to the 31st July, 1934, the exports would not exceed 110,000,000 bushels. The balance would be exported during the following months, and, if necessary, would be added to the harvest of 1934-35: which exportable balance is fixed at 108,000,000 bushels until the end of this Agreement.

This note of agreement between the Oversea Exporting Countries is initialled on the understanding that the export quota of the U.S.A. for the crop year 1933-34 is 47,000,000 bushels.

APPENDIX 5

FINAL ACT OF THE CONFERENCE OF WHEAT EXPORTING AND IMPORTING COUNTRIES

Held in London at the Offices of the High Commission for Canada
from the twenty-first day to the twenty-fifth day of August,
one thousand nine hundred and thirty-three

The Governments of GERMANY, AUSTRIA, BELGIUM, BULGARIA, FRANCE, the UNITED KINGDOM of GREAT BRITAIN and NORTHERN IRELAND, GREECE, HUNGARY, IRISH FREE STATE, ITALY, POLAND, ROUMANIA, SPAIN, SWEDEN, CZECHOSLOVAKIA, SWITZERLAND, the UNION OF SOVIET SOCIALIST REPUBLICS, and YUGOSLAVIA, having accepted the invitation extended to them by the Secretary-General of the Monetary and Economic Conference on behalf of the Governments of ARGENTINE, AUSTRALIA, CANADA and the UNITED STATES OF AMERICA, to take part in a Conference to consider the measures which might be taken in concert to adjust the supply of wheat to effective world demand and eliminate the abnormal surpluses which have been depressing the wheat market and to bring about a rise and stabilisation of prices at a level remunerative to the farmers and fair to the consumers of breadstuffs, have agreed as follows:

Article 1

The Governments of Argentine, Australia, Canada and the United States of America agree that the exports of wheat from their several countries during the crop year August 1st, 1933, to July 31st, 1934, shall be adjusted, taking into consideration the exports of other countries, by the acceptance of export maxima on the assumption that world import demand for wheat will amount during this period to 560,000,000 bushels.

Article 2

They further agree to limit their exports of wheat during the crop year August 1st, 1934, to July 31st, 1935, to maximum figures 15 percent less in the case of each

Source: *Dominion of Canada Treaty Series*, 1933, No. 11.

country than the average outturn on the average acreage sown during the period 1931-33 inclusive after deducting normal domestic requirements. The difference between the effective world demand for wheat in the crop year 1934-35 and the quantity of new wheat from the 1934 crop available for export will be shared between Canada and the United States of America as a supplementary export allocation with a view to the proportionate reduction of their respective carry-overs.

Article 3

The Governments of Bulgaria, Hungary, Roumania and Yugoslavia agree that their combined exports of wheat during the crop year August 1st, 1933, to July 31st, 1934, will not exceed fifty million bushels. This undertaking is made on the understanding that the aggregate may be increased to a maximum of fifty-four million bushels if the Danubian countries find that such a supplementary quota is required for the movement of the exportable surplus of the 1933 crop.

Article 4

They further agree that their combined exports of wheat during the crop year 1934-35 will not exceed a total of fifty million bushels and recognise that the acceptance of this export allocation will not allow any extension of the acreage sown to wheat.

Article 5

The Government of the Union of Soviet Socialist Republics, while unable to give any undertaking in regard to production of wheat, agree to limit their exports for the crop year 1933-34 to a figure which will be arrived at upon the completion of negotiations, with the Governments of the overseas wheat exporting countries. They also agree that the question of their export of wheat during the crop year 1934-1935 shall be the subject of further negotiations with the wheat exporting countries represented on the Advisory Committee.

Article 6

The Governments of the wheat-importing countries in signing this instrument:

I. Agree henceforth not to encourage any extension of the area sown to wheat and not to take any governmental measures, the effect of which would be to increase the domestic production of wheat;

II. Agree to adopt every possible measure to increase the consumption of wheat and are prepared to bring about the progressive removal of measures which tend to lower the quality of breadstuffs and thereby decrease the human consumption of wheat;

III. Agree that a substantial improvement in the price of wheat should have as its consequence a lowering of customs tariffs, and are prepared to begin such adjustment of customs tariffs when the international price of wheat reaches and maintains for a specified period an average price to be fixed. It is understood that the rate of duty necessary to assure remunerative prices may vary for different countries, but will not be sufficiently high to encourage their farmers to expand wheat acreage.

Appendix A contains the agreed definitions relating to the technical points mentioned in this paragraph;

IV. Agree that in order to restore more normal conditions in world trade in wheat the reduction of customs tariffs would have to be accompanied by modification of the general regime of quantitive restrictions of wheat imports and accept in principle the desirability of such a modification. The exporting countries for their part agree that it may not be possible to make substantial progress in these modifications in 1933-1934, but the importing countries are prepared to make effective alterations in 1934-1935 if world prices have taken a definitely upward turn from the average price of the first six months of the calendar year 1933. The objective of these relaxations of the various forms of quantitive restrictions will be to restore a more normal balance between total consumption and imports, and thereby to increase the volume of international trade in wheat. It is understood that this undertaking is consistent with maintaining the home market for domestic wheat grown on an area no greater than at present. It is obvious that fluctuations in the quantity and quality of the wheat harvest resulting from weather conditions may bring about wide variations in the ratio of imports to total consumption from season to season.

The obligations of the importing countries under this Agreement are to be interpreted in the light of the following declaration:

It is recognized that measures affecting the area of wheat grown and the degree of protection adopted are primarily dependent upon domestic conditions within each country, and that any change in these measures must often require the sanction of the legislature.

The intention of this Agreement is nevertheless that the importing countries will not take advantage of a voluntary reduction of exports on the part of the exporting countries by developing their domestic policies in such a way as to frustrate the efforts which the exporting countries are making, in the common interest, to restore the price of wheat to a remunerative level.

Article 7

The countries participating in the Conference agree to set up a Wheat Advisory Committee to watch over the working and application of this Agreement. The functions, organisation and financial basis of this Committee are set out in Appendix B.

DONE at London, the twenty-fifth day of August, one thousand nine hundred and thirty-three, in a single copy which shall be deposited in the archives of the Secretariat of the League of Nations and of which authenticated copies shall be delivered to all Members of the League of Nations and non-member States represented at the Conference of Wheat Exporting and Importing Countries.

GERMANY—ALLEMAGNE
E. H. Ruter
ARGENTINE—ARGENTINE
T. E. Le Breton
AUSTRALIA—AUSTRALIE
S. M. Bruce
AUSTRIA—AUTRICHE
L. Wimmer
BELGIUM—BELGIQUE
C. Bastin
FRANCE—FRANCE
Halgouet
GREECE—GRECE
D. Caclamanos
HUNGARY—HONGRIE
de Winchkler

BULGARIA—BULGARIE
P. H. Mischeff
CANADA—CANADA
R. B. Bennett
M. A. McPherson
SPAIN—ESPAGNE
Luis Calderon
Agustin Velarde
UNITED STATES OF AMERICA—
ETATS UNIS D'AMERIQUE
Frederick E. Murphy
SWEDEN—SUEDE
K. Lundberg
ad referendum
SWITZERLAND—SUISSE
Ernest Laur

IRISH FREE STATE—
ETAT LIBRE D'IRLANDE
John W. Dulanty
ad referendum
ITALY—ITALIE
G. B. Ceccato
POLAND—POLOGNE
T. Goeppert
ROUMANIA—ROUMANIE
E. Marian
UNITED KINGDOM—
ROYAUME—UNI
H. F. Carlill

CZECHOSLOVAKIA—
TCHECOSLOVAQUIE
Z. Konecny
ad referendum

UNION OF SOVIET SOCIALIST
REPUBLICS—UNION DES
REPUBLIQUES SOVIETISTES
SOCIALISTES
A. Gourevitch

YUGOSLAVIA—YOUGOSLAVIE
M. Pilja

APPENDIX 6

A HISTORY OF THE WHEAT POSITION

The most difficult agricultural problem in Canada relates to wheat. It is the most difficult because more farmers depend upon wheat for their economic existence than depend upon the production and sale of any one other product. About 250,000 farmers are dependent upon the production and sale of wheat. High grade spring wheat can only be grown in comparatively dry areas and where the nights are cool. Wheat of a kind can be grown in almost every country in the world. Because the United States market is closed to Canadian wheat, Canadian farmers are farther away from a possible market for a considerable part of its wheat than any other country unless it be Argentina and Australia. The only natural market for Canadian wheat off this continent is the United Kingdom and every other wheat producing area claims part of that market in return for purchasing British manufactured goods.

Wheat production, therefore, is subject to all the pests of drought and frost. Wheat marketing is subject to all the difficulties of distance and competition.

1930's DIFFICULT

Prior to the war we were confronted from 1930 to 1939 with all the difficulties at one time. We had seven years of drought with two almost complete failures in that period. We had grasshoppers and cutworm. All European countries were attempting to produce their own at any cost. The United States increased their own production by putting on a prohibitive duty of 42 cents a bushel and guaranteeing a parity price. They then dumped part of their surplus on markets we were dependent upon.

This brought us to the shooting war period which began in 1939 with our wheat farmers in the most difficult circumstances they had ever experienced and in the greatest financial suffering of any of our farmers.

CO-OPERATIVES FORMED

To meet these difficulties they had organized the greatest co-operative marketing organizations in Canada. These organizations have the active support of more than

---

Source: *Cabinet Document 44-51, October 11, 1950,* Privy Council office files. This document was written by J. G. Gardiner. (see p. 1027 of the text)

half the wheat farmers in the Prairie Provinces and their views are agreed with by at least 75% of the farmers. Their whole system and trading technique is based on the idea that there should be no speculation in the grain trade and particularly in the marketing of the wheat of Western Canada. The only farmers who disagree are those who are financially strong enough to do for themselves what the pools undertake to do for all others.

CO-OPERATIVES vs. GRAIN EXCHANGE

The bitterest battle ever waged between the farmers led by the co-operators and the speculators led by the Grain Exchange was from 1929 to 1940.

The five year contract pools had broken down along with all other organizations dependent upon enormous financial obligations in 1929.

GRAIN EXCHANGE WON IN 1935

The first part of their battle ended on the floor of the Commons in 1935 when the Wheat Board Act of 1935 was passed. It ended with victory on the side of the Grain Exchange. The Pools had asked for compulsory delivery of grain to a Wheat Board. Mr. Bennett brought in a Bill granting their request. The opposition proposed that the Bill be withdrawn and one substituted which made delivery to the Board optional. Mr. Bennett submitted the question to a small committee of which he was chairman. This committee recommended that the Bill providing for compulsory delivery of grain to a Board be withdrawn and one substituted which made delivery of wheat to a Board optional. This turned out to be a triumph for the advocates of a continuance of the speculative method of trading in wheat.

It should be recorded that during the period from 1930 to 1935 the open market was in control. The records indicate United States farmers received 15 cents per bushel more for their wheat at the farm than Canadian farmers, at a time from 1930 to 1935 when the United States farmers only obtained 61 cents a bushel. It should also be recorded that during the five years from 1935 to 1939 the United States farmer received 23 cents a bushel more than the Canadian at a time when the United States farmer obtained $1.10 a bushel.

The delivery of prairie wheat to those who sold it in the markets of the world was carried out under this system until 1940.

TRADE RECEIVED PROFITS - GOVERNMENT TOOK LOSSES

The result was that when the Board set an initial payment which turned out to be above the "world price" the Board got all the wheat and paid a subsidy to the producer equal to the difference between the "world price" and the Board payment; when the Board payment was lower than "world price" the Board got no wheat and the trade received all the wheat and hence all the profit.

This resulted in the Treasury covering all the deficits and the trade taking all the profits. This is what I mean by saying the legislation obtained in 1935 was a triumph for the advocates of speculation.

LITTLE CONTROVERSY 1940 to 1945

There is a period from 1940 to 1945 when there was very little controversy between the trade and the pools or co-operatives. This was due to the fact that we were at war and neither party could see their way through the financing of the purchase of wheat which might not be marketed for five years and the ownership of which at the end of the war might be uncertain. The practice was, therefore, for the trade and co-operatives to meet the Wheat Committee of the Government together and agree upon what should be done.

THE GOVERNMENT ASSUMED COSTS AND RISKS

The Government assisted in the construction of special storage. The Wheat Board took delivery of wheat and paid an advance of 90 cents a bushel basis No. 1 Northern Fort William until September, 1943, when it was raised to $1.25 a bushel on the same basis and the Wheat Board took over all wheat held by the trade and pools. In 1941 the Government had put on price control. The price of wheat to the mills was set at 77⅜ cents. Because the initial payment on wheat was 90 cents from August 1st, 1942, until September, 1943, and $1.25 from September, 1943, until September, 1945, the difference was paid out of the Treasury to keep down the cost of bread. Such action would subsidize the consumer not the producer.

VICTORY BROUGHT INCREASED PRICES

From 1943 until 1945 inclusive the price of wheat on the world markets rose constantly until September of 1945 when it was selling at $1.55 a bushel.

From 1940 until 1943 the Wheat Board was selling wheat to the United Kingdom at approximately the initial payment plus other costs and to others at the world price. From September, 1943 on, all wheat was delivered to the Wheat Board. From September, 1943, until September, 1945, wheat was sold to Great Britian at $1.25 basis No. 1 Northern, Fort William. From September, 1942, until September, 1945, constantly rising prices were available and during that period about 160,000,000 bushels were sold to the United States at world prices.

WHEAT BOARD SETTLED THE POOL

At the end of the war, the Wheat Board calculated the farmers' position from the setting up of the Board in 1935. They made a cut-off as of the end of the 1939 crop year. This indicated that the Board had paid out in advances to farmers approximately $61,000,000 more than had been realized from sales. This amount was paid from consolidated revenue by the Government.

The wheat delivered from all succeeding crops was settled for down to July 31, 1945, from returns received from the sale of wheat after deducting all costs. The final participation payments for the 1940-41-42-43 and 44 crops amounted to approximately $125,000,000.

CONTROVERSY REOPENED

Immediately the war ended the controversy between the Grain Exchange and the Wheat Pools reopened. The Grain Exchange maintained that wheat should be put back on the market and the farmer allowed to take advantage of the higher prices. The Wheat Pools took the position that compulsory delivery to the Wheat Board should continue.

At this stage the Minister of Trade and Commerce, with the concurrence of the Minister of Agriculture, recommended that unless the Government was prepared to give some guarantee of returns over a period to farmers the market should be thrown open and the farmer allowed to take his chances. The suggestion was that we should not sell his wheat for $1.55 a bushel basis No. 1 Northern, Fort William, when he could sell for $1.93 unless we were prepared to give him some guarantee over a period.

It was reported to Council that the Prices Board had taken the position that to allow prices to run wild on a product so important in the economic structure as wheat would render it impossible to maintain controls on inflation. Council finally decided that we must continue the policy of selling wheat to Britain at $1.55 a bushel and providing wheat to the mills for Canadian consumption at $1.25.

Discussions were going on in London in an attempt to arrange a multilateral wheat agreement. The terms proposed were a floor price of $1.00 and a ceiling price of $1.50. It was thought that if a 5-year agreement on these terms with regard to price were in existence it might be considered sufficient guarantee. We cabled London and received the reply that agreement could not be reached.

COUNCIL DECIDED

Council then decided to give the Canadian farmers a guarantee of a floor of $1.00 a bushel for five years provided they would be satisfied with a ceiling of the price then being charged the United Kingdom, $1.55. The Minister of Trade and Commerce announced the Government's policy in that regard in the House of Commons on September 19, 1945.

His statement was in part as follows:
"It is in the interest of Canada and of Canadian wheat growers that the importing countries should continue to obtain Canadian wheat at prices not in excess of those prevailing at the end of hostilities. Accordingly the government, by Order-in-Council, has instructed the Canadian Wheat Board to offer wheat for sale for export overseas (this eliminated the United States) at prices not higher than the current export price of $1.55 per bushel, basis No. 1 Northern, in store Fort William/Port Arthur or Vancouver. In asking Canadian producers to forego such benefits as might be realized in the short run through higher export prices, the government recognizes the paramount need for relative stability of income to wheat producers. Toward this end, the government undertakes that in the five-year period ending July 31, 1950, producers will receive not less than $1 per bushel, basis No. 1 Northern, in store Fort William/Port Arthur or Vancouver on the authorized deliveries for each crop year. For the balance of the 1945-46 crop year, at least, the Canadian Wheat Board initial advance will continue at $1.25, where it was set two years ago. By providing a long-term floor price of not less than $1.00 the government will protect producers against the consequences of any sharp reversal in the world wheat position during the next five-year period.
The government, in adopting this policy of a maximum price for overseas shipments for the present and a floor price for five years, is asking the producers, in their own interests, to forego exceptional short-run advantages in favour of a long-run stability of income. In arriving at its decision on this policy, the government had the following fundamental considerations in mind:
Any further increase in wheat prices now would aggravate the problems of economic and political readjustment of the liberated areas to Canada's detriment in future trade with those areas. There is a moral obligation not to take advantage of our recent allies in their time of compelling need. Higher wheat prices would encourage the importing countries in a hurried return to wheat production and pre-war wheat policies very directly to the detriment of the wheat exporting countries, particularly Canada. Moreover, production in a number of exporting countries would be unduly encouraged."
The experiences of the intervening years have proven the views expressed in the last three paragraphs to be wrong. I think it is fair to admit that the wheat producers have received none of the benefits anticipated and that the variations in price which might have been injurious to farmers had they been on a lower level have been on such high level that the setting of a ceiling price of $1.55 a bushel has resulted in low returns to the wheat producers. It should be said that Marshall Aid was not heard of when this decision was reached. Marshall Aid pushed the price of American wheat to high levels and maintained it there.

SUMMARY

It is evident from this record:
1. That no subsidies were paid to wheat producers on account of wheat during the period of war.

2. That there were no ceilings placed upon the price of wheat prior to September, 1945.

3. That the Wheat Board took over all stored wheat in September of 1943 at the then market price of $1.25 a bushel basis No. 1 Northern Ft. William and that the delivery of wheat to the Board was compulsory from then on.

4. That the Board sold the wheat in bulk sales, mostly to Great Britain, from 1940 until the end of the war in September 1945 at prices which were during the early years approximately the initial payments made to the farmers, or from 1943 on were approximately the prices prevailing on a rising American market adjusted to Canadian conditions on the day the sale was made. This would result, in the last two years of the period, in Britain getting her wheat on an average below the market. The estimates are that the Canadian farmers received over the five years preceding the British-Canadian agreement about 23 cents a bushel less for their wheat than the United States farmers.

5. That the Wheat Board was able out of these receipts to make participation payments over the years from 1940 to 1944 inclusive amounting to $125,000,000. These payments were not subsidies.

6. That the Government decided on September 19, 1945,

   (a) That the United Kingdom and our other European allies were not to be asked to pay more than $1.55 a bushel basis No. 1 Northern Ft. William for wheat and instructed the Wheat Board to offer wheat at that price.

   (b) To give to the farmers in return a guarantee that at no time within the period from August 1, 1945, and July 31, 1950, would the wheat producers be asked to accept less than $1.00 a bushel but that for the time being the advance would remain at $1.25.

   (c) That any further increase in wheat prices at that time would aggravate the problems of economic and political readjustment of the liberated areas to Canada's detriment in future trade with those areas.

   (d) That higher wheat prices would encourage the importing countries in a hurried return to wheat production.

7. It was agreed by the Government that the Minister of Trade and Commerce and the Minister of Agriculture negotiate with the British or any other allied governments in an effort to make agreements which would maintain the price at as near as possible $1.55 a bushel throughout the entire five years. The Minister of Trade and Commerce agreed that the Minister of Agriculture should conduct negotiations on occasions when he was overseas regarding the marketing of other farm products or at F.A.O. conferences. In actual fact the Minister of Trade and Commerce was present in London during some of the negotiations.

THE GOVERNMENT MADE DECISIONS

The fact is that none of these decisions was discussed prior to the decision on September 19, 1945, with farm or any other organizations. The opinion of the Minister of Trade and Commerce and Minister of Agriculture was that the price should be allowed to advance now that war was over. The opinion of the Prices Board, as expressed by the Minister of Finance, was that "Any further increase in wheat prices would aggravate the problems of economic and political readjustment of the liberated areas to Canada's detriment in future trade with those areas". The government agreed there should be no further increase and further agreed that the Minister of Agriculture should discuss the announced policy and proposed agreements with the Wheat Pools.

DISCUSSIONS WITH POOLS

My discussions with the Pools satisfied me that the Pools would have no objection to the $1.55 price being made a ceiling provided it could be maintained throughout the five years or agreements entered into which would insure approximately that price being obtained for the greater part of our wheat over five years, and provided further that prices of what the wheat producer requires did not get out of line. I gathered from my discussions that they had more doubt about our being able to get more than 120 million bushels written into a four or five year agreement than about the price we might be able to obtain. When I convinced them that we could sell 600,000,000 bushels to the United Kingdom under a four year contract I think it is correct to say they were all for it. It is only fair to say, however, that we sold the idea to them, not they to us.

THE FIVE YEAR POOL

The first decision taken by the Government in September, 1945, when the war ended, was that wheat in common with other products should have a ceiling placed upon sales for consumption within Canada and sales to Europe. The ceiling placed upon sales for consumption in Canada was $1.25 a bushel No. 1 Fort William and overseas $1.55. It was agreed that the Government should guarantee a floor of $1.00 a bushel until July 31, 1950.

The first variation of this decision came on July 26, 1946, when the Four Year Wheat Contract with the United Kingdom was announced. This contract grew out of the discussions of September, 1945, when the Minister of Trade and Commerce and the Minister of Agriculture were authorized to attempt to maintain the price of wheat at the ceiling price of $1.55 a bushel over as great a part of the five year period as possible through long time government to government contracts similar to those we had with the United Kingdom on other farm products.

DISCUSSIONS IN LONDON

I arrived in London on December 22, 1945, Mr. Biddulph, representative of the Wheat Board in London, arranged for me to have lunch with Mr. James Rank and Mr. Hooker of the Cereals Committee of the Food Ministry on December 26.

My notes indicate that we discussed for two hours the possibility of a five year agreement on wheat. Mr. Rank expressed the view that because of the attitude taken by Canada throughout the war Britain should make an attempt to meet any marketing needs Canada might have and seemed sympathetic to a five year contract. Mr. Hooker, on the other hand, seemed favourable to getting back to the open market as soon as possible.

We explored many possibilities, including the United Kingdom buying all our wheat to be distributed in Europe at a price and reselling it either as wheat or flour.

Sir Ben Smith, the Minister of Food, had gone to the United States for two weeks, and Mr. MacKinnon was expected in London in January, 1946. It was agreed that we would continue the discussions at that time. Following the middle of January these discussions took place.

In the meantime Mr. Biddulph and I went to Paris, Belgium and Holland. We found France required more wheat and that Belgium and Holland were well supplied. None of them were ready to discuss contracts.

We returned to London in mid-January, 1946. We met there Mr. MacKinnon. He and Mr. Biddulph, together with Dr. Barton and me, had some discussions with the British. My memory is that Mr. MacKinnon and I reached certain understandings as to continued discussions, after which Mr. MacKinnon left and agreed that I should continue the discussions if possible to understandings which could be recommended to the Canadian Government.

The final meeting was between me and Sir Ben Smith, Minister of Food in the Atlee government. Dr. Barton and Mr. Biddulph were with me, and Sir Ben had Mr. James Rank, Mr. Hooker, and Mr. Pilman with him.

In previous meetings we had pointed out to the British that we were anxious to have a five year contract which would assure our farmers $1.55 a bushel basis No. 1 Northern Fort William on a quantity sufficiently large to bring the total receipts as nearly as possible to an average of $1.55 over the five-year period ending July 31, 1950.

On the occasion of this last meeting Sir Ben stated that they had considered the suggestion and had concluded that they could not agree to a contract for longer than two years. They were prepared to discuss a contract for 120,000,000 bushels a year at $1.55 for two years.

I replied to this that there was nothing to be gained by our discussing the matter further on that basis. I could not recommend that to our Government, and I was quite satisfied they would not accept it if I did.

Sir Ben then asked me if we would recommend to our Government that the negotiations be continued in Canada provided the United Kingdom Government undertook to consider along with an offer to purchase 120,000,000 bushels at $1.55 an undertaking to accept a similar amount and also responsibility for the Canadian Government guarantee of $1.00 a bushel under two more years. The United Kingdom was buying 1945 wheat at $1.55. The proposal was that we take as a basis of discussion two more years at $1.55 for increased amounts and $1.00 as a minimum price for the last two years.

I agreed to recommend to the Canadian Government that they invite the Minister of Food and any officials he might care to bring to come to Ottawa to discuss a four year contract. The Government agreed to this, and in the spring of 1946 the delegation arrived in Ottawa, under the leadership of Mr. E. G. Harwood, Under-Secretary of the British Ministry of Food.

My memory is that when they arrived the Honourable J. A. MacKinnon had gone to Mexico and that before he left he arranged with me and with the Government that I should conduct the negotiations.

When the delegation arrived they were adamant in maintaining that they could not agree on a price for more than two years. They were most anxious to receive high quantities during the first two years and were prepared to pay $1.55. They were most anxious to reduce the quantities to 100,000,000 bushels during the last two years and did not want a fixed price. They were prepared to guarantee $1.25 as a floor for the third year and $1.00 for the fourth year.

We stated we would not consider a contract for anything under 120,000,000 bushels as of any value to us at any time because Britain would be compelled by necessity to take that much from us for four years. We finally persuaded the British to agree to 160,000,000 for the first two years and 140,000,000 for each of the last two with the possibility of delivering an additional 40,000,000 during the first two years. This was later asked and refused.

We finally agreed to their suggestion that there be no set price for the last two years but that a price be agreed to at least six months before the opening of the crop years 1948 and 1949, provided there would be a floor of $1.25 a bushel for 1948 and $1.00 for 1949 as proposed by the British, and provided further that there would be no ceiling on the price which might be agreed to and that whatever that price was it would take care of any losses sustained by Canada accepting $1.55 during the first two years by adding such losses to the world price in each of the last two years.

The above is the meaning of the understanding reached before an attempt was made to put it in the form of an agreement.

The British later, when the agreement was being drawn, raised the question as to whether it would be possible to determine a mathematical calculation of the position. I stated that I was not concerned with holding them to a mathematical calculation; that so long as the British understood what the understanding was I was satisfied they would carry it out in spirit and I was also satisfied the Canadian Government would not be unreasonable.

MR. STRACHEY CAME OVER

Mr. Strachey, who had recently been appointed Minister of Food succeeding Sir Ben Smith, came to Canada at the end of these discussions to sign the contract. He was not able to do so because some question had been raised in Washington as to whether the contract was in contradiction of the terms of the Geneva Trade Agreements. The signing of the contract was delayed a month until this point was cleared. It was cleared and the agreement was signed on behalf of Canada by the Minister of Trade and Commerce, the Honourable J. A. MacKinnon, and on behalf of the United Kingdom by the High Commissioner, Sir Alexander Clutterbuck, on the 24th day of July, 1946.

There were discussions across Canada immediately as to what the "have regard to" clause meant. Critics said that in law it meant nothing. I stated in reply that whether it meant anything legally or not our experience had taught us that the United Kingdom always acknowledged her obligations in spirit and I was satisfied she would do so in this case. The Right Honourable John Strachey, Minister of Food for the United Kingdom, was in Canada in February, 1947, when this discussion was at its height. He spoke in Winnipeg on February 25, 1947, and is reported in the Winnipeg Tribune, a disinterested publication, as having said: "British opposition, he said, was that in the end the British people would have to pay millions of pounds more for their wheat. Canadian criticism was that higher prices could be obtained now.

He termed as 'utterly' unwarranted and 'monstrous' the suggestion that any British government would break the terms of the agreement when prices fell."

After stating that the essence of the agreement was floor prices to protect Canada in case of rapidly decreasing prices in the last two years, he stated:

"Should the price not fall as sharply as all that, the agreement provided precise negotiations for fixing prices in the third and fourth years." "This means", continued Mr. Strachey, "that the fact that we have bought our wheat from you this year below world prices and that we may do so again next year will be one of the factors in negotiating the actual prices to be paid in the third and fourth years."

This is what we had always claimed the "have regard to" clause meant.

The first discussions to arrange prices under the above provisions of the agreement took place between me, supported by Mr. Buddulph representing the Wheat Board and Dr. Wilson representing Trade and Commerce, and Mr. Strachey supported by Mr. J. R. Rank and Mr. Hooker of the Cereals Committee who were the chief advisers of the Food Ministry throughout the negotiations of the agreement.

Mr. King was leaving for Toronto on his private car the night before I left for London. Mr. Howe had just returned from London. Mr. King called us to his car and we discussed fully the representations to be made. It was agreed that I might accept $2.00 as payment for 1948 wheat provided that was not considered full and final settlement under the "have regard to" clause.

I went to London and found everyone we met accepted the interpretation we placed on the meaning of the "have regard to" clause, namely, that the losses sustained by Canada in selling at $1.55 from 1946 and 1947 crops should in some part be made up in the price paid above the world price by the United Kingdom for wheat obtained from 1948 to 1949 crops.

Those, among others, who specifically accepted that point of view were Mr. Rank, Mr. Hooker, Mr. Strachey and the Chancellor of the Exchequer, Lord Dalton. My memory is that Mr. Abbott was in London at the time and Lord Dalton stated to him that Canada was entitled to consideration on this point.

After discussions among officials, Mr. Strachey invited me to dinner when we discussed the matter fully. The suggestion that we were entitled to consideration was never questioned. We finally agreed that it would be impossible to make any calculation which could be considered final until the end of the contract owing to the fact that wheat was selling on the market at more than $2.00 a bushel and there was no sign of it going down in price. We finally agreed on the understanding reached before I left Ottawa, namely, that the payment throughout the 1948 crop year should be $2.00 but that it could only be considered to have partially taken care of the agreement under the "have regard to" clause provided wheat dropped below $2.00 at some time in that year.

Wheat prices did not drop below $2.00 during that crop year. On December 9, 1948, Mr. Max MacKenzie, Dr. Charles Wilson, Mr. McCubbin and I took off from Montreal to conduct negotiations re the price to be paid in the 1949 crop year.

My notes state: "Our mission was to conduct negotiations as provided for under clause 2(b) of the United Kingdom-Canada wheat agreement. In September of 1947 we had agreed that with wheat at over three dollars a bushel there was no possibility of reaching an agreement on the third year as compared with the first. It was admitted by the United Kingdom that a final settlement at less than $2.00 was not likely and, therefore, they would agree to pay $2.00 for the third year with the understanding that any settlement provided for in clause 2(b) would be applied in the light of all the circumstances then existing both with regard to the crop of 1948 and that of 1949.

MET MR. STRACHEY

On Saturday, December 11, 1948, we met Mr. Strachey and officials of the Department of Food among whom were Mr. Rank and Mr. Hooker as well as officials of the Chancellory. The chief change in these we had to confer with was that there was a new Chancellor who did not appear in person but whose views were emphasized by the Minister of Food.

Mr. Strachey outlined the attitude of the United Kingdom Government which was to the effect that they could not accept further responsibility for any losses we had sustained than might materialize from payment of $1.75 a bushel basis No. 1 Northern at Fort William in 1949-50 and an undertaking to place a floor of $1.40 a bushel under 100,000,000 bushels of wheat to be delivered in 1950-51 at Canada's option, which option must be declared before April 30, 1950.

It was suggested in the discussions that this was approximately what they were prepared to advocate in the conference shortly to be held in relation to a proposed multilateral contract and that they were suggesting that as proposed in the contract we both be governed in 1949-50 by the terms of the multilateral contract.

We stated that this proposal did not "have regard to" losses sustained during the 1946 and 1947 crop years. Conferences of officials were arranged for and held.

A further conference was held which was attended by Mr. Strachey and me. Mr. Strachey was accompanied by a considerable panel of Ministry of Food and Chancellory officials. I was accompanied by our officials and Mr. McCubbin. Mr. Strachey emphasized that he was speaking for the Chancellor as well as himself and was sorry to say that he could not assume responsibility for going any further than he had gone in our first meeting. He stated that the position was very strongly taken that they were not under obligation to make an arithmetical calculation of any losses but to "have regard to" the differences between the world price and the $1.55 a bushel basis Fort William which was received for the 1946 and 1947 crops.

He went further to state that they were of opinion that the floor was to be taken as the point from which any advance would be made rather than the world price of wheat which they claimed could not be determined.

I pointed out that if it were calculated on that basis it would be considerably more than we were suggesting.

I was out of London for two days during which a small committee of four worked upon a possible agreement. It was submitted on my return and proposed that the payment for 1949 crop be $2.00 and that if the average price for wheat that year fell below $1.50, two dollars for 1949 wheat be considered a full and final settlement of the "have regard to" clause. This acknowledged our right to further claims to the extent of 50 cents a bushel on 140,000,000 bushels, or $70,000,000. There were other proposals should other things happen, but they do not change the fundamental proposal.

I met Mr. Strachey later and he stated to me that it did not appear possible to come to agreement. I proposed a meeting between myself and the Chancellor. He agreed it might have possibilities and arranged it.

DISCUSSIONS WITH SIR STAFFORD CRIPPS

During my discussions with Mr. Cripps, I submitted to him a method of consideration based upon what the American farmer and the Canadian farmer had received which would place the lowest possible valuation upon the claims of Canadian farmers which would amount in total to $133,000,000. I stated I was quite prepared to recommend to the Canadian Government that the settlement be on a basis of $100,000,000 and that this be subject to any further reduction resulting from the fact that the world price was under $2.00, provided $2.00 was paid for 140,000,000 bushels of 1949 wheat.

Sir Stafford stated the proposal could not be accepted because they had not agreed to take care of losses.

I answered that the agreement stated that they were called upon to have regard to the difference between $1.55 a bushel basis Fort William for 1946 and 1947 crops and the world price in determining what ought to be paid for the 1948 and 1949 crops. I went on to state (as this memorandum verifies) that this interpretation of the clause had been agreed to by the previous Chancellor, by the Minister of Food, speaking in Winnipeg, and later when he and I discussed the 1948 crop payment, and that no question of this interpretation was raised in December of 1947, when his delegation was in Ottawa and it was suggested by us we drop the contract, and again when he was in Ottawa in September of 1948.

On each of these occasions we could have benefited by dropping the contract but it had been retained in all its terms at the request of the United Kingdom.

He replied to this that in any case it was not accepted that they would be required to pay a calculated loss. I pointed out the calculation was only made to determine how low we could justify to farmers making the claim. I stated the Government might consider cutting off another $25,000,000, but in my opinion that is the limit I should go in any recommendation made the Government.

He then refused the proposal and submitted one of his own which was essentially the same as the committee had discussed the previous day.

I submit that this proposal admits a loss of $70,000,000 and then states we would only obtain the $70,000,000 if we accepted $2.00 a bushel for our 1949 wheat and the average price for the year turned out to be $1.50 a bushel or less.

It was stated by Sir Stafford Cripps that if his offer was not satisfactory they would be prepared to send out a team to discuss the matter further.

The offer was discussed by Cabinet here, accepted in principle but not in detail. Details which would be acceptable were submitted but were refused by Britain. It was finally decided that the British would pay $2.00 during the 1949-50 crop year and that final settlement of the "have regard to" clause would be further discussed in the light of developments before July 31, 1950.

SIR STAFFORD REVERSES HIMSELF

Sir Stafford Cripps apparently changed his mind with regard to this whole matter before February 23, 1949. On that date he gave an interview to the Canadian Press in London which was circulated across Canada. With regard to this matter he said:

"As regards wheat, we shall continue to depend on Canada for the greater part of our supplies. The four year contract negotiated in 1946 will expire in 1950 and we have recently agreed upon a price of $2.00 a bushel for the 1949-50 season. We think there is every probability of the world price falling below the $2.00 level before the end of the contract, either because of the general improvement in the supply position or as a condition of any international wheat agreement which may be concluded in the near future. If this should be the case, the Canadian farmer will enjoy a favoured position by virtue of the fixed price on which we have agreed. This might prove to be a fair compensation for the earlier years when he was selling us wheat at below the world price; it depends, of course, upon how far prices actually fall. But in any case we have agreed to discuss this matter further with the Canadian Government some time towards the middle of 1950."

Sir Stafford says they agreed to pay $2.00 a bushel expecting the price would go down for one or both of two reasons and that if this should be the case he might receive a fair compensation for having sold Britain wheat below the world price depending on how far prices fall. He goes on to say that in any case this matter is to be further discussed.

He admits in this statement that Canadian farmers did take a loss. The world prices did not go below $2.00 in 1949-50. Therefore, the farmer received nothing on that basis. Canadian wheat under the international agreement sold at $1.98 or 2 cents below the $2.00 price. This could not be claimed to be compensation. He states that in any case this matter would be further discussed. He not only refused to discuss it but makes Canada's insistence upon that a reason for refusing to consider doing what in the first sentence of the paragraph he states Britain will do, namely, take the greater part of her supplies from Canada. 110,000,000 bushels is not the greater part of her supplies.

RECOMMENDATION

I think I have shown beyond a shadow of a doubt that Britain agreed to pay the Canadian farmer more for the 600,000,000 bushels of wheat she secured between 1946 and 1949 inclusive under the Canadian-United Kingdom four year contract than she has yet paid.

I think she should be asked to re-open the discussions and that this Government should press the farmers' claims to at least $100,000,000 and that we should refuse to agree to less than $65,000,000. If she pleads shortage of dollars, then I recommend that she be asked to agree to the utilization of the remainder of the loan to make the payment.

If we agree the matter is closed as between this Government and the British Government, then I submit that I think we have assumed the obligation and should proceed to consider the amount which should be paid to the Wheat Board to cover the farmers' claims.

APPENDIX 7

EXCERPTS FROM
MR. GEORGE McIVOR'S
LETTER OF NOVEMBER 18, 1974

MR. McIVOR'S APPOINTMENT AS ASSISTANT CHIEF COMMISSIONER AND LATER AS CHIEF COMMISSIONER OF THE CANADIAN WHEAT BOARD

Referring to your reference on page 511 to my appointment as Assistant Chief Commissioner, and your further reference on page 540 to my appointment as Chief Commissioner, I would like to make the following comment. First, it was a matter of surprise to me when the government approached me and asked me to become Assistant Chief Commissioner. Mr. McFarland and the government were already locked in an argument, and as I had been associated with him for five years, I had not expected to be asked to serve a new Board. I was agreeably surprised to learn that Mr. Murray had strongly urged the government to approach me. I discussed the matter with Mr. McFarland, and without hesitation he said I should carry on with the Board as I had never become involved with the political side. James R. Murray was a remarkable man. Some of my friends warned me that he was hard to get along with, but I did not find this was the case. He was hot tempered and did not suffer fools gladly, but for sheer ability I have met very few to match him. Although he was tough he was exceedingly fair, and I certainly enjoyed my association with him and was sorry when it had to come to an end. He continued to advise me after I succeeded him as Chief Commissioner. Sometimes these interviews were not too pleasant when he pointed out my shortcomings, but they were of great benefit. I think Canada was fortunate in attracting men of the calibre of Mr. John I. MacFarland and Mr. James R. Murray, and each in their own way served Canada well.

SOURCE: Mr. McIvor's letter of above date addressed to the author. The page references in the letter have been changed to refer to the present text.

CANADIAN WHEAT BOARD HANDLING OF RELIEF SEED WHEAT FOR THE GOVERNMENT OF SASKATCHEWAN, 1937-38

In early June 1937, Mr. Murray requested me to go to the United Kingdom to clear up a number of matters concerning the Board. The future of the Board was uncertain and the government had not made up their minds definitely as to how the Board would operate. I knew that Mr. Murray had recommended me to the government as his successor, but so far I had not received any approach from Mr. Euler, Minister of Trade and Commerce, so that I was quite uncertain about my future plans. I received word from Mr. Euler to return to Canada by the first boat and to go to Ottawa en route to Winnipeg. I had heard reports that the wheat crop was going badly, but as this was early in the crop year, I had discounted them. When I reached Ottawa about the middle of July, it was clear that we had experienced a disaster of a major proportion. The crop was planted in the dry spring and without rain of any kind and day after day of heat. The deterioration was rapid and complete. Total production in western Canada was in the nature of 175 million bushels, with the bulk of these bushels produced in the province of Alberta. Saskatchewan alone produced 37 million bushels of wheat, or an average of 2½ bushels per acre.

An immediate decision was made by the government that no further wheat would be sold, the quantity on hand represented by futures contracts being 6,964,000 bushels. After discussion with the Wheat Committee of the Cabinet, it was considered desirable to retain the futures contracts referred to and to exchange them for actual wheat suitable for seed requirements in the province of Saskatchewan. This wheat was ultimately sold to the government of the province of Saskatchewan. The first job of the Wheat Board was to locate desirable wheat for seed, and shipping orders were halted from the province of Saskatchewan, and as much as possible of desirable seed wheat was retained in country elevators in preparation for distribution in the spring. This quantity was limited and the bulk of the purchases were made for shipment from southern Alberta where a good crop had been harvested. These stocks were stored in the various interior government elevators, and where possible the stocks were maintained in the country elevators in southern Alberta.

In accordance with arrangements made with the Honourable J. G. Taggart, Minister of Agriculture for the province of Saskatchewan, the Board not only undertook to purchase all the seed requirements for wheat in the province of Saskatchewan, but also agreed to act in a similar capacity for the Saskatchewan government's requirements of coarse grains for seed and feed. In addition purchases were made of seed oats for the government of the province of Quebec. With a very limited staff, the Board found this task one of major proportions, but considering all the difficulties, it developed into a smooth operation. It is pleasing to report that nature was kind to western Canada in the 1938/39 crop year, and Canadian production of 350 million bushels of wheat was the largest crop since 1932. It should be noted that, in spite of the financial difficulties experienced in the western provinces, and particularly Saskatchewan, the Federal Department of Finance under Dr. W. C. Clark, once again came to the rescue of the west by guaranteeing, through the banks, the Saskatchewan government's account. It should also be reported that the western producer repaid these loans over a period of time.

THE INITIAL PAYMENT IN 1938

I would now like to refer to page 561-565 in which the question of the fixation of the initial price for wheat in the 1938/39 crop year is dealt with by you in detail. I have a fairly clear recollection of the events at that time, particularly in view of the fact that it was my first year as Chief Commissioner in which the Board resumed operations as the seller of Canadian wheat under the Canadian Wheat Board Act. The fixation of this price was a serious problem for both the Board and the government. Under the requirements of the Act instructions to the Board were clear as it was the intention of Parliament when the Act was written that the initial price would bear proper relationship to the world's situation and that the price would be simply as it was stated, an initial price, with a strong inference that additional payments would follow. It was inevitable that the initial operations of the Board in the 1938/39 crop year would be carried out under world wide surplus conditions. Wheat production in the 1938/39 crop year reached a new record level of about a half billion bushels above the previous record production of 1928. Substantial yields in European importing countries resulted in restriction of imports until the need for security stocks later in the crop year. The Danubian countries produced about 100 million bushels more than in the crop year 1937/38, and Argentina produced a record crop of over 336 million bushels. Australia had a moderate crop, but the United States crop of 932 million was the largest since 1931. In spite of the fact that the selection of seed, by the very nature of things, for planting in the spring of 1938 in Canada, had to be fairly haphazard, under favourable weather conditions Canadian production, however, was 350 million bushels, the largest crop since 1932. It followed, therefore, that there was keen competition for the limited available markets, and both Argentina and the United States employed subsidy methods to dispose of their surplus.

As you will see it was, therefore, under a state of very difficult conditions that the Board were required to recommend to the government the fixing of the minimal price. There was certainly nothing in the situation to indicate an advance in world prices — on the contrary the possibility of a substantial decline was very much on the cards. Based on these facts the Board originally recommended a price of 60¢ a bushel, but the judgment of the Board was sound as evidenced by the fact that in July 1939 wheat broke below 50¢ a bushel. The recommendation of the Board of 60¢ created a serious problem for the government. The government felt, however, that the Board had no alternative but to recommend a price based on world conditions at that time. The government, however, had a responsibility of providing western producers with a liveable price which certainly was above 60¢ a bushel. We must bear in mind that the western producer was in bad shape financially as a result of the disastrous crop of 1937/38. Mr. Dunning, the Minister of Finance, was particularly concerned with the financial position of the western producer, and the writer was asked if he would have any objection to revising the initial price to 80¢ a bushel. I said "No, I was sure the Board under no circumstances wished to deny this additional payment to the western producer, but that I would have to inform them that it probably would mean a loss of over 60 million dollars as it was the intention of the Board to dispose of this wheat at the world price and not to attempt in any way to hold up movement of wheat in order to try and gain a price which would bring the government out even". My recollection is that I wrote a letter to Mr. Euler incorporating the above view and that he replied accepting the judgment of the Board. We therefore proceeded to sell wheat at the market, and my recollection is that the ultimate loss to the government was something in the neighborhood of $63 million. In retrospect it would appear that the judgment of the Board in selling the wheat at the market was sound because, in spite of the fact that we offered wheat competitively with other sellers, we ended up with a substantial carryover, and in the fall of 1939 war broke out and, as a result of the collapse of the countries of western Europe after the fall of the Maginot Line, wheat was practically unsaleable except to the United Kingdom. The position of the board in this kind of a situation was not a happy one. Temptation was great that we should try to boost the market by holding wheat for a higher price. This temptation was resisted, however, by the Board and wheat was offered freely every day at the world price.

MR. CRERAR'S ATTEMPT TO NEGOTIATE A
LONG TERM CONTRACT WITH BRITAIN

With reference to your outline of the ill-fated negotiations with respect to a long term contract with Britain, which is well outlined on pages 643 to 646, I have quite a clear recollection of the discussions in London. First, the fact that the British government were not buying in quantity in the open market in Canada was a matter of deep concern to myself and Mr. Crerar, and later to other members of the delegation such as Mr. Wilgress.

The idea that the British might be receptive to a long term contract first came to me through Mr. R. V. Biddulph, the European Commissioner of the Canadian Wheat Board located in London. Biddulph had some discussions with Sir Norman Vernon, an important official on the administrative side of the Ministry of Food. The gossip was that Vernon was on very friendly terms with Prime Minister Chamberlain. He put the query forward to Biddulph as to why it would not be in the best interests of the United Kingdom and ourselves to enter into a long term agreement so that the matter could be settled with regard to wheat supplies, and both governments could confine their attention to many of the problems which were considered more timely and important. I had a definite feeling that our government would not be receptive because I felt that they would strongly object to the closing of the Winnipeg futures market, and I did not see how the market could operate satisfactorily once such a long term contract was made. I discussed the matter with Mr. Crerar in the early stages and he at first was quite reluctant to go ahead for the reasons I have stated. He felt that we should still persist in endeavouring to get the British government to buy a good round lot of wheat through market channels and the Board would assist in this type of operation which you have referred to in your recital by offering certain quantities of wheat in the market from day by day. The matter lay dormant for a few days and I did not press for a decision because of the uncertainty in my own mind as to what we should do. It again came to a head after the return of Mr. Crerar on a week-end visit to France where he and the other leaders of delegations to the Empire War Conference were given a first hand look at the Maginot Line. He came back quite concerned about the situation. His words, as I recall them, were: "I am just a farm boy from Manitoba, but I am afraid the Germans will go around that Line". Unfortunately he proved to be correct. This led to some further thinking and discussions between Biddulph and myself as to what would happen in the event of such a disaster and we were deeply worried that such an event would mean the loss of some of our better wheat markets and the almost complete confinement of sales to the United Kingdom. I again opened the matter with Mr. Crerar and by this time he was deeply concerned about the situation and his concern led to the cable to the Prime Minister on December 2nd which you refer to. You have also made reference to the cable of December 5th from Ottawa in which the Canadian government recommended the withdrawal of our offer. Needless to say the government's decision was a matter of deep concern to Mr. Crerar and myself, and also to Mr. Wilgress who by this time had fully agreed that a long term contract was the only way out of our problem. A letter was written to the British government and the matter was closed. We sailed for home about the 15th of December and during our passage we had no way of knowing what the course of the market was. When we arrived at St. John we found that there had been a serious break in the price of wheat at Winnipeg. I think, looking back, that the difficulties of communication had more to do with the break-down in thinking between Ottawa and ourselves, but the two environments entered into this breakdown. We were close to the situation in London and our deepest concern related to the possibility of a collapse in the Continent. No one was talking about this, but it could not help but be in the back of our minds. Another thing that entered into my own thinking was that there seemed to be an opinion in North America that, like all wars prior to this one, wheat was bound to go up, and if you apply this to wars generally, this was not a faulty opinion, but this was a different kind of a war, and any setback would simply have the effect of reducing the available markets for wheat. This generally was the thinking of our delegation at the time and was a driving force behind our anxiety to have a contract for a period of time. We did not hold with the view that came from Ottawa that prices were low based on the world position because there was plenty of wheat in the world, except that Canada had a preferred position due to the shipping difficulties from elsewhere. The irony of the situation was that I personally was very close to Mr. Rank who was the Chairman of the Imported Cereals Division of the Ministry of Food responsible for all grain imports under the Ministry of Food. Mr. Rank was very opposed to a long term contract as he felt that prices were bound to go lower. As is well known now his judgment in this regard was correct.

THE INTRODUCTION OF DELIVERY QUOTAS

The development of the quota system on the delivery of grain is one of the most interesting stories concerning grain marketing during the period of the war. Reference had been made at various farm meetings concerning the probable difficulties which would arise in the delivery of grain due to the shortage of elevator space. The Canadian Wheat Board was asked by the Wheat Committee of the Cabinet to work out a system whereby an opportunity to deliver would be available to every producer, irrespective of delivery point and irrespective of area of delivery. This task was delegated to Dr. Grindley, the Secretary of the Canadian Wheat Board, and the writer. Needless to say there was the closest consultation between Grindley and myself and the other members of the Wheat Board. Various proposals had been made over the years in a general way by the producers' organizations, but discussions had not reached the point where a definite plan had been proposed. Time was running out, and it was necessary for Grindley and myself to apply ourselves immediately to the problem. As a result a new quota system was evolved, and you make reference to this on pages 661-662.

The important point in regard to the quota system is that, over the years the quota system was to change completely the method of delivery of grain. Prior to the adoption of the quota system the railways moved grain in what they considered the most efficient manner from the standpoint of transportation. Consequently they first gave preference in the distribution of their box cars to Manitoba, then Saskatchewan, then Alberta. I doubt that Grindley and I realised at the time the fact that not only were we putting forward a system which would control deliveries to the primary country elevator points, but the end result was control of deliveries from the Lakehead clear up to the Peace River area — in fact the whole expanse of territory in which grain was grown. The reason for this was that a quota would be fixed initially for each grain elevator point. Each producer carried a permit delivery book and when that quota was finished, box cars were cut off at that point and switched to other points where quotas had not been delivered. As time went on quotas were raised again, and this resulted in a perpetual increase for quotas as transportation presented itself, but perhaps the most interesting development was the fact that a producer in Manitoba whose delivery point was tributary to the Lakehead lost the advantage which he had always enjoyed, and was put on an equal basis with the producer — we will say at Grande Prairie in the Peace River country. In other words the delivery of grain was equalized at the country point, and eventually over the whole of western Canada grain growing area. Needless to say, at the outset the Manitoba farmers protested vigorously, and I was aked to attend a meeting to explain the situation to them. This meeting was held in Winnipeg and was well attended. Conditions in the United Kingdom were very much in my mind and I did not pull any punches. I said that this was a very small price for the grain producer to pay in western Canada compared to the hardships of these people in the United Kingdom and surely we were all in the war effort together. Someone got up and moved a vote of confidence in the Board and there the matter ended. It is interesting to note that apart from some changes which the Board made, not in principle but in the variations in the system which they felt were required, in principle the system is the same as it was when it first came into being. It is interesting to note too that nearly all the changes in marketing came about as a result of various crises, and many of these changes were required to be set up to deal with a situation which arose from time to time and, of course, most of these changes were authorised under the War Measures Act, and as they did not require the usual long debate in Parliament, decisions were made quickly and firmly.

THE CLOSING OF THE WHEAT FUTURES MARKET AND THE TAKEOVER OF COMMERCIAL STOCKS

It is not necessary to repeat the very full account which you have given of the conditions which led to the closing of the futures market. On Monday evening, September 27th, 1943, I requested Gordon Smith and D. A. Kane, my two associates on the Board, to leave for Winnipeg because I felt that a decision was imminent on the question of the closing of the market and that the decision would be that the futures market would be closed effective September 27th, 1943. Gordon Smith and Dan Kane left for Winnipeg that night and, therefore, both of them were available on the floor of the Exchange when the Minister's telegram was read instructing that the Exchange would be closed. This was a most fortunate turn of events from the standpoint of the Board, and undoubtedly did a great deal to smooth out the transition from one form of marketing to the other. It was felt generally that the closing of the market was a temporary war action and it was hard to believe that the market was still closed after 31 years.

At this point I would like to pay tribute to Gordon Smith and the late D. A. Kane for the masterful job that they accomplished in the take-over of over 200 million bushels of wheat. There were thousands of contracts outstanding and millions of bushels of grain had been sold through the futures market. For several weeks the Board's offices were crowded with anxious buyers who wondered whether they were going to get delivery of the grain they had bought. Every contract was considered by the Board, and after several weeks of almost round the clock operations, the job was finished. The remarkable thing was that to my knowledge there was not one single complaint of unfair treatment, and while the trade generally did not react favourably to the closing of the market which is understandable, they did feel that the Board had acted properly in the winding up of these various contracts.

REFERENCES

STATUTES OF CANADA

1801   An Act to authorize appointment of Inspectors of Flour, 41 George III, Chap. VII.

1820   Amendment to Act to appoint Inspectors of Flour, 1 George IV, Chap. V.

1835   An Act to establish a Standard Weight . . . for Grain, etc., 5 William IV, Chap. VII.

1853   An Act to establish a Standard Weight for the different kinds of Grain and Pulse, 16 Vict., Cap. CXCIII.

1863   An Act respecting the Inspection of Wheat and other Grain. 26 Vict., Cap. III.

1868   Rupert's Land Act, 31-32 Vict., Cap. CV.

1869   An Act for the temporary Government of Rupert's Land and the North-Western Territory when united with Canada. 32-33 Vict., Cap. III.

1870   An Act . . . to establish and provide for the Government of the Province of Manitoba, 33 Vict., Cap. III.

1873   An Act to provide for the establishment of "The Department of the Interior", 36 Vict., Chap. 4.
        An Act respecting the Administration of Justice and for the Establishment of a Police Force in the North West Territories, 36 Vict., Chap. 35.

1874   An Act respecting Inspection of certain Staple Articles of Canadian Produce, 37 Vict., Chap. 45.

1881   An Act respecting the Canadian Pacific Railway, 44 Vict., Chap. 1.

1886   The General Inspection Act, 49 Vict., Chap. 99.

1889   An Act to amend the General Inspection Act, 52 Vict., Chap. 16.

1891   An Act to amend the General Inspection Act, 54-55 Vict., Chap. 48.

1892   An Act to amend the General Inspection Act, 55-56 Vict., Chap. 23.

1897   An Act to authorize a Subsidy for a Railway through the Crow's Nest Pass, 60-61 Vict., Chap. 5.

1899   An Act to amend the General Inspection Act, 62-63 Vict., Chap. 25.

1900   The Manitoba Grain Act, 63-64 Vict., Chap. 39.

1902   An Act to amend the Manitoba Grain Act, 1900, 2 Edward VII, Chap. 19.

1903   An Act to amend the Manitoba Grain Act, 1900, 3 Edward VII, Chap. 33.
        The National Transcontinental Railway Act, 3 Edward VII, Chap. 71.

1904   The Grain Inspection Act, 4 Edward VII, Chap. 15.

1908	The Inspection and Sale of Grain Amendment Act, 7-8 Edward VII, Chap. 36.
	The Manitoba Grain Inspection Act, 7-8 Edward VII, Chap. 45.
1912	The Canada Grain Act, 2 George V, Chap. 27.
1919	The Board of Grain Supervisors Act, 10 George V, Chap. 5.
	The Canadian Wheat Board Act, 10 George V, Chap. 9.
	An Act to amend the Canada Grain Act, 9-10 George V, Chap. 40.
1920	The Canadian Wheat Board Act, 10-11 George V, Chap. 40.
1922	The Canadian Wheat Board Act, 12-13 George V, Chap. 14.
1925	The Canada Grain Act, 15-16 George V, Chap. 33.
	An Act to amend the Railway Act, 1919, 15-16 George V, Chap. 52.
1927	An Act to amend the Canada Grain Act, 17 George V, Parts I-II.
1929	An Act to amend the Canada Grain Act, 19-20 George V, Chap. 9.
1930	The Canada Grain Act, 20-21 George V, Chap. 5.
1931	An Act Respecting Wheat, 21-22 George V, Chap. 60.
1935	The Canadian Wheat Board Act, 25-26 George V, Chap. 53.
1936	The 1930 Wheat Crop Equalization Payments Act, 1 Edward VIII, Chap. 12.
1939	The Agricultural Products Co-operative Marketing Act, 3 George VI, Chap. 28.
	The Grain Futures Act, 3 George VI, Chap. 31.
	The Wheat Co-operative Marketing Act, 3 George VI, Chap. 34.
	An Act to amend the Canadian Wheat Board Act, 1935, 3 George VI, Chap. 39.
	The Prairie Farm Assistance Act, 3 George VI, Chap. 50.
1940	An Act to amend the Canadian Wheat Board Act, 1935, 4 George VI, Chap. 25.
1942	The Wheat Acreage Reduction Act, 6 George VI, Chap. 10.
1943	The War Appropriation (United Nations Mutual Aid) Act, 7 George VI, Chap. 17.
1944	The Agricultural Prices Support Act, 8 George VI, Chap. 29.
1945	The National Emergency Transitional Powers Act, 9-10 George VI, Chap. 25.
1946	The United Kingdom Financial Agreement Act, 10 George VI, Chap. 12.
1947	An Act to amend the Canadian Wheat Board Act, 1935, 11 George VI, Chap. 15.
1948	An Act to amend the Canadian Wheat Board Act, 1935, 11-12 George VI, Chap. 4.
1950	An Act to amend the Canadian Wheat Board Act, 1935, 14 George VI, Chap. 31.
1951	An Act to amend the Canadian Wheat Board Act, 1935, 15 George VI, Chap. 3.

STATUTES OF SASKATCHEWAN

1948	The Coarse Grains Marketing Control Act, 12 George VI, Chap. 66.

ORDERS IN COUNCIL

1901	P.C. 1509, July 26, transferring to Department of Trade & Commerce responsibility for administering The Manitoba Grain Act, 1900, and also the General Inspection Act.
1906	P.C. 1475, July 19, appointing a Royal Commission to investigate matters in connection with the Grain Trade of Canada.

1915 P.C. 2874, December 4, authorizing $10 million to finance commandeered wheat, and authorizing Robert Magill to countersign cheques and certify transfers.

1917 P.C. 1604, June 11, establishing the Board of Grain Supervisors.

P.C. 1605, June 11, appointing the members of the Board of Grain Supervisors.

P.C. 2867, October 12, amending P.C. 1604 and authorizing the Carrying Charge Fund to be administered by the Board of Grain Supervisors.

1918 P.C. 2153, September 5, amending and enlarging powers of the Board of Grain Supervisors.

1919 P.C. 1589, July 31, establishing the Canadian Wheat Board.

P.C. 1751, August 22, establishing Wheat Board initial prices.

P.C. 2518, December 20, approving an honorarium of $10,000 to Robert Magill.

1921 P.C. 1270, April 12, appointing the Hyndman Royal Grain Inquiry Commission.

1923 P.C. 774, May 1, appointing a Royal Commission to inquire into grain handling and marketing in particular the grading and weighing of wheat, etc.

1931 P.C. 853, April 10, appointing a Royal Commission to enquire into and report upon what effect, if any, the dealing in grain futures has upon the price received by the producer.

P.C. 2238, September 12, providing a guarantee on bank loans made to Canadian Co-operative Wheat Producers Limited against 1930 crop deliveries to the pools.

P.C. 2239, September 12, furnishing guarantees to permit the three provincial pools to operate small voluntary pools on grain delivered to them from the 1930 crop.

1932 P.C. 1576, July 11, reviewing the government's guarantee under the provisions of the Unemployment and Farm Relief Act.

1935 P.C. 2497, August 14, appointing Mr. John I. McFarland as chief commissioner, Mr. David L. Smith as assistant commissioner and Dr. Henry C. Grant as commissioner of the Canadian Wheat Board.

P.C. 2518, August 14, appointing Messrs. C. H. G. Short, Sidney T. Smith, Robert McKee, L. C. Brouillette, P. F. Bredt, Lew Hutchison and Brooks Catton, as members of the Advisory Committee to the Canadian Wheat Board.

P.C. 3199, October 10, relating to the acquisition of wheat from Canadian Co-operative Wheat Producers Limited.

P.C. 3455, October 31, appointing the Wheat Committee of the Cabinet.

P.C. 3756, December 3, retiring the McFarland Wheat Board and appointing the Murray Board.

1936 P.C. 1577, June 27, appointing Royal Grain Inquiry Commission.

1937 P.C. 1770, July 27, rendering the 87½ cent initial payment effective only if the market price fell below 90 cents.

1940 P.C. 4214, appointing members of the Advisory Committee to the Canadian Wheat Board.

1941 P.C. 3047, April 30, establishing regulations for wheat acreage reduction payments.

P.C. 3849, May 30, establishing maximum delivery quota regulations.

P.C. 8527, November 1, establishing general maximum prices regulations.

1942   P.C. 1800, March 9, designating the Canadian Wheat Board as a sole
        buyer of flaxseed.
        P.C. 9692, October, creating the Food Requirements Committee.
1943   P.C. 2894, April 9, authorizing the Canadian Wheat Board to purchase
        sunflower seed and rapeseed.
        P.C. 7942, October 12, providing for the discontinuance of wheat trading,
        the creation of the crown account, and the marketing of all 1943-44
        deliveries through the Canadian Wheat Board.
1945   P.C. 1116, February 20, replenishing the crown account.
        P.C. 6122, September 19, instructing the Canadian Wheat Board to
        maintain the wheat export price ceiling.
        P.C. 6338, September 27, increasing the oats and barley equalization pay-
        ments.
1949   P.C. 3713, July 20, extending Parts III and IV of the Canadian Wheat
        Board Act to Oats and Barley.

GOVERNMENT DOCUMENTS, PUBLICATIONS AND REPORTS

1867-
1951   DEBATES OF THE HOUSE OF COMMONS OF CANADA

        JOURNALS OF THE HOUSE OF COMMONS OF CANADA

1919   Report of Special Commission on Cost of Living, Jnls. of H/C, Part II,
        Vol. LV, Appendix No. 7, July 2, 1919.
1931   Report of Mr. H. Tooley, Secretary, Board of Grain Supervisors for
        Canada (letter dated Sept. 11, 1919) Jnls. of H/C, 22 George V, June 23,
        1931.

        SESSIONAL PAPERS

1870   Report of S. J. Dawson, Civil Engineer, to the Hon. William McDougall,
        C. B., Minister of Public Works, &c., Ottawa, May 1, 1869, Sess. Paper No.
        12, 33 Vict., 1870.
1900   Report of the Royal Commission on Shipment and Transportation of
        Grain, Sess. Papers No. 81 and 81a, 63 Vict., 1900.
1908   Report of Royal Commission on the Grain Trade of Canada, 1906, Sess.
        Paper No. 59, 7-8 Edward VII, 1908.
1913   Report of the Board of Grain Commissioners for Canada, Sess. Paper No.
        10d, 3 George V, 1913.
1921   Report of the Canadian Wheat Board, Sess. Paper No. 54, 11 George V,
        1921.

        COMMITTEES OF THE HOUSE OF COMMONS

1931   Select Standing Committee on Agriculture and Colonization, Proceed-
        ings and Evidence.
1934   Select Standing Committee on Banking and Commerce, Proceedings and
        Evidence
1935   Special Committee on Bill 98, Canadian Grain Board Act, Proceed-
        ings and Evidence.
1936   Special Committee on the Marketing of Wheat and Other Grains,
        Proceedings and Evidence.

        REPORTS OF SECRETARY OF STATE, 1868-1877

1872   Report from J. Stoughton Dennis, Surveyor-General, Dominion Lands
        Office, to the Hon. J. C. Aikens, Secretary of State for Canada, dated
        March 1st, 1872, Appendix C.

1917-
1920   REPORTS OF DEPARTMENT OF TRADE AND COMMERCE
        Reports for fiscal year 1917 and 1918, and for the fiscal year 1920.

1908-
1950   REPORTS OF DOMINION BUREAU OF STATISTICS
        Annual Reports on the Grain Trade of Canada, 1919-1950.
1933-
1940   Monthly Review of the Wheat Situation.

1913-
1950   ANNUAL REPORTS OF THE BOARD OF GRAIN COMMISSIONERS FOR CANADA.

1935-
1951   ANNUAL REPORTS OF THE CANADIAN WHEAT BOARD. 1935-36 — 1950-51.

        CANADIAN LAW REPORTS
1924   Exchequer Court of Canada, June 24, 1924.
1925   Supreme Court of Canada, March 9, 10 and May 5, 1925.

        REPORTS OF ROYAL COMMISSIONS
1900   Report of the Royal Commission on Shipment and Transportation of
        Grain, 1900, *see* under Sessional Papers, p. 1668.
1908   Report of the Royal Commission on the Grain Trade of Canada, 1908, *see*
        under Sessional Papers, p. 1668.
1925   Report of the Royal Grain Inquiry Commission, King's Printer, Ottawa,
        1925
1931   Report of the Commission to Enquire into Trading in Grain Futures,
        King's Printer, Ottawa, 1931.
1935   Report of the Royal Commission on Price Spreads, King's Printer, Ottawa,
        1935.
1938   Report of the Royal Grain Inquiry Commission, King's Printer, 1938.
1940   Report of the Royal Commission on Dominion-Provincial Relations,
        King's Printer, Ottawa, 1940.

OTHER REPORTS

1943   Advisory Committee on Reconstruction, Agricultural Policy, Final Report
        of the Subcommittee, Ottawa, December 16, 1943.

PUBLIC ARCHIVES OF CANADA

1915-
1921   Foster Diaries.
1915-
1921   Foster Papers.
1919   White Papers.
1929   Malcolm Papers.
1930-
1936   Bennett Papers.
1934   Stevens Papers.
1935-
1949   King Papers.
1935-
1948   King Diary (by special permission)

DEPARTMENTAL FILES IN THE PUBLIC ARCHIVES OF CANADA

DEPARTMENT OF TRADE AND COMMERCE

1917-
1931   The Board of Grain Supervisors, File T-14-144.
1917   Memoranda of the Board of Grain Supervisors for Canada, File T-14-144.
1917   Report on Price of Wheat by the Board of Grain Supervisors for Canada, File T-14-144.
1918   Report by the Secretary, Board of Grain Supervisors for Canada, File T-14-144.
1919   Movement of the Grain Crop, 1918-1919, (The Board of Grain Supervisors for Canada, Winnipeg, Manitoba, March 19, 1919), File T-14-144.
1919-
1923   The Canadian Wheat Board, File 24181A.
1920   Operations of the Board of Grain Supervisors for Canada, June 11, 1917, to January 31, 1920, File T-14-144.
1921   Hyndman Royal Grain Inquiry Commission, File T-14-124.
1922   Canadian Council of Agriculture, "Memorandum to the Dominion Government Regarding the Reestablishment of the Canadian Wheat Board," File 24181A.
1933   Note of Agreement between the Overseas Exporting Wheat Countries, June 30, 1933, (reproduced as Appendix 3.) Annex of August 21, 1933 to June 30, Note of Agreement, (reproduced in Appendix 4), File 26204:14.
1933-
1944   Wheat Advisory Committee and International Wheat Council, File 26204:14.
1940   Canadian Wheat Board Advisory Committee, File 1-17-187.

WARTIME PRICES AND TRADE BOARD

1941   Grain File.

PRIVY COUNCIL OFFICE

1943   Cabinet Conclusions.

DEPARTMENTAL FILES STILL WITHIN THE DEPARTMENTS

DEPARTMENT OF TRADE AND COMMERCE

1944-
1949   International Wheat Council, File 26204:14.
1946-
1949   United Kingdom Grain and Flour, File 20-141-U2.
1950   Memorandum to the Right Honourable C. D. Howe re Settlement of Obligations under the Canada-United Kingdom Agreement, May 5, 1950, File 20-141-U2.
1950   Supporting Documents, Canada-United Kingdom Wheat Discussions, May 1950, File 20-141-U2.
1942-
1948   Cabinet Wheat Committee, File 20-141-11.
1945   Memorandum Re 1945 Grain Production, File 20-141-11.
1945   Notes on Treasury Proposals, File 20-141-11.
1946   Observations on Proposed United Kingdom Wheat Contract, File 20-141-11.

PRIVY COUNCIL OFFICE

1946-
1951   Files C-20-2, D-10-1 and G-70 (by special permission).

CANADIAN WHEAT BOARD. 1935

1935-
1950   Reports of the Canadian Wheat Board, 1935-36 — 1950-51.
1940-
1950   Minutes of the Advisory Committee to the Canadian Wheat Board.
1942-
1948   Minutes of the Wheat Committee of the Cabinet.
1939   United Kingdom Food Control Plans in the Event of War.
1939   Memorandum re Measures to Control the Prices and Movement of Wheat in the United Kingdom and Canada in Time of War.
1942   Recommendations of the Canadian Wheat Board re 1942-43 Wheat Policy, January 17, 1942.
1942   Report of the Inter-Departmental Committee on Wheat Policy, February 11, 1942.
1943   Canadian Wheat Board Memorandum re Transportation of Grains, February, 1943.

CANADA: TREATY SERIES

1933   Treaty Series, 1933, No. 11:
        Conference of Wheat Exporting and Importing Countries, Final Act signed at London, August 25, 1933 (reproduced in Appendix 5).
1942   Treaty Series, 1942, No. 11:
        Memorandum of Agreement and Draft Wheat Convention.
1949   Treaty Series, 1949, No. 10:
        International Wheat Agreement.

OTHER OFFICIAL PUBLICATIONS

1921   First Report of the Royal Commission on Wheat Supplies, London, 1921.
1921   Report to the Government of Saskatchewan on Wheat Marketing, James Stewart and F. W. Riddell, Regina, 1921.
1932   Memorandum on Wheat and Flour Methods of Empire Preference with Special Reference to the Quota, prepared by the General Economic Committee of the Preparatory Organization for the Imperial Economic Conference, 1932.
1933   League of Nations, Monetary and Economic Conference, Draft Annotated Agenda submitted by the Preparatory Commission of Experts, Geneva, January 20, 1933.
1933   United States Department of State Treaty Information Bulletin No. 48, September, 1933.
1934   The World Wheat Problem and the London Agreement, Ottawa, 1934.
1938   Proceedings of the Conference on Markets for Western Farm Products, Winnipeg, 1938.
1939   Memorandum of the Preparatory Committee of the International Wheat Conference and draft International Wheat Agreement, P.C. 1 and 2, January 28, 1939.
        Draft of International Wheat Agreement P.C. 22, April 24, 1939.
        Submission of the Western Committee on Markets and the Agricultural Re-adjustment to the Dominion Government, March 1, 1939.

1939   Second Submission of the Western Committee on Markets and Agricultural Re-adjustment to the Dominion Government, April 24, 1939.

1941-
1942   Washington Wheat Meeting, Minutes.

1942-
1949   International Wheat Council, Minutes.

1945   Department of External Affairs Conference Series 1945, No. 3, Proposals for Expansion of World Trade and Employment.

1947   Draft Wheat Agreement, March 29, 1947.

1947   Resumé of Proceedings of Committee I, London Wheat Conference.

1948   Province of Manitoba: Manitoba's Position on Oats and Barley Marketing.

1949   International Wheat Conference, Washington, Minutes.

OTHER REPORTS

1934-
1950   Directors' Reports, Canadian Co-operative Wheat Producers Limited, included in the Annual Reports of Saskatchewan Co-operative Wheat Producers Limited 1934-35 to 1949-50.

1942   Canadian Federation of Agriculture Submission to the Prime Minister of Canada and Members of the Government, Ottawa, February 2, 1942.

1943   Canadian Federation of Agriculture Submission to the Prime Minister of Canada and Members of the Government, Ottawa, March 5, 1943.

1945-
1950   Canadian Federation of Agriculture, Ottawa: Farmers meet the Cabinet.

1935-
1943   Minutes of the Council of the Winnipeg Grain Exchange.

PERIODICAL PUBLICATIONS

1900-
1950   Annual Reports of the Winnipeg Grain Exchange.

1902-
1938   Canadian Annual Review of Public Affairs.

1924-
1940   Wheat Studies of the Food Research Institute, Vols. 1 to 18, Stanford University Press.

GENERAL WORKS

Beaverbook, Lord, *Friends* (Heineman, Toronto, 1959).

Berton, Pierre, *The National Dream — The Great Railway, 1871-1881* (Pierre Berton Enterprises Ltd., McClelland and Stewart Ltd., Toronto, 1970).

The Last Spike (McClelland and Stewart Ltd., Toronto, 1971).

Borden, Robert Laird, *His Memoirs* (MacMillan, Toronto 1938).

Britnell, G. E., *The Wheat Economy* (University of Toronto Press, 1939).

— and Fowke, V. C., *Canadian Agriculture in War and Peace* (Stanford University Press, 1962).

Colquette, R. D., *The First Fifty Years (A History of the United Grain Growers Ltd.)* (Modern Press, Winnipeg, 1957).

Davis, J. S. *Wheat and the AAA* (Brookings Institution, Washington, D.C., 1935).

Dawson, R. M., *William Lyon Mackenzie King, 1874-1923* (University of Toronto Press, 1958).

Fowke, Vernon C., *Canadian Agricultural Policy, The Historical Pattern* (University of Toronto Press, 1946).

References 1117

— *The National Policy and the Wheat Economy* (University of Toronto Press, 1957).
— (with George E. Britnell, as above).
Galbraith, J. K., *The Great Crash* (Houghton Mifflin, Boston, 1955).
Hammond, R. J., *Food,* Vols. I to IV (History of the Second World War, U.K. Civil Series).
Hancock, W. K., and Gowing, M. M., *British War Economy* (History of the Second World War, U.K. Civil Series, 1947).
Hudson's Bay Company, *Charters, Statutes and Orders in Council, Etc., Relating to the Hudson's Bay Company* (London, 1931).
Innis, Harold A., *A History of the Canadian Pacific Railway* (University of Toronto Press, 1923).
— *The Diary of Alexander James McPhail* (University of Toronto Press, 1940).
Keynes, J. M., *The Economic Consequences of the Peace* (Harcourt, Brace and Howe, New York, 1920).
— *General Theory of Employment Interest and Money* (Harcourt, Brace and Howe, 1936).
MacGibbon, Duncan Alexander, *The Canadian Grain Trade* (The MacMillian Company of Canada Ltd., Toronto, 1932).
— *The Canadian Grain Trade 1931-1951* (University of Toronto Press, 1952).
Mackintosh, W. A., *Agricultural Co-operation in Western Canada* (Queen's University, Kingston, The Ryerson Press, Toronto, 1924).
McDougall, J. Lorne, *Canadian Pacific* (McGill University Press, Montreal, 1968).
Moorehouse, Hopkins, *Deep Furrows* (George J. McLeod Ltd., Toronto and Winnipeg, 1918).
Morton, W. L., *The Progressive Party in Canada* (University of Toronto Press, 1930).
Parish & Heimbecker *The Personal Factor in a Nation-Wide Business* (Parrish & Heimbecker Ltd., Toronto, 1949).
Patton, Harald S., *Grain Growers' Co-operation in Western Canada* (Harvard University Press, Cambridge, 1928).
— *The Canadian Wheat Pool in Prosperity and Depression, Essays in Honour of T. N. Carver* (Harvard University Press, Cambridge, 1935).
Pearson, the Right Honourable Lester B., *The Memoirs of the Right Honourable Lester B. Pearson, Volume I, 1897-1948* (University of Toronto Press, 1972).
Robbins, L., *The Great Depression* (MacMillian, 1934).
Roll, Eric, *The Combined Food Board* (Stanford University Press, 1956).
Rolph, William Kirby, *Henry Wise Wood of Alberta* (University of Toronto Press, 1950).
Ruble, Kenneth D., *The Peavey Story* (The Peavey Company, Minneapolis, 1963).
Stevens, G. R., *Canadian National Railways* (Clarke, Irwin & Co., Ltd., Toronto and Vancouver, 1960).
Strange, H. G. L., *A Short History of Prairie Agriculture* (Searle Grain Company Ltd., Winnipeg, 1954).
Surface, Frank M., *The Grain Trade during the World War* (The MacMillian Company, New York, 1928).
Swanson, W. W. and Armstrong, P. C., *Wheat* (MacMillan, Toronto, 1930).
United Grain Growers Ltd., *The Grain Growers Record 1906 to 1943* (The Public Press Ltd., Winnipeg, 1944).
Watkins, Ernest, *R. B. Bennett* (Secker and Warburg, London, 1963).
Wood, Louis Aubrey, *A History of Farmers' Movements in Canada* (Ryerson Press, Toronto, 1924).

BULLETINS, PAMPHLETS AND ARTICLES

Bawlf, W. R., *The Marketing of Canadian Grain under War Conditions*, Presidential Address to Winnipeg Grain Exchange, September 11, 1918.

Booth, J. F., *Agricultural Co-operation in Canada*, Conference on Agricultural Co-operation, Ontario Agriculture College, Guelph, September 20-22, 1938.

— *Co-operative Marketing of Grain in Western Canada*, U.S. Department of Agriculture, Technical Bulletin No. 63, January, 1928.

Clark, W. C. "The Country Elevator in the Canadian West", *the Bulletin of the Department of History and Economic Science*, Queen's University, Kingston, 1916.

Dafoe, J. W., "The Economic History of the Prairie Provinces 1870-1913", *Canada and Its Provinces, The Prairie Provinces, Part II* (Shortt, Adam and Doughty, Arthur G., editors, publisher: Publishers' Association of Canada Ltd., 1914), Vol. 20, Chap. XX.

Lambert, Norman P., "Review of W. L. Morton, The Progressive Party in Canada", *the Winnipeg Free Press*, July 15, 1950.

Magill, Dr. Robert, "Secretary's Report on the Wheat Situation", *Winnipeg Grain Exchange Annual Report*, August 20, 1919.

Morrison, J. W., "Marquis Wheat — A Triumph of Scientific Endeavor", *Agricultural History*, Vol. 34, No. 4.

Sharp, Mitchell W., "Allied Wheat Buying in Relationship to Canadian Marketing Policy, 1914-18", *Canadian Journal of Economics and Political Science*, August, 1940.

Taylor, Alonzo E., "The International Wheat Conferences during 1930-31", *Wheat Studies of the Food Research Institute*, Stanford University, California, Vol. VII, No. 9. August, 1931.

NEWSPAPERS

The Calgary Albertan
The Calgary Herald
The Country Guide
The Edmonton Journal
The Financial Post
The Manitoba Free Press
The New York Times
The Ottawa Citizen
The Ottawa Journal
The Regina Leader-Post
The Toronto Telegram
The Toronto World
The Winnipeg Free Press
The Winnipeg Telegram
The Winnipeg Tribune

INDEX

A CENTURY OF CANADIAN GRAIN

In *A Century of Canadian Grain* Dr. Charles F. Wilson provides a single, continuous account of the decision-making process and resultant policy, written from the policy-maker's standpoint and for the use of future policy-makers and advisers, as well as students embarking on careers in various sectors of the industry. The excellent index, bibliography and inclusion of a wealth of material from original sources increase the book's value to government, industry and the academic community.

Wilson himself was at the center of policy formulation from 1938 to 1951 and writes from that unique vantage point. He concentrates on exposition rather than appraisal of policy decisions. The review is enlivened by his record of the interplay of the principal personalities involved. Thus, he unites policy decisions and the persons who made them.

COVER PHOTO BY GIBSON PHOTOS LTD.
COVER DESIGN WARREN CLARK